International Bibliography of Business History

Edited by
Francis Goodall,
Terry Gourvish
and
Steven Tolliday

London and New York

First published 1997
by Routledge
11 New Fetter Lane, London EC4P 4EE
29 West 35th Street, New York, NY 10001

Typeset by Routledge

Printed and bound in England by TJ Press (Padstow) Ltd, Cornwall

British Library Cataloguing in Publication Data
A catalogue record for this book is available from the British Library

Library of Congress Cataloging in Publication Data
A catalogue record for this book has been requested

ISBN 0-415-08641-8

Table of Contents

General Editors

Subject Editors

Introduction

Business History is a dynamic and changing area of study; and as it changes, it inspires a considerable debate about its definition, roots, and ambitions. Its origins can be traced to German scholarship in the nineteenth century, but it was shaped into a discipline in the United States in the first half of the twentieth century, notably by Edwin Gay and Norman Gras at the Harvard Business School. At first, business history had a strong emphasis upon the case study. Since then, however, it has broadened out until in the 1990s it is eclectic, drawing upon the theoretical and empirical approaches of many disciplines: history, economics, economic history, sociology, political science, social psychology and management studies. In this bibliography we provide material which reflects the changing scope and direction of the subject, indicates the richness and diversity of the scholarship which claims to be business history, and identifies theoretical and descriptive works which business historians customarily find useful in framing their analyses.

The idea of compiling an International Bibliography for Business Historians emerged in a discussion between Sue McNaughton of Routledge and Francis Goodall and Terry Gourvish of the Business History Unit, LSE in 1991. They agreed that the existing British bibliographies of business history compiled by Goodall (Gower, 1987) and Zarach (Macmillan, 1987, new edition, 1994), while useful were rather limited in scope. They focused mainly upon histories of individual firms and their coverage was almost exclusively British. Above all, they provided no critical assessment of the entries they included. Henrietta Larsen's Guide to Business History (Harvard University Press, 1948) was a courageous single-handed attempt to cover similar ground within the contemporary limits of the discipline, but was now seriously out of date. Routledge agreed to commission a wide-ranging but selective bibliography, and contracts were signed in June 1992. A team of nine subject specialists was then appointed, and the compilation of entries proceeded in stages concluding in January 1995. We should like to thank all those at Routledge who were concerned at various stages with the project: Shan Millie, Tara Montgomery, and at the later, critical stages, Mark Barragry, Seth Denbo, Alasdair Ogg and Denise Rea.

Entries were commissioned from the subject specialists, who acted as editors for the individual chapters, and drew upon the advice and assistance of a team of business history experts from all over the world. We should like to express our sincere thanks to the subject specialists who provided chapters for the bibliography in the order in which they appear; Maurice Kirby of Lancaster University (Primary and Extractive Industries); James Smyth and Alan McKinlay of Stirling University (Traditional and Heavy Industries); Steven Tolliday, Leeds University (Light Manufacturing Industries, and the Motor Industry), who subsequently joined the general editorial team; Keith Burgess of Roehampton Institute (Trade and Distribution); Youssef Cassis, Business History Unit, LSE (Banking and Finance); John Armstrong, Thames Valley University (Utilities, Transport and other Services); Leslie Hannah, LSE (Strategy and Structure: Approaches to Business History); David Jeremy, of Manchester Metropolitan University (Entrepreneurship and Management, including Technology and Labour). Takeshi Yuzawa (assisted by Satoshi Sasaki) covered Japan's impressive contributions to the subject, which are divided between the other chapters following the general arrangement. Clearly, in a work of this nature, it was necessary to restructure chapters, introduce additional material, and relocate entries contributed by editors to other chapters. We trust that the chapter editors will be happy with our judgement, for which we take full responsibility.

We also were extremely fortunate to enjoy the help offered by the Business History Unit's network of specialist scholars, together with those who responded so generously with annotations sent direct to our subject specialists. To all these, then, our sincere thanks: Margot Adams-Webber, Brock University, Ontario; Peter Alter, German Historical Institute, London; Franco Amatori, Bocconi University, Milan; Rolv Amdam, Norwegian School of Management; Ted Ashworth, Nottingham Trent University; Bill Aspray, Rutgers University; Stefano Battilossi, Bologna University; Susan Becker, Bonn University; Alain Beltran, CNRS, Paris; Sergio Birchal, PUC-Minas Gerais; Frankie Bostock, Reading University; Frank Broeze, University of Western Australia; Martin Campbell-Kelly, Warwick University; Francesca Carnevali, Birmingham University; Alfred D. Chandler, Jr., Harvard Business School; Tim Coles, Exeter University; Richard Coopey, BHU/University College, Aberystwyth; Philip Cottrell, Leicester University; François Crouzet, Paris-Sorbonne; Carlos Davila, Los Andes University, Bogota; David DeRamus, University of Massachusetts-Amherst; Marc Dierikx, Utrecht University; Margarita Dritsas, Crete University; J.R. Edwards, Cardiff Business School; Roy Edwards, LSE; Douglas Farnie, Manchester University; Wolfram Fischer, Free University, Berlin; Elena Frangakis-Syrett, CUNY; Telmo Frantz; Michael French, Glasgow University; Patrick Fridenson, EHESS–CNRS, Paris; Till Geiger, Queen's University, Belfast; Domingos Giroletti, Federal University of Minas Gerais; M. E. Gomez Roso, Malaga University; Howard Gospel, Pembroke College, Oxford; Robert Greenhill, London Guildhall University; Janet Grenier, BHU/Warwick University; Per Hansen, Odense University; Sven Hansen, Norwegian School of Management; Naveed Hasan, LSE; John Hassan, Manchester Metropolitan University; William Hausman, William & Mary College, Williamsburg; Ginette Kurgan van Hentenryk, Free University, Brussels; Katrina Honeyman, Leeds University; Vapu Ikonen, Bank of Finland; Kris Inwood, Guelph University; Ryoichi Iwauchi, Meiji University; Finn Johannessen, Norwegian School of Management; Charles Jones, Warwick University; Geoffrey Jones, Reading University; Joost Jonker, Amsterdam; Hartmut Kaelble, Humboldt University, Berlin; Sverre Knutsen, Norwegian School of Management; Masako Kurohane, Tsukuba University; David Kynaston, BHU; Colin Lewis, LSE; Håkan Lindgren, Uppsala University; José Lopes Cordeiro, Minho University; Ra Lundström, Uppsala University; Martin Lynn, Queen's University Belfast; Peter Lyth, BHU/Tel-Aviv University; David Mackenzie, Toronto University; Gregory Marchildon, Saskatchewan; James Maybury, CUNY; Michèle Merger, Paris; Rory Miller, Liverpool University; Alois Mosser, Economics University, Vienna; Timo Myllyntaus, Helsinki University; Daniel Nelson, Akron University; Ayodeji Olukoju, Lagos University; Jan Ottosson, Uppsala University; Manuel Peláez, Malaga University; Richard Perren, Aberdeen University; Gordon Pirie, Witwatersrand University; Dil Porter, BHU/Worcester College; Jon Press, Bath College; Harald Rinde, Norwegian School of Management; José Navia Rojas, Antioquia University; Michèle Ruffat, CNRS, Paris; Harm Schröter, Free University, Berlin; Michael Schudson, University of California–San Diego; Richard Seebohm, London; Masachika Shinomiya, Takachino University; John Singleton, Victoria University of Wellington; John Skeie, Norwegian School of Management; Tsuneo Suzuki, Gakushuin University; Richard Sylla, Leonard N. Stern School of Business, New York; Jacob Tanner, Basel University; Mikulas Teich, Cambridge University; Alice Teichova, BHU; Keith Telford, IBM UK; Nick Tiratsoo, BHU/Warwick University; Laurent Tissot, Swiss National Research Council, Lausanne; Pier Angelo Toninelli, Milan University; Gabriel Tortella, Alcala University; Dwijendra Tripathi, Indian Institute of Management, Ahmedabad; Geoffrey Tweedale, Sheffield University; Kersti Ullenhag, Uppsala University; Jesus Valdaliso, Pais Vasco University; Désirée Verdonk, Vienna; Simon Ville, ANU; Margaret Walsh, Nottingham University; Keiichi Watanabe, St Paul's University; Mira Wilkins, Florida International University, Miami; John F. Wilson, Manchester University; Harald Wixforth, Bielefeld University; Vera Zamagni, Bologna University; and Dieter Ziegler, Bielefeld University. We are most grateful for the help given by Chikage Hidaka of BHU Musashi University with Japanese company names. Many other scholars have encouraged us with their support and advice; if we have inadvertently missed the names of any who have provided entries we hope they will accept our apologies and thanks.

Our aim has been to assemble an authoritative international bibliography containing much of the best work in business history, written mainly in book form. We have tried to confine the contents to books which are: i) high quality scholarly works; ii) works of a lesser quality which nevertheless are essential reading for students of the specific topic; and iii) important primary materials (autobiographies, journalism, bibliographies, etc.). Postgraduate theses and journal articles were included only where they were considered to be seminal to a particular subject. We have not sought to provide an exhaustive listing. Selectivity, with the emphasis on quality, was our watchword. Here, of course, we faced a considerable intellectual challenge. Perceptions of quality vary with the state of scholarship, and these in turn vary from country to country and from subject area to subject area. Inevitably, our coverage reflects the strengths of certain countries in the field, and notably the strong Anglo-Saxon and Japanese interest in the subject; inevitably too, we mirror the different stages of research reached in particular fields. There is, for example, more on textiles, where scholarship is abundant, than on retailing, where it is not. In new and fast-changing fields such as computers, telecommunications and biotechnology we have tried to include the best available work, even where it may be less scholarly than in other fields. The problem of defining what is and what is not 'business history' was an additional challenge. As noted earlier, this is a much debated issue. A great deal of scholarship is wide-ranging, drawing upon economic, political and social history, or upon economics, management studies, sociology and philosophy; and many books are extremely difficult to categorize. We have generally deferred to the position taken by each of our chapter editors, but as general editors we took the view that the bibliography should take a broad definition of the subject and should also include a selection of the more important general and theoretical works which have stimulated and continue to stimulate work in business history. And since not every business history title fits into the generic framework, we have provided a short general chapter covering these works.

We considered it to be vitally important to avoid producing a mere listing of titles. Instead, we decided to include short but informative critical annotations for each work. We also regarded cross-referencing as a vital aid to usage. Works which are of relevance in more than one area are cross-referenced. Where a work makes an equally important contribution to two or more areas of business history, it is given a dual or multiple entry. The titles of entries which have been published in languages other than English are listed in their original form with a brief English translation. Of course some imperfections remain in a volume of this scale and ambition. We see the bibliography as an on-going venture, which will be improved, expanded and corrected in subsequent editions. We acknowledge that our treatment of some areas, e.g. Eastern Europe and the Far East (except for Japan) is rather weak. Our coverage of the business history literature in languages other than English also varies in quality. Scholars in some countries were not able to give us the assistance we asked for in the time available. Readers who find omissions are invited to draw our attention to them c/o Business History Unit, London School of Economics, London WC2 2AE e.mail: T.R.Gourvish@lse.ac.uk. Coverage extends to works published to 1994 (with a few exceptions).

The overall arrangement of the bibliography is based on broad chapters: for example, the section covering primary and extractive industries, includes agriculture and mining. But even a simple subdivision such as this brought its difficulties. Many entries on, for example, the oil industry, could as easily fall elsewhere, e.g. with multinational enterprise, entrepreneurship or the role of government regulation. To overcome this problem we have tried to provide extensive cross-references to other areas where related entries might be found. Users will be aware that firms often change their names and their sector of their operations over time; it would have been impossible to follow all of these up in a general bibliography such as this.

Within individual chapters we have first subdivided entries by industry. Where necessary, most notably with banking and finance, entries have been divided geographically to provide more manageable sub-sections. Again it must be remembered that business does not operate to facilitate the systems of the bibliographer. We have endeavoured to give the user a selection of related books as a starting point. If the reader is more interested in works by a particular author or about an individual firm, the indexes provide assistance.

This bibliography is aimed at undergraduates, postgraduates, business historians or would-be business historians, and those from the business world who wish to learn something of the international scholarship in the field. We hope that the general arrangement will help the reader who is looking for a specific title, and that he/she will then be encouraged to browse further into a wider literature.

FG
TG
ST
August 1995

General Sources

Bibliographies

1

ABC-Clio Information Services

Corporate America: A Historical Bibliography

1984 ABC-Clio *Santa Barbara, CA*

A substantial 300 page annotated bibliography organized on an industry by industry basis and covering books and, in particular, periodical articles and extensively indexed. It includes works in several languages.

2

Bain, G. S.; Bennett, J. D. (Editors)

Bibliography of British Industrial Relations, 1971–9

1985 Cambridge University Press *Cambridge*

A supplement to Bain and Woolven (qv).

3

Bain, G. S.; Woolven, G. B. (Editors)

A Bibliography of British Industrial Relations

1979 Cambridge University Press *Cambridge*

A massive bibliography of over 15,000 items aiming 'to bring together all the secondary source material, except that of an ephemeral or strictly propagandist nature, published in English between 1880 and 1970 on British industrial relations'. It includes books, articles, pamphlets, theses and government reports. It covers trade unions, labour–management relations, and the wider field of job regulation, and is interdisciplinary across industrial relations, industrial sociology, labour economics, labour history, labour law, industrial psychology, and social administration.

4

Bellamy, Joyce M. (Editor)

Yorkshire Business Histories: A bibliography

1970 Bradford University Press *Bradford*

A standard work of reference (425 pages) comprising a comprehensive analysis of material relating to all traceable Yorkshire businesses available in Yorkshire libraries and records offices, arranged under SIC classifications.

5

Benson, John; Neville, Robert G.; Thompson, Charles H. (Editors)

Bibliography of the British Coal Industry: Secondary literature, parliamentary and departmental papers, mineral maps and plans, and a guide to sources

1981 National Coal Board/Oxford University Press *Oxford*

A comprehensive survey (650 pages) organized on a regional basis. It includes an especially thorough guide to published literature and parliamentary papers but does not cover archives.

6

Bloomfield, Gerald T.; Bloomfield, Elizabeth

Canadian Industry in 1871 [CANIND71]

1989 University of Guelph *Guelph, Canada*

This book reports on a Canadian database accessible to researchers. The information retrieval system, CANIND71, contains 45,000 records of industrial firms listed in Canada's first national census taken in 1871. The 1970 SIC was used to classify the 1871 schedules into major industry groups and specific industry types. The original French and English terminology is included and the SIC codes are based on reported outputs of the businesses.

7

Boger, Karl (Editor)

Japanese Direct Foreign Investments: An annotated bibliography

1989 Greenwood Press *Westport, CT*

670 items on Japanese direct foreign investment, all in English language. Mainly covers press and periodical articles in the 1970s and 1980s.

8

Brealey, Richard; Edwards, Helen (Editors)

A Bibliography of Finance

1991 MIT Press *Cambridge, MA*

An enormous bibliography of over 12,000 items, mainly from academic periodicals. A resource for practitioners, but also useful for business historians.

9

Burt, Roger; Waite, Peter

Bibliography of the History of British Metal Mining

1988 University of Exeter *Exeter*

A comprehensive bibliography of all theses, books and articles about British metalliferous mining published since 1945 (modelled on Benson et al on coal, qv). It is not annotated but contains c.500 books and theses and 2,000 articles.

10

Business Archives Council

Business Archives Council Library Catalogue

1993 Business Archives Council *London*

This microfiche of the Business Archives Council Library Catalogue is indexed by company and sorted by main business activity. The Library contains a substantial collection of over 4,500 business histories, a large number of which have been privately produced and are not available elsewhere. The catalogue is updated annually.

11

Catterall, Peter (Editor)

British History, 1945 to 1987: An annotated bibliography

1990 Institute of Contemporary British History/Basil Blackwell *Oxford*

A comprehensive annotated bibliography and guide to the literature on all aspects of British history since 1945. The section on Economic History (150 pages) is of particular interest to business historians. Catterall covers books, theses and articles and aims to be inclusive rather than selective. A source well worth consulting.

12

Chao, Sheau-Yueh J.

The Japanese Automobile Industry: An annotated bibliography

1994 Greenwood Press *Westport, CT*

601 items, including documents, monographs and articles (scholarly and journalism) published between 1980 and 1992, with selective coverage of earlier work. It also covers Japanese transplants in the USA.

13

Collazzo, Charles (Editor)

The Foot and the Shoe: A bibliography

1988 Bata Shoe Museum Foundation *Boston, MA*

Collazzo's comprehensive bibliography covers all aspects of the shoe industry, including industrial and company histories and archives.

14

Geahigan, Priscilla C.

US and Canadian Businesses, 1955 to 1987: A bibliography

1988 Scarecrow Press *London*

An extensive listing of company histories and biographical studies arranged by two-digit SIC classification with extensive indexes. Extensive coverage of the ephemeral and in-house histories as well as better-quality studies.

15

Goodall, Francis

A Bibliography of British Business Histories

1987 Gower *Aldershot*

This provides a simple listing of company histories with no attempt to assess quality. It provides indexes of company names and SIC classifications.

16

Habgood, Wendy

Chartered Accountants in England and Wales: A guide to historical records

1994 Manchester University Press *Manchester*

This guide provides information on the present location of the archives of firms of chartered accountants in England and Wales, a few of which originated in the late eighteenth century. It features brief histories of almost 200 firms, together with lists of their surviving records, and includes many of the old practices which, through merger, now form part of today's major national and international firms. The guide is prefaced by essays on the development of the accountancy profession and the nature and use of the historical records of accountants.

17

Hopkins, A. G.

Imperial Business in Africa

Journal of African History, vol. 17, no. 1–2, 1976: pp 29–48, 267–90

These two articles provide the seminal review of the subject up to the mid-1970s, pointing out the limitations of existing scholarship. The first surveys some fifty histories of European companies in West, Central and East Africa.

18

Hudson, Patricia

The West Riding Wool Textile Industry: A catalogue of business records from the 16th to the 20th centuries

1975 Pasold Research Fund *Edington*

An invaluable firm by firm survey of the surviving business records of some 120 firms.

19

Japan Business History Institute

Kaisha-shi Sogo Mokuroku [A Complete Bibliography of Company History in Japan]

1986 Maruzen Kabushiki Kaisha *Tokyo, Japan*

This book is an overall bibliography which includes 6,127 company histories and 783 histories of economic organization. Also covered are histories of individual factories and branch offices. Since publication of the book, supplements have been issued by Japan Business History Institute.

20

Jones, Charles A.

Britain and the Dominions: A guide to business and related records in the United Kingdom concerning Australia, Canada, New Zealand and South Africa

1978 G. K. Hall *Boston, MA*

An excellent descriptive guide to the records of British companies overseas.

21

Lane, Joan (Editor)

Register of Business Records of Coventry and Related Areas

1987 Department of Politics and History, Lanchester Polytechnic *Coventry*

A useful regional guide.

22

Larson, Henrietta M.

Guide to Business History: Materials for the study of American Business History and suggestions for their use

1948 Harvard University Press *Cambridge, MA*

A pioneering work of over 1,200 pages and 5,000 entries, fully annotated. It covers the historical background of American business, biographies, business history of companies, industrial histories and general topics in business history, including ethics, labour, technology, wealth, failures, and business and economic conditions. Compilation began under Miss Elva C. Tooker around 1931 and was brought to completion in 1948. As N. S. B. Gras says in his Preface, it was the result of 'years of drudgery' motivated by the idea of 'service to the other fellow'. An unsurpassed work of scholarship.

23

Linton, David; Boston, Ray

The Newspaper Press in Britain: An annotated bibliography

1987 Mansell Publishing *London*

An indispensable pioneering work of bibliography. It contains 2,900 mostly annotated entries on books, articles, research papers and newspapers with a comprehensive index, Appendices include a chronology of the British newspaper industry, 1476–1986 and a guide to the location of archives.

24

Mathias, Peter; Pearsall, A. W. H.

Shipping: A survey of historical records

1971 David & Charles *Newton Abbot*

The result of an extensive survey, this book provides brief histories and details of the archives of all traceable British shipping companies as well as details of relevant materials in record offices. Because of its vintage it is now in great need of updating, being now far from comprehensive.

25
McConville, James; Rickaby, Glenys (Editors)
Shipping Business and Maritime Economics: An annotated international bibliography
1995 Mansell *London*

Though designed primarily as a resource for shipping practitioners, this 3,000 item annotated bibliography contains a limited amount of historical material but is a thorough guide to post 1970 publications on the industry.

26
Morris, Peter J. T.; Russell, Colin A. (Editors)
Archives of the British Chemical Industry, 1750–1914: A handlist
1988 British Society for the History of Science *Faringdon*

An invaluable work based on an extensive survey covering the archives of over 200 firms.

27
Nakagawa, Keiichiro (Editor)
Union Catalog on Enterprise Histories and Biographies of Businessmen in the World Outside of Japan
1979 Yushodo *Tokyo, Japan*

This bibliography was produced to mark the 10th anniversary of the Business History Society of Japan. It includes around 6,000 entries on businesses and businessmen in Europe, America and Russia held in Japanese university libraries, plus almost 500 entries in the V.I. Lenin Library, Moscow. Entries are subdivided by country and industrial classification. Many titles are uncritical, in-house publications. This might, however, direct researchers to little-known books and pamphlets.

28
Nasrallah, Wahib
United States Corporation Histories: A bibliography, 1965–1990
1991 Garland Publishing *New York, NY*

A 511 page bibliography including a great deal of ephemera and slight in-house historical pieces.

29
Ostrye, Anne T.
Foreign Investment in the American and Canadian West, 1870–1914: An annotated bibliography
1986 Scarecrow Press *London*

A comprehensive scholarly bibliography of nearly 600 items, covering scholarly and popular works and business and personal archival collections on companies and individuals investing in these areas. Careful annotations and an excellent archival guide.

30
Ottley, George (Editor)
A Bibliography of British Railway History
2nd Edition
1983–8 HMSO *London*

This is the authoritative two volume bibliography, first published as a single volume in 1966. Containing nearly 13,000 entries, it includes most of the works on the business history of British railways, both scholarly and antiquarian.

31
Pech, E.
Manuel des Sociétés Anonymes fonctionnant en Turquie [A Manual of Private Companies Active in Turkey]
5th Edition
1911 Girard Frères *Constantinople, Turkey*

This is a contemporary work of reference that ran through several editions, the above-cited being of the more accessible and complete ones given the rate of growth of the Ottoman Empire by 1911. It includes useful data on a very considerable array of banks and other companies in such areas as infrastructure, transportation and public utilities.

32
Pressnell, L. S.; Orbell, John
A Guide to the Historical Records of British Banking
1985 Gower *Aldershot*

This volume describes in detail the surviving records of over 600 active and defunct British banks. These include the present-day clearing banks, old established London private banks such as Coutts, Drummonds, Childs and Hoares, country banks established in the eighteenth and nineteenth centuries, joint stock banks, merchant banks such as Barings and Rothschilds, and discount houses. There are useful introductions to banking history and the nature of bank archives.

33
Richmond, Lesley; Turton, Alison
Directory of Corporate Archives
2nd Edition
1987 Business Archives Council *London*

This gives potted histories of each company, details of holdings and access and information on published materials.

34
Richmond, Lesley; Turton, Alison (Editors)
The Brewing Industry: A guide to historical records
1990 Manchester University Press *Manchester*

This collection presents the results of the first national survey of brewing archives, covering nearly 650 breweries. It includes potted histories of each company and comprehensive details of archives. The introductory chapters by Richard Wilson and Peter Mathias are succinct summaries of scholarship on the subject. Altogether an indispensable guide for researchers.

35
Ritchie, L. A.
The Shipbuilding Industry: A guide to historical records
1992 Manchester University Press *Manchester*

Shipbuilding has long been of importance to Britain and during the nineteenth century the British industry dominated world markets. This volume facilitates study of shipbuilding by making available information on the present location of the industry's archives. It features brief histories of some 200 businesses along with lists of their surviving records. There are introductions on the history of the industry and the nature and value of shipbuilding archives.

36
Rowe, D. J. (Editor)
Northern Business Histories: A bibliography
1979 Library Association *London*

An alphabetical unannotated bibliography which lists holdings of business archives. To be used in conjunction with Bellamy (qv).

37
Royal Commission on Historical Manuscripts
Records of British Business and Industry, 1760–1914: Textiles and leather
1990 HMSO *London*

Describes the records of 1,200 companies, partnerships and individuals active in the manufacture and finishing of textiles, clothing, and leather. It is based on a comprehensive survey and is published as part of the Royal Commission on Historical Manuscripts Guides to Sources for British History.

38
Salond, J. L.
Small Business: A bibliography
1969 University of Aston *Birmingham*

A classified bibliography of British and American books, reports, articles, theses and working papers which has been periodically updated.

39
Storey, Richard; et al
Consolidated Guide to the Modern Records Centre
1986 University of Warwick *Coventry*

This guide together with a supplement published in 1992 covers the holdings of one of the most important depositories of British business records, including notable company, employer association and trade union collections.

40
Whitten, David O. (Editor)
Manufacturing: A historiographical and bibliographical guide (Series Title: Handbook of American Business History)
1990 Greenwood Press *New York, NY*

This 500 page volume (the first in a planned series) covers 23 manufacturing industries, with each chapter giving concise histories of the industry supported by bibliographical essay and a bibliography.

41
Young, Stephen C.
An Annotated Bibliography on Relations Between Government and Industry in Britain, 1620–1982
1984 Economic and Social Research Council

A complex and full two volume bibliography. There is a lengthy introduction and each section is introduced in detail. Lacks indexes.

42
Zarach, Stephanie
British Business History: A bibliography
2nd Edition
1994 Macmillan *Basingstoke*

Like Goodall (qv), this provides a simple listing arranged by business sector and with a company index.

Guides to Business Information

43
Armstrong, John; Jones, Stephanie
Business Documents: Their origins, sources, and uses in historical research
1987 Mansell *London*

This book is structured around an introduction to and interpretation of fifteen of the most commonly found types of business documents, explaining how they came into existence and how they may be used in research. The documents include: prospectuses, articles of association, board minutes, letter books, registers, bookkeeping records, balance sheets, licenses, patents and dealer agreements. The book is based on the authors' experience with England's Business Archives Council.

44
Daniels, Lorna M. (Editor)
Business Information Sources
3rd Edition
1993 University of California Press *Berkeley, CA*

A comprehensive guide to contemporary business sources.

45
Haythornthwaite, Jo
The Business Information Maze: An essential guide
1990 Aslib *London*

A good starting point for contemporary business information sources.

46
Noda, Nobuo
Nippon Keiei-shi Nenpyo [A Chronological Table of Japanese Business History]
1981 Diamond-sha *Tokyo, Japan*

This wide-ranging chronological table covers Japanese business history from 1868 to 1968.

47
Norkett, Paul
Guide to Company Information in Great Britain
1986 Longman *Harlow*

A handbook showing how and where to find information on British companies and how to interpret the data.

48
Times Books
The Times 1000
Times Books *London*

An annual statistical compilation of Britain's, Europe's and the world's leading industrial and financial companies, with basic data (in recent years much enhanced) on turnover, capital, profits, employees, etc.

49
Turton, Alison (Editor)
Managing Business Archives
1991 Butterworth Heinemann *London*

Managing Business Archives deals with the specific professional duties and responsibilities of archivists working in a business environment. In addition to the major archival functions of appraisal, arrangement and description, use of computers, repository design and environment, access policy and conservation, the book deals with many subjects of special interest to business archivists. These include the history of business and office technology in Britain, the nature and value of statutory and accounting corporate records, the public relations uses of business archives, and the archivist as manager. It is intended as a work of reference for the professional as well as an introduction to the administration of business archives for the beginner.

Critical Writings in Business History/Elgar

50
International Library of Critical Writings in Business History
1991 to date Edward Elgar *Aldershot*
This ongoing series, edited by Geoffrey Jones, brings together key articles on the major themes of modern business history, making material for research and reference readily available.

51
Burgess, Giles H. Jr (Editor)
Antitrust and Regulation
1992 Edward Elgar *Aldershot*
Concerned with government's regulation of business and chiefly in the USA, this collection of 28 reprinted articles deals with the emergence, growth and reversal of regulation.

52
Cassis, Youssef (Editor)
Business Elites
1994 Edward Elgar *Aldershot*
This book reprints 27 articles or chapters published between 1950 and 1992 dealing with the social origins and social mobility of business elites; their education, culture and mentality; their social profiles; and their wealth and high society. Elites in Britain, the USA, France, Germany and Japan are treated in these writings, some of which (like D. C. Coleman's on 'Gentlemen and Players' (qv) are much quoted.

53
Hollander, Stanley C.; Rassuli, Kathleen M. (Editors)
Marketing
1993 Edward Elgar *Aldershot*
The business history of marketing and retailing, compared to manufacturing, is relatively neglected so this two volume reprint collection of 81 articles is a very valuable resource. Topics treated include marketing thought, education, policy, market research, consumer behaviour, advertising, channels of distribution, price, product and marketing management.

54
Jeremy, David J. (Editor)
Technology Transfer and Business Enterprise
1994 Edward Elgar *Aldershot*
This collection of articles covers the theory and process of technology transfer and the agencies including the state, private business and multinationals. It ranges from the 18th century to the present and includes Asian countries as well as the UK and USA.

55
Jones, Geoffrey
Coalitions and Collaboration in International Business
1993 Edward Elgar *Aldershot*
Organized under the headings of concepts, international cartels, non-equity forms of international collaboration and equity forms of international collaboration, the reprint of these 28 articles and excerpts valuably illuminates the recent phenomenon of cross-border strategic alliances.

56
Lazonick, William; Mass, William (Editors)
Organisational Capability and Competitive Advantage
1995 Edward Elgar *Aldershot*
This book brings together scholarly contributions to the debates over the origins and characteristics of organizational capabilities that bring competitive advantage. Included are case studies on textiles, chemicals, cars, computers and agriculture.

57
Livesay, Harold (Editor)
Entrepreneurship and the Growth of Firms
1995 Edward Elgar *Aldershot*

A two volume collection of articles, the first dating from 1928, exploring the role of the entrepreneur as a prime mover of economic invigoration.

58
Marchildon, Gregory P. (Editor)
Mergers and Acquisitions
1991 Edward Elgar *Aldershot*

The collection of 27 reprinted pieces is organized around the impact of mergers on economic development, the decision to merge, concentration policy and the causes of merger waves. Included are classic articles by Nelson, Hannah, Tilly and Utton.

59
Supple, Barry E. (Editor)
The Rise of Big Business
1992 Edward Elgar *Aldershot, London*

A convenient compendium of the classic articles on the corporate economy. Berle and Means, Schumpeter, Drucker, Galbraith, Coase, Williamson and Chandler are all here, as are the major empirical contributions to the debate from the US, Great Britain, Germany, France and Japan.

60
Tolliday, Steven W. (Editor)
Government and Business
1991 Edward Elgar *Aldershot*

This reprint collection of 25 articles spans the contribution of government policies to industrialization and the business framework, and the interaction of business and politics. The collective political organizations of employers and the response of business to war, depression and decolonization are topics also represented.

61
Wilkins, Mira (Editor)
The Growth of Multinationals
1991 Edward Elgar *Aldershot*

A collection of 25 articles, this volume reprints classic articles and excerpts covering surveys, theory and case studies of multinationals. Authors such as Dunning, Stopford, Geoffrey Jones and Wilkins herself are well represented. Coase, Penrose, Williamson, Casson and Chapman are among those in the 'New Perspectives' section. The editor's introduction is a valuable bibliographic essay.

Industrial Revolutions/Blackwell; Economic History Society

62
The Industrial Revolutions
1994 Basil Blackwell *Oxford*

The eleven volumes of this set, published simultaneously under the auspices of the Economic History Society, each include around 25 important articles together with editorial introduction surveying research progress over the last 50 years, and a critical bibliography. The series includes both topical volumes dealing with individual industries or areas of economic activity and volumes covering the industrial revolutions in particular countries or continents, notably Great Britain, North America, Japan and Western Europe. The series editors are R. A. Church and E. A. Wrigley.

63
Chartres, J. A. (Editor)
Pre-Industrial Britain (Series Title: The Industrial Revolutions, Volume 1)
1994 Basil Blackwell *Oxford*

Chartres covers the period where Britain became differentiated from other European countries through the development of trade, transport and industry, and the effective integration of its economy as a whole, becoming more urban and industrial than its neighbours.

64
Church, R. A. (Editor)
The Coal and Iron Industries (Series Title: The Industrial Revolutions, Volume 10)
1994 Basil Blackwell *Oxford*

Britain led the world in coal and iron production, helped critically by the emergence of mineral fuel technology. Other countries had different natural resource endowments, cost structures, domestic markets and commercial policies. There were differing patterns of development and timing in the heavy industries. The roles of entrepreneurs and government are also examined.

65
Hoppit, Julian; Wrigley, E. A. (Editors)
The Industrial Revolution in Britain (Series Title: The Industrial Revolutions, Volumes 2 and 3)
1994 Basil Blackwell *Oxford*

These two volumes examine the concept of the Industrial Revolution and the central themes of land, labour and capital. Further sections examine technical change and the state of supply and demand.

66
Jenkins, D. T. (Editor)
The Textile Industries (Series Title: The Industrial Revolutions, Volume 8)
1994 Basil Blackwell *Oxford*

Textiles have played an important role in industrial transition. Here are brought together articles on the industries in Britain, Europe, Japan and the United States dealing with technical advance, changes in society and how textiles provide a paradigm for theories of industrialization and development.

67
Macpherson, William J. (Editor)
The Industrialization of Japan (Series Title: The Industrial Revolutions, Volume 7)
1994 Basil Blackwell *Oxford*

This collection of papers examines the complex interactions between political, socio-cultural and economic forces which lay behind the transformation of the Japanese economy particularly during the Meiji period, 1868–1912.

68
Michie, R. C. (Editor)
Commercial and Financial Services (Series Title: The Industrial Revolutions, Volume 11)
1994 Basil Blackwell *Oxford*

Here the importance of services that facilitated matching supply and demand in the market place are emphasized. These included the growth of trade, the role of communications, including railway, steamship and telegraph systems, as well as financial networks.

69
O'Brien, Patrick K. (Editor)
The Industrial Revolution in Europe (Series Title: The Industrial Revolutions, Volumes 4 and 5)
1994 Basil Blackwell *Oxford*

Here the diverse experiences in varied parts of Europe are drawn together to provide a unified frame of reference. Volume 4 adopts a conceptual and comparative approach, while Volume 5 includes sixteen national case studies.

70
Pollard, Sidney (Editor)
The Metal Fabrication and Engineering Industries (Series Title: The Industrial Revolutions, Volume 9)
1994 Basil Blackwell *Oxford*

This volume looks behind the 'American system of manufacture' to what made it possible, the development of simple tools, improvements to steam engines, development of machine tools and the diffusion of engineering technology among major producing countries, all leading towards the development of mass production.

71
Temin, Peter (Editor)
Industrialization in North America (Series Title: The Industrial Revolutions, Volume 6)
1994 Basil Blackwell *Oxford*

This study starts with an examination of income growth and distribution, covers the institution of slavery and its place in the early American economy. It then deals with agriculture which provided the context within which industrialization began, proceeding to iron, railroads, the growth of large firms and banks and financial markets.

Encyclopedias and Textbooks

72
Ackrill, Margaret
Manufacturing Industry since 1870
1987 Philip Allan *Oxford*

A survey of British manufacturing over the period 1870–1980, with cameo accounts of the major sectors and attention paid to the experience of some of the leading firms.
Firms: British Celanese; Courtaulds; EMI; GEC; ICI; Vickers

73
Becker, William H. (Editor)
Encyclopedia of American Business History and Biography
1988 to date Facts on File *New York, NY*

This is an ongoing series (9 volumes published so far) chronicling American business history and business leaders. Each volume focuses on a particular industry and the profiles on companies and business leaders are written by subject specialists. Most articles are 1-3 pages in length and contain guides to further reading.

74
Blackford, Mansel G.; Kerr, K. Austin
Business Enterprise in American History
3rd Edition
1994 Houghton Mifflin *Boston, MA*

Blackford and Kerr are well known for this major textbook which covers the history of American business from the colonial period. The third edition provides extensive coverage of the post-1945 period, with chapters on government–business relations, restructuring and the competitive environment.

75
Bryant, Keith L. Jr; Dethloff, Henry C.
A History of American Business
2nd Edition
1990 Prentice-Hall *Englewood Cliffs, NJ*

This is a simple general historical survey focusing on individuals and key firms with helpful suggestions for further reading.

76
Buchheim, Christoph
Industrielle Revolution: Langfristige Wirtschaftsentwicklung in Grossbritannien, Europa und Übersee [Industrial Revolution Long term development of industry in Great Britain, Europe and elsewhere]
1994 *Munich, Germany*

This book surveys the characteristic features of the industrial revolution in different countries. It primarily discusses the reasons why some of the countries under review managed to industrialize successfully while others did not. As it is, at the same time, concerned with the problem of development policy it combines a historical approach towards the industrial revolution with current problems.

77
Business History Society of Japan
Keiei-shi-gaku no Niju-nen [Twenty Years of Business History in Japan: Retrospect and prospect]
1985 Tokyo Daigaku Shuppan-kai *Tokyo, Japan*

Reviewing the development of academic research on business history in Japan up to 1985, this book discusses the major results of research into various issues, such as entrepreneurship and managers, business ideologies, zaibatsu, government and industry, finance and Japanese-style management.

78
Chandler, Alfred D. Jr; Tedlow, Richard S. (Editors)
The Coming of Managerial Capitalism: A casebook on the history of American economic institutions
1985 Richard D. Irwin Inc. *Homewood, IL*

A useful textbook of business history cases from the Harvard Business School, ranging from John Jacob Astor, through Samuel Slater, J. P. Morgan, Standard Oil and Du Pont to the modern multinational.

79
Cochran, Thomas C.
American Business in the 20th Century
1972 Harvard University Press *Cambridge, MA*

This general work gives an overview of American business history from 1900 to 1971, seeing essential turning points in 1930 and 1945. It provides an alternative to the case-laden accounts of Al Chandler (qv).

80
Comín, F.; Martín Aceña, P. (Editors)
Empresas y empresarios en la Historia de España [Firms and Entrepreneurs in Spain's History]
1995 Civitas *Madrid, Spain*

This book is probably the most comprehensive general survey of Spanish business history in the nineteenth and twentieth centuries. It covers a large variety of themes and industries.

81
Derdak, Thomas (Editor)
The International Directory of Company Histories
1988 to date St. James Press *Chicago, IL*

The nine volumes of this directory consist of two to five page profiles of 1,800 of the world's largest and most influential companies. It is arranged by industry. Volume 1 covers subjects from Advertising to Drugs; Volume 2, Electrical and Electronics to Food Processing; Volume 3, Health and Personal Care Products to Materials; Volume 4, Mining and Metals to Real Estate; Volume 5, Retail to Waste. Indexed by company and person and with a helpful guide to subsidiaries. Subsequent volumes form appendices covering additional companies. The collection has been prepared on the basis of publicly-available material and tends to be uncritical. However, it provides much useful information in a convenient format.

82
Dunning, John H.; Pearce, Robert D.
The World's Largest Industrial Enterprises 1962–1983
1985 Gower *Aldershot*

This study presents critical data for business historians on the world's largest industrial enterprises for 1962, 1967, 1972, 1977, 1982 and 1983.

83
Hon'iden, Sachio
Keiei-shi: Kigyo Hatten no Hoko [Business History A guide to the development of business]
1966 Nippon Hyoron-sha *Tokyo, Japan*

This business history of Europe, America, Russia and Japan covers the period from ancient times to the 1960s including subsistence agriculture, craft guilds, guild merchants and modern enterprises.

84
Jeremy, David J.; Shaw, Christine (Editors)
Dictionary of Business Biography
1984–6 Butterworths *London*

The first five volumes (in alphabetical sequence of subjects' names) present the business biographies of 1,181 individuals active in Britain (outside Scotland) in the period from the 1860s to the 1960s, written by 447 contributors. Individuals included have been selected by subjective rather than objective criteria. The sixth paperback volume provides indexes to industries, companies and people. While there are omissions, and entries vary in length and quality, the *DBB* itself fills many gaps in the *Dictionary of National Biography*. To be used in conjunction with Slaven & Checkland (qv).

85
Jeremy, David J.; Tweedale, Geoffrey
Dictionary of Twentieth Century British Business Leaders
1994 Bowker-Saur *Sevenoaks*

Useful new dictionary of business leaders, tending to focus on those working in large firms, but including more contemporary material than in the *Dictionary of Business Biography* and *Scottish Dictionary of Business Biography* (qqv).

86
Kurita, Shinzo
Keiei-shi-gaku [Business History]
1971 Maruzen Kabushiki Kaisha *Tokyo, Japan*

This book gives an outline of the mainstream studies in business history mainly in America, Germany and Japan from the 1920s to 1960s.

87
Morikawa, Hidemasa (Editor)
Businessman no tameno Sengo Keiei-shi Nyumon [A Primer of Postwar Japanese Business History for Businessmen]
1992 Nippon Keizai Shinbun-sha *Tokyo, Japan*

Covering the period 1945 to 1990s, this book discusses key factors determining the development of postwar Japanese business including postwar business groups, the iron and steel industry, the computer industry, the general trading company, the automobile industry and so on.

88
Porter, Glenn (Editor)
Encyclopedia of American Economic History: Studies of the principal movements and ideas
1980 Charles Scribner's Sons *New York, NY*

A massive compilation including many significant contributions by leading business historians on important subjects in business history. The three volumes contain around 70 essays contributed by experts providing an introduction to the framework of American growth (Volume 1), the institutional framework (Volume 2) and the social framework (Volume 3). Each essay has a short bibliography to support a fine discussion of the current state of scholarship in the various fields. This provides an excellent starting point for the student of American business history.

89
Sakudo, Yotaro; Mishima, Yasuo; Yasuoka, Shigeaki; Inoue, Yoichiro
Nippon Keiei-shi [Japanese Business History]
1980 Mineruva Shobo *Kyoto, Japan*

Following an introduction on the development of academic approaches to business history, this book gives an outline of Japanese business history from the sixteenth century (the Tokugawa period) to the 1960s. A chronological table of Japanese business history from 1590 to 1978 is included at the end of the book.

90
Slaven, Anthony; Checkland, Sydney (Editors)
Dictionary of Scottish Business Biography
1986–90 Aberdeen University Press *Aberdeen, Scotland*

Nearly 400 individuals active in Scottish industry in the century before 1960 are included in these two volumes. They have been selected because they headed major companies, which in turn have been chosen on the basis of firm size and industry weighting. Entries have been arranged by industry, volume 1 covering the staple industries (mining, metal manufacture, engineering, shipbuilding, chemicals, textiles), volume 2, processing, distribution and services.

91
Wilson, John F.
British Business History, 1720–1994
1995 Manchester University Press *Manchester*

A pioneering textbook that focuses on the manufacturing sector from 1720 to the present day, explaining the development of British industry and its subsequent decline. Wilson argues that company culture has been crucial to the evolution of business organizations and management practices. The Chandler thesis that Britain failed to develop the kind of managerial hierarchies typified by American and German corporations is critically examined.

92
Yasuoka, Shigeaki
Zaibatsu no Keiei-shi [Business History of Zaibatsu]
1978 Nippon Keizai Shinbun-sha *Tokyo, Japan*

After a general discussion on entrepreneurship and strategy of prewar Zaibatsu, this work compares them to family businesses. This is a very informative introduction for scholars who intend to undertake comparative studies.

93
Yonekawa, Shin'ichi
Keiei-shi-gaku: Seitan, Genjo, Tenbo [Business History Origins: The present situation and prospects for the future]
1973 Toyo Keizai Shinpo-sha *Tokyo, Japan*

This book is an excellent summary of the growth and development of various approaches to business history in the USA, UK and Germany from the 1920s to 1960s. This is still highly rated by Japanese business historians as one of the pioneering studies on the history of academic approaches to business history.

94
Yui, Tsunehiko (Editor)
Kogyo-ka to Kigyo-sha Katsudo: Nippon Keiei-shi Koza, vol. 2 [Industrialization and Entrepreneurial Activities: Japanese Business History Series, vol. 2]
1976 Nippon Keizai Shunbun-sha *Tokyo, Japan*

This wide-ranging entrepreneurial history

covers the early years of the Meiji Era (1868–1912). There are chapters on Tomoatsu Godai, the disposal of government-run business, the capital of noblemen and management by descendants of samurai, modern industrial technologies, trade in the concession, corporation law and accounting.

Fuji Conferences

95
Fuji Conferences
Tokyo University Press *Tokyo, Japan*

The Japan Business History Society (founded in 1964) inaugurated, in 1974, a series of international conferences for Japanese researchers and invited foreign scholars to the Fuji Education Center, Shizuoka, Japan. The proceedings of the International Conferences on Business History, known as the Fuji Conferences, mark the progression of the discipline in internationally comparative perspectives and form an excellent introduction to the understanding of both Japanese and Western businesses. Further conferences are planned. The proceedings of the various conferences are listed below.

96
Abe, Etsuo; Suzuki, Yoshitaka (Editors)
Changing Patterns of International Rivalry: Some lessons from the steel industry (Seventeenth Fuji Conference)
1991 Tokyo University Press *Tokyo, Japan*

Changes in the competitive advantage of nations provide the unifying theme for this assessment of a basic staple of industrialization. Useful introduction and conclusion.

97
Kawabe, Nobuo; Daito, Eisuke (Editors)
Education and Training in the Development of Modern Corporations (Nineteenth Fuji Conference)
1993 Tokyo University Press *Tokyo, Japan*

Useful compilation of papers on the significance of education and training systems in the development of modern corporations.

98
Kobayashi, Kesaji; Morikawa, Hidemasa (Editors)
Development of Managerial Enterprise (Twelfth Fuji Conference)
1986 Tokyo University Press *Tokyo, Japan*

As is usual with conference volumes this volume contains a mixed bag. It has especially interesting essays on management training and on large enterprises in small countries.

99
Kudo, Akira; Hara, Terushi (Editors)
International Cartels in Business History (Eighteenth Fuji Conference)
1992 Tokyo University Press *Tokyo, Japan*

Analyses the operations of international cartels in the chemical and electrical industries (see also Sixth Conference) in the interwar period. Strong on factual information, weaker on broader perspectives.

100
Nakagawa, Keiichiro (Editor)
Strategy and Structure of Big Business (First Fuji Conference)
1976 Tokyo University Press *Tokyo, Japan*

The early Japanese attempts at conference book production contained examples of extremely shoddy Japanese workmanship: typesetting and editing quality improve in the later volumes! This is appropriately (if somewhat nominally) linked to a discussion of Chandler's (qv) pathbreaking model and sets the scene for the conference's role in internationally comparative business history.

101
Nakagawa, Keiichiro (Editor)
Social Order and Entrepreneurship (Second Fuji Conference)
1977 Tokyo University Press *Tokyo, Japan*

This contains an interesting set of papers on a difficult subject, which saw some of the best discussion at these conferences. It does not, however, always come out well in this volume.

102
Nakagawa, Keiichiro (Editor)
Marketing & Finance in the Course of Industrialism (Third Fuji Conference)
1978 Tokyo University Press *Tokyo, Japan*

This is a miscellaneous collection which is not clearly focused, though it contains interesting papers on Japan, the USA, France and Britain.

103
Nakagawa, Keiichiro (Editor)
Labor and Management (Fourth Fuji Conference)
1979 Tokyo University Press *Tokyo, Japan*

This is a useful corrective to 'cultural' explanations of labour/management differences, emphasizing the historical process of industrialization and its changing influence on industrial relations, not only in Japan but also in the USA, Britain and Germany.

104
Nakagawa, Keiichiro (Editor)
Government and Business (Fifth Fuji Conference)
1980 Tokyo University Press *Tokyo, Japan*

This volume does not approach the issue of whether Japanese government industrial policy differed from that in the USA, Germany or Britain as directly as political scientists such as Chalmers Johnson but it does provide some useful empirical material.

105
Okochi, Akio; Inoue, Tadakatsu (Editors)
Overseas Business Activities (Ninth Fuji Conference)
1984 Tokyo University Press *Tokyo, Japan*

This volume contains an important collection of essays on international direct and portfolio investments.

106
Okochi, Akio; Simokawa, Koichi (Editors)
Development of Mass Marketing: The automobile and retailing industries (Seventh Fuji Conference)
1981 Tokyo University Press *Tokyo, Japan*

A rather loose collection of essays, dominated by an examination of production and marketing differences in motor manufacturing in the United States and Japan.

107
Okochi, Akio; Uchida, Hoshimi (Editors)
Development and Diffusion of Technology (Sixth Fuji Conference)
1980 Tokyo University Press *Tokyo, Japan*

Examines technological innovation in the chemical and electrical industries in four countries: Japan, Britain, Germany, and the United States.

108
Okochi, Akio; Yasuoka, Shigeaki (Editors)
Family Business in the Era of Industrial Growth: its Ownership and Management (Tenth Fuji Conference)
1984 Tokyo University Press *Tokyo, Japan*

This volume contains excellent essays on family firms in Japan, France, Germany, Britain and the USA, though it is hard to detect common definitions of the phenomenon.

109
Okochi, Akio; Yonekawa, Shin'ichi (Editors)
The Textile Industry and its Business Climate (Eighth Fuji Conference)
1982 Tokyo University Press *Tokyo, Japan*

Despite its title, focuses on the cotton industry and its business climate, here defined as 'the human and natural environmental factors surrounding an enterprise'.

110
Yamazaki, Hiroaki; Miyamoto, Matao (Editors)
Trade Associations in Business History (Fourteenth Fuji Conference)
1988 Tokyo University Press *Tokyo, Japan*

This is perhaps one of the best of the Fuji Conference volumes, containing much material which cannot readily be found elsewhere on a subject generally ignored by business historians.

111
Yonekawa, Shin'ichi; Yoshihara, Hideki (Editors)
Business History of General Trading Companies (Thirteenth Fuji Conference)
1987 Tokyo University Press *Tokyo, Japan*

The aim of this conference was to place Japan's *sogo shosha* or general trading companies in a broader comparative and historical perspective, with case studies of American, British and German as well as Japanese firms. The venture was not entirely successful since these institutions have no direct parallels outside Japan.

112
Yui, Tsunehiko; Nakagawa, Keiichiro (Editors)
Business History of Shipping: Strategy and structure (Eleventh Fuji Conference)
1985 Tokyo University Press *Tokyo, Japan*

Deals with shipping in the nineteenth and early twentieth centuries, with reference to Britain, the USA, Japan, Germany and Denmark. Most contributors concern themselves with issues at the industry level rather than with the problems of individual firms. Topics covered include ownership, finance, impact on world trade, and entrepreneurship.

113
Yui, Tsunehiko; Nakagawa, Keiichiro (Editors)
Japanese Management in Historical Perspective (Fifteenth Fuji Conference)
1989 Tokyo University Press *Tokyo, Japan*

Unlike most Fuji conferences, this one concentrated on Japan, though six foreign experts were invited to review organizational aspects of twentieth-century enterprise, with cultural factors played down.

114
Yuzawa, Takeshi; Udagawa, Masaru (Editors)
Foreign Business in Japan Before World War II (Sixteenth Fuji Conference)
1990 Tokyo University Press *Tokyo, Japan*

These are essays drawn from a Fuji Conference which, like its predecessor, concentrated on a Japanese theme - foreign business operations in Japan.

Business History Review - special issues

115
Business in Latin America
Business History Review, vol. 59, no. 4, 1985

With an introductory essay by H. V. Nelles, this contains studies of Argentinian tobacco trade (Whigham), W. R. Grace in Peru (de Secada), British business in Mexico (Randall), and Enrique Creel's Mexican businesses.

116
Competitiveness and Capital Investment: The restructuring of US industry, 1960–1990
Business History Review, vol. 68, no. 1, 1994

Chandler provides an introductory overview and a major article on the competitive performance of US industrial enterprises since the Second World War. The other articles cover capital budgeting and US investment since 1945 (Baldwin and Clark), and corporate restructuring in the US in the 1970s and 1980s (Hall).

117
Entrepreneurs in Business History
Business History Review, vol. 63, no. 1, 1989

Harold Livesay surveys the literature on entrepreneurship in an introductory essay. The other papers cover black-owned businesses in the nineteenth century South (Schweninger, Kenzer), Rockefeller and the development of Brazilian capital markets (Cobbs), the Guggenheims in Chile (O'Brien). Ed Perkins contributes a review article on entrepreneurship in colonial America.

118
Financial Services
Business History Review, vol. 65, no. 3, 1991

The principal articles cover money and credit in 15th century Yorkshire (Kermode), Rhode Island bankers in the age of Jackson (Lamoreaux and Glaisek), the American life insurance industry after the Civil War (Merkel), and German banking between the Wars (Balderston). Larry Schweikart contributes a historiographical review of the literature on US commercial banking.

119
Government and Business
Business History Review, vol. 64, no. 1, 1990

The principal articles cover corporate liberalism and electric power in the 1920s (DeGraaf), the development of mass consumption of electrical goods in the USA in the 1930s (Field), airline regulation and deregulation (Vietor), and government industry relations in British railways under Thatcher (Gourvish).

120
High-Technology Industries
Business History Review, vol. 66, no. 1, 1992

The principal articles deal with external economies in the microcomputer industry (Langlois), the rivalry of VHS and Beta video systems (Cusumano, Mylonadis and Rosenbloom), Theodore Vail and innovation in the Bell system (Galambos), and intellectual property in the chicken-breeding industry (Bugos).

121
Multinational Enterprise
Business History Review, vol. 62, no. 3, 1988

The principal articles cover family partnerships and international trade in early modern Europe (Mathers), the chartered trading companies as predecessors of modern multinationals (Carlos and Nicholas), interwar German business in Scandinavia (Schröter), Norton Company under the Third Reich (Cheape) and multinational competition in the British advertising agency business (West).

122
Real Estate in Business History
Business History Review, vol. 63, no. 2, 1989

There is an extensive introductory overview of the literature on real estate history by Marc Weiss, followed by articles on the redevelopment of Baltimore after the Fire of 1904 (Rosen), Henry Huntington and the growth of Southern California (Fredericks), city development in Columbus, Ohio (Stach) and terminating building societies in Quebec City (Paterson and Shearer).

123
Resource Based Industries
Business History Review, vol. 62, no. 4, 1988

The principal articles cover the decline of US whaling (Davis, Gallman and Hutchins), conservation in the Maine lobster industry (Judd), mechanization in the Pacific salmon-canning industry (Newell), and medical screening in the tri-State Zinc-Lead industries (Derickson).

124
Small Business and Its Rivals
Business History Review, vol. 65, no. 1, 1991

Mansel Blackford's introductory essay surveys the historiography of small business. The other articles deal with flexible production during American industrialization (Scranton), the American corset trade (Smith), and dime store chains (Raucher).

125
The Automobile Industry
Business History Review, vol. 65, no. 4, 1991

The principal articles deal with marketing and manufacturing in the interwar US auto industry (Raff), the modernization of the interwar French automobile industry (Cohen), supplier relations in the US auto industry (Helper), Bruce Barton and the revolution in marketing at General Motors (Marchand), and determinants of multinational entry into the Brazilian auto industry in the 1950s (Shapiro).

126
Transportation
Business History Review, vol. 58, no. 1, 1984

Contains an introductory essay by Albro Martin, and studies of technological innovation on the railroads (Usselman), government and highway building (Seeley), Hoover and commercial aviation (Lee), and the English coal trade (Ville, Hausman).

Business History - special issues

127

Abe, Etsuo; Fitzgerald, Robert (Editors)
The Origins of Japanese Industrial Power: Strategy, institutions and the development of organizational capability
Business History, vol. 37, no. 2, 1995

Seven articles by Japanese business historians examine the timing of industrialization and economic development, the influence of national culture on management and the industrial system, and the development of competitive advantage.

128

Davenport-Hines, R. P. T.; Jones, Geoffrey (Editors)
The End of Insularity: Essays in Comparative Business History
Business History, vol. 30, no. 1, 1988

This is an important collection of essays, including contributions from Howard Gospel, Robert Locke and Mira Wilkins.

128/1

Davenport-Hines, R. P. T.; Jones, Geoffrey (Editors)
Entrepreneurship, Management and Innovation in British Business 1914–80
For main entry, see 3706

129

Harvey, Charles (Editor)
Business History: Concepts and measurement
Business History, vol. 31, no. 3, 1989

Through a series of case studies, this collection demonstrates how simple statistical analysis can illuminate source-driven research.

130

Harvey, Charles; Jones, Geoffrey (Editors)
Organisational Capability and Competitive Advantage
Business History, vol. 34, no. 1, 1992

A series of papers set in the perspective of the views of Chandler and Porter, sharply pointed up by Tweedale's description of the failure of Ferranti to capitalize on its early lead in computers.

131

Harvey, Charles; Press, Jon (Editors)
International Competition and Industrial Change: Essays in the history of mining and metallurgy 1800–1950
Business History, vol. 32, no. 3, 1990

Within the context of the industry, this collection examines topics as diverse as the role of multi-national enterprise, raising capital, labour relations, and the influence of engineers and advancing technology.

132

Harvey, Charles; Turner, John (Editors)
Labour and Business in Modern Britain
Business History, vol. 31, no. 2, 1989

This provides a series of studies of episodes in British industrial relations covering, among others, railways, engineering, car manufacture and flour milling.

133

Jones, Geoffrey (Editor)
Banks and Money: International and comparative finance in history
Business History, vol. 33, no. 3, 1991

Includes contributions by Perkins, Cottrell, Cassis, Marchildon, Lamoreaux, Sjögren, Geiger & Ross, Bostock and Burke, this deals with both financial systems and international banking.

134

Jones, Geoffrey (Editor)
The Making of Global Enterprise
Business History, vol. 36, no. 1, 1994

A set of essays providing important insights on the history of international businesses.
Firms: Bell Telephone; Vickers; Du Pont; ICI; IG Farben; Ford

135

Jones, Geoffrey; Rose, Mary B. (Editors)
Family Capitalism
Business History, vol. 35, no. 4, 1993

A series of studies of family-owned businesses in a wide range of environments and from the eighteenth century onwards demonstrate flexibility and entrepreneurial drive, directly confronting the Chandler/Lazonick argument that family enterprise is inappropriate in the second industrial revolution.

136
Marchildon, Gregory P.; McDowall, Duncan (Editors)
Canadian Multinationals and International Finance
Business History, vol. 34, no. 3, 1992

This series of studies examines the important role of Canadian banks in international business and investment.

137
Rose, Mary B. (Editor)
International Competition and Strategic Response in the Textile Industries since 1870
Business History, vol. 32, no. 4, 1990

Contains a long essay by Mass and Lazonick reviewing the debate on the sources of competitive advantage or decline. Robertson, Dupree and Singleton describe complacency and pessimism leading to disaster, Jenkins and Malin, a rather different outcome in the woollen industry, Farnie, the textile machine business and Chapman, changes in merchanting.

138
Ullenhag, Kersti (Editor)
Nordic Business in the Long View: On control and strategy in structural change
Business History, vol. 35, no. 2, 1993

Largely concerned with Swedish industry, the authors find departures from the Chandler three-stage model; in many cases owners and/or financiers have retained control, as shown in industry case-studies.

Journals on Business History

139
Accounting, Business and Financial History
Routledge (3 issues per year) *London*

Published since 1990, this journal seeks to link business history and accounting history. It contains good quality academic articles and selective book reviews.

140
Annali Di Storia Dell'Impresa
Fondazione Assi/Franco Angeli (annual)
Milan, Italy

First published in 1984, this is the yearbook for business history in Italy.

141
Business and Economic History
Business History Conference (2 issues per year) *Williamsburg, VA*

This is the journal of the American Business History Conference and has been published since 1971. It is based on the publication of selected articles presented at the Conference's annual meeting.

142
Business Archives
Business Archives Council (2 issues per year)
London

Published since 1934, this is the bulletin of the Business Archives Council. It contains articles, details of recent deposits, book reviews and a regular bibliography.

143
Business History
F. Cass & Co. (4 issues per year) *London*

Published since 1958, this is the principal British journal of business history. Since 1990 it has carried an extensive annual review of new publications in British business history. It published frequent special issues, several of which have been republished as books (qv).

144
Business History Review
Harvard Business School Press (4 issues per year) *Boston, MA*

Published continuously since 1926, this is the leading American journal of business history. It has published numerous special issues (qv) and its book review section is very comprehensive.

145
Economic History Review
Basil Blackwell (4 issues per year) *Oxford*

The journal of the Economic History Association regularly carries articles of interest to business historians. Since 1950 it has carried a regular annual listing of books and articles on the economic history of Britain and Ireland (with a section on business history) published in the preceding year. It also publishes annual reviews of periodical literature, and has an extensive book review section.

146
Entreprises et Histoire
Editions ESKA *Paris, France*

A new French journal launched in 1992, specializing in the business history of France and other industrializing countries from the eighteenth century.

147
Essays in Economic and Business History
University of Southern California, Economic and Business Historical Society (annual) *Los Angeles, CA*

Published since 1982, this is an annual volume based on articles presented to the annual meeting of the Economic and Business Historical Society. A wide variety of subjects is covered in each issue and the articles are often short or based on work in progress.

148
Financial History Review
Cambridge University Press (2 issues per year) *Cambridge*

First published in 1994, this is an international journal designed for scholars in all areas of the history of banking, finance and monetary matters. It covers all historical periods and encourages international and comparative studies as well as those focused on national, regional and local affairs.

149
German Yearbook on Business History
German Society for Business History and Institute for Bank-Historical Research (annual) *Frankfurt, Germany*

Annual (since 1985) publication providing vital information on work in the business history field.

150
Industrial and Corporate Change
Oxford University Press (4 issues per year) *Oxford*

Published since 1992, this is an innovative interdisciplinary journal, publishing work on competition and industrial structure, technical change, strategy, the sociology of management, the labour process, and business history with an emphasis on contributions to theoretical and analytic issues. It has been particularly strong on the analysis of technical change and industrial structure.

151
Japanese Yearbook on Business History
Japan Business History Institute *Tokyo, Japan*

Annual series (since 1984) which provides an extremely useful compendium of Japanese publications in the field. The Yearbook is published in English.

152
Journal of Economic History
Cambridge University Press (4 issues per year) *New York, NY*

The journal of the American Economic History Association publishes high quality articles, with a particular emphasis on quantitative economic history. It contains many articles of interest to business historians and an extensive book review section.

153
Journal of European Economic History
Banco di Roma (3 issues per year) *Rome, Italy*

Published since 1972, this journal regularly carries articles on European business history as well as wider coverage of European economic history. It publishes selective, extended book reviews.

154
Technology and Culture
University of Chicago Press (4 issues per year) *Chicago, IL*

First published in 1959 and supported by the Smithsonian Institute, this journal has paid increased attention to business and institutional features of technological change since the 1970s and is now an important forum for the history of business and technological change. It has played an important role in the emergence of 'socio-technical' interpretation of technical change. It contains an extensive book review section and regular historiographical review essays.

155
Zeitschrift für Unternehmensgeschichte
Franz Steiner Verlag (3 issues per year)
Stuttgart, Germany

First published as *Tradition* in 1956, this is the journal of the German Society of Business History.

Accounting Histories

156
Baxter, W. T. (Editor)
Studies in Accounting Theory
1950 Sweet & Maxwell *London* 1990 Garland Publishing *New York and London*

This book was prepared on behalf of the then newly established association of university teachers of accounting. Together with Littleton and Yamey (1956) and Solomons (1952) (qqv), it represents a landmark in the development of British literature on accounting.

157
Chatfield, Michael
A History of Accounting Thought
1977 Robert E. Krieger Publishing *New York and London*

This book is mainly a history of ideas rather than a chronicle of events for a factual study. Relevance to contemporary problems was a primary test for the inclusion of material. The writing style is designed to enable the text to be read by those with no more than an elementary knowledge of accounting.

158
Edwards, John Richard
A History of Financial Accounting
1989 Routledge *London and New York*

This is the first book to examine in detail the development of British financial accounting practices. It deals with the evolution of accounting from earliest times, and gives particular attention to corporation accounting development since the industrial revolution. The author seeks to identify the various sources of accounting practices employed by British companies, to demonstrate the main changes which have taken place, when they occurred, and why.

159
Edwards, John Richard (Editor)
Twentieth-Century Accounting Thinkers
1994 Routledge *London*

This is the first major international review of accounting theory to focus on the contributions of its leading thinkers. It is a reflection of the nature of accounting as a practical discipline that each of the thinkers discussed shows concern to use accounting theory to help solve practical thinking problems. Each entry is written by an expert on his/her subject.

160
Garrett, Alexander A.
History of the Society of Incorporated Accountants, 1885–1957
1961 privately published, Oxford University Press *Oxford*

This is a standard descriptive account of the foundations and growth a major British professional body until its liquidation. It was written by its secretary (1919–49).

161
Howitt, Harold
The History of the Institute of Chartered Accountants in England and Wales 1880–1965: And of its founder accountancy bodies 1870–1880
1966 Heinemann *London* 1984 Garland Publishing *New York*

This work narrates the history of the ICAEW and then details students' societies and overseas activities, examinations and education, discipline, membership, founder firms and past presidents. The book contains a useful bibliography.

162

Jones, Rowan Harrison

The History of the Financial Control Function of Local Government Accounting in the United Kingdom

1992 Garland Publishing *London and New York*

This book explains why local governments in the United Kingdom adopted various financial accounting techniques, examining the history of local government accounting from the Middle Ages onwards. It argues that the techniques used today date from the nineteenth century, having been imposed as part of the financial control of elected local governments by the central government. It is probably the best overview of accounting developments in the local government sector.

163

Kedslie, Moyra J.

Firm Foundations: The development of professional accounting in Scotland

1990 Hull University Press *Hull*

The Scots are proud of the fact that professional accounting bodies were first established in that country. This book discusses their development from 1850 to 1900 and examines their monopolistic success in several areas of professional work. It explores the cooperation and competition amongst them and their fruitless attempts to provide for the registration of accountants.

164

Lee, T. A. (Editor)

The Evolution of Audit Thought and Practice

1988 Garland Publishing *New York and London*

This is a volume of reprinted articles which comprise a detailed overview of the changes which have occurred in audit thinking and practice during the last two centuries. The material covers general and specific issues, and examines the influences and pressures of individuals, legislation and regulation, and organizations.

165

Lee, T. A. (Editor)

The Closure of the Accounting Profession

1990 Garland Publishing *New York and London*

Using historical writings, this text examines the development of accounting in society - particularly the creation of an organizational structure to maintain a monopoly of service by control of its body of knowledge. The analysis presents accounting as the social system involving closures through institutionalizing and legitimating processes. It provides a historical context for understanding contemporary issues in accounting.

166

Littleton, Ananias Charles

Accounting Evolution to 1900

1933 American Institute Publishing Co. *New York, NY* 1988 Garland Publishing *New York and London*

Written in 1933, this is undoubtedly the best wide-ranging study of the development of accounting up to 1900.

167

Littleton, Ananias Charles; Yamey, Basil (Editors)

Studies in the History of Accounting

1956 Arno Press *New York, NY*

The principal focus of this book is to illuminate major aspects of the long history of double entry bookkeeping, but it also gives attention to certain nineteenth-century developments in financial reporting. It is still the best single text on bookkeeping developments.

168

Mepham, M. J.

Accounting in Eighteenth-Century Scotland

1988 Garland Publishing *New York and London*

This comprehensive study documents the appearance of an embryonic Scottish accounting profession and the achievements of the Scottish enlightenment. It is a meticulous work, packed with informative detail.

169

Parker, R. H.; Yamey, B. S. (Editors)

Accounting History: Some British contributions

1994 Clarendon Press *Oxford*

This brings together contributions by major British scholars in the field of accounting history research, grouped under the following headings: the ancient world; before double entry; double entry corporate accounting; local government accounting; cost and management accounting, notably in the shipping, railway and textile industries; accounting theory; and accounting in context.

170
Previts, Gary John; Merino, Barbara Dubis
A History of Accounting in America: An historical interpretation of the culture significance of accounting
1979 Ronald Press *New York, NY*

Each chapter tackles, chronologically, the social, political, economic and personal elements of important eras - from Puritan to modern times. The breadth of coverage precludes in-depth analysis of any single factor, but attempts to portray the humour, anecdotes, warm friendships, and bitter controversies that underlay the progression of events.

171
Solomons, David
Studies in Costing
1952 Sweet & Maxwell *London*

This is a wide-ranging study of costing practices in the 1950s, which is introduced by a substantial historical section containing David Solomons's classic paper on 'The Historical Development of Costing'.

172
Stacey, Nicholas A. H.
English Accountancy 1800–1954: A study in social and economic history
1954 Gee *London*

This is the first major study of the development of the 'English' accountancy profession. It places developments in a social and economic context and was written at an American university with the aid of an award by the American government.

173
Yamey, B. S.; Edey, H. C.; Thompson, Hugh W.
Accounting in England and Scotland, 1543–1800
1963 Sweet & Maxwell *London* 1982 Garland Publishing *New York, NY*

The first section of this reference book contains over 100 extracts from 32 books on accounting up to 1818. It contains a representative selection of the content of early accounting treatises. The second part contains a survey of books in English up to 1800 and an analysis of eight sets of extant account-books dating from the seventeenth and eighteenth centuries.

174
Zeff, Stephen A.
Forging Accounting Principles in Five Countries: A history and an analysis of trends
1972 Stipes Publishing *Champaign, IL*

This major study of the development of accounting principles during the present century contains a comparative analysis of developments in five countries.

Primary and Extractive Industries

Agriculture, Europe

175
Brown, Jonathan
Agriculture in England: A survey of farming, 1870–1947
1987 Manchester University Press *Manchester*
Brown gives a succinct account of English farming development covering organization and technology and the changing pattern of markets. State intervention is also discussed.

176
Cooper, Andrew Fenton
British Agricultural Policy, 1912–36: A study in conservative politics
1989 Manchester University Press *Manchester*
This is a valuable study of British agricultural policy focusing on that of the Conservative Party between the wars. The book conveys well the different strands of thinking and reaction to left-radical policy prescriptions.

177
Dewey, Peter
British Agriculture in the First World War
1989 Routledge *London*
This is the definitive account of state–industry relations during the First World War, notable for its conclusion that the war did not mark a significant discontinuity in agriculture's sectoral decline.

178
Farquharson, J. E.
The Plough and the Swastika: The NSDAP and agriculture in Germany, 1928–1945
1976 Sage *Beverly Hills, CA*
This book examines peasant support for the Nazis and the impact of Nazi autarky policies. The Nazis significantly aided German farmers 1933–6, but thereafter farmers suffered from price controls. The emphasis throughout is on peasant agriculture rather than the Junkers.

179
Holderness, B. A.
British Agriculture since 1945
1985 Manchester University Press *Manchester*
This book gives a concise account of the postwar development of British agriculture, focusing on the record of state intervention in general and activities of marketing boards in particular. The book also analyses price and productivity movements and the pattern of investment.

180
Holderness, B. A.; Turner, Michael (Editors)
Land, Labour and Agriculture, 1700–1920: Essays for Gordon Mingay
1991 Hambledon Press *London*
A valuable collection of essays including coverage of the decline of small landowners, the origins of high farming, information and innovation in early Victorian farming, landlord investment and developments in agricultural technologies. It also covers labour themes extensively.

181
Koning, Niek
The Failure of Agrarian Capitalism: Agrarian politics in the UK, Germany, the Netherlands and the USA, 1840–1916
1994 Routledge *London*
A comparative examination of the failure of agriculture to establish itself as a profitable industry in northern Europe and the United States from the Corn Laws to the First World War.

182
Kuuse, Jan
Interaction Between Agriculture and Industry: Studies of farm mechanisation and industrialisation in Sweden and the United States 1830–1930
For main entry, see 1389

183
Loubère, Leo A.
The Red and the White: A history of wine in France and Italy in the nineteenth century
For main entry, see 1863

184
Mingay, G. E. (Editor)
The Agrarian History of England and Wales: Vol. 6, 1750–1850
1989 Cambridge University Press *Cambridge*

A colossal work that contains an enormous amount of information about the business of agriculture. Topics covered include markets and marketing, the agricultural servicing and processing industries, land ownership and estate management, and rural labour. A high scholarly standard is maintained throughout.

185
Moeller, Robert G.
German Peasants and Agrarian Politics, 1914–1924: Rhineland and Westphalia
1986 University of North Carolina Press *Chapel Hill, NC*

Moeller traces the roots of peasant hostility to the Weimar Republic to the structures of the agricultural economy, especially the suspension of functioning markets after the First World War, and prolonged state intervention which created a mass of grievances.

186
Moeller, Robert G. (Editor)
Peasants and Lords in Modern Germany: Recent studies in agricultural history
1986 Allen & Unwin *Winchester, MA*

This book presents a sequence of essays by German, British and American scholars on aspects of German agricultural history in the first half of the twentieth century. It is of interest to business historians principally on account of the chapters on the political economy of estate ownership.

187
Perren, Richard
The Meat Trade in Britain 1840–1914
For main entry, see 2051

188
Perry, P. J.
British Farming in the Great Depression, 1870–1914: An historical geography
1974 David & Charles *Newton Abbot*

A thorough study of farming in a crucial period, especially concentrating on land ownership, farm finance, legislation, and the changing practice of farming.

189
Self, Peter; Storing, H. J.
The State and the Farmer
1962 University of California Press *Berkeley, CA*

A good study of the state and the farmer in Britain in the 1950s, outstanding on the role of the farmers in influencing agricultural policy and on relations with farm workers.

190
Smith, Martin J.
The Politics of Agricultural Support in Britain: The development of the agricultural policy community
1990 Gower *Dartmouth*

Smith questions the view that the level of state support for agriculture in Britain can be explained by the organization and resources of the National Farmers' Union. He traces the links between the NFU and the Ministry of Agriculture from the 1930s, when relations were not very close, through its institutionalization in the Second World War, and through the threats posed by the Common Agricultural Policy.

191
Tracy, Michael
Government and Agriculture in Western Europe, 1880–1988
3rd Edition
1989 New York University Press *New York, NY*

Tracy presents an authoritative analysis of the fluctuating fortunes of agriculture in Western Europe from the 1880s to the inception of the Common Agricultural Policy. Whilst sympathetic to the plight of farmers, the author is generally critical of government policies.

192
Verhulst, A.; Vandenbroeke, C. (Editors)
Landbouwproduktiviteit in Vlaanderen en Brabant, 14 de–18 de eeuw/ Productivité agricole en Flandre et en Brabant, 14e–18e siècle [Agricultural Productivity in Flanders and Brabant 14th–18th Century]
1979 Rijksuniversiteit te Gent *Ghent, Belgium*

This is a collection of seven essays by Belgian historians on the agricultural history of the Low Countries from the fourteenth to the eighteenth centuries. The approach is quantitative which serves to confirm the record of static productivity in relation to the limited sample of evidence offered.

193
Whetham, Edith H. (Editor)
The Agrarian History of England and Wales: Vol. 8, 1914–1939
1978 Cambridge University Press *Cambridge*

While there is less on business aspects of agriculture in this volume than in the earlier one edited by Mingay (qv) there is still substantial material on government policies, pricing, and technological and other changes in farming practice in the interwar years.

Agriculture, North America

194
Atack, Jeremy; Bateman, Fred
To Their Own Soil: Agriculture in the antebellum north
1987 Iowa State University Press *Ames, IA*

This is an authoritative analysis of farming and the farming community in the northern USA in the antebellum period. The book emphasises the pre-war role of agriculture in American economy and society and points to the non-pecuniary attractions of rural life.

195
Badger, Anthony J.
Prosperity Road: The New Deal, tobacco and North Carolina
For main entry, see 1809

196
Breen, David H.
The Canadian Prairie West and the Ranching Frontier 1874–1924
1983 University of Toronto Press *Toronto, Canada*

A history of the Canadian range cattle industry is given here, offering contrasts and comparisons with its US counterpart, especially with regard to the differing roles of government in determining land occupancy.

197
Broehl, Wayne G. Jr
Cargill: Trading the World's Grain
For main entry, see 3934

198
Brunson, B. R.
The Texas Land Development Company
For main entry, see 2641

199
Carlson, Paul H.
Texas Woollybacks: The range sheep and goat industry
1982 Texas A & M University Press *College Station, TX*

An excellent account is given here of sheep and goat farming in Texas from the period of Spanish occupation to 1940.

200
Clark, John G.
The Grain Trade in the Old Northwest
1966 University of Illinois Press *Urbana, IL*

Clark's is a valuable study of the grain trade in the north-western United States in the period 1815 to 1860. It provides an excellent discussion of the impact of transport improvements and this is neatly complemented by extensive analysis of changing patterns of demand.

201
Clarke, Sally H.
Regulation and the Revolution in US Farm Productivity
1994 Cambridge University Press *Cambridge*

Clarke argues that regulation acted in tandem with farmers' competitive markets to create a dynamic process for productivity growth.

In particular, it stimulated large-scale investment in tractors by stabilizing prices and introducing new sources of credit. Rapid growth in productivity was followed by a shake-out in favour of aggressive farmers investing in land and technology.
Firms: International Harvester; Ford; Metropolitan Life Insurance Co.; Northwestern Mutual Life Insurance Co.

202
Clingerman, Harold Bennett
Field Man: The chronicle of a bank farm manager in the 1940s
1989 Iowa State University Press *Ames, IA*

This revealing account of the state of agriculture in Nebraska in the 1940s is written from the perspective of a bank employee responsible for the management and liquidation of firms taken over by banks in consequence of the Great Depression of the 1930s. The author presents a good case for the sympathetic attitude of bankers to farmers in financial difficulty.

203
Cochrane, Willard W.; Ryan, Mary E.
American Farm Policy, 1948–1973
1976 University of Minnesota Press *Minneapolis, MN*

A survey of aspects of US farm policy emphasizing their New Deal roots, this book is notable for its defence of farming interests.

204
Danbom, David B.
The Resisted Revolution: Urban America and the industrialization of agriculture, 1900–1930
1979 Iowa State University Press *Ames, IO*

A study of the Country Life Movement and its attempts at reform and modernization of rural America in the early 20th century, and the resistance by farmers to urban attempts to import radical social change into the countryside. It is argued that it was increased productivity in US farming rather than political resistance which ultimately made the 'reform' movement effective.

205
Danhof, Clarence H.
Changes in Agriculture: The northern United States, 1820–1870
1969 Harvard University Press *Cambridge, MA*

Danhof has made a useful study of the transition from semi-subsistence to commercial farming in the USA, concentrating on financial issues and the management of agricultural enterprise.

206
Daniel, Pete
Breaking the Land: The transformation of cotton, tobacco, and rice cultures since 1880
1985 University of Illinois Press *Champaign, IL*

An analysis of the fluctuating fortunes of southern agriculture is made here, focusing on structural evolution and the resulting human dislocation. Effective comparisons and contrasts are offered on each of the sectors covered. A subsidiary theme is provided by federal policies for agriculture, notably through the work of the Agricultural Adjustment Administration and its successors.

207
De-Canio, Stephen J.
Agriculture in the Postbellum South: The economics of production and supply
1974 MIT Press *Cambridge, MA*

This highly competent quantitative study (based on previously published work) of the Southern cotton farming industry after 1865, focuses on the alleged exploitation of agricultural labour, productivity differences, relative prices and the development of alternative crops.

208
Dethloff, Henry C.
A History of the American Rice Industry, 1685–1985
1988 Texas A & M University Press *College Station, TX*

A succinct account is given here of the development of the American rice industry, noting its geographical spread and market penetration, both at home and abroad.

209
Dorel, Gérard
Agriculture et grandes entreprises aux États-Unis [Agriculture and Large Businesses in the United States]
1985 Economica *Paris, France*

Based on a Doctorat d'État, this book explores the role of big agribusiness in North American agriculture. Case studies of Florida and California show the pressure put on small family enterprises (the traditional mainstay of US agriculture) by the big companies.

210
Drache, Hiram M.
Beyond the Furrow: Some keys to successful farming in the twentieth century
1976 Interstate Printers and Publishers *Danville, IL*

This is a detailed account of farming development in north-central USA emphasizing technology and the farmer's role as a business manager.

211
Ebeling, Walter
The Fruited Plain: The story of American agriculture
1980 University of California Press *Berkeley, CA*

This is a thoughtful study of American agricultural history which questions the modern technological base of the farm sector, most notably in California.

212
Ferleger, Lon (Editor)
Agriculture and National Development: Views on the nineteenth century
1990 Iowa State University Press *Ames, IA*

This is an edited and authoritative collection of essays on US farming in the nineteenth century focusing on farm life and society. Organizational issues are discussed with respect both to northern and southern agriculture.

213
Fite, Gilbert C.
Beyond the Fence Rows: A history of Farmland Industries Inc. 1929–1978
1978 University of Missouri Press *Columbia, MO*

This is a history of the Consumers Cooperative Association (Farmland Industries Inc. after 1966), a highly successful farmers' cooperative, in American agriculture, notable for its focus on the corporate-style activities of the corporation in relation to competition, labour disputes and relations with government.
Firms: Consumers Cooperative Association; Farmland Industries Inc; Union Oil Co.

214
Fitzgerald, Deborah
The Business of Breeding: Hybrid corn in Illinois, 1890–1940
1990 Cornell University Press *Ithaca, NY*

This is a pioneering study that uses the invention and development of hybrid corn as a stepping off point for an exploration of US agribusiness and the process of turning science into technology. It provides a detailed analysis of the relationship between the major companies and the universities and the process of technological innovation that enabled the giant companies to dominate the industry through the development of hybridization technology.
Firms: Funk Brothers; DeKalb Agricultural Association; Pfister Hybrids

215
Friedberger, Mark
Farm Families and Change in Twentieth Century America
1988 U Press of Kentucky *Lexington, KY*

An examination of family farming enterprise in twentieth-century America is made here, set against a background of technological change, ownership concentration and periodic credit crises. The analytical focus is on the Iowa Corn Belt and the Central Valley of California.

216
Havens, A. Eugene; Hooks, Gregory; Mooney, Patrick H.; Pfeffer, Max J.
Studies in the Transformation of US Agriculture
1986 Westview Press *Boulder, CO*

The historical development of US agriculture is discussed by several contributors from the point of view of critical rural sociology. The book covers the accumulation process, changes in the class structure on the land, state agricultural policies, and changes in the labour process.

217
Hoag, W. Gifford
The Farm Credit System: A history of financial self-help
1976 Interstate Printers and Publishers *Danville, IL*

This informed account of the farm credit system covers its role in financing US agriculture from its inception in 1916.

218
Holden, Frances Mayhogh
Lambshead Before Interwoven: A Texas range chronicle, 1848–1878
1982 Texas A & M University Press *College Station, TX*

This book is an informed synthesis of the early development of ranching in West Texas.

219
Holden, William Curry
The Espuela Land and Cattle Company
1970 Texas State Historical Association *Austin, TX*

A study is made here of company-based ranching activity in Texas during the nineteenth and early twentieth centuries, of use to business historians for its account of ranch management and other economic aspects of ranch operations.

Firms: Espuela Land and Cattle Co.

220
McGregor, Alexander Campbell
Counting Sheep: From open range to agribusiness on the Columbia plateau
1982 University of Washington Press *Seattle, WA*

McGregor has made a detailed study of livestock farming on the Columbia plateau in Washington, Oregon and Idaho from the 1850s to the 1970s. The book focuses on the McGregor Land and Livestock Company's role as a family enterprise committed to sheep, cattle and hog-raising as a precursor to diversification into other agricultural sectors.

Firms: McGregor Land and Livestock Company

221
McInnis, R. Marrin
Perspectives on Ontario Agriculture
1992 Langdale Press *Gananoque, Ont., Canada*

A collection of essays on the history of agriculture in Upper Canada in the nineteenth and twentieth centuries, useful to business historians for its commentary on the changing market and productive structures.

222
Moore, John H.
The Emergence of the Cotton Kingdom in the Old Southwest: Mississippi, 1770–1860
1988 Louisiana State University Press *Baton Rouge, LA*

Moore examines the cotton economy in Mississippi, emphasizing the technical changes that transformed cotton plantations into the equivalent of factories, and slaves into skilled and highly productive farm workers. Moore argues that Mississippi was a pioneer in progressive farm methods. He also considers the role of steamboats and railroads and local banking structures.

Firms: Gullett Gladney & Co.; Mississippi Manufacturing Co.

223
Pisani, Donald J.
From the Family Farm to Agribusiness: The irrigation crusade in California and the West, 1850–1931
1984 University of California Press *Berkeley, CA*

This book studies Californian agriculture through the prism of irrigation, linking issues of land monopoly and concentration, social and economic reform, and agricultural progress. The key theme is the persistent mismanagement and ineffectiveness of both private enterprise and government in regulating the use of water, and the role of business lobbies.

Firms: Fresno Canal and Irrigation Co.; Kern County Land and Water Co.; San Joaquin and King's River Canal Co.; Southern Pacific Railroad

224
Saloutos, Theodore
The American Farmer and the New Deal
1982 Iowa State University Press *Ames, IA*

An authoritative account of the origins of, and impact of, New Deal policies on American farms in the interwar period is presented here. The organizational structure is exceptionally lucid, based on a firm appreciation of demand and supply factors and relevant interlinkages. Whilst sympathetic to the New Deal the author qualifies his judgements carefully by reference to its limited provision for tenants, sharecroppers and farm labourers.

225
Scarborough, William Kauffman
The Overseer: Plantation management in the Old South
For main entry, see 4226

226
Schlebecker, John T.
Whereby We Thrive: A history of American farming, 1607–1972
1975 Iowa State University Press *Ames, IA*

Schlebecker's is an informed, narrative account of the development of American agriculture from the colonial period onwards, of interest to business historians mainly for its detailed description of technological developments.

227
Schwartz, Marvin
Tyson: From farm to market
For main entry, see 1640

228
Scott, Roy V.
The Reluctant Farmer: The rise of agricultural extension to 1914
1970 University of Illinois Press *Urbana, IL*

This is a first-rate study of the spread of technical education in US farming in the period to 1914. Concentrating on the extension movement, the book highlights the role of businessmen in disseminating technical and scientific knowledge to farmers.

229
Skaggs, Jimmy M.
The Cattle Trailing Industry: Between supply and demand, 1866–1890
1973 U Press of Kansas *Lawrence, KS*

This is a useful account of the development of cattle trailing from Texas to Kansas in its post-Civil War heyday. Individual entrepreneurial strategies are reviewed effectively.
Firms: Lythe, McDaniel, Schreiner and Light Cattle Co.

230
Walsh, Margaret
The Rise of the Midwestern Meat Packing Industry
For main entry, see 1645

231
Whitaker, James W.
Feedlot Empire: Bay cattle feeding in Illinois and Iowa, 1840–1900
1975 Iowa State University Press *Ames, IA*

Whitaker gives a competent account of the development of beef cattle feeding which concentrates on technological and market developments. The role of the railroad is viewed as critical to the industry's expansion, especially after the innovation of the refrigeration car in the late 1870s.

232
Wik, Reynold M.
Steam Power on the American Farm
For main entry, see 1395

233
Williams, Robert C.
Fordson, Farmall and Poppin' Johnny: A history of the farm tractor and its impact on America
1987 University of Illinois Press *Urbana, IL*

This highly readable study of the diffusion of the tractor describes its impact on the economic and social life of American farmers in the twentieth century. It is of use to business historians for its commentary of the evolving structure of the tractor industry and the sources of productivity and market advantage.
Firms: Allis-Chalmers; Fordson; International Harvester Co.; John Deere

234

Wines, Richard A.

Fertilizer in America: From waste recycling to resource exploitation

1985 Temple University Press *Philadelphia, PA*

A history of the shift from recycling wastes to the development of commercial fertilizers in response to market pressures from the growth of East Coast cities in the USA during the 19th century. Cities resulted in increased demand and produced problems for the recycling of organic wastes from farms. The result was a turn first to Peruvian guano and then to the manufacture of superphosphates. Wines sees fertilizers as part of a technology system involving manufacturers, farms and mass consumers and argues that it is an example of the evolutionary development of a complex technological system. This is a far broader study than the title suggests.

Firms: Pacific Guano Co.; Antony Gibbs and Sons; Baugh and Sons

235

Wood, Charles L.

The Kansas Beef Industry

1980 Regents Press of Kansas *Lawrence, KS*

Wood's well-researched study of the Kansas beef-cattle industry covers the period from the 1890s to the 1970s. It charts innovations in breeding, entrepreneurial origins, and organizational developments. The main focus of the book is an analysis of the Kansas Livestock Association, representing the state's leading producers.

Firms: Kansas Livestock Association

Agriculture, Rest of World

236

Abbott, G. J.

The Pastoral Age: A re-examination

1971 Macmillan *Melbourne, Australia*

Abbott gives an intelligent assessment of the growth of raw wool production and export from the time of European settlement to the middle of the nineteenth century. Areas of focus include sheep-breeding, station finance, labour shortages, profitability, government policy and the place of wool production in the early economic development of Australia.

237

Barnard, A.

The Australian Wool Market

1958 Melbourne University Press *Melbourne, Australia*

This is an excellent study of the institutions of the wool export market from Australia to Britain in the nineteenth century. The study focuses on the change from small scale wool sales to colonial merchants at the beginning of the century, to an organized consignment trade to London in mid-century and finally the relocation of the wool market to Australia at the end of the period and the growth of large wool-trading firms.

Firms: Australian Agricultural Co.; Bank of New South Wales; Dalgety; Elder Smith; Gibbs Ronald & Co.; Goldsborough Mort

238

Bejarano, Jesús A. (Editor)

El Siglo XIX en Colombia Visto por Historiadores Norteamericanos [The Nineteenth Century in Colombia: The American historians' view]

For main entry, see 2957

239

Bergquist, Charles

Café y Conflicto en Colombia, 1886–1904: La guerra de los mil dias: sus antecedentes y consecuencias [Coffee and Conflict in Colombia, 1886–1904: Origins and outcomes of the war of the thousand days]

1978 Duke University Press *Durham, NC*

This volume is focused on the political consequences of the expansion of Colombia's coffee export economy during the 1886–1910 period. In analysing the economic interests among different business groups related to the coffee economy, the author disputes other politically based explanations of Colombia's longest civil war during the nineteenth century and its consequences. It is carefully written and based on thorough research both in primary and secondary sources.

240
Cardoso de Mello, Zélia Maria
Metamorfoses de riqueze: São Paulo, 1895 [Changes in Wealth São Paulo]
1990 Editoria Hucitec *São Paulo, Brazil*

Using inventories, wills and other legal documents, this book charts changing patterns of investment in the dynamic coffee region of Brazil during the second half of the nineteenth century, de Mello shows how planters' (*fazendeiros*) portfolios shifted gradually from an overwhelming concentration in agriculture (land and slaves) to substantial holdings in railway and utility companies, banking and finance and manufacturing. The work makes a substantial contribution to the study of entrepreneurial history by providing short biographies of key businessmen.

241
Davies, Peter N.
Fyffes and the Banana: Musa Sapientum. A Centenary History, 1888–1988
1990 Athlone *London*

This book is a scholarly official centenary history which examines the foundations of the international banana trade in the Canaries and Jamaica by the pioneer entrepreneurs Alfred Jones and Edward Fyffe and the development of the international Fyffes Group. The study is written against a background of the world banana industry, including provision for its seabourne carriage and Fyffe's principal competitors, Geest and Jamaica Producers. It has the merit of setting the company's West Indian activities on the context of US operations in Central America.
Firms: Elder Dempster; Fyffes; Geest; Jamaica Producers; Standard Fruit Co.; United Fruit Co.

242
Dean, W.
Rio Claro: A Brazilian plantation system, 1820–1920
1976 Stanford University Press *Stanford, CA*

This is an excellent work about the coffee plantation system in the county of Rio Claro, in the state of São Paulo in Brazil. It examines the establishment and decline of coffee growing in the county during the hundred-year period 1820–1920.

243
Evans, B. L.
A History of Agricultural Production and Marketing in New Zealand
1969 Keeling and Mundy *Palmerston North, New Zealand*

This wide-ranging study of New Zealand agriculture draws extensively upon earlier work by H. G. Philpott. It gives emphasis to the pattern of land settlement, the development of different forms of agricultural production and the impact of government policy.

244
Font, Mauricio
Coffee, Contention and Change in the Making of Modern Brazil
1990 Basil Blackwell *Oxford*

This study of the political economy of coffee production in interwar Brazil focuses on the contentious relationship between the 'old coffee elite' and a new class of small scale proprietors, and immigrant industrialists. The book provides key insights into the decline of large coffee plantations.

245
Frantz, Telmo Rudi
Cooperativismo Empresarial e Desenvolvimento Agricola [Entrepreneurial Co-operatives and Agricultural Development]
1982 Cotrijui - Fidene *Ijui (RS), Brazil*

Cotrijui was set up by a group of small and medium-sized farmers as a cooperative based on mutual interests to supply goods and provide credit; as it developed, it changed characters into a major entrepreneurial organization with a large export trade in wheat and soya. Frantz is particularly interested in the social implications of this transformation.
Firms: Cooperativa Regional Triticola Serrana (Cotrijui); FIDENE

246
Griffiths, Sir Percival
The History of the Indian Tea Trade
For main entry, see 1607

247
Harrison, Godfrey
Borthwicks: A century in the meat trade, 1863–1963
For main entry, see 1633

248
Hayami, Yujiro; Yamada, Saburo
The Agricultural Development of Japan: A century's perspective
1991 University of Tokyo Press *Tokyo, Japan*

The standard work on Japanese agriculture which focuses on technial change (improved rice varieties, fertilizer, crop changes and mechanization). Tremendous statistical underpinning.

249
Lind, C. A.
A Cut Above: Early history of the Alliance Freezing Company (Southland) Ltd
For main entry, see 1635

250
May, Stacy; Plaza, Galo
The United Fruit Company in Latin America
1958 National Planning Association *Washington, DC*

This useful study is packed with data on the operations of United Fruit and its impact on local economies, especially in the 1940s and 1950s. There is no index.
Firms: United Fruit

251
McCann, Thomas
An American Company: The tragedy of United Fruit
1976 Crown Publishing *New York, NY*

This sensationalized history of United Fruit and its activities, political and economic, covers Central America, mainly in the 1950s and 1960s.
Firms: United Brands; United Fruit

252
Meer, Cornelis L. J. van der; Yamada, Saburo
Japanese Agriculture: A comparative economic analysis
1990 Routledge *London*

An examination of the stagnation and high prices of Japanese agriculture through a sustained comparison with the Netherlands. An excellent work to be used in conjunction with Hayami and Yamada (qv).

253
Nagahara, Keiji; Nakamura, Masanori; Nishida, Yoshiaki; Matsumoto, Hiroshi
Nihon Jinushi Sei no Kosei to Dankai [The Structure and Development of Japanese Landownership]
1972 Tokyo University Press *Tokyo, Japan*

The authors cover landownership in the Yamagata prefecture from 1880 to 1937. They describe the silk-raising business and the process of enlargement of capital employed. Yamagata provides an example of general patterns of change in Japanese land tenure.
Firms: Nezu Family

254
Ochi, Tsutomu
Nihon Nogyo Ron [The Study of Japanese Agriculture]
1978 Iwanami shoten *Tokyo, Japan*

Ochi describes the features of Japanese agriculture from 1920 to 1973, and refers to technologies, working conditions for agricultural labourers, the agrarian business, decision mechanisms of price setting and agricultural policy.

255
Ogura, Takekazu
Can Japanese Agriculture Survive?: A historical and comparative approach
1979 Agricultural Policy Research Centre *Tokyo, Japan*

A massive (870 pages) study of all aspects of Japanese agriculture, including taxation, ideology, food policy, co-operative organizations, land reforms and agrarian structure. Encyclopedic and essential, though short on analysis.

256
Palacios, Marco
Coffee in Colombia (1850–1970): An economic, social and political history
1980 Cambridge University Press *Cambridge*

This book studies the evolution of Colombia's main export crop – coffee, concentrating on its role in foreign trade, and in the social, productive and political structure of the country. The chapters on the coffee 'haciendas' and the formation of an oligarchy are particularly useful for the business historian. It is lucidly written and based on a wide range of sources.

257
Sabato, Hilda
Agrarian Capitalism and the World Market: Buenos Aires in the Pastoral Age, 1840–1940
1990 University of New Mexico Press *Albuquerque, NM*

A valuable account is given here of Argentinian agriculture in the twentieth century, which highlights the role of sheep farming in the overall agrarian structure. The book is especially useful for its insights into international commercial relationships.

258
Saes, Flávio Azevedo Marques de
A grande empresa de serviços públicos na economiá cafeeira 1850–1930 [A Great Enterprise of Public Service in the Coffee Economy 1850–1930]
For main entry, see 2952

259
Smith, Peter H.
Politics and Beef in Argentina: Partners of conflict and change
1969 Columbia University Press *New York, NY*

A study of the Argentine beef industry is made here shedding considerable light on the relationship between the state and foreign-owned packing houses. It also provides a valuable discussion of the fraught relationship between breeders and fatteners.
Firms: Armour; Swift; Vestey

260
Stein, S. J.
Vassouras: A Brazilian coffee county, 1850–1900
1957 Harvard University Press *Cambridge, MA*

This book is an excellent and important reference work for the study of the coffee economy in the Paraiba Valley in Brazil. The work examines the coffee plantation economy in the county of Vassouras, in the state of Rio de Janeiro, chronicling the years of establishment, prosperity and decline of coffee growing in the county during the 50-year period from 1850 to 1900.

261
Tohata, Seiichi; Kozo, Uno (Editors)
Nihon Shihonsyugi to Nogyo [Japanese Capitalism and Agriculture]
1958 Iwanami Shoten *Tokyo, Japan*

This work covers the changing relationships between landowners and tenant farmers during the development of the Japanese economy from 1860 to 1956. It also refers to working conditions and lifestyles of farmers.

Agriculture, Rubber

262
Barlow, Colin
The Natural Rubber Industry: Its development, technology and economy in Malaysia
1978 Oxford University Press *Oxford*

A dense and thorough study of the economics and industrial organization of Malaysian rubber plantations is made here, giving substantial historical content. The book is especially strong on technology, industrial structure, distribution and the international market.

263
Bauer, P. T.
The Rubber Industry: A study in competition and monopoly
1948 Longmans, Green & Co. *London*

This is a detailed study of the economics of the global rubber industry which pays special attention to business cycles, cartels and attempts to regulate production.

264
Coates, Austin
The Commerce in Rubber: The first 250 years
1987 Oxford University Press *Singapore*

Coates makes a competent survey of the development of rubber growing and marketing in South-East Asia with emphasis on European and Asian plantation and trading companies.
Firms: B.F. Goodrich; Dunlop; Firestone; Goodyear; United States Rubber Co.

265
Dean, Warren
Brazil and the Struggle for Rubber: A study in environmental history
1987 Cambridge University Press *Cambridge*

This is a major study of the global rubber industry focusing on why Brazil lost its original dominant position in the industry and has struggled unsuccessfully to regain it ever since.

266
Drabble, John H.
Rubber in Malaya, 1876–1922: The genesis of the industry
1973 Oxford University Press *Kuala Lumpur, Malaya*

This excellent study of the early development of the rubber industry in Malaya takes the narrative up to the introduction of the Stevenson restriction scheme. It adds to earlier accounts by illuminating the extent of rubber research and the political origins of the Stevenson scheme. Particular emphasis is placed on European investment.

267
Drabble, John H.
Malaysian Rubber: The interwar years
1991 Macmillan *London*

This is a careful study of the period based on government sources. It is strong on industry structure (estates v. smallholders), and attempts to cope with fluctuating prices via restrictive schemes. Drabble also carefully documents the interaction of producers in Malaysia with British colonial and metropolitan governments. The Stevenson scheme (1928) is discussed as a prelude to an examination of the International Rubber Regulation Agreement of 1934–41.

268
Kenney, Martin; Florida, Richard
Beyond Mass Production: The Japanese system and its transfer to the US
For main entry, see 947

269
Nihon Gomu Kogyoshi
Nihon Gomu Kogyoshi [The History of the Japanese Rubber Industry]
For main entry, see 1917

270
Weinstein, Barbara
The Amazon Rubber Boom, 1850–1920
1983 Stanford University Press *Stanford, CA*

This sophisticated account of Brazil's rubber economy covers the seventy-year 'extractive boom'. The book analyses the reasons for the limited impact of the rubber trade on the Amazonian economy and explains the decline of the industry in the face of South-East Asian competition. It also provides excellent insights into the persistence of primitive production methods.

Agriculture, Sugar

271
Albert, Bill
An Essay on the Peruvian Sugar Industry, 1880–1920: And the letters of Ronald Gordon, Administrator of the British Sugar Company in Canete, 1914–1920
1976 UEA School of Social Studies *Norwich*

A useful survey is made here of the fluctuating fortunes of the Peruvian sugar industry in the late-nineteenth and twentieth centuries, enlivened by selective correspondence of a senior estate manager of the British Sugar Company.
Firms: British Sugar Company

272
Albert, Bill; Graves, Adrian (Editors)
Crisis and Change in the International Sugar Economy, 1860–1914
1984 ISC Press *Norwich*

This collection of 20 papers analyses the development of the sugar industry in its tropical and European contexts. Themes covered include competitive and market forces, state intervention, labour and technology.

273
Albert, Bill; Graves, Adrian (Editors)
The World Sugar Economy in War and Depression, 1914–40
1988 Routledge *London*
This is a collection of 18 papers, 17 of which are country case-studies. The principal themes are the socio-political aspects of sugar production and distribution.

274
Chalmin, Philippe
The Making of a Sugar Giant: Tate and Lyle, 1859–1989
For main entry, see 1596

275
Craton, Michael; Walvin, James
A Jamaican Plantation: The history of Worthy Park, 1670–1970
1970 University of Toronto Press *Toronto, Canada*
This detailed history of one of the oldest sugar plantations in Jamaica is notable for its accounts of the slave labour system and the technical and organizational rejuvenation which proceeded after the First World War.
Firms: Worthy Park

276
Eichner, Alfred S.
The Emergence of Oligopoly: Sugar refining as a case study
For main entry, see 1599

277
Eisenberg, Peter L.
The Sugar Industry in Pernambuco: Modernization without change, 1840–1910
1974 University of California Press *Berkeley, CA*
Eisenberg's book is a detailed study of the sugar industry in the north eastern Brazilian State of Pernambuco in the context of increasingly effective European and Caribbean competition from the 1840s, technological modernization and the shift from slave to free labour. It presents a stimulating analysis of the social and economic barriers to effective modernization of the industry.

278
Galloway, J. H.
The Sugarcane Industry: An historical geography from its origins to 1914
1989 Cambridge University Press *Cambridge*
This is a broad ranging survey of the development of the sugarcane industry. The geographical coverage is global.

279
Graves, Adrian
Cane and Labour: The political economy of the Queensland sugar industry, 1862–1906
1993 Edinburgh University Press *Edinburgh, Scotland*
This is an intelligent and informative study of the rise of the Queensland sugar industry which explains the growth of the plantation system and then its replacement by central milling in the final three decades of the nineteenth century.
Firms: Colonial Sugar Refinery Co.; Melbourne Mackay Sugar Co.

280
Heitmann, John A.
The Modernization of the Louisiana Sugar Industry, 1830–1910
1987 Louisiana State University Press *Baton Rouge, LA*
A contribution to the new economic history of the South, this study examines the scientific and technical, as well as the social, bases of industrialization. It shows the importance of trade associations and educational institutions, and is enriched by a deep grasp of the technology. Heitmann argues that the technical infrastructure paved the way for Louisiana's transition from sugar to petroleum. This book places the industry in its international context.

281
Heston, Thomas J.
Sweet Subsidy: The economic and diplomatic effects of the US Sugar Acts, 1934–1974
For main entry, see 4352

282
Higuchi, Hiroshi
Nihon Togyo shi [The History of the Japanese Sugar Industry]
1956 Naigai Keizaisha *Tokyo, Japan*

Higuchi covers the production, marketing and export of sugar from 1610 to 1895. He also examines policy during the Tokugawa Shogunate and the diffusion of the technology of sugar refining in the Meiji era.
Firms: Nisho-Iwai

283
Rojas, José Mariá
Empresarios y Tecnología en la Formación del Sector Azucarero en Colombia, 1860–1980 [Entrepreneurs and Technology in the Colombian Sugar Industry, 1860–1980]
1983 Universidad del Valle/Banco Popular *Cali, Colombia*

This is a sectoral history (sugar industry), conducted at the regional level (Cauca Valley, Colombia), and organized around the evolution of the social division of labour (from sugar plantation to agribusiness), entrepreneurial types, capital concentration and centralization. It is based on limited access to leading companies' archives, interviews and varied secondary sources.

Forestry & Timber, North America

284
Cox, Thomas R.
Mills and Markets: A history of the Pacific coast lumber industry to 1900
1974 University of Washington Press *Washington, DC*

This study of the cargo mill trade focusing on San Francisco as a commercial centre is strong on the competitive structure of the industry and the efforts of entrepreneurs to control market fluctuations. It places the industry in the context of international trade and synthesizes earlier more narrow studies, though it is limited on labour and contains less economic data than might be desirable.
Firms: Northwestern Lumber; Pope & Talbot

285
Ficken, Robert E.
Lumber and Politics: The career of Mark E. Reed
1980 University of Washington Press *Seattle, WA*

This is a study of the life and work of Mark Reed in the Pacific North-West lumber industry and his role in Washington State politics in the 1920s. The book stresses Reed's contribution to integration in the lumber industry and his campaigns for workers' welfare legislation.

286
Ficken, Robert E.
The Forested Land: A history of lumbering in western Washington
1987 University of Washington Press *Seattle, WA*

A detailed history of Washington's major industry is given here, from its inception in the 1850s to the 1930s. The emphasis is on industrial structure and markets and industry relations with federal and state governments.
Firms: West Coast Lumbermen's Association

287
Fickle, James E.
The New South and the 'New Competition': Trade association development in the southern pine industry
1980 University of Illinois Press *Champaign, IL*

Fickle has made a detailed study of the southern pine lumber industry in the USA from the 1880s to the 1950s. The core of his analysis deals with trade association activity on the part of the Southern Pine Association. Issues covered include marketing, afforestation, labour relations and government regulation.
Firms: Southern Pine Association

288
Hidy, Ralph W.; Hill, Frank E.; Nevins, Allan
Timber and Men: The Weyerhaeuser story
1963 Macmillan *New York, NY*

This is a large-scale scholarly official history of the Weyerhaeuser timber empire (research associates on the project included Vincent Carosso and Mira Wilkins). It covers many of the

major logging regions, and is especially strong on conservation, labour, technology and the role of government. There are excellent statistical appendices and this book is an essential starting point for the history of the industry.
Firms: Boise Cascade Lumber Co.; Clearwater Timber Co.; Potlatch Lumber Co.; Weyerhaeuser Co.

289
Kohlmayher, Fred W.
Timber Roots: The Laird, Norton story, 1855–1905
1972 Winona County Historical Society *Winona, MN*

A detailed account is given here of the contribution of the Laird, Norton company to the development of the logging industry in the USA, focusing on Minnesota. The growth and diversification of the company is well narrated, as is the role of the railroad in facilitating market expansion.
Firms: Laird, Norton; Potlatch Lumber Co.; Weyerhaeuser

290
Lower, Arthur R. M.
The North American Assault on the Canadian Forests: A history of the lumber trade between Canada and the US
1938 Ryerson Press *Toronto, Canada*

This extensively researched study of the Eastern Canadian timber industry and its shift from dependence on Britain to dependence on US markets is still an important source. It gives a powerful presentation of links between the international economy and the shaping of a new region and nation.

291
Lower, Arthur R. M.
Great Britain's Woodyard: British America and the timber trade 1763–1867
1973 McGill-Queen's University Press *Montreal, Canada*

This book is the culmination of a lifetime's study of the colonial origins of the Canadian timber industry by a leading Canadian economic and social historian. It is a deeply researched study of the role of tariffs and naval politics in shaping the industry.

292
MacKay, Donald
Empire of Wood: The Macmillan Bloedel story
1982 Douglas & McIntyre *Vancouver, Canada*

This is a company-sponsored history of a multinational forest products firm, Macmillan Bloedel Limited, based in British Columbia. It provides a detailed narrative account of mergers and acquisitions, and the company's diversification into the southern USA after 1960.
Firms: Alberta West Forest Products Corp.; Bloedal Stewart & Welch; H. R. Macmillan Export Co.; Macmillan Bloedel; Powell River Co.; United Fruit

293
Maunder, Elwood R.
Twentieth Century Businessman: An oral history interview with Walter Samuel Johnson
1974 Forest History Society *Santa Cruz, CA*

This book studies the contribution of Walter Samuel Johnson to the development of box lumber manufacturing in the USA. Based on oral interviews, the book sheds much light on the industry's contribution to the successful marketing of Californian agricultural produce.

294
Maxwell, Robert S.; Baker, Robert D.
Sawdust Empire: The Texas lumber industry, 1830–1940
1983 Texas A & M University Press *College Station, TX*

This is an authoritative study of the Texas lumber industry from its inception to 1940. The chronological focus is on the bonanza era (1880–1930). Marketing systems are evaluated and there are good descriptions of technological developments.

295
Mayor, Archer H.
Southern Timberman: The legacy of William Buchanan
1988 Georgia University Press *Athens, GA*

Heavily based on oral history, this book gives interesting insights into the culture and community of the Southern timber industry and its personalities, though it is weak on statistical and financial data.

296
Petersen, Keith
Company Town: Potlatch, Idaho, and the Potlatch Lumber Company
1987 Washington State University Press *Pullman, WA*

This is a high quality scholarly history of the Washington/Idaho based company. It has a twin focus on the issue of the 'company town' and Potlatch's relationship with the wider Weyerhaeuser empire.
Firms: Potlatch Lumber Co.; Weyerhaeuser

297
Radforth, Ian
Bush Workers and Bosses: Logging in Northern Ontario, 1900–1980
1987 University of Toronto Press *Toronto, Canada*

The author traces mechanization, increasing concentration and other changes in the Ontario logging industry with a particular focus on labour.

298
Robbins, William G.
Lumberjacks and Legislators: Political economy of the U.S. lumber industry, 1890–1941
1982 Texas A & M University Press *College Station, TX*

Robbins's book is a thoroughly researched study of the US lumber industry which addresses a range of economic and poltical issues. It sheds much light on the evolution of trade associations and the subsequent emergence of large scale enterprise leading to corporate monopoly. An essential work.
Firms: National Lumber Manufacturers' Association; Weyerhaeuser

299
Robbins, William G.
American Forestry: A history of national, state and private cooperation
1985 University of Nebraska Press *Lincoln, NB*

A detailed and authoritative account of the development of cooperative forestry programmes is given here, from the late nineteenth century to the 1980s. Commissioned by the US Forest Service, the book offers a critical interpretation of its achivements.
Firms: US Forest Service

300
Robbins, William G.
Hard Times in Paradise: Coos Bay, Oregon, 1850–1986
1988 University of Washington Press *Seattle, WA*

This is one of the most sophisticated of numerous local studies of the US timber industry, using extensive oral history to depict the timber community from bosses to workers. It is especially strong on labour and technology, and places the story in a broader national context.
Firms: C. A. Smith & Co.; Coos Bay Lumber Co.; Georgia-Pacific Co.; Weyerhaeuser Timber Co.

301
Smith, David
A History of Lumbering in Maine, 1861–1960
1972 University of Maine Press *Orono, ME*

Smith's book is a well-researched and very detailed study of the lumber industry in Maine, which is especially strong on conservation, the big companies and links with the paper industry. Technological and market developments are analysed clearly and the book is notable for its sympathetic account of conservation movements after 1900.
Firms: Great Northern Paper; International Paper; S. D. Warren

302
Twining, Charles E.
Phil Weyerhaeuser, Lumberman
1985 University of Washington Press *Seattle, WA*

This useful and well-researched business biography supplements Hidy et al.'s book (qv). It is especially good on the role of the family and on the transition from a company that dealt in timber to vertically integrated lumber and wood products.
Firms: Weyerhaeuser Timber Co.

Forestry & Timber, Rest of World

303
Ahvenainen, Jorma
Suomen sahateollisuuden historia [History of Finnish Sawmilling]
1984 Werner Söderström Osakeyhtiö
Helsinki, Finland

The sawmill industry was the principal branch of industry in Finland from the eighteenth century until the 1930s. The book is a coherent presentation of that industry from its very modest beginnings at the end of the Middle Ages to the process-controlled production lines of the 1980s. The work gives a comprehensive account of the sawmill industry and the closely connected forest economy, its companies and entrepreneurs. The scope also extends to foreign trade and international competition.

304
Bergh, Trond; Lange, Even
Foredlet virke, historien om Borregaard, 1889–1989 [The History of Borregaard 1889–1989]
1989 Ad Notam A/S *Oslo, Norway*

This book covers the first hundred years of one of the largest Norwegian industrial firms, Borregaard Industries. The company was based on technical innovations, foreign capital and two of the main Norwegian natural resources: forests and water power. The core activity has been wood conversion (pulp and paper), but since the late 1950s Borregaard has developed into an industrial conglomerate.
Firms: Borregaard Industries

305
Chew, Sing C.
Logs for Capital: The timber industry and capitalist enterprise in the nineteenth century
1992 Greenwood Press *Westport, CT*

A long-run socio-historical analysis of timber in the world economy and the role of competition and the state in the industry. It is strong on international economic networks and trade.

306
Dargavel, J. (Editor)
Sawing, Selling and Sons: Histories of Australian timber firms
1988 Centre for Resource and Environment
Canberra, Australia

This brief but informative study describes the history of timber-milling. It traces the expanding size and improving technology of the industry and attempts to explain why most production units remain small scale except in Western Australia.

307
Fukao, Seizo
Ringyo Keiei no Tenkaikatei [The Development of the Forestry Business]
1988 Mineruva Shobo *Kyoto, Japan*

Covering the forestry business in Japan from 1890 to 1970, Fukao mainly focuses on patterns of afforestation and cutting and on changes of ownership and business behaviour.
Firms: Moroto Family

308
Healy, B.
A Hundred Million Trees: The story of New Zealand Forest Products Limited
1982 Hodder & Stoughton *Auckland, New Zealand*

Healy's book contains much valuable information about the unusual financing of afforestation companies beginning in the 1920s and 1930s. It also analyses the competition with Tasman Pulp and Paper and the growth paths pursued by both firms since 1945.
Firms: Afforestation; NZ Paper Mills; NZ Perpetual Forests; New Zealand Forest Products (NZFP); Smith Wylie Australia; Tasman Pulp and Paper

309
Kuisma, Markku
Metsäteollisuuden maa: Suomi, metsät ja kansainvälinen järjestelmä 1620–1920 [A Country of the Forest Industries: Finland, forests and the international system, 1620–1920]
1993 Finnish Historical Society and the Association of the Forest Industries
Jyväskylä, Finland

The main theme of this book is the emergence of forest-based capitalism in Finland. The transformation of an agrarian periphery into a major exporter of timber and paper is described as a result of the interaction between internal factors and external circumstances emphasizing the world trade of forest products, such as tar, sawn timber, pulp and paper. The author employs a synthetic approach, applies the perspective of business history to macroeconomic change and writes in a narrative, journalistic style. The book contains a summary in English.

310
Lange, Even
Fra Linderud til Eidsvold Vaerk vol. IV
1985 Dreyer *Oslo, Norway*
This volume covers the period 1895 to 1979 in the company history of Mathiesen-Eidsvold, Vaerk. In this period the old forest and sawmill company developed into a wood-processing industry firm, manufacturing chemical pulp and paper, before returning to sawmilling and the timber trade in the 1960s.
Firms: Mathiesen-Eidsvold Vaerk

311
Nihon Gohan Kogyokai
Gohan 50 Nen Shi [Fifty Years of Japanese Plywood]
1959 Nihon Gohan Kogyokai *Tokyo, Japan*
This history of the Japanese plywood industry from 1905 to 1955, describes technological development, management, marketing, importing raw materials, and exports.

312
Sejersted, Francis
Fra Linderud til Eidsvold Vaerk, vol.III
1979 Dreyer *Oslo, Norway*
This volume covers the period 1842 to 1895 in the company history of Mathiesen-Eidsvold Vaerk when the railway, the steamship and the steamsaw brought great changes in the activities of the forest company.
Firms: Mathiesen-Eidsvold Vaerk

313
Sejersted, Francis; Schou, August
Fra Linderud til Eidsvold Vaerk, vol.II
1972 Dreyer *Oslo, Norway*
This is a part of the company history of Mathiesen-Eidsvold Vaerk, a large forest company in Norway. The first volume was written by Andreas Holmsen and published by Dreyer in 1946. The second volume covers the period 1792–1842, when export of planks was the basic activity. England was the dominant market until around 1830 when France became more important.
Firms: Mathiesen-Eidsvold Vaerk

314
Shiomi, Toshitaka (Editor)
Nihon Ringyo to Sanson Syakai [Japanese Forestry and Society in the Mountainous District]
1962 Tokyo University Press *Tokyo, Japan*
The work examines two issues: a historical analysis of landownership and the sale of national property to the private sector, and family and political structures in the mountainous district.

Fisheries

315
Blackford, Mansel G.
Pioneering a Small Business: Wakefield Seafoods and the Alaskan frontier
1979 JAI Press *Greenwich, CT*
This is one of the few high-quality business histories concerned with an individual small firm. The study is based on business and public records, many interviews and solid personal understanding. While setting the progress of the firm in the American pioneering tradition, Blackford also sets it firmly in context with government involvement, labour and environmental influences.
Firms: Wakefield Seafoods

316
Dewar, Margaret E.
Industry in Trouble: The federal government and the New England Fisheries
1983 Temple University Press *Philadelphia, PA*
This is a thoughtful analysis of the fluctuating fortunes of the New England fishing indus-

try since 1945. The book focuses on the record of federal intervention and offers good insights into the formulation of official policy for declining industries.

317
Gray, Malcolm
The Fishing Industries of Scotland, 1780–1914: A study in regional adaptation
1978 Oxford University Press *Oxford*

This history of Scottish fisheries in the industry's heyday is rooted in primary sources. The book provides key insights into the industry's contribution to regional and national income and Aberdeen's role as a trading port is expertly analysed.

318
Johannessen, Finn Erhard
Challenge and Change: The history of Protan from 1939 to 1989
For main entry, see 1915

319
McEvoy, Arthur F.
The Fisherman's Problem: Ecology and law in the California fisheries, 1850–1980
1990 Cambridge University Press *Cambridge*

This is a detailed analysis of the decline of the California fisheries from the later nineteenth century onwards. It provides an exemplary account of the depletion of fish stocks, both inland and coastal.

320
Mishima, Yasuo
Hokuyo Gyogyo no Keieishiteki Kenkyu [The Business History of the Northern Fishery (revised)]
1985 Mineruva Shobo *Kyoto, Japan*

Mishima describes the development of fishing in the northern territorial waters belonging to the USSR between 1900 and 1937 and the foreign affairs implications. He also covers the business history of Nichiro Gyogyo Co. from the aspect of business organization and labour management.

Firms: Nichiro Gyogyo

321
Nerheim, Gunnar; Utne, Bjorn S.
Under samme stjerne: Rederiet Peder Smevig 1915–1990 [Smedvig: A story of canning, shipping and contract drilling from western Norway]
For main entry, see 3097

322
Newell, Dianne (Editor)
The Development of the Pacific Salmon Canning Industry: A grown man's game
For main entry, see 1637

323
Ommer, Rosemary
From Outpost to Outport: A structural analysis of the Jersey-Gaspé cod fishery, 1767–1886
1991 McGill-Queen's University Press
Kingston and Montreal, Canada

Ommer gives an analysis of the cod fishery's place in a pattern which secured success for Jersey at the expense of underdevelopment in the Gaspé.

324
Solhaws, Trygve
De Norske Fisheries Historie, 1815–80 [The History of Norwegian Fisheries 1815–80]
1976 Universitetsforlaget *Bergen, Oslo, Tromsø, Norway*

This highly detailed two-volume study of the Norwegian fisheries in the pre-industrial period, emphasises the critical role of the fishing industry in the Norwegian economy. The books provide excellent accounts of employment patterns and financial aspects.

325
Vamplew, Wray
Salvesen of Leith
For main entry, see 3078

Coal Mining, UK

326
Ashworth, William
The History of the British Coal Industry: Volume 5, 1946–1982: The nationalised industry
1986 Clarendon Press *Oxford*

Ashworth gives the definitive account of the British coal industry in the nationalization era. Whilst he is exceptionally good at analysing technological developments, his book also provides good insights into marketing and pricing problems, the conduct of labour relations, and investment strategies. The reader gains a fine impression of the nature of decision-making at upper managerial levels.
Firms: National Coal Board

327
Baldwin, George B.
Beyond Nationalization: The labor problems of British coal
1955 Harvard University Press *Cambridge, MA*

A detailed study of early reforms in labour relations following the nationalization of the British coal industry. It focuses on case studies of key problems such as collective bargaining, absenteeism, wage structure, technological change and the effects of incentive wage systems.
Firms: National Coal Board

328
Beckett, J. V.
Coal and Tobacco: The Lowthers and the economic development of west Cumberland, 1660–1760
1987 Cambridge University Press *Cambridge*

This study of the contribution of Sir John and Sir James Lowther to economic development in west Cumberland is based on estate papers. It traces the Lowthers' role as colliery entrepreneurs and coal shippers and also their activities in the tobacco trade. As both a local and regional study the book is excellent. It is less successful in explaining Glasgow's success in the tobacco trade at the expense of Whitehaven, and it offers few insights into the Lowthers' limitations as entrepreneurs.

329
Benson, John; Neville, Robert G.; Thompson, Charles H. (Editors)
Bibliography of the British Coal Industry: Secondary literature, parliamentary and departmental papers, mineral maps and plans, and a guide to sources
For main entry, see 5

330
Church, Roy
The History of the British Coal Industry: Volume 3: 1830–1913: Victorian pre-eminence
1986 Clarendon Press *Oxford*

This is the definitive account of the British coal industry in its Victorian and Edwardian heyday. Church provides an exceptionally clear treatment of the structure and organization of the industry and ranges over capital formation, wage determination, profitability and the quality of entrepreneurship. Technological developments are also highlighted.

331
Cooper, David; Hopper, Trevor (Editors)
Debating Coal Closures: Economic calculation in the coal dispute, 1984–5
1988 Cambridge University Press *Cambridge*

This sequence of studies concentrates on the industrial restructuring issues which precipitated the British coal dispute of 1984–5. The common theme is the interface between economic and social criteria in the management decision making process.
Firms: British Coal

332
Dintenfass, Michael
Managing Industrial Decline: Entrepreneurship in the British coal industry between the wars
1992 Ohio State University Press *Columbus, OH*

Taking four companies representing ranges of difference in geological conditions, firm size, ownership type, sources of management and markets, this study finds evidence of growth and profits in three companies in the volatile

and shrinking markets of the 1920s and 1930s. Success came from 'second-best' strategies in technology and marketing. The study is a useful empirical test of the Elbaum-Lazonick explanation of Britain's relative industrial decline and confirms entrepreneurial failing.
Firms: Ashington Coal Co.; Henry Briggs, Son & Co.; Throckley Coal Co.; Waterloo Main Colliery Co.

333
Duckham, Baron F.
A History of the Scottish Coal Industry: Vol. 1, 1700–1815
1970 David & Charles *Newton Abbot*
Duckham's is a detailed account of the early development of the Scottish coal industry with excellent coverage of technological issues. The book is notable also for its analysis of the diffusion of English mining practice.

334
Fine, Ben
The Coal Question: Political economy and industrial change from the nineteenth century to the present day.
1990 Routledge *London*
This sequence of essays, mostly pre-published, focuses on industrial structure, mineral property rights, technology and productivity, and public ownership in the British coal industry. The book reveals the need for further research on critical aspects of the industry's economic performance and structure.
Firms: British Coal; National Coal Board

335
Flinn, Michael
The History of the British Coal Industry: Vol. 2: 1700–1830: The Industrial Revolution
1984 Clarendon Press *Oxford*
A definitive account is given here of the development of the British coal industry in its formative phase. The book comments in depth on labour and technology, capital formation and profitability, and provides excellent insights into the industry's evolving structure and organization.

336
Gilbert, David
Class, Community, and Collective Action: Social change in two British coalfields, 1850–1926
1992 Clarendon Press *Oxford*
A study of mining communities in Ynysybwl in South Wales and Hucknall in Nottinghamshire in the period culminating in the General Strike 1926. The main focus is on the balance of local power between mineowners and miners.
Firms: Barber Walker Company; Hucknall Colliery Co.; Ocean Co.

337
Grayling, Christopher
The Bridgewater Heritage: The story of Bridgewater Estates
1983 Bridgewater Estates *Manchester*
Grayling gives a narrative account of the history of the Bridgewater Estates, their changing ownership, and the merger of the colliery interests in Manchester Collieries Limited in 1929. The book was published to mark the sixtieth anniversary of the company founded to acquire the Earl of Ellesmere's coal and land interests at Worsley.
Firms: Bridgewater Estates; Manchester Collieries Limited

338
Hatcher, John
The History of the British Coal Industry: Vol. 1: Before 1700: Towards the age of coal
1993 Clarendon Press *Oxford*
One of Britain's leading early modernists provides a thorough analysis of the progress of Britain's coal industry to 1700. This is the first (though published last) in an impressive five-volume account, commissioned by the National Coal Board (British Coal).

339
Jaffe, James A.
The Struggle for Market Power: Industrial relations in the British Coal Industry, 1800–1840
1991 Cambridge University Press *New York, NY*

This valuable analysis of labour relations in the British coal industry focuses on the north east of England during the first half of the nineteenth century. The book is at its best in explaining the miners' early acceptance of the immutability of market forces.

340
Kirby, Maurice W.
Men of Business and Politics: The Rise and Fall of the Quaker Pease Dynasty of North-East England, 1700–1943
For main entry, see 3820

341
Kirby, M. W.
The British Coalmining Industry, 1870–1946: A political and economic history
1977 Macmillan *London*

This book provides an analysis of the record of state intervention across the First World War until nationalization. The analytical focus is on the development of collusion and the working of the statutory cartel system in the 1930s. It comments also on the failure of statutory reorganization via mergers.

342
Mee, Graham
Aristocratic Enterprise: The Fitzwilliam industrial undertakings 1795–1857
1975 Blackie *London*

This is an account of the fourth Earl Fitzwilliam's development of his Elsecar collieries, which focuses on managerial practices and the Earl's paternalistic labour management.

343
Morris, J. H.; Williams, L. J.
The South Wales Coal Industry, 1841–1875
1958 University of Wales Press *Cardiff, Wales*

The authors give a detailed account of the rise to prominence of coalmining in the Welsh industrial economy. The book also focuses on the growth of the steam coal export trade and its interactions with the domestic market.

344
Riden, Philip
The Butterley Company 1790–1830
2nd Edition
1990 Derbyshire Record Society *Chesterfield*

A brief, but scholarly account of the development of the largest coal and iron making concern in the East Midlands is given here. Original documents are reproduced in an appendix.
Firms: Butterley Company

345
Robens, Alfred
Ten Year Stint
For main entry, see 3915

346
Supple, Barry
The History of the British Coal Industry: Vol. 4, 1913–1946: The political economy of decline
1987 Clarendon Press *Oxford*

This indispensable account of a crucial chapter in the history of the British coal industry, covers the period from undiluted private ownership through mounting state intervention. It is the latter theme which looms large and the book provides a fine analysis of trends in industrial organization focusing on cartelization during the inter-war period. Industrial relations issues are also well treated.

347
Waller, R. J.
The Dukeries Transformed: The social and political development of a 20th century coalfield
1983 Oxford University Press *Oxford*

Waller provides a detailed account of the emergence of the new Nottinghamshire coalfields between 1913 and 1951. His focus is on labour, but the central role of company villages and employer paternalism is fully examined, in the context of the economics of the development of new coalfields.
Firms: Butterley Company; Stanton Company

Coal Mining, USA

348
Binder, Frederick Moore
Coal Age Empire: Pennsylvania coal and its utilization to 1860

1974 Pennsylvania Historical and Museum Commission *Harrisburg, PA*

This detailed study of the early years of the coal industry in Pennsylvania, is of interest to business historians for its account of technical and marketing developments.

349
Bowman, John R.
Capitalist Collective Action: Competition, cooperation and conflict in the coal industry
1989 Cambridge University Press *New York, NY*

This study of the evolving structure of the US bituminous coal industry from the 1880s to the 1940s is written from a Marxist standpoint and rooted in 'new industrial organization' theory.

350
Dix, Keith
What's a Coal Miner to Do?: The mechanization of coal mining
1989 University of Pennsylvania Press *Pittsburgh, PA*

This book studies the impact of mechanization on the mining workforce from the end of the nineteenth century onwards. The author analyses the reasons for worker opposition to technological advance and also the changing stance of the United Mine Workers of America on the issue of mechanization.

351
Eller, Ronald D.
Miners, Millhands and Mountaineers: Industrialisation of the Appalachian South, 1880–1930
1982 University of Tennessee Press *Knoxville, TN*

This book gives a detailed history of an industrializing region of the USA focusing on the interconnections between the railroad, timber, and coalmining industries. It ranges over government–industry relations, marketing structures and the formation and culture of company towns.

Firms: J. P. Morgan and Co.; Pennsylvania Railroad; US Steel

352
Fishback, Price V.
Soft Coal, Hard Choices: The economic welfare of bituminous coal miners, 1890–1930
1992 Oxford University Press *New York, NY*

This detailed study of wages and working conditions in the US bituminous coalmining industry is grounded in economic theory and quantitative techniques of analysis. The author demonstrates, convincingly, that labour market competition was an active factor in constraining employers' bargaining power.

353
Gardner, A. Dudley; Flores, Verla R.
Forgotten Frontier: A history of Wyoming coal mining
1989 Westview Press *Boulder, CO*

A valuable study is made here of the coalmining industry in Wyoming in the nineteenth and twentieth centuries. The book evaluates the role of the Union Pacific Railroad in early mining development and comments in depth on labour relations issues and traces technological and production trajectories.

Firms: Union Pacific Railroad

354
Gitelman, Howard M.
The Legacy of the Ludlow Massacre: A chapter in American industrial relations
1988 University of Pennsylvania Press *Philadelphia, PA*

An excellent study is made by Gitelman of the Colorado coal strike of 1914 and its consequences for the conduct of labour relations. The latter is analysed with reference to the Rockefeller family's Colorado Fuel and Iron Company and the adoption of industrial relations reforms devised by the Canadian liberal politician, Mackenzie King.

Firms: Colorado Fuel and Iron Co.

355
Graebner, William
Coal-Mining Safety in the Progressive Period: The political economy of reform
1976 University Press of Kentucky *Lexington, KY*

This is an excellent account of the limited achievements of coal-mining safety campaigners in the progressive era (1910–20) in the United States. The author focuses on the structure of the industry as an impediment to enhanced safety and presents cogent arguments to explain the opposition of both mine owners and miners to progressive legislation.

356
Hevener, John W.
Which Side Are You On?: The Harlan County coal miners, 1931–1939
1978 University of Illinois Press *Urbana, IL*

Hevener presents an authoritative study of labour disputes in the coalfields of Harlan County, Kentucky in the 1930s. Strong on the economic and social context of strike activity, the book is notable for its scholarly objectivity.

357
Johnson, James P.
The Politics of Soft Coal: The bituminous industry from World War I through the New Deal
1979 University of Illinois Press *Urbana, IL*

This detailed study of the US bituminous coal industry is written from the standpoints of state–industry relations and labour issues. The book emphasises the interaction between the industry's decentralized structure and the general political environment.

358
Long, Priscilla
Where the Sun Never Shines: A history of America's bloody coal industry
1989 Paragon House *New York, NY*

Long's book is a detailed work of synthesis on the history of the US coal industry, concentrating on class relations and the transition from small scale organization to 'corporate liberalism'. Although national in geographical coverage, the book focuses on the Rocky Mountain West mining region.

359
Munn, Robert F.
The Coal Industry in America: A bibliography and guide to studies
1977 West Virginia University Library *Morgantown, WV*

This is an indispensable guide to the history of coalmining in the USA.

360
Palladino, Grace
Another Civil War: Capital, labour and the state in the anthracite regions of Pennsylvania, 1840–68
1990 University of Illinois Press *Urbana, IL*

Palladino has made an excellent study of the coalmining industry in Pennsylvania across the divide of the Civil War. She focuses attention on the emergence of big business and its adverse consequences for the bargaining power of the mining workforce.

Firms: Lehigh Coal and Navigation Co.

361
Powell, H. Benjamin
Philadelphia's First Fuel Crisis: Jacob Cist and the developing market for Pennsylvania anthracite
1978 Pennsylvania State University Press *University Park, PA*

This account of the early development (1800–1830) of coal mining in Philadelphia focuses on the pioneering role of Jacob Cist in the marketing of anthracite fuel.

Firms: Lehigh Coal Mine Co.

362
Scamehorn, H. Lee
Mill and Mine: The CF and I in the twentieth century
1992 University of Nebraska Press *Lincoln, NE*

This sponsored history of the Colorado Fuel and Iron Company in the nineteenth and twentieth centuries portrays the firm as in the vanguard of advanced welfare and labour relations practices – despite its involvement in the Ludlow Massacre of 1913/14. Allowing for the author's bias, the book provides valuable insights into the transition from labour–management conflict to collective bargaining in the 1930s.

Firms: Colorado Fuel & Iron Co.

363
Seltzer, Curtis
Fire in the Hole: Miners and managers in the American coal industry
1985 University Press of Kentucky
Lexington, KY

Seltzer's book is a highly detailed history of the United Mine Workers of America, which is useful to business historians for its analysis of national negotiations with employers. Sympathetic to the union, the author argues for public planning of energy policy.

Coal Mining, Rest of World

364
Abelshauser, Werner
Der Ruhrkohlenbergbau seit 1945 [Coalmining in the Ruhr since 1945]
1984 C. H. Beck *Munich, Germany*

This study is a comprehensive history of German coal mining since 1945. Written by a leading economic historian, it sets the industry in a wider economic context of energy crises, re-organization and decline.
Firms: Ruhrkohle AG

365
Aso Hyakunen Shi Hensan Iinkai
Aso Hyakunenshi [A Centenary of Aso]
1975 Aso Cement Co. *Fukuoka, Japan*

This book describes the development of Aso which started as a coal mining company, and its diversification into the cement industry. It presents numerous charts and illustrations. The documentation is good and there are several contributions from authorities within the firm.
Firms: Aso Cement Co.

366
Caulier-Mathy, N.
La Modernisation des Charbonnages Liègois pendant la première moitié du XIXe Siècle: Techniques d'Exploitation [Modernization of the Liège Coalmines]
1971 Société d'Édition 'Les Belles Lettres
Paris, France

A highly detailed study is made here of the technical development of coalmining in the area of Liège during the nineteenth century. It is at its best in discussing the process of technological diffusion from the 1830s and 1840s.

367
Coll, S.; Sudria, C.
El carbón en España (1770–1961): Una historia económica [Coal in Spain (1770–1961): An economic history]
1987 Turner *Madrid, Spain*

This is the best monograph published on the Spanish coal mining industry. It concentrates on the industry as a whole, but there is much information on the major firms engaged in the sector.

368
Culver, William W.; Greaves, Thomas C. (Editors)
Miners and Mining in the Americas
1985 Manchester University Press *Manchester*

This is an eclectic collection of essays on the differing attributes of miners and their social and economic environments in various American locations, from Ontario and West Virginia to Mexico and Chile. The accent is on South America.

369
Feldman, Gerald D.; Tenfelde, Klaus (Editors)
Workers, Owners and Politics in Coal Mining: An international comparison of industrial relations
1990 Berg *Oxford*

This collection gives a valuable cross-country survey of labour relations structures in western coalmining since the later nineteenth century. Individual chapters are written by acknowledged authorities and they provide key insights into employers' labour strategies.

370
Geiger, Reed G.
The Anzin Coal Company, 1800–1833: Big business in the early stages of the French industrial revolution
1975 Temple University Press *Philadelphia, PA*

Established in the early eighteenth century, close to the Franco-Belgian border, the Anzin

Coal Company was the largest coal undertaking in France. This is an excellent study of its transition from a traditional to a new technology.
Firms: Anzin Coal Co.

371
Gillet, Marcel
Les Charbonnages du Nord de la France au XIXe Siècle [Coalmining in the North of France in the Nineteenth Century]
1973 Mouton *Paris, France*
Gillet's history of the development of the Nord-Pas-de-Calais coal industry in the nineteenth century focuses on company formation, competition for concessions, and the rise of political pressure groups and marketing associations. It is useful to business historians for its insights into the role of family capitalism in industrial development.

372
Gillingham, John
Industry and Politics in the Third Reich: Ruhr coal, Hitler and Europe
1985 Columbia University Press *New York, NY*
This book is a study of the relationship between Ruhr coal industrialists and the National Socialist state. Focusing on the records of investment, productivity and marketing, the book emphasizes the caution and pessimism of the industry in the face of Nazi schemes of territorial expansion and self-sufficiency. It also stresses industry continuities from the International Steel Cartel of 1926 to the European Coal and Steel Community of 1951.

373
Guillaume, Pierre
La Compagnie des Mines de la Loire, 1848–54: Essai sur l'apparition de la grande industrie capitaliste en France [The Compagnie des Mines de la Loire 1848-54: A study of the appearance of big capitalist industry in France]
1966 Presses Universitaires de France *Paris, France*
Guillaume describes the attempts to build a national coal monopoly in France and its destruction by Napoleon III's government.
Firms: Compagnie des Mines de la Loire

374
Hein, Laura E.
Fueling Growth: The energy revolution and economic policy in postwar Japan
1990 Harvard University Press *Cambridge, MA*
This study examines Japan's post-war economic development through the prism of the energy sector. It studies Japan's shift from primary reliance on domestic coal and hydroelectricity to imported oil and the debates over energy policy, and the intense struggles between government and business interests that resulted.
Firms: Electric Power Development Company; Hokkaido Colliery and Steamship Co.; Kansai Electric Power Co.; Mitsubishi; Mitsui; Nippon Hassoden Kabushiki Gaisha

375
Honeyman, Katrina
Origins of Enterprise: Business Leadership in the Industrial Revolution
For main entry, see 3814

376
Ogino, Yoshihiro (Editor)
Senzenki Chikuho Tankogyo no Keiei to Rodo [Business and Labour in the Chikuho Coal-Mining Industry Before the Second World War]
1990 Keibunsya *Kyoto, Japan*
This work covers the business behaviour of the coal-mining industry in the Kyusyu district, dealing with the introduction of machinery, the labour–management relationship, transportation problems and exports to South-East Asia.
Firms: Aso Sangyo; Kaijima Tankou

377
Pounds, N. E.; Parker, W. N.
Coal and Steel in Western Europe: The influence of resources and techniques on production
For main entry, see 637

378
Shoda, Makoto
Kyushu Sekitan Sangyo Shiron [A Study of

the Coal-Mining Industry in the Kyushu District of Japan]
1987 Kyushu University Press *Fukuoka, Japan*

This work deals with the history of working conditions, the introduction of machinery and the output of coal, comparing big companies with small ones before the Second World War. It also highlights the problems of a declining industry and unemployment after the Second World War.

379
Sumiya, Mikio
Nihon Sekitan Sangyo Bunseki [A Study of the Japanese Coal-Mining Industry]
1968 Tokyo University Press *Tokyo, Japan*

Covering the period 1703–1906, this work deals with the developing process of obtaining monopolistic power. It also applies a historical approach to the coal-mining industry, considering mainly technical innovation and marketing.
Firms: Mitsui Kozan

380
Tanaka, Naoki
Kindai Nihon Tanko Rodoshi Kenkyu [A Historical Study of Labour-Management Relations in the Modern Japanese Coal-Mining Industry]
For main entry, see 4236

381
Torres, Eugenio
Ramón de la Sota: Historia económica de un empresario (1857–1936) [Ramon de la Sota: The economic history of an entrepreneur (1857–1936)]
For main entry, see 4038

382
Whitmore, R. L.
Coal in Queensland: The late nineteenth century, 1875–1900
1985 University of Queensland Press *Brisbane, Queensland, Australia*

This is the definitive account of the Queensland coal industry in its late nineteenth century heyday. The book concentrates on geology, industry structure, technology and markets.

383
Wright, Tim
Coal Mining in China's Economy and Society, 1895–1937
1984 Cambridge University Press *Cambridge*

This important study of the Chinese coal mining industry is useful to business historians for its assessment of foreign concerns and their relationship with state authorities.

384
Yoshimura, Sakio
Nihon Tankoshi Shichu [The History of the Japanese Coal-Mining Industry: A note]
1984 Ochanomizu Shobo *Tokyo, Japan*

This work covers the payment systems of the workers engaged in the coal-mining industry before the Second World War and also contrasts working conditions and competition with oil and other energy industries after the war.
Firms: Mitsui Kozan

Energy Policy

385
Balogh, Brian
Chain Reaction: Expert debate and public participation in American commercial nuclear power, 1945–1975
1991 Cambridge University Press *Cambridge*

A well-documented study of nuclear policy making in the USA which highlights the importance of experts in early decision-making in the development of commercial nuclear power and the reason for their subsequent decline.
Firms: General Electric; Yankee Atomic Electric Company

386
Burn, Duncan
Nuclear Power and the Energy Crisis: Politics and the atomic industry
1978 Macmillan *London*

Analyses the politics and economics of nuclear decision-making in the 1960s and 1970s, especially under the impact of the oil crisis.

Detailed research and insider knowledge make this an invaluable study.
Firms: Atomic Power Construction Co.; Babcock & Wilcox; British Nuclear Fuel Ltd; Central Electricity Generating Board; General Electric

387
Clark, John G.
Energy and the Federal Government: Fossil fuel policies, 1900–1946
1987 University of Illinois Press *Urbana, IL*
Clark has made a major study of US Federal Government policy with respect to oil, gas and coal. The focus is on regulatory mechanisms and industry responses. Weaknesses in policy are analysed with particular reference to short term commercial gain and political compromise.

388
Gillingham, J.
Coal, Steel and the Rebirth of Europe, 1945–1955: The Germans and French from Ruhr conflict to economic community
For main entry, see 629

389
Gustafson, Thane
Crisis Amid Plenty: The politics of Soviet energy under Brezhnev and Gorbachev
1989 Princeton University Press *Princeton, NJ*
A rare case study of Soviet industrial policy-making. Analyses the paradox that the Soviet Union had abundant energy resources (oil, gas and coal) and yet experienced a major energy crisis in the 1970s and 1980s resulting from runaway costs, abysmal inefficiency and repeated shocks and surprises. Concludes that energy policy has been the single most disruptive factor in Soviet industry since the mid 1970s and one of the main causes of the economic slowdown of the 1980s.

390
Harris, Richard A.
Coal Firms Under the New Social Regulation
For main entry, see 4351

391
Hein, Laura E.
Fueling Growth: The energy revolution and economic policy in postwar Japan
For main entry, see 374

392
Kawamura, Taiji
Enerugi Sangyo [The Energy Industry]
1960 Iwanami Shoten *Tokyo, Japan*
Covering coal-mining, petroleum, and the electricity industry from 1880 to 1960, Kawamura describes the history of these related industries and changes in their technologies.
Firms: Mitsui Kozan; Nihon Sekiyu

393
Nelson, Robert H.
The Making of Federal Coal Policy
1983 Duke University Press *Durham, NC*
This study of US federal government coal leasing policy between 1971 and 1981 is written by a policy analyst for the Interior Department. The book concludes that the failure of policy was the product of conflicting ideologies both within and between pressure groups.

394
Sapelli, G.; Carnevali, F.
Uno sviloppo fra politica e strategia: ENI (1953–1985) [Development Between Politics and Strategy: ENI (1953–1985)]
For main entry, see 2730

395
Vietor, Richard H. K.
Environmental Politics and the Coal Coalition
1980 Texas A & M University Press *College Station, TX*
Vietor makes an authoritative analysis of the politics of coal in the USA, focusing on environmental controversies and legislative responses, mainly in the 1970s.
Firms: Occidental Petroleum; Pacific Power & Light

396
Vietor, Richard H. K.
Energy Policy in America Since 1945: A study of business–government relations
1984 Cambridge University Press *Cambridge*

This detailed and critical appraisal of US energy policy since 1945 sheds much light on government–industry relations. It combines a theoretical approach with empirical testing, the latter stressing the human element in the vagaries of policy making.

397
Williams, Roger
The Nuclear Power Decisions: British policies, 1953–1978
1980 Croom Helm *London*
A helpful study of policy-making in the industry, focusing on rising public concerns about safety and the consequent erosion of Whitehall's monopoly on decision-making power with the rise of public inquiries.
Firms: British Nuclear Fuels

398
Wynne, Brian
Rationality and Ritual: The Windscale Inquiry and nuclear decisions in Britain
1982 British Society for the History of Science *Chalfont St Giles*
A good account of decision-making in nuclear energy, examining the Windscale public inquiry of 1977 into the application by British Nuclear Fuels to build a thermal oxide reprocessing plant on the site.
Firms: British Nuclear Fuels

Oil, Politics & General

399
Anderson, Irvine H. Jr
The Standard Vacuum Oil Company and United States East Asian Policy 1933–1941
1975 Princeton University Press *Princeton, NJ*
This is an interesting study of the evolution of a vertically integrated oil company focusing on its role in US–Japanese political relations in the 1930s and early 1940s. The book sheds considerable and objective light on State Department–business relations at a critical period in East Asian diplomacy.
Firms: Standard Vacuum Oil Company (Stanvac)

400
Blair, John M.
The Control of Oil
1977 Pantheon Books *New York, NY*
Written from a US perspective, this is an authoritative study of the international oil industry which offers cogent comments on a range of demand and supply issues from the 1920s to the 1970s. The book contains an exceptionally clear analysis of the 1973–4 energy crisis.
Firms: BP; Exxon; Gulf; Shell; Socal; Texaco

401
Clark, John G.
The Political Economy of World Energy: A twentieth century perspective
1990 Harvester Wheatsheaf *London*
This study focuses on oil as the pre-eminent energy industry in the twentieth century. Despite its uncritical approach to the left-of-centre critique of multi-national oil enterprise, it provides a readable account of the development of the international industry. The temporal focus is on the post-1945 period.

402
Clarke, Angela
Bahrain Oil and Development, 1929–1989
1990 International Research Center for Energy and Economic Development *Boulder, CO*
This lavishly produced history of the oil industry in Bahrain is of use to business historians for its analysis of the early rivalries between British and American enterprise and the involvement of governments in attempting to secure productive advantages.
Firms: American Gulf Oil Corporation; Anglo Persian Oil Company; Bahrein Oil Company; Bahrein Petroleum Corporation (BAPCO); Standard Oil (California)

403
Copp, E. Anthony
Regulating Competition in Oil: Government intervention in the US refining industry, 1948–1975
1976 Texas A & M University Press *College Station, TX*
An excellent, critical analysis of US federal

oil policy is given here, which emphasizes the interplay between national security and economic efficiency considerations. The book offers good insights into the lack of co-ordination in federal energy policy which promoted increasing dependence on foreign oil supplies.

404
Crystal, Jill
Oil and Politics in the Gulf: Rulers and merchants in Kuwait and Qatar
1990 Cambridge University Press *Cambridge*
Crystal has made a scholarly study of the domestic impact of oil wealth in two conservative Arab states in the twentieth century, concentrating on the evolution of state bureaucracies.

405
Engler, Robert
The Brotherhood of Oil: Energy policy and the public interest
1977 University of Chicago Press *Chicago, IL*
This somewhat polemical account of US oil politics in the 1960s and 1970s, is notable for its accusations of 'regulatory capture' on the part of 'big oil' and the duplicity of public officials.

406
Ferrier, R. W.; Fursenko, A.
Oil in the World Economy
1989 Routledge *London*
This is an eclectic collection of studies on the international oil industry in the twentieth century, embracing North and South America, the Middle East, Europe and the USSR. The chapters on the USA contain excellent insights into demand and supply-side responses.
Firms: Paribas; Standard Oil of California (SOCAL); Union Oil Co.

407
Johnson, Arthur M.
The Development of American Petroleum Piplines: A study in private enterprise and public policy, 1862–1906
For main entry, see 2959

408
Johnson, Arthur M.
Petroleum Pipelines and Public Policy 1906–1959
For main entry, see 2960

409
Karshenas, Messoud
Oil, State and Industrialisation in Iran
1990 Cambridge University Press *Cambridge*
Although this is a rather narrowly conceived account of the political economy of oil in Iran, it is of use to business historians mainly for its discussion of state intervention in the period 1953–1977.
Firms: Anglo-Persian Oil Company

410
Miller, Aaron David
Search for Security: Saudi Arabian oil and American foreign policy, 1939–1949
1980 University of North Carolina Press *Chapel Hill, NC*
A meticulously researched study of American oil policy in Saudi Arabia in the trans-World War Two period. US domestic oil needs are discussed in the context of external strategic considerations as perceived by the State Department.
Firms: Arabian American Oil Company

411
Painter, David S.
Private Power and Public Policy: Multinational oil corporations and U.S. foreign policy 1941–1954
1987 I. B. Tauris *London*
This 'corporatist' interpretation of government–industry relations covers a wide geographical compass, including Latin America. It stresses the notion of 'a public-private partnership' in the evolution of US foreign oil policy.

412
Penrose, Edith T.
The Large International Firm in Developing Countries: The international petroleum industry
1969 MIT Press *Cambridge, MA*
This is an exceptionally erudite study of the spread of western oil enterprise to developing

countries, notably from the Second World War. The book provides a valuable account of demand and supply-side interactions between oil companies, producing countries and oil importers.

413
Randall, Stephen J.
United States Foreign Oil Policy, 1919–1948: For profits and security
1985 McGill-Queen's University Press *Toronto, Canada*

Randall's is a well documented study of US foreign oil policy which, in explaining the cooperative relationship between government and business, rejects both leftist interpretations and analyses grounded in the notion of conflict.

414
Sampson, Anthony
The Seven Sisters: The great oil companies and the world they made
1975 Hodder & Stoughton *London*

This popularized and somewhat polemical account of the political economy of the world oil industry concentrates on the activities of the West's leading oil companies. The focus is on events in the 1960s and 1970s.

Firms: BP; Exxon (Esso); Gulf; Mobil; Shell; Socal (Chevron); Texaco; Esso (Chevron)

415
Sayigh, Yusif A.
Arab Oil Policies in the 1970s
1982 Johns Hopkins University Press *Baltimore, MD*

This excellent study of OPEC price and production policy is written from an Arab standpoint. The author espouses the case for government intervention and collaborative policies in the production of oil as a non-renewable resource.

416
Schneider, Steven A.
The Oil Price Revolution
1983 Johns Hopkins University Press *Baltimore, MD*

In a detailed factual study of the international oil market from 1945 to 1980 this book explains the basis of US hegemony until the OPEC-sponsored price revolutions of the 1970s. For the business historian the book's main interest lies in its effective refutation of the 'corporate conspiracy thesis' as an explanation of the 1970s energy crisis.

417
Sklar, Martin J.
The Corporate Reconstruction of American Capitalism, 1890–1916: The market, the law, and politics
For main entry, see 4392

418
Stocking, George W.
Middle East Oil: A study in political and economic controversy
1970 Vanderbilt University Press *Nashville, TN*

This is now an outdated analysis of the political economy of the Middle East oil industry. It does, however, possess the merit of a detailed account of oil exploration and production, highlighting the role of western enterprise and the emergence of political and economic controversies. The early history of OPEC is also discussed.

419
Stoff, Michael B.
Oil, War and American Security: The search for a national policy on foreign oil, 1941–1947
1980 Yale University Press *New Haven, CT*

Stoff gives an excellent account of American foreign oil policies during the Second World War, focusing on the Anglo-American oil agreement delimiting Middle Eastern interests. The book relates foreign oil diplomacy to corporate vested interests within the USA.

420
Venn, Fiona
Oil Diplomacy in the Twentieth Century
1986 St Martin's Press *New York, NY*

This brief but stimulating account of the role of oil in international relations is notable for its extended chronological coverage and soundly based judgements, especially in the period to 1939.

421
Yergin, Daniel
The Prize: The epic quest for oil, money and power
1991 Simon & Schuster *New York, NY*

A brilliantly written history of the global oil industry, later made into a film series for American television. Yergin is superb on the characters and conflicts of the industry and has produced a highly readable epic that does justice to the drama of its subject as well as containing a mountain of original research.
Firms: Anglo-Persian Oil Co.; Arabian-American Oil Co. (Aramco); British Petroleum (BP); Compagnie Française des Petroles (CFP); Exxon (Standard Oil of New Jersey); Gulf Oil; Iraq Petroleum Co. (IPC); Royal Dutch; Shell; Standard Oil

Oil, Europe

422
Arnold, Guy
Britain's Oil
1978 Hamish Hamilton *North Pomfret, VT*

This is a journalistic but useful account of the vicissitudes of British national oil policy in the 1970s. It is of interest to business historians mainly for its focus on the conflict of interests between international corporations and the host government.
Firms: Anglo-Dutch Shell Group; BP; British National Oil Corporation

423
Bamberg, J. H.
The History of the British Petroleum Company: Vol. 2: The Anglo-Iranian years, 1928–1954
1994 Cambridge University Press *Cambridge*

Bamberg presents an insightful study of BP's corporate history focusing on its Middle Eastern activities across the divide of the Second World War. The book is essential reading on international cartel developments and on the consequences, both diplomatic and economic, of the nationalization of the Iranian oil industry. The author also analyses in depth BP's evolving relationship with successive British governments. The earlier history is covered by Ferrier (qv).
Firms: British Petroleum

424
Beaton, Kendall
Enterprise in Oil: A history of Shell in the United States
1957 Appleton-Century Crofts *New York, NY*

This general history of Shell's activities in the USA also gives information on early development of the 'Koninklijke' and 'Shell' in the Netherlands and Britain. It draws mainly on American sources.
Firms: American Gasoline Co.; Roxana Petroleum Co.of Oklahoma; Roxana Petroleum Corp.; Shell Co. of California; Shell Oil Company Inc.; Shell Petroleum Corp.; Shell Union Oil Corp.; Koninklijke Nederlandsche Petroleum Maatschappij

425
Corley, T. A. B.
A History of the Burmah Oil Company: Vols. 1 and 2
1983-88 Heinemann *London*

A highly detailed analysis of the growth and development of Britain's oldest oil company from its late nineteenth-century inception. These volumes offer substantial insights into the evolution of the British petroleum industry in general, ranging over a variety of issues of interest to business historians. Management strategies are analysed confidently, as are the industry's technological trajectories and relations with a variety of incumbent governments in the developing and developed worlds. Corley's work is essential reading for students of the international oil industry.
Firms: Anglo Persian Oil Co.; British Petroleum Co. (BP); Burmah Oil Co.

426
Ferrier, R. W.
The History of the British Petroleum Company: Volume 1: The developing years, 1901–1932
1982 Cambridge University Press *Cambridge*

This definitive history of the early years of the British Petroleum Company is exceptionally detailed in content and coverage and provides fine insights into Persian history and Anglo-Persian relations. Financial and institutional factors are analysed in depth, as are scientific and technological developments. The book is at its best in recounting business and political negotiations both in London and Teheran. Later years are covered by Bamberg (qv).

Firms: Anglo-Iranian Oil Co.; Anglo-Persian Oil Co.; British Petroleum Co. (BP)

427

Förster, Fren

Geschichte der deutschen BP, 1904–1979 [A History of BP in Germany, 1904–1979]

1979 Reuter & Klöckner *Hamburg, Germany*

This book traces the history of the German operations of British Petroleum from its beginnings as a petroleum importer formed by an Austrian entrepreneur. After the failed attempts of the original company to win oil concessions in the Middle East, the Anglo-Iranian Oil Company acquired a controlling interest in the firm. After 1945 the company expanded its production into petro-chemical processes. This is a well-written, sponsored company history. It lacks annotation but contains a detailed bibliography and index.

Firms: Anglo-Iranian Oil Co.; British Petroleum Co. (BP); Deutsche Erdöl-AG, Berlin; Deutsche Petroleum-Verkaufsgesellschaft, Berlin; Erdölchemie GmbH; Europäische Petroleum Union, Bremen; Europäische Tanklager- und Transport-AG; Östereichische und ungarische Mineralöprodukte AG, Wien

428

Gerretson, F. C.

History of the Royal Dutch

1953 E. J. Brill *Leiden, The Netherlands*

Despite its age and being long out of print, this four-volume work is, for lack of a more recent study, the authoritative account of the development of the Royal Dutch Shell Group. It provides a detailed analysis of the origins of the Dutch and British oil trading businesses, their merger in 1907, and inter-war developments.

Firms: Anglo Saxon Petroleum Co.; Asiatic Petroleum Co.; Bataafsche Petroleum Maatschappij; Koninklijke Nederlandsche Petroleum Maatschappij; Koninklijke Nederlandsche Maatschappij tot Exploitatie; Shell Transport and Trading Co.

429

Hanisch, Tore Jørgen; Nerheim, Gunnar

Norsk oljehistorie: Fra vantro til overmot? (vol. I) [History of the Norwegian Oil Industry]

1992 Leseselskapet *Oslo, Norway*

The book covers the history of the exploitation of Norwegian oil and gas resources in the North Sea, from the first contact between a multinational oil company and Norwegian authorities in 1962 until the mid-1970s. Hanisch discusses political aspects as well as the influence of oil on the Norwegian economy, whereas Nerheim concentrates on technology transfer and the development of a Norwegian oil industry.

Firms: Aker Offshore a.s.; Amoco Norway Oil Company; Conoco Norway Inc.; Elf Petroleum Norge A/S; Esso Norge A.S.; Fina Exploration Norway U.a.s.; Mobil Exploration Norway Inc.; Norsk Hydro a.s.; Saga Petroleum a.S.; Statoil

430

Henriques, Robert

Marcus Samuel: First Viscount Bearsted and founder of the Shell Transport and Trading Company, 1853–1927

1960 Barrie & Rockliff *London*

This is a highly detailed narrative of Marcus Samuel's entrepreneurial role in the early oil industry, focusing on the period from 1890 to the end of the First World War. It sheds much light on the marketing of Far Eastern oil.

Firms: Koninklijke Nederlandsche Petroluem Maatschappij; Royal Dutch-Shell Group; Shell Transport & Trading Co.

431

Huré, Joseph

De la naissance de la S.G.H.P. à la S.F.B.P. d'aujourd'hui: Histoire de cinquante années [From the Birth of SGHP to the SFBP of Today: A history of 50 years]

1971 Société française des Pétroles B.P. *Courbevoie, France*

This book is a business history of the French subsidiary of BP by its former CEO.
Firms: British Petroleum (BP); Société Française des Pétroles B.P.

432
Jenkin, Michael
British Industry and the North Sea: State intervention in a developing industrial sector
1981 Macmillan *London*
Government intervention was initially prompted by the failure of British industries to respond to the opportunities of the North Sea. This is a fine study of the development of government policy to try and encourage a greater British role in the supply of the offshore oil industry, particularly the work of the Offshore Supplies Office.

433
Jones, Geoffrey
The State and the Emergence of the British Oil Industry
1981 Macmillan *London*
This is an indispensable account of the early relationship between the state and British oil companies. Attention is focused on fuel-oil requirements in an imperial, and especially Middle Eastern context. In these respects the core of the book focuses on the developing relationship after 1914 between the state and the Anglo-Persian Oil Company.
Firms: Anglo-Persian Oil Co.; British Petroleum (BP); Burmah Oil Co.; Mexican Eagle; Royal Dutch; Shell Transport & Trading

434
Kennedy, K. H.
Mining Tsar: The life and times of Leslie Urquhart
1987 Allen & Unwin *London*
This is the biography of a Scottish oil and mining entrepreneur active in Russia up to the 1920s. It provides a good account of the impact of the Russian Revolution on foreign entrepreneurs and subsequent claims for compensation.
Firms: Inter-Russian Syndicate; Kyshtim Corp.; Russo-Asiatic Corp.; Scibaieff Petroleum; Tanalyk Corp.

435
Kent, Marian
Oil and Empire: British policy and Mesopotamian oil, 1900–1920
1976 Macmillan *London*
Kent gives a detailed account of the evolution of British oil policy in relation to Iraq. Based on archival research, the book highlights the interplay of interests between the Foreign Office, Admiralty and the government of India, and comments lucidly on the rivalry between the Anglo-Persian Oil Company and Royal Dutch Shell.
Firms: Anglo-Persian Oil Co.; Royal Dutch Shell

436
Longhurst, Henry
Adventure in Oil: The story of British Petroleum
1959 Sidgwick & Jackson *London*
This narrative account of the development of the British Petroleum Company takes it from its origins in the Anglo-Persian Oil Company to the 1950s. The focus is firmly on the individual entrepreneur.
Firms: Anglo-Iranian Oil Co.; Anglo-Persian Oil Co.; British Petroleum Co. (BP)

437
Pearton, Maurice
Oil and the Romanian State
1971 Clarendon Press *Oxford*
This factual account of the development of Romania's oil industry is notable mainly for its discussion of foreign direct investment.
Firms: Creditul Minier; Industria Romȃna de Petrol (IRDP)

438
Tolf, Robert W.
The Russian Rockefellers: The saga of the Nobel family and the Russian oil industry
1976 Hoover Institution Press *Stanford, CA*
A good account is given here of the contribution of the Nobel family to the development of the oil industry in nineteenth-century Russia. The book provides insights into business organization, finance and technology, and presents interesting comparisons with the US industry.

Firms: Nobel Brothers Petroleum Production Co.

439
Ultramar
A Golden Adventure: The first 50 years of Ultramar
1985 Hurtwood Press *London*

This is an in-house history of a British-based oil exploration company in the period after its inception in 1935. Although mainly descriptive, the book provides useful insights into Ultramar's global expansion and diversification from its Venezuelan origins.
Firms: Ultramar Exploration Co.

Oil, North America

440
Akin, Edward N.
Flagler: Rockefeller partner and Florida baron
1988 Kent State University Press *Kent, OH*

A scholarly biography of one of Rockefeller's leading managers at Standard Oil, based on the company's archives, which sheds significant light on the emergence and early rise of the company. It also deals extensively with Flagler's important 'second career' in Florida real estate development and railroad building.
Firms: Standard Oil; Baltimore & Ohio Railroad; New York Central; Pennsylvania Railroad; Florida East Coast Railway

441
Anderson, Irvine H.
Aramco, the United States and Saudi Arabia: A study of the dynamics of foreign oil policy, 1933–50
1981 Princeton University Press *Princeton, NJ*

A careful reconstruction of US foreign oil policy before and after the Second World War, focusing on the role of the leading US oil company in Saudi Arabia. He shows that a de facto coalition of government agencies and oil companies coalesced around the rapid development of Saudi Oil, though policy implementation was left in private hands.
Firms: Aramco; Anglo-Iranian Oil Co.; Compagnie Française des Petroles; Caltex; Gulf Oil; Socony-Vacuum Oil Co.; Standard Oil Co. (New Jersey); Standard Oil Co. of California

442
Breen, David H. (Editor)
William Stewart Herron: Father of the petroleum industry in Alberta
1984 Historical Society of Alberta *Calgary, Canada*

This is an edited collection of documents highlighting W. S. Herron's pioneering role in the Alberta oil industry. It is of interest to business historians for the insights provided into Herron's severe limitations as a man of business.

443
Bringhurst, Bruce
Antitrust and the Oil Monopoly: The Standard Oil cases, 1890–1911
1979 Greenwood Press *Westport, CT*

An excellent narrative account is given here of the legal suits launched by public officials against Standard Oil of New Jersey in the period 1890–1911. The book emphasizes the political context of the antitrust process and provides good insights into the constraints on an effective public policy. It supersedes previous accounts.
Firms: Buckeye Pipelines; Indiana Standard; Kansas Standard; Kentucky Standard; Louisiana Standard; Ohio Oil; Prairie Oil & Gas; Solar Refining; Standard Oil of New Jersey

444
Foster, Peter
Other People's Money: The banks, the government and Dome
1984 Totem *Toronto, Canada*

This book gives a popularized account of the spectacular rise and fall of Canada's Dome Petroleum Company in the 1970s and 1980s.
Firms: Dome Petroleum

445
Gibb, George S.; Knowlton, Evelyn H.
The Resurgent Years, 1911–1927: History of the Standard Oil Company (New Jersey) Vol. 2
1956 Harper & Brothers *New York, NY*

The second volume of this huge authorized

history follows the organization and operations of the broken-up companies derived from Standard Oil. The book examines the structure of domestic supplies, the quest for foreign oil, war and government relations, technical innovation and the rise of foreign competition.
Firms: Anglo-Persian Oil Co.; Carter Oil Co.; Deutsche-Americanische Petroleum-Gesellschaft; Humble Oil & Refining Co.; International Petroleum Co.; Oklahoma Pipeline Co.; Royal Dutch Shell; Standard Oil; Vacuum Oil Co.

446
Giebelhaus, August W.
Business and Government: A case study of Sun Oil, 1876–1945
1980 JAI Press *Greenwich, CT*
This excellent history of a medium-sized US oil company is written in the context of state–industry relations. It focuses on family management and provides good insights into the relatively late adoption of a multidivisional organization.
Firms: British Sun Co.; Sun Oil Co.

447
Herbert, John H.
Clean Cheap Heat: The development of residential markets for natural gas in the United States
1992 Praeger *New York, NY*
Herbert provides a historical survey of the use of natural gas in US residential markets which analyses a range of demand and supply factors. The author offers cogent comment on the impact of fuel prices on household use and welfare.

448
Hidy, Ralph W.; Hidy, Muriel E.
Pioneering in Big Business, 1882–1911: History of Standard Oil Company (New Jersey) Vol. 1
1955 Harper & Brothers *New York, NY*
A massive study (800 pages) of the rise of Standard Oil from the chaos and depression of unrestrained competition in the 1870s to the controlled centralization under a giant holding company. The book focuses on top-level decision making and covers the functional organization of the company in enormous depth. The study is based on Rockefeller and other archives and Hidy and Hidy carry the story up to the break-up of the company by the US government in 1911.
Firms: American Petroleum Co.; Anglo-American Oil Co.; Atlantic Refining Co.; Deutsche-Americanische Petroleum-Gesellschaft; National Transit Co.; Ohio Oil Co.; Pacific Coast Oil Co.; Standard Oil; Vacuum Oil Co.

449
Hutchinson, W. H.
Oil, Land and Politics: The California career of Thomas Robert Bard
For main entry, see 3955

450
Johnson, Arthur M.
The Challenge of Change: The Sun Oil Company, 1945–1977
1983 Ohio State University Press *Columbus, OH*
This excellent business history of the Sun Oil Company relates the firm's activities to the contemporary political and economic environment. The study focuses on entrepreneurial decision-making in investment, marketing, and commercial strategies.
Firms: Sun Oil Co.

451
Jones, Charles S.
From the Rio Grande to the Arctic: The story of the Richfield Oil Corporation
1972 University of Oklahoma Press *Norman, OK*
This valuable account of the development of a large domestic US oil company is written by the company president. The pre-history of Richfield is analysed as a precursor to an authoritative account of the company's role in Californian and Alaskan oil production. The book provides good insights into financial issues, as well as corporate strategy and organization.
Firms: Richfield Oil Co.; Richfield Oil Corp.; Rio Grande Oil Co.

452
Kilbourn, William
Pipeline: Trans-Canada and the great debate: a history of business and politics
1970 Clarke, Irwin *Toronto, Canada*

This excellent study of the construction and operation of the trans-Canada natural gas pipeline is written from the perspective of the founding company, Trans-Canada Pipelines, from the mid 1950s onwards. The main focus is on financial issues and the relationship between government and business.

Firms: Trans-Canada Pipelines; Western Pipelines

453
King, John O.
Joseph Stephenson Cullinan: A study of leadership in the Texas petroleum industry, 1897–1937
1970 Vanderbilt University Press *Nashville, TN*

This is a sympathetic account of one of the leading pioneers of oil production in Texas. Cullinan's early relationship with Standard Oil affiliates is described in detail as a precursor to analysis of his role in the development of the Texas (Oil) Company.

Firms: Texas (Oil) Company

454
King, Judith (Editor)
An Oilman's Oilman: A biographical treatment of Walter W. Lechner as told to James A. Clark
1979 Gulf Publishing *Houston, TX*

The story of a pioneer oilman in the east Texas oilfield in the first half of the twentieth century is recounted here. The book is notable for its discussion of oil wildcatting and resistance to government intervention on the part of independent producers.

455
Larson, Henrietta M.; Knowlton, Evelyn H.; Popple, Charles S.
New horizons, 1927–1950: History of Standard Oil Company (New Jersey) Vol. 3
1971 Harper & Row *New York, NY*

This third volume of the history of Standard Oil covers a period which witnessed its development as a truly multinational enterprise. Domestic and overseas product and market developments are analysed in detail and the book presents a fine account of managerial strategies in relation to financial issues and administrative structures.

Firms: Standard Oil (New Jersey)

456
Larson, Henrietta M.; Porter, Kenneth Wiggins
History of the Humble Oil and Refining Company
1959 Harper *New York, NY*

A detailed account of the development of the Humble Oil and Refining Company is given here, from its foundation in 1919 to 1948. Problems of structure and organization are examined in depth, as are technical developments. Relationships with the Standard Oil Company of New Jersey are also covered.

Firms: Humble Oil and Refining Co.; Standard Oil Co.

457
Loos, John L.
Oil on Stream!: A history of Interstate Oil Pipe Line Company, 1909–1959
For main entry, see 2961

458
Massie, Joseph L.
Blazer and Ashland Oil: A study in management
1960 University Press of Kentucky
Lexington, KY

This is a detailed study of Paul G. Blazer's role as chief executive of the Ashland Oil and Refining Company of Kentucky from the 1920s to the 1950s.

Firms: Ashland Oil and Refining Co.; Ashland Oil and Transportation Co.; Ashland Refining Co.

459
Nash, Gerald D.
United States Oil Policy, 1890–1964: Business and government in twentieth century America
1968 University of Pittsburgh Press
Pittsburgh, PA

This is a dated but nevertheless indispensible account of government–business relations in the US oil industry, notable for its clarity and objectivity.

460
Olien, Roger M.; Olien, Diana Davids
Wildcatters: Texas Independent Oilmen
1984 Texas Monthly Press *Austin, TX*

This book is a study of 'independent' entrepreneurship in the drilling and testing for oil and gas in west Texas in the twentieth century. It draws attention to the conservation of major oil companies in encouraging 'wildcatters' to undertake exploration and drilling risks.

461
Olien, Roger M; Olien, Diana Davids
Easy Money: Oil promoters and investors in the Jazz Age
1990 University of North Carolina Press *Chapel Hill, NC*

A valuable study of oil promotion in the USA, focusing on the 1920s. The book provides critical insights into the adverse impact of fraudulent schemes on the industry, and also highlights the role of small-scale business in the oil industry.

462
Pratt, Joseph A.
The Growth of a Refining Region: Industrial development and the social fabric
1980 JAI Press *Greenwich, CT*

This book is a detailed study of the contribution of the oil industry to the economic development of the US Texas gulf coast region. The book places the region in its national context in relation to markets and decision-making, and provides an incisive account of government regulation and promotion.

463
Schruben, Francis W.
Wea Creek to El Dorado: Oil in Kansas, 1860–1920
1972 University of Missouri *Columbia, MO*

A brief but useful study of the early development of the Kansas oil industry. It is of use to business historians for its account of the contentious relationship between local producers and the Standard Oil Company, focusing on crude oil prices.

Firms: Forest Oil Company; Prairie Oil and Gas Co.; Standard Oil Co. (New Jersey)

464
Scott, Otto J.
The Exception: The story of the Ashland Oil and Refining Company
1968 McGraw-Hill *New York, NY*

Written for a popular audience, this sponsored history describes the corporate growth of one of America's smaller oil refining companies from its foundation after the First World War.
Firms: Ashland Oil and Refining Co.

465
Wall, Bennett H.
Growth in a Changing Environment: A history of Standard Oil (New Jersey) 1950–1972 and Exxon Corporation 1972–1975. History of Standard Oil (New Jersey), Vol. 4
1988 McGraw-Hill *New York, NY*

This authoritative study of a major oil company analyses Exxon's strengths and weaknesses at the global level. The analytical focus is provided by the evolution of corporate strategy and the contribution of individual executives.
Firms: Exxon; Humble Oil Co.; Standard Oil Co. (New Jersey)

466
Wall, Bernard H.; Gibb, George S.
Teagle of Jersey Standard
1974 Tulane University *New Orleans, LA*

This is a detailed biography of Walter C. Teagle, president of the Standard Oil Co. (New Jersey) (1917–1937) and subsequently its chairman (1937–1942). The book highlights Teagle's organizational reforms, especially the adoption of a holding company structure and provision for research and development. Documentation and bibliography are, however, not included.
Firms: Imperial Oil Co. of Canada; Republic Oil Co.; Standard Oil Co. of Ohio; Standard Oil Co. (New Jersey)

467
Williamson, Harold F.; Andreano, R. L.; Daum, Arnold R.; Klose, G. C.
The American Petroleum Industry: Volume II. The age of energy, 1899–1959

1963 North Western University Press
Evanston, IL

This highly-detailed history of the US petroleum industry covers the first half of the twentieth century, providing an excellent account of technical developments. For business historians the book is useful for its commentary on organizational issues, from production to retailing.

468
Williamson, Harold F.; Daum, Arnold R.
The American Petroleum Industry: Volume I. The age of illumination 1859–1899
1959 North Western University Press
Evanston, IL

This monumental account of the early history of the US petroluem industry has excellent coverage of the technological aspects, including transport and relations with the coal industry. The book is of interest to business historians mainly on account of its discussion of the Standard Oil Company as the dominant producer.
Firms: Standard Oil

Oil, Rest of World

469
Brown, Jonathan C.
Oil and Revolution in Mexico
1993 University of California Press *Berkeley, CA*

This study provides insights into entrepreneurship in difficult environments in Mexico between 1880 and 1920 but it does not fully confront the political and economic outcomes in Mexico of the activities of the international oil companies.
Firms: Huasteca Petroleum Co.; El Aguila (Compañiá Mexicana del Petróleo El Aguila); Pemex (Petróleos Mexicanos); Penn Mex Fuel Co.; Royal Dutch-Shell; Standard Oil (New Jersey); Waters-Pierce Oil Co.

470
Brown, Jonathan C.; Knight, Alan (Editors)
The Mexican Petroleum Industry in the 20th Century
1992 University of Texas Press *Austin, TX*

An important collection of essays covering all aspects of the Mexican oil industry, including the impact of foreign investment, oil workers, and the history of PEMEX, the state-owned oil enterprise.
Firms: PEMEX

471
Bullard, Fredda Jean
Mexico's National Gas: The beginnings of an industry
1968 Bureau of Business Research, University of Texas *Austin, TX*

This is a descriptive and uncritical study of the role of Pemex in exploiting Mexico's hydrocarbon resources from its foundation in 1935. It offers a brief, but useful account of Pemex's pricing policies in relation to natural gas and petroleum products.
Firms: Pemex (Petrolus Mexicanus)

472
Grayson, George W.
The Politics of Mexican Oil
1981 University of Pittsburgh Press
Pittsburgh, PA

An account is given here of the development of the oil industry in Mexico by foreign firms until their expropriation in 1938 and the founding of Pemex as a state oil producer. The book is at its best in dealing with policy developments in the 1970s.
Firms: Pemex

473
Grayson, George W.
Oil and Mexican Foreign Policy
1988 University of Pittsburgh Press
Pittsburgh, PA

Grayson gives an analysis of the role of oil in determining the course and conduct of Mexican foreign policy in the twentieth century. Domestic political consequences are also analysed.
Firms: Pemex

474
Iguchi, Tosuke
Sekiyu [The Oil Industry]
1963 Kojunsha *Tokyo, Japan*

Covering not only the development of the Japanese petroleum industry, but also the strategy of the international petroleum cartel from 1868 to 1960, Iguchi describes three issues: first the development of the petroleum industry as a whole, second competition and cooperation among the Japanese firms as well as between the foreign cartels, and third the industrial policy of MITI.
Firms: Nihon Sekiyu; Tonen

475
McBeth, B. G.
Juan Vincente Gomez and the Oil Companies in Venezuela, 1908–1935
1983 Cambridge University Press *Cambridge*

This is a detailed study of the role of J. V. Gomez, Venezuelan dictator from 1908 to 1935, in the development of the country's oil industry. It offers fine insights into the relationship between governments and multinational companies and a useful assessment of the impact of oil on the domestic economy.

476
Meyer, Lorenzo
Mexico and the United States in the Oil Controversy, 1917–1942
1977 University of Texas Press *Austin, TX*

This account of Mexican–US oil diplomacy is written from a Mexican standpoint. The book contains some penetrating analysis of the contentious relationship between the Mexican government and US oil companies.
Firms: Mexican Eagle Oil Co. (El Aguila); Pemex; Pan American Petroleum & Transport; Waters-Pierce Oil Co.

477
Nihon Sekiyu
Nihon Sekiyu 100 Nen shi [A Hundred Years of Nihon Sekiyu Co.]
1988 Nihon Sekiyu Co. *Tokyo, Japan*

This work deals not only with the history of Nihon Sekiyu Co. over 100 years, but also that of the Japanese oil industry as a whole, especially technological change and related companies.
Firms: Nihon Sekiyu

478
Okabe, Akira
Sekiyu Sangyo [The Oil Industry]
1986 Nihon Keizai Hyoron-sha *Tokyo, Japan*

Covering the Japanese oil industry from 1900 to 1980, this work deals with imports from major international oil companies and links with the Navy before the Second World War. It also describes the reconstruction and development process of the post-war era.
Firms: Kyodo Sekiyu; Nihon Sekiyu

479
Philip, George
Oil and Politics in Latin America: Nationalist movements and state companies
1982 Cambridge University Press *Cambridge*

This is a comprehensive account of the history and politics of oil production in Latin American states from the 1890s to 1970s. It is of interest to business historians for its critical assessment of the role of state oil companies in petroleum affairs.
Firms: Pemex; Petrobrás; Petroperu; Petroven; VPF (Argentina); VPFB (Bolivia)

480
Randall, Laura
The Political Economy of Venezuelan Oil
1987 Praeger *New York, NY*

A useful study of the evolution of the Venezuelan oil industry, especially focused on the lead-up to and aftermath of the 1975 nationalization.
Firms: Petroleos de Venezuela SA (PDVSA)

481
Randall, Laura
The Political Economy of Mexican Oil
1989 Praeger *New York, NY*

Randall gives an in-depth study of Pemex, Mexico's state-owned oil monopoly, valuable for its critical comparisons with similar organizations in Brazil and Venezuela. The book offers a favourable conclusion on Pemex's contribution to the Mexican economy.
Firms: Pemex

482
Randall, Laura
The Policial Economy of Brazilian Oil
1993 Praeger *New York, NY*

A study of Brazil's pursuit of self-sufficiency in oil and the internal planning and operations of PETROBRAS, the state-owned oil company.

Firms: PETROBRAS

483
Sekiyu Renmei
Sengo Sekiyu Sangyo-shi [The Oil Industry in Post-War Japan]
1985 Sekiyu Renmei *Tokyo, Japan*

This work covers the development of the Japanese oil industry from 1945 to 1984, describing the policy of GHQ (General Headquarters) and the Japanese government. It also describes the development of industrial policy in the oil industry in post-war Japan.

484
Smith, Peter Seaborn
Oil and Politics in Modern Brazil
1976 Macmillan Company of Canada
Toronto, Canada

This book contains an account, based mainly on domestic sources, of oil industry development in Brazil during the twentieth century. The book is of interest to business historians selectively, on issues such as government responses to Standard Oil (NJ) and the role of internal interest groups.

Firms: Petrobrás; Standard Oil (N.J.)

485
Solberg, Carl E.
Oil and Nationalism in Argentina: A history
1979 Stanford University Press *Stanford, CA*

This is a concise study of state involvement in oil production and distribution in Argentina in the period 1907–1939. It focuses on the state petroleum agency, Yacimientos Petroliferos Fiscales, which acted as a model for similar organizations elsewhere in Latin America.

Firms: Yacimientos Petroliferos Fiscales (YPF)

486
Tonen
Tonen 50 Nen Shi [50 Years of Tonen Co.]
1991 Tonen Co. *Tokyo, Japan*

Covering Tonen Oil Co. from 1939 to 1989, this book describes the relationship with its parent SVOC (Standard Vacuum Oil Co.), negotiations with MITI and more generally on the problems where Japanese firms have close links with foreign businesses.

Firms: Tonen; Stanvac

487
Vedavalli, R.
Private Foreign Investment and Economic Development: A case study of petroleum in India
1976 Cambridge University Press *Cambridge*

A penetrating study is made here of the role of foreign oil companies in relation to India's balance of payments from the 1950s. It also sheds much light on the behaviour patterns of multinational companies in less developed economies. The author concludes that a naive Indian government presided over an unduly lax regulatory regime which permitted the oil companies to reap maximum advantage from favourable price movements and falling transport costs.

Firms: Burmah Shell; Caltex; Standard Vacuum

488
Wirth, John D. (Editor)
Latin American Oil Companies and the Politics of Energy
1985 University of Nebraska Press *Lincoln, NB*

This book contains a sequence of studies on the history of the oil industry in Argentina, Brazil, Mexico and Venezuela. The collection also includes an account of the activities of Jersey Standard in Latin America. The accent is on the politics of oil with a particular focus on the role and functions of state oil companies.

Firms: Jersey Standard Oil Co.

Mining, General

489
Baldwin, William
The World Tin Market: Political pricing and economic competition
1983 Duke University Press *Durham, NC*

This analysis of the international tin market focuses on patterns of supply and demand, ownership and mining costs. The overriding theme is the regulation of prices at the international level, ending with the collapse of the International Tin Council.

490
Bunting, David
Statistical View of the Trusts: A manual of large American industrial and mining corporations active around 1900
1974 Greenwood Press *Westport, CT*

This indispensable financial dataset covers 242 of the largest industrial and mining corporations in existence in the USA in the period 1896–1905. Statistical tables embrace dividend rates, stock market prices, growth rates and other key indicators.

491
Eckes, Alfred E. Jr
The United States and the Global Struggle for Minerals
1979 University of Texas Press *Austin, TX*

This detailed survey of official US concerns over mineral resources (excluding oil) during the twentieth century focuses on conservation, defence strategy, security of supply and price structures. It is of use to business historians for its insights into the political forces and foreign policy influences moulding US multinational policy in mineral exploitation.

492
Harvey, Charles; Press, Jon (Editors)
International Competition and Industrial Change: Essays in the history of mining and metallurgy, 1800–1950
1990 Cass *London*

An edited collection of essays on various aspects of the history of mineral mining, this book is international in its coverage. There are excellent commentaries on labour and production issues, corporate (including multinational) structures and finance.

493
Nash, George H.
The Life of Herbert Hoover: The engineer, 1874–1914
For main entry, see 3974

Mining, Europe

494
Blanchard, Ian
Russia's Age of Silver: Precious metal production and economic growth in the eighteenth century
1989 Routledge *London*

This wide ranging account of non-ferrous mining both inside and outside Russia covers the period from the sixteenth to the eighteenth centuries. The focus is on silver and the book provides a good analysis of the relationship between silver production and economic growth in Russia.

495
Burt, Roger (Editor)
Cornish Mining: Essays on the organisation of Cornish mines and the Cornish mining economy
1969 David & Charles *Newton Abbot*

This collection of nineteenth-century papers on the Cornish mining industry concentrates on labour organization and remuneration.

496
Burt, Roger
John Taylor, Mining Entrepreneur and Engineer, 1779–1863
1977 Moorland Publishing *Hartington*

This book is a concise biography of a key figure in British mineral exploitation during the first half of the nineteenth century. It is especially useful in charting Taylor's role in the diffusion of advanced mining practices beyond Cornwall.

497
Burt, Roger
The British Lead Mining Industry
1984 Dyllanow Truran *Redruth*

Burt presents an economic history of the British lead mining industry in the eighteenth and nineteenth centuries, which is especially strong on the geological and technical aspects of the industry. The book also touches on organizational and financial issues, as well as the remuneration of labour. It forms a useful complement to D. J. Rowe's 1983 study of lead manufacturing (qv).

498
Burt, Roger; Waite, Peter
Bibliography of the History of British Metal Mining
For main entry, see 9

499
Checkland, S. G.
The Mines of Tharsis
1967 George Allen & Unwin *London*

This is a history of the Glasgow-based Tharsis company and its pyrites mining interests in Southern Spain in the century after 1866. It is a detailed study of Scottish entrepreneurship in the mining and chemical industries and sheds much light on the firm's limitations. Technological and locational factors are highlighted, as are the difficulties of operating an expatriate company in an underdeveloped country.

Firms: Tharsis Sulphur & Copper Co.; United Alkali Co.; Tennant & Sons Ltd; Société des Mines de Cuivre d'Huelva

500
Delhaes-Guenther, Dietrich von
Kali in Deutschland: Vorindustrien, Produktions-techniken und Marktprozesse der Deutschen Kaliwirtschaft ins 19 Jahrhundert [Potash in Germany]
1974 Neue Wirtschaftgeschichte *Wien: Böhlau*

This is a valuable study of potash mining and manufacture in nineteenth-century Germany. It is useful to business historians for its commentaries on entrepreneurship and business organization.

501
Dumielle-Chancelier, Isabelle
La Compagnie du Boléo [The Boléo Company]
1993, PhD Thesis, University of Paris

This dissertation studies a French small mining multinational, operating a copper mine in Spain.

502
Forbes, R. J. (Editor)
Het Zout der Aarde [The Salt of the Earth]
1968 Koninklijke Nederlandsche Zoutindustrie *Hengelo, Netherlands*

This book provides a general history of salt mining, consumption and usage through the ages by nine specialist authors. Although it concentrates on salt as a mineral, the book contains two chapters in which attempts are made to offer a concise history of the Koninklijke Nederlandsche Zoutindustrie Hengelo.

Firms: Koninklijke Nederlandsche Zoutindustrie Hengelo

503
Gomez Mendoza, Antonio
El "Gibraltar económico": Franco y Riotinto, 1936–1954 [The "economic Gibraltar": Franco and Rio Tinto, 1936–1954]
1994 Rio Tinto *Madrid, Spain*

This book analyses the least known stage of the firm, from 1936 to its nationalization by the Spanish Government in 1954. The author focuses on the harassment of the firm by Franco's government for political and economic reasons, and questions the benefits of nationalization for the Spanish economy as a whole.

Firms: Rio Tinto Co.

504
Harris, J. R.
The Copper King: A biography of Thomas Williams of Llanidan
1964 Liverpool University Press *Liverpool*

This detailed study of Thomas Williams's role in developing the copper industry in Britain covers the later eighteenth century. It sheds much light on structure and organization, with a particular focus on the collusive agreement between Williams's Anglesey interests and the Cornish Metal Company.

Firms: Cornish Metal Co.; Thomas Williams

505
Harvey, C. E.
The Rio Tinto Company: An economic history of a leading international mining concern, 1873–1954
1981 Alison Hodge *Penzance*

This is a thematic study of the Rio Tinto Company from the company's formation in 1873 by an Anglo-German syndicate. Strong on theoretical insights, the book ranges over the Company's activities in sulphur and copper production, principally in Spain, but also in the Northern Rhodesian copper belt. It places the history of the company firmly in its Spanish context, both economically and politically.
Firms: Rio Tinto Co.

506
Kennedy, K. H.
Mining Tsar: The life and times of Leslie Urquhart
For main entry, see 434

507
Lindsay, Jean
A History of the North Wales Slate Industry
1974 David & Charles *Newton Abbot*

Lindsay gives a narrative account of the development of the slate industry in North Wales. She is especially informative on labour and social issues.

508
Rowe, D. J.
Lead Manufacturing in Britain: A history
1983 Croom Helm *London*

The definitive account of the development of lead manufacturing in Britain from the eighteenth century is given here. Based on company archives, the book focuses on organization and marketing. Of particular interest is the account of cartel developments from the 1890s onwards.
Firms: Associated Lead Manufacturers; Walkers Parker and Co.

509
Sudrià Carles
El INI en el sector de la minería: Orígenes y evolución [INI in the Mining Sector Origins and development]
1994 Fundación Empresa Pública *Madrid, Spain*

This book describes the activities of the main mining businesses within the INI group during Franco's period.
Firms: Instituto Nacional de Industria

510
Whately, Christopher A.
The Scottish Salt Industry 1570–1850: An economic and social history
1987 Aberdeen University Press *Aberdeen, Scotland*

This is an authoritative account of the development of the salt industry in Scotland covering technology, organization and the labour force. It is particularly useful for its analysis of the relationship between the salt and coal industries.

Mining, North America

511
Blakey, Arch Frederic
The Florida Phosphate Industry: A history of the development and use of a vital mineral
1973 Harvard University Press *Cambridge, MA*

This detailed study of the Florida phosphate industry, traces the mineral's market expansion as a chemical fertiliser. Technological developments are analysed effectively and the book ends with an informed commentary on the industry's response to environmental concerns.

512
Bothwell, Robert
Eldorado: Canada's national uranium company
1984 University of Toronto Press *Toronto, Canada*

This is a highly readable account of the history of Eldorado Gold Mines Limited and its involvement in the Canadian uranium industry from its inception in the 1930s.
Firms: Eldorado Gold Mines

513
Chaput, Donald
The Cliff: America's first great copper mine

1971 Sequoia Press *Kalamazoo, MI*

This brief but useful study of the development of Cliff copper takes the story from the inception of exploitation in the 1840s to its demise in 1870. The focus is on the mining community in its social and economic context.

514
Davis, John H.
The Guggenheims: An American epic
1978 William Morrow & Co. *New York, NY*

This book is a generational history of the Guggenheim family from the mid-nineteenth century, containing insights into the control and operation of the US minerals industry.

Firms: American Smelting and Refining Co.; Guggenheim

515
Dempsey, Stanley; Fell, James E. Jr
Mining the Summit: Colorado's Ten Mile District, 1860–1960
1986 University of Oklahoma Press *Norman, OK*

This is a useful account of mining developments in Colorado which highlights the evolving pattern of mineral exploitation, from gold and silver to molybdenum.

516
Fahey, John
The Ballyhoo Bonanza
1971 University of Washington Press *Seattle, WA*

Fahey gives an excellent study of Charles Sweeney's career as a mining promoter in the Coeur d'Alenes during the 'buccaneering age'. The book is useful to business historians for its focus on financial and legal manoeuvrings.

517
Fell, James E. Jr
Oils to Metals: The Rocky Mountain smelting industry
1980 University of Nebraska Press *Lincoln, NB*

This detailed study of mining and smelting in Colorado covers the later nineteenth century. Narrative-based, the book provides a good description of technological developments and of the market and competitive forces which promoted integration.

Firms: American Smelting & Refining Co.; Consolidated Kansas City; Meyer Guggenheim; Omaha and Grant; United Smelting & Refining Co.

518
Gibson, Arrell M.
Wilderness Bonanza: The Tri-State District of Missouri, Kansas and Oklahoma
1972 University of Oklahoma Press *Norman, OK*

This is a somewhat outdated, but useful study of mineral exploitation in the Tri-state district in the nineteenth and twentieth centuries. The book concentrates on the production of lead and zinc and is useful to business historians for the insights offered into the delayed arrival of corporate mining in the district.

519
King, Joseph E.
A Mine to Make a Mine: Financing the Colorado mining industry, 1859–1902
1977 Texas A & M University Press *College Station, TX*

King's book is a study of the role of eastern capital in financing the mining of precious metals in Colorado. He explains why few fortunes were made and emphasizes the contribution of capital imports to economic diversification.

520
Navin, Thomas R.
Copper Mining and Management
1978 University of Arizona Press *Tucson, AZ*

This critical evaluation of the US copper mining industry focuses on technical developments and managerial standards from the 1880s onwards. The book emphasizes the technological imperatives in the industry which have inhibited commercial success.

Firms: Anaconda; Calumet; Hecla

521
Newell, Dianne
Technology on the Frontier: Mining in old Ontario
1986 University of British Columbia Press *Vancouver, Canada*

Newell gives a detailed and authoritative study of mining development in nineteenth-century Ontario. The emphasis is on technology in relation to a wide range of mining endeavours, including salt, brine, petroleum and phosphate.

522
Norris, James D.
AZn: A history of the American Zinc Company
1969 State Historical Society of Wisconsin
Madison, WI

This is a useful study of a US mineral corporation in the twentieth century, concentrating on entrepreneurship in relation to a variety of demand and supply-side issues, including company organization and labour relations.
Firms: American Zinc Co. (AZn)

523
Peterson, Richard H.
The Bonanza Kings: The social origins and business behaviour of western mining entrepreneurs, 1870–1900
For main entry, see 3856

524
Rohrbough, Malcolm J.
Aspen: The history of a silver mining town, 1879–1893
1986 Oxford University Press *New York, NY*

This highly-focused study of a leading silver mining town covers its late nineteenth century heyday. The arrival of the railroad is noted as the critical factor in facilitating Aspen's commercial and social diversification.

525
Smith, Duane A.
Song of the Hammer and Drill: The Colorado San Juans, 1860–1914
1982 Colorado School of Mines Press *Golden, CO*

Smith's book is a study of mineral exploitation in the San Juan mining region of south western Colorado. The book conveys well the numerous obstacles in the way of successful mining enterprise, from transport deficiencies to turbulent labour relations.

526
Spence, Clark C.
The Conrey Placer Mining Company: A pioneer gold-dredging enterprise in Montana, 1897–1922
1990 Montana Historical Society Press
Helena, MT

This factual study of a pioneering company in the Montana gold mining industry, concentrates on technical developments and provides an excellent account of dredging technology.
Firms: Conrey Placer Mining Co.

527
Suggs, George G. Jr
Colorado's War on Militant Unionism: James H. Peabody and the Western Federation of Miners
1972 Wayne State University Press *Detroit, MI*

This authoritative account of labour disputes in the Colorado mining and refining industry in the years 1903 and 1904 highlights the extent of economic and physical coercion at the hands of employers and politicians intent upon the pursuit of repressive labour policies.

528
Whiteman, Maxwell
Copper for America: The Hendricks family and a national industry, 1755–1939
1971 Rutgers University Press *New Brunswick, NJ*

This is an account of the contribution of a Sephardic Jewish family to the development of the early copper industry in America. It is of use to business historians principally for its description of a family firm's transition from merchanting to manufacturing in the period 1755–1830.
Firms: Soho Copper Co.

529
Young, Otis E. Jr
Western Mining: An informal account of precious metals prospecting, placering, lode mining, and milling on the American frontier from Spanish times to 1893
1970 University of Oklahoma Press *Norman, OK*

This is an eclectic account of mining practice with a focus on the history of technology.

530
Young, Otis E. Jr
Black Powder and Hand Steel: Miners and machines on the old western frontier
1976 University of Oklahoma Press *Norman, OK*

Young presents a useful study of the technology of hard-rock mining in the American West, providing good insights into the way of life of frontier prospectors.

Mining, Latin America

531
Bernstein, Marvin D.
The Mexican Mining Industry 1890–1950: A study of the interaction of politics, economics and technology
1964 State University of New York Press *Albany, NY*

This is a detailed account of base metal mining in Mexico tracing the record of foreign investment and relations with the Mexican state. The role of the USA as an importer is also assessed.

532
Brew, Roger
El Desarrollo Económico de Antioquia Desde la Independencia Hasta 1920 [The Economic Development of Antioquia (Colombia) from 1820–1920]
1977 Banco de la República *Bogotá, Colombia*

This regional history examines the interweaving of capital, technology, labour markets and entrepreneurship in Antioquia's pioneering industrialization. Sectoral analysis shows the key role played by gold mining, then commerce and later on the coffee economy in propelling mountain-locked Medellín ('the Manchester of Colombia') into the industrial era. It constitutes a master work based on thorough research in primary and secondary sources.

533
Dore, Elizabeth
The Peruvian Mining Industry: Growth, stagnation and crisis
1988 Westview Press *Boulder, CO*

A study of the Peruvian mining industry in the twentieth century which offers a well informed critique of dependancy theory. Based on secondary sources, the book provides insights into government–industry relations and the mobilization of mine labour.

Firms: Cerro de Pasco Corp.; Peruvian Corp.; Southern Peru Copper Corp. (ASARCO)

534
Eakin, Marshall C.
British Enterprise in Brazil: The St John d'El Rey Mining Company and the Morro Velho Gold Mine, 1830–1960
1989 Duke University Press *Durham, NC and London*

This evaluation of the economic and social impact of foreign enterprise in the Brazilian gold mining industry, starts with the founding of the St John d'El Rey Company in 1839 to its transfer to US ownership in 1960. The 'business history' component is narrative-based. Relations with local, state and central governments are analysed.

Firms: St John d'El Rey Mining Company

535
Gootenburg, Paul
Between Silver and Guano: Commercial policy and the state in post-independence Peru
1989 Princeton University Press *Princeton, NJ*

This is a well-documented study of the political economy of the Peruvian guano industry in the nineteenth century.

536
Libby, D. C.
Trabalho escravo e capital estrangeiro no Brasil: o caso de Morro Velho [Slave labour and foreign capital in Brazil: The Morro Velho case]
1984 Editora Itatiaia *Belo Horizonte, Brazil*

This work examines the history of the St John d'El Rey Mining Company, from its establishment in the 1830s until the last years of slavery in Brazil in the 1880s. It analyses the

ability of slaves to adapt to industrial enterprises.
Firms: St John d'El Rey Mining Co.

537
Libby, D. C.
Transformacão e trabalho em uma economia escravista: Minas Gerais no século XIX [Transformation and Work in a Slave Economy: Nineteenth-century Minas Gerais]
For main entry, see 662

538
Lopez-Toro, Alvaro
Migracíon y Cambio Social en Antioquia, Colombia, durante el Siglo XIX [Migration and Social Change in Antioquia, Colombia During the Nineteenth Century]
1970 Universidad de los Andes *Bogotá, Colombia*
This short yet authoritative book preceded the abundant scholarly literature of the last two decades on Antioquia–the region in Colombia well known for its entrepreneurial activity. It masterfully combines economic analysis and historial interpretation. It offers a series of suggestive hypotheses on the complex web linking gold mining, colonization, and entrpreneurial resources. It relies exclusively on secondary sources.

539
Moran, Theodore H.
Multinational Corporations and the Politics of Dependence: Copper in Chile
1974 Princeton University Press *Princeton, NJ*
This excellent study of the post-1945 Chilean copper industry offers first-rate comparisons and contrasts between the US owned Kennecott and Anaconda companies. Entrepreneurial strategies are discussed in detail, as are corporate–government relations.
Firms: Anaconda; Kennecott

540
O'Brien, Thomas F.
The Nitrate Industry and Chile's Crucial Transition: 1870–1891
1982 New York University Press *New York, NY*
Grounded in a Marxian and dependency framework, this is a study of the impact of the foreign-dominated nitrate industry on Chilean economic and social development in the later-nineteenth century. The analysis of labour systems and local credit networks is of interest to business historians.
Firms: J. D. Campbell & Co.; Tarapaca Nitrate Co.; Associated Banks; Banco Nacionale de Chile; Antofagasta Nitrate & Railway Co.

541
Randall, Robert W.
Real del Monte: A British mining venture in Mexico
1972 University of Texas Press *Austin, TX*
Based on archive sources, this is a detailed study of the Company of Adventurers in the Mines of Real del Monte (1824–1849), a British-owned silver mining concern. The book analyses the reasons for the Adventurers' financial failure and provides useful insights into the diffusion of mining technology.
Firms: Real del Monte

542
Sonnichsen, C. L.
Colonel Greene and the Copper Skyrocket
1976 University of Arizona Press *Tucson, AZ*
This is a detailed account of the role of William Cornell Greene as a leading entrepreneur in the copper mining industry of Mexico and the South Western United States. The book draws effective links between Greene's ambitious plans for expansion and his limited access to capital. It also sheds light on the nationalistic forces which precipitated a major strike by Greene's Mexican labourers in 1906, an event which led to his departure from the industry in the following year.
Firms: Cananea Consolidated Copper Co.; Greene Cananea Copper Co.

543
Twinam, Ann
Miners, Merchants, and Farmers in Colonial Colombia
1982 University of Texas Press *Austin, TX*
Relying on local and national archives, this volume traces the origins of the entrepreneurial tradition of a Colombian region (Antioquia). It concentrates on gold mining, commerce and

agriculture during the late colonial period (1760–1810). The author provides a revisionist interpretation of Antioqueño entrepreneurship focusing on the regional elite's conduct framed by high risk, liquidity and reinvestment.

Mining, Rest of World

544
Blainey, G.
The Rise of Broken Hill
1968 Macmillan *Melbourne, Australia*
Blainey gives an accurate and descriptive early history of Broken Hill Proprietary Co. Ltd and other companies which emerged from the vast silver and lead discoveries made at Broken Hill from 1883. The book contains interesting comments on the technological and organizational challenges facing mining companies before 1914.
Firms: Broken Hill Proprietary (BHP)

545
Blainey, Geoffrey
The Peaks of Lyell
3rd Edition
1970 Melbourne University Press *Melbourne, Australia*
This is a history of mineral exploitation, and of copper in particular, in north-western Tasmania from the late-nineteenth century onwards.

546
Blainey, Geoffrey
The Rush That Never Ended: A history of Australian mining
2nd Edition
1970 Melbourne University Press *Melbourne, Australia*
A highly readable account of the history of metal mining in Australia, this book emphasizes the industry's contribution to overall economic growth.

547
Cartwright, A. P.
Gold Paved the Way: The story of the Gold Fields Group of companies
1967 Macmillan *London*
This book is a popular and narrative history of Consolidated Gold Fields Limited.
Firms: Consolidated Gold Fields; Gold Fields of South Africa; New Consolidated Gold Fields

548
Cartwright, A. P.
Golden Age: The story of the industrialization of South Africa and the part played in it by the Corner House Group of companies
1968 Purnell and Sons *Cape Town and Jo'burg, South Africa*
This is a company-sponsored narrative history of Rand Mines and the Central Mining and Investment Corporation in the twentieth century.
Firms: Central Mining Investment Corporation; Rand Mines

549
Chilvers, H. A.
The Story of de Beers
1939 Cassell *London*
A pioneer and authoritative study.
Firms: De Beers

550
Coleman, Francis L.
The Northern Rhodesia Copperbelt 1899–1962
1971 Manchester University Press *Manchester*
This account of the early development of copper mining focuses on exploration and technology.

551
Cunningham, Simon
The Copper Industry in Zambia: Foreign mining companies in a developing country
1981 Praeger *New York, NY*
This history of foreign enterprise in the development of Zambia's copper industry focuses on corporate diplomacy and managerial decision making.
Firms: Anglo Metal; Climax Molybdenum; Rhodesian (Roan) Selection Trust

552
Davenport-Hines, Richard P. T.; Van Helten, Jean-Jacques
Edgar Vincent, Viscount d'Abernon, and the Eastern Investment Company in London, Constantinople and Johannesburg
For main entry, see 2320

553
Dowa Mining Co.
Sogyo 100 Nen Shi [A Centenary of Dowa Mining Co.]
1985 Dowa Mining Co. *Tokyo, Japan*

Dowa, one of the oldest Japanese mining companies, originated in 1884 as Fujita Gumi and was reorganized as Dowa Kogyo after the Second World War. The first half of the book mainly deals with the development of Fujita and the latter half describes the mining business as a whole as well as Dowa's diversification. It is essential for the study of the development of the Japanese mining industry.
Firms: Dowa Mining Co.; Fujita

554
Emden, P. H.
The Rand Lords
1935 Hodder & Stoughton *London*

This is still the best introduction to the business history of the Witwatersrand, written with inside information and in a superb style.
Firms: A. Beit; B. V. Barnato; C. Rhodes; Consolidated Gold Fields; J. B. Robinson

555
Freund, Bill
Capital and Labour in the Nigerian Tin Mines
1981 Longman *London*

This study of western tin mining interests in Nigeria from the early exploitation by the Royal Niger Company to the post-1939 development of the Amalgamated Tin Mines of Nigeria, is written from a Marxist perspective. It offers particular insights into the development of the tin share market in London and the process of company consolidation which led to the formation of the Anglo-Oriental Financial Trust, the predecessor to Amalgamated Tin Mines. The most penetrating sections offer incisive comment on the formation and control of the native labour force.
Firms: Amalgamated Tin Mines of Nigeria; Anglo-Oriental Financial Trust; Bisichi Tin Co.; Gold & Base Metals Mining Co.; Royal Niger Company; United Africa Co.

556
Furukawa Co.
Sogyo 100 Nen Shi [100 Year History of Furukawa Company Limited]
1976 Furukawa Co. *Tokyo, Japan*

Furukawa, one of the Zaibatsu, grew from its origins in copper mining in 1875. It developed rapidly with the industrialization in the Meiji era, and diversified into related industries. This book is a well-balanced business history, written with advice from famous business historians. It includes sections on strategies, functional changes, technical developments, diversification policies and so on, with a historical background of the industry.
Firms: Furukawa Co.

557
Greenhalgh, Peter
West African Diamonds 1919–83: An economic history
1985 Manchester University Press *Manchester*

The main focus of this study is on the activities of the Consolidated African Selection Trust (now part of BP Minerals) in southern Ghana and the eastern province of Sierra Leone. Based on archival research the book describes company development thematically, covering such issues as labour, profits, government intervention, marketing and African diggings. It notes the financial failure of West African diamond mining which followed state takeovers of European operations after 1960.
Firms: BEYLA; BP Minerals; Consolidated African Selection Trust Ltd; Diamond Corporation; National Diamond Co. (Sierra Leone); Sierra Leone Selection Trust; SOGUINEX; West African Diamond Syndicate

558
Gregory, Sir Theodore
Sir Ernest Oppenheimer and the Economic Development of Southern Africa
1962 Clarendon Press *Oxford*

A detailed account is given here of Sir Ernest Oppenheimer's activities in the financial organ-

ization of diamond mining in Southern Africa up to the 1950s. Based on archive material, the book focuses on the operation of the diamond market and the attempts at monopolization.
Firms: Anglo-American Corporation; Diamond Corporation; De Beers Consolidated Mines

559
Innes, D.
Anglo-American and the Rise of Modern South Africa
1984 Heinemann Educational Books *London*

Innes updates and expands Gregory's book on Oppenheimer (qv), setting Anglo-American in the context of South Africa's economic and political life and describing its international industrial linkages. Although particularly concerned with social change, this study explores the history and dominance of the company.
Firms: Anglo-American Corporation of South Africa; De Beers Industrial Corporation

560
Jeeves, Alan H.
Migrant Labour in South Africa's Mining Economy: The struggle for the gold mines' labour supply, 1890–1920
1985 McGill-Queen's University Press *Montreal, Canada*

A first-rate study of labour supply and demand in the early development of South African gold mining. The book describes the extent of inter-firm competition for labour, the role of neighbouring colonial authorities and that of the Rand-based Native Recruiting Corporation after 1919.

561
Johnson, Paul
Gold Fields: A centenary portrait
1987 Weidenfeld & Nicolson *London*

This is a company-sponsored history of Consolidated Gold Fields, published to mark the firm's centenary.
Firms: Consolidated Gold Fields

562
Kubicek, Robert V.
Economic Imperialism in Theory and Practice: The case of South African gold mining finance, 1886–1914
1979 Duke University Press *Durham, NC*

This is a well-researched study of the early financing of gold mining in South Africa. The 'economic imperialism' theme is well sustained and the book offers a fine commentary on the relevant historiography.

563
Langen, Godehard
The History of Diamond Production and the Diamond Trade
1970 Praeger *New York, NY*

This history of diamond production and trade from the earliest times, is of use to business historians for its focus on the South African experience after 1870. The role of Cecil Rhodes is evaluated, but principally from a demand-side perspective.
Firms: De Beers Mining Co.

564
Lind, C. A.
Super in the South: The early history of the Southland Cooperative Phosphate Co. Ltd
1983 Southland Cooperative Phosphate Co. *Invercargill, New Zealand*

This company was established in 1947 to avoid long transport haul of fertilisers from Otago. It is an interesting example of a cooperative and the book highlights conflicts over 'dry' (non-farmer) shareholders.
Firms: Dominion Fertiliser; Kempthorne-Prosser; Southland Cooperative Phosphate Co.

565
Newbury, Colin
The Diamond Ring: Business, politics and precious stones in South Africa, 1867–1947
1989 Clarendon Press *Oxford*

This analysis of the development of the South African diamond industry is based upon the inter-linkages between political, social, geological and technological factors. It provides a good account of the forces promoting concentration and vertical integration. The role of the individual entrepreneur is placed in a wide-ranging context.
Firms: De Beers Consolidated Mines; Anglo-American Corporation

566
Nippon Mining Co. Ltd
A Company History: 1956–1985
1989 Nippon Mining Co. *Tokyo, Japan*
This work charts the growth and development of the firm with a particular stress on the business environment and business strategy.
Firms: Nippon Mining Co.

567
Perrings, Charles
Black Mineworkers in Central Africa: Industrial strategies and the evolution of an African proletariat in the Copperbelt 1911–1941
1979 Holmes & Meier *New York, NY*
This book is a study of the exploitation of copper deposits in Zambia and Zaire by British and French enterprise. Comparisons and contrasts are drawn via strategies for the recruitment and control of labour.
Firms: Union Minière

568
Takeda, Haruhito
Nihon Sandogyo Shi [A History of the Japanese Copper Industry]
1987 University of Tokyo Press *Tokyo, Japan*
This work is a detailed study of the development of copper mining in Japan between 1870 and 1930. It examines how the developing copper mining industry established a capitalist managerial system and a consolidated and distinctive industrial structure.
Firms: Furukawa Co.

569
Turrell, R. V.
Capital & Labour on the Kimberley Diamond Fields 1871–90
1987 Cambridge University Press *Cambridge*
A study of the Kimberley diamond mines, with particular reference to the colour bar, race and labour. The role of Cecil Rhodes is included.
Firms: De Beers Consolidated

570
Williams, M.; MacDonald, B.
The Phosphateers: A history of the British Phosphate Commissioners and the Christmas Island Phosphate Commission
1985 Melbourne University Press *Melbourne, Australia*
The Commission was established by the UK, Australia and New Zealand in 1920 to provide primary producers with a regular supply of high grade fertilizers at low cost. Illustrating cooperative activity by farmers, this is a lengthy and somewhat indigestible account.

571
Worger, William H.
South Africa's City of Diamonds: Mine workers and monopoly capitalism in Kimberley, 1867–1896
1987 Yale University Press *New Haven, CT*
This book gives an analysis of the recruitment of immigrant labour and the emergence of joint-stock organization in South African diamond mining, focusing on the formation of De Beers. The labour issues are handled more effectively than matters of structure and organization.
Firms: De Beers

Traditional and Heavy Industries

Iron & Steel, UK

572
Abe, Etsuo; Suzuki, Yoshitaka (Editors)
Changing Patterns of International Rivalry: Some lessons from the steel industry (Seventeenth Fuji Conference)
For main entry, see 96

573
Abromeit, H.
British Steel: An industry between the State and the Private Sector
1986 Berg *Leamington Spa and Heidelberg, Germany*

Somewhat ironically, given that it was written during the privatisation of the British Steel Corporation, this is a study of the meaning of nationalisation; how nationalised industries are expected to operate and how they actually operate in practice. The book is based primarily on interviews of individuals in the steel industry (private and public) and in Whitehall.
Firms: British Steel

574
Addis, John P.
The Crawshay Dynasty: A study in industrial organization and development 1765–1867
1957 University of Wales Press *Cardiff, Wales*

Based on contemporary business papers, this excellent study of the South Wales iron industry sets it in an economic context of costs and demand, though there is little on the labour force and its management.
Firms: Crawshay; Cyfartha Works

575
Andrews, P. W. S.; Brunner, E.
Capital Development in Steel: A study of the United Steel Companies Ltd
1952 Basil Blackwell *Oxford*

Benefiting from full access to company records and to individuals in United Steel, this is a very detailed account of investment decisions in mnufacturing industry. The book charts the progress of the company since its formation in 1918 but the main focus is on capital development in the 1930s and after the War up to 1950.
Firms: United Steel Companies; Appleby-Frodingham Iron & Steel Co.; Samuel Fox & Co.; Workington Iron and Steel Co.; Steel, Peech & Tozer

576
Ashton, T. S.
Iron and Steel in the Industrial Revolution
1924 3rd edn 1963 Manchester University Press, *Manchester*

Although first published in 1924, Professor Ashton's classic study can still be regarded as a necessary text in understanding the British iron and steel industry. The period covered is the eighteenth century through to c.1820 and Ashton deals with the various technical discoveries, the inventors and entrepreneurs, foreign competition and policy among the capitalists and the conditions of the industry's labour force.
Firms: Boulton & Watt; Carron Co.; Coalbrookdale Co.; Ambrose & John Crowley; Ebbw Vale Co.

577
Atkinson, Michael; Baber, Colin
The Growth and Decline of the South Wales Iron Industry 1700–1880: An industrial history
1987 University of Wales Press *Cardiff, Wales*

The authors provide a detailed overview of the fortunes of the South Wales iron industry. The introduction of coke-fired furnaces in the mid-eighteenth century established the industry which, by the 1820s, was dominant within the British iron trade. The collapse of the industry in the 1880s, it is argued, would likely have occurred even without the emergence of steel.
Firms: Dowlais Co.; Ebbw Vale Co.; Monmouthshire Iron & Steel Co.; Pontypool Bar Iron & Tinplate Co.; Pentwyn Iron & Coal Co.

578

Barraclough, K. C.

Steelmaking: 1850–1900

1990 The Institute of Metals *London*

Barraclough provides a very detailed, technical account of steelmaking in Europe and the USA in the second half of the nineteenth century. The story told is how the inventions of Bessemer, Siemens and Thomas revolutionized the world of steel production and how the small-scale, specialized steel industry of mid-century was transformed by the massive output and dramatically cheaper costs of 'bulk steel'.

Firms: John Brown & Co.; Barrow Haematite Steel Co.; Bolton Iron & Steel Co.; Brown, Bailey & Dixon Ltd; Hoesch; Krupp; Nashua Iron & Steel Co., New Hampshire; New Russian Iron Co.; Petia, Gaudet et Cie; Steel Company of Scotland

579

Beynon, Hugh; Hudson, Ray; Sadler, David

A Place Called Teesside: A locality in a global economy

1994 Edinburgh University Press *Edinburgh, Scotland*

Traces the fate of a region of north-east England dominated by the chemical and steel industries from the mid nineteenth to late twentieth centuries. The core argument is that this is not a region based on low-technology, staple industries but one for which the roots of decline are not technological but strategic choices made by corporations in an increasingly global economy. The social and political impact of economic change on this locality are assessed.

Firms: British Steel Corporation; Imperial Chemical Industries

580

Birch, Alan

The Economic History of the British Iron & Steel Industry 1784–1879

1967 Frank Cass *London*

This book sets out to be a reappraisal of the history of the iron and steel industry from the eighteenth to the later nineteenth centuries. Although a series of essays the volume provides a coherent chronological account. The themes running through the book are the development of technology and the role of innovation and enterprise.

Firms: Carron Co.; Coalbrookdale Co.; Dowlais Co.; Siemens

581

Boswell, Jonathan S.

Business Policies in the Making: Three steel companies compared

1983 George Allen & Unwin *London*

Using managerial insights, Boswell examines three steel firms between the wars, focusing on decision-making processes, growth and efficiency policies, responses to shrinking markets, problems of managerial succession, and social action. Differences in executive decision-making resulted in quite different developmental trajectories based on implicit and explicit trade-offs between growth and efficiency.

Firms: Dorman Long; Stewarts & Lloyds; United Steel Companies

582

Boyce, Gordon

The Development of the Cargo Fleet Iron Company, 1900–1914: Entrepreneurship, costs and structural rigidity in the northeast coast steel industry

Business History Review, vol. 63, no. 4 1989: pp 839–75

Boyce makes an analysis of the response of firms in the North East of England in the early-twentieth century to technological challenges. Through an examination of one company's efforts it is argued that firm-specific rather than managerial characteristics were more important in defining corporate strategy.

Firms: Cargo Fleet Iron Co.; Consett Iron Co.; Dorman Long; Furness, Withy & Company; Skinningrove Iron Co.; South Durham Steel Co.

583

Bryer, R. A.; Brignall, T. J.; Maunders, A. R.

Accounting for British Steel: A financial analysis of the failure of the British Steel Corporation 1967–80

1982 Gower *Aldershot*

This book traces the evolution of business strategy and capital structure of the nation-

alized British Steel Corporation from 1967–80 and concludes that disastrous performance was the result of poor strategic choices rather than nationalization. The political limits on BSC's activities, confined to bulk steel making, interference on pricing policy, and disastrous capital investment decisions combined to produce massive cumulative losses for the public corporation.
Firms: British Steel Corporation

584
Burk, Kathleen
The First Privatisation: The politicians, the City, and the denationalisation of steel
1988 Historians' Press *London*
The 'privatization' of the British steel industry between 1953–61 was a process beset by ambivalence among politicians, bankers, industrialists and the public. Both labour opposition and Conservative government recognized that, irrespective of ownership, a high degree of state regulation would be exercised over the steel industry. The share offers of the various steel companies revealed a public more interested in realizing quick profits than in becoming permanent investors.
Firms: Baring Brothers; British Steel; Morgan Grenfell; United Steel Co.

585
Burn, Duncan L.
The Economic History of Steelmaking 1867–1939: A study in competition
1940 Cambridge University Press *Cambridge*
Burn's book is the classic study of competition in the British steelmaking industry to 1939. The central themes are competitiveness, entrepreneurship, company structure and technical change.
Firms: United Steel Co.; Steel Company of Scotland; Colvilles

586
Burn, Duncan L.
The Steel Industry, 1939–59: A study in competition and planning
1961 Cambridge University Press *Cambridge*
A continuation of Burn's major work on the steel industry covering nationalization, de-nationalization and the expansion of the supervised industry in the 1950s. Plentiful comparative material on European steel industries. Strong on planning and industry–government relations and rich in insider detail.
Firms: Colvilles; United Steel; Richard Thomas; Dorman Long; GKB

587
Burnham, T. H.; Hoskins, G. O.
Iron and Steel in Britain 1870–1930
1943 George Allen & Unwin *London*
Although published during the war this study was begun in 1931. The book provides a comparative perspective in which the relative and absolute decline of the British steel industry is viewed over the period from 1870 to 1930. The authors contend that the industry itself was greatly responsible for that decline.

588
Campbell, R. H.
Carron Company
1961 William & Boyd *Edinburgh, Scotland*
This business history of a Scottish iron company covers the period to 1914 with notable depth on eighteenth century developments.
Firms: Carron Co.

589
Carr, J. C.; Taplin, W.
History of the British Steel Industry
1962 Basil Blackwell *London*
This book provides a thorough and detailed study of the history of the British steel industry between 1856 and 1939, with a prologue and epilogue covering the pre 1856 years and the situation from 1940 to 1960. The authors provide a comprehensive account with particular insights into the post 1918 years due to access to the archives of the British Iron and Steel Federation.
Firms: Barrow Hematite Steel Co.; William Beardmore & Co.; Colvilles; Consett Iron Co.

590
Dew, Charles B.
Iron Maker to the Confederacy: Joseph R. Anderson and the Tredegar Iron Works
For main entry, see 3945

591
Dudley, G. F.; Richardson, J. J.
Politics and Steel in Britain 1967–1988: The life and times of the British Steel Corporation
1990 Dartmouth *Aldershot*

The authors provide a study of the relationship between the British steel industry and the Government. The book begins with the ill-fated decision behind the massive investment programme decided in 1967, charts the depression of steel's main markets and the of the industry, and also with the creation of the newly-privatised British Steel plc in 1988.
Firms: British Steel Corporation; British Steel plc; Rover; Ford UK; Vauxhall; Nissan

592
Elsas, Madeleine (Editor)
Iron in the Making: Dowlais Iron Company letters 1782–1860
1960 Glamorgan County Council/Guest Keen and Nettlefold *Cardiff, Wales*

This selection of letters gives a vivid picture of the business, exports and labour problems of the business,together with others on social concerns of the day.
Firms: Dowlais Iron Co.; Guest Keen Iron & Steel Co.

593
Erickson, Charlotte
British Industrialists: Steel and hosiery, 1850–1950
For main entry, see 3811

594
Flinn, M. W.
Men of Iron: The Crowleys in the Early Iron Industry
1962 Edinburgh University Press *Edinburgh, Scotland*

This is a fine study of a major iron business in the eighteenth and early nineteenth centuries dealing not only with family partners but with commercial and industrial organization and the concern with industrial welfare.
Firms: Crowley

595
Harris, J. R.
The British Iron Industry, 1700–1850
1988 Macmillan *London*

Produced as part of the Economic and Social History Society's series of student texts, this pamphlet is a concise and informative survey of the British iron industry and its historiography.

596
Heal, D. W.
The Steel Industry in Post War Britain
1974 David & Charles *Newton Abbot*

This is a study of industrial geography which examines the issue of location in the British steel industry from the end of the Second World War up to the second nationalisation in 1967. Arguing that locational change is just as important as technological and organisational change, the author illustrates why, nevertheless, there has been a greater continuity in the location of the industry.
Firms: British Steel Corporation; Colvilles; Consett Iron Co.; Dorman Long & Co.; Richard Thomas & Baldwins; United Steel Companies; Stewarts & Lloyds; South Durham Steel & Iron Co.

597
Horsfall, John
The Iron Masters of Penns 1720–1970
1971 Roundwood Press *Kineton*

Horsfall provides a history of 250 years of a family-run business, with more on family dynamics than details of the business but interesting on tensions and change.
Firms: Webster & Horsfall; Latch & Bachelor

598
Hume, J. R.; Moss, M. S.
A Bed of Nails: The history of P. MacCallum and Sons Ltd: A study in survival
1981 Lang & Fulton *Greenock, Scotland*

This is a standard business history commissioned by the company to celebrate its bicentenary. The origins of the company lie in providing materials to the Clyde shipbuilding industry and for most of its history its main activity has been steel stockholding with periodic involvement in tramp shipping. Overshadowed by larger, more famous local companies such as Lithgows, the interest of MacCallum and Sons lies in how a small to medium-sized enterprise has managed to thrive for so long.

Firms: P. MacCallum & Sons; Lang & Fulton; Colvilles; Shipping Co.; William Beardmore & Co.

599
Hyde, Charles
Technological Change and the British Iron Industry 1700–1870
1977 Princeton University Press *Princeton, NJ*

This study of technological change in the British iron industry ranges from the early days of charcoal furnaces to the introduction of cheap steel. The author's main concern is with the diffusion of new technologies rather than their invention. Rather unsurprisingly, it is shown that relative cost was the determining factor in the British ironmasters' choice of processes.

Firms: Coalbrookdale Co.; Dowlais Co.; Ebbw Vale Co.; Backbarrow Co.; Carron Co.

600
Jones, Edgar
Guest, Keen & Nettlefolds: vol. 1: Innovation and Enterprise 1759–1918; vol. 2: The Growth of a Business 1918–45
For main entry, see 1360

601
Keeling, B. S.; Wright, A. E. G.
The Development of the British Steel Industry
1964 Longmans *London*

This is an account of the British steel industry covering the period from 1939 to 1963 and, as such, provides a continuation of the *History* by Carr and Taplin (qv). The book was commissioned by the British Iron and Steel Federation and is intended as a general rather than overly technical history.

Firms: William Beardmore; British Steel Corporation; Colvilles; English Steel Corporation; Steel Company of Wales; United Steel Companies

602
Lloyd, Godfrey I. H.
The Cutlery Trades: An historical essay on the economics of small-scale production
1913 Longmans, Green & Co. *London*

A superb early study of an industrial district in the Sheffield cutlery industry from the seventeenth to twentieth centuries. Massively researched, it provides detailed coverage of each specialized sub-sector of the trade.

603
McCloskey, Donald N.
Maturity and Entrepreneurial Decline: British iron and steel, 1870–1931
1973 Harvard University Press *Cambridge, MA*

This seminal work analyses the investment and productivity records of late-Victorian British businessmen. The central conclusion is that there is no evidence of entrepreneurial failure but rather of a realistic appraisal of technological alternatives, given the constraints of markets, revenues and royalties.

604
McEachern, D.
A Class Against Itself: Power and the nationalisation of the British Steel industry
1980 Cambridge University Press *Cambridge*

This is not so much a study of the steel industry as an analysis of the nature of class power in a capitalist society, as illustrated by the debates and struggles over nationalisation and denationalisation between 1945 and 1967. The conclusion that the industry was unlikely ever to be returned to the private sector has proved mistaken.

Firms: British Steel Corporation; Colvilles; Richard Thomas & Baldwins; Steel Company of Wales; United Steel Companies

605
Minchinton, W. E.
The British Tinplate Industry: A history
1957 Clarendon Press *Oxford*

The history of the British tinplate industry was characterised by small production units, low investments, over-capacity and a reliance on craft labour. Structural features hindered modernisation of the industry before 1939 relative to the rapid expansion of the American tinplate market, which responded to the boom in canned food.

Firms: Baldwins; Richard Thomas & Co.; Guest Keen & Baldwins

606
Ovenden, Keith
The Politics of Steel
1978 Macmillan *London*

This book provides a detailed account of the process of the renationalisation of steel under the Wilson Government in the 1960s. The interest of the author lies in the study of politics rather than business history; nonetheless this is a useful addition to the literature on the steel industry.
Firms: British Steel Corporation; Colvilles; Richard Thomas & Baldwins; Steel Company of Wales; United Steel Companies

607
Payne, Peter L.
Colvilles and the Scottish Steel Industry
1979 Oxford University Press *London*

This major case study traces the rise of Scotland's premier steelmaking firm from 1861 and the dominance of the founding family. Family control was exercised directly and, perhaps more importantly, indirectly through trusted managerial stewards. The prime objectives of the professional managers after 1918 were the firm's survival and the protection of the Colville family interests. Familial control and complex debt structures lay behind the failure to modernize and rationalize the industry in the 1930s.
Firms: Colvilles; Lithgows; Steel Company of Scotland

608
Pugh, Arthur
Men of Steel By One of Them: A chronicle of eighty-eight years of trade unionism in the British iron and steel industry
1951 Iron and Steel Trades Confederation *London*

This is a monumental study of the various unions active in the British steel industry. The book is of interest both for insights into the industry and the union's involvement in the labour movement. It is essentially an insider's view, the author having been the General Secretary of the Confederation.
Firms: Colvilles; Steel Company of Scotland; Richard Thomas & Co.; Dowlais Steelworks; United Steel Companies Ltd; Stewart & Lloyds; South Durham Steel Co.; Dorman Long & Co.; Consett Iron Co.

609
Raistrick, Arthur
Dynasty of Iron Founders: The Darbys and Coalbrookdale
1953 Longmans, Green *London*

This covers the first 150 years (and five generations) of this Quaker family business to the mid-nineteenth century, providing a compelling history of trade against the backdrop of the industrial revolution, to which the company made a significant contribution.
Firms: Coalbrookdale Co.; Boulton & Watt; Allied Ironfounders

610
Roberts, C. W.
A Legacy from Victorian Enterprise: The Briton Ferry Ironworks and the daughter companies
1983 Alan Sutton *Gloucester*

This is a detailed study, written by a member of the family and based on extensive private records of the various iron and steel-making companies of Briton Ferry in South Wales. The records utilised cover the period 1845 to 1930 though there is some treatment of the period from the late eighteenth century and down to 1978 when the last productive unit closed. The interest of the book lies in the role of small to medium-sized enterprises in the industrial process.
Firms: Briton Ferry Works; Albion Steel Co.; Villiers Tinplate Co.; Tinplate Co,; Whitford Steel Sheet & Galvanising Co.

611
Roepke, Howard
Movements of the British Iron and Steel Industry, 1720–1951
1956 University of Illinois Press *Urbana, IL*

This is a study of the location of the British iron and steel industry going back to the early eighteenth century and covering the early postwar years of 1945–51. As such it overlaps with, but acts as a companion piece to Heal (1974) (qv). Locational inertia is seen as part of the explanation for the British industry's difficulties in meeting foreign competition.

612
Scopes, Frederick
The Development of Corby Works
1968 Stewarts & Lloyds *London*

Published by the company, this is very much an insider's view of Stewarts and Lloyds, the author having been one of the Managing Directors of the company. Although the period covered goes back to 1880 the major concern of the book is with the decision behind the construction and early development of the new iron and steel works at Corby in the 1930s.
Firms: Stewarts & Lloyds Ltd; Barkers Industrial Development Ltd; H. A. Brassert & Co. Ltd; Clydesdale Iron & Steel Works; Colville & Sons Ltd; Frodingham Iron & Steel Co. Ltd; Lancashire Steel Corporation; Lloyds Ironstone Co. Ltd; Scottish Tube Co. Ltd; Steel Company of Scotland Ltd

613
Tolliday, Steven
Business, Banking, and Politics: The case of British Steel, 1918–1939
1987 Harvard University Press *Cambridge, MA*

Between 1918 and 1939 the British steel industry confronted collapsing markets with a largely antiquated capital stock. Indeed, profitability, however intermittent, was possible only for those companies with archaic equipment whose value had been fully amortized rather than those firms with modern equipment but carrying interest charges. The inherent difficulties of reorganizing a fragmented industry and rationalizing its capacity were compounded by a gridlock of competing political and financial interests. The failure to restructure the industry laid the ground for the decline of British steel after 1945.
Firms: Beardmore, William & Co.; Bolckow Vaughan & Co.; Colville, David & Sons; Consett Iron Co.; Dorman Long & Co.; Lithgows; Richard Thomas & Co.; Steel Company of Scotland; Stewarts & Lloyds; United Steel

614
Tweedale, Geoffrey
Sheffield Steel and America: A century of commercial and technological interdependence, 1830–1930
1987 Cambridge University Press *London*

Tweedale examines the interaction of the British and American specialist steel industries. British investment in American manufacturing in the late-nineteenth century was the starting point for a complex pattern of reciprocal technology transfer.
Firms: Edgar Allen & Co.; Hadfields Ltd; Sanderson Bros; Thomas Firth & Sons

615
Tweedale, Geoffrey
Steel City: Entrepreneurship, Strategy and Technology in Sheffield 1743–1993
1995 Oxford University Press *Oxford*

Tweedale looks at the Sheffield special steel trades and the cluster of related industries in cutlery, tools and engineering. Drawing on business records, the book reveals a remarkably enduring and successful steel producing region that does not fit easily into historical theories of entrepreneurial failure and big business.

616
Vaizey, John
The History of British Steel
1974 Weidenfeld & Nicolson *London*

As the first person allowed access to the British Steel archive, the author is able to provide a detailed narrative of the history of the industry from 1918 to the 1960s. Three periods are identified: 1918 to 1932 and the introduction of the tariff; recovery from 1933 to the early 1950s; and the great boom from the Korean War on.
Firms: British Steel Corporation; Colvilles Ltd; Dorman Long; Ebbw Vale Steel, Iron and Coal Co.; English Steel Corporation; Richard Thomas and Baldwins; United Steel; Steel Company of Wales; Stewarts and Lloyds

617
Wainwright, David
Man of Steel: The history of Richard Thomas and his family
1986 Quiller Press *London*

This book details the history of one of the many smaller enterprises which became part of the British Steel Corporation. Attention is given mainly to Richard Thomas, the founder, and to the years from 1884 to 1944. Thomas became expert in the latest processes for

tinplate and steel manufacture and established mills in South Wales and the Forest of Dean.
Firms: Richard Thomas & Co.; Richard Thomas & Baldwins; British Steel Corporation

618
Walshaw, E. R.; Behrendt, C. A.
The History of Appleby-Frodingham
1950 Appleby-Frodingham Steel Co. *London*
This is a company history written by two employees. The book is a narrative account unencumbered by either bibliography or index. Nonetheless it does contain some interesting detail on what was one of the largest integrated steel makers in Britain and which became part of the United Steel Companies Ltd.
Firms: Appleby-Frodingham Steel Co.; United Steel Companies; Frodingham Iron Co.; Appleby Iron Co.

619
Warren, Kenneth
The British Iron and Steel Sheet Industry Since 1840: An economic geography
1970 G. Bell & Sons *London*
The concern of this book is with industrial location. Examined over a period of 130 years the industry has experienced three distinct phases: the growth of small-scale sheet metal manufacture in the West Midlands; the emergence and concentration of the industry in the coastal area of South Wales; the replacement of the old hand mills by modern, strip mills.
Firms: Baldwins; Frederick Babt & Co.; Colvilles Ltd; Ebbw Vale Steel, Iron & Coal Co.; John Lysaght & Co.; Steel Company of Wales

620
Warren, Kenneth
Armstrongs of Elswick: Growth in engineering and armaments to the merger with Vickers
1989 Macmillan *Basingstoke*
Warren describes the competitive rivalry and complex interlinkages between the firms in the British armament sector, 1850–1939. Insulated from commercial pressures by international tensions and the Great War, Armstrongs was plunged into debt after 1920. It was indebtedness which led to Armstrongs' merger with Vickers in 1927 and the subsequent rationalization of the armaments sector.
Firms: Sir W. G. Armstrong & Co.; Armstrong-Whitworth; Beardmore; Vickers

621
Warren, Kenneth
Consett Iron, 1840–1980: A study in industrial location
1990 Oxford University Press *Oxford*
Warren describes the history of the Consett Iron Co., in its commercial, technical, and community setting from 1840 to closure in 1980.
Firms: British Steel Corporation; Consett Iron

622
Wurm, Clemens A.
Politics and International Relations: Steel, cotton and international cartels in British politics, 1924–1939
For main entry, see 4410

Iron & Steel, Europe (excl. UK)

623
Abe, Etsuo; Suzuki, Yoshitaka (Editors)
Changing Patterns of International Rivalry: Some lessons from the steel industry (Seventeenth Fuji Conference)
For main entry, see 96

624
Baudant, Alain
Pont-à-Mousson (1918–1939): Stratégies industrielles d'une dynastie lorraine [Pont-à-Mousson, 1918–1939: Industrial strategies of a Lorraine family]
1980 Publication de la Sorbonne *Paris, France*
This is a detailed study of a large firm in Lorraine, which dominated the French market for cast-iron pipes and tubes. It is based on business records.
Firms: Pont-à-Mousson

625
Bonelli, Franco
Lo sviluppo di una grande impresa in Italia: La Terni dal 1884 al 1962 [The Development of a Great Enterprise in Italy: The history of Terni, 1884–1962]
1975 Einaudi *Turin, Italy*

The history of one of the largest Italian steel producers, a company that epitomizes Italian industrial development because of its close and continuous relationship with the State, which offered tariffs, orders, financial support, and periodically came to the rescue. More than for economic (i.e., to cut costs per unit) the company's growth occurred above all for strategic reasons–i.e. to put it in a better bargaining position with the political powers.
Firms: Terni Banca Commerciale Italiana, IRI

626
Feldenkirchen, Wilfried
Die Eisen- und Stahlindustrie des Ruhrgebiets, 1879–1914: Wachstum, Finanzierung, und Struktur ihrer Grossunternehmen [The Iron and Steel Industry of the Ruhr, 1879–1914]
1982 Steiner *Wiesbaden, Germany*

This is a massive and learned study of the leading concerns in the Ruhr's iron and steel industry before 1914, based on company archives. It provides a very useful statistical database.
Firms: Bochumer Verein; Deutsch-Luxemburg; Gutehoffnungshütte; Hoesch; Krupp; Phoenix; Rheinishe Stahlwerke; Thyssen; Union

627
Feldman, Gerald D.
Iron and Steel in the German Inflation 1916–1923
1977 Princeton University Press *Princeton, NJ*

Feldman charts the rise and demise of a form of 'collective capitalism' in the heavy industries of the Ruhr 1916–23. Hyper inflation, however, convinced the iron and steel masters of the need to evade state controls over their pricing policies.
Firms: AEG; Krupp; MAN; Siemens

628
Fritz, Sven
AB Åkers Styckebruk 1942–1966: Rutger von Seths tid [Aker's Gun Factory Ltd, 1942–1966: The age of Rutger von Seth]
1974 Norstedt & Söner *Stockholm, Sweden*

This work analyses the expansion of AB Åkers Styckebruk – a family concern in the hands of Rutger von Seth, a modern 'ironmaster' ('brukspatron') – during the decades following the Second World War. The emphasis is on technical development and labour conditions. The company's expansion demonstrated a capacity for technical change. This meant specializing in drain pipes and rollers for the iron and steel industry.
Firms: AB Åkers Styckebruk

629
Gillingham, J.
Coal, Steel and the Rebirth of Europe, 1945–1955: The Germans and French from Ruhr conflict to economic community
1991 Cambridge University Press *Cambridge*

This sophisticated study of the German and French coal and steel industries focuses on the post-1945 decade, but is set in the historical context of the Versailles settlement. It provides an excellent account of the political and economic background to the formation of the European Coal and Steel Community in May 1950.
Firms: Krupp AG; Vereinigte Stahlwerke; Thyssen AG

630
Kleinschmidt, Christian; Welskopp, Thomas
Amerika aus deutscher Perspektive: Reisseeindrucke deutscher Ingenieure über die Eisen- und Stahlindustrie der USA 1900–1930 [America from a German Perspective: Impressions of the American iron and steel industry 1900–1930]
Zeitschrift fur Unternehmensgeschichte, 1994: pp 73–103

This article claims that German engineers had a distorted perception of the US iron and steel industry (1900–1930). They conclude that technological transfer from the USA to Germany was hampered by the engineers' biased concern with production and industrial relations problems back home. On the contrary, the visits of German engineers to the USA seem to have been utilized in order to promote the Germans' technological self-consciousness and to reinforce their prevailing idealistic concept of a 'workplace community' which was understood to be essentially a non-union system.

631

Locke, Robert R.

Les fonderies et forges d'Alais à l'époque des premiers chemins de fer, 1829–1874 [The Foundries and Forges of Alais During the Era of the First Railways, 1829–1874]

1978 Marcel Rivière et Cie *Paris, France*

This history of an iron-making company (in south-eastern France), describes how it was established to introduce the English techniques of coke-smelting and puddling into France. The company met with many difficulties and eventually ceased operating in 1874. An interesting correspondence between members of the ironmasters' family is published in the appendix. The book was published in French by an American historian.

632

Lungonelli, M.

Magona d'Italia: Enterprise, labour and technology over a century of Tuscan iron and steel industry (1865–1975) (Original Title: La Magona d'Italia: Impresa, lavoro e tecnologia in un secolo di siderurgia toscana (1865–1975)

1991 Il Mulino–ASSI *Bologna, Italy*

Through the history of one of Italy's private steel works over more than a century, from the unification of the country to the oil crisis, for the first time the private sector's contribution to the Steel and Iron industry is studied. An important contribution of this book is the emphasis placed on the strategies followed by a private steel company in a country where steel and iron were considered to be the responsibility of the state.

Firms: Magona d'Italia

633

Maschke, Erich

Es entsteht ein Konzern: Paul Reusch und die GHH [Paul Reusch and the Growth of a Business]

1969 Rainer Wunderlich Verlag *Tübingen, Germany*

Focusing on the role of its major entrepreneur, Paul Reusch, this is an account of the growth of the iron and steel concern Gutehoffnungshütte into a diversified, vertically integrated group.

Firms: Gutehoffnungshütte; M.A.N.

634

Mény, Yves; Wright, Vincent (Editors)

The Politics of Steel: Western Europe and the steel industry in the crisis years (1974–1984)

1987 de Gruyter *Berlin, Germany*

This massive well-documented work sets national steel industries, with their particular problems, in a European and world context. Separate chapters cover the industries in the UK, Italy, France, Germany and Belgium.

635

Mioche, Philippe

La sidérurgie et l'Etat, 1938–1978 [Iron and Steel and the State 1938–1978]

1992, PhD thesis, University of Paris IV

This general business history describes the decline of the French steel companies and their relationship to the State.

636

Omnès, Catherine

De l'atelier au groupe industriel: Vallourec, 1882–1978 [From Workshop to Industrial Group: Vallourec, 1882–1978]

1980 Presses Universitaries de Lille *Lille, France*

This study of concentration in the steel tubes industry in France, resulted in its dominance by one very large firm–Vallourec. The book is based on a wide range of business and other records.

Firms: Vallourec

637

Pounds, N. E.; Parker, W. N.

Coal and Steel in Western Europe: The influence of resources and techniques on production

1957 Faber & Faber *London*

This book provides a long term history of the coal, iron and steel industries of western Europe. The area studied is essentially that of the original membership of the European Community and the period dealt with covers the eighteenth century origins up to the creation of the European Coal and Steel Community.

Firms: Krupp; Gelsenkirchener Bergwerks A.G.; Deutsche-Luxemburgisch Bergwerks-und-Hütten A.G.; Thyssen; Dugree-Marihaye; Châtillon-Commentry; Mannesmann

638
Sédillot, René
La maison de Wendel de mille sept cent quatre à nos jours [The House of Wendel From 1704 to the Present]
1958 Riss et Cie.-Editions *Paris, France*

This is a book for the general public, about the longest-lived and best-known dynasty of French ironmasters; they were pioneers of new technology, but successive changes in the Franco-German border in Lorraine created serious problems.
Firms: Wendel

639
Seebold, Gustav-Hermann
Ein Stahlkonzern im Dritten Reich: Die Bochumer Verein 1927–1945 [A Steel Firm During the Third Reich: Bochumer Verein 1927–1945]
1981 Hammer *Wuppertal, Germany*

This is a history of the Bochumer Verein, a major German iron and steel company, during the late Weimar years, when it was integrated into the giant Vereinigte Stahlwerke (United Steel), and the Third Reich period. The emphasis is predominantly upon the position of labour and labour-management relations.
Firms: Bochumer Verein; Vereinigte Stahlwerke

640
Spencer, Elaine Glovka
Management and Labor in Imperial Germany: Ruhr industrialists as employers 1896–1914
1984 Rutgers University Press *New Brunswick, NJ*

This is a study of industrial relations in the Ruhr before 1914, which focuses on the strategies and tactics of the heavy industrialists in their fight against political and industrial democracy in Germany. Contains useful introductory chapters on the development of the region and its industries, corporate growth, the entrepreneurial elite, the working class as well as the industry's relations with the government.
Firms: Bochumer Verein; Deutsch-Luxemburg; Gelsenkirchener Bergwerks AG; Gutehoffnungshütte; Harpener Bergbau; Hibernia; Hoesch; Krupp; Phoenix; Thyssen

641
Torres, Eugenio
Ramón de la Sota: Historia económica de un empresario (1857–1936) [Ramon de la Sota The economic history of an entrepreneur (1857–1936)]
For main entry, see 4038

642
Treue, Wilhelm
Die Geschichte der Ilseder Hütte [The Story of the Ilseder Iron and Steel Works]
1960 Peine *Munich, Germany*

This centenary (1858–1958) company history focuses largely on production but sets the business in historical perspective.
Firms: Ilseder Hütte; Peiner Walzwerk

643
Treue, Wilhelm
Die Feuer verlöschen nie: August-Thyssen Hütte Vol. I: 1890–1926, Vol II: 1926–1966 [The Fires Never Went Out]
1966 Econ-Verlag *Düsseldorf, Germany*

This work is well known as the standard business history of Thyssen, one of Germany's largest steelmakers.
Firms: Thyssen

644
Uebbing, Helmut
Wege und Wegmarken: 100 Jahre Thyssen [Ways and Directions]
1991 Siedler *Berlin, Germany*

This book was written by a journalist about one of Germany's most important companies. It lacks references and analysis but provides useful background material.
Firms: Thyssen; Vereinigte Stahlwerke

645
Vichniac, Judith Eisenberg
The Management of Labor: The British and French iron and steel industries, 1860–1980
For main entry, see 4244

646
Vorsteher, Dieter
Borsig: Eisengießerei und Maschinenbauanstalt zu Berlin [Borsig: Iron foundry and mechanical engineering in Berlin]
1983 W. T. J. Siedler Verlag *Berlin, Germany*

This is a company history of Borsig, iron founders and mechanical engineers, in nineteenth-century Germany. The book covers the period to 1887 but is poorly referenced.
Firms: A. Borsig

647
Weisbrod, Bernd
Schwerindustrie in der Weimarer Republik: Interessenpolitik zwischen Stabilisierung und Krise [Heavy Industry During the Weimar Republic]
1978 Hammer *Wuppertal, Germany*

This is an important history of heavy industry in the Weimar period. The emphasis is predominantly upon the industry's political influence.
Firms: Hoesch; Klöckner-Werke; Krupp; Mannesmannröhren; Vereinigte-Stahlwerke

648
Welskopp, Thomas
Arbeit und Macht im Hüttenwerk: Arbeits- und industrielle Beziehungen in der deutschen und amerikanischen Eisen- und Stahlindustrie von den 1860er bis zu den 1930er Jahren Eisen- und Stahlindustrie von den 1860er bis zu den 1930er Jahren [Work and Power in the Steel Industry]
1992 PhD Thesis, Free University of Berlin

This is an excellent dissertation in comparative business history. Welskopp investigates the organization of work on the shopfloor in the German and American Iron and Steel industries. He examines its relevance for social relations within the factory as well as its implications for political and unionized labour associations. By means of comparison between the "Team"-system, the "Drive"-system and the "Crew"-system, Welskopp looks at the factory as a variable system of work and power structures.
Firms: August Thyssen-Hütte; Duisburg-Ruhrort; Fried. Krupp GmbH, Essen; Gutehoffnungshütte AG; Hoesch AG, Dortmund; Mannesmann AG, Düsseldorf

649
Wengenroth, Ulrich
Enterprise and Technology: The German and British steel industries 1865–95 (Original Title: Unternehmensstrategien und technischer Fortschritt: die deutsche und die britische Stahlindustrie)
1994 Cambridge University Press *Cambridge*

This is a translation by Sarah Hanbury Tenison of a key monograph, published by Vandenhoeck & Ruprecht of Göttingen in 1986. The book greatly enhances our understanding of steel technology and product markets on the one hand and British and German firms' strategies on the other. In the process it provides a valuable contribution to the 'decline of Britain' debate.
Firms: Bochumer Verein; Bolckow Vaughan & Co.; Dortmunder Union; Hörder Verein; Krupp; Osnabrücker Stahlwerk; Phönix works; Rheinische Stahlwerke; Rhineland-Westphalian works; Steel Co. of Scotland

Iron & Steel, America

650
Abe, Etsuo; Suzuki, Yoshitaka (Editors)
Changing Patterns of International Rivalry: Some lessons from the steel industry (Seventeenth Fuji Conference)
For main entry, see 96

651
Blackford, Mansel G.
A Portrait Cast in Steel: Buckeye International and Columbus, Ohio, 1881–1980
1982 Greenwood Press *Westport, CT*

This comprehensive study of the growth of a small local business examines its place in its industry and community, the risks of complacency and its technological and marketing innovation. It demonstrates that small enterprises may be as interesting as large corporations.
Firms: Buckeye International

652
Eschwege, W. L. von
Pluto Brasiliensis [Brazilian iron]
1979 Editora Itatiaia Editoria da USP *Belo Horizonte, Brazil*

This is a biographical account of the establishment and development of the iron industry in Brazil in the first three decades of the last century. The author was a German engineer who lived in Brazil from 1811 to the 1820s and established one of the first iron foundries in Minas Gerais.

Firms: Fabrica de Ferro de São Joao do Ipanema; Fabrica de Ferro do Prata; Real Fabrica do Morro do Pilar

653
Gomes, F. M.
História da siderurgia no Brasil [The History of the Iron and Steel Industry in Brazil]
1983 Editoria Itatiaia Editoria da USP *Belo Horizonte, Brazil*

This work examines the several stages in the development of the iron and steel industry in Brazil, from primitive small-scale domestic production during colonial times, leading up to the modern large-scale industrial production of the 1970s. It is an important reference work for the study of the Brazilian iron and steel industry.

654
Gregory, Frances W.; Neu, Irene D.
The American Industrial Elite in the 1870s: Their social origins
For main entry, see 3842

655
Hessen, Robert
Steel Titan: The Life of Charles M. Schwab
1975 Oxford University Press *Oxford*

This is the definitive biography of the President of United States Steel and Bethlehem Steel who ranked second only to Andrew Carnegie as a pioneer in the American steel industry. The book shows how he undercut his stature by taking shortcuts that plunged him into scandal and controversies.

Firms: Bethlehem Steel; Carnegie Steel; United States Steel; Midvale Steel Company

656
Hoerr, John P.
And the Wolf Finally Came: The decline of the American steel industry
1988 University of Pittsburgh Press *Pittsburgh, PA*

Hoerr places poor labour-management relations at the centre of an analysis of the long-run loss of competitive advantage by the American steel industry.

Firms: Kaiser Steel; National Steel Corporation; US Steel; USX; Jones & Laughlin

657
Ingham, John N.
The Iron Barons: A social analysis of an American urban elite, 1874–1965
For main entry, see 3844

658
Ingham, John N.
Making Iron and Steel: Independent mills in Pittsburgh, 1820–1920
1991 Ohio State University Press *Columbus, OH*

A revisionist study of the Pittsburgh iron and steel industry stressing the persistence of small independent ironmakers who refused to compete head-on with the powerful steelmakers but instead focused on carving out profitable niche markets where they were highly successful until the 1930s.

659
Inwood, Kris E.
The Canadian Charcoal Iron Industry, 1870–1914
1986 Garland Publishing *New York, NY*

Inwood explores causal forces influencing the vicissitudes of a declining industry which was reborn at the end of the nineteenth century.

660
Kenney, Martin; Florida, Richard
Beyond Mass Production: The Japanese system and its transfer to the US
For main entry, see 947

661
Kuniansky, Harvey Richard
A Business History of the Atlantic Steel Company, 1901–1968
1976 Arno Press *New York, NY*

Throughout the period covered by this volume the Atlantic Steel Company remained a specialist regional company in America. This niche strategy was designed to insulate the company from competition from the national steel companies but, from the mid-1950s, the mini-mill was also a potent threat.
Firms: Atlantic Steel Company; United States Steel Company

662
Libby, D. C.
Transformacão e trabalho em uma economia escravista: Minas Gerais no século XIX [Transformation and Work in a Slave Economy: Nineteenth-century Minas Gerais]
1988 Brasiliense *São Paulo, Brazil*

This excellent work examines the economy, demography, and employment of slave labour in three key industrial sectors (iron, textiles, and gold-mining) of nineteenth-century Minas Gerais in Brazil. It is an essential reference work for the study of the economy of Minas Gerais.
Firms: Companhia Cedro e Cachoeira; St. John d'El Rey Mining Company

663
Livesay, Harold C.
Andrew Carnegie and the Rise of Big Business
1975 Little, Brown & Co. *Boston, MA*

This book describes the life and career of Andrew Carnegie, from manager of the Pennsylvania Railroad to the creation of the Carnegie Steel Company.
Firms: Carnegie Steel Company; Pennsylvania Railroad

664
McDowall, D.
Steel at the Sault: Francis H. Clergue, Sir James Dunn, and the Algoma Steel Corporation, 1901 –1956
1984 University of Toronto Press *Toronto, Canada*

This book traces the rise of one of Canada's largest steel companies and the relationship between the founders and Canadian politcal leaders. Decades of insolvency compounded locational, technological and managerial weaknesses which were offset only by government aid. The Second World War cemented the company's dependence on Canadian government subsidies and protection.
Firms: Algoma Steel Corporation; Steel Company of Canada; US Steel

665
McHugh, Jeanne
Alexander Holley and the Makers of Steel
1980 The Johns Hopkins University Press *Baltimore, MD*

A detailed business biography of a pioneer of US steelmaking technology. Though short on interpretation, the book is painstaking on Holley's role in the development of the Bessemer process and his work at the Pennsylvania Steel Co. and the Edgar Thomson Steel Works.
Firms: Bessemer Steel Co.; Carnegie Steel

666
Norrell, Robert J.
James Bowron: The autobiography of a New South industrialist
1991 University of North Carolina Press *Chapel Hill, NC*

This is a valuable edited autobiography of a leading steelworks manager at the Tennessee Coal and Iron Co. in the 1880s and 1890s. It contains insights on problems of overcapacity, stock manipulation, and an internal view of the TCI's exploitative policies towards black labour.
Firms: Tennessee Coal & Iron

667
Paskoff, Paul F.
Industrial Evolution, Organization, Structure and Growth of the Pennsylvania Iron Industry, 175 0–1860
1983 The Johns Hopkins University Press *Baltimore, MD*

A detailed look at the firms active in the formative years of the industry. The book investigates individual firms and documents the process of learning by doing by industry managers.

Firms: Baltimore Co.; Hopewell Forge; Speedwell Forge

668
Reutter, Mark
Sparrows Point. Making Steel: The rise and ruin of American industrial might
1988 Summit Books *New York, NY*

This book uses a history of the Sparrow Point steel mill in Maryland (once the biggest singly owned industrial complex in the world) as a stepping off point to analyse the history of the US steel industry. It uses archival material to analyse the role of Charles Schwab in the late nineteenth century and later is particularly good at using oral history to develop an account of the changing fortunes of the steelworkers in the industry.
Firms: Bethlehem Steel

669
Santos, M. W.
Labouring on the Periphery: Managers and workers at the A. M. Byers Company, 1900–1956
Business History Review, vol. 61, no. 1, 1987: pp 113–33

This is a study of management and labour relations in a medium-sized wrought-iron manufacturer in Pittsburgh in early twentieth-century USA. Contrasted to the growing corporate structure of big business, it is argued that in this instance, as elsewhere in the industrial economy, forms of 'simple control' continued, based on existing family control and the history of the firm.
Firms: A. M. Byers Co.

670
Temin, Peter
Iron & Steel in Nineteenth Century America: An economic inquiry
1964 MIT Press *Cambridge, MA*

This study provides an economic analysis of the American iron and steel industry between 1830 and 1900. Considerable attention is paid to the production of rails and the use of the Bessemer converter as influences upon change in the industry.
Firms: United States Steel Corporation; Bessemer Steel Company; Carnegie Steel Company; Bethlehem Iron Company; Pennsylvania Steel Company; Trenton Iron Company

671
Tiffany, Paul A.
The Decline of American Steel: How management, labor and government went wrong
1988 Oxford University Press *New York, NY*

Severely handicapped by limited access to corporate archives, Tiffany examines the sharp decline of the American steel industry since the mid-1970s. He maintains that the roots of contemporary failure lie in the defensive policies pursued by labour, management and government between 1945 and 1960.
Firms: Bethlehem Steel; United States Steel

672
Warren, Kenneth
The American Steel Industry 1850–1970: A geographical interpretation
1973 Clarendon Press *Oxford*

Warren's book is a historical geography of the expansion of the American iron and steel industry 1850–1970. Initial locational choices hinged on the availability of vital raw material. From 1900 onwards technological changes in processing and the growth of consumer durables, especially automobiles, fundamentally altered locational choice by the steel makers. Steel production became concentrated in the Manufacturing Belt by 1945 and, from c.1960, was exposed to a growing volume of steel imports as the industry became increasingly global.
Firms: Bethlehem Steel Corporation; Carnegie Steel Co.; Kaiser Steel Corporation; National Steel Corporation; Pennsylvania Steel Co.; US Steel

Iron & Steel, Japan

673
Abe, Etsuo; Suzuki, Yoshitaka (Editors)
Changing Patterns of International Rivalry: Some lessons from the steel industry (Seventeenth Fuji Conference)
For main entry, see 96

674
Horikiri, Yoshio
Nippon Tekkogyo Shi Kenkyu: Tekko Seisan Kozo no Bunseki o Chusin to Shite [A Study in The History of The Japanese Steel Industry]
1987 Waseda Daigaku Shuppan Bu *Tokyo, Japan*

This book is a detailed study of the development of the Japanese steel industry, and examines the structure of steel manufacturing with particular emphasis on its production technology.

675
Iida, Ken-ichi
Nippon Tekko Gijutsu Shi [Technical History of Iron and Steel in Japan]
1979 Toyo Keizai Shinpo-sha *Tokyo, Japan*

This wide-ranging technical history of the modern iron and steel industry stresses the role of engineers in the industry.

676
Japan Iron Manufacturing Corporation; Nihon Seitetsu Kabushi, ki Kaisha
Nippon Seitetsu Kabushiki Kaisha Shashi [A History of Japan Iron Manufacturing Corporation]
1959 Japan Iron Manufacturing Corporation *Tokyo, Japan*

Covering the period 1934 to 1950, this work describes the establishment of the Japan Iron Manufacturing Corporation and gives a short history of the firm and its dissolution after the Second World War.
Firms: Nippon Seitetsu

677
Japan Steel Manufacturing Association
Sengo Tekko Shi [The Postwar History of the Japanese Steel Industry]
1959 Japan Steel Manufacturing *Tokyo, Japan*

Covering the period 1945 to 1955, this work explains the process of reconstruction in the Japanese steel industry after the Second World War. This analysis provides for an understanding of the strength and secrets of the industry.

678
Nakura, Bunji
Nippon Tekkogyo Shi no Kenkyu: 1910 Nendai kara 30 Nendai Zenhan no [The History of the Japanese Steel Industry: Structural characteristics from the 1910s to the first half of the 1930s]
1984 Kondo Shuppan *Tokyo, Japan*

Nakura describes the development of the Japanese steel industry from the 1910s to the first half of the 1930s. In particular, he emphasizes the role of the steel industry in the development of Japanese capitalism.

679
Nippon Light Metal Co.
Nippon Keikinzoku 20 Nen Shi [20-Year History of Nippon Light Metal Co.]
1959 Nippon Light Metal Co. *Tokyo, Japan*

Covering the period 1939 to 1959, this book explains the growth and development of Nippon Light Metal Co. Ltd, with particular emphasis on its business strategy. This work also includes a description of the development of the Japanese aluminium industry in general.
Firms: Nippon Light Metal Co.

680
Yonekura, Seiichiro
The Japanese Iron and Steel Industry 1850–1990: Continuity and discontinuity
1994 Macmillan *Basingstoke*

This book provides a detailed history of the Japanese iron and steel industry from its beginnings to the present day. The main thrust of the study, however, is to explain the phenomenal success of the Japanese industry since 1945. The author eschews a simplistic 'Japan Inc' explanation but argues that this success was rooted in a new business-government relationship whereby competition and co-operation coexisted within the private enterprise system.
Firms: Nippon Steel Corporation; Fuji Steel Corporation; Nippon Steel Corporation; Yawata Steel Corporation; Sumitomo Metal Industries; Kobe Steel

Heavy Engineering

681
Campbell, R. H.
The Rise and Fall of Scottish Industry, 1707–1939
1980 John Donald *Edinburgh, Scotland*

Campbell presents a long-term analysis of the decline of Scottish industrial leadership, concentrating on the west of Scotland and the traditional heavy industries with much of the detail taken from the records of individual firms.

Firms: David Colville and Sons; Fairfield Shipbuilding and Engineering Company; John Brown and Company; North British Locomotive Company; Steel Company of Scotland; William Beardmore and Company

682
Cocks, Edward J.; Walters, B.
A History of the Zinc Smelting Industry in Britain
1968 George G. Harrap *London*

This history of the Imperial Smelting Corporation takes the story from its inception as the National Smelting Company in 1917. The book concentrates on technological developments, including the adoption of American inventions, as well as the company's strategy of product diversification, especially during the 1930s.

Firms: Imperial Smelting Corporation; National Smelting Co.; New Jersey Zinc Company

683
Coe, W. E.
The Engineering Industry of the North of Ireland
For main entry, see 1346

684
d'Angio, Agnès
La politique des travaux publics du groupe Schneider de 1895 à 1949 [The Politics of Public Works in the Schneider Group 1895–1949]
For main entry, see 4330

685
Davenport-Hines, Richard P. T.
Dudley Docker: The life and times of a trade warrior.
For main entry, see 1348

686
Doria, M.
Ansaldo: L'impresa e lo Stato [Ansaldo: The enterprise and the state]
1989 Franco Angeli *Milan, Italy*

Ansaldo's history mirrors with a special clarity the contradictions and the patterns of industrial development in Italy. This book reconstructs the central role played by the state in the birth, survival and development of the heavy engineering industry from 1852 up to the 1960s, through private ownership to direct state control. Managerial decisions and technological change are also analysed, showing how Ansaldo has been central in the development of the industrial structure of the country.

Firms: Ansaldo

687
Epkenhans, Michael
Die wilhelminische Flottenrüstung 1908–1914: Weltenmachstreben, industrieller Fortschrift, soziale Integration [Wilhelmine Naval Support 1908–1914 World powerhouse, industrialists progress and social integration]
1991 Oldenbourg, Beiträge *Munich, Germany*

The author describes the commercial, technical and personal links between German heavy industry, notably Krupps, and the Admiralty before 1914.

Firms: Krupp; Rheinmetall

688
Evans, Harold
Vickers: Against the odds 1956–1977
For main entry, see 1406

689
Frese, Matthias
Betriebspolitik im Dritten Reich: Deutsche Arbeitsfront, Unternehmer und Staatsbürokratie in der Westdeutschen Grossindustrie 1933–1939 [Business Politics in the Third Reich: German labour front,

employers and town bureaucracy in the major industries of West Germany]
1991 Ferdinand Schöningh *Paderborn, Germany*

The Nazis' abolition of trade unions in 1933 and the formation of a 'Labour Front' did not eliminate conflict between the new body, the state and industry. These conflicts, especially over welfare and training, are analysed through the experience of the Ruhr steel industry.
Firms: Glanzstoff-Fabriken; Gutehoffungshütte; Krupp; Mannesmann; Siemens; Vereinigte Stahlwerke

690
Goldbeck, Gustav
Kraft für die Welt: Klöckner-Humboldt-Deutz A.G. 1864–1964 [Power for the World]
1964 *Düsseldorf, Germany*

This is a basic though reliable and informative history of the mechanical engineering firm Klöckner-Humboldt-Deutz and its constituent companies.
Firms: Klöckner-Werke A.G.; Maschinenfabrik-Anstalt Humboldt; Gasmotoren-Fabrik Deutz; Klöckner-Humboldt-Deutz A.G.

691
Hentschel, Volker
Wirtschaftsgeschichte des Maschinenfabrik Esslingen AG 1846–1918 [Economic History of the Esslingen Engineering Works 1846–1918]
1971 Ernst Klett *Stuttgart, Germany*

This is a company history with a strong emphasis on financial performance.
Firms: Maschinenfabrik Esslingen AG

692
Hume, John R.; Moss, Michael S.
Beardmore: The history of a Scottish industrial giant.
For main entry, see 1358

693
Joest, Hans-Josef
Pionier im Ruhrgebiet: Gutehoffnungshütte: Vom altesten Montan-Unternehmen Deutschlands zum grössten Maschinenbaukonzern Europas [Gutehoffnungshütte: A Pioneer in the Ruhr]
For main entry, see 1359

694
Jones, Edgar
Guest, Keen & Nettlefolds: vol. 1: Innovation and Enterprise 1759–1918; vol. 2: The Growth of a Business 1918–45
For main entry, see 1360

695
Klass, Gert von
Krupps: The story of an industrial empire
1954 Sidgwick & Jackson *London*

While more a journalistic history of the Krupp family and its achievements than a business history, this provides insights into the development and vicissitudes of the business over several generations. This is an English translation, by James Cleugh, of a German original.
Firms: Krupp

696
Magnusson, Lars
Arbetet vid en svensk verkstad: Munktell, 1900–1920 [Labour in a Swedish Factory: Munktell 1900–1920]
For main entry, see 4208

697
Manchester, William
The Arms of Krupp 1587–1968
1969 Michael Joseph *London*

This is a journalistic account of the Krupp dynasty and its steel and armaments with strong emphasis on the years just before and during the Second World War. The book includes a controversial interpretation which seeks to rehabilitate the firm and the family's role during the Second World War.
Firms: Krupp; Vickers; Volkswagen; W. G. Armstrong

698
Maschke, Erich
Es entsteht ein Konzern: Paul Reusch und die GHH [Paul Reusch and the Growth of a Business]
For main entry, see 633

699
McCreary, Eugene C.
Social Welfare and Business: The Krupp welfare program, 1860–1914
For main entry, see 4211

700
Mitsubishi Jukogyo
Mitsubishi Jukogyo Kabushiki Kaisha Sha Shi [A History of Mitsubishi Heavy Industries Co. Ltd]
1956 Mitsubishi Jukogyo *Tokyo, Japan*
Covering the period 1875–1950, this book describes the growth of the company and outlines changing patterns of management control.
Firms: Mitsubishi Jukogyo

701
Myllyntaus, Timo
Finnish Industry in Transition, 1885–1920: Responding to Technological Challenges
For main entry, see 4285

702
Pierenkemper, Toni
Die westfälischen Schwerindustriellen 1852–1913: Soziale Struktur und unternehmerischer Erfolg [Westphalian Heavy Industry 1852–1913: Social structure and entrepreneurial success]
For main entry, see 3797

703
Pogge von Strandmann, Hartmut
Unternehmenspolitik und Unternehmensführung: Der Dialog zwischen Aufsichtsrat und Vorstand bei Mannesmann 1900 bis 1919
1978 *Düsseldorf, Germany*
This is an account of the relationships between the chairman of the supervisory board and the chairman of the executive board in the German firm of Mannesmann, which provides a valuable insight into the operation of German corporate structure and the relationships between banks and industry.
Firms: Mannesmann

704
Schybergson, Per
Verkar och dagar: Ahlströms historia 1851–1981 [Works and Days: A history of Ahlström Ltd, 1851–1981]
For main entry, see 1667

705
Scott, John D.
Siemens Brothers 1858–1958: An essay in the history of industry
For main entry, see 1538

706
Scott, John D.
Vickers: A history
1962 Weidenfeld & Nicolson *London*
Written by a former member of the Cabinet Office and author of part of the Official History of the Second World War, this is an insightful business history which focuses on the relationship between a private arms manufacturer and the government, using full official access to company archives. The study covers the company from its origins to the 1950s and is strong on the financial intricacies and the technical side of the industry (notably the designing of the Spitfire and Wellington aircraft). It also provides a detailed history of the company's rival, Armstrong Whitworth, which ultimately merged with Vickers in the 1920s.
Firms: Armstrong Whitworth; Vickers

707
Slaven, Anthony; Aldcroft, Derek H. (Editors)
Business, Banking and Urban History: Essays in honour of S. G. Checkland
For main entry, see 2231

708
Tolliday, Steven; Zeitlin, Jonathan (Editors)
The Power to Manage?: Employers and industrial relations in comparative-historical perspective
For main entry, see 4241

709
Trebilcock, Clive
The Vickers Brothers: Armaments and enterprise, 1854–1914
1977 Europa Publications *London*

This is a commercial evaluation of Vickers' shift from steel-making to armaments production from the late 1880s onwards. Before 1914 Vickers expanded its capital base to acquire a comprehensive range of armament companies. The internationalization of the company's business activities was complemented by its pursuit of technical leadership through the purchase of patents and licences. Trebilcock's book is a valuable short synthesis which is archivally based. Themes include management structures, manufacture and finance. The company's expansion rested more on the managerial structure adopted than the swashbuckling personalities of the two Vickers brothers.
Firms: Vickers

710
Uebbing, Helmut
Wege und Wegmarken: 100 Jahre Thyssen [Ways and Directions]
For main entry, see 644

711
Young, Gordon
The Fall and Rise of Alfred Krupp
1960 Cassell *London*

This is a biography of the leading (and controversial) German entrepreneur.
Firms: Krupp (Friedrich)

Chemicals and Pharmaceuticals, Europe

712
Amatori, F.; Bezza, B. (Editors)
Montecatini 1888–1966: Capitoli di storia di una grande impresa [Montecatini 1888–1966: Chapters in the history of a large firm]
1990 Il Mulino–ASSI *Bologna, Italy*

This work covers the history of Montecatini, one of Italy's first and most important companies in the chemical sector, from its beginnings in 1888 to the 1960s. Starting from the role played by Guido Donegani as a 'Schumpeterian' entrepreneur, this work studies the stages that made this firm one of the world leaders in the production of fertilizers. The advantages deriving from an almost monopolistic position, the firm's close links with the government, and technological innovations are closely analysed.

713
Beynon, Hugh; Hudson, Ray; Sadler, David
A Place Called Teesside: A locality in a global economy
For main entry, see 579

714
Bürgin, Alfred
Geschichte des Geigy Unternehmens von 1758–1939: Ein Beitrag zur Basler Unternehmer- und Wirtschaftsgeschichte, Basel 1958 [History of Geigy]
1958 Geigy *Basel, Switzerland*

The author offers a social history of the Geigy chemical company, located in Basel, describing the genesis of a modern enterprise. Since 1758, the Geigy family, members of the Basler upper-class, have run a worldwide drugs company, which, a century later, began the production of aniline dyes and expanded in the twentieth century into the agrobusiness and pharmaceuticals. The study offers a broad picture of factory discipline, work force recruitment, and strategies of social control in a very traditional enterprise.
Firms: J. R. Geigy AG

715
Cayez, Pierre
Rhône-Poulenc: Contribution à l'étude d'un groupe industriel [Rhône-Poulenc]
1988 Armand Colin *Paris, France*

This is an excellent history of the largest chemical and drugs company in France, which developed from modest beginnings near Lyon.
Firms: Rhône-Poulenc

716
Davenport-Hines, Richard P. T.; Slinn, Judy
Glaxo: A history to 1962

1992 Cambridge University Press *Cambridge*

This is a fine company history, particularly on Glaxo's research and development push into pharmaceuticals from 1920 onwards and its development of an international business especially after 1945. In terms of product and geographic scope, this volume details Glaxo's place as a highly successful multinational company.
Firms: Allen & Hanburys; Evans Medical; Glaxo; Joseph Nathan & Co.

717
Fieldhouse, D. K.
Unilever Overseas: The anatomy of a multinational 1895–1965
1978 Croom Helm *London*

This study complements Wilson's earlier history by focusing on the activities of Unilever's overseas subsidiary companies. It demonstrates how the latter increased the firm's turnover far beyond the limits of the European market.
Firms: Unilever

718
Fischer, Wolfram
Henning, Berlin: Die Geschichte eines pharmazeutischen Unternehmens, 1913–1991 [Henning, Berlin: The history of a pharmaceutical company, 1913–1991]
1992 Duncker & Humblot *Berlin, Germany*

This book covers the lifespan of a family firm up to its takeover by a multinational. The study looks at prospects for innovation by a small firm. Special attention is paid to constraints caused by the Second World War, the Cold War and the firm's location (Berlin), and their contribution to its special competitiveness.
Firms: Henning

719
Fox, M. R.
Dye-Makers of Great Britain 1856–1976: A history of chemists, companies, products and changes
1987 Imperial Chemical Industries *London*

This work is a detailed record of individual chemists and entrepreneurs and British dye-making firms. It charts the role of Ivan Levinstein and his successive companies which formed the core of the British dye-making industry from 1845 to his death in 1916. The slow decline of the dye-making industry and its dependence on German materials became a national scandal during the First World War. Incorporated into ICI in 1926, the dye-making became closely linked with marketing under Harry McGowan.
Firms: Imperial Chemical Industries; British Alizarin Co.; British Dyes; Du Pont; Holliday & Sons; Levinstein & Co.

720
Godfrey, John F.
Capitalism at War: Industrial policy and bureaucracy in France 1914–1918
1987 Berg *Leamington Spa*

The chemical industry was at the centre of the French state's control of business between 1914 and 1918. Despite the opposition of industrialists, however, wartime state control provided the investment and technological platform for the post-war dominance of the Saint-Gobain company.
Firms: Saint-Gobain

721
Haber, L. F.
The Chemical Industry During the Nineteenth Century: A study of the economic aspects of applied chemistry in Europe and North America
1958 Clarendon Press *Oxford*

In the first of his two books, Haber concentrates on two areas, Leblanc soda and coal tar dyestuffs, to characterize changes in the industry from empirical to scientific as the work of academic research and education diffused into the processes of the chemical industry with major consequences for the economy as a whole.

722
Haber, L. F.
The Chemical Industry 1900–1930: International growth and technological change
1971 Clarendon Press *Oxford*

This major study of the world chemical industry covers academic chemistry and new technology, international rivalry, cartels, research and labour relations. It has an excellent bibliography.

Firms: ***Bayer; Brunner, Mond & Co.; CIBA; Castner-Kellner Alkali Co.; Du Pont; Geigy; ICI (Imperial Chemical Industries); IG Farbenindustrie AG; Sandoz; Solvay***

723

Hanscher, Leigh

Regulating for Competition: Government, law and the pharmaceutical industry in the United Kingdom and France

1990 Clarendon Press *Oxford*

Hanscher presents an examination of the relationship between patterns of state regulation and business strategy in the British and French pharmaceutical industry since 1945.

Firms: ***Glaxo; Hoechst; Hoffman La Roche; Wellcome; ICI***

724

Hardie, D. W. F.

A History of the Chemical Industry in Widnes

1950 Imperial Chemical Industries *London*

Hardie's book is a business history of Widnes, England, as a chemical manufacturing town. Although covering the development of the industry to 1950, the text focuses on the late nineteenth century. It is particularly interesting on the relationship between the host of chemical companies, legitimate concern over the control of dumping and emissions, and local elite politics.

Firms: ***Golding Davis & Co.; Gaskell-Deacon & Co.; Imperial Chemical Industries; United Alkali Co.; Pilkington Bros***

725

Harvey-Jones, John

Getting It Together

For main entry, see 3894

726

Hassbring, Lars

The International Development of the Swedish Match Co., 1917–24

For main entry, see 1679

727

Hayes, Peter

Industry and Ideology: IG Farben in the Nazi era

1987 Cambridge University Press *Cambridge*

This major monograph examines the attitude of the leaders of a major German corporation to the changing political events in twentieth-century Germany, and the productive support given to the Nazi regime.

Firms: ***IG Farben***

728

Henneking, Ralf

Chemische Industrie und Umwelt: Konflikte um Umweltbelastungen durch die chemische Industrie am Beispiel der schwerchemischen, Farben- und Dungemittelindustrie in der Rheinprovinz (ca. 1800-1914) [Chemical Industry and Environment: Conflicts over environmental costs]

1994 Steiner *Stuttgart, Germany*

Ralf Henneking's book describes the history of environmental problems up to 1914, their perception as well as legislative and industrial reactions. In particular he examines the most important branches of the chemical industry in the Rhineland from about 1800 up to 1914. Based on thorough and extensive case studies he concludes that environmental concern was generally of little importance to the authorities. The companies' concern was profit maximization, whereas the public seemed to accept environmental damages as the price it had to pay for technological progress. Only those people directly affected by chemical plants protested against them; a general environmental concern was therefore non-existent. Henneking observes that environmental damages were due to the entrepreneurs' sometimes careless and even thoughtless attitude rather than to technological necessities.

729

Hohenberg, Paul M.

Chemicals in Western Europe 1850–1914: An economic study of technical change

1967 Rand McNally *Chicago, IL*

Hohenberg examines the role of the chemical industry as a technical catalyst with effects throughout the economy as its research and products influenced other industries. He focuses on France, Germany and Switzerland and contrasts performance and market environments in each.

730
Johannessen, Finn Erhard
Challenge and Change: The history of Protan from 1939 to 1989
For main entry, see 1915

731
Kennedy, Carol
ICI: The company that changed our lives
2nd Edition
1993 Paul Chapman Publishing *London*

This book's primary focus is on products and innovation rather than business strategy and structures. It includes commentary on the major changes in ICI in the late 1980s.

Firms: Brunner Mond; ICI; IG Farben; United Alkali Company; Zeneca

732
Kudo, Akira; Hara, Terushi (Editors)
International Cartels in Business History (Eighteenth Fuji Conference)
For main entry, see 99

733
Lindgren, Håkan
Corporate Growth: The Swedish match industry in its global setting
For main entry, see 1681

734
Lischka, J. R.
Ludwig Mond and the British Alkali Industry
1985 Garland *New York, NY*

Lischka describes the entry and impact of Ludwig Mond into the British alkali industry from 1862. By focusing on the elimination of waste through process improvements, Mond initiated a series of technical innovations which allowed his company to rationalize an industry traditionally dominated by small family firms.

Firms: Brunner Mond & Co.; Imperial Chemical Industries; Magadi Soda Company

735
Lundström, Ragnhild
Alfred Nobel som internationell företagare: Den nobelska sprängämnesindustrin 1864–1886 [Alfred Nobel as International Entrepreneur: The Nobel explosives industry, 1864–1886]
1974 Acta Universitatis Upsaliensis *Uppsala, Sweden*

This is a history of the new explosives industry that grew up on the basis of Nobel's patents for the industrial use of nitroglycerine. Based on archival research in the various European firms, it gives a comparative account of their financing, markets, production and financial results. It analyses the factors that led to the establishment of a European dynamite trust. Summary in English.

Firms: Dynamit-Actien Gesellschaft; Dynamite Nobel; La Société Centrale de Dynamite; La Société Générale pour la Fabrication de la Dynamite; Nitroglycerin AB; Nobel's Explosives Co. Ltd; Anonyme Espagnole de Dynamite; Nobel-Dynamite Trust Co. Ltd

736
Michelsen, Karl-Erik
Sähköstä ja suolasta syntynyt: Finnish Chemicals Oy–Nokia Chemicals 1937–1987 [Made of Electricity and Salt: Finnish Chemicals Ltd–Nokia Chemicals, 1937–1987]
1989 Nokia Chemicals *Helsinki, Finland*

Michelsen's book deals with the supply of chlorine to the Finnish paper industry. To prevent the rise of Finnish competitors, the international cartel of the German IG Farben, the British ICI and the Belgian Solvay decided in the mid-1930s to set up a joint chlorine factory in the country. Despite friction between the owners, the company grew quickly and greatly benefited from the success of Finnish papermaking. The book contains a summary in English.

Firms: Finnish Chemicals; ICI; IG Farben; Nokia Chemicals; Nokia Oy; Solvay

737
Morris, Peter J. T.; Russell, Colin A. (Editors)
Archives of the British Chemical Industry, 1750–1914: A handlist
For main entry, see 26

738
Musson, A. E.
Enterprise in Soap and Chemicals: Joseph Crosfield & Sons, Limited 1815–1965
1965 Manchester University Press *Manchester*

A company history of Joseph Crosfield & Sons Ltd which straddled the soap and chemical industries for over a century until its eventual assimilation within Unilever in the 1950s. Particularly interesting on the shift from manufacturing to brand management in the first half of the twentieth century.
Firms: Joseph Crosfield & Sons; Brunner Mond & Co.; Erasmic Co.; Imperial Chemical Industries; Unilever; United Alkali Co.; Proctor & Gamble

739
Okochi, Akio; Uchida, Hoshimi (Editors)
Development and Diffusion of Technology (Sixth Fuji Conference)
For main entry, see 107

739/1
Pettigrew, Andrew
The Awakening Giant: Continuity and change in Imperial Chemical Industries
For main entry, see 4094

740
Plumpe, Gottfried
I. G. Farben: Business, technology and politics, 1904–1945
1990 Duncker & Humblot *Berlin, Germany*
This revisionist business history argues that I. G. Farben were driven by economic rationality rather than ideology during the years 1933–45. The company's rise from 1904 onwards and its stagnation after 1919 forms the backdrop to fateful managerial decisions after 1933. The book contains a careful analysis of the firm's approach to competition.
Firms: BASF; Bayer; Hoechst; I. G. Farben

741
Reader, William J.
Imperial Chemical Industries: A History: Vol. 1, The forerunners 1870–1926; Vol. 2, The first quarter century 1926–1952
1970–5 Oxford University Press *Oxford*
Reader charts the amalgamations of British chemical and dynamite companies in the late nineteenth century and the role of major managerial figures such as Alfred Mond and Harry McGowan in amalgamating their firms as ICI in 1926. Thereafter the emphasis is on the personal and political dynamics of the international cartel controlling the global chemical industry.
Firms: Brunner Mond; Du Pont; I. G. Farben; Imperial Chemical Industries (ICI); Nobel Industries; United Alkalai Co.

742
Saviotti, P. P.; Simonin, L.; Zamagni, V.
From Ammonia to New Materials: The history of the Institute for Chemical Research Guido Donegani in Novara (Original Title: Dall'ammoniaca ai nuovi materiali: Storia dell'Istituto de Richerche Chimiche Guido Donegani de)
1991 Il Mulino–ASSI *Bologna, Italy*
The history of Donegani Institute, from its origins at the beginning of the century up to the 1990s, while describing the results obtained and the difficulties encountered also shows how investments in organization, human resources and technology have allowed chemical research to be innovative and successful even in a non-leader country like Italy.

743
Smith, John Graham
The Origins and Early Development of the Heavy Chemical Industry in France
1979 Clarendon Press *Oxford*
This is a history of the transformation of the French chemical industry from scattered artisanal production to large scale manufacture between 1760 and 1820. It is notably strong on changes in technology and production technologies.
Firms: Baccarat; Chaptal

744
Stokes, Raymond G.
Divide and Prosper: The heirs of IG Farben under allied authority, 1945–1951
1988 University of California Press *Berkeley, CA*
This is a major study of IG Farben's postwar recovery. Policy uncertainties between the occupying powers left space for the rebuilding of German corporate strength. Continuity in management personnel allowed the German chemical companies to re-establish the techno-

logical and trading links vital to their later success in export markets.
Firms: BASF; Bayer; Hoechst; IG Farben

745
Stokes, Raymond G.
Opting for Oil: The political economy of technological change in the West German chemical industry 1945–1961
1994 Cambridge University Press *Cambridge*

An excellent book on the shift from coal to oil feedstocks, setting case studies of the major firms in a historical, technical, economic and political context.
Firms: BASF (Badische Anilin- und Soda-Fabrik); Bayer; Hoechst; Hüls; Shell; IG Farben; BP

746
Tausk, Marius
Organon: de geschiedenis van een bijzondere Nederlandse onderneming [Organon: The story of an unusual pharmaceutical enterprise]
1978 Dekker & Van de Vegt *Nijmegen, The Netherlands*

This is a detailed, but rather uncritical history of this pharmaceutical company. Attention is focused on pharmaceutical research practices and results, but the business aspects of Organon are neglected.
Firms: Akzo Pharma; Koninklijke–Zout Organon; Koninklijke Zwanenberg Organon; Organon

747
Travis, Anthony S.
The Rainbow Makers: The origins of the synthetic dyestuffs industry in Western Europe
1993 Lehigh University Press *Bethlehem, PA*

This is a fine, archivally-based study of the emergence of the European coal-tar dye industry. The focus is principally on Britain and Germany and the evolution of key synthetic dyes. Travis traces both the technical innovations themselves, and in particular the work of Perkins and Caro and the commercialization process. He rejects the notion that organized industrial research in Germany played a significant role in these developments.

748
Warren, Kenneth
Chemical Foundations: The alkali industry in Britain to 1926
1980 OUP Clarendon Press *Oxford*

Thoroughly researched and written with the insights of a geographer who is keenly aware of business dimensions, this is particularly good for the Leblanc side of the alkali industry.
Firms: United Alkali Co.; Salt Union; Castner-Kellner Co.

749
Wetzel, Walter
Natural Science and the Chemical Industry in Germany
1991 Franz Steiner *Stuttgart, Germany*

This detailed study describes the close links between university research and the German chemical industry, particularly between 1850 and 1914.
Firms: Bayer; Hoechst; IG Farben

750
Wikander, Ulla
Kreuger's Match Monopolies, 1925–30: Case studies in market control through public monopolies
For main entry, see 1684

751
Wilson, Charles
The History of Unilever: A study in economic growth and social change
1954 Cassell *London*

This impressive two volume study of one of the world's major conglomerates did much to establish the reputation of business history as an academic discipline. It is invaluable on the process of competition, cartels and mergers in the oils and fats industries. Originating in an amalgamation of British soap manufacturers, the firm diversified into many other activities, notably the Niger Company, and acquired its Dutch interests in 1929.
Firms: Unilever; Lever Bros; Margarine Union; Van den Bergh

752
Wilson, Charles
Unilever 1945–1965: Challenge & response in the post-war industrial revolution
1968 Cassell *London*

The final volume of the Unilever history, published fourteen years after the first two, follows the same themes and gives considerable detail on the company, but it is less insightful and critical than the first two volumes.
Firms: Unilever; Lever Bros; Margarine Union; Van den Bergh

753
Wimmer, Wolfgang
"Wir haben fast immer was Neues": Gesundheitswesen und Innovation der Pharmaindustrie in Deutschland 1870–1939 ["We Almost Always Have Something New": Health and innovation in the German pharmaceutical industry 1870–1939]
1994 Duncker & Humblot *Berlin, Germany*

Wimmer is interested in the innovation process in three of the largest German pharmaceutical companies between 1850 and 1935. His book on Bayer, Hoechst and Schering attempts to compensate for the lack of studies on industrial research and development organization which persists in German historiography. By comparing the innovative capabilities of these three companies he shows that Bayer was able to take the lead thanks to its early internalization of research and development activities. Moreover, a typical historical development could be traced which moves from a kind of 'personalized' research organization to an 'institutional' one and finally reaches the state of an 'organized' innovation process. Yet, as Wimmer himself concedes, an international approach is necessary to fully comprehend this modern industry which operated multinationally from its early beginnings.
Firms: Bayer; Hoechst; Schering

Chemicals and Pharmaceuticals, Japan

754
Ajinomoto Co.
Ajinomoto Kabushiki Kaisha Shashi [A Company History of Ajinomoto]
1971–72 Ajinomoto Co. *Tokyo, Japan*

This is an excellent company history of Ajinomoto, the Japanese inventor of an artificial food flavouring – glutamic acid. The book is well documented and illustrated with several contributions from authorities on biochemicals and ethnology. Vol. 1 deals with the prewar period and Vol. 2 the postwar period.
Firms: Ajinomoto

755
Amano, Masatoshi
Awa Ai Keizaishi Kenkyu [An Economic History of Indigo in Awa District, Kochi Prefecture]
1986 Yoshikawa Kobunkan *Tokyo, Japan*

Covering the history of indigo production in Awa, the most flourishing district in Japan, between 1750 to 1899, the book describes the production system, technological change and distribution by analysing the case of the largest firm Miki Shoten (Miki & Co.).
Firms: Miki Shoten

756
Brock, Malcolm
Biotechnology in Japan
1989 Routledge *London*

A study of Japanese 'targeting' of biotechnology, considering the relationship between public and private sectors.

757
Iijima, Takashi
Nihon no Kagaku Gijutu [The Technology of the Japanese Chemical Industry]
1981 Kogyo Chosakai *Tokyo, Japan*

Covering mainly technological change in the Japanese chemical industry from 1871 to 1972, this book describes how the incorporation of foreign with local technologies is based on the corporate history of individual firms.
Firms: Chisso; Hodogaya Kagaku; Idemitsu

Kosan; Mitsui Kozan; Mitsui Sekiyu Kagaku; Nihon Zeon; Sumitomo Kagaku; Teijin

758
Kamatani, Shinzen
Nihon Kindai Kagaku Kogyo no Seiritsu [The Establishment of the Modern Chemical Industry in Japan]
1989 Asakura Shoten *Tokyo, Japan*

This work mainly focuses on the formative period of the Japanese chemical industry from 1822 to 1894, and describes the role of foreign engineers, the development of training for technicians and government assistance.
Firms: Nissan Kagaku Kogyo

759
Kawade, Tsunetada; Bono, Mitsuo
Sekiyu Kagaku Kogyo (sintei han) [The Petrochemical Industry (revised)]
1970 Toyo Keizai Shinpo-sha *Tokyo, Japan*

Covering the origins and development of the Japanese petrochemical industry after the Second World War from 1949 to 1967, compared with those of America and Europe, the authors discuss the influence of the industrial policies of MITI in the development of the industry.
Firms: Mitsui Sekiyu Kagaku; Mitsubishi Yuka; Nihon Sekiyu Kagaku; Sumitomo Kagaku

760
Molony, Barbara
Technology and Investment: The preWar Japanese chemical industry
1990 Harvard University Press *Cambridge, MA*

Molony studies the interwar history of electrochemicals and fertilizers in Japan with particular emphasis on Noguchi Jun, one of Japan's best known entrepreneurs. Noguchi's firm developed from a fertilizer company into a diversified chemicals company while he forged ties with politicians and military leaders. The book examines entrepreneurship, the links between technology and investment, the emergence of a class of scientific managers and the relationship of business strategy and imperialism before the Second World War.
Firms: Nippon Chisso Hiryo [Nichitsu]; Chosen Chisso Hiryo; Mitsubishi; Mitsui; Sumitomo

761
Nihon Ryuan Kogyokai
Nihon Ryuan Kogyo Shi [The History of the Japanese Ammonium-Sulphate Industry]
1968 Nihon Ryuan Kogyokai *Tokyo, Japan*

Covering the formative and developmental periods of the Japanese ammonium-sulphate industry from 1896 to 1967, this book describes corporate history from the point of view of introducing new technologies, management and relations with government.
Firms: Chisso; Denki Kagaku Kogyo; Mitsubishi Kasei Kogyo; Mitsui Toatsu Kagaku Kogyo; Nissan Kagaku Kogyo; Sumitomo Kagaku Kogyo

762
Nihon Soda Kogyokai
Nihon Soda Kogyo Hyaku-nenshi [One Hundred Years of the Japanese Alkali Industry]
1982 Nihon Soda Kogyokai *Tokyo, Japan*

Covering the formative period in the Japanese alkali industry to 1980, this work examines many problems such as technology, salt, pollution and R&D, and includes short histories of the firms involved.
Firms: Asahi Glass; Hodogaya Kagaku; Nissan Kagaku; Tokuyama Soda

763
Osaka Enogu Senryo
Enogu Senryo Shoko Shi [The Commercial and Industrial History of the Paint and Dyestuff Industry]
1938 Osaka Enogu Senryo Dogyo Kumiai *Osaka, Japan*

The formative period of the Japanese dyestuff industry from 1770 to 1935 is discussed here. The development of the Japanese dyestuff industry as a whole is described and the leading importers are covered. This book also examines the affiliates of the German dyestuff companies in Japan.
Firms: Hodogaya Kagaku; Mitsui Kozan; Mitsui Toatsu Kagaku Kogyo; Nihon Kayaku; Sumitomo Kagaku Kogyo

764
Sekiyu Kagaku Kogyo
Sekiyu Kagaku Kogyo Junenshi [Ten Years of the Petrochemical Industry]
1971 Sekiyu Kagaku Kogyo Kyokai *Tokyo, Japan*

Covering mainly the formative period of the Japanese petrochemical industry from 1949 to 1968, this work describes the establishment of new ventures, from their planning stages to completion and the industrial policy of MITI.
Firms: Daikyowa Sekiyu Kagaku; Idemitsu Sekiyu Kagaku; Maruzen Sekiyu Kagaku; Mitsubishi Kasei Kogyo; Mitsubishi Yuka; Mitsui Sekiyu Kagaku; Nihon Sekiyu Kagaku; Sumitomo Kagaku; Tonen Sekiyu Kagaku

765
Shibamura, Yango
Nihon Kagaku Kogyo Shi [A History of the Japanese Chemical Industry]
1943 Kurita Shoten *Tokyo, Japan*

This work describes the character of the Japanese chemical industry and the development of alkali, fertilizer, dyestuffs and chemical fibre manufacture with reference to the leading firms.
Firms: Asahi Glass; Chisso; Mitsui Kozan; Nissan Kagaku Kogyo; Showa Denko; Sumitomo Kagaku; Taki Kagaku

766
Shimotani, Masahiro
Nihon Kagaku Kogyo Shiron [A Historical Study of the Japanese Chemical Industry]
1982 Ochanomizu Shobo *Tokyo, Japan*

Shimotani covers four sections of the chemical industry from 1888 to 1945: calcium-phosphate, electrochemicals, ammonium-sulphate and dyestuffs. He describes technological developments and how the chemical industry was developed largely by new Zaibatsu until after the First World War when old Zaibatsu, seeing profitable opportunities, moved to invest in this new industry.
Firms: Chisso; Denki Kagaku Kogyo; Hodogaya Kagaku; Mitsubishi Kasei Kogyo; Mitsui Toatsu Kagaku Kogyo; Nihon Kayaku; Nissan Kagaku Kogyo; Sumitomo Kagaku Kogyo

767
Watanabe, Tokuji (Editor)
Kagaku Kogyo [The Chemical Industry]
1959 Iwanami Shoten *Tokyo, Japan*

This work covers four divisions of the chemical industry comprising alkali, ammonium sulphate, dyestuff and plastics from 1870 to 1955, and gives full details of the introduction of new technologies and diversification.
Firms: Chisso; Denki Kagaku Kogyo; Mitsui Toatsu Kagaku; Sumitomo Kagaku

768
Watanabe, Tokuji (Editor)
Kagaku Kogyo Jou [The Chemical Industry]
1968 Kojunsha Shuppankyoku *Tokyo, Japan*

This book is wide-ranging in its approach, covering, from 1880 to 1945, the traditional products such as matches and indigo as well as modern ones such as synthetic dyestuffs and ammonium-sulphate. The book describes technological change, trading, industrial policy as a whole and the important engineers. Altogether, it is an excellent study.
Firms: Asahi Glass; Chisso; Mitsui Kozan; Nihon Soda; Nissan Kagaku; Sumitomo Kagaku; Teijin; Toray

769
Watanabe, Tokuji (Editor)
Sengo Nihon Kagaku Kogyo Shi [The History of the Japanese Chemical Industry Since the Second World War]
1973 Kagaku Kogyo Nippousha *Tokyo, Japan*

Covering the technological and main product changes from fertilizers to petrochemicals, 1945 to 1970, Watanabe describes the industry from the perspectives of technologies introduced, acquisition of raw materials, the industrial policy of MITI and technical cooperation with foreign firms.
Firms: Asahi Kasei; Bridgestone; Kyowa Hakko; Mitsui Sekiyu Kagaku; Nihon Gosei Gomu; Nissan Kagaku Kogyo

Chemicals and Pharmaceuticals, USA and rest of world

770
Aftalion, Fred
A History of the International Chemical Industry
1991 University of Pennsylvania Press *Philadelphia, PA*

This is an important overview of the history of the chemical industry, viewed from an international perspective.

771
Burk, Robert F.
The Corporate State and the Broker State: The du Ponts and American national politics, 1925–1940
1990 Harvard University Press *Cambridge, MA*

Burk gives a detailed analysis of the 'corporate conservatism' of the du Pont family and their closest business associates. Their deep opposition to federal taxation of business profit and personal income and the New Deal was coupled with an advocacy of the application of business principles to public administration. Political donations and extensive propaganda, however, failed to save the du Ponts from political marginalization through the 1930s.
Firms: Du Pont; General Motors

772
Butrica, Andrew J.; Douglas, Deborah G.
Out of Thin Air: A history of Air Products and Chemicals Inc., 1940–1990
1990 Praeger *New York, NY*

This company was a late entrant into the chemical sector, and an equally late arrival as a major enterprise in the 1960s. Diversification out of industrial gas products into chemicals followed a change in leadership and strategy.
Firms: Air Products and Chemicals

773
Chandler, Alfred D. Jr; Salsbury, Stephen
Pierre S Du Pont and the Making of the Modern Corporation
For main entry, see 3939

774
Cheape, Charles W.
Strictly Business: Walter Carpenter at Du Pont and General Motors
For main entry, see 3941

775
Collins, Douglas
The Story of Kodak
For main entry, see 1576

776
Dorian, Max
The du Ponts: From gunpowder to nylon
1962 Little, Brown *Boston, MA*

This is a history of the Du Pont corporation as a family firm, and describes tensions within the family and between generations.
Firms: Dow Chemical Company; Du Pont; Union Chloride Corporation

777
Haynes, Williams
American Chemical Industry
1945–54 Van Nostrand *New York, NY*

This is the classic work on the American chemical industry surveying its development from 1609 to the early 1950s. The book includes short histories of over 200 firms.
Firms: Du Pont (E.I. Du Pont de Nemours & Co.)

778
Hochheiser, Sheldon
Rohm and Haas: History of a chemical company
1986 University of Pennsylvania Press *Philadelphia, PA*

Consistent pursuit of a strategy focused on speciality chemicals, such as acrylics, linked Rohm and Haas with the most dynamic sectors of the American economy after 1945, notably automobiles and aircraft.
Firms: Dow; Du Pont; Monsanto; Rohm and Haas

779
Hollander, S.
The Sources of Increased Efficiency: A study of Du Pont rayon plants
1965 MIT Press *Cambridge, MA*

This is an intensely detailed microeconomic study which confirms that technical change is the major factor in reducing unit costs of production. The research was based on viscose-rayon manufacture at five Du Pont factories in North America over the period 1929–60, supplemented by interviews with company personnel.
Firms: Du Pont

780
Hounshell, David A.; Smith, John Kenly
Science and Corporate Strategy: Du Pont R&D, 1902–1980
1988 Cambridge University Press *Cambridge*
The authors examine the role of research and internal development in Du Pont's growth to 1980 against the background of the dynamics of the world chemical industry. The main foci are the development of new products and the corporation's shifts between centralized and decentralized control over R&D.
Firms: Du Pont

781
Jenkins, Reese
Images and Enterprise: Technology and the American photographic industry, 1839–1925
For main entry, see 1580

782
Juma, Calestous
The Gene Hunters: Biotechnology and the scramble for seeds
For main entry, see 4275

783
Kenney, Martin
Biotechnology: The university-industrial complex
1986 Yale University Press *New Haven, CT*
This is the first serious history of the US biotechnology industry examining its growth and structure, and presents a critical analysis of its interactions with the universities.
Firms: Genentech Inc; Cetus Corporation; Monsanto Co.

784
Kudo, Akira; Hara, Terushi (Editors)
International Cartels in Business History (Eighteenth Fuji Conference)
For main entry, see 99

785
Liebenau, Jonathan
Medical Science and Medical Industry: The formation of the American pharmaceutical industry
1987 Macmillan *London*
Using a case study of the Mulford Company of Philadelphia, Liebenau builds a comprehensive picture of the American pharmaceutical industry, from the early-nineteenth century to 1939. Underlying concentration, increasingly complex patterns of government regulations, and patent and licence agreements was the emergence of the sector's distinctive pattern of scientific commercialism.
Firms: Eli Lilly; Hoechst; Mulford Co.; Parke Davis & Co.; Smith Kline & French

786
Madison, James H.
Eli Lilly: A life, 1885–1977
1989 Indiana Historical Society *Indianapolis, IN*
This business biography of Eli Lilly describes him as a successful and innovative industrialist, philanthropist and idiosyncratic religious and social thinker.
Firms: Eli Lilly and Company

787
Okochi, Akio; Uchida, Hoshimi (Editors)
Development and Diffusion of Technology (Sixth Fuji Conference)
For main entry, see 107

788
Orsenigo, Luigi
The Emergence of Biotechnology
1989 St Martin's Press *New York, NY*
A comparative study of the emergence of the biotechnology industry in six advanced economies. Orsenigo studies the processes of learning and competition and the integration of new and old technological capabilities. The focus is on how a complex commercial research system

was established following scientific discoveries in genetic engineering.
Firms: Merck; Upjohn; Eli Lilly; Ajinomoto; Hoechst; Glaxo

789
Spitz, Peter H.
Petrochemicals: The rise of an industry
1988 John Wiley *New York, NY*

Written from a technical viewpoint, this nevertheless gives a wide-ranging picture of an important industry whose growth dates largely from the Second World War but whose profitability has never matched its innovation.

790
Sturchio, Jeffrey L. (Editor)
Values and Visions: A Merck Century
1991 Merck & Co. Inc. *Rahway, NJ*

This is a commissioned history of a major pharmaceutical, written to mark its centenary as an American business. Its coffee-table appearance obscures the fact that part one, on 'Visions', was contributed by Louis Galambos. It therefore provides some useful insights into entrepreneurship, research style, technology and marketing.
Firms: Merck & Co. Inc.; Merck Sharp & Dohme

791
Taylor, G. D.
Management Relations in a Multinational Enterprise: The case of Canadian Industries Limited, 1928–1948
Business History Review, vol. 55, no. 3, 1981: pp 337–58

Taylor presents a case study of management autonomy in a multinational subsidiary in Canada between 1928 and 1948. Canadian Industries Ltd was owned jointly by Du Pont and ICI, but the argument here is that local management enjoyed a remarkable degree of independence and autonomy in strategy and decision-making.
Firms: Canadian Industries; Du Pont; Imperial Chemical Industries

792
Taylor, G. D.; Sudnik, Patricia E.
Du Pont and the International Chemical Industry
1984 Twayne *Boston, MA*

This book traces the transformation of a relatively small, technically backward explosives firm, founded in the early-nineteenth century, into an international corporation. Family control did not hinder the adoption of pioneering management strategies and structures. International cartelization allowed Du Pont to match the research efforts of its German rivals, exemplified by the huge commercial success of nylon in the 1940s and 1950s.
Firms: Du Pont; ICI; IG Farben

793
Teitelman, Robert
Gene Dreams: Wall Street, academia, and the rise of biotechnology
1989 Basic Books *New York, NY*

This is a journalist's account of the optimism of scientists, technologists and especially of investors, exemplified through the development of a small Seattle company, Genetic Systems, and how the potential revolution of biotechnology encountered limits to technology and entrepreneurship.
Firms: Genetic Systems; Genentech; Bristol-Myers

794
Temin, Peter
Taking Your Medicine: Drug regulation in the United States
1980 Harvard University Press *Cambridge, MA*

Temin's book is a history of the regulation of the pharmaceutical industry in the USA from 1906, and the relationship of business and the state in this managed environment.
Firms: Eli Lilly

795
Wall, Joseph Frazier
Alfred I. du Pont: The man and his family
For main entry, see 3991

796
Wilkinson, Norman B.
Lammot du Pont and the American Explosives Industry, 1850–1884
1984 University of Virginia Press
Charlottesville, VA

Lammot du Pont's university education combined with extensive travel to maintain his company at the leading edge of technical change in the explosive sector. Du Pont's cultivation of the military in the second half of the nineteenth century ensured his company's predominance and a powerful role in the cartelization of the industry
Firms: Du Pont

797
Wines, Richard A.
Fertilizer in America: From waste recycling to resource exploitation
For main entry, see 234

Motor Industry, UK

798
Adeney, Martin
The Motor Makers: The turbulent history of Britain's car industry
1988 Fontana *London*

Written by an industrial correspondent, this book provides a single volume history of the British road vehicle industry from the late nineteenth century to the malaise of the 1980s. The author attacks the 'myth' that the British ever built great cars and points out that the situation in the 1980s reflected the years prior to 1914: the British industry expanded less than its competitors and was reliant upon other countries for equipment and technique.
Firms: Austin Motor Co.; British Leyland Motor Corporation; British Motor Corporation; Ford Motor Co.; General Motors; Morris Motor Co.; Rootes Group; Standard Motor Co.; Vauxhall Motor Co.; Rover Co.

799
Adeney, Martin
Nuffield: A biography
1993 Robert Hale *London*

A full-scale biography which draws on Nuffield's papers and describes his early career, his flirtation with fascism and his philanthropy rather more than the business side of his affairs.
Firms: Morris Motors; Nuffield Organization

800
Andrews, P. W. S.; Brunner, Elizabeth
The Life of Lord Nuffield: A study in enterprise and benevolence
1955 Basil Blackwell *Oxford*

This presents a business biography of William Morris within the context of his company's strategy and structure to 1945. It clearly contrasts the success of Morris the entrepreneur with his difficulties in coming to terms with the challenge of management of a large organization.
Firms: Morris Motors; MG Car Co.; Austin Motor Co.; Ford

801
Barker, Theo (Editor)
The Economic and Social Effects of the Spread of Motor Vehicles: An international centenary tribute
1987 Macmillan *Basingstoke*

This is a genuine international collection of essays looking at different aspects of the impact of motor vehicles since the turn of the century. The issues and periods covered are disparate but it is welcome to have such a range of countries covered: UK, USA, Canada, Japan, France, Germany, Czechoslovakia, USSR and Zaire.
Firms: Berr and Co.; British Daimler Motor Co.; Ford Co.; General Motors; Greyhound Corporation; Panhard et Levassor; Skoda; Nippon Automobile Co.

802
Beynon, Huw
Working for Ford
1984 Penguin *Harmondsworth*

This is a classic sociological account of working in a British car factory in the late 1960s and early 1970s. It is particularly strong on the interaction of union and management strategies from the shop floor through to the multinational boardroom. This edition includes an afterward which considers the impact

of Ford's move to an involvement strategy in labour relations, albeit tempered by a strong adherence to the principle of management's right to manage.
Firms: Ford

803
Carr, Christopher
Britain's Competitiveness: The management of the vehicle components industry
1990 Routledge *London*

The best survey available of the development of the British vehicle components sector, a field seriously neglected by business historians.
Firms: BL; Automotive Products; Bosch; GKN; Quinton Hazell; RHP; SKF; Smiths; Tenneco; TI

804
Church, R. A.
Innovation, Monopoly and the Supply of Vehicle Components in Britain, 1880–1913: The growth of Joseph Lucas Ltd
Business History Review, vol. 52, no. 2, 1978: pp 226–49

One of the very few studies of the development of automobile components that considers the interaction of assemblers and component makers.
Firms: Lucas; Austin

805
Church, Roy
Herbert Austin: The British motor car industry to 1941
1979 Europa *London*

This is a detailed study of an entrepreneur whose firm embodied his technical excellence and disdain for finance and marketing matters. Church highlights the importance of external creditors in the modernization of British business structures between the wars. It is valuable for comparisons made between Austin, William Morris and Ford's Percival Perry.
Firms: Austin; Ford UK; Morris; Rootes; Standard Motors; Vauxhall

806
Church, Roy
The Rise and Decline of the British Motor Industry
1994 Macmillan *Basingstoke*

This is a concise history of the British car industry, especially the British-owned manufacturers. Although focussed on the rise and decline of British-owned car firms, Church places these issues in the context of the European industry and current trends towards globalization. It presents an economic history which places the strategies of individual firms at the centre of its analysis.
Firms: Austin Motor Co.; British Leyland; British Motor Corporation; Chrysler UK; Ford; Rootes Group; Vauxhall; Morris Motors; Standard Co.

807
Collins, Paul; Stratton, Michael
British Car Factories from 1896: A complete historical, geographical, architectural and technological survey
1993 Veloce Publishing *Godmanstone*

An invaluable study of the industrial archaeology of the car industry which sheds light on the plants, their construction and the changes in technology over a century.

808
Demaus, A. B.; Tarring, J. C.
The Humber Story, 1868–1932
1989 Alan Sutton *Gloucester*

A careful company and technical history of the Humber company from its origins in the cycle making industry in the 1870s, through its move into motor manufacturing and up to its acquisition by Rootes Limited in 1932. Lavishly illustrated and technically detailed, this is an invaluable chronicle of the early years of the motor industry.
Firms: Humber; Rootes

809
Dunnett, Peter J. S.
The Decline of the British Motor Industry: The effects of government policy, 1945–1979
1980 Croom Helm *London*

This presents a review of the impact of government policies on the British motor industry 1945–79, including demand management, state investment, and intervention in industrial relations. Dunnett concludes that in the long-run government intervention did nothing to in-

crease profits, productivity or competitiveness and that this failure had jaundiced all major parties against national industrial strategies by 1980.
Firms: British Leyland; British Motor Corporation; Ford; General Motors; Vauxhall

810
Edwardes, Michael
Back from the Brink
For main entry, see 3883

811
Foreman-Peck, James; Bowden, Sue; McKinlay, Alan
The British Motor Industry
1995 Manchester University Press *Manchester*
A concise single volume history of the British motor industry with particular emphasis on demand, competition, industrial relations and government policy.
Firms: Austin; BMC; BL; Chrysler; Ford; Morris; Vauxhall; Rootes; Rover

812
Friedman, Andrew L.
Industry and Labour: Class struggle at work and monopoly capitalism
1977 Macmillan *London*
An influential study in the course of the 'labour process' debate, which focused on the Coventry car industry as a crucial case study. Though the theory has been much criticized, there is still much of value on the history of the production process and organization of labour in this study.
Firms: Standard Motors; Rootes Group; British Leyland Motor Corporation

813
Friedman, Henry; Meredeen, Sander
The Dynamics of Industrial Conflict: Lessons from Ford
1980 Croom Helm *London*
Written by a former senior trade union convenor at Dagenham and a former senior member of Ford's central industrial relations staff, this is a highly unusual and fascinating look back at the crucial Ford Sewing Machinists' equal pay dispute of 1968. The book takes the form of a dialogue between the two authors with alternative views of the same events presented.
Firms: Ford

814
Garrahan, Phillip; Stewart, Paul
The Nissan Enigma
1992 Mansell *London*
A study of Nissan's British transplant factory in Sunderland. Highly critical of the company and its methods, but effectively exposes the weaknesses or more optimistic interpretations like those of Wickens (qv).
Firms: Nissan

815
Gray, Robert
Rolls on the Rocks: The history of Rolls-Royce
1971 Compton Press *Salisbury*
A workmanlike history of Rolls-Royce covering both the cars and aero-engine operations. A particular focus is on the events leading up to the company's bankruptcy in 1971.
Firms: Rolls-Royce; Lockheed

816
Hodge, Michael
Multinational Corporations and National Governments: A case study of the UK's experience, 1964–1970
For main entry, see 3401

817
Jack, Doug
Beyond Reality: Leyland Bus - the twilight years
1994 Venture Publications *Glossop, Derbyshire*
This is the story, written by a participant, of the Leyland bus plant at Workington, Cumbria, from its inception in the early 1970s to its closure in 1991. It is strong on the role of government, technology, and the changes in the market place, and committed.
Firms: British Leyland; Leyland Bus; British Commercial Vehicles; Eastern Coach Works; Cummins

818

Lancaster, Bill; Mason, Tony (Editors)

Life and Labour in a Twentieth Century City: The experience of Coventry

1986 Cryfield Press *Coventry*

A collection of high quality essays on aspects of the business and social history of Coventry. Studies of Alfred Herbert, the Coventry car companies, Courtaulds and GE are of particular interest to business historians.

Firms: Alfred Herbert; Standard Motors; Jaguar; Rootes; Courtaulds; GE

819

Langworth, Richard; Robson, Graham

Triumph Cars: The complete 75-year history

1979 Motor Racing Publications *Surrey*

Langworth and Robson have produced a definitive technical history of the cars that also includes masses of business history information on an important British manufacturer of light, sports and luxury cars, 1903–1978. The book is particularly strong on the early years of the company and its great successes in the post Second World War boom. Contains much material on the Standard Motor Co. unavailable elsewhere.

Firms: Triumph Cards; Austin; MG; Standard Motors; Austin-Healey

820

Lewchuk, Wayne

American Technology and the British Vehicle Industry

1987 Cambridge University Press *Cambridge*

Lewchuk studies technical change in the context of the 'effort bargain' (a game-struggle between managers and workers over labour effort). He argues that the collapse of the British motor vehicle industry followed the adoption of American mass production techniques after 1945, when employers lost control over labour effort.

Firms: AEC; Austin; British Leyland; British Motor Corporation; Ford; Humber; Morris; Rover; Vauxhall

821

Lloyd, Ian

Rolls-Royce: Vol. I The growth of a firm; Vol. II The years of endeavour, Vol. III The Merlin at war

For main entry, see 1364

822

Marsden, David; Morris, Timothy; Willman, Paul; Wood, Stephen

The Car Industry: Labour relations and industrial adjustment

1985 Tavistock Press *London*

A wide-ranging study of the British motor industry in the late 1970s and early 1980s, concentrating on new developments in management strategy and labour relations, but also reaching widely into technology, skills, working practices, strikes and trade union strategy.

Firms: BL; Ford

823

Maxcy, George; Silberston, Aubrey

The Motor Industry

1959 George Allen & Unwin *London*

This presents an economic analysis of the demand and, in greater detail, the supply of cars in Britain. It concludes that greater efficiency in the 1960s could only be achieved through fewer models produced in greater volume by fewer companies.

Firms: Austin Motor Co.; British Motor Corporation; Ford UK; Standard Motor Co.; Vauxhall; Volkswagen

824

McComb, F. W.

MG

1978 Osprey *London*

Aiming to be 'the definitive analysis of the world's best known sports car', this is a detailed labour of love, chronicling the rise and decline of Britain's leading sports car manufacturer from the 1920s to the 1970s, paying particular attention to the technical side, but also with extensive details on personalities, the boardroom and marketing. Fully illustrated with detailed production data.

Firms: MG; Morris Motors; Austin-Healey; BMC

825
Melman, Seymour
Decisionmaking and Productivity
1958 Basil Blackwell *Oxford*

A detailed case study of management and production methods at the Standard Motor Co. in the 1950s focusing on the decentralized gang system of labour management. Argues that a wide-ranging practice of bilateral decision-making was the key to high productivity. Much criticized in retrospect, this remains a seminal study with many controversial ideas.

Firms: Standard Motors; Massey-Harris-Ferguson

826
Montagu of Beaulieu, Lord
Lost Causes of Motoring
1966 Cassell *London*

A wonderful study of the great failures of the auto industry, full of evocative lost names. Written with panache and insight. Why did so many inspired ideas fail? What was the difference between success and failure? This volume, a revised edition of an original 1960 publication, concentrates on Britain. A second volume (qv), published in 1971, deals with Continental Europe.

Firms: Albion Cars; Argyll Cars; Arrol-Johnston; BSA; Clyno; Crossley Motors; Enfield-Allday; GWK; Invicta; Jowett

827
Montagu of Beaulieu, Lord
Rolls of Rolls-Royce: A biography of the Hon. C. S. Rolls
1967 Motoraces Book Club *Derby*

A useful biography of Charles Rolls. An excessive focus on motor-racing mars the book, but there is also significant information on the business side.

Firms: Rolls-Royce

828
Morewood, Steven
Pioneers and Inheritors: Top Management in the Coventry Motor Industry, 1896–1972
For main entry, see 3822

829
Nicholson, T. R.
The Birth of the British Motor Car: Vol. 1, A new machine, 1769–1842; Vol. 2, Revival and defeat, 1842–1893; Vol. 3, The last battle, 1894–7
1982 Macmillan *London*

A detailed history of the invention and evolution of the passenger car. The third volume is especially useful on the early industry and its political, legislative struggles for acceptance at the turn of the century.

Firms: British Motor Syndicate; Daimler; De Dion; Great Horseless Carriage Company; Humber & Co.; New Beeston Cycle Co.; Panhard

830
Nickols, Ian; Karslake, Kent
Motoring Entente: The story of Sunbeam, Talbot, Darracq and Sunbeam Talbot Cars
1956 Cassell *London*

This is a history of the Sunbeam company from the production of its first model in 1899 to the takeover by the Rootes Group in 1936. The main interest of this book lies in the sudden decline of the company in the 1930s from a position of dramatic success in the 1920s.

Firms: Sunbeam Motor Car Co.; S.T.D. Motors; Rootes Securities; A. Darracq & Co.; Clément-Talbot

831
Nixon, St John C.
Daimler 1896–1946: A record of fifty years of the Daimler Company
1948 Foulis *London*

This is an uncritical narrative of 'a Great British Institution' rather than a company history. Unfortunately, the company papers were mostly destroyed during an air raid on Coventry, but the author does provide the basic information on the company, its directors and its cars.

Firms: Daimler Motor Co.; Daimler Co.

832
Nixon, St John C.
Wolseley: A saga of the motor industry
1949 Foulis *London*

The author provides a celebratory narrative

of fifty years of Wolseley Cars. The story covers the beginning of car production in the 1890s through to the company's war time efforts between 1939 and 1945. Although lacking bibliography and index, there is plenty for the enthusiast.
Firms: Wolseley Co.; Siddeley Autocar Co.; Morris Motors Ltd

833
Oliver, Nick; Wilkinson, Barry
The Japanization of British Industry
For main entry, see 3749

834
Overy, Richard J.
William Morris, Viscount Nuffield
For main entry, see 3906

835
Plowden, William
The Motor Car and Politics in Britain
1973 Penguin *Harmondsworth*
Plowden's book (first published as *The Motor Car and Politics in Britain 1846–1970*) is an examination of piblic policy towards the motor car. It is not the story of the car's impact upon society bût, rather, the story of society's response to the car.

836
Rhys, D. G.
The Motor Industry: An economic survey
1972 Butterworths *London*
This provides a structural analysis of the British motor industry, c.1945–70. It includes reviews of supply, demand, competition, and finance, as well as overseas competitors. It stresses the compex, inter-related factors which shaped British performance in this sector.
Firms: British Leyland; Chrysler; Ford UK; Vauxhall; Rootes; Rover

837
Richardson, Kenneth
The British Motor Industry 1896–1939
1977 Macmillan *London*
Richardson describes the transformation of the British motor car industry from the luxury market to mass production and documents the growth of middle-class ownership.
Firms: Austin; Daimler; Ford; Morris; Rover

838
Robson, Graham
The Rover Story
1977 Patrick Stephens *Cambridge*
A well-informed account of the entire history of the company from its formation as a bicycle firm to its absorption by British Leyland. Although it is not footnoted, the author has used company records and interviewed extensively to produce a fascinating account of the company.
Firms: Rover Co.; British Leyland; Triumph

839
Ryerson, Barry
The Giants of Small Heath: The history of BSA
1980 Foulis *Yeovil*
An informative company history with an emphasis on strategy and decision-making and the shifting course of top management. Covers the entire history of the company with particular detail on the decline and collapse of the company in the 1960s and 1970s. Though there is plenty of technical detail this is not a narrowly technical history and is one of the few good histories of the British motorcycle industry.
Firms: Birmingham Small Arms Co. Ltd; BSA

840
Terry, Michael; Edwards, Paul K. (Editors)
Shopfloor Politics and Job Controls: The post War engineering industry
For main entry, see 4239

841
Thomas, Miles
Out on a Wing: An autobiography
1964 Michael Joseph *London*
Written by one of the leading managers of the Nuffield Organization (Morris Motors) this is an inside view of internal management tensions within the Morris empire and of business–government relations before and during the Second World War. Thomas is also informative on the history of British airlines. He became chairman of BOAC in 1949.
Firms: Morris Motors; Ford; Nuffield Organization; BOAC

842
Thoms, David; Donnelly, Tom
The Motor Industry in Coventry Since the 1890s
1985 Croom Helm *London*

This is a study of a British car city which combined a powerful craft tradition of work organization with firms' ambitions to become, or remain, volume producers. The weakness of the city's smaller car firms was clear before 1939 but concentration only occurred in the 1950s and decline in the 1970s. The period from 1970 has also witnessed the loss of industrial control from Coventry to national government and multinational corporations.

Firms: Alvis; Armstrong-Siddeley; Daimler; Humber; Jaguar; Peugeot; Rootes Group

843
Tolliday, Steven; Zeitlin, Jonathan (Editors)
The Automobile Industry and its Workers: Between Fordism and flexibility
1986 Polity Press *Oxford* 2nd edn., 1992, Berg, *Oxford*

This international collection of essays covers historical and contemporary developments in the global automobile industry. It includes a wide-ranging introduction on the uneven diffusion of mass production and Fordist management techniques.

Firms: British Leyland; Citroen; Fiat; Ford; General Motors; Mazda; Toyota; Volkswagen

844
Turner, Graham
The Leyland Papers
1971 Eyre & Spottiswoode *London*

Prepared with full co-operation from the company, this racy account of the creation of British Leyland as the standard-bearer of the British motor industry abounds with details of managerial problems and failures, far removed from the professional management pioneered by Sloan (qv) at General Motors. Turner's *The Car Makers* (1963) includes some details of European competition.

Firms: British Leyland; BMC (British Motor Corporation); Austin; Morris; Leyland Motors; Jaguar; ACV (Associated Commercial Vehicles); Standard-Triumph; AEC (Associated Equipment Co.)

845
Turner, H. A.; Clack, G.; Roberts, G.
Labour Relations in the Motor Industry: A study of industrial unrest and an international comparison
1967 George Allen & Unwin *London*

A superb detailed analysis, using comparative statistics and case studies of the labour relations problem in the British motor industry in the 1950s and 1960s on which all subsequent researchers in the field must rely heavily.

Firms: Ford; BMC; Standard; Rootes; Vauxhall; Jaguar

846
Underwood, John
The Will to Win: John Egan and Jaguar
For main entry, see 3928

847
Whipp, Richard; Clark, Peter
Innovation and the Auto Industry: Product, process and work organisation
1986 Frances Pinter *London*

This study of innovation and design in the Rover car company covers the period from 1896 to 1982. It is particularly strong on Rover's abortive attempt to marry its tradition of high-quality, speciality products to mass production.

Firms: British Leyland; British Motor Corporation; Ford UK; General Motors; Rover

848
Whisler, Timothy R.
At the End of the Road: The rise and fall of Austin-Healey, MG, and Triumph sports cars
1995 JAI Press *Greenwich, CT*

An important study of the much neglected, and for a time very successful, British sports car industry, comparing the major producers. The study covers design, development and production relations and also stretches far into issues of significance for the volume producers.

Firms: Austin-Healey; Triumph; MG; Austin; BL; BMC; Standard-Triumph

849
Whiting, R. C.
The View from Cowley: The impact of industrialization upon Oxford, 1918-1939
1983 Clarendon Press *Oxford*

Essentially a work of labour history with an interest in the impact of increasing factory employment on politics. The value to business history lies in the author's description of the growth of the British motor industry during this period in Oxford, its impact on the city, and his argument that informal methods of labour resistance acted as a constraint upon management.
Firms: Austin; Ford; Morris Motors; Pressed Steel; Vauxhall

850
Whyte, Andrew
Jaguar: The history of a great British car
1980 Patrick Stephens *Cambridge*

A very detailed history, covering the early development of the company by a small group of engineers in Blackpool, the move to Coventry, and its years of maturity and success. The book has a particular focus on the career of the company's founder Sir William Lyons. It is extensively illustrated and does full justice to the technical history of the company.
Firms: Jaguar; Standard Motors; Triumph

851
Wickens, Peter
The Road to Nissan: Flexibility, quality, teamwork
1987 Macmillan *London*

Written by the Director of Personnel and Information Systems at Nissan Motor Manufacturing (UK) Ltd, this is an account of Nissan's approach to the establishment of its transplant plant at Sunderland in the 1980s. It is a highly partisan piece, but it embodies the vision of the early Japanese auto transplants, in particular in relation to quality, teamwork and trade unions.
Firms: Nissan

852
Wilks, Stephen R. M.
Industrial Policy and the Motor Industry
1988 Manchester University Press *Manchester*

This book is a review of the detrimental impact of government intervention in the British car industry from c.1945–85: a tale of the 'triumph' of pragmatism over planning.
Firms: British Leyland; British Motor Corporation; Chrysler; Ford; General Motors; Rover Group

853
Williams, Karel; Williams, John; Haslam, John
The Breakdown of Austin Rover: A case study in the failure of business strategy and industrial policy
1987 Berg *Leamington Spa*

This is a critical evaluation of the performance of Austin Rover under Michael Edwardes. The authors conclude that Edwardes's product-led recovery strategy was doomed to failure given the inheritance of Austin Rover's poor management, marketing, product range and productivity. They contrast this with Ford's careful policies which harvested consistent profits in the UK.
Firms: Austin Rover; British Leyland; British Motor Corporation; Ford UK

854
Willman, Paul; Winch, Graham
Innovation and Management Control: Labour relations at BL Cars
For main entry, see 4245

855
Wood, Jonathan
Wheels of Misfortune: The rise and fall of the British motor industry
1988 Sidgwick & Jackson *London*

Written by a motor car journalist, this is an accessible one-volume history of the British motor industry from its beginnings in 1896. In its approach and the book concentrates upon the principal participants. The author locates the industry's spectacular decline in the two decades after 1945 when critical management failings were masked by the seller's market.
Firms: Austin Motor Co.; Ford Motor Co.; General Motors; Morris Motors; Rootes; Rover Group; Standard Motor Co.; Vauxhall; British Leyland Motor Corporation

856
Wyatt, R. J.
The Austin, 1905–52
1981 David & Charles *Newton Abbot*

A complete history of Austin Motor Co., focusing on the planning, design and marketing of the models. A thorough piece of work and an essential reference book for historians of the industry, containing extensive production and financial detail.

Firms: Austin; Ford; Morris; Rover; Vauxhall; Wolseley Co.

857
Young, S.; Hood, N.
Chrysler UK: A corporation in transition
1977 Praeger *New York, NY*

The tortuous relationship between the British government and the weakest of the 'big three' American multinational car producers is described here. The book focuses primarily on the crisis of 1975 and the government's temporary bail-out of the company in 1976.

Firms: British Leyland; Chrysler; DAF; Ford; General Motors; Vauxhall; Volvo

Motor Industry, Europe (excl. UK)

858
Bardou, J.-P.; Chanaron, J. J.; Fridenson, P.; Laux, J. M.
The Automobile Revolution: The impact of an industry
1982 University of North Carolina Press *Chapel Hill; NC*

Probably the best single volume history of the international automobile industry. The study covers not only business and technological developments, but also the social impact of the industry.

Firms: Austin; Benz; GM; Chrysler; Citroen; Fiat; Ford; Nissan; Olds; Opel

859
Bellon, Bernard P.
Mercedes in Peace and War: German automobile workers, 1903–45
1990 Columbia University Press *New York, NY*

Bellon combines a detailed study of the daily lives of factory workers at Daimler-Benz and their relations and conflicts with factory management with a broader discussion of the role of the auto industry in German economic development. In particular, he examines how the labour struggles of the 1920s gave way to Nazism in the factory in the 1930s, and to close ties between Daimler-Benz and the Nazi leadership, leading up to the use of slave labour and concentration camp inmates during the Second World War.

Firms: Daimler-Benz

860
Berggren, Christian
Alternatives to Lean Production: Work organization in the Swedish auto industry
1992 ILR Press *Ithaca, NY*

A fine discussion of the distinctive organizational and productive practices of the Swedish automobile industry from the 1970s to the 1990s. Berggren argues that the Swedish model of teamwork increased independent decision-making and elicited strong union commitment. [The British edition is entitled: 'The Volvo Experience'].

Firms: Volvo; Saab

861
Bigazzi, Duccio
Il Portello: Operai, tecnici e imprenditori all'Alfa Romeo 1906–1926 [Portello: Workers, technicians, managers and entrepreneurs in Alfa Romeo, 1906–1926]
1988 Angeli *Milan, Italy*

This is a combination of business and social history, covering the early years of one of the most famous Italian automobile manufacturers. Based on the company's archives, the book follows the stories of the different social components of the company: entrepreneurs, managers, workers, technicians, both independently and together. The outcome is a fresco of the relationship between a factory and the city where it is located (Milan).

Firms: Alfa Romeo; Ansaldo; Banca Italiana Di sconto

862
Brandhuber, Klaus
Die Insolvenz eines Familien-Konzernes: Der wirtschaftliche Niedergang der Borgward-Gruppe [The Economic Collapse of Borgward, a family business]
1988 Muller Botermann Verlag *Cologne, Germany*

Based on a massive doctoral thesis, this is a detailed analysis of the Borgward company, an important smaller German auto producer, which pays particular attention to the role of the family and the financial problems that led to the downfall of the company in the 1960s.
Firms: Borgward

863
Busch, K. W.
Strukturwandlungen der Westdeutschen Automobilindustrie [The Structure of the West German Car Industry]
1966 Duncker & Humblot *Berlin, Germany*

Still the most reliable account and source of information on the structure and development of the West German auto industry and its markets from the 1940s to the 1960s. Extensive statistical analysis.
Firms: VW; Ford; Opel; Borgward

864
Castronovo, Valerio
Giovanni Agnelli: La Fiat dal 1899 al 1945 [Giovanni Agnelli: Fiat between 1899 and 1945]
For main entry, see 4002

865
Doleschal, R.; Dombois, R. (Editors)
Wohin lauft VW?: Automobilproduktion in der Wirtschaftkrise [Whither VW? Car production and economic crisis]
1982 Reinbek *Hamburg, Germany*

An extremely valuable collection of essays on the history of Volkswagen which supplements the less academic work of Nelson (qv).
Firms: Volkswagen

866
Duncan, H. O.
World on Wheels
1926 H. O. Duncan *Paris, France*

Part autobiography of a cycling and motoring pioneer, part reportage, part business analysis, this massive (1,200) pages and profusely illustrated tome is a bible for historians of the early motor industry in Britain, France and Germany. It is hard to obtain, but indispensable.

867
Duruiz, Lale; Yenturk, Nurhan
Facing the Challenge: Turkish automobile, steel and clothing industries' response to the post-Fordist restructuring
1992 Duruiz & Yenturk *Istanbul, Turkey*

A comparative study of the Turkish automobile, steel and clothing sectors, considering industrial responses to changing international conditions of competition from the 1970s to 1990s.
Firms: Oyak-Renault; Toyota; Erdemir

868
Dyer, Davis; Salter, Malcolm S.; Webber, Alan M.
Changing Alliances: The Harvard Business School project on the automobile industry and the American economy
For main entry, see 924

869
Enrietti, Aldo; Fornengo, Graziella
Il Gruppo Fiat: Dall'inizio degli anni Ottanta alle prospettive del mercato del 1992
1989 La Nuova Italia Scientifica *Rome, Italy*

This is a study of the restructuring of Fiat in the 1980s concentrating on markets and product strategy.
Firms: The Fiat Group

870
Faith, Nicholas
The Wankel Engine: The story of the rotary engine
1976 George Allen & Unwin *London*

This book focuses on the revolutionary Wankel engine, its development and commercialization. Of particular interest is the impact of the engine (for both good and ill) on two major companies that adopted the technology - NSU in Germany and Mazda in Japan.
Firms: NSU; Mazda

871
Fridenson, Patrick
Histoire des usines Renault: La Naissance de la grande entreprise, 1898–1939 [A History of Renault: Volume I Birth of a great enterprise, 1898–1939]
1972 Editions du Seuil *Paris, France*

This is a serious history of a firm which was a pioneer of the automobile industry and which rose from workshop to the first rank of carmakers in Europe. The company was nationalized after the Second World War, for alleged collaboration by Louis Renault with the Nazis. The book is based firmly on company records.
Firms: Renault

872
Friedman, Alan
Agnelli and the Network of Italian Power
For main entry, see 4010

873
Giacosa, Dante
Forty Years of Design with Fiat
1979 Automobilia *Milan, Italy*

A rare insight into the internal life of auto design studios by one of Fiat's leading design engineers who played a leading role in Fiat's post-war small car projects until the early 1970s. Full of technical drawings and photos and fascinating on the rhythms of work and the commercialization of design ideas and insights.
Firms: Fiat

874
Glimstedt, Henrik
Mellan teknik och samhälle: Stat, marknad och produktion i svensk bilindustri, 1930–1960 [Between Technology and Society: State, markets and production in the Swedish transport industry, 1930–1960]
1993 Göteborg University Press *Göteborg, Sweden*

This book describes how the Swedish transport market was politically constructed in the interwar years. Transport policies protected the railway system and forced the truck industry to adjust to marginal markets demanding specialized products. Hence, Volvo developed versatile non-Fordist practices and extensive subcontracting relations with the highly flexible and innovative general engineering sector in Sweden. This is an important contribution to explaining the distinctive characteristics of the Swedish automobile industry.
Firms: Volvo

875
Hatry, Gilbert
Louis Renault: Patron absolu [Louis Renault: Absolute boss]
1991 Éditions JCM *Paris, France*

A huge archivally researched business biography. It emphasizes Renault's dominant personal role in the company, his role in planning plants and products, and his personality. It also gives a full account of the controversies over his collaboration with the Nazis during the Second World War.
Firms: Renault

876
Hopmann, Barbara; Spoerer, Mark; Weitz, Birgit; Bruninghaus, Beate
Zwangsarbeit bei Daimler-Benz [Forced Labour at Daimler-Benz]
1994 Zeitschrift für Unternehmensgeschichte *Stuttgart, Germany*

This is an unusual case study. The authors based their study on almost 300 interviews with former concentration camp inmates, which were supplemented by the records of Daimler-Benz and various other archives. They are concerned not so much with the economic effects of forced labour, but with those aspects relevant to social history, most of all, the working and living conditions of the forced labourers. Moreover, they try to evaluate how far Daimler-Benz was able or willing to alleviate the conditions for 'their' forced labourers. Apart from only marginal exceptions, this study is remarkable for its thorough implementation and impartial judgement.
Firms: Daimler-Benz

877
Jemain, Alain
Les Peugeot: Vertiges et secrets d'une dynastie [The Peugeots Excitements and secrets of a dynasty]
1987 J.C. Lattes *Paris, France*

This is an attempt by a journalist to probe the

affairs of the secretive Peugeot dynasty. Though superseded by Loubet (qv) in terms of business history, it gives a very different view of the internal workings of the company.

878
Jürgens, Ulrich; Malsch, Thomas; Dohse, Knuth
Breaking from Taylorism: Changing forms of work in the automobile industry
1993 Cambridge University Press *Cambridge*

A dense and difficult text that examines the restructuring of the global automobile industry in the 1980s, based on case studies of leading (but anonymous) car companies in the United States, UK, and Germany. The authors argue that the different strategies employed by firms and trade unions, and different national institutional systems, have had a major impact on the dismantling of Fordism and Taylorism.
Firms: Ford; Volkswagen; Toyota

879
Kimes, Beverly Rae
The Star and the Laurel: The centennial history of Daimler, Mercedes and Benz, 1886–1986
1986 Mercedes Benz of North America *Montvale, NJ*

An enormous centenary history with over 850 photographs and 350 pages of large format text. Full of technical detail on the early development of the companies and their contribution to the technical history of the industry. It prefers to cover the motor racing achievements of the 1930s rather than any serious history of the industry under the Hitler era, but used with care it has much useful information.
Firms: Daimler-Benz; Mercedes

880
Kugler, Anita
Arbeitsorganisation und Produktionstechnologie der Adam Opel Werke (von 1900 bis 1929) [Work Organization and Production Technology at Opel]
1985 Wissenschaftzentrum *Berlin, Germany*

A rare detailed study of production organization and technological change at firm level in the German auto industry up to the 1920s. Densely researched.
Firms: Opel

881
Lagendijk, Arnoud
The Internationalization of the Spanish Automobile Industry and Its Regional Impact: The emergence of a growth-periphery
1993 Thesis Publishers *Amsterdam, The Netherlands*

Though heavily concerned with economic and locational theory, the second half of the book contains an extensive review of the post-war development of the Spanish auto industry and is the fullest work available in English on the Spanish industry.
Firms: Ford; General Motors; Chrysler; Volkswagen; SEAT

882
Laux, James
The European Automobile Industry
1992 Twayne *New York, NY*

Laux gives a comprehensive general account of the development of the European automobile industry from 1892 to the present day. An excellent starting point.
Firms: Fiat; Ford; General Motors; Renault; Volkswagen

883
Laux, James M.
In First Gear: The French automobile industry to 1914
1976 Liverpool University Press *Liverpool*

Laux analyses the development of the French automobile industry in Paris and the provinces and the performance of French pioneer firms in international markets.
Firms: Bugatti; Citroen; Delage; Peugeot; Renault; Simca; Talbot

884
Loubet, Jean-Louis
Automobiles Peugeot: Une réussite industrielle, 1945–1974 [Peugeot: An industrial success 1945–74]
1990 Economica *Paris, France*

This is a massive archivally-based study of Peugeot, analysing how the most provincial of

the French car companies reconstructed itself after the Second World War, around the strategy of 'le modèle moyen' and the development of a large range of cars. The company showed a remarkable capacity for change and adaptation.
Firms: Peugeot; Citroen; Renault

885
Ludvigsen, Karl
Opel: Wheels to the world
1975 Princeton University Press *Princeton, NJ*
In the absence of anything better, this is a useful quasi-official single volume history of Opel.
Firms: Opel; Volkswagen; GM

886
McLintock, J. Dewar
Renault: The cars and the charisma
1983 Patrick Stephens *Cambridge*
The only available English language company history of Renault. Though clearly the work of a motoring journalist and lacking the depth of Fridenson's history (qv), it covers a longer period (until 1979) and provides plentiful information on design and development of the cars. Fully illustrated.
Firms: Renault

887
Midler, Christophe
L'auto qui n'existait pas: Management des projets et transformation de l'entreprise [The car which didn't exist: project management and the transformation of the enterprise]
1993 InterEditions *Paris, France*
One of the most detailed studies of design and project development in the auto industry, focusing on the history of the Twingo project at Renault in the late 1980s and the dilemmas of creativity and production economy.
Firms: Renault

888
Mönnich, Horst
The BMW Story: A company in its time
1991 Sidgwick & Jackson *London*
Although written in dreadful, verbose style and often rambling, this does contain a full story of the Bavarian Motor Works, from its foundation in 1916, covering its motorcycling, aviation and automobile interests. Written with access to company archives, it covers the origins, the Nazi era, the revival and near collapse of the company in the 1950s and the revival under new ownership in the 1960s. Lacks an index.
Firms: BMW; Daimler-Benz

889
Montagu of Beaulieu, Lord
Lost Causes of Motoring: Vol. 2, Europe
1971 Cassell *London*
A companion to the author's study of great failures in the British car industry (qv).
Firms: Darracq; De Dion-Bouton; Delahaye; Hispano-Suiza; Hotchkiss; Lorraine-Dietrich; Mathis; Minerva; Voisin

890
Naville, Pierre; Bardou, Jean-Pierre; Brachet, Philippe; Lévy, Catherine
L'État Entrepreneur: Le cas de la régie Renault [The state as Entrepreneur: The case of Renault]
1971 Editions anthropos *Paris, France*
A study of the impact of public ownership on the operation of Renault in the 1950s and 1960s. It is particularly concerned with financial and employment issues.
Firms: Renault

891
Nelson, Walter Henry
Small Wonder: The amazing story of the VW
1970 Little, Brown *Boston, MA*
Still the best business history of Volkswagen from the 1930s to 1970s. Wood (qv) is superior on the technical side, but Nelson is fuller on management and corporate strategy.
Firms: VW; Porsche

892
Pohl, Hans; Habeth, Stephanie; Bruninghaus, Beate
Die Daimler-Benz AG in den Jahren 1933-1945: Eine Dokumentation [Daimler-Benz in the Years 1933–1945 A documentation]
1986 Steiner *Wiesbaden, Germany*
This contains 180 pages of text and 200 pages

of documents fully covering the history of the company in the Nazi era. It covers entrepreneurship, production, products and the company's involvement in the Nazi war economy.

893
Reich, Simon
The Fruits of Fascism: Postwar prosperity in historical perspective
1990 Cornell University Press *Ithaca, NY*

A controversial work that argues that the West German economic miracle may be best understood as a result of the discriminatory economic policies of the Nazi regime. Reich uses detailed comparisons of the German and British auto industries to argue that the key factor in their divergent performance was the willingness and capability of the state to discriminate in favour of particular producers.
Firms: Ford; Austin; Volkswagen; BMW

894
Rosellen, Hanns-Peter
Ford-Schritte in Deutschland, 1945–1970 [Ford Progress in Germany]
1988 Zyklam Verlag *Frankfurt, Germany*

An official history published on behalf of the company, but containing considerable detail and extensive statistical appendices.
Firms: Ford; Opel; VW

895
Sabates, Fabien; Schweitzer, Sylvie
André Citroën: Les chevrons de la gloire [André Citroën: Chevrons of glory]
1980 EPA *Paris, France*

A gloriously illustrated official history that also contains serious scholarship. Its strengths are its coverage of the evolution of the production process, Citroën's marketing innovations, and the biography of the company's complex founder, focusing on the early years of the company from 1911 to 1933.
Firms: Citroën

896
Schweitzer, Sylvie
Des engrenages à la chaîne: Les usines Citroën, 1915–1935 [Setting Up the Assembly Line: The Citroën factories, 1915–1935]
1982 Presses Universitaires de Lyon *Lyons, France*

This study of Citroën from its origins until the takeover by Michelin focuses on the production processes and the factories as well as on the labour relations of the company. A detailed archival study.
Firms: Citroën; Michelin

897
Seherr-Thoss, H. C. Graf von
Die Deutsche Automobilindustrie: Eine Dokumentation von 1886 bis 1979 [The German Motor Industry Documents 1886–1979]
1979 Deutsche Verlags-Anstalt *Stuttgart, Germany*

This is a massive 750 page compilation of factual data on the German auto industry, presented in the form of annals. An essential reference work.

898
Seidler, Edouard
Let's Call it Fiesta: The autobiography of Ford's Operation Bobcat
1976 Patrick Stephens *Cambridge*

A lively and well-informed journalistic account of one of Ford's most important industrial projects, the creation of a wholly new small car (the Fiesta), to be built at a huge new industrial complex in Spain in the 1970s. Seidler enjoyed privileged access to engineers, planners and managers throughout.
Firms: Ford

899
Seidler, Edouard
Olé, Toledo!: The saga of SEAT and the car which is giving it a new dimension
1991 Editions J. R. Piccard *Lausanne, Switzerland*

Despite its very 'popular' appearance, this is one of the few useful sources of information on SEAT and the Spanish car industry. Written by a quality journalist, the book covers the nationalized era of SEAT, and then concentrates on the takeover by Volkswagen and the design and development of SEAT's new Toledo car in the early 1990s. Much fascinating information on

design and development and the internal history of the merger.
Firms: SEAT; Volkswagen; Fiat

900
Siegfried, Klews-Jörg
Rüstungsproduktion und Zwangsarbeit im Volkswagenwerk 1939–1945 [Arms Production and Forced Labour in the Volkswagen plant 1939–1945]
1987 Campus Verlag *Frankfurt, Germany*

This is a documentary account of wartime arms production and forced labour in Volkswagen's operations during the Second World War.
Firms: Volkswagen

901
Starkey, Ken; McKinlay, Alan
Strategy and the Human Resource: Ford and the search for competitive advantage
1993 Basil Blackwell *Oxford*

This is a historically informed study of changes in management strategy, structure and process in the Ford Motor Company from the mid-1970s to the present.
Firms: Ford Motor Company; Ford of Europe; General Motors; Honda; Vauxhall

902
Streeck, Wolfgang
Industrial Relations in West Germany: A case study of the car industry
1984 Heinemann/PSI *London*

Actually much narrower than its title suggests, this is a detailed study of the industrial relations system at Volkswagen, focused particularly on the company's crisis and revival in the early 1970s. Streeck argues that co-operative labour relations, embodied in both national and corporate institutions, were crucial to the success of the company.
Firms: Volkswagen; Audi-NSU; Opel

903
Thomas, Donald E. Jr
Diesel: Technology and society in industrial Germany
For main entry, see 4303

904
Touraine, Alain
L'Évolution du Travail Ouvrier aux Usines Renault [The Evolution of Manual Labour in the Renault Factories]
1955 CNRS *Paris, France*

This is a classic study of changes in the technical, managerial and manual division of labour within the Renault factory, 1920–54.
Firms: Renault

905
Wood, Jonathan
The VW Beetle, including Karmann Ghia
1983 Motor Racing Publications *London*

An excellent technical history of Volkswagen which also contains valuable information on the business side of the company.
Firms: Volkswagen

Motor Industry, America

906
Abernathy, William J.
The Productivity Dilemma: Roadblock to innovation in the automobile industry
For main entry, see 4247

907
Amberg, Stephen
The Union Inspiration in American Politics: The autoworkers and the making of a liberal industrial order
1994 Temple University Press *Philadelphia, PA*

An important study in the political economy of the New Deal industrial order. Amberg's main interest is the politics of the AFL-CIO and its links to the Democratic Party, but the book contains an extensive case study of the impact of this system on competitive failure at Studebaker.
Firms: Studebaker; Ford; GM; Chrysler

908
Arteaga, Arnulfo (Editor)
Proceso de trabajo y relaciones laborales en la industria automotriz en Mexico

1993 Friedrich Ebert Stiftung *Iztapalpa, Mexico*

A collection of comparative studies of changing labour relations in major Mexican auto firms from the 1970s to 1990s.

Firms: Nissan; GM; DINA; Volkswagen

909

Bardou, J.-P.; Chanaron, J. J.; Fridenson, P.; Laux, J. M.

The Automobile Revolution: The impact of an industry

For main entry, see 858

910

Bayley, Stephen

Harley Earl and the Dream Machine

1983 Knopf *New York, NY*

Written by a design historian, this is a study of General Motors' most famous designer in the Sloan era, focusing on the work of the famous Art and Color Section. Earl was the pioneer of the 'styled' car for the masses whose use of sculpture and symbol transformed the American car into the 'befinned, chromed, bejewelled, decorated, naugahyde upholstered.... Detroit cruiser' of the 1950s and 1960s. An incisive and lavishly illustrated text.

Firms: GM

911

Belasco, Warren James

Americans on the Road: From auto camp to motel, 1910–45

1981 Harvard University Press *Cambridge, MA*

A fascinating study of the impact of motorization on American travel and leisure activities. Belasco investigates both business and social aspects of the development of autocamps, motels, gas stations, roads and national parks.

912

Bennett, Douglas C.; Sharpe, Kenneth E.

Transnational Corporations versus the State: The political economy of the Mexican auto industry

1985 Princeton University Press *Princeton, NJ*

Bennett and Sharpe focus on bargaining conflicts between the Mexican state and transnational auto companies between 1959 and the 1980s. They concentrate on the shift from import substitution to export-led growth and on Mexico's power to modify the actions of transnationals. The theoretical approach that they develop has been influential.

Firms: Fabricas Auto-Mex; Ford; GM; Chrysler; Nissan; Volkswagen

913

Brennan, James P.

The Labor Wars in Cordoba, 1955–1976: Ideology, work and labor politics in an Argentine industrial city

1994 Harvard University Press *Cambridge, MA*

Examines the industrial development of Cordoba and the labour conflicts that followed the establishment of IKA-Renault and Fiat in Argentina. The domination of the local economy by a single industry and the prominent role played by the auto workers' unions brought about the greatest working-class protest in postwar Latin American history, the 1969 Cordobazo.

Firms: IKA-Renault; Fiat

914

Chandler, Alfred D. Jr (Editor)

Giant Enterprise: Ford, General Motors and the automobile industry

1964 Harcourt, Brace & World *New York, NY*

Chandler has collected together a series of extracts from internal documents, annual reports and contemporary comments on strategy, structure, management processes and labour relations in General Motors and Ford to 1945.

Firms: Ford Motor Company; General Motors

915

Chandler, Alfred D. Jr; Salsbury, Stephen

Pierre S Du Pont and the Making of the Modern Corporation

For main entry, see 3939

916

Cheape, Charles W.

Strictly Business: Walter Carpenter at Du Pont and General Motors

For main entry, see 3941

917
Clark, Kim B.; Fujimoto, Takahiro
Product Development Performance: Strategy, organisation and management in the world auto industry
For main entry, see 995

918
Cray, Ed
Chrome Colossus: GM and its times
1980 McGraw-Hill *New York, NY*

A mammoth, colourful chronicle of GM and its leading personalities from the beginnings to 1973.
Firms: GM; Ford

919
Dassbach, Carl
Global Enterprises and the World Economy: Ford, General Motors, and IBM, the emergence of the transnational enterprise enterprises
For main entry, see 4058

920
Davis, Donald Findlay
Conspicuous Production: Automobiles and élites in Detroit, 1899–1933
1988 Temple University Press *Philadelphia, PA*

The luxury car-makers of turn of the century Detroit disdained Henry Ford's efforts to create a mass market for what they regarded as a prestige product. Ford's exclusion from the Detroit élite confirmed his determination to build a car for the masses.
Firms: Chrysler; Dodge; Ford; General Motors; Hudson; Packard

921
Dicke, Thomas S.
Franchising in America: The development of a business method, 1840–1880
For main entry, see 2032

922
Drucker, Peter F.
The Concept of the Corporation
For main entry, see 4059

923
Dunham, Terry B.; Gustin, Lawrence R.
The Buick: A complete history
1980 Automobile Quarterly *Princeton, NJ*

An encyclopedic history of one of the key companies that made up General Motors. An intensively researched study of the technology and management of the company, it is an essential work for understanding the evolution of GM.
Firms: Buick Motor Co.; Cadillac Motor Co.; GM; Olds Motor Co.

924
Dyer, Davis; Salter, Malcolm S.; Webber, Alan M.
Changing Alliances: The Harvard Business School project on the automobile industry and the American economy
1987 Harvard Business School Press *Boston, MA*

The result of a collaborative project by a team from Harvard Business School, this book analyses the changing nature of international competition in the automobile industry. Its main concerns are the strategy of the Big Three in the USA, the role of the UAW, and evaluation of the European national industries, the development of globalization, and the Japanese challenge. Well-informed and insightful, though at times wayward on the history of the more distant past, this is an excellent survey of developments in the 1970s and early 1980s.
Firms: Ford; GM; Chrysler; Volkswagen; Fiat; Toyota; Nissan

925
Eastman, Joel W.
Styling vs Safety: The American automobile industry and the development of automotive safety, 1900–60
1984 University Press of America *Lanham, MD*

The best academic study to date on the American automobile industry's response to pressures for greater safety. It examines the responses at the levels of corporate strategy, technical change and political lobbying.
Firms: Ford; Chrysler; GM

926
Edsforth, Ronald W.
Class, Conflict and Cultural Consensus: The making of a mass consumer society in Flint, Michigan
1987 Rutgers University Press *New Brunswick, NJ*

Flint was the birthplace and largest production centre of General Motors and was an early centre of both mass production and mass consumption. Edsforth traces the development of Flint through the twentieth century analysing the impact of GM on work and politics. His attention is on class formation and the development of unions as well as on business culture and its interaction with local politics.
Firms: GM

927
Edwards, Charles E.
Dynamics of the United States Automobile Industry
1965 University of South Carolina Press *Columbia, SC*

This is a fine study of the final phase of competition between the Big Three and the 'Independents' in the 1950s. It shows how economies of scale, marketing and financial strength were brought to bear by the giant companies.
Firms: Ford; General Motors; Chrysler; American Motors; Studebaker-Packard; Nash; Hudson

928
Epstein, Ralph C.
The Automobile Industry: Its economic and commercial development
1928 A. W. Shaw & Co. *Chicago, IL*

An early study of the evolving industry which contains much original information on the development of mass production and consumption, and the rise and fall of firms with much statistical analysis. An important work.
Firms: Ford; REO; Packard

929
Flink, James J.
America Adopts the Automobile, 1895–1910
1970 MIT Press *Cambridge, MA*

A detailed study of the formative years of the American auto industry concentrating on the social history of the emergence of a mass market. Strong on issues such as road development, regulation, promotion and institutional responses, and on the key design innovations in steam, electric and gasoline cars.
Firms: Buick Motor Co.; Cadillac; Electric Vehicle Company; Ford; Locomobile Company of America; Maxwell-Briscoe Motor Co.; Old Motor Works; REO Motor Co.; Studebaker

930
Flink, James J.
The Car Culture
1975 MIT Press *Cambridge, MA*

Flink gives an analysis of the development of a mass market for automobiles and a 'car culture' in America from the early twentieth century to the 1970s.
Firms: Ford; General Motors

931
Flink, James J.
The Automobile Age
1988 MIT Press *Cambridge, MA*

This presents a social history of the American car industry covering corporations, competitiveness and consumption. It is a highly suggestive overview placing the American experience in a comparative context, particularly for the period from 1960–80.
Firms: Chrysler; Ford Motor Co.; General Motors; Mitsubishi; Adam Opel; Toyota

932
Ford, Henry; Crowther, Samuel
My Life and Work
1922 Heinemann *London*

Henry Ford reflects on the organization of mass production both in his own company and its wider applicability. This provides an illuminating mixture of morality, homespun managerialism and authoritarianism.
Firms: Ford Motor Co.

933
Fucini, J.; Fucini, S.
Working for the Japanese
1990 Macmillan *New York, NY*

A brilliant investigation of the establishment and operation of Mazda's Flat Rock plant in

Detroit in the 1980s, destroying many myths about Japanese management methods.
Firms: Ford; Mazda

934
Gartman, David
Auto Opium: A social history of American automobile design
1994 Routledge *London*

A pioneer study of the profession and aesthetics of American automobile design. Gartman ambitiously attempts to link the symbols and design aspects of the car as an embodiment of the American dream to wider social struggles in American society. Though this broader project may not convince, the detailed material on the organizational processes of design remains invaluable.
Firms: Ford; GM; Chrysler

935
Graham, John D.
Auto Safety: Assessing America's performance
1989 Auburn House Publishing Co. *Dover, MA*

A detailed study of the interaction of big business and Washington politics over the question of auto safety, unravelling the interests and pressure groups involved.
Firms: Chrysler; Ford; GM

936
Halberstam, David
The Reckoning
1986 Avon Books *New York, NY*

In a 'masterful storytelling style' this Pulitzer Price winning journalist tells the story of US-Japanese auto rivalry through twin narrative of the Ford Motor Company and Nissan. It is superb on personalities like Iacocca and Katayama, and with a rare level of insight on the inside working of a Japanese firm.
Firms: Ford; General Motors; Nissan; Toyota

937
Harris, Howell
The Right to Manage: Industrial relations policies of American business in the 1940s
For main entry, see 4190

938
Hayes, Walter
Henry: A life of Henry Ford II
1990 Weidenfeld & Nicolson *London*

Hayes gives an insider's account of the Ford Motor Company under Henry Ford II.
Firms: Chrysler; Ford Motor Company; General Motors

939
Humphrey, John
Capitalist Control and Workers' Struggle in the Brazilian Auto Industry
1982 Princeton University Press *Princeton, NJ*

An important study of the Brazilian auto industry under the Brazilian military dictatorship, focusing on the emergence of worker militancy, the role of the state, and management use and control of labour in large auto plants. Differences in the shopfloor relations between companies are stressed.
Firms: Ford; Volkswagen; GM; Fiat

940
Iacocca, Lee; Novak, William
Iacocca
For main entry, see 3956

941
Jardim, Anne
The First Henry Ford: A study in personality and business leadership
1970 MIT Press *Cambridge, MA*

This is an unconventional business biography which relates Henry Ford's personality to the development of his company. Ford's obsession with maintaining his personal power within the company lay behind the disdain for effective administration which brought the company to near collapse.
Firms: Ford; General Motors

942
Jefferys, Steve
Management and Managed: Fifty years of crisis at Chrysler
1986 Cambridge University Press *Cambridge*

A detailed account is given here of the evolution of Chrysler's approach to organized labour in its Dodge Main plant. Chrysler's neglect of any strategic approach to labour

management was a major source of labour unrest and competitive disadvantage.
Firms: Chrysler; Ford; General Motors

943
Jenkins, Rhys
Transnational Corporations and the Latin American Automobile Industry
1987 Macmillan *London*

Jenkins gives a historical analysis of the role of multinational automobile companies in the industrialization of Latin America after 1945. In this period government policies selected the automobile sector as a key element in industrial modernization.
Firms: Fiat; Ford Motor Company; General Motors; Volkswagen

944
Katz, Harold
The Decline of Competition in the Automobile Industry, 1920–1940
1977 Arno Press *New York, NY*

A reprint of a PhD thesis, this is an important work concentrating on the implications of developments in economies of scale for the competitive structure of the American auto industry after the Second World War. It is especially interesting on the costs of tooling, model changes and the impact of styling competition.
Firms: Ford; General Motors; Chrysler

945
Katz, Harry C.
Shifting Gears: Changing labor relations in the US automobile industry
1985 MIT Press *Cambridge, MA*

A major study of the partial breakdown in the period 1979–1983 of the collective bargaining system that had dominated the American auto industry since the 1940s, focusing on concession bargaining and changes in work organization. Combines historical, case and statistical analysis.
Firms: Ford; GM; Chrysler

946
Keller, Maryann
Rude Awakening: The rise, fall and struggle for recovery of General Motors
1989 William Morrow & Co. *New York, NY*

Written by a leading auto journalist and financial analyst, this book draws on hundreds of interviews to examine the crisis of top management at GM in the 1970s and 1980s. Its cumbersome management systems disabled it in face of the Japanese challenge and only a series of internal cathartic shocks enabled it to begin to respond partially through initiatives such as the NUMMI joint venture and the Saturn project.
Firms: GM; Toyota; NUMMI (New United Motor Manufacturing Inc.); EDS (Electronic Data Systems); Ford

947
Kenney, Martin; Florida, Richard
Beyond Mass Production: The Japanese system and its transfer to the US
1993 Oxford University Press *New York, NY*

A controversial analysis of Japanese transplant factories in the USA in the automobile, steel and rubber industries. The authors argue that a new model of production and work organization has emerged in Japan, centred on a synthesis of intellectual and physical labour (which they label 'Fujitsuism'). This model is now being transferred to the USA. Based on a mass of field studies, this is an impressively-researched book which still seems to have failed to convince.
Firms: Armco Steel Co.; Bridgestone-Firestone; Canon Corporation; Diamond Star; Fujitsu; Hitachi; Honda; IN Tek; Matsushita; Mazda

948
Kronish, Rich; Mericle, Kenneth C. (Editors)
The Political Economy of the Latin American Motor Vehicle Industry
1984 MIT Press *Cambridge, MA*

An important collection of essays covering the evolution of the auto industry in Brazil, Argentina, Mexico and Colombia, within a framework of radical political economy.
Firms: IKA-Renault; Chrysler; Fiat; Ford; Mercedes-Benz; Nissan; Volkswagen

949

Kuhn, Arthur J.

GM Passes Ford, 1918–1938: Designing the General Motors performance-control system

1986 Pennsylvania State University Press *University Park, PA*

The creation and extension of quantitative controls over all aspects of decision-making was vital to General Motors's rise to supremacy in the American automobile industry from 1918 to 1938. Conversely, Henry Ford's highly personalized control over a divided management structure was a crippling source of competitive weakness.

Firms: Chrysler; Ford; General Motors

950

Lacey, Robert

Ford: The men and the machine

1987 Little, Brown *Boston, MA*

A monumental and fascinating 800-page history of the Ford family and its management of the Ford Motor Company. A popular biography (by the author of the best-selling *Majesty*!) but exhaustively-researched, and full of wonderful detail, illuminating the continuing role of the owning family in modern big business.

Firms: Ford; GM; Chrysler

951

Langworth, Richard M.

Kaiser-Frazer. The Last Onslaught on Detroit: An intimate behind the scenes study of the postwar American car industry

1975 Automobile Quarterly *Princeton, NJ*

A rare and detailed study of one of the largest surviving US minors and its struggle to survive alongside the Big Three auto companies. Rich in technical detail and perceptive on strategic dilemmas.

Firms: Kaiser-Frazer; Ford; GM

952

Leland, Mrs Wilfred C.; Millbrook, Minnie Dubbs

Master of Precision: Henry M. Leland

For main entry, see 3965

953

Leslie, Stuart W.

Boss Kettering: Wizard of General Motors

1983 Columbia University Press *New York, NY*

A good business biography of the inventor of the electric self-starter and prolific engineering inventor. At GM Kettering contributed to a host of innovations – leaded gasoline, high-compression engines, four-wheeled brakes – that converted the automobile from plaything to big business. A fascinating inquiry into the interaction of innovation and corporate bureaucracy.

Firms: GM

954

Levin, Doron P.

Irreconcilable Differences: Ross Perot versus General Motors

1990 Penguin *New York, NY*

A valuable insider account of the upheavals within GM following the takeover of Ross Perot's Electronic Data Systems. A huge internal clash of egos and cultures resulted in a massively costly buyout of Perot's stake in the company. The book illuminates the crisis of GM in the 1980s.

Firms: GM; EDS (Electronic Data Systems)

955

Lewis, David L.

The Public Image of Henry Ford

1976 Wayne State University Press *Detroit, MI*

The policies of Henry Ford's company and his personal nostrums on all manner of things were at the centre of American public life until his death in 1947. Lewis analyses the multi-faceted public persona of Henry Ford and its role in corporate public relations.

Firms: Ford

956

Lichtenstein, N.; Meyer, S. (Editors)

On the Line: Essays in the history of auto work

1989 University of Illinois Press *Urbana, IL*

This is a collection of essays on the dynamics of management and trade unionism in the American automobile industry.

***Firms:* Chrysler; Ford Motor Co.; General Motors; Studebaker Corporation**

957
Macdonald, Norbert
Henry J. Kaiser and the Establishment of an Automobile Industry in Argentina
Business History, vol. 30, no. 3, 1988: pp 329–45

Macdonald argues that the expansion of Kaiser-Frazer–a marginal player in the American domestic automobile market–into Argentina in 1954 was born of financial chaos rather than strength.

***Firms:* Chrysler; Ford; General Motors; Kaiser Aluminium & Chemicals Co.; Kaiser-Frazer Automobile Co.; Mercedes-Benz; Renault**

958
MacDonald, Robert M.
Collective Bargaining in the Automobile Industry: A study of wage structure and competitive relations
1963 Yale University Press *New Haven, CT*

A classic study of the institutions of pattern bargaining in the American auto industry in the 1950s.

***Firms:* Ford; GM; Chrysler; Studebaker; Willys Motors Inc.**

959
May, George S.
A Most Unique Machine: The Michigan origins of the American automobile industry
1975 William B. Erdmans *Grand Rapids, MI*

May traces the early history of the American automobile industry in Michigan to 1909. The book is particularly interesting on the many companies which failed at this early stage of the industry's development.

***Firms:* Buick; Cadillac; Dodge; Ford; General Motors; Oldsmobile**

960
May, George S.
R. E. Olds, Auto Industry Pioneer
For main entry, see 3973

961
Meyer, Stephen
The Five Dollar Day: Labour management and social control in the Ford Motor Company, 1906–1921
1981 University of New York Press *Albany, NY*

From its introduction of the five dollar day basic wage in 1914 Ford Motor Company extended its range of welfare services to deepen its social control over labour. Through its Sociological Department, Ford attempted to 'Americanize' the immigrant labour employed on the company's assembly lines. Meyer concludes that this corporate paternalism was a signal failure and effectively ended in 1921.

***Firms:* Ford Motor Company**

962
Montiel, Yolanda
Proceso de trabajo, accion sindical y nuevas tecnologias en Volkswagen de Mexico
1991 Miguel Othon *Tlalpan, Mexico*

A detailed study of the operations of Volkswagen (the leading producer) in Mexico concentrating on technical change and labour relations.

***Firms:* Volkswagen**

963
Neimark, Marilyn Kleinberg
The Hidden Dimension of Annual Reports: Sixty years of conflict at General Motors
1992 Markus Wiener Publishing *New York, NY*

Neimark has an innovative approach to understanding organizational change and industrial conflict in General Motors through the twentieth century.

***Firms:* Chrysler; Ford Motor Company; General Motors**

964
Neimeyer, Glenn A.
The Automotive Career of Ransom E. Olds
1963 Michigan State University Press *East Lansing, MI*

This is a detailed business biography, based on the Olds papers, of an early leader of the American automobile industry and his role in

the bitter struggle for control of Old's second company, REO, in 1932.
Firms: Dodge; Durant Motors; Ford; General Motors; Hudson Motor Car Co.; Maxwell Motor Car Co.; Old Motor Vehicle Co.; Pierce-Arrow; REO Motor Car Co.

965
Nevins, Allan
Ford: The times, the man, the company
1954 Scribner *New York, NY*

Part business history, part biography, Nevin's text remains the essential starting point for any survey of the development of the American automobile industry and the Ford Motor Company to c.1914. Best for its description of mass production techniques, this book is unfortunately weak in underusing the business papers and tells us little about James Couzen's administration (he was the sole supervisor of all except production and design until 1915).
Firms: Chrysler; Ford Motor Company; General Motors

966
Nevins, Allan; Hill, Frank Ernest
Ford: Decline and Rebirth, 1933–1962
1963 Scribner *New York, NY*

This traces the history of Ford Motor Company from 1933-62. The decline of the company under Henry Ford is linked to his refusal to redefine his product strategy or modernize corporate structure. Restructuring on the General Motors model proceeds after 1945 under Henry Ford II and the most famous of the 'Whiz Kids', Robert McNamara.
Firms: Ford; General Motors

967
Nevins, Allan; Hill, Frank Ernest
Ford: Expansion and Challenge, 1915–1933
1957 Scribner *New York, NY*

With monumental coverage of Ford, the company, this volume runs from the First World War through the construction of the Rouge plant and the Model A and then the impact of the Depression. The erosion of the company's domination of the American mass market is a key feature of the period.
Firms: Chrysler; Ford; General Motors

968
Nofal, Maria Beatriz
Absentee Entrepreneurship and the Dynamics of the Motor Vehicle Industry in Argentina
1989 Praeger *New York, NY*

A case study of the Argentinian automobile industry focusing critically on the role of multinational companies. Argentina abandoned import protection and export promotion in the 1970s and attempted a free market, free trade strategy with negative effects which the author attributes to relying on multinationals rather than indigenous firms to develop an infant industry.
Firms: Ford; Fiat; GM; Renault; IKA

969
Okochi, Akio; Simokawa, Koichi (Editors)
Development of Mass Marketing: The automobile and retailing industries (Seventh Fuji Conference)
For main entry, see 106

970
Oliveira, F. de; Popoutchi, M.
El Complejo Automotor en Brasil
1979 ILET/Nueva Imagen *Sacramento, Mexico*

A comprehensive study of the development of the Brazilian sector with particular attention to industry structure, the role of the state, international trade, the supply sector and distribution. A basic work.
Firms: Ford; GM; VW; Fiat

971
Olney, Martha
Buy Now, Pay Later: Advertising, credit and consumer durables in the 1920s
1991 University of North Carolina Press *Chapel Hill, NC*

A pioneering study of the rise of consumer durables in 1920s America. Olney uses a comprehensive data set to examine patterns of consumer spending and shifts in the allocation of family income. In particular she analyses the role of consumer credit, especially in the expansion of demand for automobiles. She also examines the upsurge in expenditure on advertising in this period.

Firms: GM; GMAC (General Motors Acceptance Corporation)

972
Rae, John B.
American Automobile Manufacturers: The first forty years
1959 Chilton *Philadelphia, PA*

This is a narrative history underpinned by the theme that technical education or workshop experience was a vital formative influence on the leading entrepreneurs of the early American automobile industry.
Firms: Buick; Cadillac; Chevrolet; Chrysler; Ford Motor Company; General Motors; Studebaker; White Motor Co.

973
Rae, John B.
Nissan/Datsun: A history of Nissan Motor Corporation in USA 1960–1980
1982 McGraw-Hill *New York, NY*

Rae describes the establishment of a foreign distribution subsidiary to market Japanese Nissan cars. Based on company sources, it provides much detail of operations but lacks wider analysis and comparisons.
Firms: Nissan; Nissan Motor Corporation in USA; Datsun; Chrysler; Mitsubishi; Ford; American Motors; General Motors; Volkswagen; Fiat

974
Reich, Robert B.; Donahue, John D.
New Deals: The Chrysler revival and the American system
1985 Times Books *New York, NY*

This is a historically informed account of the financial, market and managerial collapse of Chrysler 1979–81 and its spectacular recovery by 1983.
Firms: Chrysler Corporation; Ford; General Motors

975
Roos, Daniel; Jones, Daniel T.; Womack, James P.
The Machine that Changed the World
1990 Rawson Associates *New York, NY*

This volume popularizes the MIT study of the world automobile industry and the concept of 'lean production'.

976
Samuels, Barbara C.
Managing Risk in Developing Countries: National demands and multinational responses
1990 Princeton University Press *Princeton, NJ*

This focuses on the interaction of host country demands and multinational responses in the Brazilian and Mexican automobile industries from the 1960s to the 1980s. It contrasts and compares the strategies of various multinationals.
Firms: Chrysler; Ford; General Motors; Mercedes Benz; Nissan; Saab-Scania; Volkswagen

977
Schiffer, Michael Brian
Taking Charge: The electric automobile in America
1994 Smithsonian Institution Press *Washington, DC*

Schiffer charts the history of the electric automobile from the 1890s to the 1920s and argues that its failure had as much to do with money and gender as technological shortcomings. Electric cars were better adapted to the needs of in-town drivers, but the champions of power and speed and the masculine attributes of cars won out. The demise of the electric car was a slow process and owed more to culture than technology.
Firms: Baker Motor Vehicle Co.; Electric Vehicle Co. (EVC); Ford; GM

978
Seltzer, Laurence
A Financial History of the Automobile Industry: A study of the ways in which the leading American producers have met their capital requirements
1928 Houghton Mifflin *Boston, MA*

A comprehensive study of the financing of the early American automobile industry which, though old, is still valuable.
Firms: Ford; GM; Studebaker; Dodge Brothers; Packard; Nash; Hudson; Reo

979
Serrin, William
The Company and the Union: GM and the UAW
1970 Knopf *New York, NY*
Focusing on the giant auto strike of 1970, Serrin probes the 'civilized relationship' between GM and the UAW and the struggles for power and profit behind the surface of pattern bargaining. First rate investigative journalism with a historical dimension.
Firms: Ford; GM; Chrysler

980
Shapiro, Helen
Engines of Growth: The state and transnational auto companies in Brazil
1993 Cambridge University Press *Cambridge*
A study of Brazil's successful exercise in sectoral state planning in the automobile industry in the 1950s. In 1956 the Brazilian government banned all car imports and forced all foreign automobile companies either to invest in Brazil or abandon the market. The success of these policies led to Brazil developing the largest LDC car industry in the world. A detailed archivally-based study that links the issue to wider debates on state and multinationals.
Firms: Ford; Volkswagen; Fiat; GM; Fabrica Nacional de Motores (FNM); Vemag

981
Shapley, Deborah
Promise and Power: The life and times of Robert McNamara
For main entry, see 3982

982
Silva, Elizabeth Bortolaia
Refazendo a Fabrica Fordista: Contrastes da Industria Automobilistica no Brasil e na Gra-Bretanha [Remaking the Fordist Factory: Contrasts in the Brazilian and British automobile industries]
1991 HUCITEC *São Bernardo, Brazil*
A plant-level study which compares Ford's production strategies in manufacturing similar cars in British (Dagenham) and Brazilian (São Bernardo) factories in the 1970s and 1980s. A rare attempt at international plant-level comparison.
Firms: Ford

983
Sloan, Alfred Pritchard Jr.
My Years with General Motors
1963 Sidgwick & Jackson *London*
This is the classic account of the imposition of a single coordinated structure, run by a general office and a hierarchy of executives, on a sprawling collection of production units. Part 1 gives an historical account of General Motors (of which Sloan was executive or chairman for 45 years from 1918), Part 2 gives accounts of the transformation of the company's function.
Firms: General Motors; Chevrolet; Pontiac; Oldsmobile; Buick; Cadillac; GNC Truck & Coach; Vauxhall; Adam Opel; GM-Holdens

984
Sobel, Robert
Car Wars: The untold story
1984 McGraw-Hill *New York, NY*
An overview of international corporate competition in the car industry since the Second World War by one of the leading American writers of popular business history ('the models, the men....' etc). A good read.
Firms: Ford; GM; VW; Toyota; Nissan

985
Sorensen, Charles E.
My Forty Years with Ford
For main entry, see 3984

986
Tedlow, Richard S.
New and Improved: The story of mass marketing in America
1990 Basic Books *New York, NY*
A lengthy chapter of this study of mass marketing compares the marketing strategies of Ford and General Motors.
Firms: Ford; General Motors

987
Warnock, C. Gayle
The Edsel Affair: What went wrong?
1980 ProWest *Paradise Valley, AZ*
Written by the former Public Relations Director of the Edsel Division, this is a fascinating chronicle of one of the great marketing disas-

ters of business history - Ford Motor Co's launch of the Edsel. Warnock was provoked to write the book by the disappearance of crucial Edsel material from Ford company files. A hard hitting and extremely entertaining narrative.
Firms: Ford

988
White, Lawrence J.
The Automobile Industry since 1945
1971 Harvard University Press *Cambridge, MA*
White's book is particularly strong on the development of the American automobile market from 1945. He includes material on dealer networks and pricing policy, as well as more conventional issues such as scale economies.
Firms: Chrysler; Ford Motor Company; General Motors; Packard; Studebaker

989
Wilkins, Mira; Hill, Frank Ernest
American Business Abroad: Ford on six continents
1964 Wayne State University Press *Detroit, MI*
This is the case study which launched Mira Wilkins on her distinguished career as the doyenne of multinational historians. It spans pre-1914 licencing arrangements, satellite producers and moves to make Ford a fully-integrated global corporation.
Firms: Ford

990
Williams, Karel; Haslam, Colin; Johal, Sukhdev; Williams, John
Cars: Analysis, history, cases
1994 Berghahn Books *Providence, RI*
A collection of the controversial essays of the group of researchers directed by Karel Williams who have used the techniques of radical accountancy to rethink key issues in the history of the industry such as the nature of mass production and the roots of international competitive advantage. Contains the most persuasive critique of the view of the IMVP (qv Womack et al) on the challenge of 'lean production' and a reconsideration of the methods of Henry Ford.
Firms: Ford; Toyota; Renault; Volvo; BL

991
Yates, Brock
The Decline and Fall of the American Automobile Industry
1984 Random House *New York, NY*
An insightful, journalistic account of the origins of Detroit's crisis in the 1970s, especially strong on the excesses of product and design in the 1950s, and the weaknesses of top corporate management.
Firms: Ford; GM; Chrysler

Motor Industry, Japan and rest of world

992
Amagai, Syogo
Nippon Jidosha Kogyo no Shiteki Tenkai [Historical Development of the Japanese Automobile Industry]
1982 Aki Shobo *Tokyo, Japan*
Amagai provides a useful introduction to the development of the Japanese car industry, including comparisons with the US industry.

993
Bloomfield, Gerald
The World Automotive Industry
1978 David & Charles *Newton Abbot*
This is a geographical study of the development of the work automobile industry from 1945 to the mid 1970s. A strength is the text's concern to analyse strategy, manufacture and distribution. It reflects the dominance of the American multinationals in the period but does offer material on initial internalization of Japanese car workers.
Firms: Ford; Renault; General Motors; Chrysler; Volkswagen; Fiat

994
Chao, Sheau-Yueh J.
The Japanese Automobile Industry: An annotated bibliography
For main entry, see 12

995
Clark, Kim B.; Fujimoto, Takahiro
Product Development Performance: Strategy, organisation and management in the world auto industry
1991 Harvard Business School Press *Boston, MA*

Drawing on a study of twenty auto firms in Europe, Japan and North America, the authors study the capabilities that lead to superior performance in lead time, engineering productivity, and total product quality. A study that is both prescriptive and analytic and that explores a much neglected area of competition in depth.
Firms: Chrysler; Ford; GM; Nissan; Toyota

996
Cole, Robert
Work, Mobility and Participation: A comparative study of Japanese and American industry
For main entry, see 3650

997
Cusumano, Michael A.
The Japanese Automobile Industry: Technology and management at Nissan and Toyota
1985 Harvard University Press *Cambridge, MA*

This is a monumental study of the rise of the Japanese car industry from its inter-war origins. It links the post-1950 emergence of Japanese car manufacturers with their assimilation of Western technologies with indigenous production systems geared to speed, flexibility, and quality. Cusumano dispels the myth that Japanese companies are essentially similar in organization, by contrasting Nissan's more capital-intensive production with the more labour-intensive techniques of Toyota.
Firms: Nissan; Toyota

998
Doner, Richard F.
Driving a Bargain: Automobile industrialization and Japanese firms in Southeast Asia
1991 University of California Press *Berkeley, CA*

Doner describes the complex negotiated relationship between host nations and Japanese motor companies in Southeast Asia, c.1960–1990.
Firms: Chrysler; Ford; Hyundai; Mitsubishi Motor Corporation; Nissan; Toyota

999
Duncan, William Chandler
US–Japan Automobile Diplomacy: A study in economic confrontation
1973 Ballinger *Cambridge, MA*

This is an analysis of American diplomatic pressure on Japan between 1967 and 1971 in order to allow American investment in Japanese industry. This crucial moment in the liberalization of trade and capital movements is located in the context of the development of the Japanese motor industry.
Firms: Chrysler; Ford; General Motors; Honda; Isuzu; Mitsubishi; Nissan; Toyota

1000
Dyer, Davis; Salter, Malcolm S.; Webber, Alan M.
Changing Alliances: The Harvard Business School project on the automobile industry and the American economy
For main entry, see 924

1001
Fucini, J.; Fucini, S.
Working for the Japanese
For main entry, see 933

1002
Genther, Phyllis
A History of Japan's Government–Business Relationship: The passenger car industry
1990 Center for Japanese Studies, University of Michigan *Ann Arbor, MI*

Genther provides a detailed study of state–industry relations in the Japanese car industry from the 1930s to the 1980s. In particular it considers the exclusion of American multinationals before the War, MITI's abortive merger plans, and the state's role in the internationalization of the industry.
Firms: Toyota; Nissan; Mazda; Ford; GM

1003
Halberstam, David
The Reckoning
For main entry, see 936

1004
Harwit, Eric
China's Automobile Industry: Policies, problems, and prospects
1995 M. E. Sharpe & Co. *New York, NY*
A detailed analysis of the history of four foreign joint ventures in China, and of China's state-owned auto industry since 1949. Volkswagen's success is particularly contrasted with the failures and difficulties of others.
Firms: Beijing Jeep; Shanghai-VW; Guangzhou Peugeot; Panda Motors

1005
Isuzu Jidosha
Isuzu Jidosha 50 Nen Shi [50-Year History of Isuzu Motors]
1988 Isuzu Motors *Tokyo, Japan*
This work explains the growth and development of Isuzu Motors, with particular emphasis on its business strategy and organization, including a description of the Isuzu-General Motors partnership.
Firms: General Motors; Isuzu Motors Co.

1006
Itami, Hiroyuki; Kagono, Tadao; Kobayashi, Takao; Sakakibara, Kiyonori
Kyoso to Kakusin: Jidosha Sangyo no Kigyo Seicho [Competition and Innovation: The growth of firms in the Japanese automobile industry]
1990 Toyo Keizai Shinpo-sha *Tokyo, Japan*
A detailed analytical study of the growth of the Japanese motor industry. There are chapters on entrepreneurship, the Toyota system, product strategy and industrial policy.
Firms: Nissan Motor Co.; Toyota Motor Co.

1007
Kamata, Satoshi
Japan in the Passing Lane
1983 Pantheon *New York, NY*
A remarkable first-hand account of life in a Japanese auto factory (Toyota) in the early 1970s. It stresses the dark side of employment for temporary and marginal workers. A superbly written and devastating account.
Firms: Toyota

1008
Kenney, Martin; Florida, Richard
Beyond Mass Production: The Japanese system and its transfer to the US
For main entry, see 947

1009
Kodaira, Katsumi
Jidosha [Automobiles]
1968 Aki Shobo *Tokyo, Japan*
This is a general study of the development of the Japanese motor industry, with particular emphasis on management including finance, purchasing, production, sales and labour relations.

1010
Mair, Andrew
Honda's Global Local Corporation
1994 Macmillan *London*
Honda sought to circumvent its more powerful domestic rivals by moving quickly to invest in the United States and then in the UK. This is a thorough study of Honda's management methods and a detailed comparison of the process of transplantation in the USA and UK.
Firms: Honda; Rover

1011
Mann, Jim
Beijing Jeep: How Western business stalled in China
1990 Simon & Schuster *New York, NY*
A vigorous journalistic account of the attempts of American Motors to penetrate the Chinese market when China first opened its doors to the West in the 1970s. Beijing Jeep was an American-Chinese joint venture, closely watched by politicians in both countries. Mann argues that China eventually acquired valuable new technology at virtually no expense to themselves.
Firms: American Motors; Beijing Jeep

1012

Maruyama, Yoshinari; Fujii, Mitsuo

Toyota, Nissan

1991 Otsuki Shoten *Tokyo, Japan*

This book provides a comparison of the growth and development of Toyota and Nissan in the postwar period. It describes Toyota's mass production technology and Nissan's international competitiveness.

Firms: Nissan Motor Co.; Toyota Motor Co.

1013

Mason, Mark

American Multinationals and Japan: The political economy of Japanese capital controls, 1899–1980

For main entry, see 3410

1014

Maxcy, George

The Multinational Motor Industry

1981 Croom Helm *London*

Arguably still the best single volume overview of the development of the global auto industry. The focus is on multinationals and apart from a general narrative, the book contains case studies of the UK, USA, Canada, Australia, Brazil and India.

Firms: BL; Chrysler; Citroën; Daimler-Benz; Fiat; Ford; GM; Nissan; Renault; Toyota

1015

Nakamura, Seiji

Nihon Jidosha Kogyo Hattatsu Shi Ron [A History of the Japanese Automobile Industry]

1953 Keisho Shobo *Tokyo, Japan*

This comprehensive study describes the role of the car industry in the development of Japanese capitalism. It includes chapters on the car industry during the wartime and postwar periods and its structure and characteristics.

Firms: Nissan Motor Co.; Toyota Motor Co.

1016

Narayana, D.

The Motor Vehicle Industry in India: Growth within a regulatory policy environment

1989 Oxford and IBH Publishing Co. *Bombay, India*

The nearest thing to a history of the Indian auto industry, but really more a survey of the state of the industry in the 1970s and 1980s.

Firms: Ashok Leyland; Bajaj Auto; Hindustan Motors; Mahindra & Mahindra; Standard Motor Products; TELCO

1017

Nihon Jidosha Kogyokai

Nihon Jidosha Sangyo Shi [A History of the Japanese Motor Industry]

1988 Japan Automobile Manufacturers Association *Tokyo, Japan*

This work describes the growth and development of the Japanese motor industry in general and in particular focuses on government–industry relations.

Firms: Nissan Co.; Toyota Co.

1018

Nishiguchi, Toshihiro

Strategic Industrial Sourcing: The Japanese advantage

1994 Oxford University Press *Oxford*

A detailed exploration of the evolution of supply chains and subcontractors in the auto parts industry. Nishiguchi explores the development of inter-firm collaboration and mutual problem-solving between suppliers and assemblers. The first half of the book is a historical study of the system, the second is a theoretical and analytic study of the contemporary working of the system. His book should be read in conjunction with Smitka (qv).

Firms: Fuji Electric; Hitachi; Matsushita; Mitsubishi Electric; NEC; Nissan; Toshiba; Toyota

1019

Nissan Jidosha

Nissan Jidosha 30 Nen Shi [30-Year History of Nissan Motor Co. Ltd]

1965 Nissan Jidosha *Tokyo, Japan*

Covering the period 1934 to 1964, this book describes the growth and expansion of Nissan. It includes labour disputes in the postwar period, production facilities, the Nissan–Austin collaboration, etc.

Firms: Austin Motor Co.; Nissan Motor Co.

1020
Odaka, Konosuke; Ono, K.; Adachi, F.
The Automobile Industry in Japan: A study of ancillary firm development
1988 Oxford University Press *Oxford*

This is a historically informed analysis of the relationship between primary assemblers and ancillary firms in the Japanese car industry to the late 1970s.
Firms: Aisan Industrial Co.; NGK Spark Plug Co.; Nippondenso Co.; Nissan; Toyota; Yazaki Group

1021
Ohno, Taichi
Toyota Production System: Beyond large-scale production
1988 Productivity Press *Cambridge, MA*

A personal account of the development of the Toyota Production System by its originator, the 'founding father' of Just-In-Time, kanban, Autonomation, Poka-Yoke, and Single Minute Exchange of Dies (SMED). Anecdotal and didactic, but still fascinating.
Firms: Toyota; Ford

1022
Okochi, Akio; Simokawa, Koichi (Editors)
Development of Mass Marketing: The automobile and retailing industries (Seventh Fuji Conference)
For main entry, see 106

1023
Oshima, Taku; Tamaoka, Shigeki
Jidosha [Automobiles]
1987 Nihon Keizai Hyoron-Sha *Tokyo, Japan*

This general study of the Japanese car industry deals with industrial policy and the move into world markets.

1024
Rae, John B.
Nissan/Datsun: A history of Nissan Motor Corporation in USA 1960–1980
For main entry, see 973

1025
Rennard, Jean-Philippe
Industrialisation tardive et nouvelles approches de l'économie mondiale: Le cas de l'industrie automobile en Republique de Coree [Late Industrialization: The case of the Korean car industry]
1993 IREPD *Grenoble, Switzerland*

The best available study of the rise of the South Korean automobile industry. Rennard's detailed study considers the market, technology transfer, and the international extension of the Korean industry.
Firms: Shinjin Auto Co.; Hyundai Motor; Asia Motor; Kia Motor; Mitsubishi Motor; Daewoo

1026
Sakiya, Tetsuo
Honda Motor: The men, the management, the machines
1982 Kodansha International *Tokyo, Japan*

A corporate biography of an unusual Japanese firm, dominated by idiosyncratic entrepreneurs, an obsession with motor racing, dramatic product innovations, and disorganized labour relations.
Firms: Honda

1027
Shimokawa, Koichi
The Japanese Automobile Industry: A business history
1994 Athlone Press *London*

The best single volume history of the Japanese auto industry, though it is stronger on data than analysis.
Firms: Toyota; Nissan; Honda; Mazda; Mitsubishi Motors

1028
Smitka, Michael J.
Competitive Ties: Subcontracting in the Japanese automotive industry
1991 Columbia University Press *New York, NY*

Smitka argues that Japan's distinctive pattern of supplier relations has been central to its competitive success in autos. He shows how the system was stimulated by responses to labour militancy in the 1940s and then evolved in distinct phases. He uses detailed case studies. His work parallels and contrasts with Nishiguchi (qv).
Firms: Kato Shatai Group; Mitsubishi Motors; Nissan; Toyota; Mazda

1029
Toyo Kogyo
Toyo Kogyo 50 Nen Shi: 1920–1970 [A 50-Year History of Toyo Kogyo: 1920–1970]
1972 Toyo Kogyo *Hiroshima, Japan*

This book describes the growth of Toyo Kogyo with particular emphasis on business strategy. It details the research and development leading to the introduction of the rotary engine.

Firms: Mazda Motor Corporation; Toyo Kogyo Co.

1030
Toyoda, Eiji
Toyota: Fifty years in motion
1987 Harper & Row *New York, NY*

This is a highly personal account of the rise of Toyota and the pragmatic, often financial reasoning behind the company's innovations in production organization, including Just-in-Time.

Firms: General Motors; Nissan; Toyota

1031
Toyota Jidosha
Sozo Kagirinaku: Toyota Jidosha 50 Nen Shi [A 50-Year History of Toyota Motor Corporation]
1987 Toyota Motor Co. *Toyota, Japan*

One of the best company histories on the Japanese motor industry. It describes Toyota's activities from the beginning with an explanation of the introduction of the 'Kanban' and 'Just in Time' systems.

Firms: Toyota Motor Company

1032
Venkataramani, Raja
Japan Enters Indian Industry: The Maruti-Suzuki joint venture
1990 Sangam Books *New Delhi, India*

This book studies the antecedents, evolution and performance of this important joint venture, focusing on state intervention, technology transfer and attempts to promote a Japanese-style work culture in the plant.

Firms: Maruti Udyog; Suzuki

1033
Wickens, Peter
The Road to Nissan: Flexibility, quality, teamwork
For main entry, see 851

1034
Yamaoka, Shigeki
Nihon no Jizeru Jidosha [The Japanese Diesel Motor Car]
1988 Nihon Keizai Hyoron Sha *Tokyo, Japan*

This is a study of diesel engine technology for cars and how diesel cars made an impact on Japanese society.

Shipbuilding, UK & General

1035
Banbury, Philip
Shipbuilders of the Thames and Medway
1971 David & Charles *Newton Abbot*

Short business histories of the many private shipyards of the Thames and Medway. The lack of deep water hindered the development of the large scale facilities necessary for the larger vessels which emerged in the industry in the late nineteenth century.

Firms: John Thornycroft; Thames Ironworks; Yarrow & Co.

1036
Carvel, John L.
Stephen of Linthouse: A record of two hundred years of shipbuilding 1750–1950
1950 Alexander Stephen & Sons *Glasgow, Scotland*

Carvel gives a detailed history of the ships produced by Stephens, a key British shipyard until the 1960s.

Firms: Alexander Stephen & Sons; Stephens

1037
Dougan, David
The History of North East Shipbuilding
1968 George Allen & Unwin *London*

Dougan relates the history of one of the key shipbuilding regions of Britain and Europe, on the rivers Tyne and Wear. Shipbuilding was the capstone of a highly specialized regional economy which based its competitive advantage, and, ultimately, disadvantage, on a set of structurally interlocked heavy industries.

Firms: Doxfords; Hawthorn Leslie & Co.; Palmers Shipbuilding; Swan, Hunter and Wigham Richardson

1038

Foster, Mark S.

Henry J. Kaiser: Builder in the modern American West

For main entry, see 3948

1039

Jones, Leslie

Shipbuilding in Britain: Mainly between the two world wars

1957 University of Wales Press *Cardiff, Wales*

This is the classic outline history of British shipbuilding 1900–50.

Firms: Armstrong-Whitworth; Palmers Shipbuilding and Iron Co.; Swan, Hunter and Wigham Richardson

1040

Lorenz, Edward H.

Economic Decline in Britain: The shipbuilding industry, 1890–1970

1991 Clarendon Press *Oxford*

The low trust industrial relations which developed during Britain's zenith between 1870 and 1914 as shipbuilder to the world underlay the industry's post-1945 relative and absolute decline. Britain's retention of craft-based production methods is contrasted with the French adoption of mass production.

Firms: Armstrong-Whitworth; Beardmores; Cammell Laird; Fairfields; Govan Shipbuilders; Lithgows; Scott-Lithgow; Swan, Hunter and Wigham Richardson

1041

Melling, Joseph

Non-Commissioned Officers: British employers and their supervisory workers, 1880–1920

For main entry, see 4212

1042

Moss, Michael; Hume, John R.

Shipbuilders to the World: 125 years of Harland and Wolff, Belfast 1861–1986

1986 Blackstaff Press *Belfast, N. Ireland*

Lavishly illustrated and authoritative, this is a commissioned history of Harland and Wolff. It is illuminating on the relationship between the Belfast shipbuilder and its main customers, including the British Admiralty and the Royal Mail Group.

Firms: Blue Star Line; Harland and Wolff; Royal Mail Group

1043

Parkinson, J. R.

The Economics of Shipbuilding in the UK

1960 Cambridge University Press *Cambridge*

A systematic study of the postwar British shipbuilding industry which is a basic work for historians of the industry.

Firms: Blythswood Shipbuilding Co.; John Brown & Co.; Cammell Laird & Co.; William Doxford & Sons Ltd; Fairfield Shipbuilding & Engineering Co.; Furness Shipbuilding Co.; Harland & Wolff Ltd; Lithgows Ltd; Swan, Hunter and Wigham Richardson Ltd; Vickers-Armstrong Ltd

1044

Peebles, Hugh

Warshipbuilding on the Clyde: Naval orders and the prosperity of the Clyde shipbuilding industry, 1889–1939

1987 John Donald *Edinburgh, Scotland*

This is a careful reconstruction of the finances of key British shipbuilders before 1939. The viability of Clydeside's increasingly uncompetitive merchant shipyards rested on their ability to attract profitable naval contracts.

Firms: Armstrong-Whitworth & Co.; Fairfield Shipbuilding & Engineering Co.; Scotts & Co.; Yarrows

1045

Pollard, Sidney; Robertson, Paul

The British Shipbuilding Industry, 1870–1914

1979 Harvard University Press *Cambridge, MA*

This seminal study of the rise of British shipbuilding covers the period of global dominance before 1914. The fragmented nature of an industry populated by fiercely independent family firms and the intense cyclicality of demand combined to limit capital investment or the modernization of management structures. The roots of late twentieth-century collapse were established during the industry's nineteenth-century zenith.

Firms: Alexander Stephen & Sons; Charles Connell & Co.; Fairfield Shipbuilding; John Brown & Co.; Lithgows; William Denny & Bros

1046

Reader, William J.

The Weir Group: A centenary history

For main entry, see 1372

1047

Reid, J. M.

James Lithgow: Master of work

1964 Hutchinson *London*

This business biography is unencumbered by the use of company archives or insight. Lithgow was, however, a crucial figure in the restructuring of British industry 1919-39.

Firms: Fairfield Shipbuilding and Engineering Co.; Lithgows; National Shipbuilders Securities

1048

Ritchie, L. A.

The Shipbuilding Industry: A guide to historical records

For main entry, see 35

1049

Slaven, A.

A Shipyard in Depression: John Browns of Clydebank 1919–1938

Business History, vol. 19, no. 2, 1977: pp 192–217

This presents a case study of the severe constraints imposed on the management of an important British shipyard, John Browns, 1919–38.

Firms: John Browns; Fairfields; Harland and Wolff; Cammell Laird; Royal Mail Group; Vickers; Swan Hunter; Cunard

1050

Strath, Bo

The Politics of Deindustrialisation: The contraction of the west European shipbuilding industry

1987 Croom Helm *London*

This comparative study of west European business covers union and political responses to the contraction of shipbuilding and the collapse of European competitiveness in global markets.

Firms: British Shipbuilders; Cammell Laird; FNV; Govan Shipbuilders; John Brown; Thyssen; Krupp

1051

Todd, Daniel

Industrial Dislocation: The case of global shipbuilding

1991 Routledge *London*

A detailed study of changing competitive advantage in the post-1945 global shipbuilding industry, this contrasts the decline of Western shipbuilding nations with the rise of, first, Japan and then other newly industrializing countries.

Firms: General Dynamics; HDW; Hitachi Zosen; IHI; Krupp; Mitsubishi

1052

Wadia, Ruttorijee A.

The Bombay Dockyard and the Wadia Master Builders

For main entry, see 3200

Shipbuilding, Japan

1053

Chida, Tomohei

Nippon Kaiun no Kodo Seicho: Showa 39nen kara 48nen made [The High Growth of Japanese Shipping: 1964–1973]

For main entry, see 3129

1054

Chida, Tomohei; Davies, Peter N.

The Japanese Shipping and Shipbuilding Industries: A history of their modern growth

1990 Athlone Press *London*

The authors review the rapid rise of Japan from the devastation of 1945 to its position as the world's leading shipbuilding nation by the mid-1960s. Based on competitive advantage in large tanker production, the Japanese industry was ruthlessly rationalized after the oil crisis of 1974. A notable feature of this study is its dissection of the intricate ties between the corporate players in Japanese shipping and shipbuilding.
Firms: Idemitsu Kodan; Ishikajima Hirano Zosenjo; Kawasaki Kisen; Mitsubishi Heavy Industries; Nippon Yusen Kaisha

1055
Fukasaku, Yukiko
Technology and Industrial Development in Pre-War Japan: Mitsubishi Nagasaki Shipyard 1884–1934
1992 Routledge *London*
Fukasaku gives a fine-grained account of the assimilation of imported technology by Japanese scientists, managers and workers. Investment in manual skills and technical expertise in the late nineteenth century developed the 'improvement engineering' capability characteristic of Japanese manufacturing in the twentieth century.
Firms: Mitsubishi

1056
Inoue, Yoichiro
Nippon Kindai Zosen-gyo no Tenkai [Evolution of the Japanese Shipbuilding Industry in Modern Japan]
1990 Minerba Shobo *Kyoto, Japan*
Covering the period 1800s to 1945, Inoue describes the development of the Japanese shipbuilding industry, with a particular focus on the interrelation between the shipbuilding and shipping industries.

1057
Nihon Zosen Gakkai
Showa Zosen Shi [A History of the Japanese Shipbuilding Industry in the Showa Era]
1978 Hara Shobo *Tokyo, Japan*
This work charts the growth and development of the Japanese shipbuilding industry during the Showa period, with particular emphasis on engineering and technology, training and industrial policy.

1058
Teratani, Takeaki
Nippon Kindai Zosen Shi Josetsu [Modern History of the Shipbuilding Industry in Japan]
1979 Gannando Shoten *Tokyo, Japan*
This is one of the authoritative studies on the development of the Japanese shipbuilding industry, which places particular emphasis on the business activities of individual firms: Kawasaki Shipyard, Osaka Ironworks, Mitsubishi Shipyard, Asano Shipyard, Uraga Dockyard, Harima Shipyard, Yokohama Dockyard, etc.
Firms: Asano Shipyard; Harima Shipyard; Kawasaki Shipyard; Mitsubishi Shipyard; Osaka Ironworks; Uraga Dockyard; Yokohama Dockyard

1059
Wray, William D.
Mitsubishi and the NYK 1870–1914: Business strategy in the Japanese shipping industry
For main entry, see 3145

1060
Yamashita, Yukio
Kaiun to Zosen-gyo [Shipping and the Shipbuilding Industry]
1984 Nihon Keizai Shimbun sha *Tokyo, Japan*
This work charts the development of the Japanese shipbuilding industry. It provides a valuable analysis of the links between shipbuilders and the shipping industry.

Railway Equipment

1061
Bagwell, P. S.
Doncaster: Town of train makers, 1853–1990
1991 Doncaster Books *Doncaster*
Bagwell describes the history of the locomotive workshops in Doncaster, England. He traces the story from the original works of the Great Northern Railway, through two world wars, nationalization and privatization. The

book is produced in a large scale format and is lavishly illustrated.
Firms: British Rail Engineering Ltd (BREL); British Railways; Great Northern Railway; North British Locomotive Company

1062
Clark, E. K.
Kitsons of Leeds, 1837–1937: A firm and its folk by one of them
1938 The Locomotive Publishers Co. *London*

This book gives a standard, insider's view of the history of an English company of locomotive builders, Kitson & Co. of Leeds. The book is written by the grandson of the founder, James Kitson, and traces the story of the firm from its foundations to its rescue from liquidation in the 1930s.
Firms: Kitson & Co.

1063
Johnson, J.; Long, R. A.
British Railways Engineering 1948–80
1981 Mechanical Engineering Publications *London*

This is an extremely thorough and detailed study of the developments in and contributions of engineering in British Rail from nationalization to 1980. Essentially an in-house production, the book deals with the challenge of maintaining a system that is constantly changing; the coming of diesel and then electrification being the two most obvious examples of change.
Firms: British Rail Engineering Ltd (BREL); British Railways; London and North Eastern Railway (LNER); London, Midland and Scottish Railway (LMS)

1064
Larkin, E. G.; Larkin, J. G.
The Railway Workshops of Britain, 1823–1986
1988 Macmillan *Basingstoke*

This is an authoritative history of the railway workshops of Great Britain. The study deals with all the main workshops in operation when the railways were amalgamated in 1921. However, the period covered is much longer, stretching from Stephenson and the early days of steam, the heyday of the railways, nationalisation and eventual contraction.
Firms: British Rail Engineering (BREL); Great Western Railway (GWR); London Midland & Scottish Railway (LMS); London & North Eastern Railway (LNER); Southern Railway (SR)

1065
Reed, B.
Crewe Locomotive Works and Its Men
1982 David & Charles *Newton Abbot*

Reed gives a history of one of the major locomotive builders in Britain. Like many railway companies the London and North Western Railway manufactured, as well as repaired, their own locomotives. This is altogether a well-illustrated book which pays considerable attention to the role of individuals in the firm.
Firms: British Rail Engineering Ltd; Grand Junction Railway; L & CR; Liverpool & Manchester Railway; LMS; LNWR

1066
Rolt, L. T. C.
A Hunslet Hundred: One hundred years of locomotive building by the Hunslet Engine Company
1964 David & Charles *Dawlish*

Rolt's is an interesting study of one of Britain's major locomotive builders. Based in Leeds, the company – a family run concern – exported widely and was a pioneer in diesel engines. As an in-house history, however, the book tends towards a celebratory narrative rather than analysis.
Firms: Avonside Engine Company; Hunslet Engine Company; Kerr, Stuart Company

1067
Tetsudo Sharyo Kogyo Kai
Tetsudo Sharyo Kogyo 20 Nen no Ayumi [A 20-Year History of the Rolling Stock Industry]
1968 Japan Rolling Stock Manufacturers' Association *Tokyo, Japan*

This work describes the growth and development of the rolling stock industry in Japan, from 1948 to 1968 and describes the activities of the association.

Aircraft, General

1068
Mowery, David C.
Alliance Politics and Economics: Multinational joint ventures in commercial aircraft
1987 Ballinger Publishing Co. *Cambridge, MA*

This volume is not so much a company history, more an important contribution to one aspect of modern business strategy, the joint venture, in commercial airframe and aero engine manufacture. Although concentrating on American examples there is some discussion of British Aerospace, Airbus Industrie, and Brazilian, Japanese and Swedish examples. It is analytic and policy orientated.
Firms: Airbus Industrie; Boeing; British Aerospace; Embraer; Fairchild; General Electric; McDonnell Douglas; Saab

1069
Todd, Daniel; Simpson, J.
The World Aircraft Industry
1986 Croom Helm *London*

This study describes the recent international situation of the producers of airframes. Coverage is given to the USA, Europe, Japan, the old Soviet Bloc and the newly industrializing countries. Attention is paid to the importance of the industry as a major employer in manufacturing, the link between technological development and demand, and the crucial role of the state.
Firms: Aerospatiale; Boeing Co.; British Aerospace; Dassault; Fuji; Rolls-Royce

Aircraft, USA

1070
Adams, Gordon
The Politics of Defense Contracting: The iron triangle
For main entry, see 1403

1071
Bauer, Eugene E.
Boeing: In peace and war
1991 TABA Publishing *Enumclaw, WA*

Bauer follows Boeing from its foundation by William Boeing in 1916 through its precarious existence in the inter-war period. From 1940 to 1970 Boeing's fate was bound up with government agency contracts and further complicated by rapid innovation in fundamental product design and technologies.
Firms: Boeing; Douglas; Lockheed; Pan American Airlines; United Aircraft & Transportation Co.

1072
Bilstein, R. E.
Flight in America 1900–1983: From the Wrights to the astronauts
1984 The Johns Hopkins University Press *Baltimore, MD*

This single volume history of aviation in the USA takes the story from the first manned flight by the Wright brothers to the Space Shuttle. It is essentially a narrative account that deals with the social, economic and political aspects, but it also outlines the principal technological trends within the aerospace industry.
Firms: Boeing Co.; Douglas Aircraft Co.; Grumman Aerospace; Lockheed Aircraft Co.; McDonnell Douglas Corporation; Pan American World Airways

1073
Bluestone, Barry; Jordan, Peter; Sullivan, Mark
Aircraft Industry Dynamics: An analysis of competition, capital and labor
1981 Auburn House *Boston, MA*

This is a solid, scholarly study of the modern US aircraft manufacturing industry concentrating on the nature of the market, the capital investment and plant location, labour relations and the interface between government and industry. It has a useful couple of chapters on the history of the industry.
Firms: Boeing; Lockheed; McDonnell Douglas; Pratt & Whitney

1074

Bright, C. D.

The Jet Makers: The aerospace industry from 1945 to 1972

1978 Regents Press of Kansas *Lawrence, KS*

This book provides an account of the fortunes of the American aircraft industry after the Second World War. The story revolves around the interaction between new technology and political pressure which permitted the manufacturing companies to prosper during the Cold War. As an academic work it is seriously flawed by a lack of primary material and references.

Firms: Boeing Co.; Grumman Aerospace; Lockheed Corporation; McDonnell Douglas Corporation; Pratt & Whitney

1075

Discalla, R. V.

The Development of the Aerospace Industry on Long Island: Volume III, A chronology, 1833–1965

1968 Hofstra University *New York, NY*

This is the final volume of a three-volume history (see Kaiser) of the aerospace industry in New York. This volume is basically a calendar record of significant events in the history of the industry and contains little of any significance, although it is a useful companion to the first two volumes.

Firms: Brewster; Fairchild; Grumman; Republic; Sperry

1076

Kaiser, W. K. (Editor)

The Development of the Aerospace Industry on Long Island: Volume I, 1904–1964

1968 Hofstra University *New York, NY*

This is the first of a three volume, multi-authored history (see also Kaiser & Stonier, Discalla) of the American aerospace industry in a regional setting. This volume is divided roughly into a series of narrative histories of the various companies on Long Island, and coverage of different aspects of the influence of government policy on the industry.

Firms: Brewster; Fairchild; Grumman; Republic; Sperry

1077

Kaiser, W. K.; Stonier, C. F. (Editors)

The Development of the Aerospace Industry on Long Island: Volume II, Financial and related aspects

1968 Hofstra University *New York, NY*

This, the second of a three volume history of the aerospace industry in New York, has a more analytical approach and the issues covered by different authors include finance and investment, labour relations, the impact of the industry on related industries and the local economy, and problems such as noise and air pollution.

Firms: Brewster; Fairchild; Grumman; Republic; Sperry

1078

Kuter, L. S.

The Great Gamble: The Boeing 747

1973 University of Alabama Press *Tuscaloosa, AL*

This presents a detailed and somewhat breathless account of the joint venture between Boeing and Pan Am which led to the development of the 'jumbo jet', the Boeing 747. It is written with an insider's knowledge, the author having been a General in the US Airforce and an Executive Vice-President of Pan Am.

Firms: Boeing; Pan American Airways

1079

Lotchin, Roger W.

Fortress California, 1910–1961: From warfare to welfare

For main entry, see 1408

1080

Newhouse, J.

The Sporty Game

1982 Knopf *New York, NY*

This provides a history of the development and marketing of wide bodied aircraft. A rather journalistic account which relies upon information from private sources, it does contain interesting detail on the growing competitiveness between American and European aircraft manufacturers.

Firms: Airbus Industrie; Boeing Co.; Lockheed Aircraft Corporation; McDonnell Douglas Corporation; Pratt & Whitney; Rolls-Royce

1081
Phillips, A.
Technology and Market Structure: A study of the aircraft industry
1971 D. C. Heath & Company *Lexington, MA*

This study of the American aircraft manufacturing industry covers the period from the 1920s to the mid-1960s. The author's main interest lies in the relationship between changes in industrial technology and changes in market structure. He illustrates a process of increasing concentration over the forty-year period.
Firms: Boeing Co.; Douglas Aircraft Co.; Fairchild Engine & Airplane Corp.; Fokker Aircraft Corp. of America; Ford Motor Co.; Lockheed Aircraft Co.

1082
Rae, J. B.
Climb to Greatness: The American aircraft industry, 1920–1960
1968 MIT Press *Cambridge, MA*

This is a study of the history of the American aircraft manufacturing firms and the entrepreneurs of the industry. Rae begins his narrative after the First World War and ends it in the late 1950s with the arrival of the jet era. The post-war years are not dealt with as substantially as the earlier decades but it is a valuable book nonetheless.
Firms: Bell Aerospace; Boeing; McDonnell Douglas

1083
Rae, John B.
Financial Problems of the American Aircraft Industry, 1906–1940
Business History Review, vol. 39, no. 1, 1965: pp 99-114

Rae describes the perilous finances of the pioneers of the American aircraft industry and the gradual rise of the state as the key customer for military and civilian aircraft.
Firms: Corvair; General Dynamics; Wright Company; Curtiss-Herring Company; Lockheed Aircraft Company; Curtiss Aeroplane & Motor Corporation; Dayton-Wright Airplane Company; National Cash Register Company; Boeing Aircraft & Transport Corporation; Pratt & Whitney

1084
Simonson, G. R. (Editor)
The History of the American Aircraft Industry: An anthology
1968 MIT Press *Cambridge, MA*

This collection of readings on the American aircraft industry covers the period from 1903 to 1965. Although described by the editor as 'classics', the article selected are variable in quality. The scope of the contributions is attractive, ranging from Orville Wright's 'How We Invented the Airplane' to studies of the impact of guided missiles and the space race on the industry.

1085
Stekler, H. O.
The Structure and Performance of the Aerospace Industry
1965 University of California Press *Berkeley, CA*

This is a standard text on the American aerospace industry up to the early 1960s. The historical development of the industry is somewhat sketchy, but the author's treatment of the structure of the industry is more substantial. Of most interest is the discussion of firm entry into and exit from the industry.
Firms: American Telegraph & Telephone Co. (A.T. & T.); Bell Aircraft; Boeing Aircraft Co.; Douglas Aircraft Co.; Grumman Aircraft Engineering Corp.; Lockheed Aircraft Corp.

1086
Trimble, W. F.
The Naval Aircraft Factory, the American Aviation Industry, and Government Competition, 1918–1928
Business History Review, vol. 60, no. 1, 1986: pp 175–98

This essay describes the American aircraft manufacturing industry in the 1920s. Faced with cuts in military orders and little or no demand for civilian aircraft, the private manufacturers focused their hostility on 'government competition', especially as represented by the Naval Aircraft Factory at Philadelphia. Eventually, an uneasy partnership between the navy and business was established.

1087
Trimble, William F.
High Frontier: A history of aeronautics in Pennsylvania
1982 University of Pittsburgh Press *Pittsburgh, PA*

A comprehensive study of the aeronautics industry in a major state of the USA. The story ranges from the early hot air balloonists of the late eighteenth century to the modern aerospace industry. The impact of the First World War, the role of big business, state regulation of air travel and technological developments are all covered.

Firms: AGA Aviation Group; G. & A. Aircraft Inc.; Westinghouse Electric Corp.; Curtis-Wright Corp.; Pitcairn Aircraft co.; Transworld Airlines (TWA)

Aircraft, Europe & Japan

1088
Carlier, Claude
Marcel Dassault: Le Légende d'un siècle [Marcel Dassault Legend of a century]
1992 Perrin *Paris, France*

This is a comprehensively researched business biography, examining Dassault's diversified industrial empire and political connections as well as his core aircraft business and the creation of the Mirage jet.

1089
Chadeau, Emmanuel
Latécoère
1990 Olivier Orban *Paris, France*

This is a biography and also a business history of Pierre-Georges Latécoère (1883–1943), who was a pioneer both of the French aircraft industry and of commercial air transport. The book is based on business and private records.

1090
Chapman, H.
State Capitalism and Working Class Radicalism in the French Aircraft Industry
For main entry, see 4171

1091
Costello, John; Hughes, Terry
The Battle for Concorde
1971 Compton Press *Salisbury*

This is not so much a business history as the history of a particular project, the first and only Anglo-French supersonic commercial aircraft. It is particularly strong on the political machinations, the technological problems encountered and the escalating costs, though all written in simple terms. Sadly, it lacks the usual academic paraphernalia of sources, notes, a bibliography and even an index.

Firms: Aerospatiale; British Aircraft Corporation; BOAC

1092
Edgerton, David
Technical Innovation, Industrial Capacity and Efficiency: Public ownership and the British military aircraft industry, 1935–48
Business History, vol. 26, no. 3, 1984: pp 247–79

This article describes the relations between the state and the British military aircraft sector in war and peace, 1935–48. It is particularly strong on the importance of the design capability of individual firms during a period of rapid technical innovation.

Firms: D. Napier & Son; English Electric Co.; Fairey Aviation Co.; Harland and Wolff; Power Jets; Short Bros

1093
Edgerton, David
England and the Aeroplane: An essay on a militant and technological nation
1991 Macmillan *Basingstoke*

Edgerton has written a provocative history of aviation and the aircraft industry in England from the birth of the aeroplane to the present day. He presents a picture of a large and successful industry actively promoted by government. This thesis cuts across the consensus of England's industrial decline and suggests instead a technological, industrial and militant nation.

Firms: Aircraft Manufacturing Company; Armstrong-Whitworth; British Aerospace; British Aircraft Corporation; Hawker Siddeley; Rolls-Royce; Vickers; de Havilland

1094
Fearon, Peter
The Vicissitudes of a British Aircraft Company: Handley Page Ltd, between the wars
Business History, vol. 20, no. 1, 1978: pp 63–86

This presents the experience of the Handley Page airframe manufacturers, 1919–39, as a case study of a limited market hampering innovation in product and process technologies.
Firms: Handley Page; Barclays Bank; Imperial Airways; Short Bros; Douglas; Lockheed

1095
Feldman, E. J.
Concorde and Dissent: Exploring high technology project failures in Britain and France
1985 Cambridge University Press *Cambridge*

Feldman makes a detailed examination of three highly prestigious projects in Britain and France: Concorde, and the attempts to build new international airports for London and Paris. Although primarily a comparative study of policy making, the book does throw some interesting light on the aircraft and air transport industries.
Firms: Air France; Airbus Industrie; British Aircraft Corporation; British Airports Authority; British Airways; British Overseas Airways Corporation

1096
Gardner, C.
British Aircraft Corporation: A history
1981 Batsford *London*

Gardner gives an insider's view of the history of the British Aircraft Corporation (formed 1960). The period covered stretches from Whitehall's ultimatum on rationalization of the British aircraft industry in 1957 to BAC's eventual (though short lived) nationalization in 1977 as British Aerospace. Not surprisingly the book has a considerable amount to say on relations between industry and government.
Firms: Bristol Aircraft; British Aerospace; British Aircraft Corporation; English Electric Aviation; Hunting Aircraft

1097
Hayward, Keith
Government and British Civil Aerospace: A case study in post-war technology policy
1983 Manchester University Press *Manchester*

Hayward gives a comprehensive account of the relationship between the British civil aircraft industry and government. The book covers the impact of the jet engine in the Second World War, Concorde, European and international joint ventures. The account goes up to 1981 and the 'privatization' of British Aerospace.
Firms: Bristol Siddeley Engines; British Aerospace; British Aircraft Corporation; Hawker Siddeley Group; Rolls-Royce

1098
Hayward, Keith
International Collaboration in Civil Aerospace
1986 Francis Pinter *London*

This book examines international cooperation and competition in the civil aircraft industry. Although covering the period from 1945, the focus falls largely on the post-1970 period when international collaborative projects began to emerge. America, Europe and Japan are dealt with but the book is most informative on the European scene and the growing US–European rivalry.
Firms: Airbus Industrie; Boeing Co.; General Electric; Japanese Aero-Engine Co.; McDonnell Douglas Corporation; Rolls-Royce

1099
Hayward, Keith
The British Aircraft Industry
1989 Manchester University Press *Manchester*

Hayward argues that the creation of the aircraft industry owed everything to military demands; state–industry relations have remained paramount, even after privatization. The British aerospace industry has failed to match American might and has moved increasingly towards joint European ventures. This is a coherent and comprehensive analysis of an extremely complex sector.
Firms: British Aerospace; British Aircraft Corporation; Hawker Siddeley Group; Rolls-Royce; Vickers-Armstrong; Westland Aircraft

1100

Higham, Robin

Quantity vs Quality: The impact of changing demand on the British aircraft industry, 1900–1960

Business History Review, vol. 42, no. 4, 1968: pp 443–66

This covers the transfer of technical and design specifications between the British and American aircraft industries from 1900–60. The differing demands of military production - quantity - versus the quality requirement of civil aviation hampered the British manufacturers' progress.

Firms: Imperial Airways; De Havilland; Rolls Royce

1101

Homze, Edward L.

Arming the Luftwaffe: The Reich Air Ministry and the German aircraft industry 1919–39

1976 University of Nebraska Press *Lincoln, NE*

Homze makes a forensic examination of the extent of Nazi investment and management under the veneer of private ownership in the German aircraft industry from 1933. His book is particularly strong on the deterioration of the initially close working relationship within the Nazi military-industrial complex. He also reveals the growing chaos, as an authoritarian state proved incapable of coordinating production for 'total war'.

Firms: Bayerische Flugzeugwerke (BFW); Bayerische Motorenwerke (BMW); Focke-Wulf; Heinkel; Henschel; Junkers; Messerschmitt

1102

Knight, Geoffrey

Concorde: The inside story

1976 Weidenfeld & Nicolson *London*

This slim volume is really the history of a specific project, the Anglo-French supersonic Concorde, written by someone closely involved in the process, latterly as vice chair of the British manufacturing firm, British Aircraft Corporation. It lacks sources and references, tends to downplay opposition to the aircraft, and is frankly personal, nonetheless it is of value as a sound narrative account, strong on personalities.

Firms: British Aircraft Corporation; British Aerospace Co.; Aerospatiale; BOAC; Air France; Rolls Royce

1103

Lloyd, Ian

Rolls-Royce: Vol. I The growth of a firm; Vol. II The years of endeavour; Vol. III The Merlin at war

For main entry, see 1364

1104

Minowa, Tetsu (Editor)

Nihon no Koku Uchu Kogyo Sengo no Ayumi [The Post War History of the Aerospace Industry in Japan]

1985 Society of Japanese Aerospace Companies *Tokyo, Japan*

This book provides a general explanation of the growth and development of the Japanese aerospace industry with particular emphasis on government industrial policy. For a European comparison see Mönnich on BMW (qv).

1105

Mönnich, Horst

The BMW Story: A company in its time

For main entry, see 888

1106

Morow, J. H.

German Air Power in World War I

1982 University of Nebraska Press *Lincoln, NE*

This military–industry history argues that aircraft were not peripheral to the conduct of the First World War. The emphasis is on the industrial mobilization of the aircraft industry by the military commands of Imperial Germany and Austro-Hungary, with their requirements for increased production and technological innovation.

Firms: AEG; BMW; Benz Motor Company; DFW; Daimler Motor Company; Fokker Aircraft Works

1107
Reader, W. J.
Architect of Air Power: The life of the first Viscount Weir of Eastwood 1877–1959
For main entry, see 1371

1108
Robertson, Alan
Lion Rampant and Winged: A commemorative history of Scottish Aviation Ltd, predecessor company of British Aerospace plc, Civil Aircraft Division, Prestwick
1986 Alan Robertson *Barassie, Scotland*

This privately printed history is profusely illustrated and narrates the history of Scottish Aviation from its inception in 1935 to provide flying training under contract to the Air Ministry largely financed by De Havilland, to its incorporation in the nationalized British Aerospace, via aircraft maintenance during the Second World War. It is rather narrative and anecdotal, but contains much useful information. It lacks an index.
Firms: British Aerospace; Scottish Aviation

1109
Samuels, Richard J.
'Rich Nation, Strong Army': National security and the technological transformation of Japan
1994 Cornell University Press *Ithaca, NY*

From 1868 to 1945 the Japanese economy linked technological development to national security under the slogan 'Rich Nation, Strong Army'. Following the War, planners reversed these assumptions and promoted instead the development of commercial technology and infrastructures. The system of innovation that resulted enabled Japan to become an innovator in both civilian and military technologies, including aerospace. The book contains detailed studies of Japan's aircraft and armaments industries.
Firms: Fuji Heavy Industries; Hitachi; Ishikawajima-Harima Heavy Industries; Kawasaki Heavy Industries; Lockheed; Mitsubishi Heavy Industries; Mitsubishi Aircraft; Mitsubishi Electric; Nakajima Aircraft; Shin Meiwa Industries

1110
Smith, M.
British Air Strategy Between the Wars
1984 Clarendon Press *Oxford*

This is an informative study of the process of developing a military air strategy by Britain between the First and Second World Wars. It is primarily a military and political history but does have some value to business historians, notably in the area of how to implement strategies after they have been decided.
Firms: Fairey Aircraft Co.; Handley Page Aircraft Co.; Hawkers Aircraft Co.; Rolls-Royce; Shorts Aircraft Co.; Vickers Aircraft Co.

1111
Takahashi, Yasutaka
Nakajima Hikoki no Kenkyu [A Study of Nakajima Aircraft Company]
1988 Nihon Keizai Hyoron Sha *Tokyo, Japan*

This book is a detailed study of the Nakajima Aircraft Company with emphasis on the prewar period. There are chapters on its growth, the wartime aircraft industry, management and the operation of the Nakajima factories during the war.
Firms: Nakajima Aircraft Co.

1112
Wilson, A.
The Concorde Fiasco
1973 Penguin *Harmondsworth*

This is an impassioned account, by an Associate Editor of the *Observer* newspaper, of why the Concorde project was an unforgivable failure. Written as an exposé of government secrecy and failure properly to investigate the costs, financial and environmental, of supersonic aircraft, the book contains a considerable amount of significant information.
Firms: British Aircraft Corporation; British Overseas Airways Corporation; Dassault; Hawker Siddeley; Rolls-Royce; Sud Aviation

Textiles, Early Modern

1113

Braumann, W. R.

The Merchant Adventurers and the Continental Cloth Trade (1560s–1620s)

1990 Walter de Gruyter *Berlin, Germany*

This is an informative study of the trade in English wool on the Continent and the finishing of the imported cloth. Originally, the trade was concentrated in Antwerp but for a variety of reasons it shifted to the ports and cities of northern Germany.

1114

Bythell, Duncan

The Handloom Weavers: A study of the English cotton industry during the Industrial Revolution

1969 Cambridge University Press *Cambridge*

This is a valuable book which provides the first detailed study of the history of the cotton handloom weavers in Lancashire between 1780 and 1850. The author throws much-needed light on a number of issues such as weavers' earnings, technological progress in the cotton industry, and the role played by weavers in radical politics.

Firms: M'Connel & Kennedy; Richard Arkwright & Co.

1115

Edwards, M. M.

The Growth of the British Cotton Trade, 1780–1815

1967 Manchester University Press *Manchester*

Continuing the work of Wadsworth and Mann (qv) this is a comprehensive study of the British cotton industry during a critical period. The author provides a useful examination of the contribution of the domestic and foreign markets to the trade, the supply of American cotton, and the provision of capital in the industry.

1116

Harte, N. B.; Ponting, K. G. (Editors)

Textile History and Economic History: Essays in honour of Miss Julia de Lacy Mann

1973 Manchester University Press *Manchester*

This collection of fifteen essays covers some four centuries of English textile history. The period stretches from 1500 to the later nineteenth century and covers topics as disparate as fashion in the stocking industry 1500 to 1700, an analysis of the assets of pre-industrial textile entrepreneurs, and the Manchester cotton trade in the 1860s. In due recognition of Mann's interests, wool, linen and cotton are all included.

Firms: Boulton & Watt; Bush, Newton & Bush; John Cartwright; Divett Price Jackson & Co.; ICI; Joyce Cooper & Co.; Samuel Salter & Co.; Yerbury Tugwell & Esmonds

1117

Heaton, Herbert

The Yorkshire Woollen and Worsted Industries: From the earliest times to the Industrial Revolution

2nd Edition

1965 Oxford University Press *Oxford*

This is the second edition of a volume first published in 1920. The author provides a detailed chronology of the woollen industry in Yorkshire from the fourteenth century to the eighteenth century. The treatment of the organization of the industry and of the state efforts at regulation are particularly valuable.

1118

Kerridge, Eric

Textile Manufacturers in Early Modern England

1985 Manchester University Press *Manchester*

This study of the English textile industry as a whole covers the range of sectors and regions from the sixteenth to the early eighteenth century. While the scope and detail of the book are impressive it is lacking in comparative analysis and is of limited use to business historians.

Firms: Dutch East India Company; East India Company; Eastlands Company; French Company; Hatter's Company; Russell's Company

1119

Lloyd, T. H.

The English Wool Trade in the Middle Ages

1977 Cambridge University Press *Cambridge*

This is an extensive survey of England's wool export trade. The author provides new insights into the nature of the merchant companies and associations and their financial dealings with the Crown. Although it does not attempt to measure the overall importance of the wool trade upon the economy as a whole, it remains a valuable addition to the history of the English wool trade.

1120
Lowe, N.
The Lancashire Textile Industry in the Sixteenth Century
1972 Manchester University Press *Manchester*

This study published for the Chetham Society deals with an area of the English textile trade which pre-dates the cotton era and the work of Wadsworth and Mann (qv). Textiles in sixteenth-century Lancashire meant wool and linen and both were dominated by the independent weaver. Only toward the end of the century did more capitalist-type development occur.

1121
Mazzaoui, M. F.
The Italian Cotton Industry in the Later Middle Ages, 1100–1600
1981 Cambridge University Press *Cambridge*

This is a path-breaking study which charts the early production of cotton by Italian merchants (borrowing heavily from the Islamic world), the dominance of the Italian export industry and its gradual displacement by southern German rivals. The author identifies the shift of economic power from the Mediterranean to the Atlantic seaboard and the transition to the modern economic system.

1122
Ponting, K. G.
The Woollen Industry of South-West England
1971 Adams & Dart *Bath*

This general overview of the wool textile industry of south-west England stretches from the very earliest times to the beginning of the nineteenth century. The author's main concern, however, lies in the impact that the industrial revolution had upon the lives of the workforce. Following the Hammonds, Ponting shows the determination of the handloom weavers not to go into the mills.

Firms: Boulton & Watt; East India Company

1123
Thomson, J. K. J.
Clermont-de-Lodeve, 1633–1789: Fluctuations in the prosperity of a Languededocian cloth-making town
1982 Cambridge University Press *Cambridge*

This is a revised version of a PhD thesis examining the fortunes of one of the three cloth-making centres of the Languedoc. It is a welcome addition to the history of proto-industry in France. Thomson focuses on the critical role of the entrepreneur and illustrates the rise of the industry and the crisis it faced after 1750 with the removal of mercantile regulations.

1124
Wadsworth, A. P.; Mann, Julia de L.
The Cotton Trade and Industrial Lancashire 1600–1780
1931 Manchester University Press *Manchester*

This is a classic account of the development of the cotton industry in Lancashire, England, before the factory age. The book charts the emergence of a country textile industry, the place of cotton goods in European commerce and the growing firms of capitalist organization of the industry. Despite its age this is a work which remains unsurpassed.

Textiles, UK - Cotton

1125
Baines, Edward
History of the Cotton Manufacture in Great Britain
2nd Edition
1966 Frank Cass *London*

This is the second edition of Baines's great work on the British cotton industry first published in 1835. The study ranges from ancient Egypt to Britain in the early nineteenth century. Along the way Baines deals with European, Asian, African and American cottons. The crucial period dealt with is the 'era of invention' beginning in the early eighteenth century. Baines provides useful material on technology, the commercial significance of the industry and the conditions of the labour forces.

1126
Boyson, Rhodes
The Ashworth Cotton Enterprise: The rise and fall of a family firm 1818–1880
1970 Clarendon Press *Oxford*

This important if sometimes disappointing history of a nineteenth-century British cotton firm, includes a biography of Henry Ashworth, the leading partner in the family firm. The business was rural-based rather than an urban enterprise and Henry Ashworth was a leading Liberal manufacturer, a representative of the Manchester School, opposed to the Corn Laws and deeply opposed to factory legislation.
Firms: Edmund Ashworth & Son; H. & E. Ashworth; Henry Ashworth & Sons

1127
Catling, Harold
The Spinning Mule
1970 David & Charles *Newton Abbot*

This is both a technical and social history of the spinning mule and its long dominance within the British cotton industry. Samuel Crompton's invention of 1779 was an immediate success and spinning mules were enthusiastically adopted throughout the industry. Although no new mules were built after 1914 it was only in the 1950s that the British industry eventually shifted to using spindles.
Firms: M'Connel & Kennedy; Platt Brothers; Dobson & Barlow

1128
Chapman, Stanley D.
The Early Factory Masters: The transition to the factory system in the Midlands textile industry
1967 David & Charles *Newton Abbot*

This study of the emergence of factory production in the English Midlands covers the critical period spanning the late eighteenth and early nineteenth centuries. Although a regional study, the book makes a valuable contribution to debates on entrepreneurial responses in the early industrial revolution in Britain, and the role played by cotton.

1129
Chapman, Stanley D.
The Cotton Industry in the Industrial Revolution
1972 Macmillan *London* 1987 Macmillan *Basingstoke*

This book is part of the well-known series commissioned by the Economic History Society, and provides a well-balanced overview of the British cotton industry during the industrial revolution, c.1760–1850. One of its merits is its wide coverage (it includes references to Scotland and the Midlands as well as to Lancashire). It also deals with consumption as well as production.
Firms: David Dale & Co.; M'Connel & Kennedy; Robert Peel & Co.; Robinson & Co.; Samuel Greg & Co.; William Douglas & Co.

1130
Chapman, Sydney J.
The Lancashire Cotton Industry: A study in economic development
1973 Manchester University Press *Manchester*

Chapman's study is a detailed examination of the internal structure of the Lancashire cotton industry from the early eighteenth century to the end of the nineteenth century. His concerns lie in the fields of production, marketing and the distribution of income within the industry. On the last point Chapman provides interesting material on both worker and employer organizations. This is a facsimile reprint of the 1904 edition.

1131
Daniels, G. W.
The Early English Cotton Industry: With some unpublished letters of Samuel Crompton
1920 Manchester University Press *Manchester*

This deals with the origins of the cotton industry until around 1825, describing the introduction of machinery and use of patents to protect new technology.

1132
Dupree, Marguerite (Editor)
Lancashire and Whitehall: The diary of Sir Raymond Streat
1987 Manchester University Press *Manchester*

This edition of the weekly diary of the secre-

tary of the Manchester Chamber of Commerce, 1920–40, and chairman of the Cotton Board, 1940–57, spans the period 1931–57. Streat illuminates our view of the Lancashire cotton industry in decline, particularly its internal tensions and its interactions with the government's bureaucratic and political machinery.
Firms: Manchester Chamber of Commerce

1133
Dutton, H. I.; King, J. E.
Ten Per Cent and No Surrender: The Preston Strike, 1853–1854
1981 Cambridge University Press *Cambridge*

This book provides a very detailed account of the forty-week strike by Preston's cotton operatives in 1853–4. The cause of the strike and subsequent lock-out was the attempt to regain the ten per cent cut in wage rates made by the employers in 1847. The authors provide a very revealing snapshot of the time and place by looking at both workers and employers, as well as the local authorities and the press.
Firms: Mannex and Co.; Slater and Pollard

1134
Ellison, Thomas
The Cotton Trade of Great Britain: Including a history of the Liverpool cotton market and of the Liverpool Cotton Brokers' Association
1886 Effingham Wilson *London*

The intention of this volume was to provide a useful reference manual of historical and contemporary information to the British cotton industry. Part one provides a general history of the industry from c.1780 while part two examines the history of the Liverpool cotton market. Much of the information and statistics collected can still be used by historians today.

1135
Farnie, D. A.
The English Cotton Industry and the World Market, 1815–1896
1979 Clarendon Press *Oxford*

Farnie's book is a study of the English, and primarily Lancashire, cotton industry in the period of maturity. The coverage is more uneven than the title suggests and includes chapters on 'The Localization of the Industry in Lancashire', and 'The Growth of the World Market', where the trade figures refer to Britain. Farnie is more concerned with factory communities than individual firms.
Firms: Du Fay & Co.; J. & P. Coats; Jardine, Matheson & Co.; Kingston Cotton Mill Co.; Rochdale Cotton Spinning Co.; Sun Mill Co.

1136
Fishwick, F.; Cornu, R. B.
A Study of the Evolution of Concentration in the United Kingdom Textile Industry
1975 Commission of the European Community *Luxembourg*

One of a series of studies of the evolution of concentration in the EC. Contains a detailed statistical analysis of concentration between 1963 and 1974, analysing the continuing defensive reorganization of the industry in response to increasing uncertainty among its customers and increasing import penetration.
Firms: Courtaulds; ICI; Coats-Paton; Illingworth-Morris; Carrington-Viyella; Tootal

1137
Fitton, R. S.
The Arkwrights: Spinners of fortune
1989 Manchester University Press *Manchester*

Fitton presents a major biography of one of the most important business families in the history of British industry. It is a fascinating account of the dispersal of a fortune and the gentrification of a business family, made vivid by the generous quotation of sources. The narrative concentrates on the first two generations, covering the late eighteenth and early nineteenth centuries. The original Arkwright is credited as the inventor of the factory system. Despite limited primary sources the author has provided a significant contribution to business biography.
Firms: Ancoats Twist Co.; Boulton & Watt; M'Connel & Kennedy; Sir Richard Arkwright & Co.

1138
Fitton, R. S.; Wadsworth, A. P.
The Strutts and the Arkwrights 1758–1830: A study of the early factory system
1958 Manchester University Press *Manchester*

This book takes a biographical approach to the study of the early factory system in the

British cotton industry. The authors utilize the Strutt Collection at Derby Public Library and the records of the English Sewing Cotton Company. Most of this material deals with the Strutt family and their businesses are the main concern of the book, although Jedediah Strutt and Richard Arkwright were partners for a period.
Firms: English Sewing Cotton Company; Boulton & Watt; W. G. & J. Strutt; Sir Richard Arkwright & Co.; East India Company; M'Connel & Kennedy

1139
Hidaka, Chikage
Eikoku Mengyo Suitai no Kozu [The Decline of the British Cotton Industry]
1995 University of Tokyo Press *Tokyo, Japan*
This book examines the collapse of the British cotton industry between the two Wars from a new perspective, proposing that financial restructuring, which increased the industry's fixed costs, was the crucial factor rather than technological backwardness.

1140
Jeremy, David J.
Transatlantic Industrial Revolution: The diffusion of textile technologies between Britain and America, 1790–1830s
For main entry, see 4270

1141
Jeremy, David J. (Editor)
Strategies of the Declining Lancashire Textile Industry
Textile History, vol. 24, no. 2, 1993
The five case studies in this issue span companies operating in Lancashire between the 1880s and the 1980s and were assembled in order to explore generalizations about Britain's industrial decline. The authors are: J. S. Toms, D. A. Farnie, David J. Jeremy, D. M. Higgins and John A. Blackburn.
Firms: Bleachers' Association (Whitecroft); Carrington & Dewhurst; Coats Viyella; Courtaulds; Crewdson; Horrocks; ICI; Lancashire Cotton Corporation; Platt Bros; Viyella International

1142
Jewkes, J.; Gray, E. M.
Wages and Labour in the Lancashire Cotton Spinning Industry
1935 Manchester University Press *Manchester*
This book is one of the numerous inquiries undertaken by the Economics Research Section of the Department of Economics at Manchester University. The concern of this study is the system of remuneration in cotton spinning in Lancashire and the authors' main contribution lies in their clear exposition of the notoriously complex Spinning Wage Lists.

1143
Joyce, Patrick
Work, Society and Politics: The culture of the factory in later Victorian England
For main entry, see 3739

1144
Kirby, Maurice W.
Men of Business and Politics: The Rise and Fall of the Quaker Pease Dynasty of North-East England, 1700–1943

For main entry, see 3820

1145
Lazonick, William
Competitive Advantage on the Shop Floor
For main entry, see 3458

1146
Lee, C. H.
A Cotton Enterprise 1795–1840: A history of M'Connel & Kennedy, fine cotton spinners
1972 Manchester University Press *Manchester*
In this study of the early history of one of Manchester's most famous textile firms, Lee describes how M'Connel & Kennedy concentrated on fine spinning, made its own machinery, and did not move into weaving. The author's concentration on a single leading firm illustrates the relationship between spinning and engineering and the expansion of markets.
Firms: M'Connel & Kennedy

1147

Lemire, Beverly

Fashion's Favourite: The cotton trade and the consumer in Britain, 1660–1800

For main entry, see 1900

1148

Lloyd-Jones, R.; Lewis, M. J.

Manchester and the Age of the Factory: The business structure of Cottonopolis in the Industrial Revolution

1988 Croom Helm *London*

This is a study of the business system operating in Manchester during a vital stage in the industrial revolution, c.1815–1825. The authors are not concerned with providing another history of the cotton industry. Rather, their concern lies with the ordinary overall business structure of 'cottonopolis' and the business relationship between factory and warehouse in particular.

Firms: Haig, Marshall & Co.; John Heywood & Son; T. C. Hewes; Houldsworth; M'Connel & Kennedy; O. Owens & Son

1149

Longmate, N.

The Hungry Mills

1978 Maurice Temple Smith *London*

Longmate gives a descriptive account of the Lancashire 'cotton famine' of the 1860s when the American Civil War cut off the supply of cotton to Britain. Mainly a social history of the attendant distress of the mill workers, there is some interesting material on the Liverpool and Manchester Cotton Exchanges and the attempts to secure an alternative supply of cotton from India.

Firms: Anglo-Confederate Trading Company; East India Company; Fraser, Trenholm & Co.; Manchester Cotton Co.

1150

Miles, Caroline

Lancashire Textiles: A case study of industrial change

1968 Cambridge University Press *Cambridge*

This is an excellent study of the Lancashire textile industry from 1945 to the mid-1960s looking both at the decline of cotton and the growth of man-made fibres. The author's concern lies with technical progress with industry and the heart of this book lies in a detailed examination of the impact of the 1959 Cotton Industry Act which deliberately sought to accelerate the process of scrapping old and replacing with new machinery.

1151

Okochi, Akio; Yonekawa, Shin'ichi (Editors)

The Textile Industry and its Business Climate (Eighth Fuji Conference)

For main entry, see 109

1152

Roberts, David

Paternalism in Early Victorian England

For main entry, see 3755

1153

Robson, R.

The Cotton Industry in Britain

1957 Macmillan *London*

This is a detailed study of the British cotton industry over a forty-year span from the First World War to the mid-1950s. While producing a narrative of the developments and changes over this period, the author also illustrates the structure of the industry, regulation by the industry itself and government involvement, as well as providing some international background.

Firms: J. & P. Coats; English Sewing Cotton Co.; Lancashire Cotton Corporation; Winterbottom Book Cloth Company; Fine Spinners and Doublers

1154

Rose, Mary B.

The Gregs of Quarry Bank Mill: The rise and decline of a family firm, 1750–1914

1986 Cambridge University Press *Cambridge*

This is an interesting case study of a family firm spanning 150 years and five generations. Opening their first spinning mill in 1784, the Gregs were a giant in the industry by 1830, though they went into gradual decline thereafter. The focus on Quarry Bank illustrates why rural, water-powered mills gave way to urban, steam-powered mills in the nineteenth-century English textile industry. Quarry Bank is now

the finest textile museum in the north west of England.
Firms: Gregs

1155
Rose, Mary B. (Editor)
International Competition and Strategic Response in the Textile Industries since 1870
1991 Frank Cass *London*

This collection of essays first appeared in *Business History* (October 1990). Although the main focus of the book is on the Lancashire cotton industry, there are also chapters on the European woollen industry, textile machinery, and textile merchanting.
Firms: Dai Nippon; Fukushima; Kanegafuchi; Kishiwada Kurashiki; Lancashire Cotton Corporation; Mitsui; Nippon Neukwa; Osaka Godo; Platt Bros; Toyo

1156
Sandberg, L. G.
Lancashire in Decline: A study in entrepreneurship, technology and international trade
1974 Ohio State University Press *Columbus, OH*

Sandberg's book is a study of the decline of the British cotton industry which argues against the widely held view of entrepreneurial failure. The author goes back to the 1880s and explains the 'failure' of the Lancashire owners to adopt ring-spinning as a rational choice in terms of profit-maximization. The decline of the industry is located in the context of international trade and specialization.
Firms: Ashton Brothers; Amoskeag Manufacturing Co.; Lancashire Cotton Corporation

1157
Shapiro, S.
Capital and Cotton in the Industrial Revolution
1967 Cornell University Press *Ithaca, NY*

Shapiro makes a significant contribution to the extensive literature on the British cotton industry. His main concern lies in examining the growth of the industry against the limitations of the long-run capital market. The study shows the importance of the entrepreneur's own savings and the plough-back of profits for the development of the industry.
Firms: Arkwright, Toplis & Company; Bank of England; British Linen Company; East India Company; M'Connel & Kennedy

1158
Silver, A. W.
Manchester Men and Indian Cotton, 1847–1872
1966 Manchester University Press *Manchester*

This study of the Lancashire cotton industry describes its efforts to achieve an alternative to American supplies of cotton from within the British Empire during the heyday of free trade. This work is of value in illustrating the relationship between government and industry, the imperialism of free trade, and Anglo-Indian relations generally.

1159
Singleton, John
Lancashire on the Scrapheap: The cotton industry 1945–1970
1991 Pasold Research Fund/Oxford University Press *Oxford*

This is a pioneering study of the decline of the British cotton industry. There are two subperiods: 1945–51, when the industry prospered under a Labour Government's planned export drive; and the years after 1951, when socialist reconstruction was forgotten and foreign competition revived. An examination of the 'merger mania' of the 1960s – when the giant artificial fibre makers appeared on the scene – is of particular interest.
Firms: Combined English Mills; Courtaulds; English Sewing Cotton; Fine Spinners and Doublers; Imperial Chemical Industries; Lancashire Cotton Corporation; Tootals

1160
Timmins, Geoffrey
The Last Shift: The decline of handloom weaving in nineteenth century Lancashire
1993 Manchester University Press *Manchester*

This book makes a contribution to the continuing debate on the extent and pace of technological change in nineteenth-century British industry. The author focuses on the cotton industry – usually seen as a leading sector in technological development – and points at the

continuing significance of handloom weaving in early to mid-nineteenth-century Lancashire.
Firms: Gregs; Horrocks & Co.; Tootal, Broadhurst & Lee; Watson & Co.

1161
Tippett, L. H. C.
A Portrait of the Lancashire Textile History
1969 Oxford University Press *London*
This book provides a general history of the Lancashire textile industry – cotton and man-made fibres – for the fifty years, after the First World War. The author worked for four decades in the Shirley Institute (the industry's research organization) and although most aspects of the industry are covered the study is strongest on the technology side.
Firms: Empire Cotton Growing Corporation; Horrockses, Crewdson & Co.; ICI; Lancashire Cotton Corporation; Tootal, Broadhurst & Lee; Umella International

1162
Unwin, George
Samuel Oldknow and the Arkwrights: The Industrial Revolution at Stockport and Marple
1968 Manchester University Press *Manchester*
This is the second edition (with a preface by W. H. Chaloner) of a work first published in 1924. The title is somewhat misleading as the book's overwhelming concentration is on Oldknow. His fame and significance in textile history lies in being the first manufacturer able to produce fine cottons that stood comparison with Indian muslins. Oldknow's successful business career spanned only a relatively short period in the 1780s and 1790s, though he spent many more years as a paternalist community builder.
Firms: East India Company; Boulton & Watt; Richard Arkwright & Co.; Samuel Oldknow & Co.; S. & W. Salte

1163
Wurm, Clemens A.
Politics and International Relations: Steel, cotton and international cartels in British politics, 1924-1939
For main entry, see 4410

Textiles, UK - Wool

1164
Clapham, J. H.
The Woollen and Worsted Industries
1907 Methuen *London*
This is a study of the woollen industry in Britain in the late nineteenth and early twentieth centuries ('worsted' is simply a finer and lighter wool fabric). Clapham provides detail on the manufacturing process, raw materials, the organization of the industry, the labour force, the woollen industries abroad and the international trade in woollens.

1165
Crump, William B. (Editor)
The Leeds Woollen Industry 1780–1820
1931 Thoresby Society *Leeds*
This volume provides a history of the transformation of the Leeds woollen industry between 1780 and 1820. The editor provides a general introduction, but the heart of the book lies in the reprinting of, and commentaries upon, a series of historical documents. The main figure is Benjamin Gott, a merchant-manufacturer whose papers are deposited in Leeds University Library. The use of these documents allows a view of the industry 'from the inside', and they can be quarried usefully by other researchers.
Firms: Benjamin Gott & Sons; Rogerson & Lord; Boulton & Watt; J. Sturges & Co.

1166
Crump, William B.; Ghorbal, Gertrude
History of the Huddersfield Woollen Industry
1935 Tolsen Memorial Museum *Huddersfield*
Although described as a 'handbook' this slim volume provides a valuable history of the woollen industry in the Pennines from the beginning of the fourteenth century to the early nineteenth century. The authors deal with both the long history of the domestic industry and the transformation post 1760 to modern conditions. The story continues to the Great Exhibition of 1851 and a list of Huddersfield manufacturers at the Exhibition is appended.

1167

Hudson, Pat

The Genesis of Industrial Capital: A study of the West Riding wool textile industry c. 1750–1850

1986 Cambridge University Press *Cambridge*

This revised and extended version of a PhD thesis throws welcome light on the role of the wool textile industry during the industrial revolution in England. Hudson provides both an additional empirical building block and theoretical insights into the emergence of industrial capitalism. This is a significant contribution both to economic and business history.

Firms: B. & W. Mariner; Benjamin Gott & Co.; Hague, Cook & Wormald; John Foster & Son Ltd; Jowitt & Co.; Lupton & Co.

1168

Hudson, Patricia

The West Riding Wool Textile Industry: A catalogue of business records from the 16th to the 20th centuries

For main entry, see 18

1169

Jenkins, D. T.; Ponting, K. G.

The British Wool Textile Industry 1770–1914

1982 Heinemann Educational Books *London*

The authors give a thorough overview of a complex industry, dealing with the various sectors and regional specializations. There is a considerable amount of technical detail on the changing processes of production. The authors' treatment of the industry locates it both within the British economy and the world market.

Firms: Crombies; J. & T. Clark; Marshalls; Platt Brothers; Pringle

1170

Jenkins, J. G.

The Welsh Woollen Industry

1969 National Museum of Wales *Cardiff, Wales*

A welcome addition to the literature on Welsh industry. This is a general overview of the industry which gives considerable attention to the technical side of woollen production, and discusses the different centres of the industry, particularly focusing on the mid nineteenth-century shift from north and mid- to west Wales.

Firms: W. A. Madouls; Shrewsbury Drapers Co.; Welsh Flannel, Tweed and Woolstapling Co.

1171

Jenkins, J. G. (Editor)

The Wool Textile Industry in Great Britain

1972 Routledge & Kegan Paul *London*

This is a large collection of seventeen essays ranging from prehistoric times to 1960. The volume is divided into three sections: historical studies; detailed examination of the more important technical innovations; and specific studies of the major wool-producing regions.

Firms: Blanket Weavers Company; W. & J. Crighton; East India Company; Hattersley and Sons

1172

Mann, Julia de L.

The Cloth Industry in the West of England from 1640 to 1880

1971 Clarendon Press *Oxford*

This is the definitive study of two and a half centuries of cloth (narrowly but precisely defined) in the English counties of Gloucestershire, Wiltshire and Somerset. The author traces the fortunes of the industry from its transitional position during the English Civil War to its ultimate decline in the Victorian age. Particular attention is paid to production techniques and to labour and marketing.

Firms: East India Company; H. & G. Austin; Hamburg Company; Merchant Adventurers' Company; Messrs Hanson & Mill; Messrs J. & T. Clark

1173

Randall, A.

Before the Luddites: Cotton, community and machinery in the English woollen industry, 1776–1809

1991 Cambridge University Press *Cambridge*

Randall makes a comparative study of the advent of a machine economy in the West Riding of Yorkshire and the west of England. The author is primarily concerned with the reaction by labour to the introduction of the spinning jenny in the wool industry. The differing responses are explained largely by the pre-existing organization of work in the two areas.

1174

Reynolds, J.

The Great Paternalist: Titus Salt and the growth of nineteenth century Bradford

1983 Maurice Temple Smith/University of Bradford *London* and *New York, NY*

This is a study of Titus Salt (1803–1876) widely regarded as the epitome of the enlightened Victorian capitalist. Salt, who made his fortune in the English worsted textile industry, is most famous for the creation of the industrial community, Saltaire. Although not a conventional business biography this is an illuminating account of one entrepreneur during the process of industrialization.

Firms: Daniel Salt & Son; Edward Ripley & Co.; J. G. Horsfall & Co.; Titus Salt & Co.

1175

Sigsworth, Eric M.

Black Dyke Mills: A history

1958 Liverpool University Press *Liverpool*

A valuable study of the Yorkshire woollen industry. Based on company records, Sigsworth studies the development of the worsted industry in the nineteenth century, factory building, productive capacity, finance, and trade in different raw materials and products.

Firms: Black Dyke Mills; John Foster and Sons

Textiles, UK - Finished Goods etc.

1176

Bartlett, J. N.

Carpeting the Millions: The growth of Britain's carpet industry

1978 John Donald *Edinburgh, Scotland*

This comprehensive history of the British carpet industry covers the period 1850–1914, although there is also some material about events before and after these dates. The author provides valuable information on the introduction of mechanization, the organization of the industry, and on the workforce and employers.

Firms: A. F. Stoddard & Co.; Chlidema Carpet Co.; J. Bright & Brothers; James Templeton & Co.; John Crossley & Sons; Tomkinson & Adam

1177

Butt, John; Ponting, Kenneth (Editors)

Scottish Textile Industry

1987 Aberdeen University Press *Aberdeen, Scotland*

This is an interesting collation of ten essays on different aspects of the textile industry in Scotland stretching from the early eighteenth century through to the twentieth century. Most of the contributions examine a particular industry within a specific geographical location though there are valuable chapters on aspect of design and on trade unions and industrial relations.

Firms: British Linen Co.; East India Company; United Turkey Red Co.

1178

Cairncross, A. K.; Hunter, J. B. K.

The Early Growth of Messrs J. & P. Coats, 1830–83

Business History, vol. 29, no. 2, 1987: pp 157–77

Provides a quantitative analysis of the expansion of the thread company, J. & P. Coats in the nineteenth century. The essential context for an understanding of this company's multinational expansion is given here.

Firms: Clark Thread Co.; Conant Co.; J. & P. Coats; J. & J. Clark

1179

Chapman, Stanley D.; Chassagne, S.

European Textile Printers in the Eighteenth Century: A study of Peel and Oberkampf

1981 Heinemann Educational Books *London*

This is a comparative study of two textile printing firms – one British, one French – in eighteenth- and early nineteenth-century Europe. Although Peel and Oberkampf operated at different ends of the market, they shared much in common. This book is a welcome contribution not only to the history of textile printing but also of entrepreneurial activity in Britain and France.

Firms: Howarth, Peel & Yates; Oberkampf & Cie; Peel, Aisworth & Co.; Peel, Wilkes & Co.; Peel, Yates & Co.; Sarassin, Oberkampf & Cie

1180

Clark, W.

Linen on the Green: An Irish mill village, 1730–1982

1983 Universities Press *Belfast, N. Ireland*

This is a study of the history of a linen firm – Clarks of Uplands – through successive generations. The dominance of linen in the Northern Ireland economy and the relative lack of published works make this a valuable contribution. The book only deals with the period to 1960 and, being written by a member of the owning family, tends to be uncritical of its subject.

Firms: William Clark & Sons Ltd

1181

Coleman, D. C.

Courtaulds: An economic and social history: 1. The Nineteenth Century: Silk and crape; 2. Rayon; 3. Crisis and Change, 1940–1965

1969/80 Clarendon Press *Oxford*

This is a monumental study of one of Britain's major conglomerates. Courtaulds pioneered and came to dominate the manufacture of rayon fibre in the UK, and extended its activities worldwide. It was also involved in nylon and, misguidedly, in cotton in Lancashire. Although an official company history, the author provides an unusually critical and lively account. The focus is very much on the internal dynamics of the firm and the crucial role played by the individual personalities in the boardroom.

Firms: American Viscose Corporation; British Nylon Spinners; Courtaulds Ltd; Du Pont Rayon Co.; Imperial Chemical Industries; Samuel Courtauld & Co.

1182

Durie, A. J.

The Scottish Linen Industry in the Eighteenth Century

1979 John Donald *Edinburgh, Scotland*

Durie has made an important study of the linen industry, the main manufacture of Scotland in the eighteenth century. The book starts with the Act of Union between Scotland and England in 1707 and ends in 1815. Particular attention is paid to the efforts of the British Linen Company and the Scottish Board of Trustees for Fisheries and Manufacturers in stimulating and developing the industry.

Firms: British Linen Bank; British Linen Company

1183

English, W.

The Textile Industry: An account of the early inventions of spinning, weaving and knitting machines

1969 Longmans, Green & Co. *London*

English gives an excellent account of technical developments in the early textile industry in Britain. Beginning with household spinning, the study moves on to Lee's stocking frame and covers the various machine inventions over twenty-six chapters. Very well illustrated, the book also places the inventions within their business context.

1184

Gulvin, C.

The Tweedmakers: A history of the Scottish fancy woollen industry 1600–1914

1973 David & Charles *Newton Abbot*

A thorough account is given here of an important though relatively neglected Scottish industry. The period dealt with is from 1600 to 1914. The Scottish woollen industry changed from a concentration on rough woollens to high-quality, internationally renowned fabrics. Though small-scale, the industry was crucial to the economy of certain parts of Scotland, such as the Borders.

1185

Gulvin, C.

The Scottish Hosiery and Knitwear Industry, 1680–1980

1984 John Donald *Edinburgh, Scotland*

This book follows on from the author's earlier study (qv) of the manufacture of tweed in Scotland. Here, Gulvin concentrates on another specialization of Scottish textile production, knitwear and hosiery. In the late nineteenth century, in response to English competition, Scottish firms moved into the luxury end of the market in which their reputation remains unsurpassed.

Firms: Braemar Knitwear Ltd; Dawson Interna-

tional; Innes, Henderson & Company; Lyle and Scott; Pringle and Son; William Watson & Sons

1186
Honeyman, Katrina
Origins of Enterprise: Business Leadership in the Industrial Revolution
For main entry, see 3814

1187
Jowitt, J. A.; McIvor, A. J. (Editors)
Employers and Labour in the English Textile Industries, 1850–1939
1988 Routledge *London*

This richly detailed and interesting collection of essays is grouped around three themes: employers and employers' organizations, trade unions and labour, and women in textiles. While there is much of value in all three sections, business historians will find the first of most use, especially as employers have tended to be neglected in much textile history.

Firms: Ashton Brothers; English Sewing Cotton Co.; Hepburn & Co.; Musgrave Spinning Co.; Slater & Co.; United Turkey Red Co.

1188
Knight, Arthur
Private Enterprise and Public Intervention
For main entry, see 4079

1189
Knox, W. W.
Hanging by a Thread: The Scottish cotton industry, c. 1850–1914
1994 Carnegie *Preston*

Knox contrasts the success of Scottish threadmakers with the failure of cotton markets, outcomes ascribed to different patterns of industrial relations and control of product markets.

Firms: Dunlop; Houldsworths; J. & P. Coats; J. & J. Clark

1190
Morton, J.
Three Generations in a Family Textile Firm
1971 Routledge & Kegan Paul *London*

This narrative account of a family business, Morton Sundour Fabrics, was written by its last independent chairman. Beginning in the 1860s with the founder Alexander Morton, a Scottish handloom weaver, the business grew and diversified into the whole range of textile production. Eventually taken over by Courtaulds in 1963, the author poses the question of the relationship between ownership, control and innovation.

Firms: Alexander Morton & Co.; Courtaulds; FNF Ltd; Imperial Chemical Industries; Morton Sundour Fabrics

1191
Pasold, Eric W.
Ladybird, Ladybird: A story of private enterprise
For main entry, see 1904

1192
Plummer, A.; Early, R. F.
The Blanket Makers: A history of Charles Early & Marriott (Witney) Ltd
1969 Routledge & Kegan Paul *London*

Although the English woollen industry was dominated by the West Riding of Yorkshire, certain enclaves, such as Witney in Oxfordshire, have managed to survive through specialization. This is a useful study of a family firm and its response to changing circumstances. Nonconformist and paternalist, the families only allowed 'outside' directors into the companies in the 1950s.

Firms: Company of Blanket Weavers, Witney; Courtaulds; Early & Co.; Early & Marriott (Witney) Ltd; Marriott & Sons

1193
Rimmer, W. G.
Marshall's of Leeds, Flax Spinners, 1788–1886
1960 Cambridge University Press *Cambridge*

This is a detailed account of the firm's origins, rise and decline and provides a vivid picture of the family which in three generations made and lost the largest flax-spinning business in Europe.

Firms: Marshall's

1194
Smith, L. D.
Carpet Weavers and Carpet Masters: The hand loom carpet weavers of Kidderminster, 1780–1850
1986 Kenneth Tomkinson *Kidderminster*

Kidderminster was the centre of the carpet industry in early nineteenth-century Britain, and the town was dominated by the industry. As such, this study is a political and social as well as a business history. The main theme is that the expansion of carpet manufacture in Kidderminster occurred through an expanded 'domestic' system rather than through the application of steam power.
Firms: G. P. Simcox; G. Talbot and Sons; H. J. Dixon; James Holmes; Morton and Son; Pardoe, Hooman & Pardoe

1195
Wells, F. A.
Hollins and Viyella: A study in business history
1968 David & Charles *Newton Abbot*

This account of William Hollins & Company describes its foundation in 1784 in the English East Midlands, to its eventual position as part of Viyella International formed in 1961. It adds substantially to Pigott's (1949) earlier history of the firm. Wells provides interesting material on vertical integration within the industry, use of natural and man-made fibres, and links to the chemical industry.
Firms: ICI; Viyella International; William Hollins & Co.

1196
Wells, F. A.
The British Hosiery and Knitwear Industry: Its history and organisation
1972 David & Charles *Newton Abbot*

This is a revised and extended version of a book first published in 1935. The period dealt with stretches from Lee's invention of the stocking frame in 1589 to the state of the industry in the latter part of the twentieth century. Despite some gaps this remains the best general history of the hosiery industry in Britain.

1197
Whatley, C. A.
Onwards From Osnaburgs: The rise and progress of a Scottish textile company: Don & Low of Forfar, 1792–1992
1992 Mainstream *Edinburgh, Scotland*

This commissioned company history charts the fortunes of a textile firm on Tayside, Scotland. The book's main contribution lies in its examination of a declining sector–linen and jute–and one company's successful shift into man-made fibres. Now a wholly owned subsidiary of Shell UK, the company is one of the major European producers of polypropylene-based textile products.
Firms: Don & Co.; Don & Low Ltd; Don Brothers, Buist & Co.; Low Brothers & Co. (Dundee) Ltd; Shell UK Ltd; William and John Don & Co.

1198
Yonekawa, S.
Flotation Booms in the Cotton Spinning Industry: A comparative study
Business History Review, vol. 61, no. 4, 1987: pp 551–81

This is an international comparative study of the burst in formation of cotton spinning companies in the late nineteenth century in the major cotton exporting economies–Britain, the USA, India and Japan–are detailed. In this period the public limited company is seen to establish itself in the cotton spinning industry. The expansion of mills is seen, in turn, to increase international competition.

Textiles, Europe (excl. UK)

1199
Bruland, Kristine
British Technology and European Industrialisation: The Norwegian textile industry in the mid nineteenth century
1989 Cambridge University Press *Cambridge*

This important study of the process of technology transfer from Britain to Europe describes its impact upon industrial growth on the Continent. Bruland's concern is with the acquisition of new technology by individual firms and, as such, she has made a substantial contribution to the history of technological change and to European industrialization.

Firms: Anderston Foundry; Arne Fabriker; Fruhling & Goschen; Hjula Weavery; J. Hetherington & Son; Nydalen Spinnery

1200
Burger, Roelf A.
100 Jaar G. en H. Salomonson: kooplieden-entrepreneurs, fabrikanten en directeuren van de Koninklijke Stoomweverij te Nijverdal [100 Years of G. & H. Salomonson: Merchants, manufacturers and managers of the Royal Mills, Nijverdal]
1954 Stenfert Kroese *Leiden, The Netherlands*

This is a traditional and uncritical account of the rise of the prominent Dutch cotton firm of Godfried and Hein Salomonson, 1816–1918 (i.e. Koninklijke Stoomweverij Nijverdal), and of their exports to The Netherlands East Indies.
Firms: G. & H. Salomonson; Koninklijke Stoomweverij Nijverdal

1201
Caspard, Pierre
La Fabrique-Neuve de Cortaillod, 1752–1854: Entreprise et profit pendant la Révolution industrielle [La Fabrique-Neuve de Cortaillod.1752–1854: Enterprise and profit during the Industrial Revolution]
1979 Sorbonne *Paris, France*

The Swiss calico printing industry played an important role in European industrialization. Based largely on company archives, this introspective work analyses the evolution of a leading enterprise located in the Canton of Neuchâtel. Dealing with all the aspects of the manufacturing process, it is a major contribution to an under-researched field.
Firms: Fabrique-Neuve de Cortaillod

1202
Chassagne, S.
La Manufacture de Toiles Imprimées de Tournemine-les-Angers (1752–1820): Étude d'une Entreprise et d'une Industrie au XVIII Siècle [The Manufacture of Printed Cotton at Tournemine-les-Angers (1752–1820): Study of a company and an industry in the eighteenth century]
1971 Klincksieck *Paris, France*

This is a study of a cotton printing firm in Western France, though lacking the company records, it is more a study of the industry and the economic history of the Angers region. The imaginative use of other sources makes this a valuable examination of early, small-scale industrialization in France.
Firms: Tournemine

1203
Chassagne, Serge
Oberkampf: un entrepreneur capitaliste au siècle des Lumières [Oberkampf: A capitalist entrepreneur in the Age of the Enlightenment]
1980 Aubier-Montaigne *Paris, France*

This is an excellent monograph on the leading cotton-printer in late eighteenth- and early nineteenth-century France and the large works he developed at Jouy-en-Josas, near Versailles. For an intefirm comparison, see Chapman & Chassagne (qv).
Firms: Oberkampf & Cie.

1204
Chassagne, Serge
Le coton et ses patrons: France, 1760–1840 [Cotton and Factorymasters: France 1760–1840]
1991 Éditions de l'École des Hautes Étude *Paris, France*

This is the basic work on the origins of the French cotton industry, focusing on the evolution of its techniques and the entrepreneurs involved during the transition from protofactories to factory production. Detailed analysis of successive 'generations' of entrepreneurs and especially of the role of family and religion is included.

1205
Fischer, Eric J.
Fabriqueurs en fabrikanten: de Twentse Kabennijverheid en de onderneming S. J. Spanjaard te Borne tussen circa 1800 en 1930 circa 1800 en 1930 ["Fabriqueurs" and manufacturers: Twentse's cotton industry and the firm of S. J. Spanjaard in Borne between about 1800 and 1930]
1983 Matrijs *Utrecht, The Netherlands*

This wide-ranging dissertation, focuses on industrialization in The Netherlands, taking the Spanjaard firm as an example. At the micro-level, the study analyses finance, mechaniza-

tion and infrastructure developments, and their effects on labour.
Firms: S. J. Spanjaard

1206
Fohlen, Claude
Une affaire de famille au XIXe siècle: Méquillet-Noblot [A Nineteenth Century Family Business: Méquillet-Noblot]
1955 Armand Colin *Paris, France*
This is a pioneer work in French business history, dealing with a medium-sized family firm in eastern France. It developed from domestic manufacture to the factory system and it engaged in cotton spinning, weaving and printing. It declined after 1871 and this book, based on the firm's records, ends in 1897–though the firm was still active when the book was written.
Firms: Méquillet-Noblot

1207
Freudenberger, H.
The Waldstein Woolen Mill: Noble entrepreneurship in eighteenth century Bohemia
1963 Harvard Business School *Boston, MA*
This is an important and illuminating account of an aristocratic family enterprise. The study makes a valuable contribution to the history of industry in the Hapsburg Empire and to the role of the aristocracy in business development. The research is based upon family business records and a unique set of engravings depicting every stage of the production process.

1208
Honeyman, Katrina; Goodman, Jordan
Technology and Enterprise: Isaac Holden and the mechanization of woolcombing in France, 1848–1914
1986 Scolar Press / Pasold Research Fund *Aldershot*
An examination of the process of mechanization of the wool combing industry in nineteenth-century France through the activities of Isaac Holden. Ironically, Holden and his partner, Samuel Lister, wished to impede the development of rival technology. This makes the book a particularly revealing study of technological diffusion, as well as a thorough business history.
Firms: Donisthorpe & Crofts; Holden Company; Lister & Holden

1209
Kisch, Herbert
From Domestic Manufacture to Industrial Revolution: The case of the Rhineland textile districts
1989 Oxford University Press *Oxford*
This is the English language edition of a work first published in German in 1981. Kisch died in 1978 and this volume is a collection of well-known articles. One of the first historians to emphasise the importance of rural manufacture and proto-industrialization, these studies by Kisch are all intensely detailed.
Firms: Andrea Brothers; Dutch East India Company; Hill, Cazalet & Co.; Von der Leyen

1210
La Force, J. C. Jr
The Development of the Spanish Textile Industry, 1750–1800
1965 University of California Press *Berkeley, CA*
This is a pioneering study of the Spanish textile industry in the later eighteenth century. The author's principal concern is with the question of economic development and the role played by the state. As elsewhere in Europe the Spanish monarchy operated within a mercantilist framework of establishing large enterprises and recruiting skilled workers from abroad.

1211
Lomüller, Louis-Marie
Guillaume Ternant, 1763–1833: créateur de la première intégration industrielle française [Guillaume Ternant, 1763–1833: Founder of the first French industrial empire]
1978 Édition de la Cabzo d'Oz *Paris, France*
Lomüller was one of the earliest 'captains of industry' in France. He built up an empire in the woollen industry under Napoleon, but was ruined after the Emperor's fall.

1212
Nijhuis, H. D.
De structurele ontwikkeling van de Nederlandse Katoen-, Rayon- en Linnenindustrie [The Structural Development of the Dutch Cotton, Rayon and Flax Industries]
1950 Gouda Quint *Arnhem, The Netherlands*

Dealing mainly with the prewar period, this book provides a long-term economic analysis of the gradual demise of these industries in The Netherlands.

1213
Reitsma, G. W.
Economische ontwikkeling in de katoenindustrie van 1918 tot 1957 [Economic Development of the Cotton Industry from 1918 to 1957]
1957 State University, Sociological Institute *Leiden, The Netherlands*

This extensive report was issued in the context of a sociological research project on the textile and cotton industry in the eastern provinces of The Netherlands. It focuses on the economic problems caused by rising international competition.

Firms: H. ten Cate Hzn. & Co.; Koninklijke Stoomweverij Nijverdal (KSW)

1214
Roverato, Giorgio
Una casa industriale: I Marzotto [An Industrial House: The Marzotto family]
For main entry, see 4031

1215
Thomson, J. K. J.
A Distinctive Industrialization: Cotton in Barcelona, 1728–1832
1992 Cambridge University Press *Cambridge*

Thomson presents a study of the cotton industry of Catalonia (overwhelmingly concentrated in Barcelona) in the century prior to mechanized, factory production. It is an ambitious work with a multiplicity of themes – including the regional element in European industrialization, and the comparative study of the textile industry – it also provides an admirable account of business activity.

1216
Veyrassat, Béatrice
Négociants et fabricants dans l'industrie cotonnière suisse, 1780–1840: Aux origines financières de l'industrialisation [Merchants and Manufacturers in the Swiss Cotton Industry, 1780–1840: The financial origins of industrialisation]
1982 Payot *Lausanne, Switzerland*

Through the history of a wide range of small enterprises, this study explores the financing of the Swiss cotton industry in connection with the technical and commercial changes which occurred in this sector. It underlines the intervention of commercial capital in industrial activities.

1217
Vleesenbeek, Hubert H.
De eerste grote industriële fusie in Nederland na de Tweede Wereldoorlog: het ontstaan van Nijverdal-Ten Cate–een bedrijfshistorische analyse [The First Big Industrial Merger in The Netherlands after the Second World War: The formation of Nijverdal-Ten Cate–a business history analysis]
1981 Privately published *Rotterdam, The Netherlands*

The author contrasts traditional (nineteenth-century style) entrepreneurial mentality in the Dutch cotton industry with changing industrial and market conditions, necessitating rationalization, industrial co-operation, and economies of scale, which resulted in the merger of Koninklijke Stoomweverij Nijverdal and H. ten Cate Hzn. & Co. in 1957. The book contains a summary in English.

Firms: G. & H. Salomonson; H. ten Cate Hzn. & Co.; Koninklijke Stoomweverij Nijverdal (KSW); Nijverdal-Ten Cate

Textiles, USA

1218
Armstrong, J. B.
Factory Under the Elms: A history of Harrisville, New Hampshire, 1774–1969
1969 MIT Press *Cambridge, MA*

This book describes the history of a mill town in New Hampshire, USA. It is not a standard company history for, while the focus is largely on the workforce and townspeople, it is the business of the company which provided the raison d'être of the town. The most remarkable fact is the continuing survival of woollen manufacture by the original firm.
Firms: B. Harris & Co.; Milan Harris & Co.

1219
Cohen, Isaac
American Management and British Labor: A comparative study of the cotton spinning industry
1990 Greenwood Press *Westport, CT*

A comparative study to assess why American cotton industrialists and workers responded to industrialization in a different fashion to British millowners and operatives between the 1780s and 1880. It contrasts workers' control in England with management control in the United States, and the triumph of craft production in England with the victory of mass production in the United States. It covers mainly Lancashire and New England.
Firms: American Linen Co.

1220
Copeland, Melvin T.
The Cotton Manufacturing Industry of the United States
1912 Harvard University Press *Cambridge, MA*

One of the earliest and most detailed studies of the American cotton manufacturing industry. Copeland's history runs from 1800 to the turn of the twentieth century and his main concern is an international comparison between the American and European industries of geographical factors, technical methods, labour conditions and industrial and commercial organization.
Firms: American Thread Co.; English Sewing Cotton; International Cotton Mills Corp.; New England Cotton Yarn Co.; United States Finishing Co.

1221
Crockett, N. L.
The Woolen Industry of the Mid West
1970 University Press of Kentucky *Lexington, KY*

This is a valuable study of industrial development in the mid-west states of the USA. The book examines four woollen mills in four different states from the 1860s to the industry's demise after 1900. Among the issues dealt with are problems of marketing and of securing supplies of raw material and labour.

1222
Cudd, J. M.
The Chicopee Manufacturing Company, 1823–1915
1974 Scholarly Resources *Wilmington, DE*

This large American cotton manufacturing company based in Massachusetts was founded in 1823 and was taken over by Johnson and Johnson in 1916. Seriously hampered by the relative paucity of company records, the author nevertheless provides an intelligent narrative history.
Firms: Boston and Springfield Co.; Chicopee Manufacturing Co.; Johnson and Johnson Co.

1223
Ewing, John S.; Norton, Nancy P.
Broadlooms and Businessmen: A history of the Bigelow-Sanford Carpet Company
1955 Harvard University Press *Cambridge, MA*

This is an early, but impressive case study of a leading American carpet manufacturer and its predecessor companies. It covers the period from 1820 to the early 1950s.
Firms: Bigelow Carpet Co. (later Corp.); Bigelow-Hartford Carpet Co.; Bigelow-Sanford Carpet Co.; Hartford Carpet Co. (later Corp.); E. S. Higgins & Co.; Lowell Manufacturing Co.; Stephen Sanford & Sons; Tariff Manufacturing Co.; Thompsonville Carpet Manufacturing Co.

1224
Gerstle, G.
Working Class Americanism: The politics of labour in a textile city
1989 Cambridge University Press *Cambridge*

This is an original work examining the alliance of socialist Franco-Belgian immigrants and conservative French Canadians in Woonsocket, New England, which created one of the

strongest textile unions in the 1930s. An intelligent treatment of ethnicity and labour, it is limited somewhat by lack of detail on the local firms and industrialists.
Firms: American Woolen Company; Amoskeag Manufacturing Company; Branch River Wool Combing Company; Guerin Mills; Manville Jenckes Corporation

1225
Hareven, Tamara K.
Family Time and Industrial Time: The relationship between the family and work in a New England industrial community
1982 Cambridge University Press *Cambridge*

A continuation of Hareven's earlier co-authored work *Amoskeag* (qv), this study continues her concern with the textile town of Manchester, New Hampshire. Much of the material is the same but this is a more theoretical treatment of the relationship between family time and work time. The use of company records and arguments on labour strategies are of interest.
Firms: Amoskeag Manufacturing Company

1226
Hareven, Tamara K.; Langenbach, R.
Amoskeag: Life and work in an American factory village
1978 Pantheon Books *New York, NY*

A fascinating oral history of the Amoskeag Manufacturing Company of Manchester, New Hampshire (1837–1936), once the largest textile factory in the world. This is not simply an elegiac description of working conditions but a multi-layered chronicle of the company and of mill life.
Firms: Amoskeag Manufacturing Company

1227
Hedges, James B.
The Browns of Providence Plantation: Vol. 1: The Colonial Years; Vol. 2: The Nineteenth Century
For main entry, see 3788

1228
Jeremy, David J.
Transatlantic Industrial Revolution: The diffusion of textile technologies between Britain and America, 1790–1830s
For main entry, see 4271

1229
Killick, J. R.
The Transformation of Cotton Marketing in the Late Nineteenth Century: Alexander Sprunt and Son of Wilmington, N.C., 1884–1956
Business History Review, vol. 55, no. 2, 1981: pp 143–69

This significant essay further challenges the view of the southern USA as economically backward. The focus is on one particularly successful firm and the argument is that there was an effective revolution in the marketing of cotton between the 1880s and the 1920s which permitted the South to continue to dominate the international cotton market.
Firms: Alexander Sprunt and Son

1230
Kulik, G.; Parks, R.; Penn, T. Z.
The New England Mill Village
1982 MIT Press *Cambridge, MA*

This is the second volume of the series Documents in American Industrial History. It is a well-edited collection of important and representative documents which throw considerable light on the early mechanized cotton industry and the small textile mill villages of New England where the industry was located.
Firms: Boston Manufacturing Co.; Pomfret Manufacturing Co,; Ramapo Cotton Factory; Sturbridge Manufacturing Co.; Thompsonville Manufacturing Co.; Ware Manufacturing Co.

1231
Lander, F. M. Jr
The Textile Industry in Antebellum South Carolina
1969 Louisiana State University Press *Baton Rouge, LA*

Lander gives a comprehensive account of the textile industry in the southern USA in the pre-Civil War years. The picture is one of few successes but many company failures. Mainly small-scale, the mills had to contend with problems of production, marketing and labour supply. Despite this the author contends that the

period set 'many precedents' for the much larger post-war industry.
Firms: Batesville; Graniteville; Waltham Mill

1232
Lomax, A. L.
Later Woolen Mills in Oregon: A history of the woolen mills which followed the pioneer mills
1974 Binfords and Mort *Portland, OR*

A sequel to the same author's earlier, *Pioneer Woolen Mills in Oregon*, this book covers the period 1880 to 1910. The tendency to examine each woollen mill in isolation limits the implications of the work. Nevertheless, it provides another regional study of industrial development in the USA.
Firms: Eugene Mills; Pendleton Woolen Mills; Union Mills

1233
McGouldrick, P. F.
New England Textiles in the Nineteenth Century: Profits and investment
1968 Harvard University Press *Cambridge, MA*

McGouldrick gives a quantitative analysis of profits, dividends and investment in the nineteenth-century textile industry in the USA. The period covered is 1830–1880, i.e. before the locus of the industry shifted to the South. The data is taken from the extant records of a number of individual companies.
Firms: Boston Co.; Dwight Co.; Hamilton Co.; Lawrence Co.; Merrimack Co.; Nashua Co.; Suffolk Co.; Trenant Co.

1234
McHugh, C. L.
Mill Family: The labour system in the southern cotton textile industry, 1880–1915
1988 Oxford University Press *Oxford*

An examination is made here of the strategies adopted by the mill owners of the southern USA in order to recruit a stable labour force. The system adopted was that of family labour which is related to the depressed state of agriculture and lack of alternative employment. A concluding chapter offers contrasts with the labour system employing single females found in New England and Japan.
Firms: Alamance Mill; Odell Manufacturing Co.

1235
McLaurin, M. A.
Paternalism and Protest: Southern cotton mill workers and organized labour, 1875–1905
1971 Greenwood Press *Westport, CT*

McLaurin's work challenges the traditional view of industrial relations in the textile industry of the southern States of the USA as harmonious and the mill worker as docile and tractable. The author shows the efforts made by textile workers to organize themselves and the successful anti-union strategies adopted by the mill-owners which defeated the unions by 1905.
Firms: Eagle and Phoenix Manufacturing Co.; Fulton Bag and Cotton Mills; Graniteville Manufacturing Co.; Holt Manufacturing Co.; Piedmont Mills

1236
O'Connor, Thomas H.
Lords of the Loom: The cotton Whigs and the coming of the Civil War
1968 Scribner *New York, NY*

This study of the cotton textile manufacturers of Massachusetts, USA covers the period before the Civil War. It is very much a social and political history of a group of conservative businessmen who are seen, contrary to the traditional historiography, as one of the more influential forces trying to avoid bloodshed between North and South.

1237
Prude, J.
The Coming of Industrial Order: Town and factory life in rural Massachusetts, 1810–1860
1983 Cambridge University Press *Cambridge*

This book studies the growth and transformation of three towns in rural Massachusetts. The concentration on the developments brought by the introduction of water-powered textile mills introduces a rural contrast to previous studies of industrial change in urban settings. Although it is somewhat weak on the business histories of the firms dealt with it is an

important addition to the historiography of early American industrialization.
Firms: Dudley Woolen Manufacturing Company; Providence Steam Cotton Company; Samuel Slater & Sons

1238
Roddy, Edward G.
Mills, Mansions and Mergers: The life of William M. Wood
For main entry, see 3978

1239
Rosenberg, Nathan (Editor)
The American System of Manufactures: The report of the committee on the machinery of the United States, 1855; and the special reports of George Wallis and Joseph Whitworth, 1854
For main entry, see 4293

1240
Scranton, Philip
Figured Tapestry: Production, markets, and power in Philadelphia textiles, 1885–1941
1989 Cambridge University Press *Cambridge*

A sequel to the author's earlier work (1983, qv) on Philadelphia's textile industry, this volume charts the decline of that industry. Again, much of the interest lies in Philadelphia's family-firm capitalism, as opposed to the 'modern', corporate enterprises of New England. It is an extensively researched book which is of value to business and textile historians.
Firms: American Viscose Company; American Woollen Company; Apex Hosiery Company; Archibald Campbell & Co.; Middlesex Co.; Quaker Lace Company

1241
Scranton, Philip
Proprietary Capitalism: The textile manufacturers at Philadelphia 1800–1885
1983 Cambridge University Press *Cambridge*

This is a thorough study of the vast and complex textile industry of nineteenth-century Philadelphia. Heavily influenced by the 'New Labour History', the book is concerned with the variety of paths towards the development of manufacturing. Of particular interest is the contrast between Philadelphia's multiplicity of small, specialized firms, and the mass-production, corporate giants of the Lowell system.
Firms: Archibald Campbell & Co.; Charles Spencer & Co.; Imperial Woollen Company; Lowell Manufacturing Company; Middlesex Company

1242
Scranton, Philip B. (Editor)
Silk City: Studies on the Paterson Silk Industry, 1860–1940
1985 New Jersey Historical *Newark, NJ*

This edited volume looks at the industrial history of a city dominated by small, proprietary firms, rather than the large, integrated corporations so beloved of the Chandler school. Much of the book concentrates on struggles over control of the production process. Its importance lies in further illustrating the complexity of America's industrial and business past.
Firms: Pelgram and Meyer

1243
Shelton, C. J.
The Mills of Manayunk: Industrialisation and social conflict in the Philadelphia region, 1787–1837
1986 The Johns Hopkins University Press *Baltimore, MD*

Shelton makes an important contribution to the growing literature on the industrialization process in the north-east states of America. The main cocern is with the migration of English and Irish workers and the export of popular radicalism from Lancashire to Philadelphia. This adds to the list of areas where the organization of textile production varied from the pattern established at Lowell, Massachusetts.
Firms: Bank of the United States; J. J. Bowie; Joseph Ripka

1244
Siegenthaler, H.
Das Gewicht monopolistischer Elemente in der Amerikanischen Textilindustrie, 1840–1880 [The Significance of the Monopolistic Element in the American Textile Industry, 1840–1880]
1972 Duncker & Humblot *Berlin, Germany*

This is a fresh and independent view of the American textile industry between 1840 and

1880. The author argues that the market in textile goods, which appears to have been fully competitive was, in fact, monopolistic. In this view the crucial role was played by the independent commission houses who enjoyed a crucial advantage due to their general knowledge of the market and of changing fashions.

1245
Tucker, B. M.
The Merchant, the Manufacturer, and the Factory Manager: The Samuel Slater case
Business History Review, vol. 55, no. 3, 1981: pp 297–313

This significant article covers the rise of management in the expanding factory system of early nineteenth-century America. The cotton textile industry and the firm of Samuel Slater is examined to illustrate the growing difficulties facing family firms and the way in which they turned to salaried agents to manage their mills.
Firms: Samuel Slater and Sons

Textiles, Latin America

1246
Arango, Luz Gabriela
Mujer, Religión e Industria: Fabricato 1923–1980 [Women, Religion and Industry: Fabricato 1923–1982]
1991 Editorial Universidad de Antioquia *Medellín, Colombia*

This book focuses on labour relations in one of Colombia's leading textile firms. It describes paternalistic management strategies implemented to halt a decline in female recruitment set against the strategies for survival by workers' families.
Firms: Fabricato

1247
Gamboa Ojeda, Leticia
Los empresarios de ayer: El grupo dominante en la industria textil de Puebla, 1906–1929 [Yesterday's Entrepreneurs: The dominant group in the textile industry of Puebla]
1985 Universidad Autónoma *Puebla, Mexico*

A comprehensive study of the textile entrepreneurs of Puebla, related particularly to the sources of their capital, investment strategy and relations with other entrepreneurs.

1248
Giroletti, Domingos A.
Modernização Capitalista em Minas Gerais: A Formacão do Operariado Industrial e de uma nova Cosmovisão [Capitalist Modernization of Minas Gerais: The creation of an industrial workforce and a new view of the world]
1987 Museu Nacional/UFRJ *Rio de Janeiro, Brazil*

This book examines the economic development of Minas Gerais during the second half of the nineteenth century, with reference to the textile business. Entrepreneurs had to overcome technical, disciplinary and ideological problems in creating a proletarian workforce. The factory, tied housing and training in lay convents and the primary schools were the main institutions used to transform slaves and poor freemen into industrial workers in Brazil from the 1870s on.
Firms: Cedro and Cachoeira Company; Cedro, Cachoeira and St Vicente Textile Factories

1249
Giroletti, Domingos A.
Fabrica Convento Disciplina [Factory Convent Discipline]
1991 Imprensa Oficial of Minas Gerais *Belo Horizonte, Brazil*

The book focuses on the entrepreneurial strategies used to transform slaves and free men, women and children, peasants and craftsmen into industrial workers in Brazil, covering technical, disciplinary and ideological aspects. It is based on the archives of three textile factories set up with British machinery in the last quarter of the nineteenth century. British supervisors were engaged to train workers. A lay convent, organized like a religious house, was used by industrialists to recruit and discipline orphans, single girls and widows.
Firms: Cedro and Cachoeira Company (CCC)

1250
Martins, I. L.
Empreendedores e investidores em industria textil no Rio de Janeiro: 1878–1895: Uma contribuiçao para o Estudo do Capitalismo no

Brasil [Entrepreneurs and Financiers in the Textile Industry in Rio de Janeiro: 1878–1895: A contribution to the study of capitalism in Brazil]
1985 ICHF/Universidade Federal Fluminens *Niteroi, Brazil*

This work examines the establishment of the textile industry in the city of Rio de Janeiro in the last quarter of the nineteenth century. It examines the sources of the capital invested in the establishment and expansion of the industry.

Firms: Fabrica de Tecidos Pau Grande; Fabrica de Tecidos Sao Lazaro; Fabrica de Tecidos do Rink

1251
Salvucci, R. J.
Textiles and Capitalism in Mexico: An economic history of the Obrajes, 1539–1840
1987 Princeton University Press *Princeton, NJ*

This is a study of the wool textile industry in colonial Mexico. The *obrajes* were large workshops, employing on average forty workers, which produced the bulk of Mexico's cloth. Most of the focus of the book is on the eighteenth century, though Salvucci also details the destruction of the *obrajes* through civil war and foreign imports in the early nineteenth century.

Firms: Ansaldo; Panzacola

1252
Stein, S. J.
Origens e evolução da industria textil no Brasil, 1850–1950 [Brazilian Cotton Manufacture: Textile enterprise in an underdeveloped area, 1850–1950]
1979 Editora Campus *Rio de Janeiro, Brazil*

A reference work on the study of the textile industry in Brazil, this excellent book covers the first century of the industry's history. It examines the conditions in which the Brazilian textile industry was established and developed until the 1950s.

1253
Vaz, A. M.
Cia. Cedro e Cachoeira: história de uma empresa familiar, 1883–1987 [Cedro and Cachoeira Company: The story of a family enterprise, 1883–1987]
1990 Cia. Cedro e Cachoeira *Belo Horizonte, Brazil*

This commissioned history celebrates the 100th anniversary of the Companhia de Fiaçao e Tecidos Cedro e Cachoeira, based on the author's PhD thesis ('Companhia de Fiaçao e Tecidos Cedro e Cachoeira: l'evolution d'une affaire familiale, 1872–1972') and later extended to 1987.

Firms: Companhia de Fiaçao e Tecidos Cedro e Cachoeira

Textiles, Rest of World

1254
Abe, Takeshi
Nihon niokeru Sanchi Men-orimono-gyo no Tenkai [The Development of the Local Cotton Weaving Industry in Japan]
1989 Tokyo University Press *Tokyo, Japan*

Covering the local cotton weaving areas such as Osaka and Hyogo prefectures from 1920 to 1937, Abe describes the mechanization of manufacture and the development of design, selling and distribution functions.

Firms: Itoh Chu; Obitani Shoten

1255
Chandavarkar, Rajnarayan
The Origins of Industrial Capitalism in India: Business Strategies and the Working Classes in Bombay, 1900–1940
1994 Cambridge University Press *Cambridge*

Chandavarkar explores the development of the Bombay cotton-textile industry, its problems in the 1920 and 1930s, and the millowners' and state's responses to them. He also investigates how an industrial labour force was formed in Bombay.

1256
Chao, K.
The Development of Cotton Textile Production in China
1977 East Asian Research Center, Harvard *Cambridge, MA*

This is an ambitious single volume history of cotton production in China. First introduced 2,000 years ago, cotton penetrated inland

China in the eleventh century and had become the major industry after agriculture by the fourteenth century. This study goes on to cover nineteenth-century imports, foreign manufacturers, and China's indigenous modern cotton industry.
Firms: East India Company; Ewo Cotton Spinning and Weaving Co.; Hongkong Cotton Spinning, Weaving and Dyeing Company; Hongkong and Shanghai Banking Corporation; Jardine, Matheson Co.

1257
Fujii, Mitsuo
Nihon Sen-i Sangyo Keiei Shi [The Business History of the Japanese Textile Industry]
1971 Nihon Hyoron Sha *Tokyo, Japan*

Covering the development of the fibre industry from cotton to synthetics between 1945 and 1970, Fujii explores the reasons and methods adopted by cotton and/or artificial (cellulose) fibre makers in diversifying into the synthetic (petrochemical) fibre industry.
Firms: Asahi Kasei; Kanebo; Kurabo; Kurashiki Boseki; Nisshin Boseki; Teijin; Toray; Toyobo; Unitika

1258
Hossain, H.
The Company Weavers of Bengal: The East India Company and the organization of textile production in Bengal, 1750–1813
1988 Oxford University Press *Delhi, India*

This study of the weavers of Bengal covers the period of stagnation and decline in the cotton export industry. Hossain argues that the decline was due, not to the mechanization of production in Britain, but to the ill-conceived strategy of the East India Company itself. Although a difficult read, this is an important contribution to the economic history of India.
Firms: English East India Company

1259
Husband, W. B.
Revolution in the Factory: The birth of the Soviet textile industry 1917–1920
1990 Oxford University Press *Oxford*

Husband gives a fascinating account of the textile mills in the central industrial region around Moscow during the revolutionary and civil war period. A contribution to the growing literature on workers' experiences in the Revolution, this study throws light on the aspirations of the labour force, tensions between the centre and the periphery, and the development of managerial structures.

1260
Ishii, Kanji
Nippon Sanshi-gyo-shi Bunseki [A Historical Study of the Japanese Raw Silk Industry]
1972 Tokyo University Press *Tokyo, Japan*

This work presents two types of raw silk firms: those producing ordinary raw silk and those producing fine silk. It covers the development of the industry from 1870 to 1907, dealing with the production process, distribution, credit, female labour, and exports.
Firms: Gunze; Katakura

1261
Ito, Kotaro
Nihon Yomo Kogyo Ron [The Study of the Japanese Woollen Industry]
1957 Toyo Keizai Shinpo-sha *Tokyo, Japan*

Covering the development of the Japanese woollen industry from 1868 to 1955. Ito deals with the import of raw wool, dyeing, weaving, exporting and competition from other fabrics.
Firms: Daido Keori; Nihon Keori

1262
Kajinishi, Mitsuhaya (Editor)
Seni Jou [The Fibre Industry, Vol. I]
1974 Kojunsha Shuppankyoku *Tokyo, Japan*

This excellent work covers the whole range of the Japanese fibre industry between 1860 and 1940 from silk to synthetic fibres. It also examines technical problems, the import of raw materials as well as the export of final goods, labour management and foreign affairs.
Firms: Asahi Kasei; Kanebo; Kurashiki Boseki; Nissin Boseki; Teijin; Toray; Toyobo; Unitika

1263
Kelly, M.
Mill in the Valley: A centennial history of Arthur Ellis and Co. Ltd
1977 Arthur Ellis & Co. Ltd *Dunedin, New Zealand*

Kelly gives a brief descriptive survey of one

company's expansion and growth strategies. It began business using an imported flock machine and sold flock to retailers who made up mattresses. Thereafter they vertically integrated forwards and also diversified into related products. The study provides evidence of reactions to external events such as war, new technology and changes in company law.
Firms: Arthur Ellis & Co. Ltd

1264
Kuwahara, Tetsuo
Kigyo Kokusaika no Shiteki Bunseki [Japanese Business Abroad in Historical Perspective: Foreign Direct Investment of Japanese Cotton-Spinning Firms in China before World War I]
For main entry, see 2575

1265
Leadbeater, S. R. B.
The Politics of Textiles: The Indian cotton-mill industry and the legacy of Swadeshi, 1900–1985
1993 Sage *New Delhi, India*
This is a study of relations between the Indian government and the country's leading textile businesses. Leadbeater argues that the mill sector had more influence under British rule. Since 1947 the government has discriminated against the mill sector and in favour of the handloom and small workshop sectors.

1266
Li, L. M.
Silks by Sea: Trade, technology and enterprise in China and Japan
Business History Review, vol. 56, no. 2, 1982: pp 192–217
This is a comparative examination of the East Asian silk trade from the 1850s to the 1930s. Starting at comparable levels and sharing the same basic technology, the relative performance of the Chinese and Japanese silk industries diverged widely. The Chinese industry did not perform badly but it was the Japanese who dominated the world market in silk in the early twentieth century.

1267
Lucas, K. G.
A New Twist: A centennial history of Donaghy's Industries
1979 Donaghy's Industries *Dunedin, New Zealand*
This history of Donaghy's, which began as ropemakers in 1876, highlights the policies of a company which faced a frequently shifting market. It concentrated for some time on developing and publicizing new ideas for cordage, but by the 1970s adopted a diversification strategy, embracing linen and jute based goods, nylon and polyester ropes, a variety of synthetic fibres, and food products.
Firms: Andrews Twine Co.; BNZ Estates Co.; Donaghy's Industries; Nixon Industries Ltd; Severnside Foods (NZ) Ltd

1268
McLean, G. J.
Spinning Yarns: A centennial history of Alliance Textiles Ltd and its predecessors, 1881–1981
1981 Alliance Textiles *Dunedin, New Zealand*
McLean looks at the development of the three companies, dating back to the 1870s, which combined to form Alliance Textiles in 1960. The book also covers the early years of Alliance and the move to specialization at each of the sites.
Firms: Alliance Textiles; Bruce Woollen Manufacturing Co.; Oamaru Woollen Factory Co.; Oamaru Worsted & Woollen Mills; Timaru Worsted & Woollen Co.; Timaru Worsted Spinning and Manufacturing Co.

1269
Nihon Boseki Kyokai (Editor)
Sengo Boseki Shi [The History of the Japanese Cotton Industry Since the Second World War]
1962, 79 Nihon Boseki Kyokai *Tokyo, Japan*
Covering the Japanese cotton industry as a whole from 1945 to 1977, this work especially refers to the structural depression affecting the industry, the industrial policy developed by MITI and the agreement to encourage exports from Japan.

1270
Nihon Choki Shinyo Ginko
Gosei Sen-i [The Synthetic Fibre Industry]
1960 Nihon Choki Shinyo Ginko *Tokyo, Japan*

This work is mainly concerned with the formative years of the Japanese synthetic fibre industry from 1945 to 1960. It describes the growth of vertically-integrated firms dealing with all aspects of manufacture from processing the raw fibre to dyeing and weaving.
Firms: Asahi Kasei; Kurare; Nihon Exlan; Teijin; Toray

1271
Nihon Kagaku Sen-i Kyokai
Nihon Kagaku Sen-i Sangyo Shi [The History of the Japanese Artificial Fibre Industry]
1974 Nihon Kagaku Sen-i Kyokai *Tokyo, Japan*

Covering not only the formative and developmental stages of the Japanese artificial fibre industry in the prewar years, but also the development of the synthetic fibre industry after the Second World War, this excellent book examines many problems such as strategies, industrial policies, the introduction of foreign patents and marketing.
Firms: Asahi Kasei; Kanebo; Kurare; Mitsubishi Rayon; Teijin; Toho Rayon; Toray; Toyobo; Unitika

1272
Nihon Yomo Bosekikai
Nihon Yomo Boseki Ryakushi [A Short History of the Japanese Woollen Industry]
1987 Nihon Yomo Bosekikai *Tokyo, Japan*

This work covers the course of development of the Japanese woollen industry as a whole prior to the Second World War, and in particular, describes relations with government concerning industrial policies such as the import of raw wool and abolition of excess capacity.
Firms: Daido Keori; Kanebo; Nihon Keori; Unitika

1273
Nishikawa, Hiroshi
Nihon Teikokusyugi to Mengyo [The Japanese Empire and the Cotton Spinning Industry]
1987 Mineruva Shobo *Kyoto, Japan*

Nishikawa describes the formation of big business in the cotton spinning industry between 1914 and 1934 and focuses mainly on exports to China and investment there, and the problems experienced with exporting to India.
Firms: Kanebo; Kurashiki Boseki; Nisshin Boseki; Tyobo; Unitika

1274
Ohara, Soichiro
Kagaku Sen-i Kogyoron [A Study of the Japanese Artificial Fibre Industry]
1961 Tokyo University Press *Tokyo, Japan*

Set in context with the world-wide artificial fibre industry, this book describes the history of the Japanese artificial fibre industry from 1846 to 1960, dealing with technological change, the trends in consumption, exports, importing raw materials, processing and business behaviour.
Firms: Asahi Kasei; Kanebo; Kurare; Mitsubishi Rayon; Teijin; Toray

1275
Okochi, Akio; Yonekawa, Shin'ichi (Editors)
The Textile Industry and its Business Climate (Eighth Fuji Conference)
For main entry, see 109

1276
Otsuka, K.; Ranis, G.; Saxonhouse, G.
Comparative Technology Choice in Development: The Indian and Japanese cotton textile industries
1988 Macmillan *Basingstoke*

This study emerged out of Yale University's Economic Growth Center and a major research effort in the early 1980s looking at technology choice in less developed countries. The authors provide a historical account of the development of the cotton textile industries of Japan and Indian between 1880 and c.1935. Their approach emphasizes the domestic industrial structure and the extent of protectionism offered to the industries by national governments.
Firms: Bank of Japan; Platt Brothers; Toyoda Automatic Loom Co.

1277

Sastry, D. U.

The Cotton Mill Industry in India

1984 Oxford University Press *Delhi, India*

Sastry gives a concise study of the textile industry in modern India, concentrating on the period 1950–81. The book is part of a series–Studies in Economic Development and Planning–issued by the Institute of Economic Growth. The author concentrates on three aspects of the industry: capacity utilization; productivity; and demand. His findings are directed towards policy-makers and the industry itself.

Firms: National Textile Corporation

1278

Stewart, P. J.

Patterns on the Plain: A Centennial History of Mosgiel Woollens Limited

1975 Mosgiel *Dunedin, New Zealand*

The firm had its origins in 1870 when it employed imported labour and machinery. Stewart concentrates on the challenges of rapidly changing technology and the impact this had upon the size of the firm and its capital requirements.

Firms: Kaipoi Textiles Ltd; Mosgiel Woollens; Otago & Southland Investment Co.; Shepherd Wools Ltd

1279

Takamura, Naosuke

Bosekigyoshi Josetsu [A Historical Study of the Japanese Cotton Spinning Industry]

1971 Hanawa Shobo *Tokyo, Japan*

The Japanese cotton spinning industry between 1870 and 1914, is described here. Important issues, such as introducing new technologies, importing raw cotton, the employment of women, the distribution of finished goods and exporting are all discussed. Takamura also examines the formation of the six major companies in this excellent study.

Firms: Kanebo; Kurashiki Boseki; Nissin Boseki; Toyobo; Unitika

1280

Tanaka, Minoru

Nihon Gosei Sen-i Kogyo Ron [A Study of the Japanese Synthetic Fibre Industry]

1967 Miraisha *Tokyo, Japan*

This book describes the Japanese synthetic fibre industry from 1935 to 1965. It focuses on the strategies employed to decide what kind of fibres and what kind of technologies should be introduced.

Firms: Asahi Kasei; Kanebo; Kurare; Nihon Exlan; Teijin; Toray; Unitika

1281

Tsurumi, E. Patricia

Factory Girls: Women in the thread mills of Meiji Japan

1990 Princeton University Press *Princeton, NJ*

Tsurumi investigates the experience of women cotton textile workers in the period of Japanese industrialization. She documents the hardships and exploitation of the country girls and captures their struggles by imaginative use of diaries and songs. The regime of the thread mills is superbly drawn.

Firms: Dojima; Kanegafuchi; Mie; Osaka Cotton Spinning Co.; Tenma; Tomioka

1282

Uchida, Hoshimi

Gosei Sen-i Kogyo (Shintei Han) [The Synthetic Fibre Industry (revised)]

1970 Toyo Keizai Shinpo-sha *Tokyo, Japan*

Uchida describes the development of the Japanese synthetic fibre industry between 1938 and 1970. He discusses the strategies of firms adopting new fibre such as nylon and the competition with eath other, contrasted with the experience of American and European companies.

Firms: Kurare; Teijin; Toray; Unitika

1283

Ward, C.

Russia's Cotton Workers and the New Economic Policy: Shop floor culture and state policy 1921–1929

1990 Cambridge University Press *Cambridge*

Ward gives a fascinating account of Russia's textile workers during the period of the New Economic Policy. Rationalization is seen to have had a limited impact due to the complexities of the manufacturing process and to the culture of the workers–their continuing peasant links and organization around the family unit.

Firms: Anglo Russian Cotton Company; Asa Lees and Co.; Chase National Bank; Platt Bros

1284
Yamaguchi, Kazuo (Editor)
Nihon Sangyo Kinyushi Kenkyu: Boseki Kinyu Hen [The History of the Japanese Industrial Finance: The finance of the cotton spinning industry]
1970 Tokyo University Press *Tokyo, Japan*

This work covers the main problems faced by the Japanese cotton industry between 1867 to 1914. First, financing for investment and import and second, the relations between trading companies and exchange banks. It also provides an analysis of the leading cotton firms.
Firms: Kanebo; Mitsui Bussan; Tokyo Ginko; Toyobo; Unitika

1285
Yamazaki, Hiroaki
Nihon Kasen Sangyo Shiron [A Historical Study of the Japanese Artificial Fibre Industry]
1975 Tokyo University Press *Tokyo, Japan*

This excellent work describes the history of the Japanese artificial fibre industry and compares it with the development of the industry in Europe and America from 1903 to 1937. It covers technological change, R&D, marketing and labour management.
Firms: Asahi Kasei; Kurare; Mitsubishi Rayon; Teijin; Toho Rayon; Toray; Unitika

Construction

1286
Barjot, Dominique
Fougerolle: Deux siècles de savoir-faire [Fougerolle: Two centuries of savoir-faire]
1992 Éditions dy Lys *Caen, France*

Barjot describes the remarkable history of a small building firm of central France, founded by a family of stonemasons. It eventually became one of the largest building and public work groups in France and has operated worldwide; a management buy-out was recently achieved. This book is based on business records.
Firms: Fougerolle

1287
Burnel, Anne
La société des Batignolles de 1914 à 1939, histoire d'un déclin [Batignolles 1914–1939: A Story of decline]
1992, PhD Thesis, École des Chartres

This dissertation describes the decline of a large Paris-based public works company.
Firms: Batignolles

1288
Clarke, Linda
Building Capitalism: Historical change and the labour process in the production of the built environment
1991 Routledge *London*

Clarke describes the transformation of the English building industry from independent artisan to contractor, c. 1800–30 and its impact on employment and work organization.

1289
Coad, R.
Laing: The biography of Sir John W. Laing, CBE (1879–1978)
For main entry, see 3877

1290
d'Angio, Agnès
La politique des travaux publics du groupe Schneider de 1895 à 1949 [The Politics of Public Works in the Schneider Group 1895–1949]
For main entry, see 4330

1291
Doughty, M. (Editor)
Building the Industrial City
1986 Leicester University Press *Leicester*

One of the 'Themes in Urban History' series published by Leicester University Press, this volume brings together four studies on the physical creation of the Victorian city in England and Scotland. Although they are somewhat uneven in quality and disparate in coverage the essays do, however, illuminate the relationship between land, finance, and the building industry itself.
Firms: Bradford Building Society; Halifax Building Society; John Brown & Co.; Leeds Per-

manent Building Society; William Beardmore & Co.

1292
Foster, Mark S.
Henry J. Kaiser: Builder in the modern American West
For main entry, see 3948

1293
Middlemas, R. K.
The Master Builders: Thomas Brassey; Sir John Aird; Lord Cowdray; Sir John Norton-Griffiths
For main entry, see 3902

1294
Morrell, David
Indictment: Power and politics in the construction industry
1987 Faber & Faber *London*

Written by the former chairman of Mitchells, a major construction company that was forced into bankruptcy in 1973 by disastrous problems during the construction of the Kariba Dam. The book is a ferocious but documented attack on the role of the World Bank and the British government in these events, and of the wider issues of politics and the construction industry.
Firms: British Steel Corporation; McAlpine; Mitchell Construction Co.; Prudential Assurance Co.

1295
Poulson, John
The Price: The autobiography of John Poulson, architect
For main entry, see 3910

1296
Powell, C. G.
An Economic History of the British Building Industry, 1815–1979
1980 Architectural Press *London*

This illuminating general history of the building industry in Britain covers the last 150 years. An architect and social historian, the author has provided a descriptive account based mainly on secondary sources. Despite its compressed style, the book provides much of interest in discussing the nature of continuity and change in a conservative industry.
Firms: Costain; Laing; Sir Robert McAlpine & Sons; Thomas Cubitt; William & Francis Radford; Wimpey

1297
Price, R.
Masters, Unions and Men: Work control in building and the rise of labour, 1830–1914
1980 Cambridge University Press *Cambridge*

Price's book is a stimulating examination of industrial relations and class struggle in nineteenth-century Britain. Although largely unaffected by any new developments in technology, the building industry was still greatly affected by industrial capitalism. The author's interest lies in the continuing struggle between workers and employers over control of the work process.

1298
Rainbird, Helen; Syben, Gerd (Editors)
Restructuring a Traditional Industry: Construction employment and skills in Europe
1991 Berg *New York, NY*

An examination of organizational and technological change in construction in historical and comparative perspective. Studies of small and medium firms in France and technological change in interwar Germany are particularly valuable for the business historian. The second half of the book focuses on pressures for change in the 1980s and the run up to 1992.

1299
Robinson, M.
James Fletcher: Builder
1970 Hodder & Stoughton *London*

This personal and business biography of New Zealand's most successful builder begins shortly before the First World War. The book examines the company's growth through vertical integration and diversification.
Firms: Colonial Sugar Refining Co.; Fletcher; Tasman Pulp & Paper; Wright Stephenson

1300
Rosenberg, Nathan
Economic Planning in the British Building Industry, 1945–9
1960 Pennsylvania University Press
Philadelphia, PA

An account of the impact of government economic planning on the industry in this period.

1301
Smyth, Hedley
Property Companies and the Construction Industry in Britain
1985 Cambridge University Press *Cambridge*

This is a study of Britain's construction industry in the years 1939–79. Concerned with the agents who produce and control the built environment, the author shows how the largest contractors have maintained their dominant position. The critical period was during the Second World War when the government's massive building programme was entrusted to a few major companies.
Firms: Bovis; Costain; Laing; McAlpine; Taylor Woodrow; Wimpey

1302
Warner, Sam Bass
Streetcar Suburbs: The process of growth in Boston, 1870–1900
For main entry, see 3271

Construction, Building Materials

1303
Aso Hyakunen Shi Hensan Iinkai
Aso Hyakunenshi: A Centenary of Aso
For main entry, see 365

1304
Bowley, M.
Innovations in Building Materials: An economic study
1960 Gerald Duckworth & Co. *London*

Part of the *Industrial Innovations Series*, this volume is concerned with innovations in the building materials industry in Britain before and after the First World War. The book is concerned with the relationship between innovation and the structure of industry, and also provides a valuable piece of economic history.
Firms: British Plaster Board Ltd; Cellactite and British Uralite Co.; Imperial Chemical Industries; John Laing & Son; London Brick Co.; Marley Tile Co.

1305
Bowley, M.
The British Building Industry: Four studies in response and resistance to change
1966 Cambridge University Press *Cambridge*

A companion volume to Bowley's earlier work (1960, qv) on building materials in Britain, this book is concerned with innovations in structure and design in the building industry. The period covered is the same – from before 1914 to 1956 – as is the main hypothesis, that the attitude of an industry to innovations is largely determined by the structure and organization of the industry.
Firms: Bristol Aeroplane Co.; Cubitts & Co.; G. & J. Weir Ltd; Imperial Chemical Industries; John Laing & Son; Orlit Ltd

1306
Brodeur, Paul
Outrageous Misconduct: The asbestos industry on trial
1985 Pantheon Books *New York, NY*

A rare study of the asbestos industry, this book concentrates primarily on the wave of worker injury litigation that brought the Manville Corporation, one of the US Top 200, to bankruptcy in 1982. Although it is rivetting on legal, medical and ethical issues it lacks important aspects on the organization and economics of the business.
Firms: Manville Corp.

1307
Dubois, Léon
Lafarge Coppée, 150 ans d'industrie: Une mémoire pour demain [Lafarge Coppée, 150 Years of Industry: A memoir]
1988 Belfond *Paris, France*

The leading company in the French cement industry is described in this business history by a company man.
Firms: Lafarge-Coppée

1308
Earle, James Basil Foster
Black Top: A history of the British flexible roads industry
1974 Basil Blackwell *London*

Written by someone who worked in the industry for many years, this is a single volume history of the use of tar, asphalt and bitumen (rather than concrete) for road making in Britain. Apart for the occasional snippet of interesting detail it is of little use to the business historian.

Firms: Limmer & Trinidad Lake Asphalt Co.; Tarmac

1309
Earle, J. B. F.
A Century of Road Materials: The history of the Roadstone Division of Tarmac Ltd
1971 Basil Blackwell *Oxford*

This, with the same author's *Black Top* (qv), describes the use of tarmac in British roads with particular emphasis on technical developments, but also covering raw materials, amalgamations and the impact of government policy on the industry. There is little on finance but these books provide an invaluable insight into a little researched area.

Firms: Tarmac

1310
Francis, A. J.
The Cement Industry, 1796–1914: A history
1977 David & Charles *Newton Abbot*

Francis gives a comprehensive account of the history of cement manufacture in Britain from the end of the eighteenth century to the First World War. Down to the middle of the nineteenth century Roman cement was predominant but, thereafter, Portland cement displaced it. Despite the serious lack of business records, this is a useful contribution to the history of the construction industry.

Firms: Aspdin, Ord & Co.; Associated Portland Cement Manufacturers; British Portland Cement Manufacturers; Francis & Whyte; Imperial Chemical Industries; Parker & Wyatt

1311
Heerding, A.
Cement in Nederland [Cement in The Netherlands]
1971 Cementfabriek Ymuiden *Ymuiden, The Netherlands*

This general history of cement-making in The Netherlands has its emphasis on the formation (in 1930) and subsequent development of the ENCI-CEMY cement-manufacturing conglomerate as a daughter company of the Hoogovens Ymuiden steelworks.

Firms: Cementfabriek Ymuiden (CEMY); Eerste Nederlandsche Cement Industrie (ENCI); Hoogovens Ymuiden

1312
Johansen, Hans Chr.
Gennem forandring til fremskridt: Aalborg Portlands udvikling 1972–89 [Through Change Towards Progress: Restructing at Aalborg Portland, 1972–1989]
1989 Aalborg Portland *Aalborg, Denmark*

This book describes the development of the largest Danish cement works 1972–89. The central theme is the restructuring which took place when demand declined dramatically because of the fall in the general investment level in Denmark during the oil crises. Remedies were centralization of production, new technology, and energy saving measures.

Firms: A/S Aalborg Portland-Cement-Fabrik

1313
Loescher, Samuel M.
Imperfect Collusion in the Cement Industry
1959 Harvard University Press *Cambridge, MA*

Loescher describes the development of oligopoly and absence of price competition in this industry; the existence of a strong market limited the impact of an anti-trust decision. This is an important study on pricing behaviour.

Firms: General Portland Cement Co.; Lehigh Portland Cement Co.; Penn-Dixie Cement Corp.; Universal Atlas Cement Co.

1314
Routley, J.; Mattingly, H.
A Saga of British Industry: The story of the British Plaster Board Group
1959 The British Plaster Board (Holdings *London*

Published privately by the company, this is a history of the British Plaster Board Group: the parent company, the multitude of associated companies and, of course, of gypsum plasterboard itself. The original company was founded privately in 1917 and grew massively through takeovers and amalgamations.
Firms: British Plaster Board; Gypsum Mines; Gyproc Products

1315
Shashi Hensan Iinkai
Hyakunenshi [A Centenary]
1983 Nihon Cement Co. *Tokyo, Japan*

This story of Nihon Cement Co., the oldest and the largest in Japan, which started as Asano Cement gives a detailed treatment of technology, supply of raw materials, marketing, personnel and labour relations and plenty of tables and charts.
Firms: Asano Cement; Nihon Cement Co.

1316
Turner & Newall
Turner & Newall Limited: The first fifty years, 1920–1970
1970 Turner & Newall *Manchester*

This is an uncritical house history of a leading British asbestos manufacturer, published in celebration of the firm's Golden Jubilee. The book does, however, provide useful information on the company's development.
Firms: Turner & Newall

1317
Whipp, Richard
Patterns of Labour: Work and social change in the pottery industry
1990 Routledge *London*

A study of work in the British pottery industry from the late nineteenth century to the interwar years. Very much concerned with labour, gender, and community, but also shedding light on industry structure, industrial relations, and management.
Firms: Furnival Co.; Johnson Co.; Wedgwood Co.

Construction, Glass

1318
Amdam, Rolv Petter; Hanisch, Tore Jørgen; Pharo, Ingvild Elisabeth
Vel blåst!: Christiania Glasmagasin og norsk glassindustri 1739–1989 [Everything OK!: An Oslo glass workshop in the Norwegian glass industry, 1739–1989]
1989 Gyldendal *Oslo, Norway*

The Christiania Glasmagasin in one of the oldest glassworks in Norway, founded in 1739. In this book the industry is seen in its political – economic context from mercantilism to the present. The development in art and style is also covered, and the book is generously illustrated.
Firms: Christiania Glasmagasin

1319
Barker, T. C.
The Glassmakers: Pilkington: The rise of an international company 1826–1976
1977 Weidenfeld & Nicolson *London*

This is a revised and extended version of the author's earlier *Pilkington Brothers and the Glass Industry* (1960), a pioneering study of the flat glass industry of Britain which was also a company history and a history of the Pilkington family. Where the first book dealt in detail to 1918 only, this version covers the inter-war years, with a rather cursory epilogue taking the story to 1976.
Firms: Greenall and Pilkingtons; Pilkington Brothers; St Helen's Crown Glass Company

1320
Daviet, Jean-Pierre
Une multinationale à la française: Saint-Gobain 1665–1989 [A French Multinational: Saint-Gobain, 1665–1989]
1989 Fayard *Paris, France*

Daviet gives a full history of the famous glass and chemicals company, during its three-centuries history. He had previously written a detailed history of the firm, from 1830 to 1939, [*Un destin international, la Compagnie de Saint-*

Gobain de 1830 à 1989, Montreux-Paris, Éditions des archives contemporaires, 1988], which continues the work by Pris (qv) on the pre-1830 period. This is an excellent work of synthesis, based on primary material.
Firms: Saint-Gobain

1321
Davis, P.
The Development of the American Glass Industry
1949 Harvard University Press *Cambridge, MA*

This history of the glass industry in the USA covers the period from colonial times to the twentieth century. Produced within the Harvard Economic Studies series, the book provides a basic economic history of the industry, an examination of the rise of organized labour and an analysis of the impact of tariff protection on the industry.
Firms: American Window Glass Co.; Boston and Sandwich Glass Co.; Ford Motor Co.; Imperial Window Glass Co.; Independent Glass Co.; New England Glass Co.

1322
Lippert, Frank
Industrielle Rationalisierung in der Weimarer Republik: Die Flaschenglasinsdustrie [Industrial Rationalization in the Weimar Republic The bottle glass industry]
Zeitschrift fur Unternehmensgeschichte, 1994: pp 166–92

The German bottle glass industry is examined to determine whether rationalization was fully exploited during the Weimar Republic. In his very detailed article, Lippert suggests that although rationalization was only partial, it had still gone too far as it was costly and resulted in price increases. Also, decreasing demand did not permit its full utilization.

1323
Merley, Jean; Luirard, Monique; et al
Histoire d'une entreprise forézienne: La verrerie BSN de Veanche [History of a Forézienne Business: The BSN Glassworks of Veanche]
1983 Université de Saint-Etienne *Saint-Etienne, France*

This centenary history of a glass-works in central France, which was established in 1882, for making bottles, is a serious and scholarly study. The company is now part of the large BSN group of companies. The book is based on the firm's records.
Firms: BSN

1324
Pris, Claude
La manufacture royale des glaces de Saint-Gobain, 1665–1830: Une grande entreprise sous l'ancien régime [The Royal Plate Glass Factory of Saint-Gobain, 1665–1830]
1975 University of Lille *Lille, France*

Pris presents a detailed and very scholarly history of a famous firm, which is one of the oldest still in existence, after continuous activity for over three centuries. It is based on the company's surviving records and on an exhaustive search into archival materials. Another book, by J. E. Daviet (q.v.), brings the story up to the present. Saint-Gobain was established to make plate-glass, but diversified into chemicals from the early nineteenth century onwards. A shorter version, also in French, was published by Arno Press, New York in 1981.
Firms: Saint-Gobain

1325
Scoville, W. C.
Revolution in Glassmaking: Entrepreneurship and technological change in the American industry, 1880–1920
1948 Harvard University Press *Cambridge, MA*

This study of the American glassmaking industry covers a period of rapid expansion and change. Between 1880 and 1920 the industry was transformed from a handicraft, family-owned industry to a modern, technological industry dominated by large corporations. Considerable attention is paid to the pre-1880 period while the main focus is on the men and firms of Toledo, Ohio where the major technological breakthroughs were made.
Firms: American Bottle Co.; American Window Glass Co.; Libbey Glass; Libbey-Owens-Ford Glass Co.; Toledo Glass Co.

Light Manufacturing Industries

Engineering - General

1326
Buchanan, Robert A.
The Engineers: A history of the engineering profession in Britain, 1750–1914
For main entry, see 4108

1327
Cheape, Charles W.
Family Firm to Multinational: Norton Company, a New England enterprise
1985 Harvard University Press *Cambridge, MA*

The Norton company, founded in 1880, provided the abrasives and grinding machinery necessary to the mechanical revolution of 1880–1914. Within forty years it had bought or built plants worldwide and licensed its products in markets where it had no direct presence. The firm remained family owned and controlled until diversification in the 1960s brought a managerial transformation. This is a valuable, archivally-based study which covers the whole span of the company's history.

Firms: Behr-Manning Co.; Carborundum Co.; Cincinatti Milling Machinery Co.; Norton Co.

1328
Friedman, David
The Misunderstood Miracle: Industrial development and political change in Japan
1988 Cornell University Press *Ithaca, NY*

A controversial and important book which uses a densely researched study of the Japanese machine-tool industry as a stepping-off point to argue a revisionist case on the role of the Japanese state in economic development. MITI's strategy for machine-tools is argued to have been largely misconceived and ineffective, whilst the role of small business is shown to have been vital and much neglected.

1329
Glimstedt, Henrik
Mellan teknick och samhalle: Stat, marknad och produktion i svensk bilindustrie, 1930–1960 [Between Technology and Society: State, markets and production in the Swedish transport industry, 1930–1960]
For main entry, see 874

1330
Habakkuk, H. J.
American and British Technology in the Nineteenth Century: The search for labour saving inventions
For main entry, see 4263

1331
Hoke, Donald R.
Ingenious Yankees: The rise of the American system of manufactures in the private sector
1990 Columbia University Press *New York, NY*

This book examines the origins of mass-produced consumer durables in the USA through detailed studies of four industries: wooden movement clocks, axes, watches, and typewriters. Issues discussed include the economic reasoning of nineteenth-century entrepreneurs, the economic and technical forces behind new product design, the economics of mass production, and market responses to product innovation. Hoke traces the development of the 'American system' of manufacturing and argues that its origins can be found more in the synergy between entrepreneurs and engineers than in the adaptation of manufacturing processes first developed in the public and armoury sectors.

Firms: American Writing Machine Co.; Remington Typewriter Co.; Waltham Watch Co.

1332
Hounshell, David A.
From the American System to Mass Production, 1800–1932: The development of manufacturing technology in the United States
1984 Johns Hopkins University Press *Baltimore, MD*

This is a splendidly-researched and written analysis of the development of production technologies, from interchangeability to Fordism. It demonstrates how armory methods of production spread to the production of other light consumer durables like sewing machines, reapers, bicycles, and cards.
Firms: Colt; Ford; General Motors; McCormick; Singer; Wilcox & Gibbs; Brown & Sharpe

1333
Huck, V.
Brand of the Tartan: The 3M story
1955 Appleton-Century-Croft *New York, NY*

Huck relates the story of the first half-century of '3M' or, the Minnesota Mining and Manufacturing Company. Founded in 1901 to mine corundum, the company made an enforced shift into artificial abrasives when their mine turned out to be worthless. These were the unlikely beginnings of what was to become a major corporation with an extensive range of products.
Firms: Carborundum Company; Durex Corporation; Minnesota Mining and Manufacturing Co.; United States Sandpaper Company

1334
Mauersberg, Hans
Deutsche Industrien im Zeitgeschehen eines Jahrhunderts [Germany Industry over a Century]
1966 Gustav Fischer Verlag *Stuttgart, Germany*

This examines the growth of a range of major German firms over the 100 years up to 1960 and contrasts their experiences, in order to develop a model of the growth process.
Firms: BASF; Brown, Boveri & Cie AG; Daimler-Benz AG; Erba, Hoesch AG; MAN

1335
McGuffie, Chris
Working in Metal: Management & labour in the metal industries of Europe & the USA 1890–1914
1986 Merlin Press *London*

This book focuses on the industrial transformation of the metal industries in Britain, France, Germany and the USA around the turn of the century. It examines moves towards systematic management, changes in methods of work, industrial education, and the rise of professional management. A rare comparative study which contributes to the social history of work and the history of management, but which is sometimes superficial in its research and, in the tradition of the 'labour-process debate', tends to over-emphasize the role of deskilling and the technical fragmentation of work.

1336
Musson, A. E.
Joseph Whitworth and the Growth of Mass-Production Engineering
For main entry, see 4284

1337
Nerheim, Gunnar
Growth Through Welding: Perspectives on the history of a Norwegian welding firm–Norgas AS, 1908–1983
1983 Universitetsforlaget *Oslo, Norway*

This book explores the development of the welding industry in Norway, and particularly the development of Norgas AS. Major themes are the breakthrough in welding production methods in the 1930s, the transfer of new American welding techniques after the Second World War, and the company's subsequent expansion in step with the metalworking industries.
Firms: Norgas AS; Norsk Aktieselskab Gasaccumulator (NAG); Norsk Surstof et Vandstoffabrik AS (NSV)

1338
Pierenkemper, Toni
Entrepreneurs in Heavy Industry: Upper Silesia and the Westphalian Ruhr region, 1852–1913
For main entry, see 3798

1339
Tolliday, Steven; Zeitlin, Jonathan (Editors)
The Power to Manage?: Employers and industrial relations in comparative-historical perspective
For main entry, see 4241

1340
Torres, Félix (Editor)
Une histoire pour l'avenir: Merlin-Gérin 1920–1992 [A History for the Future: Merlin-Gérin 1920–1992]
1992 AlbinMichel *Paris, France*

Torres describes the history of this large, initially regional mechanical and electronic company.

Firms: Merlin-Gérin

Mechanical Engineering

1341
Blaich, Fritz
Amerikanische Firmen in Deutschland, 1890–1918: US-Direktinvestitionen im deutschen Maschinenbau [American Companies in Germany 1890–1918: US direct investment in the German engineering industry]
1984 F. Steiner *Wiesbaden, Germany*

A scholarly examination of US direct investment in the German machinery industry during the period of Kaiser Wilhelm II. Examines the direct investments of US firms in the machine-tool, sewing machine, office machinery, leather and textile machinery, and agricultural machinery industries. Discusses the effects of these investments on the development of German industries within the context of the political debate over the fear of American trusts.

1342
Broehl, Wayne G. Jr
Precision Valley: The machine tool companies of Springfield, Vermont: Jones and Lamson Machine Company, Fellows Gear Shaper Company, [and] Bryant Chucking Grinder Company
1959 Arno Press *New York, NY*

A study of three machine tool firms in Springfield, Vermont: two of which were spin-offs from Jones and Lamson. Rather narrowly focused on the internal history of the firms, but based on archives and carries the story to 1957.

Firms: Bryant Chucking Grinder Co.; Fellows Gear Shaper Co.; Jones & Lamson

1343
Cantrell, J. A.
James Nasmyth and the Bridgewater Foundry: A study of entrepreneurship in the early engineering industry
1985 Manchester University Press *Manchester*

Solidly based on archives, this book charts the rapid growth of an innovative capital goods manufacturer in mid-nineteenth century Britain. Technical innovation in steam-driven machine tools was matched by financial acumen and marketing flair. Cantrell argues that Nasmyth played an important but neglected role in the development of standardization and interchangeability.

Firms: Bridgewater Foundry

1344
Carstensen, Fred V.
American Enterprise in Foreign Markets: Singer and International Harvester in Imperial Russia
1984 University of North Carolina Press *Chapel Hill, NC*

Based on the Singer and International Harvester archives, this study examines the two largest foreign multinational exterprises in Russia before 1914. Both firms built big factories in Russia and came to depend heavily on the Russian market for sales growth. The business history of the firms is told within the context of the changing Russian political and economic structures of the period utilizing Russian language sources.

Firms: International Harvester; Singer

1345
Church, R. A.
Kenricks in Hardware: A family business 1791–1966
1969 David & Charles *Newton Abbot*

This book describes the vicissitudes of a family-controlled business, how it adapted to changing markets in the twentieth century and

how it introduced professional managers. Regarded as a worthy exception to the customary obsession of business historians with large-scale enterprise.
Firms: Archibald Kenrick & Sons

1346
Coe, W. E.
The Engineering Industry of the North of Ireland
1967 David & Charles *Newton Abbot*
This examines the various strands of the Northern Irish engineering industry within its wider context as it evolved through textile machine making, marine engineering and vehicle construction. The history of well known firms is interwoven into the analysis which illustrates industrial relations, management and industrial organisation.
Firms: Harland & Wolff; Short Bros; Workman Clark

1347
Dane, E. Surrey
Peter Stubs and the Lancashire Hand Tool Industry
1973 Sherratt *Altrincham*
This provides much detail on commercial practices, distribution and settlement before 1840 for a business which straddled the transition from cottage industry to factory manufacture.
Firms: Peter Stubs

1348
Davenport-Hines, Richard P. T.
Dudley Docker: The life and times of a trade warrior
1984 Cambridge University Press *Cambridge*
A well-controlled business biography of an ambitious and eclectic industrialist, financier, political dabbler and newspaper proprietor whose influence on the merger movement is legendary. While set in the context of Britain's relative decline after 1890, the author fails to identify the connection between his subject and economic failure.
Firms: BSA; British Westinghouse; Daimler Motor Car Co.; Metropolitan Carriage & Finance Co.; Metropolitan-Vickers Electrical Co.; Vickers

1349
Davies, Robert Bruce
Peacefully Working to Conquer the World: Singer sewing machines in foreign markets, 1854–1920
1976 Arno Press *New York, NY*
A reprint of an important Ph.D. thesis which considers Singer's formation, early development and the establishment of a worldwide sales and marketing organization, and the company's pioneer role in the development of mass marketing.
Firms: Singer

1350
Dick, Rolf
Die Arbeitsteilung zwischen Industrie- und Entwicklungsländern im Maschinenbau [Mechanical Engineering in Industrialized and Less-Developed Countries]
1981 J. C. B. Mohr (Paul Siebeck) *Tübingen, Germany*
An economic study of the determinants of the competitive position of the machinery industry in the industralized countries *vis-à-vis* less-developed countries. The primary goal of the study is to come to conclusions regarding future locational determinants for the industry. The central focus is on West German industry in the 1970s, although comparative data (notably statistical) is included for the USA, Sweden and less developed countries.

1351
DiFilippo, Anthony
Military Spending and Industrial Decline: A study of the American machine tool industry
1986 Greenwood Press *New York, NY*
DiFilippo argues that sustained high levels of military expenditure have been detrimental to the US machine-tool industry. Contains a brief history of the industry in the twentieth century and focuses in depth on structure and developments between 1958 and 1982. Strong on trade, industry structure, and technology this book provides important information on government–industry relations, though many readers may not swallow the whole of its argument.

1352
Dummett, G. A.
From Little Acorns: A history of the A.P.V. Company Limited
1981 Hutchinson Benham *London*

This is a wide-ranging history of one of Britain's major brewery equipment manufacturers, APV. Founded by Richard Seligman, the firm led the way in several technical developments, ranging from the heat exchanger of 1923 to the continuous-flow methods and giant fermenting vessels of the 1960s and 1970s.
Firms: A.P.V. Co.

1353
Eibert, Georg
Unternehmenspolitik Nürnberger Maschinenbauer 1835–1914 [Engineering in Nurenberg 1835–1914]
1979 Klett-Cotta *Stuttgart, Germany*

This book describes the history of the mechanical engineering firms in the Nurenberg region. It is strongly archivally based. See also Jacob-Wendler and Kabisch for other aspects of the firms' development outside Germany.
Firms: Klett; MAN; Spaeth; Sigmund Schuckert

1354
Floud, Roderick
The British Machine Tool Industry, 1850–1914
1976 Cambridge University Press *Cambridge*

A computerized econometric analysis of the business records of Greenwood & Batley of Leeds, this study is more interested in company performance, evaluated from the viewpoint of the rational economist, than in the business dilemmas facing generations of managers. Evidence of mismanagement at the end of the nineteenth century emerges from this rigorous quantitative approach.

1355
Fritz, Martin; Gårdlund, Torsten
Ett världsföretag växer fram: Alfa-Laval 100 år [The Growth of a Multinational Company: Alfa-Laval]
1983 EFI, Alfa-Laval AB *Stockholm, Sweden*

An extensive history of one of Sweden's earliest and largest multinationals, during most of its existence the world market leader in separators and heat exchangers for fluids, and suppliers of complete systems and processes within those fields. The importance of market pull versus technical push and R&D for the company's growth is thoroughly discussed. There is a statistical appendix of 150 pages.
Firms: Alfa-Laval; Bergedorfer Eisenwerk AG; DeLaval Separator Co.; Monza (Italy); STAL Refrigeration; Titan (Denmark); Vulcan-Laval (India); AB Separator

1356
Hofmann, Hannes
Die Anfange der Maschinenindustrie in der deutschen Schweiz 1800–1875 [The Origins of the Mechanical Engineering Industry in German Switzerland 1800–1875]
1962 Fretz und Wasmuth Verlag *Zurich, Switzerland*

The only authoritative study of the growth of the machinery industry in Switzerland (with special emphasis on textile machinery). Based on company archives, the work studies product innovation, the organization of production and the structures of the Swiss metal and machinery industry.

1357
Holland, Max
When the Machine Stopped: A cautionary tale from industrial America
1989 Harvard Business School Press *Cambridge, MA*

A fascinating inside story of the development, success and crisis of Burg Tools, later the Burgmaster Division of Houdaille Industries, and the pressures and problems of international competition. An insightful and well-written post mortem.
Firms: Burg Tools; Houdaille Industries

1358
Hume, John R.; Moss, Michael S.
Beardmore: The history of a Scottish industrial giant
1979 Heinemann *London*

A detailed company history based on company, government and bank archives which is also beautifully produced and illustrated. Very strong on industry structure and product and technical developments, and equally at home in

the financial affairs of the company, this is an unusually well-balanced company history.
Firms: Beardmore

1359
Joest, Hans-Josef
Pionier im Ruhrgebiet: Gutehoffnungshütte: Vom altesten Montan-Unternehmen Deutschlands zum grössten Maschinenbaukonzern Europas [Gutehoffnungshütte; A Pioneer in the Ruhr]
1982 Seewald *Stuttgart, Germany*

This company history recounts the development of this firm from the oldest iron and steel producer to a vertically integrated concern, and after 1945, following decontrol, to the largest machine tool producer in Europe. The author provides a vivid picture of the economic and social conditions within the firm as well as within the region.
Firms: Gutehoffnungshütte AG; Maschinenfabrik Augsburg Nürnberg AG

1360
Jones, Edgar
Guest, Keen & Nettlefolds: vol. 1: Innovation and Enterprise 1759–1918; vol. 2: The Growth of a Business 1918–45
1987–90 Macmillan *London*

The official company history based on full access to company archives. Describes the rise of the company from a small partnership in Dowlais to one of the world's largest manufacturing groups. Particularly strong on the entrepreneurs who led the company, on the woodscrew monopoly in the nineteenth century, and on the early ironmaking industry. But it is weaker and often apologetic on labour and social issues. The book is impressively produced and profusely illustrated, often in colour.
Firms: Dowlais Iron Co.; Guest, Keen & Nettlefolds; Lysaght, John & Co.; Patent Nut & Bolt Co.; Birmingham Screw Co.; Nettlefolds

1361
Kampmann, Tobias
Vom Werkzeughandel zum Maschinenbau: Der Aufstieg des Familienunternehmens W. Ferd. Klingelnberg Söhne 1900–1950 [From Toolmaking to Mechanical Engineering: The rise of the Klingelnberg family business]
1994 Zeitschrift fur Unternehmensgeschichte, Beiheft 82 *Stuttgart, Germany*

This is a rare case study of a medium-sized engineering company: W. Ferd. Klingelnberg, a family firm which developed into an important company of this branch of industry. Initially, its trade in tools was expanded before Klingelnberg integrated into the production of tools and machinery. Kampmann attributes the company's success largely to Adolf Klingelnberg, who ran the company for most of the time under review and whom he describes as a prototypical Schumpeterian entrepreneur. Although this study is highly valuable because it offers insights into one of the most important branches of German industry as well as in its predominant type of enterprise, a more comparative approach would have further enhanced its value.
Firms: W. Ferd. Klingelnberg Söhne

1362
Kaysen, Carl
United States v. United Shoe Machinery Corporation: An economic analysis of an anti-trust case
1956 Harvard University Press *Cambridge, MA*

The documentation of the 1952–4 antitrust case provides the basis for this scholarly examination of the structure, competition and performance of the industry, written by the Clerk to the investigation who went on to become an academic. There is also much insight into the antitrust process and its limitations.
Firms: United Shoe Machinery Corporation

1363
Lifshey, Earl
The Housewares Story: A history of the American housewares industry
1973 National Housewares Manufacturers Association *Chicago, IL*

A valuable summary of the history of the development of a wide variety of household technologies, from pots and pans to baths and brooms, from gadgets to electrics to plastics. The book pulls together much diverse information. Though concerned mainly with technology and products, it contains invaluable detail on many small or transient firms. Profusely illustrated.

1364

Lloyd, Ian

Rolls-Royce: Vol. I The growth of a firm; Vol. II The years of endeavour; Vol. III The Merlin at war

1978 Macmillan *London*

Lloyd describes the transition of Rolls-Royce from prestige car maker to manufacturer of aero engines, particularly for military use. He highlights the concomitant shift from handicraft production triggered by increasingly cost-sensitive markets to comprehensive militarization of aero-engine production during the Second World War.

Firms: Rolls-Royce

1365

Mahan, Ernest

The History of McNally Pittsburg

1972 McCormick-Armstrong Co. *Wichita, KS*

This business history describes the largest builder of coal preparation plants in the western hemisphere from its inception in 1906, focusing on the company's diversification strategy at home and abroad.

Firms: McNally Pittsburgh Manufacturing Co.

1366

Marburg, Theodore F.

Small Business in Brass Manufacturing: The Smith & Griggs Co. of Waterbury

1956 New York University Press *New York, NY*

This provides a valuable study of a small brass-fabricating business whose hard driving entrepreneurs carved out niches in speciality products, pioneered new production technologies and developed close relations with wholesalers during the firm's period of greatest prosperity between 1865 and 1908. The erosion of those factors led to decline and failure by 1936.

Firms: Smith & Griggs Co.

1367

Moss, M. S.; Hume, J. R.

Workshop of the British Empire: Engineering and Shipbuilding in the West of Scotland

1977 Heinemann *London*

Focusing on the period from the 1850s to 1914, the authors stress the technical and productive resilience of the west of Scotland engineering and shipbuilding industries in face of foreign competition. This is both an essay in economic history and a detailed photographic exploration of technology and work organization in the factories and shipyards, stressing the diversity of the industrial base. The book is based on the authors' work for the Western Survey of the National Register of Archives, Scotland.

Firms: Andrew Barclay & Sons; Fairfield Shipbuilding and Engineering Co.; John Brown

1368

Pelet, Paul-Louis

Les Usines Metallurgiques de Vallorbe, 1899–1974: Tradition et technique de pointe [Metal Manufacture in Vallorbe, 1899–1974: Tradition and advanced technology]

1974 Impr. Réunies *Lausanne, Switzerland*

A case study of file manufacture in the industrial complex of the Swiss Jura, with particular emphasis on technical linkages.

Firms: Usines metallurgiques de Vallorbe

1369

Plumpe, Gottfried

Die württembergische Eisenindustrie im 19 Jahrhundert: Eine Fallstudie zur industriellen Revolution in Deutschland [The Württemberg Iron Industry in the 19th Century]

1982 Steiner *Wiesbaden, Germany*

A detailed analysis of technological development in the southern German machine tool industry. It tries to place the development into the wider context of German industrialization. An important though flawed work.

1370

Reader, W. J.

Metal Box: A history

1976 Heinemann *London*

This is not his best work, perhaps, but it remains an authoritative outline history of a major British manufacturing enterprise with a dominant hold on the tin container sector.

Firms: Barclay & Fry; Metal Box & Printing

Industries (Metal Box Co); Continental Can Co.; Hudson Scott & Sons

1371
Reader, W. J.
Architect of Air Power: The life of the first Viscount Weir of Eastwood 1877–1959
1968 Collins *London*

This presents a biography of one of Scotland's foremost industrial figures of the twentieth century. Weir rose to national prominence during the First World War and was partly responsible for the continuing independence of the Royal Air Force. From his business base in the Scottish heavy industry complex Weir played an active role as a government adviser, notably over efforts to reorganize the steel industry and particularly over the rearmament programme of the 1930s.
Firms: Weir Group; Bristol Aeroplane Co.; Blackburn Aeroplane Co.; Colvilles

1372
Reader, W. J.
The Weir Group: A centenary history
1971 Weidenfeld & Nicolson *London*

A workmanlike centenary history of the Group 1870–1970. Not one of Reader's best, but still a careful and balanced account of the company from archival sources.
Firms: Weir Group

1373
Roll, Eric
An Early Experiment in Industrial Organisation: Being a history of the firm of Boulton & Watt
1968 Frank Cass *London*

This early and brilliant industrial history analyses such features of Boulton and Watt's business as the organization of the work process, the accounting procedures, and the licensing and patenting of engines. The multifarious activities of Boulton and Watt are neatly integrated within a discussion of the commercial and technical environment.
Firms: Boulton & Watt

1374
Roth, Matthew W.
Platt Brothers and Company: Small business in American manufacturing
1994 University Press of New England
Hanover, NH

Like Blackford (qv), Roth examines the role of a smaller firm in the American business world. Happy to remain a small niche supplier of speciality brass and zinc items, Platt Brothers survived over five generations where other more entrepreneurial firms failed. Studies such as this will encourage a reassessment of the role of smaller firms to counterbalance the general emphasis on the business giants.
Firms: Platt Brothers

1375
Siegrist, Hannes
Vom Familienbetrieb zum Managerunternehmen: Angestellte und industrielle Organisation am Beispiel der Georg Fischer AG in Schaffhausen (1797–1930) [From Family Firm to Corporate Enterprise: Georg Fischer AG 1797–1930]
1981 Vandenhoeck & Ruprecht *Göttingen, Germany*

The study presents a history of Georg Fischer AG at Schaffhausen from its inception and explores the development from a small factory at the beginning of the period of industrialization in Switzerland to a modern corporate enterprise. It offers a social history of the management (human capital building, salaries, organizations).
Firms: Georg Fischer AG

1376
Taber, Martha
A History of the Cutlery Industry in the Connecticut Valley
1955 Smith College *Northampton, MA*

A scholarly collective biography of the group of small firms that dominated America's leading cutlery region from the 1830s to the Second World War.

1377
Tann, Jennifer (Editor)
The Selected Papers of Boulton & Watt: Vol 1–The engine partnership 1775–1825
1981 Diploma *London*

A small and carefully chosen sample (213 documents from a total of many thousands) of letters between Boulton & Watt and their customers. The content of the correspondence, which is placed within an explanatory framework, indicates the complex organization of the business, and illustrates the prolonged process of perfecting the steam engine.
Firms: Boulton & Watt

1378
Usher, Abbot P.
A History of Mechanical Inventions
For main entry, see 4304

1379
Vetterli, Rudolf
Industriearbeit Arbeiterbewusstsein und gewerkschaftliche Organisation: Dargestellt am Beispiel der Georg Fischer AG (1890–1930) [Production, Workers and Workplace Organization Georg Fischer AG, 1890–1930]
For main entry, see 4243

1380
Wagoner, Carless D.
The US Machine Tool Industry from 1900 to 1950
1968 MIT Press *Cambridge, MA*

A thorough analysis of the development of the industry by an industrial economist, with particular stress on location, business cycles and managerial problems, and the industry's readiness and response to the Second World War.

1381
Wilson, Charles; Reader, W. J.
Men and Machines: A history of D. Napier and Son Engineers, Ltd. 1808–1958
1958 Weidenfeld *London*

An examination of 150 years of the Napier dynasty's business activities, within the context of the dynamic engineering industry. It emphasizes the context of the continuity of craft, as the company shifted production from printing presses to automobiles and aeroplanes and to mid-twentieth-century instruments of destruction.
Firms: Napier

1382
Wohlert, Klaus
Framvaxten av svenska multinationella foretag [The Emergence of Swedish Multinational Corporations]
1981 Almqvist and Wiksell International *Uppsala, Sweden*

A case-study of Alfa-Laval and the Swedish separator industry, 1876–1914, against the background of theories of direct foreign investment. Analyses the prerequisites for, and causes of, internationalization. There is an English summary.
Firms: AB Separator; Alfa-Laval; Bergedorfer Eisenwerk AG; DeLaval Separator Co.; Svenska Centrifug

1383
Yoshida, Michio
Sengo Nihon Kosaku Kikai Kogyo no Kozo Bunseki [The Structural Analysis of the Japanese Machine Tool Industry in the Post-Post-War Period]
1986 Miraisha *Tokyo, Japan*

Yoshida describes the development and characteristics of the Japanese machine tool industry in the post-war period with special emphasis on comparisons with the United States and Europe.

Agricultural Engineering

1384
Broehl, Wayne G. Jr
John Deere's Company: A history of Deere & Company and its times.
1984 Doubleday *New York, NY*

A massive narrative based on company records by a leading American business historian. The emphasis is on entrepreneurial and managerial activities.
Firms: John Deere

1385
Carstensen, Fred V.
American Enterprise in Foreign Markets: Singer and International Harvester in Imperial Russia
For main entry, see 1344

1386
Cook, Peter
Massey at the Brink: The story of Canada's greatest multinational and its struggle to survive.
1981 Collins *Toronto, Canada*

A readable and well-researched study with much insider insight into the rise and crisis of the Canadian agricultural machinery giant.
Firms: Massey-Ferguson

1387
Grace, D. R.; Phillips, D. C.
Ransome's of Ipswich: A history of the firm and a guide to its records
1975 University of Reading *Reading*

An excellent introductory outline of the firm's development, stressing the company's marketing flexibility and product diversification, followed by a succinct guide to the best surviving records of a British agricultural engineering firm. The book is well illustrated.
Firms: Ransome's

1388
Hutchinson, William T.
Cyrus Hall McCormick: vol. 1 Seed-Time 1809–1856; vol. 2 Harvest, 1856–1884
1968 Da Capo Press *New York, NY*

A monumental study (1200 pages) of the founder of McCormick-International Harvester, based on company records and personal correspondence, which covers his technical innovations and developments in harvest machinery, and also his role in religious, political and philanthropic affairs.
Firms: International Harvester; McCormick-International Harvester

1389
Kuuse, Jan
Interaction Between Agriculture and Industry: Studies of farm mechanisation and industrialisation in Sweden and the United States 1830–1930
1974 Universitet, Economisk-historiska *Gothenburg, Sweden*

Starting from the demand side and usage patterns, this book contains much valuable business history on both large and small agricultural machinery firms in Sweden and the USA (especially data on technology, finance, output and international marketing). Scholarly and valuable.
Firms: AB Separator; Broderna Anderssons; International Harvester; Lilla Harrie; McCormick-International Harvester; Mekaniska Verkstad

1390
Marsh, Barbara
A Corporate Tragedy: The agony of International Harvester Company
1985 Doubleday *Garden City, NY*

A well-written narrative of crisis at International Harvester which emphasizes managerial problems and labour conflict.
Firms: International Harvester

1391
Neufeld, Edward P.
A Global Corporation: A history of the international development of Massey-Ferguson Limited
1969 University of Toronto Press *Toronto, Canada*

A scholarly, analytical history of Massey (with financial and production data that Cook (qv) lacks) dealing with the company's strategy and evolution, with especial attention to the changing international environment. It concentrates on the post-Second World War period, mergers, managerial reorganization and internationalization and uses much internal documentation.
Firms: Massey-Ferguson

1392
Ozanne, Robert W.
A Century of Labor-Management Relations at McCormick and International Harvester
1967 University of Wisconsin Press *Madison, WI*

A uniquely detailed account of a century of

labour-management relations, based on company archives that detail managerial deliberations on these issues, together with analysis of a remarkably complete set of payroll records. An important work.
Firms: International Harvester; McCormick

1393
Ozanne, Robert W.
Wages in Practice and Theory: McCormick and International Harvester 1860–1960
1968 University of Wisconsin Press *Madison, WI*

A study linked to Ozanne's 1967 work which analyses wage determination on the basis of International Harvester's payroll records.
Firms: International Harvester; McCormick

1394
Peterson, Walter F.; Weber, C. Andrew
An Industrial Heritage: Allis-Chalmers Corporation
1976 Milwaukee County Historical Society *Milwaukee, WI*

A substantial company history, narrowly focused, but strong on technology, management and mergers. It carries the story to the 1970s. Well illustrated.
Firms: Allis Chalmers

1395
Wik, Reynold M.
Steam Power on the American Farm
1950 University of Pennsylvania Press *Philadelphia, PA*

An important scholarly study of early agricultural machinery technology and the companies involved. It studies innovation, manufacture, distribution and industrial structure and the benefits of agricultural machinery to the farm sector.
Firms: Case Company; Frick Co.; Geiser Co.; Huber Manufacturing Co.; Nichols & Shepard Co.

Textile Engineering

1396
Catling, Harold
The Spinning Mule
For main entry, see 1127

1397
Gibb, George Sweet
The Saco-Lowell Shops: Textile machinery building in New England, 1813–1949
1950 Harvard University Press *Cambridge, MA*

A massively thorough academic history of the USA's leading textile machinery maker based on free access to the firm's records. Taking the boardroom perspective, and as much interest in technical change as in entrepreneurial and corporate issues, the study includes an analysis of its rescue from near-failure in the 1920s.
Firms: Lowell Machine Shop; Otis Pettee & Co.; Saco Water Power Machine Shop; Saco-Lowell Shops

1398
Hills, Richard L.
Power in the Industrial Revolution
1970 Manchester University Press *Manchester*

An archive-based study of the great inventions in the English cotton industry from that of Wyatt (1733) to that of Crompton (1779), supplemented by a study of horse power, water wheels and steam engines. Written by the founder of the Manchester Museum of Science and Industry.
Firms: Boulton & Watt; Richard Arkwright

1399
Honeyman, Katrina; Goodman, Jordan
Technology and Enterprise: Isaac Holden and the mechanisation of woolcombing in France 1848–1914
1986 Scolar Press *Aldershot*

This book traces the innovative and entrepreneurial activities of Isaac Holden, inventor of one of several competing woolcombing technologies of the mid-nineteenth century. It considers the dynamic role of the patent in technical change and identifies the impact of

invention on the growth of larger scale enterprise and concentration of production.
Firms: Holden; Lister & Holden

1400
Jeremy, David J.
Transatlantic Industrial Revolution: The diffusion of textile technologies between Britain and America 1790–1830s
For main entry, see 4270

1401
Navin, Thomas R.
The Whitin Machine Works since 1831
1950 Harvard University Press *Cambridge, MA*
A carefully-researched company history of a major American textile machinery maker distinguished by its long survival as a family firm. Adopting a boardroom view, this study is as much concerned with technological change as with corporate affairs.
Firms: Whitin Machine Works

1402
Rose, Mary B. (Editor)
International Competition and Strategic Response in the Textile Industries since 1870
For main entry, see 1155

Ordnance/Weapons Engineering

1403
Adams, Gordon
The Politics of Defense Contracting: The iron triangle
1981 Transaction Books, Council on Economics Priorities *New Brunswick, NJ*
A valuable sourcebook on defence contracting and business–government relations in the USA, looking at the political power of the defence industry through case studies of procurement in eight firms in the 1970s.
Firms: Boeing; General Dynamics; Grumman; Lockheed; McDonnell-Douglas; Northrop; Rockwell International; United Technologies

1404
Bradley, Joseph
Guns for the Tsar: American technology and the small arms industry in 19th century Russia
1990 Northern Illinois University Press *De Kalb, IL*
A study of the transfer of US technology to Russia in arms and machine tools, especially looking at management, technology and relations with the state. Serious and detailed.
Firms: Colt Patent Firearms Manufacturing Co.

1405
Davenport-Hines, Richard P. T.
Dudley Docker: The life and times of a trade warrior.
For main entry, see 1348

1406
Evans, Harold
Vickers: Against the odds 1956–1977
1978 Hodder & Stoughton *London*
Evans uses company sources to extend Scott's history (qv) in a more popular and accessible fashion. This book is especially strong on business-government relations and diversification.
Firms: Vickers

1407
Kolodziedj, Edward A.
Making and Marketing Arms: The French experience and its implications for the international system
1987 Princeton University Press *Princeton, NJ*
A heavyweight study of the French military-industrial complex, investigating the centrality of military production in the French system. While its main focus is on politics and the state, it is also a book on the structure and operation of the arms industry itself.
Firms: Dassault Corporation; Matra Corporation; Thomson

1408
Lotchin, Roger W.
Fortress California, 1910–1961: From warfare to welfare
1992 Oxford University Press *Oxford*
An important study of relations between the defence industry and urban development in

California. A regional study of the military-industrial complex including the Los Angeles aircraft industry and the San Francisco and San Diego naval-linked industries, and their links to the universities.
Firms: Boeing; Douglas Aircraft Co.; Lockheed

1409
Rosenberg, Nathan (Editor)
The American System of Manufactures: The report of the committee on the machinery of the United States, 1855; and the special reports of George Wallis and Joseph Whitworth, 1854
For main entry, see 4293

1410
Sampson, Anthony
The Arms Bazaar
3rd Edition
1988 Hodder & Stoughton *London*

Vivid coverage of personalities and politics in the international arms industry from the nineteenth century to Irangate. The book contains many insights.
Firms: Krupp; Lockheed; Northrop; Vickers

1411
Samuels, Richard J.
'Rich Nation, Strong Army': National security and the technological transformation of Japan
For main entry, see 1109

1412
Scott, John D.
Vickers: A history
For main entry, see 706

1413
Smith, Merritt Roe
Harper's Ferry Armory and the New Technology: The challenge of change
1977 Cornell University Press *Ithaca, NY*

Smith's book focuses on the day-to-day operations of the US armoury at Harper's Ferry, Virginia, from 1798 to 1861, to show what the introduction of mechanized production meant in terms of organization, management and worker morale. It is strong on conflicts between the craft tradition and mechanization and on the social and political context of management decision-making. Of particular importance is a sustained comparison with the national armoury at Springfield, Massachusetts which led to the adoption of mechanized methods. Smith shows that the new technology flowed from north to south only, and that the local culture of the Virginia factory was a formidable barrier to the adoption of new technology. Elegantly written and thoroughly researched, this is an important study of much more than local interest. To be read with Hounshell (qv).

1414
Smith, Merritt Roe
Military Enterprise and Technological Change: Perspectives on the American experience
1985 MIT Press *Cambridge, MA*

A collection of specialized chapters dealing with military R&D, technology, and mass production in the United States. There is a useful piece on the Corps of Engineers and modern management in the 19th century, and diverting chapters on Ford's ill-fated attempt to mass-produce Eagle boats in the First World War, and the development of transistor technology by the Army Signal Corps after the Second World War.
Firms: Bell Telephone; Ford Motor Co.

1415
Sumida, Jon Tetsuro
In Defence of Naval Supremacy: Finance, technology and British naval policy, 1889–1914
1989 Routledge *London*

Though primarily a study of policy and strategy, this book provides much information on naval procurement and the armaments industry, drawing on the papers of Arthur Hungerford Pollen who was a managing director of two companies, Linotype and Machinery Ltd. and Argo, which developed the instruments for a new naval gunnery system. Sumida places the companies and their technology in the context of long-run developments in naval technology and the financial constraints of procurement.
Firms: Linotype and Machinery; Argo

1416
Trebilcock, Clive
The Vickers Brothers: Armaments and enterprise, 1854–1914
For main entry, see 709

1417
Williamson, Harold F.
Winchester, the Gun that Won the West
1952 Combat Forces Press *Washington, DC*

A fine, neglected study of the firearms industry from the 1850s to the 1930s, focusing on Winchester. It has much detail on marketing, competition, finance, technology and business–government relations. Well illustrated.
Firms: Colt; Winchester

1418
Young, Gordon
The Fall and Rise of Alfred Krupp
For main entry, see 711

Electrical & Computers, Computer Predecessors & General

1419
Aspray, William (Editor)
Computing Before Computers
1990 Iowa State University Press *Ames, IA*

This is a useful companion to Williams (qv), on the history of computing technology.

1420
Austrian, Geoffrey D.
Herman Hollerith: Forgotten Giant of information processing
1982 Columbia University Press *New York, NY*

A serious business biography dealing with entrepreneurship and innovation in the punch-card tabulating machine industry by the founder of a predecessor company of IBM.
Firms: Hollerith; IBM

1421
Borrus, Michael G.
Competing for Control: America's stake in microelectronics
1988 Ballinger *Cambridge, MA*

A valuable survey of US electronics in an international context in the 1970s and 1980s. It is especially strong on the military and government role in US industry and on Japanese and European competition. Borrus argues that government policy and industry structure are the keys to competitive advantage. Clear and theoretically informed.

1422
Braun, Ernest; MacDonald, Stuart
Revolution in Miniature: The history and impact of semiconductor electronics
1982 Cambridge University Press *Cambridge*

The evolution of semiconductors and the microprocessor chip was a prelude to the emergence of the personal computer, and Silicon Valley became the cultural centre for these developments in the USA. This is an excellent and well-balanced study by two academics, which prepares the ground for other serious studies of the computer industry.
Firms: Intel; Motorola

1423
Cortada, James W.
A Bibliographic Guide to the History of Computing, Computers and the Information Processing Industry
1990 Greenwood Press *New York, NY*

An indispensible bibliography on information technology, which includes many entries on the office machinery and computer industries. The huge selection of entries is occasionally eclectic and annotations are uneven.

1424
Crandall, Richard L.; Robins, Sam
The Incorruptible Cashier: Vol. 1: The formation of an industry 1876–1890
1988 Vestal Press *Vestal, NY*

This profusely illustrated history of the early US cash register industry–aimed at collectors–contains significant reprints of early company documents and important technical information.

1425
Darby, Edwin
It All Adds Up
1968 Victor Comptometer Corp.

This is a typical example of the many company histories produced in-house, in this case by the Victor Comptometer Corp.
Firms: Comptometer Corp.; Victor Adding Machines Corp.; Victor Comptometer

1426
Dorlay, John S.
The Roneo Story
1978 Roneo Vickers *Croydon*

A straightforward commissioned company history, which celebrates the firm's centenary. The book is an essential source on a little-researched sector. It is excellent on products and marketing but contains little on finance and strategy. Profusely illustrated.
Firms: Roneo

1427
Dosi, Giovanni
Technical Change and Industrial Transformation: The theory and an application to the semiconductor industry
For main entry, see 4255

1428
Ende, Jan van den
Knopen, kaärten en chips
1991 Uitgave Centraale Bureau voor Statistick *Voorburg/Heerlen, The Netherlands*

This general history of computing places a special emphasis on Dutch computing.
Firms: PTT Netherlands; Philips

1429
Flamm, Kenneth
Targetting the Computer
1987 Brookings Institution *Washington, DC*

An excellent international comparison of the impact of government support for the computer industries in the USA, Japan and Europe.

1430
Flamm, Kenneth
Creating the Computer
1988 Brookings Institution *Washington, DC*

An excellent account of the origins (especially the military origins) of the computer, and the interactions between government and the computer industry in the USA, Europe and Japan.

1431
Hyman, Anthony
Charles Babbage: Pioneer of the computer
1984 Oxford University Press *Oxford*

National philosopher and polymath, Babbage (1791–1871) conceived and built punched-card controlled mechanical computers, stimulated the production of precision machine tools and commended improved factory layout (ie operational research). The disregard of his practical science-based research is symptomatic of much criticism of British industry.

1432
Ichbiah, D.; Knepper, S. L.
The Making of Microsoft: How Bill Gates and his team created the world's most successful software
1991 Prima Publishing *Rocklin, CA*

A detailed account of the development of Microsoft from a start-up company serving the hobbyist market into an international software producer, and of its intriguing involvement with IBM. Probably the best journalistic account of the rise of Miscrosoft and the personal-computer software industry.
Firms: Digital Research; IBM; Lotus; Microsoft

1433
Langlois, Richard N.; Pugel, Thomas A.; Haklisch, Carmela S.; Nelson, Richard R.; Eglehoff, William G.
Microelectronics: An industry in transition
1988 Unwin Hyman *London*

An important book on the global semiconductor industry. It concentrates on strategic dilemmas posed by the simultaneous need for innovation and large-scale mass production, arising from an industry that is both R&D and capital intensive. An essential starting point.
Firms: Fairchild; Fujitsu; Hitachi; IBM; Intel; Motorola; Philips; Siemens; Texas Instruments

1434
Leslie, Stuart W.
The Cold War and American Science: The military-industrial-academic complex at MIT and Stanford
For main entry, see 4278

1435
Linvill, John G.; La Mond, Annette M.; Wilson, Robert W.
The Competitive Status of the US Electronics Industry: A study of the influences of technology in determining international industrial competitive advantage
1984 National Academy Press *Washington, DC*

A valuable summary of the debate on competition in high technology industries by a government committee containing both leading academics and businesspeople. It focuses on barriers to international trade and covers semiconductors, computers, telecoms, and consumer electronics. It contains many valuable mini-sector case studies.

1436
Littman, Jonathan
Once Upon a Time in Computerland: The amazing billion dollar tale of Bill Millard's computerland empire
For main entry, see 2041

1437
Metropolis, N.; Howlett, J.; Rota, G-C. (Editors)
A History of Computing in the 20th Century
1980 Academic Press *New York, NY*

A valuable collection of essays drawing together recollections of academic and business participants in the development of the computer. Especially good on the academic/R&D interface.

1438
Morris, P. R.
A History of the World Semiconductor Industry
1990 Peregrinus/IEE *Hitchin*

This worldwide history of the semiconductor industry focuses on the evolution of the science and technology and the patterns of development in different national industries. Starting with detailed studies of the evolution of thermionic valve and transistor technologies, it also deals with the evolution of the major technical processes in the fabrication of semiconductor devices. At each stage it contrasts and compares developments in Japan, the USA, and Europe.
Firms: Bell Telephone Labs; Fairchild; Texas Instruments; Toshiba

1439
Okimoto, Daniel; Sugano, Takuo; Weinstein, Franklin B. (Editors)
Competitive Edge: The semiconductor industry in the US and Japan
1984 Stanford University Press *Stanford, CA*

The result of lengthy research by a multidisciplinary team of US and Japanese scholars the book analyses the strengths and weaknesses of each country's semiconductor industry in three areas: technological innovation, the role of the government, and the influence of financial institutions. It assesses the threat to US supremacy in one of its last bastions of industrial leadership.
Firms: Fairchild; Hitachi; Intel; Motorola; NEC; Texas Instruments

1440
Petzold, Hartmut
Rechnende Maschinen: Eine Historische Untersuchung ihrer Herstellung und Anwendung vom Kaiserreich bis zur Bundesrepublik [Calculating Machines: A historical study]
1985 VDI Verlag *Düsseldorf, Germany*

This long, detailed monograph focuses on technical development in the German calculating machine industry to c.1960.

1441
Proudfoot, William Bryce
The Origin of Stencil Duplicating
1972 Hutchinson *London*

An interesting study of developments in office technology centred around the Gestetner Co., with the focus on technology and products. Well illustrated. This book partly fills a major gap in the literature.
Firms: Gestetner

1442
Sciberras, Edmond
Multinational Electronics Companies and National Economic Policies
1977 JAI Press *Greenwich, CT*

A careful study of the economics of the electronics industry, focusing on the reasons for the

oligopolistic power of large firms, especially in terms of technology, business–government relations and industry structure. It contains many helpful short case studies of individual firms.
Firms: Fairchild; Ferranti; GEC; Hughes Aircraft; ITT; Motorola; Mullard; Philips; Plessey; RCA

1443
Todd, Daniel
The World Electronics Industry
1990 Routledge *London*

A global overview of the industry covering structural and geographical issues and the interlinkages between subsectors. It covers the civilian as well as the military sides of the industry. A valuable reference book.

1444
Wallace, James; Erickson, Jim
Hard Drive: Bill Gates and the making of the Microsoft empire
1992 Wiley *New York, NY*

This is a biography of Bill Gates, founder and chairman of Microsoft, now the dominant personal computer software producer in the world. It is based on an investigative series published by the *Seattle Post-Intelligencer*, and undertaken 'without the help and co-operation of Microsoft', though based on interviews with over 150 people associated with the company. Altogether this is a well-written, fascinating account, with plenty of anecdotal detail.
Firms: Apple; Digital Research; IBM; Microsoft

1445
Williams, Michael R.
A History of Computing Technology
1985 Prentice-Hall *Englewood Cliffs, NJ*

The best book on computer history–but contains little on business.

Electrical & Computers, UK

1446
Adamson, Ian; Kennedy, Richard
Sinclair and the Sunrise Technology: The deconstruction of a myth
1988 Penguin *Harmondsworth*

A fascinating and densely researched investigation by two journalists into the myths surrounding Sir Clive Sinclair and his role in the early British computer industry (the early development of the miniaturised low-cost computer). The book argues that his role was boosted by assiduous self-promotion and an uncritical press. Despite the incredible success of a handful of products the story is one of mismanagement and shortsighted business practices which resulted in products plagued by technical faults and poor customer service, both of which have much in common with British failures in other industries.
Firms: Sinclair Radionics

1447
Campbell-Kelly, Martin
ICL. A Business and Technical History: The official history of Britain's leading information systems company
1989 Clarendon Press *Oxford*

Based on full access to company archives, this study sheds new light on the British punched card industry and its oppressive transatlantic ties with IBM. It analyses the transition to the modern computer industry in the 1950s and the important role of government and merger policies in the subsequent evolution of the industry, leading to the formation of ICL in 1968. The book is particularly strong on the interaction of politics, technology and business strategy. The study also covers ICL's attempt to build a new range of computers which brought it close to crisis by the early 1980s.
Firms: British Tabulating Machine Co.; English Electric; IBM; ICL; Powers-Samas

1448
Hendry, John
Innovating for Failure: Government policy and the early British computer industry
1989 MIT Press *Cambridge, MA*

Hendry describes the attempt by the British National Research Development Corp. to foster a British computer industry in the 1950s. Written by a leading scholar of the subject.
Firms: EMI (Electric & Musical Industries); Elliott Brothers; English Electric; Ferranti; IBM; ICT (International Computers and Tabu-

lators); National Research Development Corp.; Powers-Samas; STC (Standard Telephones & Cables)

1449
Hodge, Michael
Multinational Corporations and National Governments: A case study of the UK's experience, 1964–1970
For main entry, see 3401

1450
Kelly, Tim
The British Computer Industry: Crisis and development
1987 Croom Helm *London*

This book analyses the structure of both hardware and software industries in Britain at the time of ICL's financial collapse in the early 1980s. It focuses on the history and geography of the industry, the evolution of the leading firms, new firm formation, trade patterns, and the role of the technology policies of successive governments.

Firms: Acorn Computers; Amstrad; Burroughs; Elliott Brothers; Honeywell; IBM; ICT (International Computers and Tabulators); STC International Computers

1451
Lavington, S. H.
Early British Computers
1980 Manchester University Press *Manchester*

A short, reliable and readable account of the development of the computer in Britain and the early computer industry.

Firms: Elliott Brothers; English Electric; Ferranti

1452
Oakley, Brian; Owen, Kenneth
Alvey: Britain's strategic computing initiative
1989 MIT Press *Cambridge, MA*

An account of Britain's attempt to revitalize its information-technology research base, written by the director of the programme (Oakley) and a leading science journalist (Owen).

1453
Thomas, David
Alan Sugar: The Amstrad story
For main entry, see 2062

Electrical & Computers, USA

1454
Angel, David P.
Restructuring for Innovation: The remaking of the US semiconductor industry
1994 Guilford Press *New York, NY*

During the 1980s, the United States rapidly lost its world leadership position in semiconductors to Japan. But starting in the late 1980s firms like Motorola and Texas Instruments led a remarkable recovery. Angel's study examines the strengths and structural weaknesses of the US industry and argues that a profound restructuring enabled the firms to break down old barriers between innovation and production. The book draws on detailed case studies and survey research.

Firms: Motorola; Texas Instruments; Fairchild Semiconductor

1455
Bashe, C. et. al.
IBM's Early Computers
1985 MIT Press *Cambridge, MA*

A very detailed and authoritative account of IBM's electro-mechanical punched-card machines and early computers, written as an internal IBM history project.

Firms: IBM

1456
Belden, Thomas G.; Belden, Marva R.
Lengthening Shadow: The life of Thomas J. Watson
1962 Little, Brown *Boston, MA*

An authorized biography of the founder of IBM by two journalists, which is still a valuable source for historians.

Firms: IBM

1457
Brock, G. W.
The US Computer Industry: A study of market power
1975 Ballinger *Cambridge, MA*

An important study of the development of the US industry, focusing on economies of scale, barriers to entry, and industry structure, using a Structure-Conduct-Performance framework.

1458
Carroll, Paul
Big Blues: The unmaking of IBM
1994 Weidenfeld & Nicolson *London*

An investigation of why IBM, so widely admired and seen as a model corporation in the 1980s, fell into crisis and enormous losses in the 1990s. A fine complement to Sobel (qv).

1459
Chposky, James; Leonsis, Ted
Blue Magic: The people, power and politics behind the IBM personal computer
1988 Facts on File *New York, NY*

A study of the introduction of the IBM personal computer and its subsequent impact on IBM. More concerned with personalities and politics than with technology, the book is nevertheless a well-written example of the genre, drawing on a wide range of interviews.
Firms: Apple; IBM; Microsoft

1460
Connolly, J.
A History of Computing in Europe
1967 IBM World Trade Corp. *New York, NY*

An uninspiring account of IBM's European operations, rumoured to have been suppressed by the company. Withdrawn by IBM, there are only a few bootlegged copies of this book around. It contains some interesting tidbits not available elsewhere, but otherwise is disappointing and unreliable.
Firms: IBM

1461
Cortada, James W.
Before the Computer: IBM, NCR, Burroughs and Remington Rand and the industry they created 1865–1956
1993 Princeton University Press *Princeton, NJ*

A study of the US data processing industry from its inception down to the period when the computer became its primary tool. A well-researched and well-written account of the industry as a whole.
Firms: Burroughs; IBM; NCR; Remington Rand

1462
Cortada, James W.
The Computer in the United States: From laboratory to market, 1930–1960
1993 M. E. Sharpe *Armonk, NY*

This is a straightforward account of the development and commercialization of computer technology.

1463
Dassbach, Carl
Global Enterprises and the World Economy: Ford, General Motors, and IBM, the emergence of the transnational enterprises
For main entry, see 4058

1464
Delamarter, Richard T.
Big Blue: IBM's use and abuse of power
1988 Macmillan *London*

More detailed than Sobel (qv) but with less context, this is an excellent, accessible account by a journalist of the rise and operation of IBM.
Firms: IBM

1465
Dodds, Gordon B.; Wollner, Craig E.
The Silicon Forest: High Tech in the Portland area
1991 Oregon Historical Society Press
Portland, OR

The authors describe the evolution of a smaller cousin of Silicon Valley in Oregon's Washington County, focusing on the development of Electro-Scientific Industries (ESI) and Tektronix in the 1940s and Floating Point Systems in the 1970s and their spin-off companies. The book emphasizes the role of large firms in spinning off the entrepreneurs and skills that form the foundations of networks of small firms.
Firms: ESI; Tektronix; Floating Point Systems

1466
Engelbourg, Saul
International Business Machines: A business history
1976 Arno Press *New York, NY*

The outstanding early history of IBM; a 1976 printing of the author's 1954 PhD thesis from Columbia University.

Firms: IBM

1467
Fisher, Franklin M.; McGowan, John J.; Greenwood, Joen E.
Folded, Spindled, and Mutilated: Economic analysis and US vs IBM
1983 MIT Press *Cambridge, MA*

A detailed analysis of the US antitrust case against IBM that ran from 1969 to 1982, one of the longest and costliest of such cases in history. It argues that the case against IBM failed because of the government's inability to define the nature of competition and monopoly. The book develops a rigorous economic analysis of competition in the computer industry, covering issues of market share, entry barriers, technical change, predatory behaviour and profitability.

Firms: Digital Equipment Corporation (DEC); GE; Honeywell; IBM; NCR; RCA; Univac

1468
Fisher, Franklin M.; McKie, James W.; Mancke, Richard B.
IBM and the U.S. Data Processing Industry: An economic history
1983 Praeger Publishers *New York, NY*

A massive basic study of IBM and the industry largely based on US vs. IBM antitrust case documents. A systematic study of competition, marketing and barriers to entry.

Firms: AT&T; Burroughs; Control Data Corporation; Digital Equipment Corporation; GE; Honeywell; IBM; NCR; Sperry Rand

1469
Fishman, Katherine Davis
The Computer Establishment
1981 McGraw Hill *New York, NY*

A collection of articles profiling the major US computer companies (as of the 1970s).

Firms: Burroughs; Control Data; DEC; IBM; NCR; RCA; Sperry Rand

1470
Freiberger, Paul; Swaine, Michael
Fire in the Valley: The making of the personal computer
1984 Osborne/McGraw-Hill *Berkeley, CA*

A fine account of the evolution of the personal computer industry. Covers the emergence of the hobbyist microcomputer trade in the mid-1970s with the introduction of the Altair; the growth of companies such as Apple, Digital Research and Microsoft; and the entry of IBM into the field in 1981. A well-researched book with a wealth of business and cultural information: essential reading.

Firms: Altair; Apple; Digital Research; IBM; Microsoft

1471
Kidder, Tracy
The Soul of a New Machine
1981 Little, Brown *Boston, MA*

Vivid journalistic description of the human dynamics and management of a team of engineers designing a new computer, sharply contrasting with conventional approaches to labour management.

Firms: Data General

1472
Levy, Steven
Hackers: Heroes of the computer revolution
1984 Doubleday *New York, NY*

Despite its off-putting title this book contains much information on the early development of the personal computer. 'Hacker' in the title is used not in the familiar sense of someone who breaks into computer networks, but in the more 'traditional' sense of describing those with an irresistible urge to engross themselves in exploring the potential of the computer. Essential background reading.

Firms: Apple; Xerox

1473
Lundstrom, David E.
A Few Good Men From UNIVAC
1987 MIT Press *Cambridge, MA*

This personal account, from an engineer's perspective, covers product development and management in the US computer industry.

Firms: Control Data; Remington Rand; Sperry Rand; UNIVAC

1474

Maisonrouge, Jacques

Inside IBM: A European's story

1988 Collins *London*

An autobiography of the first non-American to join IBM's top management. The book covers the period of IBM's pre-eminence in the world's computer industries.

Firms: IBM

1475

Malone, Michael S.

The Big Score: The billion dollar story of Silicon Valley

1985 Doubleday *New York, NY*

Written by an 'insider' journalist, this is a survey of the Valley from its early days, dealing principally with Atari and Apple. It tries to get to grips with the culture and environment of the 'T-Shirt Tycoons' as well as the technological phenomenon of the Valley.

Firms: Apple; Atari; Intel

1476

Mowery, David C.; Rosenberg, Nathan

Technology and the Pursuit of Economic Growth

For main entry, see 4283

1477

Nerheim, Gunnar; Nordvik, Helge W.

Not Only Machines: The history of IBM in Norway 1935–1985

1987 IBM *Oslo, Norway*

A translation of a commissioned history of IBM's Norwegian subsidiary written by two respected academic economic historians. Emphasis is on the relationship between the parent company and its Norwegian subsidiary. It covers the major technical advances and shifts in products and markets, from selling and leasing typewriters, to punch card machines and time control equipment and, finally, computers.

Firms: IBM

1478

Pugh, Emerson

Memories That Shaped an Industry

1984 MIT Press *Cambridge, MA*

This history describes core memory development at IBM and elsewhere and its effect on IBM product development.

Firms: IBM

1479

Pugh, Emerson W.; Johnson, Lyle R.; Palmer, John H.

IBM's 360 and Early 370 Systems

1991 MIT Press *Cambridge, MA*

Written by IBM employees, this is the official (though nevertheless critical) account of one of IBM's greatest commercial and technical triumphs–the launch in 1964 of the IBM System/360 family of compatible computers. Technological developments are described in detail, but so too are the management practices that made the IBM 360 such a landmark event.

Firms: IBM

1480

Rifkin, Glenn; Harrar, George

The Ultimate Entrepreneur: The story of Ken Olsen and Digital Equipment Corporation

1988 Contemporary Books *Chicago, IL*

DEC was IBM's most serious challenger in the world computer market after the 1960s, with its founder Ken Olsen acclaimed as the most successful entrepreneur of his generation. An unauthorized study by two Computerworld journalists making extensive use of their contacts, this book analyses DEC's uncomfortable handling of the personal computer and its failure to understand the new market until too late.

Firms: Apple; Digital Equipment Corporation; IBM

1481

Rodgers, William H.

Think: A biography of the Watsons and IBM

1969 Stein and Day *New York, NY* 1974 New American Library *New York, NY*

This is a first-rate journalistic investigation of the origins of IBM whose publication the company wanted to stop in favour of the book by the Beldens (qv). A classic paternalistic com-

pany and its business leaders stand revealed. The revised edition contains important additional information.
Firms: IBM

1482
Rogers, Everett M.; Larson, Judith K.
Silicon Valley Fever: Growth of high-technology culture
1984 Basic Books *New York, NY*

Written by a Stanford professor and a Silicon Valley consultant, and based largely on interviews and the local press, this book attempts to give a picture of the culture of Silicon Valley, typified by the story of Apple. Rather more worshipful than the similar study by Malone (q.v.) but worthy of reference.
Firms: Apple; Atari; Hewlett-Packard; IBM

1483
Rose, Frank
West of Eden: The end of innocence at Apple Computer
1989 Hutchinson Business Books *London*

This book covers Apple's history between 1983 and 1986, when the company changed from 'being a pirate' to 'joining the navy'. In this period John Sculley was brought in from Pepsi-Cola to guide the company towards maturity, and Steve Jobs, the co-founder of the company, was forced to leave. The title is an apt summary of the theme of the story.
Firms: Apple

1484
Rubin, Michael Rogers; Huber, Mary Taylor
The Knowledge Industry in the United States, 1960–1980
1986 Princeton University Press *Princeton, NJ*

The authors present an economic analysis of US industry in computers and communications. This can be read as a follow-up volume to Fritz Machlup's *The Production and Distribution of Knowledge in the United States*, Princeton University Press, 1962.

1485
Saxenian, Annalee
Regional Advantage: Culture and Competition in Silicon Valley and Route 128
1994 Harvard University Press *Cambridge, MA*

A comparative analysis of the development of the two leading centres of the US electronics industry. Despite similar histories and technologies, Silicon Valley developed a decentralized industrial system that encouraged experimentation, collaboration and collective learning, blurring the boundaries between customers, suppliers and competitors and giving it a 'regional advantage'. In contrast, Route 128 came to be dominated by a few self-sufficient corporations and found it hard to adjust its skills and technologies to changing markets. Based on hundreds of interviews, this is a pioneering and important work.
Firms: Data General Corp.; Digital Equipment Corp.; Hewlett-Packard; IBM; Raytheon; Apple

1486
Sculley, John; Byrne, John A.
Odyssey. Pepsi to Apple: A journey of adventure, ideas, and the future
1987 Harper & Row *New York, NY*

Sculley's account of how he came to leave Pepsi-Cola for a chance to 'change the world' at Apple, where he replaced Steve Jobs, its co-founder. It covers Apple's transition from small start-up business into a Fortune 500 Corporation. This is also 'the story of ideas which have changed my life', and each chapter ends with an appropriate tutorial.
Firms: Apple; Pepsi Co.

1487
Smith, Douglas K.; Alexander, Robert C.
Fumbling the Future: How Xerox invented, then ignored, the first personal computer
1988 William Morrow *New York, NY*

Xerox PARC (Palo Alto Research Centre) was an imaginative investment in the future, which developed the personal computer, automated office and desktop publishing, amongst other things. But Xerox did not have the confidence to exploit the technology, which consequently passed on to other companies. An absorbing account of an important phase for both Xerox and the personal computer.
Firms: Apple; Xerox

1488
Sobel, Robert
I.B.M., Colossus in Transition
1981 Times Books *New York, NY*

Still the most accessible academic but non-technical history of IBM's origins and development this book is particularly good on personalities, business strategy and marketing.
Firms: IBM

1489
Stern, N. B.
From ENIAC to UNIVAC: An appraisal of the Eckert-Mauchly computers
1981 Digital Press *Bedford, MA*

This is by far the best account of Remington Rand's entry into the computer industry, together with a solid account of the invention of the computer.
Firms: Remington Rand

1490
Watson, Thomas J. Jr
A Business and Its Beliefs: The ideas that helped build IBM
For main entry, see 3994

1491
Watson, Thomas J. Jr; Petre, Peter
Father, Son & Co: My life at IBM and beyond
1990 Bantam Press *London*

The author was CEO of IBM from 1956 to 1971. Watson gives a fast-moving and frank account of his relationship with his father (the first President of IBM) and the restructuring of IBM into a computer company. The book is particularly illuminating on the personalities and business strategies surrounding the development of the landmark IBM System/360 computers.
Firms: IBM

1492
Young, Jeffrey S.
Steve Jobs: The journey is the reward
For main entry, see 3997

Electrical & Computers, Rest of World

1493
Anchordoguy, Marie
Computers Inc: Japan's challenge to IBM
1989 Harvard University Press *Cambridge, MA*

This book describes the building of the Japanese computer industry from the 1950s when Japan was wholly reliant on IBM and other foreign suppliers. Anchordoguy covers the role of protectionism, financial aid, cooperative R&D, and the establishment of a quasi-public computer rental company, and argues that government intervention avoided risks of technical sluggishness by encouraging keen competition among computer firms.
Firms: Fujitsu; Hitachi; IBM; Japan Electronic Computer CO (JEC); Nippon Electric Company (NEC); Toshiba

1494
Barreau, Jocelyne; Mouline, Abdelaziz
L'industrie électronique française: 29 ans de relations État-groupes industriels, 1958–1986 [The French Electronics Industry: 29 years of state-industry relations, 1958–1986]
1987 LGDJ *Paris, France*

A study of the relations between the French electronics sector and successive government regimes (De Gaulle, Pompidou, Giscard, Mitterand), especially in relation to assistance and planning and the mixture of negotiation, compromise and confrontation with the industry groups. There is no index.
Firms: Thomson; Bull

1495
Ciborra, Claudio
Le Affinita Asimmetriche: Il Caso Olivetti-AT&T [Asymmetrical Affinity Olivetti and AT&T]

A study of the cooperation agreement between AT&T and Olivetti, providing a general overview of the global information and office automation industries, along with more detailed examinations of AT&T, IBM, and Olivetti, including their products and market positions. A separate section examines organ-

izational changes, both in management structures and the nature of work, and the impact of technology.
Firms: AT&T; IBM; Olivetti

1496
Cusumano, Michael
Japan's Software Factories: A challenge to US management
1991 Oxford University Press *New York, NY*

Although Japan has successfully competed with US companies in the manufacturing and marketing of computer hardware, it has been much less successful in the development of computer programs. Cusumano's study is a detailed analysis of attempts to redress this imbalance by the use of 'software factories' which apply skills in engineering and production management to software development. A feature of the book is comparative chapters on Hitachi, Fujitsu, Toshiba and NEC.
Firms: Fujitsu; Hitachi; NEC (Nippon Electric Co.); Toshiba

1497
Ferguson, Charles H.; Morris, Charles R.
Computer Wars: How the West can win in a post-IBM world
1993 Times Books *New York, NY*

The authors describe the rise and decline of IBM, then set IBM in context with its competitors, especially major Japanese electronic firms and the Third Force–small highly innovative companies. It covers the impact of government policy on the computer industry both in the United States and elsewhere.
Firms: DEC (Digital Equipment Corp.); Fujitsu; Hitachi; IBM; NEC (Nippon Electric Co.); Toshiba

1498
Fransman, Martin
The Market and Beyond: Co-operation and competition in information technology in the Japanese system
1990 Cambridge University Press *Cambridge*

Fransman discusses the exceptional innovative capacity of the Japanese system, focusing on the interaction of cooperating private companies, government policy-makers and universities. He stresses the central role of government in innovation in computers, and provides a detailed analysis of major national projects including: VLSI, Optical Measurement and Control, Supercomputers, Fifth Generation Computers.
Firms: Hitachi; IBM; NEC; Oki; Toshiba

1499
Gregory, Gene
Japanese Electronics Technology: Enterprise and innovation
1985 Japan Times Inc. *Tokyo, Japan*

This book collects together numerous articles by the author, written from the mid-1970s to the mid-1980s in scientific and management journals. It provides valuable detail not available elsewhere, and effectively offers a continuous narrative of the rise of the industry. There is no index.
Firms: Fujitsu; Hitachi; NEC; NTT

1500
Mason, Mark
American Multinationals and Japan: The political economy of Japanese capital controls, 1899–1980
For main entry, see 3410

1501
Sheff, David
Game Over: Nintendo's battle to dominate an industry
1993 Hodder & Stoughton *London*

An insightful journalistic study of Japan's most successful company in the early 1990s, a computer games giant that earned more than IBM, Apple or Microsoft. Sheff follows the company and its entrepreneurs from its origins as a playing card manufacturer in Kyoto in the early twentieth century to its huge success with SuperMario. Based on interviews with leading figures in the company, it is especially strong on innovation and strategy.
Firms: Nintendo; Sega

1502
Tyson, Laura D'Andrea
Who's Bashing Whom?: Trade conflict in high-technology industries
1992 Institute for International Economics *Washington, DC*

A series of well-researched case studies of crucial trade disputes between the USA and Japan in aircraft, semiconductors, supercomputers, telecommunications and electronics.
Firms: Motorola; Cray; Airbus Industrie; ATT; Boeing; Fujitsu; Lockheed; McDonnell-Douglas; NTT; Texas Instruments

multinationals. The scope is broad and the work is published in three volumes. Two volumes present economic development, focusing on financing, owner influence, production and markets. The third is dedicated to the technology of telecommunications.
Firms: LM Ericsson

Electrical Engineering, Europe

1503
Andrews, H. H.
Electricity in Transport: Over Sixty Year's Experience, 1883–1950
1951 English Electric Co. *London*
This is essentially a public relations exercise by English Electric, advertising their expertise in the field of electrical traction since the 1880s as Dick, Kerr & Co. It is worth reading for the factual content, but the analytical content is negligible.
Firms: Dick, Kerr & Co.; English Electric; Siemens

1504
Arnold, Erik
Competition and Technological Change in the Television Industry: An empirical evaluation of the theories of the firm
1985 Macmillan *London*
A detailed study of the UK television manufacturing industry, focusing on the role of viewdata (videotext), which uses the empirical material to attack conventional industry economics theory. Good data is provided and the study is strong on technology and marketing issues.
Firms: Granada; Radio Rentals; Rediffusion; Thorn Television Rentals

1505
Attman, Artur; Kuuse, Jan; Olsson, Ulf; Jacobaeus, Christian
LM Ericsson: 100 years
1977 LM Ericsson *Örebro, Sweden*
This history of LM Ericsson, the telecommunications company, was written by a group of authors to celebrate one hundred years of production within one of the first Swedish

1506
Baker, W. J.
A History of the Marconi Company
For main entry, see 3213

1507
Blanken, Ivo J.
Geschiedenis van de Philips Electronics NV, 1922–34: De ontwikkeling van de N. V. Philips Gloeilampenfabrieken tot elektrotechnisch concern [The History of Philips Electronics NV. 1922–34: The development of the NV Philips Gloeilampenfabrieken into an electrotechnical concern]
1992 Martinus Nijhoff *Leiden, The Netherlands*
This is the third volume of the official history of Philips. The first two volumes by Heerding (q.v.) have been translated into English but this one is only available in Dutch. This volume deals with Philips' changeover from being a specialized producer of incandescent lamps, and part of the international Phoebus cartel, into a vertically integrated group of companies encompassing many different areas of activity, particularly sound technology (radio and gramophone).
Firms: Philips

1508
Broder, Albert; Torres, Félix
Alcatel Alsthom: Histoire de la Compagnie Générale d'Electricité [Alcatel Alsthom: History of the Compagnie Générale d'Electricité]
1992 Larousse *Paris, France*
This book charts one hundred years of the largest French company in electronics.
Firms: Alcatel; Alsthom; Compagnie Générale d'Electricité

1509
Byatt, Ian C. R.
The British Electrical Industry 1875–1914: The economic returns to a new technology
1979 Oxford University Press *Oxford*

Based on a doctoral thesis, this book provides a detailed insight into the performance and development of British electricity undertakings and their main suppliers (British and foreign). Statistical backing is given on both the industry and the main companies, making it essential reading.

Firms: British Thomson-Houston; British Westinghouse; Brush Electrical Engineering Co.; Dick, Kerr & Co.; Ferranti Ltd; GEC; London Electricity Supply Co.

1510
Cawson, Alan; Morgan, Kevin; Webber, Douglas; Holmes, Peter; Stevens, Anne
Hostile Brothers: Competition and closure in the European electronics industry
1990 Clarendon Press *Oxford*

This book is the result of a large-scale research project on government–industry relations in the consumer electronics and telecommunications industries of Britain, France and West Germany, analysing how these industries have adapted to technical change and international competition in the 1970s and 1980s. In particular, it describes the emergence of multinational firms as the major political actors engaged in negotiations with governments and the EC, stressing variance in patterns of market closure and trade liberalization.

1511
Church, R. A.
Innovation, Monopoly and the Supply of Vehicle Components in Britain, 1880–1913: The growth of Joseph Lucas Ltd
For main entry, see 804

1512
Clayton, Robert; Algar, Joan
The GEC Research Laboratories 1919–1984
1989 Peregrinus, Science Museum *London*

This book covers in painstaking technical detail developments in the history of GEC's research activities from the First World War to the 1980s, based largely on technical reports produced within the company's laboratories. Analysis of R&D is almost wholly from a technical point of view but the book is nevertheless most valuable for the study of R&D and science-based enterprises.

Firms: GEC

1513
Corley, Thomas Anthony B.
Domestic Electrical Appliances
1966 Jonathan Cape *London*

Corley analyses in detail how the domestic appliance market operates, and how the major electrical appliance manufacturers develop their products. Information on market shares is provided, as well as an analysis of market trends in a highly competitive industry affected by government stop-go policies in the fifteen years after the Second World War.

Firms: GEC; Hotpoint

1514
Czada, Peter
Die Berliner Elektroindustrie in der Weimarer Zeit [The Electrical Industry in Berlin During the Weimar Period]
1969 Colloquium Verlag *Berlin, Germany*

A scholarly study of the Berlin electrical machinery industry with much valuable information on Siemens and its suppliers.

Firms: Siemens

1515
Dore, Ronald
British Factory - Japanese Factory
For main entry, see 3651

1516
Feldenkirchen, Wilfried
Werner von Siemens: Inventor and international entrepreneur
1994 Ohio State University Press *Columbus, OH*

This is a concise study of the entrepreneurship and business strategies of the founder of Siemens (1816–1892). Published to commemorate the 100th anniversary of its subject's death, it is, however, a scholarly study.

Firms: Siemens

1517

Ferranti, Gertrude Ziani de; Ince, Richard

The Life and Letters of Sebastian Ziani de Ferranti

1934 Williams & Norgate *London*

Based on the diaries and letters of S. Z. de Ferranti, mixed in with his wife's reminiscences, this book provides an insight into the character of a leading British electrical engineer. Extensive extracts are provided from original documents, with little editing, but other works are better on his companies and technical ventures.

Firms: Ferranti; J & P Coats; Vickers

1518

Freyburg, Thomas von

Industrielle Rationalisierung in der Weimarer Republik: Untersucht an Beispielen aus dem Maschinenbau und der Elektroindustrie [Industrial Rationalization in the Weimar Republic]

1989 Campus *Frankfurt, Germany*

Taking mechanical and electrical engineering as examples, this sociological study examines the impact of changing working practices on the workforce, on management and ultimately on German national policies.

Firms: AEG; Siemens

1519

Glete, Jan

ASEA under hundra ar 1883–1983 [ASEA Centenary 1883–1983]

1983 EHF-Stockholm School of Business *Stockholm, Sweden*

A study of the organizational, technical and economic development of ASEA, the Swedish counterpart of General Electric or AEG. Now half-owner of the international combine ABB.

Firms: ABB; ASEA

1520

Hautsch, Gert

Das Imperium AEG-Telefunken [The AEG-Telefunken Empire]

1979 Marxistische Blätter *Frankfurt, Germany*

Hautsch provides a marxist view of AEG as a multinational and its oligopolistic links with other companies together with much financial detail.

Firms: AEG-Telefunken; Siemens

1521

Heerding, A.

The History of N. V. Philips' Gloeilampenfabrieken: Vol. 1 The origins of the Dutch incandescent lamp industry. Vol. 2 A company of many parts

1986–9 Cambridge University Press *Cambridge*

Immensely detailed (720 pages) history of the company, that is especially strong on technology and personnel management, and on the early development of the company and the field of electric lighting. It is, however, marred by rather obscure writing and excessively technical descriptions and occasionally slips towards hagiography. Nevertheless, an essential work. Particular attention is paid to patents and to international alliances.

Firms: Philips

1522

Heuss, Theodor

Robert Bosch: His life and achievements

1994 Henry Holt & Co. *New York, NY*

An authorized life by a former President of the Bundestag and founder of the FDP, a personal friend of Robert Bosch. It was written during the Second World War, and is generally apologetic, but it draws extensively on Bosch's personal papers to tell of his life, philanthropy and labour policies, and to provide useful data on innovation and strategy in the firm.

Firms: Robert Bosch

1523

Hoffman, Kai

Sähkötekniikan taitaja: Strömberg 1889–1989 [An Expert in Electrical Engineering: Strömberg, 1889–1989]

1990 ABB Strömberg Oy *Vaasa, Finland*

Hoffman describes the history of the largest Finnish electrical engineering company which developed from a tiny workshop into a major producer of heavy electrical equipment. The book deals with the company's linkages to the forest industries, the government and rivals. The competition with multinationals led to a merger with the Swedish firm ASEA in 1986 and later it became part of the giant ABB concern.

Firms: ABB Strömberg Oy; ASEA; Gottfrid, Strömberg Oy

1524

Jacob-Wendler, Gerhart

Deutsche Elektroindustrie in Lateinamerika: Siemens und AEG 1890–1914 [German Electrical Firms in Latin America: Siemens and AEG]

1982 Klett-Cotta *Stuttgart, Germany*

After describing the origins of the world electricity industry, this book covers both exports and the establishment of local branches in the countries of Latin America.

Firms: AEG; Siemens

1525

Jones, Robert; Marriott, Oliver

Anatomy of a Merger: A history of GEC, AEI & English Electric

1970 Jonathan Cape *London*

The most comprehensive study of the three British electrical engineering companies from their origins in the 1880s up to the late 1960s merger. Fascinating detail is provided on the main characters, their businesses and the impact American corporations had on the development of British electrical engineering. It is essential reading for all business historians.

Firms: AEG; Associated Electrical Industries; British Thomson-Houston; British Westinghouse; English Electric; GEC; General Electric; Metropolitan-Vickers Electrical Co.; Siemens; Westinghouse

1526

Kaarsted, Tage; Boje, Per

Thomas B. Thrige, primus motor: Fra el-industriens barndom [Thomas B. Thrige, Prime Mover: From the infancy of the electrical industry]

1983 Odense University Press *Odense, Denmark*

The book is in two parts. The first part is a biography of Thomas B. Thrige, the founder of one of the first large Danish factories in electrical engineering. It describes his early years, including three years in Edison's laboratories in the United States, and his social position in his years as an entrepreneur. The second part is an analysis of his Danish business, covering the period from 1894 to 1938, with special emphasis on technological development, marketing and labour relations.

Firms: Thrige, Thomas B.

1527

Kocka, Jürgen

Unternehmensverwaltung und Angestelltenschaft am Beispiel Siemens 1847–1914: Zum Verhältnis von Kapitalismus und Bürokratie in der deutschen Industrialisiering [Siemens: The administation of a business and its employees: Capitalism and bureaucracy during German industrialisation]

For main entry, see 3568

1528

Kudo, Akira; Hara, Terushi (Editors)

International Cartels in Business History (Eighteenth Fuji Conference)

For main entry, see 99

1529

Marchi, Alves; Marchionetti, Renato

Montedison, 1966–1989: L'evoluzione di una grande impresa al confine tra pubblico e privato [Montedison 1966–1989: The development of a great industry between public and private enterprise]

1992 Franco Angeli *Milan, Italy*

This is a major archivally-based study of the leading Italian electrical company.

Firms: Montedison

1530

Millard, Andre J.

A Technological Lag: Diffusion of electrical technology in England, 1879–1914

For main entry, see 2726

1531

Morgan, R. M.

Callender's 1882–1945

1982 BICC plc *Prescot*

This is a useful commissioned history of the major British cable manufacturer, which merged with British Insulated Cables in 1945 to form British Insulated Callender's Cables (BICC).

Firms: British Insulated Cables; Callender's Cable & Construction Co.

1532

Newfarmer, Richard S.

Transnational Conglomerates and the Economics of Dependent Development: A case study of the international electrical oligopoly and Brazil's electrical industry

1980 JAI Press *Greenwich, CT*

An important book which, within a broad theoretical context, explores relations between global oligopolies and host countries. It follows the history through the periods of cartels, rivalry and direct foreign investment from 1880 to the 1970s, focusing on market power, industrial structure and trade in order to illuminate structural dependence.

Firms: AEG; ASEA; Brown Boveri; Ericsson; General Electric; Hitachi; ITT; NEC; Osram; Philips

1533

Nockolds, Harold

Lucas: The First Hundred Years: Vol. 1 The king of the road. Vol. 2 The successors.

1976–8 David & Charles *Newton Abbot*

A detailed official company history based on the archives of Lucas and extensive interviewing, but unfortunately lacking any footnotes. It provides little financial or output data, but does give an excellent picture of the company's early years, its leading entrepreneurs and a sound outline of the company's evolution and business strategy.

Firms: CAV; Lucas

1534

Ochetto, Valerio

Adriano Olivetti

For main entry, see 4025

1535

Okochi, Akio; Uchida, Hoshimi (Editors)

Development and Diffusion of Technology (Sixth Fuji Conference)

For main entry, see 107

1536

Peschke, Hans-Peter von

Elektroindustrie und Staatsverwaltung am Beispiel Siemens, 1847–1914 [The Electrical Industry and State Control: The case of Siemens 1847–1914]

1981 Peter D. Lang *Frankfurt, Germany*

Based on a thesis, this book examines the growth of the electrical industry and the political framework in which it operated using Siemens as a case study.

Firms: Siemens

1537

Philips, Frederik

45 Years with Philips: An industrialist's life

For main entry, see 4029

1538

Scott, John D.

Siemens Brothers 1858–1958: An essay in the history of industry

1958 Weidenfeld & Nicolson *London*

An interesting analysis of how a German-owned company established a subsidiary in Britain and developed it over 100 years. Detailed information on performance and an analysis of company structure is at times lacking, but the book is still useful for students of the electrical industry and those interested in the evolution of multinational subsidiaries.

Firms: Dick, Kerr & Co.; English Electric; GEC; Siemens

1539

Teulings, A.

Philips: Geschiedenis en praktijk van een wereldconcern [Philips: History and practice of a multinational]

1977 Van Gennep *Amsterdam, The Netherlands*

A highly critical, and somewhat journalistic history of Philips, 1891–1976, written from a sociological viewpoint. Based mainly on published sources, the emphasis is on wartime company policy and post Second World War labour relations in The Netherlands.

Firms: Philips

1540

Trevor, Malcolm

Toshiba's New British Company: Competitiveness through innovation in industry

1988 Policy Studies Institute *London*

This provides a fascinating insight into how a Japanese multinational invaded and dominated the British television market, contrasting the global strategies of this type of company and the more limited approach of its British counterparts. Important links with government regional and industrial policies are also made.
Firms: Pye; Toshiba

1541
Weiher, Sigfrid von
Die englischen Siemens-Werke und das Siemens-Überseegeschäft in das Zweiten Hälfte der 19. Jahrhunderte [The English Siemens Works and Siemens Overseas Business in the Second Half of the 19th Century]
1990 Duncker & Humblot *Berlin, Germany*

This describes Siemens role in electric telegraph cables and in power engineering and the entrepreneurial role of the Siemens brothers.
Firms: Siemens Brothers; Siemens Halske & Co.

1542
Wilson, J. F.
Ferranti and the British Electrical Industry, 1864–1930
1988 Manchester University Press *Manchester*

Based on extensive research in the personal and company archive, this book describes the fascinating career of Ferranti and its impact on the electricity supply and electrical engineering industries. The aim is to examine the main constraints which prevented the full implementation of his expansive schemes, looking at political, economic and personal aspects of the story.
Firms: British Insulated Wire Co.; Ferranti; J & P Coats; Vickers

1543
Young, Peter
Power of Speech: A history of Standard Telephones and Cables 1883–1983
For main entry, see 3241

Electrical Engineering, America

1544
Carlson, W. Bernard
Innovation as a Social Process: Elihu Thomson and the rise of General Electric, 1870–1900
1991 Cambridge University Press *Cambridge*

Elihu Thomson was a prolific inventor whose inventions included arc and incandescent lighting systems, alternating-current motors and transformers, electric welding equipment and the recording wattmeter. But unlike Edison, who worked independently, Thomson developed his inventions while employed by General Electric Company and its predecessors. Carlson's pioneering study examines how technologists employ craft knowledge to create new products and the role of technology in the rise of a major corporation.
Firms: Brush Electric Light Co.; GE; Thomson-Houston Electric Co.

1545
Case, Josephine Y.; Case, Everett N.
Owen D. Young and American Enterprise: A biography
1982 David R. Godine *Boston, MA*

A massive archivally-based biography of the man who, with Gerard Swope, transformed GE from a major national to a multinational company and founded RCA. Full attention is also paid to Young's political career.
Firms: GE; RCA

1546
Friedel, Robert D.; Israel, Paul; Finn, Bernard S.
Edison's Electric Light: Biography of an innovation
1986 Rutgers University Press *New Brunswick, NJ*

This is a definitive commissioned history of the technical origins and early development of the electric light, based on the Edison archives.
Firms: Edison

1547
Graham, Margaret B.
RCA and the VideoDisc: The business of research
1986 Cambridge University Press *Cambridge*

Graham's project began as on-the-spot observation of an attempt to bring a major new consumer electronics project from the research stage to market, but it evolved into a full-scale analysis of the interaction of R&D and corporate strategy under David Sarnoff's regime at RCA. An important and insightful study of the 'business of research'.
Firms: RCA

1548
Kudo, Akira; Hara, Terushi (Editors)
International Cartels in Business History (Eighteenth Fuji Conference)
For main entry, see 99

1549
Millard, André
Edison and the Business of Innovation
For main entry, see 4281

1550
Nye, David E.
Image Worlds: Corporate Identities at General Electric, 1890–1930
1985 MIT Press *Cambridge, MA*

Unorthodox study that uses the history of GE as an avenue to explore consumption, advertising, art and culture. It has plentiful photos and sheds much light on GE's marketing and positioning of its products.
Firms: GE

1551
Okochi, Akio; Uchida, Hoshimi (Editors)
Development and Diffusion of Technology (Sixth Fuji Conference)
For main entry, see 107

1552
Passer, H. C.
The Electrical Manufacturers, 1875–1900: A study in competition, entrepreneurship, technical change and economic growth
1954 Harvard University Press *Cambridge, MA*

An essential work (by a student of Schumpeter) on the economics and development of the early electrical manufacturing industry in the USA. Still not superseded, it covers the entrepreneurs, strategy and technology of the major firms and the relationship between entrepreneurship and technical change.
Firms: GE; Westinghouse; Edison; Brush Electric Co.; Thomson-Houston; Weston Electric Light Co.

1553
Reich, Leonard S.
The Making of American Industrial Research: Science and business at GE and Bell, 1876–1926
For main entry, see 3235

1554
Schatz, Ronald W.
The Electrical Workers: A history of labor at General Electric and Westinghouse, 1923–1960
For main entry, see 4227

1555
Smith, George D.
The Anatomy of a Business Strategy: Bell, Western Electric and the origins of the American telephone industry
For main entry, see 3237

1556
Wasserman, Neil H.
From Invention to Innovation: Long distance transmission at the turn of the century
For main entry, see 3240

1557
Wise, George; Whitney, Willis R.
General Electric and the Origins of U.S. Industrial Research
1985 Columbia University Press *New York, NY*

An extensively researched, scholarly study of R&D at GE from 1900 to the 1920s, based on company archives.
Firms: GE

Electrical Engineering, Japan

1558
Aoyama, Yoshiyuki
Kaden [Home Electrical Machinery]
1991 Nihon, Keizai Hyoron-sha *Tokyo, Japan*
A good introduction to the electrification of Japanese daily life with particular emphasis on the growth and development of the home electrical appliance industry.

1559
Dore, Ronald
British Factory - Japanese Factory
For main entry, see 3651

1560
Hitachi Cable
Hitachi Densen Shi [A History of Hitachi Cable]
1980 Hitachi Cable *Tokyo, Japan*
A short descriptive history of the company's technology and products between 1956 and 1976, focusing on the growth of the company.
Firms: Hitachi Cable Co.

1561
Kudo, Akira; Hara, Terushi (Editors)
International Cartels in Business History (Eighteenth Fuji Conference)
For main entry, see 99

1562
Lyons, Nick
The Sony Vision
1976 Crown Publishers *New York, NY*
A useful company history with particular attention to leading personalities and key innovations.
Firms: Sony

1563
Mason, Mark
American Multinationals and Japan: The political economy of Japanese capital controls, 1899–1980
For main entry, see 3410

1564
Mitsubishi
Mitsubishi Denki Shashi [A Company History of Mitsubishi Electric]
1982 Mitsubishi Electric *Tokyo, Japan*
This book covers the period from 1921 to 1981 and describes the activities of Mitsubishi Electric including its products, diversification and technology.
Firms: Mitsubishi Denki; Mitsubishi Electric Co.

1565
Morita, Akio
Made in Japan: Akio Morita and Sony
For main entry, see 4024

1566
Nihon Denki Kabushiki
Nippon Denki Kabushiki Kaisha 70 Nen Shi [70-Year History of Nippon Electric Co.]
1972 Nippon Electric *Tokyo, Japan*
Covering the period from 1899 to 1969, this book explains the growth and development of the Nippon Electric Co., which started as a subsidiary of Western Electric Co. and gradually developed its own technology. A fine study of the transfer of foreign technology from a Western multinational to what became an indigenous firm.
Firms: Nihon Denki; Nippon Electric Co.; Western Electric

1567
Nihon Denki Kogyo Kai
Denki Kogyo Shinko 30 Nen no Ayumi [A History of the Japanese Electrical Industry]
1956–79 Nihon Denki Kogyo Kai *Tokyo, Japan*
A comprehensive history of the Japanese electrical industry with particular emphasis on the technology and products of heavy electrical equipment and home electric appliances. The work includes material on related businesses and trade associations.
Firms: Hitachi Co.; Matsushita Electric Co.; Nihon Denki Kogyo Kai

1568

Nihon Denshi Kogyo Shinko Kai

Denshi Kogyo Shinko 30 Nen no Ayumi [30-Year History of the Promotion of the Electronics Industry]

1988 Japan Association of the Electronics Industry *Tokyo, Japan*

A good introduction to the post-war electronics industry in Japan with particular emphasis on computers, electronic equipment, electronic parts, etc.

1569

Okochi, Akio; Uchida, Hoshimi (Editors)

Development and Diffusion of Technology (Sixth Fuji Conference)

For main entry, see 107

1570

Onishi, Katsuaki; Ohashi, Eigo

Hitachi to Toshiba [Hitachi & Toshiba]

1990 Otsuki Shoten *Tokyo, Japan*

A survey of Japanese big business through case studies of Hitachi and Toshiba. In particular it focuses on Hitachi's strategy and problems of growth and Toshiba's resolution of financial problems.

Firms: Hitachi Co.; Toshiba Co.

1571

Toshiba

Toshiba 100 Nen Shi [A Centenary of Tokyo Shibaura Electric Co.]

1977 Toshiba *Tokyo, Japan*

Covers the period 1875 to 1975 and describes the growth and development of the Tokyo Shibaura Electric Co. (Toshiba) with special emphasis on aspects of technology and production methods. The book includes material on associated companies.

Firms: Tokyo Shibaura Denki Kabushiki Kaisha; Toshiba Co.

1572

Yamashita, Toshihiko

The Panasonic Way: From a chief executive's desk

1987 Kodansha International *Tokyo, Japan*

The autobiography of the young executive catapulted into the top job at Matsushita to replace the dominant founder. Too much holy wisdom, but also insights on the company.

Firms: Matsushita

Scientific & Precision Engineering

1573

Barty-King, Hugh

Eyes Right: The story of Dollond & Aitchison, Opticians 1750–1985

1986 Quiller Press *London*

A thorough, if rather pedestrian, company history of a leading British lens maker, based on company documents.

Firms: Dollond & Aitchison; Slater Walker

1574

Blanc, Jean-François

Suisse-Hong Kong: Le défi horloger: innovation technologique et division internationale du travail [From Switzerland to Hong Kong: The watchmaking challenge: technological innovation and international division of labour]

1987 Éditions d'en bas *Lausanne, Switzerland*

A rich and clear synthesis of recent changes in the watch industry and its social dimensions, focused on three national systems: Switzerland, Japan and Hong Kong. It analyses the internationalization of production, international competition and industrial strategies in developing countries, with special emphasis on the dynamics of Hong Kong.

1575

Cattermole, M. J. G.; Wolfe, A. P.; Darwin, Horace

Horace Darwin's Shop: A history of the Cambridge Scientific Instrument Company, 1878 to 1968

1987 Hilger *Bristol*

A straightforward narrative of the rise of one of Britain's leading precision instrument makers (notably temperature measuring devices and electrocardiographs). A wealth of detail on the individuals involved, though little material after the death of the company's founder, Horace Darwin, in 1929. The book is especially strong on the technical history of the

instruments themselves. Based on company archives.
Firms: Cambridge Scientific Instrument Co.

1576
Collins, Douglas
The Story of Kodak
1990 H. N. Abrams *New York, NY*

Appropriately for the company, this is a lavish and spectacularly illustrated book. The text is a somewhat bland authorized history of the company some 400 pages long. But in this case the pictures really do tell the story, notably of the interaction between user and producer in the evolution of film and camera.
Firms: Kodak

1577
De Ferrière, Marc
Christofle: Une aventure industrielle, 1793–1940 [Christofle: An industrial adventure 1793–1940]
1991, PhD Thesis, Université, Paris IV

This duplicated thesis describes Christofle the leading French producer of silver jewellery. The company is still operating.
Firms: Christofle

1578
Gibb, George S.
The Whitesmiths of Taunton: A history of Reed & Barton, 1824–1943
1976 Arno Press *New York, NY*

A traditional business history of a firm of silversmiths, detailing slow changes in management style.
Firms: Reed & Barton

1579
Hermann, Armin
Nur der Name war geblieben: die abenteuerliche Geschichte der Firma Carl Zeiss [Only the Name Remained: The adventurous history of the Carl Zeiss Company]
1989 Deutsche Verlags-Anstalt *Stuttgart, Germany*

A political history of the firm Carl Zeiss, with an emphasis on its post-war fortunes, after its division into statised Zeiss parent company (Jena) and the Zeiss enterprise reconstituted in the Federal Republic.
Firms: Carl Zeiss

1580
Jenkins, Reese
Images and Enterprise: Technology and the American photographic industry, 1839–1925
1975 Johns Hopkins University Press *Baltimore, MD*

This book explores the business, technical and social factors that transformed the American photographic industry from the early daguerrotype to the rise of motion pictures. In particular, it traces the technical changes that culminated in George Eastman's creation of the Kodak system of amateur photography in the 1880s. An acclaimed study of industrial research in the struggle to develop commercially practical colour photography. The book is archivally based and contains plentiful technical drawings and illustrations.
Firms: Eastman Kodak; Kodak; Scovill Manufacturing Co.

1581
Jephcott, Sir Anthony
A History of Longworth Scientific Instrument Co. Ltd
1988 Regency Press *London*

A short, but instructive account of the first thirty years of a small British manufacturer (registered in 1943), written by the son of Glaxo entrepreneur, Sir Harry Jephcott (qv Davenport-Hines and Slinn, *Glaxo*). It provides financial detail as well as managerial insights.
Firms: Longworth Scientific Instrument Co.

1582
Jequier, François
Une Enterprise Horlogère du Val-de-Travers: Fleurier Watch Co. SA: De l'atelier familial du XIXe aux concentrations du XXe siècle [A Watchmaking Business in the Val-de-Travers: Fleurier Watch Co. SA]
1972 Éditions de la Baconnière *Neuchâtel, Switzerland*

The fullest history of a Swiss family watchmaking firm, this book deals with the transformation of the firm from a family company to a holding company over two centuries. A history of entrepreneurship (based on the archives of the firm and the family) integrated into a his-

tory of the Swiss watch industry which emphasizes the weight of family traditions on the development of the firm.
Firms: Fleurier Watch Co. SA

1583
Jequier, François; Schindler-Pittet, Chantal
De la forge à la manufacture horlogère (XVIIIe-XXe siècles): cinq générations d'entrepreneurs de la vallée de Joux au coeur d'une mutation industrielle [From Forge to Watchmaking: Five generations of entrepreneurs]
1983 Bibliothèque historique vaudoise *Lausanne, Switzerland*
A richly documented monograph (using the archives of the firm and the Le Coultre family) on the technological, commercial, financial and organizational evolution of a firm of the Swiss Jura (watches, munitions, speedometers, photographic apparatus) from the family firm to holding company. Social questions are prominent.
Firms: Le Coultre & Cie

1584
Landes, David
Revolution in Time: Clocks and the making of the modern world
1983 Harvard University Press *Cambridge, MA*
A passionate and magisterial synthesis devoted to the measure of time in all its aspects: cultural, scientific and technical, aesthetic, economic and social, from the origins (European monopoly of the mechanical watch) to today and across diverse national cultures. The French edition entitled *L'heure qu'il est. Les horloges, la mesure du temps et la formation du monde moderne* (Paris, Éditions Gallimard, 1987) contains an important additional chapter on the quartz revolution which represents the first attempt at synthesis on the new technologies of electronic watches.

1585
McConnell, Anita
Instrument Makers to the World: A history of Cooke, Troughton & Simms
1992 William Sessions *York*
A short but useful account of a major British scientific instruments firm. The book is stronger on products than on finance, but provides useful information on the principal entrepreneurs.
Firms: Cooke, Troughton & Simms

1586
Moore, Charles W.
Timing a Century: History of the Waltham Watch Company
1945 Harvard University Press *Cambridge, MA*
This is a minutely detailed, intensely researched company history carried out under the direction of N. S. B. Gras, of the oldest American watchmaking company, based in New England. Moore studies the process of growth and the transformation of the company from craft to industrial production, tracing company policies and leadership. An essential work.
Firms: Waltham Watch Co.

1587
Moss, Michael S.
Range and Vision: The first 100 years of Barr & Stroud
1988 Mainstream Publishing Co. *Edinburgh, Scotland*
A well researched and thoroughly documented history of an important optical and opto-electronic British instrument company, which is especially strong on its long-running collaborative links with universities and on the process of technical change and innovation.
Firms: Barr & Stroud

1588
Schomerus, Friedrich
Geschichte des Jenaer Zeisswerkes, 1846–1946 [A History of the Zeiss Business in Jena]
1952 Piscator Verlag *Stuttgart, Germany*
An extraordinarily detailed history of the firm Carl Zeiss, written for its centenary, seen from the inside (written by one of its leading managers) and placed in the context of the broad evolution of the German economy. There is special emphasis on diversification of products and the social policy of the enterprise. Its weak point is the lack of any scholarly apparatus or footnotes.

Firms: Carl Zeiss

1589
Schumann, Wolfgang (Editor)
Carl Zeiss Jena: Einst und Jetzt [Carl Zeiss Jena: Then and now]
For main entry, see 4034

1590
Suzuki, Yoshitaka
Three Decades of Fuji Xerox 1962–1992
1994 Fuji Xerox *Tokyo, Japan*

This is a polished and insightful commissioned history published in English and written by a leading business historian. It provides an outstanding example of a successful joint venture enterprise in Japan.
Firms: Xerox; Fuji Xerox

1591
Tissot, Laurent
E. Paillard & Cie, SA: Une entreprise vaudoise de petite méchanique, 1920–1945. Entreprise familiale, diversification industrielle et innovation technologique [E. Paillard & Cie, SA: A small-scale engineering firm in the Vaud region, 1920–45]
1987 DelVal *Causset Fribourg, Switzerland*

An excellent history of a Swiss Jura firm which specialized in typewriters (Hermes), cinematographic apparatus (Bolex), radios and Paillard gramophones.
Firms: E. Paillard & Cie, SA

1592
Uchida, Hoshimi
Wall Clocks of Nagoya, 1885-1925
1987 Hattori Seiko *Tokyo, Japan*

A lucid story–originally a part of Seiko's official history. It focuses on the closing of the technology gap with the West and on the pattern of industrial organization and subcontracting that facilitated it. The book is based on company archives. None of the rest of the Seiko history is as yet translated.
Firms: Seiko

1593
Williams, Mari E. W.
The Precision Makers: A history of the instruments industry in Britain and France, 1870–1939
1994 Routledge *London*

This book examines the role of small high-technology firms in changing competitive environments and the importance of government support for military applications.
Firms: Barr & Stroud; Cambridge & Paul Instrument Co.; Cambridge Scientific Instrument Co.; Carella, CF; Cooke, Troughton & Simms; Elliott Brothers; Munro, RW; Optique et Précision de Lavallois

Food Manufacture, Excluding Meat Packing

1594
Adam, James S.
A Fell Fine Baker: The story of United Biscuits
1974 Hutchinson Benham *London*

A well-written company history of United Biscuits from the early nineteenth century, focusing on the entrepreneurial history of the smaller companies that went into the 1948 amalgamation.
Firms: Carr's of Carlisle; Kemps Biscuits; Macfarlane Lang; McVitie & Price; Meredith & Drew; William Crawford and Sons

1595
Burrough, Brian; Helyar, John
Barbarians at the Gate: The fall of RJR Nabisco
For main entry, see 2644

1596
Chalmin, Philippe
The Making of a Sugar Giant: Tate and Lyle, 1859–1989
1990 Harwood Academic Publishers *Chur, NY*

A massive and detailed study of a multinational company in the world sugar economy. It describes the emergence of the two family sugar-refining businesses of Tate and Lyle in the nineteenth century and their merger and further acquisitions. The book is especially strong on the organizational and financial complexity of the developing multinational and the

technology and strategy of sugar manufacturers.
Firms: Tate & Lyle

1597
Conly, G.
Wattie's: The first fifty years
1984 J. Wattie Canneries *Hastings, New Zealand*
A history of the most successful firm in the New Zealand fruit and vegetable processing industry. It began in 1930 with the use of windfall fruit for processing in place of imported fruit pulp from Australia.
Firms: Advanced Meat; Cropper-NRM; Food Processors; General Foods Corporation (NZ); N.Z. Packing Corporation; Wattie's

1598
Corley, Thomas A. B.
Quaker Enterprise in Biscuits: Huntley & Palmers of Reading 1822–1972
1972 Hutchinson *London*
An archivally-based study of a Quaker family partnership that became a major international company. It is especially good on the process of federation and merger of family firms, product innovation and marketing, the role of social considerations in management and the day-to-day running of the business (based on an unbroken series of ledgers and accounts books).
Firms: Huntley & Palmer; Peek Frean & Co.; W. & R. Jacob & Co.

1599
Eichner, Alfred S.
The Emergence of Oligopoly: Sugar refining as a case study
1969 Johns Hopkins University Press *Baltimore, MD*
A detailed economic history of the trust movement in sugar refining, 1895–1907. An excellent study based on an extensive use of antitrust records, evaluating changes in management and economies of scale and weighing allegations of monopoly and oligopoly.
Firms: American Sugar Refining Co.; E. C. Knight & Co.; National Sugar Refining Co.

1600
Emmet, Boris
The California and Hawaiian Sugar Refining Corporation of San Francisco,: A study of the origin, business policies and management of a co-operative refining and distributing organization
1970 AMS Press *New York, NY*
This is a well-researched study of an important US sugar region which was originally published in 1928. The book is especially strong on technology and industrial organization and contains much business and financial detail not available elsewhere on the internal workings of an important sugar company.
Firms: California & Hawaiian Sugar Refining Co.

1601
Fieldhouse, D. K.
Unilever Overseas: The anatomy of a multinational 1895–1965
1978 Croom Helm *London*
This study complements Wilson's earlier history by focusing on the activities of Unilever's overseas subsidiary companies. It demonstrates how the latter increased the firm's turnover far beyond the limits of the European market.
Firms: Unilever

1602
Fierain, Jacques
Les raffineries de sucre des ports en France, XIXe–debut du XXe Siècles [Sugar Refining in French Ports, Nineteenth to the Beginning of the Twentieth Century]
1977 Arno Press *New York, NY*
A history of sugar refining in the French sea-ports during the nineteenth and early twentieth centuries which contains much data on the main firms which operated there. There is also a detailed study of the rise of several very large companies such as the Raffineries du Saint-Louis and Raffineries de la Mediterranée. Based on large quantities of archival material.
Firms: Raffineries de la Mediterranée; Raffineries du Saint-Louis

1603
Fitzgerald, Robert
Rowntree and the Marketing Revolution 1862–1969
1995 Cambridge University Press *Cambridge*

This is a major study of Rowntree's marketing of cocoa, chocolate and confectionery products, focusing upon the development of new strategies to counter Cadbury's dominance in the 1920s. The role of George Harris in setting the company on the right road, and the appearance of major brands such as KitKat and Aero are fully explored.
Firms: British Cocoa and Confectionery (Cadbury-Fry); Cadbury Brothers; J. S. Fry & Sons; Nestlé; H. I. Rowntree & Co.; Rowntree & Co.; Rowntree Mackintosh

1604
Fruin, W. Mark
Kikkoman: Company, clan and community
1983 Harvard University Press *Cambridge, MA*

A major study of one of Japan's oldest and most profitable industrial giants and its development over three hundred years, becoming the best known and most widely used manufacturer of soy sauce products in the world. Using a variety of sources, but based on the voluminous Kikkoman archives, Fruin describes the company's metamorphosis from a traditional small family business into a modern corporation based on mass production methods and places it in the social and economic context of modern Japan.
Firms: Kikkoman

1605
Gardiner, Alfred G.
The Life of George Cadbury
For main entry, see 3891

1606
Gauldie, Enid
The Scottish Country Miller 1700–1900: A history of water-powered meal milling in Scotland
1981 Bell & Bain *Glasgow, Scotland*

Gauldie uses industrial archaeology and business archives as well as oral history to reconstruct the history of rural millers–key economic actors in local economies–and the changing technology and economics of their industry. An original and insightful study.

1607
Griffiths, Sir Percival
The History of the Indian Tea Trade
1967 Weidenfeld & Nicolson *London*

A weighty and authoritative standard work on the industry from the early days to the 1960s. Particular focus is placed on labour, scientific research and technological change, the organization and finance of the industry, and international markets.

1608
Heer, Jean
World Events 1866–1966: The first hundred years of Nestlé
1966 Nestlé Co. *Rivaz, Switzerland*

A hagiographic survey: but one of the few sources of information on Nestlé. This book was published in French, English, German, Italian and Spanish
Firms: Crosse & Blackwell; Findus; La Gragnanese; Locatelli; Maggi; Nestlé; Peter Cailler, Kohler

1609
Heitmann, John A.
The Modernization of the Louisiana Sugar Industry, 1830–1910
For main entry, see 280

1610
Jenkins, Alan
Drinka Pinta: The story of milk and the industry that serves it
1970 Heinemann *London*

A popular but extensively researched history of the National Milk Publicity Council which sheds considerable light on the advertising and marketing techniques which helped to give milk its characteristic place in British social and dietary life. It has fascinating illustrations.
Firms: Milk Marketing Board

1611
Kagome
Kagome Hachi-ju Nenshi [Eighty Years of Kagome With Tomatoes]

1978 Kagome *Nagoya, Japan*

Kagome, the biggest ketchup maker in Japan, developed a new food industry in 1899 as part of the westernization of Japanese dietary life. This book explains how the local small family firm succeeded in developing nationally into a major tomato processing business, also diversifying into tomato cultivation.

Firms: Kagome Co.

1612

Kuhlman, Charles B.

The Development of the Flour-Milling Industry in the United States

1929 Houghton-Mifflin *Boston, MA* 1973 Augustus Kelley *West Caldwell, NJ*

A careful study of the history of the industry from colonial times to the 1920s, especially focusing on technical change and innovation in the Midwest and Minneapolis from the 1870s.

1613

Kuuse, Jan

Sockerbolaget Cardo, 1907–1982

1982 Cardo *Malmö, Sweden*

When the Swedish Sugar Co. was founded in 1907 as a result of a series of mergers, it was the largest joint-stock company in Sweden. Ever since it has had a virtual monopoly of sugar production in Sweden. Thus the book is the history of the entire Swedish sugar industry and its many dealings with the government regarding agricultural policy.

Firms: Svenska Sockerbolaget Cardo

1614

Lucas, K. G.

A new Twist: A centennial history of Donaghy's Industries

1979 Donaghy's Industries *Dunedin, New Zealand*

This history of Donaghy's, which began as ropemakers in 1876, highlights the policies of a company which faced a frequently shifting market. It concentrated for some time on developing and publicizing new ideas for cordage, but by the 1970s adopted a diversification strategy, embracing linen and jute based goods, nylon and polyester ropes, a variety of synthetic fibres, and food products.

Firms: Andrews Twine Co.; BNZ Estates Co.; Donaghy's Industries; Nixon Industries Ltd; Severnside Foods (NZ) Ltd

1615

Oddy, Derek J.; Miller, Derek S. (Editors)

Diet and Health in Modern Britain

1985 Croom Helm *London*

An important but neglected collection of essays which provides important information on demand, consumption and marketing in the meat, brewing, fruit and vegetable industries, as well as substantial material on the history of nutrition.

1616

Powell, Horace B.

The Original Has This Signature: W. K. Kellogg

1956 Prentice-Hall *Englewood Cliffs, NJ*

The authorized biography. Generally hagiographic, the book contains valuable information on the origins of mass marketing and the production of breakfast cereals.

Firms: Kellogg

1617

Powell, William J.

Pillsbury's Best: A company history from 1869

1985 Pillsbury Co. *Minneapolis, MN*

The authorized biography which, though pious, has much data not elsewhere available.

Firms: Pillsbury

1618

Reader, William J.

Metal Box: A history

For main entry, see 1370

1619

Reader, W. J.

Birds Eye: The early years

1963 Birds Eye *Walton-on-Thames*

A useful authorized history which has considerable insight into the evolution of the frozen food industry.

Firms: Birds Eye

1620

Sabin, Dena Markoff

How Sweet It Was!: The beet sugar industry in

microcosm, the National Sugar Manufacturing Company, 1899 to 1967
1986 Garland *New York, NY*

This is a revised version of the author's 1980 PhD thesis. It focuses on the battle of the cane sugar refiners, led by the American Sugar Refining Co. and the Sugar Trust, against the incursions of the rapidly rising beet sugar industry in the late nineteenth century. Tactics shifted from attempting to destroy the beet producers to incorporating them. The focus is on a detailed study of the National Sugar Co. of Colorado, in particular dealing with entrepreneurship, technology, marketing and business strategy.
Firms: American Sugar Refining Co.; National Sugar Co. (Colorado); Sugar Trust

1621
Smith, Chris; Child, John; Rowlinson, Michael
Reshaping Work, the Cadbury Experience
1990 Cambridge University Press *Cambridge*

The authors focus on the management of organizational change at Cadbury. The first hundred pages provide an excellent history of management at Cadbury and the rest of the book focuses in detail on the management of a major capital investment programme at Bournville in the 1980s.
Firms: Cadbury

1622
Strasser, Susan
Satisfaction Guaranteed: The making of the American mass market
For main entry, see 2060

1623
Stuyvenberg, J. H. van (Editor)
Margarine: An economic and social history, 1869–1969
1969 University of Toronto Press *Toronto, Canada*

This book is a collection of seven chapters by different authors: (1) 100 Years of the Margarine Industry; (2) Raw Materials; (3) Technology and Production; (4) Nutritional and Dietetic Aspects; (5) Research; (6) Marketing and (7) Aspects of Government Intervention. The early development of the industry in France and Holland, and then in the USA after 1880, and in Russia after 1900 is discussed.

1624
Vatin, François
L'industrie de lait: Essai d'histoire économique [The Milk Business: An economic study]
1990 L'Harmattan *Paris, France*

An extensive history of the industrialization of the French milk industry from rural industry to bio-technology, with a focus on the rural/industrial interface and its impact on rural employment and work.

1625
Vernon, Anne
A Quaker Business Man: The life of Joseph Rowntree, 1836–1925
For main entry, see 3929

1626
Wagner, Gillian
The Chocolate Conscience
1987 Chatto & Windus *London*

A useful study concentrating on the Quaker founding families, their business practices, and their welfare concerns in the British chocolate industry.
Firms: Cadbury; Fry; Rowntree

1627
Williams, Iolo A.
The Firm of Cadbury 1831–1931
1931 Constable *London*

Despite the publication of Smith et al. (qv), this remains an invaluable source for the early history of the company from 1831 to the 1920s.
Firms: Cadbury

1628
Wilson, Charles
The History of Unilever: A study in economic growth and social change
1954 Cassell *London*

This impressive two volume study of one of the world's major conglomerates did much to establish the reputation of business history as an academic discipline. It is invaluable on the process of competition, cartels and mergers in the oils and fats industries. Originating in an amalgamation of British soap manufacturers,

the firm diversified into many other activities, notably the Niger Company, and acquired its Dutch interests in 1929.
Firms: Unilever; Lever Bros; Margarine Union; Van den Bergh

1629
Wilson, Charles
Unilever 1945–1965: Challenge & response in the post-war industrial revolution
1968 Cassell *London*

The final volume of the Unilever history, published fourteen years after the first two, follows the same themes and gives considerable detail on the company, but it is less insightful and critical than the first two volumes.
Firms: Unilever; Lever bros; Margarine Union; Van den Bergh

Food Manufacture, Meat Packing

1630
Clemen, Rudolph A.
The American Livestock and Meat Industry
1923 Ronald Press Company *New York, NY*

For many years this volume was the standard reference on the American meat industry. It was written by an associate editor of a trade journal well-versed in the activities of the industry. It is now outdated in approach, but still offers a considerable body of information of traditional nature.
Firms: Armour & Co.; Morris & Co.; Swift & Co.; Wilson & Co.

1631
Critchell, James T.; Raymond, Joseph
A History of the Frozen Meat Trade
1912 Constable *London*

A lengthy international survey of all aspects of the industry from its beginnings in the mid-1870s until 1912, mentioning the pioneers and early firms of the industry. It covers all the aspects of production and marketing. The authors wrote over 4,000 letters to all concerned in the industry and also used published business reports as well as press and journal articles.

1632
Hanson, Simon G.
Argentine Meat and the British Market
1938 Oxford University Press *Oxford*

This book describes the development of the Argentine frozen meat industry and the crucial role of the British market in its growth from 1880 onwards. Although not a business history, the work contains extensive references to, and information on, a number of ranching, packing, freezing and marketing firms in the industry.
Firms: Armour & Company; British & Argentine Meat Co.; Frigorifica Uruguaya; James Nelson & Sons; La Plata Cold Storage Co.; National Packing Co.; Sansinena; Smithfield & Argentine Meat Co.; Swift & Co.; Union Cold Storage Ltd

1633
Harrison, Godfrey
Borthwicks: A century in the meat trade, 1863–1963
1963 Borthwicks *London*

A solid company history of a Lancashire firm of butchers who became importers of New Zealand meat in the 1880s and branched out to establish packing and freezing works in New Zealand (1902) and Australia (1908). Eventually they had five works in New Zealand and five in Australia and also owned sheep and cattle in those countries.
Firms: Thomas Borthwick & Sons Ltd

1634
Knightley, Phillip
The Vestey Affair
1981 Macdonald Futura *London*

A well-written, lively account by an investigative journalist that tells how the brothers William and Edmund Vestey, founders of the family fortune in the meat business, established a series of offshore holding companies to prevent themselves paying what they considered to be punitive British taxes after 1915. Their tax evasion schemes were modified over the years and were still being enjoyed in the 1970s by their descendants, who controlled the family's extensive meat businesses, yet paid hardly any taxes in Britain.
Firms: Argenta Meat Co.; Blue Star; Eastmans;

J. H. Dewhurst; Union Cold Storage; W & R Fletcher

1635
Lind, C. A.
A Cut Above: Early history of the Alliance Freezing Company (Southland) Ltd
1985 Alliance Freezing *Invercargill, New Zealand*

This study details the efforts of Southland farmers in New Zealand to set up their own freezing works in 1947. This was in response to the bankruptcy threat many had faced in the 1930s while existing freezing companies were returning good profits. An interesting example of a cooperative.
Firms: Alliance Freezing Co.; Associated NZ Farmers (UK); Ocean Beach Freezing Works; Southland Frozen Meat Co.

1636
Nerheim, Gunnar; Utne, Bjorn S.
Under samme stjerne: Rederiet Peder Smevig 1915–1990 [Smedvig: A story of canning, shipping and contract drilling from western Norway]
For main entry, see 3097

1637
Newell, Dianne (Editor)
The Development of the Pacific Salmon Canning Industry: A grown man's game
1990 McGill-Queen's University Press *Toronto, Canada*

This edited collection of original documents illuminates the development of the salmon-canning industry in British Columbia in the period 1902–1928. The Canadian experience is set helpfully within a general North American context.

1638
Pate, J'Nell L.
Livestock Legacy: The Fort Worth stockyards, 1887–1987
1992 Texas A & M University Press *College Station, TX*

An extensively-researched history of a major livestock firm from its origins through the period of heyday to postwar decentralization and decline. Based on company and town archives, it describes both everyday life and work in the stockyards (including plentiful anecdotes) and the business strategy and practices of Armour and Swift.
Firms: Armour & Co.; Swift & Co.; Union Stock Yards Co.

1639
Perren, Richard
The Meat Trade in Britain 1840–1914
For main entry, see 2051

1640
Schwartz, Marvin
Tyson: From farm to market
1991 University of Arkansas Press *Fayetteville, AR*

Though not an academic work, this book contains much helpful information on the creation of mass-marketed chickens, especially the development of farming and production methods and the marketing and redefinition of the product.
Firms: Tyson

1641
Skaggs, Jimmy M.
Prime Cut: Livestock raising and meatpacking in the United States, 1607–1983
1986 Texas A & M University Press *College Station, TX*

A useful reference work presenting the conclusions of books and journal articles on meatpacking and livestock raising, but which adds little of the author's own analysis. An extensive twenty-seven page bibliography testifies to the exhaustive research undertaken.
Firms: Armour & Co.; Cudahy & Co.; George H. Hammond Co.; Nelson Morris & Co.; Schwarschild & Sulzberger; Swift & Co.

1642
Smith, Peter H.
Politics and Beef in Argentina: Partners of conflict and change
For main entry, see 259

1643
Swift, Louis F.; Vissingen, Jr, Arthur van
The Yankee of the Yards: The biography of Gustavus Franklin Swift

1970 AMS Press *New York, NY*

This book, a reprint of a work first published in 1927, presents a rather heroic picture of one of the United States' major meatpackers. Written by Swift's son, the folksy narrative offers some insights into the hero's character and the developments in the industry.

Firms: Swift & Co.

1644

Wade, Louise C.

Chicago's Pride: The stockyards, Packingtown, and environs in the nineteenth century

1987 University of Illinois Press *Urbana, IL*

A well-researched narrative of Chicago's meat packing industry and its impact on the surrounding communities in the period from the 1850s to the 1890s. It is stronger on socio-economic history than business history.

Firms: Armour & Co.; Swift & Co.

1645

Walsh, Margaret

The Rise of the Midwestern Meat Packing Industry

1982 University Press of Kentucky *Lexington, KY*

A description of the development of pork packing in the Ohio Valley and Mississippi Valley States from a seasonal agricultural industry to city-based factory processing. This is an excellent research monograph that makes wide use of a variety of original source material including government reports, state agricultural statistics, local directories and newspapers. The analytical focus is on transport improvements and the role of individual entrepreneurs in organization and technology.

1646

Yeager, Mary

Competition and Regulation: The development of oligopoly in the meat packing industry

1981 JAI Press *Greenwich, CT*

A professional analysis of the growth and development of the leading US meat packing firms, centered on the years from 1886 to 1912. Yeager explains how the dressed beef industry emerged along oligopolistic lines in order to cope with the problems of technology and markets, but by 1912 its members had learnt to maintain price agreements without overt collusion.

Firms: Armour & Co.; Hammond & Co.; Morris & Co.; National Packing Company; Swift & Co.

Food Manufacture, Soft Drinks

1647

Kahn, E. J.

The Big Drink: An unofficial history of Coca-Cola

1950 Max Reinhardt *London*

Marginally the best of a very poor crop of popular histories of Coca-Cola.

Firms: Coca-Cola

1648

Louis, J. C.; Yazijian, Harvey Z.

The Cola Wars

1980 Everest House *New York, NY*

A useful journalistic account of the struggles between Coke and Pepsi.

Firms: Coca-Cola; PepsiCo

1649

Martin, Milward W.

Twelve Full Ounces

1962 Holt, Rinehart and Winston *New York, NY*

A little-known but fascinating book on the early history of Pepsi, which, although not footnoted, appears to be largely based on legal documents relating to the adjudication of the ownership of Pepsi-Cola in the late 1930s.

Firms: PepsiCo

1650

Muris, Timothy J.; Scheffman, David T.; Spiller, Pablo T.

Strategy, Structure and Antitrust in the Carbonated Soft-Drink Industry

1993 Greenwood Press *Westport, CT*

This book blends history and economic theory in an important analysis of the industry. It argues that strategic moves towards vertical integration into bottling by concentrate producers has been pro- rather than anti-competitive. It challenges the standard wisdom about

oligopolistic structures in the industry and the role of antitrust through an in-depth analysis of market segmentation and company strategy.
Firms: Pepsico; Coca-Cola; Seven-Up; Dr Pepper

1651
Prendergrast, Mark
For God, Country and Coca-Cola: The unauthorised history of the great American soft drink and the company that makes it
1993 Weidenfeld & Nicolson *London*

A lively journalistic history which is at its best on the early days of Coca-Cola, tracing its emergence from an environment of patent medicines, quackery and financial chicanery. It is rich in anecdotes and illuminating on the personalities involved.
Firms: Coca-Cola

1652
Riley, John J.
A History of the American Soft Drink Industry: Bottled carbonated beverages, 1807–1957
1972 Arno Press *New York, NY*

A valuable overview of the history of the industry up to the Second World War.
Firms: Coca-Cola; PepsiCo

1653
Simmons, Douglas A.
Schweppes: The first 200 years
1983 Springwood Books *London*

A valuable commissioned history. Though glossy and highly illustrated, it is a serious study, strong on product and marketing innovation, mergers, entrepreneurs and strategy, but unfortunately lacks financial data.
Firms: Cadbury; Schweppes

1654
Tedlow, Richard S.
New and Improved: The story of mass marketing in America
1990 Basic Books *New York, NY*

Tedlow provides a full and vivid case study of the Great Cola Wars–Coke vs. Pepsi–that is one of the few quality contributions to the history of the US soft drinks industry.
Firms: Coca-Cola; PepsiCo

1655
Tollison, Robert P.; Kaplan, David P.; Higgins, Richard S.
Competition and Concentration: The economics of the carbonated soft drink industry
1991 Lexington Books *Lexington, MA*

A detailed economic study of competition, performance, entry and collusion in the US soft drinks industry in the 1980s with plentiful quantitative analysis. One of the few scholarly studies of the industry–though it lacks much historical depth.
Firms: Coca-Cola; Dr. Pepper; PepsiCo

Papermaking

1656
Ahvenainen, Jorma
Paperitehtaista suuryhtiöksi. Kymin Osakeyhtiö 1918–1939 [The great paper making company. Kymin Osakeyhtiö 1918–1939]
1972 Kymmene Co. *Kuusankoski, Finland*

During the period between the two World Wars, the Finnish company Kymin Osakeyhtiö was the largest paper manufacturer in the Nordic countries and very successful financially. The book deals with the development of the company from 1872 to 1940 and describes the domestic and international environment in which the company was operating, and how it found and secured its markets. The history of the company is viewed as one part of the history of the Finnish wood-processing industry, and consequently crucial issues of the Finnish paper industry of the 1920s and the 1930s are also addressed.
Firms: Kymin Osakeyhtiö

1657
Ahvenainen, Jorma
The History of Star Paper 1875–1960
1976 Studia Historica Jyväskyläensia (University at Jyväskylä) *Jyväskylä, Finland*

The Star Paper Co. Ltd was established in 1875 in Lancaster, England with a paper mill in Blackburn. Its founders were mainly textile manufacturers from Blackburn and Darwen. In 1930, Kymin Osakeyhtiö purchased this firm when it fell on hard times and, at the same time,

also bought the bankrupt factory of the Yorkshire Paper Mills in Barnsley which had belonged to the Marsden family. The book deals with the history of the company since its establishment until the 1970s. In addition to the Star factories, the relevant history of British paper mills is also considered here.
Firms: Star Paper Co.; Kymin Osakeyhtiö

1658
Ahvenainen, Jorma
Enso-Gutzeit Oy 1872–1992
1992 Enso-Gutzeit Oy *Helsinki, Finland*

The Enso-Gutzeit operation began in 1872 and operation of the company was fairly difficult until the beginning of the 1890s but thereafter its position gradually improved as the company accumulated very extensive tracts of land. In 1918 the government of Finland purchased the majority of the shares in the company under turbulent political conditions. In dealing with the impact of a large wood-processing company on the Finnish economy, particular emphasis is placed on the issue of how the vast natural resources that had come into possession of the company were put to industrial use. The book also deals with the timber industries of British Columbia where the firm founded Eurocan Pulp and Paper Co. Ltd in 1965 (at Kitimat).
Firms: Enso-Gutzeit; Eurocan Pulp & Paper

1659
Borgis, Jean-Pierre
Histoire de la Papeterie de Moulin Vieux, 1869–1989 [A History of the Moulin Vieux Paper Mill 1869–1989]
1991 Presses Universitaires de Grenoble *Grenoble, France*

Borgis describes the history of a middle-sized paper mill.
Firms: Papeterie de Moulin Vieux

1660
Coleman, Donald C.
The British Paper Industry 1495–1860: A study in industrial growth
1958 Clarendon Press *Oxford*

Essential starting point for the history of the industry. This book is a scholarly examination of the economic and technical problems, and the structure and organization of the industry up to the end of the rag-based and beginning of the wood-pulp based industry. Substantial statistical material.
Firms: Fourdrinier Bros; John Dickinson; Longman

1661
Evans, Joan
The Endless Web: John Dickinson & Co. Ltd, 1804–1954
1955 Jonathan Cape *London*

A full-length business history based on family papers and company archives.
Firms: John Dickinson & Co.

1662
Hills, Richard L.
Papermaking in Britain, 1488–1988: A short history
1988 Athlone Press *London*

The best single volume overview of the entire history of the industry. Excellent on technology, weaker on the financial and organizational side of the industry.

1663
Mathias, Philip
Takeover: The 22 days of risk and decision that created the world's largest newsprint empire, Abitibi-Price
1976 MacLean-Hunter *Toronto, Canada*

This book reconstructs events leading to the takeover of Price Co. by Abitibi Paper Co. in 1974, covering especially the legal and financial issues, when Abitibi, an old and conservative Canadian paper company moved dramatically into the merger business. The author gives more on the takeover itself than the industry.
Firms: Abitibi Paper; Price Co.

1664
McGraw, Judith A.
Most Wonderful Machine: Mechanization and social change in Berkshire paper making, 1801–1885
1987 Princeton University Press *Princeton, NJ*

A widely-acclaimed study that uses the paper industry to look at the technical and social origins of US industrialization, stressing incremental technical change and the role of

smaller units of production in mechanization and the complex balance between hand labour and the new technology of the Fourdrinier presses. The author makes use of numerous business archives. A notable book.
Firms: Crane & Co.; L. L. Brown & Co.

1665
Ohanian, Nancy K.
The American Pulp and Paper Industry, 1900–1940: Mill survival, firm structure, and industry relocation
1993 Greenwood Press *Westport, CT*

Ohanian employs an econometric analysis as a basis for a study of business survival, growth and competition during a period of major structural change and with implications for general theories of industrial organization.

1666
Reader, W. J.
Bowater: A history
1981 Cambridge University Press *Cambridge*

A detailed and authoritative business history, concentrating on the leading roles of key personalities, the multinational expansion of the company and its merger and diversification strategies. It contains a wealth of business and financial data and is very strong on the international patterns of competition in the newsprint industry.
Firms: Bowater; Ralli-International

1667
Schybergson, Per
Verkar och dagar: Ahlströms historia 1851–1981 [Works and Days: A history of Ahlström Ltd, 1851–1981]
1992 Ahlström Ab *Vammala, Finland*

This is a business history of a large Finnish multi-industrial concern that has grown rapidly as a family enterprise since the mid-nineteenth century. It describes the expansion of the company from sawmilling to paper making, glass blowing and mechanical engineering. The main themes of the book consist of takeovers, investment projects and the decision making of the top executives.
Firms: Ahlström Oy; Karhula Oy; Paul Wahl Oy

1668
Shorter, Alfred H.
Paper Making in the British Isles: An historical and geographical study
1971 David & Charles *Newton Abbot*

A study in the historical geography of the paper industry in the British Isles from 1490 to 1900 with shorter material on the twentieth century. Particularly illuminating on the emergence of modern locational patterns.

1669
Thomson, Alistair G.
The Paper Industry in Scotland, 1590–1861
1974 Scottish Academic Press *Edinburgh, Scotland*

An extensively researched, scholarly account of the growth of Scottish papermaking from the sixteenth to twentieth centuries. Close attention is paid to technical change and shifting locations: very thorough attention to the financial side of the industry using business archives, family correspondence and official papers.

1670
Virtanen, Sakari
Kajaani Oy 1907–1982: I osa: Kainuuseen sijoitettu, II osa: Puusta elävä [Kajaani Ltd 1907–1982: Vol. I: Located in Kainuu, Vol. II: Living by means of wood]
1982–5 Kajaani Oy *Helsinki, Finland*

This describes the establishment of an integrated wood-processing mill in a remote region of Finland. The book analyses the use of abundant forest and hydropower resources in the Kainuu region as well as the company's economic performance. It also focuses on the firm's internal business culture and its relationships to the surrounding province.
Firms: Kajaani Oy

1671
Virtanen, Sakari
Lapin leivän isä 100 vuotta: Kemiyhtiön historia [The Breadwinner in Lapland A history of Kemi Ltd]
1993 Oy Metsä-Botnia Ab *Jyväskylä, Finland*

This commissioned history (1893–1993) celebrates the industrialization of the northernmost province of Finland. The main theme is the study of the relationships between owners

and management in a company that developed from three merged sawmills into a major wood-processing concern. It also gives an account of the 'forced industrialization' of postwar Lapland by the extensive intervention of the Finnish government and the fierce struggles between various owners of the company.
Firms: Kemi; Bank of Finland; Uleå; Veitsiluoto

1672
Voorn, H.
De geschiedenis van de Nederlandse papierindustrie [The History of the Dutch Papermaking Industry]
1960–73 Wormerveer *Haarlem, The Netherlands*
A wide-ranging and detailed survey of the papermaking trade and papermaking processes in The Netherlands through the ages. More an encyclopaedia of manufacturers than a historical analysis, this work gives little attention to the business side of the mills discussed.

1673
Weeks, Lyman Horace
A History of Paper-manufacturing in the United States, 1690–1916
1969 B. Franklin *New York, NY*
A detailed study of the origins of the industry by a dedicated antiquarian, completed in 1916 but now reprinted. It contains a great deal of (barely digested) information.

Furniture

1674
Garenc, Paule
L'industrie du meuble en France [The Furniture Industry in France]
1958 Presses Universitaires de France *Paris, France*
A massive, scholarly examination of the French furniture industry from the fifteenth to the twentieth century. There is systematic coverage of periods, regions and sub-sectors, of the national market. Encyclopaedic. Lacks an index.

1675
Kirkham, Pat; Mace, Rodney; Porter, Julia
Furnishing the World: The East London furniture trade, 1830–1980
1987 Journeyman Press *London*
Beautifully produced and illustrated, this book draws particularly upon the collection of the Geffrye Museum, and using the archives of numerous East End companies provides both a social and business history of the furniture trade. It pays particular attention to the craft origins and rise of the industry, marketing, and trade unionism.

1676
Linton, David; Boston, Ray
The Newspaper Press in Britain: An annotated bibliography
For main entry, see 23

1677
Oliver, John L.
The Development and Structure of the Furniture Industry
1966 Pergamon Press *Oxford*
Oliver deals with the structure and historical geography of the wooden furniture industry, with special reference to the USA and the UK. Relatively brief but an indispensable starting-point.

Wood Products, General

1678
Chew, Sing C.
Logs for Capital: The timber industry and capitalist enterprise in the nineteenth century
For main entry, see 305

1679
Hassbring, Lars
The International Development of the Swedish Match Co., 1917–24
1979 Liber Förlag *Stockholm, Sweden*
A volume in the official history of the Swedish Match Co. It investigates the transformation of the industry from a domestic to multinational one. The book concentrates

especially on Kreuger's strategic innovations and the financing of internationalization.
Firms: Swedish Match Co.

1680
Hildebrand, Karl-Gustaf
Expansion, Crisis, Reconstruction 1917–1939
1985 Liber Förlag *Stockholm, Sweden*

In this summary of the Swedish Match operations 1917–1939, Professor Hildebrand gives a dramatic history of the company's internationalization process. Authors of other books on Swedish Match history are Lars Hassbring, Håkan Lindgren, Ulla Wikander and Hans Modig (qqv).
Firms: Swedish Match Co.

1681
Lindgren, Håkan
Corporate Growth: The Swedish match industry in its global setting
1979 Liber Förlag *Stockholm, Sweden*

This is part of the important series of official history volumes commissioned by the Swedish Match Company. The volume covers the internationalization of the industry and the emergence of the Swedish Match Co. as one of the dominant match producers of the world. It focuses especially on the match markets of Britain and the Soviet Union in the 1920s and 1930s and deals with barriers to entry, product differentiation and strategy in world markets. An important work.
Firms: Swedish Match Co.

1682
Myllyntaus, Timo
Finnish Industry in Transition, 1885–1920: Responding to Technological Challenges
For main entry, see 4285

1683
Ruuskanen, Pekka
Koivikoista maailmanmarkkinoille: Suomen rullateollisuus vuosina 1873–1972 [From Birch Groves to the World Market: The rise and fall of the Finnish spool industry, 1873–1972]
1992 University of Jyväskylä *Jyväskylä, Finland*

The book relates the life cycle of both an industrial product, wooden spools for reeling cotton thread, and a Finnish wood-processing industry. In addition, it gives an interesting account of how British multinational thread trusts, J. & P. Coats and the English Sewing Cotton Company, controlled not only the international thread business but also the world trade in wooden spools. The book contains a summary in English.
Firms: Ab Tornator; Enso-Gutzeit Oy; J. & P. Coats; Kaukas Ab; Oy H. Saastamoinen; Oy Pallas Ab; English Sewing Cotton Company; Öström & Fisher Ab

1684
Wikander, Ulla
Kreuger's Match Monopolies, 1925–30: Case studies in market control through public monopolies
1979 Liber Förlag *Stockholm, Sweden*

Part of the official history of the Swedish Match Co., this volume focuses on Kreuger's strategy of 'buying' public monopolies from national governments to construct his Match Trust. This scholarly study traces a remarkable episode of financial and business/government dealings.
Firms: Swedish Match Co.

Printing & Publishing, General

1685
Altschull, J. Herbert
Agents of Power: The role of the news media in human affairs
1984 Longmans *London*

A wide-ranging and at times idiosyncratic study of news media from the First Amendment to the present day. It contains useful business history information on the commercial press in the nineteenth century; the muckrakers; the press in the Third World; and the press and the advertising industry.

1686
Bagdikian, Ben H.
The Effete Conspiracy and Other Crimes of the Press
1972 Harper & Row *New York, NY*

A controversial study that analyses relations

between the press and the advertising industry, demonstrating that most of the expansion in the size and content of newspapers in the USA between 1940 and 1965 was due to the increased volume of advertising material.

1687

Boyd-Barrett, Oliver

The International News Agencies

For main entry, see 3274

1688

Dunnett, Peter J. S.

The World Newspaper Industry

1987 Croom Helm *London*

This book surveys the state of the world newspaper industry in the 1980s, but its extensive data covers developments over time as well as current structure. Dunnett covers all the major newspaper industries and is best on the impact of new technologies and concentration of ownership.

1689

Kaldor, Nicholas; Silverman, Rodney

A Statistical Analysis of Advertising Expenditure and of the Revenues of the Press

For main entry, see 3293

1690

Kobrak, Fred; Luey, Beth (Editors)

The Structure of International Publishing in the 1990s

1992 Transaction Publishers *New Brunswick, NJ*

A mixed bag of essays with some valuable historical material. It focuses on the role of mergers, takeovers and concentration in the global publishing industry and the long-run tensions between 'mass' and 'serious' culture. It contains some good case studies of particular mergers.

Firms: Harry N. Abrams Inc.; Macmillan Inc.; Scribner Book Co.; Times Mirror

1691

Parsons, Wayne

The Power of the Financial Press: Journalism and economic opinion in Britain and America

1989 Edward Elgar *Aldershot*

Parsons focuses on economic journalism and its influence on policy-making; he incorporates a succinct account of the evolution of the financial press and comments on its contemporary role in the global information economy.

1692

Rose, Mark

Authors and Owners: The invention of copyright

1993 Harvard University Press *Cambridge, MA*

This is a scrupulous study of the emergence of the idea of authorial property in early eighteenth-century England. Its starting point is legal history, but the author is at pains to develop the implications for the structure of commercial publishing and also examines the emerging challenge of new publishing technologies for the concept of copyright.

1693

Smith, Anthony

Goodbye Gutenberg: The newspaper revolution in the 1980s

1980 Oxford University Press *New York, NY*

An excellent examination of the challenge of 'electronic newspapers' to the conventional press. It stresses the social function of newspapers, the economic 'rescue' of the newspaper by electronic technology in the 1970s, and its threat to supersede it in the 1980s. Superb on technical change.

1694

Smith, Anthony (Editor)

Newspapers and Democracy: International essays on a changing medium

1980 MIT Press *Cambridge, MA*

A valuable international comparative collection of essays on various aspects of the press, especially technology, and relations with governments. High quality material on the UK, USA, Japan, Scandinavia, France, Spain and Italy.

1695

Stark, Gary D.

Entrepreneurs of Ideology: Neoconservative publishers in Germany, 1890–1933

1981 University of North Carolina Press *Chapel Hill, NC*

A study of 'cultural entrepreneurship', focusing on links between leading publishers and political parties of the far right, and their role in the development of antimodernist and racialist theories.

Printing & Publishing, UK

1696
Andrews, W. Linton; Taylor, H. A.
Lords and Laborers of the Press: Men who fashioned the modern British newspaper
1970 Southern Illinois University Press *Carbondale, IL*

Two leading British journalists provide valuable portraits of leading newspaper editors and proprietors, including Northcliffe, Spender, Garvin, Camrose, Cudlipp and Thomson.
Firms: Amalgamated Press; Beaverbrook Newspapers; International Publishing Corp.; Kemsley Newspapers; Odhams Press; Thomson Organisation

1697
Ayerst, David G. O.
The *Manchester Guardian*: Biography of a newspaper
1971 Collins *London*

One of the better newspaper histories, written by a former Guardian staff writer. The book is thin on details of the business and financial side of the paper, and covers its development mainly in terms of the leading editorial figures, especially the Taylor and Scott families. Still the fullest account of the paper's history and can be used in conjunction with G. Taylor (qv).
Firms: Manchester Guardian

1698
Barrell, Joan; Braithwaite, Brian
The Business of Women's Magazines
1988 Kogan Page *London*

A basic work, with useful data appendices, covering the history of this important segment of the magazine market in the UK, and particularly the mushrooming growth of new launches following the success of *Cosmopolitan* in the early 1970s.
Firms: Amalgamated Press; Argus Press; International Publishing Corp. (IPC); National Magazine Co.; Newnes, George; Thomson Organisation; Thomson, D. C. Hearst Corporation; Hearst Corporation

1699
Berry, William Ewert (Lord Camrose)
British Newspapers and their Controllers
1947 Cassell *London*

A valuable source book on national and provincial papers and political periodicals by a former Chairman and editor of the *Daily Telegraph* and proprietor of the *Sunday Times* and *Financial Times*.

1700
Berry, William Michael (Lord Hartwell)
William Camrose: Giant of Fleet Street
1992 Weidenfeld & Nicolson *London*

A major biography of the great press proprietor by his second son.
Firms: Amalgamated Press; Daily Telegraph; Financial Times

1701
Bourne, Richard
Lords of Fleet Street: The Harmsworth dynasty
1990 Unwin Hyman *London*

The primary focus is on the personalities and politics of the Northcliffe–Rothermere dynasty. Much weaker than Pound & Harmsworth (qv) but it covers a much longer period.
Firms: Associated Newspapers; Daily Mail; Daily Mirror; Evening News

1702
Bower, Tom
Maxwell, The Outsider
For main entry, see 3867

1703
Boyce, George; Curran, James; Wingate, Pauline (Editors)
Newspaper History: From the seventeenth century to the present day
1978 Constable *London*

This is a collection of eighteen essays in revisionist academic history, re-examining the factors that affected the early development and political influence of the British press. It has an extensive bibliography and chronology.

1704
Briggs, Asa (Editor)
Essays in the History of Publishing in Celebration of the 250th Anniversary of the House of Longman, 1724–1974
1974 Longman *London*

A useful set of eleven scholarly essays that sets the history of Longmans in the context of the broader history of British publishing, especially in relation to issues of copyright, the paperback revolution and educational publishing. Well produced and profusely illustrated, often in colour.
Firms: Longman & Co.

1705
Brown, Lucy
Victorian News and Newspapers
1985 Clarendon Press *Oxford*

A study of the handling and distribution of news in late Victorian Britain, especially the rise of the cheap newspaper following the advent of continuous rotary presses from the mid-1860s. It focuses on the tensions between old ways of reporting news and new ways of producing papers. A fascinating and meticulous study.
Firms: Press Association; Reuters

1706
Chippindale, Peter; Horrie, Chris
Stick It Up Your Punter!: The rise and fall of *The Sun*
1990 Heinemann *London*

First-class modern muckraking which provides a superb critique of the degradation of the British tabloid press in the 1980s.
Firms: Mirror Group Newspapers (Daily Mirror); News International; Sun

1707
Chisholm, Anne; Davie, Michael
Beaverbrook: A life
1992 Hutchinson *London*

A superb biography, invaluable for details of Beaverbrook's early business ventures in Canada and for his later career as a press baron. It contains an appendix on the 'Canada Cement affair' of 1909–13.
Firms: Beaverbrook Newspapers; Canada Cement Company; Express Newspapers; Royal Securities Company

1708
Cleverley, Graham
The Fleet Street Disaster: British national newspapers as a case study in mismangement
1976 Constable *London*

This book examines the business aspects of British national newspapers, including their profits, circulation, advertising and union-management relations.
Firms: International Publishing Corporation; Thomson Organization; Daily Mirror

1709
Cross, Nigel
The Common Writer: Life in nineteenth-century Grub Street
1985 Cambridge University Press *Cambridge*

A study of the social, cultural and economic factors surrounding freelance journalism and the development of publishing in the late eighteenth and early nineteenth centuries.

1710
Cudlipp, Hugh
Publish and Be Damned!: The astonishing story of the *Daily Mirror*
1953 Dakers *London*

A fine autobiographical account of the *Daily Mirror* in its heyday as Britain's leading mass-circulation daily, and its innovations in picture-led campaigning journalism directed to a primarily working-class readership.
Firms: Daily Mirror

1711
Curran, James; Seaton, Jean
Power without Responsibility: The press and broadcasting in Britain
4th Edition
1987 Methuen *London*

A highly regarded political analysis of the media, its ownership and power and the controls within which it operates.

1712
Daniel, Richard Altick
The English Common Reader: A social history of the mass reading public, 1800–1900
1957 Chicago University Press *Chicago, IL*

A pioneering work on newspaper readership in Britain, with valuable appendices on circulation.

1713
Darton, F. J. Harvey
Children's Books in England: Five centuries of social life
1982 Cambridge University Press *Cambridge*

A classic study of the history of children's books. Though its main concern is with the content of the books, the author's scholarship leads him into the commercial considerations that shaped the writing and marketing of these works, and which provided the background for the recurring struggles between instruction and amusement, freedom and constraint, in the literature.

1714
Economist Intelligence Unit
The National Newspaper Industry: A survey
1966 EIU *London*

A massive (over 500 pages) and indispensable factual survey of management, production methods, the role of trade unions, finance, and circulation, prepared under the auspices of the Joint Board for the National Newspaper Industry as a private study but later published.

Firms: Express Newspapers; Daily Mirror; Daily Telegraph; Manchester Guardian; Sun

1715
Edwards, Ruth Dudley
The Pursuit of Reason: *The Economist* 1843–1993
1993 Hamish Hamilton *London*

A massive chronicle of the life and times of *The Economist* which, besides describing the history of the journal, is a valuable source on the development and diffusion of economic ideas and debates.

Firms: Economist

1716
Gerald, J. Edward
The British Press under Government Economic Controls
1956 University of Minnesota Press *Minneapolis, MN*

A critical evaluation of the impact of wartime and post-war economic controls on the independence of the press, especially in the context of a decline of competition between newspapers. Full of much rare and valuable data on finance and competition in the national and regional press and in book publishing. It contains useful tables on advertising, circulation and profitability.

1717
Gollin, Alfred M.
The *Observer* and J. L. Garvin, 1908–1914: A study in a great editorship
1960 Oxford University Press *Oxford*

A scholarly and archivally-based study of the role of the *Observer* in politics in the crucial pre-First World War years, which also contains useful detail on the internal management organization of the paper and its financial and circulation strategies.

Firms: Observer

1718
Goodhart, David; Wintour, Patrick
Eddy Shah and the Newspaper Revolution
1986 Coronet *Sevenoaks*

Two journalists describe the break-up of the traditional pattern of British newspaper production. Its immediacy and description of the newspaper business in the mid-1980s make up for the lack of an index and bibliographic references.

Firms: Messenger Newspaper Group; News International; News UK; Today

1719
Harris, Michael
London Newspapers in the Age of Walpole: A study of the origins of the modern English press
1987 Associated University Presses *London*

A thoroughly-researched study that casts light not only on the press but also on London's wider role in the service and industrial sectors. It stresses the role of politics and control of newspapers by booksellers. The book is rather dense, but contains much of value on the scope and organization of the industry.

1720
Hart-Davis, Duff
The House the Berrys Built
1990 Hodder & Stoughton *London*

A fascinating study of internal governance in the *Telegraph* group which links personalities and wider managerial and financial issues. Especially strong on decline and crisis in the 1970s and 1980s.
Firms: Allied Newspapers; Amalgamated Press; Daily Telegraph

1721
Hobson, H.; Knightley, P.; Russell, L.
The Pearl of Days: An intimate memoir of the *Sunday Times*, 1822–1972
1972 Hamish Hamilton *London*

An authoritative and fascinating history which focuses particularly on leading personalities such as Kemsley, Thomson, Evans and Hamilton.
Firms: Thomson Organization; Sunday Times

1722
Hollis, Patricia L.
The Pauper Press: A study in working-class radicalism of the 1830s
1970 Oxford University Press *Oxford*

Hollis uses the Carlile Papers from the Huntington Library (San Marino, CA) to produce detailed studies of the leading proprietors and authors in the radical press during the Chartist era. An important study.

1723
Hubback, David
No Ordinary Press Baron: A life of Walter Layton
1985 Weidenfeld & Nicolson *London*

An intimate biography which is especially valuable for Layton's editorship of *The Economist* from 1922–38 and for his long association with the *News Chronicle* until its demise in 1960.
Firms: Associated Newspapers; Daily News; News Chronicle; Economist

1724
Jenkins, Simon
The Market for Glory: Fleet Street ownership in the twentieth century
1986 Faber & Faber *London*

A fluent journalistic account of the whole span of Fleet Street history. It is strongest on the proprietors, but also provides a balanced view of labour relations and managerial strategies in the industry that avoids the sensationalism with which the industry is often treated.
Firms: Associated Newspapers; Beaverbrook Newspapers; Mirror Group; News International; Thomson Organisation; Daily Telegraph

1725
Koss, Stephen E.
Fleet Street Radical: A. G. Gardiner and the *Daily News*
1973 Allen Lane *London*

An accomplished biography that sheds fresh light on the working of the press in Edwardian England.
Firms: Daily News

1726
Koss, Stephen E.
The Rise and Fall of the Political Press in Britain: Vol. 1. The nineteenth century. Vol. 2. The twentieth century
1981–4 Hamish Hamilton *London*

Koss attacks the rival myths that the British press has been either a Tory-led capitalistic swindle or that it has never had much political influence. Lengthy, well-researched and authoritative.

1727
Kynaston, David
The *Financial Times*: A centenary history
1988 Penguin Viking *London*

A thoroughly-researched newspaper history which is at its best describing the long rivalry between the *Financial Times* and the *Financial News* prior to their merger in 1945, and the establishment of international publishing and distribution in the 1960s and 1970s. The book has a good eye for anecdote and personality,

but, as so often in this genre, it is relatively thin on business and financial data.
Firms: Financial News; Financial Times

1728
Leapman, Michael
Treacherous Estate: The Press after Fleet Street
1992 Hodder & Stoughton *London*
A vigorous journalistic account of the transformation of the British press from its exodus from Fleet Street to its new high-tech location in Wapping. The book focuses on personalities and is a good counterpart to Francis Williams's earlier *Dangerous Estate* (qv).
Firms: Beaverbrook Newspapers; Mirror Group Newspapers; Thomson Organisation; Times Newspapers; Daily Telegraph

1729
Lee, Alan J.
The Origins of the Popular Press in England 1855–1914
1976 Croom Helm *London*
A fine work, completed shortly before the author's early death, which argues that the industrialization of the press in the 1890s marked a shift from a family-based press concerned with public service to bigger firms concerned more to entertain than inform.

1730
Martin, Roderick
New Technology and Industrial Relations in Fleet Street
1981 Clarendon Press *Oxford*
A detailed description of attempts to introduce computerized photocomposition in British newspapers between 1975 and 1980. It covers in depth management–union negotiations at the *Financial Times*, Times Newspapers and Mirror Group where new technology was either substantially delayed or implemented without great success. The book stresses both managerial and technical obstacles to new technology as well as union resistance.
Firms: The Times; Daily Mirror; Financial Times

1731
McAleer, Joseph
Popular Reading and Publishing in Britain, 1914–1950
1992 Clarendon Press *Oxford*
An important work on the commercialization of popular fiction and the structure of the children's, adult and religious book markets.
Firms: Amalgamated Press; D. C. Thomson; Mills & Boon

1732
Musson, Alfred E.
The Typographical Association: Origins and history up to 1949
1954 Oxford University Press *Oxford*
Musson primarily describes the development of trade unionism in the provincial letterpress industry from the earliest chapels to the national Association, based on the Association's records. But it also includes a massive amount of detail on employers, the organization of the industry and technological change which make it an indispensable source for any work on the nineteenth-century printing industry.

1733
Nelson, Elizabeth
The British Counter-Culture, 1966–73: A study of the underground press
1989 Macmillan *London*
A rare scholarly study of an important period for the alternative press, which studies both political/cultural struggles and circulation and the more mundane struggles for survival.

1734
Political and Economic Planning (PEP)
Report on the British Press
1938 PEP *London*
The result of three years' research by a PEP team, this work covers production, finance, structure, personnel and law, and is still a landmark publication.

1735
Pound, Reginald; Harmsworth, A. Geoffrey
Northcliffe
1959 Cassell *London*
A massive biography based on free access to

the Northcliffe archives, including private diaries, correspondence and notebooks. It lacks footnotes, but there are often indications of sources in the text itself. Especially strong on the use of mass media as a weapon of social and political power. The authors argue that Northcliffe and his papers exercised a powerful influence over Asquith, Lloyd George and others.
Firms: Associated Newspapers; Daily Mail; Daily Mirror; Evening News; The Times

1736
Raven, James
Judging New Wealth: Popular publishing and responses to commerce in England, 1750–1800
1992 Clarendon Press *Oxford*

Although this is primarily an innovative study of attitudes to businessmen and business life in eighteenth-century novels and popular literature, this book also contains an excellent history of the development of the eighteenth-century book trade.

1737
Shawcross, William
Rupert Murdoch: Ringmaster of the information circus
1992 Chatto & Windus *London*

The best and fairest of numerous journalistic biographies of Murdoch. Along with excellent biographical detail, the book provides extensive information on Murdoch's dealings in the newspaper, television and film industries and a detailed account of the near collapse of News Corporation and the Murdoch empire in the early 1990s. The story is firmly placed in the context of the information revolution.
Firms: British Satellite Broadcasting (BSB); Cruden Investments Pty; Fox; News Corporation; Sky TV; Twentieth Century Fox; Sun

1738
Simpson, D. H.
Commercialization of the Regional Press: The development of monopoly, profit and control
1981 Gower *Aldershot*

Simpson argues that the revolution in British provincial newspapers led by the Thomson Group has resulted in a downgrading of journalists and editors and domination by a new breed of commercial managers. The book lacks an index.
Firms: Thomson Organisation

1739
Tarapoorevala, Russi Jal
Competition and Control in the British Book Trade, 1850–1939
1973 Pitman *London*

A useful study of the long history of controls on competition in the British book industry, including the Net Book Agreement. Strong on the legal and financial side and the tug-of-war between organized booksellers and organized book publishers.

1740
Taylor, Alan J. P.
Beaverbrook
1972 Hamish Hamilton *London*

A massive, fully-documented work with an extensive bibliography, by a onetime friend of Beaverbrook and famous historian. The most complete biography of Beaverbrook that fully describes his remote but direct control of his newspapers.
Firms: Beaverbrook Newspapers; Express Newspapers; Daily Express

1741
Taylor, Geoffrey
Changing Faces: A history of the *Guardian*, 1956–88
1993 Fourth Estate *London*

A detailed but reticent account of managerial manoeuvres and the rivalries over the control and direction of the paper. It contains interesting accounts of disputes over editorial policy, failed takeover attempts and the crucial move from Manchester to London. Particular focus is placed on the editorships of Alistair Hetherington (who launched the *Guardian* women's page and *Education Guardian*) and Peter Scott, who was in charge during the government prosecution of the paper over the cruise missile 'leaks'.
Firms: Guardian; Manchester Guardian

1742
The Times
The History of *The Times*
1935-93 *The Times* and Times Books *London*
Six published volumes to date cover the paper's history in monumental detail from 1785 to 1981. Editorial policy is to the fore, but the business history of *The Times* and its owners from the Walter family to Northcliffe, Astor and Thomson is also covered.
Firms: Thomson Organisation; Times Newspapers; The Times

1743
Whale, John
The Politics of the Media
1980 Manchester University Press *Manchester*
A good study of the development of the media and the relations between the media and government since 1945.

1744
Whates, H. R. G.
The *Birmingham Post* 1857–1957: A centenary history
1957 *Birmingham Post and Mail, Birmingham*
This lucid narrative contains much useful detail on the ownership, management and editorial policy of Birmingham's most important newspaper. The *Post* is firmly located in the political culture of Britain's 'second city'.
Firms: Birmingham Post and Mail

1745
Williams, Francis
Dangerous Estate: The anatomy of newspapers
1957 Longmans, Green *London*
A classic journalistic account of British newspapers from the earliest years to the 1950s.

1746
Williams, Raymond
The Long Revolution
1961 Chatto & Windus *London*
A major work of cultural analysis that devotes substantial space to British newspapers, in particular stressing the deep roots of mass readership, stretching back far before the *Daily Mail*.

1747
Wilson, Charles
First With the News: The history of W. H. Smith, 1792–1972
For main entry, see 2067

1748
Wintour, Charles
The Rise and Fall of Fleet Street
1989 Hutchinson *London*
A broad and well-written series of biographical portraits of key figures covering the whole history of Fleet Street, by a former editor of the *Evening Standard*. More on personalities than business.

1749
Woods, Oliver; Bishop, James
The Story of *The Times*
1983 Michael Joseph *London*
A quasi-official history covering the period to 1945 with a brief postwar summary.

Printing & Publishing, Rest of Europe

1750
Amaury, Francine
Histoire du plus grand quotidien de la IIIè République: *Le Petit Parisien* 1876–1944 [History of the Greatest Daily of the Third Republic]
1972 P.U.F. *Paris, France*
A substantial business history of a major mass-circulation newspaper. The firm (renamed *Le Parisien*) is still in existence.
Firms: Le Parisien; Le Petit Parisien

1751
Barbier, Frédéric
Trois cents ans de librairie et d'imprimerie: Berger-Levrault 1676–1830 [300 Years of Bookselling and Printing: Berger-Levrault 1676–1830]
1980 Droz *Geneva, Switzerland*
This business history describes a company which is both a printer and a publisher and is still in existence.
Firms: Berger-Levrault

1752
Bellanger, Claude; Godechot, Jacques; Guiral, Pierre; Tarrou, Fernand (Editors)
Histoire Générale de la Presse Française [A History of the French Press]
1970 Presses Universitaires de France *Paris, France*
An enormous standard work which covers all aspects of the French press from the seventeenth century to the present day, including substantial detail on industry structure, technology and marketing.

1753
Bouffanges, Serge
Casterman jusqu'en 1910 [Casterman up to 1910]
1991, PhD Thesis, École des Chartes
This dissertation describes the history of a middle-sized Franco-Belgian publisher and printer which is still operating.
Firms: Casterman

1754
Freiberg, J. W.
The French Press: Class, state and ideology in the period from 1945 to 1980
1981 Praeger Publishers *New York, NY*
Dedicated to Nicos Poulantzas, this is a Marxist study of the tendency towards monopoly in the press–though France is seen as an outlier in having a less monopolized press. The state's role as subsidizer, rule-maker and enforcer is stressed. The book also includes case study material on *Le Monde.*
Firms: Le Monde

1755
Freyburg, W. Joachim; Wollenberg, Hans (Editors)
Hundert Jahre Ullstein, 1877–1977 [One Hundred Years of Ullstein, 1877–1977]
1977 Ullstein *Berlin, Germany*
A major multi-volume edited history of a Berlin publishing company. The history is covered from a wide variety of perspectives ranging from business to editorial policy. The contributors range from former employees to the publisher's authors. The contributors place the history of Ullstein in the context of general historical developments.
Firms: Springer; Ullstein Verlag

1756
MacReynolds, Louise
The News Under Russia's Old Regime: The development of a mass-circulation press
1991 Princeton University Press *Princeton, NJ*
This book describes the origins and development of the Russian commercial newspaper industry, following the theme of shifts in communications needs arising from industrialization, as well as the political and socio-economic changes reflected in the press.

1757
Marchetti, Ada Gigli
I Tre Anelli: Mutualita, resistenze, cooperazione diei tipografi milanesi 1860–1925 [The Three Connections: Mutual assistance, co-operation and resistance of Milanese printers 1860–1925]
1983 Franco Angeli *Milan, Italy*
A historical study of the typographical workers' associations in Milan from 1860 to 1925. It provides a detailed look at the typographical industry, the conditions of work and life for the typographical workers, and the organization of the unions and their struggles, examining whether the typographical workers' union was a vanguard organization or a labour aristocracy. The book focuses on the relationship between technological progress and the organization of work, union militancy and new forms of workers' associations.

1758
Muller, Hans Dieter
Press Power: A study of Axel Springer
1969 Macdonald *London*
Written by a former Springer journalist, this book stresses the monopolistic and political aspects of the Springer Group. However, it is a rare English-language source and contains useful information on the structure, organization and management of the Group.
Firms: Springer Group

1759

Sarkowski, Heinz

Der Springer-Verlag: Stationen Seiner Geschichte Teil 1, 1842–1945 [Springer-Verlag: Stages in its history, Vol. I 1842–1945]

1992 Springer-Verlag *Berlin, Germany*

This is a substantially archivally based commissioned history. Springer evolved out of a leading scientific and technical publisher in Berlin, and became an important and unusually export-oriented publisher before the Second World War. The book documents the business history of the firm, including an account of the problems of a 'half-Jewish' firm under the Hitler regime.

Firms: Springer-Verlag

1760

Tunstall, Jeremy; Palmer, Michael

Media Moguls

1991 Routledge *London*

A study of the small number of media moguls who dominate much of the west European media industries. The study also covers the invasion of Hollywood programming, the transformation of news agencies and the role of advertising.

Firms: Agence Presses-France; Associated Press-Dow Jones; Burlusconi Group; Maxwell Group; Murdoch Group; Benedetti; Reuters; Springer Group

1761

Vissink, H. G. A.

Economic and Financial Reporting in England and the Netherlands: A comparative study over the period 1850 to 1914

1985 Van Gorcum *Assen, The Netherlands*

This rambling, inadequately-edited survey of the financial press has been ill-served by its English translation. Its bibliography, covering English and Dutch sources, is useful.

Printing & Publishing, USA

1762

Baughman, James L.

Henry R. Luce and the Rise of the American News Media

1987 Twayne *Boston, MA*

A highly acclaimed biography of the man who revolutionized US publishing with the first news magazine (*Time*); the leading business monthly (*Fortune*); the original photoweekly (*Life*); and the production of the newsreel 'March of Time'. The author analyses these major journalistic innovations drawing on extensive archival data and focuses on both business and political activities (especially in relation to the Cold War). The book is an excellent introduction to the foundations of the twentieth-century news media.

Firms: Time Inc.

1763

Baughman, James L.

The Republic of Mass Culture: Journalism, filmmaking and broadcasting in America since 1941

1992 Johns Hopkins University Press *Baltimore, MD*

A serious study of inter-media competition in the USA since the War. Baughman argues that publishers of newspapers and periodicals failed to recognize the long-term threat of television, and that as a result television was able to capture a core mass market and push its rivals to pursue 'niche audiences': in the process, TV indirectly influenced what its rivals produced.

1764

Berger, Meyer

The Story of the *New York Times*, 1851–1951

1951 Simon & Schuster *New York, NY*

A good historical account of the development of an individual newspaper in the context of the history of the nineteenth-century penny press.

Firms: New York Times

1765
Byron, Christopher
The Fanciest Dive: What happened when the giant media empire of Time/Life leaped without looking into the age of high-tech
1986 W. W. Norton *New York, NY*
Insightful coverage of *Time*'s financial setbacks in the 1980s.
Firms: Time Inc.

1766
Cazden, Robert E.
A Social History of the German Book Trade in America to the Civil War
1984 Camden House *Columbia, SC*
A formidably detailed study of the German book trade in America, tracing the spread of the German retail trade following the westward course of German settlement and the evolution of German-American publishing.

1767
Cloud, Barbara
The Business of Newspapers on the Western Frontier
1992 University of Nevada Press *Reno, NV*
This valuable monograph covers 1846–1890, studying the life and death of newspapers in the frontier region from a business point of view. It covers markets, development and funding; sources of income; expenditures and balance sheets and draws together rare and scattered data.

1768
Coser, Lewis; Kadushin, Charles; Powell, Walter
Books
1986 Basic Books *New York, NY*
An overview of the modern US publishing industry by three sociologists. Not historically rich, but the best contemporary snapshot of the structure and nature of the industry.

1769
Elson, Robert T.; Prendergast, Curtis
Time Inc: The intimate history of a publishing enterprise
1968–86 Atheneum *New York, NY*
An occasionally critical and unusually well-documented three volume study which relies extensively on oral histories and full access to the *Time* archives which otherwise remain closed to scholars.
Firms: Time Inc.

1770
Emery, Edwin; Smith, Henry Ladd
The Press and America
1954 Prentice-Hall *New York, NY*
The standard textbook on the history of American newspapers from their beginnings to the early 1950s, when radio and TV began to compete. At times this work is rather adulatory.

1771
Forsyth, David P.
The Business Press in America, 1750–1865
1964 Chilton Books *New York, NY*
An uninspiring but methodical chronicle of this important sector of the US newspaper industry, from the shipping lists and bank-note reporters of the late eighteenth and early nineteenth centuries, to the railroad, mining and promotional papers of the mid-nineteenth century. It contains detailed information on costs, distribution, advertising, circulation and subscriptions.

1772
Frasca, Ralph
The Rise and Fall of the *Saturday Globe*
1992 Susquehanna University Press *Toronto, Canada*
A well-researched book on an early 'national' US newspaper. It is especially strong on product and visual innovations and on innovations in distribution and competition with the sensationalism and chequebook journalism of the Hearsts.
Firms: Hearst Corporation; Saturday Globe

1773
Friedrich, Otto
Decline and Fall: The struggle for power at a great American magazine – *The Saturday Evening Post*
1970 Harper & Row *New York, NY*
An insider account by a former foreign affairs editor of the 1960s collapse of the Curtis Publishing Co. and its *Saturday Evening Post* in Philadelphia, focusing on the problems of

changing a corporate culture and dealing with the predatory interests of Wall Street. This is high-class narrative journalism, with good pickings for the careful historian.
Firms: Curtis Publishing Co.; Saturday Evening Post

1774
Gilmore, William J.
Reading Becomes a Necessity of Life: Material and cultural life in rural New England, 1780–1835
1989 University of Tennessee Press *Knoxville, TN*

This book offers more on the consumer end than on the industry, but provides excellent data on the distribution of printed matter in the USA.

1775
Hage, George S.
Newspapers on the Minnesota Frontier, 1849–60
1967 Minnesota Historical Society *St Paul, MN*

A careful archival study of the role of the press in the pre-telegraph West. It is strong on the transient newspaper pioneers and their links with early promoters, though most of the text focuses on the press and politics.

1776
Irwin, William
The American Newspaper
1969 Iowa State University Press *Ames, IA*

A classic muckraker, first published in 1911, which mounts an attack on the role of financial interests in the rise of the press. The book is based on a series of articles in *Colliers Magazine*. An impressive and heavily emotional analysis.

1777
Juergens, George I.
Joseph Pulitzer and the *New York World*
1966 Princeton University Press *Princeton, NJ*

The best account of Pulitzer, with substantial information on the business as well as the man, and his competitive success through the development of a new style of popular journalism in the 1880s.
Firms: New York World

1778
Kielbowicz, Richard
News in the Mail: The press, post office and public information, 1760–1860s
1989 Greenwood Press *Westport, CT*

This scholarly study describes the role of the US post office in the development of press and newspapers in the late colonial and antebellum periods. Kielbowicz shows how political debates about national communication had a powerful influence in the institutionalization of congressional subsidies to the press. He is also strong on postal technology in the pre-telegraph era.

1779
Kluger, Richard
The Paper: The life and death of the *New York Herald-Tribune*
1984 Athenaeum *New York, NY*

A very good and recent history of the *New York Herald-Tribune*. A rich mine of information on a great metropolitan daily.
Firms: New York Herald-Tribune

1780
Lyons, Louis M.
Newspaper Story: One hundred years of the *Boston Globe*
1971 Harvard University Press *Cambridge, MA*

One of the better institutional histories, fully researched and especially strong on the role of the Taylor family, late-nineteenth-century marketing, and post-Second World War repositioning.
Firms: Boston Globe

1781
McLee, Alfred
The Daily Newspaper in America
1937 Macmillan *New York, NY*

A valuable scholarly analysis. It is outstanding in its examination of the financial basis of early newspapers and in correcting the adulatory bias of much newspaper history (e.g. Mott, qv). The book contains painstaking quantitative material on relations between advertising and the press.

1782
Meeker, Richard H.
Newspaperman: S. I. Newhouse and the business of news
1983 Ticknor and Fields *New Haven, CT*
A useful study of a major US chain newspaper owner.

1783
Mott, Frank Luther
History of American Magazines: Vol. 1 1741–1850; Vol. 2 1850–1865; Vol. 3 1865–1885; Vol. 4 1885–1905; Vol. 5 1905–1930
1957-68 Harvard University Press *Cambridge, MA*
A monumental standard work (3,548 pages) which, while mainly concerned with literary and publishing aspects, also contains much on circulation, entrepreneurship and business affairs.

1784
Mott, Frank Luther
American Journalism: A history, 1690–1960
1962 Macmillan *New York, NY*
A standard history of American newspapers. Nine hundred pages of an indispensable source of basic data on the industry.

1785
Peterson, Theodore
Magazines in the Twentieth Century
1956 University of Illinois Press *Urbana, IL*
Peterson traces the history of the popular magazine from the nineteenth century to 1955, with strong emphasis on the business and economic side of the industry. It is especially strong on the links of magazines to consumer goods marketing and to broad social and economic forces such as shifts in leisure time and the redistribution of income. The book is also good on competition in the industry. A sound and scholarly work based on a PhD thesis which is much superior to Mott (qv).

1786
Schudson, Michael
Discovering the News: A social history of American newspapers
1978 Basic Books *New York, NY*
A valuable and provocative book which examines the scope for objectivity in journalism against the background of American newspapers in the nineteenth and twentieth centuries.

1787
Steinberg, Salme Harju
Reformer in the Marketplace: Edward W. Bok and the *Ladies' Home Journal*
1979 Louisiana State University Press *Baton Rouge, LA*
A sophisticated and scholarly history of an editor and a pioneer mass magazine in the context of developments in big business and mass markets. The author analyses the rise of mass advertising and the 'feminization' of American purchasing. Technical change made cheap mass magazines feasible, but the creation of a durable link between readers and advertisers required sophisticated entrepreneurship. The book ranges widely over audiences, circulation, finance and strategy.
Firms: Curtis Publishing Co.; Ladies' Home Journal

1788
Stillman, Richard J.
Dow Jones Industrial Average: History and role in an investment strategy
1986 Dow Jones-Irwin *Homewood, IL*
Stillman describes the establishment of the Dow Jones Company, their *Wall Street Journal* and how the Dow Jones Industrial Average has become an indispensable aid to financial planning.
Firms: Dow Jones & Co.

1789
Swanberg, W. A.
Citizen Hearst: A biography of William Randolph Hearst
1967 Bantam *New York, NY*
An entertaining, but not very reliable bio-

graphy of a major figure. It contains excellent gossip.
Firms: Hearst Corporation

1790
Swanberg, W. A.
Luce and His Empire
1972 Scribners *New York, NY*
A big comprehensive biography of Luce. While Baughman (qv) is fuller on the business side, this is not wholly superseded.
Firms: Time Inc.

1791
Tebbel, John W.
The Life and Good Times of William Randolph Hearst
1962 Paperback Library *New York, NY*
Perhaps the most 'balanced' of the many biographies of Hearst.
Firms: Hearst Corporation

1792
Tebbel, John W.
The Compact History of the American Newspaper
1963 Hawthorn Books *New York, NY*
The standard short history of US newspapers covering the transition from the newspaper as personal instrument to the newspaper as business institution.

1793
Tebbel, John W.
Between Covers: The rise and transformation of book publishing in America
1987 Oxford University Press *New York, NY*
A one volume version of Tebbel's four volume *History of Book Publishing in the United States*. A massive but wholly internally focused chronicle of trade publishing, and the great houses and publishers.

1794
Tebbel, John; Zuckerman, Mary Ellen
The Magazine in America, 1741–1990
1991 Oxford University Press *New York, NY*
This book provides a comprehensive history of magazines in America, from their elite origins to the current mass media. It is encyclopaedic in its coverage of different sectors of the market (magazines for women, sport, TV, etc.), and full of fascinating detail on the entrepreneurs, but is less adequate on the business and financial side of the industry.

1795
Trimble, Vance H.
The Astonishing Mr Scripps: The turbulent life of America's penny press lord
1992 Iowa State University Press *Ames, IA*
Based on full access to Scripps's archives, and written by a Pulitzer prize-winning journalist, this is a massive and well-written biography of a key figure in the penny press. While it contains huge amounts of information, it is disappointingly unsystematic on key business aspects of the story.

1796
Wendt, Lloyd
***Chicago Tribune*: The rise of a great American newspaper**
1979 Rand McNally *Chicago, IL*
One of the most thorough studies of the organization and history of a major American newspaper.
Firms: Chicago Tribune

1797
Whited, Charles
Knight: A publisher in the tumultuous century
1988 E. P. Dutton *New York, NY*
One of the few items to cover the important sector of chain-building across the US local press system.
Firms: Knight-Ridder Corporation

Printing & Publishing, Rest of World

1798
Day, Patrick
The Making of the New Zealand Press: A study of the organizational and political concerns of New Zealand newspaper controllers 1840-1880
1990 Victoria University Press *Wellington, New Zealand*
Day studies the origins and early ownership of the New Zealand press in the context of the

role of newspapers in colonial society. The book analyses evolving forms, functions and readership of the New Zealand press in the mid-nineteenth century and the shift of newspapers from political discussion forums to profit-oriented businesses.

1799
Fetherling, Douglas
The Rise of the Canadian Newspaper
1990 Oxford University Press *Oxford*

A concise study of the Canadian newspaper industry from its origins as an instrument of government, through the era of control by political parties. Only after the supremacy of newspapers was broken by the challenge of TV and other media did the press break from political control. The book is especially strong on the distinctive concept that political parties should found, control and own newspapers and on the role of the editor/politician, as well as the recent supersession of this system by the growth of chain ownership.

1800
Goldenberg, Susan
The Thomson Empire
1985 Sidgwick & Jackson *London*

This work contains valuable coverage of Roy Thomson's Anglo-Canadian news empire which owned 200 papers by the 1980s. By this date it was the leading UK non-London newspaper owner, the second largest newspaper owner in the USA, and the leader in Canada. The author focuses on its global acquisitions, the role of the family, and diversification. It is also very good on the origins of the Ontario radio industry and on the paradoxes of Thomson's empire: it was internally pennypinching but freespending in acquisitions; it pursued a monopolist strategy in news but took a competitive stance in the travel industry, and in its oil and gas interests. Thoroughly researched.
Firms: Hudson's Bay Co.; Thomson Organisation; Times Newspapers

1801
Hons, André de Seguin des
Le Brésil: Presse et histoire, 1930–1985
1985 L'Harmattan *Paris, France*

A valuable study of one of the most developed Third World press establishments. It focuses on the press's relations with political regimes, but also devotes substantial space to ownership structure, press groups, and the economics of the industry (especially in relation to advertising and literacy).

1802
Kasza, Gregory J.
The State and the Mass Media in Japan, 1918–1945
1993 University of California Press *Berkeley, CA*

A case study of public policy towards radio, film, newspapers and magazines and how the media was drawn into supporting mobilization for war. It also studies issues of monopoly and industrial structure in the media.
Firms: NHK

1803
Kesterton, W. K.
A History of Journalism in Canada
1967 McClelland & Stewart *Toronto, Canada*

The basic survey of journalism in Canada, 1752–1966. Covers the newspaper production process and technological changes; freedom of press during the period; qualitative developments in reporting; and the impact of radio and television.
Firms: Globe and Mail; La Presse; Le Devoir; Toronto Star; Vancouver Sun; Winnipeg Free Press

1804
Lent, John A. (Editor)
The Asian Newspapers' Reluctant Revolution
1971 Iowa State University Press *Ames, IA*

A useful collection of essays providing historical outlines by numerous contributors of the development of the press in nineteen Asian countries (including Japan, China (pre- and post-1949), Korea, Taiwan, India, Malaysia, etc.). A basic starting point for work in this area.

1805
Omu, Fred I. A.
Press and Politics in Nigeria, 1880–1937
1978 Longman *London*

Though the press in Nigeria at this time consisted primarily of political organs, this book provides a thorough coverage of the ownership and organization of the industry and its patterns of readership.

1806
Rutherford, Paul
A Victorian Authority: The daily press in late nineteenth century Canada
1982 University of Toronto Press *Toronto, Canada*

Rutherford covers the late nineteenth century, when fierce rivalry between party organs, sectarian dailies and upstart peoples' journals fashioned a popular journalism for mass urban audiences. By the late 1890s there were more daily and weekly editions than there were Canadian families! While primarily about culture and nationbuilding, the book contains much about personnel, business routines and competition for circulation.

1807
Sommerlad, E. Lloyd
The Press in Developing Countries
1966 Sydney University Press *Sydney, Australia*

The core of this book is a statistical analysis of the founding, financial performance and failure of newspapers in developing regions. It covers the links of newspaper ventures to politics, literacy and popular communications (especially the role of letters columns). Contains much valuable data.

1808
Westney, D. Eleanor
Imitation and Innovation: The transfer of Western organizational patterns to Meiji Japan
1987 Harvard University Press *Cambridge, MA*

Meiji Japan adopted a wide range of Western institutions in a very short space of time. Westney focuses on the police, postal system and mass circulation newspapers to analyse the transfer of social technologies across cultures.
Firms: Osaka Asahi Shumbun; Osaka Mainichi; Japanese Post Office; Yomiuri Shimbun; Yubin Hochi Shimbun

Tobacco, USA

1809
Badger, Anthony J.
Prosperity Road: The new deal, tobacco and North Carolina
1980 University of North Carolina Press *Chapel Hill, NC*

The first full-scale study of the impact of New Deal policies on the North Carolina tobacco industry. It reassesses the impact of crop control programmes and their differential impact on large and small producers.

1810
Burrough, Brian; Helyar, John
Barbarians at the Gate: The fall of RJR Nabisco
For main entry, see 2644

1811
Cooper, Patricia
Once a Cigar Maker: Men, women and work culture in American cigar factories, 1900–1910
1987 University of Illinois Press *Urbana, IL*

Cooper makes extensive use of oral history to study the interaction of new technology, skill and gender in the US cigar business. Though mainly concerned with labour history and work culture it provides useful business context and invaluable detail on technology and employment.
Firms: American Cigar Co.; American Tobacco Co.; United Cigar Manufacturers

1812
Cox, Reavis
Competition in the American Tobacco Industry, 1911–1932: A study of the effects of the partition of the American Tobacco Company by the United States Supreme Court
1968 AMS Press *New York, NY*

A thorough study by an economist of the impact of the break-up of American Tobacco on scale economics, integration, purchasing and price and non-price competition.
Firms: American Tobacco Co.

1813
Nicholls, William H.
Price policies in the Cigarette Industry: A study of "Concerted Action" and its social control, 1911–1950
1951 Vanderbilt University Press *Nashville, TN*

A valuable and very detailed empirical study of oligopolistic pricing, branding, industry structure and business strategy in the US tobacco industry and its relationship with government antitrust policies.
Firms: American Tobacco Co.; Brown & Williamson; Liggett & Myers; Lorillard Tobacco Co.; Philip Morris & Co.; R.J. Reynolds

1814
Siegel, Frederick F.
The Roots of Southern Distinctiveness: Tobacco and society in Danville, Virginia, 1780–1865
1987 University of North Carolina Press *Chapel Hill, NC*

Siegel focuses on booms and busts in one region and how its economic choices created a structural dependence on tobacco that inhibited development.

1815
Tennant, Richard C.
The American Cigarette Industry: A study in economic analysis and public policy
1950 Yale University Press *New Haven, CT*

Though dated in some respects, this book is a scrupulous study of the economics of the industry, which contains much rich historical detail not found elsewhere.

1816
Tilley, Nannie M.
The Bright-Tobacco Industry, 1860–1929
1972 Arno Press *New York, NY*

A broad and well-balanced history of the production, marketing and manufacture of Bright Tobacco through the period of its early growth to maturity and the eve of the New Deal. This is a detailed study of technical change, regional culture, and small versus large manufacturers.
Firms: American Tobacco Co.; Continental Tobacco Co.; Liggett & Myers Tobacco Co.; R. J. Reynolds Tobacco Co.

1817
Tilley, Nannie M.
The R. J. Reynolds Tobacco Company
1985 University of North Carolina Press *Chapel Hill, NC*

The authorized history of one of the world's largest tobacco companies which retained its strong Southern roots and identity. It is based on company archives and is especially strong on the industry's links with North Carolina (Winston-Salem), technical change, and labour organization. Detailed and dull–a fascinating contrast with Burrough and Helyar's *Barbarians At The Gate* (qv).
Firms: Liggett & Myers; R. J. Reynolds

1818
White, Lawrence J.
Merchants of Death: The American tobacco industry
1988 Beech Tree Books *New York, NY*

Along with Peter Taylor's *Smoke Ring* (qv), this is a useful overview of the health implications of tobacco and the industry's long and dogged resistance to recognizing them.

Tobacco, Rest of World

1819
Alford, Bernard W. E.
W. D. & H. O. Wills and the Development of the UK Tobacco Industry 1786–1965
1973 Methuen *London*

A massive company history based on the company archives. It is particularly strong on the company's response to the American invasion in the 1900s and the formation by merger of the Imperial Tobacco Company. It also traces the loss of Wills's dominant position in the industry as one of the constituent firms of Imperial.
Firms: Gallaher; Imperial Tobacco Co.; John & Sons; Lambert & Butler; Ogden & Co.; Player; W. D. & H. O. Wills; American Tobacco Co.

1820
Blaich, Fritz
Der Trustkampf (1901-1915): ein Beitrag zum Verhalten der Ministerialbürokratie genenüber Verbandsinteressen im Wilhelmin Deutschland [The Trust Battle, 1901–1915: An example of government relations with trade interests in Wilhelmine Germany]
1975 Duncker & Humblot *Berlin, Germany*

A major study of government policy in relation to the German cigarette trusts in the early twentieth century, carefully documented from government archives.

1821
Cochran, Sherman
Big Business in China: Sino-foreign rivalry in the cigarette industry, 1890–1930
1980 Harvard University Press *Cambridge, MA*

The first major study in Chinese business history based largely on business records. It focuses on the battle for the cigarette market in China between the British-American Tobacco Company and its leading Chinese rival, Nanying Brothers Tobacco Company of Hong Kong and Shanghai, when the latter attempted to breach the former's lucrative monopoly. It is especially strong on Chinese entrepreneurial innovation and the business practices of Chinese companies, as well as the political and diplomatic context.
Firms: British-American Tobacco Co.; Nanying Brothers

1822
Corina, Maurice
Trust in Tobacco: The Anglo-American struggle for power
1975 Michael Joseph *London*

This is still the best and most accessible general history of all aspects of the Anglo-American tobacco industry.
Firms: American Tobacco; British-American Tobacco; Carreras; Gallaher; Imperial Tobacco Co.; Liggett & Myers; Molins; Philip Morris; Player & Son; R. J. Reynolds

1823
Devine, T. M.
The Tobacco Lords: A study of the tobacco merchants of Glasgow and their trading activities, c.1740–90
1990 Edinburgh University Press *Edinburgh, Scotland*

This book studies the growth of the great merchant families of Glasgow who played a key role in the eighteenth-century transatlantic tobacco trade. It focuses on who the merchants were, their profits and their investments. It is especially strong on their trading methods, their impact on the Scottish domestic economy and the reasons for their eventual demise.
Firms: Buchanan-Hastie & Co.; John Glassford & Co.; Spiers Bowman & Co.; William Cunninghame & Co.

1824
Jesus, E. C. De
The Tobacco Monopoly in the Philippines: Bureaucratic enterprise and social change, 1766–1880
1980 Ateneo de Manila University Press *Quezon City, Philippines*

A business and economic history of the Philippine tobacco industry which breaks from Eurocentric traditions in business history to study the relationship between the Spanish Tobacco Monopoly and the indigenous economy and local cultivators.

1825
Price, Jacob M.
France and the Chesapeake: A history of the French tobacco monopoly, 1674–1791, and of its relationship to the British and American tobacco trades
1973 University of Michigan Press *Ann Arbor, MI*

A huge (1,235 pages) study of the French tobacco monopoly, written over a 25-year period. It contains detailed quantification of markets and mechanisms of trade and its impact on Glasgow, St. Domingue, Louisiana and the Chesapeake.

1826
Sluyterman, Keetie E.
Ondernemen in sigaren: analyse van bedrijfsbeleid in vijf Nederlandse sigarenfabrieken in de perioden 1856–1865 en 1925–1934 [Manufacturing Cigars: An

analysis of company management in five Dutch cigar factories in the period 1856–1865 and 1925–1934]
1983 Stichting Zuidelijk Historisch Contect *Tilburg, The Netherlands*

A blend of entrepreneurial and business history, which follows the development of the Dutch cigar industry during a period of rapid expansion (1856–65) and during a period of contraction (1925–34), during the transition from manual to mechanized production.
Firms: Agio Sigarenfabrieken; Boex-Hoefnagels & Co.; Elisabeth Bas; Fa. A. Wintermans; G. Ribbius Peletier Jr; Gebr. van Schuppen; H. Jos Van Susante; Koninklijke Tabak - en Sigarenindustrie

1827
Stubbs, Jean
Tobacco on the Periphery: A case study in Cuban labour history, 1860–1958
1985 Cambridge University Press *Cambridge*

A concise scholarly study of the Cuban tobacco industry. The focus is on labour, but the book also deals fully with the role of international capital and mechanization.

1828
Taylor, Peter
Smoke Ring: The politics of tobacco
1984 Bodley Head *London*

A trenchant and insightful account by a leading journalist of the protective circle of political and economic interests around the British tobacco industry. Based on extensive interviews it casts much light on the health, taxation and sponsorship elements of the industry.
Firms: British American Tobacco (BAT); Gallaher; Imperial Tobacco; Philip Morris; R. J. Reynolds & Co.

Beer, UK

1829
Barnard, Alfred
The Noted Breweries of Great Britain and Ireland
1889–91 Sir J. Causton & Sons *London*

The essential compendium of brewing companies at the beginning of the stock exchange 'mania'. It contains basic information on a selection of 113 of the large and medium-sized enterprises of the day.

1830
Donnachie, Ian
A History of the Brewing Industry in Scotland
1979 John Donald *Edinburgh, Scotland*

A major reference work on the development of the brewing industry in Scotland. Good on the eighteenth and nineteenth centuries, but provides only twenty or so pages on the period after 1914.

1831
Gourvish, T. R.
Norfolk Beers from English Barley: A history of Steward & Patteson, 1793–1963
1987 Centre of East Anglian Studies, University of East Anglia *Norwich*

A study of a major provincial brewery located in Norwich, which grew to quasi-national size before being taken over by Watney Mann in 1963. Better on the twentieth century than the nineteenth.
Firms: Steward & Patteson; Steward, Patteson, Finch & Co.; Watney Mann

1832
Gourvish, T. R.; Wilson, R. G.
The British Brewing Industry, 1830–1980
1994 Cambridge University Press *Cambridge*

The first full-length account of the modern British brewery industry. Commissioned by the Brewers' Society, it pays considerable attention to the business strategies of brewing companies. This comprehensive, readable work is primarily a business history, but it also explores the political and social dimensions of brewing.

1833
Gutzke, David W.
Protecting the Pub: Brewers and publicans against temperance
1989 Royal Historical Society/The Boydel Press *Woodbridge*

Gutzke uses the archives of national and regional brewer and publican pressure groups to show that their reputation as a monolithic pressure group has been exaggerated. Instead they were beset by serious cleavages and only briefly able to unite to defeat the threat of prohibition in the 1890s. By 1914 their political influence was largely spent. The book sheds light on the economics of the pub as well as social and political aspects of the temperance issue.

1834
Harman, C. L.
Cheers, Sir!: From the vicarage to the brewery
1987 Tallis Press *Cheddar*

A wickedly irreverent account of management life at Hunt Edmunds & Co. of Banbury in the mid-twentieth century.
Firms: Bass, Mitchells & Butlers; H.E.H. Ltd; Hitchman & Co.; Hunt Edmunds & Co.

1835
Hawkins, Kevin H.
The Conduct and Development of the Brewing Industry in England and Wales, 1880–1938
1981, PhD Thesis, University of Bradford

This doctoral thesis is a little-used but vital source for the comparative development of the industry since 1880. However, the thesis is based on only a handful of firms – notably Allsopp of Burton and Tetley of Leeds.
Firms: Joshua Tetley & Co.; Samuel Allsopp & Co.

1836
Hawkins, Kevin H.
A History of Bass Charrington
1978 Oxford University Press *Oxford*

Printed but not formally published by Oxford University Press, this commissioned study provides a great deal of information on some of the major companies of the late nineteenth and early twentieth centuries. Not intended for circulation to the public, it lacks an index. However, it contains important insights into corporate strategies, merger activity, and investment.
Firms: Bass Charrington; Bass Mitchells & Butlers; Bass, Ratcliff & Gretton; Charrington & Co.; Charrington United Breweries; Hope & Anchor; Mitchells and Butlers; Worthington & Co.

1837
Janes, Hurford
The Red Barrel: A history of Watney Mann
1963 John Murray *London*

A journalistic chronicle of the rise and emergence of Watney Mann from the eighteenth century Stag Brewery. Popular and unfootnoted, it is often vivid and strongest when dealing with personalities.
Firms: Elliot, Watney & Co.; Watney & Co.; Watney Combe Reid; Watney Mann

1838
Lynch, Patrick; Vaizey, John
Guinness's Brewery in the Irish Economy 1759–1876
1960 Cambridge University Press *Cambridge*

This book is more impressive in weaving the early history of this major international brewer into Ireland's economic and social history than in its business history, but is required reading for all that.
Firms: Guinness, Arthur, Son & Co.

1839
Mathias, Peter
The Brewing Industry in England 1700–1830
1959 Cambridge University Press *Cambridge*

A masterly account of the English brewing industry before 1830, focusing upon the experience of the great London porter brewers. Impressive in its exploration of the integrative relationship of brewing with agriculture, but weak on brewing outside London and the South-East.
Firms: Anchor Brewery; B. Truman; Barclay Perkins; Calverts; Courage; J. Lacon & Co.; Meux Reid; S. Whitbread

1840
Monckton, H. A.
A History of the English Public House
1969 Bodley Head *London*

Useful general account in an under-researched area – the business of drink-retailing.

1841
Nevile, Sir Sydney O.
Seventy Rolling Years
1958 Faber & Faber *London*

A rare autobiography of one of the leading

brewery managers of the twentieth century. It contains valuable insights into the 'political' activities of brewing leaders.
Firms: Brandon's Putney Brewery; Whitbread & Co.

1842
Owen, C. C.
The Development of Industry in Burton upon Trent
1978 Phillimore *Chichester*
A careful study of brewing in Burton during the eighteenth and nineteenth centuries which places the industry in the context of other local industries and regional development.
Firms: Allsopp, Samuel & Sons; Bass, Ratcliff & Gretton; Marston, Thompson and Evershed; Peel, Yates & Co.; Trent Navigation

1843
Owen, C. C.
The Greatest Brewery in the World: A history of Bass, Ratcliff & Gretton
1992 Derbyshire Record Society *Chesterfield*
Drawing on his earlier (1978) study of Burton upon Trent, Owen provides a workmanlike factual account of the progress of Bass, Burton's best-known brewer. The book is supported by valuable statistical appendices.
Firms: Bass Charrington; Bass Mitchells & Butlers; Bass, Ratcliff & Gretton

1844
Reader, W. J.
Grand Metropolitan: A history, 1962–1987
1988 Oxford University Press *Oxford*
A short history of the brewing to hotelier leisure industry group.
Firms: Grand Metropolitan

1845
Richmond, Lesley; Turton, Alison (Editors)
The Brewing Industry: A guide to historical records
For main entry, see 34

1846
Sheppard, Francis
Brakspear's Brewery, Henley-on-Thames, 1779–1979
1979 Brakspear *Henley*
A model for the more modest commissioned history of a brewing enterprise. Succinct, but within its limits a sound analysis of an independent company.
Firms: Brakspear

1847
Vaizey, John E.
The Brewing Industry 1886–1951: An economic study
1960 Isaac Pitman & Sons *London*
An economist's view of the British brewing industry in the early 1950s with short chapters on the previous seventy years. Useful sections on mergers and the relationship between production, distribution and retailing.

1848
Williams, Gwylmor Prys; Brake, George Thompson
The English Public House in Transition
1982 Edsall *London*
The most thorough examination of the public house in the postwar period.

1849
Wilson, Richard G.
Greene King: A business and family history
1983 Jonathan Cape and Bodley Head *London*
Probably the best account of a single brewery enterprise, bringing together the motivations of family, political aspiration, social expression and the solid foundations of a well-run enterprise.
Firms: Greene King

Beer, Rest of World

1850
Baron, Stanley W.
Brewed in America: A history of beer and ale in the United States
1962 Little, Brown *Boston, MA*
An important and wide-ranging survey of the American brewing industry from its seventeenth-century origins to around 1950.

1851
Boje, Per; Johansen, Hans Chr.
Altid pa vej.....Albani Bryggeriernes historie, 1859–1984 [History of the Albany Brewery 1859–1984]
1989 Odense University Press *Odense, Denmark*

A comprehensive history of one of the largest provincial Danish breweries, the Albany Breweries in Odense, from its start in 1859 to 1984, analysed in an industry-wide context. Topics covered are investment, technology, marketing and profitability.
Firms: Albani Bryggerierne A/S

1852
Cochran, Thomas C.
The Pabst Brewing Company: The history of an American business
1975 Greenwood Press *Westport, CT*

A seminal study of a major US brewing company, first published in 1948. It is especially strong on entrepreneurship, marketing and finance, and written by a leading US business historian. The book is based on company archives.
Firms: Anheuser-Busch; Pabst

1853
Downard, William L.
The Cincinnati Brewing Industry: A social and economic history
1973 Ohio University Press *Athens, OH*

A study of the origins and development of the industry, mainly between 1860 and 1920, focusing on the social and economic milieu from which the industry developed, especially the context of urban life and the German community, drawing heavily on local press sources.
Firms: Christian Moerlin Brewing Co.; Windisch-Muhlhauser Brewing Co.

1854
Glamann, Kristoff
Jacobsen of Carlsberg: Brewer and philanthropist
1991 Gyldendal *Copenhagen, Denmark*

Written by a major authority on brewing (chairman of the Carlsberg foundation and Carlsberg Ltd from 1976, and Professor of Economic History at Copenhagen, 1960–81), this is a biography of the founder of Carlsberg brewery. It is authoritative on the contribution made to technological change in brewing, but also provides insights into the nature of entrepreneurship.
Firms: Carlsberg; Tuborg (United Breweries)

1855
Ogliastri, Enrique
Cien Años de Cerveza Bavaria [One Hundred Years of Cerveza Bavaria]
1990 Universidad de los Andes *Bogota, Columbia*

This monograph traces the evolution of a leading Colombian brewery's business policies and strategies during its first century (1888–1988) against the backdrop of the Colombian economy and government economic policies. Particular attention is paid to the period from 1959 to 1989. The company's annual reports are the main source utilized.
Firms: Cerveza Bavaria

1856
Sedlmayr, Fritz
Geschichte der Spatenbrauerei unter Gabriel dem Älteren und dem Jüngeren 1807–1874 sowie Beiträge zur bayerischen Brauereigeschichte dieser Zeit [A History of the Spaten Brewery 1807–1874 as an Example of Bavarian Brewing History]
1934 Piloty and Loehle *Munich, Germany*
1951 Hans Carl *Nuremberg, Germany*

Surprisingly, the German brewing industry has received little serious attention from economic and social historians. Indeed, these two volumes - published 61 and 44 years ago respectively - retain their indispensable value to our understanding of nineteenth-century brewing in Bavaria before it became a fully-fledged industry. Most remarkably, the author was not a trained historian but a brewer who based his invaluable case study of the then most important Munich brewery on family and business records, and other diverse archival and literary sources.
Firms: Spatenbrauerei

1857

Weck, Helene-Alix De

La Brasserie du Cardinal de 1877 à 1907 [The Cardinal Brewery 1877 to 1907]

1986 Institut d'histoire moderne et contemporaine *Fribourg, Switzerland*

This book describes the development of a family brewing firm. It explores the changing patterns of entrepreneurial behaviour and the strategic choices of management, production, and distribution.

Firms: Brasserie Cardinal

1858

Welborn, S.

Swan: The history of a brewery

1987 University of Western Australia Press *Nedlands, WA, Australia*

This excellent history of a leading Western Australian brewery takes the story from its mid- nineteenth-century origins. Its rise to market domination, through technical leadership and forward vertical integration are intelligently analysed.

Firms: Fosters Brewery Co.; Stanley Brewery Co.; Swan Brewery Co.

1859

Werf, J. van der

Heineken, 1949–1988

1991 Heineken *Amsterdam, The Netherlands*

A commissioned, rather glossy history of postwar developments in this Dutch brewing giant with the emphasis on international marketing. Very little attention is paid to financial matters.

Firms: Amstel; Heineken

Wine & Spirits

1860

Bartoli, P. (Editor)

L'économie viticole française [The French Wine Business]

1987 INRA *Paris, France*

A comprehensive survey of the industry, including extensive historical sections on industrial organization, technology, consumption, distribution, politics and global markets. The book contains extensive statistics and factual documentation, though it is limited on interpretation.

1861

Lachiver, Marcel

Vins, vignes et vignerons: Histoire du vignoble français [History of the French Wine Industry]

1988 Fayard *Paris, France*

Probably the best single-volume economic history of the French wine industry from the Middle Ages to the present day.

1862

Laurent, Robert

Les vignerons de la 'Côte d'Or' au XIXe siècle [Winemaking in the Côte d'Or in the Nineteenth Century]

1957 Belles Lettres *Paris, France*

An encyclopaedic study based on a three-volume doctoral thesis which documents almost every detail of the organization, technology and marketing of this important wine region before the phylloxera crisis. The book contains copious statistics.

1863

Loubère, Leo A.

The Red and the White: A history of wine in France and Italy in the nineteenth century

1978 *New York, NY*

This book provides a good survey of the development of wine manufacture in France and Italy before the First World War, outlining its importance for smaller producers in sustaining agrarian incomes. Also covers the disastrous phylloxera plague which from 1863–4 destroyed much of Europe's vines.

1864

Loubère, Leo A.

The Wine Revolution in France: The twentieth century

1990 Princeton University Press *Princeton, NJ*

A continuation of *The Red and the White* for the twentieth century, but excluding coverage of Italy because all the author's notes on Italy were stolen from his car, parked at the University of Bordeaux! Nevertheless, a profound study of the technical and productive transformation of French wine in the twentieth century.

Loubère argues that the artisanal phase ended in 1914 and was followed by a period of revolutionary technical transformation. He covers political and social as well as business aspects. An essential work.

1865
Marrus, Michael A.
Samuel Bronfman: The life and times of Seagram's Mr. Sam
1991 University Press of New England *Waltham, MA*

The authorized biography of the leader of Canada's Jewish community. The book has fascinating insights into Canadian anti-Semitism and its periodic waves of prohibitionism. This rounded biography of the founder of one of the world's dominant liquor groups shows the importance of his key business policies of competing through quality (which distinguished him from most of his rivals) which gave birth to brands like Chivas Regal. The book is weaker on technical aspects of the industry but good on the problems arising from Bronfman's personal management.
Firms: Seagram

1866
Moss, M. S.; Hume, J. R.
The Making of Scotch Whisky: A history of the Scotch whisky distilling industry (Bruichladdich Distillery, Islay 1881–1981
1981 James & James *Edinburgh, Scotland*

Superbly illustrated and scrupulously documented, this is a model history of a single company, though it is comparatively brief on its coverage after 1945.
Firms: Bruichladdich Distillery

1867
Saunders, James
Nightmare: The Ernest Saunders story
For main entry, see 3920

1868
Unwin, P. T. H.
Wine and the Vine: An historical geography of viticulture and the wine trade
1991 Routledge *London*

A wide-ranging study of the development of viticulture from ancient society to the present day, with a global sweep and an eye to political and social conditions as well as economics. This is essential background for any more specific study of the wine industry, and contains detailed material on technical change and distribution.

1869
Warner, Charles K.
The Winegrowers of France and the Government since 1875
1960 Columbia University Press *New York, NY*

Starting from the threat to one of France's largest export industries posed by the phylloxera epidemic of 1875, this book shows that wine-growers were the 'spoiled child' of French government and legislation, with rising costs to the rest of the economy.

1870
Weir, Ronald B.
The History of the Malt Distillers' Association of Scotland 1874–1974
1974 Malt Distillers' Association *Elgin, Scotland*

An in-depth study of a key employers' association in the whisky industry from 1874–1974, based on full access to excellent archives. Especially strong on legal regulation of the industry and taxation policies.
Firms: Malt Distillers' Association of Scotland

Leather & Footwear

1871
Blewett, Mary H.
Men, Women, and Work: Class, gender, and protest in the New England shoe industry, 1780–1910
1988 University of Illinois Press *Urbana, IL*

While primarily a study of work and gender, the book is also a rich study of the transition from rural outwork to factory production in the New England shoe industry.

1872
Blim, Michael L.
Made in Italy: Small-scale industrialization and its consequences
1990 Praeger *New York, NY*

Though a much broader study of small business clusters in central Italy, this book has essential material on the shoemaking artisans of San Lorenzo (Marche) who typify many of the reasons for Italian success in the shoe industry.

1873
Dawley, Alan
Class and Community: The Industrial Revolution in Lynn
1976 Harvard University Press *Cambridge, MA*

A study of the shoemakers of Lynn and their search for equality. A thorough reconstruction of factory life and the economics of entrepreneurship in the period of the Industrial Revolution in New England.

1874
Ellsworth, Lucius F.
The American Leather Industry
1969 Rand McNally & Co. *Chicago, IL*

This is a useful outline history of the industry from the Revolutionary war to the 1960s, concentrating on shifts in technology, industrial structure and labour.

1875
Ellsworth, Lucius F.
Craft to National Industry in the Nineteenth Century: A case study of the transformation of the New York State tanning industry
1975 Arno Press *New York, NY*

This is a reprint of a 1971 PhD thesis. It covers the nineteenth-century development of the industry and the transition from craft to industrial methods. It is strong on the role of the New York leather merchants and their dominance of the industry via control of the foreign hide market and a modified putting-out system which was later followed by backward integration.

1876
Ensslin, Ernst
Entwicklungsanalyse und -perspektive der schweizerischen Schuh- und Lederindustrie im Lichte weltwirtschaftlicher Strukturänderungen [Analysis of the Development of the Swiss Shoe and Leather Industry in the Light of Global Change]
1981 Ruegger *Dissenhofen, Switzerland*

An immensely detailed structural analysis of the organization, technology and markets of the Swiss shoe and leather industry, covering the 1950s to the 1970s and looking towards future trends. Comprehensive statistics.

1877
Foggi, Franco (Editor)
Nel segno di Saturno: origini e sviluppo dell'attivita conciaria a Santa Croce sull'Arno [In the Sign of Saturn: Origins and development of leather tanning at Santa Croce sull'Arno]
1987 Alinea *Florence, Italy*

A fascinating, detailed study of the regional leather-tanning industry drawing on company records and a superb oral history investigation.

1878
Hazard, Blanche E.
The Organization of the Boot and Shoe Industry in Massachusetts Before 1875
1969 A. M. Kelley *New York, NY*

A major scholarly study of the economics of the transition from craft to factory methods based on much insider and local knowledge and research. An essential work.

1879
Hoover, Edgar M.
Location Theory and the Shoe and Leather Industries
1937 Harvard University Press *Cambridge, MA*

A study of industrial organization (originally a Harvard economics PhD) which contains an enormous amount of business detail for the 1890s to 1930s. It covers location, industrial structure, marketing and technical change.

1880
Hudson, Kenneth
Towards Precision Shoemaking: C & J Clark and the development of the British shoe industry
1968 David & Charles *Newton Abbot*

Despite the title, this is a rather old-fashioned company history of C & J Clark, not an industry study. It covers the whole of the firm's history from 1821 to 1967, providing the only published study of Clark's rise to market leadership in the twentieth century. However, there are numerous omissions to frustrate the business historian–such as no real analysis of profitability.
Firms: C & J Clark

1881
Jonell-Ericsson, Britta
Skinnare i Malung: Fran hemarbete till fabriksindustrie [Leather and Fur Workers in Malung: From domestic work to manufacturing industry]
1975 Almqvist & Wiksell International, Uppsala Studies in Economic History
Stockholm, Sweden

Written in Swedish with a summary in English, this book is the story of the transition from domestic work to manufacturing industry in Swedish fur and leather production. The focus is on working conditions in AB S. P. Persson. This corporation, founded in 1888, was based solely on domestic labour until 1942, when factory premises were established. Domestic workers, however, stayed on as a buffer. Interviews and questionnaires are used as a complement to written source material.
Firms: Persson, S. P.

1882
Kaysen, Carl
United States v. United Shoe Machinery Corporation: An economic analysis of an anti-trust case
For main entry, see 1362

1883
Klaus, Fred
Le Pied dans la Porte: Le Match Bally/Bührle [A Foot in the Door: Bally and Bührle]
1986 Éditions Zoe *Geneva, Switzerland*

Klause focuses on the 1976 takeover of Bally high quality shoes, and the financial dealings involved. His style is journalistic but the book contains useful insights into the world of 'cordonniers'.
Firms: Bally; Bührle

1884
Lombardi, Waldo J.
The Italian Footwear Industry: An empirical analysis
1971 Herbert Lang & Co. *Berne, Switzerland*

Lombardi's careful historical survey covers the historical background, concentration, manufacturing processes, distribution and consumption patterns of the industry. The book is especially oriented to the analysis of economies of scale and the size of the firm, and the role of smaller establishments in the remarkable growth rates of the Italian industry in the 1950s and 1960s. The author provides extensive statistics and stresses the role of non-price competition.

1885
Mack, Ruth P.
Consumption and Business Fluctuations: A case study of the shoe, leather and hide sequence
1956 National Bureau of Economic Research
New York, NY

A large, dense study of the structure of these related industries in the 1920s to 1950s, based on statistical analysis. It especially concentrates on cyclical fluctuations, market structure, vertical integration and retailing.

1886
Mounfield, P. R.
The Footwear Industry of the East Midlands
1968 University of Nottingham Press
Nottingham

A detailed historical geography of the industry from medieval times to the twentieth century. It contains much detail on technical and locational change and on small firms. There are plentiful maps and statistics,but the book lacks an index.

1887
Nafziger, E. W.
African Capitalism: A case study in Nigerian entrepreneurship
For main entry, see 3794

1888
Press, Jon
The Footwear Industry in Ireland 1922–1973
1989 Irish Academic Press *Dublin, Ireland*

Press surveys the emergence of the Irish footwear industry after political independence in 1922. Important themes are the relationship with British footwear producers and the effects of government intervention. The book examines the ways in which policies of protectionism and self-sufficiency encouraged or constrained the growth of the industry.
Firms: C & J Clark; Clarks Ireland; Joan Halliday & Sons

1889
Royal Commission on Historical Manuscripts
Records of British Business and Industry, 1760–1914: Textiles and leather
For main entry, see 37

1890
Sutton, George B.
A History of Shoemaking in Street, Somerset: C & J Clark, 1833–1903
1979 William Sessions *York*

Originally a 1959 MA thesis, this is a highly competent survey, which is essential reading on C & J Clark in the nineteenth century. The book is heavily based on archives, with useful sections on production, technology, marketing and family biography. There is, however, little consideration of Clark's place in the UK footwear industry as a whole.
Firms: C & J Clark

1891
Tanaka, Hiroshi
Personality in Industry: The human side of a Japanese enterprise
1988 Pinter *London*

A detailed study of the leading Japanese footwear and sports apparel company ASICS and its founder entrepreneur Kihachiro Onitsuka. Although uncritical it is a rare detailed study of a medium-sized Japanese company over time.
Firms: ASICS

1892
Thomson, Ross
The Path to Mechanized Shoe Production in the United States
1989 University of North Carolina Press *Chapel Hill, NC*

An important scholarly work on the transition from craft to mechanized shoe production in the USA which addresses important theoretical questions concerning technological change, and places the industry in the broader context of the US economy. Especially strong on technical history.
Firms: Goodyear; McKay

1893
Zahavi, Gerald
Workers, Managers, and Welfare Capitalism: The shoeworkers and tanners of Endicott Johnson, 1890–1950
1988 University of Illinois Press *Urbana, IL*

A detailed study of Endicott-Johnson's labour policies and the company trade union, which argues that workers 'negotiated loyalty'.
Firms: Endicott Johnson

Clothing Industry

1894
Carpenter, Jesse T.
Competition and Collective Bargaining in the Needle Trades 1910–1967
1972 School of Industrial and Labor Relations, Cornell *Ithaca, NY*

A massively-documented, 900 page study of collective bargaining in the needle trades which argues that organized bargaining both increased profits for organized manufacturers and provided more jobs and a better standard of living for organized workers. Though legalistic and proceduralist in its approach it has nevertheless quarried union archives and the trade press and casts much light on the employers, their associations and the business practices of the trade.

1895
Cray, Ed
Levi's
For main entry, see 3943

1896
Erickson, Charlotte
British Industrialists: Steel and hosiery, 1850–1950
For main entry, see 3811

1897
Ferry, Claude
La Blanchisserie et Teinturerie de Thaon 1872–1914 [The Thaon Laundry and Dye-works 1872–1914]
1992 Presses Universitaires de Nancy *Nancy, France*

This book describes the history of a large regional dye and laundry business.
Firms: Blanchisserie et Teinturerie de Thaon

1898
Field, John W.
Fig Leaves and Fortunes: A fashion company named Warnaco
1990 Phoenix Publishers *West Kennebunk, ME*

Field presents a careful history of an important middle-sized fashion-apparel company, especially concentrating on competition in the fashion industry from the 1880s to the 1980s.
Firms: Warnaco

1899
Guppy, Alice
Children's Clothes 1939–1970: The advent of fashion
1978 Blandford Press *Poole*

Guppy studies the shift of children's clothing from the private and domestic sphere to high fashion and international competition and describes the 'death of class distinction in children's clothing'.

1900
Lemire, Beverly
Fashion's Favourite: The cotton trade and the consumer in Britain, 1660–1800
1992 Oxford University Press *Oxford*

Though many may doubt the thesis of an eighteenth-century mass market, this book is a fine study of the burgeoning demand for versatile and popular textiles, and, in particular the role of 'fashionable' clothing and second-hand clothes.

1901
Pasold, Eric W.
Ladybird, Ladybird: A story of private enterprise
1977 Manchester University Press *Manchester*

Pasolds was one of the world's largest manufacturers of children's clothing with its famous Ladybird brand name. This book by the founder blends autobiography and a considerable amount of business history, describing the rise and growth of the firm, starting from its origins as an offshoot of a family knitwear firm in Czechoslovakia, its rise in interwar Britain, and the division of the firm as a result of war in Central Europe. A fascinating study of entrepreneurship. There is, however, only one brief chapter on post Second World War developments.
Firms: Pasolds

1902
Redmayne, Ronald (Editor)
Ideals in Industry, Being the Story of Montague Burton Ltd 1900–1950
1951 Montague Burton *Leeds*

Redmayne describes a clothing retailer who integrated vertically into manufacture. Particular emphasis is placed on Burton's paternalistic management, which was very unusual in the clothing business.
Firms: Montague Burton

1903
Schmiechen, James A.
Sweated Industries and Sweated Labor: The London clothing trades 1860–1914
1984 University of Illinois Press *Urbana, IL*

This book studies the spread of non-factory outwork in the London clothing trades. It focuses especially on employment practices, such as the subcontracting and switching of work into and out of factory production, and on the implications for the labour force (mainly women and immigrant Jews) and the response of trade unions.

1904
Sigsworth, Eric M.
Montague Burton: The tailor of taste
1990 Manchester University Press *Manchester*
Starting out as an immigrant from Lithuania, Montague Burton came to dominate retail and wholesale men's clothing in Britain. This archivally-based study of the firm covers not only the business strategy and structure, but also Burton's distinctive benevolent employment practices, and the impact of the firm on modern fashion and retailing until the early 1950s.
Firms: Montague Burton

1905
Waldinger, Roger David
Through the Eye of the Needle: Immigrants and enterprise in New York's garment trades
1986 New York University Press *New York, NY*
Based on a doctoral dissertation, this study follows the evolution of the industry from tenement sweatshops to global trade, with a focus on immigrant entrepreneurs, origins of businesses, the role of management in small firms and ethnicity at work.

1906
Westphal, Uwe
Berliner Konfektion und Mode: Die Zerstörung einer Tradition, 1836–1939 [Ready-To-Wear and Fashion in Berlin: The destruction of a tradition]
1986 Edition Hentrich *Berlin, Germany*
This history of Berlin fashion houses particularly examines the role of Jewish businesses and their destruction under Hitler and the emigrant connections resulting.

1907
Wray, Margaret
The Women's Outerwear Industry
1957 Duckworth *London*
A study of competition and innovation in the industry from the 1930s to the 1950s by an economist, which analyses both shifts in the product and the growing importance of new distribution channels and consumer advertising. Much case study material on individual small businesses is included.
Firms: Marks & Spencer

Rubber & Tyres (World excl. USA)

1908
Anelli, P.; Bonvini, G.; Montenegro, A.
Pirelli, 1914–80: Strategia aziendale e relazioni industriali nella storia di una multinazionale [Pirelli, 1914–80: Business strategy and industrial relations in the history of a multinational]
1985 Franco Angeli *Milan, Italy*
A full-scale study of the company with special attention to internationalization, industrial relations and business–government relations. The first volume deals with the origins of the company and its distinctive industrial relations, and its relations with Fascism. The second volume covers the 1960s to the 1980s and deals especially with new technology, mergers and corporate reorganization in the 1970s. There is no index.
Firms: Dunlop; Pirelli

1909
Barrière, Antoine
Michelin vu de l'intérieur: Ce que j'ai véçu de 1950 a 1961: témoignage de vie ouvrière [Michelin: A View from the Inside: What I lived through 1950 to 1961: story of the worker's life]
1983 Éditions Creer *Nonette, France*
This study of Michelin takes the point of view of a leading trade union activist – and deals especially with trade unions and the labour policies of the firm.
Firms: Michelin

1910
Bridgestone Tire Co.
Bridgestone Tire Goju-nenshi [Fifty Years of Bridgestone Tire Company]
1982 Bridgestone Tire Co. *Tokyo, Japan*

Bridgestone Tire Company originated in 1906 as a maker of Japanese footwear, *Tabi*, and diversified in 1931 into tyremaking, first adopting American technology and then developing its own technology during wartime. This book is important in understanding the development of the Japanese tyre industry.
Firms: Bridgestone Tire Co.

1911
Donnithorne, Audrey G.
British Rubber Manufacturing: An economic study of innovation
1958 Duckworth *London*

This book deals with the structure and changing technology of the major sectors of the UK rubber industry. The innovations in production and products after 1945 are well covered, but the main strength is in dealing with non-tyre sectors better than most studies of the industry.
Firms: Avon India Rubber Co.; BF Goodrich; BTR (British Tyre and Rubber) Co.; Dunlop; Firestone; Goodyear; Michelin; North British Rubber; Pirelli

1912
Du Cros, Arthur P.
Wheels of Fortune: A salute to pioneers
1938 Chapman & Hall *London*

Written by the son of the founder of Dunlop's predecessor company, this is a broad resumé of the development of the leading British rubber company.
Firms: Dunlop

1913
Jemain, Alain
Michelin: un siècle de secrets [Michelin: A century of secrets]
1982 Calmann-Lévy *Paris, France*

A useful study of this secretive family empire by a journalist. It concentrates on the family and the strategy and structure of the company. There are few citations or statistics.
Firms: Michelin

1914
Jennings, Paul F.
Dunlopera: The works and workings of the Dunlop Rubber Company
1961 Dunlop Rubber Co. *London*

This is something of a 'snapshot' of Dunlop's activities with a rather piecemeal historical account, but is useful for its outline of production methods and products in the late 1950s. A company publication. Less complete than McMillan (qv).
Firms: Dunlop

1915
Johannessen, Finn Erhard
Challenge and Change: The history of Protan from 1939 to 1989
1989 Thorsrud *Lillehammer, Norway*

The book covers the history of Protan, an enterprising company founded in 1939 to produce lifejackets. Fifty years later the company was the leader in Scandinavia in plastic-coated textiles and the second largest in the world in alginate, a thickening agent produced from seaweed.
Firms: Protan

1916
McMillan, James
The Dunlop Story: The life, death, and rebirth of a multinational
1989 Weidenfeld & Nicolson *London*

The only full history of Britain's major rubber company and, as such, a vital source. A competent analysis of the firm's early years, but the book's strength is in its description of the post-1945 history of the firm, based on interviews with leading executives.
Firms: Dunlop

1917
Nihon Gomu Kogyoshi
Nihon Gomu Kogyoshi [The History of the Japanese Rubber Industry]
1950 Nihon Gomu Kogyokai *Tokyo, Japan*

The development of the Japanese rubber industry from 1870 to 1945 is described here, covering issues such as the import of raw materials, plantations, processing, marketing and foreign trade.
Firms: Bridgestone; Yokohama Gomu

1918
Payne, Peter L.
Railways and Rubber in the Nineteenth Century: A study of the Spencer Papers 1853–1891
1961 Liverpool University Press *Liverpool*

A clearly-written and expert history of a small rubber company which explains changing technology and product development very well. Of interest for the insights into transatlantic technology transfer/information flows in the nineteenth century.
Firms: Hancock; Moulton; Spencer

1919
Treue, Wilhelm
Gummi in Deutschland: Die deutsche Kautschukversorgung und Gummi-Industrie im Rahmen weltwirtschaftlicher Entwicklungen [Rubber in Germany: The German rubber industry in the context of world economic developments]
1955 Bruckmann Verlag *Munich, Germany*

A scholarly and detailed study of the German tyre and rubber industry, especially focused on the Continental Gummi-Werke AG. An essential reference work.
Firms: Continental Gummi-Werke AG

1920
West, Peter J.
Foreign Investment and Technology Transfer: The tire industry in Latin America
1984 JAI Press *Greenwich, CT*

The best account of the multinational activities and impact of tyre manufacturers, with good descriptions of changing tyre designs and production methods. It is essential reading for its comparisons of different firms and of the principal Latin American markets. There is an excellent bibliography, especially for trade journal sources.
Firms: BF Goodrich; Dunlop; Firestone; General Tire; Goodyear; Michelin; Pirelli; US Rubber (Uniroyal)

1921
Woodruff, William
The Rise of the British Rubber Industry During the Nineteenth Century
1958 Liverpool University Press *Liverpool*

The only detailed general history of British rubber manufacture, based on the author's PhD thesis. It is based largely on papers relating to the Moulton, MacIntosh and North British Rubber companies. The leading personalities and major technological developments are described well. This is a basic source, but weakened by the very limited account of the shift to tyre-making in the 1890s.
Firms: James Lyne Hancock; MacIntosh; Moulton; North British Rubber

Rubber & Tyres, USA

1922
Allen, Hugh
Rubber's Home Town: The real-life story of Akron
1949 Stratford House *New York, NY*

A journalistic account of the growth of the major tyre manufacturing centre in the USA by a Goodyear public relations official. Emphasis on the colourful and episodic. A book that is still of value in identifying leading Akron personalities and conveying a sense of the rapid change between 1900 and 1940.
Firms: BF Goodrich; Diamond Rubber; Firestone; Goodyear

1923
Allen, Hugh
The House of Goodyear: A story of rubber and of modern business
1976 Arno Press *New York, NY*

A traditional company history by an 'authorized' writer, first published in 1943. Useful for events and personalities, it is colourfully written.
Firms: Goodyear Tire & Rubber

1924
Babcock, Glenn D.
History of the United States Rubber Company: A case study in corporation management
1966 Indiana University Press *Bloomington, IN*

An excellent company history to 1945, covering all aspects of the company's creation via

mergers and its transition from footwear to tyre and chemicals production. Written by a retired executive of a US Rubber subsidiary, management policies are analysed in the context of the changing industry.
Firms: U.S. Rubber Co.; Uniroyal

1925
Chalk, Frank Robert
The United States and the International Struggle for Rubber, 1914–1941
1970, PhD Thesis, University of Wisconsin

An unpublished thesis, this is the most perceptive account of the tensions between rubber manufacturers and the suppliers of the principal raw material. Good in tracing the attitudes of US firms toward pricing policies and plantation investments, and efforts to obtain government support.
Firms: BF Goodrich; Firestone; Goodyear; US Rubber

1926
French, M. J.
The U.S. Tire Industry: A history
1990 Twayne Publishers *Boston, MA*

A brief but scholarly introduction to the history of the tyre industry from the 1870s to the present. It includes essential information on industry trends, firms, and leading executives.

1927
Herbert, Vernon
Synthetic Rubber: A project that had to succeed
1985 Greenwood Press *Westport, CT*

A detailed account of the US synthetic rubber programme in the Second World War, based largely on federal sources. The most complete study of the topic; strongest on technology and government–industry relations, but less good than Morris on research styles/cultures.
Firms: IG Farben; Standard Oil

1928
Lief, Alfred
Harvey Firestone: Free man of enterprise
1951 McGraw-Hill *New York, NY*

The standard biography of the founder of the Firestone company written by the company historian. Though excellent on the firm's early years and the family background, the book is rather uncritical and less complete for the 1930s. It has no bibliography but utilizes extensive Harvey Firestone correspondence, now deposited at the University of Akron.
Firms: Firestone Tire and Rubber

1929
Lief, Alfred
The Firestone Story: A history of the Firestone Tire and Rubber Company
1951 Whittlesey House *New York, NY*

An official history by the company historian dealing in detail with all aspects of the firm and its place in the industry. Essential reading; strongest on technology and marketing and weakest on labour relations. The book has a good bibliography.
Firms: Firestone Tire and Rubber

1930
Litchfield, Paul W.
Industrial Voyage: My life as an industrial lieutenant
1954 Doubleday & Co. *New York, NY*

The autobiography of a long-serving and senior Goodyear executive which complements the official company histories in tracing the firm's rise to dominance in US tyre manufacturing. An essential source for management thinking; of greatest value for organizational change, 1908–1916, welfare policy, and multinational growth. It is, however, unrevealing on 1930s labour relations.
Firms: Goodyear Tire and Rubber

1931
McKenney, Ruth
Industrial Valley
1992 ILR Press *Ithaca, NY*

A fascinating, semi-fictional account of class conflict in Akron, Ohio, America's centre of tyre production, in the 1930s. A Popular Front perspective by a well-known author and communist.

1932
Nelson, Daniel
American Rubber Workers and Organized Labor, 1900–1941
1988 Princeton University Press *Princeton, NJ*

A thorough and detailed analysis of changing labour relations in the US tyre manufacturing industry, concentrating on the major Akron firms and US Rubber. Interesting comparisons are made between plants and firms, particularly in relation to 1920s 'welfare capitalism' and 1930s management–union conflicts. Nelson emphasizes relations between economic and technological changes and worker behaviour.
Firms: BF Goodrich; Firestone; General Tire; Goodyear; US Rubber

1933
O'Reilly, Maurice; Keating, James T. (Editors)
The Goodyear Story
1983 Benjamin *Elmsford, NY*
An official company history which provides an extensive account of all aspects of the firm. The pre-1919 section simply reprints Allen's 1943 company history, but the remainder of the book is an indispensable source on Goodyear's multinational growth, diversification, and the switch to radial tyres.
Firms: Goodyear Tire and Rubber

1934
Roberts, Harold S.
The Rubber Workers: Labor organisation and collective bargaining in the rubber industry
1944 Harper *New York, NY*
Although superseded in many respects by Nelson (qv), this older institutional-style account of tyre industry unionization is still useful for its detailed discussion of 1930s union history. It contains some valuable material on wages, hours and employment.
Firms: Goodyear; Firestone; US Rubber; General Tire

1935
Taylor, Wayne C.
The Firestone Operations in Liberia
1976 Arno Press *New York, NY*
Taylor describes Firestone's development of rubber plantations after 1926, by agreement with the Liberian government and its efforts to integrate its operations in an underdeveloped economy.
Firms: Firestone

1936
Wolf, Howard; Wolf, Ralph
Rubber: A story of glory and greed
1936 Covici Friede *New York, NY*
Journalistic in style, this book deals ably with rubber-growing, chemistry, manufacture, the Akron firms and union growth. Later studies are more detailed, but this is a good starting point and better than other works in imparting a sense of the social changes in Akron. The Wolfs were Akron residents.
Firms: BF Goodrich; Diamond Rubber; Firestone; General Tire; Goodyear; US Rubber

Musical Instruments, Toys

1937
Brown, Kenneth D.
The Children's Toy Industry in Nineteenth-Century Britain
Business History, vol. 32, no. 2, 1990: pp 180–97
Almost nothing has been written about the business history of the toy industry. This is one of several articles by the author designed to rectify the situation.
Firms: Britains; Meccano

1938
Brown, Kenneth D.
The Collapse of the British Toy Industry, 1979–1984
Economic History Review, vol. 46, no. 3, 1993: pp 592–606
Poor management, poor marketing, resistance to change, elements of the UK's 'industrial disease', are explored in this useful article.
Firms: Lines Brothers; Mettoy; Meccano; Lesney; Britains

1939
Ehrlich, Cyril
The Piano: A history
1976 Dent *London*
A fine general study, showing how improved technology and manufacture allied with effective marketing and the growth of consumer credit transformed the industry. The story is well set in its social context.
Firms: Steinway & Sons

1940
Formanek-Brunell, Miriam
Made to Play House: Dolls and the commercialization of American girlhood, 1830–1930
1993 Yale University Press *New Haven, CT*

This is a study of the creation of the material culture of 'dollhood' that the author argues profoundly shaped the lives of American women from the mid nineteenth century. Using business records, advertisements and literature, the book charts the changing product and marketing in great detail. The treatment of business strategy, however, often verges towards the conspiratorial.

1941
Fuller, Roland
The Bassett-Lowke Story
1984 New Cavendish *London*

The story of a typical family business run for over 50 years by enthusiasts for enthusiasts. Despite close contacts with Bing, the German toymakers, Bassett-Lowke fatally preferred promoting craft skills rather than creating mass markets.
Firms: Bassett-Lowke; Bing

1942
Hillier, Mary
Dolls and Dollmakers
1968 Weidenfeld & Nicolson *London*

This illustrated narrative of the evolution of the doll from the earliest times to the 1960s is stronger on technical processes and patents than on institutional business history. It offers a serious and informative survey and can offer more suggestions than collectors' guides.

1943
Kaye, Marvin
A Toy is Born
1973 Stein and Day Publishers *New York, NY*

Written by a journalist insider in the toy business, this book offers a kaleidoscopic view of the American industry focusing on the success stories of famous toys and games. It also looks at new trends in products and at new issues in the industry in the late 1960s and early 1970s.

1944
McClintock, Inez; McClintock, Marshall
Toys in America
1961 Public Affairs Press *Washington, DC*

This standard history of American toys is an encyclopedic narrative written mainly for the general reading audience and for enthusiasts. It offers a wide range of information on traditional toys and includes a useful listing of nineteenth-century toy manufacturers in the United States.

1945
Nisbet, Peggy
The Peggy Nisbet Story
1988 Hobby House Press *Cumberland, MD*

An informal but instructive account of the author's experiences in founding and running one of Britain's well-known doll companies. Illustrated.
Firms: Peggy Nisbet

1946
O'Brien, Richard
The Story of American Toys: From the Puritans to the present
1990 Abbeville Press *New York, NY*

This delightfully illustrated volume is a labour of love, written by one of the experts in the field. The author deals mainly with the twentieth century, recording the expansion of the industry in terms of variety of output, size of firms and the nature of the market. Information is available on companies, technological changes, products and sales patterns. The book is aimed at toy collectors and the general reading public, but academics will find much of value about an industry which has received scant attention.

1947
Sheff, David
Game Over: Nintendo's battle to dominate an industry
For main entry, see 1501

1948
Singer, Aaron
Labor Management Relations at Steinway & Sons 1853–1896
1986 Garland *New York, NY*

Although the main emphasis is on labour relations, this book is an invaluable and well contextualized study of the growth of Steinways to become the largest and most prestigious piano manufacturer in America.
Firms: Steinway & Sons

1949
Wainwright, David
Broadwood By Appointment: A history
1982 Quiller *London*

Based on a rich family archive and profusely illustrated, this is a serious historical study as well as a labour of love. It closely follows the family origins and leadership of the company and its rise to being the largest piano-maker in the world, and its subsequent struggle for survival in the twentieth century as it responded slowly to technological change and foreign challenges.
Firms: Broadwood

Trade and Distribution

Merchants & Trading

1950
Anderson, B. L.; Latham, A. J. H. (Editors)
The Market in History
1986 Croom Helm *London*

This collection of essays focuses on the role of markets in history. The scope of markets is not restricted to their narrowly economic functions, but attention is also given to their effect on issues like public morality and political freedom. Perhaps not suprisingly, given the climate of opinion when this book was published, these essays offer a generally positive assessment of the effects of free markets, unencumbered by government intervention and manipulation.

1951
Bailyn, Bernard
The New England Merchants in the Seventeenth Century
1955 Harvard University Press *Cambridge, MA*

This pioneering study defines the role of the merchants in transforming the seventeenth-century Bible Commonwealth into the eighteenth-century hub of commerce placed on one side of the triangular Atlantic trading network. It investigates the social origins of the transplanted London businessmen, shows the wide variety of goods in which they dealt and describes their relations with colonial administrations during the period.

1952
Baxter, W. T.
The House of Hancock: Business in Boston 1724–1775
1945 Harvard University Press *Cambridge, MA*

This pioneering business history examines how a firm of independent booksellers was transformed into one of the leading New England merchant houses during this period. Baxter shows that the basis of the firm's success lay in its exploitation of the lucrative triangular trade involving land, commerce and the London market. Baxter demonstrates how the firm became expert at arranging transfers of credit between suppliers and customers, establishing a practice that was similar in principle to bill-of-exchange transactions.
Firms: Hancock's of Boston

1953
Benson, John
The Penny Capitalists: A study of nineteenth-century working-class entrepreneurs
For main entry, see 2015

1954
Bergeron, Louis
Banquiers, Négociants et Manufacturiers Parisiens du Directoire à l'Empire [Parisian Bankers, Merchants and Manufacturers from the Director to the Empire Empire]
For main entry, see 2349

1955
Broeze, Frank
Mr Brooks and the Australian Trade: Imperial business in the 19th century
For main entry, see 4000

1956
Brown, Hilton
Parry's of Madras
1954 Parry & Co. *Madras, India*

This is an official history of the Madras-based merchant house, established at the end of the eighteenth century. It is not uninformed but lacks sophistication in its treatment of the firm's investment decisions.
Firms: Parry & Co.

1957
Bruchey, Stuart W.
Robert Oliver, Merchant of Baltimore, 1783–1819
1956 The Johns Hopkins Press *Baltimore, MD*

This case study focuses on the career of a wholesale and retail merchant, importer and exporter, who became one of the first self-made millionaires of the new American republic. It shows how this enormous fortune was acquired from active trading in fashionable commodities, especially coffee during the early nineteenth century, and from successful speculation in South American markets. It was the comprehensive nature of the services offered by the firm, including wares of many kinds, and the provision of loans, insurance and storage facilities, which made the success of the firm possible.
Firms: Oliver's of Baltimore

1958
Carande, Ramón
Carlos V y sus banqueros [Carlos V and his Bankers]
1967 Sociedad de Estudios y Publicaciones *Barcelona, Spain*

A clear analysis of the relations between the most powerful European monarchy in the sixteenth century and its bankers. Although it is, above all, a work of economic history, the author draws a brilliant portrait of the business methods and activities of the bigger merchants and bankers of Europe in that age.

1959
Carlos, Ann M.
The North American Fur Trade, 1804–1821: A study in the life cycle of a duopoly
1986 Garland Publishing *New York, NY*

Carlos's survey and analysis of market structure and firm behaviour draws upon archival materials and economic analysis.

1960
Chan, Wellington K. K.
Merchants, Mandarins and Moslem Enterprise in Late Ch'in China
1977 Harvard University Press *Cambridge, MA*

This study focuses on how China's old Ch'in empire tried to accommodate itself to the rise of modern commerce and industry. It shows how the mandarins sought initially to make use of the merchants and their new activities, but by degrees some officials found it more expedient to become entrepreneurs themselves. Although the mandarin class was committed to economic modernization as a national goal, Chan demonstrates that their efforts were generally a failure since they showed little understanding of the need to transform the traditional values and institutions of Chinese society.

1961
Chapman, Stanley D.
Merchant Enterprise in Britain from the Industrial Revolution to World War I
For main entry, see 3784

1962
Crone, Patricia
Meccan Trade and the Rise of Islam
1987 Princeton University Press *Princeton, NJ*

This original study traces the links between the growth of the classical spice trade of the Middle East and the rise of the Islamic religion. The growth of commerce is shown to have been incompatible with the tribal divisions rife in the early Arab world. Islam was both a monotheist and an ancestral religion that sought to overcome these divisions and provide the Arab world with a new political mission, in response to the spread of a cosmopolitan commerce.

1963
Davis, Ralph
Aleppo and Devonshire Square: English traders in the Levant in the eighteenth century
1967 Macmillan *London*

This study tells the story of the London merchants who developed trade routes to Turkey and the Middle East during the eighteenth century and their representatives or 'factors' in Aleppo. Based largely on cloth and especially silk, the author shows how the widening range of English manufactures created demand for new types of silk during this period. It also highlights the importance of inherited wealth

and personal contacts for one of Britain's mercantile elites in the pre-industrial era.
Firms: R & E Radcliffe; Radcliffe & Stratton; Barker & D'Aeth; H J & T March

1964
Doerflinger, Thomas M.
A Vigorous Spirit of Enterprise: Merchants and economic development in revolutionary Philadelphia
1986 University of North Carolina Press *Chapel Hill, NC*

This is a wide-ranging study of the development of the merchant community on the North American eastern seaboard from the late eighteenth century until the 1840s. It examines the social structure and recruitment patterns of merchants during this period, the emergence of specialization between dry goods and provision trades, and the political role of merchants during the Revolutionary period. The author demonstrates that in their various roles as marketer, financier and founding industrialist, the Philadelphia merchants became the catalyst of the Industrial Revolution in the USA.

1965
Dumett, R. E.
John Sarbah, the Elder and African Mercantile Entrepreneurship on the Gold Coast in the Late 19th Century
Journal of African History, vol. 14, no. 4, 1973: pp 653–79

This study describes one of the major African merchants to emerge in West Africa in the nineteenth century: John Sarbah (1834–1892). It considers the reasons for the emergence of such merchants and the limits to their success.
Firms: John Sarbah

1966
Dumett, R. E.
African Merchants of the Gold Coast 1860–1905: Dynamics of indigenous entrepreneurship
Comparative Studies in Society and History, vol. 25, 1983: pp 661–93

This is a general study of the African merchants who emerged on the Gold Coast in the nineteenth century, the reasons for their success and the limits to their development.
Firms: R. J. Ghartey; William Ocansey

1967
Egashira, Koji
Ohmi Shonin no Kenkyu [A Study of Nakai Merchant House–Ohmi Merchant]
1965 Yuzankaku *Tokyo, Japan*

This is a superb case study of Ohmi merchant, a local merchant group near lake Biwa, covering the Edo to the early Meiji periods. It describes Nakai's diversification from merchanting to finance, brewing and property development, examining finance, personnel policy, and the expansion of outlets, in addition to the management structure.
Firms: Nakai Merchant House

1968
Fawas, Leila Tarazi
Merchants and Migrants in Nineteenth-Century Beirut
1983 Harvard University Press *Cambridge, MA*

This is a detailed account of the spectacular growth of the eastern Mediterranean port during the nineteenth century. It shows how a combination of foreign and indigenous entrepreneurs was able to exploit the advantageous geographical and political position of Beirut, transforming it into a major trading centre. The social costs, however, included a very uneven distribution of wealth among the various ethnic communities, which impeded the formation of a fully integrated urban society.

1969
Field, Michael
The Merchants: The big business families of Arabia
1984 John Murray *London*

The stories are told here of some of the largest and richest business families of the Arabian oil states–the elite of the merchants who made their fortunes from trade. Through this narrative, the evolution of Saudi Arabia and the Gulf States is traced, and the workings of Arab society and its business environment today are described.
Firms: Ahmed Hamad Algosaibi & Bros (Saudi Arabia); Alghanim Industries (Kuwait); E. A. Juffali & Bros (Saudi Arabia); Haji Abdullah

Alireza & Co. (Saudi Arabia); Kassem & Abdullah Sons of Darwish Fahkroo (Qatar); Khalifa Algosaibi Group (Saudi Arabia); Rezayat Group (Kuwait); W. J. Towell & Co. (Oman and Kuwait); Yusuf Ahmed Alghanim & Sons (Kuwait); Yusuf bin Ahmed Khanoo Companies (Saudi Arabia/Bahrain)

1970
Fieldhouse, D.K.
Merchant Capital and Economic Decolonization: The United Africa Company 1929–1989
1994 Clarendon Press *Oxford*

Fieldhouse has written an 820 page classic of modern business history. The UAC was the largest commercial organization in West Africa for half a century, and Fieldhouse traces its workings in the classic age, during decolonization and in the era of independent Africa. He recognizes the implicitly political character of big business in this arena throughout the period and also develops an approach to the broader study of 'merchant capital'. The scope is huge and the research, based on full access to company records is definitive.
Firms: African Timber & Plywood Co.; Compagnie Française de l'Afrique Occidentale; Elder Dempster; G.B. Ollivant; Heineken; J. Holt & Co.; Lever Bros.; Société Commerciale de l'Ouest Africaine; Unilever; United Africa Co.

1971
Frangakis-Syrett, Elena
The Commerce of Smyrna in the Eighteenth Century (1700–1820)
1992 Centre of Asia Minor Studies *Athens, Greece*

In the course of the eighteenth century, Smyrna (Izmir) emerged as the most important port in the trade of the Ottoman Empire with the West. This book examines this commercial rise and analyses the nature and organization of the trading activities and credit mechanisms of British, French and Dutch merchants established in Smyrna and trading with the West.
Firms: Levant Company

1972
Fyfe, C.
Charles Heddle, An African 'Merchant Prince'
1983 Laboratoire 'Connaissance du tiers-monde' *Paris, France*

This is a study of an African businessman involved in the groundnut and palm products trade from West Africa to France and Britain in the mid-nineteenth century.
Firms: Charles Heddle

1973
Garlick, Peter C.
African Traders and Economic Development in Ghana
1971 Clarendon Press *Oxford*

This is a carefully researched monograph based upon the study of this west African state during the 1950s and 1960s. It focuses on the importance of the importing activities undertaken by its indigenous black merchants during this period. The social background to their businesses is stressed, especially customary inheritance patterns, and their objectives are related, in turn, to the economic policies pursued by the Nkrumah government. It shows how Ghanaian merchants were at a disadvantage in relation to overseas multinationals in not being able to spread their risks inter-territorially.

1974
Gies, Joseph; Gies, Frances
Merchants and Moneymen: The commercial revolution, 1000–1500
For main entry, see 3787

1975
Hao, Yen'ping
The Comprador in Nineteenth Century China: Bridge between East and West
For main entry, see 3710

1976
Hayashi, Reiko
Edo tonya nakama no kenkyu [A Study of the Merchant Guilds in the Edo Period]
1967 Ochanomizu Shobo *Tokyo, Japan*

This book describes the distribution systems of the Edo period focusing on the merchant guilds, known as Tonya nakama. It uses a business history methodology to analyse distributive mechanisms, citing the cases of, for example, Shirokiya, Echigoya (Mitsui), Daimaru and Nishikawa.

1977
Henriques, Robert
Marcus Samuel: First Viscount Bearsted and founder of the Shell Transport and Trading Company, 1853–1927
For main entry, see 430

1978
Hindle, Tim
The Sultan of Berkeley Square: Asil Nadir and the Thatcher years
For main entry, see 3896

1979
Hopkins, A. G.
R. B. Blaize 1845–1904: Merchant prince of West Africa
Tarikh, vol. 1, 1966: pp 70–9

This is a study of a West African businessman and newspaper publisher in late nineteenth-century Nigeria. It examines the reasons why such figures faced increasing difficulties in the early twentieth century.
Firms: R. B. Blaize

1980
Ibrahim, Mahmoud
Merchant Capital and Islam
1990 University of Texas *Austin, TX*

This is a comprehensive study of the relationship between the development of merchant capital in Mecca and the rise of Islam from the earliest times until the present day. In contrast to the European experience of the transition from feudalism to capitalism, the author shows that in Mecca merchant capital and its accumulation gave way to the growth of feudalism and military rule. He concludes that Islam as a religion is orientated neither towards capitalism nor socialism, but adapted itself to the unique imperatives of Arabic merchant capital.

1981
Innis, Harold A.
The Fur Trade in Canada
1956 University of Toronto Press *Toronto, Canada*

This is the classic study, first published in 1930, by Canada's most distinguished economic historian, whose trademark approach is a broad vision that emphasizes geographic and technical influences.

1982
Kaplow, S. B.
African Merchants of the 19th Century Gold Coast
1971, PhD thesis, Columbia University

This unpublished PhD thesis studies the African merchants of the Gold Coast and their relations with European firms. It stresses the development of racism in the late nineteenth century as a factor in the problems they faced.
Firms: G. B. Williams; George Blankson; Henry Barnes; James Bannerman; John Sarbah; R. J. Ghartey; Robert Hutchison; William Ocansey

1983
King, Blair P.
Partner in Empire: Dwarkanath Tagore and the age of enterprise in eastern India
For main entry, see 4018

1984
Laan, H. L. van der
The Lebanese Traders in Sierra Leone
1975 Mouton & Co. *The Hague, The Netherlands*

This is a study of the role of Lebanese traders in the general economic history of Sierra Leone between c.1895–1970s.

1985
Maixe Altes, J. C.
Comercio y banca en la Cataluña del siglo XVIII: La compañía Bensi and Merizano de Barcelona (1724–1750) [Trade and Banking in 18th Century Catalonia: The firm of Bensi and Merizano of Barcelona (1724–1750)]
1994 Publicaciones Universitarias *La Coruña, Spain*

A detailed business history of a trade and banking firm in the mid-eighteenth century in Catalonia. The author analyses carefully the origins and activities of the company and its owners.

Firms: Bensi and Merizano

1986

McCalla, Douglas

The Upper Canada Trade 1834–1872: A study of the Buchanans' business

1979 University of Toronto Press *Toronto, Canada*

This is a study of a wholesale dry goods business, established originally in Glasgow in 1834 to supply the Canadian market. It is a well-researched monograph that emphasizes the dependence of family businesses on fragile credit networks in the uncertain frontier of nineteenth-century Canada.

Firms: Buchanans

1987

Miyamoto, Mataji

Nihon Kinsei Tonyasei no Kenkyu [A Study of the Japanese Wholesale System in the Edo Period]

1971 Tokoshoin *Tokyo, Japan*

This famous study is written by the authority in this field, concentrating on the Edo period, though partly covering the ancient and Meiji periods. Miyamoto analyses the development of distribution systems, the role of wholesalers, their organization, mechanisms of the trading system, and so on.

1988

Ocampo, José Antonio

Colombia y la Economía Mundial, 1830–1910 [Colombia and the World Economy, 1830–1910]

1984 Siglo XXI *Bogotá, Colombia*

This is the fullest history of Colombian foreign trade during the nineteenth century based on statistical data and abundant qualitative materials. It describes in detail Colombia's weak articulation into the world's economy and the succession of short-lived exports of agricultural commodities until the coffee market began to develop steadily after 1870. In this context, the Colombian businessmen of the period are portrayed as speculators.

1989

Origo, Iris

The Merchant of Prato: Francesco di Marco Datini, 1335–1410

For main entry, see 4027

1990

Ospina-Vasquez, Luis

Industria y Protección en Colombia, 1810–1930 [Industry and Protection in Colombia, 1810–1930]

1955 Editorial Sante Fe *Bogotá, Colombia*

This is a classic work on Colombian economic history in which the evolution of industrialization in different Colombian regions is linked to economic policy, especially industrial protection. It deals with the 1810–1930 period, in which, according to the author, industry in Colombia was more an adventure than a business. The book is based on a careful scrutiny of a wealth of primary and secondary sources.

1991

Papenfuse, Edward C.

In Pursuit of Profit: The Annapolis merchants in the era of the American Revolution, 1763–1805

For main entry, see 3796

1992

Pointon, A. C.

Wallace Brothers

For main entry, see 2335

1993

Reynolds, E.

The Rise and Fall of an African Merchant Class on the Gold Coast, 1830–74

Cahiers d'Études Africaines, vol. 54, 1974: pp 253–64

Reynolds looks at the changing position over time of African merchants on the Gold Coast and their competition with European traders.

Firms: George Blankson; James Bannerman; R. J. Ghartey

1994

Rodriguez, Manuel; Restrepo, Jorge

Los Empresarios Extranjeros de Baranquilla, 1820–1900 [Foreign Entrepreneurs in Barranquilla, Colombia, 1820–1900]

1982 Desarrollo y Sociedad, Universidad *Bogotá, Colombia*

This is a study of the leading role of foreign businessmen in the development of Barranquilla (Colombia). Their highly diversified activity (commerce, river navigation, railroads and industry) is linked to their ability to respond to economic opportunities and the potential for social mobility. It relies strongly on consular dispatches from the British and United States governments.

1995

Ruber, Vera Blinn

British Mercantile Houses in Buenos Aires 1810–1880

1979 Harvard University Press *Cambridge, MA*

A detailed analysis of the operations, activities and economic functions of the private mercantile houses in nineteenth-century Argentina.

Firms: Banco de Descuentos y Banco de Buenos Aires; Baring Brothers; Owen Owens & Sons

1996

Ruiz Martin, Felipe

Pequeño capitalismo, gran capitalismo: Simón Ruiz y sus negocios en Florencia [Small Capitalism, Large Capitalism. Ruiz and his businesses in Florence]

1990 Crítica *Barcelona, Spain*

Taking the business of a major Spanish merchant as his starting point, the author gives an insight into the operation of the Castilian economy in the sixteenth century.

1997

Rutter, Owen

At the Three Sugar Loaves and Crown

1938 Davison & Newman *London*

This brief in-house history of the Davison & Newman firm of City of London grocers begins with its establishment in 1650. Based on trade in spices with the West Indies, it had evolved into the West Indian Produce Association by the end of the nineteenth century.

Firms: Davison & Newman

1998

Seaburg, Carl; Paterson, Stanley

Merchant Prince of Boston: Colonel T. H. Perkins, 1764–1854

For main entry, see 3981

1999

Smithies, Edward

The Black Economy in England since 1914

1984 Gill & Macmillan *Dublin, Ireland*

A continuous history of the underground economy since the First World War, including pilfering, tax evasion and a whole range of effectively marginal small businesses (though he does not cover the drug-dealing industry). Smithies stresses that many black market transactions had motives other than financial gain, and that in recent years the growth of tax evasion has dwarfed all other underground economic activities.

2000

Steven, Margaret

Merchant Campbell 1769–1846

For main entry, see 4036

2001

Stone, R. C. J.

Young Logan Campbell

1982 Auckland University Press *Christchurch, New Zealand*

This is the story of the Scots born New Zealand merchant whose business activities flourished during the first half of the nineteenth century. Beginning as an importer of manufactured goods, Campbell's later career also involved land development and cattle dealing, as well as an active role in local politics. His success owed much to his shrewd investment decisions in a still capital-scarce frontier society.

Firms: Logan Campbell

2002

Svoronos, Nicolas

Le Commerce de Salonique au XVIIIe siècle [The Commerce of Salonica in the 18th Century]

1956 Presses Universitaires de France *Paris, France*

This is a pioneering work that examines the conditions and organization of trade of the

Ottoman Balkan port of Salonica (Thessaloniki), and of its factors - the European mercantile communities - with the West in the eighteenth century.

2003

Tooker, Elva

Nathan Trotter: Philadelphia Merchant, 1787–1853

For main entry, see 3988

2004

Tripathi, Dwijendra

Dynamics of A Tradition: Kasturbhai Lalbhai and his entrepreneurship

1981 Manohar Publications *New Delhi, India*

This book traces the history of one of the oldest business families in India and its transition from trade to industry. Based on archival material, company records, and participants' observation, it offers an authoritative account of the rise of an important industrial group in India.

Firms: Lalbhai Group of Industries

2005

Tripathi, Dwijendra; Mehta, M.

Business Houses in Western India: A study in entrepreneurial response, 1850–1956

1990 Manohar Publications *New Delhi, India*

The book traces the histories of nine major Indian business houses, operating from their headquarters in old Bombay Presidency. Analysing how the leaders of these groups perceived industrial opportunities and exploited or ignored them, it seeks to explain the entrepreneurial dynamics–variations and commonalities in occupational choices and strategic decisions–informed by a comprehensive conceptual framework.

Firms: Amins; Khataus; Kirloskars; Lalbhais; Larsen & Toubro; Mafatlals; Ranchhodlal Chhotalal; Tatas; Walchands

2006

Veyrassat, Béatrice

Reseaux d'affaires internationaux emigrations et exportations en Amerique Latine au XIXe siècle: Le commerce suisse aux Ameriques [International Business Networks, Emigration and Exports to Latin America in the Nineteenth Century: Swiss trade with the Americas]

1994 Droz *Geneva, Switzerland*

This book examines a basic feature of the Swiss economy in the nineteenth century: its opening to the world. The emergence in Switzerland of dynamic social networks - those of migration, business and financial alliances - at the end of the eighteenth century and their international development in the nineteenth, resulted not only in the progressive building of a worldwide marketing force but also in the growth of the export sector and in the creation of the sociopolitical and institutional pillars of an outward-looking economy. This analysis proposes a new approach by integrating the migratory perspective into the study of Swiss trade expansion, and by investigating the relations established with Latin American states, without, however, losing sight of the other American continent, the English-speaking one.

2007

Westerfield, Ray Bert

Middlemen in English Business

1915 Yale University Press *New Haven, CT*

This pioneering example of business history investigates the origins and development of the organization of middlemen who served English business before the Industrial Revolution. It is a wide-ranging study of how the growth of domestic and foreign markets led to increasing specialization in merchanting in the period 1660–1760, which developed the commercial practices and institutions indispensable to industrialization.

2008

White, E. F.

Sierra Leone's Settler Women Traders: Women on the Afro-European frontier

1987 University of Michigan Press *Ann Arbor MI*

A study of women traders in Sierra Leone in the nineteenth and early twentieth centuries, stressing their early success and later difficulties.

2009

Yamaguchi, Kazuo

Ryutsu no Keieishi- Kahei. Kinyu Unyu. Boeki

[A Business History of Distribution–money, finance, transport and trade]
1989 Nihon Keieishi Kenkyusho *Tokyo, Japan*
This is an authoritative collection of essays on distribution, trading, finance and transport. The coverage is mainly of the Meiji and Edo periods.

2010
Yogev, Gedalia
Diamonds and Coral: Anglo-Dutch Jews and eighteenth-century trade
1978 Leicester University Press *Leicester*
This is a study of the role of the major Jewish merchants of London during the eighteenth century. It is shown how they were especially active in developing London as a market for precious metals, as importers and buyers, as sellers and exporters, and as brokers. The author describes how the trade in bills of exchange grew out of the trade in precious metals between London and Amsterdam. The House of the Prager Brothers, which focused its activities on colonial commodities traded in London, is studied to illustrate the wider shift in the relative importance of London and Amsterdam as trading centres in this period.
Firms: Prager Brothers

Retail Trading

2011
Allingham, E. G.
A Romance of the Rostrum
1924 H. T. & G. Witherley *London*
This early history of the Covent Garden auction house of Henry Stevens tells how the firm owed its success to its ability to respond quickly to changing consumer fashions in nineteenth-century Britain. Flowers, animals, wines and historical relics were some of the many items sold through this London sales room. The illustrations provide insight into the shopping culture of the period.
Firms: Stevens, Henry

2012
Assael, Henry (Editor)
The Politics of Distributive Trade Associations: A study in conflict resolution
1967 Hofstra University *Hempstead, NY*
This collection of essays examines how trade associations in US retailing sought to resolve conflict between the discount and more traditional firms during the 1950s and 1960s. It is especially useful in its stress on the legislative framework of business activity.

2013
Atherton, Lewis E.
The Southern Country Store 1800–1860
1949 Louisiana State University Press *Baton Rouge, LA*
This is a social and economic study of the development of the retail trade in the Old South. It shows how the retail store played a unique role in southern society, functioning both as a source of goods and as a marketing agent for farm crops. It was also prominent in encouraging the development of local artisan manufacturing, and the author shows how the southern storekeeper attained a unique position of wealth and status in a largely agrarian society.

2014
Beaver, Patrick
A Pedlar's Legacy: The origins and history of Empire Stores 1831–1981
1981 Henry Melland *London*
This official history tells the story of the well-known British mail order firm. Its origins are traced back to the shop of watchmakers and jewellers established by an Italian immigrant in Harrogate during the 1840s. It describes how purchasing clubs led to mass buying in credit, which prefigured the beginnings of mail order retailing in Britain during the 1890s.
Firms: Empire Stores

2015
Benson, John
The Penny Capitalists: A study of nineteenth-century working-class entrepreneurs
1983 Rutgers University Press *New Brunswick, NJ*
As late as the beginning of the twentieth

century, more than 40% of working families engaged in some form of 'penny capitalism': selling goods with a horse and cart, taking in sewing and laundry, acting as a moneylender, selling in the street, or running a small shop or beerhouse. Benson's study considers the local economies which sustained these activities, the amount of employment it provided, the type of people it attracted, and its functioning as an economic sub-system.

2016

Benson, J.; Shaw, G. (Editors)

The Evolution of Retail Systems, c.1800–1914

1992 Leicester University Press *Leicester*

With a geographical flavour, this book examines the shift from traditional small and localized retailing to large scale retailing, with some discussion on German and Canadian examples, with their slower rate of change, as well as British. It looks particularly at cooperative retailing and department stores.

2017

Berekoven, Ludwig

Geschichte der Deutschen Einzelhandels [The History of German Retailing]

1987 Deutscher Fachverlag *Frankfurt am Main, Germany*

One of the few books on the recent evolution of retailing, this is notable for the emphasis on the post-war years and recent trends, supermarkets, discounting, out-of-town shopping, etc.

2018

Birchall, Johnston

Co-op: The people's business

1994 Manchester University Press *Manchester*

Published to celebrate the 150th anniversary of the movement, this is a careful and detailed history of the Co-op from the Rochdale Pioneers to the present International Co-operative Alliance. It covers not only retailing, but also Co-op activities in housing, fishing, agriculture and credit. Well produced and illustrated, it places the businesses firmly in their social and political contexts.

Firms: Co-operative Wholesale Society (CWS); Rochdale Equitable Pioneers' Society

2019

Bradley, Keith; Taylor, Simon

Business Performance in the Retail Sector: The experience of the John Lewis Partnership

1992 Clarendon Press *Oxford*

A study of the human relations strategies of John Lewis in the 1990s examining its application of democratic principles. The book also includes an analysis of the company's commercial success over several decades and the wider business context.

Firms: John Lewis Partnership

2020

Briggs, Asa

Wine for Sale: Victoria Wine and the liquor trade 1860–1984

1985 Batsford *London*

This is an officially commissioned history of one of Britain's leading wine retailers. Its growth is traced from modest beginnings in the Victorian era to the period of rapid growth after 1945. This lavishly-produced study shows that the firm's success owed much to clever marketing and its ability to influence the changing tastes of consumers during the consumer boom of the 1950s and 1960s.

Firms: Victoria Wine

2021

Burton, C. L.

A Sense of Urgency: Memoirs of a Canadian merchant

1952 Clarke, Irwin *Toronto, Canada*

This autobiography examines the career of a leading Canadian wholesaler and retailer, beginning in the early twentieth century. It is a social history centred on an individual, rather than a strict business history, but it sheds light on working life in the wholesale and retail trade in North America during the first half of this century.

Firms: C. L. Burton

2022

Bush, George

The Wide World of Wickes: An unusual story of an unusual growth company

1976 McGraw-Hill *New York, NY*

This is an officially commissioned history of how a Chicago-based manufacturer of lathes

transformed itself into the world's largest retailer of timber and building supplies. It shows how a US conglomerate used its market dominance at home as a means to becoming a worldwide trading concern. The book contains interesting personal material on the firm's leading executives.
Firms: Wickes

2023
Caplovitz, David
The Merchants of Harlem: A study of small business in a black community
1973 Sage *London*

This study of black business in New York was undertaken during the 1960s, based upon interviews with 259 Harlem businessmen. It shows how the black business community was confined to low-cost retail services, rather than high value-added merchandise or services.

2024
Cassau, Theodor
The Consumer Co-operative Movement in Germany
1925 Co-operative Union *Manchester*

Although now over half a century old, this volume still represents the definitive history of the German consumers' co-operative. Well informed, it systematically deals with each facet of their evolution from the middle of the nineteenth century and special reference is made to their cooperative and business organization.

2025
Cazden, Robert E.
A Social History of the German Book Trade in America to the Civil War
For main entry, see 1766

2026
Channon, Derek F.
The Service Industries: Strategy, structure and financial performance
1978 Macmillan *London & Basingstoke*

An important overview of an under-represented section of business activity with detailed consideration of the retail distribution, property, insurance and other sectors, bringing all into a theoretical framework.

2027
Chapman, Stanley
Jesse Boot of Boots the Chemists
1974 Hodder & Stoughton *London*

This study of the British firm of retail chemists focuses on the policies and ideology of the entrepreneur who created it. The firm's success is attributed to high-pressure salesmanship, aggressive advertising, and faith in the value of the popular market. This is a well-researched and wide-ranging business history.
Firms: Boots

2028
Corina, Maurice
Pile it High, Sell it Cheap: The authorised biography of Sir John Cohen, founder of Tesco
1971 Weidenfeld & Nicolson *London*

This popular biography of one of Britain's leading retailers shows how the firm evolved from the London street markets of the 1920s. It highlights the importance of the abolition of retail price maintenance in 1964 in providing the firm with the opportunity to develop its range of low-cost branded merchandise.
Firms: Tesco

2029
Cullen, L. M.
Eason & Son: A history
1989 Eason & Son *Dublin, Ireland*

This commissioned history tells the story of the Dublin firm of newspaper and book wholesalers, established in the mid-nineteenth century. It is a comprehensive study of a business strategy based on successful diversification which eventually came to include publishing, printing and manufacture. The firm's success is attributed to marketing innovations like railway bookstalls that achieved important economies of scale in distribution.
Firms: Eason & Son

2030
Davenport-Hines, R. P. T. (Editor)
Markets and Bagmen: Studies in the history of marketing and British industrial performance 1830–1939
1986 Gower *Aldershot*

This edited collection contains seven essays on the contrasting marketing methods used by

British firms in overseas markets. These historical studies draw on theoretical work on planning, pricing and branding, and show how obsolete selling methods contributed to Britain's relative industrial decline during this period.
Firms: Burroughs Wellcome; GKN; Mulford, HK; Rowntree; Vickers; Wellcome

2031
Davies, George
What Next?
For main entry, see 3880

2032
Dicke, Thomas S.
Franchising in America: The development of a business method, 1840–1880
1992 University of North Carolina Press *Chapel Hill, NC*
A pioneering historical study of the use of franchising in the United States. Dicke uses case studies of five major industries to show how franchising helped resolve the problems of distribution posed by high-volume production. He analyses how sales procedures were standardized and the 'packaged' franchise opportunity created, and considers the changing rights and obligations of parent companies and franchise owners.
Firms: Singer; McCormick; Ford; Sun Oil; Domino's Pizza

2033
Grislain, Jacqueline; Le Blan, Martine
La Redoute: Une histoire au quotidien [La Redoute: An everyday story]
1985 La Redoute *Roubaix, France*
This is a history of the largest French mail-order firm, based in northern France, which is still operating.
Firms: La Redoute

2034
Gutknecht, C.
Zur Entwicklung der innernen und verbandsmässigen Willensbildung der deutschen Konsumgenossenschaften von deren Anfängen bis zum Jahre 1922 [Decision-Making in German Consumer Co-operatives]
Zeitschrift für Unternehmensgeschichte, vol. 27, no. 3, 1982: pp 168–91
Gutknecht examines the internal decision making process within early German consumer cooperatives from the middle of the nineteenth century to 1922. Clearly illustrated by individual examples, this article examines the extent to which the democratic situation and politics within a society were able to influence decisions regarding the undertaking of business.

2035
Herrmann, Frank
Sotheby's: Portrait of an Auction House
1980 Chatto & Windus *London*
This is an in-house history of one of Britain's most famous firms of auctioneers. It shows how the firm diversified from a specialist dealer in books and prints, until by the 1920s it had become a major dealer in antiquities and works of art of all kinds.
Firms: Sotheby's

2036
Hoffman, Kai
K-kaupan historia [A History of Kesko Ltd]
1983 Kesko Oy *Helsinki, Finland*
This is a commissioned history on the joint economic efforts of Finnish retail shopkeepers and the rise of a large wholesale company. The book covers the period from the late nineteenth century to the early 1980s.
Firms: Kesko Oy

2037
Jefferys, J. B.; McColl, M.; Levett, G. L.
The Distribution of Consumer Goods: A factual study of methods and costs in the United Kingdom in 1938
1950 Cambridge University Press *Cambridge*
In a relatively neglected area, this book examines both the structure and costs of the distribution of consumer goods and also provides twenty case studies of separate commodity groups such as foods, clothing, toiletries, etc.

2038
Johnson, Laurence A.; Ray, Marcia
Over the Counter and On the Shelf: Country storekeeping in America, 1620–1920

1961 Charles E. Tuttle *Rutland, VT*

This splendidly illustrated history of US retailing from colonial times to the advent of the supermarket sheds interesting light on the effects of brand names and mass advertising in shaping the development of modern retailing.

2039
Le Blan, Martine
Histoire de la Blanche Porte depuis 1806 [History of La Blanche Porte Since 1806]
1992 La Blanche Porte *Roubaix, France*

This is a typical mail-order company in the north of France which is quite strong on clothing.

Firms: La Blanche Porte

2040
Lerner, Harry
Currys: The first 100 years
1984 Woodhead-Faulkner *Cambridge*

This is an official history of one of Britain's leading electrical retailers, which originated in the bicycle boom of the 1880s. It is a story of successful product diversification, ending with the firm's entry into the micro-computer market in 1981.

Firms: Curry's

2041
Littman, Jonathan
Once Upon a Time in Computerland: The amazing billion-dollar tale of Bill Millard's computerland empire
1987 Price Stern Sloan *Los Angeles, CA*

Despite its overwritten and breathless style this is a valuable journalistic source on the mushroom growth of one of the first retail computer franchising chains in the USA, which made its founder one of the richest men in America before sinking into scandal and the lawsuits which provide the rich raw material for this book. A rare account of the important outlet side of the industry (see also Thomas, *Sugar*).

Firms: Computerland; IMSAI

2042
Mahoney, Tom; Sloane, Leonard (Editors)
The Great Merchants: America's foremost retail institutions and the people who made them great
1949 Harper & Row *New York, NY*

This is very much a celebratory business history. It surveys the rise of some of the most famous US retailers, but is a superficial treatment of the real historical reasons for the expansion of America's retail giants.

2043
Mai, Ulrich; Buchholt, Helmut
Peasant Peddlars and Professional Traders
1987 Institute of Southeast Asian Studies *Singapore*

This is a study of subsistence trade in the rural markets of Indonesia. Focusing primarily on the post-1945 period, it highlights the role of traders in a subsistence economy in promoting the market principle and creating social and economic differentiation. It is shown how this is made possible by a strictly controlled family economy based on the exploitation of women and children.

2044
Marshall, Alan
The Gay Provider: The Myer story
1961 F. W. Cheshire *Melbourne, Australia*

This is a narrative account of Australia's leading fashion retailer from its establishment at the beginning of this century. Much of its success was owed to the firm's successful advertising campaigns and its careful management of staff relations.

Firms: Myer

2045
Mathias, Peter
Retailing Revolution
1967 Longmans *London*

This is a commissioned history of the Allied Suppliers Group of Companies, founded originally on the Thomas Lipton chain of grocery shops. It is a wide-ranging study which situates the origins of chain store grocery in Britain in the context of the rise in living standards during the second half of the nineteenth century. It is shown how new methods of purchasing and packaging standard items made possible the rise of mass retailing in the grocery sector.

Firms: Allied Suppliers

2046
Morris, Jonathan
The Political Economy of Shopkeeping in Milan 1886–1922
1993 Cambridge University Press *Cambridge*

This is a wide-ranging economic and social history of shopkeeping in the Italian city during its period of economic resurgence. The changing composition and fortunes of Milan's retailers are related, in turn, to the social movements of the period. Morris concludes that Milan's shopkeepers were prepared to support a variety of political strategies and he casts doubt on the current orthodoxy that stresses this stratum's autonomy in relation to other social classes.

2047
Mui, Hoh-Cheng; Mui, Lorna H.
Shops and Shopkeeping in Eighteenth-Century England
1989 Routledge *London*

This pioneering study focuses on a neglected period in the history of retailing in England. It shows how retailing was affected by the hierarchical character of English society in the eighteenth century but then demonstrates how this was modified by the emergence of a substantial middling group. The latter led to the phenomenon of competitive emulation which extended to all groups with the exception of the most deprived. It is shown that this was the outcome of rising per capita incomes, leading to the spread of newspapers to the provinces and the publication of magazines showing the latest fashions.

2048
Murray, Alison J.
No Money, No Honey: A study of street traders and prostitutes in Jakarta
1991 Oxford University Press *Oxford*

This is a personally observed study of the links between street traders and prostitutes in the Indonesian capital of Jakarta during the 1980s. Prostitution is analysed in the context of the movement from anarchic subsistence communities to individual consumer society. It is shown how the exploitation of women by women is an intrinsic part of the way urban classes are defined and, in turn, define themselves in perhaps the oldest form of retail trading.

2049
Nathan, L. D.
As Old As Auckland: The history of L. D. Nathan & Co. Ltd
1984 Benton Ross *Auckland, New Zealand*

This is a history of one of Auckland's oldest and most important firms. From general trading activities in the 1840s, Nathan's emerged as a leading wholesaler for many years before integrating into retailing in 1878. The book is written in personal terms but is full of interesting detail.
Firms: Associated Wholesalers; Blue & White Stores; Consolidated Hotels; L. D. Nathan & Company; Marriotts Stores; Woolworths (not UK/US)

2050
Parish, William J.
The Charles Ilfield Company: A study of the rise and decline of mercantile capitalism in New Mexico
1961 Harvard University Press *Cambridge, MA*

This is a case study of the transition from petty to mercantile capitalism in the southwestern USA during the nineteenth century. It is a detailed investigation of how the merchant credit system developed in the absence of specialist banks in this region at the time. It shows how a system of wholesaling and branch warehouses came to dominate the economy of the region until well into the present century, and anticipated the advent of the cash and carry warehouses of the modern era.
Firms: Charles Ilfield

2051
Perren, Richard
The Meat Trade in Britain 1840–1914
1978 Routledge & Kegan Paul *London*

This standard reference work draws on a scattered and disparate group of sources to described the nineteenth-century meat trade primarily from the supply side. The study covers a period of major change in the growth of meat imports to Britain.

Firms: National Federation of Meat Traders' Associations

2052
Pollon, Frances
Shopkeepers and Shoppers: A social history of retailing in New South Wales from 1788
1989 Retail Traders' Association of New South Wales *Sydney, Australia*

This officially commissioned history traces the rise and changing character of retailing in New South Wales, beginning with the bonded warehouses and bazaars of the colonial period. It is not a systematic business history and does not extend beyond 1900, but it does offer some interesting insights into this early phase of Australian history.

2053
Powell, David
Counter Revolution: The Tesco story
1991 Grafton Books *London*

An authorized history of Tesco with particular focus on the life of Sir Jack Cohen. Covers the rise of the firm from street markets in the 1920s through corner shop, self-service, supermarket and superstore. The author had full access to Tesco archives and shows that behind the apparent continuous record of success is a history of internal feuding as well as strategic innovation.
Firms: Tesco

2054
Reader, W. J.
Grand Metropolitan: A history, 1962–1987
For main entry, see 1844

2055
Ritchie, Berry
A Touch of Class: The story of Austin Reed
1990 James & James *London*

This officially commissioned history tells the history of one of Britain's leading clothes retailers. The firm owed much of its success to the introduction in Britain of American bulk-purchasing and pricing systems in the early 1900s.
Firms: Austin Reed

2056
Roddick, Anita; Miller, Russell
Body and Soul
For main entry, see 3916

2057
Sebba, Anne
Laura Ashley: A life by design
For main entry, see 3921

2058
Sieff, Marcus
Don't Ask the Price: The memoirs of the president of Marks & Spencer
For main entry, see 3922

2059
Sigsworth, Eric M.
Montague Burton: The tailor of taste
For main entry, see 1904

2060
Strasser, Susan
Satisfaction Guaranteed: The making of the American mass market
1989 Random House *New York, NY*

A fine study of the emergence of mass marketing in the USA, covering branding, distribution, product development and design and the politics of packaged products. Complements the work of Tedlow (qv).
Firms: Gillette; Great Atlantic and Pacific Tea Company (A&P); Ingersoll Watch Co.; W. K. Kellogg Co.; National Biscuit Co. (Nabisco); Procter and Gamble; Quaker Oats Co.; United Cigar Stores; Montgomery Ward; Sears, Roebuck & Co.

2061
Tedlow, Richard S.
New and Improved: The story of mass marketing in America
1990 Basic Books *New York, NY*

An important study of the revolution in retailing and the growth of supermarkets and mail order. Tedlow also examines the creation of markets for cars and soft drinks.
Firms: A & P (Great Atlantic & Pacific Tea Co.); Sears, Roebuck; GE (General Electric); Frigidaire; Montgomery Ward

2062
Thomas, David
Alan Sugar: The Amstrad story
1990 Century *London*

Alan Sugar is the famed British entrepreneur who revolutionized the sale of personal computers (and before that, hi-fi equipment) at prices that people can afford. This biography tells the 'rags to riches' story of the man who has built Amstrad into one of the best-known European consumer electronics companies. It is an interesting and readable account, though a little hackneyed in its approach.
Firms: Amstrad

2063
Thomas, John Birch
Shop Boy
1983 Century *London*

This is an autobiography of a shop worker in Peckham in south-east London between 1860 and 1885. It graphically depicts working life in a small shop before the retailing revolution of the late nineteenth century, and interesting light is cast on the appalling conditions for those 'living in' and working in retailing during this period.

2064
Walton, John K.
Fish and Chips and the British Working-Class, 1870–1940
1992 Leicester University Press *Leicester*

This is not only a social history but also a valuable history of the trade and its organization, including much on small businesses and trade associations.

2065
Willan, N. J.
Tradesmen in Early Stuart Wiltshire
1960 Wiltshire Archaeological & Natural History Society *Devizes*

This local study of retail trading in the agricultural south-west of England is based on various Exchequer records. It shows how retail trading was regulated by statute, proclamation and administrative order in early seventeenth-century England.

2066
Willan, T. S.
An Eighteenth-Century Shopkeeper: Abraham Dent of Kirkby Stephen
1970 Manchester University Press *Manchester*

This carefully researched study of shopkeeping in a north of England village is a story of successful marketing. Beginning as a wine merchant and brewer, Abraham Dent took up the hosiery business in the 1760s, and started to supply markets as far away as London. The author sheds interesting light on the origins of national credit markets and networks in pre-industrial England.
Firms: Dent, Abraham

2067
Wilson, Charles
First With the News: The history of W. H. Smith, 1792–1972
1985 Cape *London*

Wilson covers the rise of the newspaper retail from scruffy touts and furtive publications in the eighteenth century to mass retailing. He concentrates on marketing and product innovations and on leading personalities. The book is good on the relationship of the firm to broader social and economic change.
Firms: W. H. Smith

2068
Yoshino, M. Y.
The Japanese Marketing System: Adaptation and Innovation
1971 MIT Press *Cambridge, MA*

This is still the most useful survey of the rise of mass retailing in Japan. It shows how the structure of retailing in this country was shaped not only by the emergence of a mass consumption market but also by cultural factors like the decline of traditionally collectivist values. It shows how the 'demonstration effect' of the American system was especially influential in creating the egalitarian character of Japanese retailing.

Department Stores, UK

2069
Bentall, Rowan
My Store of Memories
1974 W. H. Allen *London*

This autobiography of the grandson of one of the leading department stores in south-west London begins in the 1920s. It shows how a family firm evolved into a group of stores worth £25 millions by the 1970s, based upon innovative marketing and successful product diversification.
Firms: Bentall's

2070
Briggs, Asa
Friends of the People: The centenary history of Lewis's
1956 Batsford *London*

This is a social history of the Liverpool-based chain of department stores, rather than a conventional business history, but it does illuminate the transformation of retailing in Britain since the nineteenth century. It was one of the first retailers in Britain to sell its own branded goods based on bulk-purchasing.
Firms: Lewis's

2071
Corina, Maurice
Fine Silks and Oak Counters: Debenhams 1778–1978
1978 Hutchinson Benham *London*

This well-produced popular history tells the story of the London-based chain of department stores. It is shown how Debenhams was one of the first British retailers to establish close and regular contacts with its manufacturers in the late nineteenth century. During the twentieth century, its success owed more to shrewd takeovers of rival firms. The latter is illustrative of a wider trend in post-1945 British business history.
Firms: Debenhams

2072
Flanders, Allan; Pomeranz, Ruth; Woodward, Joan
Experiment in Industrial Democracy
1968 Faber & Faber *London*

This influential study of the John Lewis retail partnership focuses on how the firm's successful attempts to implement democratic management distinguished it from the majority of British companies. It analyses in detail the firm's profit-sharing scheme and its complex structure of consultative committees.
Firms: John Lewis

2073
Herbert, Charles
A Merchant Adventurer: Being the biography of Leonard Hugh Bentall Kingston-on-Thames
1936 Waterlow *London*

This book is a personal biography of one of the leading retailers in the London area. The firm's growth is related to the suburban growth of London, and its successful exploitation of the new consumer goods of the inter-war period.
Firms: Bentall's

2074
Honeycombe, Gordon
Selfridges Seventy-Five Years: The story of the store 1909–1984
1984 Park Lane Press *London*

This is an official history of the famous London department store. The firm owed much of its success to its innovative use of displays, which subsequently influenced retailing throughout Britain.
Firms: Selfridges

2075
Kinloch, James; Butt, John
History of the Scottish Co-operative Wholesale Society Limited
1980 Co-operative Wholesale Society
Glasgow, Scotland

This official history of the Scottish co-operative movement is a carefully-researched study and includes an examination of its wider social and political aims, in addition to its retailing activities.
Firms: Scottish Co-operative Wholesale Society

2076
Lambert, Richard S.
The Universal Provider: A study of William Whiteley and the rise of the London department store
1938 Harrap *London*

This early business history of retail trading in Britain centres on the growth of department stores in London. It is more a social history of shopping than a systematic business history, and it does not extend beyond 1900.
Firms: William Whiteley

2077
Moss, Michael; Turton, Alison
A Legend of Retailing: House of Fraser
1989 Weidenfeld & Nicolson *London*

Although focused on the original Glasgow-based department store, this is a wide-ranging study of the transformation of shopping in Britain since the late nineteenth century. The main trends in retailing are outlined but there is little detail on buying and marketing strategies.
Firms: House of Fraser

2078
Pottinger, George
The Winning Counter: Hugh Fraser and Harrods
1971 Hutchinson *London*

This is a popular biography of the head of the House of Fraser retailing empire. It focuses on the firm's strategy of successful product diversification during the inter-war period, showing how its astute policy of takeovers transformed Fraser's into one of Britain's largest department chains by the 1950s.
Firms: House of Fraser

2079
Pound, Reginald
Selfridge: A biography
1960 Heinemann *London*

This biography of the founder of the famous London department store examines how novel advertising methods contributed to the firm's success. Original photographs testify to innovations like 'mood music' and the introduction of a 'running letter' sign over the front of the store, combining news and advertisements. It is lavishly produced for a popular audience.
Firms: Selfridges

2080
Redfern, Percy
The New History of the Co-operative Wholesale Society
1938 Dent *London*

This was an officially commissioned history of the co-operative movement in England and Wales. Although detailed, it is very much a celebratory history and ignores the challenge posed by the private sector to many of the movement's retailing activities during the 1920s and 1930s.
Firms: Co-operative Wholesale Society of England and Wales

2081
Rees, Goronwy
St Michael: A history of Marks & Spencer
1973 Pan *London*

This comprehensive study of one of Britain's leading retailers begins with the establishment of the original partnership during the 1890s. It shows how the firm created a new kind of relationship with its suppliers, beginning in the 1930s, which led to the large-scale production of goods of high quality.
Firms: Marks & Spencer

2082
Sieff, Marcus
Don't Ask the Price: The memoirs of the president of Marks and Spencer
1986 Weidenfeld & Nicolson *London*

This autobiography of one of Britain's leading retailers contains some fascinating insights into the social and political concerns of this family business. Sieff's broad sympathies and wider outlook made him one of the pioneers in Britain of the human relations school of management.
Firms: Marks & Spencer

2083
Tse, K. K.
Marks and Spencer: Anatomy of Britain's most effectively managed company
1985 Pergamon *Oxford*

This study focuses on the unique managerial style that has made Marks & Spencer one of Britain's leading department stores. The firm pioneered what today would be called 'total quality control', bringing 'upper-class quality' products to people with modest incomes.
Firms: Marks & Spencer

Department Stores, Europe (excl. UK)

2084
Amatori, Franco
Proprietà e direzione: La Rinascente 1917–1969 [Ownership and Management: La Rinascente 1917–1969]
1989 Franco Angeli *Milan, Italy*

The history of the 'Rinascente', the outstanding Italian department store, with a particular focus on the evolution of its top management. Utilizing the family's private papers, the author focuses on the conflicts between various stakeholders.
Firms: La Rinascente

2085
Faraut, François
Histoire de La Belle Jardinière [A History of La Belle Jardinière]
1987 Belin *Paris, France*

This is a history of one of the leading Paris department stores, which was founded in 1824, moved to monumental premises in 1867, declined after the Second World War and was closed in the 1970s. The firm was also a pioneer in the rise in France of the ready-made clothing industry. A short, but serious book, based upon primary sources.
Firms: La Belle Jardinière

2086
Fuchs, Konrad
Zur Geschichte des Warenhaus Konzerns. I. Schocken Söhne. Unter besondere Berücksichtigung der Jahre seit 1933 [The History of the Schocken Söhne Department Store Business]
Zeitschrift für Unternehmensgeschichte, vol. 33, no. 4, 1988, pp 232–52

This is one of the relatively few studies which examine a German department store concern (Schocken Söhne) following the First World War. It provides a unique insight into the extreme pressure exerted by the Nazi Government on a Jewish-owned business and the subsequent postwar struggles of the Schocken family to regain control of their business.
Firms: Schocken Söhne

2087
Gellately, Robert
An der Schwelle der Moderne Warenhäuser und ihre Feinde in Deutschland
1993 Vandenhoeck & Ruprecht *Göttingen, Germany*

This article in *Im Banne der Metropolen. Berlin und London in der Zwanziger Jahren*, edited by Peter Alter, reviews the significance of changes in retailing in Germany. It pays particular reference to the emergence of Jewish-owned department stores.

2088
Gerlach, Siegfried
Das Warenhaus in Deutschland: Seine Entwicklung bis zum ersten Weltkrieg in historisch-politischer Sicht [The Department Store in Germany]
1988 Franz Steiner Verlag Wiesbaden *Stuttgart, Germany*

The most thorough publication to deal with the emergence of the German department store before the First World War, this discussion analyses systematically each facet of its evolution. Its status as a key reference work is emphasized by the inclusion of an exhaustive bibliography.
Firms: A. Wertheim; Hertie (H. Tietz); Jandorf; KaDeWe (Kaufhaus des Westens); Karstadt; L. Tietz; Shocken Söhne

2089
Göhre, Paul
Das Warenhaus [The Department Store]
1907 Rütten & Loening *Frankfurt am Main, Germany*

This is the most complete account of the way in which the turn of the century German department store undertook its business and furthermore gained its importance in the national

economy. The account draws heavily on the author's experience of Wertheim stores in his home town of Berlin.
Firms: A. Wertheim

2090
Lux, Käthe
Studien über die Entwicklung der Warenhäuser in Deutschland [The Development of Department Stores in Germany]
1910 Gustav Fischer *Jena, Germany*

Amongst a proliferation of studies published at the turn of the century dealing with German department store evolution, Lux's stands out by virtue of its unique approach. Methodologically, confidential questionnaire data from the earliest German department stores enables the most intimate discussion of the development of their businesses. Similarly unparalleled is the author's subsequent account of their wider impact on manufacturing industry.

2091
Miller, Michael B.
The Bon Marché: Bourgeois culture and the department store, 1869–1920
1981 Princeton University Press *Princeton, NJ*

This thoroughly researched study of the Parisian department store examines how innovations in finance, purchasing and organization led to the mass market revolution in retailing at the end of the nineteenth century. An interesting aspect of this book is the way in which it combines business history with the wider process of middle-class formation in western Europe.
Firms: Bon Marché

2092
Tietz, Georg
Hermann Tietz: Geschichte einer Familie und ihrer Warenhäuser [Hermann Tietz: History of a family and its department stores]
1965 Deutsche Verlags-Anstalt *Stuttgart, Germany*

This volume, although essentially biographical in nature, documents the Tietz family and the growth of their 'Hertie' department store empire in Germany. Although technically not a professional business history (there are no footnotes or index), it is important in that it stresses the inextricable relationship between idiosyncratic personal circumstances and their business growth.
Firms: Hermann Tietz (Hertie); Hertie (H. Tietz)

Department Stores, North America

2093
Asher, Louis; Heal, Edith
Send No Money
1942 Argus *Chicago, IL*

This book was written by colleagues of Richard Sears, the founder of the US retailer Sears, Roebuck. It is based on extensive personal correspondence and describes how the firm developed its methods of buying by mail and marketing goods by picture and description. There is some fascinating personal detail included on the founder of the firm.
Firms: Sears, Roebuck & Co.

2094
Biggart, Nicole Worsley
Charismatic Capitalism: Direct selling organizations in America
1989 University of Chicago Press *Chicago, IL*

This is a study of the economic and social origins of direct selling organizations in the USA during the twentieth century. It is shown that whereas bureaucratic firms seek to exclude social relations in order to control workers, the direct selling industry pursues profit in the opposite way, by making social networks serve business ends. This emphasis on the creation of social bonds and the management of existing ones to support economic activity is related, in turn, to the crisis of 'organized capitalism' in the post-1945 period.

2095
Blythe, LeGette; Belk, William Henry
Merchant of the South
1950 University of North Carolina *Chapel Hill, NC*

This is a study of the growth of the Belk chain of department stores in the southern states of the USA during the inter-war period. The suc-

cess of the firm rested on the opening of branches in smaller towns and cities whose potential trading area was increased enormously by the spread of the automobile during the 1920s and 1930s. This book contributes to an understanding of the beginnings of the wider transformation of the American South during the present century.
Firms: Belk

2096
Brough, James
The Woolworths
1982 McGraw-Hill *New York, NY*
This popular history tells how fixed price retailing methods transformed the face of American shopping at the end of the nineteenth century. It also examines the process whereby Woolworths became the retail personification of big business America by the early 1900s.
Firms: Woolworths

2097
Emmet, Boris; Jeuck, John E.
Catalogues and Counters: A history of Sears, Roebuck & Co.
1950 University of Chicago Press *Chicago, IL*
This is a thoroughly researched and comprehensive study of the US retailing enterprise. It covers every aspect of the firm's development, including its methods of central buying, management structure, employee relations, and its stress on cultivating good public relations. It is an early model of a fine tradition of American business history.
Firms: Sears, Roebuck & Co.

2098
Hendrickson, Robert
The Grand Emporium: The illustrated history of America's great department stores
1979 Stein and Day *New York, NY*
As thick as a Sears' catalogue and profusely illustrated, this book provides an enormous amount of information on the history of US department stores. Thin on analysis, but still an essential reference work.
Firms: Marshall Field & Co.; Sears, Roebuck & Co.; Wanamaker's; Woolworths

2099
Hower, Ralph M.
History of Macy's of New York, 1858–1919
1946 Harvard University Press *Cambridge, MA*
This authoritative history of the famous New York department store is one of the finest early examples of American business history. It is comprehensive in scope, examining not only the firm's marketing methods and entrepreneurial strategies, but also labour relations and working conditions.
Firms: Macy's of New York

2100
Johnson, Robert E. L.
Woodward & Lothrop: Portrait of a Corporate Institution
1963 Newcomen Society of North America *New York, NY*
This brief account of the history of the Washington-based department store illustrates the effectiveness of 'one-price' advertising, which transformed the face of US retailing at the end of the nineteenth century.
Firms: Woodward & Lothrop

2101
Katz, Donald R.
The Big Store: Inside the crisis and revolution at Sears
1987 Viking Penguin *New York, NY*
A superb in-depth journalistic account of the history of Sears, Roebuck, particularly of the crisis that rocked the company in the 1970s and its recovery in the 1980s. Based on full access to Sears documentation.
Firms: Sears, Roebuck & Co.; Montgomery Ward

2102
LaDame, Mary
The Filene Story: A study of employees' relations to management in a retail store
1930 Russell Sage Foundation *New York, NY*
This wide-ranging study of the Boston-based department store focuses on one of the first attempts to implement democratic management structures in US retailing. It demonstrates

how profit-sharing and comprehensive staff training underpinned the success of the firm.
Firms: Filene

2103
Macpherson, Mary-Etta
Shopkeepers to a Nation: The Eatons
1963 McClelland & Stewart *Toronto, Canada*

This history of one of Canada's leading department stores explains how a small shop selling dry goods and haberdashery, founded in 1869, had grown to become a major retail emporium by the 1960s. It shows how systematic catalogue-selling led to the creation of a nationwide chain of outlets.
Firms: Eaton's

2104
Marcus, Stanley
Minding the Store: A memoir
1975 Hamish Hamilton *London*

This is a personal history of the Dallas-based department store of Neiman-Marcus. Much of the firm's success was a result of its clever advertising of the latest style European fashions to the North American market.
Firms: Neiman-Marcus

2105
Rhoads, Webster S. Jr
Miller & Rhoads: Seventy-five years of growth
1960 Newcomen Society of North America *New York, NY*

This is a personal history of the leading department store in Richmond, Virginia. The firm's success owed very much to its efforts to present itself as a 'public institution', in the historic traditions of the American South.
Firms: Miller & Rhoads

2106
Rosenberg, Leon Joseph
Dillard's: The first fifty years
1988 University of Arkansas *Fayetteville, AR*

This officially commissioned history focuses on the rise of the chain of department stores in the south-eastern states of the USA. The firm did not open its first store until 1938, yet there were more than 100 branches by the late 1980s, based on the successful retailing concept of suburban malls. It offers insight into the growth of modern retailing outside large towns and cities.
Firms: Dillard's

2107
Santink, Joy L.
Timothy Eaton and the Rise of His Department Store
1990 University of Toronto Press *Toronto, Canada*

More a study of the store than of Eaton, this book is nevertheless scholarly in both respects.
Firms: Eaton's

2108
Stephenson, William
The Store That Timothy Built
1969 McClelland & Stewart *Toronto, Canada*

This lavishly produced official history was written to celebrate the centenary of Eaton's, the Canadian chain of department stores. Based on successful marketing of its catalogue business, this study contains interesting insights into changing trends in popular advertising.
Firms: Eaton's

2109
Twyman, Robert W.
History of Marshall Field & Co. 1852–1906
1954 University of Pennsylvania Press *Philadelphia, PA*

This is an official history of the Chicago-based department store, which came to dominate retail trading in the US midwest during the second half of the nineteenth century. It sheds interesting light on one of the pioneers of mail order retailing, selling high-quality products at reasonable prices.
Firms: Marshall Field & Co.

2110
Wendt, Lloyd; Kogan, Herman
Give the Lady What She Wants
1952 Rand McNally *Chicago, IL*

This popular and well-illustrated history traces the rise of the Chicago-based retailing business of Marshall Field. It shows how the innovative marketing of European fashions led to the growth of one of the most successful US retailers during the last quarter of the nine-

teenth century. Its extensive use of graphic materials captures the atmosphere of the period.
Firms: Marshall Field & Co.

2111
Worthy, James C.
Shaping an American Institution: Robert E. Wood and Sears, Roebuck
1984 University of Illinois Press *Chicago, IL*
Covers Robert E. Wood's thirty years' leadership of Sears, Roebuck, focusing on the role of the leading entrepreneur in shaping the company and on his managerial philosophy and practices. Also provides an important account of the strategy and development of the company from the 1910s to the 1950s.
Firms: Sears, Roebuck; Montgomery Ward

Department Stores, Rest of World

2112
Brasch, Charles; Nicolson, C. R.
Hallensteins: The first century 1873–1973
1973 Hallensteins *Dunedin, New Zealand*
This officially commissioned history was written to celebrate the centenary of one of New Zealand's leading department stores. The firm was a pioneer in the introduction of modern advertising methods to Australasia during the 1930s.
Firms: Hallensteins

2113
Davies, S. W.
Foy's Saga
1945 Foy's *Perth, Australia*
This in-house history was written to celebrate the fiftieth anniversary of the leading department store in Western Australia. It shows how a small family business evolved into a major public company.
Firms: Foy's

2114
Kay, M.
Inside Story of Farmers': First complete record of the marvellous growth of Laidlaw Leeds and the Farmers Trading Co. Ltd
1954 Farmers' *Auckland, New Zealand*
This book traces the history of a firm which began as a mail order enterprise for the farming community in 1909. Expansion came through forward vertical integration into retail outlets and backwards into factory production of its own goods.
Firms: Farmers' Trading Co.; Laidlaw Leeds

2115
Pasdermadjian, H.
The Department Store: Its origins, evolution and economics
1954 Newman Books *London*
Although severely dated this is an interesting study of the competitive niche of department stores in retailing.

2116
Tucker, K. A.
Milne and Choyce: A one hundred year business history 1867–1967
1968 Milne & Choyce *Auckland, New Zealand*
This is an in-house history of one of New Zealand's leading department stores. It is especially informed on the financial growth of the firm and its relationship to the wider development of the New Zealand economy.
Firms: Milne and Choyce

International Trading Companies, UK

2117
Bacha, E.; Greenhill, R. G.
150 Años de Cafe [150 Years of Coffee]
1992 Salamanda Consultoria *Rio de Janeiro, Brazil*
This book celebrates the 150th anniversary of the founding of the British merchant house, E. Johnston & Co. in 1842, which became one of the largest coffee shippers from Brazil during the nineteenth and twentieth centuries. It contains a business history of the company and its successors, an analysis of Brazilian coffee policy over the 150 years and a comprehensive statistical section.
Firms: Brazilian Warrant Agency & Finance Co.; E. Johnston & Co.

2118

Cheong, W. E.

Mandarins and Merchants: Jardine Matheson & Co.

1979 Curzon Press *London*

This is a study of the origins of the firm of Far Eastern British merchants. It shows how Jardine Matheson emerged from the disintegration of the East India Company early in the nineteenth century. Based on extensive use of the firm's archives, the author sets out the firm's successful policy of product diversification away from opium to textiles and teas. It thus contributed to the beginnings of China's integration into the international economy of the nineteenth century.

Firms: East India Company; Jardine Matheson & Co.

2119

Davies, K. G.

The Royal African Company

1957 Longmans *London*

This is the definitive study of the activities of the English Royal African Company during the seventeenth and eighteenth centuries. It is shown how the company was created in order to assume responsibility for an essential link in the Imperial economy. This attempted fusion of public responsibility and private interest was characteristic of commercial development during this period. Combining these objectives often proved difficult, but the company ultimately failed because it was unable to control effectively employees thousands of miles away.

Firms: Royal African Company

2120

Drage, Charles

Taikoo

1970 Constable *London*

This is an officially commissioned history of John Swire & Sons, the Liverpool-based trading company. It is a wide-ranging narrative account of the firm's growth, and it focuses, in particular, on the impact of war and civil strife on the company's activities in the Far East.

Firms: John Swire & Sons

2121

Flint, J. E.

Sir George Goldie and the Making of Nigeria

1960 Oxford University Press *London*

This study of George Goldie's career on the River Niger covers the period between the 1870s and 1900s, his creation of the Royal Niger Co. in 1886 and its role in the conquest of northern Nigeria.

Firms: Royal Niger Co.

2122

Galbraith, J. S.

Mackinnon and East Africa 1878–1895: A study in the 'new imperialism'

1972 Cambridge University Press *Cambridge*

This book studies the career of Sir William Mackinnon and his involvement in the Imperial British East Africa Co., its role in the spread of British influence in East Africa and its eventual failure.

Firms: Imperial British East Africa Co.

2123

Galbraith, J. S.

Crown and Charter: The early years of the British South Africa Co.

1974 University of California Press *Berkeley, CA*

This company was the vehicle for Rhodes's political and industrial expansionist policies between 1884 and 1897 and his dominance was encouraged by the cupidity of investors and the passivity of politicians in London.

Firms: British South Africa Company

2124

Gertzel, C. J.

John Holt: A British merchant in West Africa in the era of imperialism

1959, PhD thesis, Oxford University

John Holt (1841–1915) was one of the major traders in West Africa in the late nineteenth/early twentieth centuries and founder of John Holt & Co. Included in this unpublished D.Phil. thesis is material on his political campaigns over the future of southern Nigeria.

Firms: John Holt & Co.

2125

Griffiths, Sir Percival

A License to Trade: A history of the English chartered companies

1974 Ernest Benn *London*

This is a wide-ranging survey of Britain's major overseas trading companies. Written by a retired Indian civil servant, it focuses on overseas trade, colonization and administration. It constitutes an informed introduction to this area accessible to the general reader.

Firms: East India Company; Levant Company; Royal African Company; Russia Company

2126

Hunt, W. G.

Heirs of Great Adventure: The history of Balfour Williamson & Company Limited. Vol. I (1851–1901) and Vol. II (1901–1951)

1951–60 Jarrold & Sons *Norwich*

Based upon the company's extensive archive, this book was published to celebrate the firm's centenary. Its two volumes describe the development of the business from its origins as a small commission house working on the west coast of Latin America, to its twentieth-century role as a multinational with interests in the United States as well as Chile and Peru. The company diversified from its interests in commodity trades to financial services, property management and industrial investment.

Firms: Balfour Williamson & Co.; Lobitos Oilfields; Williamson, Balfour & Co.

2127

Hyde, Francis E.

Far Eastern Trade 1860–1914

1973 Adam & Charles Black *London*

This study documents the opening up of the Far East to western commercial interests in the age of high imperialism. It consists of a wide-ranging analysis of the growth of the staple products in the Far Eastern trade, and offers an optimistic appraisal of their contribution to the growth of the indigenous economies. Hyde concludes that the links between trade and capital accumulation played an especially important role in promoting the growth of this region.

2128

Insh, George Pratt

The Company of Scotland Trading to Africa and the Indies

1932 Charles Scribner *London*

This is a narrative history of Scotland's attempt to establish itself as a colonial power at the end of the seventeenth century. It sheds interesting light on how overseas trading expeditions were organized in this period, and how private interests were merged with the ambitions of governments. The Company's short-lived existence ended with the Act of Union in 1707.

Firms: Company of Scotland

2129

Ishii, Kanji

Kindai Nihon to Igirisu Shihon [Modern Japan With Special Relation with British Capital: The case of Jardine Matheson Co.]

1984 Tokyo University Press *Tokyo, Japan*

This book examines the great influence of foreign merchants on the modernization of the Japanese economy, especially focusing on the Jardine Matheson Co. The influence of this company was gradually reduced as a result of Meiji government policy.

Firms: Jardine, Matheson & Co.

2130

Jones, Stephanie

Merchants of the Raj: British managing agency houses in Calcutta yesterday and today

1992 Macmillan *London*

This is an officially commissioned history of the managing agency houses in Calcutta by the Inchcape group of companies. The managing-agency system is traced back to the 1830s when the East India Company lost its monopoly, and individual private trading was permitted. It is shown how former East India Company personnel formed partnerships and created agency houses, trading in indigo, sugar, cotton, silks, spices and opium. This authoritative study also contains an appendix providing useful biographies of the leading merchants involved.

Firms: Balmer Lawrie; Begg Dundas; Bird's; Gillanders; James Finlay; Jardine Henderson; Lovelock and Lewes; Mackinnon; Macrieill & Barry; McLeod

2131
Jones, Stephanie K.
Two Centuries of Overseas Trading: The origins and growth of the Inchcape Group
For main entry, see 3059

2132
Jones, Stephanie K.
Trade and Shipping: Lord Inchcape, 1852–1932
For main entry, see 3060

2133
Leubuscher, Charlotte
The West African Shipping Trade, 1909–1959
For main entry, see 3136

2134
Longhurst, Henry
The Borneo Story: The history of the first 100 years of trading in the Far East by the Borneo Company Limited
1956 Newman Neame *London*

This in-house history, officially commissioned by the company, tells the story of the London-based trading firm from the mid-nineteenth century. It is a lavishly illustrated celebratory history, containing a useful appendix listing the company's principal officers.
Firms: Borneo Company

2135
Macaulay, R. H.
History of the Bombay Burmah Trading Corporation Ltd. 1864–1910
1934 Spottiswoode & Ballantyne *London*

This early business history focuses on the formative years of one of Britain's colonial trading companies to the Far East. No systematic attempt is made to appraise the firm's business strategy, although some light is shed on the primitive methods of forestry in tropical areas in the period before 1914.
Firms: Bombay Burmah Trading Corporation

2136
Marriner, Sheila
Rathbones of Liverpool, 1845–1873
1961 Liverpool University Press *Liverpool*

Marriner presents a pioneering study of a major Liverpool merchant house, which opened a branch in the City of London in 1867. Her book is illuminating on the traditional merchants' working techniques, which were to decline in the late-nineteenth century following, in particular, the introduction of the telegraph.
Firms: Rathbone Brothers & Co.

2137
Marriner, Sheila; Hyde, Francis E.
The Senior: John Samuel Swire, 1825–98: Management in Far Eastern shipping trades
1967 Liverpool University Press *Liverpool*

This biography of the dominant personality in John Swire & Sons and the architect of the Shipping Conferences (cartels) between Europe and the Far East shows him as an able manager whose defects are not spared. This volume was a pioneering work on the role of shipping agents. It covers the work of John Swire & Sons, later Butterfield & Swire, who were agents for the Blue Funnel Line and built up trade and industry in the Far East. It is strong on their role as agents, the work of the conference system, and their part in promoting local enterprise. Hyde and Falkus (1990) (qqv) are complementary sources.
Firms: Butterfield & Swire; China Navigation Co.; John Swire & Sons; Ocean Steamship Co.

2138
Mathew, W. M.
The House of Gibbs and the Peruvian Guano Monopoly
1981 Royal Historical Society *London*

This work focuses upon the relationship between the British merchant house of Antony Gibbs & Sons and the Peruvian Government over the management of the guano trade on the west coast of South America. It is not merely a business history but contributes to debates on such issues as informal imperialism and business control. The period covered is broadly the 1840s to 1870s.
Firms: Antony Gibbs & Sons

2139
McGrath, Patrick
The Merchant Venturers of Bristol and Society of Merchant Venturers of the City of Bristol

1975 Merchant Adventurers of the City of Bristol *Bristol*

This is an official history of the Bristol merchant community from the late seventeenth century until the post-1945 period. Based upon the Society's own archives, it shows how the city's economic fortunes changed during this period. It examines how a group of would-be trading monopolists was transformed into a broadly-based public enterprise, providing technical education as well as carrying out charitable work.

Firms: Merchant Venturers of Bristol

2140

Neil-Tomlinson, B.

The Nyassa Chartered Company 1891–1929

Journal of African History, vol. 18, no. 1, 1977: pp 109–28

This is a study of the operations of the Nyassa Co. at ground level, its use as a conquering force and its role as a supplier of migrant labour.

Firms: Nyassa Co.

2141

Newbury, C.

Trade and Technology in West Africa: The case of the Niger Co. 1900–20

Journal of African History, vol. 19, no. 4, 1978: pp 551–75

This is a study of the Niger Company between the surrender of its charter and its takeover by Lever Bros. Newbury stresses its expansion into new activities and the role of technological adaptation in business performance.

Firms: (Royal) Niger Co.; Lever Bros

2142

Pedler, Frederick

The Lion and the Unicorn in Africa: A history of the origins of the United Africa Company 1787–1931

1974 Heinemann *London*

This study was undertaken by one of the directors of this British trading company. It is a lengthy narrative, not without interest, but there is little systematic analysis of either business strategy or management control.

Firms: United Africa Company

2143

Perham, M. (Editor)

Mining, Commerce and Finance in Nigeria

1948 Faber & Faber *London*

This is an old, but otherwise useful, text on trading and mining firms in colonial Nigeria. It covers the period 1900 to 1945 and gives useful insights into mining, commerce and banking in colonial Nigeria–business methods, profitability, competition among firms and relations, with the colonial government and Africans. J. Mars's chapter on extraterritorial firms remains the best treatment ever of the expatriate merchant houses in the period up to the end of the Second World War.

Firms: CFAO; John Holt & Co.; Lever Bros; Paterson Zochonis; Raccah; United Africa Company

2144

Platt, D. C. M. (Editor)

Business Imperialism 1840–1930: An inquiry based on British experience in Latin America

1977 Clarendon Press *Oxford*

This multi-authored compilation examines the Latin American experience of firms engaged in finance, public utilities including transport and trade. There is also an important section on government-business relations. The contributors are leading British specialists in their field.

Firms: Baring Brothers; Fray Bentos; Antony Gibbs & Sons; F. Johnston & Sons; Leibig; James Nelson & Sons; Pacific Steam Navigation Co.; S. Pearson & Sons; River Plate Trust Loan & Agency Co.; Royal Mail Steam Packet Co.

2145

Rabb, Theodore K.

Enterprise and Empire: Merchants and gentry investment in the expansion of England 1575–1630

1967 Harvard University Press *Cambridge, MA*

This is a painstaking study of the social composition of those involved in England's first joint-stock companies. It shows that most of these enterprises rested primarily on merchant capital and adventurers, but they also drew vital support from the gentry. In the process, they helped to create a sense of national identity and mission for England overseas, which did so much to promote its subsequent economic development. This study is also of interest as an early example of computer-assisted business history.

2146
Robert, Rudolph
Chartered Companies and their Role in the Development of Overseas Trade
1969 Bell *London*

This introductory survey tells the story of the major British trading companies since the seventeenth century. The generally informed narrative illuminates the activities of the most significant concerns. It is shown how these firms became a means for building empires, administering colonies, and developing overseas trade.
Firms: British North Borneo Company; Eastland Company; Falkland Island Company; Levant Company; Merchant Adventurers; Royal Niger Company

2147
Webb, John
Great Tooley of Ipswich: Portrait of an early Tudor merchant
1962 Suffolk Records Society *Ipswich*

This study centres on the Ipswich-based merchant Henry Tooley, who played a prominent role in promoting English trade with northern Europe during the first half of the fifteenth century. It is shown how Tooley organized imports of salt, iron, woad and wine, in addition to a wide range of other items. Insight is provided into accountancy practices during this early period, as well as the social position more generally of merchants in early modern England.
Firms: Henry Tooley

2148
Willan, T. S.
The Early History of the Russia Company 1553–1603
1956 Manchester University Press *Manchester*

This study of the London-based trading company illustrates the new directions that were established for England's foreign trade during the second half of the sixteenth century. It describes the structure of joint-stock companies in this period, and the uncertain financial methods in operation at the time. The firm exchanged English cloth for raw materials like hides and fur, although its impact on the two countries at the time seems to have been minimal.
Firms: Russia Company

2149
Wood, Alfred C.
A History of the Levant Company
1964 Frank Cass *London*

This new edition of a study published originally by Oxford University Press in 1935, examines the development of England's trading relations with Turkey via the Levant Company from its establishment in 1583 until it was wound up in 1825. It sheds light on the intricate links that drew together private and public interests in the pre-industrial period, together with insight into the life of the Levant factories and how joint-stock companies were organized in this period.
Firms: Levant Company

International Trading Companies, UK (East India Company)

2150
Chaudhuri, K. N.
The Trading World of Asia and the English East India Company 1660–1760
1978 Cambridge University Press *Cambridge*

This is the definitive study of the formative years of the English East India Company. Input-output theory is applied in analysing the company's operations which are related, in turn, to its management structures. The various aspects of the firm's trading operations in the Far East are comprehensively studied, and its accountancy methods are analysed to yield estimates of the firm's long-term profitability during this period.
Firms: East India Company

2151
Dhar, Niranjan
The Administrative System of the East India Company in Bengal 1714–1786
1964 Eureka *Calcutta, India*

This is a detailed study of the way the British East India Company organized its operations during the eighteenth century. It provides insight into the management structure of one of the leading trading concerns of its time, including means of communication, as well as the working conditions of the firm's employees.
Firms: East India Company

2152
Foster, Sir William
John Company
1926 Bodley Head *London*

This early history of the British East India Company is a narrative account of the firm's activities from its inception until the early nineteenth century. It highlights the wide range of the company's activities and its impact more generally on the social life of the period.
Firms: East India Company

2153
Foster, William
The East India House: Its history and associations
1924 Bodley Head *London*

This lavishly produced early history of the London-based trading concern focuses on the activities of its officers and its impact on the life of the metropolis more generally during the eighteenth century. It sheds light on the way the firm was organized and the methods of work of its employees.
Firms: East India Company

2154
Fry, Howard T.
Alexander Dalrymple (1737–1808) and the Expansion of British Trade
1970 Cass *London*

This is a biography of one of the leading servants of the British East India Company. It is a detailed study of how the Company sought new commodity trade in the Far East during the late eighteenth century. Interesting light is shed on the close links that were forged between international traders and government during this period.
Firms: East India Company

2155
Hossain, H.
The Company Weavers of Bengal: The East India Company and the organization of textile production in Bengal, 1750–1813
For main entry, see 1258

2156
Marshall, P. J.
East Indian Fortunes: The British in Bengal in the eighteenth century
1976 Clarendon Press *Oxford*

This is a detailed study of the British merchant community in the east Indian state of Bengal under the rule of the East India Company. It is shown how British merchants succeeded in entrenching themselves in certain commodity markets like silk and piece-goods, enabling them to charge high prices relative to those paid to domestic producers. Only in banking were native capitalists able to emulate the fortunes that accrued to British merchants.

2157
Mui, Hoh-cheung; Mui, Lorna H.
The Management of Monopoly: A study of the English East India Company's conduct of its tea trade 1784–1833
1984 University of British Columbia
Vancouver, Canada

This essay in business history deals with the conduct of the English East India Company in the management of its exclusive privilege to import tea into Britain between 1784 and 1833. The firm's commercial bureaucracy is described in detail and is related, in turn, to how it enforced its tea monopoly. The firm's directors carefully regulated supply to produce regular profits, whilst at the same time ensuring that customers remained satisfied with the final product. The authors conclude by observing that during the half century of monopoly the tea trade with China was conducted largely in peace and harmony, but in the subsequent period, free trade was prosecuted under the shadow of guns.
Firms: East India Company

2158
Nightingale, Pamela
Trade and Empire in Western India 1784–1806
1970 Cambridge University Press *Cambridge*

This study examines the influence of commercial interests on the growth of the British Empire in western India in the age of Cornwallis and Wellesley. It shows that the East India Company retained the initiative in promoting territorial expansion during this period, and was still largely independent of the authorities in Bengal and London. This expansion was in response chiefly to local conditions which were restricting the commercial interests of private British traders.
Firms: East India Company

2159
Philips, C. H.
The East India Company 1784–1834
1940 Manchester University Press *Manchester*

This detailed monograph examines how Britain's leading trading company was gradually relieved of its long-held privileges in the East. It shows that the advantages enjoyed by the home government, together with divisions inside the India House itself, led to the Company's surrender of many of its monopolies by the early 1830s. This illustrates the wider changes to a free trade outlook in Britain during this period.
Firms: East India Company

2160
Robinson, F. P.
The Trade of the East India Company from 1709 to 1813
1912 Cambridge University Press *Cambridge*

This early history of Britain's leading trading company in the pre-industrial period is often critical of the principle of monopoly control. But the author argues that the firm endeavoured by all its means to promote trade with India that would benefit its shareholders, the English nation, and India itself. This generally celebratory history offers an interesting comparison with more recent studies of the firm.
Firms: East India Company

2161
Sutherland, Lucy S.
The East India Company in Eighteenth-Century Politics
1952 Clarendon Press *Oxford*

The British East India Company was in important respects the precursor of today's international trading concerns. This definitive study highlights the company's significance for Britain's growing economy in the eighteenth century.
Firms: East India Company

International Trading Companies, Rest of World

2162
Arasaratnam, Sinnappah
Merchants and Companies on the Coromandel Coast 1650–1740
1986 Oxford University Press *Delhi, India*

This highly detailed monograph tells the story of the penetration of the trade of India's Bay of Bengal by European merchants in the early modern period. Based largely on trade in cloth, dyes and spices, the author shows how Dutch aggressiveness, superior shipping technology and the declining profitability of overseas trade had led to the impoverishment of many indigenous merchants by the mid-eighteenth century. Only those Indian merchants who abandoned joint family enterprises for joint-stock associations seemed to have prospered in the face of European competition.

2163
Blussé, L.; Gaastra, F. (Editors)
Companies and Trade: Essays on overseas trading companies during the *Ancien Régime*
1981 Leiden University Press *Leiden, The Netherlands*

This collection of essays provides a comparative perspective on the activities of European trading companies during the seventeenth and eighteenth centuries. It highlights the tensions between the commercial priority of maintaining liquidity and the efforts by governments to pursue their strategic ambitions. The consequently unplanned losses of these firms became

unexpected investments in the process that led from the discoveries to the creation of a modern world market.
Firms: Brandenburg Overseas Trading Company; Danish East India Company; Dutch East India Company; East India Company

2164
Bonin, Hubert
C.F.A.O. Cent ans de compétition [C.F.A.O. A Hundred Years of Competition]
1987 Economica *Paris, France*

This is an official, but serious centenary history of the Compagnie française de l'Afrique occidentale, a trading company which operated in French West Africa. It is still active there, but since decolonization, it has diversified into Europe.
Firms: Compagnie française de l'Afrique occidentale (CFAO)

2165
Cavignac, Jean
Jean Pellet, commerçant de gros, 1694–1772: Contribution à l'étude du région bordelais au XVIIIe siècle [Jean Pellet, International Merchant of Bordeaux, 1694–1772: A contribution to the study of the Bordelais region of the 18th Century]
1967 S.E.V.P.E.N. *Paris, France*

This is a detailed study of the career and business of an eighteenth-century merchant of Bordeaux, who traded with the French West Indies, with northern Europe, with Spain and her colonies. The book is based particularly on Pellet's papers, which are preserved in the Bordeaux record office.
Firms: Jean Pellet

2166
Clayton, L.
Grace: W. R. Grace & Co., the formative years, 1850–1930
1985 University of Illinois Press *Ottawa, IL*

The book describes the development of the American trading house, W. R. Grace & Co. Its business was at first chiefly in the trades of the west coast of Latin America where, in the nineteenth century, it was a major rival of such British houses as A. Gibbs & Co. and Balfour, Williamson. By the early decades of the twentieth century the firm had developed, commercially and organizationally, into a fully-fledged US multinational.
Firms: W. R. Grace & Co.

2167
Coquery-Vidrovitch, C.
L'Impact des intérets coloniaux: S.C.O.A. et C.F.A.O. dans l'ouest Africain, 1910–65
Journal of African History, vol. 16, no. 4, 1975: pp 595–621

A study of the two main French firms in western Africa.
Firms: La société commerciale de l'ouest Africain (SCOA); La compagnie Française de l'Afrique occidentale (CFAO)

2168
Hieke, E.
Das Hamburgische Handelshaus: Wm O'Swald & Co. Teil I 1831–70 [The Hamburg Trading House: Wm O'Swald & Co. Vol. I 1831–70]
1939 Verlag Hans Christians *Hamburg, Germany*

This study describes one of the earliest German firms involved in the Africa trade. Initially a firm trading to China, its interest switched to Africa in the 1840s.
Firms: Wm O'Swald & Co.

2169
Hieke, E.
G. L. Gaiser: Hamburg–Westafrika: Hundert Jahre Handel mit Nigeria [G. L. Gaiser: Hamburg–West Africa: One hundred years of trade with Nigeria]
1949 Hoffman & Campe Verlag *Hamburg, Germany*

This is a study of one of the earliest German firms involved in the Africa trade.
Firms: G. L. Gaiser

2170
Hussey, R. D.
The Caracas Company, 1728–1784
1934 Cambridge University Press *Cambridge, MA*

In spite of its age, this study on a Spanish

chartered company in the colonial trade has not yet been superseded.
Firms: Real Compañía Guipuzcoana de Caracas

2171
Karnes, Thomas L.
Tropical Enterprise: The Standard Fruit and Steamship Company in Latin America
1978 Louisiana State University Press *Baton Rouge, LA*

A pioneering business history, this investigates the role of US multinationals in Latin America, especially Honduras, Nicaragua, Mexico and Haiti. Written with full access to the archives of Standard Fruit ("Dole"), the book carries the story to 1964.
Firms: Standard Fruit & Steamship Company; United Fruit Co.

2172
Léon, Pierre
Marchands et spéculateurs dauphinois dans le monde antillais au XVIIIe siècle: Les Dolle et les Raby [Merchants and Speculators in the French West Indies in the Eighteenth Century: The Dolle and Raby families]
1963 Les Belles Lettres *Paris, France*

A study of two merchant families of Grenoble (France), which traded extensively with the French West Indies, became plantation owners in Santo Domingo, but were ruined as a consequence of the French Revolution.
Firms: Dolle; Raby

2173
Nash, E. Gee
The Hanse: Its history and romance
1929 Bodley Head *London*

This study of north German merchant houses tells the story of their rise in the Middle Ages until the beginnings of decline in the mid-seventeenth century. It provides insight into the close links between overseas trade and rivalry among nation states during this period.
Firms: Hanse

2174
Prakash, Om
The Dutch East India Company and the Economy of Bengal, 1630–1720
1985 Princeton University Press *Princeton, NJ*

This well-researched monograph is the authoritative history of one of Europe's leading international trading concerns during the early modern period. Based mainly on unpublished material held in the firm's archive in The Hague, it shows how the company's activities affected levels of output, income and employment in the Bengali economy in this period.
Firms: Dutch East India Company

2175
Shenton, Robert W.
The Development of Capitalism in Northern Nigeria
1986 University of Toronto Press *Toronto, Canada*

This book provides a thorough-going analysis of the interaction of big business and the colonial state in northern Nigeria. It covers the period from about 1900 to 1939 with a discussion of the pre-1900 period and contains much insight into the origins and transformation of merchant capitalism–tin mining, merchandise trading and shipping–as it relates to this landlocked area of Nigeria.
Firms: Ambrosini and Co.; Elder Dempster Lines; Lever Brothers; London and Kano Co.; United Africa Co.; Woermann Line

2176
Vail, L.
Mozambique's Chartered Companies: The rule of the feeble
Journal of African History, vol. 17, no. 3, 1976: pp 389–416

This article studies the role of chartered companies in governing parts of Mozambique between the 1890s and the 1920s. It stresses the failure of such companies to provide the development capital needed for such areas and the role of Britain and Germany in using these companies as proxies for their own interests.
Firms: Companhia de Moçambique; Companhia do Niassa; Nyassa Consolidated Co.

2177
Waszkis, Helmut
Philipp Brothers: The history of a trading giant 1901–1985
1987 Metal Bulletin Books *London*

This is an official history of Philipp Brothers,

the international metal trader founded originally in Hamburg in 1901. This study highlights the vulnerability of even well-diversified firms in the uncertain world of international commodity markets.
Firms: Philipp Brothers

Japanese Zaibatsu and Sogo Shosha

2178
Asajima, Shoichi
Senkanki Sumitomo Zaibatsu Keiei-shi Kenkyu [A Business History of the Sumitomo Zaibatsu in the Inter-war Period]
1983 Tokyo Daigaku Shuppan-kai *Tokyo, Japan*
Covering the period from 1921 to 1945, the author analyses archival records dealing with the ownership and management of the Sumitomo Zaibatsu, with particular reference to financial accounts of receipts and outgoings.
Firms: Sumitomo

2179
Hashimoto, Juro; Takeda, Haruhito (Editors)
Nippon Keizai no Hatten to Kigyo Shudan [The Development of the Japanese Economy and Business Groups]
1992 Tokyo Daigaku Shuppan-kai *Tokyo, Japan*
This wide-ranging history of Japanese business groups includes prewar Zaibatsu covering the period from the 1860s to the 1980s. There are chapters on the privileged merchant and Zaibatsu, the diversification, the Konzern, the war economy, the dissolution of Zaibatsu and the formation of business groups.

2180
Hatakeyama, Hideki
Sumitomo Zaibatsu Seiritsu-shi no Kenkyu [A History of the Formation of the Sumitomo Zaibatsu]
1988 Dobunkan Shuppan *Tokyo, Japan*
Covering the period from the 1590s to the 1950s the author gives a very detailed study of the development of the Zaibatsu as a whole and its constituent companies. This is a full study of Sumitomo in prewar Japan.
Firms: Sumitomo

2181
Holding Company Liquidation Committee
Nippon Zaibatsu to sono Kaitai [Japanese Zaibatsu and their Dissolution]
For main entry, see 3656

2182
Kawabe, Nobuo
A Study of Sogo Shosha (General Trading Companies): The case of the Mitsubishi Trading Co. in prewar America
1982 Jikkyo Shuppan *Tokyo, Japan*
This book has been developed from a PhD dissertation presented to the Ohio State University in 1980. It describes the history of the San Francisco and Seattle branches of the Mitsubishi Trading Co., looking at the changing strategy and structure of the firm.
Firms: Mitsubishi Trading Co.

2183
Kuwahara, Tetsuya
Kigyo Kokusaika no Shiteki Kenkyu [Historical Analysis of the Internationalization of Japanese Firms]
1990 Moriyama Shoten *Tokyo, Japan*
This book provides an analysis of the Japanese firms which made direct investments in mainland China before the Second World War, comparing eight major cotton spinning companies. Different patterns of motivation and behaviour were found, related to the products of each firm.
Firms: Dainihon-boseki Co.; Fuji Gas-boseki Co.; Kanegafuchi-boseki Co.; Toyoboseki Co.

2184
Matsumoto, Hiroshi
Mitsui Zaibatsu no Kenkyu [A Study of the Mitsui Zaibatsu]
1979 Yoshikawa Kobunkan *Tokyo, Japan*
This work is an authoritative study of the structure of the Mitsui Zaibatsu and its accumulation of capital in the prewar period, with particular focus on Mitsui & Co., which was the holding company of Mitsui Zaibatsu, and the

Mitsui Corporation, which was a general trading company.
Firms: Mitsui

2185
Mishima, Yasuo (Editor)
Nippon Zaibatsu Keiei-shi: Mitsubishi Zaibatsu [A Japanese Business History of Zaibatsu: Mitsubishi Zaibatsu]
1981 Nippon Keizai Shinbun-sha *Tokyo, Japan*

This is a detailed account of the Mitsubishi Zaibatsu for the period from the 1860s to the 1950s which includes its reorganization as a contemporary business group. The introduction presents the main features of the company's history.
Firms: Mitsubishi

2186
Mishima, Yasuo
Nippon Zaibatsu Keiei-shi: Hanshin Zaibatsu [A Japanese Business History of Zaibatsu: Zaibatsu in the Osaka-Kobe region]
1984 Nippon Keizai Shinbun-sha *Tokyo, Japan*

This study features the three Zaibatsu in the Osaka-Kobe area: Nomura, Yamaguchi and Kawasaki during the period from the 1850s to 1945. Mishima describes how these provincial Zaibatsu developed into national Zaibatsu.
Firms: Kawasaki; Nomura; Yamaguchi

2187
Mitsui
The House of Mitsui
1937 Mitsui Gomei Kaisha *Tokyo, Japan*

This is an early in-house history of one of the pioneer Japanese conglomerates. It explains how a network of family capitalists had transformed themselves into a diversified and international trading company by the 1930s. It uses company records to shed light on the distinctively Japanese strategies pursued by firms during the first half of the twentieth century.
Firms: Mitsui

2188
Mitsui
The 100 Year History of Mitsui and Co. Ltd. 1876–1976
1976 Mitsui *Tokyo, Japan*

This is an official history of one of Japan's leading international trading concerns. It emphasizes the importance of government–business relations in the Japanese context, although there is little discussion of labour and training.
Firms: Mitsui

2189
Morikawa, Hidemasa
Zaibatsu no Keiei-shi-teki Kenkyu [A Business History of Zaibatsu]
1980 Toyo Keizai Shinpo-sha *Tokyo, Japan*

This book is a business history of prewar Japanese Zaibatsu with particular reference to Mitsui, Mitsubishi, Sumitomo and Furukawa. The author reviews the changing pattern of strategy and structure of these four Zaibatsu.
Firms: Furukawa; Mitsubishi; Mitsui; Sumitomo

2190
Morikawa, Hidemasa
Nippon Zaibatsu Keiei-shi: Chiho Zaibatsu [A Business History of Japanese Zaibatsu: Local Zaibatsu]
1985 Nippon Keizai Shinbun-sha *Tokyo, Japan*

The author defines the Zaibatsu as a diversified family business based on closed ownership by family members including local business. This work is a case study of sixteen local Zaibatsu and five local family businesses in prewar Japan.

2191
Morikawa, Hidemasa
Zaibatsu: The rise and fall of family enterprise groups in Japan
1992 University of Tokyo Press *Tokyo, Japan*

This is an extremely useful account in English of those major Japanese enterprises, the *zaibatsu*. Written by a leading business historian, it examines the changing fortunes of ten such business groups, focusing on the elements of 'family exclusiveness' which disappeared after the post-war dissolution.
Firms: Asano; Fujita; Furukawa; Okura; Mitsui; Mitsubishi; Sumitomo; Suzuki; Yasuda

2192
Roberts, J. G.
Mitsui: Three centuries of Japanese business
1989 Weatherill *New York, NY*

Roberts gives a detailed history of the sprawling Japanese conglomerate with interests stretching from iron/steel, chemicals, construction, and textiles to transportation. The book is especially interesting on the heavy financial backing given to Toyota in the 1930s and 1950s.

Firms: Japan Steel Works Ltd; Mitsui Construction; Mitsui Pharmaceuticals; Showa Aircraft; Toshiba; Toyota Motor Corporation

2193
Saito, Satoshi
Shinko Konzern Riken no Kenkyu: Okouchi Masatoshi to Riken Sangyo Shudan [A Study of the Growth of Riken: Masatoshi Okouchi and the Riken Industrial Group]
1987 Jicho-sha *Tokyo, Japan*

The author examines closely the formation and development of the newly-established Riken Zaibatsu covering the period from the 1910s to the 1940s from many points of view. This is an excellent case study on Riken in pre-war Japan.

Firms: Riken

2194
Sakudo, Yotaro (Editor)
Nippon Zaibatsu Keiei-shi: Sumitomo Zaibatsu [A Japanese Business History of Zaibatsu: Sumitomo Zaibatsu]
1982 Nippon Keizai Shinbun-sha *Tokyo, Japan*

This work charts the evolution and development of the Sumitomo Zaibatsu from the 1850s to 1945. The book is a detailed history of the Sumitomo group in the prewar period.

Firms: Sumitomo

2195
Shibagaki, Kazuo
Nippon Kin'yu Shihon Bunseki [An Analysis of Japanese Financial Capital]
1965 Tokyo Daigaku Shuppan-kai *Tokyo, Japan*

This is an excellent research work on Japanese oligopolistic capital for the affiliated businesses of prewar Zaibatsu, or the cotton-spinning industry which was outside the Zaibatsu. Though the framework is based on the theory of economic development stages rather than the perspective of entrepreneurial or management history, the work analyses the financial structure of the prewar business groups.

2196
Suzuki, Yoshitaka; Abe, Etsuo; Yonekura, Seiichiro
Keiei-shi [Business History]
For main entry, see 3632

2197
Tamaki, Hajime
Nippon Zaibatsu-shi [A History of Japanese Zaibatsu]
1976 Shakai Shiso-sha *Tokyo, Japan*

This wide-ranging business history of Japanese Zaibatsu covers the period from the 1910s to the 1950s which includes the businesses of Mitsui, Mitsubishi, Sumitomo, Yasuda, Nissan, Nicchitsu, Nisso, Mori and Riken.

Firms: Mitsubishi; Mitsui; Mori; Nicchitsu; Nissan; Nisso; Riken; Sumitomo; Yasuda

2198
Tamaki, Hajime
Chiho Zaibatsu to Dozoku Ketsugo [Local Zaibatsu and Family Combinations]
1981 Ochanomizu Shobo *Tokyo, Japan*

Tamaki's book is a study of Japanese provincial Zaibatsu. These are diversified family businesses based on closed ownership, some of which are relatively small. The book describes the relationship between management and ownership. There are chapters on 'family constitutions', the Matsuzakaya Zaibatsu, and the Kamino Zaibatsu.

Firms: Kamino; Matsuzakaya

2199
Togai, Yoshio
Mitsui Bussan Kaisha no Keieishi teki Kankyu: Moto Mitsui Buss an kaisha no teichaku, hatten, kaisan [A Business History of the Mitsui Trading Co: Origin, development and the dissolution of the old Mitsui Co.]
1974 Toyokeizai shinposha *Tokyo, Japan*

This book clarifies the characteristics of a

general trading company from the Meiji period to the dissolution of the firm in 1947 immediately after the war. Particular emphasis is placed on the role of Mitsui as a general trading company, bringing together information, finance, technical expertise and managerial skills in new areas of business.
Firms: Mitsui Trading Co.

2200
Udagawa, Masaru
Nippon Zaibatsu Keiei-shi: Shinko Zaibatsu [A Business History of Japanese Zaibatsu: New Zaibatsu]
1984 Nippon Keizai Shinbun-sha *Tokyo, Japan*
This work is a case study of five new Zaibatsu: Nissan, Nicchitsu, Nisso, Mori and Riken with particular focus on the period from the 1920s to 1940s. This informative volume describes features of the structure and the scope of the diversified business of these new Konzerns.
Firms: Mori; Nicchitsu; Nissan; Nisso; Riken

2201
Yasuoka, Shigeaki
Zaibatsu Keisei-shi no Kenkyu [A Study of the Formation of Zaibatsu]
1970 Mineruva Shobo *Kyoto, Japan*
This author gives a detailed description of the evolution of the Konoike and Mitsui businesses with particular reference to the Tokugawa period and the early days of Meiji era. This is a comparative case study contrasting Konoike, which declined after the Meiji Restoration with Mitsui, which overcame the difficulties.
Firms: Konoike; Mitsui

2202
Yasuoka, Shigeaki (Editor)
Nippon no Zaibatsu: Nippon Keiei-shi Koza, Vol. 3 [The Japanese Zaibatsu: Japanese Business History, Vol. 3]
1976 Nippon Keizai Shinbun-sha *Tokyo, Japan*
This is a wide-ranging business history of Zaibatsu in prewar Japan. There are chapters on the four big Zaibatsu, the industrial Zaibatsu, the late-coming Zaibatsu, the local Zaibatsu, on the Suzuki Shoten whose plan for the formation of Zaibatsu miscarried, the general trading companies, and the dissolution of Zaibatsu.

2203
Yasuoka, Shigeaki (Editor)
Zaibatsu-shi Kenkyu [Business History of Zaibatsu]
1979 Nippon Keizai Shinbun-sha *Tokyo, Japan*
This is a collection of eight wide-ranging papers on the business history of Zaibatsu. There are papers on the industrial structure and types of Zaibatsu, the provincial Zaibatsu, Mitsui and shipping, Sumitomo and chemicals, the financial structures, Ogura Masatsune of Sumitomo, and the Tata Zaibatsu in India.
Firms: Mitsui; Sumitomo; Tata

2204
Yasuoka, Shigeaki (Editor)
Nippon Zaibatsu Keiei-shi: Mitsui Zaibatsu [A Japanese Business History of Zaibatsu: Mitsui Zaibatsu]
1982 Nippon Keizai Shinbun-sha *Tokyo, Japan*
This, the fullest history of the Mitsui Zaibatsu, covers the period from the seventeenth century to the 1950s which includes the reorganization of Zaibatsu as a contemporary business group. The editor's scholarly introduction sets out highlights in the history of Mitsui.
Firms: Mitsui

2205
Yasuoka, Shigeaki; Fujita, Teiichiro; Ishikawa, Kenjiro
'Oumi' Shonin no Keiei Isan: Sono Sai-hyoka [The Managerial Legacy of 'Oumi' Merchants: A reassesment]
1992 Dobunkan *Tokyo, Japan*
This work reviews the activities of 'Oumi' Merchants with reference to their influence on personnel management, business ideology and entrepreneurship.

2206
Yonekawa, Shin'ichi (Editor)
Sekai no Zaibatsu Keiei [Business Management of the Big Family Business in a World Context]

1981 Nippon Keizai Shinbun-sha *Tokyo, Japan*

This comprehensive work includes ten papers on big family business in industrially advanced countries such as the UK, France, Germany and the USA, and in developing countries like India, the Philippines, Korea, Brazil and Argentina.

2207

Yonekawa, Shin'ichi; Shimokawa, Koichi; Yamazaki, Hiroaki (Editors)

Sengo Nippon Keiei-shi; Dai Nikan [Postwar Japanese Business History, Vol. II]

1990 Toyo Keizai Shinpo-sha *Tokyo, Japan*

This book discusses the development and restructuring in various industries: electrical machine, automobile, machine tool, petroleum, petrochemical and electric power.

2208

Yonekawa, Shin'ichi; Shimokawa, Koichi; Yamazaki, Hiroaki (Editors)

Sengo Nippon Keiei-shi; Dai Ikkan [Postwar Japanese Business History, Vol. I]

1991 Toyo Keizai Shinpo-sha *Tokyo, Japan*

Following the changes in net profit in the bigger 50 companies before and after the Second World War, this work describes the development and restructuring of the cotton spinning industry, the synthetic fibres industry, the shipbuilding industry, and the iron and steel industry.

2209

Yonekawa, Shin'ichi; Shimokawa, Koichi; Yamazaki, Hiroaki (Editors)

Sengo Nippon Keiei-shi; Dai Sankan [Postwar Japanese Business History, Vol. III]

1991 Toyo Keizai Shinpo-sha *Tokyo, Japan*

This book describes the development and restructuring of industries such as distribution, banking, trading companies, shipping and foreign-run industry. In the last chapter of this volume, the editors outline various approaches to postwar Japanese business history.

2210

Yonekawa, Shin'ichi; Yoshihara, Hideki (Editors)

Business History of General Trading Companies (Thirteenth Fuji Conference)

For main entry, see 111

2211

Yoshihara, Kunio

Sogo Shosha: The vanguard of the Japanese economy

1982 Oxford University Press *Oxford*

Yoshihara traces the history of the big Japanese general trading companies (notably Mitsui Bussan and Mitsubishi Shoji) and analyses their structure and prospects in the 1980s. A thorough and useful study.

Firms: Ataka; C. Itoh; Gosho; Iwai & Co.; Kanematsu; Marubeni; Mitsubishi Shoji; Mitsui Bussan; Nichimen; Nissho

2212

Yoshino, M. Y.; Lifson, Thomas B.

The Invisible Link: Japan's Sogo Shosha and the organization of trade

1986 MIT Press *Cambridge, MA*

This well-documented analysis examines the historical development of the corporate strategies and organizational culture of Japanese conglomerates. It combines management theory with an account of the growth of these firms in their historical context, based on original sources.

2213

Young, Alexander K.

The Sogo Shosha: Japan's multilateral trading companies

1979 Westview Press *Boulder, CO*

This is an authoritative study of the behaviour and development of Japanese conglomerates. It explains how their core business of trade intermediation evolved into the wider function of increasing long-term demand and supply in the Japanese economy in the post-1945 period. It is essential reading for an understanding of the Japanese economy more generally in this period.

2214
Yui, Tsunehiko (Editor)
Nippon Zaibatsu Keiei-shi: Yasuda Zaibatsu [A Japanese Business History of Zaibatsu: Yasuda Zaibatsu]
1986 Nippon Keizai Shinbun-sha *Tokyo, Japan*

This book analyses the development of the Yasuda Zaibatsu from the 1830s to 1945. It is the most complete history of Yasuda, the predecessor of the contemporary Fuyo group, and there are sections on the Zaibatsu's non-financial business.
Firms: Fuji Bank; Yasuda

Banking and Finance

General

2215
Born, Karl Erich
International Finance in the Nineteenth and Twentieth Centuries
1983 Berg Publishers *Leamington Spa*

This is one of the very rare existing textbooks on international banking and financial history.

2216
Cameron, Rondo
Banking in the Early Stages of Industrialisation: A study in comparative economic history
1967 Oxford University Press *London*

This collection of articles explores the finance of economic development, largely by applying the theoretical framework of Gurley and Shaw. The contributors consider the experience of the emerging major industrial European economies before 1870, while this is counterpointed by chapters devoted to Russia and Japan during the late nineteenth century. This seminal collection is brought together by a common approach, a purposeful introduction and an effective conclusion, which is more than a summary of the major findings. O. Crisp, H. T. Patrick and R. Tilly collaborated with Cameron on this book.

2217
Cameron, Rondo (Editor)
Banking and Economic Development: Some lessons of history
1972 Oxford University Press *London*

Alexander Gerschenkron's explanation of the role played by banks within economies that industrialized 'relatively late' is explored in this collection through contributions which consider the experience of eastern and southern Europe over the course of the nineteenth century. The arising findings are set against comparable explorations of financial trends in the United States and in Japan, although in the latter case over the period from the mid-nineteenth century until the early twentieth century. These various studies are welded into a whole by a forceful introduction reviewing the appropriate contextual literature.

2218
Cassis, Y.; Feldman, G. D.; Olssen, V. (Editors)
The Evolution of Financial Institutions and Markets in Twentieth Century Europe
1995 Scolar Press *Aldershot*

This is an important collection of essays assessing the relationship between the evolution of financial markets and institutions and overall economic development in twentieth-century Europe, covering central, commercial and savings banks, stock markets and other capital markets in nine European countries.

2219
Cassis, Youssef (Editor)
Finance and Financiers in European History, 1880–1960
1992 Cambridge University Press *Cambridge*

A collection of essays offering a comparative analysis of the role of finance in six European countries (the United Kingdom, France, Germany, Belgium, Sweden and Switzerland) and approaching the problem from the economic, social, political and international points of view.

2220
Cottrell, P. L.; Lindgren, Håkan; Teichova, Alice (Editors)
European Industry and Banking Between the Wars: A review of bank–industry relations
1992 Leicester University Press *Leicester*

This is an important collection of essays focusing on the role of banks in the industrialization process of the less developed countries of Europe, with particular attention to Austria, Hungary and Sweden.

Firms: Allgemeine Österreichische Boden-Credit Anstalt; Anglo-Austrian Bank; Bohemian Discount Bank and Society of Credit; Bohemian Union Bank; Deutsche Bank; Goldman Sachs; Mendelssohns (Amsterdam and Berlin); Midland Bank; Stockholms Enskilda Bank

2221
European Association for Banking History (Editor)
Handbook on the History of European Banks
1994 Edward Elgar Publishing *Aldershot*

This is a useful reference work containing historical notices on nearly 200 banks in 18 European countries, and surveys, written by distinguished scholars, of the history of banking in these countries. The book also contains information on established banking archives.

2222
Hilferding, Rudolf
Das Finanzkapital [Finance Capital]
1968 Europaïsche Verlagsanstalt *Frankfurt, Germany*

This is a reprint of one of the most influential studies on the relations between banks and industry, first published in 1910. Based on marxian theory, it stresses the dominance of the banks over industry, which results in the rule of the 'Finanzkapital' in capitalist economies. This work was regarded by contemporaries as the fourth volume of *Das Kapital.*

2223
James, Harold; Lindgren, Håkan; Teichova, Alice (Editors)
The Role of Banks in the Interwar Economy
1991 Cambridge University Press *Cambridge*

This is a major collection of essays on bank–industry relations between the wars, written by scholars from seven countries and including comparative studies of political disputes, universal banking. It contains valuable information on banking operations in Britain, the USA, Canada, Germany, Scandinavia, Belgium and the Netherlands, Austria, Hungary, Italy, Greece and Japan.

2224
Jones, Charles A.
International Business in the Nineteenth Century: The rise and fall of a cosmopolitan bourgeoisie
1987 Columbia University Press *New York, NY*

This book is the story of an important yet little known nineteenth-century business group, the international merchants, described by Jones as a 'cosmopolitan bourgeoisie', which emerged on the remnants of the established merchants of the eighteenth century and reached its apogee in the mid-nineteenth century. The study focuses on two peripheral zones, Argentina and India, and on the centre of world trade, London.

2225
Jones, Geoffrey (Editor)
Banks as Multinationals
1990 Routledge *London*

This important collection of essays investigates, in an international comparative perspective, the origins and business strategies of multinational banks and suggests a conceptual framework in which this development can be understood.

Firms: Anglo-South American Bank; Australia and New Zealand Bank; Bank of New South Wales; Barclays Bank; Barings; Chartered Bank of India, Australia and China; Citybank; Crédit Suisse; Deutsche Bank; Diskonto-Gesellschaft

2226
Jones, Geoffrey (Editor)
Banks and Money: International and comparative finance in history
For main entry, see 133

2227
Kindleberger, C. P.
A Financial History of Western Europe
1984 George Allen & Unwin *London*

This is an essential tool for anyone interested in financial history, which provides a wealth of information and no less illuminating insights.

2228
Lévy-Leboyer, Maurice
Les banques et l'industrialisation internationale dans la première moitié du dix-neuvième siècle [Banks and International Industrialization in the First Half of the Nineteenth Century]
1964 Presses Universitaires de France *Paris, France*

This is a magisterial study, which provides a proper reassessment of the role of the banks in the industrialization of France and the Continental powers, combining economic insight and historical sensitiveness, and relying on an extremely wide range of sources.

2229
Moran, Michael
The Politics of the Financial Services Revolution: The USA, UK and Japan
1991 Macmillan *London*

A comparative study of the financial services revolution in the 1970s and 1980s in the USA, UK and Japan, which argues that 'deregulation' has often concealed important state-centred sources of competitive advantage.

2230
Sampson, Anthony
The Money Lenders: Bankers in a dangerous world
1981 Hodder & Stoughton *London*

This is an important account of the politics of international finance in the 1960s and 1970s written by a highly respected journalist.

2231
Slaven, Anthony; Aldcroft, Derek H. (Editors)
Business, Banking and Urban History: Essays in honour of S. G. Checkland
1982 John Donald *Edinburgh, Scotland*

Part one contains empirical studies of Halbeth Colliery and Saltworks (Peter Payne), management and shipbuilding on the Clyde (Anthony Slaven), Clyde shipbuilding between the wars (Roy Campbell), and the supply of aircraft (Alex Robertson). Part two contains contributions on banking history from Rondo Cameron, Charles Munn and Philip Cottrell.

2232
Teichova, Alice; Gourvish, Terry; Pogány, Agnes (Editors)
Universal Banking in the Twentieth Century: Finance, industry and the state in north and central Europe
1995 Edward Elgar Publishing *Aldershot*

This collection of 19 essays draws upon a major international research project to explore the relationship between banks and industry in nine countries, viz. Austria, Czechoslovakia, Denmark, Greece, Hungary, Norway, Slovenia, Sweden and the UK.
Firms: Boden-Credit-Anstalt; Credit-Anstalt; Danish Central Bank; Hungarian General Credit Bank; Niederösterreichische Escompte-Gesellschaft; Wiener Bank-Verein; Zivnostenkenká Banka

2233
Truell, Peter; Gurwin, Larry
BCCI: The inside story of the world's most corrupt financial empire
1992 Bloomsbury *London*

This is a detailed inquiry into one of the late twentieth-century's major banking scandals by two experienced financial journalists.
Firms: BCCI

2234
Wee, H. van der; Bogaert, R.; Kurgan van Hentenryk, G. (Editors)
La banque en occident [Banking in the West]
1991 Fonds Mercator *Antwerp, The Netherlands*

This is a history of banking from the Ancient World to the present. The very long-term perspective is particularly stimulating. Superb iconography.

UK - General

2235
Bellman, Sir Harold
Cornish Cockney: Reminiscences and reflections
For main entry, see 3865

2236
Bermant, Chaim
The Cousinhood: The Anglo-Jewish gentry
1971 Eyre & Spottiswoode *London*

A highly readable genealogical study of the leading British Jewish families, which played a major role in finance.

2237
Cadbury, Sir Adrian
Report of the Committee on the Financial Aspects of Corporate Governance
For main entry, see 4052

2238
Cassis, Youssef; Van Helten, Jean-Jacques (Editors)
Capitalism in a Mature Economy: Financial institutions, capital exports and British industry, 1870–1939
1990 Elgar *Aldershot*

This useful collection of essays addresses the much debated question of the relationships between finance and industry in Britain.

Firms: Bank of England; Baring Brothers; Bovril; Industrial Development Co.; Consolidated Gold Fields; Forest Land Timber and Railway Co.; Kleinwert, Sons & Co.; Lloyds Bank; Midland Bank

2239
Davenport, N.
Memoirs of a City Radical
1974 Weidenfeld & Nicolson *London*

Nicholas Davenport combined a career in the City with various posts in financial journalism (he was financial correspondent of the *New Statesman* and then *The Spectator*). This gossipy, polemical but perspicacious autobiography charts his varied experiences from the 1920s to the 1970s and provides important insights on Labour's attitude to the City.

Firms: National Mutual Life Assurance Society

2240
Davies, Peter N.
Business Success and the Role of Chance: The extraordinary Philipps Brothers
For main entry, see 3882

2241
Fraser, William Lionel
All to the Good
For main entry, see 3890

2242
Kynaston, David
The City of London: Vol. I: A World of Its Own, 1815–1890
1994 Chatto & Windus *London*

This, the first of a three-volume history of the City of London, is based on a wealth of primary sources. Combines a lively narrative conveying the 'atmosphere' of the Square Mile with a worthy discussion of the issues raised by its long-term development.

2243
Offer, Avner
Property and Politics, 1870–1914: Landownership, law, ideology and urban development in England
For main entry, see 3254

2244
Pressnell, L. S.; Orbell, John
A Guide to the Historical Records of British Banking
For main entry, see 32

2245
Saunders, James
Nightmare: The Ernest Saunders story
For main entry, see 3920

2246
Smithies, Edward
The Black Economy in England since 1914
For main entry, see 1999

UK - Banking

2247
Attali, Jacques
A Man of Influence: Sir Siegmund Warburg, 1902–82
1986 Weidenfeld & Nicolson *London*

Attali's book has been much criticized, even ridiculed, for its windy prose style, but it is still

an important work. It is the only full length study of the outstanding City of London figure since Nathan Rothschild. According to some who knew Warburg, an accurate portrait of his complex character.
Firms: S. G. Warburg & Co.

2248
Bagehot, Walter
Lombard Street: A description of the money market
1873 Kegan Paul and Co. *London*
A classic study of British money markets in the 1870s.

2249
Barclays Bank
A Banking Centenary: Barclays Bank (Dominion, Colonial & Overseas), 1836–1936
1938 Barclays Bank *Plymouth*
This is a pioneer study of a British overseas bank.
Firms: Barclays Bank (DC&O)

2250
Baster, A. S. J.
The Imperial Banks
1929 King *London*
An outstanding account of the history of the British overseas banks which were founded to operate in the British Empire from their nineteenth-century origins until the 1920s. The book is useful on the government regulations under which the banks were founded, and it also contains a still useful account of the development of central banking in the British Commonwealth.
Firms: Bank of Australasia; Bank of British North America; Bank of New South Wales; Chartered Bank of India, Australia and China; Colonial Bank; Standard Bank of South Africa; Union Bank of Australia

2251
Baster, A. S. J.
The International Banks
1935 King *London*
Baster's essential supplement to his 1929 volume which deals with the history of the British overseas banks which operated mainly outside the British Empire. The book includes a chapter on the Eastern Exchange Banks. As in the case of the earlier volume, this book must be supplemented by the more recent bank histories, such as FHH King's history of the Hongkong Bank, and by Jones's *British Multinational Banks 1830–1990* (qqv). Nevertheless, Baster's work remains a lucid and well-informed starting point for all research in this area.
Firms: Anglo-Austrian Bank; Anglo-Californian Bank; Anglo-Egyptian Bank; Anglo-South American Bank; Hongkong and Shanghai Banking Corporation; Imperial Bank of Persia; Ionian Bank; London and Brazilian Bank; London and River Plate Bank

2252
Bolitho, Hector; Peel, Derek
The Drummonds of Charing Cross
1967 Allen & Unwin *London*
This is the story of the family and the bank, one of the oldest private banks in London, from its foundation in 1717 to its takeover by the Royal Bank of Scotland in 1924.
Firms: Coutts & Co.; Messrs Drummonds; Hoare & Co.; N. M. Rothschild & Co.; Smith, Payne & Smiths; Royal Bank of Scotland

2253
Boyle, Andrew
Montagu Norman
1967 Cassell *London*
This book was written to meet the family's dissatisfaction with the biography by Henry Clay (qv) of the City's dominant inter-war figure. Although unreliable on financial policy and detail, Boyle unravels much more of the enigma of Norman's elusive and strange personality.
Firms: Bank of England; Brown, Shipley & Co.

2254
Bramsen, Bo; Wain, Kathleen
The Hambros 1779–1979
1979 Michael Joseph *London*
A reliable, although at times slightly superficial, history of one of London's earliest merchant banks. Based on the bank's internal archives, the book also pays attention to its Danish origins and connections.
Firms: Hambros Bank

2255
Burk, Kathleen
Morgan Grenfell 1838–1988: The biography of a Merchant Bank
1989 Oxford University Press *Oxford*

A high quality anniversary volume written by a professional historian on the basis of the bank's internal archives. For a contrasting view of the bank, see Hobson's *The Pride of Lucifer*.
Firms: George Peabody & Co.; J. S. Morgan & Co.; Morgan Grenfell

2256
Cassis, Youssef
La City de Londres, 1870–1914 [The City of London, 1870–1914]
1987 Belin *Paris, France*

A history of the City of London in its golden years, which pays attention to both financial institutions and key individuals.

2257
Cassis, Youssef
City Bankers, 1890–1914
1994 Cambridge University Press *Cambridge*

Through a social analysis of the banking community of London, the book provides insights about important aspects of British banking and finance in the Edwardian age. This is a major work.

2258
Chandler, Charles
Four Centuries of Banking
1968 Batsford *London*

This is a history of Martins Bank, a British joint stock bank taken over by Barclays in 1968, and its constituent banks. Very informative on both London and provincial banks in the nineteenth century.
Firms: Bank of Liverpool; Cocks, Biddulph & Co.; Equitable Bank Limited; Halifax Commercial Banking Company; Lancashire and Yorkshire Bank; North Eastern Banking Company; Martins Bank

2259
Chapman, Stanley D.
The Rise of Merchant Banking
1984 Allen & Unwin *London*

A pioneering study of the development of merchant banking in nineteenth-century Britain, mostly based on archival material. It pays attention to both individual firms and the banking speciality as a whole.

2260
Checkland, S. G.
Scottish Banking: A history 1695–1973
1975 Collins *Glasgow, Scotland*

Drawing upon substantial archival research, this is a scholarly work published to commemorate the centenary of the foundation of the Institute of Bankers in Scotland. It focuses upon three major themes: the importance of innovations in business practice developed by Scottish banks and bankers, their impact upon Scottish industrialization, and monetary debate and policy. The discussion proceeds chronologically through chapters each devoted to about half a century, aided by available, published bank data from 1865.

2261
Chernow, Ron
The Warburgs: A family saga
For main entry, see 2432

2262
Clapham, Sir John
The Bank of England: A history: I, 1694–1797; II, 1797–1914
1944 Cambridge University Press *Cambridge*

This book is written from internal papers collected during the Second World War, and at the Bank's behest in order to celebrate its 250th birthday. Although not an official history, the book analyses the 'public' business of the 'Old Lady' to complement Acre's *Bank of England from Within* (1931). The first volume, after considering the origins of the Bank, addresses eighteenth-century developments with a broad division in 1764. By necessity, the second volume moves at a slower pace and, generally, each of its eight chapters is concerned with trends over two decades, although even greater attention is paid to the debate behind the 1844 Bank Charter Act, and the Baring Crisis and its consequences. Both volumes are buttressed by appendices.
Firms: Bank of England

2263
Clay, Henry
Lord Norman
1957 Macmillan *London*

Though dated and of a somewhat hagiographic character, Clay's study remains a reliable source of information and is still the best available biography of the longest serving Governor of the Bank of England (1920–44), in a period of intense monetary turbulence.
Firms: Bank of England; Bankers' Industrial Development Corporation; Federal Reserve Bank of New York; Morgan, J. P. & Co.; Reichsbank

2264
Cleaver, George; Cleaver, Pamela
The Union Discount: A centenary album
1985 Union Discount *London*

This book is a frustratingly incomplete history of London's most important discount house, but it is strong on atmosphere and characters.
Firms: Union Discount

2265
Coleman, Donald C.
Sir John Banks, Baronet and Businessman: A study of business, politics and society in later Stuart England
For main entry, see 3878

2266
Collins, Michael
Money and Banking in the UK: A history
1988 Croom Helm *London*

This book is concerned with three main developments between 1826 and 1986–domestic commercial banking, monetary policy, and the international financial position of the United Kingdom. These themes provide the analytical structure for each of the book's three chronological sections - 1826–1913; 1914–39; and 1939–86. The main emphasis is upon English financial institutions, but due consideration is given to the unique features of Irish and Scottish developments.

2267
Collins, Michael
Banks and Industrial Finance in Britain 1800–1939
1991 Macmillan *Basingstoke*

This is a concise and clear survey, with a detailed bibliography, of the controversies surrounding the contribution of banks to British industrial development from the early nineteenth to the mid-twentieth century.

2268
Coopey, Richard; Clarke, Donald
3i: Fifty years investing in industry
1995 Oxford University Press *Oxford*

An innovative commissioned history of ICFC/3i, this book contains a historical assessment supplied by a business historian (Coopey) and the insider's view of Don Clarke. A major study of a unique British investment bank.
Firms: 3i (Investors in Industry); Finance Corporation for Industry (FCI); Finance for Industry (FFI); Industrial and Commercial Finance Corporation (ICFC)

2269
Cope, S. R.
Walter Boyd: A merchant banker in the age of Napoleon
1983 Alan Sutton *Gloucester*

Cope's is a pioneering and somewhat neglected study of a key financial figure during the French Wars. The author was himself a banker, and this biography is informed with the understanding of a banker's problems.
Firms: Boyd, Benfield & Co.; Boyd, Ker et Cie.

2270
Cottrell, P. L.
Industrial Finance 1830–1914: The finance and organization of English manufacturing industry
1979 Methuen *London*

A pioneering study of the much-debated question of the relationships between banks and industry in England, contains some case studies based on provincial banks' archives and a chapter on the development of company law. The author emphasizes the importance of the regional, sometimes informal, capital markets and of internal and private sources of funds.

2271

Crick, W. F.; Wadsworth, J. E.

A Hundred Years of Joint Stock Banking

1958 Hodder & Stoughton *London*

Written by the staff of its economic advisory unit (who brought together the archival base), to commemorate the centenary of the Midland Bank, this volume provides a valuable outline of the modern development of English banking, coupled with an intensive treatment of the emergence of the then largest joint stock bank in the world. The evolution of the Midland is considered through chapters each devoted to a study, on a regional basis, of the development of the banks which it acquired. Furthermore, there are biographies of major bankers who played key roles in the growth of the English domestic banking system. At the time of its publication it was a groundbreaking work, and in many respects still remains unsurpassed.

Firms: Belfast Banking Co.; Clydesdale and North of Scotland Bank; London Joint City and Midland Bank; Midland Bank

2272

Dayer, Roberta Allbert

Finance and Empire: Sir Charles Addis, 1861–1945

1988 Macmillan *Basingstoke*

This is a meticulously researched biography of an important banker who was much involved with Montagu Norman in the financial reconstruction of Europe in the 1920s. Dayer's book is stronger on the political and diplomatic aspects than the strictly financial, but is generally a top-class study.

Firms: Bank of England; Hongkong & Shanghai Bank

2273

Dickson, P. G. M.

The Financial Revolution in England: A study in the development of public credit, 1688–1756

1967 Macmillan *London*

Pioneering, magisterial and yet elegantly written, this is one of the few really outstanding books in British financial history. Almost thirty years after publication, Dickson's interpretation continues to hold the field.

Firms: Bank of England

2274

Fforde, John

The Bank of England and Public Policy 1941–1958

1992 Cambridge University Press *Cambridge*

This is a continuation of the official history of the Bank of England which covers the period from the Second World War to sterling's formal return to convertibility. Contrary to previous volumes, it has been written by an insider rather than a professional historian. Based on ample archive material and not uncritical to the Bank, the book provides a mine of information, but primarily remains a Bank account of events with few references to non-Bank literature.

Firms: Bank of England

2275

Fraser, William Lionel

All to the Good

1963 Heinemann *London*

The rather staid memoirs of an important figure from the 'meritocratic' wing of merchant banking are presented here. There are too many punches pulled, but it is helpful in certain areas, such as the rapid development of London's foreign exchange market in the 1920s.

Firms: Max Bonn & Co.; Helbert, Wagg & Co.; J. Henry Schroder, Wagg & Co.

2276

Fulford, Roger

Glyn's 1753–1953: Six generations in Lombard Street

1953 Macmillan *London*

Though a little old-fashioned, this is an informative book about the most important and most successful of the London private banks, today part of the Royal Bank of Scotland. Glyn's was one of the pioneers of domestic railway finance and contributed to the foundation of several overseas banks in Australasia, Latin America, South-eastern Europe and the Ottoman Empire.

Firms: Glyn, Mills & Co.; Royal Bank of Scotland

2277

Goodhart, C. A. E.

The Business of Banking, 1891–1914

1972 Weidenfeld & Nicolson *London*

This work provides an analysis of the business undertaken by the increasingly dominant London-based joint stock banks at the turn of the century. It draws upon their published annual and half-yearly balance sheets, monthly reports and unpublished data contained in their surviving papers; these are described in Section I, with new statistical time series given in Appendices. The banks' major assets and liabilities are discussed in Section II, in terms of the functioning of the system, with emphasis on portfolio policies. Lastly, the role of the domestic banking system, with respect to the international adjustment mechanism under the gold standard, is investigated in Section III.

2278
Gregory, T. E.; Henderson, Annette
The Westminster Bank Through a Century
1936 Westminster Bank *London*

This is a commemorative work written by a distinguished economist who had a scholarly interest in financial and monetary history. The first volume considers the London & Westminster Bank's development during the nineteenth century and contains a chapter devoted to the London & County Bank. The second volume addresses three themes: the history of the Westminster from the 1900s until the late 1930s; the development of Parr's Bank; and lastly, a biographical analysis of important bankers who contributed to the growth of English banking, as well as having played a part in the development of either the Westminster or its constituents.
Firms: London & County Bank; London & Westminster Bank; Parr's Bank; Westminster Bank

2279
Hennessy, Elisabeth
A Domestic History of the Bank of England
1992 Cambridge University Press *Cambridge*

This is a study of the Bank of England's internal organization, dealing with matters such as increased professionalism or the introduction of modern technology, rarely touched on by Clapham, Sayers and Fforde in their respective volumes (qqv) on the Bank's history. Based on the Bank of England's business records, it is a contribution to our knowledge of the evolution of the modern business enterprises.
Firms: Bank of England

2280
Hidy, Ralph
The House of Baring in American Trade and Finance: English merchant bankers at work, 1763–1861
1949 Harvard University Press *Cambridge, MA*

Despite its age, this remains one of the best accounts of the activities of a top British merchant bank. Starting with the firm's foundation in 1763, the story unfortunately stops in 1861.
Firms: Baring

2281
Hobson, Dominic
The Pride of Lucifer: Morgan Grenfell 1838–1988; the unauthorized biography of a Merchant Bank
1990 Hamish Hamilton *London*

Concentrating particularly on the 1970s and 1980s, this book provides a racy account of the role of City advisers in takeover battles, notably the acquisition of Distillers by Guinness.
Firms: Distillers Group; Guinness; Morgan Grenfell

2282
Holmes, A. R.; Green, Edwin
Midland: 150 years of banking business
1986 Batsford *London*

This is a sequel, and complementary, to Crick and Wadsworth's study of 1936 (qv), compiled by a former general manager of the Midland and the bank's archivist to celebrate the institution's 150th jubilee. The emphasis is upon the Midland itself, from its origins in Birmingham in the mid-1830s to its restructuring as an international banking group during the first half of the 1970s. The final decade is considered through an outline table, listing developments by month until April 1986. The historical analysis is supported by a set of appendices.
Firms: Midland Bank

2283

Jones, Geoffrey

British Multinational Banking 1830–1990

1993 Oxford University Press *Oxford*

This major study traces the history of British overseas, or multinational, commercial banks from their origins in the 1830s until 1990. It is based on every surviving bank archive. The focus is on the competitive advantages and performance of the banks, and a feature of the work is a detailed analysis of bank profitability based on 'real' profit figures.

2284

King, W. T. C.

History of the London Discount Market

1972 Frank Cass *London*

Although heavily reliant on evidence to Parliamentary inquiries, and tailing off from the late nineteenth century, and despite first being published in 1936, this is still an indispensable narrative account of the evolution of the modern London money market and its relationship to the banking system. It is a remarkable achievement by a working journalist.

2285

Kinross, John

Fifty Years in the City: Financing small business

1982 John Murray *London*

This is a less than modest, but engaging account by a founding father of ICFC (the modern 3i). It sheds much light on the often difficult relationship between finance and industry and in particular the problems of filling the 'Macmillan Gap'. There is a more recent assessment in Coopey & Clarke (qv).

Firms: Arthur Wheeler & Co.; Cheviot Trust; Industrial and Commercial Finance Corporation (ICFC)

2286

Kirby, Maurice W.

Men of Business and Politics: The Rise and Fall of the Quaker Pease Dynasty of North-East England, 1700–1943 1943

For main entry, see 3820

2287

Kynaston, David

Cazenove & Co: A history

1991 Batsford *London*

This is the best account of a stockbroking firm yet produced, based on the firm's records and elegantly written by one of the most knowledgeable historians of the City of London. It is particularly strong on the interwar years, where the author traces the growing involvement of the firm, and London stockbrokers in general, in the domestic issue market.

Firms: Cazenove & Co.

2288

Leighton-Boyce, J.

Smiths the Bankers 1658–1958

1958 National Provincial Bank *London*

This provides an unexciting though informative account of a fabulous banking dynasty, at the very heart of the City aristocracy. Although the family banks were taken over in 1902 by the Union Bank of London, now integrated into the National Westminster Bank, successive generations of Smiths continued to head major financial institutions.

Firms: National Provincial Bank; National Westminster Bank; Smith, Payne & Smiths; Union Bank of London

2289

Malcolm, Charles A.

The Bank of Scotland 1695–1945

1945 R. & R. Clark *Edinburgh, Scotland*

Although old-fashioned, this is nevertheless a useful survey of this leading Scottish bank, written to mark its 250th anniversary.

Firms: Bank of Scotland

2290

Michie, Ranald C.

The City of London: Continuity and change, 1850–1990

1991 Macmillan *Basingstoke*

This is a valuable attempt to interpret the development of the City of London in a long-term perspective. The book underlines in particular the resilience of the City's commercial activities.

2291
Moran, Michael
The Politics of Banking: The strange case of competition and credit control
1986 Macmillan *Basingstoke*

A case study of the transformation of British banking in the 1970s, including, in the second edition, an analysis of the collapse of the Johnson Matthey bank.

Firms: Bank of England; Johnson Matthey

2292
Munn, Charles W.
The Scottish Provincial Banking Companies, 1747–1864
1981 John Donald *Edinburgh, Scotland*

This is a scholarly history of the Scottish provincial banks whose innovation and international reputation was enormous during the period.

2293
Munn, Charles W.
Clydesdale Bank: The first hundred and fifty years
1988 Collins *London*

This is a professionally written history of one of the major Scottish joint stock banks, affiliated to the Midland Bank in 1919.

Firms: Bank of England; Bank of Scotland; Clydesdale Bank; Midland Bank; National Bank of Scotland; Royal Bank of Scotland; Union Bank of Scotland

2294
Nevin, Edward; Davis, E. W.
The London Clearing Banks
1970 Elek Books *London*

This is a useful survey of the history of the London clearing banks from the origins to the 1960s.

Firms: Barclays Bank; Childs Bank; Glyn, Mills & Co.; Lloyds Bank; Martins Bank; Midland Bank; National Provincial Bank; Westminster Bank

2295
Ollerenshaw, Philip
Banking in Nineteenth Century Ireland: The Belfast banks, 1825–1914
1987 Manchester University Press *Manchester*

A scholarly study of the Belfast banks in the nineteenth century, which fills a major gap, the Irish banks having attracted far less attention than their English and Scottish counterparts. The author assesses their contribution to economic development in the period 1880–1914, challenging the traditional view that they were conservative in their lending policies and unwilling to finance the Ulster economy.

Firms: Allied Irish Bank; Bank of Ireland; Belfast Bank; Northern Bank; Provincial Bank of Ireland; Ulster Bank

2296
Orbell, John
Baring Brothers & Co. Limited: A history to 1939
1985 Baring Brothers & Co. Limited *London*

This is a short but reliable and informative account of one of Britain's top merchant banks.

Firms: Baring Brothers & Co.

2297
Pressnell, Leslie S.
Country Banking in the Industrial Revolution
1956 Oxford University Press *Oxford*

This magisterial monograph remains the only concerted consideration of the development of the modern English financial sector during its nascent stage. It is the product of painstaking research, the results of which are written in an elegant and careful style so that every word on the page has a precise and important meaning. Over the 40 years since its appearance, no other scholar has attempted to produce such a thorough and exhaustive study.

Firms: Barnard & Co.; Beckett & Co.; Cocks, Biddulph & Co.; Glyn, Mills & Co.; Gurney & Co.; Heywood & Co.; Jones, Loyd & Co.; Leyland, Bullins & Co.; Praed & Co.; Smith & Co.

2298
Roberts, Richard
Schroders: Merchant and bankers
1992 Macmillan *Basingstoke*

This thoroughly researched and professionally written book is a history of one of London's leading merchant banks since the early nineteenth century. It is possibly the best study to date of an individual City firm with its detailed

and closely argued analysis of the actual business, especially the accepting side.
Firms: Schroders; Helbert, Wagg & Co.

2299
Sayers, R. S.
Lloyds Bank in the History of English Banking
1957 Clarendon Press *Oxford*

Written by one of the most distinguished English financial historians at the invitation of the bank, this volume covers the development of Lloyds, primarily over the course of the nineteenth century. Whilst the available archival base was limited, the author provides a perceptive picture of the growth and development of the bank from the perspective of its staff, in terms of relations with customers, other banks and the Bank of England. The chapters are arranged thematically and supported by three extensive and detailed appendices.
Firms: Lloyds Bank

2300
Sayers, R. S.
Gilletts in the London Money Market, 1867–1967
1968 Oxford University Press *Oxford*

This is the most detailed study of a London discount house - but a shame that the doyen of British financial historians did not choose a more major force in the money market.
Firms: Gillett Brothers

2301
Sayers, R. S.
The Bank of England, 1891–1944
1976 Cambridge University Press *Cambridge*

The classic three-volume history of the Bank of England during that period by a distinguished financial economist and historian. Although starting in 1891, the bulk of the book is devoted to Montagu Norman's reign as Governor from 1920 to 1944.
Firms: Bank of England

2302
Sykes, J.
The Amalgamation Movement in English Banking
1926 *London*

Despite its age, this book remains the standard account of the amalgamation movement in English banking, which had been nearly completed by the time the book was written.

2303
Tamaki, Norio
The Life Cycle of the Union Bank of Scotland, 1830–1954
1983 Aberdeen University Press *Aberdeen, Scotland*

A very good account, based on a wealth of archival data, of one of the most interesting Scottish banks set up in the late-nineteenth century and which played a significant role in the development of the Scottish economy during the mid-nineteenth century.
Firms: Union Bank of Scotland

2304
Thomas, W. A.
The Finance of British Industry 1918–1976
1976 Methuen *London*

A sequel to Cottrell's *Industrial Finance 1830–1914* (qv) (though published two years earlier), this book provides a useful and detailed examination of the main sources of funds, both long term and short term, to British industry, and the passage from an international to a predominantly domestic new issue market. In contrast to more recent, and still unpublished, studies the book relies on official reports and secondary literature rather than on banks' archives.
Firms: Bank of England; Barclays Bank; Industrial and Commercial Finance Corporation; Lloyds Bank; Midland Bank

2305
Truptil, R. J.
British Banks and the London Money Market
1936 Jonathan Cape *London*

A detailed study that is still of interest for its accounts of the activities of joint stock banks, discount houses, and acceptance houses.

2306
Tuke, A. W.; Gillman, R. J. H.
Barclays Bank Limited, 1926–1969
1972 Barclays Bank *London*

A disappointing book written by an ex-chairman and an ex-employee of the bank. Its main

interest derives from the description of individual events and how they were viewed from Lombard Street, as well as from the presentation of the balance sheet throughout the period in a clear and graphic form.
Firms: Barclays Bank

2307
Wainwright, David
Government Broker: The story of an office and of Mullens & Co.
1990 Matham Publishing *East Molesey*
This is a disappointingly unambitious and uncritical history of a key stockbroking firm, but it is important for anyone interested in British public finance.
Firms: Mullens & Co.

2308
Winton, J. R.
Lloyds Bank 1918–1969
1982 Oxford University Press *Oxford*
A sequel to Sayers's history by the bank's economic advisor, this is a consideration of the institution's development from its amalgamation in 1918 with the Capital & Counties Bank until the failure of its attempt to take over Martins Bank in 1968/9. The ananlysis is largely concerned with the bank's domestic business, arranged in broad chronological chapters, but also incorporates a valuable study of branches in Egypt, India and Burma, resulting from the acquisition in 1923 of Cox & Co., ailing Army Agents, at the behest of the authorities.
Firms: Capital & Counties Bank; Cox & Co.; Lloyds Bank

2309
Ziegler, Dieter
Central Bank, Peripheral Industry: The Bank of England and the provinces, 1826–1913
1990 Leicester University Press *Leicester*
Translated from the German, this is an important contribution to English banking history, based on the archive material of the Bank of England's branch records. Through an analysis of the Bank's provincial offices, the book controversially argues that the bank restricted its responsibilities to maintaining its own liquidity and was unwilling to give more support to industry.
Firms: Bank of England

2310
Ziegler, Philip
The Sixth Great Power: Barings 1762–1929
1988 Collins *London*
An elegantly written history of one of Britain's most distinguished banking dynasties, this is useful and informative, although not strictly speaking an academic study.
Firms: Baring Brothers & Co.

UK - Insurance, Stock Market etc.

2311
Bernard, R. W.
A Century of Service: The story of the Prudential 1848–1948
1948 Prudential *London*
Although old fashioned, this is still the only available history of the UK's largest insurance company which dominated the life insurance market.
Firms: Prudential Assurance

2312
Boddy, Martin
The Building Societies
1980 Macmillan *London*
A useful overview of the history of the building societies, focused particularly on their expansion since the First World War. The book covers their financial and organizational structure and their role in the financial markets and housing system. Boddy is particularly interested in the expansion of home-ownership and its economic and social implications. Good statistical appendix.
Firms: Halifax Building Society; Nationwide Building Society

2313
Boleat, Mark
The Building Society Industry
1982 George Allen & Unwin *London*
Written by a leading figure in the Building Societies Association, this is an analysis of the

economics of building societies and the major policy issues within the industry. Mostly concerned with the 1970s and 1980s it contains useful statistical material over longer periods.

2314

Burton, H.; Corner, D. C.

Investment and Unit Trusts in Britain and America

1968 Elek *London*

A study of investment companies (investment trusts) in the UK and their role in channeling collective savings into stock exchange securities. The historical sections of the book examine the growth of the industry from the 1860s, changes in the capital structure and portfolio composition of trusts, and the response of the industry to major crises in the 1890s and 1930s. It also discusses the rather different history of Scottish companies. About half of the book is a review of the structure of the industry in the early 1960s. Comprehensive and valuable.

Firms: Foreign & Colonial Government Trust

2315

Cassell, Michael

Inside Nationwide: One hundred years of co-operation, 1884–1984

1984 Nationwide Building Society *London*

An attractively produced and illustrated authorized history of the Nationwide (until 1970 the Co-operative Permanent Building Society). A good straightforward company history. The index is a supplement not bound in to the book.

Firms: Nationwide Building Society; Co-operative Permanent Building Society; Southern Co-operative Permanent Building Society

2316

Channon, Derek F.

The Service Industries: Strategy, structure and financial performance

For main entry, see 2026

2317

Cleary, E. J.

The Building Society Movement

1965 Elek Books *London*

A careful and detailed history of the British building societies from the 1830s to the 1960s. It covers their growth, organizational development, legal regulation, responses to crises and their expansion in the twentieth century. A basic work.

Firms: Bradford Third Equitable Building Society; Co-operative Building Society; Greenwich Union Building Society; Halifax Building Society; Leeds Permanent Building Society; Temperance Building Society; Woolwich Equitable Building Society

2318

Cockerell, H. A. L.; Green, Edwin

The British Insurance Business 1547–1970

1994 Heinemann *London*

A survey of the insurance business archives, which also contains an abundance of information about the insurance business in Great Britain, in particular a brief history of each of the major lines of insurance – marine, fire, life and accident–and an outline of the history and records of some 300 British companies.

2319

Corbett, Donald

Before the Big Bang: Tales of the old Stock Exchange

1986 Milestone Publications *Portsmouth*

The genial recollections of a stockbroker-cum-journalist provide little analysis, but much valuable period detail.

2320

Davenport-Hines, Richard P. T.; Van Helten, Jean-Jacques

Edgar Vincent, Viscount d'Abernon, and the Eastern Investment Company in London, Constantinople and Johannesburg

Business History, vol. 28, no. 1, 1986: pp 35–61

This article examines the career of Sir Edgar Vincent as international civil servant, banker and mining company promoter in Egypt, Constantinople - he was Director-General of the Imperial Ottoman Bank, 1889–1897 - South Africa, Paris and the City of London, and his active involvement in the speculation in the 'kaffir' market (dealing in South African mining shares).

Firms: Imperial Ottoman Bank; Eastern Investment Company

2321
Dickson, P. G. M.
The Sun Insurance Office 1710–1960: The history of two and a half centuries of British insurance
1960 Oxford University Press *Oxford*

This is a pioneering study in the history of British insurance by a distinguished financial historian. Mostly concerned with the eighteenth and nineteenth centuries.
Firms: Alliance Assurance Co.; Globe Insurance; London Assurance Corporation; Lloyd's of London; Phoenix Assurance Co.; Royal Exchange Assurance Co.; Royal Insurance Co.; Sun Insurance Office

2322
Dodds, James Colin
The Investment Behaviour of British Life Insurance Companies
1979 Croom Helm *London*

A critical analysis of the investment policies of these companies between 1962 and 1976.

2323
Doughty, M. (Editor)
Building the Industrial City
For main entry, see 1291

2324
Drake, Leigh
The Building Society Industry in Transition
1989 Macmillan *Basingstoke*

A very thorough study of the Building Societies in the 1980s, examining the building pressures for change in this decade. Drake concentrates on the impact of regulatory change and a new competitive environment including the new role of the wholesale market, changed supervision, the new role of the high-street banks, and changing consumer demand for mortgage finance.
Firms: Abbey National Building Society; Alliance & Leicester Building Society; Bank of England; Barclays Bank; Bristol & West Building Society; Halifax Building Society; Midland Bank; National Home Loans Corporation (NHLC); Nationwide Anglia Building Society; Trustee Savings Bank (TSB)

2325
Franklin, Peter J.; Woodhead, Caroline
The UK Life Assurance Industry: A study in applied economics
1980 Croom Helm *London*

Though primarily a study in applied economics, this book contains useful series of data going back to the 1950s and occasionally to the early twentieth century.
Firms: Commercial Union Assurance Co.; Eagle Star Insurance Co.; Guardian Royal Exchange Assurance; Hambro Life Assurance; Norwich Union Life Insurance Society; Prudential Assurance Co.; Royal Insurance Co.; Sun Alliance and London Assurance Co.

2326
Gibb, D. E. W.
Lloyd's of London: A study in individualism
1957 Macmillan *London*

Although dated, this is still a useful account of the insurance market.
Firms: Lloyds of London

2327
Hannah, Leslie
Inventing Retirement: The development of occupational pensions in Britain
1986 Cambridge University Press *Cambridge*

This is a short but sophisticated history of the development of pension funds in Britain, with particular reference to the most entrepreneurial firm in the field, the Legal and General.
Firms: Legal and General

2328
Hobson, O. R.
A Hundred Years of the Halifax: The history of the Halifax Building Society, 1853–1953
1953 Batsford *London*

A rather stuffy in-house history which nevertheless provides a continuous chronicle of one of Britain's largest building societies.
Firms: Halifax Building Society

2329
Hodgson, Geoffrey
Lloyd's of London: A reputation at risk
1984 Allen Lane *London*

Though not primarily a history book, this

journalistic account is useful in the absence of a proper historical study of Lloyds.
Firms: C.T. Bowring; Alexander Howden; C. E. Heath; Pearson Webb Springbett; Postgate & Denby; Hogg Robinson; Sedgwick Group; Shell Oil; Lloyds of London

2330
Jones, Edgar
Accountancy and the British Economy: The evolution of Ernst and Whinney
For main entry, see 3248

2331
Kitchen, J.; Parker, R. H.
Accounting Thought and Education: Six English pioneers
For main entry, see 3250

2332
Michie, Ranald C.
The London and New York Stock Exchanges 1850–1914
1987 Allen & Unwin *London*

This is an important comparative study of the two leading stock exchange institutions before 1914. The book also attempts to relate these institutions to wider world markets.

2333
Michie, R. C.
Money, Mania and Markets: Investment, company formation and the Stock Exchange in nineteenth century Scotland
1981 John Donald *Edinburgh, Scotland*

This is an important study of the development of the Scottish Stock Exchanges in the nineteenth century and their involvement in company formation and capital investment both at home and overseas.

2334
O'Hagan, H. Osborne
Leaves From My Life
1929 John Lane *London*

This two-volume work is arguably the best of all business autobiographies. O'Hagan represented the acceptable face of late-Victorian company promoting and his voluminous, highly readable memoirs–broadly accurate, despite being written wholly from memory– continue to be a treasure trove.

2335
Pointon, A. C.
Wallace Brothers
1974 Oxford University Press *Oxford*

A rather dull, but solid account of a major firm of merchants and merchant bankers with interests in India and Burmah, this is particularly illustrative of the successful transition from a merchant house to an investment group, that is a firm deriving the bulk of its income from financing a variety of enterprises rather than from the pyhsical trade in merchandise.
Firms: Wallace Brothers

2336
Raynes, Harold E.
A History of British Insurance
1948 Pitman *London*

Despite its age, Raynes's work remains the only comprehensive history of British commercial insurance from the thirteenth to the twentieth century, and can still offer valuable services to the student of the industry.

2337
Reader, William J.
A House in the City: A study of the City and the Stock Exchange based on the records of Foster and Braithwaite, 1825–1975
1979 Batsford *London*

This provides a good initiation into the world of the Stock Exchange through a rather descriptive history of a major firm of stockbrokers.
Firms: Foster & Braithwaite; London Stock Exchange

2338
Redden, Richard
A History of the Britannia Building Society, 1856–1985
1985 Franey & Co. *London*

A careful and well-researched history of the Britannia, mainly focused on its predecessor the Leek and Moorlands Building Society until reorganization and name change in 1975. Good on the local origins and regional roots of this important Society.

Firms: Britannia Building Society; Leek and Moorlands Permanent Benefit Building Society

2339
Reid, Margaret
All-Change in the City: The revolution in Britain's financial sector
1988 Macmillan *Basingstoke*

A senior financial journalist gives the best account of the origins and early developments of 'Big Bang' – the opening up of the Stock Exchange to outside ownership, restructuring and the shift from floor to screen trading.
Firms: London Stock Exchange

2340
Supple, Barry E.
The Royal Exchange Assurance: A history of British insurance, 1720–1970
1970 Cambridge University Press *Cambridge*

An important contribution to British insurance history; despite the destruction of most of the early records in the fire of 1838, the author has produced a well-structured work of corporate development set in the context of more general trends in the performance of the insurance industry and the economy as a whole.
Firms: Royal Exchange Assurance

2341
Trebilcock, Clive
Phoenix Assurance and the Development of British Insurance: Vol. I, 1782–1870
1986 Cambridge University Press *Cambridge*

A magisterial business history which casts significant and corrective light on areas of business activity both within and beyond Phoenix Assurance and the insurance industry.
Firms: Phoenix Assurance

2342
Westall, Oliver M. (Editor)
The Historian and the Business of Insurance
1984 Manchester University Press *Manchester*

This is a multi-authored volume which demonstrates the diversity and importance of the insurance function in post-industrial economies. Case studies cover fire, life, and marine insurance, and broking, and there is an introduction from Barry Supple. The book deals mainly with the UK.
Firms: Hogg Robinson; Indemnity Marine Insurance; Norwich Union; Standard Life Assurance

2343
Westall, Oliver M.
The Provincial Insurance Company 1903–38: Family, markets and competitive growth
1992 Manchester University Press *Manchester*

This is a model business history of an insurance company written by the leading historian of insurance in the UK. It is particularly strong in illuminating the market environment in which firms traded in the inter-war years.
Firms: Provincial Insurance Co.

2344
Wright, Charles; Fayle, C. Ernest
A History of Lloyds
1928 Macmillan *London*

Though dated, this is a still a useful account of the insurance market.
Firms: Lloyds of London

France

2345
Allinne, Jean-Pierre
Banquiers et Bâtisseurs: un siècle de Crédit Foncier, 1852–1940 [Bankers and Builders: A century of Crédit Foncier 1852–1940]
1984 Editions du C.N.R.S. *Paris, France*

The major bank for access to finance for housing, this business is still in operaiton.
Firms: Crédit Foncier

2346
Andrieu, Claire
La Banque sous l'Occupation: Paradoxes de l'histoire d'une profession, 1936–1946 [French Banks Under the Occupation: Paradoxes of the history of a profession, 1936–1946]
1990 Presses de la Fondation Nationale *Paris, France*

This is a history of the relationships between banking and the state in France between 1936 and 1946. Particular attention is paid to the banking legislation of the Popular Front, the Banking Act promulgated by the Vichy government in 1941 and the nationalization of the deposit banks in 1946. The book also discusses the problems raised by the relationships between bankers and the occupying power.

2347
Autin, Jean
Les Frères Péreire: Le bonheur d'entreprendre [The Péreires: The satisfactions of entrepreneurship]
1984 Perrin *Paris, France*

A sympathetic account of the rise and fall of the Péreire brothers with a wealth of detail on the principles, activities and influence of the Crédit Mobilier, both in France and abroad.
Firms: Crédit Mobilier

2348
Barbier, Frédéric
Finance et Politique: Le dynastie des Fould XVIIIe–XXe siècle [Finance and politics: The dynasty of the Fould family]
1991 Armand Colin *Paris, France*

The story of a Jewish family from Eastern France; one of its members became a banker in Paris and his bank played an important role, especially under Napoleon III. The Foulds gave up banking eventually, but remained active both in business and politics. They had business or family connexions with several leading Jewish banking families. The book is based on primary sources.
Firms: Fould

2349
Bergeron, Louis
Banquiers, Négociants et Manufacturiers Parisiens du Directoire à l'Empire [Parisian Bankers, Merchants and Manufacturers from the Director to the Empire Empire]
1978 École des Hautes Études en Sciences *Paris, France*

This is a penetrating study of the Parisian business community at the end of the eighteenth and early years of the nineteenth centuries, a period when bankers often functioned as merchants and merchants became involved in manufacturing. Based on a wealth of new material, with miniature histories of scores of enterprises, this is a key study for the understanding of France's economic history during the period of the country's early industrialization.

2350
Bergeron, Louis
Les Rothschild et les Autres: la gloire des banquiers [Rothschilds and others: The glory of bankers]
1991 Librairie academique Perrin *Paris, France*

A learned yet vivid and accessible history of the Parisian 'Haute banque' and its role in French economy and society from the late eighteenth to the mid-nineteenth century.
Firms: Rothschild

2351
Bonin, Hubert
Suez: du canal à la finance (1858–1987) [Suez: From canal to finance]
1987 Economica *Paris, France*

The first part of this book deals with the history of the Suez Canal Company up to its nationalization by Nasser in 1956; most of the work is devoted to the post-1956 mutation and reconversion of the firm, which diversified into finance, real estate, industry and banking. Moreover, in the 1980s, it was nationalized and then privatized. An 'official' history, but serious and based upon primary sources.
Firms: Suez Canal Company

2352
Bonin, Hubert
L'Argent en France depuis 1880: Banquiers, financiers, épargnants dans la vie économique et politique [Money in France Since 1880: Bankers, financiers and savers in economic and political affairs]
1989 Masson *Paris, France*

This is a valuable survey of the development of the multifaceted aspects of French finance between 1880 and 1980.

2353
Bonin, Hubert
Histoire de la Société Bordelaise de Crédit Industriel et Commercial: 1880 –1990 [A History of the Société Bordelaise de Crédit Industriel et Commercial, 1880–1990]
1991 Horizon Chimérique *Bordeaux, France*

The history of a typical French regional bank is described by Bonin.
Firms: Société Bordelaise de Crédit

2354
Bonin, Hubert
Le Crédit Agricole de la Gironde: La passion d'une région 1901–1991 [Crédit Agricole de la Gironde The passion of a region 1901–1991]
1992 Ed L'horizon chimérique *Bordeaux, France*

Bonin describes the development of Crédit Agricole from numerous local financial co-operatives into a strong regional bank against a background of changing local needs.
Firms: Crédit Agricole de la Gironde

2355
Bouvier, Jean
Etudes sur le Krach de l'Union Générale (1878–1885) [A Study of the Failure of Union Générale (1878–1885)]
1960 Presses Universitaires de France *Paris, France*

The failure of a Catholic bank, and its lasting consequences for French banks are analysed in this book.
Firms: Union Générale

2356
Bouvier, Jean
Le Crédit Lyonnais de 1863 à 1882: Les années de formation d'une banque de dépôts [The Crédit Lyonnais from 1863 to 1882: The early years of a joint stock bank]
1961 Imprimerie nationale *Paris, France*

This is a landmark in French business history. A detailed account of the early history of one of the joint-stock commercial banks, which were started during the Second Empire. Unlike many others, the *Crédit Lyonnais* (which soon moved its headquarters from Lyon to Paris) prospered and grew fast to become one of the largest French banks.
Firms: Crédit Lyonnais

2357
Bouvier, Jean
Les Rothschild [The Rothschilds]
1967 Club français du livre *Paris, France*

The story of the famous dynasty within the context of French banking in the nineteenth and twentieth centuries.
Firms: Rothschild

2358
Bouvier, Jean
Un Siècle de Banque Française: Les contraintes de l'État et les incertitudes du marché [A Century of French Banking: State constraints and market uncertainties]
1973 Hachette *Paris, France*

Bouvier's book is an early, yet still thought-provoking historical essay on the history of French banking from the mid-nineteenth century to the 1960s.

2359
Bussière, Eric
1872–1992. Paribas, l'Europe et le Monde [1872–1992. Paribas, Europe and the World]
1992 Fonds Mercator *Antwerp, Belgium*

A short, but serious history of the leading French merchant bank (*banque d'affaires*), from its foundation. It is based on the bank's records, plus interviews with some of the recent CEOs. This is published in French and English.
Firms: Banque de Paris et des Pays-Bas; Paribas

2360
Gille, Bertrand
La Banque et le Crédit en France de 1815 à 1848 [Banking and Credit in France, 1815–1848]
1959 Presses Universitaires de France *Paris, France*

This is a pioneering study of French banking history in the first half of the nineteenth century, based on the archives on the Bank of France as well as those of a number of private banks, including Neuflize Schlumberger, Mallet, Rothschild.
Firms: Banque de France; Neuflize Schlumberger; Mallet; Rothschild

2361
Gille, Bertrand
Histoire de la maison Rothschild: Vol. I: Des origines à 1848; Vol II: 1848–1870 [A History of the House of Rothschild]
1965/67 Droz *Geneva, Switzerland*

A mammoth work on the history of the

French Rothschilds; based on the bank's records, and on other archival materials. A very detailed and precise study, the author's untimely death prevented the continuation of the story after 1870. See also: Jean Bouvier, *Les Rothschild*, Paris, Fayard, 1967; much shorter but covers all the family's history.
Firms: Rothschild

2362
Gille, Bertrand
La Banque en France au XIXᵉ siècle [Banking in Nineteenth-Century France]
1970 Droz *Geneva, Switzerland*
A collection of articles written by the author and dispersed in journals which are often hard to get, which includes a study of the Crédit Mobilier and two studies of the Société Générale.
Firms: Crédit Mobilier; Société Générale

2363
Grand, Christian
Trois Siècles de Banque: De Neuflize, Schlumberger, Mallet, 1667–1991 [Three Centuries of Banking: De Neuflize, Schlumberger, Mallet 1667–1991]
1991 Éditions E/P/A *Paris, France*
A short history of a merchant bank, which was created in 1969 as a result of a number of mergers. Two of its 'ancestors' had been active since the seventeenth century and are well-known examples of 'protestant banking' (*haute banque protestante*).
Firms: Neuflize Schlumberger Mallet

2364
Grosskreutz, Helmut
Privatkapital und Kanalbau in Frankreich, 1814–48: Eine Fallstudie zur Rolle der Banken in der französischen Industrialisierung [Private Capital and Canal Building in France 1814–48: A case study of the role of banks in French industrialization]
For main entry, see 3023

2365
Gueslin, André
Le Crédit Mutuel: de la caisse rurale à la banque sociale [Crédit Mutuel From rural bank to social bank]
1983 Copru *Strasbourg, France*
Gueslin studies a major bank which is still operating, and started first for farmers, then for wage earners.
Firms: Crédit Mutuel

2366
Gueslin, André
Histoire des crédits agricoles: Vol. I: L'envol des caisses mutuelles, 1910–1960, Vol II: Vers la banque universelle [A History of the Crédits Agricoles]
1984 Economica *Paris, France*
A massive study of a group of banks, which had started as farmers' 'friendly societies', and which recently became a giant undertaking, with assets which place it among the world's leading banks.
Firms: Crédits Agricole

2367
Koch, Henri
Histoire de la Banque de France et de la Monnaie sous la IVe République [History of the Bank of France and Monetary Policy Under the Fourth Republic]
1983 Dunod *Paris, France*
This is a history of the Bank of France and of French monetary policy under the Fourth Republic, from 1946 to 1958.
Firms: Banque de France

2368
Lévy-Leboyer, Maurice (Editor)
La Position Internationale de la France: Aspects économiques et financiers. XIXe–XXe siècles [France's International Position in the 19th and 20th Centuries: Economic and financial aspects]
1977 École des Hautes Études en Sciences *Paris, France*
This collection of 34 studies deals with various aspects of France's international financial position, in particular capital exports, inward foreign investments, financial co-operation, as well as the relationships between financial interests and foreign and imperial policies.

2369
Lüthy, Herbert
La Banque Protestante en France: de la Revocation de l'Edit de Nantes à la Révolution [The Protestant Bank in France: From the revocation of the Edict of Nantes to the Revolution]
1959/61 S.E.V.P.E.N. *Paris, France*

This is a classic, masterly analysis of the international networks of the Protestant bank in the eighteenth century.

2370
Marguerat, Philippe
Banque et Investissement Industriel: Paribas, le pétrole roumain et la politique française 1919–1939 [Bank and Industrial Investment: Paribas, Romanian oil and French politics 1919–1939]
1987 Droz *Geneva, Switzerland*

An archivally-based study of the interests of the bank Paribas in Romanian oil, this raises interesting questions about the relationships between banks and industry and between finance and state politics.
Firms: Paribas

2371
Meuleau, Marc
Des Pionniers en Extrême-Orient: Histoire de la Banque de l'Indochine (1875–1975) [Pioneers in the Far East: The Bank of Indochina]
1990 Fayard *Paris, France*

A detailed study of a 'colonial bank', which diversified outside Indochina and was thus able to survive the colonies' independence. It eventually merged with another refugee-firm, the Suez Canal Company.
Firms: Banque de l'Indochine

2372
Moreau, Émile
The Golden Franc. Memoirs of a Governor of the Bank of France: The stabilization of the Franc (1926–1928)
1991 Westview Press *Boulder, CO*

This is the diary of the Governor of the Bank of France from June 1926, when the Franc plunged to its low of the decade, to 1930. It is revealing on the negotiations between the French Treasury and the Bank about the rate at which the Franc should be stabilized, the personality clashes between Moreau and the 'regents' (directors) of the bank, especially the two strongest personalities, François de Wendel and Edouard de Rothschild, as well as clashes between Moreau and Montagu Norman. Translated by Stephen D. Stoller and Trevor C. Roberts.
Firms: Banque de France

2373
Morin, François
La Structure Financière du Capitalisme Français [The Financial Structure of French Capitalism]
1974 Calmann-Lévy *Paris, France*

This provides a valuable study of the ownership of the 200 largest French companies, the role of financial houses and trends towards concentration and centralization, and the creation of strategic alliances.

2374
Plessis, Alain
La Banque de France sous le Second Empire: Vol. 1: La Banque de France et ses deux cents actionnaires, Vol. 2: Régents etc, Vol. 3: La politique de la Banque de France de 1851 à 1870 [The Bank of France During the Second Empire]
1982/85 Droz *Geneva, Switzerland*

A detailed and scholarly history, based upon company records, of the Bank of France in the 1850s and 1860s, with a particular attention to its 200 largest shareholders, who had the privilege to elect the board of directors.
Firms: Banque de France

2375
Rivoire, Jean
Le Crédit Lyonnais: Histoire d'une banque [Crédit Lyonnais The story of a bank]
1989 Cherche-Midi *Paris, France*

Written by one of the bank's former executives, the book stresses in particular the bank's internal organization and the relationships between its senior executives.
Firms: Crédit Lyonnais

2376
Ruffat, Michèle; Caloni, Edouard-Vincent; Laguerre, Bernard
L'U.A.P. et l'Histoire de l'Assurance [UAP and the History of Insurance]
1990 Editions Lattès *Paris, France*
This is a preliminary historical survey of a major French insurance company, privatized in 1994.
Firms: Union des Assurances de Paris

2377
Sabouret, Anne
MM. Lazard Frères & Cie: Une saga de la fortune [Lazard Frères & Cie: A saga of fortune]
1987 Olivier Orban *Paris, France*
This is a journalistic account of one of the most successful French private investment banks in recent years. Half of the book is devoted to the years before 1950.
Firms: Lazard Frères, New York; Lazard Brothers, London; Rothschilds; I.T.T.; B.S.N.; Saint-Gobain; L'Air Liquide; Boussac; Compagnie Générale d'Électricité; Moët Hennessy

2378
Siegel, Michel
Les Banques en Alsace, 1870–1914 [Banks in Alsace 1870–1914]
1991, PhD Thesis, Université de Strasbourg II
This doctoral thesis examines how regional banks in Alsace evolved under German occupation.

2379
Thobie, Jacques
Intérêts et Impérialisme Français dans l'Empire ottoman, 1895–1914 [French Interests and French Imperialism in the Ottoman Empire, 1815–1914]
For main entry, see 2555

2380
Torres, Félix (Editor)
L'Assurance: De la Royale au GAN [Insurance: From the Royale to GAN]
1992 Editions Tchou *Paris, France*
This is a preliminary historical survey of a major French insurance company.
Firms: Groupement des Assurances Nationales (GAN)

Spain

2381
Banco de España (Editor)
El Banco de España: Una historia económica [The Bank of Spain: An economic history]
1970 Banco de España *Madrid, Spain*
A collective work on modern economic and banking history by several leading authors. Aside from a chapter on medieval and early modern banking history, the book covers the modern period, some chapters dealing with general economic history, others with the history of the Bank of Spain.
Firms: Banco de España

2382
Cabana, Francesc
Història del Banc de Barcelona [History of the Bank of Barcelona]
1978 Edicions 62 *Barcelona, Spain*
Written in Catalan, this is the history of Spain's leading nineteenth-century commercial bank, which went bankrupt after the First World War.
Firms: Banc de Barcelona

2383
Cordones Ramírez, Mercedes; Aurioles Martín, Adolfo
La quiebra en las Ordenanzas consulares de Málaga [The Ordenanzas of Málaga]
1987 T.A.T. *Granada, Spain*
This is an interesting book on insolvency and bankruptcy at the Ordenanzas of Málaga (1825–1829), with special comparative references to the Código de Comercio (Spanish Commercial Act of 1829) and the French Code de commerce of 1807. With respect to bankruptcy, the authors take up such topics as the significance of issuance regulation and various institutions for maintaining trust relationships. All the problems taken up in this monograph are indispensable to a proper understanding of Spanish insolvency. The volume also contains the principal chapters of the Ordenanzas of

Málaga, with the theoretical formulation of Málaga's economic growth in the nineteenth century.

2384
Cuervo, Alvaro
La crisis bancaria en España, 1977–1985 [The Banking Crisis in Spain]
1988 Ariel *Barcelona, Spain*

A thorough study of the recent banking crisis, which was particularly serious in Spain, and coincided with a period of deregulation and revamping of monetary institutions. It includes an estimate of the total cost of the crisis.

2385
Fanjul, Oscar; Maravall, Fernando
La eficiencia del sistema bancario español [The Efficiency of the Spanish Banking System]
1985 Alianza Editorial *Madrid, Spain*

A group of econometric, though readable, studies on the banking sector during 1950–1980 concentrating mainly on competition, profits, and productivity. The authors' main conclusion is that competition and productivity have increased moderately.

2386
Lacomba, Juan Antonio; Ruiz, Gumersindo
Una historia del Banco Hipotecario de España (1872–1986) [History of the Banco Hipotecario de España]
1990 Alianza Editorial *Madrid, Spain*

The history of the official mortgage bank, competently written but perhaps excessively uncritical towards a monopolistic, bureaucratic institution.
Firms: Banco Hipotecario de España

2387
Martín Aceña, Pablo
La política monetaria en España, 1919–1935 [Monetary Policy in Spain, 1919–1935]
1984 Instituto de Estudios Fiscales *Madrid, Spain*

The definitive work on monetary policies during the interwar period, making use of monetary theory to interpret and assess the effects of the different measures, especially of the complicated exchange rate policies followed during the depression by a country that never was on the gold standard.

2388
Muñoz, Juan
El poder de la banca en España [The Power of the Banks in Spain]
1969 Editorial ZYX *Algorta, Vizcaya, Spain*

A study of the banking system from the standpoint of structure, interbank and bank–industry connections. Although somewhat denunciatory of the banks' monopolistic structure and power, it is based on solid research.

2389
Nadal, Jordi; Sudrià, Carles
Història de la Caixa de Pensions [History of the Caixa de Pensions]
1981 Edicions 62 *Barcelona, Spain*

The history of the largest savings bank in Spain. Written in Catalan, the Castilian (Spanish) translation is also available.
Firms: Caixa de Pensions

2390
Otazu, Alfonso
Los Rothschild y sus Socios en España (1820–1850) [The Rothschilds and their Agents in Spain 1820–1850]
1987 OHs Ediciones *Madrid, Spain*

A history of Daniel Weisweiller, the Rothschilds' agent in Madrid during the first half of the nineteenth century. Sticking closely to its archival sources, it gives a good description of the Madrid business circles at the time.
Firms: Rothschild

2391
Peláez, Manuel (Editor)
Historia Económica y de las Instituciones Financieras [Economic History of Financial Institutions]
1989 University of Málaga *Barcelona, Spain*

A collection of papers giving an integrated analytical approach to the history of economic relations from the eleventh century to the 1960s, covering agriculture, transport, financial institutions, etc., mainly focused on Spain.

2392
Sard , Juan
La Política Monetaria y las Fluctuaciones de la Economía Española en el Siglo XIX siglo XIX [Monetary Policy and Economic Fluctuations in 19th Century Spain]
1948 Consejo Superior de Investicaiones *Madrid, Spain*

The classic, though considerably dated, work on Spanish monetary and banking history, which emphasizes the role of governmental monetary policy and the development of the banking system. It contains a price index which is still used by economic historians.

2393
Tedde de Lorca, Pedro
El Banco de San Carlos (1782–1829) [The Bank of San Carlos 1782–1829]
1988 Banco de España/Alianza Editorial *Madrid, Spain*

The monumental, definitive work on the history of the first official Spanish bank, the forerunner of the Bank of Spain.
Firms: Banco de España; Banco de San Carlos

2394
Titos Martínez, Manuel
La Caja General de Ahorro y Monte de Piedad de Granada, 1891–1978
1979 Caja General de Ahorros y Monte de Piedad de Granada *Granada, Spain*

A well written, thorough history of one of the oldest savings banks in Spain.
Firms: Caja General de Ahorros y Monte de Piedad de Granada

2395
Tortella, Gabriel (Editor)
La Banca Española en la Restauración [The Bank of Spain in the Restoration Period]
1974 Banco de España *Madrid, Spain*

A thorough collective study of the banking system during the 1874–1914 period, based upon the Bank of Spain's collection of banking publications and documents, newspapers and other archival sources. The main topics studied are a prosopography of finance ministers and monetary authorities, the Bank of Spain, the banking system, and the monetary aggregates. Vol. 2 is a statistical appendix.
Firms: Banco de España

2396
Tortella, Gabriel
Banks, Railroads, and Industry in Spain, 1829–1874
1977 Arno Press *New York, NY*

This book studies the development of the Spanish banking system in the mid-nineteenth century which evolved in a cycle of slow growth, rapid growth, boom and crash due to over-investment in public debt and railroads. The interrelations between banks and government receive considerable attention.

2397
Tortella, Gabriel; Jiménez, Juan Carlos
Historia del Banco de Crédito Industrial [History of the Banco de Crédito Industrial]
1986 Alianza Editorial *Madrid, Spain*

This is the state industrial credit bank created in the aftermath of the First World War. Its history covers the period of intense industrialization in Spain. Although publicly owned, the BCI worked in tandem with the private banking sector.
Firms: Banco de Crédito Industrial

Netherlands

2398
Buist, M. G.
At spes non fracta: Hope & Co. 1770–1815
1974 Bank Mees & Hope *Rotterdam, The Netherlands*

A masterly account in English of the most prominent Dutch merchant bank, and the money market around it, from the last years of world leadership into decline and fall. The detailed yet clear account of the continuing close interrelationship between trade and finance alone are essential reading for the period.
Firms: Bank Mees & Hope; Hope & Co.

2399

De Nederlandsche Bank

Financiële instellingen in Nederland 1900–1985: balansreeksen en naamlijst van handelsbanken [Financial Institutions in The Netherlands 1900–1985]

1987 De Nederlandsche Bank *Amsterdam, The Netherlands*

A very useful and well-thought out compilation of the balance sheets of the Dutch banks according to sector, including pension funds, with separate tables detailing the ongoing concentration. The alphabetical and chronological tables of companies at the back are unfortunately less than complete.

2400

Eisfeld, C.

Das niederländische Bankwesen [Banking in The Netherlands]

1916 Martinus Nijhoff *The Hague, The Netherlands*

Eisfeld's analysis of Dutch banking around 1911 is still a useful introduction for non-Dutch speakers. The approach may be somewhat dated because of its built-in expectation that all banking would follow the German pattern, but the extensive data arranged in tables are worthwhile.

2401

Jong, A. M. de

Geschiedenis van de Nederlandsche Bank, 1814–1914 [History of the Nederlandsche Bank 1814–1914]

1929/67 De Nederlandsche Bank *Amsterdam, The Netherlands*

A magisterial work in four volumes, covering the first 100 years of the central bank, but also offering a good account of monetary policy and fair glimpses of Dutch economic development and banking from that vantage point. The statistical data and bibliography at the back also make it an essential start for every student of the period. The first two volumes, published separately in 1929, now show their age.

Firms: Nederlandsche Bank

2402

Jongman, C. D.

De Nederlandse geldmarkt [The Netherlands Money Market]

1960 Stenfert Kroese *Leiden, The Netherlands*

After defining the money market, its instruments and working, Jongman gives an exemplary account of, and data on, the development of the Dutch money market from 1813 to about 1960. The book is unsurpassed as an overall view, but leaves room for a more critical analysis.

2403

Laar, Paulus Th. van de

Financieringsgedrag in de Rotterdamse maritieme sector, 1945–1960 [Financial Behaviour in the Rotterdam Maritime Sector, 1945–1960]

1991 Tinbergen Institute *Rotterdam, The Netherlands*

A comparative history of finance and investment in the port of Rotterdam. Attention focuses on capitalization of a number of Dutch maritime companies, and on their selection of funds for investment. The book analyses which underlying considerations determined the selection of the observed finance pattern.

Firms: Holland America Line (HAL); Koninklijke Rotterdamsche Lloyd (KRL); Van Nievelt Goudriaan & Co. Stoomvaart Maatschappij; Phs. van Ommeren; Wm. H. Müller & Co.; Wijklijn; Maatshappij Zeevaart; Houtvaart

2404

Nederlansch Economisch-Historisch Archief; (NEHA)

Historische bedrijfsarchieven, een geschiedenis en een bronnenoverzicht [A History and Overview of Amsterdam Archives]

1988/92 NEHA *Amsterdam, The Netherlands*

With this series NEHA aims to take stock of Dutch company records sector by sector. In 1988 the series was heralded by B. P. A. Gales and J. L. J. M. van Gerwen, *Sporen van leven en schade, een geschiedenis en een bronnenoverzicht van het Nederlandse verzekeringswezen* Amsterdam: NEHA (1988), containing an excellent introductory essay on the insurance sector from Gales. In 1992 volume 1 appeared

(*Bankwezen, een geschiedenis en een bronne-noverzicht* Amsterdam: NEHA (1992)), with Joh. de Vries giving a somewhat tired survey of Dutch banking. Since the books are compiled on the basis of questionnaires supplemented by limited further research, the data are incomplete so the user should prepare himself for disappointments as well as surprises.

2405
Renooij, D. C.
De Nederlandse emissiemarkt van 1904 tot 1939 [The Netherlands Stock Exchange 1904–1939]
1951 J. H. de Bussy *Amsterdam, The Netherlands*

In many ways the companion volume to Jongman's book (qv) presenting an overview of the flotations on the stock exchange, together with an analysis of the factors influencing them.

2406
Vries, Joh. de
1811–1961: Met Amsterdam als brandpunt. Honoervijftig jaar Kamer van Koophandel en Fabrieken [1811–1961: Amsterdam at the centre. One hundred and fifty years of the Chamber of Commerce]
1961 Kamer van Koophandel en Fabrieken *Amsterdam, The Netherlands*

A voluminous survey of 150 years of the Amsterdam Chamber of Commerce's activities, with special attention paid to the economic and commercial environment in which the Chamber functioned. The emphasis is on post-war industrialization and economic recovery.
Firms: Amsterdam Kamer van Koophandel

2407
Vries, Joh. de
De Coöperatieve Raiffeisen-Boerenleenbanken in Nederland 1948–1973: van exponent tot component [The Cooperative Raiffeisen-Boerenleenbanken in The Netherlands 1948–1973]
1973 Coöperatieve Raiffeisen-Boerenleenbank *Utrecht, The Netherlands*

The only book covering Dutch post-war banking in some detail. The first chapter covers the history of the cooperative agricultural banks from 1896 to 1940; the focus then shifts to encompass the banks' broadening activities from the late fifties onwards, extending to the development of Dutch banking as a whole.
Firms: Coöperatieve Raiffeisen-Boerenleenbank

2408
Vries, Joh. de
Een eeuw vol effecten: Historische schets van de Vereniging voor de Effectenhandel en de Amsterdamse Effectenbeurs, 1876–1976 [A Century Full of Stock: A historical sketch of the Association for the Trade in Stock and the Amsterdam Stock Exchange, 1876–1976]
1976 Vereniging voor de Effectenhandel *Amsterdam, The Netherlands*

A global description in economic terms of the history and growth of the trade in stocks and the stock market in Amsterdam, with special emphasis on the Association's role as supervisor of the Amsterdam Stock Exchange since 1876.
Firms: Vereniging voor de Effectenhandel

2409
Vries, Joh. de
Geschiedenis van de Nederlandsche Bank, 1914–1948 [A History of the Nederlandsche Bank, 1914–1948]
1989/93 De Nederlandsche Bank *Amsterdam, The Netherlands*

As a continuation of De Jong's work these two volumes are disappointing. They lack the sure grip on quantitative data about the bank's development and its position in the money market, and as a result the analysis often sacrifices structural factors to long stretches of documents in synopsis. The wealth of anecdotes offers some compensation.
Firms: Nederlandsche Bank

Belgium

2410
La Banque en Belgique 1830–1980 [The Bank in Belgium 1830–1980]
Revue de la Banque, Special Issue, 1980

This volume includes several studies on the evolution of financial institutions, monetary policy, international financial relations and the role of the banks in the economy.

2411
Chlepner, B. S.
Le marché financier belge depuis cent ans [One Hundred Years of Belgian Financial Markets]
1930 Falk fils *Brussels, Belgium*

Although a little dated, this is still a very useful book for the history of the Belgian banks and financial market in the nineteenth and early twentieth centuries.

2412
Clerq, G. De (Editor)
A la Bourse. Histoire du marché des valeurs en Belgique de 1300 à 1990 [A History of Belgian Stock Exchanges from 1300 to 1990]
1992 Duculot *Brussels, Belgium*

The result of a collaboration between historians, journalists and economists, this volume includes several chapters devoted to the history of the Stock Exchange in the nineteenth and early twentieth centuries which entirely revise Chlepner's work (qv).

2413
CRISP
Morphologie des groupes financiers: Répertoire permanent des groupes d'enterprises (1967–1978)
1962 CRISP *Brussels, Belgium*

Since 1962, CRISP (Centre de recherche et d'information socio-politique) has been studying the structure of 'groups' of companies from the point of view of the relationships between ownership and control in banking and insurance as well as holding companies.

2414
Daems, H.
The Holding Company and Corporate Control
1978 Martinus Nijhoff *Leiden, The Netherlands*

Following Alfred Chandler's work, this book analyses the strategy and structure of the Belgian holding companies, in particular the Societé Générale de Belgique, in the twentieth century.
Firms: Société Générale de Belgique

2415
Durviaux, R.
La banque mixte, origine et soutien du développement économique et social de la Belgique [Clearing Banks and the Economic and Social Development of Belgium]
1947 Emile Braylant *Brussels, Belgium*

Although mostly descriptive, this is an invaluable source of information on the evolution of the banking system and its major financial institutions.

2416
Jacquemyns, G.
Langrand-Dumonceau: promoteur d'une puissance financière [Langrand-Dumonceau Financial promoter]
1960-75 Éditions de l'Université de Bruxelles *Brussels, Belgium*

This monumental biography is devoted to a financial adventurer whose objective was the 'christianization of capital' through the mobilization of the savings of the aristocracy and the Catholic middle classes. The book offers a detailed picture of the Belgian and foreign financial world and of the relationships between finance and politics in the 1850s and 1860s.

2417
Janssens, V.
Le Franc Belge: Un siècle et demi d'histoire monétaire [The Belgian Franc: One and a half centuries of monetary history]
1976 Edition et Imprimerie *Brussels, Belgium*

Janssens covers 150 years of monetary history from the perspective of Belgium's central bank.

2418
Kauch, P.
La Banque Nationale de Belgique: I 1850–1918 [The Belgian National Bank]
1950 Banque Nationale de Belgique *Brussels, Belgium*

The first of three books (the others are Janssens and Van der Wee and Tavernier (qqv)), based on the archives of the Belgian National Bank, which are essential reading for the study of the central bank and its relation-

ships with the other banks as well as with the State.
Firms: Banque Nationale de Belgique

2419
Minguet, A.
Les Marchés Financiers Belges [The Belgian Financial Markets]
1990 Office International de Librairie *Brussels, Belgium*
A descriptive account of Belgium's financial markets.

2420
Put, A. Van; Nose, Ch. (Editors)
Les Banques d'Épargne Belges: Histoire, droit, fonction économique, institutions [Belgian Savings Banks: History, law, economic function, institutions]
1986 Lannoo *Tielt, Belgium*
This collective volume includes several well-researched chapters written by historians on savings banks in the nineteenth and early twentieth century.

2421
Ranieri, L.
Emile Francqui ou l'Intelligence Créatrice 1863–1935 [Emile Francqui–Creative Intelligence 1863–1935]
1985 Duculot *Brussels, Belgium*
Although only marginally dealing with the workings of the financial system, the biography of this central figure of Belgian finance in the interwar period is essential to the study of national and international networks of the time.

2422
Thielmans, M.-R.
La Grande Crise et le Gouvernement des Banquiers [The Great Crisis and the Bankers' Government]
1980 Institut de Science Politique *Brussels, Belgium*
This study throws new light on the interplay between finance and politics during the 1934 crisis.

2423
Timmermans, A. P.
Les Banques en Belgique 1946–1968 [Banks in Belgium, 1946-1968]
1969 Groeninghe *Courtrai, Belgium*
A general study of Belgian banks in the twenty years after the Second World War.

2424
Vincent, A.
Banques et Assurances: Les groupes présents en Belgique [Banks and Insurance: Existing groups in Belgium]
1993 CRISP *Brussels, Belgium*
The author emphasizes the complexity of financial networks and their internationalization on the eve of the European single market.

2425
Wee, H. Van der; Tavernier, K.
La Banque Nationale de Belgique et l'Histoire Monétaire entre les deux Guerres Mondiales [The Banque Nationale de Belgique and Monetary History Between the Two World Wars]
1975 Banque Nationale de Belgique *Brussels, Belgium*
Based on the Bank's archives, this book deals with the history of the central bank in the inter-war period.
Firms: Banque Nationale de Belgique

2426
Wee, H. Van der; Verbeyt, M.
Mensen maken Geschiedenis: De Kredietbank en de Economische Opgang van Vlaanderen 1935–1985 [The Kredietbank and Economic Growth in Flanders 1935–1985]
1985 Kredietbank *Brussels, Belgium*
A commissioned history of the Kredietbank, written to mark its fiftieth anniversary. This is an important landmark in that it was based on internal archives and authored by professional historians. A shortened version was published in French under the title *Les hommes font l'histoire: La Kredietbank et l'essor économique de la Flandre 1935–85.*
Firms: Kredietbank

2427
Witte, E.; Preter, R. De
Histoire de l'Épargne Sociale à travers l'Évolution de la Banque Codep et de ses Prédécesseurs [The History of Social Savings through the Evolution of the Banque Codep and its Predecessors]
1989 Éditions Labor *Brussels, Belgium*

A commissioned history of Codep, based on access to company archives.
Firms: Banque Codep

Germany

2428
Anon.
A History of German Banking
1982 Knapp *Frankfurt am Main, Germany*

The only general history of German banking (including savings banks and credit cooperatives) available. The volumes are chronologically organized, beginning with the Middle Ages. The third volume includes a short descriptive history of banking in National Socialist Germany.

2429
Barrett Whale, P.
Joint Stock Banking in Germany: A study of the German Creditbanks before and after the war
1968 Frank Cass *London*

A reprint of a book originally published in 1930, on the eve of the 1931 disaster. It is valuable as a testimony, but also provides a wealth of material from printed sources. The author moderates the oversimplified monolithic view of German banks and industrial finance.
Firms: Deutsche Bank; Disconto-Gesellschaft; Dresdner Bank; Darmstädter Bank; National Bank für Deutschland; Danat Bank (Darmstädter und National Bank); Commerz-und Privat Bank; Mitteldeutsche Creditbank; Berliner Handelsgesellschaft

2430
Bayerische Hypotheken- und Wechselbank
Eine hochwichtige, vaterländische Anstalt, 1835–1985: Geschichte der HYPO-BANK im Spiegel der Geschäftsberichte [A History of the HYPO-BANK, 1835–1985]
1985 Bayerische Hypotheken- und Wechselbank *Munich, Germany*

A small illustrated history of a major Bavarian bank. Despite its coffee-table character, this book offers real insight in the development of one of Germany's major regional banks.
Firms: Bayerische Hypotheken- und Wechselbank; HYPO-BANK

2431
Born, Karl Erich
Die deutsche Bankenkrise 1931 [The German Banking Crisis 1931]
1967 Piper *Munich, Germany*

The most important study on the causes and the development of the 1931 German banking crisis, for which reparation policies are largely held responsible.

2432
Chernow, Ron
The Warburgs: A family saga
1993 Chatto & Windus *London*

Chernow has written an absorbing, though overlong, family saga of a major German and international banking dynasty.
Firms: S.G. Warburg & Co.

2433
Deutsche Bundesbank
Währung und Wirtschaft in Deutschland 1876–1975 [Currency and the Economy in Germany 1876–1975]
1976 Knapp *Frankfurt am Main, Germany*

A collection of articles celebrating the centenary of the German Banking Law of 1875, which created the Imperial Bank ('Reichsbank') as the central bank of the new Empire. Knut Borchardt's article about 'Währung and Wirtschaft vor dem Ersten Weltkrieg' is the most authoritative account of Reichsbank policy before the First World War.
Firms: Reichsbank

2434

Donaubauer, Klaus

Privatbankiers und Bankenkonzentration in Deutschland von der Mitte des 19. Jahrhunderts bis 1932 [Private Banks and Bank Concentration in Germany from the mid-Nineteenth Century to 1932]

1988 Knapp *Frankfurt am Main, Germany*

The only study of provincial and mostly small-scale private banks in Germany based on archival sources. Apart from a general account of the concentration process, the scope of the study is limited to the Bavarian private banks which merged with the Bavarian Hypotheken- und Wechselbank.

Firms: HYPO-BANK

2435

Eistert, Ekkehart

Die Beeinflussung des Wirtschaftswachstums in Deutschland 1880–1913 durch das Bankensystem [The Influence of the Banking System on Economic Growth in Germany 1880–1913]

1970 Duncker & Humblot *Berlin, Germany*

This study analyses the influence and impact of the German universal banking system on economic development during the last decades of the Kaiserreich by econometric measurement.

2436

Fürstenberg, Carl

Die Lebensgeschichte eines deutschen Bankiers [The Life of a German Banker]

1968 Econ-Verlag *Düsseldorf, Germany*

These are the memoirs of one of the most prominent bankers in Imperial Germany (Fürstenberg was managing director of the Berliner Handelsgesellschaft), edited by his son. It was first published in 1931.

Firms: Allgemeine Electricitäts-Gesellschaft; Berliner Handelsgesellschaft; Deutsche Bank; Disconto-Gesellschaft

2437

Gerhards, Michael

Die Industriebeziehungen der westdeutschen Banken [Bank-Industry Relations in West Germany]

1982 Sendler *Frankfurt am Main, Germany*

This work is the first attempt to analyse the relations between banks and industry in the Federal Republic from the 1950s to the beginning of the 1980s. The study is focused on Hilferding's 'Finanzkapital' and tries to affirm this theoretical concept with some modifications for the case of the Federal Republic. Unfortunately it completely lacks archival sources.

2438

Gossweiler, Kurt

Großbanken-Industriemonopole-Staat 1914–1932 [Banks, Industry and the State, 1914–1932]

1971 Deutscher Verlag des Wissens *Berlin, Germany*

A study of the relations between banks, industry and the state in Germany during the First World War and up to the seizure of power by the Nazis. It is focused on the 'Stamokap' theory and provides a simplified and one-sided interpretation of this subject, emphasizing the importance of 'monopoly groups' led by the major German banks.

2439

Hagemann, Wilhelm

Das Verhältnis der deutschen Großbanken zur Industrie [The Influence of German Banks on Industry]

1931 Wilhelm Christians *Berlin, Germany*

One of the first attempts to analyse the relations between banks and industry during the Kaiserreich and the Weimar Republic, which provides plenty of information from a contemporary point of view. The details are still useful for an analysis of this subject today.

2440

Hauf, Reinhard

Von der Armenkasse zum Universal-Kreditinstitut: 125 Jahre Kreis- und Stadtsparkasse Neu-Ulm, 1860–1985 [125 Years of the Neu-Ulm Savings Bank]

1985 Kreis- und Stadtsparkasse Neu-Ulm *Neu-Ulm, Germany*

This is a well-researched, fully annotated history of a small municipal savings bank. It documents the growing importance of these small banking institutions in public ownership for local and regional economic development. This

study offers an insight into this neglected sector of German financial institutions.
Firms: Kreis- und Stadtsparkasse Neu-Ulm

2441
Horstmann, Theo
Die Alliierten und die deutschen Großbanken: Bankenpolitik nach dem Zweiten Weltkrieg in Westdeutschland [The Allies and the Major German Banks: Bank policies in West Germany after the Second World War]
1988 Bouvier *Bonn, Germany*

An important study of post-war government banking policy. The main focus of this study is the failed attempt of the Allied military governments to break up the large German banks after the Second World War. A very readable, well-researched and documented study.
Firms: Commerzbank; Deutsche Bank; Dresdner Bank

2442
James, Harold
The Reichsbank and Public Finance in Germany 1924–1933
1985 Knapp *Frankfurt am Main, Germany*

This work covers the crucial period of Reichsbank history between the Weimar stabilization and the banking crisis of 1931, for which the Bank was partly held responsible.
Firms: Reichsbank

2443
Jeidels, Otto
Das Verhältnis der deutschen Großbanken zur Industrie [The Relationship Between the Major German Banks and Industry]
1905 Duncker & Humblot *Leipzig, Germany*

A classic contemporary study of the bank–industry relationship in Imperial Germany. Contrary to Hilferding (qv), Jeidels stresses the lively competition between the great banks which prevented any bank dominance over industry.

2444
Kluge, Arnd Holger
Geschichte der deutschen Bankgenossenschaften [A History of German Bank Co-operatives]
1991 Knapp *Frankfurt am Main, Germany*

The fullest history of the development of the credit cooperatives from the beginnings–based on conservative, Christian and liberal ideologies–to the present day, when the credit cooperatives had adopted conventional banking practices. The study includes a short description of the cooperative 'central banks' such as the Deutsche Genossenschaftsbank (DG Bank) founded in 1975.
Firms: Deutsche Genossenschaftsbank (DG Bank)

2445
Krüger, Alfred
Das Kölner Bankiergewerbe vom Ende des 18. Jahrhunderts bis 1875 [Banking in Cologne From the End of the Eighteenth Century to 1875]
1925 Baedeker *Essen, Germany*

The classic text on the early development of the Cologne private banks which pioneered the universal banking principle in Germany. Cologne private banks (such as Oppenheim, Schaaffhausen, Herstatt and later Deichmann) were essential both for the financing of the early railway companies in Western Germany and for the building up of Ruhr heavy industry.
Firms: Deichmann; JD Herstatt; Sal. Oppenheimer Jr. & Cie; Schaaffhausenscher Bankverein

2446
Marsh, David
The Bundesbank: The bank that rules Europe
1992 Heinemann *London*

This is a journalistic though well informed account of the role of the Bundesbank in German and European monetary policy, set in its proper historical and institutional context.
Firms: Bundesbank

2447
Meyen, Hans G.
120 Jahre Dresdner Bank: Unternehmens-Chronik, 1872 bis 1992 [120 Years of the Dresdner Bank: 1872–1992]
1992 Dresdner Bank *Frankfurt am Main, Germany*

A comprehensive study of one of the major German banks written by the bank's former chief economist. An interesting and well

presented account offering insight into the development of the bank's operations. This book stands out among similar studies of this type.
Firms: Darmstädter und National-Bank; Dresdner Bank

2448
Neuburger, Hugh
German Banks and German Economic Growth from Unification to World War I
1977 Arno Press *New York, NY*

Although addressing the much wider topic of the efficiency of the German universal banking system, the more valuable part of this book is the documentation of the involvement of the Frankfurt private banking house Bethmann in industrial finance, based on archival research.
Firms: Bethmann

2449
Neumann, Regina
Der deutsche Privatbankier: Seine Stellung im deutschen Kreditgewerbe nach 1948 [German Private Banking After 1948]
1965 Gabler *Wiesbaden, Germany*

A valuable study of the role and significance of private bankers in the German economy.

2450
Pohl, Manfred
Konzentration im deutschen Bankwesen [Concentration in German Banking]
1980 Knapp *Frankfurt am Main, Germany*

A detailed study of the causes and development of the concentration process in German banking, based on extensive material from bank archives.

2451
Pohl, Manfred
Entstehung und Entwicklung des Universalbanksystems [Origins and Development of the Universal Banking System]
1986 Knapp *Frankfurt am Main, Germany*

A short survey of the development of the universal banking principle and of joint stock banks (including savings banks and credit cooperatives) from the earliest years to the present day. This is essential reading.

2452
Pohl, Manfred
Hamburger Bankengeschichte [A History of Banking in Hamburg]
1986 V. Hase & Koehler *Mainz, Germany*

This is a valuable study of banking in a major trading community, covering local savings banks as well as merchant banks and the largest banks with their overseas connections set against the changing needs of the community.
Firms: Joh. Berenberg, Gossler & Co.; Commerzbank; Deutsche Bank; Deutsche Schiffsbeleihungs-Bank; Disconto Gesellschaft; Norddeutsche Bank; Schröder Gebr. & Co.; Vereinsbank in Hamburg; M. M. Warburg-Brinckmann, Wirtz & Co.; Hypothekenbank in Hamburg

2453
Poschinger, Heinrich von
Bankwesen und Bankpolitik in Preußen [Banks and Banking Policy in Prussia]
1971 Auvermann *Glashütten, Germany*

A reprint of the classic text of 1878. The first volume covers the period 1765–1846, concentrating on the development of the Royal Bank and the Seehandlung. The second and third volumes cover the period 1846–1870, and deal with the establishment and further development of the Prussian Bank as the central (note-issuing) bank and with the state's attitude towards credit mobilier bank projects.
Firms: Preussische Seehandlung

2454
Radtke, Wolfgang
Die Preußische Seehandlung zwischen Staat und Wirtschaft in der Frühphase der Industrialisierung [The Preußische Seehandlung Between State and Industry in the Early Phase of Industrialization]
1981 Colloquium *Berlin, Germany*

This work covers the period from the late 1820s to the early 1840s when the Prussian state bank attempted to become a 'development bank' and to initiate industrial development in distressed areas. This is essential reading for students of German industrialization.
Firms: Preussische Seehandlung

2455
Riesser, Jacob
Die deutschen Großbanken und ihre Konzentration [The Great Banks and their Concentration]
1912 Gustav Fischer *Jena, Germany*

Although written from a contemporary point of view by the former chairman of the German Bankers' Association, this work is still the most influential analysis of the concentration process in German banking before the First World War, as it is based on an insider's information. The book is also available in English as part of the material gathered by the United States National Monetary Commission for its 1911 inquiry into European banking systems (Washington DC, 1911).

Firms: A. Schaaffhausen & Co.; J.R. Bischoffsheim; Darmstädter Bank; Disconto-Gesellschaft; Von der Heydt-Kersten & Sons; J.D. Herstatt & Co.; J.H. Stein & Co.; J.W. Fischer & Co.; M.A. Rothschild & Co.; Sal Oppenheim Jr & Co.

2456
Rosenbaum, E.; Sherman, A. J.
MM. Warburg & Co. 1798–1938, Merchant Bankers of Hamburg
1979 C. Hurst & Co. *London*

This is a competent history of one of the leading German private banks, from its origins until its liquidation in 1938 and subsequent 'Aryanisation', under the name of Brinckmann, Wirtz & Co. in 1941.

Firms: Warburg; Brinckmann, Wirtz & Co.

2457
Stürmer, Michael; Teichmann, Gabrielle; Treue, Wilhelm
Wägen und Wagen: Sal. Oppenheim Jr. & Cie: Geschichte einer Bank und einer Familie [Oppenheim: History of a bank and a family]
1989 Piper *Munich, Germany*

A competent history of a major private bank in Germany written by a team of leading German historians. The authors successfully place the bank's development in the general historical context. Very readable, well researched and superbly indexed. It does, however, lack annotations.

Firms: Sal. Oppenheim Jr. & Cie

2458
Tilly, Richard
Financial Institutions and Industrialization in the Rhineland 1815–1870
1966 University of Wisconsin Press *Madison, WI*

The fullest history of the early development of the bank–industry relationship in Germany. In particular, Tilly examines the Cologne private bankers who–despite a rather hostile state attitude–were already pioneering the mixed banking principle in the 1840s.

Firms: A. Schaaffhausen & Co.; J.R. Bischoffsheim; Darmstädter Bank; Disconto-Gesellschaft; Von der Heydt-Kersten & Sons; J.D. Herstatt & Co.; J.H. Stein & Co.; J. W. Fischer & Co.; M.A. Rothschild & Co.; Sal. Oppenhiem Jr & Co.

2459
Tilly, Richard
Kapital, Staat und sozialer Protest [Capital, State and Social Protest]
1980 Vandenhoeck & Ruprecht *Göttingen, Germany*

A collection of articles dealing with the role of banks and the state in the industrialization process and with the development of large-scale enterprise.

Firms: Königliche Bank zu Berlin; Preussische Bank; Reichsbank; Schaaffhausen'scher Bankverein

2460
Trende, Adolf
Geschichte der deutschen Sparkassen [History of German Savings Banks]
1957 Deutscher Sparkassenverlag *Stuttgart, Germany*

The classic text about the development of savings banks from their beginnings to the early twentieth century. Since savings banks were (and still are) local institutions, the book is organized on a regional rather than chronological basis.

2461
Untersuchungsausschuß für das deutsche Bankwesen
Untersuchungen des deutschen Bankwesens 1933 [Investigations into German Banking, 1933]
1933 Reimund Hobbing *Berlin, Germany*

A most important collection of studies, submitted by an official enquiry committee after the German banking crisis of 1931, on the situation of German banking in the 1920s. It also contains a huge amount of statistics.

2462
Wallich, Paul
Die Konzentration im deutschen Bankwesen [Concentration in German Banking]
1905 Cotta *Berlin, Germany*

One of the first attempts to analyse the concentration process in German banking and the role of the great (universal) banks before the First World War.

2463
Weber, Adolf
Depositenbanken und Spekulationsbanken [Deposit Banks and Investment Banks]
1908 Duncker & Humblot *Munich, Germany*

A contemporary comparison between the German and English banking systems and capital markets. The author praises the German system of mixing financial services as cheaper (as regards the issuing of stock) and less risky (by portfolio diversification) than the English division of function system.

2464
Wellhöner, Volker
Großbanken und Großindustrie im Kaiserreich [Banks and Industry in the German Empire]
1989 Vandenhoeck & Ruprecht *Göttingen, Germany*

A recent analysis of the relations between banks and industry before the First World War, based on sources and material from different archives. This study disproves Hilferding's theory of bank dominance over industry before the War (qv).
Firms: Berliner Handelsgesellschaft; Darmstädter Bank; Deutsche Bank; Disconto-Gesellschaft; Dresdner Bank; Gutehoffnungshütte; Mannesmann; Phoenix; Rheinische Stahlwerke; Schaaffhausen'scher Bankverein

2465
Wysocki, Josef
Untersuchungen zur Wirtschafts- und Sozialgeschichte der deutschen Sparkassen im 19. Jahrhundert [Essays on the History of the German Savings Banks in the Nineteenth Century]
1980 Deutscher Sparkassenverlag *Stuttgart, Germany*

This book is not meant as a full history of the development of savings banks in the nineteenth century, but concentrates on specific topics, such as the social composition of savings bank customers (savers), the structure of savings and the contribution of savings banks to economic growth.

Switzerland

2466
Banque Nationale Suisse
Banque Nationale Suisse: Vol. 1, 1907–1932; Vol. 2, 1907–1957; Vol. 3, 75e anniversaire de la Banque Suisse Nationale Suisse. Les années 1957–1982 [The Swiss National Bank]
1932–82 Banque Nationale Suisse *Zurich, Switzerland*

Three volumes published by the Swiss National Bank to celebrate its twenty-fifth, fiftieth and seventy-fifth anniversaries. Their official character does not prevent them from being seriously written and informative on both the Bank's policy and its internal organization.
Firms: Banque Nationale Suisse

2467
Bänziger, Hugo
Die Entwicklung der Bankaufsicht in der Schweiz seit dem 19. Jahrhundert [The Development of Banking Supervision in Switzerland Since the Nineteenth Century]
1986 Lang *Bern, Switzerland*

A good account of the evolution of banking supervision in Switzerland from the informal agreements which lasted until the 1930s to the regulation imposed by the 1934 Banking Act.

2468

Bauer, Hans

Société de Banque Suisse 1872–1972

1972 Société de Banque Suisse *Basel, Switzerland*

A good centenary account, written by an insider, of one of the three Swiss 'big' banks.

Firms: Société de Banque Suisse; Swiss Banking Corporation

2469

Blattner, N.; Genberg, H.; Swoboda, A. (Editors)

Competitiveness in Banking: Banking in Switzerland

1992 Physica-Verlag *Heidelberg, Germany*

Part of a wide research project on the position and perspectives of the Swiss financial sector, these two collections of mostly economic studies provides useful historical retrospectives on the 1970s and 1980s.

2470

Braillard, Philippe

La place financière suisse: Politique gouvernementale et compétitivité internationale [The Swiss Financial Marketplace: Government policy and international competitiveness]

1987 Georg *Geneva, Switzerland*

This is a useful study of the competitive position of Switzerland as an international financial centre in the late 1970s and early 1980s, set in an international comparative perspective.

2471

Cassis, Youssef; Tanner, Jakob (Editors)

Banken und Kredit in der Schweiz/Banques et Crédit en Suisse, 1850–1930 [Banks and Credit in Switzerland 1850–1930]

1993 Chronos *Zurich, Switzerland*

A collection of original essays, mostly written by young researchers, dealing with the history of Switzerland as a financial centre, the development of its banking institutions and aspects of the relationships between banks and industry.

Firms: Banque Cantonale de Neuchâtel; CEG-Genève; Crédit Suisse; Swiss Banking Corporation; Zürcher Kantonal Bank

2472

Christensen, Benedicte Vebe

Switzerland's Role as an International Financial Center

1986 International Monetary Fund *Washington, DC*

This is a short (40 pages) but thoughtful and well-informed analysis of Switzerland's role as an international financial centre, mostly dealing with the early 1980s, but containing a few retrospective statistical tables.

2473

Guex, Sébastien

La politique monétaire et financière de la Confédération suisse 1900–1920 [The Monetary and Financial Policy of the Swiss Confederation 1900–1920]

1993 Payot *Lausanne, Switzerland*

Although this is a well-researched study of Switzerland's monetary policy in the early twentieth century, the analysis is weakened by the uncritical use of out-dated theories such as 'the interests of Swiss finance capital'.

2474

Hartmann, Alfred

Der Konkurrenzkampf zwischen den schweizerischen Grossbanken und Kantonalbanken [Competition Between the Big Swiss Banks and the Cantonal Banks]

1947 Kommerzdruck- und Verlags *Zurich, Switzerland*

Based on the banks' published balance sheets and covering the period from the mid-nineteenth to the mid-twentieth century, this book analyses the development of competition between the two major categories of Swiss banks, the cantonal banks, mainly owned by the cantons and benefiting from a state guarantee, and the privately owned 'universal' big banks.

2475

Hiler, David

CEG Genève: De la Caisse d'Épargne à la banque universelle [CEG Genève: From Savings Bank to Universal Bank]

1992 CEG *Geneva, Switzerland*

A valuable monograph on the savings bank

of one of Switzerland's major financial centres, which makes a good use of oral sources.
Firms: CEG Genève

2476
Iklé, Max
Switzerland as an International Banking and Financial Center
1972 Dowden, Hutchinson & Ross *Striudsber, PA*

This is an English translation of a book originally written in German by a former director of the Swiss National Bank. A good overview of the major aspects of what was then the third international financial centre behind New York and London.

2477
Jöhr, W. A.
Schweizerische Kreditanstalt 1856–1956: Hundert Jahre im Dienste der schweizerischen Volkwirtschaft [Schweizerische Kreditanstalt 1856–1956: A hundred years of service to the Swiss economy]
1956 Schweizerische Kreditanstalt *Zurich, Switzerland*

Although written by an insider, this is a good account of one of the three Swiss 'big' banks.
Firms: Crédit Suisse; Schweizerische Kreditanstalt

2478
Körner, Martin H.
Solidarités Financières Suisses au seizième siècle [Swiss Financial Solidarity in the Sixteenth Century]
1980 Editions Payot *Lausanne, Switzerland*

This book is a major study of financial activity in Switzerland in the sixteenth century.

2479
Ritzmann, Franz
Die Schweizer Banken: Geschichte–Theorie–Statistik [Swiss Banks: History–theory–statistics]
1973 Haupt *Bern, Switzerland Stuttgart, Germany*

The only comprehensive analysis of the development of Swiss banking institutions from the eighteenth century to the 1960s. Written by an economist with theoretical inclinations, it does not, however, neglect the historical context and contains invaluable statistical data, a chronology covering the period 1702–1966 and an excellent bibliography.

2480
Schneider, Ernest
Die schweizerischen Grossbanken im zweiten Weltkrieg 1939–1945 [The Big Swiss Banks During the Second World War 1939–1945]
1951 Brunner & Bodmer *Zurich, Switzerland*

An analysis of the activities of the big Swiss banks during the Second World War, based on the banks' published balance-sheets. The book is useful despite its limitations. It does, however, tend to underplay the impression of the dawn of a new era given by the growth of the banks' total assets during the war.
Firms: Basler Handelsbank; Crédit Suisse; Federal Bank; Leu & Cie; Schweizerische Volksbank; Swiss Banking Corporation; Union Bank of Switzerland

2481
Zimmermann, Rolf
Volksbank oder Aktienbank?: Parlamentsdebatten, Referendum und zunehmende Verbandsmacht beim Streit um die Nationalbankgrün dung, 1891–1905 [Popular Bank or Joint Stock Bank?: Parliamentary debates, referendum and the increased power of interest groups in the controversies surrounding the foundation of the National Bank]
1987 Chronos *Zurich, Switzerland*

This is a study of the political debates surrounding the late foundation of the Swiss National Bank in 1905. The author is primarily concerned with the economic and financial discourse, and the mechanism of the Swiss politics, in particular the growing influence of interest groups at the expense of Parliament at the turn of the century.
Firms: Nationalbank (Switzerland)

Austria

2482
Baltzarek, Franz
Die Geschichte der Wiener Börse: Öffentliche Finanzen und privates Kapital im Spiegel einer österreichischen Wirtschaftsinstitution [The History of the Vienna Stock Exchange]
1973 Verlag der österreichischen Akademie *Vienna, Austria*

The only existing account of the history of the Vienna Stock Exchange from its beginnings in 1771 to 1971.

2483
März, Eduard
Österreichische Industrie- und Bankpolitik in der Zeit Franz Josephs I [Austrian Industry and Banking in the Reign of Franz Joseph I]
1968 Europa Verlag *Vienna, Austria*

This work covers the period 1848 to 1913 and not only deals with the establishment of the credit mobilier system in Austria but also traces the inter-twining of industrial development and the rise of the banking system in Austria-Hungary.

2484
März, Eduard
Austrian Banking and Financial Policy: Credit Anstalt at a Turning Point 1913-1923
1981 Weidenfeld & Nicolson *London*

A detailed and lengthy sequel to März (qv). The author here concentrates on the policy of the Creditanstalt, Austria's largest and most important bank at the time, and puts it within the overall economic framework. The book includes a full account of Austria-Hungary's wartime economy and its problems and the subsequent inflation and stabilization.
Firms: Creditanstalt

2485
Michel, Bernard
Banques et banquiers en Autriche au début du vingtième siècle [Banks and Bankers in Austria at the Beginning of the Twentieth Century]
1976 Presses de la Fondation Nationale *Paris, France*

A study of both banks and the activities of bankers, including the latter's social status (middling, for most), and political role (negligible) between 1898 and 1914, based on extensive archival research.

2486
Pressburger, S.
Österreichische Notenbank. 1816–1966: Geschichte des österreichischen Noteninstituts [The Austrian National Bank 1816–1966]
1966 Österreichischen Nationalbank *Vienna, Austria*

A comprehensive history of the Austrian National Bank written by the bank's librarian. It covers the very beginning from 1816 to 1878, deals at length with the bank's role during the Dual Monarchy as well as during the First Austrian Republic and resumes its detailed account in 1945 leading up to the publishing date in 1966. This is the only detailed account of the Austrian National Bank.
Firms: Österreichische Notenbank

2487
Roloff, Marita; Mosser, Alois
Wiener Allianz. Gegrundet 1860 [Wiener Allianz: Established 1860]
1991 Wiener Allianz Versicherungs-Aktien gesellschaft *Vienna, Austria*

A commissioned history (1860–1990) to celebrate the 150th anniversary of this important insurance company. This work places the history of the Wiener Allianz within a general economic context. It also provides a historical balance-sheet analysis and a social history of the staff from 1860 to the present.
Firms: Wiener Allianz

2488
Rudolph, Richard L.
Banking and Industrialization in Austria-Hungary: The role of banks in the industrialization of the Czech crownlands, 1873– 1914
1976 Cambridge University Press *Cambridge*

An analysis of the role of the banks in developing the Austro-Hungarian empire's principal industrial area. It plays down the role of the banks in industrial finance.

Greece

2489
Dertilis, George
To zetema ton Trapezon 1871–1873 [The Banking Question 1871–1873]
1980 National Bank of Greece *Athens, Greece*

The book deals with the first significant investment in Greece in the nineteenth century of 'diaspora' capital and the creation of the General Credit Bank. This event is used to highlight the strategies of competing groups in securing the issuing monopoly and through it important privileges conceded by the government. The analysis also focuses on the social and political situation of Greece at the time. Extensive use is made of primary sources, economic, diplomatic and political.
Firms: National Bank of Greece

2490
Dertilis, George (Editor)
Banquiers, Usuriers et Paysans: Réseaux de Crédit et Stratégies du Capital en Grèce 1780–1930 [Bankers, Usurers and Peasants: Networks of credit and investment strategies in Greece 1780–1930]
1988 Fondation des Treilles, Editions la Découverte *Paris, France*

A collection of papers presented at the Treilles Colloquia on the general theme of the evolution of the Greek economy. Particular emphasis is placed on the credit system and the presence of financial networks inside and outside Greece.

2491
Dritsas, Margarita
Viomihania kai Trapezes sten Hellada tou mesopotemou [Banking and Industry in Interwar Greece]
1990 National Bank of Greece *Athens, Greece*

This book assesses the role of banking in the process of development and industrialization. More specifically it looks at the relationship between the banks especially the National Bank of Greece, and the secondary sector of the economy. It focuses not only on credit flows to industry, comparing them with credit flows to other sectors of the economy, but also examines the policy of attracting foreign capital to Greece in the form of direct investment, the process of forming mergers and cartels, and the attempt of the Bank to introduce the idea of 'rationalization' to the management of firms.
Firms: National Bank of Greece

2492
Dritsas, Margarita; Lindgren, Håkan; Teichova, Alice (Editors)
L'Entreprise en Grèce et en Europe XIXe-XXe siècles [Business in Greece and in Europe, Nineteenth and Twentieth Centuries]
1991 Association Interdisciplinaire Français *Athens, Greece*

A collection of both theoretical and empirical articles, presented at the First Greek Business History Symposium held in Athens. It deals with the general themes of relations between business history and other disciplines, as well as with questions regarding the margins of freedom open to business firms, government action, modes and strategies of financing business enterprises and ways of adjusting to social environment.

2493
Exertzoglou, Haris
Prosarmostikotita kai politiki imogeniakon kefalaion: Hellines Trapezites stin Konstantinoupoli: to katastema Zarifis Zafiropoulos 1871–1881 [Politics and Adaptability of Diaspora Capital: Greek bankers in Constantinople: The case of Zarifis Zafiropoulos 1871–1881]
1989 Commercial Bank of Greece *Athens, Greece*

The book examines the behaviour of a banking house belonging to the wider group known as Greek Galata Bankers who lived and operated within the Ottoman Empire in the 1870s at the time of profound changes brought about in Constantinople's capital market, due to the influx of European capital. While working closely with foreign capitalists Greek bankers directed their attention towards the emerging Greek nation-state.
Firms: Zafiris & Zafiropoulos

2494
Ionian Bank
Ionian Bank Limited: A history
1953 Ionian Bank *London*

This slim volume was produced by the bank to celebrate its centenary in 1939–a project delayed by the outbreak of the Second World War. It covers briefly the origins of the project for a State bank for the Ionian Islands which were under British suzerainty at the time, the bank's foundation in London, its launch in the Islands, its transformation into an Anglo-Greek bank when the Islands were ceded to Greece in 1864, and the successful diversification of its activities to Egypt in 1907. Never large, the bank nevertheless had a significant role in the political and economic development of both the Islands and the mainland. Although the book is an 'in-house' publication and very short, it is archivally-based and accurate.
Firms: Ionian Bank; Ionian State Bank

2495
Kostis, Kostas
Oi Trapezes kai e Krisi 1929–1932 [Banks and the Crisis 1929–1932]
1986 Commercial Bank of Greece *Athens, Greece*

Essentially a chronology of the economic crisis of 1929–1932 and its impact on the banking sector of Greece. The banking system experienced a considerable transformation and a State Central Bank, the Bank of Greece, was created. This affected the regulation of the montary system, the gold exchange standard, and the structure and functions of the credit system. The study is based on the personal archives of leading Greek politicians of the time.
Firms: Commercial Bank of Greece

Italy

2496
Balletta, Francesco
Il Banco di Napoli e le rimesse degli emigranti (1914–1925) [The Bank of Naples and Remittances From Emigrants]
1979 Institut international d'histoire *Naples, Italy*

An examination of the remittances sent to the Bank of Naples between the First World War and the mid-1920s by Italian emigrants, estimated by the author to amount to about 3 per cent of the Italian GNP. Entrusted by law in 1901 with the administration of these remittances, the Bank of Naples was only concerned with the technical problems arising from the transfer of money.
Firms: Banco di Napoli

2497
Balletta, Francesco
Il Banco di Napoli in Calabria al tempo della prima guerra mondiale [The Bank of Naples in Calabria at the Time of the First World War]
1979 Droz *Geneva, Switzerland*

An analysis of the Bank of Naples in Calabria during the period of the First World War which throws light on the complexities of the crisis affecting much of rural Italy in these years.
Firms: Banco di Napoli

2498
Basini, Gian Luigi; Forestieri, Giancarlo
Branche Locali e Sviluppo Dell'Economia: Parma e la Cassa di Risparmio [Local Banks and Economic Development]
1989 Cassa di Risparmio di Parma *Milan, Italy*

Four essays on the impact of Parma's savings banks on the economic development of the city between 1860 and 1960. Despite its strictly local and microeconomic character, it provides a useful contribution on the role played by financial intermediaries in the process of economic development and the internal working of a bank.
Firms: Cassa di Risparmio di Parma

2499
Castronovo, Valerio
Storia di una banca: La Banca Nazionale del Lavoro e lo sviluppo economico italiano 1913–1983 [History of a Bank: The Banca Nazionale del Lavoro and the economic development of Italy]
1983 Einaudi *Turin, Italy*

This is a history of the most important state-owned bank in Italy. Born as an institute for land and building credit to cooperative societies, it was captured by the fascist government and transformed into a regime bank for all the public authorities and the corporative organizations. From the 1930s BNL's peculiar structure was based on several sections of special credit for the movie industry, hotels and tourism and the fishing industry. In the postwar period it developed industrial credit by entering into preferential relations with major groups such as Fiat in the private sector or the state-owned ENI. It also expanded its operations into mid-term credit to medium and small concerns and to the Southern industries. Based on documents of the bank's directorate, the book focuses on both the BNL's vicissitudes and the political and economic history of Italy at the time.
Firms: Banca Nazionale del Lavoro; Istituto nazionale di credito per la cooperazione; Fiat; ENI

2500
Cesarini, Francesco
Alle origini del credito industriale: l'IMI negli anni trenta [The Origins of Industrial Credit: The IMI in the 1930s]
1982 Il Mulino *Bologna, Italy*

Cesarini's work is a detailed examination of the activity of the IMI during its early period. This book demonstrates the inability of this industrial credit institute to contribute effectively towards the financial reorganization of big industry after the crisis of 1931–34, especially because of its unwillingness to finance new investments, its strict preference for mortgage loans and its overconcetration on financing the electric industry.
Firms: Istituto Mobiliare Italiano

2501
Confalonieri, Antonio
Banca e Industria in Italia (1894–1906)
1980 Il Mulino *Bologna, Italy*

An invaluable three volume study on the evolution of the Italian banking system during the 'industrial revolution' of the country, which stresses the role of universal, German-type banks in the process of capital formation and the economic development of Italy. The book is largely based on rich archive sources.
Firms: Banca Commerciale Italiana; Banco di Roma; Credito Italiano

2502
Confalonieri, Antonio
Banca e crisi in Italia dalla crisi del 1907 all'agosto 1914 [Banking in Italy from the Crisis in 1907 to 1914]
1982 Banca Commerciale Italiana *Milan, Italy*

The growth and evolution of the two Italian largest universal banks, Banca Commerciale and Credito Italiano in the pre-First World War period. This study follows up the monograph by the same author (qv) on the Italian banking system before the 1907 crisis.
Firms: Banca Commerciale Italiana; Banco di Roma; Credito Italiano; Società Bancaria Italiana

2503
Confalonieri, Antonio
Banche miste e grande industria in Italia 1914–1933 [Mixed Banks and Big Industry in Italy]
1994 Banca Commerciale Italiana *Milan, Italy*

This book, based on original archive sources, concludes Confalonieri's twenty-year research on the role played by universal banks in the industrial development of Italy. The author focuses on the evolution of the Italian banking system between the inflationary crisis following the First World War and the financial stabilization in 1925–7, then on the question of industrial credit and the crucial role played in this field by the Bank of Italy. Two broad monographic chapters finally deal with the vicissitudes of the two large Milanese mixed banks, and analyse the long-term causes of the crisis of 1931–1933. A rich statistical appendix concludes the volume.
Firms: Banca Commerciale Italiana; Credito Italiano; Banco di Roma; Cassa di Risparmio delle Provincie Lombarde

2504
Conti, Giuseppe
La politica aziendale di un istituto de credito

immobiliare: Il Monte dei Paschi de Siena dal 1815 al 1872 [The Corporate Policy of a Land Loan Bank]
1985 Olschki *Florence, Italy*

This analysis of the evolution of the operational, organizational and managerial structure of the bank is made from a strictly corporate point of view. The book demonstrates the persistent resistance offered by the management of the Sienese nobility to innovations in land and mortgage loans. A statistical appendix includes accounting tables based on the historical series of balance sheets.
Firms: Monte dei Paschi di Siena

2505
Cova, Alberto; Galli, Anna Maria
La Cassa di Risparmio delle Provincie Lombarde dalla fondazione al 1940 [The Lombardy Savings Bank 1823–1940]
1992 CARIPLO Laterza *Milan-Bari, Italy*

This detailed and well-documented history of the most important Italian savings-bank from its foundation in 1823 is described within the framework of the economic and financial evolution of the Lombardy region, the most prosperous district of Italy.
Firms: Cassa di Risparmio delle Provincie Lombarde

2506
Credito Italiani
Il Credito Italiano e la fondazione dell'IRI [The Credito Italiano and the Founding of IRI]
1990 Scheiwiller *Milan, Italy*

Proceedings of the Congress organized in 1989 to inaugurate the historical archives of the Credito Italiano. The essays concentrate on the relations between universal banks and big industry: Antonio Confalonieri deals with the case of the Credito Italiano from 1914 to 1933, Sabino Cassese and Gianni Toniolo focus on the crisis of 1931–1934, the banking salvages and the creation of IRI.
Firms: Credito Italiano

2507
De Rosa, Gabriele
Una banca cattolica tra cooperazione e capitalismo: la Banca Cattolica del Veneto [A Catholic Bank Between Cooperative System and Capitalism]
1991 Laterza *Rome-Bari, Italy*

This is a history of one of the most important Catholic banks, deeply rooted in the rural credit banks and the white cooperative movement in north-eastern Italy, active in small low-interest loans to farmers and small entrepreneurs. Involved in the crisis which led several minor banks to bankruptcy during the 1930s, the bank was rescued by an agreement between the fascist regime and the ecclesiastic hierarchies in Rome, and, thanks to an operative policy of mergers, it became the mainstay of the Catholic credit system in Veneto. Includes an appendix of documents from the bank's archives and the Vatican Secret Archives.
Firms: Banca Cattolica del Veneto

2508
De Rosa, Luigi
Banche e lavori pubblici in Italia tra le due guerre (1919–1939) [Banks and Public Works in Italy between the Two Wars]
1979 Giuffré *Milan, Italy*

This provides an analysis of the role played by the banking system in financing public works between the first post-war period and the Great Crisis. The book focuses on the history of Crediop, established in 1919 by Alberto Beneduce. This special credit institute was able to create a state-guaranteed bond market and to mobilize savings collected by the savings banks; its mortgage loans contributed to the modernization of Italian infrastructures (ie the electrification of the railways and the growth of the merchant fleet), and to the realization of the fascist integral reclamation policy. Crediop also took a part in the foundation of IRI.
Firms: Crediop (Consorzio di credito per le opere pubbliche); IRI

2509
De Rosa, Luigi; De Rosa, Gabriele
Storia del Banco di Roma [History of the Bank of Rome]
1982–4 Banco di Roma *Rome, Italy*

This is a history of the large Catholic and Italian universal bank (in contrast with the two German banks, Banca Commerciale and

Credito Italiano) from its origins to the period following the Second World War. Rescued from bankruptcy in 1922 by the Bank of Italy and in 1934 by IRI, the Bank of Rome was fascistized and became the favourite bank of the regime, especially because of its wide international expansion in the Mediterranean area and the Near East. The study is based on the rich historical archives of the bank.
Firms: Banco di Roma; IRI

2510
Falchero, Anna Maria
La Banca Italiana di Sconto 1914–1921: Sette anni di guerra [The Banca Italiana di Sconto 1914–1921: Seven years of war]
1990 Angeli *Milan, Italy*

This is a history of the brief and adventurous life of the most Italian of banks, established by the Perrone brothers of Ansaldo with the aim of ousting the German banks from their leading role in the banking system. Serving the ambitious cause of Italy's economic independence and its transformation into a real international great power, the BIS aspired to establish both a big integrated concern (the Ansaldo vertical system) and an Italianized banking system headed by the State, to direct savings towards the development of the national industry. This study of Italian imperialism is based on wide-ranging research carried out by the author in a large number of archives.
Firms: Banca Italiana di Sconto; Ansaldo

2511
Polsi, Alessandro
Alle origini del capitalismo italiano: Stato, banche e banchieri dopo l'Unità [At the Origins of the Italian Capitalism: State, banks and bankers after the Unification]
1993 Einaudi *Turin, Italy*

This is an original and archive-based study on the growth and the organization of the private banking system in Italy during the nineteenth century. The author focuses on the spread of *Credit Mobilier* banks in the Savoy Piedmont and, during the banking boom of the 1870s, in the main business centres of the rest of the country. Special attention is also paid to the movement of the popular banks, local credit institutes inspired by mutual solidarity principles which later became important deposit banks. An accurate analysis of the shareholders who invested their capital in banking concludes the study.

2512
Rodano, Giorgio
Il credito all'economia: Raffaele Mattioll alla Banca Commerciale Italiana [Credit to the Economy: Raffaele Mattioli at the Banca Commerciale Italiana]
1983 Ricciardi *Milan, Italy*

Based on the rich documents held in the personal archives of Raffaele Mattioli and in the historical records of the bank, this study examines the vicissitudes of the large Milanese bank from the interwar crisis to the economic boom of the 1960s. Many interesting documents are widely or entirely quoted and commented on by the author, dealing with crucial questions like the bank's rescue in 1931–1933, the establishment of Mediobanca, the links between commercial and investment credit, the Comit's role in the banker's syndicate, and the relations with its main shareholder IRI.
Firms: Banca Commerciale Italiana; Mediobanca

2513
Sassi, Salvatore
La vita di una banca attraverso i suoi bilanci: Il Banco di Roma dal 1880 al 1933 [The Life of a Bank Through its Balance Sheets]
1986 Il Mulino *Bologna, Italy*

This is an analysis of the historical series of the Bank of Rome's balance sheets (financial statements and profit and loss accounts), with a detailed explanation of the bank's policy on deposits and investments.
Firms: Banco di Roma

2514
Segreto, Luciano
La City e la *dolce vita* romana: La storia della Banca Italo Britannica 1916–1930 [The City and the Roman *dolce vita*: The history of the British Italian Bank]
Passato e Presente, no. 13, 1987: pp 63–95

This essay, based on wide research in Italian and foreign archives, tells the history of an ambitious project by English banks (Lloyds

Bank, London County & Westminster Bank, National Provincial Bank) to conquer leading positions in the Italian finance system: a project swept away by risky speculations and concluded with the banks' rescue by the Bank of England.
Firms: Banca Italo Britannica; Credito Italiano; Lloyds Bank; London County and Westminster Bank; National Provincial Bank; Bank of England

2515
Toniolo, Gianni
One Hundred Years 1894–1994: A short history of the Banca Commerciale Italiana
1994 Banca Commerciale Italiana *Milan, Italy*
This is a short but insightful commissioned history of an important universal bank. Not very critical, but does include useful material on managers.
Firms: Banca Commerciale Italiana

Denmark

2516
Danmarks Statistik
Statistiske Undersøgelser nr. 24. Kreditmarkedsstatistik [Statistical Investigations No. 24. Credit-Market Statistics]
1969 Danmarks Statistik *Copenhagen, Denmark*
This collection of data is indispensable for any student of Danish banking and finance. It contains balance-sheet information for all commercial banks before 1920. The data are also presented on a regional and national basis. Besides the information on commercial banks, the book contains statistical information on the savings banks to 1920, credit associations 1851–1965, the bond market, 1810–1965 and the public debt, 1750–1965.

2517
Gejl, Ib
Indenfor Snorene, Fondsbørsvekselerernes historie - isaer til 1945 [A History of the Stock Exchange Brokers]
1989 Erhvervsarkivet *Aarhus, Denmark*
This history of stock exchange brokers from 1800 to 1990 lays special emphasis on the pre-1930 period. Though somewhat superficial in its coverage, it contains much useful information concerning trading on the stock-exchange, the relative importance of shares and bonds respectively and the passage from virtually unregulated markets to the introduction of regulation after 1914.

2518
Glud, Troels
Kreditforeningsinstitutionen i Danmark [Mortgage-Institutions in Denmark]
1951 De Danske Kreditforeninger *Copenhagen, Denmark*
Though somewhat dated, this is the only comprehensive history of the Danish mortgage institutions. It describes the background for the first credit-associations, and the regulation concerning their establishment and functioning. In addition, the evolution of the associations and their importance to the Danish credit market before 1950 are analysed.

2519
Hansen, Svend Aage
Pengevaesen og kredit, 1813–1860 [Money and Credit, 1813–1860]
1960 *Odense, Denmark*
The foundation and early development of the Danish savings banks and commercial banking systems are analysed against the background of European monetary and financial development. Likewise the early history of the central bank, the 'Nationalbanken', is covered. This book is a fine introduction to the early history of banking in Denmark.

2520
Hansen, Svend Aage
Early Industrialization in Denmark
1970 Department of Economic History *Copenhagen, Denmark*
Inspired by the approach of Rondo Cameron in his *Banking in the Early Stages of Industrialization* (qv) the author investigates early industrialization in Denmark to 1914. Included in this short book (77 pp.) is a useful examination of the role of credit institutions and general

monetary and credit policies in the industrialization process. The book remains an important source of information on industrial finance.

2521
Johansen, Hans Chr.
En koncern i udvikling 1942–92: Alm. Brand af 1792 [A Business Making Progress: Alm. Brand]
1992 Gyldendal *Copenhagen, Denmark*

The history of the largest Danish fire insurance company, Alm. Brand, assessed in relation to the development of the insurance business in Denmark. The period 1792–1942 is only treated in outline whereas there is a detailed analysis of the history over the last 50 years, when there was a major restructuring of Danish insurance.
Firms: Alm. Brand af 1792

2522
Mordhorst, Kirsten (Editor)
Dansk pengehistorie: Vol. III. Bilag [Danish Monetary History: Vol. III. Appendixes]
1968 Danmarks Nationalbank *Copenhagen, Denmark*

This volume provides data on the discount rate 1818–1967, balance sheet data for the Nationalbanken 1900–1960 and information about bank failures and reconstructions in the banking crises of the 1920s. It is a necessary companion to studies of the macro- and micro-economic functions of the Danish Central Bank after 1900.
Firms: Danmarks Nationalbank

2523
Olsen, Erling; Hoffmeyer, Erik
Dansk Pengehistorie: Vol. II, 1914–1960 [Danish Monetary History: Vol. II, 1914–1960]
1968 Danmarks Nationalbank *Copenhagen, Denmark*

This volume covers Danish monetary history from 1914 to 1960. Part one covers the problems of the gold standard from 1914 to 1927, when Denmark returned to gold. In part two, increased regulation, and monetary policy are analysed. This book is indispensable for those interested in Denmark's monetary policy in the first half of the twentieth century.
Firms: Danmarks Nationalbank

2524
Skrubbeltrang, Fridlev
Den Sjaellandske Bondestands Sparekasse 1856–1958 [The Zealand Farmers' Savings Bank, 1856–1958]

Published in 1959, in connection with the 100th anniversary of one of the largest Danish savings banks, this is a comprehensive, contextualized study of the savings bank. In spite of its micro-oriented approach, it is pertinent to any study of the savings banks in Denmark, which were a major source of credit in the Danish economy.
Firms: Sjaellandske Bondestands Sparekasse

2525
Svendsen, Knud Erik; Hansen, Svend Aage
Dansk Pengehistorie: Vol. I, 1700–1914 [Danish Monetary History: Vol. I, 1700–1914]
1968 Danmarks Nationalbank *Copenhagen, Denmark*

This is volume one in a three volume study commissioned by the Danish central bank, the 'Nationalbanken' to commemorate its 150th anniversary. Based on primary source material, part one concentrates on the period 1700 to 1818, covering mercantilist monetary policy, the foundation of the first Danish bank, and the introduction of bank notes in Denmark. Part two covers the period 1818–1914 and describes the evolution of the central bank, the savings banks, and the commercial banks. The evolution of the financial system is set in the context of Denmark's economic development. This book is a necessary starting point.
Firms: Danmarks Nationalbank

Norway

2526
Jahn, Gunnar; et al
Norges Bank gjennom 150 år [The Bank of Norway Through 150 Years]
1966 Norges Bank *Oslo, Norway*

This monograph covers 150 years of the history of Norges Bank, the central bank of Norway. It is not an analytical work, but gives

important material about the activities of the central bank.
Firms: Norges Bank

2527
Jensen, Arne; et al (Editors)
Studier i Sparing og Sparebankvesen i Norge 1822–1972 [Essays on Saving and Savings Banks in Norway 1822–1972]
1972 Gyldensdal *Oslo, Norway*

This is a collection of essays on the development of savings banks in Norway. Covering the period 1822–1972, the essays describe both the institutional development and the role of savings banks in Norwegian economic development.

2528
Nordvik, Helge W.; et al
Penger spart-Penger tjent: Sparebanker og økonomisk utvikling på Sør-Vestladent fra 1839 til 1989 [Money Saved–Money Earned: Savings banks and economic development in South-West Norway 1839–1989]

This work focuses on the development of the savings banks and their contribution to economic development and growth at a regional level, namely the south-western part of Norway during the period 1830–1989.

2529
Petersen, Kaare
Bankkriser og valuta-uro: Forretningsbankenes historie i mellomkrigsårene [Banking Crises and Currency Problems: The history of the commercial banks during the inter-war years]
1982 A/S Hjemmet-Fagpresseforlaget *Oslo, Norway*

A commissioned history of commercial banking in Norway during the inter-war and post-war periods. This work was published with the financial support of the Norwegian Bankers Association. It gives a non-analytical and descriptive survey of commercial banking in Norway, but contains essential material for students of the subject.

2530
Sejersted, Francis (Editor)
En storbank i blandingsøkonomien: Den norske Creditbank 1957–1982 [A Major Bank in the Mixed Economy: The Norske Creditbank 1957–1982]
1982 Gyldendal *Oslo, Norway*

This is a commissioned collection of essays published on the 125th anniversary of the Norske Creditbank, the largest commercial bank in Norway during the period concerned. Five Norwegian scholars analyse and describe several aspects of the development of the bank and its activities during the period 1957–82. There are essays on lending policy, development of management and organization, international activities, financing of the oil industry and adaptation to the regulation of financial markets and institutions during the period.
Firms: Norske Creditbank

2531
Skånland, Hermod
Det Norske Kredittmarked Siden 1900 [The Norwegian Credit Market Since 1900]
1967 The Central Bureau of Statistics *Oslo, Norway*

The author, Governor of the Bank of Norway since 1985, presents a historical account of credit market statistics since the turn of the century. An analysis of the data is provided, setting the development of financial markets in economic and political context.

Finland

2532
Blomstedt, Yrjö
Kansallis-Osake-Pankki 1889–1939 [The History of Kansallis-Osake-Pankki]
1989 Kansallis-Osake-Pankki *Helsinki, Finland*

An anniversary history of the second largest commercial bank in Finland during its first stormy decades. The author (a former professor of history) ably describes the troubles of the bank and also its important role in Finnish financial markets and society. The author pinpoints especially the role of the managers of the Kansallis-Osake-Pankki.
Firms: Kansallis-Osake-Pankki

2533
Pipping, Hugo
Banklivet Genom Hundra År: Föreningbanken i Finland 1862–1962 [One Hundred Years of Banking: The history of the Union Bank of Finland]
1962 Föreningbanken *Helsinki, Finland*

An anniversary history of the first and biggest commercial bank in Finland. The author (a former professor of economics) describes the development of financial markets, the clients of the Union Bank of Finland and of course the great success of the Bank.
Firms: Föreningsbanken i Finland

2534
Saarinen, Veikko
Liikepankkien Keskuspankkirahoituksen Ehdot, Määrä Ja Kustannukset 1950–1984 [Terms, Volume and Cost of Commercial Banks' Central Bank Financing 1950–1984]
1986 Bank of Finland *Helsinki, Finland*

A quantitative analysis of the relationship between the commercial banks and the central bank during the period of regulation in Finland. The book contains a summary in English.

2535
Schybergson, Emil
Suomen Pankki 1811–1911 [The Bank of Finland 1811-1911]
1914 Bank of Finland *Helsinki, Finland*

This is the first book to celebrate the history of the Bank of Finland. The author describes the way in which the Bank's functions changed in response to the development of financial markets in the nineteenth century. The paradigm is mostly institutional and concentrates on Bank directors.
Firms: Bank of Finland

2536
Tudeer, A. E.
The Bank of Finland 1912–1936
1940 Bank of Finland *Helsinki, Finland*

An insider's view of the Bank of Finland's history during its troubled years. Between the years 1912–36 Finland had to face the First World War, the declaration of independence and civil war, the Great Depression and two serious banking crises. The author (a former head of department of BOF) describes the Central Bank's solution to these problems, adopting a sympathetic stance towards its policies.
Firms: Bank of Finland

2537
Urbans, Runar
Suomen Säästöpaakkilaitos 1822–1922 [The Finnish Savings Banks 1822–1922]
1963 Finnish Savings Banks Association *Vammala, Finland*

A descriptive and narrative outlook of the development of the saving banks in Finland.

Sweden

2538
Englund, Karl
Försäkring och fusioner, Skandia, Skåne, Svea, Thule, Öresund, 1855–1980 [From Skandia to the Skandia Group, 1855–1980]
1982 Försäkrings AB Skandia *Stockholm, Sweden*

This solid and penetrative study analyses the development of the Swedish insurance industry from the foundation of the first joint stock insurance company, Skandia, in 1855 up to the 1980s. It covers the intense merger movement at the beginning of the 1960s, when five large Swedish insurance groups (with origins in 53 independent companies) merged into one, to form the Skandia Group, with a market share of more than 25 per cent. The analysis focuses on the causes and effects of the various merger waves in the insurance business. The book includes an extensive English summary.
Firms: Folksam (Folket och Samarbete); Försäkrings AB Skandia; Försäkrings AB Svea; Hansa Ömsesidig Sakförsäkring; Lifförsäkrings AB Thule; Livförsäkrings AB Skåne; Sjöförsäkrings AB Öresund; Städernas Allmänna Försäkringsbolag; Trygg Ömsesidig Livförsäkring

2539
Gasslander, Olle
History of Stockholms Enskilda Bank to 1914
1962 Stockholms Enskilda Bank *Stockholm, Sweden*

An excellent monograph of a private Swedish bank, concerned with its business behaviour and its function and importance in the economy as a whole. It was owned by the Wallenberg family, which was actively involved in industrial development not only in Sweden but also in other Nordic countries, above all Norway. Its importance, analysed in this volume, was based both on exceptional, cautious banking practices, adopted after the financial crisis in 1878/79 with the aim of piling up hidden reserves, and on the considerable support it gave to the development of new industries and the restructuring and modernization of the economy, via credits, venture capital, ownership and managerial governance.
Firms: AB Providentia; Allmänna Svenska Elektriska AB/ASEA; Badische Anilin- & Soda-Fabrik; Banque de Paris et des Pays-Bas; Banque des Pays du Nord; Centralbanken for Norge; Crédit Lyonnais; Danske Landmandsbank; Stockholms Enskilda Bank; British Bank of Northern Commerce

2540
Hildebrand, Karl-Gustaf
I omvandlingens tjänst. Svenska Handelsbanken 1871–1955 [Banking in a Growing Economy. Svenska Handelsbanken since 1871]
1971 Svenska Handelsbanken *Stockholm, Sweden*

An impressive 'model' study for business history research, combining micro- and macroeconomic analysis and integrating the analysis of banking activities into the general social, political and economic framework. The study focuses on bank–industry relations in the 1920s. It shows clearly that the bank, being the biggest commercial institution in Sweden with a market share of about 25 per cent not only took responsibility for its industrial clients in restructuring the firms financially, but also made huge efforts to reorganize them industrially.
Firms: AB Industrivärden; AB Ytterstford-Munksund; Skandinaviska Banken/Skan dinaviska Kredit AB; Stockholms Enskilda Bank; Stora Kopparbergs; Svenska Cellulosa AB/SCA; Svenska Emissions AB; Svenska Handelsbanken; Svenska Sockerfabriks AB; Svenska Tändsticks AB/Swedish Match AB

2541
Lindgren, Håkan
Bank, Investmentbolag, Bankirfirma: Stockholms Enskilda Bank 1924–1945 [Commercial Bank, Investment Company, Banking Firm: Stockholms Enskilda Bank 1924–1945]
1988 EHF Institute, Stockholm School of Economics *Stockholm, Sweden*

As the title suggests, the business of this important Swedish bank extended to more than retail banking. Through its network of closely related financial companies the bank was the most important instrument in the Wallenberg family's business activities. The bank, its industrial clients and its affiliated investment companies formed a strong combine, in which ownership, entrepreneurial and creditor functions of the leading members of the family were applied to develop new areas of investments and strong financial–industrial development blocks. The expansion of these activities, and the increasing influence on Swedish business life of the Wallenberg family to the end of the Second World War is thoroughly researched in this weighty study, which relates the activities within the Wallenberg Group to developments on the national and international level. The book contains an extensive English summary.
Firms: AB Custos; AB Industrivärden; AB Investor; Bankifirman C G Cervin; Banque Internationale à Luxembourg SA; Banque des Pays du Nord; Firma Albert Bonnier/Bonnier Group of Companies; Skandinaviska Banken/Skandinaviska Kredit AB; Stockholms Enskilda Bank; Svenska Diesel

2542
Nilsson, Göran B.
Banker i brytningstid [Banking in Pioneer Times]
1981 EHF Institute, Stockholm School of Economics *Stockholm, Sweden*

An impressive study, approaching the question of the foundation of a modern banking system in Sweden 1850–1864 in a holistic perspective, integrating economic, political, social and ideological explanatory variables and

using a business history methodology. It is convincingly shown that the formation of the 'model' banking system in Sweden was based on the Scottish system, though it developed and changed according to local Swedish requirements. It is also clearly shown that the 'banking question' was one of the main issues for the new 'association-liberals' in their policy of promoting the growth of a backward Swedish economy. The book contains an extensive English summary.
Firms: Banque de Belgique; Société Générale de Belgique; Stockholms Enskilda Bank; Stockholms Filialbank; English and Swedish Bank Co.; Gellivara Company; Östergötlands Enskilda Bank

2543
Olsson, Ulf
Bank, Familj och Företagande. Stockholms Enskilda Bank 1946–1971 [Bank, Family and Entrepreneurship]
1986 EHF Institute, Stockholm School of Economics *Stockholm, Sweden*

In this last volume of the Stockholm Enskilda Bank series, its business during the years of tight Keynesian regulation of financial markets is dealt with, up to the merger of 1972 when the S.E. Bank was formed. In the main part of the book, the growth of the Wallenberg group of companies and its increasing importance in the Swedish economy after the Second World War is discussed. Using an apposite example from the pulp and paper industry the entrepreneurial activities of the Wallenbergs are discussed, and the interdependence of bank and industry is analysed. In comparison with other big banks in Sweden, the Stockholms Enskilda Bank relied heavily on deposits from industrial firms–especially those belonging to the Wallenberg sphere of interest. It is clearly shown that the 1960s meant increasing problems for the bank, as the liquidity of the business sector diminished and credit control measures were enforced by the Central Bank.
Firms: AB Electrolux; AB Investor; ASEA AB; Atlas Copco AB; Förvaltnings AB Providentia; IG Farbenindustrie AG; Robert Bosch GmbH/Bosch Group of Companies; Skandinaviska Banken; Stockholms Enskilda Bank; Svenska Handelsbanken

2544
Söderlund, Ernst
Skandinaviska Banken i det svenska bankväsendets historia: Vol. I. 1864–1914; Vol II. 1914–1939 [Scandinavska Banken in the History of Swedish Banking]
1954–78 Almqvist & Wiksell *Uppsala, Sweden*

This two-volume edition contains the history of one of the major Swedish commercial banks up to the Second World War. Its activities – mainly in retailing – are compared with those of other banks, which means that the reader will also obtain a thorough knowledge of developments in the commercial banking sector as a whole. The book also contains a comprehensive account of the merger movement, 1908–1926, and of changes in Sweden's banking laws, and the duties of the Banking Inspectorate.
Firms: AB Kreuger & Toll/Kreuger Group of Companies; Bankirfirman C G Cervin; Centralgruppens Emissions AB; Gamlestadens Fabrikers AB; M M Warburg & Co.; Skandinaviska Banken/Skandinaviska Kredit AB; Svenska Sockerfabriks AB; Svenska Tändsticks AB/Swedish Match AB; Swedish American Investment Corp.; Trafik AB Grängesberg-Oxelösund Gränges

Middle East

2545
Anan'ich, B. V.
Rossiiskoi samoderzhaviei vyvoz kapitalov [Export of Capital by the Russian State]
1975 *Leningrad, USSR*

This important book gives a history of the Russian bank founded to operate in Iran in 1890, known as the Société des Prêts. Considerable information is provided on this bank's business activities and its close relationship with the Tsarist government before the 1917 Revolution.
Firms: Société des Prêts

2546
Badrud-Din, Abdul-Amir
The Bank of Lebanon: Central banking in a financial centre and entrepot
1984 Frances Pinter *London*

This study provides a history of the Bank of Lebanon, the Lebanese central bank founded in 1964. There is also discussion of Lebanon's banking history prior to that date, and especially the important quasi-government role of the Banque de Syrie et du Liban.
Firms: Bank of Lebanon; Banque de Syrie et du Liban

2547
Bostock, Frances; Jones, Geoffrey
Planning and Power in Iran: Ebtehaj and economic development under the Shah
1989 Frank Cass *London*
This book is a business biography of Abol Hassan Ebtehaj. Ebtehaj was the senior employee of the British-owned Imperial Bank of Persia in Iran until 1936. Subsequently he became Governor of the government-owned central bank, the Bank Melli. This book provides new evidence on the political and business context in the early years of Iranian banking, using a range of Iranian, British and American sources.
Firms: Bank Melli; Imperial Bank of Persia

2548
Clay, Christopher
The Imperial Ottoman Bank in the Later Nineteenth Century: A multinational 'national' bank?
1990 Routledge *London*
This article, in *Banks and Multinationals* (ed. G. Jones, qv), studies the Imperial Ottoman Bank, the state bank of the Ottoman Empire and an Anglo-French financial concern, from the point of view of its multinational activities which it concludes were, with some exceptions, rather circumspect.
Firms: Imperial Ottoman Bank

2549
Clay, Christopher
The Origins of Modern Banking in the Levant: The branch network of the Imperial Ottoman Bank, 1890–1914
International Journal of Middle East Studies, vol. 26, no. 4, 1994: pp 589–614
This article argues that although the Imperial Ottoman Bank had probably the biggest network of branches in the Ottoman Empire than any other bank, it created such a network cautiously and completed it only in the final years before the First World War, following rather than leading economic growth.
Firms: Imperial Ottoman Bank

2550
Davis, Eric
Challenging Colonialism: Bank Misr and Egyptian industrialization, 1920–1941
1983 Princeton University Press *Princeton, NJ*
This book is a study of the first purely Arab bank and its place in Egypt between the two World Wars, including its sponsorship of Egypt's industrialization movement.
Firms: Bank Misr

2551
Jones, Geoffrey
Banking and Empire in Iran
1986 Cambridge University Press *Cambridge*
This is the first of a two-volume history of the British Bank of the Middle East. It traces the history of the Bank from its foundation in 1889 as the state bank of Iran, and its development of modern banking in that country, to the ending of its links with Iran in 1952. The book is based on the confidential archives of the bank and has been widely praised for its critical and objective approach to the subject.
Firms: British Bank of the Middle East; Hongkong Bank

2552
Jones, Geoffrey
Banking and Oil
1987 Cambridge University Press *Cambridge*
This is the second of a two-volume history of the British Bank of the Middle East. This volume covers its history since 1940, its pioneering of banking in the Arabian Gulf in the 1940s and 1950s, and the acquisition of the bank by the Hongkong Bank in 1960. This study is unusual because the author had unrestricted access to confidential banking archives, including financial records, up to the 1960s.
Firms: British Bank of the Middle East; Hongkong Bank

2553

Landes, David S.

Bankers and Pashas: International Finance and Economic Imperialism in Egypt

2nd Edition

1979 Harvard University Press *Cambridge, MA*

This is a pioneering study in banking history, based on the discovery in the vaults of the Bank of France of a unique correspondence between two bankers in the 1860s. It highlights in particular the role of high finance in European expansion and contains a still unsurpassed chapter on the world of European private bankers in the mid-nineteenth century.

Firms: Anglo-Egyptian Bank; Baring Brothers & Co.; Comptoir d'Escompte de Paris; Crédit Mobilier (Paris); Dervieu, Edouard & Cie; Fould-Oppenheim & Cie; Frühling & Goschen; Imperial Ottoman Bank; International Financial Society; Marcuard, André & Cie

2554

National Bank of Egypt

National Bank of Egypt 1898–1948

1948 National Bank of Egypt *Cairo, Egypt*

This book is a history of the first fifty years of the National Bank of Egypt. It is not footnoted, but it does provide a considerable amount of information about the bank. It is the only study of the National Bank.

Firms: National Bank of Egypt

2555

Thobie, Jacques

Intérêts et impérialism français dans l'Empire ottoman, 1895–1914 [French Interests and French Imperialism in the Ottoman Empire, 1815–1914]

1977 Sorbonne *Paris, France*

This is a comprehensive work on the strategy and activities of French capital in the Ottoman Empire in such areas as state financing, commercial banking, infrastructure, transportation, mining and public utilities and it thus includes short histories of a number of companies where French capital participated.

Firms: Banque Impériale Ottomane; Banque du Liban; La Régie co-intéressée des tabacs de l'Empire ottoman; La Compagnie du Gaz da Beyrouth; La Société d'Héraclée

2556

Thobie, Jacques

Les choix financiers de l' 'Ottomane' en Méditerranée orientale de 1856 à 1939 [The Financial Choices of the 'Ottoman' in the Eastern Mediterranean from 1856 to 1939]

1985 Chambre de Commerce et d'Industrie *Marseilles, France*

This article in *Banque et Investissements en Méditerranée à l'époque contemporaine* studies the role and activities of the Imperial Ottoman Bank as a state bank, financier of the Ottoman state and as a holding company and, in the latter role, it examines its participation in various companies covering the period c.1880–1914.

Firms: Banque Impériale Ottomane

2557

Wilson, Rodney

Banking and Finance in the Arab Middle East

1983 Macmillan *London*

This book provides a short history of commercial banking in the Arab world. It begins with traditional money lending, examines the growth of modern banking, and the emergence of financial centres in the region.

Firms: Bank Misr

Asia (excl. Japan)

2558

Bagchi, A. K.

The Evolution of the State Bank of India: Vol. I The Roots, 1806–1876 Part I The early years, 1806–1860; Part II Diversity and regrouping, 1860–1876

1987 Oxford University Press *Bombay, India*

The first volume of a comprehensive commissioned history of the State Bank of India from its origins in the Bank of Calcutta, 1806, through the founding of the three Presidency banks of Bengal, Bombay and Madras and the passing of the co-ordinating legislation in 1876 where volume I ends. The banks were subsequently amalgamated in the Imperial Bank of India in 1921 and reorganized as the State Bank of India in 1955.

Firms: Bank of Calcutta; Imperial Bank of India; State Bank of India

2559

Checkland, Olive; Nishimura, Shizuya; Tamaki, Norio (Editors)

Pacific Banking, 1859-1959: East meets West

1994 St Martin's Press *New York, NY*

This volume explores the implications of colonialism in Pacific banking. It includes, inter-alia, studies of the role of the Yokohama Specie Bank in Japanese imperialism; attempts by Chinese entrepreneurs to break into Pacific banking; and the dominance of the Hongkong and Shanghai Bank in the region.

Firms: Yokohama Specie Bank; Hongkong and Shanghai Bank; Banque de l'Indochine; Bank of Italy; James Finlay & Co.; John Lean & Sons

2560

King, Frank H. H. (Editor)

Eastern Banking: Essays in the history of the Hongkong and Shanghai Banking Corporation

1983 Athlone Press *London*

Scholars from twelve countries have contributed the thirty-three essays in this innovative work in the field of international banking and financial history. While the main focus is on the worldwide activities of the Hongkong Bank from the middle of the nineteenth century to the 1980s, other contributions deal with related banks and with various banking problems in a historical context. This collection of essays reflects a multi-archival approach, including oral history. The book's biggest disadvantage is its size and weight.

Firms: Hang Seng Bank; Hongkong & Shanghai Banking Corporation; Imperial Bank of Persia; Marine Midland Bank; Mercantile Bank; Wells Fargo Bank; British Clearing Banks

2561

King, Frank H. H.

The History of the Hongkong and Shanghai Banking Corporation

1987–91 Cambridge University Press *Cambridge*

This comprehensive four-volume history, based on extensive archival and oral research, provides an unusually complete picture of the activities of a major Eastern exchange bank. It is also essential reading for anyone interested in the developing financial history of the East. The bank was a key player throughout the period, and, in making the transition from a regional to a multinational institution, reflected the increasing significance of the East on the world stage. These four volumes have both breadth and depth. They range from the provision of political finance and the maintenance of a presence through revolutions and rebellions to the decline in the price of silver and the problems faced by the international gold standard; from descriptions of the bank's management structures and the division of power between its Hong Kong and London offices to details of its extensive branch network, its local staff and the lifestyle of its young expatriate bankers.

Firms: British Bank of the Middle East; Hongkong Bank; Hongkong and Shanghai Banking Corporation; Marine Midland Bank; Mercantile Bank; The Hongkong Bank Group

2562

Mackenzie, Compton

Realms of Silver: One hundred years of banking in the East

1954 Routledge & Kegan Paul *London*

This is a history of the Chartered Bank from its foundation in London in 1853 until 1953. It was founded by the man who started *The Economist*. Although a fairly general history, it provides a useful background on one of the most important of the British overseas banks. There are no footnotes, but much of the information can be cross-referred in the Public Record Office.

Firms: Chartered Bank; Chartered Bank of India, Australia and China; P & O Banking Consortium

2563

Sithi-Amnuai, Paul

Finance and Banking in Thailand: A study of the commercial system, 1888–1963

1964 Thai Watana Panich *Thailand*

This is probably still the most comprehensive, if not the only, attempt to analyse and describe the financial structure of Thailand in a historical perspective. It has sections on the general characteristics of the Thai economy,

early finance and banking, the banking system during the Second World War, post-war developments in currency and banking, the commercial banks and the Bank of Thailand, branch banking, commercial banking law, and the modern banking system. The author, at the time of writing, was Vice-President of the Bank of Bangkok, and some of the chapters were written or co-authored by members of his staff.
Firms: Bank of Bangkok; Bank of Thailand

2564
Tripathi, Dwijendra; Misra, Priti
Towards a New Frontier: History of the Bank of Baroda
1985 Manohar Publications *New Delhi, India*
The book traces the genesis and growth of the largest nationalized commercial bank in India. Discussing how a small company originating in a princely state developed into a giant with extensive operations in India and abroad, it provides valuable insights into the transition from a feudal financial structure to modern banking in the country.
Firms: Bank of Baroda

2565
Tyson, Geoffrey
100 Years of Banking in Asia and Africa
1963 National and Grindlays Bank Ltd *London*
This is a history of National and Grindlays Bank from its earliest days in the nineteenth century as the National Bank of India to the merger with Grindlays in 1948 and the acquisition of Lloyds Eastern Branches in 1961. Although this is a sponsored, centenary history, its author has sufficient relevant experience of both Asia and of finance and economics to ensure that it is more than merely an apologia for the bank.
Firms: Cox & Co.; Grindlays; Henry S. King; Lloyds Eastern Branches; National Bank of India; National and Grindlays

Japan

2566
Alletzhauser, Albert J.
The House of Nomura: The inside story of the legendary Japanese financial dynasty
1991 Little, Brown *New York, NY*
The story of how a small Osaka money-changing firm founded in 1872 grew to be a dominant force in world finance. Based on access to Nomura family papers, the book describes how Nomura pioneered retail stockbrokerage in Japan, developed door-to-door selling techniques in the 1950s, and came to benefit from a peculiarly close relationship with top politicians. A valuable study that covers not only the single firm but the 'big four' brokerage houses as a whole.
Firms: Nomura Securities; Daiwa; Nikko; Yamaichi

2567
Aoki, Masahiko; Patrick, Hugh (Editors)
The Japanese Main Bank System: Its relevance for developing and transforming economies
1994 Clarendon Press *Oxford*
A massive collective study of the evolution and operation of the Japanese main bank system. This is a definitive description of the system which traces the system's roots, its heyday in the era of rapid growth, and its responses to deregulation and liberalization.
Firms: Bank of Japan; Japan Development Bank; Mitsui

2568
Asakura, Kokichi (Editor)
Ryo-Taisenkan ni okeru Kin-yu Kozo [Financial Structures Between the Wars]
1980 Ochamonizu Shobo *Tokyo, Japan*
The contributors examine the radical changes in the monetary system and financial structures between the First and Second World Wars, focusing on the behaviour of regional banks. The book explores the *Keiretsu* or special relationship among regional banks and certain Zaibatsu banks, savings banks and trust companies.
Firms: Bank of Japan

2569
Calder, Kent E.
Strategic Capitalism: Private business and public purpose in Japanese industrial finance
1993 Princeton University Press *Princeton, NJ*

A major reinterpretation of Japanese capitalism focusing on the allocation of credit and its relationship to industrial policy. Calder puts state and private banking in the forefront and downplays the role of the state in favour of private sector initiatives.

Firms: Bank of Japan; Dai-Ichi Kangyo Bank; Industrial Bank of Japan; Japan Development Bank; Japan Electronic Computer Corporation (JECC); Mitsubishi; Mitsui Bank; Nippon Steel; Sasebo Heavy Industries; Kawasaki Steel

2570
Imuta, Toshimitsu
Meijiki Kin-yu Kozo Bunseki Josetsu [An Analysis of Financial Structures in the Meiji Era, 1867–1912]
1976 Hosei University Press *Tokyo, Japan*

Seven chapters examine the modern financial system and development of corporations, financial policy as to overseas trade, the monetary policy of the Bank of Japan, loans of national banks and the business activities of Seishu Iwashita and his bank, covering the period 1867 to 1914.

Firms: Kawase Kaisha; First National Bank; Bank of Japan

2571
Imuta, Toshimitsu (Editor)
Senji Taiseika no Kin-yu Kozo [The Financial Structure of Japan on a War-time Footing, 1933–1945]
1991 Nihon Hyoron Sha *Tokyo, Japan*

This book examines the process of creating the Yen currency block and its failures in the Great East Asia Economic Block (Dai Toa Kyoei Ken). It also covers financial institutions under a wartime footing, changes in the roles of special banks and the reorganization of commercial banks under a controlled economy, covering the period 1931–45.

2572
Kato, Toshihiko
Honpo Ginkoshi-ron [Banking History and Theory of Japan]
1957 Tokyo University Press *Tokyo, Japan*

This book examines the monetary system and banking business in the course of the industrialization of Japan. The theory developed by Kato in this book, especially Kikan-ginnkoron or banking status of the private financial institutions of certain firms, has become widely accepted.

Firms: Daiichi Bank; Mitsubishi Bank; Mitsui Bank; Sumitomo Bank; Yasuda Bank

2573
Kato, Toshihiko (Editor)
Nihon Kin-yuron no Shi-teki Kenkyu [Historical Studies in Japanese Monetary Policy and Theory]
1983 Tokyo University Press *Tokyo, Japan*

This book analyses monetary policies and theories relating to Japanese monetary history, covering the period from the Meiji era (1867–1912) to the present. The thirteen chapters examine twelve different financial institutions including agricultural and industrial banks, trust companies, credit co-operatives, commercial and savings banks. It also aims to introduce recent significant books and articles on Japanese monetary history to students in this field.

Firms: Bank of Japan; Hokkaido Colonial Bank; Industrial Bank of Japan; Mutual Finance (Mujin); Deposit Bureau of Ministry of Finance; Yokohama Specie Bank

2574
Kato, Toshihiko; Ouchi, Tsutomu (Editors)
Kokuritsu Ginko no Kenkyu [Studies of National Banks]
1963 Keisho Shobo *Tokyo, Japan*

This volume examines seven national banks in Japan, focusing on the establishment of their business, their shareholders, banking activities shown on their financial statements and relationship to the local industries. One chapter contrasts the Japanese pattern with the national bank system in the USA.

Firms: Fifteenth National Bank; First National

Bank; Fourth National Bank; One Hundred and seventeenth National Bank; Seventy-seventh National Bank; Thirty-seventh National Bank

2575

Kuwahara, Tetsuo

Kigyo Kokusaika no Shiteki Bunseki [Japanese Business Abroad in Historical Perspective: Foreign Direct Investment of Japanese Cotton-Spinning Firms in China before World War I]

1990 Moriyama *Tokyo, Japan*

This book describes an early example of foreign direct investment, the entrepreneurial background to the decision by some firms (and why other firms followed different strategies) and the way Japanese management systems were introduced. The book provides a paradigm for the transplants by Toyota and Nissan in recent years.

Firms: Toyota; Nissan

2576

Kyowa Bank (Editor)

Honpo Chochiku Ginkoshi [History of Savings Banks in Japan]

1969 Kyowa Bank *Tokyo, Japan*

This book describes the history of savings banks from their origins in 1880 up to 1948. It examines the effect of the Savings Bank Act of 1893, policy and control by the government over savings banks' business, management policy, the activities of individual banks and amalgamation movements. The book makes use of the archives of the various banks.

Firms: Daiichi Sogo Savings Bank; Fudo Savings Bank; Naikoku Savings Bank; Nihon Savings Bank; Nihon Sogo Savings Bank; Osaka Savings Bank; Setsu Savings Bank; Tokyo Savings Bank; Yasuda Savings Bank

2577

Pressnell, L. S. (Editor)

Money and Banking in Japan: (By the Bank of Japan Economic Research Department)

1973 St Martin's Press *New York, NY*

Pressnell provides a useful introduction to a major study prepared by the Economic Research Department of the Bank of Japan. The study itself considers the evolution of the modern Japanese financial system, the money supply and flow of funds, and a detailed discussion of eleven types of financial institution, including banks, securities companies and specialist financial institutions. There is extensive statistical information throughout.

Firms: Bank of Japan; Industrial Bank of Japan

2578

Sugiyama, Kazuo

Kaiun Fukko-ki no Shikin Mondai: Josei to Shichu Shikin [Financing of Japanese Shipping in the Reconstruction Period: Grants and the money market]

For main entry, see 3142

2579

Suzuki, Toshio

Japanese Government Loan Issues on the London Capital Market 1780–1913

1994 The Athlone Press *London*

This is a pioneering study of Japanese borrowing in London before the First World War, with useful information on the operations of banks and banking syndicates.

2580

Teranishi, Juro

Nihon no Keizaihatten to Kin-yu [Economic Development and Monetary Policy in Japan]

1982 Iwanami Shoten *Tokyo, Japan*

This study examines the financial mechanisms that encouraged the industrial development of the Japanese economy, covering the period 1874 to 1975. It focuses on money flow and capital accumulation, using econometric tools, i.e. time-series and cross-section analyses for historical analysis.

Firms: Fifteenth National Bank; First National Bank; Fourth National Bank; One Hundred and Seventeenth National Bank; Seventy-seventh National Bank; Thirty-seventh National Bank

2581

Tsutsui, William M.

Banking Policy in Japan: American efforts at reform during the Occupation

1988 Routledge *London*

The Japanese banking system was reshaped under the American Occupation: yet it maintained continuity and avoided attempts at democratization. This book explores why the

Americans were committed to reform and why they failed. The maintenance of the financial status quo was an important element in Japan's subsequent recovery.
Firms: Bank of Japan

2582
Watanabe, Sahei; Kitahara, Michitsura (Editors)
Ginko: Gendai Nihon Sangyo Hattatsusi XXVI [The Bank: A history of modern industrialization in Japan, vol. 26]
1966 Kojunsha Shuppankyoku *Tokyo, Japan*

This examines all banks and banking institutions in Japan in the period from 1867 to the 1960s. It provides fundamental knowledge and historical material for students of Japanese banking history and focuses on the process of industrialization and its financing.
Firms: Bank of Japan; Hypothec Bank

2583
Yamaguchi, Kazuo (Editor)
Nihon Sangyo Kin-yushi Kenkyu [Studies in the History of Industrial Finance in Japan]
1966-74 Tokyo University Press *Tokyo, Japan*

The authors examine the financial management of textile firms and the roles of banks and wholesale merchants in industrial finance during the early industrialization of Japan (Meiji and Taisho era, 1880s to 1910s). Based on primary materials of individual firms and banks, it explores how early entrepreneurs financed their businesses.
Firms: Nineteenth National Bank; Yokohama Specie Bank; Kishiwada Boseki Kaisha; First Bank; Mitsui Biessan

Africa

2584
Amphlett, G. T.
History of the Standard Bank of South Africa Ltd, 1862–1913
1914 Maclehose *Glasgow, Scotland*

This jubilee history is now somewhat dated but it includes valuable statistical series absent from Henry & Siepmann's (qv) centenary history.
Firms: Standard Bank

2585
Crossley, Julian; Blandford, John
The DCO Story: A history of banking in many countries 1925–71
1975 Barclays Bank International *London*

This is a useful survey of the history of DCO since its establishment in 1925 as a result of the amalgamation of the Colonial and Anglo-Egyptian Banks and the National Bank of South Africa, written by a former chief executive and an in-house historian and archivist. It is not footnoted, but it does have some useful appendices on the growth of the balance sheet, the directors and the geographical spread of the branches.
Firms: Anglo-Egyptian Bank; Barclays Bank DCO; Barclays Bank (Dominion, Colonial and Overseas); Barclays Bank (London and International); Barclays Bank International; Barclays Group; Colonial Bank; National Bank of South Africa

2586
Fry, Richard
Bankers in West Africa
1976 Hutchinson Benham *London*

Despite its lack of footnotes and references, this is an authoritative and accurate history of the Bank of British West Africa (later the Bank of West Africa) from its foundation in Liverpool in 1893, as a department of the Elder Dempster shipping line, until its merger with The Standard Bank of Africa in 1965. The bank overcame initial opposition and difficulties to play a prominent part in the economic development of British West Africa.
Firms: Bank of British West Africa; Bank of West Africa; Standard Bank of West Africa; Elder Dempster

2587
Henry, J. A.; Siepmann, H. A.
The First Hundred Years of the Standard Bank
1963 Oxford University Press *London*

This history of the Standard Bank traces its development from its local establishment in Port Elizabeth, South Africa, in the 1850s, through its foundation in London to serve British South Africa as an overseas bank in 1862,

and its diversification into neighbouring territories and East Africa in the late nineteenth and early twentieth centuries. Although not footnoted, this book is firmly based on the bank's archives. Moreoever, it has been checked and edited by a former director of the Bank of England, a fact which lends the chapters on the gold standard crisis and exchange and central banking added interest. Useful appendices, chronologies and maps are included.
Firms: African Banking Corporation; London & South African Bank; Standard Bank; Standard Bank of British South Africa; Standard Bank of South Africa

2588
Jones, Stuart (Editor)
Banking and Business in South Africa
1988 Macmillan *London*

A collection of essays on the history and operation of capitalist enterprise in South Africa, ranging from the foundation of the Eastern Province Bank in the Cape in 1838 to an assessment of the top 100 companies in South Africa in the latter decades of the twentieth century and an analysis of the multinational corporations in the SADCC (Southern African Development Coordination Conference) area.
Firms: Eastern Province Bank; Nedbank; South African Reserve Bank

2589
Kock, G. de
A History of the South African Reserve Bank, 1920–1952
1954 Van Schaik *Pretoria, South Africa*

This is the definitive study, by the son of the pioneer economic historian of South Africa, M. H. de Kock.
Firms: South African Reserve Bank

2590
Mabin, Alan; Conradie, Barbara (Editors)
The Confidence of the Whole Country: Standard Bank reports on economic conditions in Southern Africa 1862–1902
1987 Standard Bank Investment Corp. *Johannesburg, South Africa*

This book uses the rich resource of the bank's official correspondence to illuminate a fascinating period in the economic history of South Africa–a period which included the discovery of diamonds and gold, successive booms and slumps, droughts and plagues of locusts, and which culminated in the upheaval of the Boer War. The letters comment on the history, economy and politics of the country, as well as describing the activities of the bank, the largest financial institution in South Africa during the period, and its decision-making process. They are also a mine of information on such specific topics as legislation, railway extension, climatology, and irrigation. The book is an invaluable primary source.
Firms: Standard Bank of South Africa

2591
Selm, R. van
History of the South African Mutual Life Assurance Society 1845–1945
1946 South African Mutual *Capetown, South Africa*

This history of South Africa's most enduring life assurance firm (Die Oud Mutual) has a valuable statistical appendix.
Firms: South African Mutual Life Assurance Society; Oud Mutual

USA - Banking

2592
Adams, Donald R. Jr
Finance and Enterprise in Early America: A study of Stephen Girard's Bank, 1812–1831
1978 University of Pennsylvania Press *Philadelphia, PA*

One of the leading merchant capitalists of the early USA, Girard took over the Philadelphia office of the first Bank of the United States after Congress voted not to recharter it, and converted it to a private bank. The author presents a detailed picture of the Girard bank's operations over two decades, based on surviving bank records.
Firms: Bank of the United States; Girard Bank

2593
Adams, Eugene H.; Dorsett, Lyle W.; Pulcipher, Robert S.
The Pioneer Western Bank: First of Denver 1860–1980
1984 First Interstate Bank of Denver *Denver, CO*

This book represents a fine example of public corporate history based on internal documents. Together with Noel (qv) it makes a substantial contribution to an understanding of Colorado banking.
Firms: First Interstate Bank of Denver

2594
Bogue, Allan G.
Money at Interest: The farm mortgage on the middle border
1955 Cornell University Press *Ithaca, NY*

The settling of the American west in the nineteenth century created an excess demand for farm mortgage loans in newly settled areas. The author shows how specialized financial intermediaries arose to transfer funds from eastern investors to frontier farmers.

2595
Brandeis, Louis D.
Other People's Money and How the Bankers Use It
1914 Frederick A. Stokes Co. *New York, NY*

A classic expression of the American distrust of large institutions, especially large financial institutions. Brandeis railed against Wall Street's 'financial oligarchs'. Two decades later, in the wake of the Great Depression, his concerns and proposals were embodied in public policy.

2596
Buenger, Walter L.; Pratt, Joseph A.
But Also Good Business: Texas Commerce Banks and the financing of Houston and Texas, 1886–1986
1986 Texas A & M University Press *College Station, TX*

This is a comprehensive history of Texas Commerce Banks with particular attention to the role of real estate lending.

2597
Burr, Anna R.
Portrait of a Banker: James Stillman, 1850–1918
1927 Duffield and Co. *New York, NY*

A biography of the man who, at the turn of the century, transformed New York's National City Bank (today's Citibank) from a small bank serving one entrepreneur's business empire into an innovative powerhouse and, for a time, the world's largest bank.
Firms: Citibank; National City Bank

2598
Carosso, Vincent P.
Investment Banking in America: A history
1970 Harvard University Press *Cambridge, MA*

A study of the evolution of a specialized financial intermediary–the investment banking house–in US history. The primary function of such intermediaries is to raise long-term capital funds for non-financial firms, mostly by underwriting and distributing bond and stock issues. Among other things, Carosso demonstrates that specialized investment banking was as much the product of US regulations that segmented the provider of financial services, as of a Smithian division of labour.

2599
Carosso, Vincent P.
The Morgans: Private international bankers, 1854–1913
1987 Harvard University Press *Cambridge, MA*

Carosso was granted access to the records of the Morgan bank, and as a result he is able to tell more of an inside story than was possible for other writers who previously examined this celebrated firm. The book offers fresh insights into the achievements and the occasional failures of the firm and its dominant personality, J. Pierpont Morgan.
Firms: J. P. Morgan & Co.; Morgan, Stanley & Co.

2600
Chandler, Lester V.
Benjamin Strong: Central banker
For main entry, see 3940

2601

Chernow, Ron

The House of Morgan: An American banking dynasty and the rise of modern finance

1990 Atlantic Monthly Press *New York, NY*

An award-winning study of the Morgan bank, from its 1830s origins as an American merchant bank in London to the 1980s, by which time parts of the old organization had gone their separate ways and had even started to compete with one another.

Firms: J. P. Morgan & Co.; Morgan, Stanley & Co.

2602

Cleveland, Harold van B.; Huertas, Thomas

Citibank, 1812–1970

1985 Harvard University Press *Cambridge, MA*

A scholarly study of the development of one of the USA's leading banks by two 'insiders', officers of the bank. By the early twentieth century, the National City Bank was one of the largest and most innovative banks in the world. Although hampered by tighter US banking regulations dating from the New Deal, the bank built on its innovative tradition, especially in international banking, where it was a US pioneer.

Firms: Citibank; National City Bank

2603

Doti, Lynne Pierson; Schweikart, Larry

Banking in the American West From the Gold Rush to Deregulation: From the Gold Rush to Deregulation

1991 University of Oklahoma Press *Norman, OK*

This is a detailed study ranging from the earliest frontier banks through recession and boom, regulation and opening up of the business to international competition after the 1960s.

2604

Erickson, Erling A.

Banking in Frontier Iowa, 1836–1865

1971 Iowa State University Press *Ames, IA*

Banking was a politically-charged issue in the young United States. Some states, such as Iowa, even went so far as to ban banking corporations from operating within their borders. The author shows how unincorporated banks and corporate banks in other states prevented Iowa from fully experiencing 'the blessed state of banklessness'.

2605

Forbes, Jack Douglas

J. P. Morgan, Jr, 1867–1943

1981 University Press of Virginia *Charlottesville, VA*

A pleasant biography, although at times frustrating–particularly as far as business decisions are concerned–of the younger Morgan, son of the famous John Pierpont Morgan.

Firms: J. P. Morgan & Co.; Morgan, Stanley & Co.

2606

Friedman, Milton; Schwartz, Arma J.

A Monetary History of the United States, 1867–1960

1963 Princeton University Press *Princeton, NJ*

Money is the root of all financial services. This path-breaking work demonstrated what money was, how it behaved, and what were the consequent economic effects for nearly a century.

2607

Goodhart, C. A. E.

The New York Money Market and the Finance of Trade, 1900–1913

1969 Harvard University Press *Cambridge, MA*

This is a study of the workings of the New York money market prior to the advent of the Federal Reserve System. Periods of strain and ease in the money market were caused by fluctuations in the US balance of trade connected with the agricultural cycle. The author shows that the market and the banking system handled seasonal patterns quite well, undercutting the basis of some arguments favouring the establishment of the Federal Reserve System.

2608

Gras, Norman S. B.

The Massachusetts First National Bank of Boston

1937 Harvard University Press *Cambridge, MA*

Gras, a pioneer of business history, here studies the development of one of the United States's oldest banks, founded in 1784. The Bank of Boston, as it is now known, is well into its third century.

Firms: Bank of Boston

2609

Greef, Albert O.

The Commercial Paper House in the United States

1938 Harvard University Press *Cambridge, MA*

Historically, a market in commercial paper, the short-term, unsecured debts of large business firms, was unique to the United States. It was a product of peculiar banking laws that made it difficult for large firms to obtain large loans from US banks. The author studies the development of the financial intermediaries that arose to overcome this drawback of US banking arrangements.

2610

Greenberg, Dolores

Financiers and Railroads, 1869–1889: A study of Morton, Bliss & Company

1980 University of Delaware Press *East Brunswick, NJ*

This important work examines the relationship between private bankers and the promotion, finance and reorganization of railroad companies in late nineteenth-century USA. It draws on the papers of George Bliss but also contains insights into other financiers' activities, such as J. P. Morgan, Jay Gould and the Seligmans.

Firms: Chesapeake & Ohio Railroad; J. P. Morgan & Co.; Morton, Bliss & Co.

2611

Greider, William

Secrets of the Temple: How the Federal Reserve runs the country

1987 Simon & Schuster *New York, NY*

The author, a journalist and something of a 'populist' in the traditions of American politics, surveys twentieth-century US financial services and financial interests. He contends that the system, especially the central bank, is set up to protect financial interests at the expense of the larger public interest. In the process he provides a stimulating account of the financial developments of recent decades.

2612

Haeger, John Denis

The Investment Frontier: New York Businessmen and the Economic Development of the Old Northwest

1981 State University of New York Press *Albany, NY*

This work is a study of the business strategies of Eastern capitalists who transferred capital to the American west before the civil war.

2613

Hammond, Bray

Banks and Politics in America, from the Revolution to the Civil War

1957 Princeton University Press *Princeton, NJ*

Bray's book is a magisterial account of the origins and early development of banking in the USA from the 1780s to the 1860s. The focus is on the politics of banking, especially the politics of central banking as embodied in the first and second Banks of the United States, whose passing from the scene the author, from his pro-central banking perspective, much laments.

Firms: Bank of the United States

2614

Hidy, Muriel E.

George Peabody: Merchant and financier, 1829–1854

For main entry, see 3953

2615

James, F. Cyril

The Growth of Chicago Banks

1938 Harper *New York, NY*

Chicago was a wilderness village in the 1830s and the United States's second largest city and financial centre a century later. James studies the key role of banking in that transformation.

2616

James, John A.

Money and Capital Markets in Postbellum America

1978 Princeton University Press *Princeton, NJ*

A study of the regional and national integration of local money and banking markets in the United States between the 1860s and the 1910s. Financial integration over a large geographical area is difficult to achieve in any case. In the US case, it was made more difficult by laws and regulations that fragmented the financial system. Nonetheless, financial firms and markets in great measure overcame these barriers during the period.

2617

James, Marquis; James, Bessie Rowland

Biography of a Bank: The story of Bank of America N.T. and S.A.

1954 Harper and Brothers *New York, NY*

This is the story of A. P. Giannini and his bank. Giannini founded the Bank of Italy early in the century to serve Italian-American clients in California. Half a century later, when this book was written, the bank had become Bank of America, the (then) largest bank in the world. Giannini was one of the great innovators of modern banking.

Firms: Bank of America

2618

Johnson, Arthur M.; Supple, Barry E.

Boston Capitalists and Western Railroads: A study in the nineteenth century railroad investment process

For main entry, see 3790

2619

Kabisch, Thomas R.

Deutsches Kapital in den USA [German Capital in the USA]

1982 Klett-Cotta *Stuttgart, Germany*

Many German companies established American subsidiaries in the years before 1914. This study examines the reasons for and mechanisms of capital transfer to support this business, and German investment in American companies.

2620

Klebaner, Benjamin J.

American Commercial Banking: A history

1990 Twayne Publishers *Boston, MA*

Although brief and intended primarily for students, this is the most up-to-date survey of the whole history of US commercial banking.

2621

Koskoff, David E.

The Mellons: The chronicle of America's richest family

For main entry, see 3962

2622

Lamoreaux, Naomi

Insider Lending: Banks, personal connections, and economic development in industrial New England, 1789–1912

1994 Cambridge University Press *Cambridge*

Lamoreaux documents a transition in US banking that parallels the move from family firms to managerial capitalism in manufacturing. Early New England banks were the financial arms of the small groups of entrepreneurs who organized them. As the New England economy matured, these small banks became less competitive and were merged into larger units operated by professional bank managers.

2623

Larson, Henrietta M.

Jay Cooke, Private Banker

1936 Harvard University Press *Cambridge, MA*

This is a study of the business career of one of the greatest US financiers. Cooke introduced the mass marketing of securities during the American Civil War. His firm became overextended in US railway finance and went down in flames during the financial crisis of 1873.

2624

Noel, Thomas J.

Growing Through History with Colorado: The Colorado National Banks, the first 125 years 1862–1987

1987 Colorado National Banks and the Colorado Studies Center *Denver, CO*

This is a fine corporate history based on internal documents.
Firms: Colorado National Banks

2625
Payne, Peter Lester; Davis, Edwin Lance
The Savings Bank of Baltimore, 1818–1866: A historical and analytical study
1956 The Johns Hopkins University Press *Baltimore, MD*

This is a model case-study of one of America's largest savings banks from its formation to the Civil War.
Firms: Savings Bank of Baltimore

2626
Perkins, Edwin J.
Financing Anglo-American Trade: The House of Brown, 1800–1880
1975 Harvard University Press *Cambridge, MA*

With branches in England, the Baltimore-based Browns managed to overtake and surpass the Barings in Anglo-American trade financing during the period of this study.
Firms: Brown

2627
Redlich, Fritz
The Molding of American Banking - Men and Ideas
1968 Johnson Reprint Corporation *New York, NY*

An encyclopedic study of virtually all aspects of US banking development from 1781 to 1910. The author read and digested every piece of banking literature on which he could lay his hands, which makes the book valuable as a reference work. But he slights quantitative measures of banking development. The two parts, covering 1781–1840 and 1840–1910, were published separately in 1947 and 1951. The reprint edition adds a long introduction surveying work on the subject from 1950 to 1968.

2628
Reich, Cary
Financier: The Biography of André Meyer: A story of money, power and the reshaping of American business
For main entry, see 3977

2629
Rockoff, Hugh
The Free Banking Era: A re-examination
1978 Arno Press *New York, NY*

The free banking movement, a liberalization of bank chartering, swept through the United States in the 1840s and 1850s. Older, orthodox financial writers identified it with reckless, wild-cat banking. In this analytical study, Rockoff demonstrates that free banking worked rather well, with losses to bank creditors that were quite small.

2630
Schweikart, Larry
Banking in the American South from the Age of Jackson to Reconstruction
1987 Louisiana State University Press *Baton Rouge, LA*

The antebellum South experienced some of the best, and some of the worst, banking in the early United States. Schweikart associates good banking with minimal government involvement and bad banking with too much such involvement. But the stage of development also mattered: the good banking was in the older states while bad banking was experienced in the newer, frontier states.

2631
Sobel, Robert
The Life and Times of Dillon Read
1991 Penguin Books *Harmondsworth*

This is a history of one of the oldest investment banking houses on Wall Street from 1832 to the present day. Strong on leading personalities like Clarence Dillon, on Dillon Read's role as the premier financier of Weimar Germany and on the nature of 'relationship banking' in one of the more traditionalist Wall Street firms.
Firms: Dillon Read; Kidder Peabody; Lehmann Bros; Lee Higginson; Morgan Stanley; Vereinigte Stahlwereke

2632
Supple, Barry E.
A Business Elite: German Jewish financiers in nineteenth century New York
For main entry, see 3805

2633
Sylla, Richard
The American Capital Market, 1846–1914: A study of the effects of public policy on economic development
1975 Arno Press *New York, NY*

Sylla's book is a study of how the federal government's banking reforms of the civil war era (1861–65) inadvertently retarded the growth of banking in agricultural and newly settled regions while at the same time concentrated financial capital in money centres, particularly New York City.

2634
Trescott, Paul B.
Financing American Enterprise: The story of commercial banking
1963 Harper & Row *New York, NY*

This book is a survey of the history of American banking from the perspective of banks' contributions to capital formation and economic development, rather than from the more usual concern with the relationship of banks to the monetary system.

2635
West, Robert Craig
Banking Reform and the Federal Reserve, 1863–1923
1977 Cornell University Press *Ithaca, NY*

This is a study of the financial reform ideas and movements that flourished in the United States in the late nineteenth and early twentieth centuries. The long debate finally resulted in a central banking system in 1914.

2636
White, Eugene N.
The Regulation and Reform of the American Banking System, 1900–1929
1983 Princeton University Press *Princeton, NJ*

White views US banking reforms of the early twentieth century, including the Federal Reserve System, as ill-conceived. Instead of changing the rules to allow more branch banking as in other countries, the United States preserved its system of thousands of independent 'unit' banks and attempted to shore up that system's weakness with new institutions, e.g. the Fed and deposit insurance.

2637
Wilkins, Mira
The History of Foreign Investment in the United States to 1914
1989 Harvard University Press *Cambridge, MA*

This is a detailed study of how the American economy, its industries, and even particular firms raised capital from overseas as the United States grew from a small agricultural economy to an industrial colossus in little more than a century. A second volume on post-1914 developments is in preparation.

USA - Insurance, Stock Market, etc.

2638
Anders, George
Merchants of Debt: KKR and the mortgaging of American business
1992 Jonathan Cape *London*

This is the best of the journalistic accounts of the 1980s Wall Street merger boom, chronicling the rise of Kohlberg, Kravis, Roberts & Co., the most successful leveraged buy-out company.
Firms: Kohlberg, Kravis, Roberts & Co.; RJR Nabisco; Safeway; Duracell; Motel 6

2639
Bernstein, Peter L.
Capital Ideas: The improbable origins of modern Wall Street
1992 The Free Press *New York, NY*

An intellectual history of the development of modern finance theory and the impact that it has had on American and world investment markets. When money is involved, as the author shows, academic ideas can rather quickly be translated into real-world financial practice.

2640
Broehl, Wayne G. Jr
Cargill: Trading the World's Grain
For main entry, see 3934

2641
Brunson, B. R.
The Texas Land Development Company
1970 University of Texas *Austin, TX*
This is a study of a Texas land development company from its inception in 1912 to the mid-1950s. The focus is on financial issues and problems.
Firms: Empire Trust; Old Colony Trust; Prairie Lands Trust; Stalked Plains Trust; Texas Land Development Co.

2642
Buley, R. Carlyle
The Equitable Life Assurance Society of the United States, 1859–1964
1967 Appleton-Century-Crofts *New York, NY*
A business history of one of the leading insurance companies in the United States.
Firms: Equitable Life Assurance Society

2643
Burk, James
Values in the Market Place: The stock market under Federal Securities law
1988 Walter de Gruyter *Berlin, Germany*
1988 Walter de Gruyter *New York, NY, USA*
The New Deal securities laws, by creating a level playing field for investors and improving the flow of financial information, greatly enhanced the viability and importance of the stock market in American economic life. The author argues that the laws did not go far enough, and so further problems arose in the 1960s, 1970s, and 1980s that only recently have been straightened out, to some extent.

2644
Burrough, Brian; Helyar, John
Barbarians at the Gate: The fall of RJR Nabisco
1990 Jonathan Cape *London*
A journalistic tour-de-force that reads like a thriller, but which provides a mass of first-hand testimony on the behind-the-scenes turmoil involved in the largest takeover in Wall Street history. While it has to be used with considerable caution, it provides an unprecedentedly detailed look at how giant leveraged buyouts were conducted.
Firms: Kohlberg, Kravis, Roberts & Co.; Nabisco; RJR Nabisco; Reynolds, RJ, Tobacco Co.

2645
Burton, H.; Corner, D. C.
Investment and Unit Trusts in Britain and America
For main entry, see 2314

2646
Cowing, Cedric B.
Populist, Plungers, and Progressives: A social history of stock and commodity speculation, 1890–1936
1965 Princeton University Press *Princeton, NJ*
A study of the tensions that were created in the United States as the nation's financial development outpaced even its rapid economic development. Farmers, for example, found it difficult to understand how financiers could buy and sell several times the amount of grain they grew each year.

2647
Eichler, Ned
The Thrift Debacle
1989 University of California Press *Berkeley, CA*
This book is a good analysis of the origins and course of the crisis in the United States savings and loans industry from the 1890s to 1987. Eichler concludes that the 1980s crisis was 'the greatest financial regulatory fiasco in American history'.

2648
Grant, James
Money of the Mind: Borrowing and lending in America from the Civil War to Michael Milken
1992 Farrar Strauss Giroux *New York, NY*
Credit is money of the mind, according to the author, a Wall Street professional. In his iconoclastic view, credit has become too easy to get during most of the twentieth century. The demonstration of credit and the socialization of risk have caused financial irresponsibility and dis-

aster. It's a Jeremiad, but the author gives good support to his case.

2649

Keller, Morton

The Life Insurance Enterprise, 1885–1910: A study in the limits of corporate power

1963 Harvard University Press *Cambridge, MA*

Life insurance companies were among the most important financial intermediaries in the USA around the turn of the century. The author studies how they used and abused the funds entrusted to them, and how they were reined in by laws and regulations.

2650

Klein, Maury

The Life and Legend of Jay Gould

For main entry, see 2871

2651

Krooss, Herman E.; Blyn, Martin

A History of Financial Intermediaries

1971 Random House *New York, NY*

A study of the many types of financial institutions that developed in US history. The complexity of financial intermediaries is partly the result of the complexity of the American economy. But it is also the result of laws and regulations that consciously fragmented financial services.

2652

Michie, Ranald C.

The London and New York Stock Exchanges 1850–1914

For main entry, see 2332

2653

Myers, Margaret G.

The New York Money Market: Origins and development

1931 Columbia University Press *New York, NY*

Despite its age, Myers's study remains the fullest historical account of how New York became America's and the world's leading financial centre. The short-term credit needs of New York's securities markets played a large role. Meeting that credit demand enabled New York's banks to attract the reserve funds of banks throughout the United States.

2654

Rapone, Anita

The Guardian Life Insurance Company, 1860–1920: A history of a German-American enterprise

1987 New York University Press *New York, NY*

This is the first book in a proposed two volume history of the company established by German immigrants in New York City, which at first concentrated on the insurance needs of ethnic Germans until this strategy failed during the First World War. Although based on company records,the book's focus remains relatively narrow.

Firms: Guardian Life Insurance

2655

Rappaport, A.

Creating Shareholder Value: A new standard for business performance

For main entry, see 3623

2656

Seligman, Joel

The Transformation of Wall Street: The history of Securities and Exchange Commission and modern corporate finance

1982 Houghton Mifflin *Boston, MA*

A history of the New Deal agency that 'cleaned up' Wall Street and did much to promote the great breadth and depth of US capital markets.

2657

Sobel, Robert

The Big Board: A history of the New York Stock Market

1965 The Free Press *New York, NY*

Although now dated and rather more anecdotal than analytical, this remains a good survey of the history of an institution that played a large role in the development of the US economy. From the early days of the country, the stock market has reflected the achievements and failures as well as the aspirations and fears of American business. Sobel captures its spirit.

2658
Sobel, Robert
Dangerous Dreamers: The financial innovators from Charles Merrill to Michael Milken
1993 John Wiley & Sons *New York, NY*

This is a fascinating account of financial innovators on Wall Street in the twentieth century and the narrow road they trod between financial innovation and criminality. Generally sympathetic to the financiers, but intelligible to non-specialists and throwing much light on the junk bond boom and the Savings & Loans debacle.

2659
Stillman, Richard J.
Dow Jones Industrial Average: History and role in an investment strategy
For main entry, see 1788

2660
Werner, Walter; Smith, Steven T.
Wall Street
1991 Columbia University Press *New York, NY*

The bulk of this study deals with the early decades of the Wall Street capital markets, 1790–1840. The authors argue, however, that the functional roles of the markets that developed in those early years persisted down to the present day.

2661
White, Lawrence J.
The S&L Debacle: Public policy lessons for bank and thrift regulation
1991 Oxford University Press *New York, NY*

A balanced and historical account of how America's savings and loan associations and other depository institutions failed in large numbers during the 1980s, at considerable expense to investors and taxpayers. White presents a case study of how questionable financial regulation can interact with questionable macroeconomic policies to produce financial disaster.

2662
Zartman, Lester
Investments of Life Insurance Companies
1906 Henry Holt *New York, NY*

Insurance companies were the most important non-bank financial intermediaries in the United States at the turn of the twentieth century. The author studies how they invested their huge assets in this era, before their latitude for investing was reduced by stringent regulation.

Canada

2663
Darroch, James
Canadian Banks and Global Competitiveness
1994 McGill-Queen's University Press *Montreal, Canada*

This is an original analysis of Canada's four largest chartered banks: the Royal Bank, the Canadian Imperial Bank of Commerce, the Bank of Nova Scotia, and the Bank of Montreal. Presenting case studies on each bank from their founding to the present, the author explores the long-term impact of corporate strategies and public policy on this regulated industry.
Firms: Royal Bank; Canadian Imperial Bank of Commerce; Bank of Nova Scotia; Bank of Montreal

2664
Denison, Merrill
Canada's First Bank: A history of the Bank of Montreal
1966–7 McClelland & Stewart *Toronto, Canada*

This is a commissioned history of Canada's first commercial bank which was founded in 1817. Based upon bank records but lacking footnote or endnote attribution, this study is of limited use to the historian.
Firms: Bank of Montreal

2665
Jamieson, A. B.
Chartered Banking in Canada
1953 Ryerson Press *Toronto, Canada*

Almost one-half of this book is devoted to a history of Canada's largest banks–the so-called 'chartered' banks in Canada–which were given special legislative powers under successive 'Bank Act' legislation.

2666
McDowall, Duncan
Quick to the Frontier: Canada's Royal Bank
1993 McClelland & Stewart *Toronto, Canada*

This history of Canada's largest bank begins with its establishment as the Merchants Bank of Halifax and ends with the bank's contemporary international strategy. The author carefully documents the bank's expansion from eastern Canada into central and western Canada, as well as the Caribbean, Latin America and the United States, making it the largest bank in the country by the 1920s.

Firms: Royal Bank

2667
Neufeld, E. P.
The Financial System of Canada: Its growth and development
1972 Macmillan of Canada *Toronto, Canada*

This is a broad survey of the evolution of Canadian financial institutions based upon both primary and secondary sources. Banks and insurance companies form an important part of the study.

2668
Ross, Victor; Trigge, A. St. L.
A History of the Canadian Bank of Commerce
1920–34 Oxford University Press *Toronto, Canada*

This three-volume book is a scholarly history of the Bank of Commerce including the banks which it absorbed over a century. Based upon primary sources, this study provides a valuable wealth of detail on the bank's evolution and bank practices more generally.

Firms: Canadian Bank of Commerce

2669
Rudin, Ronald
Banking en français: The French Banks of Québec, 1835–1925
1985 University of Toronto Press *Toronto, Canada*

From the Banque de Peuple to the Banque Nationale, French-Canadian commercial banks offered a vigorous alternative to the large Anglo-Scottish Canadian banks for the French-speaking investors, managers, and entrepreneurs of Quebec who preferred to do business in their native language.

Firms: Banque de Peuple; Banque Nationale

2670
Rudin, Ronald
In Whose Interest: Quebec's Caisses Populaires
1990 McGill-Queen's University Press *Montreal, Canada*

An historical survey of Quebec's credit unions, an institution which supplanted the commercial banks as the single largest recipient of the savings of both working and middle class francophones in the province. This study is useful as both a political history and a business history of a movement which produced significant change in saving and borrowing practices among ordinary Quebecers in the twentieth century.

2671
Schull, Joseph
100 Years of Banking in Canada: A history of the Toronto-Dominion Bank
1958 Copp Clark *Toronto, Canada*

This is a history of the Bank of Toronto and the Dominion Bank which were amalgamated into the Toronto-Dominion Bank in 1954, one of the big five chartered banks in Canada. Although based on bank records, this study lacks endnotes and of all the business histories of Canada's largest banks, is the least helpful to the professional historian.

Firms: Bank of Toronto; Dominion Bank; Toronto-Dominion Bank

2672
Schull, Joseph
The Century of the Sun: The first hundred years of Sun Life Assurance Company of Canada
1971 Macmillan of Canada *Toronto, Canada*

This is a commissioned history of the Sun Life Assurance Company of Canada published on the centenary of the firm's establishment. Although lacking endnotes, the history is based almost entirely upon primary sources and remains the only business history of a Canadian

insurance company and is valuable for this reason alone.
Firms: Sun Life Assurance Co. of Canada

2673
Schull, Joseph; Gibson, J. Douglas
The Scotiabank Story: A history of the Bank of Nova Scotia, 1832–1982
1982 Macmillan of Canada *Toronto, Canada*
This, a scholarly study of the Bank of Nova Scotia, begins with the bank's establishment in Halifax in 1832 and its development into one of Canada's largest commercial banks eventually headquartered in Toronto.
Firms: Bank of Nova Scotia

Latin America

2674
Bett, Virgil M.
Central Banking in Mexico: Monetary policies and financial crises, 1864–1940
Michigan Business Studies, vol. 13, no. 1, 1957
A pioneering study of abiding value.

2675
Buzzetti, José L.
Historia economica y financiera del Uruguay [An Economic and Financial History of Uruguay]
1969 *Montevideo Uruguay*
A single volume account of banking and finance in one of the more sophisticated of the smaller republics.

2676
Cardoso de Mello, Zélia Maria
Metamorfoses de riqueze: São Paulo [Changes in Wealth: São Paulo]
1990 Editora Hucitec *São Paulo, Brazil*
Using inventories, wills and other legal documents, this book charts changing patterns of investment in the dynamic coffee region of Brazil during the second half of the nineteenth century. Cardoso de Mello shows how planter (*fazendeiros*) portfolios shifted gradually from an overwhelming concentration in agriculture (land and slaves) to substantial holdings in railway and utility companies, banking and finance, and manufacturing. The work makes a substantial contribution to the study of entrepreneurial history by providing short biographies of key businessmen.

2677
Drake, Paul
The Money Doctor in the Andes: The Kemmerer missions, 1923–33
1989 Duke University Press *Durham, NC*
This is a superb study of the banking, monetary, and fiscal reforms resulting from missions by Princeton economics professor Edwin Kemmerer to Colombia, Chile, Ecuador, Bolivia, Peru, Mexico, and Guatemala between 1923 and 1931. Drake's book is essential to any understanding of the transition from British to United Sates economic and ideological hegemony in Latin America.

2678
Joslin, David
A Century of Banking in Latin America: Bank of London and South America Limited 1862–1962
1963 Oxford University Press *London*
Background chapters on the general economic and financial history of Latin America are interwoven with an archivally-based though unreferenced, account of the several Anglo-South American banks eventually absorbed into the Lloyds group.
Firms: Anglo South American Bank; Bank of London and South America; Bank of Tarapac and London; Brazilian and Portuguese Bank; London Bank of Mexico and South America; London and Brazilian Bank; London and River Plate Bank

2679
Lough, William H.
Banking Opportunities in South America
1915 US Department of Commerce
Washington, WA
An extremely useful account of prevailing business practice addressed, like several other United States official publications of this period, to North American bankers who might be induced to challenge the position of the British in Latin America.

2680
Ludlow, Leonor; Marichal, Carlos (Editors)
Banca y poder en Mexico (1800–1925) [Bank and Power in Mexico 1800–1925]
1985 Editorial Grijalbo *Mexico City, Mexico*

A very good collection of essays describing the development of banking throughout the country.

Firms: Banco Nacional de México

2681
Marchant, Anyda
Viscount Maua and the Empire of Brazil: A biography of Irineu Evangelista de Sousa (1813–1889)
1965 University of California Press *Berkeley, CA*

This is a thoughtful biography of Irineu Evangelista de Sousa, who drew both on Saint Simon and his practical experience as confidential clerk to an English merchant in order to develop a spectacular though ill-fated banking and business empire extending from Brazil to the River Plate.

Firms: Banco Mau ; Compania Pastoril, Agrícola e Industrial; London, Brazilian and Mau Bank; Mau , MacGregor & Co.

2682
Marichal, Carlos
A Century of Debt Crises in Latin America: From independence to the Great Depression
1989 Princeton University Press *Princeton, NJ*

This is the best summary of the repeated cycles of enthusiasm for Latin American investment and subsequent disillusion in European capital markets during the century following independence.

2683
McCaleb, Walter F.
Present and Past Banking in Mexico
1920 Harper *New York, NY*

This is a classic study, which is still of value.

2684
Platt, D. C. M. (Editor)
Business Imperialism, 1840–1930: An inquiry based on British experience in Latin America
1977 Clarendon Press *Oxford*

This book covers several sectors, but does include chapters by Charles Jones on commercial banks and mortgage companies and on fire insurance.

Firms: London and Brazilian Bank; London and River Plate Bank

2685
Quintero Ramas, Angel M.
A History of Money and Banking in Argentina
1965 University of Puerto Rico *Rio Piedras, Puerto Rico*

This book is a sturdy and reliable account of money and banking in Argentina from independence, institutional rather than economic in emphasis.

2686
Quiroz, Alfonso W.
Banqueros en conflicto: estructura financiera y economia peruana, 1884–1930 [Bankers in conflict: Financial institutions and the Peruvian economy 1884–1930]
1989 Universidad del Pacifico *Lima, Peru*

An archivally-based study, of particular value for its treatment of the Bank of Peru and London, an institution over which control moved from foreign to local hands during the period of study.

Firms: Bank of Peru and London

2687
Rippy, J. Fred
British Investments in Latin America, 1822–1949: A case study in the operation of private enterprise in retarded regions
1959 University of Minnesota Press *Minneapolis, MN*

Rippy surveys all sectors, and does offer some figures for amounts invested in commercial banking and the returns on this investment, but his statistical methods are not entirely satisfactory.

2688
Subercaseaux, Guillermo
Monetary and Banking Policy of Chile
1922 Carnegie Endowment *Oxford*

This work is a rather descriptive account of public policy by a former finance minister.

Australasia

2689
Appleyard, R. T.; Schedvin, C. B. (Editors)
Australian Financiers: Biographical essays
1988 Macmillan Australia *South Melbourne, Australia*

This collection contains nineteen chapters dealing with individual financiers or clusters of financiers over the period 1788–1988. It is comprehensive and unique in its coverage of different kinds of finance and banking and also shows many personal links between the financial and other sectors of the Australian economy.

2690
Bailey, J. D.
A Hundred Years of Pastoral Banking: A history of the Australian Mercantile, Land and Finance Company 1863–1963
1966 Clarendon Press *Oxford*

London-based company involved in Australian finance, which initially focused on land but soon specialized in advances to wool growers. In due course the company became owner of many wool stations, and then diversified into meat and the Argentine. Excellent company history based on extensive research in rich company archives.
Firms: Gibbs Ronald & Co.; Australian Mercantile, Land and Finance Co.

2691
Beever, E. A.
Launceston Bank for Savings, 1835–1970: A history of Australia's oldest savings bank
1972 Melbourne University Press *Melbourne, Australia*

A commissioned but full and critical company history, this book is highly commendable for placing the developments of the Launceston Bank for Savings in the context of the history of the city and northern Tasmania. Since the Launceston bank is one of only two privately-owned banks of this kind, this study is more important than the size of the bank would suggest.
Firms: Launceston Bank for Savings

2692
Blainey, G. N.; Hutton, G.
Gold and Paper: A history of the National Bank of Australasia Limited
1983 Macmillan *Melbourne, Australia*

This is the first of the excellent range of Australian banking histories, first published in 1958 and revised and updated by Hutton. Although commissioned and conservative it is not uncritical. The style is narrative rather than quantitative and financially analytical and sets the bank's history against the backdrop of Australia's general history.
Firms: Ballarat Banking Co.; Colonial Bank of Australasia; National Bank of Australasia; Queensland National Bank

2693
Broeze, Frank
Mr Brooks and the Australian Trade: Imperial business in the 19th century
For main entry, see 4000

2694
Burns, P.
Fatal Success: A history of the New Zealand Company
1989 Heinemann Reed *Auckland, New Zealand*

A history of the land company, formed in 1839, which played an important role in early New Zealand colonization and developed Edward Gibbon Wakefield's theories of settlement. This intelligent and wide-ranging study also details previous settlement attempts and the demise of the company in 1850.
Firms: New Zealand Company

2695
Butlin, S. J.
Australia and New Zealand Bank: The Bank of Australasia and the Union Bank of Australia Limited 1828–1951
1961 Longmans *London*

This is probably still the best of the many Australian bank histories, written by the country's foremost financial historian of his generation. The Bank of Australasia was the first 'imperial' bank, with headquarters in London and operations abroad. The account focuses on the operations of the two constituent

banks of the ANZ Bank (the merger occurred in 1951) in Australia and New Zealand within the context of their economic development. Both before and after 1951 there were several other mergers.
Firms: Australia and New Zealand Bank (ANZ); Bank of Australasia; Bank of New Zealand; Colonial Bank of New Zealand; National Bank of New Zealand; Oriental Bank; Union Bank of Australia

2696
Chappell, N. M.
New Zealand Banker's Hundred: A history of the Bank of New Zealand, 1861–1961
1961 Bank of New Zealand *Wellington, New Zealand*

A worthwhile but rather descriptive history of the leading New Zealand bank, established by a group of Auckland entrepreneurs in reaction to the proliferation of Australian and British banks.
Firms: ANZ (Australia and New Zealand Bank); Bank of Australasia; Bank of New South Wales; Bank of New Zealand; Oriental Bank; Union Bank of Australia

2697
Cooch, A.
The State Savings Bank of Victoria: Its place in the history of Victoria
1934 Macmillan *Melbourne, Australia*

This now dated history of the government-owned Savings Bank of Victoria covers the period 1842–1934 and was written by its then General Manager. It gives a succinct overview of the development of the bank and its operations, especially in housing, but is uncritical and lacking in detail.
Firms: Savings Bank of Victoria

2698
Diamond, Marion
The Seahorse and the Wanderer: Ben Boyd in Australia
1988 Melbourne University Press *Carlton, Victoria, Australia*

This is an excellent account of a flamboyant entrepreneur who was active in many fields in the 1840s. Boyd was highly controversial in using the funds of his own Royal Bank of Australia to finance his manifold operations in coastal steam shipping, agriculture, whaling and trade. The study is based on the bank's archives.
Firms: Royal Bank of Australia

2699
Gollan, R.
The Commonwealth Bank of Australia: Origins and early history
1968 Australian National University Press *Canberra, Australia*

This is a revisionist history of the CBA during the period 1911–24 in the context of contemporary political and economic conditions and debates. It also provides a discussion of the genesis of the bank out of the great depression of the 1890s. Less attention is given to the actual operations and performance of the bank itself. Intended as the country's central bank, the CBA later was transformed into a government-owned trading bank when its original functions were taken over by the Reserve Bank of Australia.
Firms: Commonwealth Bank of Australia; Reserve Bank of Australia

2700
Hawke, G. R.
Between Government and Banks: A history of the Reserve Bank of New Zealand
1973 A. R. Shearer (for NZ Government) *Wellington, New Zealand*

Hawke looks at the background to the establishment of a central banking authority in New Zealand in 1934 and its subsequent operation. This is a policy-oriented study rather than an analysis of the bank's organizational structure.
Firms: BNZ (Bank of New Zealand); Bank of Australasia; Development Finance Corporation [in N.Z.]; RBNZ (Reserve Bank of New Zealand); Union Bank

2701
Holder, R. F.
Bank of New South Wales: A history
1970 Angus & Robertson *Sydney, Australia*

This is a commissioned but not uncritical company history of Australia's oldest bank. It is informative and useful in placing the bank in the context of Australia's economic develop-

ment and also pays attention to political elements. Holder is very clear on financial matters but also interested in the influence of individual leaders.
Firms: Bank of New South Wales; Western Australian Bank

2702
Irving, J. C.
A Century's Challenge: Wright, Stephenson & Co. Limited, 1861–1961
1961 Wright, Stephenson & Co. *Wellington, New Zealand*

This is a rather pedestrian study of a leading New Zealand stock and station agent which is now part of the Fletcher Challenge group.
Firms: Abraham & Williams; Fletcher Challenge Group; H. Matson & Co.; Wright Stephenson

2703
Maclean, F. J.
River of Experience: The story of a New Zealand accounting firm
1980 Wilkinson Wilberfoss *Dunedin, New Zealand*

Maclean traces the path of acquisition and merger, dating back to the 1880s, which led to the establishment of the large accounting firm, Wilkinson Wilberfoss, in 1976. The book is mostly descriptive in nature.
Firms: Wilberfoss & Co.; Wilkinson Wilberfoss; Wilkinson, Nankervis & Stewart

2704
Merrett, D.
ANZ Bank: A History of the Australia and New Zealand Banking Group
1985 Allen & Unwin *Sydney, Australia*

Merrett's book is an official yet not uncritical history of the ANZ Banking group since the merger of the Bank of Australasia and the Union Bank of Australia (1951). A period of rapid change and several more mergers, including the takeover of Grindlays Bank, followed. The bank relocated its headquarters to Melbourne and moved into many new financial services, including hire purchase and development finance. This is an excellent study with the emphasis on bank–government relations.
Firms: ANZ (Australia and New Zealand Bank); BNSW (Bank of New South Wales); BNZ (Bank of New Zealand); Bank of Australasia; English, Scottish and Australian Bank; Grindlays Bank; National Bank of Australasia; Union Bank of Australia

2705
Moore, B.
A Superior Kind of Savings Bank: Perth Building Society 1862–1987
1989 Challenge Bank/Centre for Western *Perth, Australia*

This is a commissioned yet critical study based on extensive archival material. It is unique in its focus on a building society and set in the context of the fluctuating fortunes of the Western Australian economy. The book is also important for the description of the history of housing and, more recently, the deregulation of the Australian financial system, as the PBS transformed itself into the Challenge Bank with a far greater range of operations.
Firms: Challenge Bank; Perth Building Society

2706
Parry, G.
NMA: The story of the first hundred years of the National Mortgage Agency Company of New Zealand Ltd, 1864–1964
1964 The National Mortgage and Agency Co. *Dunedin, New Zealand*

N.M.A. was one of New Zealand's leading stock and station agents. This study analyses the firm's role in financing and advising immigrant smallholders, and includes its response to rural depression between the wars.
Firms: Albion Shipping Co.; H. Matson & Co.; NMA (National Mortgage Agency Co. of New Zealand); New Zealand Shipping Co.; Russell, Le Gren & Co.; Russell, Ritchie & Co.

2707
Parry, G.
Underwriting Adventure: A centennial history of the National Insurance Company of New Zealand Limited
1973 National Insurance Co. of New Zealand *Dunedin, New Zealand*

This book presents a history of National Insurance, from its establishment in Dunedin in 1873 in response to domination of foreign or

North Island insurance companies. The author carefully analyses rapid overseas expansion.
Firms: National Insurance Co. of New Zealand; National Mortgage Association; New Zealand Insurance; Russell, Le Gren & Co.; Standard Insurance Co.; Williams & Kettle

2708
Schedvin, C. B.
In Reserve: Central banking in Australia, 1945–75
1992 Allen & Unwin *Sydney, Australia*

Australia's leading financial historian presents an authoritative and comprehensive history of the country's central banking. The narrative starts in 1945 when the Commonwealth Bank Act gave this function to the Commonwealth Bank; in the reorganization of 1959 the new Reserve Bank of Australia was created to continue the central bank function and the Commonwealth Bank Corporation became a government-owned trading bank. This is a strongly-written and well-defined picture of Australia's central bank during the transition from Keynesianism to monetarism and the first traces of more flexible policies and deregulation. Monetary and banking policies are set in full ideological and political context and deal specifically with the interaction of institutions, markets, politics and individuals.
Firms: Commonwealth Banking Corporation; Reserve Bank of Australia

2709
Sinclair, K.; Mandle, W. F.
Open Account: A history of the Bank of New South Wales in New Zealand 1861–1961
1961 Whitcombe & Combs *Wellington, New Zealand*

This informative commissioned history of the New Zealand branch of Australia's oldest bank makes extensive use of archival material but does not present a detailed financial analysis. It is strong on its discussion of debates between the bank's leaders on strategic or policy matters and its economic performance. Altogether, this is a pioneering work which matches the scholarship of the Australian banking histories.
Firms: Australia and New Zealand Bank (ANZ); Bank of New South Wales; Bank of New Zealand; Colonial Bank; National Bank of New Zealand; Oriental Bank

2710
Spillman, K.
Horizons: A history of the Rural and Industries Bank of Western Australia
1989 University of Western Australia Press *Nedlands, Australia*

The bank of the title was state-owned until 1944 and solely dedicated to the development and diversification of Western Australia's economy. It was later transformed into a general banking institution, albeit with the continued emphasis on rural operations, and maintained a close relationship with the Western Australian government. This book is an excellent example of modern corporate history.
Firms: Rural and Industries Bank of Western Australia

2711
Vennell, C. W.
Risks and Rewards: A Policy of Enterprise, 1872–1972: A centennial history of the South British Insurance Company Ltd
1972 Wilson and Horton for the Company *Auckland, New Zealand*

Like New Zealand Insurance and National Insurance, this company was formed as part of a drive to keep the insurance of New Zealand property in the country. The study traces the South British Insurance Company's successful growth to a national and international firm.
Firms: New Zealand Insurance Co. Ltd; New Zealand Shipping Co. Ltd; South British Insurance Co. Ltd; Union Steam Ship Co. Ltd

Utilities, Transport & other Services

Utilities

2712

Armstrong, Christopher; Nelles, Henry V.
Monopoly's Moment: The organisation and regulation of Canadian utilities, 1830–1930
1986 Temple University Press *Philadelphia, PA*

This is not really a business history but rather an analysis of the evolution of the publicly owned utility sector in Canada and the reasons for and nature of regulation of these monopolies. It is wide in its coverage of utilities, extensively referenced and strong on the technology, economics and regulatory framework. As such it is indispensable for an understanding of these utility businesses.
Firms: Bell Telephone (Canada); Consumers' Gas Co. Toronto; Montreal City Passenger Railway Co.; Toronto Hydro Electric Co.

Electricity, Europe

2713

Beltrain, Alain; Picard, J. F.; Bungener, M.
Histoire d'E.D.F: Comment se sont prises les décisions de 1946 à nos jours [The History of E.D.F: How decisions were taken from 1946 to our times]
1985 Dunod Bordas *Paris, France*

The authors study the National Electric Enterprise (Électricité de France) which was created in France after the Second World War by the nationalization of private electricity companies.
Firms: Électricité de France

2714

Byatt, Ian C. R.
The British Electrical Industry, 1875–1914: The economic returns to a new technology
1979 Oxford University Press *Oxford*

Based on a doctoral thesis, this book provides a detailed insight into the performance and development of British electricity undertakings and their main suppliers (British and foreign). Statistical backing is given on both the industry and the main companies, making it essential reading.
Firms: British Westinghouse; British Thomson-Houston; Brush Electrical Engineering Co.; Ferranti Ltd; GEC; London Electricity Supply Co.; Dick, Kerr & Co.

2715

Caron, François; Cardot, Fabienne (Editors)
Histoire de l'Électricité en France: Tome premier: Espoirs et conquêtes 1881–1918 [History of Electricity in France: Vol. 1: Hopes and conquests 1881–1918]
1991 Fayard *Paris, France*

This is a huge multi-authored, lavishly illustrated volume, which is intended to be the first in a series of books on the history of electricity in France. It draws on a range of scholarly authors, is fully referenced and authoritative. It deals with technological developments, distribution and marketing, the role of hydroelectric, and the adoption of electricity in modes of transport.
Firms: Électricité de France

2716

Fischer, E. J.
Stroom Opwaarts: De electriciteitsvoorziening in Overijssel en Zuid-Drenthe tussen circa 1895 en 1986 [Running Current: Electricity supply in Overijssel and South Drenthe between circa 1895 and 1986]
1986 Electriciteits Maatschappij Yssel Centrale *Zwolle, The Netherlands*

This is a lavishly produced history of seventy-five years of electricity production in the northeastern Netherlands by the Ysselcentrale. It is based mainly on the company's annual reports. The book focuses on the

economics of demand for and supply of electricity.
Firms: Twentsch Centraal-Station; Ysselcentrale

2717
Frost, Robert L.
Alternating Currents: Nationalised power in France, 1946–1970
1991 Cornell University Press *Ithaca, NY*

This book is a comprehensive history of the first twenty-five years of the nationalized electricity generating firm, Électricité de France, using a Marxist framework to show the shift to technical corporatism. It is based on solid documentary evidence and is determinedly sociological.
Firms: Électricité de France

2718
Giannetti, Renato
La conquista della forza: Risorse, tecnologia ed economica nell'industria elettrica italiana, 1883–1940 [The Conquest of Power: Resources, technology and economy in the Italian electrical industry 1883–1940]
1985 Franco Angeli *Milan, Italy*

This book provides the history of the Italian electric sector, with a special focus on technical innovation, the firm's specialization in hydroelectric power-plants and the emergence of regional electric systems.
Firms: Società Idrolettrica Piemontese; Società Edison; Società Adriatica de Elettricità; Società Meridionale di Elettricità

2719
Hannah, Leslie
Electricity Before Nationalisation: A study of the development of the electricity supply industry in Britain to 1948
1979 Macmillan *London*

This commissioned volume traces the history of British electricity supply from the numerous small local firms and municipal enterprises of the late nineteenth century, to the formation of the Central Electricity Board in 1926, and its work down to full nationalization. It is lucidly written and strong on government–industry relations, but rather thin on the market and demand.
Firms: Central Electricity Board; Central Electricity Generating Board; British Electricity Authority; NESCO (North Eastern Electricity Supply Co.)

2720
Hannah, Leslie
Engineers, Managers and Politicians: The first fifteen years of nationalised electricity supply in Britain
1982 Macmillan *London*

This is a commissioned history of the period 1947–1962 when investment in electricity supply in Britain took eight per cent of GDP. It is particularly strong on decision making and business strategy, the changes in fuel sources and the relations with government.
Firms: Central Electricity Board; Central Electricity Generating Board

2721
Hawkley, L. J.
The Story of the Jersey Electricity Company Ltd
1983 Jersey Electricity Company *Jersey, Channel Islands*

This is a sponsored history written by an employee to celebrate half a century of this firm which was established in 1924 to provide St Helier with electric power. It is strong on the technical aspects and their changes but concentrates on personalities rather than management structure and finance. It draws on the extensive archive of the firm.
Firms: Jersey Electricity Co.

2722
Hughes, Thomas P.
Networks of Power: Electrification in western society, 1880–1930
1983 Johns Hopkins University Press *Baltimore, MD*

This is Hughes's magnum opus on the technical, social and economic history of the electric utility industry in its formative decades. Although not a comprehensive history of western electrification, the author makes very detailed comparisons of several systems in the US, Britain and Germany. This rates as the premier work in the field.
Firms: General Electric Co.; Westinghouse

Electric Co.; Thompson-Houston Electric Co.; Commonwealth Edison Co.; Allgemeine Elektrizitäts-Gesellschaft (AEG); Berliner Elektrizitätswerke; North Eastern Electric Supply Co.; Pacific Gas & Electric Co.; Pennsylvania Power & Light Co.; Rheinsh - Westfälisches Elektrizitätswerke

2723
Johannessen, Finn Erhard
I støtet: Oslo Energi gjennom 100 år 1892–1992 [In Power: 100 years of Oslo Energi, 1892–1992]
1992 Ad Notam Gyldendal *Oslo, Norway*

This is the history of the first hundred years of electricity in Oslo. Starting with a coal-fired central station in 1892, hydro-electricity played a dominant role by the turn of the century. The use of gas, kerosene and coal gradually decreased and the gasworks was finally closed in 1978. The book pays considerable attention to the electrification of the town, with its street lights, its industry and particularly its use in the home.
Firms: Oslo Energi A/S

2724
Kuisel, Richard F.
Ernest Mercier, French Technocrat
1967 University of California Press *Berkeley, CA*

This is more a business biography than a business history, of an engineer in the electrical power industry in France in the twentieth century. The book is good in explaining the secret of his success and his organizational abilities and also charts his forays into politics.

2725
Luckin, Bill
Questions of Power: Electricity and environment in inter-war Britain
1990 Manchester University Press *Manchester*

This book features a detailed description of the struggle between those advocating an all-electric Britain (the 'Triumphalists') and conservationists who opposed the construction of the National Grid between 1927 and 1934. There are interesting sections on the Electrical Development Association and the Electrical Association for Women.
Firms: Central Electricity Board

2726
Millard, Andre J.
A Technological Lag: Diffusion of electrical technology in England, 1879–1914
1987 Garland *London*

This is a reprint of a 1981 PhD thesis. Millard focuses on institutional and engineering barriers to technical development in the early electricity supply industry. He stresses that contemporary ideas of lag were much exaggerated and that, after a slow start, the British industry recovered strength before 1914.

2727
Myllyntaus, Timo
Electrifying Finland: The transfer of a new technology into a late industrialising economy
1991 Macmillan Academic and Professional *London*

This comprehensive account of the electrification of Finland covers the period 1877–1977, from the importation of the earliest steam-driven dynamo to the commissioning of the first nuclear power-plant. The book also examines the transfer of electrical technology in a comparative cross-national perspective, while highlighting some of the main trends in the rapid economic transformation of the country.
Firms: AEG; ASEA; Brown Boveri; Imatran Voima Oy; Siemens; Teollisuuden Voima Oy; Westinghouse

2728
Pantelakis, Nikos
O Exelectrismos tis Helladas: Apo ten idiotiki protovoulia sto kratiko monopolio 1889–1956 [The Electrification of Greece: From private initiative to state monopoly 1889–1956]
1991 MIET *Athens, Greece*

This concise yet detailed study traces the introduction and development of electrical energy in Greece by distinguishing three periods: (i) 1889–1922, when energy production and distribution belonged to private firms struggling to conquer the Greek market; (ii) 1922–40, a period marked by the fast growth of small local production units; and (iii) after the Second World War, when the production and distribution of electricity was nationalized. The work is based on extensive archival research.

2729
Payne, Peter L.
The Hydro: A study of the development of the major hydro-electric schemes undertaken by the North of Scotland Hydro-Electric Board
1988 Aberdeen University Press *Aberdeen, Scotland*

This book is a commissioned history of the Hydro-Electric Board of Scotland from 1943 to 1975 concentrating on the political and technical problems of construction and the effects this had on capital costs. It is not primarily a business history, but rather the story of technical difficulties overcome in a harsh climate and geography, and the impact of large civil engineering projects. It is based on the Board's voluminous archives and well illustrated.
Firms: North of Scotland Hydro-Electric Board

2730
Sapelli, G.; Carnevali, F.
Uno sviloppo fra politica e strategia: ENI (1953–1985) [Development Between Politics and Strategy: ENI (1953–1985)]
1992 Franco Angeli *Milan, Italy*

A careful analysis made here of the connections between governmental political pressures and managerial strategies describes the history of Italy's state owned energy holding company. The growth of the structure of the holding company has been studied in the light of the Italian government's desire to rescue failing firms and the management's attempts to integrate different sectors in a way coherent to the original mission of the holding company.
Firms: Energy National of Italy (ENI)

2731
Self, Sir Henry; Watson, Elizabeth M.
Electricity Supply in Great Britain: Its development and organisation
1952 George Allen & Unwin *London*

A brief but authoritative coverage of the rise of the electricity supply industry from the 1880s until the Second World War. Still a basic work.

2732
Toninelli, P. A.
La Edison: Contabilità e bilanci di una grande impresa elettrica (1884–1916) [Edison: The accounts and the balance sheets of a large electricity company (1884–1916)]
1990 Il Mulino–ASSI *Bologna, Italy*

This is an unusual study of a firm's history through the analysis of its accounts and balance sheets. A rigorous work, it describes the beginnings of this Italian electrical company in 1884 up to 1916, when there was a change in the management, placing special emphasis on the investments which followed the decision to expand through the construction of large hydroelectric plants and the acquisition of other companies and the impact this strategy had on the financial structure of the firm.
Firms: Edison Electric

2733
Williams, Roger
The Nuclear Power Decisions: British policies, 1953–1978
For main entry, see 397

2734
Wilson, J. F.
Ferranti and the British Electrical Industry, 1864–1930
1988 Manchester University Press *Manchester*

Based on extensive research in the personal and company archive, this book describes the fascinating career of Ferranti and its impact on the electricity supply and electrical engineering industries. The aim is to examine the main constraints which prevented the full implementation of his expansive schemes, looking at political, economic and personal aspects of the story.
Firms: Ferranti; J. & P. Coats; Vickers; British Insulated Wire Co.

Electricity, North America

2735
Adams, John A.
Damming the Colorado: The rise of the Lower Colorado River Authority 1933–39

1990 Texas A & M University Press *College Station, TX*

This is a history of the political and economic events that led to the establishment of the LCRA to dam the river for flood control and to produce and transmit electricity under the New Deal. It is not really business history but is good on the construction and effects of the scheme on Central Texas.

Firms: Lower Colorado River Authority

2736

Biggar, E. B.

Hydro-Electric Development in Ontario: A history of water-power administration under the Hydro-Electric Power Commission of Ontario

1920 Biggar Press *Toronto, Canada*

Although a very early example of institutional history and arguing the case for public ownership of utility companies, this book still has some value as a source for business historians. It narrates the growth of hydro-electric technology and the organizational forms evolved to administer it in Ontario.

Firms: Hydro-Electric Power Commission of Ontario

2737

Bothwell, Robert

Nucleus: The history of Atomic Energy of Canada Ltd

1988 University of Toronto Press *Toronto, Canada*

This is a history of Atomic Energy of Canada Ltd, the government-owned corporation at the centre of development of Canada's nuclear industry from the Second World War to the present. Special emphasis is given to the use of nuclear energy as a power resource and, more generally, to the changing attitudes of Canadians to the uses of nuclear energy.

Firms: Atomic Energy of Canada

2738

Dales, John H.

Hydro Electricity and Industrial Development, Quebec 1898–1940

1957 Harvard University Press *Cambridge, MA*

This volume traces the growth of hydro-electric production in central Canada and the impact this had on local industrial development. It is well referenced and draws on the records of many power companies. It is good on the technological developments, and the linkages with certain power-using industries but is not really a business history and says little about the organizational, financial and other business aspects.

Firms: Gatineau Power Co.; Montreal Light Heat & Power Co.; Shawnigan Water & Power Co.; Southern Canada Power Co.

2739

Fleming, Keith R.

Power at Cost: Ontario Hydro and rural electrification, 1911–1958

1992 McGill-Queen's University Press *Montreal, Canada*

The volume mainly discusses how electric power was brought to rural farms and hamlets by the Hydro-Electric Power Corporation of Ontario. In so doing Fleming covers aspects of marketing policy, business strategy, entrepreneurship, accountability and pricing. The work is thorough and well organized.

Firms: Hydro-Electric Power Corp. of Ontario

2740

Friedel, Robert D.; Israel, Paul; Finn, Bernard S.

Edison's Electric Light: Biography of an innovation

For main entry, see 1546

2741

Hirsh, Richard F.

Technology and Transformation in the American Electric Utility Industry

1989 Cambridge University Press *Cambridge*

This book focuses on technological and economic stagnation in the US electric utility industry in the 1960s and 1970s. Much of the blame is placed on complacent management, which was content to extrapolate historical trends rather than to anticipate the future.

Firms: American Electric Power Co.; Babcock and Wilcox Co.; Commonwealth Edison Co.; Consolidated Edison Co. of NY; Duke Power Co.; Electric Bond & Share Co.; General

Electric Co.; Middle West Utilities Co.; Pacific Gas & Electric Co.; Tennessee Valley Authority

2742
Hughes, Thomas P.
Networks of Power: Electrification in western society, 1880–1930
For main entry, see 2722

2743
McDonald, Forrest
Insull
1962 University of Chicago Press *Chicago, IL*

This volume contains a detailed biography of Samuel Insull and the electric utility empire he created. It goes a long way toward redressing the reputation of Insull as an evil and corrupt utility magnate. It is highly readable.
Firms: Chicago Edison Co.; Commonwealth Edison Co.; Middle West Utilities Co.

2744
Miller, Raymond C.
The Force of Energy: A business history of the Detroit Edison Company
1971 Michigan State University Press
E. Lansing, MI

This is a commissioned but independent history written by a historian drawing on company documents and interviews and is fully referenced. It tells the story of the firm from about 1900, and is good on the technical side, marketing of electricity, the personalities involved and financial data.
Firms: Detroit Edison Co.

2745
Nelles, Henry V.
The Politics of Development: Forests, mines and hydro-electric power in Ontario, 1849–1941
1974 Macmillan Company of Canada
Toronto, Canada

Nelles examines the role and involvement of the state in the development and regulation of natural resources in Ontario from 1849 to 1941, with particular emphasis on hydro-electric power. This work is a path-breaking study of staple production, resource development, and business–state relations in Canada.
Firms: Ontario Hydro-Electric Power Commission

2746
Platt, Harold L.
The Electric City: Energy and the growth of the Chicago area 1880–1930
1991 University of Chicago Press *Chicago, IL*

This book traces the history of the growth of electric supply in Chicago from many competing companies to a monopoly, which move was largely engineered by Samuel Insull. It is good on the marketing methods used to achieve mass consumption and rates and rate structure but thin on organizational structure and financing methods.

2747
Wollner, Craig
Electrifying Eden: Portland General Electric 1889–1965
1990 Oregon Historical Society Press
Portland, OR

This is a solid commissioned company history detailing problems with the electric railway division, ultimately sold, and the financial catastrophe narrowly escaped as a result of speculative frenzy in the early 1930s. Wollner is less successful with social issues and wider challenges to utilities. These may be tackled in the prospective successor volume.
Firms: Portland General Electric; Central Public Service Corporation of Chicago; Bonneville Power Administration

Electricity, Rest of World

2748
Armstrong, Christopher; Nelles, H. V.
Southern Exposure: Canadian promoters in Latin America and the Caribbean, 1896–1930
1988 University of Toronto Press *Toronto, Canada*

This volume analyses the activities of Canadian promoters and financiers who established operations in Latin America and the Caribbean in utilities in the early years of the twentieth century. Individuals such as William Van

Horne, Max Aitken, William McKenzie and James Dunn are dealt with.
Firms: Brazilian Traction; Demerara Electric; Jamaica Electrical Light; Mexican Light and Power; Porto Rico Railways; Trinidad Electric

2749
Christie, Renfrew
Electricity, Industry and Class in South Africa
1984 Macmillan *London*

This volume traces the growth of concentration in power supply in South Africa from numerous municipal and private companies to a state-controlled monopoly. It is more a study of energy politics and is thin on internal developments within the industry and the sources of capital.
Firms: Electric Supply Commission; Victoria Falls & Transvaal Power Co.

2750
Chugoku Denryoku
Chugoku Chiho Denki Jigyo-shi [History of Electric Utilities in Chugoku District]
1974 Chugoku Denryoku *Hiroshima, Japan*

Compiled to mark 20 years of the Chugoku Electric Power Co. Ltd, the heart of this book consists of a history of electric utilities in the Chugoku district during the period 1893–1951.
Firms: Chugoku Denryoku (Chogoku Electric Power Co.); Hiroshima Denki (Hiroshima Electric Enterprise Co.); Izumo Denki (Izumo Electric Enterprise Co.)

2751
Dias, R. F. (Editor)
Panorama do setor de energia eletrica no Brasil [The Electric Power Industry in Brazil]
1988 Centro da Memoria da Eletricidade no Brasil *Rio de Janeiro, Brazil*

This commissioned history celebrates the 100th anniversary (1889–1989) of electricity generation in Brazil and the 25th anniversary (1962–1987) of the establishment of the Centrais Eletricas Brasileiras S.A.–Eletrobras company.
Firms: Centrais Eletricas Brasileiras; Eletrobras

2752
Hendrickson, Kenneth E.
The Waters of Brazos: A history of the Brazos River Authority 1929–1979
For main entry, see 2775

2753
Japan Electric Generating and; Transmission Co. (Nippon Hassoden)
Nippon Hassoden Shashi [A History of Japan Electric Generating and Transmission Co.]
1954 Nippon Hassoden *Tokyo, Japan*

This is a history of Japan Electric Generating and Transmission Co. Ltd (Nippon Hassoden) as a state-controlled company from 1939 to 1951. It emphasizes the consolidation of the main power companies and the establishment of nine regionally integrated companies. The three volumes cover history, technology and operations.
Firms: Japan Electric Generating and Transmission Co.

2754
Kansai Electric Power Co. (Kansai Denryoku)
Kansai Chiho Denki Jigyo Hyakunen-shi [Centenary History of Electric Utilities in Kansai District]
1987 Kansai Denryoku *Osaka, Japan*

This is a comprehensive history of electric utilities in the Kansai district where many firms are established. It is a very reliable work, based on business history methodology.
Firms: Daido Electric Power Co. (Daido Denryoku); Kansai Electric Power Co. (Kansai Denryoku); Nippon Electric Power Co. (Nippon Denryoku); Ujigawa Electric Enterprise Co. (Ujigawa Denki)

2755
Kurihara, Toyo
Denry oku: Gendai Nippon Sangyo Hattatsu-shi; Dai 3-kan [Electric Utilities: History of their development in modern Japanese industry; Vol. 3]
1964 Kojun-sha *Tokyo, Japan*

This is a valuable work giving a complete history of Japanese electrical utilities. With a great number of statistics and illustrations, detailed chronological tables, and annotated bibliographies, this is an indispensable book for the study of Japanese electric utilities.

2756
McDowall, Duncan
The Light: Brazilian Traction, Light and Power Company Limited, 1899–1945
1988 University of Toronto Press *Toronto, Canada*

This is the history of a Canadian-organized business, established in 1899, which provided São Paulo and Rio de Janeiro with electric light, power, street railways, and telephones and owned hydro-electric plants. It was acquired by the Brazilian government in 1979. It is strong on business strategy and politics, and the technical and financial problems.
Firms: Brascan; Brazilian Traction Light & Power Co.

2757
Minami, Ryoshin
Power Revolution in the Industrialization of Japan, 1885–1940
1987 Kinokuniya *Tokyo, Japan*

An intensely detailed analysis of the impact of electrification on the pattern of Japanese industrialization, looking at the impact on economies of scale, concentration and technical change.

2758
Newfarmer, Richard S.
Transnational Conglomerates and the Economics of Dependent Development: A case study of the international electrical oligopoly and Brazil's electrical industry
For main entry, see 1532

2759
Pedraja, René de la
Historia de la Energía en Colombia 1537–1930 [The History of Energy in Colombia 1537–1930]
1985 El Ancora *Bogotá , Colombia*

This volume traces the history of Colombia's energy supply particularly during the 1890–1930 period, with a short background on its evolution during the colonial period and the past century. The focus is on a brief overview of the early stages of electricity companies in several regions of the country, pointing out the three different 'models' that came into existence. A chapter on the expansion of coal and another on oil are also worth looking at. The book pioneered the use of electricity company sources.

2760
Tokyo Electric Light Co. (Tokyo Dento)
Tokyo Dento Kabushiki Kaisha Kaigyo 50 nen-shi [Fiftieth Anniversary of the Tokyo Electric Light Co. Ltd]
1936 Tokyo Dento *Tokyo, Japan*

Published to celebrate the 50th anniversary of Tokyo Electric Light Co. (Tokyo Dento) this book describes in detail the process of merger and acquisition of smaller electric light firms in the Kanto district.
Firms: Tokyo Dento; Tokyo Electric Light Co.

2761
Tokyo Electric Power Co. (Tokyo Denryoku)
Tokyo Denryoku 30 nen-shi [Thirty Years of Tokyo Electric Power Co. Ltd]
1983 Tokyo Denryoku *Tokyo, Japan*

This is a business history of Tokyo Electric Power Co. (Tokyo Denryoku), from 1951 to 1981, set in the context of Japanese economic growth and technological innovation.
Firms: Tokyo Electric Power Co. (Tokyo Denryoku)

2762
Trédé, Monique (Editor)
Électricité et Électrification dans le Monde [Electricity and Electrification in the World 1880–1980]
1991 Presses Universitaires de France *Paris, France*

This volume contains over forty essays on the history of electricity and electrification in more than a dozen countries by leading scholars in the field. It originated as a set of conference papers presented in July 1990 and covers a wide range of technical, economic and business areas.

Gas

2763
Beltrain, Alain; Williot, Jean-Pierre
Le Noir et le Bleu: 40 Ans d'Histoire de Gaz de France [The Black and the Blue: Forty years of Gaz de France]
1992 Belfond *Paris, France*

This book starts with the nationalization of the run-down French gas industry in 1946 and the political and competitive pressures of the time. It deals with the transition from coal feedstocks to natural gas and the place of France in world energy markets, importing gas and selling expertise. It relies largely on oral sources. Nevertheless, this is one of the very few scholarly books on the gas industry.
Firms: Gaz de France

2764
Berlanstein, Leonard R.
Big Business and Industrial Conflict: A social history of the Parisian Gas Company
1991 University of California Press *Berkeley, CA*

This wide-ranging volume contains a brief business history of the Parisian Gas Company but concentrates on the firm's impact on labour, management and class division and conflict. Hence it is more a work on class and labour history, but is of some value to the business historian.
Firms: Parisian Gas Company

2765
Castaneda, Christopher James
Regulated Enterprise: Natural gas pipelines and northeastern markets, 1938–1954
1993 Ohio State University Press *Columbus, OH*

This book covers the early years of federal regulation of the interstate gas pipeline industry, showing how the regulatory process fostered growth and promoted intense competition among entrepreneurs to win government authorizations to transmit southwestern-produced natural gas to the major metropolitan areas of the northeast.
Firms: Brooklyn Union Gas Co.; Eastern Gas and Fuel Associates; Northeastern Gas Transmission Co.; Tennessee Gas Transmission Co.; Texas Eastern Transmission Co.

2766
Everard, Stirling
The History of the Gas Light and Coke Company 1812–1949
1949 Ernest Benn *London*

Although rather dated, and hence thin on the concerns of modern business historians, this book remains one of the few full length histories of a gas concern. Falkus (qv) continues the story beyond 1949. This volume is strong on narrative and the leading personalities and the various amalgamations.
Firms: British Gas; Gas Light & Coke Co.; North Thames Gas

2767
Falkus, Malcolm
Always Under Pressure: A history of North Thames Gas
1988 Macmillan *London*

This is a commissioned history of the nationalized firm, North Thames Gas, from 1949 to 1986 when it was privatized. It continues the work of Everard (qv) as the Gas Light & Coke Co. was the largest component of North Thames. It is strong on technology and relations with government, and is a first class study.
Firms: British Gas; Gas Light & Coke Co.; North Thames Gas

2768
Herranen, Timo
Kaasulaitostoimintaa Helsingissä 1860–1985 [The Helsinki Gasworks, 1860–1985]
1985 Energy Utility of Helsinki *Helsinki, Finland*

The book is a history of the biggest of the three urban gasworks in Finland. It deals with the adoption of gas technology, the setting up of industrial and urban works and the municipalization of the private gasworks at the turn of the century. Furthermore, the expansion and operation of the distribution network and the changes in technology and consumption patterns are also studied.
Firms: Kaasulaitostoimintaa Helsingissä

2769

Hutchison, Sir Kenneth

High Speed Gas: An autobiography

1987 Duckworth *London*

A useful autobiographical account of the transformation of the postwar British gas industry from a coal-based industry to natural gas, by a former Deputy Chairman of the Gas Council (retired 1966). Especially good on research and development.

Firms: British Gas

2770

Tokyo Gas Co.

Tokyo Gas Hyakunen-shi [100 Years of Tokyo Gas Co.]

1986 Tokyo Gas Co. *Tokyo, Japan*

This centenary history of Tokyo Gas Co. 1885–1985, concentrates mainly on the post-Second World War period. For a study of the management of prewar days, see *50 Years of Tokyo Gas Co.* (Tokyo, 1935) or *70 Years of Tokyo Gas Co.* (Tokyo, 1956).

Firms: Tokyo Gas

2771

Vietor, Richard H. K.

Contrived Competition: Regulation and deregulation in America

For main entry, see 4406

2772

Williams, Trevor I.

A History of the British Gas Industry

1981 Oxford University Press *Oxford*

This volume is a good general guide to the history of the industry as a whole rather than a specific business history. It covers the prehistory through to the 1970s and is strong on the technical, organizational and labour relations aspects, as well as industry–government relationships. It deals with the customer relations and marketing side but is thin on the financial aspects.

Firms: British Gas; Gas Light and Coke Co.; South Metropolitan Gas Co.

2773

Wilson, John T.

Lighting the Town: A study of management in the north west gas industry 1805–1880

1991 Paul Chapman *London*

This book traces the history of the more than one hundred gas production and supply companies active in north-west England before the advent of competition from electricity. The book is good on entrepreneurs, sources of capital, customers, management organization, pricing and financial strategies. It does not always contextualize the region and could explore managerial policies to a greater extent.

Water

2774

Barty-King, Hugh

Water: The book

1992 Quiller Press *London*

This book was commissioned by the (British) Water Services Association, and provides an attractive narrative of the emergence of the modern water industry. It is well supported by lavish visual materials. Although historical developments in water are outlined from the fifteenth century, emphasis is upon technical developments in the last 100 years, and upon the achievements of water undertakings in the post-privatization period. The detailed narrative does not allow space for a more critical evaluation of the industry's performance, or of the wider economic, social and environmental implications of its development.

Firms: Anglian Water; Dior Cymru Water; North West Water; Northumbrian Water; Severn Trent Water; South West Water; Southern Water; Thames Water; Wessex Water; Yorkshire Water

2775

Hendrickson, Kenneth E.

The Waters of Brazos: A history of the Brazos River Authority 1929–1979

1981 Brazos River Authority *Waco, TX*

This book is a commissioned history by a professional historian of a public authority established to dam the Brazos to aid flood control, produce electricity and retail water. It is well-researched and particularly strong on the

politics of dam construction and opposition to it, but rather weak on contextualization.
Firms: Brazos River Authority

2776
Nippon Suido Kyokai
Nippon Suido-shi [Japanese Water Service History]
1967 Nippon Suido Kyokai *Tokyo, Japan*

A complete history of the Japanese water industry is given from 1887. The spread of water services, changes in waterworks and equipment, history and management of water service in specific places, are all described in 5 volumes.

2777
Pisani, Donald J.
From the Family Farm to Agribusiness: The irrigation crusade in California and the West, 1850–1931
For main entry, see 223

2778
Rennison, Robert W.
Water to Tyneside: A history of the Newcastle and Gateshead Water Company
1978 Newcastle & Gateshead Water Co. *Newcastle*

This book is a rare example of a history of an independent water supply company which was established in 1845 and was still surviving in 1978. It is strong on technical change and the diplomacy required in dealing with the local community to raise finance and avoid municipalization.
Firms: Newcastle & Gateshead Water Co.

2779
Rudden, Bernard
The New River: A legal history
1985 Clarendon Press *Oxford*

This does not claim to be a business history, despite the importance of the company in water supply and land holdings in north London over three centuries. Rather it is concerned with the complex legal situation of the company and the precedents it set. It does, however, in passing, shed some light on the business aspects of this early and convoluted firm.
Firms: New River Co.

Transport

2780
Bonavia, Michael R.
The Nationalisation of British Transport: The early history of the British Transport Commission, 1948–53
1987 Macmillan *London*

This thin volume is more an institutional history than a true business history but it is important as it details the one attempt to integrate all modes of transport in Britain. It is particularly good on internal structure and relations between government and business. It is based on the extensive official records of government and the BTC, and written by someone involved at the time.
Firms: British Railways; British Road Services; British Transport Commission; London Transport

2781
Glazebrook, George P. de T.
A History of Transportation in Canada: Vol. I: Continental Strategy to 1867; Vol II: National Economy, 1867–1936
1938/64 McClelland & Stewart *Toronto, Canada*

This is the pre-eminent general survey of Canadian inland transport. The first volume deals with the continent before Confederation in 1867, describing various methods of transport and the conditions determining their use. The second volume (1867–1936) examines rail, water and air transport with much emphasis on the railways. It is not really a business history per se but deals with many firms in the transport business.
Firms: Canadian National Railways; Canadian Pacific Railway; St Lawrence Seaway

2782
Lepetit, B.
Chemins de Terre et Voies d'Eau: Réseaux de Transport et Organisation de l'Espace en France 1740–1840 [Roads and Inland Waterways: Transport systems and spatial organization in France 1740–1840]
1984 École des Hautes Études en Sciences Sociales *Paris, France*

This is an important and pioneering work which draws on a wealth of scattered sources to reassess the evolution of the road network and the role of rivers and canals. Lepetit's methodology is original and scientific and his conclusions iconoclastic.

2783
Platt, D. C. M. (Editor)
Business Imperialism 1840–1930: An inquiry based on British experience in Latin America
For main entry, see 2144

2784
Tominaga, Yuji
Kotsu ni okeru Shihonshugi no Hatten: Ninon Kotsu-gyo no Kindaika Katei [The Penetration of Capitalism into the Japanese Transport Sector: A process of modernisation]
For main entry, see 2941

Railways, UK

2785
Bagwell, Philip S.
The Railway Clearing House in the British Economy 1842–1922
1968 Allen & Unwin *London*

This is the standard work on the Railway Clearing House, established by the mainline British railway companies to apportion receipts from through tickets, pools and conferences and to settle inter-company disputes. It is meticulously researched and based on primary sources, and covers well the internal organization in addition to the wider impact on the economy.

2786
Behrend, George
Pullman in Europe
1962 Ian Allen *London*

This volume tells the story of the Pullman car in Europe from 1874 to the 1950s. It concentrates on the British services and is good on the cars, the operational details, the services and the entrepreneurs and is well-illustrated. Although full of factual material, it is thin on the business aspects and rather unanalytical.

Firms: Cie Internationale des Wagons-Lits; Pullman Car Co.

2787
Bonavia, Michael R.
The Four Great Railways
1980 David & Charles *Newton Abbot*

This volume looks at the four British railway companies which emerged after rationalization from 1923 down to their nationalization in 1948 on a thematic basis. It has useful chapters on each company, the technology, degree of competition between railway companies and their response to road transport, safety and operations, and the personalities involved.

Firms: Great Western Railway; Southern Railway; London & North Eastern Railway; London Midland & Scottish Railway

2788
Bonavia, Michael R.
Railway Policy Between the Wars
1981 Manchester University Press *Manchester*

This book is based on oral history: interviews carried out by the author with former railway company managers on the policies pursued by the four regional groupings between the wars. It is good on investment and commercial policy and brings out the diversity among the firms. There may be a bias among those interviewed to defend the actions and policies of their own companies.

Firms: Great Western Railway; London & North Eastern Railway; London Midland & Scottish Railway; London Transport; Southern Railway

2789
Bonavia, Michael R.
A History of the LNER
1982–3 Allen & Unwin *London*

Although primarily aimed at the enthusiast market, this study contains interesting insights for the academic. It is lavishly illustrated but lacks footnotes or even a bibliography. It is strong on managerial style and structure, shows the problems of a slow shift to standardize practices, and the reasons for poor financial performance. Personally involved in nationalization, the author is less objective on the causes and consequences of this policy.

Firms: London & North Eastern Railway

2790
Bonavia, Michael R.
The History of the Southern Railway
1987 Unwin Hyman *London*

This book gives a very competent history of the regional grouping which emerged in 1921 down to its nationalization in 1947. It is good on the costs, benefits and technology of electrification and also covers well the non-railway activities such as road, sea and air services. It bridges the gap between enthusiast and academic history but is thin on management style and structure and a touch eulogistic.
Firms: British Railways; Southern Railway

2791
Boyd, James I. C.
The Wrexham, Mold & Connah's Quay Railway
1991 Oakwood Press *Oxford*

This well-illustrated book tells the story of the railway from its inception in 1861 to its absorption by the Great Central in 1905. The approach is determinedly chronological providing much detail on this small railway business, but the larger picture and important themes are often lost in the detail.
Firms: Wrexham, Mold & Connah's Quay Railway; Great Central Railway

2792
Broadbridge, Seymour R.
Studies in Railway Expansion and the Capital Market in England, 1825–1873
1970 Frank Cass *London*

This book is a financial analysis of the Lancashire and Yorkshire Railway Company, examining the traffic and capital statistics, the profits and dividend policy and the sources of capital. It is based on the author's thesis, is fully referenced, thorough and scholarly.
Firms: Lancashire & Yorkshire Railway

2793
Carlson, R. E.
The Liverpool and Manchester Railway Project 1821–31
1969 David & Charles *Newton Abbot*

This is an in-depth study of the legal and political problems encountered in establishing a railway requiring joint stock limited liability and the need to compel land sales. It is less strong on the construction stage and financing and needs to be complemented by Donaghy (qv) on operations and finances.
Firms: Liverpool & Manchester Railway

2794
Cookridge, E. H.
Orient Express: The life and times of the world's most famous train
1980 Penguin *Harmondsworth*

This is a popular history of the promotion, financing, construction and operations of the Orient Express using external sources rather than company archives. Sadly there are no footnotes and the book is anecdotal and unanalytical but it is useful, given the absence of a scholarly history.
Firms: Orient Express

2795
Donaghy, Thomas J.
Liverpool and Manchester Railway Operations 1831–1845
1972 David & Charles *Newton Abbot*

Although it has useful material on the parliamentary and organizational events leading up to the Act, its main strength lies in the finances of the company and its operational details as a pioneer of railway transport. It is good on labour recruitment and motivation, pricing, safety aspects, and the returns to investors.
Firms: Grand Junction Railway; Liverpool & Manchester Railway; London & North Western Railway

2796
Gourvish, Terry R.
Mark Huish and the London & North Western Railway: A study of management
1972 Leicester University Press *Leicester*

This book provides an excellent study of the problems of managing railways in Britain in the nineteenth century by examining Huish's career from the 1830s to 1860s. It is strong on management policy and railway politics, the organizational structure of the firm and the

impact of competition. It is based on a broad range of archival sources.
Firms: Grand Junction Railway; London & North Western Railway

2797
Gourvish, Terry R.
British Railways 1948–73: A business history
1986 Cambridge University Press *Cambridge*

This is a substantial commissioned history of the first quarter century of the nationalized railway industry in Great Britain. Its strengths are its depth of analysis, its holistic coverage of business practices and the relationship between business and government. It is based on the archives of the industry and of the government and written by a leading transport and business historian.
Firms: British Railways Board; British Transport Commission

2798
Hawke, Gary R.
Railways and Economic Growth in England and Wales 1840–1870
1970 Clarendon Press *Oxford*

This is not a business history but a pioneering attempt to apply cliometric techniques, as formulated by Fogel in the USA, to the English mid-Victorian railway industry. It estimates the work performed by the railway system and its significance in terms of overall national income. It is well researched, stimulating and challenging.

2799
Hughes, Geoffrey
LNER
1986 Ian Allen *London*

This book, with its large format and lavish illustrations, is primarily intended for the enthusiast market. Nevertheless, it does have some very useful material on the organization and management, personalities, technical change, including electrification, financial performance and capital structure of this railway formed in 1923 as a result of parliamentary diktat, down to the 1947 nationalization.
Firms: London & North Eastern Railway (LNER)

2800
Irving, Robert J.
The North Eastern Railway Company 1870–1914
1976 Leicester University Press *Leicester*

This is one of the best business histories of a British railway company. It is particularly strong on all aspects of business policy–labour, pricing, finance and management–and also deals well with the impact of competition on the railway. It is based on a wide range of archival sources.
Firms: North Eastern Railway Co.

2801
Kirby, Maurice W.
Men of Business and Politics: The Rise and Fall of the Quaker Pease Dynasty of North-East England, 1700–1943
For main entry, see 3820

2802
Kirby, Maurice W.
The Origins of Railway Enterprise: The Stockton and Darlington Railway, 1821–1863
1993 Cambridge University Press *Cambridge*

This book re-examines the role of a pioneering business in railway development in the UK from the project's original conception through to its merger into the North Eastern Railway in 1863. Surprisingly no full scale history of this railway has been written since 1875, compared to many on the Liverpool–Manchester Railway opened five years later. The volume is strong on a range of business aspects such as the entrepreneurs, directors and managers, the nature and scale of the traffic, sources of capital, revenues, profitability and returns. It is an important work.
Firms: North Eastern Railway; Stockton and Darlington Railway

2803
Kostal, Rande W.
Law and English Railway Capitalism 1825–1875
1994 Clarendon Press *Oxford*

This impressive volume, based on the author's doctoral dissertation, is scholarly and pioneering. It analyses the relationship between the legal system and the new technology of railways

in terms of the need for rights of incorporation and land purchase. It then considers the legal constraints placed upon the railway as a going operation in terms of accidents, taxation and competition. It has a large bibliography and is fully referenced.
Firms: Liverpool–Manchester Railway; Great Western Railway; London & North Western Railway

2804
Larkin, E. G.; Larkin, J. G.
The Railway Workshops of Britain, 1823–1986
For main entry, see 1064

2805
MacDermot, E. T.; Clinker, C. R.
History of the Great Western Railway, 1833–1921
1989 Ian Allan *London*

The original work was published by MacDermot in 1927, this edition has been much revised. It was a pathbreaker in its field and is good on the politics, technical and financial problems of construction, the organisation structure and management, the strategic mergers and the technicalities of operation. This volume stops in 1921, but the story is continued by Nock (qv).
Firms: Great Western Railway

2806
Mather, F. C.
After the Canal Duke: A study of the industrial estates administered by the trustees of the third Duke of Bridgewater in the age of railway building, 1825–1872
For main entry, see 3029

2807
Morel, Julian
Pullman: The Pullman Car Company–its services, cars, and traditions
1983 David & Charles *Newton Abbot*

This volume was written by one of the company's managers active in the business from the 1960s to 1980s, and is a combination of his personal reminiscences and the history he had gathered. It is not analytic of the business history, but is useful as a source of information if rather descriptive, on English Pullman activities.
Firms: Pullman Car Co.

2808
Nock, O. S.
History of the Great Western Railway: Volume Three 1923–1947
1989 Ian Allan *London*

This third volume carries the history commenced by MacDermot and Clinker (qv) from grouping to nationalization. It takes a chronological, narrative approach and is strong on operations, technical change, the directors and managers and the politics of the railway. It has a number of useful appendices.
Firms: Great Western Railway

2809
Ottley, George (Editor)
A Bibliography of British Railway History
For main entry, see 30

2810
Parker, Peter
For Starters: The business of life
For main entry, see 3907

2811
Parris, Henry
Government and the Railways in Nineteenth-Century Britain
1965 Routledge & Kegan Paul *London*

This is not a business history per se, but examines the relationship between government and the railway industry. It is strong on the reasons for governmental involvement, the internal workings of the railway department, and the implications for this on the theory of government. It concentrates on the period up to 1867, is well researched and scholarly.

2812
Reed, Malcolm C. (Editor)
Railways in the Victorian Economy: Studies in finance and economic growth
1969 David & Charles *Newton Abbot*

This collection of essays covers a number of important aspects of British railway business history, such as their impact on the capital market, accounting and pricing policies, railway contractors, railway towns, backward and forward linkages and their impact on specific industries. They are thoroughly researched, scholarly and important.

2813

Reed, Malcolm C.

Investment in Railways in Britain: 1820–1844: A study in the development of the capital market

1975 Oxford University Press *Oxford*

This is a treasury of statistics nicely organized in a clear, crisp analysis of the role of investment in British railways. The author explores the various forms of investment, the people associated, and the legislation that regulated charters. Thorough research and attention to detail make this work essential reading for those interested in railway development.

Firms: Liverpool & Manchester Railway; Stockton and Darlington Railway

2814

Robertson, Charles J. A.

The Origins of the Scottish Railway System, 1722–1844

1983 John Donald *Edinburgh, Scotland*

This volume examines and explains the prehistory of the Scottish railway system from the early horse-drawn wagonways through the coal-carrying railways down to the railway mania of 1844. It is meticulously researched, thorough and painstaking, and includes a long bibliography. It is a first-class piece of scholarship.

2815

Rolt, Lionel T. C.

Isambard Kingdom Brunel: A biography

For main entry, see 3917

2816

Semmens, Peter

History of the Great Western Railway 1923–1948

1985 Allen & Unwin *London*

This is a competent history of the railway from rationalization in 1921 to nationalization in 1948. It appeals to both the enthusiast and the academic, covering well the operations of the trains, as well as port, road and hotel activities. It endeavours to contextualize the railway, looking at the impact of government policy, competition, and economic fluctuations. It also examines the complexities of the capital structure and relative profitability of the activities.

Firms: British Railways; Great Western Railway

2817

Simmons, Jack

The Railway in Town and Country 1830–1914

1986 David & Charles *Newton Abbot*

This volume examines the impact of the British railway system on society and economy. It is detailed, demonstrates the diversity of experiences and stresses the role of the railway as an agent of social change. It is not a business history per se, but analyses the impact of an industry on the host country. It is thoroughly researched and demonstrates deep understanding.

2818

Thomas, R. H. G.

The Liverpool and Manchester Railway

1980 Batsford *London*

One of many works on the pioneering railway's incorporation, construction and operation, it is well-illustrated but there is no bibliography and very scanty footnotes and some odd omissions. It deals well with the struggle to gain incorporation, the technology of building the railway, the Rainhill locomotive trials, the opening ceremonies, and relations with other railways. It is thin on the finances, and some social aspects, such as Sunday travel and free passes.

Firms: Liverpool & Manchester Railway

2819

White, H. Patrick

A Regional History of the Railways of Great Britain: 2, Southern England

1961 David & Charles *Newton Abbot* 1992 David St John Thomas *Nairn, Scotland*

Although nominally a history of railways in the region, this is really the story of the Southern Railway, its precursors, and Southern Region of British Rail. It is authoritative and well written giving a good overview of amalgama-

tions, business strategy, technological change and the important personalities involved.
Firms: Southern Railway; British Rail; Network South East

2820
Williams, Roy
The Midland Railway: A new history
1988 David & Charles *Newton Abbot*

This book provides a straightforward narrative history of the Midland Railway from the predecessor companies through Hudson's amalgamation and the 1923 regrouping to nationalization. It is well-illustrated and good on the technology, personalities, traffic, routes, and amalgamations but thin on the financial aspects and more purely business matters.
Firms: British Railways Board; London Midland & Scottish Railway; Midland Railway

Railways, Europe (excl. UK)

2821
Anon.
Le ferrovie in Padania [Railways in the Po Valley–Padania]
Padania, vol. 4, no. 7, 1990

This special issue of the Italian Review 'Padania' presents twelve articles dealing with the formation of the railway network and its forward linkages.

2822
Broeke, Willem van den
Financiën en financiers van de Nederlandse Spoorwegen, 1837–1890 [Finance and Financiers of the Dutch Railways, 1837–1890]
1985 Waanders *Zwolle, The Netherlands*

This book provides an in-depth financial analysis of nineteenth-century railway capitalization and development in The Netherlands.
Firms: Hollandsche Yzeren Spoorweg Maatschappij; Maatschappij tot Exploitatie van Staatsspoorwegen; Nederlandsche Centraalspoorweg Maatschappij; Nederlandsche Rhijunspoorweg Maatschappij

2823
Caron, François
Histoire de l'Exploitation d'un Grand Réseau: La Compagnie des Chemins de Fer du Nord [History of the Exploitation of a Great Network: The Northern Railway Company 1846–1937]
1973 Mouton *Paris, France*

This is an excellent history of a French railway company which was one of the earliest and most important in France. This analytical study looks at the role of government, the sources of capital, the management of costs, rates, relations with suppliers, and the effects of the company on the wider economy. It is based on exhaustive archival research, including those of the company. It was an epoch-making work for French business history.
Firms: Compagnie des Chemins de Fer du Nord

2824
Faber, J. A. (Editor)
Het Spoor: 150 jaar spoorwegen in Nederland [The Track: 150 years of railroads in The Netherlands]
1989 Meulenhoff *Amsterdam, The Netherlands*

This volume takes a multi-disciplinary approach in capturing various technical and economic aspects of a century and a half of Dutch railroad development by eight authors in nine chapters.
Firms: Hollandsche Yzeren Spoorweg Maatschappij; Maatschappij tot exploitatie van Staats-Spoorwegen; Nederlands(ch)e Spoorwegen

2825
Fremdling, Rainer
Eisenbahnen und deutsches Wirtschaftswachstum, 1840–79: Ein Beitrag zur Entwicklungstheorie und zur Theorie der Infrastruktur [Railways and German Economic Growth, 1840–79: A contribution to development theory and the theory of infrastructure]
1975 Gesellschaft für Westfälische Wirtschaftsgeschichte *Dortmund, Germany*

This important study draws on new sources to analyse the importance of railways to German economic development. Fremdling is particularly good on investment, the role of the state, and the part played by wage payments in industrialization.

2826
Gisevius, Hans F.
Zur Vorgeschichte des Preussisch-Sächsischen Eisenbahn-krieges: Verkehrspolitische Differenzen zwischen Preussen und Sachsen im Deutschen Bund [The Prehistory of the Prussian-Saxon Railway Wars: Trade policy disagreements between Prussia and Saxony in the German confederation]
1971 Duncker & Humblot *Berlin, Germany*

This study draws on previously unused sources to describe the complex negotiations between Prussia and Saxony over railway construction policy and routes, which was itself part of economic rivalry and competition. Gisevius shows the problems and consequences of this rivalry and separate development policy.

2827
Gomez Mendoza, Antonio
Ferrocarriles y Cambio Económico en Espana (1855–1913): Un Enfoque de Nueva Historia Económica [Railways and Economic Change in Spain 1855–1913: A new economic history analysis]
1982 Alianza Editorial *Madrid, Spain*

This is not really a business history per se, but rather an exercise in estimating the role of the railways in cliometric terms on Spanish economic growth. It is strong on backward and forward linkages, social saving, government policy, and their role on internal markets. This is a significant and ingenious book.

2828
Jonckers Nieboer, J. H.
Geschiedenis der Nederlandsche Spoorwegen, 1832–1938 [A History of the Netherlands Railways, 1832–1938]
1988 Nederlandsche Spoorwegen *Utrecht, The Netherlands*

This is a photomechanical reprint of a classic work. The first edition appeared in 1907 and the second edition in 1938. Though dated, this is still the authoritative account of the first hundred years of railway history and development in The Netherlands.

Firms: Hollandsche Yzeren Spoorweg Maatschappij; Maatschappij tot Exploitatie van Staatsspoorwegen; Nederlandsche Centraalspoorweg Maatschappij; Nederlandsche Rhijunspoorweg Maatschappij; Nederlandsche Spoorwegen

2829
Kurgan-van Hentenryk, Ginette
Rail, finance et politique: les entreprises Philippart, 1865–1890 [Rail, Finance and Politics: The Philippart enterprises, 1865–1890]
1982 Éditions de l'Université de Bruxelles *Brussels, Belgium*

This book describes and explains the work of the railway promoter, Simon Philippart, in building up railway systems in Belgium, Luxembourg and France in the late nineteenth century. It is good at showing his use of banks to foster mergers and takeovers and his ultimate failure when involved with the Crédit Mobilier. This is an important work.
Firms: Philippart

2830
Landi, P. L.
La Leopolda: La ferrovia Firenze–Livorno e le sue vicende 1825–1860 [The Leopolda: The Tuscany Railway Company 1825–1860]
1974 Pacini *Pisa, Italy*

This study analyses the creation and operations of the most important railway company in Tuscany before a united Italy existed. The railway is set well within its political and economic context.
Firms: La Leopolda

2831
Leclercq, Y.
Le Réseau impossible 1820–1852: La résistance au systeme des grandes compagnies ferroviaires et la politique économique de la France politique économique de la France [The Impossible Network 1820–1852 The resistance to the system of great railway companies and the political economy of France]
1987 Droz *Geneva, Switzerland*

This work analyses the difficulties which beset the creation of the largest railway companies in France. The book covers well the

relationship between the state and the companies, the impact of the former on the profits of the latter, and the degree to which this was an exploitative relationship.
Firms: Chemin de Fer de L'Est; Chemin de Fer du Nord; Paris-Lyon Chemin de Fer; Paris-Orléans cie

2832
Marks, Steven G.
Road to Power: The Trans-Siberian railroad and the colonisation of Asian Russia 1850–1917
1991 I. B. Tauris *London*

This is a history of the building of the Trans-Siberian railway which deals with strategic, political and social motives and effects as well as the industrial. It is very strong on the chaotic and near catastrophic construction stage, and the predominance of state interests over economic motives.
Firms: Trans-Siberian Railway

2833
Merger, Michèle
Origini e sviluppo del management ferroviario italiano 1850–1905 [The Origins and Evolution of Railway Management in Italy 1850–1905]
Annali di storia dell'Impresa, no. 8, 1992: pp 379–417

This article is important because it is the first study dealing with the organization of Italian railways, the role of the state on the strategies of the railway companies, and the formation of an industrial élite, namely the railway engineers.
Firms: Alta Italia railway; Meridionalia railway; Piedmont railway

2834
Negri, Pietro
Le ferrovie nello Stato Pontificio (1844–1870) [The Railways of the Papal State, 1844–1870]
1967 Archivio Economico *Rome, Italy*

This volume tells the story of the slow construction of railways in the Papal States in the mid-nineteenth century and explains why progress was so slow. It is good on the role of the state, the financial background and the role of concessionaires.
Firms: Strade Ferrate Romane

2835
Papagiannakis, Lefteris
Oi Hellinikoi Siderodromoi 1882–1910 [Greek Railways 1882–1910]
1982 Cultural Foundation of the National Bank of Greece *Athens, Greece*

This seminal study is an analysis of the history of railway construction and the way it materialized in Greece. It focuses on the process of financing and the behaviour of private investors–Greek and foreign–of banks and of the state. It is good on contextualization and the growth of state intervention. It is based on original archival and statistical material.

2836
RENFE
Los Ferrocarriles y el Desarrollo Económico de Europa Occidental durante el Siglo XIX [Railways and the Economic Development of Western Europe in the Nineteenth Century]
1981 RENFE *Madrid, Spain*

RENFE, the Spanish State Railway Authority, organized the conference at which these papers originated. As well as a lucid summary of the state of the 'new' railway history, there are some useful papers applying these ideas to Spanish experience, especially on the state's role, sources of finance, and performance levels.
Firms: Andalucian Railway Co.

2837
Ribeill, Georges
La révolution ferroviaire: La formation des compagnies de chemin de fer en France 1823–1870 [The Railway Revolution: The formation of railway companies in France 1823–1870]
1992 Ed. Belin *Paris, France*

This is a history of the business management of the major French railway companies from their beginnings to 1870.
Firms: Compagnie de l'Est; Compagnie de l'Orléans; Compagnie de l'Ouest; Compagnie du Midi; Compagnie du Nord; Compagnie du PLM

2838
Steitz, Walter
Die Entstehung der Köln-Mindener Eisenbahngesellschaft: Ein Beitrag zur Frühgeschichte der Deutschen Eisenbahnen und des Preussischen Aktienwesens [The Origins of the Cologne-Minden Railway: A contribution to the early history of German railways and Prussian joint stock business]
1974 Selbst Verlag *Cologne, Germany*

This volume explains the origins of the Cologne–Minden Railway in the 1830s and 1840s and sets it in the context of official thinking on private industrial activities. It deploys new evidence on both the railway and Prussian railway legislation.
Firms: Köln–Minden Railway

2839
Tortella, Gabriel
Banks, Railroads, and Industry in Spain, 1829–1874
For main entry, see 2396

2840
Wortmann, Wilhelm
Eisenbahnbauarbeiter im Vormarz: Sozial geschichtliche Untersuchung der Bauarbeiter der Köln-Mindener Eisenbahn in Minden-Ravensburg, 1844–7 [Railway Navvies in Vormarz: A social history of the building workers of the Cologne–Minden Railway in Minden–Ravensburg, 1844–7]
1972 Bohlau *Cologne, Germany*

This is a pioneering work on the role of railway navvies in Germany. The author examines a short stretch of the Rhine–Weser Railway to show their living conditions, material rewards, patterns of recruitment, leisure activities and conflicts with management. The book also looks at the structure of the railway's management, its effect on social policy and the state. This is an important work.
Firms: Köln–Minden Railway; Rhine–Weser Railway

Railways, USA

2841
Athearn, Robert G.
Rebel of the Rockies: The Denver and Rio Grande Western Railroad
1962 Yale University Press *New Haven, CT*

This is a rousing history of the railway originally intended to connect Denver and El Paso. Athearn's work is balanced, thorough, and captivating. Research done in company archives strengthens the fine bibliography. The story of the D&RG is that of a small independent railroad locked in fierce competition with larger and better established rivals. It covers the period 1871–1962.
Firms: Atchison, Topeka, and Santa Fe Railroad; Denver & Rio Grande Railroad; Rio Grande Western Railroad; Union Pacific Railroad

2842
Athearn, Robert G.
Union Pacific Country
1971 Rand McNally & Co. *New York, NY*

The author's lengthy research, especially in the Union Pacific archives, is put to good advantage in this exceptional study. Taking the subject beyond the routine history of the building of the line, Athearn ably investigates the competence of the Union Pacific leadership and the impact of the railroad on the expansion of the nation. This book is a significant contribution to railway history.
Firms: Great Northern; Kansas Pacific; Oregon Short Line; Union Pacific

2843
Baughman, James P.
Charles Morgan and the Development of Southern Transportation
For main entry, see 3931

2844
Berk, Gerald
Alternative Tracks: The constitution of American industrial order, 1865–1917
1994 Johns Hopkins University Press
Baltimore, MD

This thoughtful volume looks at the rail-

roads in America in the period 1880 to 1914 to determine how significant the modern type corporation was to economic growth and prosperity. Berk argues that corporate capitalism was not the only path, there were other less centralized, less hierarchical and more public routes. A well-referenced and important book.
Firms: Chicago Great Western Railroad

2845
Bryant, Keith L. Jr
Arthur E Stillwell: Promoter with a hunch
1971 Vanderbilt University Press *Nashville, TN*

Although more a business biography of this promoter of southern railroads than a true business history, this book is important. Stillwell was responsible for building well over 2,000 miles of railroad between the 1880s and 1912, and this book evaluates his promotional methods, financial stratagems and the impact on the local economy.
Firms: Kansas City Mexico and Orient Railway; Kansas City Pittsburgh and Gulf Railroad; Kansas City Southern Railway

2846
Bryant, Keith L. Jr
History of the Atchison, Topeka and Santa Fe Railway
1982 University of Nebraska Press *Lincoln, NB*

This book was first published in 1974 as one of the Macmillan series 'Railroads of America', and is a classic example of corporate railroad history. It is strong on the politics, personalities, finances, traffic, changes in technology and markets. It draws on an extensive archive.
Firms: Atchison Topeka and Santa Fe Railway

2847
Bryant, Keith L. Jr (Editor)
Railroads in the Age of Regulation, 1900–1980
1988 Bruccoli Clark Laymen/Facts on File *New York, NY*

This is the first in a series of volumes, the Encyclopedia of American Business History and Biography (general editor William H. Becker), concentrating on brief biographies and histories of businesses and firms. Entries are written by specialists and are accompanied by bibliographies. Valuable information is provided on post-First World War railroad managers. It is an important contribution to the study of the history of the railroad industry in the twentieth century.

2848
Chandler, Alfred D. Jr (Editor)
The Railroads: The nation's first big business. Sources and readings
1965/81 Harcourt Brace & World / Arno Press *New York, NY*

This is a volume of readings to demonstrate the impact of railroads on the American economy. All the extracts are from primary sources and each section has a commentary on the topic. This is not a business history per se, but is good at bringing out the changes in business thinking and practice which resulted from railroad construction and operation.

2849
Cochran, Thomas C.
Railroad Leaders, 1845–1890
1966 Russell & Russell *New York, NY*

Cochran addresses the evolution of the business practices of US railroads from 1845, when only one extra-local railroad existed in the country, to 1890, when most firms in the industry possessed the structure and practices that carried forward to the modern period. This sophisticated analysis based on solid empirical research is important to scholars interested in the evolution of giant firms, of which railroads were the first example.

2850
Cotroneo, R.
The History of the Northern Pacific Land Grant 1900–1952
1979 Arno Press *New York, NY*

This circumspect study offers a wealth of information on one of the largest land grants in railroad history. Land speculation, timber, mineral rights, irrigation, and the right of way through Indian territory are but a few of the factors scrutinized by Cotroneo in an expert and insightful fashion.
Firms: Northern Pacific

2851
Davis, Burke
The Southern Railway: Road of the innovators
1985 University of North Carolina Press *Chapel Hill, NC*

This railway was founded in Virginia in 1894 as a merger of a number of predecessor lines and in 1982 merged with the Norfolk & Western Railway, having made profits in the 1970s. This study is good on the technical side and the technical innovations, top management style, personalities and corporate strategies but is rather uncritical and celebratory and has no source documentation, not even a bibliography.
Firms: Norfolk & Western Railway; South Carolina Canal and Railroad Co.; Southern Railway

2852
Dilts, James D.
The Great Road: The building of the Baltimore and Ohio, the nation's first railroad 1828–1853
1993 Stanford University Press *Stanford, CA*

Dilts presents the definitive history of the planning and construction of the first regional railroad in America to provide access to the new western states. The roles of the professionals involved in the venture are described but there is little on day-to-day operations.
Firms: Baltimore & Ohio Railroad

2853
Dunlavy, Colleen A.
Politics and Industrialization: Early railroads in the United States and Prussia
1994 Princeton University Press *Princeton, NJ*

This book is a comparative study of the birth of American and Prussian railroads in the 1830s and 1840s which focuses on how contrasting political structures affected the dynamics of railroad policy making, the organization of railroad interests, and the process of technical choice.

2854
Fishlow, Albert
American Railroads and the Transformation of the Ante-Bellum Economy
1965 Harvard University Press *Cambridge, MA*

This book is an important attempt to measure productivity advances and the inputs of labour and capital in antebellum railroads.

2855
Fitch, Edwin M.
The Alaska Railroad
1967 Frederick A. Praeger *New York, NY*

This volume was written by a former employee of this government financed, sponsored and operated railroad, opened in 1923. It lacks the scholarly apparatus of references but has a useful bibliography, and is a detailed narrative of the construction, operations, management and traffic of the railroad. There is little on the financial aspects.
Firms: Alaska Railroad

2856
Fogel, Robert William
The Union Pacific Railroad: A case in premature enterprise
1960 Johns Hopkins University Press *Baltimore, MD*

This is not really a business history but is an important volume because of the author and the subject matter. It represents Fogel's early attempt to use economic theory to shed new light on an old transport problem, in this case the extent of profiteering in the construction of the Union Pacific and its economic rate of return compared to its financial problems. It covers the period 1845 to 1879 and is strong on the relationship with the Crédit Mobilier. Legislative records and reports serve as the cornerstone for the excellent research and fine bibliography. The methods and findings are novel.
Firms: Crédit Mobilier; Union Pacific Railroad

2857
Goodrich, Carter
Government Promotion of American Canals and Railroads 1800–1890
For main entry, see 4345

2858

Grant, H. Roger

The Corn Belt Route: A history of the Chicago Great Western Railroad

1984 Northern Illinois University Press *Dekalb, IL*

This is a narrative history of a small, midwestern railroad from the mid-nineteenth century to its merger with the Chicago & North Western in 1968. The book is strong on operational innovations but patchy on other aspects, especially those of interest to business historians.

Firms: Chicago & North Western Railroad; Chicago Great Western Railroad

2859

Greenberg, Dolores

Financiers and Railroads, 1869–1889: A study of Morton, Bliss & Company

For main entry, see 2610

2860

Gregory, Frances W.; Neu, Irene D.

The American Industrial Elite in the 1870s: Their social origins

For main entry, see 3842

2861

Grodinsky, Julius

Transcontinental Railway Strategy, 1869–1893: A study of businessmen

1962 University of Pennsylvania Press *Philadelphia, PA*

The author examines the tactics of the visionary men of enterprise who led the transcontinental railway industry in the late nineteenth century. Acquisition of capital and routes became their primary competitive factors. This volume is thorough and illuminating in its analyses, and comprehensive in scope.

Firms: Central Pacific Railroad; Union Pacific Railroad

2862

Harwood, Herbert H. Jr

Impossible Challenge: The Baltimore and Ohio Railroad in Maryland

1979 Barnard Roberts & Co. *Baltimore, MD*

This well-illustrated book traces the history of the Baltimore & Ohio Railroad from its foundation in 1828 to 1979. It draws on the internal archives of the firm as well as a wide range of published material and is strong on the technological and civil engineering challenges, the physical plant and the operations. It does not deal with financial, governmental or marketing matters.

Firms: Baltimore & Ohio Railroad

2863

Healy, K.

Performance of the U.S. Railroads Since World War II: A quarter century of private operation

1985 Vantage Press *New York, NY*

This is a good, scholarly source for those interested in the development of the postwar American railroad industry. Objective and thorough, the strength of this work is its examination of consolidation and financial management. It is especially strong in its analysis of the loss of freight business. The author's articulate style and expertise in railroad electrification help to give a clear picture of the industry's decline.

2864

Hidy, Ralph W.; Hidy, Muriel E.; Scott, Roy V.; Hofsommer, Don L.

The Great Northern Railway: A history

1988 Harvard Business School Press *Boston, MA*

This is the story of one of the major American transcontinentals. It covers the development of predecessors such as the Burlington Northern and the founding of the Great Northern by James J. Hill and goes through to 1970. It is strong on business strategy, changing technology and merger policy but weak on the assessment of entrepreneurs and managers.

Firms: Burlington Northern Railway; Great Northern Railway; St Paul, Minneapolis & Manitoba Railway

2865

Hilton, George W.

Monon Route

1978 Howell North Books *Berkeley, CA*

This is a model history of the Chicago, Indianapolis & Louisville Railway from its foundation until it was absorbed in 1971. It was a marginally successful railway. The volume is well-researched and good on corporate development, managerial leadership, traffic operations and financial performance, and is also well contextualized. This railway serves as a pattern for the study of independent regional railways.

Firms: Chicago Indianapolis & Louisville Railway; Indianapolis, Delphi & Chicago Railway; Louisville & Nashville Railroad; New Albany & Salem Railroad

2866

Hofsommer, Don L. (Editor)

Railroads in Oklahoma

1977 Oklahoma Historical Society *Oklahoma City, OK*

This is a noteworthy collection of essays. Significant topics include the pursuit of right of way through Indian Territory, case studies of individual railway companies, and interurban rail systems. Of singular interest are the case studies by Winters and Fike which examine the struggle of small local companies.

Firms: Fort Smith & Western Railway; Missouri, Kansas & Texas Railway; Missouri, Oklahoma & Gulf Railway; Oklahoma Railway

2867

Hofsommer, Don L.

The Southern Pacific 1901–1985

1986 Texas A & M University Press *College Station, TX*

This is a copiously illustrated volume drawing on the corporate archives and interviews with leading players. It is good on technical detail, and the contribution of the railway to the territory it served but has no systematic analysis of management structure or policies to show why, despite its economic advantages, it failed in the later-twentieth century.

Firms: Southern Pacific Railroad; St Louis Southwestern Railway; Texas & New Orleans Railroad

2868

Itzkoff, Donald M.

Off the Track: The decline of the intercity passenger train in the US

1985 Greenwood Press *Westport, CT*

In this estimable work the author lays the blame for the decline of passenger traffic on a lack of managerial imagination and innovation, as well as the failure of the federal government to invest in necessary improvements. Competition by the airlines, automobiles, and buses is also examined. Comparison of the successful European industry with the ailing American counterpart supports the thesis. Heavy emphasis is placed on the two decades following the Second World War.

Firms: Amtrak; Burlington; Interstate Commerce Commission; Southern Pacific

2869

Johnson, Arthur M.; Supple, Barry E.

Boston Capitalists and Western Railroads: A study in the nineteenth century railroad investment process

For main entry, see 3790

2870

Kirkland, Edward C.

Charles Francis Adams: The patrician at bay

For main entry, see 3960

2871

Klein, Maury

The Life and Legend of Jay Gould

1986 The Johns Hopkins University Press *Baltimore, MD*

Klein revises the conventional wisdom about Gould and argues that the image of him as a robber baron was a creation of the nineteenth-century press (qv Josephson). Klein argues that he was not the king of speculators but rather the prime mover in developing and restructuring of railroads and communications.

Firms: Atchison, Topeka & Santa Fe Railroad; Chicago, Burlington and Quincy Railroad; Erie Railroad; Missouri Pacific Railroad; Texas and Pacific Railroad; Wabash Railroad; Western Union Telegraph Co.

2872

Klein, Maury

Union Pacific: Vol. 1, Birth of a Railroad 1862–1893

1987 Doubleday *New York, NY*

This volume provides a very full account of the business history of the Union Pacific, correcting previous versions and bringing out the

lack of positive leadership, the problems of funding and relationships with government. It is usefully complementary to Williams (qv) which concentrates on the construction stage, and examines the role of prominent railroad promoters such as Jay Gould.
Firms: Union Pacific Railroad

2873
Klein, Maury
Union Pacific: Vol. 2, the Rebirth 1894–1969
1989 Doubleday *New York, NY*

In this second of a two-volume work, Klein writes a chronological account of how one of the best-managed firms in a declining industry coped with an increasingly unfriendly business environment. Relying on trade journals, archives and interviews, Klein unfolds his account as a series of biographies of key managers, intertwined with changing competitive pressures, regulatory frameworks, and technology. Unlike most histories of twentieth-century US railroads, this unsentimental account critically evaluates management, offering insight into the difficulties that an established management structure has adjusting to change.
Firms: Oregon Railroad & Navigation Co.; Oregon Short Line; San Pedro Los Angeles & Salt Lake; Union Pacific Railroad

2874
Kolko, Gabriel
Railroads and Regulation, 1877–1916
1965 Princeton University Press *Princeton, NJ*

This is a pioneering analysis of relations between railroads and federal regulators which argues the theory of 'capture'. The railroads, not the farmers or shippers, were, Kolko argues, the central advocates of the introduction of federal regulation and its staunchest supporters afterwards.

2875
Larson, John L.
Bonds of Enterprise: John Murray Forbes and western development in America's railway age
1984 Harvard University Press *Cambridge, MA*

Although primarily a business biography of Forbes, this volume contains much on the finance and construction of the Chicago, Burlington & Quincy Railroad system. It is especially good on finance and management, administrative organization, strategic planning, competition, rates and regulation. Larson's keen analysis and colourful sketches of peripheral characters add spice to the well-documented text.
Firms: Chicago, Burlington & Quincy Railroad; Michigan Central

2876
Latham, Earl
The Politics of Railroad Co-ordination, 1933–1936
1959 Harvard University Press *Cambridge, MA*

This is a detailed study of the problems of regulation and co-ordination of US railroads seen from 'the inside' via the archives and personal papers of Federal Co-ordinator of Transportation, Joseph B. Eastmann.
Firms: Interstate Commerce Commission

2877
Martin, Albro
Enterprisė Denied: Origins of the decline of American railroads, 1897–1917
1971 Columbia University Press *New York, NY*

Martin has written a highly critical account of the impact of regulation ('archaic Progressivism') on the functioning of US railroads. It argues that the effect of regulation was to starve the railroads of the capital investment that they needed. He suggests that the unwillingness of the ICC to grant general rate increases, especially following the Hepburn Act of 1906, prevented the flow of investment funds from keeping pace with demands on the system and paved the way for the collapse of railroad profitability after 1911.

2878
Martin, Albro
James J. Hill and the Opening of the Northwest
1976 Oxford University Press *New York, NY*

This well-researched biography of the financial and railroad magnate, James Hill, draws on his personal and business papers. It is sympathetic, analytical and well contextualized and

strong on the man, his personality, his business methods, alliances and antagonisms. The focus is on entrepreneurship and the constraints imposed by regulation.
Firms: Candian Pacific Railroad; Great Northern Railway; Northern Pacific Railroad; St Paul and Pacific Railroad

2879
Martin, Albro
Railroads Triumphant: The growth, rejection and rebirth of a vital American force
1992 Oxford University Press *Oxford*

This wide-ranging book tries to determine why the American railroad became the butt of political and economic discontent, despite its beneficial economic effects, and hence why 'anti-railroad' legislation ensued and what was needed to revive its image. It has a useful critical bibliography, is rigorous and thought provoking.

2880
Mercer, Lloyd J.
E. H. Harriman: Master railroader
1985 Twayne *Boston, MA*

This is an unusual work, a cliometric analysis of Harriman's railroad achievements in terms of rates of return, productivity, rates of freight and passenger fares. It is strong on the collection, use and interpretation of data as well as using literary sources and fundamentally reassesses his role.
Firms: Illinois Central Railroad; Southern Pacific; Union Pacific; Burlington Railroad; Chicago & Alton Railroad

2881
Miner, H. Craig
The Rebirth of the Missouri Pacific 1956–1983
1983 Texas A & M University Press *College Station, TX*

This thoroughly researched volume explains the success of the Missouri Pacific after it was bought by William Marbury and merged with other railroads; its management operations were reorganized and modernized, and its complex financial structure sorted out. It is strong on the application of computers to railway operations but says little on returns, operating ratios or management structure.
Firms: Missouri Pacific Railroad

2882
Overton, Richard C.
Gulf to Rockies: The heritage of the Fort Worth and Denver-Colorado and Southern Railways 1861–1898
1953 University of Texas Press *Austin, TX*

Although this volume is now rather dated by modern business history standards, it nevertheless still contains some useful insights, and was a seminal volume, being sponsored by the railroad but with scholarly freedom guaranteed. It is strong on the railway politics, the construction of the lines and amalgamations and agreements between companies.
Firms: Atchison Topeka and Santa Fe Railway; Colorado and Southern Railway; Fort Worth and Denver City Railway

2883
Overton, Richard C.
Burlington Route: A history of the Burlington Lines
1965 Alfred A. Knopf *New York, NY*

This remains the best company history of the Burlington Lines. Overton's expertise and the availability of company records result in a comprehensive and definitive study that should be required reading for railroad historians. Starting with the beginning of the system in 1849, the author analyses the abilities of company presidents and the gradual expansion of Burlington throughout the western United States.
Firms: Aurora Branch Railroad; Aurora Central Railroad; Chicago, Burlington, and Quincy Railroad Company; Galena and Chicago Union Railroad

2884
Overton, Richard C.
Perkins Budd: Railway statesmen of the Burlington
1982 Greenwood Press *Westport, CT*

Although this is not really a business history, it is an important work, as it uses speeches and memos of two presidents of the Chicago Burlington & Quincy Railroad to show how they developed strategy on competition, customers, administration, technology and government

regulation in the late nineteenth century and the 1930–49 period, respectively.
Firms: Chicago Burlington & Quincy Railroad

2885
Rae, John B.
The Development of Railway Land Subsidy Policy in the United States
1979 Arno Press *New York, NY*

This dissertation was written in 1936. It is an articulate and lively discussion of the development of the railroad land grant policy from 1850 to 1890. The author notes the successes and failures associated with the policy and its effect on the expansion westward. Excellent presentation of evidence and keen judgement make this a commendable resource.
Firms: Pacific Railway

2886
Reed, Merl E.
New Orleans and the Railroads: The struggle for commercial empire, 1830–1860
1966 Louisiana State University Press *Baton Rouge, LA*

Insufficient existing company records forced the author to work with legislative and other public documents, a difficult task, but well worth the effort. Reed's keen analytical treatment of the various railroad ventures in antebellum Louisiana is thorough and succinct. It is a positive and valuable addition to the literature of the field.
Firms: New Orleans, Jackson and Great Northern Railroad

2887
Ripley, William Z.
Railroads, Rates and Regulation
1920 Longmans, Green & Co. *New York, NY*

Still a fundamental study, Ripley's book explores the complex issues of railroad finance, ratemaking and regulation with an unsurpassed wealth of detail that continues to make the book essential for the modern historian.

2888
Rosenberger, Homer T.
The Philadelphia and Erie Railroad: Its place in American economic history
1975 Fox Hills Press *Potomac, MD*

This massive, well-illustrated volume traces the history of the 'P and E' from its predecessors, such as the Sunbury and Erie Railroad, to the formation of the P and E in 1861 down to 1907 when it was absorbed into the Pennsylvania Railroad. The book places the railroad in its regional context and provides good coverage of legal, political and technical problems, finance and construction, traffic, and promoters and personalities.
Firms: Pennsylvania Railroad; Philadelphia and Erie Railroad; Sunbury and Erie Railroad

2889
Salsbury, Stephen
The State, the Investor and the Railroad
1967 Harvard University Press *Cambridge, MA*

Using archival sources, Salsbury traces the evolution of business practices of the Boston & Albany from its inception as a local line through its transition into the United States' first inter-regional trunk railroad. The transition occurred with the completion of the subsidiary Western Railroad to Albany, New York, around 1840, forcing management to confront issues such as coordination of numerous trains over vast distances, and pricing policies to compete with New York for through traffic, while better utilizing an expensive but lightly travelled mountain railroad, coping with congestion on its eastern end, and accommodating irresistable political pressure.
Firms: Boston & Albany Railroad; New York Central Railroad; Western Railroad

2890
Salsbury, Stephen
No Way to Run a Railroad: The untold story of the Penn Central crisis
1982 McGraw-Hill *New York, NY*

This is an investigation of the biggest bankruptcy to that date (1970) written by a 'professional historian in the finest tradition of the discipline'. It is massively researched and concentrates on strategy and business leadership to show how 'executive obtuseness and incompetence at the highest level' caused the crash. It

is a classic of the genre, drawing on interviews with key officers as well as corporate records.
Firms: New York Central Railroad; Penn Central Railroad; Pennsylvania Railroad

2891
Saunders, L.
The Railroad Mergers and the Coming of Conrail
1978 Greenwood Press *Westport, CT*

Although the author is scathing in his criticism of capitalism and management, this work is a well-balanced survey, thorough in its research and treatment of the subject. Saunders's stimulating analysis begins with the Northern Securities merger of 1904. The highlight of the book is the coverage of the Penn Central failure which will satisfy the most discerning of scholars.
Firms: Amtrak; Gulf, Mobile & Ohio Railroad; Louisville & Nashville Railroad; Penn Central

2892
Sobel, Robert
The Fallen Colossus
1977 Weybright & Talley *New York, NY*

This is a well-written, scholarly analysis of the long-term reasons for the bankruptcy of the Penn Central Transportation Company in 1970. It traces the origins and history of the companies which made it up and their rivalry. It is good on the context of problems facing all railroad companies in the twentieth century and the strategic decisions which led to failure.
Firms: New York Central Railroad; Penn Central Railroad; Pennsylvania Railroad

2893
Stover, John F.
History of the Illinois Central Railroad
1975 Macmillan *New York, NY*

This is a masterly account of the promotion, construction, amalgamations and operations of the Illinois Central Railroad from the 1850s to the 1970s. It is strong on personalities and land grants, the effect of the railway on development and the finances of the business, and is based on a wide range of archives.
Firms: Illinois Central Railroad

2894
Stover, John F.
Iron Road to the West: American railroads in the 1850s
1978 Columbia University Press *New York, NY*

This is a study of the 'take-off' period in American railroad development.

2895
Stover, John F.
History of the Baltimore & Ohio Railroad
1987 Purdue University Press
West Lafayette, IN

This volume provides a competent history of an important American railroad line from its charter in 1827 to its takeover by the Chesapeake & Ohio in the late 1950s. The book is strong on the origins of the company, its role in the Civil War and the presidents of the business, but it is thin on the traffic, the management other than the presidents, and the workers. Some important incidents are treated too briefly or passed over.
Firms: Baltimore & Ohio Railroad; Chesapeake & Ohio Railroad

2896
Thompson, Gregory Lee
The Passenger Train in the Motor Age: California's rail and bus industries 1910–1941
1993 Ohio University Press *Columbus, OH*

This is an important contribution both to business and transport history. The author argues that the costing and marketing failures of California's railroad managers were primarily responsible for the losses made on passenger traffic in the 1920s and 1930s and the loss of market-share to buses and automobiles. A persuasive if sometimes exaggerated thesis which makes good use of the regulatory case material and archives of the Southern Pacific and Atchison, Topeka & Santa Fe railroads.
Firms: Southern Pacific Railroad; Atchison, Topeka & Santa Fe Railroad; Pacific Greyhound Lines

2897
Trelease, Allen W.
The North Carolina Railroad 1849–71, and the Modernisation of North Carolina

1991 University of North Carolina Press *Chapel Hill, NC*

This is a vast detailed study of the independent days of this small railroad based on a wide range of sources. Although dealing with many business aspects it rather lacks theory and analysis, but is stronger on operational details and the nature and conditions of the workforce.

Firms: North Carolina Railroad; Richmond and Danville Railroad

2898

Ward, James A.

J. Edgar Thomson, Master of the Pennsylvania Railroad

1980 Greenwood Press *Westport, CT*

This is a business biography of Thomson, who was president of the Pennsylvania Railroad between 1852 and 1874, which sheds much light on the company's management structure, adoption of new technology, financial record and overall strategy. It also illuminates his role in railroad construction as chief engineer of the Georgia Railroad as well as the Pennsylvania.

Firms: Georgia Railroad; Pennsylvania Railroad

2899

Williams, John H.

A Great and Shining Road: The epic story of the transcontinental railroad

1988 Times Books *New York, NY*

This book provides a history of the construction of the transcontinental railroad, covering the political, financial and technical aspects, and setting this story squarely within the national economic and political context. It is also strong on the personalities involved and brings out the dubious dealings between businessmen and politicians which pushed up the cost and reduced the quality.

Firms: Central Pacific Railroad; Union Pacific Railroad

2900

Wilson, William H.

Railroad in the Clouds: The Alaska Railroad in the age of steam 1914–45

1977 Pruell Publishing *Boulder, CO*

Wilson presents a history of this late-built railway which depended entirely on government finance and made losses until 1938. It is good on the impact of the railway on the economy of the state and the personalities who ran the company but thin on employees and actual operations.

Firms: Alaska Railroad

Railways, Canada

2901

Ashdown, Dana W.

Railway Steamships of Ontario

For main entry, see 3014

2902

Cruikshank, Ken

Close Ties: Railways, government and the Board of Railway Commissioners, 1851–1933

For main entry, see 4328

2903

Currie, Archibald W.

The Grand Trunk Railway of Canada

1957 University of Toronto Press *Toronto, Canada*

This is a study of the international financial and political activities involved in establishing a railroad to serve the St Lawrence basin from Portland, Maine to Upper Canada, Ontario. It was eventually extended to Michigan and parts of Indiana and Illinois and operated from 1852–1934. Poor financial management and overextension led to failure and sale to the Canadian Government.

Firms: Canadian Northern Railroad; Canadian Pacific Railway

2904

Dempsey, Hugh A. (Editor)

The CPR West: The iron road and the making of a nation

1984 Douglas & McIntyre *Vancouver, Canada*

This is a volume of essays on a wide range of aspects of the Canadian Pacific Railway by experts. Much of the book is devoted to its effects on economic development, but there are also essays on the Chinese labour force,

Thomas Shaughnessy, and some problems of construction.
Firms: Canadian Pacific Railway

2905
Dorman, Robert
A Statutory History of the Steam and Electric Railways of Canada 1836–1937
1938 Kings Printer (J. O. Patenaude) *Ottawa, Canada*

This is a very useful legislative history giving dates of incorporation and locations of all Canadian railroads. The additional notes with information not covered in the statutes are helpful. It is an invaluable reference work with indices by termini of merged lines, and by line, land, and bridge subsidies.

2906
Due, John F.
The Intercity Electric Railway Industry in Canada
1966 University of Toronto Press *Toronto, Canada*

This important study of the electrically-operated Canadian railway industry 1887–1959, covers the development characteristics, financial situation and decline as a result of road competition. It discusses all twenty-five companies in the industry.
Firms: Canadian National Railway; Canadian Pacific Railway

2907
Eagle, John A.
The Canadian Pacific Railway and the Development of Western Canada, 1896–1914
1989 McGill-Queen's University Press *Montreal, Canada*

This book is less a proper business history and more concerned to show how railway and government worked together to develop and settle the west of Canada to prevent the USA from moving in. It is a little thin on economic theory, but strong on the fears and aspirations of politicians and developers.
Firms: Canadian Pacific Railway

2908
Fleming, Rae B.
The Railway King of Canada: Sir William Mackenzie, 1849–1923
1991 University of British Columbia *Vancouver, Canada*

This biography of Sir William Mackenzie examines the life of one of Canada's most successful businessmen in the early part of the twentieth century. Mackenzie was involved in the development of gas, electric, and transit utilities (including the Toronto Transit Commission), and was the driving force behind the rise of the Canadian Northern Railway.
Firms: Canadian Northern Railway; Toronto Transit Commission; Mackenzie and Mann

2909
Innis, Harold A.
A History of the Canadian Pacific Railway
1971 University of Toronto Press *Toronto, Canada*

First published in 1923, and hence now rather dated in its being essentially narrative and with little use of formal economic theory, this volume is still valuable and not totally superseded by Lamb's 1977 work (qv). It is full of detail on the rationale for the railway, the role of government and the reasons for the need for subsidies. It stresses the developmental role of the railway and discusses the construction, operations and financial returns.
Firms: Canadian Pacific Railway; Grand Trunk Railway; Hudson Bay Co.

2910
Lamb, William Kaye
History of the Canadian Pacific Railway
1977 Macmillan *New York, NY*

Created in 1867, though not incorporated until 1881, and subsidized generously by the Canadian government, the CPR was an instrument of policy to unite and develop the country. This volume is strong on methods of finance, relations with government and the problems of construction–geographical, technical and financial. It also deals well with the business and political personalities involved in the line, having drawn on both company and personal papers.
Firms: Canadian Pacific Railway

2911
Regehr, T. D.
The Canadian Northern Railway: Pioneer road of the northern prairies 1895–1918
1976 Macmillan Company of Canada
Toronto, Canada

This is a study of the entrepreneurial activities of William MacKenzie and Donald Mann in promoting the construction of a railroad serving the Canadian prairie frontier, the Canadian Northern Railway. It later became part of the Canadian National Railway, when questionable financial transactions led to government takeover. The CNR allowed access to the records on which the history draws. It contains tables and appendices of operating statistics. The book is good on the impact of the railway on the economic development of the prairie provinces.
Firms: Canadian Bank of Commerce; Canadian National Railway; Canadian Northern Railway; Grand Trunk Railway; Intercolonial Railway

2912
Ruppenthal, Karl M.; Keast, Thomas
The British Columbia Railway: A railway derailed
1979 Centre for Transportation Studies
Vancouver, Canada

This volume is mainly concerned to examine the economics and management of a railway owned by the province rather than by private enterprise. It contains some useful historical material on the construction, finances and intentions of the railway.
Firms: Pacific Great Eastern Railway; British Columbia Railway

2913
Stevens, George R.
Canadian National Railways: Vol. 1: Sixty Years of Trial and Error. Vol. 2: Towards the Inevitable
1960–2 Clarke, Irwin & Co. *Toronto, Canada*

Volume 1 (1836–1896) presents the historical background of the Canadian National Railways; volume 2 (1896–1922) deals in detail with the hundred plus railroads which merged into the CNR. The author was given full access to the records of the constituent railroads and the result is a thorough and useful analysis. It is strong on finances, the relations between business and politics, and personalities.
Firms: Canadian National Railways; Mackenzie and Mann

2914
Stevens, George R.
History of the Canadian National Railways
1973 Macmillan *New York, NY*

This book is the standard account of the Canadian National Railways, tracing its growth into one of the largest railway systems in North America. Stevens writes in a popular style and follows the story from the origins of the various lines that were incorporated into the CNR. He links the building of the CNR with the growth and development of the Canadian nation from the mid-nineteenth century to the 1970s.
Firms: Canadian National Railways; Canadian Northern Railway; Grand Trunk Railway; Intercolonial Railway

2915
Tulchinsky, Gerald J. J.
The River Barons: Montreal businessmen and the growth of industry and transportation 1837–1853
For main entry, see 3807

2916
Young, Brian J.
Promoters and Politicians: The North Shore railways in the history of Quebec 1854–1885
1978 University of Toronto Press *Toronto, Canada*

This is a history of Quebec's railways from the first unsuccessful line, the North Shore Railway chartered in 1853, through other attempts until the line was sold to the Canadian Pacific Railway in the 1880s. It brings out the poor returns until the line became part of a transcontinental link, and the massive government finance needed to build the line, but is rather thin on the impact on the local economy. Much of the work revolves around the interplay of the interests of the state, the church, the business community and the English- and French-speaking communities in Quebec.
Firms: Canada Central Railway; Canadian Pacific Railway; Grand Trunk Railway; Montreal

Colonization Railway; North Shore Railway; Quebec, Montreal, Ottawa and Occidental Railway

Railways, Far East

2917

Aoki, Eiichi; Oikawa, Yoshinobu (Editors)

Min-tetsu Keiei no Rekis hi to Bunka: Higashinihon-hen [History and Culture in Private Railway Business: East Japan]

1992 Kokon Shoin *Tokyo, Japan*

This book describes nine private railway companies located in eastern Japan, each with its own history and personality. The book is clearly written and plentifully illustrated.

Firms: Tobu Railway Co.; Tokyo Kyuko Electric Railway Co.; Odakyu Electric Railway Co.; Keihin Kyuko Electric Railway Co.; Keio Teito Electric Railway Co.; Seibu Railway Co.; Keisei Electric Railway Co.; Sagami Railway Co.; Shin-keisei Electric Railway Co.

2918

Chosen Sotoku-fu (Government-General of Korea)

Chosen Tetsudo-shi: Dai 1-kan [Korean Railway History: vol. 1]

1929 Government-General of Korea *Seoul, S. Korea*

This volume was written by the Government-General of Korea, at the time of Japanese rule. It deals with the construction process of the Seoul–Pusan Railway and Seoul–Chemulpo (Inchon) Railway, their nationalization in 1906, and other lines for military use. The second volume was never published.

Firms: Seoul–Pusan Railway; Seoul–Chemulpo (Inchon) Railway

2919

Harada, Katsumasa

Tetsudo-shi Kenkyu Shiron: Kindaika ni okeru Gijutsu to Shakai [Trial Studies on Railway History: Technology and Society in the Course of Japanese Modernization]

1989 Nihon Keizai Hyoron-sha *Tokyo, Japan*

The author examines the process of technological innovation and how it was managed in the railway business. In his final analysis, he refers to the role of railways in the course of Japanese modernization.

Firms: Imperial Government Railways

2920

Huenemann, Ralph William

The Dragon and the Iron Horse: The economics of railroads in China, 1876–1937

1984 Harvard University Press *Cambridge, MA*

This book is a revisionist contribution to the controversy about whether railroads helped the development of the Chinese economy or were a part of imperialist exploitation. It assesses the financial performance of Western railroad builders and the impact on the Chinese economy which the author argues was mainly favourable. There is plentiful statistical analysis of industry performance.

2921

Japan Business History Institute (Editor)

Hanshin Denki Tetsudo 80 nenshi [Eighty Years of the Hanshin Electric Railway Co.]

1985 Hanshin Electric Railway Co. *Osaka, Japan*

This book is a full account of the rise and progress of the Hanshin Electric Railway Company. It is strong on strategic management, the development of the regions by the railway, and its influence on the operation, modernization, diversification and rationalization of business activities.

Firms: Hanshin Electric Railway Co.

2922

Japanese National Railways

Nihon Kokuyu Tetsudo Hyakunen-shi [A Hundred Years of Japanese National Railways]

1969–74 Japanese National Railways *Tokyo, Japan*

Compiled to celebrate the centenary of Japan's national railways, this work covers the period 1872 to 1972 and consists of 19 volumes. This is the largest and fullest history of Japanese railways. A chronological table, enchiridion and pictorial history of the 100 years are included.

Firms: Imperial Government Railways; Japanese National Railways

2923
Kaneko, Fumio
Kindai Nihon ni okeru Tai Manshu Toshi no Kenkyu [A Study of Investment to Manchuria in Modern Japan]
1991 Kondo Shuppan-sha *Tokyo, Japan*

In this detailed work, various activities of South Manchurian Railway Co. Ltd are described, including its foundation, financing, earnings and relationships with colonial financial organizations.
Firms: South Manchurian Railway Co.

2924
Keihin Kyuko Electric Railway Co.
Keihin Kyuko Hachijunen-shi [Eighty Years of Keihin Kyuko Electric Railway Co. Ltd.]
1980 Keihin Kyuko Electric Railway Co. *Tokyo, Japan*

This provides a good history of the Keihin Kyuko Electric Railway Co. Ltd from the establishment of its precedessor, the Daishi Electric Railway Co. in 1898. The book also includes much on organization, personnel and financial management.
Firms: Daishi Electric Railway Co.; Keihin Electric Railway Co.; Keihin Kyuko Electric Railway Co.

2925
Ministry of Railways
Nihon Tetsudo-sho [Japanese Railway History]
1921 Ministry of Railways *Tokyo, Japan*

This is an authentic history celebrating fifty years of Japanese railways. There are three volumes: 1. The early period: 1872–1892 and preceding histories; 2. Co-existence of Imperial Government Railways and private railway companies: 1893–1906; 3. After the nationalization of railways: 1907–1921.

2926
Nakanishi, Ken'ichi
Nihon Shiyu Tetsudo-shi Kenkyu: Toshi Kotsu no Hatten to sono Kozo [Historical Studies of Japanese Private Railways The development and structure of urban transport]
1963 Nihon Hyoron-shinsha *Tokyo, Japan*

This work marks an epoch in Japanese railway history studies. Its value lies in minute and positive analysis, not seen in former studies. Above all, its analysis of railway nationalization is outstanding.

2927
Noda, Masaho
Nihon Shoken Shijo Seiritsu-shi: Meiji-ki no Tetsudo Kaisha to Kabushiki Kaisha Kin'yu [A History of the Securities Market in Japan: Railway companies and their financing activities during the Meiji era]
1980 Yuhikaku *Tokyo, Japan*

This book was long in preparation, indicating its interest and importance in Japanese railway business history. It has two main analyses: one examines the natire of securities issued during the Meiji era in connection with private railway companies; the other clarifies the financing and refinancing mechanisms employed by private railway companies.

2928
Noda, Masaho; Harada, Katsumasa (Editors)
Nihon no Tetsudo: Seiritsu to Tenkai [Japanese Railways: Their formation and development]
1986 Nihon Keizai Hyoron-sha *Tokyo, Japan*

This is the first general study of railway history in Japan. With essays by thirteen individual authors, the most up to date railway history from the beginning to the 1980s is described. The biographical sketches of railway bureaucrats and entrepreneurs are also very useful.

2929
Noda, Masaho; Harada, Katsumasa; Aoki, Eiichi (Editors)
Meiji-ki Tetsudo-shi Shiryo: Dai 1-ki [Historical Materials for Railways in the Meiji Period: First series]
1980–81 Nihon Keizai Hyoron-sha *Tokyo, Japan*

This series contains twenty-nine volumes of materials from the Meiji period which are important for the study of Japanese railway history. It includes the annual statistics of the Railway Bureau for the period 1886 to 1907, histories of private companies (Nihon Railway

Co., San'yo Railway Co., Kyushu Railway Co. etc.), and biographies of railway entrepreneurs (Seinosuke Imamura, Hikojiro Nakamigawa, Keijiro Amemiya, etc.).
Firms: Kyushu Railway Co.; Nihon Railway Co.; San'yo Railway Co.

2930
Noda, Masaho; Harada, Katsumasa; Aoki, Eiichi (Editors)
Taisho-ki Tetsudo-shi Shiryo: Dai 1-ki [Historical Materials Relating to Railways in the Taisho Period: First series]
1983–5 Nihon Keizai Hyoron-sha *Tokyo, Japan*

This is a continuation of the series publishing important documents relating to Japanese railway history, in this case in the Taisho period. It consists of forty-four volumes including the annual statistics of the ministry of railways for the period 1908–25, reports on the nationalization of railways in 1906–7, the project on reconstructing the track gauge and histories of some of the private railway companies.
Firms: Tokyo Underground Railway Co.; Toky–Yokohama Electric Railway Co.

2931
Noda, Masaho; Harada, Katsumasa; Aoki, Eiichi; Oikawa, Yoshinobu (Editors)
Meiji-ki Tetsudo-shi Shiryo: Dai 2-ki [Historical Materials for Railways in the Meiji Period: Second series]
1987–9 Nihon Keizai Hyoron-sha *Tokyo, Japan*

This is a follow up to the first series of sources on Japanese railway history in the Meiji period (qv). It consists of forty-four volumes and includes the annual statistics of the Railway Operating Bureau for the period 1897–1907, reports of military transport, and minutes of the railway council.

2932
Noda, Masaho; Harada, Katsumasa; Aoki, Eiichi; Oikawa, Yoshinobu (Editors)
Showa-ki Tetsudo-shi Shiryo [Historical Materials Relating to Railways in the Showa Period]
1990–2 Nihon Keizai Hyoron-sha *Tokyo, Japan*

This is another set of documents relating to Japanese railway history, this time in the Showa period. This series consists of forty-five volumes and includes the annual statistics of the Ministry of Railways for the period 1926–48.

2933
Noda, Masaho; Harada, Katsumasa; Aoki, Eiichi; Oikawa, Yoshinobu (Editors)
Taisho-ki Tetsudo-shi Shiryo: Dai 2-ki [Historical Materials Relating to Railways in the Taisho Period: Second series]
1990–2 Nihon Keizai Hyoron-sha *Tokyo, Japan*

This is another series in this important set of volumes of documents relating to Japanese railway history. This series consists of seventeen volumes. It includes reports on the arrangements for the funeral of the Emperor Taisho (Yoshihito) and the coronation transport of the Emperor Showa (Hirohito) and discussion papers on the management policy of the Imperial Government Railways.

2934
Noguchi, Paul H.
Delayed Departures, Overdue Arrivals: Industrial familialism and the Japanese national railways
1990 University of Hawaii Press *Honolulu, HA*

Primarily a sociological and cultural study of the stressful and unhappy employment patterns on Japan's nationalized railways, but also one of the rare English-language works to cover the Japanese railway industry.
Firms: Japanese National Railways

2935
Oikawa, Yoshinobu
Meiji-ki Chiho Tetsudo-shi Kenkyu: Chiho Tetsudo no Tenkai to Shijo Keisei [A Study of Rural Railways History in Japan During the Meiji Era: The development of rural railways and formation of market area]
1983 Nihon Keizai Hyoron-sha *Tokyo, Japan*

This book is a published version of a thesis accepted by the St Paul's University for the degree of Doctor of Economics in 1982. It reconsiders the role and limits of railway construc-

tion in the formation of market areas at the beginning of the Meiji era.
Firms: Kyoto Railway Co.; Ryomo Railway Co.; Sobu Railway Co.

2936
Oikawa, Yoshinobu
Sangyo Kaku mei-ki no Chiiki Kotsu to Yuso [Local Transport and Traffic During the Industrial Revolution Period in Japan]
1992 Nihon Keizai Hyoron-sha *Tokyo, Japan*

This work examines the circulation of commodities and the development of industries from the viewpoint of transport and traffic problems. An excellent feature is the attention given to the interrelationships between railways and inland water transport and road transport.
Firms: Nihon Railway Co.; Ryomo Railway Co.; Joby Railway Co.; Tobu Railway Co.

2937
Oshima, Fujitaro
Kokka Dokusen Shihon toshiteno Kokuya Tetsudo no Shiteki Hatten [Historical Process of Imperial Government Railways as State Monopolistic Capital]
1949 Ito Shoten *Tokyo, Japan*

This was the first book published in the field of transport business history in Japan after the Second World War. Its analysis is based on Marxian economic theory, covering not only railway business but also forwarding and road haulage business.
Firms: Imperial Government Railways

2938
Shima, Yashuhiko
Nihon Shihonshugi to Kokuyu Tetsudo [Japanese Capitalism and Imperial Government Railways]
1950 Nihon Hyoron-shinsha *Tokyo, Japan*

This work deals with many aspects of the character and nature of Imperial Government Railways. Its analysis includes the foundation of Imperial Government Railways, railway nationalization in 1906–1907, capital investment, and problems in labour management.
Firms: Imperial Government Railways

2939
South Manchurian Railway Co.
Minami Manshu Tetsudo Kabushiki Kaisha Dai 3-ji Junen-shi [The Third Decade of South Manchurian Railway Co.]
1938 South Manchurian Railway Co. *Dalian, Manchuria*

The South Manchurian Railway Company published its company history in several volumes, the first in 1919, the second in 1928. This is the third volume covering the period 1927–1931 and describes mainly business organization, operations and financial performance.
Firms: South Manchurian Railway Co.

2940
Takechi, Kyozo
Toshi Kinko Tetsudo no Shiteki Tenkai [Historical Studies of Railway Companies in the Suburbs of Osaka]
1986 Nihon Keizai Hyoron-sha *Tokyo, Japan*

This book provides a very detailed archivally-based study of railways companies in the suburbs of Osaka.
Firms: Nishinari Railway Co. Ltd; Osaka Railway Co. Ltd; Nankai Railway Co. Ltd

2941
Tominaga, Yuji
Kotsu ni okeru Shihonshugi no Hatten: Ninon Kotsu-gyo no Kindaika Katei [The Penetration of Capitalism into the Transport Sector: A process of modernization in the Japanese transportation industry]
1953 Iwanami Shoten *Tokyo, Japan*

A classic work of transport history in Japan, which treats many transport problems from the beginnings. Its analysis of the railway nationalization process in Japan is especially influential on contemporary studies.

Railways, Rest of World

2942
Beckenham, Arthur F.
Wagons of Smoke: An informal history of the East African Railways and Harbours Administration 1948–1961
1987 Cadogan Publications *London*

This book was written by a veteran of railway work in the period covered and hence is not totally objective. It is good on the operational difficulties of running a complex railway, the growth of freight traffic, and the technical side of investment projects. However, it is descriptive, anecdotal and lacks real analysis but deserves inclusion because of its rarity value.
Firms: East African Railways and Harbours Administration

2943
Blakemore, Harold
From the Pacific to La Paz: The Antofagasta (Chili) and Bolivia Railway Company 1888–1988
1990 Lester Crook *London*

This is the history of a railway built by British capital and enterprise and run by British managers and engineers until the 1970s. It is strong on the traffic, labour, and government relations but marginally uncritical. It also contextualizes the railways's history within the broader Chilean social, economic and political climate.
Firms: Antofagasta & Bolivia Railway Co.

2944
Campbell, Edward D.
The Birth and Development of the Natal Railways
1951 Shuter & Shooter *Pietermaritzburg, South Africa*

Although this is in the tradition of the unacademic, reminiscence-based, in-company history, so little has been written on the business history of South African railways that it is worth including. It is strong on the technical, financial and political problems of construction and the operations and rolling stock.
Firms: Natal Railway Co.; Natal Government Railways; South African Railways

2945
El-Karah, A. C.
Filha Branca de mae preta: A companhia da estrada de ferro D. Pedro II, 1855–1865 [Black Mother's White Daughter: The railway company of D. Pedro II, 1855–1865]
1982 Vozes *Petropolis, Brazil*

This work examines the first eleven years of the history of one of the most important railways in nineteenth-century Brazil. The period covered in this book comprises the establishment of the railway in 1855, as a private enterprise, until the date when the company was taken over by the Imperial Government in 1865.
Firms: Companhia da Estrada de Ferro D. Pedro II

2946
Helten, Jean-Jacques van
German Capital, The Netherlands Railway Co. and the Political Economy of the Transvaal 1886–1900
Journal of African History, vol. 19, no. 3, 1978: pp 369–90

This is a study of the firm which possessed the monopoly of railways between the Transvaal and the outside world, with special focus on the company's impact on relations with Great Britain in the years before the South African War 1899-1902.
Firms: Netherlands South African Railway Co.

2947
Lewis, Colin M.
British Railways in Argentina, 1857–1914: A case study of foreign investment
1983 Athlone Press *London*

This is not a mainstream business history but rather a study of British investment in Argentinian railways which incidentally sheds light on the history of those firms. It is strong on the relationship between government and business, the quality of the service, and the profitability of the system. This is a perceptive and revisionist volume.

2948
O'Connor, A. M.
Railways and Development in Uganda
1965 East African Institute of Social Research *Nairobi, Kenya*

Although essentially a geographical study of the effect of railways on the economic development of Uganda, there is much material on the history of railways in the country, and hence its inclusion here. It is not a proper business history and hence has many gaps and omissions.
Firms: East African Railways & Harbours

2949
Ortega, Alfredo
Ferrocarriles Colombianos: Resumen Histórico [Colombian Railroads: A historical summary]
1920 Biblioteca de Historia Nacional *Bogotá, Colombia*

These two volumes include a detailed account of all railroad projects carried out in Colombia in the 1850–1920 period. The emphasis is contractual and legal; Ortega's volumes are distinctively a 'history of contractual litigations' rather than an analytical work. They have been a key source for historians of Colombian railroads.

2950
Paddison, L. I.
The Railways of New South Wales, 1855–1955
1955 Department of Railways, NSW *Sydney, Australia*

This is a historical narrative written from the archives of the railway to celebrate its centenary. It is a descriptive rather than analytical account of the construction and development of the state-owned system which took over the capital-starved private initiatives. Thus it is more a useful source than an analytic history in its own right.
Firms: Department of Railways, NSW; Hunter River Railway Co.; Sydney Railway Co.

2951
Saes, Flávio Azevedo Marques de
As ferrovias de São Paulo, 1870–1940 [The Railways of São Paulo, 1870–1940]
1981 Hucitec/INL-MEC *São Paulo, Brazil*

The author examines the decline in importance of the railways in Brazil. More specifically, he discusses the railways of São Paulo, comparing the first decades of prosperity with the situation in the 1930s, when the railway companies were faced with crisis. The work covers 70 years (1870–1940) of the existence of Paulista railways.
Firms: Companhia Mojiana; Companhia Paulista; Companhia Sorocabana

2952
Saes, Flávio Azevedo Marques de
A grande empresa de serviços públicos na economi cafeeira 1850–1930 [A Great Enterprise of Public Service in the Coffee Economy 1850–1930]
1986 Editora Hucitec *São Paulo, Brazil*

This is a general analysis of the origin and development of railway and public utility companies in the coffee economy of São Paulo. De Saes demonstrates that close links initially existed between the agricultural sector and the utilities created to service it in terms of capital flows, ownership, and a perceived unity of interest. However, as foreign capital increasingly came to dominate in the ownership and management of utilities, conflicts with the rural oligarchy ensued. This was reinforced by weakening links between agriculturalists and railways and utilities, as the latter developed corporate strategies for operation, organization and development in their own right rather than simply as service activities ancillary to coffee production and export.

2953
Stone, Russell C. J.
The Thames Valley and Rotorua Railway Company Ltd, 1882–9
New Zealand Journal of History, 1974: pp 22–43

This company was floated by land speculators in expectation of benefiting from the land grant scheme for railways, modelled on the American approach. When the company ran into trouble it was rescued by the Vogel government amid intimations of collusion.
Firms: Bank of New Zealand; New Zealand Loan and Mercantile Agency Co.; Thames Valley and Rotorua Railway Co.

2954
Winter, P. J. van
Order Krugers Hollanders: Geschiedenis van die Nederlandsche Zuid-Afrikaansche Spoorweg Maatschappij [History of the Netherlands-South Africa Railway]
1937–8 Bussy *Amsterdam, The Netherlands*

A definitive business history in two volumes.
Firms: Nederlandsche Zuid-Afrikaansche Spoorweg

2955

Williams, Cyril R.

Wheels and Paddles in the Sudan 1923–1946

1986 Pentland Press *Edinburgh, Scotland*

This large volume represents the memoirs of a long-serving expatriate engineer on the Sudan Railways and Steamers from the 1920s to the end of the Second World War. It is not strictly a business history but deals with some aspects such as technical developments, negotiations with government, and labour relations. This is a rare example of the recording of personal involvement in colonial transport history.

Firms: Sudan Railways and Steamers

2956

Wright, Winthrop R.

British-owned railways in Argentina: Their effect on the growth of economic nationalism 1854–1948

1974 University of Texas Press *Austin, TX*

During the nineteenth century, British-owned railways grew under the protection of an Argentinian ruling elite that considered railways both instruments and symbols of progress. Under this programme of support for foreign enterprise, Argentina had by 1914 built the largest railway network in Latin America. In the twentieth century these railroads increasingly acted in disregard for Argentinian economic interest and they became a major target for nationalist politics. Wright provides a detailed account up to Peron's purchase of the foreign-owned railways.

Firms: Anglo-Argentine Tramway Co.; Buenos Ayres and Pacific Railway; Central Argentine Railway; Great Southern Railway; Western Railway; Central Cordoba Railway

Inland Transport

2957

Bejarano, Jesús A. (Editor)

El Siglo XIX en Colombia Visto por Historiadores Norteamericanos [The Nineteenth Century in Colombia: The American historians' view]

1977 La Carreta *Bogotá, Colombia*

This book is a collection of chapters from ten doctoral theses in American universities dealing with the nineteenth century in Colombia. Seven of them contribute to Colombian business history by dealing respectively with export crops (tobacco, coffee), transport, especially river navigation and railroads, and protectionism. Lack of an index and poor editing hinder this volume, whose contribution is to get to Spanish-speaking readers studies otherwise unavailable in that language.

2958

Castaneda, Christopher J.; Pratt, Joseph A.

From Texas to the East: A strategic history of Texas Eastern Corporation

1993 Texas A & M University Press *College Station, TX*

A useful history in an under-researched area of oil and gas transmission, this tends to see the world from the company's point of view and fails to view critically the ill-judged diversifications and the opportunities as well as the challenges of regulation.

Firms: Texas Eastern Corporation; Brown & Root

2959

Johnson, Arthur M.

The Development of American Petroleum Pipelines: A study in private enterprise and public policy, 1862–1906

1956 Cornell University Press *Ithaca, NY*

This book is rather dated now but remains an invaluable study of the early history of the US pipeline industry, in western Pennsylvania, Indiana, Ohio and Kentucky. It demonstrates the competition with the railroads, the amalgamation movement, and their role in anti-trust developments. It is particularly strong on the implications of the industrial strategy on public policy.

Firms: Allegheny Transport Co.; Empire Transport Co.; National Transit Co.; Standard Oil; Tide Water Pipe Co.; United Pipe Lines

2960

Johnson, Arthur M.

Petroleum Pipelines and Public Policy 1906–1959

1967 Harvard University Press *Cambridge, MA*

This volume 'centres on alterations in the policies of a group of pipeline operators in response to changes in the political and regulatory climate, in technology, and in the economics of producing, transporting and marketing petroleum products in an industry which was highly vertically integrated'. It carries on the analysis begun by Johnson in his earlier volume *The Development of American Petroleum Pipelines* (qv).

Firms: Buckeye Pipe Line Co.; Prairie Oil & Gas Co.; Pure Oil Pipe Line Co.; Standard Oil

2961

Loos, John L.

Oil on Stream!: A history of Interstate Oil Pipe Line Company, 1909–1959

1959 Louisiana State University Press *Baton Rouge, LA*

This is the history of the planning, construction and operation of a major southern pipeline running from the mid-continent oilfields to the Baton Rouge refinery in Louisiana. It began as the Prairie Pipe Line Co. of Oklahoma and Standard Pipe Line Co. of Louisiana which merged into Interstate in 1944. Although commissioned, the book is scholarly and well referenced. It is strong on the technical side, and on the structure and personalities, but thin on the financial performance.

Firms: Interstate Oil Pipe Line; Prairie Pipe Line Co.; Standard Pipe Line Co.

2962

Merger, Michèle (Editor)

Les transports [Transport]

Histoire Économie et Société, vol. 9, 1990

This is a special issue of the review *Histoire Économie et Société* which presents eight articles dealing with French transport in the nineteenth and twentieth centuries. It deals with roads, railways, traffic and tramways, and competition between railway and waterways.

2963

Merger, Michèle

Les transports terrestres en Europe Continentale (XIXe. XX^{e}s) [Inland Transport in Continental Europe in the Nineteenth and Twentieth Centuries]

Histoire Économie et Société, vol. 11, 1992

This is a special issue of the review *Histoire Économie et Société* which includes twelve articles by European scholars. These studies deal with inland transport in Germany, The Netherlands, Belgium, Switzerland, Italy, Spain and Portugal. They cover the backward and forward linkages of railways, the modernization of the networks and waterway traffic.

Urban Passenger Transport

2964

Anderson, Roy C.

A History of Crosville Motor Services

1981 David & Charles *Newton Abbot*

Written by an ex-employee of the firm, this book traces the history of a bus service operating in North and Central Wales which was founded as a family business by the same family as began Crosville Motors. It is good on the people, the buses and routes served, the firms taken over and has a bibliography, but is thin on financial aspects and lacks references.

Firms: British Electric Traction Co.; Crosville Motor Co.; Crosville Motor Services; London Midland & Scottish Railway; Thomas Tilling

2965

Anderson, Roy C.

A History of The Midland Red

1984 David & Charles *Newton Abbot*

This volume gives a history of a number of bus companies operating in the Midlands of England which merged to become Birmingham & Midland Motor Omnibus Co. It is strong on the vehicles, the mergers and amalgamations, the routes served and the entrepreneurs, but is thin on financial aspects and marketing. It is well-illustrated but lacks references, sources and a bibliography.

Firms: Birmingham & Midland Motor Omnibus Co.; British Electric Traction Co.

2966

Anderson, Roy C.; Frankis, Geoffrey G. A.

A History of Western National

1979 David & Charles *Newton Abbot*

This book was written by two managers in the industry drawing on the company archives and personal memories of managers and employees. It is good on the routes served, operating companies, mergers and technical changes in bus design and operation but has little on the financial side and lacks notes, sources and even a bibliography. Hence it appeals more to the enthusiast than the academic. Western National was active in South West England from 1929 being a merger of many predecessor companies running buses, including the Great Western Railway.

Firms: British Electric Traction; Great Western Railway; Thomas Tilling; Western National

2967

Anderson, Roy C.; Frankis, Geoffrey G. A.

A History of Royal Blue Express Services

2nd Edition

1985 David & Charles *Newton Abbot*

This book traces the evolution of a family firm in horse-drawn coach and charabanc operations in the west of England in the 1880s, through its acquisition of motor buses, entry into pooling agreements and absorption by Thomas Tilling, to nationalization. It is strong on mergers and ownership, the vehicles and routes, but thin on finances. It is well illustrated but lacks references and a bibliography.

Firms: Associated Motorways; Elliott's Royal Blue; Royal Blue Express Services; Thomas Tilling

2968

Andrews, H. H.

Electricity in Transport: Over Sixty Years' Experience, 1883–1950

For main entry, see 1503

2969

Anon.

Metropolitan: L'autre dimension de la ville [The Metropolitan: Paris's other dimension]

1988 Bibliothèque Historique de la Ville *Paris, France*

This book contains several different studies which analyse the Parisian transport system before and after the construction of the subway network.

2970

Armstrong, Christopher; Nelles H. V.

Southern Exposure: Canadian promoters in Latin America and the Caribbean, 1896–1930

For main entry, see 2748

2971

Barker, Theodore C.; Robbins, Michael

A History of London Transport: Passenger travel and the development of the metropolis

1963/74 Allen & Unwin *London*

This two-volume account is the only comprehensive history of the developments in large-scale passenger transport by bus, tram, tube and rail which merged to form London Transport in 1933. It is particularly strong on changes in demand and technology and relations with government. It draws upon a wide range of archives including personal papers, official records and those of the London Passenger Transport Board.

Firms: London Passenger Transport Board; London Transport

2972

Belasco, Warren James

Americans on the Road: From auto camp to motel, 1910–45

For main entry, see 911

2973

Birks, John A.; Brittan, Yvonne; Dickie, Keith A. S.; Beetham, Tony

National Bus Company 1968–1989

1990 Transport Publishing *Glossop*

This large volume is a detailed history of the nationalized bus company until deregulation and privatization in 1985 and the first few years of independence. It is strong on relations with government and the operational side of running the firm, but is thin on analysis and is rather uncritical.

Firms: National Bus Co.

2974

Crandall, B. B.

The Growth of the Intercity Bus Industry

1954 Syracuse University College of Business *Syracuse, NY*

This rewritten PhD dissertation offers the only scholarly account of the rise of the US intercity bus industry. Crandall bases his work on published decisions of state regulatory agencies and the Interstate Commerce Commission, as well as on trade journals. Crandall offers insight into the changing structure of the industry, its market, its regulation, and its relation with steam railroads and electric interurban railways.

2975

Cudahy, Brian J.

Under the Sidewalks of New York: The story of the greatest subway system in the world

1979 Stephen Greene Press *Brattleboro, VT*

Although this volume is neither scholarly nor analytical, lacking references, sources and even a bibliography, it is well-illustrated and in the absence of a better study of the New York subway system earns its place here. It is good on the personalities and main events but does not claim to be a business history.

Firms: Brooklyn-Manhattan Transit Corp. (BMT); Independent Subway (IND); Interborough Rapid Transport System (IRT)

2976

Daumas, M.; Fontanon, C.; Jigaudon, G.; Larroque, D.

Analyse historique de l'évolution des transports en commun dans le région parisienne de 1855 à 1939 [A Historical Analysis of the Evolution of Public Transport in the Paris Region 1855–1939]

1977 Centre de documentation d'histoire *Paris, France*

This book is in two parts, the first covering the political background to and decisions on public transport from the Second Empire to the Second World War. The second part chronicles urban growth and the development of trains, buses and the underground in the same period.

2977

Freeman, James D. F.; Jowitt, Robert E.; Murphy, Richard J.

King Alfred Motor Services: The story of a Winchester family business

1984 Kingfisher Railway Productions *Southampton*

This is an enthusiastic history of a family-run bus service based in Winchester from 1920 to 1973. It is strong on routes and vehicle types, but thin on the other aspects of the business. It is lavishly illustrated but of limited use to the business historian.

Firms: Hants & Dorset; King Alfred Motor Services

2978

Herranen, Timo

Hevosomnibusseista metroon: Vuosisata Helsingin joukkoliikennettä [From Horse-Driven Omnibuses to the Underground: A century of public transport in Helsinki]

1988 Helsinki Board of Transport & City Council *Helsinki, Finland*

This history of public transport in the capital of Finland covers the period from the 1830s to the 1980s and is linked to the growth of the city. The book deals with the municipalization of tramways, the greater part of bus transport and the construction of an underground line. The debate on municipal traffic policy under the growing pressure of motoring is also a theme in this lavishly illustrated book.

Firms: Helsingin kaupungin liikennelaitos

2979

Hilton, George W.; Due, J. F.

The Electric Interurban Railways in America

1960 Stanford University Press *Stanford, CA*

This is the only exhaustive study of the US interurban railway industry. Hilton and Due examined trade journals, state and US regulatory decisions, as well as local histories of lines, often written by rail buffs, to write informed chapters on such topics as the industry's technology, its financial history, patterns of investment and disinvestment, regulation, and the decision to abandon. In the last half of the book, they present concise histories of every firm that existed in the industry.

2980

Hunter, David L. G.

From S.M.T. to Eastern Scottish

1987 John Donald *Edinburgh, Scotland*

This volume traces the history of what be-

came the Scottish Bus Group, from its inception in 1905 to 1985, when it was restructured. It is strong on the personalities, vehicle types and technology, the mergers and reorganizations, routes and services. However, it tends to be rather descriptive and lacks analysis of the businesss aspects of the firms.
Firms: Scottish Bus Group; Scottish Motor Traction

2981
Jackson, Alan A.
London's Metropolitan Railway
1986 David & Charles *Newton Abbot*
This history of the Metropolitan Railway, which became part of London Transport in 1933, is strong on the technology and business strategy aspects, has a chapter on the labour force, and covers the passengers and finances adequately. It is also good on the entrepreneurs and the interaction of railways and urban development.
Firms: Metropolitan Railway; London Transport; London Passenger Transport Board

2982
Jackson, Alan A.; Croome, Desmond F.
Rails Through the Clay: A history of London's tube railways
1962 George Allen & Unwin *London*
This pioneering volume narrates the history of London's deep level underground railway system. It concentrates on the technical, financial and political problems of construction and is strong on the entrepreneurs involved and the growth and extension of the system. It is not really a business history but is invaluable in understanding the business of London's tube network.
Firms: City & South London Railway; Waterloo & City Railway; Central London Railway; London Transport; London Passenger Transport Board

2983
Jackson, Carlton
Hounds of the Road: A history of the Greyhound Bus Company
1984 Bowling Green University Popular Press *Bowling Green, OH*
This volume is a popular history of America's premier long distance bus company. Although it has a full bibliography and referencing, it also includes anecdotes and apocryphal stories. There is a strong narrative thread covering the services offered, the competitors, the amalgamations, and the marketing techniques. The captionless illustrations are, however, frustrating.
Firms: Greyhound Corporation; Trailways

2984
Keenan, J.
Cincinnati and Lake Erie Railroad: Ohio's greatest interurban system
1974 Golden West Books *San Marino, CA*
While this is an enthusiast book and lacks footnotes, it is an excellent business history of one of the several attempts to adjust interurban service to the automobile age. A son of the company's advertising and public relations manager and himself a vice president of a New York-based international business products company, Keenan had an excellent perspective for writing the book. He proves to have been a sensitive and perceptive researcher of the company's history, part of which he experienced as a child.
Firms: Cincinnati and Lake Erie Railroad; Cincinnati, Hamilton and Dayton Railroad; Indiana Railroad; Lake Shore Electric Railroad; Ohio Electric Railroad

2985
Lowry, Goodrich
Streetcar Man: Tom Lowry and the Twin City Rapid Transit Co.
1979 Lerner Publications *Minneapolis, MN*
This is a business biography of Lowry by his grandson, hence it is not objective and tends to present no criticisms. It is good on the depiction of provincial business machinations but thin on operational details, financial and promotional strategies. It is included because of the scarcity of business historians of rapid transit systems.
Firms: Minneapolis Street Railway Co.; Twin City Rapid Transit Co.

2986
Mantegazza, Amilcare; Pavese, Claudio
L'ATM di Milano 1861–1972: Un secolo di trasporto urbano tra finalità pubbliche e

vincoli di bilancio [The ATM of Milan 1861–1972: A century of urban transport between public service and the obligation of the balance sheet]
1992 Franco Angeli/CIRIEC *Milan, Italy*

This is a detailed history of the public transport system in Milan from the unification of Italy in 1861. It analyses the evolution of the privately-owned and managed omnibus company of the 1860s operating in Milan into the powerful municipal agency, which today runs the entire city system of buses, trolleys and subways.

Firms: Azienda Tramviara Municipale

2987
Maund, T. B.
Ribble Volume 1
1993 Venture Publications *Glossop*

Although aimed at the enthusiast market rather than the academic, this well illustrated volume tells the story of one of Britain's largest provincial bus businesses based in the north-west of England. It is a clear narrative but rather short of analysis and thin on finance and management.

Firms: Ribble Motor Services; British Electric Traction; London Midland & Scottish Railway

2988
McDowell, Duncan
The Light: Brazilian Traction, Light and Power Company Limited, 1899–1945
For main entry, see 2756

2989
McKay, John P.
Tramways and Trolleys: The rise of urban mass transport in Europe
1976 Princeton University Press *Princeton, NJ*

The thirty-year period before the First World War is closely examined in this succinct history of European urban transport. Technological innovation in the late nineteenth century is shown to have revolutionized urban living. This is a stimulating and scholarly work recommended for its lucid analysis of a multifaceted subject.

2990
Papayanis, Nicholas
La prolétarianization des cochers de fiacres à Paris 1878–1889 [The Proletarianisation of Parisian Coachmen 1878–1889]
1985 Editions Ouvrières *Paris, France*

The author demonstrates that coachmen in Paris were divided into two groups, the ordinary coachmen and small cab firms which felt a commonality of interests against the larger capitalistic companies. Although not really a true business history, this work is nevertheless important to an understanding of Parisian urban transport.

2991
Papayanis, Nicholas
The Coachmen of Nineteenth Century Paris: Service workers and class consciousness
1993 Louisiana State University Press *Baton Rouge, LA*

This volume is not a business history per se but is a valuable study of the labour force operating Parisian cabs in the nineteenth century. Papayanis concentrates on class formation, consciousness and struggle among an apparently exploited and individualistic group. There is some incidental information on the nature of the cab business but the main analysis is of the labour force.

Firms: Compagnie Générale des Omnibus; Compagnie Impériale des Voitures à Paris

2992
Singleton, John
Monopolistic Tendencies in Road Passenger Transport: The rise of Ribble Motor Services Ltd 1919–1939
1993 Manchester University *Manchester*

This brief booklet examines the business policy of Ribble Motor Services which allowed it to become one of the largest operators of buses and coaches in north-west England by 1939. It deals well with its acquisition by British Electric Traction which then cartelized the market and provided capital for acquisition of local competing firms.

Firms: British Electric Traction; Ribble Motor Services; Tilling Brothers

2993
Thompson, Gregory Lee
The Passenger Train in the Motor Age: California's rail and bus industries 1910–1941
For main entry, see 2896

2994
Watson, Nigel
'United': A short history of United Automobile Services Ltd, 1912–1987
1987 United Automobile Services *Darlington*

This short volume provides a good narrative history of a major English regional bus service provider, from its inception until deregulation. It is well-illustrated, strong on the fleet and contains much operating detail but is eccentric in its presentation and lacks analysis of the major business aspects.
Firms: United Automobile Services

Road Haulage

2995
Anderson, L.
Coaches North: The story of the Hawke's Bay Motor Company
1967 A. H. & A. W. Reed *Auckland, New Zealand*

This book gives a rather disappointing history of the growth and development of this New Zealand road haulage firm. It explains the change from horse to motor transport but tends towards anecdote and 'human interest' stories.
Firms: Hawke's Bay Motor Co.

2996
Austin, Kenneth A.
The Lights of Cobb and Co: The story of the frontier coaches, 1854–1924
1967 Angus & Robertson *London*

Although rather narrative and lacking much analysis of the business, given the paucity of volumes on Australian horse transport firms, this book deserves inclusion. It tells the story of Cobb & Co. which ran horse-drawn passenger, goods and mail coaches in Australia and moved on to motor vehicles in the early twentieth century. It is strong on the origins, personalities, routes and passengers.
Firms: Cobb & Co.

2997
Barker, Theo
The Transport Contractors of Rye: John Jempson & Son: A chapter in the history of British road haulage
1982 Athlone Press *London*

This is one of the very few business histories of a road haulage firm in Britain written by an academic rather than an enthusiast. The firm's life spans the period from horse to motor, and from family firm to nationalization and then re-privatization. It is strong on the performance of the firm as well as the trades and type of loads.
Firms: John Jempson & Son

2998
Childs, William R.
Trucking and the Public Interest: The emergence of federal regulation, 1914–1940
1985 University of Tennessee Press *Knoxville, TN*

This is a case study of the complexities of the federal regulation of the American trucking industry. Events leading to government involvement in transport form the framework for this skilfully executed study in which the author presents a number of reasons for the eventual system of regulation. Organized and direct, this work provides a clearer picture of a chaotic period in business history than has previously been available.

2999
Felton, J.; Anderson, D. (Editors)
Regulation and Deregulation of the Motor Carrier Industry
1989 Iowa State University Press *Ames, IA*

This book analyses the federal regulation of the American trucking industry from 1935 to its deregulation in 1980 by the Interstate Commerce Commission. It is a well-documented collection of papers by faculty and doctoral students from the University of Nebraska at Lincoln. Close attention to historical detail as well as statistics and economics makes this a valuable contribution.

3000
Gerhold, Dorian
Road Transport before the Railways: Russell's London flying waggons
1993 Cambridge University Press *Cambridge*

A history of Russells of Exeter, which operated pack horses and horse-drawn waggons between Exeter and London from the seventeenth to the nineteenth centuries. It is based on the firm's letters and papers, is well-referenced and authoritative. It covers the partners, customers, costs of operation, prices and profits, competitors and operating methods. A first class piece of work.
Firms: Russell & Co.

3001
Giroletti, Domingos
A Companhia e a Rodovia União e Indústria e o Desenvolvimento de Juiz de Fora, 1850 a 1900 [The União e Indústria Company and Road and the Development of Juiz de Fora, 1850–1900]
1981 Federal University of Minas Gerais *Belo Horizonte, Brazil*

The book describes the organization of the União e Indústria Company and how it built a road from Juiz de Fora to Petropolis, Rio de Janeiro, between 1856 to 1861. It facilitated the export of coffee and brought in traded goods, integrating economically the federal capital with the countryside of Minas Gerais state. The Company and its road were key factors in the industrial and urban development of Juiz de Fora from the middle of the nineteenth century.
Firms: União e Indústria Company

3002
Hungerford, Edward
Wells Fargo: Advancing the American frontier
1949 Random House *New York, NY*

This is a history of the pioneering freight, mail and express company, Wells, Fargo and Company, which commenced trading in 1852 (and was incorporated in 1866) to take advantage of the gold boom in California. Although the book tends to dwell on the exciting incidents with robbers and bandits, it also provides a reasonable narrative of the company. It is thin on the business aspects, such as financial costs and returns and is generally unanalytical.
Firms: American Express; Wells, Fargo & Co.

3003
Nippon Tsu-un
Shashi: Nippon Tsu-un [A History of the Nippon Express Co.]
1962 Nippon Tsu-un *Tokyo, Japan*

Published to celebrate the 25th anniversary of Nippon Express Co. Ltd (Nippon Tsu-un) in 1963, this book describes the main predecessor companies and may be regarded as a major business history of road transport in Japan.
Firms: Kokusai Tsu-un; Naikoku Tsu-un; Nippon Tsu-un; Riku-un Moto Kaisha

3004
Paget-Tomlinson, Edward
The Railway Carriers: The history of Wordie & Co., carriers, hauliers and storekeepers
1990 Terence Dalton *Lavenham*

This volume gives a history of William Wordie & Co. of Stirling which provided transport services in Scotland and the north of Ireland from the late-eighteenth century until the 1960s. It is good on the workers and transport methods, the close association with some railway and shipping companies and the reasons for its demise.
Firms: William Wordie & Co.

3005
Reader, W. J.
Hard Roads and Highways: SPD Limited 1918–1968: A study in distribution
1969 Batsford *London*

This book provides one of the few studies of a British firm engaged in distribution of manufactured goods by road from the earliest days of road haulage, based on its archive, written by the most prolific of business historians. SPD was founded as a subsidiary of Lever Bros by William Lever to distribute the firm's soap. This book is strong on personalities, management style and structure and business policy.
Firms: Lever Bros; SPD Ltd; Unilever

3006
Rose, Mark H.
Interstate: Express highway politics 1941–1956
1979 Regents Press of Kansas *Lawrence, KS*

This volume looks briefly at US highway

policy from 1890 to 1941 but concentrates on the period 1941–56 when the interstate highway system was planned and began to be built. This study is particularly strong on the disagreements between the various interest groups who lobbied for road improvements, and their effect on planners and politicians. It is not a conventional business history but is good on government–business interrelationships.

3007
Seth-Smith, Michael
The Long Haul: A social history of the British commercial vehicle industry
1975 Hutchinson *London*

A sound outline history of the British road haulage industry.

3008
Thompson, Sir Peter
Sharing the Success: The story of NFC
1990 Collins *London*

Thompson pioneered the sensationally successful employee buy-out of the National Freight Corporation when this previously nationalized business was privatized in 1982. This is his account of how he did it and how he made some of his employees extremely wealthy when the NFC went public in 1989. Particularly interesting are his comments on the flotation overheads charged by City institutions. It is a lively account of this incident in recent business history.
Firms: National Freight Corporation

3009
Turnbull, Gerard L.
Traffic and Transport: An economic history of Pickfords
1979 George Allen & Unwin *London*

Pickfords provided long distance goods carriage from the 1750s, using horse and wagon, canal-boat, railway and finally motors. It absorbed Carter Paterson, its rival, in 1912. This is a rare example of a history of a carrying firm by an expert in road transport. It is based on the firm's archives and is a masterly study.
Firms: Carter Paterson; Pickfords

3010
Wigley, H.
The Mount Cook Way: The first fifty years of the Mount Cook Company
1979 Collins *Auckland, New Zealand*

This is a rather self-indulgent account by the son of the founder of this road haulage firm. It is anecdotal and descriptive rather than analytical and hence disappointing.
Firms: Mount Cook Co.

3011
Yamamoto, Hirofumi
Ishin-ki no Kaido to Yuso [Roads and Transport in the Meiji Restoration]
1972 Hosei University Press *Tokyo, Japan*

This is the first and only study of road transport business in the Meiji restoration period. The author analyses the management of road transport companies in various districts with plentiful business and official documents, and defines the Meiji government's road transport policy and attitude.

Canals and Inland Waterways

3012
Aitken, Hugh G. J.
The Welland Canal Company: A study in Canadian enterprise
1954 Harvard University Press *Cambridge, MA*

Aitken's book is an early example of a professional business history of the canal built to link Lakes Erie and Ontario in upper Canada which was commenced in the mid-1820s. Drawing on the papers of the canal company and of W. H. Merritt the main promoter, this book is good on the reasons for its promotion, the problems of construction and finance and how they were solved, the entrepreneurs, the role of government and sources of capital. It is not so strong on the canal as a going enterprise, but does have tables of costs, revenues and freight.
Firms: E. & R. Ellice & Co.; Erie Canal Co.; Forsyth, Richardson & Co.; Welland Canal Co.

3013

Angus, J. T.

A Respectable Ditch: A history of the Trent–Severn waterway 1833–1920

1988 McGill-Queen's University Press *Kingston and Montreal, Canada*

This is a thoroughly researched study of the interplay of political and economic forces on the development of a strategic waterway connecting Lake Ontario and Georgian Bay in Canada. It contains a chronology of the construction projects and their costs.

Firms: Canadian National Railway; Canadian Pacific Railway; Dominion Bridge Company; York Construction

3014

Ashdown, Dana W.

Railway Steamships of Ontario

1988 Boston Mills Press *Erin, Ont., Canada*

This book documents the shipping enterprises controlled by Canadian railroads in Ontario and the Great Lakes between 1850 and 1950. Many railroads acquired ships to use as ferries, to extend their freight and passenger services. Companies, facilities and vessels are well-documented and key vessel statistics, timetables and many photographs are included. There is a plethora of data but it is short on analysis.

Firms: Algoma Central Railway; Canadian Northern Railway; Canadian Pacific Railway

3015

Becnel, Thomas A.

The Barrow Family and the Barataria and Lafourche Canal: The transportation revolution in Louisiana 1829–1925

1989 Louisiana State University Press *Baton Rouge, LA*

This book tells the history of the Barataria & Lafourche Canal which began construction in 1829 to provide transport for sugar planters in Louisiana into New Orleans. The canal remained unfinished thirty years later, when it was taken over by the Barrow family of planters and personally owned until 1925 when it was incorporated into the Gulf Intracoastal Waterways. Becnel is strong on the transport needs of the area and the problems of construction but poor on costs, revenues and the impact of the canal.

Firms: Barataria & Lafourche Canal; Gulf Intracoastal Waterway

3016

Bergasse, Jean-Denis (Editor)

Le Canal du Midi: trois siècles de batellerie et des voyages [The Midi Canal Three centuries of vessels and voyages]

1983 J-D Bergasse *Millau, France*

This was one of four volumes commissioned to mark the tricentenary of the Midi Canal. This volume analyses well the operating conditions on the canal, the types of vessel which used it and their methods of construction, and some voyages made. It is less concerned with the finance or business history.

Firms: Canal Royal du Languedoc

3017

Bergasse, Jean-Denis (Editor)

Le Canal du Midi. Grands Moments et Grands Sites: Les canaux de Briare et du Lez-Roissy [The Midi Canal. Great Events and Great Sites: The Briare Canal and the Lez-Roissy Canal]

1985 J-D Bergasse *Millau, France*

This is the final volume of the four issued to mark the tricentenary of the Midi Canal. This book examines some aspects of the construction of the Midi, Lez and Briare Canals, the role of the canal in the nineteenth century and the construction of a parallel railway line and its impact on waterway traffic.

Firms: Canal du Midi; Compagnie des Chemins de fer du Midi; Canal du Lez

3018

Bonin, Hubert

Suez: Du canal à la finance, (1858–1987) [Suez: From canal to financial services, 1858–1987]

For main entry, see 3128

3019

Dickinson, J.

To Build a Canal: Sault Ste Marie, 1853–1854 and after

1981 Ohio State University Press *Columbus, OH*

This is a colourful and perceptive account of the beginnings of the canal linking Lakes Superior and Huron. The author examines the multitude of difficulties encountered in acquiring finance, labour and materials as well as the challenge of obtaining the support of the federal government. Entrepreneur Erastus Corning is a prominent figure in this history.
Firms: St Mary's Falls Ship Canal Company; Sault Ste Marie Ship Canal

3020
Faulkner, Alan H.
The Grand Junction Canal
1993 W. H. Walker & Bros *Rickmansworth*

This is a much revised edition of the original 1972 volume by the same author. Although not strictly a business history of the canal, it does contain much on the canal carriers, the construction, competition with the railways, and the entrepreneurs involved as well as the financial performance in terms of revenue and dividends. It is well illustrated.
Firms: Grand Union Canal; Grand Junction Canal; Fellows Morton and Clayton; Pickfords

3021
Goodrich, Carter
Government Promotion of American Canals and Railroads 1800–1890
For main entry, see 4345

3022
Gray, Ralph D.
The National Waterway: A history of the Chesapeake and Delaware Canal, 1769–1985
2nd Edition
1989 University of Illinois Press *Urbana, IL*

This book provides a good narrative history of this important American canal from its conception and construction in the eighteenth century to its takeover by the US Corps of Engineers in 1919, and its widening and deepening between 1954 and 1981. It is strong on the early promoters, the political dimensions of the project, the technical and legal problems, the traffic and the finances.
Firms: Chesapeake and Delaware Canal Co.

3023
Grosskreutz, Helmut
Privatkapital und Kanalbau in Frankreich, 1814–48: Eine Fallstudie zur Rolle der Banken in der französischen Industrialisierung [Private Capital and Canal Building in France 1814–48: A case study of the role of banks in French industrialization]
1977 Duncker & Humblot *Berlin, Germany*

This study examines the role of the state and private enterprise in canal construction in France in the early nineteenth century. Grosskreutz is good on the initiatives taken by the government and the role of Paris bankers and brings out the lack of local industrial support for canals. This is a very detailed account.

3024
Hadfield, Charles
The Canal Age
1968 David & Charles *Newton Abbot*

This book epitomizes the careful research and deep understanding that marks all the work of Hadfield, the premier British historian of canals. This volume deals with finance, construction, traffic, carriers, boatmen and companies. It is a classic on the British canal companies.

3025
Hahn, Thomas F.
The Chesapeake and Ohio Canal: Pathway to the nation's capital
1984 Scarecrow Press *Metuchen, NJ*

The Potomac Company tried to clear the river for navigation in the late eighteenth century, but having failed was superseded by the Chesapeake and Ohio Canal from the 1820s until it was sold to the Parks Service in 1938. This book is good on the working life on the canal and the people involved, but is essentially documentary with little interpretation.
Firms: Chesapeake and Ohio Canal; Potomac Co.

3026
Kunz, Andreas; Armstrong, John (Editors)
Inland Navigation and Economic Development in Nineteenth-Century Europe

1995 Verlag Philipp von Zabern *Mainz, Germany*

This volume contains more than a dozen essays by leading scholars of transport history covering most European countries. Although its main theme is the impact of inland navigation on economic growth, there is also much detail on business aspects of inland waterway traffic. This was the first volume to look at the topic from a European-wide perspective.

3027
Legget, Robert
Rideau Waterway
2nd Edition
1986 University of Toronto Press *Toronto, Canada*

Although the majority of this book is devoted to a modern guidebook to the Rideau Canal, it contains useful chapters on why and how the canal was built and its history. It is strong on the technical problems of construction and the personalities involved but is thinner on the finances and business aspects.
Firms: Rideau Canal

3028
Maistre, André
Le Canal des Deux Mers: Canal Royal du Languedoc 1666–1810 [The Canal Between Two Seas: The Royal Canal of Languedoc 1666–1810]
1968 Édouard Privat *Toulouse, France*

This volume traces the struggle to build the Midi or Languedoc Canal until its completion in 1681. It is strong on the promoters' problems and techniques of construction, and explains the impact of the canal on the local and regional economy.
Firms: Canal Royal du Languedoc

3029
Mather, F. C.
After the Canal Duke: A study of the industrial estates administered by the trustees of the third Duke of Bridgewater in the age of railway building, 1825–1872
1970 Clarendon Press *Oxford*

The rivalry between railway and canal transport is the theme of this intriguing work about the fate of the Bridgewater Canal after the death of its creator. The correspondence and records of the Bridgewater Trust are used to provide insight into the decisions made during the trusteeship. A singular story is told with skill and meticulous care.
Firms: Bridgewater Canal; Bridgewater Trust; Liverpool and Manchester Railway

3030
McCrae, Alistair; Prentice, Alan
Irrawaddy Flotilla
1978 James Paton *Paisley, Scotland*

This book provides a history of the Irrawaddy Flotilla and Burmese Steam Navigation Company from 1865 to nationalization in 1948. The firm ran steamers and flats on Burmese rivers to provide internal traffic and feeders to the Henderson Line between Rangoon and Glasgow. It is thin on the business aspects but good on trade and government relations.
Firms: Henderson Line; Irrawaddy Flotilla Co.; Irrawaddy Flotilla and Burmese Steam Navigation Co.; Todd, Findlay and Co.

3031
Merger, Michèle
Les mariniers au debut du XX siècle: des fourains d'une espèce particulière [French Bargemen at the Beginning of the Twentieth Century]
Le Mouvement Social, no. 132, 1985: pp 83–100

The author examines the living and working conditions on the barges, and the deterioration of waterway traffic in northern France, the fluctuations in freight rates, and the first bargemen's strikes of 1904 and 1909. Although not a thorough business history, it is an important contribution to some aspects of it.

3032
Osborne, B. S.; Swainson, D.
The Sault Ste Marie Canal: A chapter in the history of Great Lakes transport
1986 Canadian Parks Service *Ottawa, Canada*

This volume provides a history of the origins and construction of the ship canal which linked Lake Huron to Lake Superior. It also covers well the operation of the canal, the traffic which

used it and its impact on local economic and social activity. See also Passfield (1989).
Firms: Sault Ste Marie Ship Canal

3033
Passfield, Robert W.
Technology in Transition: The 'SOO' Ship Canal 1889–1985
1989 Canadian Parks Service *Ottawa, Canada*
This is a history of the canal built between Lakes Superior and Huron which gave a deep water route from Montreal to Port Arthur and was financed by the Canadian government. It is good on technological change but thin on management and operations. Osborne and Swainson (qv) cover the same enterprise.
Firms: Sault Ste Marie Ship Canal

3034
Pinsseau, Hubert
Un aspect du développement économique de la France: histoire de la construction, de l'administration et de l'exploitation du canal d'Orléans de 1676–1954 [An Aspect of French Economic Development: The history of the construction, administration and operations of the Orleans Canal 1676–1954]
1963 Raymond Clavreuil *Paris, France*
This volume analyses the main steps in the construction of the Orleans Canal, finished in 1692, outlines its technical characteristics, and explains the main developments in its traffic.
Firms: Orléans Canal

3035
Pisani, Donald J.
From the Family Farm to Agribusiness: The irrigation crusade in California and the West, 1850–1931
For main entry, see 223

3036
Sanderlin, Walter S.
The Great National Project: A history of the Chesapeake and Ohio Canal
1946 The Johns Hopkins University Press *Baltimore, MD*
This volume traces the history of one of the major canal projects in early nineteenth-century America, the Chesapeake and Ohio Canal. Although rather dated, it is still a useful book drawing on the archives of the canal company and placing the canal in its economic, political and social context. It is good on the technology, cargoes carried and causes of its demise.
Firms: Chesapeake and Ohio Canal

3037
Shaw, Ronald E.
Erie Water West: A history of the Erie Canal, 1792–1854
1966 University Press of Kentucky *Lexington, KY*
This is a comprehensive political history dealing with the origin of the Erie Canal and its impact on the surrounding area. Extensive primary research and elegant prose blend well in this conscientious and effective study. Deservedly, Shaw received the Organization of American Historian's Prize in 1965 for this book, which is entertainingly and skilfully written.
Firms: Erie Canal

3038
Shaw, Ronald E.
Canals for a Nation: The canal era in the United States 1790–1860
1990 University Press of Kentucky *Lexington, KY*
This scholarly book covers the whole history of canal construction rather than the business history of individual undertakings. It is extensively referenced and has a useful bibliography and is good on relations with government, technical problems and their solution and the role of the canal in binding the country together. It is less concerned with the exclusively business aspects.
Firms: Chesapeake and Delaware Canal; Chesapeake and Ohio Canal; Delaware and Hudson Canal; Delaware and Raritan Canal; Erie Canal; Illinois and Michigan Canal; Mainline Canal; Morris Canal

3039
Tulchinsky, Gerald J. J.
The River Barons: Montreal businessmen and the growth of industry and transportation 1837–1853
For main entry, see 3807

3040
Vries, Jan de
Barges and Capitalism: Passenger transportation in the Dutch economy: 1632–1839
1978 A. A. G. Bijdragen *Wageningen, The Netherlands*

This is an economic as well as a business history, thorough in its analysis of the extensive network of barge canals which served the Dutch for over two hundred years. De Vries has utilized a wealth of previously unexplored archival materials to produce a work of noteworthy quality.

3041
Williams, Cyril R.
Wheels and Paddles in the Sudan 1923–1946
For main entry, see 2955

Sea Transport, UK

3042
Blake, George
The Ben Line
1956 Nelson *London*

Although this book is rather dated by modern standards of business history, it is still useful on the history of the firm begun in Leith, Scotland, by the Thomson family of shipbrokers in the early nineteenth century. The firm traded mainly in the Far East but also tried the Baltic and Canada. The book is strong on the Victorian period but more anecdotal on more recent history.
Firms: Alexander & William Thomson; Ben Line Steamers

3043
Bowen, Frank C.
The Flag of the Southern Cross: The history of the Shaw, Savill and Albion Company Ltd, 1858–1945
1939/47 Shaw, Savill & Albion Co. *London*

This two-volume account gives a narrative of an important British shipping enterprise in the Pacific trade. It provides evidence of pioneering steam shipping services between Europe and the Pacific. Although now rather dated, it remains a useful source.
Firms: New Zealand Shipping Company; Shaw, Savill and Albion Co.

3044
Bowen, Frank C.
A Hundred Years of Towage: A history of Messrs William Watkins, Ltd, 1833–1933
1933 Gravesend & Dartford Reporter *Gravesend*

This volume is important as one of the oldest company histories written by an outside scholar and for being of a ship towage business. By virtue of its age the approach and format now seems very dated, being anecdotal, concentrating on interesting incidents, colourful characters and specific ships, but it still has some value though lacking analysis of most currently relevant business areas. The volume by Reynolds (qv) continues the history.
Firms: William Watkins

3045
Broeze, Frank
Mr Brooks and the Australian Trade: Imperial business in the 19th century
For main entry, see 4000

3046
Cable, Boyd
A Hundred Year History of the P. & O. Peninsular and Oriental Steam Navigation Company, 1837– 1937
1937 Ivor Nicholson & Watson *London*

This is obviously a very dated volume and does not take an analytical approach, lacks references, sources and even a bibliography. Nevertheless, it may be useful as a source of data – it has a comprehensive fleet list and a section on the capital structure – though largely superseded by volumes like that of the Howarths (qv).
Firms: P & O; BI

3047
Coppack, Tom
A Lifetime with Ships: The autobiography of a coasting shipowner
1973 T. Stephenson & Sons *Prescot*

This is one of the few histories of a firm in the

British coasting trade: Coppack Bros of Connah's Quay in North Wales. The firm spanned the shift from sail to steam and continued until the 1960s. It is strong on trades, family organization and the day-to-day operations, and has some detail on the work of agents and ship brokers.
Firms: Coppack Bros

3048
Cuthbert, Alan D.
Clyde Shipping Co. Ltd: A history
1956 Robert Maclehose *Glasgow, Scotland*

Although this book is too much of a 'company history', it is important because it is one of the few accounts of a British firm mainly in the coasting trade and across the Irish Sea. There is little analysis but much on the development of various trades, the ships used and the competing services.
Firms: Clyde Shipping Co.

3049
Davies, Peter N.
The Trade Makers: Elder Dempster in West Africa 1852–1972
1973 George Allen & Unwin *London*

This is the only detailed study of the operations of the principal shipping firm in the West African Shipping Conference, focusing on boardroom politics and organizational changes within the firm in the context of the dynamics of the Conference system and of the vagaries of the world economy. It highlights the contributions of British shipping to the economic development of West Africa. This is a business history of distinction.
Firms: African Steamship Co.; British and African Steam Navigation Co.; Elder Dempster and Company/Elder Dempster Lines Ltd; Holland West Africa Line; United Africa Co.; Woermann Line

3050
Davies, Peter N.
Sir Alfred Jones: Shipping entrepreneur par excellence
For main entry, see 3881

3051
Davies, Peter N.
Business Success and the Role of Chance: The extraordinary Philipps Brothers
For main entry, see 3882

3052
Davies, Peter N.
Fyffes and the Banana: Musa Sapientum. A Centenary History, 1888–1988
For main entry, see 241

3053
Falkus, Malcolm
The Blue Funnel Legend: A history of the Ocean Steam Ship Company 1865–1973
1990 Macmillan *London*

This study of the firm, started by Alfred Holt in 1865 to trade from Liverpool to the Far East, brings the earlier history by Hyde (qv) up to the 1970s and complements the earlier work, particularly in the role of masters and mariners and the family nature of this large scale business.
Firms: Alfred Holt & Co.; Ocean Steam Ship Co.

3054
Green, Edwin; Moss, Michael
A Business of National Importance: The Royal Mail Shipping Group 1902–1937
1982 Methuen *London*

This volume provides a detailed study of the events leading up to the dramatic crash of the Royal Mail Shipping Group in 1930 and the actions taken afterwards to keep the companies trading. It is very strong on business strategy and finance, the roles of various people in the crash and rescue and is based on detailed analysis of a wide range of documents.
Firms: Royal Mail Group; Royal Mail Steam Packet Co.

3055
Howarth, David; Howarth, Stephen
The Story of P&O: The Peninsular and Oriental Steam Navigation Company
1986 Weidenfeld & Nicolson *London*

This lavishly-illustrated volume celebrates the 150th anniversary of this important shipping business. It is a straightforward chronological account of the company, strong on

routes, ships, personalities and facilities. It has little to say on the more academic business areas, is unreferenced and has no bibliography.
Firms: P & O Steam Navigation Co.; BI Steam Navigation Co.

3056
Hyde, Francis E.
Blue Funnel: A history of Alfred Holt & Company of Liverpool 1865–1914
1957 Liverpool University Press *Liverpool*

This firm pioneered steamship services from the UK to the Far East as the Ocean Steam Ship Company. The book is strong on strategy, finance and marketing including shipping conferences, but weak on labour. The later volume by Falkus (qv) continues the story to 1973. Swires acted as their agent and were influential on strategy, so Marriner and Hyde (1967, qv) is also relevant.
Firms: Alfred Holt & Co.; Ocean Steam Ship Co.

3057
Hyde, Francis E.
Shipping Enterprise and Management 1830–1939: Harrisons of Liverpool
1967 Liverpool University Press *Liverpool*

This volume is a study of a firm, the Charente Steamship Co., which provided shipping services in South Africa, India, Central America and the Caribbean from its beginnings in the Portuguese wine and spirit trade. It is strong on shipping conferences and finance, thinner on personalities, but essentially a pioneering book on management decision-making and strategy in this shipping line.
Firms: Charente Steam Ship Co.; T. & J. Harrison; Houston Line; Ellerman Line; Bucknall Line; Brocklebanks

3058
Hyde, Francis E.
Cunard and the North Atlantic 1840–1973: A history of shipping and financial management
1975 Macmillan *London*

This work is based on the company's extensive archives and concentrates, as its title implies, on management and finance and more on the North Atlantic than the Mediterranean. It is strong on financial analysis, competing firms, and relations with government, and deals well with the personalities of the entrepreneurs, the role of mail contracts, the emigrant trade, and the conference system.
Firms: Cunard Shipping Company; White Star Line

3059
Jones, Stephanie K.
Two Centuries of Overseas Trading: The origins and growth of the Inchcape Group
1986 Macmillan *Basingstoke*

This book provides a clear account of the multitude of trading, agency and shipping firms which eventually formed the Inchcape Group. It is good on the role of Scottish expatriates in developing Britain's invisible exports and the British as merchants abroad. It is based on the company's extensive archives. See also Jones, *Trade and Shipping: Lord Inchcape*.
Firms: Australian United Steam Navigation Co.; British India Steam Navigation Co.; Inchcape Group; Peninsular & Oriental Steam Navigation Co.

3060
Jones, Stephanie K.
Trade and Shipping: Lord Inchcape, 1852–1932
1989 Manchester University Press *Manchester*

This is a biography of James Lyle Mackay, a prominent figure in the British shipping industry and active member of Parliamentary committees and commissions. Mackay's business career began in Scotland; he was active in India through the Mackinnon Mackenzie shipping house, and latterly engaged in public service in the UK.
Firms: British India Steam Navigation Company; Mackinnon Mackenzie; Peninsular & Oriental Steam Navigation Company; Inchcape Group

3061
Kirkaldy, Adam W.
British Shipping: Its history, organization and importance
2nd Edition
1970 Frank Cass *London*

This book, which was first published in 1914, almost predates the discipline of business history and is thus not one itself. It is a useful source book for historians of the shipping industry, mainly looking back over the nineteenth century, though lacking the theoretical framework modern business historians would employ.

3062
MacGregor, David R.
The China Bird: The history of Captain Killick and the firm he founded, Killick Martin & Company
1961 Chatto & Windus *London*

This book describes the history of the ship owning and operating activities of Killick Martin & Co., mainly from the 1860s to 1880s with a brief look at the later period as shipbrokers. Despite all the internal records of the firm having been destroyed by fire in the Second World War this is a useful account of the sea trade, though understandably it is thin on many business matters.
Firms: Ben Line Steamers; Killick Martin & Co.

3063
Marriner, Sheila; Hyde, Francis E.
The Senior. John Samuel Swire, 1825–98: Management in Far Eastern shipping trades
For main entry, see 2137

3064
Mathias, Peter; Pearsall, A. W. H.
Shipping: A survey of historical records
For main entry, see 24

3065
McConville, James; Rickaby, Glenys (Editors)
Shipping Business and Maritime Economics: An annotated international bibliography
For main entry, see 25

3066
McCrae, Alistair; Prentice, Alan
Irrawaddy Flotilla
For main entry, see 3030

3067
Muir, Augustus; Davies, Mair
A Victorian Shipowner: A portrait of Sir Charles Cayzer, Baronet of Gartmore
1978 Cayzer, Irvine & Co. *London*

This well-illustrated volume tells the story of Sir Charles Cayzer and the shipping line which he commenced and ran until the First World War. The volume is strong on the nature of the entrepreneur and his methods of operating, the family background, business strategies, routes served, the ships and cargoes. It is based on archival sources but sadly is not referenced and does not have a bibliography. It does have a comprehensive fleet list of the Clan Line.
Firms: Clan Line Steamers; Cayzer, Irvine & Co.

3068
Murray, Marischal
Union-Castle Chronicle, 1853–1953
1953 Longmans, Green *London*

A detailed and definitive centenary history.
Firms: Union-Castle Line

3069
Olukoju, Ayodeji
Elder Dempster and the Shipping Trade of Nigeria During the First World War
Journal of African History, vol. 33, no. 2, 1992: pp 255–71

This article is a very useful study of Elder Dempster's shipping practices in the war and the way its competitors reacted to them. It draws on previously unused material and its treatment of the reactions of African merchants and shippers to the company's policies is particularly strong.
Firms: Elder Dempster Shipping Co.

3070
Orbell, John
From Cape to Cape: The history of Lyle Shipping Company
1978 Paul Harris *Edinburgh, Scotland*

This is an excellent account of the growth of a Scottish shipping firm which started in sail and moved to motor ships via steam. It was founded by the same family as the sugar refiners Tate and Lyle (qv). It is strong on the financial and business aspects of the firm, is lavishly illustrated, has a full fleet list and is based on the firm's archives.
Firms: Lyle Shipping Co.; Tate & Lyle

3071
Porter, Andrew
Victorian Shipping, Business and Imperial Policy: Donald Currie, the Castle Line and Southern Africa
1986 Royal Historical Society *London*

This is a first-rate account of the man who built the Castle Line, his company, and the interrelations between imperial policy, business and entrepreneurship. It is particularly good on the connections between mail subsidies, the provision of shipping services, and the imperial aims of London politicians.
Firms: Castle Line; Union Castle

3072
Reynolds, John E.
Thames Ship Towage 1933–1992
1993 Pentland Press *Durham*

This volume continues the history of the firms which became in 1975 Alexandra Towing Co., from 1933 which was where the earlier volume by Bowen (qv) left off. It lacks the academic conventions of index, bibliography and sources and is narrowly a chronological account plus fleet list. There are few histories of a towage company, hence its inclusion.
Firms: Alexandra Towing; London Tugs; William Watkins; Ship Towage (London); Gravesend United Steam Tug; Elliott Steam Tug; Gamecock Tugs

3073
Savill, David
Sail to New Zealand: The story of Shaw, Savill & Co. 1858–82
1986 Robert Hale *London*

This is a history written by the founder's grandson of the establishment and pioneering days of sail from Britain to New Zealand, until the firm merged with the Albion Line in 1882. It is well illustrated and conveys the excitement and hazards of operating sailing ships. It is strong on the personalities and their motives but thin on the business history aspects.
Firms: Albion Line; New Zealand Shipping Co.; Shaw Savill & Albion; Shaw Savill & Co.

3074
Sinclair, Robert C.
Across the Irish Sea: Belfast–Liverpool shipping since 1819
1990 Conway Maritime Press *London*

This is one of the few histories of a firm engaged in the coasting trade between Northern Ireland and England. It is strong on strategy and technical specifications, but thin on finance, trade flows and marketing. It is well illustrated but not referenced, and therefore more enthusiast than academic.
Firms: Belfast Steamship Co.; Coast Lines Ltd

3075
Strachan, Michael
The Ben Line 1825–1982: An anecdotal history
1992 Michael Russell *Norwich*

This volume is written by a former chairman and chief executive of the company and is avowedly anecdotal rather than analytical, being based on his own experiences and observations. It summarizes the early history of the firm in one chapter based on Blake's earlier work (qv) and then continues the story since 1945. It is strong on the business strategy, personalities, trades served and changes in technology.
Firms: Ben Line

3076
Sturmey, Stanley G.
British Shipping and World Competition
1962 Athlone Press *London*

The aim of this volume is to explain why the British share of world shipping tonnage declined drastically between 1900 and 1960. As such it explores a number of aspects of the industry's business history such as competition, the economics of ship operations, ownership, labour relations, conferences and structure. It is a highly useful contribution.

3077
Taylor, James
Ellermans: A wealth of shipping
1976 Wilton House Gentry *London*

This well-illustrated volume traces the history of the Ellerman line from its inception to the 1970s written by a former employee. It deals with all the firms which were absorbed into the

group and has comprehensive fleet lists. It is not referenced and is aimed at the general reader rather than the academic and does not concentrate on the business aspects.
Firms: Ellerman Line; Papayanni & Co.; City Line; Hall Line; Wilson Line; George Smith & Co.; Mongomerie & Workman; Robert Alexander & Co.; Westcott & Laurance Line; Bucknalls

3078
Vamplew, Wray
Salvesen of Leith
1975 Scottish Academic Press *Edinburgh, Scotland*
This is a scholarly account of the growth of the firm founded by Norwegians but based in Scotland, which was involved in shipowning, broking, merchanting and whaling. The book is strong on the personalities, internal structure of the firm, the role of the family and its business policies. It can be vague on details of comparison with other firms.
Firms: Christian Salvesen

3079
Ville, Simon P.
English Shipowning During the Industrial Revolution: Michael Henley & Son, London shipowners 1770–1830
1987 Manchester University Press *Manchester*
This volume is a first rate study of a British shipping firm in the crucial period of industrialization. It covers overseas, coasting and government trades and is strong on financial returns, the deployment of ships, and the roles of masters and crew. It is based on the extensive papers of the family and firm and is a seminal study.
Firms: Michael Henley & Son

3080
Yui, Tsunehiko; Nakagawa, Keiichiro (Editors)
Business History of Shipping: Strategy and structure (Eleventh Fuji Conference)
For main entry, see 112

Sea Transport, Europe (excl. UK)

3081
Barbance, Marthe
Histoire de la Compagnie Générale Transatlantique: Un siècle d'exploitation maritime [History of the Compagnie Générale Transatlantique: A century of maritime endeavour]
1955 Arts et métiers graphiques *Paris, France*
This is an official history of the 'French line'– the largest of the French shipping companies, from its foundation in 1860 to the 1950s, before the decline in transatlantic passenger traffic. It is based on primary sources and is well illustrated, especially with photographs of famous liners.
Firms: Compagnie Générale Transatlantique; French Line

3082
Barbance, Marthe
Vie commerciale de la route du cap Horn au XIXe siècle: A. D. Bordes et fils [Commercial Life on the Cape Horn Route in the Nineteenth Century: A. D. Bordes et fils]
1969 SEVPN *Paris, France*
This is the story of the firm which ran ships between Chile and Peru and Europe carrying guano, copper, nitrates and emigrants from the 1840s to the 1930s. It chose to stay with sail in the 1880s, refusing steam and so lost out on the more lucrative trades. This is a useful book on a crucial aspect of maritime change.
Firms: A. D. Bordes et fils

3083
Bent, Mike
Coastal Express: The ferry to the top of the world
1987 Conway Maritime Press *London*
This book traces the history of the coastal steamer services of Norway since their inception in 1838. Although there were some early private ventures, the role of the state was crucial in establishing the service. The book is well illustrated and contains much detail on the ships, including plans, the changes in technol-

ogy, the entrepreneurs, routes and cargoes, but is thin on finances and management.
Firms: Bergen Line; Coastal Express Service

3084
Bent, Mike
Steamers of the Fjords: Bergen shipping since 1839
1989 Conway Maritime Press *London*

This well-illustrated volume tells the history of the coastal ships which plied from Bergen to service the small isolated seaside communities of Norway. It traces the early days when private enterprise vied with public services until the Hardanger Sunnhordlandske Steamship Co. emerged as a result of a merger between two rival companies in 1880. This book is strong on ships, services and changing technology.
Firms: Hardanger Sunnhordlandske Steamship Co.; Havgesunds Dampskibsselskab

3085
Broeze, Frank J. A.
***De Stad Schiedam*: De Schiedamsche Scheepsreedaerij en de Nederlandse vaart op Ost-Indie omstreeks 1840 [De Stad Schiedam: The Schiedam Shipping Company and the Dutch trade with the East Indies in 1840]**
1978 Martinus Nijhoff *The Hague, The Netherlands*

Broeze's book is a history of the Schiedam Shipping Company which began building and chartering ships to the Netherlands Trading Society for the East India trade in 1835, and was defunct by 1900. It is a rare example of a business history of a Dutch shipping company of the wood and sail era. It is strong on management, the relations between directors and shareholders, marine insurance and finance, and is based on the archives of the company and other shipowners. There is a summary in English.
Firms: de Schiedamsche Scheepsreederij

3086
Brugmans, I. J.
Tachtig jaren varen met de 'Nederland', 1870–1950 [Eighty Years of Sailing with the 'Nederland', 1870–1950]
1950 De Boer *Den Helder, The Netherlands*

This is a thorough economic history of the Amsterdam-based shipping line, concentrating on the interwar period, in which the company operated shipping routes between Holland, the Dutch East Indies and the USA.
Firms: Stoomvaart Maatschappij Nederland (SMN)

3087
Campo, J. N. F. M. à
Koninklijke Paketvaart Maatschappij: Stoomvaart en Staatsvorming in de Indonesische Archipel 1888–1914 [Royal Packet Steam Navigation Co: Steam shipping and state building in the Indonesian archipelago 1888–1914]
1992 Verloren *Hilversum, The Netherlands*

This is an innovative and stimulating book which is revisionist and full of new perspectives, using concepts such as 'power', 'market' and 'space' to analyse KPM, the Dutch colonial shipping line in the East Indies, as a socio-technical system. It argues convincingly that the company's operations helped delineate the borders and state formation of the Dutch East Indies. It uses network analysis and draws on the archives of the company.
Firms: Koninklijke Paketvaart Maatschappij (KPM); Rotterdam Lloyd

3088
Cecil, Lamar
Albert Ballin: Business and politics in Imperial Germany, 1888–1918
For main entry, see 4003

3089
Coons, Ronald E.
Steamships, Statesmen and Bureaucrats: Austrian policy towards the Steam Navigation Company of the Austrian Lloyd 1836–1848
1975 Franz Steiner Verlag *Wiesbaden, Germany*

Enterprise under the iron hand of the Austrian government is treated in a precise and scholarly manner. In addition to the administrative history of the line, Coons discusses the relationship between steam navigation and diplomacy in the era of Metternich. Extensive

primary and secondary sources are used to good advantage.
Firms: House of Rothschild; Steam Navigation Company of the Austrian Lloyd

3090
Delprat, Daniel A.
De Reeder schrijft zijn Journaal: Herinneringen van mr. D. A. Delprat [The Shipowner Keeps His Journal: Memoirs of D. A. Delprat]
1983 Martinus Nijhoff *The Hague, The Netherlands*

Though not really a business history as such, these are the memoirs of one of the captains of the Dutch transport industry. They are devoted to the history of the various shipping companies with which Delprat was involved.
Firms: Koninklijke Hollandsche Lloyd; Koninklijke Java-China Paketvaart Lijnen; Koninklijke Nederlandsche Scheepvaart Maatschappij; Koninklijke Nederlandsche-Indische Luchtvaart Maatschap; Koninklijke Paketvaart Maatschappij (KPM); Scheepvaart Maatschappij Nederland (SMN)

3091
Henningsen, Lars N.
Provinsmatadorer fra 1700-arene: Reder, kobmandsog fabrikantfamilien Otte: Eckernforde i okonomi og politik 1700–1770 [Provincial Tycoons of the Eighteenth Century The Otte Shipowning, merchant and manufacturing family of Eckernforde in economics and politics, 1700–1770]
1985 Sydslesvig Rosenkilde og Bagger *Copenhagen, Denmark*

This book traces the rise and fall of the Otte shipowning family of Schleswig's east coast in the eighteenth century. At their peak they owned twenty-three large sailing ships. The family's success was based on Schleswig's neutrality, the discovery of niche trades, e.g. to Iceland and Portugal, and careful maintenance and technological improvement of the fleet. The book is strong on freight rates, insurance and manning as well as business strategy.
Firms: Otte

3092
Hieke, Ernst
Rob M. Sloman, Jr: Errichtet, 1793 [Rob M. Sloman Jr: Founded 1793]
1968 Verlag Hanseatischer Merkur *Hamburg, Germany*

This is a work of outstanding scholarship, rich in data, and is a good supplemental text to previous histories. Hieke's survey is a comprehensive history of a family and its shipping house which became one of the most important German lines with maritime trade in Australia, Africa and America. This is the best work in its field.

3093
Hornby, Ove
'Ved rettidig Omhu...': skibsreder A P Møller 1876–1965 ['With All Due Care...': A P Møller, shipowner 1876–1965]
1988 Schultz Forlag *Copenhagen, Denmark*

This is the business biography of Denmark's leading shipowner who, from owning a single sailing ship, built up a fleet which by 1965 accounted for nearly half of all Danish tonnage. This study draws on the firm's archives and is strong on the changes in technology and trades, the world and Danish context, and entrepreneurial strategy. It also explains well the related diversification into ship repair and building and oil extraction.
Firms: Dampskibsselskabet Svendborg; Dampskibsselskabet af 1912; Maersk Group

3094
Kaukiainen, Yrjo
A History of Finnish Shipping
1993 Routledge *London*

This is more an industry history than a business history per se, but given the paucity of English language material on Finnish shipping deserves inclusion. The book places the shipping industry in the broader economic and political context, is good on the cargoes carried, the ownership and technology but thin on the organization of the industry.

3095
Laar, Paulus Th. van de
Financieringsgedrag in de Rotterdamse maritieme sector, 1945–1960 [Financial

Behaviour in the Rotterdam Maritime Sector, 1945–1960]

1991 Tinbergen Institute *Rotterdam, The Netherlands*

This book provides a comparative history of finance and investment in the port of Rotterdam. Attention focuses on the capitalization of a number of Dutch maritime companies, and on their selection of funds for investment. The book analyses the underlying considerations which determined the selection of financial instruments.

Firms: Holland America Line (HAL); Houtvaart; Koninklijke Rotterdamsche Lloyd (KRL); Maatschappij Zeevaart; Phs. van Ommeren; Van Nievelt Goudriaan & Co. Stoomvaart Maatschappij; Wijklijn; Wm. H. Müller & Co.

3096

Lange, Ole

Den hvide elefant: H. N. Andersen's eventyr og ØK 1852–1914 [The White Elephant: H. N. Andersen's adventures and the Danish East Asiatic Co. 1852–1914]

1986 Gyldendal *Copenhagen, Denmark*

This book is a business biography of H. N. Andersen, the founder of the Danish East Asiatic Co. (ØK), who rose from humble origins to become a major shipowner. The book brings out the dubious financial and accounting techniques used by Andersen and his use of political power to scupper his rival Transatlantisk Kompagni and gain publicity and allies.

Firms: Østasiatiske Kompagni; Transatlantisk Kompagni

3097

Nerheim, Gunnar; Utne, Bjorn S.

Under samme stjerne: Rederiet Peder Smedvig 1915–1990 [Smedvig: A story of canning, shipping and contract drilling from western Norway]

1992 *Stavanger, Norway*

During the First World War the former ship captain Peder Smedvig established himself as a shipowner and canning manufacturer in Stavanger, on the west coast of Norway. The book follows the company through three generations until 1990 when shipping and contract drilling formed the core of the activity.

Firms: Peder Smedvig A/S

3098

Papathanassopoulos, Constantine

Helleniki Emboriki Naftilia, 1833–1856: Exelixi kai anaprosarmoge [The Greek Merchant Navy, 1833–56: Evolution and adaptation]

1983 Cultural Foundation of The National Bank of Greece *Athens, Greece*

The author focuses on the early attempts of Greek entrepreneurs, the National Bank of Greece and the State to create Greek steamshipping firms at the time of the demise of the older form of sailing boats.

3099

Papathanassopoulos, Constantine

Etairia Hellinikes Atmoploias 1855–1872: Ta adiexodu tou prostateftismou [Hellenic Steam Ship Company 1855–1872: The impasse of protectionism]

1988 Cultural Foundation of the National Bank of Greece *Athens, Greece*

This is essentially a sequel to the first tentative work on Greek shipping by the same author (1983, qv) and includes a description of the creation and demise of the first shipping agency in Syros which benefited from an exclusive transport concession granted by the Greek State. The book highlights the tension between state development policy and private economic decisions in nineteenth-century Greece. It is good on the entrepreneurial groups and Greece's role in the eastern Mediterranean.

Firms: Hellenic Steam Ship Co.

3100

Rinman, Thorsten

Rederiet Johnson Line under 100 ar [The Johnson Line 1890–1990]

1990 Rinman and Lindén *Gothenburg, Sweden*

The Johnson Line was established in 1890 to run ships carrying coal and iron ore between Sweden and other European countries. It expanded in the early twentieth century into subsidized services to South America and after 1914 the Pacific coast of North and South America. The book is strong on technical change, the routes served, cargoes carried and

the role of the family, and is well illustrated but suffers from being descriptive rather than analytical and is poorly referenced.
Firms: Johnson Line; Nordstjernan Group

3101
Torres, Eugenio
Ramón de la Sota: Historia económica de un empresario (1857–1936) [Ramon de la Sota The economic history of an entrepreneur (1857–1936)]
For main entry, see 4038

3102
Valdaliso, J. M.
Los navieros vascos y la marina mercante en España, 1860–1935: Una historia económica [Basque shipowners and merchant shipping in Spain, 1860–1935: An economic history]
1991 Instituto Vasco de Administración Pública *Bilbao, Spain*
This book focuses on the Biscayan shipowners and shipping companies and the role that they played in the development of the Spanish merchant fleet. Although it is, above all, an industrial history, the author analyses the main business groups in the sector, the changes in the form and structure of shipping firms, the origins of capital and the patterns of investment and finance deployed.

3103
Valdaliso, J. M.
Desarrollo y declive de la flota mercante española en el siglo XX: Historia de la Compañía Marítima del Nervíon, (1907–1986) [Development and decline of Spanish merchant fleet in the 20th Century: History of the Compañía Marítima del Nervíon (1907–1986)]
1993 Fundacíon Empresa Pública *Madrid, Spain*
This work is a case study, framed into the development of the Spanish shipping industry in the twentieth century, and using an evolutionary theory approach.
Firms: Compañía Marítima del Nervíon

3104
Wentholt, A. D.
Brug over den oceaan: Een eeuw geschiedenis van de Holland–Amerika Lijn [Bridge over the Ocean: A century of Holland–America Line history]
1973 Nijgh & Van Ditmar *Rotterdam, The Netherlands*
This book surveys the worldwide development of the Holland–America Line on the occasion of the centennial of its foundation. Emphasis is placed on the company's acquisitions, operating methods and the ships employed. It is, however, rather unacademic having no annotations.
Firms: Holland–Amerika Lijn; Nederlandsch–Amerikaansche Stoomvaart Maatschappij

3105
Yui, Tsunehiko; Nakagawa, Keiichiro (Editors)
Business History of Shipping: Strategy and structure (Eleventh Fuji Conference)
For main entry, see 112

Sea Transport, North America

3106
Albion, Robert G.
Seaports South of Sahara: The achievements of an American steamship service
1959 Appleton-Century-Crofts *New York, NY*
Written by a noted authority on maritime history, this book is an admirable study of the development of American shipping enterprise in Africa. The author did research in the archives of the Farrell Line (previously the American South African Line) as well as in a number of towns on the African coast. Well-organized and methodical, it is a significant contribution to the literature of business history.
Firms: American South African Line; American West African Line; Argonaut Line; Farrell Line; Isthmian Line; Robin Line

3107
Baughman, James P.
The Mallorys of Mystic: Six generations in American maritime enterprise
1972 Wesleyan University Press *Middletown, CT*
This book takes a close look at the family who controlled a large shipping business for

125 years. Beginning with modest investments and specializing in whaling, Charles Mallory became a dominant figure in Connecticut's maritime trade. Succeeding generations of Mallorys brought the company through the turmoil of Civil War, changing technology, and into oil transport. This is an interesting account supported by extensive documentation.

Firms: Mallory & Co.

3108

Dunbaugh, Edwin L.

The Era of the Joy Line: A saga of steamboating on Long Island Sound

1982 Greenwood Press *Westport, CT*

This is a rare example of a business history of an American coastal steamship firm. The Joy Line began in 1899 and was bought out in 1905 by the New England Steamship Line, itself owned by the New Haven Railroad. New England shipping competition at the turn of the century is the primary focus of this account. Joy Line was an irritant while independent. The book is strong on overall strategy, operating problems, scheduling, routes and fares but thin on finances and returns.

Firms: Colonial Line; Joy Line; New England Steam Ship Line; New Haven Railroad

3109

Dunbaugh, Edwin L.

Night Boat to New England 1815–1900

1992 Greenwood Press *New York, NY*

This volume is a readable narrative of the overnight steamboats plying between New York and southern New England and from Boston to Maine. It is not intended as a business history but does deal with a number of aspects of competition, routes, service quality, and strategy. It is well illustrated.

Firms: Great Fall River Line; Neptune Line; Stonington Line; Merchants Navigation & Transportation Co.; Rhode Island & New York Steamboat Co.; Hartford and New York Steamboat Co.

3110

Musk, George

Canadian Pacific: The story of the famous shipping line

2nd Edition

1989 David & Charles *Newton Abbot*

This is a centenary history of the Canadian Pacific Line which began operations in 1887. It is more a history of the ships than of the company as such, though it has some information on subsidiary companies and oral and anecdotal evidence on working conditions and 'products'. It is very well illustrated.

Firms: Canadian Pacific Line

3111

Niven, John

The American President Line and Its Forbears 1848–1984

1987 University of Delaware Press *Cranbury, DE*

This is a well-illustrated volume telling the story of the line which commenced running steamers between Panama and San Francisco and went on to become a very large player. It is good on the environment of the firm–competition, trade cycles, technology and union issues–but there is not very much on strategy, structure or finance.

Firms: Pacific Mail Steamship Co.; President Line

3112

Reynolds, Erminie S.; Martin, Kenneth

'A Singleness of Purpose': The Skolfields and their ships

1987 Maine Maritime Museum *Bath, ME*

This book traces the history of the Skolfield family of Brunswick, Maine, USA who, in the eighteenth century, moved from farming to shipbuilding and shipping, initially in the coastal trade, but then using deep sea sailing ships. The family had moved out of shipping by the 1880s. The story is well told using primary sources and describes the individual firm in its national context.

3113

Sager, Eric; Panting, Gerald

Maritime Capital: The shipping industry in Atlantic Canada, 1820–1914

1990 McGill-Queen's University Press *Kingston and Montreal, Canada*

This award-winning study of a declining industry in a declining region focuses on investors, investments and the relationship between industry and region.

3114
Thomas, Miflin
Schooner from Windward
1983 University of Hawaii Press *Honolulu, HI*
This is an excellent, thorough and well-illustrated account of coasting and inter-island ship services in Hawaii from the eighteenth century. It is strong on technical changes, from paddle to sail to steam, when the service became dominated by two companies, Wilder's Steamship Co. and Inter-Island Steam Navigation Co., until their merger in 1905. The book is good on the vessels, trades, cargoes, personalities and various attempts at rivalry by outside firms.
Firms: Hawaiian Steam Navigation Co.; Inter-Island Steam Navigation Co.; Wilder's Steamship Co.

3115
Yui, Tsunehiko; Nakagawa, Keiichiro (Editors)
Business History of Shipping: Strategy and structure (Eleventh Fuji Conference)
For main entry, see 112

Sea Transport, Australasia

3116
Broeze, Frank
'A Great Frankenstein': The West Australian Shipping Association 1884–1906
1992 Centre for W. Australian History *Nedlands, Australia*
This chapter, in Broeze's book *Private Enterprise, Government and Society*, provides a critical overview of a unique enterprise: the shipping agency initiated by Fremantle merchants in order to break the monopoly of a number of London loading brokers. The West Australian Shipping Association was so successful that it soon joined the brokers and thus formed an imperial cartel. Operations were later extended to the trade from New York. Broeze's essay is based on the surviving correspondence of the company and its London manager.
Firms: Australian Shipping Association

3117
Buckley, K.; Klugman, K.
The History of Burns Philp: The Australian company in the South Pacific
1981 Burns Philp & Co. *Sydney, Australia*
This is the first volume of a solid, commissioned company history based on extensive archival material. It shows how a diversified business empire grew out of local merchandizing in North Queensland from the 1870s. Shipping was indispensable for trading operations in the South Pacific and plantations and finance soon followed. The company's leaders were well-versed in politics and lobbying. Burns Philp became the foundation of Australia's own colonial empire in the South Pacific and was also involved in the coastal trade and associated with the Mackinnon and then Inchcape groups.
Firms: Burns Philp; Inchcape Group; Mackinnon Group

3118
Buckley, K.; Klugman, K.
The Australian Presence in the Pacific: Burns Philp 1916–1946
1983 Allen & Unwin *Sydney, Australia*
This is the second part of a solid two-volume company history. Supported by rich archival material it offers unparalleled insights into the various interlocking elements of western economic domination in the South Pacific. The central field of operations remained merchanting to local customers and the purchase of local produce, but plantations, finance and investment were also important. Burns Philp was increasingly reluctant to remain involved in shipping but found its ships indispensable.
Firms: Burns Philp; Inchcape Group

3119
Diamond, Marion
The Seahorse and the Wanderer: Ben Boyd in Australia
For main entry, see 2698

3120
Kirk, Allan A.
Fair Winds and Rough Seas: The story of the Holm Shipping Company
1975 A. H. & A. W. Reed *Wellington, New Zealand*

Kirk presents a study of the single ship companies based in New Zealand which were operated by Ferdinand Holm and his family until merged into one firm in 1921. The company ran services around the coast of New Zealand and to the Pacific Islands. Although based on the firm's papers and commissioned by the company, the book is not analytical and fails to draw out the significance of events. It tends towards anecdote, relying on incidents retold by old employees, but has some material on the trades and vessels.
Firms: Dunedin-Wanganui Shipping Co.; Holm Shipping Co.

3121
Kirk, Allan A.
Anchor Ships and Anchor Men: The history of the Anchor Shipping and Foundry Company Ltd.
1977 A. H. & A. W. Reed *Wellington, New Zealand*

This volume provides a history of one of New Zealand's leading coastal shipping companies. The book is poorly organized but contains some useful material on the firm's vertical integration of iron production, ship building and ship operating. It is good on the company's response to technical change in shipping, the problems of incorporation and of delegating responsibility while senior managers were absent overseas.
Firms: Anchor Shipping & Foundry Co.

3122
McKellar, N. L.
From Derby Round to Burketown: The A.U.S.N. story
1977 University of Queensland Press
St Lucia, Qld, Australia

This book provides a very detailed, immensely well-researched history of the Australian United Steam Navigation Company and its predecessor companies from the 1870s to the 1960s. It provides a rare example of companies active in the Australian coastal trade, which diversified into related activities and prospered until 1945. Afterwards competition from rail, road, and air progressively removed its passengers and freight. It is good on the relationship with other coastal firms and the cartel created.
Firms: Australasian Steam Navigation Co.; Australasian United Steam Navigation Co.; Inchcape Group; Mackinnon Group; Queensland Steam Navigation Co.

3123
McLean, Gavin J.
The Southern Octopus: The rise of a shipping empire
1990 New Zealand Ship and Marine Society
Wellington, New Zealand

This is a thorough and critical account of the largest company in New Zealand in the late nineteenth century, the Union Steam Ship, from its inception in 1875 to its absorption by P & O in 1917. It deals well with the reasons for its growth, the management policies, the structure of the firm, the financial aspects, corporate strategy, labour relations, competitor behaviour and the entrepreneurship of the directors and managers. It is well illustrated and referenced and draws on company records.
Firms: Huddart Parker & Co.; McMeckan Blackwood & Co.; New Zealand Shipping Co.; Northern Steamship Co.; Peninsular & Oriental Steam Navigation Co.; Union Steam Ship Co.

3124
Page, M.
Fitted for the Voyage: The Adelaide Steamship Company Limited 1875–1975
1975 Rigby *Adelaide, Australia*

This is a commissioned and rather uncritical history of one of the foremost coastal steam shipping companies on the Australian coast. The main business centred on Adelaide but its services stretched from Queensland to Western Australia. It is informative but little attention is given to the economic and political context or rival companies. Soon after 1975 it was transformed into a non-maritime holding company.
Firms: Adelaide Steamship Co.

3125
Waters, Sydney D.
Clipper Ship to Motor Liner: The story of the New Zealand Shipping Company 1873–1939
1939 New Zealand Shipping Co. *London*

As might be expected given the date of publication this is not an academic business history. It contains no bibliography, references, discussion of sources or even an index, and is anecdotal and light weight. It tells in a narrative fashion the story of the company concentrating on ships, trades and personalities. The firm was established to check the powerful monopoly of Shaw Savill. It is useful for its details of merger activity in shipping prior to 1914.
Firms: Dennys; Federal Steam Navigation Co.; Hawthorn Leslie; Houlder Brothers; New Zealand Freight Co.; New Zealand Shipping Co.; Shaw Savill & Albion

3126
Waters, Sydney D.
Union Line: A short history of the Union Steam Ship Company of New Zealand Ltd 1875–1951
1951 Union Steam Ship Co. *Wellington, New Zealand*

Although largely superseded by McLean's 1990 book (qv) this earlier, thinner, and more narrative volume still has some value as a source book. It is well illustrated and has a useful fleet list but is not academic, having neither references nor an index. It is useful on the ships, trades and cargoes.
Firms: Union Steam Ship Co.

3127
Waters, Sydney D.
Richardsons of Napier: A century of coastal shipping 1859–1959
1959 Richardson & Co. *Napier, New Zealand*

Given its early age and short length this is a disappointing book, being narrative rather than analytical and concentrating on the ships, trades and personalities of the company. It is important, however, because it describes what is claimed to be the oldest New Zealand shipping company which was mainly engaged in the coastal, lighterage and stevedoring business. The book is good on the links with the export trades and stock and station agents.
Firms: Kincaid McQueen & Co.; Murray Roberts; Richardsons; Williams & Kettle

Sea Transport, Rest of World

3128
Bonin, Hubert
Suez: Du canal à la finance, 1858–1987 [Suez: From canal to financial services 1858–1987]
1987 Economica *Paris, France*

The first part of this book deals with the history of the Suez Canal Company up to nationalization by Nasser in 1956; most of the work is devoted to the post-1956 mutation and reconversion of the firm, which diversified into finance, real estate, industry and banking. Moreover, in the 1980s, it was nationalized and then privatized. This is 'official' history, but scholarly and based upon primary sources.
Firms: Suez Canal Co.

3129
Chida, Tomohei
Nippon Kaiun no Kodo Seicho: Showa 39nen kara 48nen made [The High Growth of Japanese Shipping: 1964–1973]
1993 Nippon Keizai Hyoron-sha *Tokyo, Japan*

This work covers the period 1964–73, the golden age of Japanese shipping. The author examines the causes of high growth and prosperity in that decade, and draws some interesting conclusions.

3130
Japan Business History Institute (Editor)
Sogyo Hyakunen-shi [Centenary History of Mitsui O.S.K. Lines]
1985 Mitsui O.S.K. Lines *Tokyo, Japan*

Published to celebrate the centenary of Mitsui O.S.K. Lines (Osaka Shosen Mitsui Senpaku). The predecessor firms, Osaka Shosen Kaisha, Mitsui Bussan Kaisha, Mitsui Steamship (Mitsui Senpaku), are also described in detail. A separate volume reproduces archive materials of Mitsui O.S.K. Lines and its predecessor firms.
Firms: Mitsui Bussan Kaisha; Osaka Shosen

Mitsui Senpaku; Mitsui Senpaku; Osaka Shosen Kaisha

3131
Japan Business History Institute (Editor)
Nippon Yusen Kabushiki Kaisha Hyakunen-shi [Centenary History of Nippon Yusen Kaisha]
1988 Nippon Yusen Kaisha *Tokyo, Japan*

This is the history of Nippon Yusen Kaisha, a typical Japanese shipping company. Covering the period 1885 to 1985, it attaches importance to the process of top management decision-making. In this work, many previously unpublished business documents and company archives are taken into account, giving valuable information for students. The historical materials (excluding minutes of the board of directors) have been published as a separate volume.
Firms: Nippon Yusen Kaisha

3132
Kobayashi, Masa-aki
Kaiun-gyo no Rodo Mondai: Kindaiteki Roshi Kankei no Senku [Labour Problems in the Shipping Industry]
For main entry, see 4201

3133
Kobayashi, Masa-aki
Sengo Kaiun-gyo no Rodo Mondai: Yobi-in-sei to Nippon-teki Koyo [Labour Problems in Shipping after the War: The 'yobi-in' organization and Japanese employment]
For main entry, see 4202

3134
Kudo, Masahiro
Nippon Kaiun-gyo no Tenkai to Kigyo Shudan [The Development of a Japanese Shipping and Business Group]
1991 Bunshindo *Tokyo, Japan*

The object of this work is first to define the formative process of a Japanese business group after the Second World War, and secondly to explain its logic. According to the author, the Japanese shipping industry provides a unique comparative case study.

3135
Kwang-Ching, Liu
Anglo-American Steamship Rivalry in China, 1862–1874
1962 Harvard University Press *Cambridge, MA*

The author concentrates on producing an account of the various operating lines rather than any intense study of the rivalry that may have existed. The initial focus is on Edward Cunningham, who started steamship transport in Shanghai in 1863 with Russell & Co., but equal attention is given to subsequent competitors. This is a competent and fascinating work.
Firms: Butterfield & Swire; Glover, Dow & Co.; Jardine, Matheson & Co.; Russell & Co.

3136
Leubuscher, Charlotte
The West African Shipping Trade, 1909–1959
1963 A. W. Sythoff *Leyden, The Netherlands*

This is the pioneering yet still relevant study of the West African Lines shipping conference. It gives a pathbreaking analysis of competition in the shipping business, government and traders' attitudes and the impact of expatriate shipping on West African economies. The author consulted then unclassified material and provided revealing insights into the business.
Firms: Black Star Line; Elder Dempster Lines; Holland West Africa Line; Nigerian National Shipping Line; United Africa Company; Woermann Line

3137
Miwa, Ryoichi
Senryo-ki no Nippon Kaiun: Saiken e-no Michi [Japanese Shipping in the Occupation Days: The process of reconstruction]
1992 Nippon Keizai Hyoron-sha *Tokyo, Japan*

This work describes the reconstruction of Japanese shipping during the occupation from 1945 to the beginning of the 1950s. It makes effective use of the latest work in economic and business history.

3138
Nakagawa, Keiichiro
Ryo Taisen-kan no Nippon Kaiun-gyo: Fukyo-ka no Kuto to Yakushin [Japanese

Shipping in the Interwar Period: Struggle and advance during the depression]
1980 Nippon Keizai Shinbun-sha *Tokyo, Japan*

This is an important work written by a specialist in business history. Nakagawa's analyses in each chapter are based on valuable archive material and interviews with people concerned in the management and operation of shipping during the interwar period.

Firms: Daido Kaiun; Kawasaki Line; Kokusai Kisen; Mitsui Bussan Kaisha; Osaka Shosen Kaisha; Yamashita Line

3139
Obiozor, G. C.; Ndekwu, E. C.; Opara, C. O.; Otudor, F. E.
Shipping, Trade and Development in the West and Central African Sub-Region
1989 Nigerian Shippers' Council *Lagos, Nigeria*

This is a collection of workshop papers on the shipping business in the region between Mauretania and Angola. It puts together various views on the industry and the informed comments of experts. It is the only such text in the entire region and will remain indispensable to practitioners and scholars. It is strong on shipping policies and African enterprise and has many good case studies of individual countries' experiences.

Firms: Africa Ocean Lines; Nigerian National Shipping Line

3140
Sasaki, Seiji
Nippon Kaiun Kyoso shi Josetsu: Kaiun-gyo no Dokuritsu, Kindaiteki Kaiun Seisei Katei ni okeru Kyoso [Competition in the Modern Japanese Shipping Industry]
1954 Kaiji Kenkyukai *Kobe, Japan*

This is the seminal work on Japanese shipping history. The author describes the transition of control in shipping, that is, the separation between shipping and trading, and analyses the modernization in Japan during the Meiji Era.

Firms: Kyodo Un'yu Kaisha; Mitsubishi Kaisha; Nippon Yusen Kaisha; Nippon-koku Yubin Jokisen Kaisha

3141
Sasaki, Seiji
Nippon Kaiun-gyo no Kindaika: Shagaisen Hattatsu-shi [The Modernization of Japanese Shipping: The growth of 'shagaisen']
1961 Kaibundo *Kobe, Japan*

This work considers the Japanese shipping business through the examination of 'shagaisen' (outsiders), in order to consider their formation and development process. In this book, four 'shagaisen' firms, Hiroumi Kisen (affiliated with 'Kitamae-bune'), Shimatani Kisen (Kyushu-Setouchi lines), Mitsui Bussan Kaisha (Zaibatsu), and Asano Kaiso-bu (newly established), are studied.

Firms: Asano Kaiso-bu; Hiroumi Kisen; Mitsui Bussan Kaisha; Shimatani Kisen

3142
Sugiyama, Kazuo
Kaiun Fukko-ki no Shikin Mondai: Josei to Shichu Shikin [Financing of Japanese Shipping in the Reconstruction Period: Subsidies and the money market]
1992 Nippon Keizai Hyoron-sha *Tokyo, Japan*

This book analyses the reconstruction of the Japanese shipping industry during the 1950s from the viewpoint of financing. The author stresses that earlier studies had overestimated the role of subsidies for reconstruction and concentrates on the role of the money market.

3143
Teratani, Takeaki
Kaiun-gyo to Kaigun: Taiheiyo Senso-ka no Nippon Shosen Tai [Shipping and the Navy: The Japanese merchant marine during the Pacific War]
1981 Nippon Keizai Shinbun-sha *Tokyo, Japan*

This work refers to the activities of Japanese shipping during the Pacific War in relation to the shipping policy and attitude of the Navy. As the author points out, the Navy's strategy gave no consideration to the protection of merchant ships.

3144
Tregonning, Kennedy G. P.
Home Port Singapore: A history of the Straits Steamship Co. Ltd
1967 Oxford University Press *Oxford*

This book provides a history of the Straits Steamship Co., which was founded in 1890 by local entrepreneurs to develop coastal and regional trades based on Singapore. Despite the bulk of the firm's records being destroyed in the Pacific War, this volume is good on the changes in business policy from the loose confederation at the beginning, through rapid growth and centralization in the 1920s, to consolidation in the 1930s and another period of growth from 1945 to 1965. It is sometimes thin on detail, but is nevertheless a useful history.
Firms: Straits Steamship Co.

3145
Wray, William D.
Mitsubishi and the NYK 1870–1914: Business strategy in the Japanese shipping industry
1984 Harvard University Press *Cambridge, MA*

This study traces the rise of Nippon Yusen Kaisha in the Meiji period through government encouragement and war contracts, careful use of the relationship with Mitsubishi, and capture of the cotton textile trade. It is strong on business strategy and industrial policies and is a well-documented and thoroughly analytical volume.
Firms: Mitsubishi; Nippon Yusen Kaisha

3146
Yamaguchi, Kazuo
Kaiun-gyo to Kin'yu: Fukyo-ki no Shikin Chotatsu [Financing of Shipping: Capital during the depression]
1981 Nippon Keizai Shinbun-sha *Tokyo, Japan*

This business history deals with the financing of four main Japanese shipping companies. The main topics covered are: how shipping companies were financed in times of prosperity; the period of the First World War (Nippon Yusen Kaisha, Mitsui Bussan Kaisha); the financial difficulties of newly-established shipping companies (Kokusai Kisen, Toyo Kisen); and shipbuilding and financial problems during the depression (Nippon Yusen Kaisha, Mitsui Bussan Kaisha, Kokusai Kisen).
Firms: Kokusai Kisen; Mitsui Bussan Kaisha; Nippon Yusen Kaisha; Toyo Kisen

3147
Yamashita, Yukio
Kaiun to Zosen-gyo [The Shipping and Shipbuilding Industries]
1984 Nihon Keizai Shinbun *Tokyo, Japan*

This work provides an excellent explanation of the development of the Japanese shipbuilding industry and the inter-relationship between the shipping industry and fluctuations in demand for shipping space.

3148
Yui, Tsunehiko; Nakagawa, Keiichiro (Editors)
Business History of Shipping: Strategy and structure (Eleventh Fuji Conference)
For main entry, see 112

Air Transport, Europe

3149
Banks, Howard
The Rise and Fall of Freddie Laker
1982 Faber & Faber *London*

This is the story of Laker Airways, born in 1966, died in 1982, and its founder who got his first break in the Berlin airlift and then flourished during the boom in package holidays. The author traces Laker's early years with British United Airways to his founding of Laker Airways charter service and Skytrain, the low-cost transatlantic passenger airline. The struggle with national and international civil aviation is closely examined. This is strong on the economic and political context and the finances, but it has neither index nor sources acknowledged which makes it of limited use to the academic.
Firms: British United Airways; Laker Airways; Skytrain

3150
Brown, Nick
Richard Branson, the Inside Story
For main entry, see 3870

3151
Campbell-Smith, Duncan
Struggle for Take-Off: The British Airways story
1986 Hodder & Stoughton *London*

This is the story of the struggle to privatize British Airways under the Thatcher government, written by a financial journalist. It looks at the thinking behind privatization, the problems encountered because of the Laker collapse and subsequent legal battles, and the immense lobbying to bring about privatization. It is easy to read but, sadly, lacks references. It is a good piece of contemporary reportage.
Firms: British Airways; British Caledonian; Laker Airways

3152
Chadeau, Emmanuel
Latécoère
For main entry, see 1089

3153
Costello, John; Hughes, Terry
The Battle for Concorde
For main entry, see 1091

3154
Cuthbert, Geoffrey
Flying to the Sun: Quarter century of Britannia Airways, Europe's leading leisure airline
1987 Hodder & Stoughton *London*

This book is beautifully illustrated but aimed more at the enthusiast and employee than the academic. It is a rare history of a charter/holiday airline from 1962 to 1987. Although it is thin on analysis, it is stronger on personalities and strategies, the routes and the aircraft.
Firms: Britannia Airways

3155
Dierikx, Marc L. J.
Bevlogen jaren: Nederlandse burgerluchtvaart tussen de wereldoorlogen [Years of High Flying: Dutch civil aviation between the world wars]
1986 Unieboek *Houten, The Netherlands*

This book is more a history of Dutch civil aviation, rather than a business history in the strict sense of the word. It offers a general survey of economic developments in the Dutch air transport sector based on archival sources.
Firms: Koninklijke Luchtvaart Maatschappij (KLM); Koninklijke Nederlandsche-Indische Luchtvaart Maatschap; Koolhoven Vliegtuigen; Nederlandsche Vliegtuigenfabriek (Fokker); Syndicaat voor Luchtachipverkeer

3156
Dierikx, Marc L. J.
Begrensde horizonten: De Nederlandse burgerluchtvaartpolitiek ijn het interbellum [Limited Horizons: The Netherlands' civil aviation policy in the interwar period]
1988 Tjeenk Willink *Zwolle, The Netherlands*

Although focusing on Dutch international air transport policy, this book offers a short business history of KLM and KNILM at the same time.
Firms: Koninklijke Luchtvaart Maatschappij (KLM); Koninklijke Nederlandsche-Indische Luchtvaart Maatschap

3157
Feldman, E. J.
Concorde and Dissent: Exploring high technology project failures in Britain and France
For main entry, see 1095

3158
Higham, Robin D. S.
Britain's Imperial Air Routes 1918 to 1939: The story of Britain's overseas airlines
1960 G. T. Foulis *London*

This volume is a detailed study of the development of British commercial aviation in the interwar period. It is strong on the technology, politics and personalities, looks at the routes served, the problems encountered and how they were overcome, the subsidies and the government creation and dismantling of monopoly. It was a pioneering effort and still highly informative.

Firms: Imperial Airways; British Airways; BOAC; De Havilland

3159
Knight, Geoffrey
Concorde: The inside story
For main entry, see 1102

3160
Reed, Arthur
Airline: The inside story of British Airways
1990 BBC Books *London*

This is a rather anodyne, commissioned work meant to accompany a TV series written by a senior aviation journalist. It concentrates on the 1980s and the imposition of market discipline and privatization on the firm. It brings out well the dislocating effects of government policy over the long run but is not a definitive history.
Firms: BEA; BOAC; British Airways; Imperial Airways

3161
Share, Bernard
The Flight of the Iolar: The Aer Lingus experience 1936–1986
1986 Gill & Macmillan *Dublin, Ireland*

This book chronicles the history of the national airline of Ireland from its origins to the 1980s. It is particularly strong on the relationship between government and state-owned industry, the personalities involved, and the 1960s diversification programme. It contains useful figures indicating the huge initial losses made until the 1960s.
Firms: Aer Lingus

3162
Thomas, Miles
Out on a Wing: An autobiography
For main entry, see 841

3163
Thomson, Adam
High Risk: The politics of the air
For main entry, see 3926

Air Transport, North America

3164
Ashley, C. A.
The First Twenty-Five Years: A study of Trans-Canada Air Lines
1963 Macmillan Company of Canada
Toronto, Canada

This book provides a useful short overview of the establishment in 1937 of a monopolistic Canadian Crown corporation, providing transcontinental air services for passengers, freight and mail. The material is drawn from annual reports and includes some statistics, and covers well the legislation relating to TCA's incorporation and the Government's attempts to draw the railroads into financing it. TCA became Air Canada.
Firms: Air Canada; Canadian National Railroad; Canadian Pacific Air; Canadian Pacific Railroad; Trans-Canada Airlines

3165
Blatherwick, Francis J.
A History of Airlines in Canada
1989 Unitrade Press *Toronto, Canada*

This is a field guide to Canadian regional and transcontinental airlines. It provides a brief, uncritical, history of each line, its fleet list, and routes travelled. Some information on crashes is also provided and jet charter and commuter lines are covered. It is a very useful source.
Firms: Air Canada; Canadian Airlines International; Canadian Pacific Airlines; Wardair; Trans-Canada Airlines

3166
Daley, Robert
An American Saga: Juan Trippe and his Pan American empire
1980 Random House *New York, NY*

This is a popular but well-researched history of Pan Am from its birth in 1927 until the founder's retirement in 1968. It is good on the personalities, technical innovations, relationship with the government, and strategies and has some useful data on capital and income. It is thin on employees and customers.
Firms: Pan American Airlines

3167
Fuller, G. A.; Griffin, J. A.; Molson, Kenneth M.
125 Years of Candian Aeronautics: A chronology 1840–1965
1983 Canadian Aviation Historical Soc. *Willowdale, Ontario, Canada*

This is a comprehensive chronology of all aspects of aeronautics in Canada and the entries include references to other sources. There are photographs of early civil and military aircraft and a section on the activities of the Royal Canadian Air Force.
Firms: Boeing Canada; Pratt-Whitney Canada Inc.

3168
Lewis, W. David; Newton, Wesley P.
Delta: The history of an airline
1979 University of Georgia Press *Athens, GA*

This is a vast, scholarly history drawing on the corporate archives, Civil Aeronautics Board records and interviews. It traces the rise of Delta from crop dusting origins in Louisiana in the 1920s and its first airmail contract and scheduled passenger service in 1934. It is good on strategy, ownership, methods of raising capital, and the entrepreneurial personalities. Founder Leo Woolman and his struggle with Eddie Rickenbacker of Eastern take centre stage in this exceptional work.
Firms: Chicago & Southern Air Corp.; Delta Air Corporation; Eastern Airlines; Huff Daland & Co.

3169
Lewis, W. David; Trimble, William F.
The Airway to Everywhere: A history of All American Aviation 1937–1953
1988 University of Pittsburgh Press *Pittsburgh, PA*

This firm commenced operations providing airmail services to small towns in the northwest USA, without the plane landing. It was initially financed by one of the du Ponts. In 1948 it became a passenger airline and in 1953 became Allegheny Airlines and later US Air. The book is strong on technical developments, dealing with the Civil Aeronautics Board, and managerial strategies. It was written by professional historians.
Firms: All American Aviation; Allegheny Airlines; US Air

3170
Main, J. R. K.
Voyageurs of the Air: A history of civil aviation in Canada 1858–1967
1967 Queen's Printer *Ottawa, Canada*

This book was a Canadian centennial year project commissioned by the Department of Transportation. Beginning with balloon ascents, the text traces the main course of events in building ground support, communications systems, navigation aids and traffic control systems. It presents well the problems encountered in developing aviation services in a harsh physical environment.

3171
Satterfield, Archie
The Alaska Airlines Story
1981 Alaska Northwest Publishing *Anchorage, AK*

This is a history of Alaska Airlines which came into formal existence in 1944 but traces its origins to predecessor firms from 1932. Sadly, it is not an academic work, with no references or sources, and not even a bibliography. It is well illustrated, and strong on personalities, planes and flying stories but very poor on the business aspects such as finance, organizational strategy and structure.
Firms: Alaska Airlines; Star Air Lines

3172
Serling, Robert J.
From the Captain to the Colonel: An informal history of Eastern Airlines
1980 Dial Press *New York, NY*

Sadly, as its subtitle indicates, this is not an academic work, with neither references nor a bibliography. It is an anecdotal history of Pitcairn Aviation, established in 1925 to fly air mails on the east coast, which was sold and renamed in 1930. It is good on the planes, routes and people but has almost nothing on the business aspects such as finance, profits, strategy and organization structure.
Firms: Eastern Air Transport; Eastern Airlines; Pitcairn Aviation

3173
Smith, Philip
It Seems Like Only Yesterday: Air Canada, The first 50 years
1986 McClelland & Stewart *Toronto, Canada*

This book traces the history of Air Canada from its origins as Trans-Canada Air Lines in 1937 through to the modern era. Written in a popular style, the author focuses on the people, as well as the politics and technology, in the first fifty years of Canada's largest airline.
Firms: Air Canada; Trans-Canada Airlines

3174
Trimble, W. F.
High Frontier: A history of aeronautics in Pennsylvania
1982 University of Pittsburgh Press
Pittsburgh, PA

Trimble makes a comprehensive study of the aeronautics industry in a major state of the USA. The story ranges from the early hot-air balloonists of the late eighteenth century to the modern aerospace industry. The impact of the First World War, the role of big business, state regulation of air travel and technological developments are all covered.
Firms: AGA Aviation Group; Curtis-Wright Corp.; G. & A. Aircraft, Inc.; Pitcairn Aircraft Co.; Transworld Airlines (TWA); Westinghouse Electric Corp.

Air Transport, Rest of World

3175
Brogden, Stanley
Australia's Two-Airline Policy
1968 Melbourne University Press *Melbourne, Australia*

This is not a company history per se but rather examines the development of Australia's domestic airline policy which created a duopoly, one firm private enterprise, the other a public corporation. This volume is good on the role of government regulation, has some useful tables of financial performance, and sets the context well.
Firms: Australian National Airways; Trans-Australia Airlines

3176
Corbett, David
Politics and the Airlines
1965 George Allen & Unwin *London*

This book does not claim to be business history orientated but rather is a study of aviation politics and diplomacy in Australia, Britain, Canada, India and the USA mostly in the 1950s and early 1960s with an occasional glance backward at the earlier history. It is an exercise in comparative politics and administration, and thus may be a useful source, though deficient in many business aspects.
Firms: Air India; BEA; BOAC; Imperial Airways; Qantas; Trans Australia Airlines; Trans Canada Airlines

3177
Davies, Ronald E. G.
A History of the World's Airlines
1964 Oxford University Press *Oxford*

This is an encyclopedic work, brimming with information not easily found in other texts. The author's intent was to catalogue every airline in existence at any period. That he succeeds in this effort is remarkable and a fortunate circumstance for those who need a reliable and quick reference in a single volume.

3178
Davies, Ronald E. G.
Airlines of Latin America Since 1919
1984 Smithsonian Institution Press
Washington, DC

This is a chronological survey rich in data. The subject of foreign investment and influence is addressed fully. The development of numerous companies, mergers, and the entrepreneurs responsible are treated with a thoroughness one comes to expect from this respected authority. Scholars will find this a useful and absorbing volume.
Firms: Mexicana; Pan American Airways; SCADTA-AVIANCA; TACA; VARIG

3179
Dobson, Alan P.
Peaceful Air Warfare: The United States, Britain and the politics of international aviation
1991 Oxford University Press *Oxford*

This volume is not explicitly on the topic of

business history, but rather a study of the aviation policies of the British and American governments from the beginning to the present. It is a detailed work of diplomatic relations and the interactions between them and aviation policy, and how this gave birth to the current system of modern civil aviation.

3180
Doganis, Rigas
Flying Off Course: The economics of international airlines
1985 George Allen & Unwin *London*

This is not a business history and does not even include a historical perspective on the topic. It is an analysis of the economics of airline operations, such as the costs of, and demand for, the service, the nature of regulation, pricing policies, fare structure, and the impact of deregulation. As such it provides a valuable body of theory business historians of the airline industry might wish to use.

3181
Driscoll, Ian H.
Airline: The making of a national flag carrier
1979 Shortland Publications *Auckland, New Zealand*

This is a commemorative history of Air New Zealand, the successor in 1965 of Tasman Empire Airways Ltd. It begins with the origins of civil aviation in New Zealand and concentrates on the struggle to make New Zealand an international participant in long-distance aviation. It is not very critical but places Air New Zealand neatly in competitive context with British, French, American and Australian companies. The 1978 merger with the second government-owned carrier ensured the survival of Air New Zealand.
Firms: Air New Zealand; National Airways Corporation; Tasman Empire Airways

3182
Gunn, J.
The Defeat of Distance: Qantas 1919–1939
1985 University of Queensland Press
St Lucia, Qld, Australia

Gunn's book is the first part of a multi-volume, commissioned company history. It is a warts and all account based on exhaustive archival documentation. A chronological and largely narrative approach is taken with emphasis on business–government relations on the one hand and the practical and technological problem of early civil aviation on the other. After initial growth in outback Queensland, Qantas (Queensland and Northern Territory Air Services) deliberately opted for expansion into overseas routes. In consequence the company became the political football between Australia, Britain and, to a lesser extent, The Netherlands.
Firms: Qantas

3183
Gunn, J.
High Corridors: Qantas 1954–1970
1988 University of Queensland Press
St Lucia, Qld, Australia

This third volume of a detailed company history gives an extensive overview of Qantas's growth in its competitive context, as seen from the Qantas prespective. It is highly informative and, as a case study, insightful on the rise of long-distance civil aviation during the introduction of jet-engined airplanes. The emphasis is on lines to Europe and trans-Pacific to America. It ends with the beginnings of the era of the jumbo jet.
Firms: Qantas

3184
Gunn, J.
Challenging Horizons: Qantas 1939–1954
1990 University of Queensland Press
St Lucia, Qld, Australia

This book provides a broad overview based on company material. Qantas became Australia's international carrier and, in a period of rapid technological change, grew at a fast pace. This second volume of the Qantas story also gives a good insight into the political context of government regulation and the many problems caused by technological change. It is highly informative, but with little attention to financial aspects.
Firms: Qantas

3185
Leary, William M.
The Dragon's Wings: The China National

Aviation Corporation and the development of commercial aviation in China
1976 University of Georgia Press *Athens, GA*
This prize-winning work traces the development of air transport in China during a volatile period in that country's history. The author shows that strong backing by the Chinese government, excellent American management, and the ability of Pan American to bear the financial losses, helped the aviation service to survive. CNAC's story is set against a fascinating backdrop of early twentieth century world events. This is a well-written and often amusing account.
Firms: China National Aviation Corporation (CNAC); Pan American

3186
McCormack, R. L.
Man with a Mission: Oswald Pirow and South African Airways 1933–39
Journal of African History, vol. 20, no. 4, 1979: pp 543–57
McCormack studies the origins of Africa's first national airline, established in 1934. He stresses how SAA was used to counter British influence in East and Central Africa.
Firms: South African Airways

3187
Rennie, Neil
Conquering Isolation: The first 50 years of Air New Zealand
1990 Heinemann Reed *Auckland, New Zealand*
This volume is lavishly illustrated, has a comprehensive fleet list and a list of the chief executives of the three airline companies involved. It deals chronologically with the development of Air New Zealand. It is good on incidents, colour, personalities and flights but is not analytical and thin on the business aspects.
Firms: Air New Zealand; New Zealand National Airways Corporation; Tasman Empire Airways

3188
Vietor, Richard H. K.
Contrived Competition: Regulation and deregulation in America
For main entry, see 4406

3189
Young, Gavin
Beyond Lion Rock: The story of Cathay Pacific Airways
1988 Hutchinson *London*
This is the history of Cathay Pacific which began operations in 1946 in Hong Kong and was acquired by John Swire & Son in 1948. It ran air services worldwide based on Hong Kong. The book is rather narrative and not analytical of the business aspects, but it is strong on personalities and human interest.
Firms: Cathay Pacific Airways; John Swire & Son

Ports and Shipping Services

3190
Beckenham, Arthur F.
Wagons of Smoke: An informal history of the East African Railways and Harbours Administration 1948–1961
For main entry, see 2942

3191
Condit, Carl W.
The Port of New York: A history of the rail and terminal system
1980/81 University of Chicago Press *Chicago, IL*
This claims not to be a business history, a genre the author deplores, but more a technical history of the growth in demand for port and terminal facilities, and the response to these pressures in terms of electrification, and terminal construction. It contains some useful statistics on freight and passenger movements but nothing on corporate history.
Firms: Port of New York

3192
Davies, Peter N.
Henry Tyrer: A Liverpool shipping agent and his enterprise 1879–1979
1979 Croom Helm *London*
This is a centenary history of a medium-sized firm of shipping agents in the West African trade, based in Liverpool with offices in London and Preston. It is good on the changes in

the trade and has some useful data on operations and finances. It is important as there are so few studies of shipping agents.
Firms: Henry Tyrer & Co.; James Murdoch & Co.

3193
Driel, Hugo van
Four Centuries of Warehousing: Pakhoed: The origins and history 1616–1967
1992 Royal Pakhoed NV *Rotterdam, The Netherlands*

This is a commissioned history of Pakhoed, a large Dutch warehousing, distribution and transport company, which traces its origins to the early seventeenth century. Although written by a scholar it lacks references, a bibliography and even an index but is well illustrated. It deals with the early development of the trade and is good on inter-firm rivalry and cooperation, the shift to the docks and the expansion and diversification of the business.
Firms: Koninklijk Pakhoed NV

3194
Fagg, Alan
Westrays: A record of J. B. Westray and Company Limited
1957 J. B. Westray *London*

Although this privately printed volume is rather dated, and lacks index, bibliography and sources, it is included because so few histories exist of ship broking firms. It is strong on the personalities and general direction of the business but thin on statistics, finance, and the more analytic details of a business.
Firms: J. B. Westray & Co.; New Zealand Shipping Co.; General Steam Navigation Co.

3195
Farnie, Douglas A.
The Manchester Ship Canal and the Rise of the Port of Manchester
1980 Manchester University Press *Manchester*

This volume tells the history of the 'last canal built in England', from its construction, financed largely by the Corporation of Manchester, through the establishment of trade links and resident liner companies and the development of the adjoining Trafford Park industrial estate. It is based on the records of the company.
Firms: Manchester Ship Canal Co.; Trafford Park Estates

3196
Hyde, Francis E.
Liverpool and the Mersey: The development of a port, 1700–1970
1971 David & Charles *Newton Abbot*

This book examines the growth of the trades which made Liverpool Britain's largest provincial port, and also the developments made within the docks in order to handle this increasing traffic. It draws heavily on the author's previous work, and tends to ignore the coastal and Irish trades, and the role of the labour force. However, it is a seminal work of port history, drawing together a number of themes.
Firms: Mersey Docks and Harbour Board

3197
Large, David (Editor)
The Port of Bristol, 1848–1884
1985 Bristol Record Society *Bristol*

This is not really a business history but rather a reprint of the records of The Bristol Corporation's Docks Committee which operated the port in this period. They amply illustrate all aspects of port operations but lack contextualization and commentary and as such this volume is narrow and not easy to use. Neale (qv) complements this book.
Firms: Bristol Docks

3198
Mountfield, Stuart
Western Gateway: A history of the Mersey Docks and Harbour Board
1965 Liverpool University Press *Liverpool*

The Board was created in 1858 to coordinate and plan developments in the second most important docks in the UK. The Board had continuously to expand facilities to cater for rising trade and to counter competition. This book is strong on changes in technology, the competitive environment and labour conditions.
Firms: Mersey Docks and Harbour Board

3199
Neale, W. G.
At the Port of Bristol
1968–76 Port of Bristol Authority *Bristol*

This three-volumed history of the port of Bristol covers the period from 1848, when the Docks Committee was established by the Council to take over from the Bristol Docks Co., until 1918. It is strong on personalities and politics, but is thin on the details of trade and operations until the twentieth century.
Firms: Bristol Dock Authority; Port of Bristol

3200
Wadia, Ruttorijee A.
The Bombay Dockyard and the Wadia Master Builders
1955 R. A. Wadia *Bombay, India*

This is a history of the Bombay Dockyard by a member of the Parsee family which began it and operated it for six generations. The study draws on family and official papers but is not really a business history, instead concentrating on the ships built and the family involved.
Firms: Bombay Dockyard; Wadia

Postal Services

3201
Beale, Philip O.
The Postal Service of Sierra Leone
1988 Royal Philatelic Society *London*

This meticulously-researched book traces the postal history of Sierra Leone to independence in 1961, drawing on a range of public archives. Although mostly concerned with the technical details of mail and parcel delivery, it does offer some insights into the economics of this colonial postal service and its impact on economic development. It is lavishly illustrated.
Firms: Sierra Leone Post Office

3202
Daunton, Martin J.
Royal Mail: The Post Office since 1840
1986 Athlone *London*

This is a large, commissioned history of British mail delivery and the many transport modes it used. The work is particularly strong on labour relations and the firm's attitude to changing technology and also covers well the changing scope of services offered, organizational structure, and relations with the government. It brings out admirably the relationship with the railways and steamship lines. It is heavily referenced and a classic of the genre.
Firms: General Post Office; Royal Mail

3203
Kielbowicz, Richard
News in the Mail: The press, post office and public information, 1760–1860s
For main entry, see 1778

3204
Leary, William M.
Aerial Pioneers: The U.S. Air Mail Service, 1918–1927
1986 Smithsonian Institution Press *Washington, DC*

This is one of the best available works on this subject, drawn from extensive primary and secondary sources. Skilfully utilizing correspondence and interviews, Leary stresses the role of the Postmaster Generals and their assistants in shaping the postal air transport system from its pioneering stages to its position as leader in the field.
Firms: U.S. Air Mail Service

3205
Lotz, Wolfgang
Deutsche Post Geschichte: Essays und Bilder [The History of the German Post Office]
1989 Nicolai *Berlin, Germany*

This is a major multi-authored celebration of the German postal service from its origins to the early 1950s. Some of the contributions focus more on business aspects, notably Vogt's chapters on postal services during the German Empire and the Weimar period, and Gnewuch on the rebuilding of the Berlin post after 1945. The book contains many fine illustrations.
Firms: Deutsche Reichspost

3206
Perry, Charles R.
The Victorian Post Office: The growth of a bureaucracy

1992 Boydell & Brewer *Woodbridge*

This well-researched volume examines the expansion of the Victorian Post Office in the context of the debate over the role of the Victorian state and the origins of a mixed economy in Britain. It looks at the additional functions taken on by the GPO in terms of national savings, the telegraph and telephone systems, railway and shipping contracts. It is referenced, has a useful bibliography and is scholarly and thoughtful.

Firms: GPO

3207

Pitt, Douglas

The Telecommunications Function of the British Post Office: A case study of bureaucratic adaptation

For main entry, see 3234

3208

Smith, William

A History of the Post Office in British North America

1920 Cambridge University Press *London*

This is a comprehensive account of the beginnings and growth of the Canadian Post Office. It covers the relations between the colonial postal system and the general post office in London until control was relinquished to the Canadian colony, and is based on extensive public records. It is obviously rather dated but is still a valuable source book.

Firms: Allan Line Steamers; Cunard Steamship Lines; Grand Trunk Railway; Great Western Steamship Company; Lever/Galway Company; Canadian Post Office

3209

Westney, D. Eleanor

Imitation and Innovation: The transfer of Western organizational patterns to Meiji Japan

For main entry, see 1808

3210

Yusei-sho

Yusei Hyakunen-shi [Centenary History of Postal Service]

1971 Teishin Kyokai *Tokyo, Japan*

This is a history of the Japanese postal service, 1871–1971. It also refers to subsidiary services, postal savings and postal life insurance. Archival material relating to the postal service is published separately in 30 volumes.

Firms: Teishin-sho; Yusei-sho

Telecommunications Services

3211

Ahvenainen, Jorma

The Far Eastern Telegraphs: The history of telegraph communication between the Far East, Europe, and America before the First World War

1981 Suomalainen, Tiedeakatemia *Helsinki, Finland*

This exhaustive study examines the provision of telegraph services to the Far East from the viewpoint of the providers. It is strong on the political and commercial battles and the secret ownership deals. It says little about the users or the operators. It brings out well the profitability of the system.

Firms: Commercial Pacific Cable Co.; Eastern Extension Telegraph Co.; Great Northern Telegraph Co.

3212

Attman, Artur; Kuuse, Jan; Olsson, Ulf; Jacobaeus, Christian

LM Ericsson: 100 years

For main entry, see 1505

3213

Baker, W. J.

A History of the Marconi Company

1970 Methuen *London*

This is a history of the firm which pioneered radio communication and hence opened the way to broadcasting, television and satellite communications. In 1929 some of its interests were merged into Cable and Wireless (qv). It is based on the company's archives and is stronger on the business–government relations, personalities and business strategy than on the financial or technical side. The 1946 merger with English Electric is covered, along with a review of the post-war history of the company.

Firms: Cable & Wireless; Marconi Co.; Mar-

coni Wireless Telegraph Co.; English Electric; GEC

3214
Barty-King, Hugh
Girdle Round the Earth: The story of Cable and Wireless and its predecessors to mark the group's jubilee 1929–1979
1979 Heinemann *London*

This volume is a commissioned history by the group archivist of the Victorian companies which laid international telegraph cables and which merged with the wireless providing firms in 1929 to form the Group which was nationalized in 1947. It is particularly strong on technological changes and the international politics of communications.
Firms: Cable and Wireless; Imperial and International Communications

3215
Bradley, Keith
Phone Wars: The story of Mercury Communications
1992 Century Business *London*

This book tells the story of the birth and growth of Mercury Communications, one of the competitors to British Telecom, brought into being by government and business in the light of BT's privatization. It is strong on the economic and political context, changes in technology and labour relations, and business policy. It is well referenced and an excellent example of very recent business history.
Firms: Mercury Communications; British Telecom; Cable and Wireless

3216
Brock, Gerald W.
The Telecommunications Industry: The dynamics of market structure
1981 Harvard University Press *Cambridge, MA*

This scholarly work examines the theories of how industry is determined and then applies it to the telegraph and telephone industry, primarily in America but with some regard to European practice. It is strong on the market conditions, the reasons for monopoly, regulation, changes in technology and how these affected industry structure. It is referenced and thoughtful.
Firms: AT&T; Western Union

3217
Brooks, John
Telephone: The first hundred years
1976 Harper & Row *New York, NY*

This is a centennial celebration of the Bell telephone system in America, based on the archives of the company. It takes a chronological approach, and is strong on the technological breakthroughs, important personalities, external economic conditions, and the growth of demand. It is referenced and readable.
Firms: AT&T; Bell Laboratories

3218
Deloraine, Maurice
When Telecom and ITT Were Young
1976 Lehigh Books *New York, NY*

This book covers ITT during the period from the First World War till just after the Second World War.
Firms: ITT

3219
Fagen, M. D. (Editor)
A History of Science and Engineering in the Bell System: Vol. 1, The early years, 1876–1925, Vol. 2, National Service in War and Peace, 1925–1975
1975/8 Bell Laboratories *New York, NY*

The first two volumes in a three volume series (qv Schindler) comprising a massive 2,500 pages of text, represent a massive in-house technical history of the Bell System. Replete with technical detail and illustration they are difficult books to use, but they are an utterly indispensable stepping off point for all historians of the Bell System.
Firms: AT&T; Bell Laboratories

3220
Fischer, Claude S.
America Calling: A social history of the telephone to 1940
1992 University of California Press *Berkeley, CA*

This well-researched and referenced volume analyses the spread of telephone use in the USA

from 1990 to 1940. It looks at who used them, how they were employed, and why, the differences that the telephone made, and how it advertised its services. It is thoughtful, wide-ranging and authoritative.
Firms: AT&T; Bell Telephone Co.

3221
Gabler, Edwin
The American Telegrapher: A social history, 1860–1900
1988 Rutgers University Press *New Brunswick, NJ*

This is a social history of telegraphers and their role in the American labor movement. It explores the effects of the Brotherhood of Telegraphers strike against Western Union in 1883 and the industry's ties with the military and railroads. It is valuable to the historian interested in labour–management relations and entertaining as well as informative.
Firms: Western Union

3222
Garnet, Robert W.
The Telephone Enterprise: The evolution of the Bell system's horizontal structure 1876–1909
1985 Johns Hopkins Press *Baltimore, MD*

This book traces the history of American Bell from its foundation in 1877, initially as a loose association of regional companies, through the formation of AT&T in 1885 into the 1890s when local autonomy began to give way to centralized management on functional lines. It uses the Chandlerian paradigm to explain Bell's structure and goals but is rather thin on competition and government relations. It originally served as data in the defence of US vs AT&T.
Firms: American Bell; American Telephone & Telegraph (AT&T); Western Union

3223
Goulden, Joseph C.
Monopoly
1968 G. P. Putnam & Sons *New York, NY*

A revealing journalistic investigation of the history of AT&T in the best muck-raking tradition, from a trust-busting perspective.
Firms: American Telephone and Telegraph Company (AT&T)

3224
Hills, Jim
Information Technology and Industrial Policy
1984 Croom Helm *London*

A good study of the government response to the growth of information technology and its policy in the areas of computing, telecommunications and microelectronics. Policy in each area since 1964 is analysed and compared with policies in competitor countries. British policy emerges as incoherent and complacent, leading to a weak industry and dependence on the United States.

3225
Holcombe, Arthur N.
Public Ownership of Telephones on the Continent of Europe
1911 Houghton Mifflin *New York, NY*

This volume contains in-depth studies of the reasons for, technology of, and effects of public monopolies of telephone services in a dozen mainland European countries. Although it is an old book, it is analytical and has some historical material and would be a useful source for the topic. It has a brief bibliography.

3226
Hungerford, Edward
Wells Fargo: Advancing the American frontier
For main entry, see 3002

3227
Kieve, J. L.
The Electric Telegraph: A social and economic history
1973 David & Charles *Newton Abbot*

This volume traces the telegraph in Britain from the pioneering days in the 1830s through the lines owned by railways and joint stock companies to nationalization in 1868 and becoming a monopoly under the Post Office, until challenged by the telephone in the twentieth century. The book is good on technical changes and the social context.
Firms: Electric Telegraph Company; General Post Office

3228
Lipartito, Kenneth
The Bell System and Regional Business: The telephone in the south 1877–1920
1989 Johns Hopkins University Press
Baltimore, MD

This book analyses the problems faced by the Bell Company in establishing a regional telephone network. It deals well with problems of recruiting managers and employees, commercial strategy, competition with Western Union (which eventually led to cooperation) financial needs, and the competition from the independents. It is excellent on the clash between regional and corporate culture.
Firms: Bell Telephone Co.; Western Union

3229
McDowell, Duncan
The Light: Brazilian Traction, Light and Power Company Limited, 1899–1945
For main entry, see 2756

3230
Meyer, John R.; Wilson, Robert W.; Baughcum, M. Alan; Burton, Ellen; Caouette, Louis
The Economics of Competition in the Telecommunications Industry
1980 Oelgeschlager, Gunn & Hain
Cambridge, MA

This is not a history of the industry, but rather an analysis of the economics of the industry in the USA at a crucial time, viz the late 1970s. The original report was commissioned by IBM from a commercial consultancy, this is the outcome. It is scholarly, analytical and penetrating and advocated a more openly competitive environment rather than the tightly regulated monopoly.
Firms: AT&T

3231
Moyal, Ann
Clear Across Australia: A history of telecommunications
1984 Nelson *Melbourne, Vic., Australia*

This well-illustrated volume charts the development of telecommunications in Australia from telegraphs in the 1850s to satellites. It is strong on technical change, adapting the technology to the environment, the role of government and politics in telecommunications history, the bureaucrats, politicians and entrepreneurs involved, and the effect of the cable and phone on the economy and society. It is a useful institutional and social history.
Firms: Australian Post Office; Telecom Australia

3232
Nippon Denshin Denwa Kosha
Denshin Denwa Jigyo-shi [A History of Nippon Telegraph and Telephone]
1959-60 Denki Tsushin Kyokai *Tokyo, Japan*

This is a 29-volume history of telegraph and telephone services in Japan. It also covers the development of prewar services in overseas colonies including Formosa (Taiwan), South Sakhalin (Minami Karafuto), Manchuria, and other occupied areas.
Firms: Teishin-sho; Nippon Denshin Denwa Kosha

3233
Ogle, Ed B.
Long Distance Please: The story of the Trans Canada Telephone System
1979 Collins *Toronto, Canada*

This book tells the story of the Trans Canada Telephone System which was formed in 1931. It was established to provide long-distance telephone services and hence link the many regional companies. It is strong on the changing technology and services, the personalities and the role of government. It is well illustrated and carries an extensive bibliography though no end notes.
Firms: Trans Canada Telephone System

3234
Pitt, Douglas
The Telecommunications Function of the British Post Office: A case study of bureaucratic adaptation
1980 Saxon House *Farnborough*

A political analysis of the telecommunications part of the Post Office from 1878 to the establishment of the Post Office Corporation in 1969.
Firms: Post Office (UK)

3235
Reich, Leonard S.
The Making of American Industrial Research: Science and business at GE and Bell, 1876–1926
1985 Cambridge University Press *Cambridge*

This is an interesting and well-written history of research and development in the communications industry. Reich concentrates on the contributions of Bell Telephone/AT&T and General Electric, beginning with the period prior to organization and discusses the reasons for the establishment of scientific laboratories. Farsighted executives and the technical problems encountered are skilfully analysed.
***Firms:** American Telephone & Telegraph (AT&T); Bell Telephone; General Electric*

3236
Schindler, G. E. Jr (Editor)
A History of Science and Engineering in the Bell System: Vol. 3, Switching technology (1925–75)
1982 Bell Laboratories *New York, NY*

The third volume of the massive in-house history of the Bell System. For details see Fagen (qv).
***Firms:** AT&T; Bell Laboratories*

3237
Smith, George David
The Anatomy of a Business Strategy: Bell, Western Electric and the origins of the American telephone industry
1985 Johns Hopkins University Press *Baltimore, MD*

This volume is part of the result of AT&T opening their voluminous archives to academics and encouraging them to research and publish. It is in the Chandlerian mode of enquiry, looking at business policy and organizational structure, and suggesting that the need for geographical domination compelled vertical integration through the control of technical equipment, hence Bell's acquisition of Western Electric from Western Union in 1882.
***Firms:** American Telephone & Telegraph (AT&T); Bell Telephone; Western Electric; Western Union*

3238
Stone, Alan
Wrong Number: The breakup of AT & T
1989 Basic Books *New York, NY*

This book traces the causes and course of deregulation of AT & T, showing how the political climate led to divestiture, and small intrusions by other firms paved the way to further dismemberment, as prices were lowered in particular market segments. It is not a business history per se, but has some useful material on 'Ma Bell''s policies and practices which preceded the break-up.
***Firms:** American Telephones and Telegraph (AT&T); MCI*

3239
Temin, Peter; Galambos, L.
The Fall of the Bell System: A study in prices and profits
1988 Cambridge University Press *Cambridge*

Although briefly tracing the growth of AT&T as a national monopoly, the book concentrates on the break between the government and the company from the 1960s, as technical change and new political ideas replaced a public service monopoly with competitive units. It is good on the reasons for this change and the underlying economic arguments.
***Firms:** American Telephone & Telegraph (AT&T)*

3240
Wasserman, Neil H.
From Invention to Innovation: Long distance transmission at the turn of the century
1985 Johns Hopkins University Press *Baltimore, MD*

The invention of the loading coil is the focus of this study. The device served to reduce attenuation thus improving the quality of telephonic voice transmissions. Wasserman follows the progress of Bell System's search for the solution to a specific problem. It is an estimable work, the product of considerable research in AT&T's archives.
***Firms:** American Telephone & Telegraph (AT&T); Bell Telephone*

3241
Young, Peter
Power of Speech: A history of Standard Telephones and Cables 1883–1983
1983 George Allen & Unwin *London*

This is a commissioned centenary history of a firm which started as an agency of the American Western Electric to market phone services in the UK. It also went in for manufacturing and the installation of telephone services worldwide. This study draws on the firm's archives and is well contextualized with a strong narrative thread. The close technical and managerial links with the American parent (now ITT) are explained, and performance data are provided.

Firms: GPO; ITT; Standard Telephones & Cables; Western Electric

Legal, Accountancy Services & Accounting History

3242
Adewoye, O.
The Legal Profession in Nigeria, 1865–1962
1982 Longman *Ikeja (Lagos), Nigeria*

This is the only business history of the legal profession in Nigeria. Adewoye dwells on the introduction of the British legal system consequent upon the establishment of colonial rule, and covers the period from the establishment of the colony in Lagos to the immediate post-independence period. The book includes case studies of attorneys, solicitors and barristers. It reflects upon the impact of Western legal systems on an African society.

Firms: C.A. Sapara–Williams & Co.; H. O. Davies & Co.; Kitoye Ajasa & Co.; Obafemi Awolowo & Co.; Rotimi Williams & Co.

3243
Belcher, Victor
Boodle Hatfield & Co: The history of a London law firm in three centuries
1985 Boodle Hatfield *London*

This book narrates the history of a firm of solicitors founded in 1722 which has acted as steward, attorney and solicitor to the Grosvenor estate ever since. This story is good on the partners and their personalities, how they earned their money and the reward of solid middle class respectability. The history stops in 1951 when they merged with Clowes Hickley & Heaver.

Firms: Boodle Hatfield & Co.; Clowes Hickley & Heaver

3244
Dennett, Laurie
Slaughter and May: A century in the City
1989 Granta *Cambridge*

This is one of the few histories of a British law firm. Slaughter & May began as a partnership in the City in 1889. The book is strong on the early partners and their involvement in industry and the changing economic climate in which they operated, but becomes rather anodyne in the more modern period.

Firms: Ashurst, Morris Crisp & Co.; Slaughter & May

3245
Habgood, Wendy
Chartered Accountants in England and Wales: A guide to historical records
For main entry, see 16

3246
Jackson, Christopher
A Cambridge Bicentenary: The history of a legal practice 1789–1989
1990 Morrow *Bungay*

This history of Francis & Co., a firm of Cambridge solicitors, was written by the senior partner using the firm's archives. It is a rare example of a history of an English provincial law firm, and is well contextualized, demonstrating the changing types of work undertaken and the rewards earned in status and solid financial respectability.

Firms: Francis & Co.

3247
Johnson, H. Thomas; Kaplan, R.
Relevance Lost: The rise and fall of management accounting
1987 Harvard Business School Press *Boston, MA*

This controversial and highly acclaimed study explores the evolution of management accounting in American business from the early textile mills to present-day computer-automated manufacturers. It seeks to demonstrate why modern corporations must make major changes in the way they measure and manage costs, unconstrained by their historical traditions.

3248
Jones, Edgar
Accountancy and the British Economy: The evolution of Ernst and Whinney
1981 Batsford *London*

This book is an important contribution to the history of accountancy, a much neglected area in the business history of financial services in Britain. The book goes beyond the history of Ernst & Whinney and discusses all leading firms since the mid-nineteenth century as well as their contribution to the economy. Many accounting firms have had their histories written. This is one of the few written by a professional historian and, by putting the firm's development into a social and economic context, is undoubtedly the best.
Firms: Ernst & Whinney; Turquands Barton Mayhew; Whinney Murray

3249
Jones, Edgar (Editor)
The Memoirs of Edwin Waterhouse, a Founder of Price Waterhouse
1988 Batsford *London*

This unique book comprises the memoirs of a founder and senior partner of one of today's largest accountancy firms. The book contains a substantial introduction by Edgar Jones designed to provide a perspective for the memoirs which follow.

3250
Kitchen, J.; Parker, R. H.
Accounting Thought and Education: Six English pioneers
1980 ICAEW *London*

The six accountants included here are Edwin Guthrie, Francis William Pixley, John Manger Fells, Lawrence Robert Dicksee, Sir Arthur Edwin Cutforth, and Frederic Rudolph Mackley de Paula. Each essay provides a carefully researched (though little-footnoted) biography and then an assessment of the subject's contribution to accountancy.
Firms: Institute of Chartered Accountants in England and Wales

3251
Langill, Ellen D.
Foley & Lardner: Attorneys at Law, 1842–1992
1992 State Historical Society of Wisconsin *Madison, WI*

This is the history of a Milwaukee-based law firm which grew to national coverage. The book is well researched and referenced and is particularly good at explaining the changing nature of the work performed, the roles of the partners involved, the mergers and acquisitions, and the financial performance of the firm.
Firms: Finch & Lynde; Miller, Mack & Fairchild; Foley & Lardner

3252
Lisagor, Nancy; Lipsius, Frank
A Law Unto Itself: The untold story of the law firm Sullivan and Cromwell
1988 Morrow *New York, NY*

This partnership originated in 1879 in New York and grew rich on corporate work such as advising on anti-trust legislation, mergers, New Deal legislation and pioneering new legal forms and methods of raising capital. Both J. F. and Allen Dulles were partners at one time. It is a rare example of a history of an American legal firm which is strong on personalities, the work undertaken and the organizational structure.
Firms: Sullivan & Cromwell

3253
Miranti, Paul J.
Accountancy comes of age. The development of an American profession, 1886–1940
1990 University of North Carolina Press *Chapel Hill, NC*

An important analysis of the rise of public accountancy in the USA, focusing on the development of cohesiveness among the practitioner community and attempts by the profession to persuade elite business and government leaders that the profession's skills could help to order a society in flux. Miranti compares the account-

ants' experience of professionalization with that of engineers, lawyers and doctors.
Firms: Haskins & Sells; Marwick & Mitchell; Price Waterhouse; Touche Ross; Arthur Young & Co.

3254
Offer, Avner
Property and Politics, 1870–1914: Landownership, law, ideology and urban development in England
1981 Cambridge University Press *Cambridge*

This is a well-researched, pathbreaking study which offers business historians valuable insights into property, taxation and urban/industrial change.

3255
Scott, John
Legibus: A history of Clifford Turner 1900–1980
1980 King, Thorne & Stace *Hove*

This is a rare example of the history of an English legal practice from its foundation as a small one-man business to a large multinational law firm. Written by a former partner using the firm's archives, it is strong on the personalities, the range of corporate clients serviced, and the growth of the firm in the UK and abroad. It has little on income and profits and is narrative and anecdotal rather than analytical.
Firms: Clifford Turner

3256
Slinn, Judy
A History of Freshfields
1984 Freshfields *London*

This is a commissioned history of a firm of solicitors which traces its origins back to the first half of the eighteenth century and prides itself on having been solicitors to the Bank of England from at least 1730. The history of the firm is well set in its context and is strong on the personalities of the partners and the role the firm played in the activities of the City of London.
Firms: Freshfields

3257
Slinn, Judy
Linklaters and Paines: The first one hundred and fifty years
1987 Longman *London*

This volume, one of the few on a City of London law firm, traces the history from predecessor partnerships in the 1830s to their merger in 1920 and then to date. The more distant periods are best covered, the more recent are anecdotal and anodyne. It shows well how prosperity depended on promotional booms and other periods of corporate activity.
Firms: Dods & Linklaters; Linklaters & Paines; Tyrell & Paine

3258
Stone, Russell C. J.
The Making of Russell McVeagh: The first 125 years of the practice of Russell McVeagh McKenzie Bartlett & Co., 1863–1988 and Co 1863–1988
1991 Auckland University Press *Auckland, New Zealand*

This is a commissioned history of Auckland's best-known law firm. It is handsomely produced and weaves the fortunes of the business into the larger economic history of the city. It is based on the firm's archives and oral evidence and brings out well the role of the lawyer in economic life as well as the internal changes within the organization. It deals with the merger of 1969 and has an interesting concluding chapter on the changes in the 1980s.
Firms: Russell McVeagh

3259
Swaine, Robert T.
The Cravath Firm and Its Predecessors 1819–1947: Vol. I The Predecessor Firms 1819–1906. Vol. II The Cravath Firm Since 1906
1946/48 Ad Press *New York, NY*

This vast tome runs to over 1,500 pages and was written by one of the senior partners of the law firm. Given its age and the author it does not aim to be an analytical business history, but rather draws on the firm's archives to provide

an uncritical narrative of the partnerships, personalities, and types of work undertaken.
Firms: Cravath, Henderson & de Gersdorff; Cravath, Swaine & Moore

Property Development

3260
Real Estate in Business History
For main entry, see 122

3261
Buenger, Walter L.; Pratt, Joseph A.
But Also Good Business: Texas Commerce Banks and the financing of Houston and Texas, 1886–1986
For main entry, see 2596

3262
Channon, Derek F.
The Service Industries: Strategy, structure and financial performance
For main entry, see 2026

3263
Clutterbuck, David; Devine, Marion
Clore: The man and his millions
For main entry, see 3876

3264
Eichler, Ned
The Thrift Debacle
For main entry, see 2647

3265
Erdman, Edward L.
People and Property
1982 Batsford *London*

This book contains the gossipy recollections of a host of twentieth-century property dealers and builders, mostly based in London, by one of their number.

3266
Fredericks, William B.
Henry E. Huntington and the Creation of Southern California
1992 Ohio State University Press *Columbus, OH*

Fredericks has written a scholarly biography of the urban entrepreneur who spearheaded the creation of Los Angeles and built a massive business empire based on trolleys, real estate, and utilities into a 'well-oiled development machine'.
Firms: Los Angeles Railway Company; Pacific Electric Railway; Pacific Light & Power Company; Southern Pacific Railroad

3267
Goldstock, Ronald et al.
Corruption and Racketeering in the New York State Construction Industry
1990 New York University Press *New York, NY*

This is the final report of the New York State Organized Crime Task Force set up by the Governor Mario Cuomo to investigate the intricate patterns of corrupt activities and relationships that have characterized the New York construction industry for over a century. The study documents in detail how organized extortion, bribery, illegal cartels and bid rigging operated in the industry, and shows how labor racketeering and official corruption sustained each other.

3268
Haeger, John Denis
John Jacob Astor: Business and finance in the early Republic
1991 Wayne State University Press *Detroit, MI*

Haeger uses Astor's career as a vehicle for exploring the transformation of the American economy between 1780 and 1840. Astor personified the intimate connection between westward expansion and national economic development. His career combined preindustrial elements in his fur trading and land speculation and industrial operations in city development and pioneering insurance business.
Firms: American Fur Company

3269
Reader, W. J.
To Have and to Hold: An account of Frederick Bandet's life in business
1983 Hunting Gate Group *Hitchin*

An official, well-illustrated history of the property development and investment group.
Firms: Hunting Gate Group

3270
Rose, Jack
Square Feet
1994 RICS Books *London*

This autobiography gives an unflattering and wholly convincing picture of estate agency and property development in post-war Britain by one of the notable entrepreneurs of the time.
Firms: Land Investors

3271
Warner, Sam Bass
Streetcar Suburbs: The process of growth in Boston, 1870–1900
1962 Harvard University Press *Cambridge, MA*

This is a careful examination of small house builders, large land developers, and other key institutional actors promoting urban growth in late nineteenth-century Boston.

3272
Weiss, Marc A.
The Rise of the Community Builders: The American real estate industry and urban land planning
1987 Columbia University Press *New York, NY*

Weiss focuses on the prewar evolution of the residential land development and brokerage industries in the United States. The author pays particular attention to the interaction of the industry with financial institutions and public planning and regulation.

3273
Worley, William S.
J. C. Nichols and the Shaping of Kansas City: Innovation in planned residential communities
1990 University of Missouri Press *Columbia, MO*

This, with Worley's 'Planned for Permanence' (1991), gives a detailed study of the J. C. Nichols Company, a large brokerage and development firm in Kansas City, Missouri and their city building work in the nineteenth century, pioneering in automobile-based suburban shopping centres.
Firms: J. C. Nichols Company

News Agencies

3274
Boyd-Barrett, Oliver
The International News Agencies
1980 Constable *London*

This valuable study analyses the significant dependence of the media on news agencies and shows how and why they have come to be controlled by media groups and how they have often been squeezed by these groups, resulting in a process of diversification into other news services such as teletext, databases and economic services.
Firms: Associated Press; Dow-Jones; Havas agency; L'Agence France Presse (AFP); Reuters; United Press International

3275
Brown, Lucy
Victorian News and Newspapers
For main entry, see 1705

3276
Fenby, Jonathan
The International News Services
1986 Schocken Books *New York, NY*

Fenby examines the 'Big Four' international agencies, which cover both industrialized and third world countries and describes how their role as news purveyors can come under criticism.
Firms: Agence France-Presse (AFP); Associated Press (AP); Reuters; United Press International (UPI)

3277
Huteau, Jean; Ullmann, Bernard
AFP, Une histoire de L'Agence France Presse, 1944–1990 [A History of L'Agence France Presse, 1944–1990]
1992 Robert Laffont *Paris, France*

The authors describe the development of L'Agence France Presse from its origins in a Resistance takeover of the old Havas Agency,

which had collaborated with Vichy, to its position as the world's third largest news agency. The book is especially strong on the role of state support in the 1950s and on the international structure of the Agence.
Firms: L'Agence France Presse

3278
Read, Donald
The Power of News: The history of Reuters
1992 Oxford University Press *Oxford*

This represents the official, commissioned history of Reuters, the international news agency, founded in 1851. It was written by a professional historian given full use of the company's archives and therefore is analytical and authoritative. Read's book describes the origins of Reuters as an imperial institution in the nineteenth century and follows it through its golden era as an agency to its transformation into the world's largest supplier of computerized information in the 1990s. It is strong on the people involved, changes in technology, the financial costs and policies and links with the government.
Firms: Reuters

3279
Rosewater, Victor
History of Co-operative News-Gathering in the United States
1930 Appleton *New York, NY*

Though old, this remains an invaluable study of early US newsbroking agencies. It is written by a former Associated Press editor and based on internal corporate documents.

3280
Schwarzlose, Robert A.
The Nation's Newsbrokers: Vol. 1. The formative years from pre-telegraph to 1865, Vol. 2. The push to institution, from 1865 to 1920
1989 Northwestern University Press *Evanston, IL*

This massive study of newsbroking agencies and intercity news networks covers the period from the 1840s to the First World War. It is especially strong on the early telegraphic activities of New York's Associated Press, and pursues themes of conflict, co-operation and technical change.
Firms: Associated Press

3281
Scott, George
Reporter Anonymous: The story of the Press Association
1968 Hutchinson *London*

This is a centenary history of the London news agency established in 1868 to service the provincial press. It is informative on relations with Reuters in which PA held a controlling interest between 1925 and 1941.
Firms: Newspaper Proprietors' Association; Press Association; Reuters

3282
Scott, J. M.
Extel 100: The centenary history of the Exchange Telegraph Company
1972 Ernest Benn *London*

A pioneer in the electronic transmission of stock market intelligence, the company diversified into a general news agency offering specialist services to bookmakers. This archive-based survey covers the full range of Extel's business.
Firms: Exchange Telegraph Company; Extel Communications; Press Association

3283
Stillman, Richard J.
Dow Jones Industrial Average: History and role in an investment strategy
For main entry, see 1788

3284
Storey, Graham
Reuters' Century, 1851–1951
1951 Parrish *London*

Although officially commissioned and largely based on Reuters' archives this is still a critical study. Storey describes the evolution of the firm from carrier pigeons to its rise to international pre-eminence. He is especially good on Reuters' monopolistic deals with the Press Association and its international cartel-style arrangements.
Firms: Reuters

Advertising & other Business Services

3285
Andersen, Håkon; Collett, John Peter
Anchor and Balance: Det Norske Veritas 1864–1989
1989 JW Cappelens Forlag *Oslo, Norway*

The Norske Veritas, founded in 1864 as a classification society for the Norwegian merchant fleet, is today one of the largest and most important international classification societies, and has moved into offshore oil business, land-based industry, etc. The book describes the development of Veritas as both guide and regulator, formulating and deciding on new technology.

Firms: Det Norske Veritas

3286
Bagdikian, Ben H.
The Effete Conspiracy and Other Crimes of the Press
For main entry, see 1686

3287
Chandler, Alfred D. Jr
Henry Varnum Poor, Business Editor, Analyst and Reformer
1956 Harvard University Press *Cambridge, MA*

Chandler's first book, this is scarcely a biography but more an analysis of Poor's *American Railroad Journal* and the information supplied to the railroads and to banking in the critical period 1849–61. Paralleling the industry's needs, Poor focused first on matters of technology, later on finance and then on management.

Firms: Poor's Manuals of the Railroads of the USA

3288
Fagg, Alan
Westrays: A record of J.B. Westray and Company Limited
For main entry, see 3194

3289
Fallon, Ivan
The Brothers: The rise and rise of Saatchi & Saatchi
1988 Hutchinson *London*

This is an example of very recent oral business history, being mostly based on interviews with those involved. The firm only started in 1970 yet within a decade it had become the largest advertising agency in the world ever. This book looks at the process and causes of growth but being so close to events may mar perspective.

Firms: Saatchi & Saatchi

3290
Hiebert, Ray E.
Courtier to the Crowd: The story of Ivy Lee and the development of public relations
1966 Iowa State University Press *Ames, IA*

Ivy Lee has been termed the 'Father of Modern Public Relations'. This biography is also a study of the nature of the industry and its place in American business during the first half of the twentieth century. The strengths of the text are in its splendid research, interesting data, and a fresh perspective of a neglected topic.

3291
Hower, Ralph M.
The History of an Advertising Agency: N W Ayer & Son at work 1869–1949
2nd Edition
1949 Harvard University Press *Cambridge, MA*

Although now rather dated, this was a pioneering volume on the history of an American advertising agency. It is good on the personalities, types of work undertaken, the customers served, financial results and organization and management. It also contextualizes the firm well within the industry and in terms of technological change.

Firms: N W Ayer & Son

3292
Ichbiah, D.; Knepper, S. L.
The Making of Microsoft: How Bill Gates and his team created the world's most successful software
For main entry, see 1432

3293
Kaldor, Nicholas; Silverman, Rodney
A Statistical Analysis of Advertising Expenditure and of the Revenues of the Press
1948 Cambridge University Press *Cambridge*

This is an invaluable statistical work produced for the National Institute of Economic and Social Research.

3294
Lefébure, Antoine
Havas de 1865 à nos jours [Havas From 1865 to the Present]
1992 Ed Grasset *Paris, France*

Lefébure gives a preliminary history of France's leading advertising company, also the leading news agency before 1940.
Firms: Havas

3295
Marchand, Roland
Advertising the American Dream: Making way for modernity, 1920–1940
1985 University of California Press *Berkeley, CA*

This book is a highly acclaimed study of the critical two decades in the rise of a mass advertising industry in America. A stimulating combination of business and social history.
Firms: Batten, Barton, Durstine & Osborn; General Motors; Lord & Thomas; J. Walter Thompson & Co.; Young & Rubicam

3296
Martin, Marc
Trois siècles de publicité en France [Three Centuries of Advertising in France]
1992 Ed. Odile Jacob *Paris, France*

This general business history describes the advertising sector in France, and also the attitudes of public opinion to advertising.

3297
Nevett, Terry R.
Advertising in Britain: A history
1982 Heinemann *London*

Commissioned by The History of Advertising Trust, this brief survey of British advertising begins with the Middle Ages and traces the progress of the industry up to the challenges of the twentieth-century media market. Nevett addresses the influence of government regulation and foreign competition in a competent manner. Public interest advertising and the impact of industrialization are further topics of interest.
Firms: C. Higham; Ogilvy & Mather; S. H. Benson; W. Crawford

3298
Newman, Karin
Financial Marketing and Communications
1984 Holt, Rinehart and Winston *Eastbourne*

Newman gives a lucid discussion of the history and practice of financial publicity in its various forms with particular reference to Britain. The book is also useful on the work of specialist advertising agencies.
Firms: Charles Barker; Street's Financial; Walter Judd

3299
Olney, Martha
Buy Now, Pay Later: Advertising, credit and consumer durables in the 1920s
For main entry, see 971

3300
Pollay, Richard W. (Editor)
Information Sources in Advertising History
1979 Greenwood Press *Westport, CT*

This is the most comprehensive collection of sources available. Pollay includes bibliographical essays, annotated bibliographies, and directories of archives. More than 1,700 bibliographical listings are accompanied by an easy system of cross-reference. The main focus is on Canada and the United States. Researchers of advertising history will find this work of great value.

3301
Richards, Thomas
The Commodity Culture of Victorian England: Advertising and spectacle 1851–1914
1990 Stanford University Press *Stanford, CA*

This thoughtful book explores how British capitalism produced and sustained its own culture via advertising and exhibitions. It argues that the commodity became central to Victorian culture and its dominance was aided by firms and their advertisers. It is an important piece of cultural history which contextualizes and explains the growth of marketing and advertising.

3302
Tedlow, Richard S.
New and Improved: The story of mass marketing in America
1990 Basic Books *New York, NY*

This is an important study on the development of mass marketing, covering changing retailing patterns, including the growth of mail order, and examining fierce competition in the automobile and soft drinks industries.

Firms: A & P (Great Atlantic & Pacific Tea Co.); Sears, Roebuck & Co.; General Electric (GE); Frigidaire; Montgomery Ward; Coca-Cola; Pepsi Co.; Ford; General Motors

Health Services

3303
Breckinridge, Mary
Wide Neighbourhoods: A story of the Frontier Nursing Service
1981 University Press of Kentucky
Lexington, KY

This is the story of the Frontier Nursing Service from its foundation in 1925 until the 1960s, told through the autobiography of its founder and director, Mary Breckinridge. Obviously it cannot be objective, and tends to narrative rather than analysis, but given the scarcity of books on health care services it deserves inclusion. It is vivid, direct and good on the variety of services offered and methods of fund raising.

Firms: Frontier Nursing Service

3304
Gray, J. D. Allan
The Central Middlesex Hospital: The first sixty years 1903–63
1963 Pitman Medical *London*

This slim volume traces the history of this hospital from its establishment as a workhouse infirmary under the Poor Laws, through its acquisition by Middlesex County Council, to its absorption in the National Health Service. Very few business histories exist of British hospitals and this is no exception. It is a general history but is well contextualized and with some insights into the business side.

Firms: Central Middlesex Hospital

3305
Lieburg, Marius J. van
Het Coolsingel Ziekenhuis te Rotterdam 1839–1900: De ontwikkeling van een stedelijk ziekenhuis in de 19e eeuw [The Coolsingel Hospital in Rotterdam 1839–1900: Development of an urban hospital in the nineteenth century]
1986 Rodopi *Amsterdam, The Netherlands*

This book provides a somewhat long-winded, highly detailed account of the Coolsingel Hospital in Rotterdam, one of the more prestigious Dutch hospitals in the nineteenth century. Special attention is given to the hospital as a socio-medical institution.

Firms: Coolsingel Ziekenhuis, Rotterdam

3306
Prochaska, Frank K.
Philanthropy and the Hospitals of London: The King's Fund, 1897–1990
1992 Clarendon Press *Oxford*

This book is not really a business history, but given the very few volumes on health care in England deserves inclusion. It is a commissioned history, drawing on the fund's archives, and tracing the development of this charity founded to help finance the voluntary hospitals of London. The fund is well contextualized and the work is scholarly and analytical.

Firms: King's Fund (King Edward's Hospital Fund for London)

3307
Rimmer, W. G.
Portrait of a Hospital: The Royal Hobart
1981 Royal Hobart Hospital *Hobart, Tasmania, Australia*

This study traces the hospital through three phases: initially as a convict hospital and then serving paupers and finally a public hospital, financed partly by government. The hospital is set in its local environment and well contextualized into the growth of medical services on Tasmania. It is also good on the early treatment

of patients, though becoming more patchy in more modern times.
Firms: Royal Hobart Hospital

3308
Scholte, E.; Lieburg, M. J. van; Aalbersberg, R. O.
Rijkskweekschool voor vroedvrouwen te Rotterdam, 1882–1982 [State Training School for Midwives in Rotterdam, 1882–1982]
1982 Ministry of Health and Education *Leidschendam, The Netherlands*

This book provides a concise history of the training facility for one of the more typically Dutch phenomena in the medical field: independently operating midwives. Emphasis is placed on the training itself and some institutional aspects are covered.
Firms: Rijkskweekschool voor Vroedvrouwen; Rijksopleiding voor Verloskundigen

3309
Wiggen, Gerrit J. van
In meer eerbare banen: De ontwikkeling van het tandheelkundige beroep in Nederland gedurende de periode 1865–1940 [In More Honourable Ways: The development of the dental profession in the Netherlands in the period 1865–1940]
1987 Rodopi *Amsterdam, The Netherlands*

This is an institutional history of the training of the dental profession since legal recognition of dentistry as a field of general medicine in 1865, and of the spread of professionally trained dentists across the country.
Firms: Nederlandsche Maatschappij voor Tandheelkunde

Film, Theatre & Music

3310
Balio, Tino
United Artists: The company built by the stars
1976 University of Wisconsin Press *Madison, WI*

This is a well-researched history of the film-making firm which catered for independent producers from 1919 to 1951 when it was restructured and refinanced. It is a good all-round business history, strong on structure and personalities, especially the founders who dominated strategy for several decades such as Chaplin, Pickford and Fairbanks. The story continues in Balio 1987 (qv).
Firms: United Artists

3311
Balio, Tino
United Artists: The company that changed the film industry
1987 University of Wisconsin Press *Madison, WI*

This volume continues the story from 1951 to 1978, following on from Balio's previous book (qv), covering the period when United Artists had been taken over by Krim and Benjamin. Again the author draws on the corporate archive but this time uses an explicit framework of competitive strategy drawn from Michael Porter. It is a good example of applied corporate strategy.
Firms: United Artists

3312
Balio, Tino (Editor)
The American Film Industry
2nd Edition
1985 University of Wisconsin Press *Madison, WI*

Balio draws together a broad collection of serious scholarship on successive phases in the development of the American film industry. He concentrates on the development of motion pictures from novelty to business enterprise, the evolution of oligopoly, and recent developments.
Firms: Warner Bros; United Artists; Loew's

3313
Bart, Peter
Fade Out: The calamitous final days of MGM
1990 Simon & Schuster *London*

This book tells the story of MGM from 1983 to 1989, after Kerkorian had bought United Artists and merged it with MGM. The author was personally involved as a senior executive, being brought in by Frank Yablans the new president, hence he makes his own views known trenchantly. It is more like memoirs of corporate politics and dealing than 'proper' business

history. See Balio (qv) for the previous history of United Artists.
Firms: Metro Goldwyn Mayer; United Artists

3314
Baughman, James L.
The Republic of Mass Culture: Journalism, filmmaking and broadcasting in America since 1941
For main entry, see 1763

3315
Curran, James; Porter, Vincent (Editors)
British Cinema History
1983 Weidenfeld & Nicolson *London*

This volume of essays covers a wide range of topics in British cinema history. They include articles on the early growth of the industry, the role of the state, individual studios, such as Ealing, official films and documentaries. The essays are scholarly and fully referenced and the volume has an extensive bibliography. It is a valuable volume, but sadly is not indexed.
Firms: Ealing Studios; British National Films; Gaumont British Picture Corporation; Pinewood Studios

3316
Dickinson, Margaret; Street, Sarah
Cinema and State: The film industry and the British Government 1927–84
1985 BFI Publishing *London*

This volume analyses the relationship between the government and the film industry from the 1920s to the 1980s. It examines changing government attitudes towards the industry, the reasons for intervention, the measures taken and their effectiveness. It is referenced and has a useful bibliography.

3317
Eberts, Jake; Ilott, Terry
My Indecision is Final: The rise and fall of Goldcrest Films
1990 Faber & Faber *London*

This is an example of very recent business history based on direct involvement, interviews and archives. It is a vast tome on the reasons for the growth and fall of this initially highly successful film-making firm which only existed between 1977 and 1986. The viewpoint is hardly objective, since Eberts was founder and chief executive until 1983. It is strong on the personalities and boardroom battles.
Firms: Goldcrest Films

3318
Jarvie, Ian
Hollywood's Overseas Campaign: The North Atlantic movie trade, 1920–1950
1992 Cambridge University Press *Cambridge*

This is a study of the growth, structure, and direction of trade in motion pictures between Canada, the UK, and the USA in the period 1920 to 1950. It is largely based on official documents, is detailed, referenced and has a useful bibliography. It is an excellent explanation of the rise of American movies as an export product.

3319
Low, Rachael
The History of the British Film 1906–1929
1948–9 George Allen & Unwin *London*

These three volumes continue the series begun by Low and Manvell (qv), being a listing and analysis of the main British film makers, the economic and social environment in which they worked, and the films they made, with a technical appraisal of the latter. Not intended to concentrate on business aspects, it may nevertheless be a useful source.

3320
Low, Rachael; Manvell, Roger
The History of the British Film 1896–1906
1948 George Allen & Unwin *London*

This is the first volume in a series carried on by Rachael Low alone (qv) which lists the main British film makers, the studios, and the films produced, with some comment on the technical ingenuity of the latter. It might be a useful source, though not directly aimed at business aspects.

3321
Miller, R.
The Incredible Music Machine
1982 Quartet *London*

A useful history of EMI, the record industry to electrical goods conglomerate.
Firms: EMI

3322
Perry, George
Movies From the Mansion: A history of Pinewood Studio
1976 Elm Tree *London*

This is a history of Pinewood Studio from its purchase and conversion in 1934, concentrating on the films that were made and their stars. It has some information on the corporate strategies and entrepreneurs involved, such as Boot and Rank, but is not so good on the business history aspects.

Firms: General Film Distributors; Rank Organization; Denham & Pinewood Holdings

3323
Perry, George
George Perry Presents Forever Ealing: A celebration of the great British film studio
1981 Pavilion, Michael Joseph *London*

This is not really a business history, but a lavishly illustrated celebration of the films, actors, producers and directors who worked at Ealing. There is some incidental information on the history of the site, which started in film production in 1907 and went on to 1959, and the companies who owned it. It has an exhaustive list of the films made, but no references and a rather thin bibliography.

Firms: General Film Renters; Union Studios; Associated Talking Pictures

3324
Poggi, Jack
Theater in America: The impact of economic forces, 1870–1967
1968 Cornell University Press *Ithaca, NY*

This book is more a history of the industry as a whole than the individual firms in it. It is particularly strong on the market for theatre and the competition from other types of entertainment, the diversity of forms of theatre, including politically committed groups, the problems of finance and the players themselves.

3325
Richards, Jeffrey
The Age of the Dream Palace: Cinema and society in Britain 1930–1939
1984 Routledge *London*

This important study examines British commercial cinema in the 1930s by looking at the films made, the stars, the operation of censorship, and the habit of movie-going. It is referenced and has a very useful bibliography, and places the film industry firmly in the economic, political and social context. It is thinner on the business aspects.

Firms: Associated British Picture Corporation; Gaumont British Picture Corporation

3326
Sanjek, Russell; Sanjek, David
American Popular Music Business in the Twentieth Century
1991 Oxford University Press *Oxford*

This is a formidably detailed history of the twentieth-century music business. It traces the technological and commercial innovations from Edison to CDs together with the business side of the industry, from the rise and fall of vaudeville to the development of huge entertainment conglomerates, from the sale of sheet music to the marketing of music videos by MTV, and from the early pop entrepreneurs to Michael Jackson.

Firms: Time-Warner; Thorn-EMI; Broadcast Music Incorporated

3327
Solomon, Aubrey
Twentieth Century Fox: A corporate and financial history
1988 Scarecrow Press *Metuchen, NJ*

This is an excellent example of a business history of a film-producing firm, concentrating, as its subtitle indicates, on costs of production, gross receipts, the financial mechanics of film production and the corporate personalities and decisions, from 1909 to the 1980s. It is a first class example of the genre.

Firms: Twentieth Century Fox

3328
Southall, Brian
Abbey Road: The story of the world's most famous recording studio
1982 P. Stephens *Cambridge*

Despite its title, this is actually a detailed history of the EMI studio by the company's

press officer, which provides detailed coverage of the evolution of recording techniques.
Firms: EMI

3329
Walker, Alexander
Hollywood, England: The British film industry in the sixties
1974 Harrap *London*
An attempt to cover the diversity of motives and talents in the British film industry and the interaction of economic changes, historical accident and artistic achievement in a turbulent period for the industry.

3330
Wood, Alan
Mr Rank: A study of J. Arthur Rank and British films
1952 Hodder & Stoughton *London*
As its title implies, this volume concentrates almost entirely on Rank's film business, using interviews with the directors and producers. It was written while Rank himself was still alive and therefore is rather uncritical. It is good on personalities but thin on details of the business side and over-general.
Firms: Denham & Pinewood Holdings; Gainsborough Pictures; Gaumont British Picture Corporation; Odeon Theatres; Rank Organization

Radio & Television

3331
Aitken, Hugh G. J.
Syntony and Spark: The origins of radio
1976 John Wiley & Sons *New York, NY*
This prize-winning study of the pioneers of radio technology, links the scientific changes to the process of commercialization.
Firms: Marconi Wireless Telegraph Company

3332
Aitken, Hugh G. J.
The Continuous Wave: Technology and American Radio, 1900–1932
1985 Princeton University Press *Princeton, NJ*
Aitken combines a narrative of technical progress with analysis of the impact of new technology on business and government. He describes how the US Navy Department blocked the British Marconi Company from resuming its dominance of the US market after the First World War and the events leading up to the creation of RCA as an instrument of American national policy.
Firms: Marconi; RCA; AT&T; General Electric; Westinghouse

3333
Barnouw, Erik
A Tower in Babel: A history of broadcasting in the United States
1966 Oxford University Press *New York, NY*
This is the first of several works by the author on this subject. A portion of the book deals with the pioneers who began by experiment and ended up promoting wireless communication. Attention is then directed to the leading competitors in the industry and how the present form of broadcasting evolved. Barnouw's expert handling of the matter makes this an insightful and useful text.
Firms: American Telephone and Telegraph; General Electric; Westinghouse

3334
Barnouw, Erik
The Golden Web: A history of broadcasting in the United States, 1933 to 1953
1968 Oxford University Press *New York, NY*
By analysing the development and success of network broadcasting, Barnouw has produced a thoughtful and well-written sequel to *A Tower in Babel* (qv). This work will be greatly appreciated by scholars who seek a clearer understanding of the reasons behind the power and influence of the networks. The study is further enhanced by the author's lucid style and exceptional research.
Firms: Federal Communications Commission; Federal Radio Commission

3335
Baughman, James L.
Television's Guardians: The FCC and the politics of programming, 1958–1967
1985 University of Tennessee Press *Knoxville, TN*

This monograph explores the conditions and events leading to the establishment of the Corporation for Public Broadcasting. The product of meticulous research, this well-written work is a worthwhile selection for the study of the field of broadcasting history. Heavy emphasis is placed on the federal government's hand in the industry but the roles of network programming and the viewing audience are also adequately covered.
Firms: Corporation for Public Broadcasting; Federal Communications Commission (FCC)

3336
Baughman, James L.
The Republic of Mass Culture: Journalism, filmmaking and broadcasting in America since 1941
For main entry, see 1763

3337
Bibb, Peter
It Ain't As Easy As It Looks: Ted Turner's amazing story
For main entry, see 3933

3338
Briggs, Asa
The History of Broadcasting in the United Kingdom
1962/79 Oxford University Press *Oxford*
This is a vast and detailed four-volume history from 1922 of the government-sponsored broadcast monopolist. It is very strong on listeners, personalities, competition, and the managers and directors, but has rather less detail on costs and finances.
Firms: British Broadcasting Corporation

3339
Briggs, Asa
The BBC: A short history of the first fifty years
1985 Oxford University Press *Oxford*
This history of the British Broadcasting Corporation from 1922 to 1972 puts the institution firmly in the context of national politics and culture. It is good on personalities and programming and the need to adapt to competition for audiences when the monopoly was removed.
Firms: BBC

3340
Burns, Russell W.
British Television: The formative years
1986 Peter Peregrinus *London*
This volume deals with the technical development of television in the UK before real broadcasting began, i.e. from 1923 to 1939. It is strong on the technical, political and financial aspects, drawing on a wide range of primary sources, is fully referenced, well-illustrated and authoritative.
Firms: GPO; BBC; Baird Television Ltd

3341
Bussey, Gordon
Wireless, the Crucial Decade: History of the British wireless industry 1924–34
1990 Peter Peregrinus *London*
This slim volume examines the history of the British wireless industry in its formative years, looking particularly at technical developments in valves, receiving sets, and transmitters and also broadcasting trends. It is mostly based on contemporary newspapers and trade magazines, is well illustrated and referenced but thin on the internal business aspects.
Firms: BBC

3342
Coase, Ronald H.
British Broadcasting: A study in monopoly
1950 Longmans, Green & Co. *London*
Although rather dated, this is a valuable volume tracing the origins of the monopoly in broadcasting in Britain, examining in detail the debate, and looking at the foreign commercial stations available in Britain. It is scholarly, analytical and based on primary sources. As such it is an invaluable source.
Firms: BBC; Radio Luxembourg; Radio Normandy

3343
Curran, James; Seaton, Jean
Power without Responsibility: The press and broadcasting in Britain
For main entry, see 1711

3344
Douglas, Susan J.
Inventing American Broadcasting 1899–1922
1987 Johns Hopkins University Press
Baltimore, MD

This scholarly book examines the pre-history of American commercial broadcasting when, the author argues, the basic technological, managerial and cultural template of American broadcasting was cast. A study in the 'social construction' of radio focusing on the contribution of both inventors and key institutions, the book concentrates on the technological breakthroughs, the inventors, the early uses of radio, the business aspects and the impact of radio on economy and society. It is thoroughly referenced and based on primary sources.
Firms: AT&T; General Electric; Marconi Wireless Telegraph Company; RCA

3345
Dunnett, Peter J. S.
The World Television Industry: An economic analysis
1990 Routledge *London*

Although this is not primarily a historical work, it does have a chapter on the history of television. It is, however, essentially an economic analysis of the industry at a crucial time of change, viz the late 1980s. It is strong on demand and supply, market structure, the role of government and the impact of technological change.

3346
Horwitz, Robert B.
The Irony of Regulatory Reform: The deregulation of American telecommunications
1989 Oxford University Press *New York, NY*

This highly-praised work provides impartial analyses of regulation and private ownership. The focus is on television and radio broadcasting but includes references to transport and telephones. Horwitz covers the history of regulation from the New Deal to the Reagan administration and the role of politics in the American economy.

3347
Manning, A. F.
Zestig jaar KRO: Uit de geschiedenis van een omroep [Sixty Years of KRO: The history of a broadcasting organisation]
1985 Ambo *Baarn, The Netherlands*

The development of this catholic broadcasting organization in The Netherlands is set against the background of the social and political changes there between 1922 and 1985.
Firms: Katholieke Radio Omroep (KRO)

3348
Paulu, Burton
British Broadcasting: Radio and television in the United Kingdom
1956 University of Minnesota Press
Minneapolis, MN

Although this volume is now rather dated, having largely been superseded by Asa Briggs's multi-volume history of the BBC (qv), it retains some value in throwing light on the history and current practice of the BBC and ITV, especially finances, staff, technical facilities and the audiences. It is scholarly and well referenced.
Firms: BBC; ITA

3349
Paulu, Burton
British Broadcasting in Transition
1961 Macmillan *London*

This book is a report on the effects of competition on the broadcasting services of the UK after thirty years of non-commercial monopoly. It follows on from his 1955 volume (qv), and is an excellent in-depth study of the BBC as of the 1950s and of the competitive forces at work in the entertainment industry. It is referenced and has a useful bibliography.
Firms: BBC; ITA

3350
Paulu, Burton
Radio and Television Broadcasting on the European Continent
1967 University of Minnesota Press
Minneapolis, MN

This book is a description and appraisal of radio and television broadcasting in twenty countries on the European continent. It looks at structure, finances, news and entertainment programmes. Although the approach is not historical it may be a useful source on post Second World War European broadcasting.

3351
Paulu, Burton
Radio and Television Broadcasting in Eastern Europe
1974 University of Minnesota Press *Minneapolis, MN*

This volume examines the structure and organization of programmes made by and audiences for, radio and television in eight communist bloc countries in the 1960s and 1970s. Its approach is not historical, but like his other volumes, it may be a useful source. It is scholarly, well referenced and analytical.

3352
Pegg, Mark
Broadcasting and Society 1918–1939
1983 Croom Helm *London*

This carefully-researched volume examines the impact of radio on society and how society used radio to satisfy certain needs. It is good on the technology of listening, the patterns of listening, organizations of listeners, the broadcasters, listener research, and the impact on leisure and social attitudes of the wireless. It is fully referenced and scholarly.
Firms: BBC; Radio Luxembourg; Radio Normandie

3353
Potter, Jeremy
Independent Television in Britain: vol. 3 Politics and control, 1968–80; vol. 4 Companies and programmes 1968–80
1989/90 Macmillan *London*

These two volumes complement the two volumes by Sendall (qv) whose illness prevented him from completing his original task. They carry the story on from where he left off looking at government enquiries, changing social attitudes and then each of the regional companies and the main trends in programming. The books are rather thin on finance and business performance.
Firms: Independent Broadcasting Authority; Independent Television Association

3354
Pusateri, C. Joseph
Enterprise in Radio: WWL and the business of broadcasting in America
1980 University Press of America *Lanham, MD*

This is an exhaustively researched history of this radio station, founded in 1922 by the Jesuits of Loyola University in New Orleans, which by 1940 was the most popular in the city and went into TV in 1956. It is strong on relations with government, management structure and operations.
Firms: Radio WWL

3355
Quinlan, Sterling
Inside ABC: American Broadcasting Corporation's rise to power
1979 Hastings House *New York, NY*

This book was written by an ex-employee, and therefore is not completely objective, but it is carefully researched using interviews and corporate records. Essentially it explains why and how ABC came to do so well in the 1960s and 1970s. It is strong on the personalities and various takeover bids, both successful and aborted.
Firms: American Broadcasting Co.

3356
Sanjek, Russell; Sanjek, David
American Popular Music Business in the Twentieth Century
For main entry, see 3326

3357
Schwoch, James
The American Radio Industry and its Latin American Activities, 1900–1939
1990 University of Illinois Press *Urbana, IL*

Although this book is less ambitious than its title suggests, it has some useful material on the role of American corporations, especially National Broadcasting Company, in setting up satellite stations in Latin America, and some instances of early wireless stations installed on the plantations of US multinationals in South America. It is also rather dogmatic and poorly produced.
Firms: National Broadcasting Co.; Radio Corporation of America; US Rubber; United Fruit

3358
Sendall, Bernard
Independent Television in Britain: vol. 1 Origins and foundation, 1946–62; vol. 2 Expansion and change, 1958–68
1982/3 Macmillan *London*

These volumes give an insider's view of the development of independent television from 1948 to 1968 as the author was Deputy Director General in the 1960s and early 1970s. They are authoritative and well researched, strong on the relations with government and the financing of the early programme contractors, the personalities of the key entrepreneurs and the internal politics. Potter (qv) extends the story into the 1980s.
Firms: Independent Broadcasting Authority; Independent Television Authority

3359
Tunstall, Jeremy; Palmer, Michael
Media Moguls
For main entry, see 1760

3360
Whale, John
The Politics of the Media
For main entry, see 1743

Sport & Leisure

3361
Arnold, Anthony J.
A Game that Would Pay: A business history of professional football in Bradford
1988 Duckworth *London*

This is the first attempt at a business history of a provincial professional soccer club in Britain. The author endeavours to contextualize his story, which is one of failure and stagnation rather than success. It is good on conflicting objectives, the problems of amateur boards and intransigent supporters, but there is not enough analysis of finance and who the supporters were.
Firms: Bradford City Football Club; Bradford Park Avenue Football Club

3362
Brendon, Piers
Thomas Cook: 150 years of popular tourism
1991 Secker and Warburg *London*

This volume is more a social history of the economic environment in which Thomas Cook operated than a straight business history. It is particularly strong on customers and routes and changes in income and taste. It concentrates on the latter half of the nineteenth century. It is based on access to the firm's archives and is well illustrated.
Firms: Thomas Cook

3363
Butlin, Sir Billy; Dacre, Peter
The Billy Butlin Story: A showman to the end
1982 Robson *London*

This book is more an autobiography of the showman turned holiday camp entrepreneur than a true business history. In 1935 he opened his first camp and in 1972 sold out to the Rank Organisation. It is candid, strong on entrepreneurship and changes in the leisure market, but is thin on analytical aspects of the business.
Firms: Butlins Holiday Camps; Rank Organisation

3364
Campbell, Tom; Woods, Pat
The Glory and the Dream: The history of Celtic FC, 1887–1987
1987 Grafton Books *London*

This book is a popular history of the famous Glasgow football club. It concentrates on the players, managers and other personalities and the record of sporting achievement but there are odd snippets of business history interlaced in this narrative, though it is not a full or analytical business history.
Firms: Celtic Football Club

3365
Cashman, Richard; McKernan, Michael (Editors)
Sport in History: The making of modern sporting history
1979 University of Queensland Press
St Lucia, Queensland, Australia

This collection of essays covers a wide range of sports predominantly in Australia and Britain in the nineteenth and twentieth centuries. The approaches are much broader than the business aspects, though some are mentioned in passing. It is, therefore, useful contextualization on football and cricket as leisure industries.

3366
Chinn, Carl
Better Betting with a Decent Feller: Bookmakers, betting and the British working-class, 1750–1990
1991 Harvester Wheatsheaf *Hemel Hempstead*

A pioneer study of bookmaking in its social context. The book analyses street bookies and race-course bookies, the law and politics and betting, and the image and reality of bookmakers.

3367
Clapson, Mark
A Bit of a Flutter: Popular gambling and British society, c.1823–1961
1992 Manchester University Press *Manchester*

This book examines the expansion of mass betting against the background of government prohibition and moral campaigning. It analyses off-course and racecource betting, the football pools, greyhound racing and Premium Bonds, and Clapson shows how the growth of these forms of betting was accompanied by a similar expansion in the hinterland of street gambling based on cards, coins, raffles and sweeps.

3368
Hill, Christopher
Horse Power: The politics of the turf
1988 Manchester University Press *Manchester*

A study of the tensions between racing as a sport and as an industry. Within the whole period, a particular focus is on why betting shops were legalized in 1960 and a levy on bookmakers' profits introduced, and an account of the rise of the bookmakers' lobby and the sometimes uneasy symbiosis between bookmaking and racing.
Firms: William Hill Organization

3369
Holt, Richard
Sport and the British: A modern history
1989 Clarendon Press *Oxford*

This book explains the nature of sport in modern Britain in terms of changes in society, politics and culture since the late eighteenth century. It is referenced and has a most useful bibliography, and is deeply researched and lively. One chapter considers the commercial aspects, looking at the finances, shareholders, professional players, role of the media and customers.

3370
Jackson, Stanley
The Savoy: The romance of a grand hotel
1964 Frederick Muller *London*

This is a popular social history of the famous London hotel. Its fluctuating fortunes are linked with the wider trends in tourism, the changing character of the London 'season', and the growth of business tourism.
Firms: Savoy Hotel

3371
Jones, Stephen G.
Workers at Play: A social and economic history of leisure 1918–1939
1986 Routledge & Kegan Paul *London*

This is not a business history of a particular company, but an attempt to demonstrate and analyse the growth of the commercialization of the leisure industry between the wars. It also shows how leisure was politicized and the attempts of the labour movement to retain control of working class leisure patterns. It is scholarly and provoking.

3372
Korr, Charles
West Ham United: The making of a football club
1987 Duckworth *London*

Drawing on the archives of the club and interviews, the author traces the history of this English soccer club founded in the east of London in 1900, based on a pre-existing works team. It is good on the supporters, the social context, the personalities and the playing record, but thinner on the finances and business performance.
Firms: Thames Ironworks; West Ham United Football Club

3373
Mason, Tony
Association Football and English Society, 1863–1915
1980 Harvester *Brighton*

This volume attempts to outline and analyse the main changes in the organization of the game of soccer over the period 1860 to 1915. It looks at players and directors, spectators and profits, wages and the geographical take up of the game. From thin and scattered sources the author weaves a convincing analysis.

3374
Miller, James
The Baseball Business: Pursuing profits and pennants in Baltimore
1990 University of North Carolina Press *Chapel Hill, NC*

This book provides a history of the 'Orioles' from 1954 when they were established in Baltimore. It is strong on the contract problems and the change in them in the 1970s, colour biases, and the conflicts between owners, fans and players. It is one of a growing number of academic studies of baseball.
Firms: Baltimore Orioles

3375
Tischler, Steven
Footballers and Businessmen: The origins of professional soccer in England
1981 Holmes & Meier *New York, NY*

This is an important contribution to the business history of professional soccer teams in England. It examines the growth of professionalism, the establishment of football clubs as businesses, the directors, players and spectators. It also covers the emergence of trade union activity among professional players. It is based largely on contemporary newspapers and magazines, thoroughly referenced, scholarly and analytical.

3376
Vamplew, Wray
The Turf: A social and economic history of horse racing
1976 Allen Lane *London*

This is not really a business history but, given the dearth of work on leisure industries, it deserves to be included for its high quality research and felicitous style. It attempts to deal, for a fairly general audience, with ownership, breeding, betting, and the changes in the nature of horse racing in Britain. It is interesting and informative.

3377
Vamplew, Wray
Pay Up and Play the Game: Professional sport in Britain
1988 Cambridge University Press *Cambridge*

This volume is useful as it contextualizes the very few works on individual football clubs, and also deals with cricket and horse racing. It is good on the nature of ownership, the rewards to the players, the sources and styles of the directors and the relationship between sporting success and profitability.

3378
Wagg, Stephen
The Football World: A contemporary social history
1984 Harvester *Brighton*

Contains valuable introduction to managers, players, the media and commerce in British soccer in the interwar years, and a useful section dealing with changes since 1945.

3379
Walvin, James
Football and the Decline of Britain
1986 Macmillan *Basingstoke*

This is more a social than a business history, but contains some useful historical insights into the world of UK soccer, with a good chapter on the 'Victorian Values' of soccer clubs.

3380
Ward, Andrew; Alister, Ian
Barnsley: A study in football 1953–59
1981 Crowberry *Barton-under-Needlewood*

Rare but invaluable study of the operational management of an English football club in the 1950s, with detailed insights into management, financial control mechanisms, information flows and control, and the minutiae of the profit and loss account, as well as much fascinating social history.
Firms: Barnsley Football Club

Strategy & Structure – Approaches to Business History

General

3381
Bishop, Matthew; Kay, John (Editors)
European Mergers and Merger Policy
1993 Oxford University Press *Oxford*

This contains the best survey (by Alan Hughes) of postwar British mergers, as well as broader statistical and qualitative analysis of European mergers.

3382
Blackford, Mansel G.
The Rise of Modern Business in Great Britain, the United States and Japan
1988 University of North Carolina Press *Chapel Hill, NC*

This presents a pioneering attempt at integrating national studies.

3383
Born, Karl Erich
Internationale Kartellierung einer neuen Industrie: Die Aluminium-Association 1901–1915 [International Cartelization of the New Aluminium Industry 1901–1915]
1994 Gesellschaft für Unternehmensgeschichte *Stuttgart, Germany*

This very informative study presents the conflicting arguments for and against cartelization and helps to understand the motivation of entrepreneurs and managers regarding international cartelization. Moreover, Born enquires into the organization of the two existing cartels as well as into their effect on the international aluminium industry. By also examining the impact of patents, for example, this study depicts the two international aluminium cartels before 1914 in a very balanced and differentiated way.

3384
Boswell, Jonathan
The Rise and Decline of Small Firms
1973 George Allen & Unwin *London*

This is a historically-sensitive survey analysis of the subject which parallels the contemporary Bolton Committee report on *Small Firms*.

3385
Brown, Jonathan; Rose, Mary B. (Editors)
Entrepreneurship, Networks and Modern Business
1993 Manchester University Press *Manchester*

In this collection of papers assembled by the Reading-Lancaster business history symposium, the authors explore aspects of entrepreneurship, drawing on the work of business historians and economists from several countries. The book contains several interesting chapters, including Balassubramanyam on British performance in the food and drink sector, Casson on the theory of entrepreneurship, Locke on the relationship between education and entrepreneurship, Rose on British family firms, and Singleton on the market for warships.

Firms: Sir W. G. Armstrong & Co.; Cornish Metal Co.; Coventry Ordnance Works; Lloyd's; Osaka Cotton Textile Co.

3386
Coleman, Donald C.
The Uses and Abuses of Business History
Business History, vol. 29, no. 2, 1987: pp 141–56

Seminal and influential LSE lecture of 1986 reviewing the state of business history in the UK in the mid-1980s. Donald Coleman revealed the 'Catch-22' facing business historians, who would prefer not to write 'disembodied company history' but are forced to do so in order to gain access to archives held by major corporations. He also suggested ways

in which business historians might break free of such constraints.
Firms: ICI; A.T.&T.; British Railways Board

3387
Coleman, Donald C.; Mathias, Peter (Editors)
Enterprise and History: Essays in honour of Charles Wilson
1984 Cambridge University Press *Cambridge*

This is a festschrift published to mark the 70th birthday of one of Britain's post-war pioneers in business history. Beginning with a plea for comparative business history from Alfred Chandler, it contains important contributions from Coleman and Reader on the nature of business history, a section on England and the Netherlands in the pre-industrial period, and several chapters on the modern period, including a piece on the Bank of Rome (Rosa), brewing technology (Glamann), large Belgian firms (Van der Wee) and French oil policy (Ferrier).

3388
Cowling, K.; Stoneman, P. (Editors)
Mergers and Economic Performance
1979 Cambridge University Press *Cambridge*

This volume is comprised of a selection of Warwick University essays on the effects of mergers, including useful business history case studies. It is one of the many sceptical assessments of the results of the merger waves of the 1960s and 1970s.

3389
Crosland, C. A. R.
The Future of Socialism
1956 Jonathan Cape *London*

Despite its title and its status as a bible of revisionist British socialists for some decades, this book has a lot to say about alleged transformations in the nature of capitalism as a result of the managerial revolution.

3390
Davenport-Hines, R. P. T.; Jones, Geoffrey (Editors)
British Business in Asia Since 1860
1989 Cambridge University Press *Cambridge*

The contributions in this collection focus on the progress of British business in Iran, Russian Asia, India, Thailand, Malaysia, Singapore, China and Japan. There is also an opening chapter by the editors which sets the context of British business in Asia and introduces general themes such as strategies and structures, business performance, relations between British business and the British government, impact and response, and the Asian impact on Britain.

3391
Dunning, John H.
International Production and the Multinational Enterprise
1981 George Allen & Unwin *London*

An important collection of Dunning's writings on the operations of MNEs, their relations with governments, and their impact on market structures, etc.

3392
Dunning, John H.
Japanese Participation in British Industry
1986 Routledge *London*

Based on detailed research this is a study of the extent and economic impact of Japanese participation in British industry in the 1980s focusing on control structures, supplier relations, labour and balance of payments issues.
Firms: Matsushita; Hitachi; Sony; NEC; Toshiba; NSK

3393
Dunning, John H.
Multinationals, Technology and Competitiveness
1988 Unwin Hyman *London*

This monograph explores the links between technology, competitiveness, and the role of MNEs. It includes a chapter on the historical development of firms' market power and technology transfer.

3394
Dunning, John H.
The Globalization of Business: The challenge of the 1990s
1993 Routledge *London*

This is a state of the art collection of essays by a leading scholar in the MNE field. The book, with its appeal for an interdisciplinary approach and emphasis on theory, provides useful pointers for further historical work as well as providing data on aspects of globalisation in the post-war period. It is easier to use than Dunning's longer work, *Multinational Enterprises and the Global Economy* (Addison-Wesley, 1992).

3395
Encarnation, Dennis J.
Rivals Beyond Trade: America versus Japan in global competition
1992 Cornell University Press *Ithaca, NY*

Encarnation examines the evolution of foreign investment and related trade of Japanese companies in America and American companies in Japan. He stresses that Japanese companies have been allowed first to trade and then to invest in the US with a freedom unavailable to Americans in Japan. The book complements the work of Mark Mason (qv).
Firms: Chrysler; Fairchild; Ford; GM; Honda; IBM; Matsushita; Motorola; Nissan; Sony

3396
Fairburn, James; Kay, John (Editors)
Mergers and Merger Policy
1989 Oxford University Press *Oxford*

Arising out of an Institute of Fiscal Studies project, this is a comprehensive multi-author review of the British experience of corporate mergers.

3397
Franko, Lawrence G.
The European Multinationals: A renewed challenge to American and British big business
1976 Harper & Row *London*

This is a major account of the 85 leading multinationals in continental Europe. It provides material on the emergence and development of the firms, which had their headquarters in Belgium, France, Germany, Italy, Luxembourg, the Netherlands, Sweden and Switzerland, and gives an invaluable snapshot of the position reached in the early 1970s.
Firms: Bayer; Bosch; CIBA; Fiat; Hoechst; Nestlé; Péchiney; Philips; Renault; Siemens

3398
Gerschenkron, Alexander
Economic Backwardness in Historical Perspective: A book of essays
1962 Harvard University Press *Cambridge, MA*

This is a path-breaking, if now less highly regarded, general study of latecomer status, focusing in particular upon Russia. It is of immense value to business historians in providing theoretical underpinning for an examination of latecomer countries in international competitive conditions and of both native and foreign firms operating in developing countries.

3399
Hertner, Peter; Jones, Geoffrey (Editors)
Multinationals: Theory and history
1986 Gower *Aldershot*

Sponsored by the European Science Foundation, this collection of pieces combines the theoretical approaches of Casson, Cantwell, Nicholas, Wilkins and others with case studies examining the historical development of MNEs in Britain, Germany, Sweden, and France. The result is an extremely useful guide to possibilities of further research in business history.

3400
Higonnet, Patrice; Landes, David S. (Editors)
Favourites of Fortune: Technology, growth and economic development since the Industrial Revolution
For main entry, see 4264

3401
Hodge, Michael
Multinational Corporations and National Governments: A case study of the UK's experience, 1964–1970
1974 Saxon House *Farnborough*

An informative study of the role of multinationals in the British economy and government control of and attitudes towards them. It includes case studies of the automobile and computer industries.

3402
Jones, Geoffrey (Editor)
British Multinationals: Origins, management and performance
1986 Elgar *Aldershot*

Business History Unit-inspired case studies charting the overseas activity of major British multinational firms from the mid-nineteenth century to c.1970.
Firms: Cadbury Bros; Courtaulds; Dunlop; Fry; Glaxo; Guest Keen Nettlefold; Pilkington; Rowntree; Vickers

3403
Jones, Geoffrey; Schröter, Harm G. (Editors)
The Rise of Multinationals in Continental Europe
1992 Edward Elgar *Aldershot*

This is a useful collection which demonstrates the diversity of European multinational enterprises. It contains material on Germany, Switzerland, the Netherlands, Sweden, Norway, Italy and Belgium.
Firms: AEG; Agfa-Gevaert; AKU; Asea-Brown-Boveri; Deutsche Bank; Dresdner Bank; I G Farben; Norsk Hydro; Océ van der Gunton; Arelli

3404
Kaelble, Hartmut
Industrielle Interessenpolitik in der Wilhelminischen Gesellschaft: Centralverband Deutscher Industrieller 1895–1914 [Industrial Influence in Wilhelmine Germany]
1967 Walter de Gruyter *Berlin, Germany*

This describes the development of the CVDI as a pressure group for industry and its influence with various factions in pre-First World War Germany.

3405
Kindleberger, Charles P. (Editor)
The International Corporation: A symposium
1970 MIT Press *Cambridge, MA*

The result of a symposium held in 1969, this volume of essays adopts a primarily theoretical approach, with sections on theory, finance and technology, and law and politics. There are also studies of three industries and three countries. Contributors include John Dunning, Harry Johnson and Raymond Vernon.
Firms: Chrysler Corp.; Ford Motor Co.; General Motors Corp.; IBM; Volkswagen; Volvo

3406
Kochanek, S.
Interest Groups and Development, Business and Politics in Pakistan
1983 Oxford University Press *Delhi, India*

Kochanek identifies Pakistani industrial group behaviour, from 1955 to 1968; its identity and how groups mobilised to access State largesse. He assesses the degree to which they developed complex, bureaucratised structures to articulate their demands at a time when restraints were imposed on group action by the political system. He identifies interest groups arising from the military and political elite who influenced commerce and trade policies to their advantage.

3407
Kujawa, Duane
Japanese Multinationals in the United States: Case studies
1986 Praeger *New York, NY*

A case-based analysis of the first wave of Japanese investment in the USA, contrasting it with the behaviour of non-Japanese foreign companies.
Firms: Honda; Mitsubishi; Murata; Sanyo; Ciba-Geigy; VW

3408
Luffman, George A.; Reed, Richard
The Strategy and Performance of British Industry, 1970–1980
1984 Macmillan *London*

A systematic examination of diversification strategies of the top 1000 British companies in the 1970s. Argues that diversifying companies generally outperformed non-diversifiers in profits and stability.

3409
Macrosty, Henry W.
The Trust Movement in British Industry: A study of business organization
1907 Longmans, Green & Co. *London*

Written by a Fabian civil servant, this is still the best history of the pre-First World War merger wave in the UK.

3410

Mason, Mark

American Multinationals and Japan: The political economy of Japanese capital controls, 1899–1980

1992 Harvard University Press *Cambridge, MA*

A major study of the history of American direct investment in Japan using corporate records and case studies to understand why it has been so restricted. Mason argues that Japanese business and government have combined to effectively lock out American firms in industries such as autos, chemicals, computers, semiconductors and telecommunications.

Firms: Coca-Cola; Dow Chemical; Ford; GM; IBM; Motorola; Otis Elevator; Texas Instruments; Western Electric; Victor Talking Machine

3411

Milner, Helen V.

Resisting Protectionism: Global industries and the politics of international trade

1988 Princeton University Press *Princeton, NJ*

This book examines the political and business view of protectionism by reference to case studies for individual firms within industries in the USA (1920s and 1970s) and France (1970s) including machinery, electronic goods, glass, pharmaceuticals and tyres.

Firms: Dunlop; Goodyear; IBM; Kodak; Motorola; Philips; RCA; Rhône-Poulenc-Santé; St Gobain; Texas Instruments

3412

Nakagawa, Keiichiro

Hikaki Keiei-shi Jo-setsu [An Introduction to Comparative Business History]

1981 Tokyo Daigaku Shuppan-kai *Tokyo, Japan*

This book is the first collection of the author's wide-ranging studies on comparative business history. It consists of two parts: the first examines diverse approaches to business history reviewing pioneering works. The second part discusses various subjects including a review of the Japanese-style business system.

3413

Piore, Michael J.; Sabel, Charles F.

The Second Industrial Divide: Possibilities for prosperity

1984 Basic Books *New York, NY*

A political scientist and economist combined to analyse the postwar competitive forces within advanced capitalism and their impact on the organization of work and of corporations. They emphasize the demise of mass production and the rise of 'flexible specialization'. A seminal, but controversial work, which takes a good point further than the evidence will permit.

3414

Pitelis, Christos; Sugden, Roger (Editors)

The Nature of the Transnational Firm

1991 Routledge *London*

An important theoretical prop for those contemplating research on MNEs, this includes a diverting contribution by Dunning which refines much of his earlier work on the 'eclectic MNE'.

3415

Ravenscraft, David J.; Scherer, F. M.

Mergers, Sell-offs and Economic Efficiency

1987 Brookings Institution *Washington, DC*

Using FTC line-of-business data, this study confirms earlier findings on the unprofitability of mergers.

3416

Schröter, Harm G.

Aufstieg der Kleinen: Multinationale Unternehmen aus fünf kleinen Staaten bis 1914 [Multinational enterprises in five smaller countries before 1914]

1993 Duncker & Humblot *Berlin, Germany*

Based on company material, this study examines over sixty multinationals with nearly 400 producing units abroad before the First World War. While proof is to be found on major theories, such as internationalization, a path of development distinct from the American one is worked out, concerning patterns of growth, ownership and management, technology transfer, etc. The fact of being based in a small state forced the companies to invest abroad early in their development. This is why in contrast to MNEs based in large countries, those from small ones were small, too, when investing abroad.

3416/1

Schröter, Harm G.

Kartellierung und Dekartellierung 1890–1990 [Cartelization and Decartelization 1890–1990]

Vierteljahrschrift für Sozial- und Wirtschaftsgeschichte, vol. 81, no. 4, 1994: pp 457–93

This article on cartelization and decartelization from 1890 to 1990 provides a general interpretation of the different explanatory factors of national and international cartelization and decartelization. Moreover, Schröter questions Chandler's concept of co-operative capitalism which he understands to be valid not only for Germany, but also for other European countries. Yet, he still considers Germany to be ahead of the others regarding its organizational capability which came to fruition in organizing national and international cartels.

3417

Scott, William G.

Chester I. Barnard and the Guardians of the Managerial State

1992 University Press of Kansas *Lawrence, KA*

This monograph provides a case study based on Barnard's contribution to managerial thought as one of the Harvard School in prewar America.

3418

Servan-Schreiber, Jean Jacques

Le Défi Americain [The American Challenge]

1967 Éditions Denoel *Paris, France*

Evoking the spectre of an American takeover of Europe, this thought-provoking book insisted that Europe could only avoid it by emulating America's managerial capabilities.

3419

Shepherd, David; Silberston, Aubrey; Strange, Roger

British Manufacturing Investment Overseas

1985 Methuen *London*

An important study of the causes of British manufacturing overseas in a historical perspective. It analyses the shifting location of investment, considers the main theoretical approaches, and assesses the overall consequences for the British economy of this overseas investment.

3420

Shonfield, Andrew

Modern Capitalism: The changing balance of public and private power

1965 Oxford University Press/Royal Institute of International Affairs *London*

Typical of its time in its overdrawn eulogies of French planning and pretence that Germany was unconsciously adopting similar expedients, this book remains an important interpretive reference point even though it has become somewhat outdated.

3421

Stopford, John M.; Dunning, John H.

Multinationals: Company performance and global trends

1983 Macmillan *London*

This is an indispensable statistical analysis of top 500 MNEs from the early 1970s to early 1980s, complementing *The World Dictionary of Multinational Enterprises 1982–3*. It contains full indexes to the enterprises analysed.

3422

Stopford, John; Turner, Louis

Britain and the Multinationals

1985 John Wiley *New York, NY*

An important and detailed study of postwar shifts in multinationals, examining both inward investment into Britain and the performance of British-owned multinationals. The authors examine arguments for and against Britain's heavy dependence on multinationals, and the issue of why Britain has been so attractive for foreign investors. This is a rigorous study with a great deal of information on specific companies.

Firms: British Aerospace; BAT Industries; BL; BOC; BP; Courtaulds; Dunlop; Ford; GKN; Glaxo

3423
Strange, Roger
Japanese Manufacturing Investment in Europe: Its impact on the UK economy
1993 Routledge *London*

A detailed quantitative assessment of the causes and consequences of Japanese manufacturing investment in fourteen sectors, together with case studies of twenty-seven investing companies. The material is used to draw some general conclusions about the dynamics of Japanese direct foreign investment.
Firms: Dainippon Ink and Chemicals; Fujitsu; Hitachi; Komatsu; Mitsubishi Electric; NEC; Calsonic Corporation; Nippon Seiko; Nissan; Sanyo Electric

3424
Supple, Barry E. (Editor)
The Rise of Big Business
For main entry, see 59

3425
Teichova, Alice; Lévy-Leboyer, Maurice; Nussbaum, Helga (Editors)
Historical Studies in International Corporate Business
Cambridge University Press *Cambridge*

A second volume of papers from the 1986 Economic History Congress. This volumes focuses on issues of research and development, financial operations, business-government relations and a wider geographical spread of countries.
Firms: AEG; J. & P. Coats Ltd.; GEC; Kanegafuchi Cotton Spinning Company; Mitsubishi; Mitsui; Philip Morris; Scheider; Thomson-Houston; Vickers

3426
Teichova, Alice; Lévy-Leboyer, Maurice; Nussbaum, Helga (Editors)
Multinational Enterprise in Historical Perspective
1986 Cambridge University Press *Cambridge*
Éditions de La Maison des Sciences *Paris, France*

This book contains a diverse set of essays prepared for the 1986 Ninth International Congress of Economic History in Berne.

3427
Teichova, Alice; Lindgren, Håkan; Dritsas, Margarita
L'Entreprise en Grèce et en Europe XIXe-XXe siècles [Business in Greece and in Europe Nineteenth to Twentieth Centuries]
1991 SOFHIS *Athens, Greece*

This is a collection of articles presented at a conference of Business History in 1989. Contributions are concerned with methodological questions about the relation between Business History and other disciplines, discuss the relevance of controversies on theory and empirical findings and inform about developments in the area of company archives. They also outline the basic concepts and processes regarding the margins of freedom open to business firms, such as government action, strategies of financing and processes of adjustment to the social environment.

3428
Temin, Peter (Editor)
Inside the Business Enterprise: Historical perspectives on the use of information
1991 University of Chicago Press *Chicago, IL*

The six excellent essays included here show some of the best current American work–both quantitatively and archivally based–in business history, developing new theoretical perspectives on the nature of the firm.

3429
Wilkins, Mira
The Emergence of Multinational Enterprise: American business abroad from the colonial era to 1914.
1970 Harvard University Press *Cambridge, MA*

This is the earliest and briefest of Mira Wilkins's important books on multinational investment; but is still the best treatment of American multinationals before 1914.

3430
Wilkins, Mira
The Maturing of Multinational Enterprise: American Business Abroad from 1914 to 1970
1974 Harvard University Press *Cambridge, MA*

Wilkins presents a careful scholarly analysis

of the post-1914 development of US multinationals and this remains, after 20 years, the best book on the subject.

3431
Wilkins, Mira (Editor)
The Growth of Multinationals
For main entry, see 61

Historical Approaches

3432
Acocella, N. et al (Editor)
Piccola e Grande Impresa: Una Problema Storica [Small and Large Enterprises: A historical problem]
1987 Franco Angeli *Milan, Italy*

This book is a collection of essays with a European perspective, reviewing American theories of industrial structure, sponsored by the ASSI Foundation.

3433
Bannock, Graham
The Smaller Business in Britain and Germany
1976 Wilton House *London*

Bannock presents a major piece of empirical research with plenty to offer business historians interested in comparative industrial performance in the modern period. The book contains an interesting comparison of brewing in the two countries.

3434
Bannock, Graham
The Economics of Small Firms: Return from the wilderness
1981 Basil Blackwell *Oxford*

This provides a short but provocative reassessment of the role of small firms in securing economic growth. Although more a primer for the 1980s than a piece of business history, it reviews earlier work on small firms with a historical element.

3435
Berk, Gerald
Alternative Tracks: The constitution of American industrial order, 1865–1917
For main entry, see 2844

3436
Blackford, Mansel G.
A History of Small Business in America
1991 Twayne Publishers *New York, NY*

This volume is a review of how small business in America has developed in the last 150 years. Its case studies of the development of small firms may be seen as an antidote to Chandler (qv).

3437
Bliss, Michael
Northern Enterprise: Five centuries of Canadian business
1987 McLelland and Stewart *Toronto, Ont., Canada*

This book is an overview by the dean of Canadian business historians of Canadian business from the beginning of European settlement to the present.

3438
Burch, Philip H. Jr
The Managerial Revolution Reassessed: Family control in America's large corporations
For main entry, see 3837

3439
Burn, Duncan (Editor)
The Structure of British Industry
1958 Cambridge University Press *Cambridge*

The essays collected here make this book still the best account of British industry in the 1950s, edited by an economic historian who became a *Times* leader writer and whose papers now form an important archive in the British Library of Political and Economic Science. The two volumes are excellent backing for an understanding of the Burn papers: a key source for 1950s industrial policy.

3440
Cain, P. J.; Hopkins, A. G.
British Imperialism: Vol. I, Innovation and

expansion, 1688–1914; Vol. II, Crisis and deconstruction
1993 Longmans *Harlow*

These two impressive volumes provide the definitive modern history of British imperialism viewed from the centre. Their significance for business historians lies in the thesis that the service sector was more critical to the imperialist process than manufacturing, and that the need to secure outlets for investment in the nineteenth century was a powerful motivating force, with the funds coming primarily from the 'rentier South' rather than the manufacturing North.

Firms: Baring; Hongkong and Shanghai Bank; Rothschild; Imperial Bank of Persia; East India Company; Bank of England

3441
Chandler, Alfred D. Jr
Strategy and Structure: Chapters in the history of industrial enterprise
1962 MIT Press *Cambridge, MA*

Chandler's book is the seminal work of modern business history, and the subject of several hundred tests, criticisms, validations and rejections. A classic of four case-studies establishes the major hypothesis that the multi-divisional organization form was developed in the 1920s in the USA by large, diversified enterprises and that this form spread rapidly among the largest 100 enterprises after the Second World War.

Firms: Du Pont; General Motors; Sears Roebuck; Standard Oil

3442
Chandler, Alfred D. Jr
The Visible Hand: The managerial revolution in American business
1977 Harvard University Press (Belknap Press) *Cambridge, MA*

This book must qualify for inclusion in any short list of the best books on business history ever written. Its central thesis is that the 'visible hand' – modern corporate bureaucracy – created many of the efficiency gains of twentieth-century American corporate capitalism.

3443
Chandler, Alfred D. Jr
The Emergence of Managerial Capitalism
Business History Review, vol. 58, no. 4, 1984: pp 473–503

This is one of the best of Chandler's shorter works setting out his schema for the rise of managerial capitalism, which has useful statistical tables comparing the United States with the United Kingdom, Germany and Japan.

3444
Chandler, Alfred D. Jr
Scale and Scope: The dynamics of industrial capitalism
1990 Harvard University Press (Belknap Press) *Cambridge, MA*

This is the most ambitious and also the weakest of Chandler's books. It has been heavily criticized, for example, for exaggerating the extent of Germany's early corporate development and overemphasizing the problems of British 'family capitalism'. Nonetheless it remains the most comprehensive survey of the comparative corporate development of the top 200 firms in the UK, Germany and the USA.

3445
Chandler, Alfred D. Jr; Daems, Herman (Editors)
Managerial Hierarchies: Comparative perspectives on the rise of the modern industrial enterprise
1980 Harvard University Press *Cambridge, MA & London*

In a sense a forerunner of Chandler's *Scale and Scope* (qv), this book contains general essays by Chandler, Daems, Oliver Williamson and Morton Keller, but the core of its empirical contribution are national studies of the largest firms in the UK (Hannah), Germany (Kocka) and France (Lévy-Leboyer). They take a rather more balanced view of European 'backwardness' in corporate and market organization than some later contributions to this debate.

3446
Channon, Derek F.
The Strategy and Structure of British Enterprise
1973 Macmillan *London* Harvard University Press *Cambridge, MA*

This is one of the seminal Harvard PhDs on European corporate structures since 1945, modelled on Chandler's *Strategy and Structure* (qv). Later work has unearthed rather more multidivisional corporations among the top 100 than Channon found, but his work remains an important foundation for the empirical analysis on diversification and corporate structures. Other European countries are examined by Pavan (Italy) and Dyas and Thanheiser (France and Germany) (qqv).

3447
Daems, Herman; Wee, Herman van der
The Rise of Managerial Capitalism
1974 Leuven University Press *Louvain, Belgium*

This is one of the earliest international conference volumes showing the increasing interest of foreign scholars in the work of Alfred Chandler (qv).

3448
Dyas, Gareth P.; Thanheiser, H.
The Emerging European Enterprise: Strategy and structure in French and German industry
1976 Macmillan *London*

This important comparative study of strategy and structure in post-war French and German industry serves as a useful adjunct to Chandler's *Scale and Scope* (qv).
Firms: Siemens; Thyssen; Volkswagen

3449
Fine, Ben; Harris, Laurence
The Peculiarities of the British Economy
1985 Lawrence & Wishart *London*

A Marxist analysis of the historical roots of the decline of British capitalism. Pays particular attention to the conflicting interests of finance and industry and also contains case study material on the coal industry.

3450
Hannah, Leslie
The Rise of the Corporate Economy
1983 Methuen *London*

Incorporating much material from company histories as well as from the work of economists and economic historians, and drawing on the author's doctorate on twentieth-century mergers, this has become a classic study of the UK's first three merger waves.

3451
Hayek, F. A. (Editor)
Capitalism and the Historians
1954 Routledge & Kegan Paul *London*

Seminal Cold War defence of the free market, including T. S. Ashton's piece on 'The Treatment of Capitalism by Historians', and L. M. Hacker's account of the 'Anticapitalist Bias of American Historians'.

3452
Hirst, Paul; Zeitlin, Jonathan (Editors)
Reversing Industrial Decline?: Industrial structure and policy in Britain and her competitors
1989 Berg *Oxford*

This is a multi-authored volume which highlights sources of industrial failure in advanced countries, and suggests policy prescriptions to arrest the trend, referring mainly to the UK and USA. In the process it provides some valuable insights for historians of contemporary business who are interested, for example, in flexible production systems and industrial relations.

3453
Hunt, Bishop Carleton
The Development of the Business Corporation in England 1800–1967
1936 Russell & Russell *New York, NY*

This is the classic study of the emergence of joint-stock and limited liability firms in nineteenth-century Britain. It pays due attention to the role of financial crises in stimulating reform.

3454
Johnson, Chalmers
MITI and the Japanese Miracle: The growth of industrial policy, 1925–1975
1982 Stanford University Press *Stanford, CA*

A hugely influential, though now much challenged, work on the nature of Japanese industrial policy since the 1920s and, in particular, the role of MITI in stimulating international competitiveness in Japan's post-war industries. The book contains much valuable narrative on the development of government policy, but tends to overstate the importance of MITI and other ministries in creating entrepreneurial success.

Firms: Bank of Japan; Fuji Steel Co.; Japan Development Bank; Japan Steel Corporation; Mitsubishi; Mitsui; Nissan; Teijin Textile Co.; Toyota Motor Co.; Yawata Steel Co.

3455

Kirby, Maurice W.; Rose, Mary B. (Editors)

Business Enterprise in Modern Britain from the Eighteenth to the Twentieth Century

1994 Routledge *London*

This is a multi-authored survey volume which will attract a student readership. It covers three centuries of British business history, and contains useful chapters on the corporate economy, multinational business, the competitive environment, the state and business, and investment in human capital.

3456

Kirby, M. W.

The Decline of British Economic Power since 1870

1981 Allen & Unwin *London*

A good overview of the issues surrounding Britain's relative economic decline.

3457

Lamoreaux, Naomi R.

The Great Merger Movement in American Business, 1895–1904

1985 Cambridge University Press *Cambridge and New York*

This is a refreshing reinterpretation of the merger mania which followed the Sherman Act in the United States. Market control appears at centre stage in the analysis. The concurrence of rapid industrial growth and price warfare were isolated as important variables. The steel and paper industries are given particular attention.

Firms: American Sugar Refining Co.; American Tin Plate Co.; Illinois Steel Co.; International Paper Co.; US Steel Corporation; Pennsylvania Steel Co.; Great Northern Paper Co.; Distilling & Cattle Feeding Co.; Consolidated Steel & Wire Co.; American Steel & Wire Co.

3458

Lazonick, William

Competitive Advantage on the Shop Floor

1990 Harvard University Press *Cambridge, MA*

Focusing on a comparison of the UK, Japan and the USA, Lazonick shows how technology and work organization interact to create industrial competitive advantages. He argues that co-operative relations between management and workers have in the twentieth century become critical to corporate (and national economic) success. This book includes Lazonick's important articles on the self-acting mule and the performance of the British cotton industry in the late 19th century.

3459

Lazonick, William

Business Organization and the Myth of the Market Economy

1991 Cambridge University Press *Cambridge*

Attacking the mainstream economic tradition, Lazonick develops comparisons of the UK, USA and Japan to suggest that the dynamics of capitalist development depend on organizations more than markets. This radical reinterpretation represents a more rigorous and challenging theoretical development of the work of Chandler (qv) on organizational capabilities.

3460

Lescure, Michel

Les PME dans la croissance des années 1920 [Small and Medium Enterprises in the Economic Growth of the 1920s]

1992, PhD Thesis, Université Paris X

This general business history of small and medium sized firms in the 1920s is a pioneering work.

3461

Lévy-Leboyer, Maurice (Editor)

Le Patronat de la Seconde Industrialisation [The Employers of the Second Industrialization]

1979 Les Éditions Ouvrières *Paris, France*

This collection contains an excellent set of internationally comparative essays on the recruitment of managers and the implications for national economic organization.

3462
Lieberman, Marvin B.; Montgomery, David B.
First-Mover Advantages
Strategic Management Journal, vol. 9, 1988: pp 41–58

This is a classic, indispensable summary of the theoretical and empirical literature dealing with the causes of first-mover status and its loss to second movers. It provides a very useful companion to Chandler's *Scale and Scope* thesis (qv), and a future research agenda.

3463
Livesay, Harold C.
Entrepreneurial Dominance in Businesses Large and Small, Past and Present
For main entry, see 4080

3464
McCraw, Thomas K. (Editor)
The Essential Alfred Chandler: Essays toward a historical theory of big business
1988 Harvard Business School Press *Boston, MA*

This is a collection of the published articles by the doyen of business historians which reveals the patient construction of Chandler's approach over fifty years of scholarship. Tom McCraw's finely written introduction describes a scholarly life which should be compulsory reading for graduate students seeking a role model.

3465
Newton, Scott; Porter, Dilwyn
Modernization Frustrated: The politics of industrial decline in Britain since 1900
1988 Unwin Hyman *London*

This study links low investment to the disproportionate influence of the financial sector in government circles, leading to the pursuit of policies which have favoured the City rather than manufacturing industry.

3466
North, Douglass C.
Institutions, Institutional Change and Economic Performance
1990 Cambridge University Press *New York, NY*

North's book is a Nobel-prizewinning overview of the theory of institutional change and transactions costs.

3467
Olson, Mancur
The Rise and Decline of Nations: Economic growth, stagflation and social rigidities
1982 Yale University Press *New Haven, CT*

The view of this book that growth in Western democracies is inversely related to the strength of efficiency-restricting cartels, unions and sundry collective restraints has been challenged, but this remains one of the most coherently argued discussions of the reasons for the differences in growth rates among OECD nations and their roots in business institutions.

3468
Pavan, Robert David John
The Strategy and Structure of Italian Enterprise
1973 University Microfilms *Ann Arbor, MI*

This 1972 Harvard thesis is available in microform condition. It is one of the four seminal postwar studies of Europe in the tradition of Chandler's *Strategy and Structure* (qv).

3469
Pollard, Sidney
The Genesis of Modern Management
1965 Edward Arnold *London*

Pollard presents a classic study of management in the British Industrial Revolution, based on a wide range of sources that is still the best study of British business history in that period. The emphasis is on large-scale technology and the labour organization, management and accounting which is required to exploit it.

3470
Prais, S. J.
The Evolution of Giant Firms in Britain 1909–70
1976 Cambridge University Press *Cambridge*

Here are the first fruits of Professor Prais's long and productive research at the National Institute of Economic and Social Research. While his emphasis on the Gibrat effect as a cause of increasing concentration has been disputed, this remains the best treatment of long-run changes in British industrial structure.

3471
Sapelli, Giulio
L'impresa come soggetto storico [The Enterprise as a Historical Subject]
1990 Il Saggiatore *Milan, Italy*

This book is a selection of essays by one of the founders of Italian business history as well as an intelligent critic of recent Italian socio-economic evolution. While not forgetting economic issues, Sapelli brings in some interesting anthropological and sociological perspectives.
Firms: Alfa Romeo; Edison; FIAT; Riunione Adriatica de Sicurtà (RAS)

3472
Tedlow, Richard S.; John, Richard R. (Editors)
Managing Big Business
1986 Harvard Business School Press *Boston, MA*

A selection of innovative articles from the Harvard Business School's *Business History Review* is collected together in this volume.

3473
Tolliday, Steven W. (Editor)
Review Colloquium on ***Scale and Scope***
Business History Review, vol. 64, no. 4, 1990: pp 690–758

This is an important collection reviewing and criticizing Chandler's major book. It comprises contributions assessing Chandler's approach from the perspective of four countries - the United States (Hughes), Germany (Kocka), the UK (Church) and Japan (Morikawa) - together with three studies which assess the book from the standpoint of economics (Scherer), sociology (Fligstein) and broad change in the global economy (Fishlow). Chandler responds to these criticisms in the final section.

3474
Zamagni, Vera (Editor)
Finance and the Enterprise
1992 Academic Press *London*

This book contains a series of useful essays on the interaction between financial systems and corporate organization: one of the many interesting conference volumes now emerging from the Italian ASSI foundation.

3475
Zunz, Olivier
Making America Corporate 1870–1920
For main entry, see 3768

Economic Approaches

3476
Amjad, R.
Private Industrial Investment in Pakistan
1982 Cambridge University Press *Cambridge*

This is a study of the behaviour of profitability and factors influencing investment in 34 Pakistani monopoly groups from 1960–1970. Amjad attributes investment decisions to factors in the exogenous environment, particularly the influx of foreign aid and political licensing in the 1960s. The macro-economic environment is presented in considerable detail and its effects on the capacity utilisation, price-cost margins, capital-output and concentration ratios of 25 industries in the manufacturing sector.

3477
Aoki, Masahiko (Editor)
The Economic Analysis of the Japanese Firm
1984 North Holland *Amsterdam, The Netherlands*

A pioneering collection of essays reflecting on the structures of the Japanese firm and probing cross-shareholdings, hierarchies, trust relations, and ownership from Aoki's distinctive perspective.

3478
Aoki, Masahiko; Dore, Ronald (Editors)
The Japanese Firm: Sources of competitive strength
1994 Clarendon Press *Oxford*

Ten years after Aoki's *Economic Analysis of the Japanese Firm* this book of essays takes stock of theoretical developments in the analysis of the Japanese firm and its trade-offs between equality and efficiency, and considers whether the key features are entering crisis in the 1990s.

3479
Berg, Maxine
The Age of Manufacturers 1700–1820: Industry, innovation and work in Britain
2nd Edition
1994 Routledge *London*

Berg presents an important new perspective on economic growth, emphasizing not macroeconomic change nor the factory system, but the mass of domestic industry and artisan workshops with a predominantly female and child labour force which co-existed with the introduction of mechanisation.

3480
Blackaby, Frank (Editor)
De-industrialisation
1979 Heinemann *London*

This book comprises a key set of contributions by economists to the discussion of manufacturing capabilities in a macroeconomic framework.

3481
Casson, Mark
The Economics of Business Culture: Game theory, transaction costs and economic performance
1991 Clarendon Press *Oxford*

This is an excellent study of the effects of leadership, moral, political and business, on economic performance through an examination of transaction costs and levels of trust.

3482
Coase, Ronald H.
The Nature of the Firm
Economica, vol. 4, no. 16, 1937: pp 386–405

This is the path-breaking treatise on transaction costs, which was neglected until it was resurrected by Oliver Williamson in the 1970s. Coase's article is now regarded as an important starting-point for all those interested in applying the theory to business history, and developing the 'Visible Hand' approach of Alfred Chandler (qv).

3483
Dunning, John H.
American Investment in British Manufacturing Industry
1958 George Allen & Unwin *London*

This is the first in a long line of distinguished books by this author on multinational investment. It is a careful business history of the origins of US multinational investment in Britain and an analysis of how their structure and behaviour differed from British firms.

3484
Florence, P. Sargant
The Logic of British and American Industry
1961 Routledge *London*

A revision of an earlier 1931 book (*The Logic of Industrial Organization*), Florence's book summarizes the state of the subject of empirical industrial economics in Britain in the 1950s.

3485
Florence, P. Sargant
Economics and Sociology of Industry
1964 C. A. Watts *London*

A comparison of business organization in Britain (and in the 2nd edition (1969) the USA) is made here with that of underdeveloped countries.

3486
Galbraith, John Kenneth
The New Industrial State
1967 André Deutsch *London*

This is one of the most influential of the 1960's critiques of the role of, and power wielded by, the American large-scale corporation.

3487
Hirschman, Albert O.
Exit, Voice and Loyalty: Responses to decline in firms, organization and states
1970 Harvard University Press *Cambridge, MA*
Hirschman's book is one of the seminal works of postwar social science, full of elegantly developed new ideas which have been extensively used by business historians. It put the political science ('voice') back into the economic analysis of corporate behaviour, which implied that 'exit' (bankruptcy) was the main vehicle for changing bad corporate policies.

3488
Jacquemin, Alexis
The New Industrial Organisation: Market forces and strategic behavior
1987 MIT Press *Cambridge, MA*
This book presents a broad policy-orientated survey of the new industrial economics.

3489
Johnson, H. Thomas; Kaplan, Robert S.
Relevance Lost: The rise and fall of management accounting
1987 Harvard Business School Press *Boston, MA*
Johnson and Kaplan's book is the *locus classicus* of the view that nineteenth-century management accounting techniques became progressively deformed in the post First World War era and by the 1980s were a major source of American competitive weakness.
Firms: Du Pont; General Motors

3490
Marris, Robin
The Economic Theory of Managerial Capitalism
1964 Macmillan *London*
Like Edith Penrose (qv) this economist sees the businessman as motivated by growth rather than profitability but works out the microeconomic implications more formally and comprehensively.

3491
Marsh, Robert M.; Mannari, Hiroshi
Organisational Change in Japanese Factories
1988 JAI Press *Greenwich, CT*
This is a major study in organization theory discussing links between organization and performance.

3492
Marshall, Alfred
Industry and Trade: A study of industrial technique and business organization; and of their influences on the conditions of various classes and nations
1919 Macmillan *London*
Few empirical analyses have stood the test of time as well as this one, which has been surprisingly neglected by business historians.

3493
Martin, W. E. (Editor)
The Economics of the Profits Crisis
1981 HMSO Books *London*
A review of the causes of Britain's long-run decline in profits is presented here in a series of conference papers.

3494
Meeks, G.
Disappointing Marriage: A study of the gains from merger
1977 Cambridge University Press *Cambridge*
A critical study of the objectives and effects of mergers. Meek's finds them generally unjustified and argues for greater regulation.

3495
Miller, Gary J.
Managerial Dilemmas: The political economy of hierarchy
1992 Cambridge University Press *Cambridge*
An important critique of organization theory in the light of game theory which argues that no incentive system can completely overcome the effects of information asymmetries. His arguments are attractive to many business historians.

3496
Nelson, R. R.; Winter, S. G.
An Evolutionary Theory of Economic Change
1982 Harvard: Belknap Press *Cambridge, MA*
A systematic explicit account is given here of a view often implicit in business history gener-

alizations: that only organizations well adapted to their business environment survive.

3497
Prais, S. J.
Productivity and Industrial Structure
1981 Cambridge University Press *Cambridge*

This book views British industrial performance in contrast with both Germany and the USA, using empirical statistical comparisons effectively. It has some particularly original reflections in its comparison of finance and organization, but also covers topics such as strike-proneness, shiftworking, vocational training and plant size.

3498
Pratt, John W.; Zeckhauser, Richard J. (Editors)
Principals and Agents: The structure of business
1984 Harvard Business School Press *Boston, MA*

This work is a helpful primer in the theory of principals and agents and its applications to organizational analysis.

3499
Pratten, C. F.
Labour Productivity Differentials Within International Companies
1976 Cambridge University Press *Cambridge*

Pratten's is a key work by one of Britain's most accomplished applied industrial economists, who mixes statistical analysis with first-hand observation.

3500
Rothschild, K. W. (Editor)
Power in Economics
1971 Penguin *Harmondsworth*

A useful collection of early articles is brought together here, not only on market power but on the implications of power structures within organizations.

3501
Scherer, Frederic M.; Ross, David R.
Industrial Market Structure and Economic Performance
3rd Edition
1990 Houghton Mifflin *Boston, MA*

This is an expanded version of the 1970 and 1980 classic, employing the structure-conduct-performance paradigm (see Hirschmann (1970). This is an essential text for business historians interested in industrial organisation, and specifically the relationships between market power, regulation and performance. It contains useful sections on entry barriers, economies of scale, oligopoly and antitrust and includes an index entry on companies.
Firms: General Electric; General Motors; US Steel

3502
Schumacher, E. F.
Small is Beautiful: A study of economics as if people mattered
1973 Blond & Briggs *London*

This book was an influential precursor of the 1980s re-recognition of the virtues of small enterprise and 'empowerment'.

3503
Schumann, C. G. W.
Structural Change and Business Cycles in South Africa 1806–1936
1938 P. S. King *London*

This book is the indispensable companion to any study of business history in South Africa, equivalent to Gayer, Rostow and Schwartz. It is a model example of econometric history.

3504
Schumpeter, Joseph A.
Capitalism, Socialism and Democracy
1943 Unwin *London*

A brilliant tour de force of interpretation which, though evidently wrong in its view that capitalism would be transformed into socialism, still contains valuable insights on the nature of the modern corporation.

3505
Schumpeter, Joseph A.; Swedberg, Richard (Editor)
The Economics and Sociology of Capitalism
1991 Princeton University Press *Princeton, NJ*

This selection by Swedberg from Schumpeter's writing provides the best anthology of

Schumpeter's diverse works on the nature of capitalist organization.

3506
Sheard, Paul (Editor)
International Adjustment and the Japanese Firm
1992 Allen & Unwin Pty *St Leonards, NSW, Australia*

A collection of essays considering the relationship between Japanese domestic corporate organization and international trade. Do such organizational forms constitute 'structural impediments'? Are they changing over time? The essays are all high quality ones, written by leading Japanese, American and Australian economists.

3507
Stigler, George J.
The Organization of Industry
1968 Richard D. Irwin *Homewood, IL*

With the emphasis on concentration and monopoly, antitrust policy, information and market imperfections, this collection of articles shows the best of George Stigler's contributions to economics which are of abiding interest to business historians.

3508
Sutton, John
Sunk Costs and Market Structure: Price competition, advertising and the evolution of concentration
1991 MIT Press *Cambridge, MA*

This book gives one of the first signs that the new game – theoretical approaches to industrial organization – is being embodied in empirical applied work in industrial economics. While it demonstrates how extremely modest are the claims of theory in explaining industrial structure, the modesty in the face of evidence of the contingent, historical nature of industry evolution will appeal to business historians. The author is one of the few industrial economists to have exploited the historical evidence so skilfully.

3509
Williamson, Oliver E.
Markets and Hierarchies: Analysis and Antitrust Implications: A study in the economics of internal organization
1975 Free Press *New York, NY*

This is a seminal work on the 'new institutional economics' which sought to apply transaction costs economics in developing a more satisfactory theory of the firm. This book formed the basis for Williamson's further work, and notably *The Economic Institutions of Capitalism* (qv).

3510
Williamson, Oliver E.
The Economic Institutions of Capitalism
1985 Free Press *New York, NY*

This presents a fusion of Chandlerian business history and Williamson's transaction costs economics, which inspired a spirited critique from Lazonick in *Business Organization and the Myth of the Market Economy* (qv).

Sociological Approaches

3511
Argyris, Chris; Schon, D. A.
Organisational Learning: A theory of action perspective
1978 Addison-Wesley *Wokingham*

This book is a study of the way organizations cope with contradictory goals. Argyris is the doyen of the US business school social psychologists.

3512
Barnard, Chester
Organization and Management
1948 Harvard University Press *Cambridge, MA*

Barnard's is a pioneering work in corporate culture by a full-time business executive with Bell Telephone, which lay long forgotten until the subject again recently became fashionable.

3513
Beniger, James R.
The Control Revolution: Technological and economic origins of the information society
1986 Harvard University Press *Cambridge, MA*

This major work advances the theory that modern society is dominated by systems aiming to achieve control. It deals with the growth of production and managerial systems, mass consumption and information technology.

3514
Bijker, Wiebe E.; Hughes, Thomas P. (Editors)
The Social Construction of Technological Systems: New directions in the sociology and history of technology
For main entry, see 4248

3515
Brenner, Reuven
Rivalry in Business: Science among nations
1987 Cambridge University Press *New York, NY*
Drawing on psychology, history and political science, this is a fresh, quirky, anecdotal look at rivalry.

3516
Brown, Jonathan; Rose, Mary B. (Editors)
Entrepreneurship, Networks and Modern Business
1993 Manchester University Press *Manchester*
The dozen essays in this volume originated in an annual symposium between business historians at Reading and Lancaster Universities. All relate the entrepreneur to economic, social and business contexts. Essays by Tony Corley and Mark Casson provide theoretical underpinnings. Contributions by Robert Locke and Ken'ichi Yasumuro offer contrasting American and Japanese views of the ways in which entrepreneurs have been produced.
Firms: Pease & Partners

3517
Burns, T.; Stalker, G. M.
The Management of Innovation
1961 Tavistock *London*
In the sociological tradition of contingency theory, the authors examine the match of organization and environment. The book is still a classic despite its origins in a period remarkable for its lack of innovation, for it pointed out that many contemporary models of organization were inappropriate to managing the less structured problems which a messy world of change generated.

3518
Cyert, R.; March, J.
A Behavioral Theory of the Firm
1963 Prentice-Hall *Englewood Cliffs, NJ*
This book presents a classic treatment qualifying the rationalist approach of much industrial economics. See also H. A. Simon (qv).

3519
Dore, Ronald
Flexible Rigidities: Industrial policy and structural adjustment in the Japanese economy 1970–1980
1986 Athlone Press *London*
A leading British sociologist attempts to explain why Japanese firms with apparently rigid structures were among the most successful in responding flexibly to the oil crisis of the 1970s.

3520
Fligstein, Neil
The Transformation of Corporate Control
1990 Harvard University Press *Cambridge, MA*
Fligstein presents an argument that corporate control in America has moved through four main phases, in turn dominated by direct control, manufacturing, sales and marketing, and finance. The bulk of the book is an extensive study of the final phase exploring the financial pressures to diversify and focus on limited financial goals. An interesting if overambitious project.

3521
Jacquemin, Alexis P.; Jong, Henry W. de
European Industrial Organisation
1977 Macmillan *London*
A study of European industrial organisation in the now dated 'structure-conduct-performance' framework.

3522
Jacquemin, A. P.; Jong, Henry W. de (Editors)
Welfare Aspects of Industrial Markets
1977 Martin Nijhoff *Leiden, The Netherlands*
This is a major collection of studies which

examine the welfare implications of industrial organisation. The book includes a key piece by Nyman and Silberston on ownership and control in the UK, and important papers on inflation and international trade.

3523
Kidron, Michael
Western Capitalism Since the War
1968 Weidenfeld & Nicolson *London*
Kidron's book is an exposition of the (now-discredited) thesis that the success of corporate capitalism in the postwar economy was based on arms spending.

3524
Lewis, Roy; Stewart, Rosemary
The Boss: The life and times of the British businessman
1958 Phoenix House *London* 1963 Aldine *London*
This is still the best treatment of British business attitudes in the postwar decade.

3525
Mackenzie, Donald
Inventing Accuracy: An historical sociology of nuclear missile guidance systems
For main entry, see 4279

3526
Marx, Karl
Capital: A critical analysis of capitalist production (Original Title: Das Kapital)
1887 Swann, Sonnenschein, Lowrey & Co. *London*
This translation is taken from the third German edition of Marx's work, by Samuel Moore and Edward Aveling, edited by Frederick Engels. It is altogether the most influential study of capitalism ever published.

3527
Nakagawa, Keiichiro (Editor)
Keiei Rinen: Gendai Keiei-gaku Zenshu Dai San kan [Business Ideology: The corpus of modern business economics, Vol. 3]
1972 Diamond-sha *Tokyo, Japan*
Taking into account the theories of Weber and Drucker, this work reviews Japanese modernization and business philosophy and different business ideologies in comparative perspective.

3528
Schein, E. H.
Organisational Culture and Leadership
1985 Jossey-Bass *San Francisco, CA*
A key contribution is made here by a social psychologist and US management professor to the understanding of corporate culture.

3529
Simon, Herbert A.
Administrative Behavior
2nd Edition
1961 Macmillan *New York, NY*
Simon's book is a classic exposition of the view that the firm is a series of shifting coalitions in which conflicting demands and objectives are imperfectly reconciled and decision-making is incremental. For an autobiographical account of the multi-disciplinary origins of these Nobel-prizewinning ideas see the same author's *Models of My Life* (qv).

3530
Simon, Herbert A.
Models of My Life
1991 Basic Books *New York, NY*
As well as being the best written book by any Nobel prize-winner, this autobiography throws interesting light on modern thinking about social pyschology and sociology and their application to the organizational behaviour of business firms.

3531
Stokman, Frans N.; Ziegler, Rolf; Scott, John
Networks of Corporate Power
1985 Polity Press *Cambridge*
This book takes the taxonomy of interlocking directorates about as far as it can reasonably be expected to go. Its sophisticated methodology produced few surprises: continental Europe is found to have more corporate interlocks than the USA or UK. Critics have suggested the authors tend to exaggerate the importance of the phenomenon.

3532
Takenaka, Seiichi; Miyamoto, Mataji (Editors)
Keiei Rinen no Keifu: Sono Kokusai Hikaku [A Genealogy of Business Ideology: International comparisons]
1979 Toyo Bunka-sha *Kyoto, Japan*

This is a collection of treatises on business philosophy which include four papers on Japan with particular focus on the Edo period, one on English business ideology, one on German business ideology and Christianity and one on business ideology in the southern United States.

3533
Tsuchiya, Takao
Nippon Keiei Rinen-shi [A History of Japanese Business Ideology]
1964 Nippon Keizai Shinbun-sha *Tokyo, Japan*

This work is a wide-ranging history of Japanese business philosophy that takes into account the theories of M. Weber and W. Sombart on the capitalist economy with particular focus on the Tokugawa period.

3534
Tsuchiya, Takao
Zoku Nippon Keiei Rinen-shi [A History of Japanese Business Ideology (second series)]
1967 Nippon Keizai Shinbun-sha *Tokyo, Japan*

This work on Japanese business philosophy takes into account Drucker's theories covering the Meiji (1868–1912), Taisho (1912–1926) and Showa (1926–1989) periods.

3535
Vogel, Ezra F.
Comeback: Building the resurgence of American business
1985 Simon & Schuster *New York, NY*

From the sociologist author of *Japan as No. 1*, this is a thoughtful analysis of the possibilities for American business responding to the Japanese challenge.

3536
Wallerstein, Immanuel
Historical Capitalism
1983 Verso *Thetford*

This book is a shorter version of Wallerstein's interpretation of the 'modern world-system'. The reified determinist, neo-marxist approach has often puzzled business historians.

3537
Weber, Max
The Theory of Social and Economic Organisation
1947 Free Press *New York, NY*

This is the classic text on bureaucracy, first published in Germany in 1924, four years after the author's death. The translation is by A. M. Henderson and T. Parsons.

3538
Woodward, Joan
Industrial Organisation: Theory and practice
1965 Oxford University Press *Oxford*

Woodward's book is a classic application of the insights of sociology to understanding industrial behaviour.

3539
Wurm, Clemens A.
Politics and International Relations: Steel, cotton and international cartels in British politics, 1924–1939
For main entry, see 4410

Business/Management Approaches

3540
Ansoff, H. I.
Corporate Strategy: An analytical approach to business policy for growth and expansion
1969 McGraw-Hill *New York, NY*

This book is a collection of the writings of the dean of 1960s strategy gurus in the USA.

3541
Anthony, R. N.
Planning and Control Systems: A framework for analysis
1965 Harvard Business School Press *Boston, MA*

This provides a 'state of the art' explanation of 1960s strategic planning procedures which later became unfashionable with more turbulent economic conditions, reflected in Armstrong (qv).

3542
Armstrong, J. S.
The value of formal planning for strategic decisions–a review of empirical research
Strategic Management Journal, vol. 3, 1982: pp 197–211

This article contains a sceptical assessment, at the end of a turbulent post-OPEC decade, of the effectiveness of 1960s-style corporate planning.

3543
Bartlett, C. A.; Ghoshal, S.
Managing Across Borders: The transnational solution
1989 Harvard Business School Press *Boston, MA*

An influential modern textbook of international management.

3544
Baughman, James P. (Editor)
The History of American Management: Selections from the Business History Review
1969 Prentice Hall *Englewood Cliffs, NJ*

This is a very important collection of articles dealing with America's management history, which includes contributions by Chandler, Litterer, Galambos, and Newcomer.

Firms: Baltimore & Ohio Railroad; Pennsylvania Railroad; DuPont; Ford

3545
Beck, P.
Corporate Plans for an Uncertain Future
1981 Shell *London*

An effective exposition of scenario planning is made here by its foremost European exponent, the Anglo-Dutch Shell company. Scenario planning became more popular in the turbulent decade of the 1970s. For a later exposition see A. de Geus, 'Planning as learning' *Harvard Business Review*, March-April 1988, pp 70-4.

Firms: Shell

3546
Boston Consulting Group
Perspectives on Experience
1972 Boston Consulting Group *Boston, MA*

This is the classic and highly influential consultancy work on the experience curve and the relation between increasing output and productivity. See also Buzzell and Gale (qv) and contrast with the cautions in Kay, chapter 11 (qv).

3547
Brandt, Steven C.
Strategic Planning in Emerging Companies
1984 Addison-Wesley *Reading, MA*

One of the best accounts of how management must change as a company grows.

3548
Burnham, James
The Managerial Revolution, or, what is happening in the world now
1942 Putnam *London*

This is a key book on the power of managers, as remarkable for its insights as for the now obvious errors of a reformed Trotskyite herald of a new capitalism.

3549
Buzzell, R. D.; Gale, B. T.
The PIMS Principles: Linking strategy to performance
1987 Free Press *New York, NY*

The PIMS database reflects the anonymous experience of more than 7,000 business units and is thus a useful corrective to the single case studies of corporate historians. It has been widely used to establish, for example, the correlation of high profitability with high market share, though see Kay (qv), chapter 11, for cautions on its use.

3550
Child, John
Management and Organisational Factors Associated With Company Performance: A contingency analysis
Journal of Management Studies, vol. 11, no. 3, 1974: pp 175–89

Two articles giving the classic exposition of the view that Chandler's suggestion that structure follows strategy is a partial one: rather the process should be viewed as interactive, with structure itself a determinant of strategy.

3551
Clark, K. B.; Kantrow, A. M.; Abernathy, W. J.
Industrial Renaissance: Producing a competitive future for America
1983 Basic Books *New York, NY*

This volume presents a critique of modish strategy theorists and their malign effect on US business.

3552
Drucker, Peter F.
The Concept of the Corporation
For main entry, see 4059

3553
Drucker, Peter F.
The Practice of Management
For main entry, see 4060

3554
Drucker, Peter F.
People and Performance: The best of Peter Drucker on management
1977 Heinemann *London*

A taster of the most prolific twentieth-century writer on management is given here. His fresh, well-written contributions on a wide variety of topics would themselves fill a bibliography!

3555
Drucker, Peter F.
The Frontiers of Management
1986 Heinemann *London*

A selection of recent Druckeriana.

3556
Edwards, Richard
Contested Terrain: The transformation of the workplace in the twentieth century
1979 Basic Books *New York, NY*

This is a popular account of the changing nature of the working environment and the development of managerial hierarchies in the United States, with an emphasis on social relations. It draws on case studies of several leading American corporations.

Firms: AT&T; IBM; Ford; General Electric; Pabst Brewing; Polaroid; US Steel; International Harvester; Pullman

3557
Gilmore, F. F.; Brandenburg, R. G.
Anatomy of Corporate Planning
Harvard Business Review, vol. 40, no. 6, 1962: pp 61–9

A good description of 1960s techniques of corporate planning is contained in this article.

3558
Goold, Michael; Campbell, Andrew
Strategies and Style: The role of the centre in managing diversified corporations
1987 Basil Blackwell *Oxford*

The authors distinguish three styles of control in diversified British companies: strategic planning; strategic control; and financial control. Their relative merits are discussed. While there are no great conceptual breakthroughs, the book represents a practical, commonsense approach to generalizing from case studies.

Firms: BOC; BP; BTR; Hanson Trust; ICI; Imperial Group; Plessey; STC; Tarmac; Vickers

3559
Granick, David
The Red Executive
1960 Doubleday *New York, NY* 1979 Arno Press *New York, NY,*

This is one of the few Western attempts to understand Societ management in the cold war era.

3560
Grinyer, P. H.; Al-Bazazz, S.; Yasai-Ardekani, M.
Towards a contingency theory of corporate planning: Findings in 48 UK companies
Strategic Management Journal, 1986: pp 3–28

This comprehensive case study analysis suggests that there is no 'perfect organization'–rather organization must be matched to the business environment.

3561
Hamermesh, R. G.
Making Strategy Work: How senior managers produce results
1986 John Wiley *New York, NY*

This treatment stresses the importance of strategy *implementation* and the weaknesses of approaches which, in contrast, stress strategy *formulation*.

3562
Handy, Charles
Understanding Organisations
1976 Penguin *Harmondsworth*

This is the first and most academically useful book of Britain's most famous postwar management guru. The germ of his later ideas on improving and thinning down organizations and using modern information technology can be found there.

3563
Hoffer, C. W.; Murray, E. A. (Editors)
Strategic Management: A casebook in business policy and planning
1978 West Publishing Co *St Paul, MN*

This is an excellent collection of case studies.

3564
Houlden, B. T.
Data and Effective Corporate Planning
Long Range Planning, vol. 13, 1980: pp 106–11

Houlden's article is a key explanation of the role of data in the budgeting and planning process.

3565
Kanter, Rosabeth Moss
When Giants Learn to Dance
1989 Simon & Schuster *New York, NY*

Kanter's book is a modish 1980s exposition of the strategy of 'empowerment' in the 'post-entrepreneurial' corporation. Earlier works were *Men and Women of the Corporation* (Basic Books, New York, 1977) and *The Change Masters* (Simon & Schuster, New York, 1983, also published by Allen & Unwin, London, 1984).

3566
Kay, John
Foundations of Corporate Success: How business strategies add value
1993 Oxford University Press *Oxford*

This is an influential British response to the competitive advantage concepts of Michael Porter (qv). Measuring corporate success by added value, Kay argues that corporate strategy should aim at developing key organizational capabilities: innovation; reputation (eg brands); strategic assets (eg monopoly); and 'architecture' (corporate links with employees, customers, suppliers). Arguments are supported by many contemporary corporate examples.

3567
Kennedy, Carol
Guide to the Management Gurus: Shortcuts to the ideas of leading management thinkers
1991 Business Books *London*

This is the best 'quick-fix' guide for business historians to twentieth-century management thinkers, covering 34 leading gurus.

3568
Kocka, Jürgen
Unternehmensverwaltung und Angestelltenschaft am Beispiel Siemens 1847–1914: Zum Verhältnis von Kapitalismus und Bürokratie in der deutschen Industrialisierung [Siemens: The administration of a business and its employees: Capitalism and bureaucracy during German industrialisation]
1969 Ernst Klett *Stuttgart, Germany*

Taking Siemens as his example, Kocka examines the changes necessary in employment and management in a massive and rapidly expanding business in the forefront of new technology.

Firms: Siemens & Halske

3569
Mintzberg, Henry
The Nature of Managerial Work
1973 Harper Business *New York, NY*

This book (also summarized in a *Harvard Business Review* article in 1975) was a pioneering study of how managers actually spend their time. Its conclusion that the spoken communication rather than the written one is critical to business decision-making poses interesting questions for archivally-based business historians.

3570
Mintzberg, Henry
Mintzberg on Management: Inside our strange world of organisations
1989 Free Press *New York, NY*

This book is a good sampler for business historians of a pre-eminent strategy theorist who has emphasized that management is a craft not a science.

3571
Morgan, Gareth
Images of Organisation
1986 Sage *Beverley Hills, CA*

This is a comprehensive survey of competing theories of managerial systems and organisational structure.

3572
Ohmae, Ken-ichi
Triad Power: The coming shape of global competition
1985 Free Press *New York, NY*

A classic exposition of international management from McKinsey's man in Tokyo is presented here.

3573
Ohmae, Ken-ichi
The Borderless World
1990 Harper Business *New York, NY*

This somewhat fanciful book by Ohmae about multinational brands, corporations, and managers may be a more accurate picture of the future than of the recent past which it selectively describes. The US–Japanese trade imbalance is stated to be an 'illusion created by accounting systems that are tragically out of date'.

3574
Peters, Thomas J.; Waterman, Robert H.
In Search of Excellence: Lessons from America's best-run companies
1982 Harper & Row *New York, NY*

Devoid of much systematic analysis, this was an influential work in generating the 'corporate culture' debate of the 1980s. Many of its exemplar firms later experienced serious difficulties.

3575
Political and Economic Planning (PEP)
Attitudes in British Management
1966 Penguin Books *Harmondsworth*

A much cited study of management and its failings in British industry, focusing on the wool textiles, shipbuilding, electronics, domestic appliances, earthmoving equipment, and machine-tool industries. Originally published as Anthony Gater et al, Thrusters and Sleepers, Allen and Unwin, 1965.

3576
Porter, Michael
Competitive Strategy: Techniques for analysing industries and competitors
1980 Free Press *New York, NY*

The work of probably the world's most influential business school strategy professor was rooted in the findings of industrial economics, though its analytical rigour was lightly worn in this exposition. Competitor analysis became extremely popular in the 1980s.

3577
Porter, Michael
Competitive Advantage: Creating and sustaining superior performance
1985 Free Press *New York, NY*

Porter's is a development of McKinsey's approach to business systems, emphasizing 'cost drivers' and niche advantages and their role in corporate success or failure. The assertion that being 'stuck in the middle' – concentrating neither on low cost nor product differentiation – is an unprofitable strategy has been questioned, but his 'value chain' analysis has been widely applauded as offering a basis for systematic work in corporate strategy formulation.

3578
Porter, Michael
The Competitive Advantage of Nations
1990 Macmillan *London*

Porter's book presents a challenging amalgam of deep but common-sense analysis and (in areas like the 'diamond' of national advantage) pseudo-science. While many conclusions have been challenged, this is a measure of the depth and interest of the book, as much as of its limitations. It is valuable in applying his views to numerous countries and industries.

3579
Porter, Michael E. (Editor)
Competition in Global Industries
1986 Harvard Business School Press *Boston, MA*
This collection of essays distils the thoughts of leading scholars on the impact of global competition on the modern corporation. It is comprehensive, and highly thought-provoking.

3580
Pralahad, C. K.; Hamel, G.
The core competence of the corporation
Harvard Business Review, vol. 68, no. 3, 1990: pp 79–91
This article contains an exposition by strategy theorists of concepts like organizational capability which have been stressed in work by business historians like Chandler and Lazonick (qqv).

3581
Pugh, D.; Hickson, D. J. (Editors)
Writers on Organisations
1990 Penguin *Harmondsworth*
This is a key book of readings by management gurus, now in a 4th edition.

3582
Quinn, J. B.; Mintzberg, H.; James, R. M.
The Strategy Process
1988 Prentice-Hall *Englewood Cliffs, NJ*
The best introduction to contemporary ideas on business strategy is presented here.

3583
Schendel, D. E.; Hofer, C. W. (Editors)
Strategic Management
1979 Little, Brown *New York, NY*
This is a good collection of essays from the 1970s on this subject.

3584
Schonberger, R. J.
World Class Manufacturing
1986 Free Press *New York, NY*
Schonberger's book is a study of manufacturing methods in America, Europe and Japan, which emphasizes what successful methods have in common rather than 'cultural' differences. It was extremely influential in companies like Hewlett Packard, to which Schonberger was a consultant.
Firms: Hewlett Packard

3585
Teece, D. J.
The Competitive Challenge: Strategies for industrial innovation and renewal
1987 Mosi Ballinger *New York, NY*
This is one of the best expositions of the role of appropriability problems, innovation and technology in the strategy process.

Country Studies (excluding Japan)

3586
Allen, G. C.
British Industries and Their Organization
4th Edition
1959 Longmans *London*
First published in 1933 and regularly updated, this gives a good introduction to industrial change in Britain's main industrial sectors after 1914.

3587
Amsden, Alice H.
Asia's Next Giant: South Korea and late industrialization
1989 Oxford University Press *Oxford*
A major study of the political economy of Korean industrialization which focuses in particular detail on the role of enterprise groups, the state and shopfloor relations in the auto, shipbuilding and steel industries.
Firms: Hyundai Motor; Hyundai Heavy Industries; Pohang Iron & Steel Co. (POSCO)

3588
Baudis, Dieter; Nussbaum, Helga
Wirtschaft und Staat in Deutschland Ende des 19.Jh. bis 1918/19 [Business and State in Germany]
1978 Akademie-Verlag *Berlin, Germany*
This book well illustrates the excellent empirical work that could be done under the generally stultifying intellectual conditions of Eastern Germany before reunification.

3589
Baughman, James P. (Editor)
The History of American Management: Selections from the Business History Review
For main entry, see 3544

3590
Buxton, Neil K.; Aldcroft, Derek H. (Editors)
British Industry Between the Wars: Instability and industrial development 1919–1939
1979 Scolar Press *London*
This multi-authored volume broke new ground in producing authoritative summaries of the experience of somewhat neglected British industrial sectors, i.e. mechanical engineering, electrical engineering, aircraft manufacturing and rayon, in addition to more familiar subjects, viz. cotton, coal, iron and steel, shipbuilding, chemicals, and motor manufacturing.

3591
Davila, Carlos
Historia Empresarial de Colombia: Estudios, Problems y Perspectivs [Colombian Business History: Issues, studies and perspectives]
1991 Monografías, 20, Faculted de Administración *Bogotá, Colombia*
This is a detailed survey of the Colombian business history literature. It is organized around eleven types of work. It emphasizes the small scale (over 300 works not limited to academic publications) and early development of this field. The heterogeneous quality of the works examined, the scarcity of scholarly company histories, the disproportionate representation of studies on the origins of regional entrepreneurship and the important role played by foreign researchers are some of the issues raised.

3592
Dertouzos, Michael L.; Lester, Richard K.; Solow, Robert M.
Made in America: Regaining the productive edge
1989 HarperCollins *New York, NY*
This is one of the MIT Commission on Industrial Productivity volumes, placing 1980s developments in world perspective.

3593
Dintenfass, Michael
The Decline of Industrial Britain 1870–1980
1992 Routledge *London*
This short book explores the reasons advanced for Britain's failure to employ resources as productively as other economies over the last 100 years. It provides primarily a 'business history' approach, with chapters on industrial techniques, labour skills, capital bias and entrepreneurial performance. The book is critical of British entrepreneurs and managers, but argues that much more work needs to be done. Use after consulting Wiener (qv).

3594
Elbaum, Bernard; Lazonick, William (Editors)
The Decline of the British Economy
1986 Oxford University Press *Oxford*
This collection of ten essays provides an extremely influential American contribution to the 'decline of Britain' debate. It is invaluable for business historians in provoking a response to the view that institutional failure lay at the root of Britain's difficulties. The book concentrates on circumstances in textiles, shipbuilding, steel, and motor manufacturing, but there are also useful chapters on broader issues such as the role of the state and industrial research.
Firms: Austin Motors; Bank of England; Bankers' Industrial Development Co.; British Leyland; British Thomson-Houston; Ford Motor Co.; ICI; Lancashire Cotton Corporation

3595
Foreman-Peck, James; Millward, Robert
Public and Private Ownership of British Industry 1820–1990
For main entry, see 4340

3596
Freedeman, Charles E.
The Triumph of Corporate Capitalism in France 1867–1914
1993 University of Rochester Press
Rochester, NY

A sequel to his earlier book, *Joint Stock Enterprise in France 1807–1867*, this work of meticulous scholarship describes the growth of sociétés anonymes, examines contemporary controversies over the efficiency of French capital markets and investment in French industry and discusses aspects of industrial concentration.

3597
Giroletti, Domingos
Industrialização de Juiz de Fora, 1850 a 1930 [The Industrialization of Juiz de Fora, 1850–1930]
1988 EDUFJF *Juiz de Fora, Brazil*

This book analyses the main factors (capital, labour, market and entrepreneurship) which brought about the industrialization of Juiz de Fora, from 1850 to 1930. Coffee production and the opening of the União e Indústria Road were crucial in making Juiz de Fora a commercial export entrepôt and an attractive area for industrial investment. Entrepreneurial skills came from German immigrants, Brazilian coffee producers and traders. The Juiz de Fora industrialization is compared with that of São Paulo.
Firms: Mineira Electricity Company; Real Credit Bank; União e Indústria Company

3598
Gutman, H. G.
Work, Culture and Society in Industrializing America: Essays on American working-class and social history
1976 Knopf *New York, NY*

This is a classic collection of essays on industrialising America, in the mould of E. P. Thompson.

3599
Hessen, Robert
In Defense of the Corporation
1979 Hoover Institution Press *Stanford, CA*

This seeks to provide a defence of the American corporation from its critics, specifically Berle and Means, Galbraith (qqv) and Nader.

3600
Horn, Norbert; Kocka, Jürgen (Editors)
Recht und Entwicklung der Grossunternehmen im 19. and frühen 20. Jahrhundert [Law and the Formation of the Big Enterprise in the Nineteenth and Twentieth Centuries]
1979 Vandenhoeck & Ruprecht *Göttingen, Germany*

This is a useful collection of essays in German, with English summaries, covering company law, mergers, cartels, public policy and other aspects of enterprise structure in a wide range of countries.

3601
Hughes, Jonathan R. T.
The Vital Few: The entrepreneur and American economic progress
For main entry, see 3843

3602
Janelli, Roger L.; Yim, Dawnlee
Making Capitalism: The social and cultural construction of a South Korean conglomerate
1993 Stanford University Press *Stanford, CA*

This is an anthropological study of a South Korean *chaebol* showing cultural influences on the Korean business system and management; this provides valuable insights into the Pacific rim economic miracle.

3603
Jobert, Philippe
Les Entreprises aux XIXe et XXe Siècles [Companies in the Nineteenth and Twentieth Centuries]
1991 Presses de L'École Normale Supérieure
Paris, France

This volume provides the definitive statistical compendium of French company statistics, including formations, bankruptcies, and financing.

3604
Johnson, Peter (Editor)
The Structure of British Industry
1988 Unwin Hyman *London*

This is the best industry-by-industry treatment since G. C. Allen's classic works.

3605
Jones, Geoffrey; Kirby, Maurice
Competitiveness and the State: Government and business in twentieth-century Britain
For main entry, see 4364

3606
Kocka, Jürgen
White Collar Workers in America 1890–1940: A socio-political history in international perspective
1980 Sage *London*

This is an English language translation of Kocka's important study (published in 1977 as *Angestellte zwischen Faschismus und Demokratie*). It provides a European perspective on the American lower-middle class, with information on employment, earnings, education and unionisation.

3607
Lee, W. R. (Editor)
German Industry and German Industrialisation: Essays in German economic and business history in the nineteenth and twentieth centuries
1991 Routledge *London*

A useful discussion of the 'German model' by the editor supplements this collection of interesting essays on topics as varied as tariffs, bank–industry links and political issues.

3608
Lefebvre-Teillard, Anne
La société anonyme au XIXe siècle [Limited Companies in the 19th Century]
1985 Presses Universitaires de France *Paris, France*

This is a detailed study, by an expert in the history of company law, on the status of limited companies in France, from Napoleon to the coming of free incorporation in 1867. Charles E. Freedeman (qv) has also written on French joint-stock companies 1807–1867.

3609
Levine, A. L.
Industrial Retardation in Britain 1880–1914
1967 Weidenfeld & Nicolson *London*

An early, but still valuable contribution to the debate on Britain's lag in developing the organizational and technological capabilities of the Second Industrial Revolution.

3610
Lévy-Leboyer, Maurice; Casanova, Jean-Claude (Editors)
Entre l'État et le Marché: L'Économie française des années 1880 à nos jours
1991 Gallimard *Paris, France*

This is a collective modern history of the French economy, which includes an excellent essay by M. Lévy-Leboyer on large enterprises, as well as contributions on banks, postwar industrial restructuring, and other topics.

3611
Lewis, S. R. Jr
Economic Policy and Industrial Growth in Pakistan
1969 George Allen & Unwin *London*

This is a neo-classical explanation of the study of the overall rate of growth and the pattern of the industrial investment in Pakistan. Lewis's hypothesis is that Pakistani industry commenced with a disequilibrium in her domestic production structure which was initially addressed by imposing import controls. However, the industrial structure remained inefficient in terms of world prices and any increase in value-added was a result of distortions in the price structure.

3612
McCraw, Thomas K. (Editor)
America vs. Japan: A comparative study
1986 Harvard Business School Press *Boston, MA*

McCraw presents a sector-by-sector analysis of differences between the economic organization of two leading industrial nations.

3613
Mintz, Beth; Schwartz, Michael
The Power Structure of American Business
1985 Chicago University Press *Chicago, IL*

A key contribution in the attempt to unravel the structure of power in American corporations via an analysis of inter-corporate relations and 'corporate interlocks' (overlapping directorates), with special reference to financial institutions.

3614
Mizruchi, Mark S.
The American Corporate Network, 1904–74
1982 Sage *Beverley Hills, CA*

Mizruchi presents a highly useful study of patterns created by interlocking directorships in the American business community, together with an analytical framework which business historians may employ in further research.

3615
Nadal, Jordi
Moler, tejer y fundir: Estudios de historia industrial [Milling, Weaving and Smelting: Studies in industrial history]
1992 Ariel *Barcelona, Spain*

This book is a compilation of several works already published by its author in the field of industrial history. It is very valuable for business historians because it includes various works related to firms and entrepreneurs in different Spanish industries and regions throughout the nineteenth century.

3616
Nussbaum, Manfred
Wirtschaft und Staat in Deutschlands Weimarer Republik [Business and State in the German Weimar Republic]
1978 Akademie-Verlag *Berlin, Germany*

An analysis of German business from eastern sources during the period of inflation and world economic crisis between 1919 and 1933.

3617
Papanek, Gustav F.
Pakistan's Development: Social goals and private incentives
1967 Harvard University Press *Cambridge, MA*

This is a study of government and private enterprise in Pakistan, pioneered by consultants from the Harvard Advisory group to the Planning Commission, Government of Pakistan in the 1960s. Papanek argues that Pakistan's development model articulated through its pioneering entrepreneurs in 1959, increased concentration of wealth [industrial assets] for seven families, while poverty, inequality and inefficiency afflicted overall industry.

3618
Papanek, Hanna
Pakistan's Big Businessmen, Muslim Separatism, Entrepreneurship and Partial Modernisation
Economic Development and Cultural Change, vol. 21, no. 1, 1972: pp 1–32

This is a detailed study of the background of leading Pakistani industrial families who emerged by the end of the 1950s. These industrial entrepreneurs were traders and members of the same religious sects or communities, and were directors of each other's companies. The influence of these industrial families extended beyond their companies and by the 1960s had converted their merchant capital into industrial capital.

3619
Payne, Leigh A.
Brazilian Industrialists and Democratic Change
1994 Johns Hopkins University Press *Baltimore, MD*

Payne re-examines the general view that business supports authoritarian rule to facilitate capitalist development and to repress popular protest. She suggests that business seeks above all a stable environment for investment and opportunities to make its voice heard. An interesting if not entirely persuasive work.

3620
Payne, Peter L. (Editor)
Studies in Scottish Business History
1967 Frank Cass *London*

An excellent collection of essays on Scottish business history. The first section covers sources, archives and bibliography. The second covers key Scottish industries including lead-mining, banking, herring fishing and coal and heavy engineering. The third section covers Scottish enterprise overseas.

Firms: Ben Line Steamers; William Denny & Bros; William Dixon; Fairfield Shipbuilding & Engineering Co.; Matador Land and Cattle Co.; Robert Napier & Sons; Racine & Mississippi

Railroad; Savings Bank of Glasgow; William Thomson & Co.; Western Bank of Scotland

3621
Pollard, Sidney
Britain's Prime and Britain's Decline: The British economy 1870–1914
1989 Edward Arnold *London*

This general economic history focuses on the state, science and capital exports. Its interest for business historians is its attempt to correct the argument that, industrially and technically, German business had forged ahead of Britain before the First World War.

3622
Pryke, Richard
Public Enterprise in Practice: The British experience of nationalization over two decades
1971 MacGibbon & Kee *London*

This study of British nationalized corporations produced evidence of an improvement of performance over the 1948–68 period, though the author later retracted some of his over-optimistic assessment.

3623
Rappaport, A.
Creating Shareholder Value: A new standard for business performance
1986 Free Press *New York, NY*

This is a mid-term report on the US takeover boom of the 1980s, and its impact on corporate strategy and structure. It reaffirmed the value of the 'Anglo-Saxon' approach to corporate finance at a time when more committed financial relationships in more successful economies than the US and UK were being held out by some as superior.

3624
Rungta, Radhe Shyam
Rise of Business Corporations in India, 1851–1900
1970 Cambridge University Press *Cambridge*

A study of the rise of modern business in India focused on the growth of joint-stock companies in cotton, tea, jute, coal and iron and steel. The development of the Calcutta and Bombay stock exchanges and the growth of company law in India are also examined, and the contribution of the managing agency is assessed.

Firms: East India Co.; Forbes & Co.; Greaves, Cotton & Co.; India General Steam Navigation Co.; Tata

3625
Safford, Frank
Aspectos del Siglo XIX en Colombia [Topics in Colombian Nineteenth Century History]
1977 Ediciones Hombre Nuevo *Medellín, Colombia*

This is a collection of the author's articles covering selected themes of Colombian business history in the nineteenth century. They deal with a comparison between national and foreign entrepreneurs, a critique of the application of the status-withdrawal thesis to Antioquia entrepreneurship, an account of study abroad as a means of forming a technical elite and a devastating critique on the first quantitative economic history of Colombia.

3626
Schatz, Sayre P.
Nigerian Capitalism
1977 University of California Press *Berkeley, CA*

This is an interesting and insightful survey of Nigeria's business history from 1949 to the mid 1970s, with chapters on capital, entrepreneurship, the economic environment, and political intervention. There are also specific references to oil, construction, and the Yaba Industrial Estate.

3627
Schmitz, Christopher J.
The Growth of Big Business in the United States and Western Europe, 1850–1939
1993 Macmillan *London*

This is a fine bibliographical survey of internationally comparative business history in the period, providing a useful corrective to Chandler on the relative position of Britain and Germany (and in a smaller way France and Italy).

3628
Schröter, Verena
Die deutsche Industrie auf dem Weltmarkt: Außen wirtschaftliche Strategien unter dem

Druck der Weltwirtschaftskrise 1929–1933 [German Industry in World Markets]
1984 P. Lang *Frankfurt am Main, Germany*
Examining major German firms during the world economic crisis 1929–33, this book explains attitudes of big business and government towards foreign markets. This is an interesting study of international cartelization as a tool to enhance competitiveness.
Firms: AEG; Demag; IG Farben; Siemens; Zeiss

3629
Scott, Bruce R.; Lodge, George C. (Editors)
US Competitiveness in the World Economy
1985 Harvard Business School Press *Boston, MA*
Although very much a book of its time, full of overdrawn notions of the difference between Asian and European business competition, this conference volume nonetheless contains much useful material on the nature of organizational and technological capability in the competitiveness of nations.

3630
Short, Adam; Doughty, Sir Arthur G. (Editors)
Canada and its Provinces
1913–17 Edinburgh University Press *Edinburgh, Scotland*
This comprises a twenty-three volume survey of all aspects of Canadian economic development. Although some of the articles are outdated, this set remains an invaluable reference which should not be overlooked. Volumes IX and X are devoted to industrial development in Canada after 1867 and the last volume of the series presents a chronology and a bibliography as well as the general index.

3631
Suzigan, W.
Industria brasileira: origem e desenvolvimento [Brazilian Industry Origins and development]
1986 Brasiliense *São Paulo, Brazil*
Based on the data on exports of machinery from Great Britain, France, Germany and the USA to Brazil in the period 1855–1939, this work analyses the nature of industrial development in Brazil between the middle of the nineteenth century and the end of the 1930s. The author gives special emphasis to the process of capital formation in industry.

3632
Suzuki, Yoshitaka; Abe, Etsuo; Yonekura, Seiichiro
Keiei-shi [Business History]
1987 Yuhikaku *Tokyo, Japan*
This book gives an outline of the evolution of modern corporate business in the USA from the 1880s to 1950s, in the UK from the 1840s to 1960s, and in Japan from the period of the First World War to the 1960s in comparative perspective.

3633
Thoms, David
War Industry and Society: The Midlands 1939–1945
1989 Routledge *London*
This is a useful study of a British region, covering the preparations for war, and the organisation of industry during hostilities. It contains an interesting account of labour's reactions to bombing.

3634
Turner, Graham
Business in Britain
1969 Eyre & Spottiswoode *London*
This is a provocative, idiosyncratic but indispensable account of British businessmen in variety of sectors. The book begins with a survey of the business environment from 1870, then provides very useful sketches on large-scale business, nationalised industries, family firms, and a variety of issues.
Firms: Bass Charrington; British Aircraft Corporation; British Leyland/British Motor Corporation; British Railways Board; Cadbury; Courtaulds; Electricity Council; Guest, Keen and Nettlefolds; IBM; ICI

3635
White, Lawrence J.
Industrial Concentration and Economic Power in Pakistan
1974 Princeton University Press *Princeton, NJ*
White traces the origins and effects of

concentration of wealth by leading Pakistani industrial families from 1962 to 1968. He aligns the magnitude of the business groups' net manufacturing assets with the extent of their economic power and influence. He shows that in 1968 of the 197 firms quoted on the Karachi Stock Exchange, 43 leading industrial families owned and controlled 53 percent of the net manufacturing assets of these firms.

3636

Wilkins, Mira

The History of Foreign Investment in the United States to 1914

1989 Harvard University Press *Cambridge, MA*

This is the first of two planned books on the subject, with the second on post-1914 due shortly. The same meticulous and comprehensive approach that Professor Wilkins showed in studying American business abroad makes this the third of her truly classic works which will be of abiding value.

3637

Wilkins, Mira; Hill, Frank Ernest

American Business Abroad: Ford on six continents

For main entry, see 989

3638

Williams, Karel; Williams, John; Thomas, Dennis

Why are the British Bad at Manufacturing?

1983 Routledge *London*

Examining the interactions of the enterprise with labour, government, the market and financiers, this book reached pessimistic conclusions about the causes and nature of Britain's 'de-industrialization'.

Firms: GEC; British Leyland

3639

Zumpe, Lotte

Wirtschaft und Staat in Deutschland 1933 bis 1945 [Business and State in Germany from 1933 to 1945]

1979 Akademie-Verlag *Berlin, Germany*

While suffering from the usual oversimplification of Marxist writings on the Nazi period, this work provides a useful corrective to the silence on the period by writers like Chandler.

Country Studies, Japan

3640

Abegglen, James; Stalk, George

Kaisha. The Japanese Corporation: The new competitors in world business

1985 Basic Books *New York, NY*

An extremely influential account of Japanese corporate strategiés by a renowned academic and a management consultant. The authors consider industrial structure, productive organization and relationships with banks to describe a model of Japanese superiority. A strong historical perspective is evident.

Firms: Bridgestone; Hitachi; Honda; Matsushita; NEC; Nissan; Sony; Toyota; Yanmar Diesel

3641

Allen, G. C.

Japanese Industry: Its recent development and present condition

1940 Institute of Pacific Relations *New York, NY*

Part of an inquiry into the problems facing Japanese industry as a result of the Sino-Japanese war, this book provides a useful, early assessment in English of industrial development, including technical progress.

3642

Aoki, Masahiko (Editor)

The Economic Analysis of the Japanese Firm

For main entry, see 3477

3643

Aoki, Masahiko; Dore, Ronald (Editors)

The Japanese Firm: Sources of competitive strength

For main entry, see 3478

3644

Bartholomew, James

The Formation of Science in Japan: Building a research tradition

1989 Yale University Press *New Haven, CT*

A remarkable study of the evolution of Japanese science from the Tokugawa period to the 1920s stressing that, although the Japanese often built scientific capability by importing foreign knowledge, they also promoted and generously funded domestic research, particulary in medicine.

3645
Broadbridge, Seymour
Industrial Dualism in Japan: A problem of economic growth and structural change
1966 Frank Cass *London*

Although somewhat dated, this is still a useful account of the evolution of economic dualism in Japan and the origins and shaping of subcontracting systems.

3646
Calder, Kent E.
Strategic Capitalism: Private business and public purpose in Japanese industrial finance
For main entry, see 2569

3647
Chokki, Toshiaki
Nippon no Kigyo Keiei [Japanese Business Management: A historical description]
1992 Hosei Daigaku Shuppan-kyoku *Tokyo, Japan*

A wide-ranging Japanese business management history covering the period 1880s to 1980s which includes entrepreneurial activities, strategy and structure, production management, research and development and the internationalization of Japanese business.

3648
Clark, Rodney
The Japanese Company
1979 Yale University Press *New Haven, CT*

Written by a former merchant banker, this is a penetrating scholarly analysis of the social and organizational structure of the Japanese corporation.

3649
Cole, Robert
Japanese Blue-Collar
1971 University of California Press *Berkeley, CA*

A pioneering analysis of Japanese factory workers, focusing on the employment system, job security and corporate paternalism, especially in the auto parts sector.
Firms: Gujo Auto Parts Co.; Takei Diecast Co.

3650
Cole, Robert
Work, Mobility and Participation: A comparative study of Japanese and American industry
1979 University of California Press *Berkeley, CA*

An important comparative study of American and Japanese industry, focusing on job mobility, the relationship between employer and employee in Detroit and Yokohama. Includes a detailed case study of Toyota Auto Body.
Firms: Toyota

3651
Dore, Ronald
British Factory - Japanese Factory
1973 Allen & Unwin *London*

A seminal work comparing and contrasting the workings of a British and a Japanese electrical manufacturer. Dore's work is not only careful and analytic but also captures the feel of the crucial difference in management styles, corporate culture, and union-management relations.
Firms: Hitachi; General Electric Co.

3652
Fruin, W. Mark
The Japanese Enterprise System: Competitive strategies and cooperative structures
1992 Clarendon Press *Oxford*

Inspired by his mentor, Alfred Chandler, Fruin provides a major, multifaceted study (in English) of the Japanese corporation in the twentieth century, and these are some Chandleresque listings of the top 200 Japanese firms. Focusing on the importance of the Japanese environment, inter-firm and supplier networks, and management at several levels, the author is able to show how Japanese firms are smaller,

less diversified and less multidivisional than in the 'Chandler model'.
Firms: General Electric; General Motors; Hitachi; Mitsubishi; Tokyo Electric Co.; Toshiba Group; Toyoda Group; Toyota Motor Corporation

3653
Fujii, Mitsuo; Maruyama, Yoshinari (Editors)
Gendai Nippon Keiei-shi: Nippon-teki Keiei to Kigyo Shakai [Modern Japanese Business History: Japanese-style management and corporate society]
1991 Mineruva Shobo *Kyoto, Japan*
A wide-ranging Japanese business history covering the period 1850s to 1980s which includes the development of prewar Zaibatsu, the formation of postwar business groups, labour management in big business, the general trading companies, the subcontracting system and so on.

3654
Gerlach, Michael
Alliance Capitalism: The social organization of Japanese business
1992 University of California Press *Berkeley, CA*
The most systematic attempt to date to evaluate the internal workings of keiretsu organizations in Japan. Based on a dense statistical analysis of these enterprise groups, Gerlach shows the difficulty of making categorical judgements about the workings of these groups. He exposes numerous myths about these intercorporate alliances and points the way for further research.
Firms: Dai-Ichi Kangyo Bank; Mitsubishi Group; Mitsui Group; Sanwa Bank; Sumitomo Group

3655
Hadley, Eleanor M.
Antitrust in Japan
For main entry, see 4347

3656
Hirschmeier, Johannes; Yui, Tsunehiko
The Development of Japanese Business, 1600–1980
1981 George Allen & Unwin *London*
The approach of this classic outline of Japanese business history is now considered somewhat dated and unsophisticated in its theoretical interpretation. Nonetheless it remains a useful summary of factual information about Japanese businesses.

3657
Holding Company Liquidation Committee (Editor)
Nippon Zaibatsu to sono Kaitai [Japanese Zaibatsu and their Dissolution]
1951 Holding Company Liquidation Committee *Tokyo, Japan*
An authoritative book on the dissolution of Japanese Zaibatsu after the Second World War. It provides detailed information on the changing activities of Zaibatsu in wartime and on the dissolution process after the war.

3658
Johnson, Chalmers; Tyson, Laura; Zysman, John (Editors)
Politics and Productivity: How Japan's development strategy works
1989 Ballinger *New York, NY*
An important collection of essays focused on Japanese industrial organization (keiretsus) and business–government relations by a leading group of American economists and political scientists.
Firms: NTT; Nippon Aircraft Manufacturing Co.

3659
Kanno, Wataro
Nippon Kaisha Kigyo Hassei-shi no Kenkyu [History of the Development of Companies in Japan]
1971 Keizai Hyoron-sha *Tokyo, Japan*
This is a pioneering study of the evolutionary origin of 'Kaisha' in Japan just after the Meiji Restoration of 1868. The author reviews the continuities and discontinuities between mercantile capital in the Edo period and corporate capital after the Meiji Restoration, and the origins of entrepreneurship.

3660
Koike, Kazuo
Understanding Industrial Relations in Modern Japan
1988 Macmillan *London*
A crucial work, interpreting the Japanese employment system and contrasting it with American practices. Often dense and difficult, but the essential starting point for understanding the operation of lifetime employment, seniority wage systems etc.

3661
Komiya, Ryutaro; Okuna, Masahiro; Suzumura, Kotaro (Editors)
Industrial Policy of Japan
For main entry, see 4368

3662
McMillan, Charles J.
The Japanese Industrial System
1985 de Gruyter *New York, NY*
A detailed study of Japanese management and industrial organization. Despite its use of the label 'samurai management', it is generally a fairly careful and accurate study.

3663
Miyamoto, Mataji
Kabu Nakama no Kenkyui [A Study of 'Kabu Nakama' (the Japanese Guild)]
1938 Yuhikaku *Tokyo, Japan*
This is an excellent study of 'Kabu Nakama' (the Japanese guild) in the feudal age. The author reviews Kabu Nakama's evolutionary origin, its structural features, its function and its dissolution process.

3664
Miyamoto, Mataji (Editor)
Edo Jidai no Kigyo-sha Katsudo: Nippon Keiei-shi Koza, Vol. 1 [Entrepreneurial Activities in the Edo Period: Japanese Business History Series, Vol. 1.]
1977 Nippon Keizai Shinbun-sha *Tokyo, Japan*
A wide-ranging business history in the Edo Period (1603–1867). There are chapters on merchants as managers, urban growth and markets, the accumulation of capital by merchants, intellectual developments, the social value system and bureacracy, the 'Ie' and Japanese modernization and the 'Kabu Nakama'.

3665
Morikawa, Hidemasa (Editor)
Keiei-sha Kigyo no Jidai [The Age of Managerial Enterprise]
1991 Yuhikaku *Tokyo, Japan*
This book is a collection of 10 papers written by Japanese business historians who celebrate Professor Morikawa's 60th birthday. The points at issue common to all writers are the development of managerial enterprise and the relationship between salaried managers and owners.

3666
Nakagawa, Keiichiro (Editor)
Kigyo Keiei no Rekishi-teki Kenkyu [A Historical Study of Business Management]
1990 Iwanami Shoten *Tokyo, Japan*
This book is a collection of 20 papers written by Japanese business historians who celebrate Professor Yoshitaro Wakimura's 90th birthday. Each paper treats wide-ranging issues such as Japanese management, comparative management, the international perspective on business management and the shipping and shipbuilding industries.

3667
Nakamura, Hideichiro; Akiya, Shigeo; Kiyonari, Tadao; Yamazaki, Mitshuru; Bando, Teruo
Gendai Chusho Kigyo-shi [A History of Modern Small and Medium-sized Enterprises]
1981 Nippon Keizai Shinbun-sha *Tokyo, Japan*
Covering the period 1945 to 1970s, this work describes the growth and development of small and medium-sized venture business in Japan taking account of the changes in policies and surroundings.

3668
Nester, William R.
Japanese Industrial Targeting: The neomercantilist path to economic superpower
1991 Macmillan *London*
Argues that Japan's economic success has stemmed from a dedicated pursuit of neomer-

cantilist policies including subsidies, sponsored cartels, import barriers and export incentives. The argument is based around case studies of agriculture, distribution, banking, steel, machine tools, cars, energy, computers, semiconductors and telecommunications. Despite its polemic aims it still contains much that is useful and interesting.

3669
Noda, Nobuo
Nippon Kindai Keiei-shi: Sono Shi-teki Bunseki [A Historical Analysis of Modern Japanese Management]
1988 Sangyo Noritsu Daigaku Shuppan-bu *Tokyo, Japan*

A wide-ranging history of Japanese business management covering the period from the Meiji Restoration to 1980s. This includes the development of Zaibatsu, the office and factory management system, business ideology, and marketing.

3670
Odagiri, Hiroyuki
Growth Through Competition, Competition Through Growth: Strategic management and the economy in Japan
1992 Clarendon Press *Oxford*

Odagiri analyses the Japanese economy in terms which are readily understandable to a student of western competitive corporate capitalism, but which emphasises the different Japanese approach to the human side of the firm.

3671
Pascale, R. T.; Athos, A. G.
The Art of Japanese Management
1981 Simon & Schuster *New York, NY*

Comparing the style of Konosuke Matsushita at Matsushita Electric and Harold Geneen at ITT, this book shaped the US debate on Japanese management culture in the 1980s.
Firms: ITT; Matsushita

3672
Patrick, Hugh (Editor)
Japanese Industrialization and Its Social Consequences
1976 University of California Press *Berkeley, CA*

Like Patrick and Rosovsky (qv) this is a collection of high-quality academic essays attempting to understand how Japan had emerged so suddenly as a leading global competitor. Still invaluable.

3673
Patrick, Hugh; Rosovsky, H. (Editors)
Asia's New Giant
1976 Brookings Institution *Washington, DC*

A much cited collection of papers covering all aspects of Japanese economic development. Although written in the 1970s, many of the articles are still widely used.

3674
Sakudo, Yotaro; Mishima, Yasuo; Yasuoka, Shigeaki; Inoue, Yoichiro
Nippon Keiei-shi [Japanese Business History]
1980 Mineruva Shobo *Kyoto, Japan*

Following introductory remarks on the development of academic approaches to business history, this book gives an outline of Japanese business history from the sixteenth century to the 1960s. A chronological table of Japanese business history from 1590 to 1978 is included at the end of the book.

3675
Sato, Kazuo; Hoshino, Yasuo (Editors)
The Anatomy of Japanese Business
1984 M. E. Sharpe Inc. *New York, NY*

A collection of essays reprinted from *Japanese Economic Studies* concerned with management, business groups, production systems and strategy.
Firms: Mitsubishi; Toyota; Fuji Xerox

3676
Shibagaki, Kazuo
Nippon Kin'yu Shihon Bunseki [An Analysis of Japanese Financial Capital]
1965 Tokyo Daigaku Shuppan-kai *Tokyo, Japan*

An excellent research work on Japanese oligopolistic capital for the affiliated businesses of prewar Zaibatsu on the cotton spinning industry which was outside the Zaibatsu. Though the framework is based on the theory of economic development stages rather than the perspective of entrepreneurial of management history, the work analyses minutely the financial structure of the prewar business groups.

3677
Shimotani, Masahiro (Editor)
Senji Keizai to Nippon Kigyo [The Wartime Economy and Japanese Companies]
1990 Showa-do *Kyoto, Japan*

This book treats of the actual situation of Japanese companies under the wartime economy through case studies of the special steel industry, chemical industry, manufacture of communications equipment, cotton spinning, coal mining and the electric power companies.

3678
Society for the Study of Postwar Japanese Management
Sengo Nippon no Kigyo Keiei: 'Min-shu-ka', 'Gouri-ka' kara 'Joho-ka', 'Kokusai-ka' e [Business Management in Postwar Japan: From the age of 'democratization' and 'Rationalization' to the age of 'Information-oriented' and 'Internationalization']
1991 Bunshindo *Tokyo, Japan*

A wide-ranging postwar Japanese business history covering the period 1945 to the 1980s which includes the tax system, the financial system, budget control, production management, labour management, computerization, distribution policy and the internationalization of business.

3679
Suzuki, Yoshitaka
Japanese Management Structures 1920–1980
1991 Macmillan *London*

This is a study of the management of the largest 100 Japanese industrial corporations. While rather weak on interpretation, this is a convenient round-up of facts about changes in management resources, diversification, mergers and ownership relations in large Japanese corporations. In particular it isolates fundamental divergences from the Anglo-Saxon model.

Firms: Hitachi Group; Isuzu Motors; Matsushita Electric Industrial; Mitsubishi Group; Mitsui Group; Nissan Motor; Sumitomo Group; Toyota Motor

3680
Tsuchiya, Moriaki; Morikawa, Hidemasa (Editors)
Kigyo-sha Katsudo no Shi-teki Kenkyu [A Historical Study of Entrepreneurial Activities]
1981 Nippon Keizai Shinbun-sha *Tokyo, Japan*

This book is a collection of 19 papers written by Japanese and foreign business historians to celebrate Professor Nakagawa's 60th birthday. Following an introductory paper by Professor Nakagawa, 9 papers deal with Japanese business history and 9 papers foreign or international business history.

3681
Tsuru, Shigeto
Japan's Capitalism: Creative defeat and beyond
1993 Cambridge University Press *Cambridge*

Tsuru examines Japan's progress since 1945, the regeneration of Japanese capitalism, the shift to high-added-value technological production, high investment and productivity. He considers the effects of the oil price shocks and the long-term effect of rocketing urban land prices for the future of Japan and the world economy.

3682
Vestal, James
Planning for Change: Industrial policy and Japanese economic development, 1945–1990
1993 Clarendon Press *Oxford*

With its emphasis on the dominant role of the state in the Japanese economic miracle, this book has a slightly dated air. Nevertheless, it is a useful overview of certain aspects, particularly of government relations with heavy industry.

3683
Vogel, Ezra F.
Japan as Number One: Lessons for America
1979 Harper & Row *New York, NY*

One of the most famous and influential analyses of the rise of Japan and its threat to the American system. It was a best-seller in Japan as well as the USA. Despite its popular reputation it is actually intelligent and relatively cautious.

3684
Wolferen, Karel Van
The Enigma of Japanese Power
1989 Basic Books *New York, NY*

An important and controversial attempt to challenge the arguments of Chalmers Johnson (qv) and to argue that far from a coherent organizing state, the Japanese state system has been characterized by a mass of conflicting interests that has vitiated any real control.

3685
Wray, William (Editor)
Managing Industrial Enterprise: Cases from Japan's pre-War experience
1989 Harvard University Press *Cambridge, MA*

Nine fine essays in Japanese business history by leading scholars. They cover the rise of salaried managers, the business lobby, early industrialization in key sectors, colonial investment and an extensive overview of Japanese business history by Wray himself.
Firms: Tomioka Filature; Japan National Railway; Mitsubishi; NYK; Nitchitsu; OSK; Riken Industrial Group

3686
Yasuoka, Shigeaki; Fujita, Teiichiro; Ishikawa, Kenjiro
Oumi Shonin no Keiei Isan: Sono Sai-hyoka [The Managerial Inheritance from 'Oumi' Merchants A reassessment]
1992 Dobunkan *Tokyo, Japan*

This work reviews the activities of 'Oumi' Merchants with particular focus on managerial inheritance from 'Oumi' Merchants including personnel management, business ideology, and entrepreneurship.

3687
Yonekawa, Shin'ichi (Editor)
Sekai no Zaibatsu Keiei [Management of Large Family Business in a World Context]
1981 Nippon Keizai Shinbun-sha *Tokyo, Japan*

This comprehensive work includes 10 papers on big family business in industrially advanced countries such as the UK, France, Germany and the USA and in developing countries like India, the Philippines, Korea, Brazil and Argentina.

3688
Yonekawa, Shin'ichi; Shimokawa, Koichi; Yamazaki, Hiroaki (Editors)
Sengo Nippon Keiei-shi; Dai Nikan [Postwar Japanese Business History, Vol II]
1990 Toyo Keizai Shinpo-sha *Tokyo, Japan*

This book draws the development and restructuring of the electrical mahine industry, the automobile industry, the machine tool industry, the petroleum industry, the petrochemical industry and the electric power industry.

3689
Yonekawa, Shin'ichi; Shimokawa, Koichi; Yamazaki, Hiroaki (Editors)
Sengo Nippon Keiei-shi; Dai Ikkan [Postwar Japanese Business History, Vol. 1]
1991 Toyo Keizai Shinpo-sha *Tokyo, Japan*

Following the review of change in the bigger 50 companies in net profit before and after the Second World War, this work describes the development and restructuring of the cotton spinning industry, the synthetic fibres industry, the shipbuilding industry, and the iron and steel industry.

3690
Yonekawa, Shin'ichi; Shimokawa, Koichi; Yamazaki, Hiroaki (Editors)
Sengo Nippon Keiei-shi; Vol. III [Postwar Japanese Business History, Vol. III]
1991 Toyo Keizai Shinpo-sha *Tokyo, Japan*

This book describes the development and restructuring of the distribution industry, the banking business, trading companies, and shipping and foreign-run industry. In the last chapter of the volume, the editors give an outline of various approaches to postwar Japanese business history.

3691
Yui, Tsunehiko (Editor)
Kogyo-ka to Kigyo-sha Katsudo: Nippon Keiei-shi Koza. Vol. 2 [Industrialization and

Entrepreneurial Activities: Japanese Business . History Series, Vol. 2]
1976 Nippon Keizai Shinbun-sha *Tokyo, Japan*

A wide-ranging entrepreneurial history in the early years of the Meiji Era (1868–1912). There are chapters on Tomoatsu Godai, the disposal of government-run business, the capital of noblemen, management by descendants of samurai, modern industrial technologies, corporation law and accounting.

3692
Yuzawa, Takeshi (Editor)
Japanese Business Success: The evolution of a strategy
1994 Routledge *London*

A useful collection of case studies of Japanese companies, focused on individual enterprises rather than the Japanese system as a whole. It is organized in three parts: High-Tech; Traditional; and Service industries.
Firms: Toyota; Fuji Denki; Fujitsu; Fanuc; Canon; Toray; NKK; IHI; Idemitsu Kosan; Kubota Ironworks

Entrepreneurship and Management

Entrepreneurship - General

3693
Azrael, Jeremy
Managerial Power and Soviet Politics
1966 Harvard University Press *Cambridge, MA*

Azrael studies the political role of technical managers (non apparatchiki) over the course of Soviet history, showing how they were transformed by Stalin into political conservatives with little managerial independence.

3694
Birchal, S. O.
Entrepreneurship and the Formation of a Business Environment in XIXth-Century Brazil Century Brazil: The case of Minas Gerais
1994, PhD thesis, University of London

This unpublished thesis examines the formation of businesses in nineteenth-century Minas Gerais, Brazil. It investigates the social origins of entrepreneurs and the source of their capital; the structural development of firms; the process of technology transfer; the dependence of various firms on foreign knowledge; and the limits to the development of indigenous technology; and the capital–labour relation and the formation of the labour market in Minas Gerais.
Firms: Companhia Mineira de Eletricidade; Companhia Força e Luz Cataguazes-Leopoldina; Companhia Têxtil Cachoeira de Macacos; Companhia União e Indústria; Companhia de Fiaçao Tecidos Cedro e Cachoeira; Companhia de Tecidos Santanense; Sociedade Anönima Industrial Machadense

3695
Bliss, Michael
Northern Enterprise: Five centuries of Canadian business
For main entry, see 3437

3696
Brading, D. A.
Miners and Merchants in Bourbon Mexico, 1763–1810
1971 Cambridge University Press *Cambridge*

This highly detailed examination of the last half century of Spanish rule in Mexico includes a large section on the roles of miners and merchants, examining their social structure and mobility and their function as suppliers of capital.

3697
Broehl, Wayne G. Jr
The Village Entrepreneur: Change agents in India's rural development
1978 Harvard University Press *Cambridge, MA*

This book is a discussion of the nature of entrepreneurship in fertiliser distribution and rice milling, which is strong on theoretical, if not factual, content.

3698
Brown, Jonathan; Rose, Mary B. (Editors)
Entrepreneurship, Networks and Modern Business
For main entry, see 3385

3699
Casson, Mark
The Entrepreneur: An economic theory
1982 Martin Robertson *Oxford*

Casson's book gives a diffuse treatment of the subject but is useful for its survey of the theoretical literature.

3700
Casson, Mark (Editor)
Entrepreneurship
1990 Edward Elgar Publishing *Aldershot*

This volume reprints 34 articles, most coming from the economics literature, dealing with economic theory and empirical evidence, but also some treating cultural dimensions.

Authors include J. S. Mill, Schumpeter, Kirzner and many more. Themes include risk, market process, innovation, the entrepreneur and the firm, personality and motivation, immigration and social mobility: a useful pot-pourri.

3701

Chandler, Alfred D. Jr

Strategy and Structure: Chapters in the history of the American industrial enterprise

1962 MIT Press *Cambridge, MA*

In this volume Chandler first developed some of his unifying ideas about the development of big business organization. Using case studies of Du Pont, General Motors, Standard Oil, Sears Roebuck, he argued that strategy formation, in the hands of managerial hierarchies, preceded structural change. The multidivisional structure, he concluded, was the most sophisticated structure to emerge.

Firms: Du Pont; General Motors; Sears, Roebuck; Standard Oil

3702

Chandler, Alfred D. Jr

The Visible Hand: The managerial revolution in American business

1977 Harvard University Press *Cambridge, MA*

In this classic (and Pulitzer-Prize-winning) magnum opus, Chandler reinterpreted the rise of big business in the USA in terms of ideas first explored in his *Strategy and Structure* (qv). To those he explicitly added the concept of transaction costs (derived from Coase and Williamson) as the economic mechanism underpinning the organization-building power of managerial hierarchies.

3703

Chandler, Alfred D. Jr

Scale and Scope: The dynamics of industrial capitalism

1990 Harvard University Press *Cambridge, MA*

In content and concept Chandler once again, but perhaps less convincingly, extends his earlier work (qqv). In content he here compares the USA, Britain and Germany, arguing that they, respectively, produced competitive managerial capitalism, personal capitalism and co-operative managerial capitalism. In concept he adds the idea of scope (emphasized by Michael Porter, qv) to his analytical toolbag.

3704

Chartres, John; Honeyman, Katrina (Editors)

Leeds City Business: Essays marking the centenary of the incorporation

1993 Leeds University Press *Leeds*

A compilation of eight company histories assembled by the Leeds Centre for Business History to mark the centenary of Leeds's incorporation. There are useful insights into business strategy, investment, profitability and entrepreneurship for major firms in sectors including the press, building societies, brewing, soapmaking, printing and retailing.

Firms: Montague Burton; Leeds Permanent Building Society; Joshua Tetley & Son; Chas F. Thackray; John Waddington; Joseph Watson; Yorkshire Post Newspapers

3705

Davenport-Hines, R. P. T. (Editor)

Markets and Bagmen: Studies in the history of marketing and British industrial performance 1830–1939

For main entry, see 2030

3706

Davenport-Hines, R. P. T.; Jones, Geoffrey (Editors)

Entrepreneurship, Management and Innovation in British Business 1914–1980

1988 Frank Cass *London*

This is another example of the familiar Cass book-from-journal device, an alternative printing of the October 1987 issue of *Business History*. However, on this occasion the decision has its merits since it gathers together important essays commissioned by the editors as a response to the assertion advanced by Donald Coleman in his 'uses and abuses' lecture (qv) that there should be more comparative and analytical work in business history. Contributors were asked to base their work on a 'basket' of company histories, and the topics covered range from business success and failure, organisation and management to consumer marketing and science and technology.

Firms: Bowater; British Electricity Authority; British Railways Board; Central Electricity Board; Colvilles; Courtaulds; Harland & Wolff; ICI; Kenricks; Midland Bank

3707
Davila, Carlos
El Empresariado Colombiano: Una Perspectiva Histórica [Colombian Entrepreneurship: A historical approach]
1986 Universidad Javeriana *Bogotá, Colombia*

This book has two associated themes. The first analyses the role, economic diversification and relationship with the State of eight leading Colombian entrepreneurs in two regions, at the end of the nineteenth century. The second critically reviews competing interpretations of Antioqueño's entrepreneurship. Both rely for the most part on secondary sources.

3708
Diamond, Sigmund
The Reputation of American Businessmen
1955 Harvard University Press *Cambridge, MA*

This fascinating study examines the obituaries of six leading executives in order to discover how the American public perceived their capitalist heroes. Those studied are Stephen Girard (d. 1831), John Jacob Astor (d. 1848), Cornelius Vanderbilt (d. 1877), J. P. Morgan (d. 1913), John D. Rockefeller (d. 1937) and Henry Ford (d. 1947).

3709
Gordon, Robert Aaron
Business Leadership in the Large Corporation
2nd Edition
1961 University of California Press/Brookings Institution *Berkeley, CA*

This classic study of leadership in the largest US corporations examines leadership in relation to what are now called 'stakeholders'.

3710
Hao, Yen'ping
The Comprador in Nineteenth Century China: Bridge between East and West
1970 Harvard University Press *Cambridge, MA*

This is the first book in English to deal comprehensively with the comprador (local agent) system. The first half describes the origins and development of the system; the second half considers the wider roles of the comprador, as manager, entrepreneur and facilitator of industrialization, and also non-economic aspects.

3711
Harvey, Charles E.; Press, Jon (Editors)
Studies in the Business History of Bristol
1988 Bristol Academic Press *Bristol*

This is an elegantly produced set of essays on the business history of Bristol since 1800. It not only contains useful case studies of leading firms, ranging from aeroplane manufacture to brewing, locomotive-building to footwear, and chocolate to banking, but provides insights into the changing economic fortunes of one of Britain's major cities and its sense of 'business community'.
Firms: Avonside Engine Co.; Bristol Aeroplane Co.; Bristol Tramways Co. (Bristol Tramways & Carriage Co.); Bristol & West Building Society; G. B. Britton & Sons; Fox, Walker & Co.; J. S. Fry & Sons; Georges & Co. (Bristol Brewery Georges); Great Western Railway; E. S. & A. Robinson

3712
Lévy-Leboyer, Maurice (Editor)
Le Patronat de la Seconde Industrialisation [The Employers of the Second Industrialization]
For main entry, see 3849

3713
Mant, Alistair
Leaders We Deserve
1983 Martin Robertson *Oxford*

Mant argues that the exploitative leader (who seeks to dominate others purely in order to achieve his/her personal survival) will be less successful than leaders who bring task and vision into the leaders-led relationship.

3714
Marriner, Sheila (Editor)
Business and Businessmen: Studies in business, economic and accounting history
1978 Liverpool University Press *Liverpool*

This is a festschrift in honour of Francis

Hyde, one of the pioneers of business history in post-war Britain and the first editor of *Business History*. The contributions range widely from Allen on industrial policy and economic performance in Britain and Japan to Mathias on 'Dr Johnson and the Business World'. There are also useful essays on France, by Crouzet on engineers and Harris on technology transfer.
Firms: Union Marine Insurance; Great Eastern Railway; Compagnie de Fives-Lille; Distillers Co.; Elder Dempster & Co.; Royal Mail Group

3715
McKay, John P.
Pioneers for Profit: Foreign entrepreneurship and Russian industrialization, 1885–1913
1970 Chicago University Press *Chicago, IL*

Though neglectful of the macro-dynamics of industrialization, this study carefully analyses the roles of French and Belgian banks and industrial firms in transferring western European technology, managerial experience and capital resources to Imperial Russia.

3716
McKendrick, Neil; Outhwaite, R. B. (Editors)
Business Life and Public Policy: Essays in honour of D. C. Coleman
1986 Cambridge University Press *Cambridge*

Unlike the work of the man this festschrift honours, this is a patchy collection of material. However, it includes some valuable contributions to British business history, e.g. by Reader on the engineer, Alford on the role of British businessmen in the First World War, and Trebilcock on nineteenth-century insurance.
Firms: Phoenix Fire Insurance; Royal Exchange Assurance

3717
Nakagawa, Keiichiro (Editor)
Social Order and Entrepreneurship (Second Fuji Conference)
For main entry, see 101

3718
Okochi, Akio
Keiei Kouso-ryoku: Kigyou-sha Katsudo no Shi-teki Kenkyu [Formulating a Management Plan: A historical study of entrepreneurial activities]
1979 Tokyo Daigaku Shuppan-kai *Tokyo, Japan*

The author conceptualizes the motive and process of entrepreneurial decision making as 'an ability to formulate a plan for management (Keiei Kouso-ryoku)' and based on this concept reviews various cases of home and foreign entrepreneurs.

3719
Perkins, Edwin J.
The Entrepreneurial Spirit in Colonial America: The foundations of modern business history
Business History Review, vol. 63, no. 1, 1989: pp 160–86

This is an important survey of recent literature and of the debate about whether pre-industrial society was (as non-Marxists argue) or was not (as new Left historians argue) market-oriented and therefore capitalistic.

3720
Potts, M.; Behr, P.
The Leading Edge: CEOs who turned their companies around
1987 McGraw-Hill *New York, NY*

An anthology of fashionable 1980s case studies.

3721
Rodriguez, Manuel
El Empresario Industrial del Viejo Caldas [Industry and Industrialists in Two Colombian Cities]
1983 Universidad de los Andes *Bogotá, Colombia*

This volume compares the social and economic backgrounds of the entrepreneur-founders and managers of the largest manufacturing firms in the industrialization of two neighbouring coffee-based, middle-size Colombian cities (Pereira and Manizales). It is based on interviews with local industrialists, research in the archives of the local financial company which promoted industrial projects, and on secondary sources.

3722
Schvarzer, Jorge
Empresarios del pasado: la Unión Industrial Argentina
1991 CISEA/Imago Mundi *Buenos Aires, Argentina*

This study of the Argentinian industrialists' association (the equivalent of the CBI) examines its history from 1874 to 1991. Particular attention is given to the changing membership of the Unión and the tensions this created, relations with government and internal organization.

3723
Seoka, Makoto
Kigyousha-shi-gaku Josetsu [Academic Approaches to Entrepreneurial History]
1980 Jikkyo Shuppan Kabushiki Kaisha *Tokyo, Japan*

Based upon the theoretical frameworks developed in the Research Center of Entrepreneurial History of Harvard University, the author introduces various approaches to entrepreneurial history and classifies them into four types: economic, psychological, sociological and behavioural.

3724
Tripathi, Dwijendra (Editor)
Business Communities of India: A historical perspective
1984 Manohar Publications *New Delhi, India*

This is a collection of specially written essays, dealing with the evolution of various communities which dominate the Indian business scene today. Based on solid historical data and marked by rigorous analysis, these essays throw valuable light on the emergence of the Indian business class.

3725
Tripathi, Dwijendra
Historical Roots of Industrial Entrepreneurship in India and Japan: A comparative interpretation
1986 Institute of Developing Economics *Tokyo, Japan*

Although India and Japan set off on the road to industrialization at about the same time, the latter far surpassed the former in a relatively short space of time. Analysing various forces impinging on the perception and exploitation of business opportunities in the two countries, the volume seeks to explain the factors behind their differential records.

3726
Wong, Siu-Lun
Emigrant Entrepreneurs: Shanghai industrialists in Hong Kong
1988 Oxford University Press *Hong Kong*

This is a largely sociological study of the background, attitudes and behaviour of entrepreneurs in the Hong Kong cotton spinning industry based on interviews with senior directors in the late 1970s. Coming to Hong Kong in the late 1940s, refugee Shanghai spinners used their overseas financial holdings and good links with Western banks to establish modern textile mills. Many directors had technological degrees from Western universities, but few possessed academic training in business administration. The study examines in considerable detail the structure and strategy of Shanghainese family firms.

3727
Wyllie, Irvin G.
The Self-Made Man in America: The myth of rags to riches
1954 Free Press *New York, NY*

Using quantitative research by Taussig, Miller, Gregory & Neu (qqv) and others, this book examines the myth of the self-made man, concluding *inter alia* that from Franklin to Lincoln the creed had an anti-aristocratic tone (aimed against high birth and a Harvard education) but after the Civil War the doctrine became a weapon in the hands of conservatives.

3728
Yamazaki, Hiroaki; Miyamoto, Matao (Editors)
Trade Associations in Business History (Fourteenth Fuji Conference)
For main entry, see 110

Business Culture

3729
Barnett, Correlli
The Audit of War: The illusion and reality of Britain as a great nation
1986 Macmillan *London*

Barnett argues that Britain's wartime industrial performance was handicapped by the 'British disease' (incompetent management, obstructive trade unions, technological obsolescence); that the postwar diversion of resources into housing and welfare deprived industry of the chance to restructure; and that the wartime educational reforms only confirmed biases against industry and technology. A controversial book.

3730
Berghahn, Volker R.
The Americanisation of West German Industry 1945–1973
1986 Berg *Leamington Spa*

This is the English version of a book first published in German in 1985, *Unternehmer und Politik in der Bundesrepublik*, with some changes and additions. While this book is not well written, it provides the best summary in English of the process by which American ideas on management scale, competition, antitrust and industrial relations contributed to German industry's postwar economic revival.
Firms: Gutehoffnungshütte; I.G. Farben; Krupp; RAND Corporation; Siemens; Thyssen

3731
Brown, Jonathan; Rose, Mary B. (Editors)
Entrepreneurship, Networks and Modern Business
For main entry, see 3516

3732
Coleman, D. C.
Gentlemen and Players
Economic History Review, vol. 26, no. 1, 1973: pp 92–116

This article has proved to be a classic probing of the process of 'gentrification' and the role of the public school in particular. It has been reprinted in Casson, *Entrepreneurship* (qv).

3733
Collins, Bruce; Robbins, Keith (Editors)
British Culture and Economic Decline
1990 Weidenfeld & Nicolson *London*

Conference papers triggered by the Wiener debate, these essays raise the issues and present additional evidence on entrepreneurship, cultural explanations, and German and American comparisons. Besides the editors, the authors are Peter Payne, W. D. Rubinstein and Harold James.

3734
Engelbourg, Saul
Power and Morality: American business ethics, 1840–1914
1980 Greenwood Press *Westport, CT*

This work is focused on aspiration and rationale rather than on practice, which is, perhaps, a weakness of the study. It attempts to find conflicts between (a) business sectors and business in general; and (b) between business in general and society. The issues treated are conflict of interest, restraint of trade, competitive tactics, stock watering and financial reporting.

3735
Heald, Morrell
The Social Responsibilities of Business: Company and community, 1900–1960
1970 Case Western Reserve University Press *Cleveland, OH*

After studying donations to public charities by major corporations (excluding private gifts like the Carnegie and Rockefeller bequests) the author concludes that the social achievements of business fell below society's needs.

3736
Jeremy, David J. (Editor)
Business and Religion in Britain
1988 Gower *Aldershot*

Two theoretical and six empirical essays on interactions between business and religion, mostly in the nineteenth century, make up this volume. Besides the editor, the authors are Clyde Binfield, John Briggs, Roy Campbell, Tony Corley Jane Garnett, Tony Howe and Maurice Kirby. An appendix lists the religious

affiliations of subjects in the same editor's *Dictionary of Business Biography* (qv).
Firms: Mackintosh; Pease & Partners; Ridgway

3737
Jeremy, David J.
Capitalists and Christians: Business Leaders and the Churches in Britain, 1900–1960
1990 Clarendon Press *Oxford*

Taking the collective biographies of three business elites (heads of the 100 largest employers in 1907, 1935 and 1955) this study examines the extent and ways in which business leaders related their faith to their business. Conversely the latter part of the book explores the ways in which business people played a part in the lay leaderships of the Christian denominations (excluding the Roman Catholic Church).

3738
Jeremy, David J.
British and American Entrepreneurial Values in the Early Nineteenth Century: A parting of the ways?
1991 Manchester University Press *Manchester*

This chapter in *The End of Anglo-America: Historical essays in the study of cultural divergence* edited by Robert A. Burchell, presents a comparison of business values in Britain and America before 1840 which looks at how society perceived entrepreneurs and how entrepreneurs perceived themselves.
Firms: Arkwright, Sir Richard; Slater, Samuel

3739
Joyce, Patrick
Work, Society and Politics: The culture of the factory in later Victorian England
1980 Harvester Press *Brighton*

Joyce argues that factory operatives moved from dependence to deference by the late nineteenth century. Using evidence chiefly from Lancashire and West Yorkshire, this study examines such aspects of factory culture as master–employee relations, political dimensions and religious aspects.

3740
Kinmonth, Earl H.
The Self-made Man in Meiji Japanese Thought: From samurai to salary man
1981 University of California Press *Berkeley, CA*

Kinmonth studies the transformation of elite ideology in Meiji Japan as the ideal of self-advancement through education and white collar employment spread from its samurai origins to the general populace. He challenges the common notion that 'group orientation' among Japanese employees is a carry-over from feudal traditions and argues that the very modernity of elite recruitment in Japan - its relative openness to all on the basis of schooling - combines with a chronic excess of graduates to generate tremendous pressure for conformity to group norms.

3741
Kinzley, W. Dean
Industrial Harmony in Modern Japan: The invention of a tradition
1991 Routledge *London*

A study of business ideologies in Japan and the relationship between paternalism, government propaganda and modern corporate ideas.

3742
Kirkland, Edward Chase
Dream and Thought in the Business Community, 1860–1900
1956 Cornell University Press *Ithaca, NY*

This is a pioneering attempt to enter the mind of the business community in the Progressive Era, tracing sources of the businessman's ideology and exploring businessmen's perceptions of wealth creation, education, college, government and philanthropy.

3743
Krooss, Herman E.
Executive Opinion: What business leaders said and thought on economic issues, 1920s–1960s
1970 Doubleday *Garden City, NY*

This study of business opinion over a period characterized by substantial shifts in economic theory concludes that the business interest held no concise ideology and that business people should stick to their trade and not set themselves up as social reformers.

3744
Lewis, Roy; Stewart, Rosemary
The Boss: The life and times of the British businessman
For main entry, see 3524

3745
Lincoln, James R.; Kalleberg, Arne L.
Culture, Control and Commitment: A study of work organisation and work attitudes in the United States and Japan
1990 Cambridge University Press *Cambridge*

Reporting on a large comparative survey of American and Japanese factories, this book seeks to explain the apparent Japanese advantage in workforce discipline and commitment. It argues that individual commitment is somewhat greater in Japan, but rejects claims that Japanese-style work organization consistently yields real payoffs in employee morale and motivation.

3746
Lundén, Rolf
Business and Religion in the American 1920s
1988 Greenwood Press *Westport, CT*

Lundén examines the ways in which the organized churches sanctioned business behaviour in the 'roaring twenties', how they adopted business practices, and conversely how both entrepreneurs and companies justified or clothed their behaviour in religious terms.

3747
McKendrick, Neil; Brewer, John; Plumb, J. H.
The Birth of a Consumer Society: The commercialisation of eighteenth-century England
1982 Europa *London*

This is particularly of interest for McKendrick's articles on early marketing of pottery by Wedgwood and shaving requisites by Packwood.
Firms: Wedgwood; Packwood

3748
O'Connor, Thomas H.
Lords of the Loom: The cotton Whigs and the coming of the Civil War
1968 Scribner *New York, NY*

O'Connor studies the attitudes of Massachusetts cotton manufacturers, typified by the Lawrences, between the 1830s and the Civil War, and attacks the thesis of Charles Beard, that the war was instigated by the divergent interests of the agrarian South and the industrial North.
Firms: A & A Lawrence

3749
Oliver, Nick; Wilkinson, Barry
The Japanization of British Industry
1988 Basil Blackwell *Oxford*

A study of the impact of Japanese methods on British industry in the 1980s with valuable case study material of individual firms.
Firms: Rover; Lucas; Nissan

3750
Pagnamenta, Peter; Overy, Richard
All Our Working Lives
1984 BBC Publications *London*

Based on an acclaimed television series, this book records elements of the visual and oral history materials collected from archives and the memories of managers and workers. Ten major industries, including cotton, shipbuilding and the motor industry, are each given a chapter. The book is good for atmosphere.

3751
Pessen, Edward
Riches, Class and Power Before the Civil War
1978 D. C. Heath *Lexington, MA*

This important study of Jacksonian America must be used in its revised edition, for which the author removed many of the failings found in the first (1973) edition.

3752
Political and Economic Planning (PEP)
Attitudes in British Management
1966 Penguin Books *Harmondsworth*

Based on interviews with 300 senior executives at nearly 50 firms (divided between those with high growth, those with low growth prospects) in six industries, this study records the attitudes of British managers on topics such as cost control, R&D, exporting, industrial relations, industrial training and the role of government.

3753
Prothro, James Warren
The Dollar Decade: Business Ideas in the 1920s
1954 Louisiana State University Press *Baton Rouge, LA*

This is a formal analysis of the philosophy articulated by the leaders of the very conservative National Association of Manufacturers and the US Chamber of Commerce in the 1920s.

3754
Richards, Thomas
The Commodity Culture of Victorian England: Advertising and spectacle 1851–1914
For main entry, see 3301

3755
Roberts, David
Paternalism in Early Victorian England
1979 Rutgers University Press *Rutgers, NJ*

Delineating the ideology of the first generation of factory masters and rural landlords, this book complements the volumes by Pollard, Howe and Joyce (qqv).

3756
Rubinstein, W. D.
Capitalism, Culture and Decline in Britain, 1750–1990
1993 Routledge *London*

This book contains four essays on culture and economic performance, education and entrepreneurship, and the role of elites. Rubinstein argues vigorously against the 'cultural critique' of Wiener, Correlli Barnett (qv) et al.

3757
Schein, Edgar H.
Organizational Culture and Leadership
1988 Jossey-Bass Publishers *San Francisco, CA*

This work defines culture as shared assumptions about reality and proceeds to show how company founders can embed their own values in their companies. It is essential reading for anyone writing or researching company culture.

3758
Shiels, W. J.; Wood, Diana (Editors)
The Church and Wealth
1987 Basil Blackwell *Oxford*

This series of conference papers given to the Ecclesiastical History Society is particularly useful in showing how, since the days of the early church, economics and religion have intertwined, clashed and informed each other. It should be read in conjunction with Tawney, Jeremy and Lundén (qqv).

3759
Southall, R.
African Capitalism in Contemporary South Africa
Journal of Southern African Studies, vol. 7, no. 1, 1980: pp 38–70

A study of the difficulties facing the emergence of black businesses in South Africa.
Firms: National African Federated Chambers of Commerce; African Bank of South Africa; African Development and Construction Company

3760
Steinberg, Theodore
Nature Incorporated: Industrialisation and the waters of New England
1991 Cambridge University Press *Cambridge*

Responding to the new concern for conservation, this study examines the theme of industry and the environment. The major tensions identified are: small farmers versus big businessmen; local versus regional interests; customary rights versus new law; fish stock versus dam construction; water purity versus industrial population growth.

3761
Tawney, Richard H.
Religion and the Rise of Capitalism
1926 John Murray *London*

This classic study of the Reformation and Puritan movements shows how the economic collectivism of the Middle Ages was transformed into the individualism of the late seventeenth century, continuing right up to the present.

3762
Temple, William
Christianity and Social Order
1942 Penguin Books *Harmondsworth* 1976 SPCK *London,*

This book, first published in 1942, was an enormously popular statement by an Archbishop of the Church of England of the role of the Church and of ethics in economics and business. It marked the triumph of intervention (for which see Jeremy, *Capitalists and Christians*) and has been controversially criticised by Correlli Barnett (qv).

3763
Thimm, Alfred
Business Ideologies in the Reform-Progressive Era, 1880–1914
1976 University of Alabama Press *Tuscaloosa, AL*

Intended to complement Herman Krooss's *Executive Opinion* (qv), this study examines the opinions of individuals in business rather more than the opinions of business groups.

3764
Tipple, John
The Anatomy of Prejudice: Origins of the robber baron legend
Business History Review, vol. 33, no. 4, 1959: pp 510–23

Tipple analyses 50 representative critics to expose the making of the legend.

3765
Wagner, Gillian
The Chocolate Conscience
For main entry, see 1626

3766
Wiener, Martin J.
English Culture and the Decline of the Industrial Spirit, 1850–1980
1981 Cambridge University Press *Cambridge*

Published at the beginning of the Thatcher decade and the unleashing of an enterprise (as opposed to a welfare) society, this book claimed wide media attention. Among academic economic historians it was damned as superficial: in the words of William Ashworth, 'Prof. Wiener has succumbed to the disease he claims to have diagnosed. This book is gentrified history: all *belles lettres* and no "nitty gritty."'.

3767
Wolfe, Kenneth M.
The Churches and the British Broadcasting Corporation, 1922–1956: The politics of broadcast religion
1984 SCM Press *London*

Wolfe gives a very detailed account of the interactions between the churches and the major public media organ in the UK, spanning the period from Reith to William Haley, when Christianity had a monopoly on broadcasting. It should be read in conjunction with Briggs (qv).
Firms: BBC

3768
Zunz, Olivier
Making America Corporate 1870–1920
1990 University of Chicago Press *Chicago, IL*

This is a heroic, idiosyncratic effort from maverick business historian Zunz. Its central thesis, much debated since it appeared, is that the American middle-class who staffed the Chandlerian managerial hierarchies established America's modern work culture and values. The book contains much that is novel and pertinent to a full understanding of the implications of corporate growth.
Firms: Chicago, Burlington & Quincy Railroad; E. I. Du Pont de Nemours; Ford Motor Company; General Motors Corporation; International Harvester Co.; McCormick Harvesting Machinery Co.; Metropolitan Life Insurance Co.

Entrepreneurs and Wealth

3769
Harbury, Colin D.; Hitchens, D. M. W. N.
Inheritance and Wealth Inequality in Britain
1979 George Allen & Unwin *London*

Unlike Rubinstein's studies (qv), this book traces the transmission of wealth across generations and between male and female lines. It offers aggregated data on the occupations of the wealthy in twentieth-century Britain and finds that agriculture and metal manufacturing favoured inheritors, construction and metal goods the self-made.

3770
Knightley, Phillip
The Vestey Affair
For main entry, see 1634

3771
Rubinstein, William D. (Editor)
Wealth and the Wealthy in the Modern World
1980 Croom Helm *London*

This book summarizes work by Rubinstein on Britain, Edward Pessen on the USA pre-1865, Frederick Cople Jaher on the USA since 1865, Adeline Daumard on France and Vera Zamagni on Italy. The editor makes some comparative remarks in a short introduction.

3772
Rubinstein, William D.
Men of Property: The very wealthy in Britain since the Industrial Revolution
1981 Croom Helm *London*

Based primarily on probate records, this path-breaking study examines the occupations and, equally importantly, the locations of millionaires and half-millionaires (and lesser wealthy in the early part of the period). Commerce and finance are shown to have been more lucrative than manufacturing and London rather than the provinces the place to make a fortune. Evidence on social mobility and the role of religion is also considered.

3773
Wedgwood, Josiah
The Economics of Inheritance
2nd Edition
1939 Pelican Books *Harmondsworth*

This work is a pioneering study which considered the legal, economic, and social dimensions of inheritance, wealth and inequality.

Entrepreneurship - Collective

3774
Altaf, Z.
Pakistani Entrepreneurs
1983 Croom Helm *London*

This is a study of the leading Pakistani entrepreneurs, their religion, educational background, occupational mobility and kinship patterns which determined choice, scale and location of industry. The informal bonds which exist in Pakistani extended families are compared with more formal institutions in the West which nurture the talent of pioneering entrepreneurs.

3775
Altaf, Z.
Entrepreneurship in the Third World: Risk and uncertainty in industry in Pakistan
1988 Croom Helm *London*

Altaf covers the history of Pakistani industrial entrepreneurs from 1949 to 1985. He categorizes three kinds of entrepreneurs who emerged as a response to the macro-economic environment of different political regimes; that is, the economic, political or progressive entrepreneurs. With each regime, the level of risk faced by entrepreneurs determined the direction, structure and extent of industrial investment.

3776
Bahamonde, A.; Cayuela, G.
Hacer las Américas: Las élites coloniales españolas en el siglo XIX [To Get On in America Spanish colonial elites in the nineteenth century]
1992 Alianza *Madrid, Spain*

This is a study of Spanish colonial elites in the nineteenth century, the origins of their capital and their investment strategy in the metropoli.

3777
Bailyn, Bernard
The New England Merchants in the Seventeenth Century
For main entry, see 1951

3778
Birchal, S. O.
O empresario Mineiro: cinco casos de sucesso [The Mineiro Entrepreneur: Five cases of success]
1989 FACE/Universidade Federal de Minas Gerais *Belo Horizonte, Brazil*

This work examines the careers of five successful entrepreneurs of the 1980s in Minas Gerais, Brazil. Based on interviews with the entrepreneurs themselves, the work examines their family background, lives and business careers.
Firms: Bioquimica do Brasil S/A; CEBRACTEX; COTEMINAS; COTENOR; ECONORTE; FANAPE; Nansen Instrumentos de Precisao; Tecnowatt–Industria Eletrotecnica

3779
Bliss, Michael
Northern Enterprise: Five centuries of Canadian business
1987 McClelland & Stewart *Toronto, Canada*

Bliss presents a survey of Canadian business from the beginning of European settlement to the present.

3780
Cassis, Youssef (Editor)
Business Elites
1994 Edward Elgar *Aldershot*

This book reprints 27 articles or chapters published between 1950 and 1992 dealing with the social origins and social mobility of business elites; their education, culture and mentality; their social profiles; and their wealth and high society. Elites in Britain, the USA, France, Germany and Japan are treated in these writings, some of which (like D. C. Coleman's on 'Gentlemen and Players' (qv) are much quoted.

3781
Cassis, Youssef
City Bankers, 1890–1914
For main entry, see 2257

3782
Cerutti, Mario
Burguesía, Capitales e Industria en el norte de México: Monterrey y su mbito regional (1850–1910) [Bourgeoisie, Capital and Industry in Northern Mexico: Monterrey and its region (1850–1910)]
1992 Alianza-Universidad Autónoma de Nuevo León *Mexico City, Mexico*

Although a regional study on one of Mexico's early industrializing regions, the author also examines the main business groups of Monterrey, their origins, evolution, investment strategies, and relations with other entrepreneurs and with the political power.

3783
Cerutti, M.; Vellinga, M. (Editors)
Burguesías e industria en América Latina y Europa meridional [Bourgeoisies and Industry in Latin America and Southern Europe]
1989 Alianza *Madrid, Spain*

This book offers a scholarly survey of the social origins of the bourgeoisie and its role in the economic development of several countries and regions in southern Europe and Latin America.

3784
Chapman, Stanley D.
Merchant Enterprise in Britain from the Industrial Revolution to World War I
1992 Cambridge University Press *Cambridge*

This work simultaneously synthesizes recent research and presents new work in a relatively unexplored area, looking not only at origins, types and dispersion of merchant activity and merchant families but also exploring ways of evaluating performance.
Firms: Benson; Cookes; Fielden; Finlay; Fraser; I & R Morley; Morrison; Ralli; Rathbone; Yule

3785
Devine, T. M.
The Tobacco Lords: A study of the tobacco merchants of Glasgow and their trading activities, c.1740–90
For main entry, see 1823

3786
Erice Sebares, F.
La burguesía industrial asturiana, 1885–1920 [The Asturian Industrial Bourgeoisie, 1885–1920]
1980 Silverio Cañada *Oviedo, Spain*

This book focuses on the origins and development of an industrial bourgeoisie in Asturias, a coal-mining region, dealing particularly with its origins, investment strategies and relations between members.

3787

Gies, Joseph; Gies, Frances

Merchants and Moneymen: The commercial revolution, 1000–1500

1972 Thomas Y. Crowell *New York, NY*

This study analyses the careers of outstanding merchants in twenty families in the later Middle Ages: most are Italian, some are from the Low Countries and England. It provides a comparative perspective on the expansion of commerce and includes an especially useful bibliography.

3788

Hedges, James B.

The Browns of Providence Plantation: Vol. 1: The Colonial Years; Vol. 2: The Nineteenth Century

1952 Harvard University Press *Cambridge, MA* 1968 Brown University Press *Providence, RI*

These rather sprawling multi-generational studies range from colonial merchanting to the promotion of early cotton factories, Nebraska land speculation and Far Eastern trade.

Firms: Browns

3789

Hirschmeier, Johannes

The Origins of Entrepreneurship in Japan

1964 Harvard University Press *Cambridge, MA*

Covering mostly the Meiji period, this study combines the economic and biographical dimensions of the subject and controversially emphasizes discontinuities between pre- and post-Meiji and the social characteristics of the Japanese.

3790

Johnson, Arthur M.; Supple, Barry E.

Boston Capitalists and Western Railroads: A study in the nineteenth century railroad investment process

1967 Harvard University Press *Cambridge, MA*

This book augured a new approach to business history examining the expectations, policies and rewards of several groups of capitalists who switched their investments into railroads between the 1840s and 1890s. Both qualitative and quantitative methods were deployed in the analysis.

Firms: Atchison, Topeka & Santa Fe Railroad; Chicago, Burlington & Quincy Railroad; Illinois Central Railroad; Michigan Central Railroad; Union Pacific Railroad

3791

Kennedy, P. T.

Ghanaian Businessmen: From artisan to capitalist entrepreneur in a dependent economy

1980 Weltforum *Munich, Germany*

This is a study of Ghanaian businessmen and their successes in the 1960s and 1970s.

3792

Kicza, John E.

Colonial Entrepreneurs: Families and business in Bourbon Mexico City

1983 University of New Mexico Press *Albuquerque, NM*

Kicza emphasizes the entrepreneurial abilities of the colonial elite and the structures, procedures and organization of business in Mexico City in the eighteenth century.

3793

Morikawa, Hidemasa

Nippon-gata Keiei no Tenkai: Sangyo Kaitaku-sha ni Manabu [The Development of Japanese Management: Learning from the industrial pioneers]

1980 Toyo Keizai Shinpo-sha *Tokyo, Japan*

Covering the period from the 1880s to the 1920s, this work outlines the entrepreneurial activities of the captains of Japanese industry. It provides much information on how the pioneers found a way of overcoming the difficulties which confronted them.

3794

Nafziger, E. W.

African Capitalism: A case study in Nigerian entrepreneurship

1977 Hoover Institution Press *Stanford, CT*

This study of Nigerian businessmen places special emphasis on the footwear industry.

3795
Papanek, Hanna
Pakistan's Big Businessmen, Muslim Separatism, Entrepreneurship and Partial Modernisation
For main entry, see 3618

3796
Papenfuse, Edward C.
In Pursuit of Profit: The Annapolis merchants in the era of the American Revolution, 1763–1805
1975 Johns Hopkins University Press *Baltimore, MD*

This is a prodigiously researched study of the social and economic development of Annapolis and the activities of its merchants together with a case study of the rise, decline and transformation of one house in particular.
Firms: Wallace, Davidson & Johnson

3797
Pierenkemper, Toni
Die westfälischen Schwerindustriellen 1852–1913: Soziale Struktur und unternehmerischer Erfolg [Westphalian Heavy Industry 1852–1913: Social structure and entrepreneurial success]
1979 Vandenhoeck & Ruprecht *Göttingen, Germany*

This is a collective biography of entrepreneurs in Westphalia's heavy industry before the First World War. It attempts to relate social analysis to business performance.

3798
Pierenkemper, Toni
Entrepreneurs in Heavy Industry: Upper Silesia and the Westphalian Ruhr region, 1852–1913
Business History Review, vol. 53, no. 1, 1979: pp 65–78

In comparing these two German regions the author argues that there has been a connection between social structure and entrepreneurship.

3799
Redlich, Fritz
History of American Business Leaders: A series of studies
1940–51 Edwards Brothers *Ann Arbor, MI*

These studies cover the iron and steel, iron ore mining and the banking industries, with banking in two parts (1780s–1840 and 1840–1910). While Redlich was preoccupied with theory, he declined the opportunity to synthesize and generalize from his cases.

3800
Sayigh, Yusif A.
Entrepreneurs of Lebanon: The role of the business leader in a developing economy
1962 Harvard University Press *Cambridge, MA*

This book contains the report of a study of 207 firms, unfortunately excluding traders, and finds that the Lebanese were more concerned with organizational design than with the provision of capital.

3801
Schweninger, Loren
Black-owned Businesses in the South, 1790–1880
Business History Review, vol. 63, no. 1, 1989: pp 22–60

This is a pioneering, solidly researched profile, based on census records, of black-owned businesses in the American South.

3802
Seligman, Benjamin B.
The Potentates: Business and businessmen in American history
1970 Dial Press *New York, NY*

Although this book lacks much scholarly apparatus and is in the muckraker tradition, the study is massively informed, lively and probing.

3803
Sierra Alvarez, María
La familia Ybarra: Empresarios y políticos [The Ybarra Family Businessmen and politicians]
1992 Muñoz Moya y Montraveta *Seville, Spain*

The author studies one of the most promi-

nent families of Seville in the Restoration period, its businesses and political careers, and the clientele network created around them.
Firms: Ybarra y Cía

3804
Stone, R. C. J.
Makers of Fortune: A colonial business community and its fall
1973 Auckland University Press *Auckland, New Zealand*

An outstanding piece of New Zealand business history, this study looks at the growth of business in Auckland in the 1860s and 1870s and the crises faced in the subsequent two decades. It focuses on the 'inner circle', a small group of entrepreneurs who played a dominant role in the local business community.
Firms: Bank of New Zealand; Brown & Campbell; NZ Insurance; NZ Loan and Mercantile Agency Co.

3805
Supple, Barry E.
A Business Elite: German Jewish financiers in nineteenth century New York
Business History Review, vol. 31, no. 2, 1957: pp 143–78

This article traces the economic and social influence of German-Jewish investment bankers, a group second only to those houses of Yankee origin, in the late nineteenth century.
Firms: Goldman, Sachs & Co.; Guggenheim; Hallgarten & Co.; J & W Seligman & Co.; Kuhn, Loeb & Co.

3806
Taussig, Frank W.; Joslyn, C. S.
American Business Leaders: A study in social origins and social stratification
1932 Macmillan *New York, NY*

This is a large statistical study of nearly 9,000 businessmen which undermined the American rags-to-riches myth.

3807
Tulchinsky, Gerald J. J.
The River Barons: Montreal businessmen and the growth of industry and transportation 1837–1853
1977 University of Toronto Press *Toronto, Canada*

Although mostly concerned with the business community in Montreal, as that city began to grow, this book also throws much light on the shipping, railway and freight companies that were established there as well as on the use of hydraulic power. It draws on a wide range of primary sources and is scholarly and judicious. Although not really a business history it is nevertheless a valuable source.
Firms: Champlain & St Lawrence Railway; Lachine Canal Co.; Montreal & New York Railway; St Lawrence & Atlantic Railway

Collective Biography, UK

3808
Beable, William Henry
Romance of Great Businesses
1926 Heath Cranton *London*

Although ostensibly devoted to company histories, the numerous entries in this book also contain profiles, of differing lengths, of many of the entrepreneurs behind the businesses.

3809
Copeman, G. H.
Leaders of British Industry: A study of the careers of more than a thousand public company directors
1955 Gee & Co. *London*

This survey provides a portrait of British business leadership in the early 1950s. Covering companies with shareholders' assets of more than £1 million, it surveyed 3,215 directors in 445 companies, of whom just over 36 per cent replied. Data are presented on the directors' original occupations, fathers' occupations, directors' education, age of starting work, age of marriage, age at becoming a director, and cross-classifications of these variables.

3810
Crouzet, François
The First Industrialists: The problem of origins
1985 Cambridge University Press *Cambridge*

Crouzet examines the social origins of 316 industrialists heading large firms in Britain in the period 1750–1850. This is the largest study to date of entrepreneurs in the early industrial period. Erudite and elegantly written, it demolishes the rags-to-riches myth but discovers upward mobility in the middle classes.

3811
Erickson, Charlotte
British Industrialists: Steel and hosiery, 1850–1950
1986 Gower *Aldershot*

This is a classic prosopographical study, first published in 1959. It provided the first and for a long time the only rigorous analysis of the social origins and career patterns of British industrialists. It remains a model of its kind.

3812
Fidler, John
The British Business Elite: Its attitudes to class, status and power
1981 Routledge & Kegan Paul *London*

Taking 130 chairmen, chief executives other directors from a sample of firms from the *Times 1000* of 1975, this study is particularly useful because it charts their views on their responsibilities, participation in their respective firms, class outlook and attitudes to political power.

3813
Gourvish, Terence R.
Les Dirigeants Salariés de l'Industrie des Chemins de Fer Britanniques, 1850–1922 [British Salaried Railway Managers]

This is a revised version of the author's important collective biography of chief executive managers in the British railway industry of 1850–1922, first published in *Business History Review* vol.47, no.3, 1973. It appears in Lévy-Leboyer's *Patronat de la Seconde Industrialisation* (qv).

3814
Honeyman, Katrina
Origins of Enterprise: Business Leadership in the Industrial Revolution
1982 Manchester University Press *Manchester*

Using a range of primary sources, this pioneering work tested and eroded the Smilesean myth of the self-made man by analysing the social origins of businessmen in lead mining, cotton spinning and lacemaking, together spanning the period 1700–1843. The study complements that by Charlotte Erickson (qv), on steel and hosiery leaders for the subsequent century.

3815
Howe, Anthony
The Cotton Masters, 1830–1860
1984 Clarendon Press *Oxford*

Based on a sample of 351 textile masters, this book presents a collective portrait of the second and third generations of Lancashire mill owners. It is especially strong on social origins, political influence, civic status and philanthropy.
Firms: H & E Ashworth; Horrocks, Miller & Co.; J & N Philips; M'Connel & Kennedy; Philips & Lee; Thomson, Chippendale & Co.

3816
Jeremy, David J.; Allan, Adrian (Editor)
The Prosopography of Business Leaders: Possibilities, Resources and Problems
1990 Business Archives Council *London*

This article, published in the Proceedings of the annual conference of the Business Archives Council edited by Adrian Allen, briefly surveys the development of collective biography and evaluates sources for use by business historians in attempting to reconstruct profiles of past business leaderships.

3817
Jeremy, David J.; Shaw, Christine (Editors)
Dictionary of Business Biography
1984–6 Butterworths *London*

The first five volumes (in alphabetical sequence of subjects' names) present the business biographies of 1,181 individuals active in Britain (outside Scotland) in the period from the 1860s to the 1960s, written by 447 contributors. Individuals included have been selected by subjective rather than objective criteria. The sixth paperback volume provides indexes to industries, companies and people. While there are omissions, and entries vary in length and quality, the *DBB* itself fills many gaps in the *Dictionary of National Biography*. To be used in conjunction with Slaven & Checkland (qv).

3818
Jeremy, David J.; Tweedale, Geoffrey (Editors)
Dictionary of Twentieth Century British Business Leaders
1993 Bowker-Saur *London*

This book contains entries on over 750 individuals active in Britain in the twentieth century. They have been selected by a combination of objective and subjective methods, the core being derived from Jeremy's *Capitalists and Christians*, (qv), Appendix 2 and from the heads of the largest UK firms in the early 1990s.

3819
Jones, David Lewis (Editor)
British and Irish Biographies, 1840–1940
1985–91 Chadwyck-Healey *Cambridge*

This is a microfiche reproduction of 272 biographical dictionaries, including Burke, Debrett, the Pike series, professional, denominational and county *Who's Who*, published in six parts. About 1,200 volumes on 14,000 microfiches have 6.5 million entries on 4 million people. With a single index of names, this is more than a major act of book preservation but, at £30,000 for the entire set, use is confined to national and major city libraries.

3820
Kirby, Maurice W.
Men of Business and Politics: The Rise and Fall of the Quaker Pease Dynasty of North-East England, 1700–1943
1984 George Allen & Unwin *London*

This is an absorbing and detailed, though relatively short, family biography spanning, chiefly, the three generations it took to make and lose a business empire. The themes of family, religion and business are unravelled with skill, scholarship and balanced judgement.
Firms: J. & J. W. Pease; Pease & Partners

3821
Machlow, H. L.
Gentlemen Capitalists: The social and political world of the Victorian businessman
1992 Stanford University Press *Stanford, CA*

This is a study of four important Victorian businessmen: Samuel Holland; William McArthur; Robert Fowler; and John Holms. It examines their business affairs, their role in the commercial elite, their roles in politics and voluntary associations and the transition of their families from outsiders to part of the metropolitan-oriented plutocracy.

3822
Morewood, Steven
Pioneers and Inheritors: Top Management in the Coventry Motor Industry, 1896–1972
1990 Coventry Polytechnic *Coventry*

This book is presented in two parts: a collective biography of 21 motor industry leaders; and individual biographies of eight of them (John Kemp Starley, Henry John Lawson, Reginald Walter Maudslay, Siegfried Bettmann, Lord (William Edward) Rootes, Sir John Black and Sir William Lyons. There is much material here but the volume is very poorly proofed and bound.
Firms: Hillman; Humber; Jaguar; Rootes Group; Rover Cycle; Standard Motor; Triumph

3823
Parker, Robert H. (Editor)
British Accountants: A biographical sourcebook
1980 Arno Press *New York, NY*

The editor has collected and reprinted the obituary notices of 65 accountants in this volume, prefixing them with a collective biography of the whole group. This is a useful interim reference work.

3824
Payne, Peter
British Entrepreneurship in the Nineteenth Century
1988 Macmillan/Economic History Society *Basingstoke*

This is the best introduction to the study of British entrepreneurship in the nineteenth century–when entrepreneurs apparently helped to make and lose the country's international industrial leadership. It is excellent for its summary of the debates and guide to the literature. The second edition (1988) must be used.

3825
Pike, W. T. (Editor)
Pike's New Century Series
1898-1912 W. T. Pike *Brighton*

Each volume in this series treats a county or major city and is in two parts: history, institutions and architecture; and biographies. The latter, arranged in sections, include industrialists. Though self-selected, these profiles are indispensable for any work on the Edwardian business elite. The biographical parts were reprinted with a master index by Peter Bell, Edinburgh, 1986 and in Jones, British and Irish Biographies (qv).

3826
Pollard, Sidney
The Genesis of Modern Management: A study of the Industrial Revolution in Great Britain
1965 Edward Arnold *London*

Confined to the large-scale industries of the period 1750–1830, this very detailed study uncovers much about the education, training, recruitment and performance of managers; about accounting techniques; and about the recruitment, training and disciplining of the industrial workforce.

3827
Scott, John; Griff, Catherine
Directors of Industry: The British corporate network, 1904–76
1984 Polity Press *Cambridge*

Like Scott and Hughes (qv) this work assumes that those holding multiple directorships will be more powerful the more they hold. Such a collective analysis needs to be supplemented by in-depth studies of the individuals concerned to see if in fact this has been true: to discover the kinds of power involved, and how far knowledge has been disseminated through such linkages.

3828
Scott, John; Hughes, Michael
The Anatomy of Scottish Capital: Scottish companies and Scottish capital, 1900–1979
1980 Croom Helm *London*

This is one of several studies by Scott in which he identifies the largest companies (by share capital measure) at key dates (1905, 1920, 1938, 1956, 1974) and plots interlocking directors in order to track business networks, and (by implication) businessmen of power.

3829
Slaven, Anthony; Checkland, Sydney (Editors)
Dictionary of Scottish Business Biography
1986–90 Aberdeen University Press *Aberdeen, Scotland*

Nearly 400 individuals active in Scottish industry in the century before 1960 are included in these two volumes. They have been selected because they headed major companies, which in turn have been chosen on the basis of firm size and industry weighting. Entries have been arranged by industry, volume 1 covering the staple industries (mining, metal manufacture, engineering, shipbuilding, chemicals, textiles), volume 2, processing, distribution and services.

3830
Stanworth, Philip; Giddens, Anthony (Editors)
Elites and Power in British Society
1974 Cambridge University Press *Cambridge*

This collection of essays contains a very useful one on concepts and methodology by Giddens (one of Britain's leading sociologists); another on directorships spanning the City and manufacturing, by Richard Whitley; and one on company chairmen, 1905–71 by Stanworth and Giddens. Other authors in this volume (like Colin Harbury and W. D. Rubinstein) have subsequently published books noted elsewhere in this bibliography.

3831
Trainor, Richard H.
Black Country Elites: The exercise of authority in an industrialized area, 1830–1900
1993 Clarendon Press *Oxford*

A study of the urban and industrial elites of the Victorian Black Country which is an important contribution to the study of the urban middle class and provincial industrial elites.

Collective Biography, USA and Rest of World

3832
Appleyard, R. T.; Schedvin, C. B. (Editors)
Australian Financiers: Biographical essays
For main entry, see 2689

3833
Ball, Alan M.
Russia's Last Capitalists: The Nepmen, 1921–29
1987 University of California Press *Berkeley, CA*

Though the title has been overtaken by events, this study of private entrepreneurs in the USSR under the New Economic Policy is important because it clarifies the nature of the NEP and argues (against Viola and Kuromiya) that private enterprise was successful in the USSR.

3834
Barjot, Dominique (Editor)
Les Patrons du Second Empire: Anjou, Normandie, Maine [Employers of the Second Empire: Anjou, Normandie, Maine]
1991 Picard/Editions Cenomane *Le Mans, France*

This is one of a series of regional studies of representative individual entrepreneurs and their influence on the growth of the French economy. Details of individuals include family, career, particular achievements, religious and political affiliation and contribution to local institutions. Studies include members of major dynasties as well as more modest businessmen. Each volume includes an introductory contextual essay. The whole series is under the overall direction of the CNRS. Other volumes in the series to date include Jobert on Bourgogne and Mayaud on Franche-Comté.

3835
Bergeron, Louis
Banquiers, Négociants et Manufacturiers Parisiens du Directoire à L'Empire [Parisian Bankers, Merchants and Manufacturers from the Directory to the Empire]
1978 École des Hautes Études en Sciences *Paris, France*

This important study of the big businessmen of Paris in the late eighteenth and early nineteenth century includes potted histories of numerous enterprises and a long chapter on the Oberkampf firm.
Firms: Oberkampf

3836
Berghoff, Hartmut
Aristokratisierung des Burgertums?: Zur Sozialgeschichte der Nobilitierung von Unternehmern in Preussen und Grossbritannien 1870 bis 1918 [Aristocratizing the Middle Class? The ennoblement of businessmen in Prussia and Great Britain 1870–1918]
Vierteljahrschrift für Sozial- und Wirtschaftsgeschichte, vol. 81, no. 2, 1994: pp 178–204

This article picks up the debate about the alleged decay of English and Prussian entrepreneurship during the pre-First World War era. He qualifies the widespread view that, as a result of their tendency towards aristocracy and their imitation of the latter, German and British entrepreneurs lost their essential social and economic qualities respectively. The assumption that entrepreneurs were systematically discriminated against in English society cannot be verified by this study of gentrified entrepreneurs.

3837
Burch, Philip H. Jr
The Managerial Revolution Reassessed: Family control in America's large corporations
1972 D. C. Heath *Lexington, MA*

Using the criterion of ownership of 4–5 per cent of a company's stock, Burch challenged Berle & Means (qv) arguing that between 45 and 50 per cent of the USA's largest industrial firms in 1965 were dominated by family interests. Chandler in his *Visible Hand* (qv) observes that stock ownership does not imply boardroom control and that Burch's examples reveal no convincing mechanisms of control.

3838

Chan, Wellington K. K.

Merchants, Mandarins and Moslem Enterprise in Late Ch'in China

For main entry, see 1960

3839

Clutterbuck, David; Crainer, Stuart

Makers of Management: Men and women who changed the business world

1990 Macmillan *London*

Covering 30 or so individuals, this is a mixture of loosely-constructed biographies and summaries of management thought. Among those thus briefly treated are Taylor, Mayo, Urwick, Drucker, Sloan, Porter, Peters and Waterman. Useful as an introduction.

3840

Cochran, Thomas C.

Railroad Leaders, 1845–1890: The business mind in action

1953 Harvard University Press *Cambridge, MA*

This is a pioneering study of 61 railroad leaders, comparing attitudes to innovation, relations with suppliers and customers, economics and finance, managerial techniques, labour relations, community development, public relations, government relations and social relevance.

Firms: Boston & Albany Railroad; Burlington Railroad; Illinois Central Railroad; Lackawanna Railroad; Lake Shore & Michigan Railroad; Michigan Central Railroad; NY Central Railroad; New Haven Railroad; Norfolk & Western Railroad; Southern (NYC) Railroad

3841

Dalzell, Robert F. Jr

Enterprising Elite: The Boston Associates and the world they made

1987 Harvard University Press *Cambridge, MA*

Dalzell's book is a pioneering synthesis of a large literature on the 80 or so Boston merchants (the Associates) whose shrewd investments built up the infrastructure and textile industry of New England between 1810 and 1860. Lacking a rigorous prosopographical analysis, it is stronger on the Associates' world than on the anatomy of the elite.

3842

Gregory, Frances W.; Neu, Irene D.

The American Industrial Elite in the 1870s: Their social origins

1962 Harper & Row *New York, NY*

This article, in William Miller's *Men in Business* (qv), reported an important piece of research into the origins of business leaders in three industries (textiles, railroads and steel) during a decade which saw the flowering of big business in the USA. The findings further eroded the rage-to-riches myth.

3843

Hughes, Jonathan R. T.

The Vital Few: The entrepreneur and American economic progress

1986 Oxford University Press *New York, NY*

The ten biographies presented here stretch the usual definition of entrepreneur to include William Penn and Brigham Young as well as Eli Whitney, Thomas Edison, Andrew Carnegie, Henry Ford, E. H. Harriman, J. Pierpont Morgan, and two additions to the eight in the 1966 edition, Mary Switzer and Marriner Eccles (bureaucratic types of entrepreneur). Here an economic historian uses biography as the vehicle for popularising the history of inventors and businessmen.

3844

Ingham, John N.

The Iron Barons: A social analysis of an American urban elite, 1874–1965

1978 Greenwood Press *Westport, CT*

While most studies of business elites chart only the group characteristics of the elite, this one aims to particularize the social and cultural institutions within and outside the firm that have created particular types of business leader. It is confined to six American cities (Pittsburgh, Philadelphia, Bethlehem, Cleveland, Youngstown and Wheeling) and three formative influences: family, social institutions and community.

3845
Ingham, John N.
Biographical Dictionary of American Business Leaders
1983 Greenwood Press *Westport, CT*

This book spans the whole of white American history and provides 835 entries on 1,159 individuals, subjectively chosen. Although entirely derived from secondary works, it is valuable for its compactness, its use of recent literature and its indexes (which group subjects by industry, company, birthplace, place of business activity, religion, ethnicity, birthdate and sex).

3846
Jobert, Philippe (Editor)
Les Patrons du Second Empire: Bourgogne [Employers of the Second Empire: Bourgogne]
1991 Picard/Editions Cenomane *Le Mans, France*

One of a series of regional studies of French entrepreneurs; for annotation, see Barjot, Dominique.

3847
Josephson, Matthew
The Robber Barons: The great American capitalists, 1861–1901
2nd Edition
1961 Harcourt Brace Janovich *New York, NY*

This is the muckraking classic, first published in 1934. Although rich in anecdote and antipathy, it lacks the rigour of prosopographical analysis and evidences no access to private papers.

3848
Kobayashi, Kamejiro; Yui, Tsunehiko; Shunko, Asano (Editors)
Jitsugyo-ka Jinmei Jiten [A Biographical Dictionary of Japanese Businessmen]
1911 Tokyo Jitsugyo Tsushin *Tokyo, Japan*
1990 Rittai-sha *Tokyo, Japan*

This book, first edited by Kobayashi in 1911 and revised by Yui and Shunko in 1990, is a comprehensive biographical dictionary of 3,864 businessmen including not only branch managers and section chiefs of leading companies but also other men of high repute such as landlords, medical doctors and lawyers.

3849
Lévy-Leboyer, Maurice
Le Patronat de la Seconde Industrialisation [Employers of the Second Industrialization]
1979 Editions Ouvrières *Paris, France*

This work contains a number of useful essays on business leaderships in France, Germany, Britain, Sweden and the USA. National, sectoral and international elites are treated.

3850
Mannari, Hiroshi
The Japanese Business Leaders
1974 Tokyo University Press *Tokyo, Japan*

This is a valuable work as it compares the origins of business leaders in Japan with those of American and British businessmen (using Erickson's data, qv).

3851
Mayaud, Jean-Luc (Editor)
Les Patrons du Second Empire: Franche-Comté [Employers of the Second Empire: Franche-Comté]
1991 Picard/Editions Cenomane *Le Mans, France*

One of a series of regional studies of French entrepreneurs; for annotation, see Barjot, Dominique.

3852
Michel, Bernard
Banques et banquiers en Autriche au début du vingtième siècle [Banks and Bankers in Austria at the Beginning of the Twentieth Century]
For main entry, see 2485

3853
Miller, William (Editor)
Men in Business: Essays on the historical role of the entrepreneur
2nd Edition
1962 Harper & Row *New York, NY*

This is a collection of essays by members of the Research Centre in Entrepreneurial History at Harvard (including Hugh G. J. Aitken, Alfred D. Chandler Jr and David S. Landes). William Miller's prosopographical analysis of the American business elite of 1901–10 is especially valuable, though his conclusions for the rags-to-riches myth have been challenged by

Ralph Andreano in L. P. Cain and P. J. Uselding (eds), *Business Enterprise and Economic Change* (Kent State University Press, 1973).

3854
Mills, C. Wright
The Power Elite
1956 Oxford University Press *London*

This classic analysis of elites in American life includes a chapter on CEOs. While Mills calls for elites to be placed in their institutional setting, his work leaves plenty of room for this to be done.

3855
Newcomer, Mabel
The Big Business Executive: The factors that made him, 1900–1950
1955 Columbia University Press *New York, NY*

This is the most thorough of the prosopographies of twentieth-century American CEOs of large corporations. It covers over 300 executives in each of the three years 1900, 1925 and 1950 and complements the work of William Miller (qv).

3856
Peterson, Richard H.
The Bonanza Kings: The social origins and business behaviour of western mining entrepreneurs, 1870–1900
1977 University of Nebraska Press *Lincoln, NB*

This is an informative study of fifty wealthy mine owners in the western USA in the later nineteenth century, which is valuable for its insights into their upward social mobility.

3857
Roberts, Edward D.
Entrepreneurs in High Technology: Lessons from MIT and beyond
1991 Oxford University Press *New York, NY*

Roberts analyses nearly twenty variables in the shaping of over 200 entrepreneurs in the high technology industries on greater Boston's Route 128 since the 1960s. He predictably concludes that success arose from a multitude of factors. One interesting trend was the tendency to replace the founder before super-success was achieved.

3858
Ruckman, Jo Ann
The Moscow Business Elite: A social and cultural portrait of two generations, 1840–1905
1984 Northern Illinois University Press *Dekalb, IL*

This is a closely focused study, centering on the twenty elite families of the Moscow merchant community and their social, cultural and political roles and attitudes.

3859
Scott, John (Editor)
The Sociology of Elites
1990 Edward Elgar Publishing *Aldershot*

This book reprints 60 articles, over 40 treating elites in business, in Britain, the USA, Japan and elsewhere. Among the authors are C. Wright Mills (qv), Stanworth & Giddens (qv), M. Zeitlin, M. Useem and D. Bunting. All are by sociologists.

3860
Vicens Vives, J.
Industrials i politics del segle XIX [Industrialists and Politics of the Nineteenth Century]
1972 Vicens-Vives *Barcelona, Spain*

Biography (in Catalan) of the outstanding figures of the political and business work of Catalonia in the nineteenth century.

Entrepreneurs, British

3861
Adamson, Ian; Kennedy, Richard
Sinclair and the Sunrise Technology: The deconstruction of a myth
For main entry, see 1446

3862
Adeney, Martin
Nuffield: A biography
For main entry, see 799

3863
Andrews, P. W. S.; Brunner, Elizabeth
The Life of Lord Nuffield: A study in enterprise and benevolence
For main entry, see 800

3864
Beckett, J. V.
Coal and Tobacco: The Lowthers and the economic development of west Cumberland, 1660–1760
For main entry, see 328

3865
Bellman, Sir Harold
Cornish Cockney: Reminiscences and reflections
1947 Hutchinson *London*

This book contains fascinating recollections by one of the architects of the building society movement with many glimpses and insights into the Nonconformist culture that produced him.
Firms: Abbey National Building Society; Abbey Road Building Society

3866
Berry, William Michael (Lord Hartwell)
William Camrose: Giant of Fleet Street
For main entry, see 1700

3867
Bower, Tom
Maxwell, The Outsider
1991 Mandarin *London*

Most of this biography was written while Maxwell, the biggest recent crook to rely on writs, was still alive. A revised edition (1993) appeared after Maxwell's death and contains substantial additions.
Firms: British Printing and Communication Corporation; Maxwell Communication Corporation; Mirror Group Newspapers; Pergamon Press

3868
Bower, Tom
Tiny Rowland: A rebel tycoon
1993 Heinemann *London*

A journalistic account of the man whose company's activities were described as the 'unacceptable face of capitalism'. Rowland created a huge but secretive trading organization in Africa whose activities, dominated by Rowland in person for around 30 years, Bower has partly untangled.
Firms: Lonrho (London & Rhodesian Mining and Land Co.); House of Fraser; Observer; Harrods

3869
Boyle, Andrew
Montagu Norman
For main entry, see 2253

3870
Brown, Nick
Richard Branson, the Inside Story
1989 Headline Book Publishing *London*

This is the biography of a Thatcher entrepreneur on the way up: the man behind Virgin records, condoms and airways. It is a very good read with plenty of colourful details and is strong on personalities. It is, however, thin on accounting data and financial performance and lacks scholarly apparatus beyond an index.
Firms: Virgin Group

3871
Brummer, Alex; Cowe, Roger
Hanson: A biography
1994 Fourth Estate *London*

Journalistic, but nevertheless welcome biography of a major if elusive entrepreneur who built up the Hanson company in post-war Britain.
Firms: Berec; Bowater; British Ever Ready; Hanson plc; ICI; Imperial Group (Imperial Tobacco); Peabody Coal Co.; Powell Duffryn; SCM Corporation; Slater Walker Securities

3872
Chapman, Stanley
Jesse Boot of Boots the Chemists
For main entry, see 2027

3873
Chisholm, Anne; Davie, Michael
Beaverbrook: A life
For main entry, see 1707

3874
Church, Roy
Herbert Austin: The British motor car industry to 1941
For main entry, see 805

3875
Church, Roy A.
Kenricks in Hardware: A family business, 1791–1966
1969 David & Charles *Newton Abbot*
This book adds to the empirical literature on family firms. Across five generations, and despite incorporation in 1883, family members developed this Birmingham business and saw it decline and nearly fail, not least because they knew their firm but not the wider skills of business management.
Firms: Kenricks

3876
Clutterbuck, David; Devine, Marion
Clore: The man and his millions
1987 Weidenfeld & Nicolson *London*
This is a workmanlike account of Charles Clore, the 'takeover king' who built up his Sears empire while shaking many a British business out of its 1950s torpor.
Firms: City & Central Investments; City Centre Properties; Sears

3877
Coad, R.
Laing: The biography of Sir John W. Laing, CBE (1879–1978)
1979 Hodder & Stoughton *London*
This is a study not only in business biography but also of the construction industry in Britain. Laing was a successful businessman and a committed Christian who introduced employee welfare schemes and gave much of his fortune to charity. As a company Laing's have been primarily house-builders and pioneers in new production techniques.
Firms: Burnip MacDougall & Co.; John Laing & Son; John Mowlem & Co.; Taylor Woodrow & Co.

3878
Coleman, Donald C.
Sir John Banks, Baronet and Businessman: A study of business, politics and society in later Stuart England
1963 Oxford University Press *Oxford*
Written in brilliant prose and carefully researched, this biography of a Restoration moneylender is limited by the absence of the subject's letterbooks or correspondence.

3879
Corina, Maurice
Pile it High, Sell it Cheap: The authorised biography of Sir John Cohen, founder of Tesco
For main entry, see 2028

3880
Davies, George
What Next?
1991 Arrow Books *London*
This is a retrospective account of his entrepreneurial career by the founder of the Next retail chain. Davies pioneered colourful co-ordinated merchandise, particularly younger women's clothing, in Britain's High Streets in the 1980s.
Firms: Hepworths; Next; Pippa Dee

3881
Davies, Peter N.
Sir Alfred Jones: Shipping entrepreneur par excellence
1978 Europa Publications *London*
This generally favourable and fascinating account of the man who rose from cabin boy to virtual master of the West African trade and founded the Bank of British West Africa, neglects the counterfactual question: would West Africa have developed any better without Jones? The book is excellent on the context within which Jones worked, his determination, drive and dedication to work.
Firms: Elder Dempster & Co.; African Steam Ship Co.; British African Steam Navigation Co.; Bank of British West Africa; Fletcher & Parr

3882
Davies, Peter N.
Business Success and the Role of Chance: The extraordinary Philipps Brothers
Business History, vol. 23, no. 2, 1981: pp 208-32
This fascinating admixture of family and business history uncovers the careers of six

brothers, three of whom made fortunes in business and reached the House of Lords: John, a City financier (Lord St Davids), Owen, with extensive shipping interests (Lord Kylsant) and Laurence, involved in finance and shipping (Lord Milford).
Firms: Court Line; Elder Dempster & Co.; Northern Securities Trust; Old Broad Street Group; Royal Mail Group; St Davids Group

3883
Edwardes, Michael
Back from the Brink
1984 Pan Books *London*

This book is a review by the chairman of the ways in which he claims to have turned round British Leyland, a nationalized shambles, between 1977 and 1982. It is especially useful for comments on business–government relations, business organization, and industrial relations.
Firms: British Leyland; National Enterprise Board

3884
Fallon, Ivan
The Brothers: The rise and rise of Saatchi & Saatchi
1988 Hutchinson *London*

Fallon gives a journalistic account of the Sephardic Jewish brothers whose advertising agency promoted the Conservative party in three election victories. The book contains a bibliography and index but no sources.
Firms: Saatchi & Saatchi

3885
Fallon, Ivan
Billionaire: The life and times of Sir James Goldsmith
1991 Hutchinson *London*

This is a long and detailed biography of the enormously wealthy, buccaneering and colourful international takeover bidder. It contains no scholarly apparatus beyond a short bibliography and an index, which does not include the subject of the book.
Firms: Cavenham Foods

3886
Ferranti, Gertrude Ziani de; Ince, Richard
The Life and Letters of Sebastian Ziani de Ferranti
For main entry, see 1517

3887
Fitton, R. S.
The Arkwrights: Spinners of fortune
For main entry, see 1137

3888
Fitzgerald, Robert
Rowntree and the Marketing Revolution 1862–1969
For main entry, see 1603

3889
Forte, Charles
Forte: The autobiography of Charles Forte
1986 Sidgwick & Jackson *London*

Forte's autobiography is strong on his career in its early and middle stages but weak on how his large hotel chain functioned in the 1970s and 1980s. The book contains much about Forte's tussles with Lord Crowther of Trust Houses and Sir Hugh Wontner of the Savoy Group.
Firms: Forte Co.; Trusthouses Forte

3890
Fraser, William Lionel
All to the Good
1963 Heinemann *London*

An autobiography of a merchant banker who chaired industrial companies (e.g. Thomas Tilling, Babcock & Wilcox), this book makes essential reading for anyone studying the workings of the City of London between the 1920s and the 1950s.
Firms: Babcock & Wilcox; Helbert Wagg; Tilling

3891
Gardiner, Alfred G.
The Life of George Cadbury
1925 Cassell *London*

The as-yet unsurpassed life story of the prime mover of the eponymous confectionery firm is given here, written shortly after Cadbury's death by a personal friend who had access to his papers and members of the family.

However, the book contains no scholarly apparatus beyond an index.
Firms: Cadbury

3892
Grieves, Keith
Sir Eric Geddes: Business and government in war and peace
1990 Manchester University Press *Manchester*

This is a rather uncritical biography of an important business leader of the First World War and interwar period: it lacks footnotes. He was a self-made man but ruthless administrator of the eponymous 'axe'.
Firms: Dunlop Rubber; Imperial Airways; North Eastern Railway

3893
Haines, Joe
Maxwell
1988 Macdonald *London*

This official, uncritical, biography of the corporate crook, was written before his dramatic death and exposure in 1991.
Firms: British Printing and Communication Corporation; Maxwell Communication Corporation; Mirror Group Newspapers; Pergamon Press

3894
Harvey-Jones, John
Getting It Together
1991 Heinemann *London*

Less than half of this autobiography is devoted to the subject's chairmanship of ICI, 1982–87, not least because of restraints imposed by ICI board colleagues. Despite this limitation, the work is important for the personal views expressed by the chairman of one of the UK's largest manufacturing companies. It is best read in conjunction with Harvey-Jones's *Making It Happen* (Collins, 1988).
Firms: Imperial Chemical Industries

3895
Henriques, Robert
Marcus Samuel: First Viscount Bearsted and founder of the Shell Transport and Trading Company, 1853–1927
For main entry, see 430

3896
Hindle, Tim
The Sultan of Berkeley Square: Asil Nadir and the Thatcher years
1991 Macmillan *London*

This is less an orthodox business history and more a journalistic sketch of one of the most notorious international traders of the 1980s. It offers some fascinating insights into the murky private and political worlds of what began as a modest clothing company in the East End of London.
Firms: Polly Peck

3897
Hoe, Susanna
The Man Who Gave His Company Away
1978 Heinemann *London*

This biography of Ernest Bader, the Quaker, pacifist and visionary, frankly recounts the tumultuous struggles, within himself and with others, which led him to transfer his chemical business to the common ownership of his employees. It lacks a scholarly apparatus, however, and needs a sequel recounting the vicissitudes of the Scott Bader Commonwealth since Bader's death in 1982.
Firms: Scott Bader

3898
Jones, Stephanie K.
Trade and Shipping: Lord Inchcape, 1852–1932
For main entry, see 3060

3899
Kennedy, K. H.
Mining Tsar: The life and times of Leslie Urquhart
For main entry, see 434

3900
Marriner, Sheila; Hyde, Francis E.
The Senior. John Samuel Swire, 1825–98: Management in Far Eastern shipping trades
For main entry, see 2137

3901
Marshall, John D. (Editor)
The Autobiography of William Stout of Lancaster, 1665–1752

1967 Manchester University Press *Manchester*

This is a closely edited autobiography of a relatively unimportant Quaker merchant in the retail and wholesale trade in Lancaster.

Firms: Stout, William

3902

Middlemas, R. K.

The Master Builders: Thomas Brassey; Sir John Aird; Lord Cowdray; Sir John Norton-Griffiths

1963 Hutchinson *London*

This is a study of four of the most important civil engineering contractors operating in the nineteenth and early twentieth centuries. All were British, but were critically involved in the expansion of the international economy. Although better on the individual biographies than on the contracting industry the book does contain valuable insights, not least into the nature of economic imperialism.

3903

Muir, Augustus; Davies, Mair

A Victorian Shipowner: A portrait of Sir Charles Cayzer, Baronet of Gartmore

For main entry, see 3067

3904

Nevile, Sir Sydney O.

Seventy Rolling Years

For main entry, see 1841

3905

O'Hagan, H. Osborne

Leaves From My Life

For main entry, see 2334

3906

Overy, Richard J.

William Morris, Viscount Nuffield

1976 Europa Publications *London*

This relatively short biography concentrates on Morris as entrepreneur, with little about technological or social contexts, or comparisons and links with the American motor industry.

Firms: Morris Motors

3907

Parker, Peter

For Starters: The business of life

1989 Jonathan Cape *London*

This is the very detailed, very enjoyable autobiography of one of the most energetic and enthusiastic present-day industrialists. Sir Peter's career has taken him to the chairmanship of British Rail (1976–83), where he pushed forward electrification and the Channel Tunnel. His interest in management education and Japanese links also make the book important.

Firms: British Rail

3908

Pasold, Eric W.

Ladybird, Ladybird: A story of private enterprise

For main entry, see 1901

3909

Porter, Andrew

Victorian Shipping, Business and Imperial Policy: Donald Currie, the Castle Line and Southern Africa

For main entry, see 3071

3910

Poulson, John

The Price: The autobiography of John Poulson, architect

1981 Michael Joseph *London*

Withdrawn from publication under threat of libel proceedings, copies of this book have surfaced now that the author is dead. Poulson's web of corruption, here given a self-justifying gloss, undermined public confidence in the political system and especially the Labour Party in the 1970s.

Firms: Ropergate Services

3911

Pound, Reginald; Harmsworth, A. Geoffrey

Northcliffe

For main entry, see 1735

3912
Reader, W. J.
Architect of Air Power: The life of the first Viscount Weir of Eastwood 1877–1959
For main entry, see 1371

3913
Reynolds, J.
The Great Paternalist: Titus Salt and the growth of nineteenth century Bradford
For main entry, see 1174

3914
Rimmer, W. G.
Marshall's of Leeds, Flax Spinners, 1788–1886
For main entry, see 1193

3915
Robens, Alfred
Ten Year Stint
1972 Cassell *London*

This is a sharply observed autobiographical account of ten years' chairmanship of the National Coal Board (1961–71) where Robens more than halved workforce and pits, but increased productivity, to meet declining demand and competition from alternative sources of energy.
Firms: National Coal Board

3916
Roddick, Anita; Miller, Russell
Body and Soul
1991 Ebury Press *London*

Roddick gives a personal account of her move from schoolteacher to the cosmetics business, where she exploited conservation issues and became a millionaire in the space of eight years. The story is strong on values and the environmental audit but silent on the financial audit.
Firms: Body Shop

3917
Rolt, Lionel T. C.
Isambard Kingdom Brunel: A biography
1957 Longmans *London*

This full-length, and best, biography of Brunel, the innovative nineteenth-century railway engineer, places him firmly in his engineering and social context with an admiration unclouded by adulation. A highly readable book, its main blemish is the omission of footnoted sources.
Firms: Great Western Railway

3918
Rose, Jack
Square Feet
For main entry, see 3270

3919
Rose, Mary B.
The Gregs of Quarry Bank Mill: The rise and decline of a family firm, 1750–1914
For main entry, see 1154

3920
Saunders, James
Nightmare: The Ernest Saunders story
1989 Hutchinson *London*

It is hard to tell whether this is biography or autobiography. It is valuable however for the perspectives of the CEO of Guinness who was found guilty in 1990 of share rigging and false accounting in his takeover of the Distillers group in 1986: one of the major City scandals of the Thatcher years.
Firms: Distillers; Guinness

3921
Sebba, Anne
Laura Ashley: A life by design
1990 Weidenfeld & Nicolson *London*

This is a readable biography of Laura and her husband (Sir) Bernard Ashley who transformed middle-class taste for female dress and household furnishings in the 1970s and 1980s. It is good on personal characteristics but weak on hard business data and there is no scholarly apparatus beyond an index.
Firms: Laura Ashley

3922
Sieff, Marcus
Don't Ask the Price: The memoirs of the president of Marks & Spencer
1986 Weidenfeld & Nicolson *London*

About a tenth of this book relates the author's role in Marks & Spencer: a disappointing feature. Otherwise the remainder is the fascinating story, strong on personal and public life

anecdotes, of the chairman of M&S in the 1970s and early 1980s.
Firms: Marks & Spencer

3923
Sigsworth, Eric M.
Montague Burton: The tailor of taste
For main entry, see 1904

3924
Taylor, Alan J. P.
Beaverbrook
For main entry, see 1740

3925
Thompson, Sir Peter
Sharing the Success: The story of NFC
For main entry, see 3008

3926
Thomson, Adam
High Risk: The politics of the air
1990 Sidgwick & Jackson *London*

This is the readable autobiography of an airline entrepreneur who, like Laker and Branson, ran up against British Airways. The book contains many insights into business–government relationships.
Firms: British Caledonian Airways

3927
Trebilcock, Clive
The Vickers Brothers: Armaments and enterprise, 1854–1914
For main entry, see 709

3928
Underwood, John
The Will to Win: John Egan and Jaguar
1989 W. H. Allen & Co. *London*

Underwood has written a popular biography of Sir John Egan and how he transformed Jaguar from a lame duck to a highly profitable business. Unfortunately the book has no scholarly apparatus whatsoever.
Firms: Jaguar Cars

3929
Vernon, Anne
A Quaker Business Man: The life of Joseph Rowntree, 1836–1925
1958 George Allen & Unwin *London*

This is a not yet superseded but very dated biography of the cocoa and chocolate manufacturer. The business is described by Fitzgerald (qv).
Firms: Rowntrees

Entrepreneurs, American

3930
Baughman, James L.
Henry R. Luce and the Rise of the American News Media
For main entry, see 1762

3931
Baughman, James P.
Charles Morgan and the Development of Southern Transportation
1968 Vanderbilt University Press *Nashville, TN*

Yankee-born Morgan (1795–1878) was the major developer of shipping and railroad networks in the Gulf Southwest and a champion of economic growth via spreading transport networks and hence markets. This biography details his activities and establishes both competitive and altruistic motives.
Firms: Louisiana & Texas RR; Mexican Ocean Mail & Steamship Co.; Texas & New Orleans Mail Line

3932
Belden, Thomas G.; Belden, Marva R.
Lengthening Shadow: The life of Thomas J. Watson
For main entry, see 1456

3933
Bibb, Peter
It Ain't As Easy As It Looks: Ted Turner's amazing story
1993 Birgin Publishing *London*

As sycophantic as its title, this book also contains plenty of useful detail on the founder of CNN and the creation of the business.
Firms: Cable News Network (CNN)

3934
Broehl, Wayne G. Jr
Cargill: Trading the World's Grain
1992 University Press of New England
Hanover, NH

A major business history of America's largest privately owned company combined with a biography of the family at its centre. Of particular interest is the description of trading and speculation in grain particularly in connection with the battle with the Chicago Board of Trade, responsible for regulating the grain trade for all firms involved and interested in stocks held, ledger spreads and speculative sales, while Cargill's trading success depended on confidentiality.
Firms: Cargill

3935
Bruchey, Stuart W.
Robert Oliver, Merchant of Baltimore, 1783–1819
For main entry, see 1957

3936
Bryant, Keith L. Jr
Arthur E Stillwell: Promoter with a hunch
For main entry, see 2845

3937
Carosso, Vincent P.
The Morgans: Private international bankers, 1854–1913
For main entry, see 2599

3938
Case, Josephine Y.; Case, Everett N.
Owen D. Young and American Enterprise: A biography
For main entry, see 1545

3939
Chandler, Alfred D. Jr; Salsbury, Stephen
Pierre S Du Pont and the Making of the Modern Corporation
1971 Harper & Row *New York, NY*

Part biography, part company history, this study is in four parts: family history and Pierre's early life; Pierre as treasurer of Du Pont; Pierre as public leader and chairman of Du Pont during the First World War; and Pierre as chairman and president of General Motors in the 1920s. This is a masterful work about leadership in the modern corporation.
Firms: Du Pont; General Motors

3940
Chandler, Lester V.
Benjamin Strong: Central banker
1958 Brookings Institution *Washington, DC*

Strong, who was Governor of the Federal Bank of New York, dominated the Federal Reserve System in the 1920s and worked with Montagu Norman to recreate the gold standard. This biography emphasizes his lack of training in central banking or economic theory and traces his clashes with the Federal Reserve Board governors in Washington.
Firms: Federal Reserve Bank of NY; Federal Reserve Board

3941
Cheape, Charles W.
Strictly Business: Walter Carpenter at Du Pont and General Motors
1995 Johns Hopkins University Press
Baltimore, MD

Carpenter is often seen as the embodiment of 'organization man' in early twentieth-century US big business. Using his voluminous correspondence, Cheape examines management, decision-making and competition at the highest levels of Du Pont and GM.
Firms: Du Pont; GM

3942
Chernow, Ron
The House of Morgan: An American banking dynasty and the rise of modern finance
For main entry, see 2601

3943
Cray, Ed
Levi's
1978 Houghton Mifflin *Boston, MA*

This full length business biography is by a respected journalist. It is especially strong on personality and incident, but also has a strong grasp of the dynamics of the industry.
Firms: Levi Strauss

3944
Davis, John H.
The Guggenheims: An American epic
1978 William Morrow & Co. *New York, NY*

This large journalistic biography uses interviews, secondary works and archival collections, to track five generations of a business family dominant in mining and minerals until 'daughtered out'.
Firms: Guggenheim; American Smelting and Refining Co.

3945
Dew, Charles B.
Iron Maker to the Confederacy: Joseph R. Anderson and the Tredegar Iron Works
1966 Yale University Press *New Haven, CT*

This study shows Anderson, ironmaster to the Confederacy during the American Civil War, to have been more interested in profits than innovations or patriotism.
Firms: Tredegar Iron Works

3946
Fleming, Rae B.
The Railway King of Canada: Sir William Mackenzie, 1849–1923
For main entry, see 2908

3947
Ford, Henry; Crowther, Samuel
My Life and Work
For main entry, see 932

3948
Foster, Mark S.
Henry J. Kaiser: Builder in the modern American West
1989 University of Texas Press *Austin, TX*

Based on the subject's papers, this is a biography of the road and dam builder of the interwar years and mass producer of Liberty ships during the Second World War, and cargo planes.
Firms: Kaiser Co.

3949
Grodinsky, Julius
Jay Gould: His business career, 1867–1892
1957 University of Pennsylvania Press *Philadelphia, PA*

Concerned with Gould's methods and activities in corporate negotiation and security trading which allowed him to build a railway empire, this study concludes that on balance Gould's activities benefited society.
Firms: Denver & Rio Grande Railroad; Erie Railroad; Missouri Pacific Railroad; St Louis & Western Railroad; Texas & Pacific Railroad; Union Pacific Railroad; Western Pacific Railroad; Western Union Telegraph

3950
Hacker, Louis M.
The World of Andrew Carnegie, 1865–1901
1968 J. B. Lippincott Co. *Philadelphia, PA*

This is a temperate and closely-reasoned rehabilitation of the 'Robber Barons' and a major reinterpretation, which should be used when reading the muckraking accounts of Charles Francis Adams, Matthew Josephson (qqv) and others.
Firms: Carnegie Steel; United States Steel

3951
Haeger, John Denis
John Jacob Astor: Business and finance in the early Republic
For main entry, see 3268

3952
Hessen, Robert
Steel Titan: The Life of Charles M. Schwab
For main entry, see 655

3953
Hidy, Muriel E.
George Peabody: Merchant and financier, 1829–1854
1979 Arno Press *New York, NY*

This dissertation of 1939 is a careful study of an important quarter century in the business career of George Peabody, the most important American international financier before J. P. Morgan.
Firms: Peabody, Riggs & Co.

3954
Hughes, Jonathan R. T.
The Vital Few: The entrepreneur and American economic progress
For main entry, see 3843

3955
Hutchinson, W. H.
Oil, Land and Politics: The California career of Thomas Robert Bard
1965 University of Oklahoma Press *Norman, OK*

This detailed and readable biography traces the career of the man who developed California's oil industry and ended up as a US Senator.
Firms: Union Oil Co. of California

3956
Iacocca, Lee; Novak, William
Iacocca
1985 Sidgwick & Jackson *London*

This is the autobiography of the high-profile automobile industry executive who reached the top in Ford only to be toppled by Henry Ford II. He then moved over to Chrysler and transformed that ailing firm. It is one of the best-selling business books of all time.
Firms: Chrysler; Ford

3957
Ichbiah, D.; Knepper, S. L.
The Making of Microsoft: How Bill Gates and his team created the world's most successful software
For main entry, see 1432

3958
Jardim, Anne
The First Henry Ford: A study in personality and business leadership
For main entry, see 941

3959
Johnson, Arthur M.
Winthrop W. Aldrich: Lawyer, banker, diplomat
1968 Harvard Business School Press *Boston, MA*

This is a good study of a leading New York banker of the 1930s and 1940s.
Firms: Chase Manhattan Bank; Equitable Trust Co., NY

3960
Kirkland, Edward C.
Charles Francis Adams: The patrician at bay
1965 Harvard University Press *Cambridge, MA*

Strong on Adams's career in railroad regulation and on his business career after 1870, this study complements the *Autobiography* of Adams, a paradoxical figure who was not representative of his class, even those in Boston.
Firms: Union Pacific Railroad

3961
Klein, Maury
The Life and Legend of Jay Gould
For main entry, see 2871

3962
Koskoff, David E.
The Mellons: The chronicle of America's richest family
1978 Thomas Y. Crowell *New York, NY*

Offering a more disciplined analysis than the book on the same subject by Burton Hersh, also published in 1978, this work documents the public and private lives of Judge Thomas Mellon and his 168 descendants in the worlds of business and the arts.
Firms: Alcoa; Gulf Oil; Mellon National Bank; T. Mellon & Sons

3963
Lacey, Robert
Ford: The men and the machine
For main entry, see 950

3964
Larson, John L.
Bonds of Enterprise: John Murray Forbes and western development in America's railway age
For main entry, see 2875

3965
Leland, Mrs Wilfred C.; Millbrook, Minnie Dubbs
Master of Precision: Henry M. Leland
1966 Wayne State University Press *Detroit, MI*

Though pietistic in tone, this biography is valuable for the information presented about the man who trained as a Yankee machinist and later turned motor manufacturer, running Ca-

dillac, mostly under General Motors, and in 1917 founding Lincoln.
Firms: Cadillac; General Motors; Lincoln

3966
Levin, Doron P.
Irreconcilable Differences: Ross Perot versus General Motors
For main entry, see 954

3967
Lief, Alfred
Harvey Firestone: Free man of enterprise
For main entry, see 1928

3968
Littman, Jonathan
Once Upon a Time in Computerland: The amazing billion-dollar tale of Bill Millard's computerland empire
For main entry, see 2041

3969
Lowry, Goodrich
Streetcar Man: Tom Lowry and the Twin City Rapid Transit Co.
For main entry, see 2985

3970
Madison, James H.
Eli Lilly: A life, 1885–1977
1989 Indiana Historical Society *Indianapolis, IN*

This study combines the biography of a business inheritor with company history, using company archives. Lilly's activities as industrialist and philanthropist are explored in detail.
Firms: Eli Lilly & Co.

3971
Marrus, Michael A.
Samuel Bronfman: The life and times of Seagram's Mr. Sam
For main entry, see 1865

3972
Martin, Albro
James J. Hill and the Opening of the Northwest
For main entry, see 2878

3973
May, George S.
R. E. Olds, Auto Industry Pioneer
1977 William B. Eerdmans *Grand Rapids, MI*

This is a thorough and painstaking piece of research into the career of one of the founders of the US automobile industry. Olds's career can be usefully contrasted with those of Ford, Leland and others.
Firms: Oldsmobile

3974
Nash, George H.
The Life of Herbert Hoover: The engineer, 1874–1914
1983 W. W. Norton *New York, NY*

The first of a multi-volume and definitive study of the mining engineer who became President of the USA, is strong on business history especially promotion, business and finance in the international mining industry. The second volume (1988) deals with Hoover the humanitarian, 1914–1917.

3975
Philip, Cynthia Owen
Robert Fulton: A biography
1985 Franklin Watts *New York, NY*

Promoter of the steamboat, Fulton emerges in this study as engineer, inventor, painter and entrepreneur. The book could have been stronger on his business activities.

3976
Powell, Horace B.
The Original Has This Signature: W. K. Kellogg
For main entry, see 1616

3977
Reich, Cary
Financier: The Biography of André Meyer: A story of money, power and the reshaping of American business
1983 William Morrow *New York, NY*

This is an important subject. André Meyer, partner in the Paris house of Lazard Frères, fled before the Nazi invasion and, as head of Lazard Frères in New York, 1943–77, transformed the Wall Street house, introducing European

investment bank functions. The book is based on oral interviews.
Firms: Lazard Frères

3978
Roddy, Edward G.
Mills, Mansions and Mergers: The life of William M. Wood
1982 Merrimack Valley Textile Museum *North Andover, MA*

Wood created and dominated the American Woollen Co., the largest woollen firm in the world, for a quarter of a century until his suicide in 1926. At its height the company employed 40,000 people in 60 mills in eight states.
Firms: American Woollen Co.

3979
Rodgers, William H.
Think: A biography of the Watsons and IBM
For main entry, see 1481

3980
Sculley, John; Byrne, John A.
Odyssey, Pepsi to Apple: A journey of adventure, ideas, and the future
For main entry, see 1486

3981
Seaburg, Carl; Paterson, Stanley
Merchant Prince of Boston: Colonel T. H. Perkins, 1764–1854
1971 Harvard University Press *Cambridge, MA*

This detailed study presents not only the rise to wealth of Thomas Handasyd Perkins but also the spirit and mentality of the old mercantile world.
Firms: T H Perkins

3982
Shapley, Deborah
Promise and Power: The life and times of Robert McNamara
1993 Little, Brown & Co. *Boston, MA*

This is a biography of a crucial figure in the development of post-1945 management processes in American big business, Robert McNamara. Based on extensive interviews, this work is particularly interesting on Robert McNamara's formative years at Harvard and in the armed services. His role in the modernization of Ford Motor Company after 1945 is of great interest to business historians.
Firms: Ford Motor Company; General Motors

3983
Sloan, Alfred Pritchard Jr
My Years with General Motors
For main entry, see 983

3984
Sorensen, Charles E.
My Forty Years with Ford
1956 W. W. Norton *New York, NY*

Sorensen was the only man to stay close to Ford over a long period of time. Without reticence or modesty he exposes Ford's stubborn retention of the Model T; his hounding of his only son to an early grave; and the inside story of the reconstruction of the Willow Run plant.
Firms: Ford

3985
Swift, Louis F.; Vissingen, Jr, Arthur van
The Yankee of the Yards: The biography of Gustavus Franklin Swift
For main entry, see 1643

3986
Tebbel, John W.
The Life and Good Times of William Randolph Hearst
For main entry, see 1791

3987
Tichy, N.; Charan, R.
Speed Simplicity and Self-Confidence: An interview with Jack Welch
Harvard Business Review, vol. 67, no. 5, 1989: pp 112–20

This article epitomizes the 1980s strategic vision of a GE manager with its modish references to restructuring and downsizing.
Firms: GE (General Electric)

3988
Tooker, Elva
Nathan Trotter: Philadelphia Merchant, 1787–1853
1955 Harvard University Press *Cambridge, MA*

Based on 1,000 bound volumes and 200 boxes of miscellaneous items, this product of massive and sustained research depicts the life of the early American merchant and the shift from international to internal trade after 1812.
Firms: Trotter

3989
Tucker, Barbara M.
Samuel Slater and the Origins of the American Textile Industry, 1790–1860
1984 Cornell University Press *Ithaca, NY*
Whereas Prude (qv) looks at Slater by means of class analysis, Tucker finds more convincing explanations in family and religion, generation and gender.
Firms: Samuel Slater

3990
Wall, Joseph Frazier
Andrew Carnegie
1970 Oxford University Press *New York, NY*
Massively detailed, this is the definitive biography of Carnegie which, as Edward Kirkland notes, 'pulses with life'.
Firms: Carnegie Steel Co.

3991
Wall, Joseph Frazier
Alfred I. du Pont: The man and his family
1990 Oxford University Press *New York, NY*
A detailed history of the du Pont family dynasty from 1739 to the 1930s, massively researched in the du Pont family archives.
Firms: E. I. Du Pont de Nemours & Co.; Du Pont

3992
Wallace, James; Erickson, Jim
Hard Drive: Bill Gates and the making of the Microsoft empire
For main entry, see 1444

3993
Ward, James A.
J. Edgar Thomson, Master of the Pennsylvania Railroad
For main entry, see 2898

3994
Watson, Thomas J. Jr
A Business and Its Beliefs: The ideas that helped build IBM
1963 McGraw-Hill *New York, NY*
Watson's book is the classic statement of the culture that shaped IBM into one of the USA's 'excellent' companies. It should be read in conjunction with company histories, such as those of Englebourg; Fisher, McKie & Mancke; Sobel (qqv).
Firms: IBM

3995
Worthy, James C.
Shaping an American Institution: Robert E. Wood and Sears, Roebuck
For main entry, see 2111

3996
Worthy, James C.
William C. Norris
1987 Ballinger *Cambridge, MA*
This is a biography of the founder and CEO of Control Data Corp.
Firms: Control Data Corp.; Cray Research; Engineering Research Associates

3997
Young, Jeffrey S.
Steve Jobs: The journey is the reward
1988 Scott, Foresman & Company *Glenview, IL*
Steve Jobs has attracted the attention of journalists, more than any other computing personality (although Bill Gates may yet usurp him here). As a consequence, there has been a minor profusion of books on the Apple Computer, and the creation of an Apple folklore. This biography of Jobs contributes to the legend: it should be read alongside other accounts of Apple such as those of Sculley and Freiberger (qqv).
Firms: Apple Computers

Entrepreneurs, Rest of World

3998
Autin, Jean
Les Frères Péreire: Le bonheur d'entreprendre [The Péreires: The satisfactions of entrepreneurship]
For main entry, see 2347

3999
Barnard, A.
Visions and Profits: Studies in the business career of T. S. Mort
1961 Melbourne University Press *Parkville, Australia*

This business biography of Thomas Sutcliffe Mort (1816–1878) is an excellent study of one of Sydney's leading businessmen. Best known for his promotion of the wool auction system in the colonies, Mort was involved in many other commercial activities such as mining, railways, dairying, dock-building and refrigeration. Based on exhaustive use of public and private archival material this book offers an excellent insight into the economic world of Sydney from the 1840s to the 1870s.
Firms: Goldborough, Mort & Co.; New South Wales Fresh Food & Ice Co.

4000
Broeze, Frank
Mr Brooks and the Australian Trade: Imperial business in the 19th century
1993 Melbourne University Press *Carlton, Vic., Australia*

This is a business biography of Robert Brooks (1790–1882), one of the leaders of London's Australian trade. Brooks was involved in all aspects of the Australian trade: shipping, trade, finance, banking, political lobbying, etc. Through its analysis of Brooks's changing business strategy and management within a comparative framework, this book provides new insights into imperial business in general. Of special interest are the sections on evolution of shipping enterprise and the connection between merchant finance and corporate banking (Brooks was a long-serving director of the Union Bank of Australia). This book is also a case study of principal-agent theory.
Firms: Union Bank of Australia

4001
Carlier, Claude
Marcel Dassault: Le Légende d'un siècle [Marcel Dassault Legend of a century]
For main entry, see 1088

4002
Castronovo, Valerio
Giovanni Agnelli: La Fiat dal 1899 al 1945 [Giovanni Agnelli: Fiat between 1899 and 1945]
1971 UTET *Turin, Italy*

This comprehensive biography of Agnelli sets it in the context of Fiat's development to 1945. It gives a detailed account of Agnelli's readiness to support Mussolini's regime and to impose an authoritarian management structure inside Fiat's factories after 1920. Castronovo deals with business strategy, as well as politics and social conflicts. Agnelli emerges as a twentieth-century version of Faust, continually strugglling to get his way.
Firms: Ansaldo; Fiat; Ilva

4003
Cecil, Lamar
Albert Ballin: Business and politics in Imperial Germany, 1888–1918
1967 Princeton University Press *Princeton, NJ*

This biography of Ballin, the managing director of the Hamburg-America Shipping Line, 1899–1918, emphasizes the role of business and of the businessmen in society.
Firms: Hamburg-AmericalHAPAG

4004
Chadeau, Emmanuel
Latécoère
For main entry, see 1089

4005
Cochran, Thomas C.; Reina, Ruben E.
Entrepreneurship in Argentine Culture: Torcuato di Tella and SIAM
1962 University of Pennsylvania Press *Philadelphia, PA*

This modestly researched history of a career and a company which began in 1910, making bread-making machinery and becoming a diversified industrial empire, is weak in setting

the company and the entrepreneur in the historical context of Argentine economy and society.
Firms: SIAM

4006
Diamond, Marion
The Seahorse and the Wanderer: Ben Boyd in Australia
For main entry, see 2698

4007
Dow, G. M.
Samuel Terry: The Botany Bay Rothschild
1974 Sydney University Press *Sydney, Australia*
Dow has written an effective and interesting business biography of emancipist Samuel Terry who became one of the wealthiest men in Australia before 1850 through a wide-ranging business empire and support by his shrewd and entrepreneurial wife, Rosetta.

4008
Faria, A.
Maua
1946 Companhia Editora Nacional *Rio de Janeiro, Brazil*
This is a biographical work about the most important and prominent entrepreneur in nineteenth-century Brazil. It covers Maua's life span, describing his entrepreneurial career until his bankruptcy at the end of his life.
Firms: Maua & Cia.

4009
Feldenkirchen, Wilfried
Werner von Siemens: Inventor and international entrepreneur
For main entry, see 1516

4010
Friedman, Alan
Agnelli and the Network of Italian Power
1988 Harrap *London*
This is a popular but penetrating assessment of the business empire of Gianni Agenelli. It sheds light on the post-war activities of some of Italy's major enterprises, such as Fiat and Mediobanca, as well as exposing some of the more disturbing aspects of entrepreneurial activity in the 'New Italy'.
Firms: Alfa Romeo; Fiat; Ford General Motor Corp; General Motors; IRI; Istituto Finanziano Industriale; Mediobanca

4011
Glamann, Kristoff
Jacobsen of Carlsberg: Brewer and philanthropist
For main entry, see 1854

4012
Harris, F. R.
Jamsetji Nusserwanji Tata: A chronicle of his life
1958 Blackie *Bombay, India*
This is a second edition of a 1925 biography of J. N. Tata who died in 1904, but whose legacy is the Tata organization with major interests in textiles, steel, electricity, heavy engineering, chemicals etc.
Firms: Tata Industries

4013
Hassbring, Lars
The International Development of the Swedish Match Co., 1917–24
For main entry, see 1679

4014
Hatry, Gilbert
Louis Renault: Patron absolu [Louis Renault: Absolute boss]
For main entry, see 875

4015
Heuss, Theodor
Robert Bosch: His life and achievements
For main entry, see 1522

4016
Hewins, Ralph
The Japanese Miracle Men
1967 Secker & Warburg *London*
This is a study of twenty leading Japanese business tycoons in a wide range of industries (textiles, oil, electrical, motorcycles, rubber, medical products, banking, property, shipping and the press). Hewins's biographies are based on interviews and published sources, but little

of this material is available elsewhere in English and all of it is presented in an engaging style.

4017

Jacquemyns, G.

Langrand-Dumonceau: promoteur d'une puissance financière [Langrand-Dumonceau Financial promoter]

For main entry, see 2416

4018

King, Blair P.

Partner in Empire: Dwarkanath Tagore and the age of enterprise in eastern India

1976 University of California Press *Berkeley, CA*

Focused on Calcutta during the 1840s, this biography throws light on the failure of business leaders in Calcutta, in contrast to those in Bombay, to develop the commercial and industrial life of their city.

Firms: Carr, Tagore Co.

4019

Kuisel, Richard F.

Ernest Mercier, French Technocrat

For main entry, see 2724

4020

Lomüller, Louis-Marie

Guillaume Ternant, 1763–1833: créateur de la première intégration industrielle française [Guillaume Ternant, 1763–1833 Founder of the first French industrial empire]

For main entry, see 1211

4021

Martins, J. S.

Empresario e empresa na biografia do conde Matarazzo [Count Matarazzo: entrepreneur and enterprise]

1967 Instituto de Ciencias Sociais/UFRJ *Rio de Janeiro, Brazil*

This is a biographical work about the largest and most prominent industrialist of the first half of twentieth-century Brazil. It is an important work about the industrialization in São Paulo and the role of foreigners as industrialists in the process.

Firms: Grupo Matarazzo

4022

Mascarenhas, N. L.

Bernardo Mascarenhas: o surto industrial in Minas Gerais [Bernardo Mascarenhas: The industrial upsurge in Minas Gerais]

1954 Grafica Editora Aurora *Rio de Janeiro, Brazil*

Bernardo Mascarenhas was one of the most successful and prominent entrepreneurs in nineteenth-century Minas Gerais. This biography, written by his grandson in the 1950s, is still an important reference work for the study of the industrialization of Minas Gerais in the last century.

Firms: Banco de Credito Real de Minas Gerais; Companhia Cedro e Cachoeira; Companhia Mineira de Eletricidade

4023

Maschke, Erich

Es entsteht ein Konzern: Paul Reusch und die GHH [Paul Reusch and the Growth of a Business]

For main entry, see 633

4024

Morita, Akio

Made in Japan: Akio Morita and Sony

1987 Fontana *London*

Although it should be used with caution, this is a surprisingly revealing autobiography of Sony's CEO. The book contains fascinating anecdotes.

Firms: Sony

4025

Ochetto, Valerio

Adriano Olivetti

1985 Molino *Bologna, Italy*

This general biography of Olivetti's life contains some original research but the primary focus is on his industrial-utopian thought, and his attempts at building a model community around his factory.

Firms: Olivetti

4026

Ohno, Taichi

Toyota Production System: Beyond large-scale production

For main entry, see 1021

4027

Origo, Iris

The Merchant of Prato: Francesco di Marco Datini, 1335–1410

1957 Alfred A. Knopf *New York, NY*

From the 150,000 letters in the Datini archive the author selects personal letters to gain insights into the daily life and attitudes of thought of the medieval Italian merchant, in this case showing how the scope of his activity had run beyond his control.

Firms: Datini

4028

Pfiffner, Albert

Henry Nestlé (1814–1890): Vom Frankfurter Apothekergehilfen zum Schweizer Pionierunternehmer [Henry Nestlé, 1814–1890: From pharmacy assistant to pioneering Swiss industrialist]

1993 Chronos Verlag *Zurich, Switzerland*

This book is essentially a biography of Henry Nestlé (1814–1890), the founder of the (now) biggest Swiss multinational enterprise. Nestlé started as an apprentice in pharmacy in Frankfurt and in the 1860s became a Swiss business pioneer in the food industry. His life and business were closely intertwined and the book outlines how the combination of personal ingenuity, market expansion and profitmaking worked so well together. However, Nestlé having a penchant for the good life sold the whole prospering enterpise in 1875 and withdrew from public life.

Firms: Nestlé

4029

Philips, Frederik

45 Years with Philips: An industrialist's life

1978 Sterling Publishing *New York, NY*

Although not very revealing about Philips's business (the largest in The Netherlands), this autobiography tells us something about business-state relations under the Nazis.

Firms: Philips NV

4030

Ranieri, L.

Emile Francqui ou l'intelligence créatrice 1863–1935 [Emile Francqui–Creative Intelligence 1863–1935]

For main entry, see 2421

4031

Roverato, Giorgio

Una casa industriale: I Marzotto [An Industrial House: The Marzotto family]

1986 Franco Angeli–ASSI *Milan, Italy*

Based on company archives, this book describes the development of Italy's largest wool manufacturer from its beginnings in the nineteenth century up to the 1960s. It is not only a business history but also, and most importantly, the history of an exceptional entrepreneur. Gaetano Marzotto Jr managed to transform a traditionally run family business into an international group, modifying technologies, innovating wholesale and retail distribution and integrating the core business with other sectors.

Firms: S.A. Filatura di Lana a Pettine Gaetano Marzotto (GMF); S.A. Lanificio; Vittorio Emanuele Marzotto (VEM)

4032

Sabates, Fabien; Schweitzer, Sylvie

André Citroën: Les chevrons de la gloire [André Citroën Chevrons of glory]

For main entry, see 895

4033

Santink, Joy L.

Timothy Eaton and the Rise of His Department Store

For main entry, see 2107

4034

Schumann, Wolfgang (Editor)

Carl Zeiss Jena: Einst und Jetzt [Carl Zeiss Jena: Then and now]

1962 Rutten & Loening *Berlin, Germany*

This book includes a collection of essays by Marxist historians from the University of Jena who see Ernst Abbe, the founder of the business, cast in the framework of class struggle, emphasizing his role as scientist and manager and much less his role as social reformer.

Firms: Carl Zeiss

4035

Shawcross, William

Rupert Murdoch: Ringmaster of the information circus

For main entry, see 1737

4036

Steven, Margaret

Merchant Campbell 1769–1846

1965 Oxford University Press *Melbourne, Vic., Australia*

This is an excellent, and at its time pioneering, study into the early commerce of New South Wales. Campbell was involved in a full range of colonial business operations, especially finance and later agriculture: less attention is given to his shipping interests. Campbell's career is set within the full context of contemporary economic, political and social developments. It is an indispensable and in many ways exemplary book.

Firms: Merchant Campbell

4037

Stone, R. C. J.

Young Logan Campbell, The Father and His Gift: John Logan Campbell's later years

1982–87 Auckland University Press *Auckland, New Zealand*

This is an excellent two-volume business biography of John Logan Campbell, one of the leading entrepreneurs in nineteenth-century Auckland. Among many interesting issues are Campbell's willingness to diversify in the face of adversity in the 1880s, which helped him survive when many others went bankrupt.

Firms: Bank of New Zealand; Brown & Campbell; Campbell & Ehrenfried & Co. Ltd; H. H. Willis [UK firm]; New Zealand Insurance; New Zealand Loan & Mercantile Agency Co.

4038

Torres, Eugenio

Ramón de la Sota: Historia económica de un empresario (1857–1936) [Ramon de la Sota The economic history of an entrepreneur (1857–1936)]

1989 Universidad Complutense *Madrid, Spain*

Comprehensive biography of one of the most prominent entrepreneurs of the Restoration period in Spain. Ramon de la Sota built up a powerful business group with interests in iron and coal mining and iron-making, ships and shipbuilding, banks, etc. The author also offers a detailed study of the main enterprises of the group.

Firms: Compañía Naviera Sota y Aznar; Compañía Euskalduna de Construcción y Reparacíon de Buques; Compañía Minera de Setares; Compañía Minera de Sierra Alhamilla; Compañía Minera de Sierra Menera

4039

Wasserman, Mark

Capitalists, Caciques, and Revolution: The native elite and foreign enterprise in Chihuahua, Mexico, 1854–1911

1984 University of North Carolina Press *Chapel Hill, NC*

This book is centred on the two most important entrepreneurs in northern Mexico prior to the revolution: Luis Terrazas and Enrique Creel. Their monopolization of power led to the revolutionary uprising.

4040

Wikander, Ulla

Kreuger's Match Monopolies, 1925–30: Case studies in market control through public monopolies

For main entry, see 1684

4041

Wilson, J. F.

Ferranti and the British Electrical Industry, 1864–1930

For main entry, see 1542

Management

4042

Aitken, Hugh G. J.

Taylorism at Watertown Arsenal: Scientific management in action, 1908–1915

1960 Harvard University Press *Cambridge, MA*

Excellent on both the Arsenal and Taylorism, this pioneering study demonstrates that complex social change, upsetting existing roles and behaviour patterns and establishing new

systems of authority and control, were involved in Taylorism–and not merely technical innovation. To be read in conjunction with Nelson and Braverman (qqv).
Firms: Watertown Arsenal

4043
Barnard, Chester I.
The Functions of the Executive
1938 Harvard University Press *Cambridge, MA*
This a highly influential text, at once practical and philosophical, is by a senior executive in the New Jersey Bell Telephone Co. He argued that formal organizations and the executive process rest on cooperative action.

4044
Baughman, James P. (Editor)
The History of American Management: Selections from the Business History Review
For main entry, see 3544

4045
Berle, Adolf A.; Means, Gardiner C.
The Modern Corporation and Private Property
1932 Macmillan *New York, NY*
From an analysis of the 200 largest firms in the USA, Berle plotted the separation (observed since the turn of the century by corporate lawyers) between ownership (shareholders) and control (managers) in business. This finding has been one of the pillars on which A. D. Chandler's (qv) theory of the rise of big business rests.

4046
Blake, Robert Rogers; Mouton, Jane S.
The Managerial Grid
1964 Gulf Publishing *Houston, TX*
This book is a pioneering attempt to provide a systematic analysis of situational leadership in business. The authors measure management styles on two dimensions, concern for production and concern for people, using a grid. The underlying assumption is that leadership is a matter of style. In some ways the Blake and Mouton grid is reminiscent of McGregor's Theory X and Theory Y (qv).

4047
Bloemen, E. S. A.
Scientific Management in Nederland, 1900–1930
1988 Nederlandsch Economisch-Historisch *Amsterdam, The Netherlands*
The author relies more on the approach of Daniel Nelson than that of Harry Braverman (qqv) and concludes that employers were less interested in Taylorism than in outside professionals like engineers, psychologists and accountants.

4048
Boswell, Jonathan S.
Business Policies in the Making: Three steel companies compared
For main entry, see 581

4049
Burnham, James
The Managerial Revolution: What is happening in the world
1941 John Day *New York, NY*
Burnham's book is a tract, albeit an influential one, for the times, asserting that capitalism was moving towards a managerial society.

4050
Burns, James MacGregor
Leadership
1978 Harper & Row *New York, NY*
Burns's book is a large eclectic volume packed with anecdotes and examples, ranging from Moses to Mao, and arguing that leadership is essentially transactional, entailing a dynamic reciprocity between leaders and followers.

4051
Cadbury, Sir Adrian
The Company Chairman
1990 Director Books *Cambridge*
Cadbury deals, as no other author has done, with the company chairman's roles from the practical point of view. This is a handbook which theorists among business and labour historians should read before pronouncing easy judgements on their targets.

4052
Cadbury, Sir Adrian
Report of the Committee on the Financial Aspects of Corporate Governance
1992 Gee & Co. *London*

A foundational document treating the system by which companies are directed and controlled, this report was directed at boards, auditors and shareholders. Covering financial reporting, accountability, and dealing with such matters as the roles of non-executive directors, it was prepared against a backdrop of corporate malfeasance in the 1980s (from BCCI to Maxwell) and aimed to pre-empt statutory reform of corporate governance by inaugurating a voluntary code of best practice, endorsed by the London Stock Exchange.

4053
Chandler, Alfred D. Jr; Daems, Herman (Editors)
Managerial Hierarchies: Comparative perspectives on the rise of the modern industrial enterprise
For main entry, see 3445

4054
Channon, Derek F.
The Strategy and Structure of British Enterprise
For main entry, see 3446

4055
Charkham, Jonathan
Keeping Good Company: A study of corporate governance in five countries
1994 Oxford University Press *Oxford*

This volume compares the system by which companies are directed and controlled in Germany, Japan, France, the USA and the UK. The criteria for assessing these systems are dynamism (managerial scope without undue government interference, litigation or displacement) and accountability (ensuring management is accountable for its decisions and actions). The study is especially good in its overview of the financial systems surrounding business. The book is to be used in conjunction with the Code named after Sir Adrian Cadbury (qv).

4056
Child, John
British Management Thought
1969 Allen & Unwin *London*

This is a chronological and analytical assessment of British management thought from the First World War until the 1960s: a pioneering survey of the landscape, superseding Urwick (qv).

4057
Chokki, Toshiaki
Nippon no Kigyo Keiei [Japanese Business Management: A historical description]
1992 Hosei Daigaku Shuppan-kyoku *Tokyo, Japan*

This Japanese business management history focuses on the period from the 1880s to the 1980s. It deals with entrepreneurial activities, strategy and structure, production management, R&D, and the internationalization of Japanese business.

4058
Dassbach, Carl
Global Enterprises and the World Economy: Ford, General Motors, and IBM, the emergence of the transnational enterprises
1989 Garland *New York, NY*

Dassbach reviews the evolution of three major corporations and their organizational contribution to the development of transnational enterprise. He is particularly interesting on the interchange of ideas and executive personnel between these path-breaking American transnationals.
Firms: Ford; General Motors; IBM

4059
Drucker, Peter F.
The Concept of the Corporation
1946 John Day *New York, NY*

Drucker's book is regarded by managers as a classic analysis of the managerial methods developed at General Motors by Alfred P. Sloan (qv). It looks at both the organization and management policies of GM and examines the corporation as a social institution.
Firms: General Motors

4060
Drucker, Peter F.
The Practice of Management
1955 Heinemann *London*

Using the cases of Sears, Ford, IBM, this popular study analyses management from a functional viewpoint, which is rather more human than the classic functional approach of Urwick (qv) and Henri Fayol (qv).
Firms: Ford; IBM; Sears

4061
Edwards, Ronald S.; Townsend, Harry (Editors)
Studies in Business Organisation
1961 Macmillan *London*

A supplement to the same editors' *Business Enterprise*: ten cases from the Edwards seminar.
Firms: Forte; Dowty; Mobil Oil; Elliott Automation; GKN; Vauxhall; P&O; Boots; HMSO; Royal Opera House, Covent Garden

4062
Edwards, Ronald S.; Townsend, Harry (Editors)
Business Enterprise: Its growth and organization
1966 Macmillan *London*

This reprints 26 of the nearly 450 papers given by industrialists to the Edwards seminar on industrial administration at the LSE, 1946–73. They are grouped in sections: early stages of growth, marketing and advertising, food and drink, aircraft, contracting and sub-contracting, large-scale administration, research and development.

4063
Fayol, Henri
Administration Industrielle et Générale: Prévoyance, Organisation, Commandement, Coordination, Controle [Industrial and General Administration]
1930 International Management Institute *Geneva, Switzerland*

First published in French in 1925, until the 1970s and 1980s Fayol's administrative paradigm of the manager's function predominated among concepts of managerial work. Fayol's five managerial activities (see book title) were expanded in the 1930s by Luther Gulick who added an acronym, POSDCORB, to capture what managers do: planning, organizing, staff, directing, coordinating, reporting and budgeting. See Mintzberg for the recent alternative to Fayol.

4064
Feldenkirchen, W.
Big Business in Interwar Germany: Organizational innovation at Vereinigte Stahlwerke, IG Farben and Siemens
Business History Review, vol. 61, no. 3, pp 417–51

This article describes organizational innovation in big business in Germany during the interwar period. Following Chandler's approach to the American experience, three distinct corporations in separate industrial spheres are studied and it is argued that changes in organizational structure and strategy were important in the economic success of these firms during this period.
Firms: IG Farben; Siemens; Vereinigte Stahlwerke

4065
Fujii, Mitsuo; Maruyama, Yoshinari (Editors)
Gendai Nippon Keiei-shi: Nippon-teki Keiei to Kigyo Shakai [Modern Japanese Business History: Japanese-style management and corporate society]
1991 Mineruva Shobo *Kyoto, Japan*

This covers the period from the 1850s to the 1980s and includes discussion of the development of prewar Zaibatsu, the formation of postwar business groups, labour management in big business, the general trading companies and the subcontracting system.

4066
Gillespie, Richard
Manufacturing Knowledge: A history of the Hawthorne experiments
1991 Cambridge University Press *Cambridge*

Gillespie conducts a thorough historical probing of the research methods and interpretations of the Hawthorne experiments into work study conducted by Mayo (qv). His book is a fascinating analysis, confirming that

knowledge produced by social science research reflects the power relations within which the research is conducted; and that researchers inevitably embed their own political, professional and personal values in their apparently objective knowledge claims.
Firms: Western Electric Co.

4067
Haber, Samuel
Efficiency and Uplift: Scientific management in the progressive era, 1890–1920
1964 Chicago University Press *Chicago, IL*
While the material on Taylor is largely familiar, this study is important for its exploration of the meanings of the term 'efficiency', including business efficiency.

4068
Handy, Charles B.
Gods of Management: The changing work of organizations
1985 Pan Books *London*
Very much a 'pop' management study, this is a lighthearted but perceptive introduction to the power cultures found in modern organizations. It should be read in conjunction with the author's *Understanding Organizations* (qv).

4069
Handy, Charles B.
Understanding Organizations
3rd Edition
1985 Penguin *Harmondsworth*
This book provides an excellent introduction to the issues, debates and literature preoccupying modern management theorists. Included are chapters on culture and leadership.

4070
Hannah, Leslie (Editor)
Management Strategy and Business Development
1976 Macmillan *London*
This collection of conference papers comprises company and sectoral case studies prefixed by a general one by Alfred Chandler. It is a very useful adjunct to the essays edited by Barry Supple (qv).
Firms: BP; Boots; ICI; Imperial Tobacco; Pilkington

4071
Hara, Terushi (Editor)
Kagaku-teki Kanri-ho no Donyu to Tenkai: Sono Rekishi-teki Kokusai Hikaku [The Introduction and Development of Scientific Management: A comparative historical study]
1990 Showa-do *Kyoto, Japan*
This work deals with the introduction and development of scientific management in the USA, UK, France, Italy, Germany, Soviet Union and Japan in comparative perspective. It outlines the extent of scientific management in each country.

4072
Hawkins, C. J.
Theory of the Firm
1973 Macmillan *London*
Hawkins gives an extremely useful summary of the various (mostly economic) theories that have been advanced to explain the behaviour of firms.

4073
Jones, Geoffrey; Rose, Mary (Editors)
Family Capitalism
Business History, vol. 35, no. 4, 1993
This special issue contains seven articles (by Roy Church, Sheila Smith, Ann Prior and Maurice Kirby, Stana Nenadic, Philip Scranton, Keetie E. Sluyterman & Helene J. M. Winkelman, and Emmanuel Chadeau) which examine Chandler's views on personal capitalism (qv), family firms in eighteenth-century India, Quaker family firms in Britain and the USA, small family firms in Victorian Scotland and family firms in The Netherlands and France.
Firms: Stockton and Darlington Railway; Bromley & Sons; Disston Saw; Campbell Soup; Carino; Peugeot; Michelin; Saint-Crobain

4074
Juran, Joseph Moses (Editor)
Quality Control Handbook
1951 McGraw-Hill *New York, NY*
This is the work which the Japanese applied to bringing their industrial products up to American quality standards. It is a reference work setting out the principles and statistical

techniques for achieving quality control both in general and in specific industries.

4075
Kanter, Rosabeth Moss
The Change Masters: Corporate entrepreneurs at work
1984 George Allen & Unwin *London*

Kanter presents a study of nearly fifty innovative companies (nominated by a poll of senior executives) and a similar control group in an attempt to discover how managers in the 1960s and 1970s effected organizational 'transformations'.

4076
Kaplinsky, Raphael; Posthuma, Anne
Easternisation: The spread of Japanese management techniques to developing countries
1994 Frank Cass *Ilford*

This is an important monograph in that it seeks to analyse the diffusion of Japanese management techniques in Brazil, the Dominican Republic, India and Zimbabwe from the 1970s. However, the book is not very user-friendly, in that the case studies are disguised and there is no index.

4077
Kaufman, Allen; Zacharias, Lawrence
From Trust to Contract: The legal language of managerial ideology, 1920–1980
Business History Review, vol. 66, no. 3, 1992: pp 523–72

This article examines the legal underpinning of managers' professional status, showing how management has been made and un-made as a semi-public profession.

4078
Kay, John
Foundations of Corporate Success: How business strategies add value
1993 Oxford University Press *Oxford*

This is an influential British response to the competitive advantage concepts of Michael Porter (qv). Measuring corporate success by added value, Kay argues that corporate strategy should aim at developing key organizational capabilities: innovation; reputation (eg brands); strategic assets (eg monopoly); and 'architecture' (corporate links with employees, customers, suppliers). Arguments are supported by many contemporary corporate examples.

4079
Knight, Arthur
Private Enterprise and Public Intervention
1974 George Allen & Unwin *London*

Sir Arthur Knight gives an insider's view of the impact of government on business in the 1950s and 1960s, touching on questions such as protection, subsidy, competition policy, takeover, merger, prices and incomes policy, and regional policy.
Firms: Courtaulds

4080
Livesay, Harold C.
Entrepreneurial Dominance in Businesses Large and Small, Past and Present
Business History Review, vol. 63, no. 1, 1989: pp 1–21

Livesay restores the entrepreneur to the business organization, from which he/she has been exiled by Chandler's managerial hierarchies.

4081
Mayo, Elton
The Human Problems of an Industrial Civilisation
1933 Harvard University Press *Cambridge, MA*

This is the popular report of the 'Hawthorne experiments', conducted under Mayo's guidance at the Western Electric Co., Chicago, which revealed the strength of personal attitudes and informal social organization in industrial organization. Mayo's research methods and interpretations have been the subject of much controversy: e.g. Gillespie (qv).
Firms: Western Electric Co.

4082
McCraw, Thomas K.
Prophets of Regulation
1984 Harvard University Press *Cambridge, MA*

McCraw skilfully uses history and biography to explore regulation as a process, demonstrating that institutional change does not emerge independent of human hands. The regulators are Charles Francis Adams, Louis Brandeis, James Landis and Alfred Kahn.

4083

McGuffie, Chris

Working in Metal: Management and labour in the metal industries of Europe and the USA 1890–1914

For main entry, see 1335

4084

Mintzberg, Henry

The Nature of Managerial Work

1973 Prentice-Hall *Englewood Cliffs, NJ*

Mintzberg challenges theories suggesting that the manager orchestrates an orderly organization; instead he identifies ten key roles which can be subsumed under three heads: inter-personal, informational and decision-making roles.

4085

Moss, Scott J.

An Economic Theory of Business Strategy: An essay in dynamics without equilibrium

1981 Martin Robertson *Oxford*

This is an intellectually challenging study intended to explain the conditions under which some business strategies are preferred to others.

4086

Nakagawa, Keiichiro (Editor)

Kigyo Keiei no Rekishi-teki Kenkyu [A Historical Study of Business Management]

1990 Iwanami Shoten *Tokyo, Japan*

This book is a collection of 20 papers written by Japanese business historians in celebration of Professor Yoshitaro Wakimura's 90th birthday. Each paper treats wide-ranging issues including Japanese management, comparative management, the international trends in business management and the shipping and shipbuilding industries.

4087

Nelson, Daniel

Managers and Workers: Origins of the new factory system in the United States, 1880–1920

1975 University of Wisconsin Press *Madison, WI*

With careful research and balanced judgement, Nelson provides a collection of essays that are together an important and stimulating exploration of the boundary between business and labour history.

4088

Nelson, Daniel

Frederick W. Taylor and the Rise of Scientific Management

1980 University of Wisconsin Press *Madison, WI*

This detailed biography of Taylor places him in his milieu and rescues him from the stereotype purveyed by Braverman (qv).

Firms: Midvale Steel

4089

Nelson, Daniel (Editor)

A Mental Revolution: Scientific management since Taylor

1992 Ohio State University Press *Columbus, OH*

Eight essays examine how Taylor's ideas on scientific management were applied in contradictory fashion and there can be no simple definition of his influence on management.

Firms: Joseph & Feiss; Link Belt Co.; Du Pont; Charles Bedaux

4090

Ogura, Eiichiro

Oumi Shonin no Keiei Kanri [The Business Management of "Oumi" Merchants]

1991 Chuo Keizai-sha *Tokyo, Japan*

The author focuses on business management by the 'Oumi' Merchants in the Edo period, including financial management, production management, cost accounting, purchasing and sales management, labour management, and R&D management.

4091

Okuda, Kenji

Hito to Keiei: Nippon Keiei Kanri-shi Kenkyu [Men and Management: A study of Japanese business management history]

1985 Management-sha *Tokyo, Japan*

This wide-ranging history of management in Japan covers the period from the 1900s to 1945 featuring the introduction and development of scientific management, the evolution of trade unions and management ideology.

4092
Penrose, Edith T.
The Theory of the Growth of the Firm
2nd Edition
1980 Basil Blackwell *Oxford*

This is a pioneering treatment of the firm by an economist grounded in both classical economic theory and real-world familiarity with business organizations. The book is concerned chiefly with issues of growth and entrepreneurship.

4093
Peters, Thomas J.; Waterman, Robert H.
In Search of Excellence: Lessons from America's best-run companies
1982 Harper & Row *New York, NY*

This is an attempt, remarkably popular at the time, to distil the management experience of 62 very successful (prior to 1982) American corporations into a clutch of key lessons. In retrospect this was a much weaker study than that of Kanter (qv).

4094
Pettigrew, Andrew
The Awakening Giant: Continuity and change in Imperial Chemical Industries
1985 Basil Blackwell *Oxford*

Analysing change in ICI between the 1960s and 1980s, this book focuses on the work of Organization Development specialists in enabling ICI to adjust to its changing environment: a rare example of a management specialist setting his work in a time-frame and the best source (to date) for ICI's history subsequent to the Reader (qv) volumes.
Firms: ICI

4095
Taylor, Frederick Winslow
The Principles of Scientific Management
1911 Harper Brothers *New York, NY & London*

This includes the classic paper by Taylor presented to the American Society of Mechanical Engineers in 1910. It was initially printed in confidential form for members of the society in 1911 and later sold to the public. Above all other writings, these are the foundational documents of the management revolution. For the debate over the theory and practice of 'Taylorism' see Aitken, Braverman, Nelson, etc.

4096
Thomas, Rosamund S.
The British Philosophy of Administration: A comparison of British and American ideas, 1900–1939
1978 Longman *London*

The author traces the American concern with discovering principles of administration analogous to scientific laws, in contrast to the British interest in defining, communicating and controlling.

4097
Urwick, Lyndall Fownes
The Elements of Administration
2nd Edition
1947 Pitman *London*

Urwick popularized the functional view of management, first explicated by Henri Fayol in his *Administration Industrielle et Generale* (1916) (qv), as forecasting (research), planning, coordinating, commanding, and controlling.

4098
Urwick, Lyndall Fownes
The Golden Book of Management: A historical record of the life and work of seventy pioneers
1956 Newman Neame *London*

This book is a roll-call of managers and management thinkers from Boulton & Watt through Fayol and Taylor to Rowntree and Mayo. It contains mainly potted biographies and is not always very informative about their subjects' management ideas. Presumably this volume is an abridgement of Urwick's *The Making of Scientific Management*, vol. 1 (qv).

4099
Urwick, Lyndall Fownes; Brech, Edward F. L.
The Making of Scientific Management

1948–9 Management Publications Trust *London*

This three-volume work is an early attempt by Urwick to place the development of management in historical perspective. His book now looks very dated and weak as historical analysis.

4100
Williamson, Oliver E.; Winter, Sidney (Editors)
The Nature of the Firm: Origins, evolution and development
1991 Oxford University Press *New York, NY*

This collection of economics conference papers celebrates the fiftieth anniversary of Ronald Coase's pioneering article on the nature of the firm. The theme remains unresolved: in one view the firm possesses 'distinct powers of fiat that are not easily replicated through market contracting'; in the other view, 'the firm's boundaries are defined by the set of assets placed under common ownership' (see Dow in *Business History Review*, vol.65, 1991, p. 992).

4101
Xenophon
The Economist of Xenophon
1876 Ellis & White *London*

Described by Henrietta Larson (qv) as 'One of the earliest works on the management of the economic unit'.

4102
Yates, JoAnne
Control through Communication: The rise of system in American management
1989 Johns Hopkins University Press *Baltimore, MD*

This important study of changes in corporate communication systems and technologies from 1850 to 1920 focuses on three company case studies.

Firms: Du Pont; Illinois Central Railroad; Scovill Manufacturing Co.

Education & Management

4103
Aldcroft, Derek H.
Education, Training and Economic Performance 1944 to 1990
1992 Manchester University Press *Manchester*

A provocative contribution to the education/'British decline' debate which goes too far in its damning indictment of the British education system and gives too much credence to the 'anti-industrial spirit' variable.

4104
Amdam, Rolv Petter
For egen regning: BI og den økonomisk-administrative utdanningen 1943–1993 [The History of the Norwegian School of Management: Business Education in Norway 1943–1993]
1993 Universitetsforlaget AS *Oslo, Norway*

A modest course-teaching and consulting firm in 1943, the Norwegian School of Management has become one of Europe's largest business schools in 1993. The book explores the background and effects of the growth of this privately owned and financed school, within an overall public educational system. The main topic is the interplay between the school itself, the educational system and working life.

4105
Artz, Frederick B.
The Development of Technical Education in France, 1500–1800
1966 MIT Press *Cambridge, MA*

This study considers schools of business as well as schools of engineering and mining.

4106
Babbage, Charles
The Economy of Machinery and Manufactures
1832 Charles Knight *London*

This, Babbage's most important book, was an analysis of Manchester-based production in the factory, and a discussion of social relations in industry. In order to promote British industrialization, Babbage prescribed the coherent development of education, science and technology, ie a union of scientific theory and industrial practice.

4107
Barnes, W.
Managerial Catalyst: The story of London Business School, 1964–1989
1989 Paul Chapman *London*

This account of the origins and development of one of the first two US-style graduate business schools set up in the UK to equip senior executives with MBAs should be read in conjunction with John Wilson's account of Manchester Business School (qv).

4108
Buchanan, Robert A.
The Engineers: A history of the engineering profession in Britain, 1750–1914
1989 Jessica Kingsley *London*

This is the best available survey of the rise and progress of the major (civil, mechanical, electrical) and lesser British engineering institutions and societies. Based largely on published sources, its major weakness is the absence of any prosopographical analysis.

4109
Carew, Anthony
Labour and the Marshall Plan: The politics and productivity and the marketing of management science
1987 Manchester University Press *Manchester*

This is an important study of American initiatives, and specifically Marshall Aid and the Anglo-American Council on Productivity, to encourage productivity-enhancing techniques in European industry. It focuses on the political implications rather than on the techniques themselves.

4110
Clements, R. V.
Managers: A study of their careers in industry
1958 George Allen & Unwin *London*

Based on interviews with over 600 managers in the north west of England, this study found, *inter alia*, very little evidence of the existence of discrete managerial skills or of a managerial profession in the region's industrial sector.

4111
Copeland, Melvin T.
And Mark an Era: The story of the Harvard Business School
1958 Little, Brown & Co. *Boston, MA*

This is a modestly critical account of Harvard Business School, the epitome of the American model of management education, which badly needs to be updated by a complementary volume covering the era since the 1950s. Written by an original member of staff, it has good descriptions of the case method of instruction and of the dominant figures who shaped the School.

4112
Cruikshank, Jeffrey L.
A Delicate Experiment. The Harvard Business School, 1908–1945
1987 Harvard Business School Press *Boston, MA*

A magnificently produced and illustrated coffee-table volume which is also a serious history of the School by an accomplished historian using primary sources. Cruikshank describes the origins of the institution in its wider context and is fascinating on the evolution of the culture of the school and the evolution of its curriculum.
Firms: Harvard Business School

4113
Dintenfass, Michael
The Decline of Industrial Britain 1870–1980
For main entry, see 3593

4114
Gospel, Howard F.
Industrial Training and Technological Innovation: A comparative and historical study
1991 Routledge *London*

This is a collection of essays first delivered at the Business History Unit's second Anglo-Japanese Business History Conference. These deal mainly with engineers (as is appropriate to the training of Japanese managers) rather than with the MBA route to management.
Firms: Mitsubishi

4115
Handy, Charles et al
The Making of Managers: A report on management education, training and development in the USA, West Germany, France, Japan and the UK
1987 Nat. Economic Development Office *London*

This was one of two reports (the other being *The Making of British Managers*) published on the same day in April 1987, which stirred a great deal of comment in the Press – and struck a heavy, if not fatal, blow against pragmatism. From a historical viewpoint it is extremely valuable for the comparative data provided for the five countries concerned, all pertaining to 1985.

4116
Handy, Charles; Gordon, Colin; Gow, Ian; Randlesome, Collin
Making Managers
1988 Pitman *London*

This collection of reflective essays is based on the data collected for Handy et al, *The Making of Managers* (qv).

4117
Hanisch, Tore Jørgen; Lange, Even
Vitenskap for industrien: NTH-En høyskole i utvikling gjennom 75 år [Science and Industry: The History of the Norwegian Institute of Technology]
1985 Universitetsforlaget *Oslo, Norway*

This book deals with the shaping and history of the main Norwegian institution for the education of scientifically-trained engineers, between 1910 and 1985. It surveys the historical interrelation between industrial development and the education of engineers, the development of the engineering profession and its role in production.

4118
Iwauchi, Ryoichi
Nippon no Kogyo-ka to Jukuren Keisei [Industrialization and Technical Training in Japan]
1989 Nippon Hyoron-sha *Tokyo, Japan*

This is a monograph on the history of Japanese in-company education and training systems covering the period from the 1870s to the 1930s, which includes case studies of Kamaishi Iron Works, Mitsubishi Heavy Industry, Japan National Railway, etc. The work describes a changing emphasis between in-house training and the school system.
Firms: Japan National Railway; Kamaishi Iron; Mitsubishi

4119
Japan Industrial Training Association
Nippon Sangyo Kunren Hyakunen-shi [A Centenary History of Industrial Training in Japan]
1971 Japan Industrial Training Association *Tokyo, Japan*

Covering the period from the 1860s to the 1960s, this book gives an outline of the development of Japanese industrial training which includes the complementary process of formal education with in-company training, the introduction of American training systems and training systems in small and medium-sized enterprises.

4120
Japan Productivity Center
Seisan-sei Undo Sanju-nen-shi [A 30-Year History of the Productivity Movement]
1985 Japan Productivity Center *Tokyo, Japan*

This is an authoritative history of the Japan Productivity Center and its role in the productivity movement in Japan after 1955. This book is a valuable source for information about how Japanese managers and executive engineers learned modern management methods from American and European countries after the Second World War.

4121
Kawabe, Nobuo; Daito, Eisuke (Editors)
Education and Training in the Development of Modern Corporations (Nineteenth Fuji Conference)
For main entry, see 97

4122
Keeble, Shirley P.
The Ability to Manage: A study of British management, 1890–1990
1992 Manchester University Press *Manchester*

This is a detailed examination of the ways in

which British managers have been produced, concluding that these have been very deficient. It complements Locke and Sanderson (qqv) and gives context to Wilson and Barnes (qqv).

4123
Kinmonth, Earl H.
The Self-made Man in Meiji Japanese Thought: From samurai to salary man
For main entry, see 3740

4124
Kobayashi, Kesaji; Morikawa, Hidemasa (Editors)
Development of Managerial Enterprise (Twelfth Fuji Conference)
For main entry, see 98

4125
Locke, Robert R.
The End of the Practical Man: Entrepreneurship and higher education in Germany, France and Great Britain 1880–1940
1984 JAI Press *Greenwich, CT*

Locke describes the crucial role of higher education in German industrialization, giving competitive advantage through wider access to technology and management science. He argues convincingly that national differences in business education have had a decisive bearing on comparative economic performance.

4126
Locke, Robert R.
Management and Higher Education Since 1940: The influence of America and Japan on West Germany, Great Britain and France
1989 Cambridge University Press *Cambridge*

This thoughtful series of essays analyses the 'scientific' American management paradigms and finds them wanting. The West German system of management education is seen as the most efficient in Europe and that which owed least to US models. This is a subtle and complex examination of the relationship between educational and business cultures which will not command universal agreement but cannot fail to stimulate.

4127
Marceau, Jane
A Family Business?: The making of an international business elite
1989 Cambridge University Press *New York, NY*

This prosopography of graduates of INSEAD, the International Business School at Fontainebleau, argues that MBA training has served to preserve the old business elite as the new managerial leadership. The study is weakened by neglect of non-French elites and by its confinement to the 1970s, prior to the Japanese challenge.
Firms: INSEAD

4128
Mayor, Alberto
Etica, Trabajo y productividad en Antioquia [Ethics, Work and Productivity in Antioquia, Colombia]
1984 Tercer Mundo *Bogotá, Colombia*

This book traces the role played by the National School of Mines in Colombia (NSM) as a seedbed of entrepreneurs and managers in Colombia during the first half of the twentieth century. The author examines the dissemination of NSM's ethos, a blend of scientific management and Roman Catholic ideologies, in public and private firms through its graduates. It relies on a wealth of primary and secondary sources.

4129
More, Charles
Skill and the English Working Class, 1870–1914
1980 Croom Helm *London*

More presents a study of the development of apprenticeship training and the question of skill levels in British industry.

4130
Morikawa, Hidemasa
Gijutsu-sha: Nippon Kindai-ka no Ninaite [The Engineers: The leaders in the modernization of Japan]
1975 Nippon Keizai Shinbun-ska *Tokyo, Japan*

This book focuses on the leading role of graduate engineers in the modernization of

Japanese business. It also deals with the formation of a technocracy in Japanese business.

4131

Noble, David F.

America by Design: Science, technology, and the rise of corporate capitalism

For main entry, see 4286

4132

Reader, William J.

Professional Men: The rise of the professional classes in nineteenth-century England

1966 Weidenfeld & Nicolson *London*

This book is especially useful for such matters as competitive entry to the professions, the impact of reforms in the professions on the educational system, and developments in those professions ancillary to business: accountancy, engineering and the law.

4133

Roderick, G. W.; Stephens, M. D.

Education and Industry in the Nineteenth Century: The English disease?

1978 Longman *London*

The authors give a useful introduction to the subject, setting out the basic facts and some of the controversies.

4134

Safford, Frank

The Ideal of the Practical: Colombia's struggle to form a technical elite

1976 University of Texas Press *Austin, TX*

This is an authoritative account of the efforts of Colombia's elite to inculcate technical skills and practical values in the nineteenth century. Among the barriers were stumbling economic progress, a rigid social structure and political instability. As a part of this work the origins of the engineering profession, including study abroad by young people from the upper-class, are examined.

4135

Sanderson, Michael

The Universities and British Industry, 1850–1970

1972 Routledge & Kegan Paul *London*

Sanderson examines both the supply of commercial education in the universities and the demand on the part of British industry for the products of that education. This is a wide-ranging and pioneering study that can be augmented by Keeble (qv) and institutional studies like that of Wilson (qv).

4136

Sumiya, Mikio (Editor)

Nippon Shokugyo Kunren Hatten-shi Jo-kan [A History of the Development of Vocational Training in Japan: Vol. 1]

1970 Japan Institute of Labour *Tokyo, Japan*

Covering the period from the 1850s to the 1900s, the book outlines the introduction of western techniques and their diffusion. There are chapters on the skill trainee system (Denshu-sei Seido), the system of craftsman and apprentice, and the formation and development of the apprentice system in factories.

4137

Sumiya, Mikio (Editor)

Nippon Shokugyo Kunren Hatten-shi Ge-kan [A History of the Development of Vocational Training in Japan, Vol. 2]

1971 Japan Institute of Labour *Tokyo, Japan*

This book covers the period from the 1910s to the 1940s. It outlines the process of setting up the Japanese-style training system at arsenals, Yawata Iron Works, Hitachi Works, Kobe Iron Works, Shibaura Engineering Works, etc. The authors also review the formal education system and legal matters.

4138

Sumiya, Mikio; Koga, Hiroshi (Editors)

Nippon Shokugyo Kunren Hatten-shi Sengo-hen [A History of the Development of Vocational Training in Japan: Vol. 3, The postwar period]

1978 Japan Institute of Labour *Tokyo, Japan*

This book consists of two parts. In the first part, the relationship between the development of vocational training systems and technological innovation after 1955 is reviewed. In the second part, the Japanese vocational training of skilled workers is examined theoretically.

4139
Wilson, John F.
The Manchester Experiment: A history of Manchester Business School, 1965–1990
1992 Paul Chapman *London*

This is an 'internalist' institutional history which explores the dichotomy between the academic and corporate modes of thought and action. Attempts to compromise between academia and business produced unsatisfactory results at the Manchester Business School. Wilson sets the strategy, organization and educational policies of the School in the wider context of developments in British education since the Franks Report of 1963.
Firms: Manchester Business School

Culture & Management

4140
Bruchey, Stuart W. (Editor)
Small Business in American Life
1980 Columbia University Press *New York, NY*

This is a collection of 17 essays which range widely over industry and law. The authors are historians, economists, professors of law, finance, marketing and labour studies.

4141
Calvert, Monte A.
The Mechanical Engineer in America, 1830–1910: Professional cultures in conflict
1967 Johns Hopkins University Press *Baltimore, MD*

This study explores the conflicts between shop culture (the artisan and self-made entrepreneur) and, after the American Civil War, school culture (the engineering school and formal education).

4142
Cole, Arthur H.
Business Enterprise in Its Social Setting
1959 Harvard University Press *Cambridge, MA*

Another pioneering study, this is in two parts. Part I relates enterprise to organization and then merges business administration, economics, sociology and history to achieve a large synthesis over a long period. Part II consists of vignettes drawn from the findings of the Research Centre in Entrepreneurial History.

4143
Edsforth, Ronald W.
Class, Conflict and Cultural Consensus: The making of a mass consumer society in Flint, Michigan
For main entry, see 926

4144
Hall, Peter Dobkin
The organisation of American Culture, 1700–1900: Private institutions, elites and the origins of American nationality
1982 New York University Press *New York, NY*

Centred on the Boston 'Brahmins' this book has many diverse insights including some on the training of corporation lawyers, engineers, financiers and managers.

4145
Hazama, Hiroshi
Nippon-teki Keiei: Shudan-shugi no Kouzai [Japanese-style Management: Merits and demerits of collectivism]
1971 Nippon Keizai Shinbun-sha *Tokyo, Japan*

This book gives an outline of the characteristics of Japanese-style management, taking account of group-oriented behavioural patterns and loyalty to the company.

4146
Hazama, Hiroshi (Editor)
Nippon no Kigyo to Shakai: Nippon Keiei-shi Koza, Vol. 6 [Business and Society in Japan: Japanese Business History Series, Vol. 6]
1977 Nippon Keizai Shinbun-sha *Tokyo, Japan*

This wide-ranging history discusses the relationship between business and society. There are chapters on the social value system, the educational system, the business elite, engineers, white-collar workers, blue-collar workers, urbanization and business, and Japan in the world community.

4147
Hofstede, Geert
Culture's Consequences: International differences in work-related values
1980 Sage *Beverley Hills, CA*

Hofstede's book is an influential analysis of international cultural differences based upon a large-scale survey of IBM employees around the world. Cultural differences are categorized in four dimensions: power distance, uncertainty avoidance, individualism and masculinity.

4148
Horie, Yasuzo
Nippon Keiei-shi ni okeru Ie no Kenkyu [A Study on 'Ie' (house) in Japanese Business History]
1984 Rinsen Shoten *Tokyo, Japan*

This is an authoritative study of the 'Ie' system in Japanese business history which includes a comparative study of du Pont and other foreign businesses. It also gives an outline of various academic approaches to the issue.
Firms: du Pont

4149
Jacques, Elliott
The Changing Culture of a Factory
1951 Tavistock Publications *London*

This classic study of human relations in industry was conducted by a member of the Tavistock Institute (founded in 1947 to place psychoanalytic psychiatry in the context of other social sciences) at Glacier Metals, a medium-sized British manufacturing company. This is a foundational text for the study of company culture.
Firms: Glacier Metals

4150
Jequier, François
Charles Veillon (1900–1971): Essai sur l'émergence d'une éthique patronale [Charles Veillon 1900–1971: The emergence of a business ethic]
1985 Société d'études en matière d'histoire *Zurich, Switzerland*

This is a biographical study of the Swiss Protestant manager of a mail order company, with special emphasis on the interactions between ethics and business.
Firms: Charles Veillon SA

4151
Lancaster, Bill; Mason, Tony (Editors)
Life and Labour in a Twentieth Century City: The experience of Coventry
For main entry, see 818

4152
McGregor, Douglas V.
The Human Side of Enterprise
1960 McGraw-Hill *New York, NY*

In this important behavioural view of the managerial task, McGregor distinguishes between two sets of assumptions, one suggesting coercion and control are appropriate, the other the reverse. The authoritarian approach he called Theory X, the more self-directive and creative, Theory Y.

4153
Morikawa, Hidemasa
Nippon-teki Keiei no Genryu [Origins of Japanese Management]
1973 Toyo Keizai Shinpo-sha *Tokyo, Japan*

The author sees Japanese entrepreneurial activities as an ideology of 'managerial nationalism' and examines various cases with particular emphasis on the prewar period.

4154
Nakagawa, Keiichiro (Editor)
Nippon-teki Keiei: Nippon Keiei-shi Kozan, Vol. 5 [Japanese-Style Management: Japanese Business History Series Vol. 5]
1977 Nippon Keizai Shinbun-sha *Tokyo, Japan*

This is a wide-ranging history of Japanese-style management. There are chapters on comparative perspectives, management organizations, R&D, marketing, labour management, finance, and business and the community.

4155
Nakagawa, Keiichiro; Yui, Tsunehiko (Editors)
Keiei Testugaku–Keiei Rinen [Business Philosophy and Business Ideology]

1969–70 Diamond-sha *Tokyo, Japan*

The first of these two volumes outlines the business ideologies and thoughts of the entrepeneurs who took an active part in the early stage of industrialization and modernization in Japan in the Meiji (1868–1912) and Taisho (1912–26) eras. The second volume focuses mainly in those in the Showa (1926–89) era.

4156

Schumacher, Ernest F.

Small is Beautiful: A study of economics as if people mattered

1973 Blond & Briggs *London*

This influential study by the Economic Adviser to the National Coal Board argues that small-scale units, communal ownership, regional workplaces and resources, and less labour saving technology would be appropriate to developing countries.

Firms: Scott Bader Co.

4157

Silk, Leonard; Vogel, David

Ethics and Profits: The crisis of confidence in American business

1976 Simon & Schuster *New York, NY*

Based on interviews with 360 business executives this work paints 'a poignant and in some ways tragic portrait of the American big businessman in 1976: offended, hostile, suspicious and often guilt-ridden, he neither trusts nor feels trusted' [George C. Lodge in *Business History Review*, vol.51, 1977]. The businessman wants order but fears the government intervention that this entails. He pays lip service to freedom but is suspicious of popular democracy.

4158

Wallace, Anthony F. C.

Rockdale: The growth of an American village in the early Industrial Revolution

1978 Alfred A. Knopf *New York, NY*

Written by a distinguished anthropologist, this study explores the impact of industrialization in one rural east-coast American community by applying a Kuhnian model of paradigmatic process to culture change. The result is a richly detailed and perceptive view of the first generation of millowners. Particular attention is paid to the formation of industrial classes and their struggles in the areas of technology, politics and religion.

Firms: Crozer; Riddle; Lammot; Phillips; Sellers

4159

Watts, Emily Stipes

The Businessman in American Literature

1982 University of Georgia Press *Athens, GA*

Watts presents a survey of 'serious' mainline authors from the period of the Puritans to the late twentieth century, concluding that most were hostile to capitalism. A survey of popular literature might produce a different view.

4160

Whitehill, Arthur M.

Japanese Management: Tradition and transition

1991 Routledge *London*

A general study of Japanese management systems in a historical context. Emphasis is on culture, and it is seriously over-generalized.

4161

Yamamura, K.

A Study of Samurai Income and Entrepreneurship

1974 Harvard University Press *Cambridge, MA*

A classic study of the origins of entrepreneurship in Meiji Japan, tracing its roots back into the samurai class, its education, training and income patterns. Detailed statistics bolster the case.

Labour Relations & Management

4162

Arteaga, Arnulfo (Editor)

Proceso de trabajo y relaciones laborales en la industria automotriz en Mexico

For main entry, see 908

4163

Bain, G. S.; Woolven, G. B. (Editors)

A Bibliography of British Industrial Relations

For main entry, see 3

4164
Baldwin, George B.
Beyond Nationalization: The labor problems of British coal
For main entry, see 327

4165
Beynon, Huw
Working for Ford
For main entry, see 802

4166
Blewett, Mary H.
Men, Women, and Work: Class, gender, and protest in the New England shoe industry, 1780–1910
For main entry, see 1871

4167
Braverman, Harry
Labor and Monopoly Capital: The degradation of work in the twentieth century
1974 Monthly Review Press *New York, NY*

This is a Marxist synthesis heavily reliant on secondary materials. It narrowly interprets Taylorism as a removal of skills from the worker to the manager. This work is now outdated by Nelson, Hounshell, Gospel and Littler, Lewchuk et al. (qqv).

4168
Brennan, James P.
The Labor Wars in Cordoba, 1955–1976: Ideology, work and labor politics in an Argentine industrial city
For main entry, see 913

4169
Burgess, Keith
Authority Relations and the Division of Labour in British Industry: with special reference to Clydesdale c.1860–1930
Social History, vol. 11, no. 2, 1986: pp 211–33

Burgess studies the failure to modernize management structures, particularly on the shop floor, in British heavy industry, 1860–1930.

Firms: Beardmores; Maxim-Nordenfelt

4170
Carpenter, Jesse T.
Competition and Collective Bargaining in the Needle Trades 1910–1967
For main entry, see 1894

4171
Chapman, H.
State Capitalism and Working Class Radicalism in the French Aircraft Industry
1991 University of California Press *Berkeley, CA*

Chapman examines the French aircraft industry during the crisis years of the 1930s and 1940s. His main concern is with the labour force and its transformation into one of the leading, militant sectors of the working class. The role of a highly interventionist state is also examined.

Firms: Société National d'Études et de Construction des Moteu; Société Nationale de Construction des Moteurs; Société Nationale des Constructions Aeronautiques

4172
Cole, Robert
Japanese Blue-Collar
For main entry, see 3649

4173
Cooper, Patricia
Once a Cigar Maker: Men, women and work culture in American cigar factories, 1900–1910
For main entry, see 1811

4174
Dawley, Alan
Class and Community: The Industrial Revolution in Lynn
For main entry, see 1873

4175
Dore, Ronald
British Factory - Japanese Factory
For main entry, see 3651

4176
Dutton, H. I.; King, J. E.
Ten Per Cent and No Surrender: The Preston Strike, 1853–1854
For main entry, see 1133

4177
Edwards, Richard
Contested Terrain: The transformation of the workplace in the twentieth century
For main entry, see 3556

4178
Feldman, Gerald D.; Tenfelde, Klaus (Editors)
Workers, Owners and Politics in Coal Mining: An international comparison of industrial relations
For main entry, see 369

4179
Fitzgerald, Robert
British Labour Management and Industrial Welfare, 1846–1939
1988 Croom Helm *London*

This study of company welfare schemes traces the provisions and reasons for the shift from ad hoc to systematic schemes, in a wide range of industries. The last two chapters deal with employers' involvement in labour co-partnership and social reform.

4180
Flanders, Allan; Pomeranz, Ruth; Woodward, Joan
Experiment in Industrial Democracy
For main entry, see 2072

4181
Friedman, Andrew L.
Industry and Labour: Class struggle at work and monopoly capitalism
For main entry, see 812

4182
Friedman, Henry; Meredeen, Sander
The Dynamics of Industrial Conflict: Lessons from Ford
For main entry, see 813

4183
Fucini, J.; Fucini, S.
Working for the Japanese
For main entry, see 933

4184
Gabler, Edwin
The American Telegrapher: A social history, 1860–1900
For main entry, see 3221

4185
Gerstle, G.
Working Class Americanism: The politics of labour in a textile city
For main entry, see 1224

4186
Gilbert, David
Class, Community, and Collective Action: Social change in two British coalfields, 1850–1926
For main entry, see 336

4187
Gordon, Andrew
The Evolution of Labour Relations in Japan: Heavy Industry, 1853–1955
1986 Harvard University Press *Cambridge, MA*

Based on case studies of shipyards, iron & steel, and engineering, Gordon analyses the emergence of the distinctive Japanese pattern of employment and labour relations, c.1850–1955.

Firms: Nippon Kokan (NKK); Uraga Dock Co.; Yokohama Dock Co.

4188
Gospel, Howard F.
Markets, Firms and the Management of Labour in Modern Britain
1992 Cambridge University Press *Cambridge*

This important book surveys the development of the management of industrial relations and human resources in Britain from the late nineteenth century up to the present day.

4189
Gospel, Howard F.; Littler, Craig R. (Editors)
Managerial Strategies and Industrial Relations: An historical and comparative study
1983 Heinemann *London*

A set of conference papers about employers' strategies in industrial relations, these eight chapters span a range of industries and four cultures. Most useful, perhaps, is Gospel's introductory essay outlining a framework for analysing structures and strategies in labour management.

4190

Harris, Howell

The Right to Manage: Industrial relations policies of American business in the 1940s

1982 University of Wisconsin Press *Madison, WI*

This is a study of the industrial relations policies of large manufacturing firms in the USA in the 1940s. Harris places elite business pressure groups such as the National Association of Manufacturers at the centre of institutional change.

Firms: General Motors; Allis-Chalmers; Packard Motor Co.; Chrysler; Ford

4191

Hazama, Hiroshi

Nippon ni okeru Roshi Kyocho no Teiryu [Influencing Cooperation between Management and Labour]

1978 Waseda Daigaku Shuppan-kai *Tokyo, Japan*

This work deals with Japanese labour management by reviewing the activities of Riemon Uno and the Society of Industry Education (Kogyo Kyoiku-kai) founded by him.

4192

Hazama, Hiroshi

Nippon Romu Kanri-shi Kenkyu [A History of Japanese Labour Management]

1978 Ochanomizu Shobo *Tokyo, Japan*

Covering the period from the 1870s to the 1930s, this work examines the development of labour management in the papermaking industry, cotton spinning, heavy industry, and in mining. It sees the historical tendency underlying Japanese labour management as 'managerial paternalism' (Keiei Kazoku-shugi).

4193

Hill, Stephen

Competition and Control at Work: The new industrial sociology 1981

1986 Gower *Aldershot*

An important work of general industrial sociology which provides useful insights for business historians interested in technological change and the labour process, trade unionism and class at work.

4194

Humphrey, John

Capitalist Control and Workers' Struggle in the Brazilian Auto Industry

For main entry, see 939

4195

Hyodo, Tsutomu

Nippon ni okeru Roshi Kankei no Tenkai [The Development of Industrial Relations in Japan]

1971 Tokyo Daigaku Shuppan-kai *Tokyo, Japan*

Covering the period from the 1880s to the 1920s, this work analyses the internal and external structures of industrial relations by examining the cases of the Yawata Iron Works, Yokosuka Naval Arsenal, Kure Naval Arsenal, Mitsubishi Nagasaki Shipyard, Mitsubishi Kobe Shipyard, Sumitomo Electric Wire et al.

Firms: Kure Naval Arsenal; Mitsubishi; Sumitomo; Yawata Iron; Yokosuka Naval Arsenal

4196

Jacoby, Sanford M.

Employing Bureaucracy: Managers, unions, and the transformation of work in American industry 1900–1945 -1945

1985 Columbia University Press *New York, NY*

This provides a carefully-researched account of the development of personnel management and changing corporate attitudes towards blue-collar workers in US industry in the first half of the twentieth century. It is especially strong on the period up to the 1920s. On labour management, Jacoby is more positive than Braverman (qv).

4197

Jacoby, Sanford M. (Editor)

Masters to Managers: Historical and comparative perspectives on American employers

1991 Columbia University Press *New York, NY*

This is a collection of essays searching for an alternative to Chandlerian and neo-Marxist interpretations of employment policy. Authors include Daniel Nelson, Howell Harris, Walter Licht, Daniel Ernst and Gerald Friedman.

4198

Jowitt, J. A.; McIvor, A. J. (Editors)

Employers and Labour in the English Textile Industries, 1850–1939

For main entry, see 1187

4199

Kamata, Satoshi

Japan in the Passing Lane

For main entry, see 1007

4200

Katz, Harry C.

Shifting Gears: Changing labor relations in the US automobile industry

For main entry, see 945

4201

Kobayashi, Masa-aki

Kaiun-gyo no Rodo Mondai: Kindaiteki Roshi Kankei no Senku [Labour Problems in the Shipping Industry]

1980 Nippon Keizai Shinbun-sha *Tokyo, Japan*

This work approaches the labour problems of shipping in the interwar period from various angles, for instance, training for labourers, labour organization for the shipowner and the crew, relations between labour and capital, the workplace environment, and so on.

4202

Kobayashi, Masa-aki

Sengo Kaiun-gyo no Rodo Mondai: Yobi-in-sei to Nippon-teki Koyo [Labour Problems in Shipping after the War: The 'yobi-in' organization and Japanese employment]

1992 Nippon Keizai Hyoron-sha *Tokyo, Japan*

This work considers the 'yobi-in' (reserve men) organization, featured in the employment structure of Japanese shipping. The author gives an unbiased account of the history and problems of 'yobi-in' organization from wartime to the present day.

4203

Kocka, Jürgen

Unternehmensverwaltung und Angestelltenschaft am Beispiel Siemens 1847–1914: Zum Verhältnis von Kapitalismus und Bürokratie in der deutschen Industrialisiering [Siemens: The administation of a business and its employees: Capitalism and bureaucracy during German industrialisation]

For main entry, see 3568

4204

Koike, Kazuo

Understanding Industrial Relations in Modern Japan

For main entry, see 3660

4205

LaDame, Mary

The Filene Story: A study of employees' relations to management in a retail store

For main entry, see 2102

4206

Lewchuk, Wayne

American Technology and the British Vehicle Industry

For main entry, see 820

4207

MacDonald, Robert M.

Collective Bargaining in the Automobile Industry: A study of wage structure and competitive relations

For main entry, see 958

4208

Magnusson, Lars

Arbetet vid en svensk verkstad: Munktell, 1900–1920 [Labour in a Swedish Factory: Munktell 1900–1920]

1987 Arkiv Förlag *Lund, Sweden*

This scholarly work describes the development of the work process of a Swedish factory and relates the results to those of Harry Braverman (qv) during the first two decades of the

twentieth century. For other publications from this project, see Ulla Wikander, Alf Johansson.
Firms: Munktell

4209
Majka, Linda C.; Majka, Theo J.
Farm Workers, Agribusiness and the State
1982 Temple University Press *Philadelphia, PA*

This study of the successes and failures of American farm labour organizations in the twentieth century focuses on the activities of the United Farm Workers.
Firms: United Farm Workers

4210
Marchetti, Ada Gigli
I Tre Anelli: Mutualita, resistenze, cooperazione diei tipografi milanesi 1860–1925 [The Three Connections: Mutual assistance, co-operation and resistance of Milanese printers 1860–1925]
For main entry, see 1757

4211
McCreary, Eugene C.
Social Welfare and Business: The Krupp welfare program, 1860–1914
Business History Review, vol. 42, no. 1, 1968: pp 24–49

This study investigates the Krupp company's role in pioneering social welfare programmes in the late nineteenth century, a form of patriarchal control which was increasingly challenged by unionisation and the rise of social democratic politics.
Firms: Krupp; Crucible Steel Company

4212
Melling, Joseph
Non-Commissioned Officers: British employers and their supervisory workers, 1880–1920
Social History, vol. 5, no. 2, 1980: pp 183–221

This is a classic analysis of the development of supervision and management authority in British heavy industry 1880–1920, with particular reference to shipbuilding.
Firms: Cadburys; John Browns; Langs; Singer Co.

4213
Melman, Seymour
Decisionmaking and Productivity
For main entry, see 825

4214
Musson, Alfred E.
The Typographical Association: Origins and history up to 1949
For main entry, see 1732

4215
Nakagawa, Keiichiro (Editor)
Labor and Management (Fourth Fuji Conference)
For main entry, see 103

4216
Nelson, Daniel
American Rubber Workers and Organized Labor, 1900–1941
For main entry, see 1932

4217
Nishinarita, Yutaka
Kindai Nippon Roshi Kankei-shi no Kenkyu [A Study of Modern Japanese Industrial Relations]
1988 Tokyo Daigaku Shuppan-kai *Tokyo, Japan*

This work deals with wide-ranging issues about Japanese industrial relations. These include the structural features of Japanese industrial relations, a case study of the shipbuilding companies, the changing pattern of industrial relations in the 1920s, industrial relations at the time of the Manchurian Incident, and the effect of Japanese Fascism on industrial relations.

4218
Noguchi, Paul H.
Delayed Departures, Overdue Arrivals: Industrial familialism and the Japanese national railways
For main entry, see 2934

4219
Odagiri, Hiroyuki
Growth Through Competition, Competition

Through Growth: Strategic management and the economy in Japan
For main entry, see 3670

4220
Olson, Mancur
The Rise and Decline of Nations: Economic growth, stagflation and social rigidities
For main entry, see 3467

4221
Ozanne, Robert W.
A Century of Labor-Management Relations at McCormick and International Harvester
For main entry, see 1392

4222
Ozanne, Robert W.
Wages in Practice and Theory: McCormick and International Harvester 1860–1960
For main entry, see 1393

4223
Price, R.
Masters, Unions and Men: Work control in building and the rise of labour, 1830–1914
For main entry, see 1297

4224
Saguchi, Kazuro
Nippon ni okeru Sangyo Minshushugi no Zentei: Roshi Kondan Seido kara Sangyo Hokok-kai e [The Early History of Industrial Democracy in Japan: From roundtable with labour and management to the Industry Patriotic Society]
1991 Tokyo Daigaku Shuppan-kai *Tokyo, Japan*

The author sees the development of industrial relations in Japan between the wars as the basis of industrial democracy in Japan. He reviews the cases of Miike Coal Mining, Kure Naval Arsenal and the formation of the Industry Patriotic Society.
Firms: Kure Naval Arsenal; Miike Coal

4225
Sakuma, Ken
Kokusai Keiei to Nihongata Roshi Kankei [International Management and Japanese Labour Relations]
1987 Yuhikaku *Tokyo, Japan*

This book describes the historical background of Japanese labour relations after the Second World War, describing changing patterns and current problems arising out of foreign direct investment by Japanese companies. There are many useful tables and charts.

4226
Scarborough, William Kauffman
The Overseer: Plantation management in the Old South
1966 Louisiana State University Press *Baton Rouge, LA*

Scarborough presents an intensive study from an extensive sample and a wide range of sources. This work discusses topics such as managerial duties and responsibilities, social and contractual relations, discords between overseer and planter, and the overseer elite.

4227
Schatz, Ronald W.
The Electrical Workers: A history of labor at General Electric and Westinghouse 1923–1960
1983 University of Illinois Press *Urbana, IL*

An account of union organizing and bargaining at GE and Westinghouse from the 1930s to 1950s. It emphasizes large locals and workers' interest in surmounting rules.
Firms: GE; Westinghouse

4228
Schiffmann, Dieter
Von der Revolution zum Neunstundentag: Arbeit und Konflikt bei BASF, 1918–1924 [From the Revolution to the Nine-Hour Day: Work and conflict at BASF, 1918–1924]
1983 Campus *Frankfurt am Main, Germany*

This wide-ranging study covers the introduction of the eight-hour day in the German chemical industry after 1918. It documents the breakdown of industrial relations within the Badische Anelin- und Soda-Fabrik as the management tried to reassert its managerial prerogative. It is a very good study of industrial relations during the early years of the Weimar Republic.
Firms: Badische Anelin- und Soda-Fabrik AG (BASF)

4229
Schmiechen, James A.
Sweated Industries and Sweated Labor: The London clothing trades 1860–1914
For main entry, see 1903

4230
Seltzer, Curtis
Fire in the Hole: Miners and managers in the American coal industry
For main entry, see 363

4231
Serrin, William
The Company and the Union: GM and the UAW
For main entry, see 979

4232
Spencer, Elaine Glovka
Management and Labor in Imperial Germany: Ruhr industrialists as employers 1896–1914
For main entry, see 640

4233
Streeck, Wolfgang
Industrial Relations in West Germany: A case study of the car industry
For main entry, see 902

4234
Stubbs, Jean
Tobacco on the Periphery: A case study in Cuban labour history, 1860–1958
For main entry, see 1827

4235
Suggs, George G. Jr
Colorado's War on Militant Unionism: James H. Peabody and the Western Federation of Miners
For main entry, see 527

4236
Tanaka, Naoki
Kindai Nihon Tanko Rodoshi Kenkyu [A Historical Study of Labour Relations in the Modern Japanese Coal-Mining Industry]
1984 Sohukan *Tokyo, Japan*

This work covers the changes in labour–management relations in the Japanese coal-mining industry 1872–1945, which was occasioned by the introduction of machinery into the industry. It focuses especially on the state of the working-class in Kyusyu District.
Firms: Mitsubishi Material; Mitsui Kozan

4237
Tanaka, Shin'ichiro
Senzen Romu Kanri no Jittai: Seido to Rinen [A Case Study of Prewar Labour Management: Institutions and ideas]
1984 Japan Institute of Labour *Tokyo, Japan*

In the first part, the author, who worked at Oji Paper Manufacturing Company as a director, reviews the labour management system of Oji with particular focus on the 1930s. In the second part, he examines executives' ideas and measures on labour management during the period from the 1910s to the 1940s.

4238
Tanner, Jakob
Mahlzeit in der Fabrik: Ernährungswissenschaft, Industriearbeit und Volksernährung in der Schweiz 1890–1950 [Mealtime in the Factory: Food science, industrial work and nutrition in Switzerland 1890–1950]

This study explains the relationships between changes in food habits, nutritional science and industrial work in Switzerland up to the mid-twentieth century. The main chapters concentrate on the Swiss Association for People's Service, a nonprofit organization which started in the First World War. After the war, this SAPS, founded originally in order to support the army, changed emphasis and by the early 1920s operated dozens of factory canteens. Research carried out by SAPS serves as general survey of the tendencies and problems in Swiss industry in general.

4239
Terry, Michael; Edwards, Paul K. (Editors)
Shopfloor Politics and Job Controls: The post War engineering industry
1988 Basil Blackwell *Oxford*

An important collection of essays on the history of industrial relations in the various sectors of the Coventry engineering industry from the Second World War to the 1980s.

4240
Tolliday, Steven; Zeitlin, Jonathan (Editors)
Shopfloor Bargaining and the State: Historical and comparative perspectives
1985 Cambridge University Press *Cambridge*

A collection of articles centred on the persistent importance and contradictory impact of state policies on the forms and outcomes of shopfloor bargaining. Articles cover the interaction of employers and shopfloor organization in the British shipbuilding, docks, motor and aerospace industries, the impact of federal bureaucracy on American labour relations before and after the New Deal, and the interaction of politics, law and shopfloor bargaining in postwar Italy.

4241
Tolliday, Steven; Zeitlin, Jonathan (Editors)
The Power to Manage?: Employers and industrial relations in comparative-historical perspective
1991 Routledge *New York, NY*

This collection of essays is designed to show that employers in engineering had the opportunity to choose alternatives to mass production techniques and work relations.
Firms: Fiat; Ford UK; Armstrong-Whitworth; John Brown; British Leyland; Siemens; Pirelli; US Steel; General Electric

4242
Turner, H. A.; Clack, G.; Roberts, G.
Labour Relations in the Motor Industry: A study of industrial unrest and an international comparison
For main entry, see 845

4243
Vetterli, Rudolf
Industriearbeit, Arbeiterbewusstsein und gewerkschaftliche Organisation: Dargestellt am Beispiel der Georg Fischer AG (1890–1930) [Production, Workers and Workplace Organization: Georg Fischer AG, 1890–1930]
1978 Vandenhoeck & Ruprecht *Göttingen, Germany*

The book explores the Georg Fischer AG at Schaffhausen (Switzerland), an enterprise in the metal/machine-branch. It describes the production process, the different kind of workplaces and the social situation of the workforce, focusing both on individual attitudes and the collective behaviour of workers. Starting from an analysis of the conflicts in the factory, the study aims at explaining how unions and employer's associations were built up, bridging the gap between business history and history of the labour movement.
Firms: Georg Fischer AG

4244
Vichniac, Judith Eisenberg
The Management of Labor: The British and French iron and steel industries, 1860–1980
1991 JAI Press *Greenwich, CT*

Vichniac contrasts the labour management strategies of French and British iron and steel industries 1860–1918. French authoritarianism and paternalism persisted whilst British employers accepted that collective bargaining was inevitable.

4245
Willman, Paul; Winch, Graham
Innovation and Management Control: Labour relations at BL Cars
1985 Cambridge University Press *Cambridge*

A detailed study of management strategy and labour relations during a period of radical technical change and reform of collective bargaining institutions. Stresses the tension between an established strategy based on increased union participation and an increasingly assertive management determined to pursue rapid productivity gains.
Firms: Ford UK; British Leyland; Vauxhall

4246
Zahavi, Gerald
Workers, Managers, and Welfare Capitalism: The shoeworkers and tanners of Endicott Johnson, 1890–1950
For main entry, see 1893

Technology

4247
Abernathy, William J.
The Productivity Dilemma: Roadblock to innovation in the automobile industry
1978 Johns Hopkins University Press *Baltimore, MD*

Pathbreaking study of the relationship between product innovation and efficiency in the American car industry. The rise of mass production, centring on incremental gains in efficiency, displaced the stress on product innovation which had stimulated the infant industry before 1914. The 'productivity dilemma' was crucial to the US industry's development c.1920–80.
Firms: Chrysler; Ford Motor Company; General Motors

4248
Bijker, Wiebe E.; Hughes, Thomas P.; Pinch, Trevor (Editors)
The Social Construction of Technological Systems: New directions in the sociology and history of technology
1987 MIT Press *Cambridge, MA*

This influential collection of 13 papers, assembled for a Twente University workshop in 1984, pioneered the application of the methodology of the sociology of scientific knowledge to technology. While some of the sociologists see technology as just another form of knowledge, Hughes, following up his *Networks of Power* (qv), argues that technology is the dominant element in a network of competing groups. The other historians contributing are Ruth Cowan and Edward Constant.

4249
Born, Karl Erich
Internationale Kartellierung einer neuen Industrie: Die Aluminium-Association 1901–1915 [International Cartelization of the New Aluminium Industry 1901–1915]
For main entry, see 3383

4250
Carlson, W. Bernard
Innovation as a Social Process: Elihu Thomson and the rise of General Electric, 1870–1900
For main entry, see 1544

4251
Clayton, Robert; Algar, Joan
The GEC Research Laboratories 1919–1984
For main entry, see 1512

4252
Constant, Edward W.
The Origins of the Turbojet Revolution
1980 Johns Hopkins University Press *Baltimore, MD*

This work interprets the transition from the piston and propeller-driven aircraft to the jet engine in terms of perception of the inadequacies of prevailing systems (a notion partly derived from Kuhn's scientific paradigms). Individuals, communities, and goverments are embraced in this fine study.

4253
Coopey, Richard; Uttley, Matthew (Editors)
Defence Science and Technology: Adjusting to change
1994 Harwood *Reading*

This, the third volume in a series of studies in defence economics, explores the position of the defence sector in advanced economies and its relationship to the civil industrial economy. The book examines issues such as the political economy of R&D and technological dependence, procurement strategies, spinoffs, crowding out, dual use technologies, and conversion.
Firms: Westland

4254
David, Paul A.
Technical Choice, Innovation and Economic Growth: Essays on American and British experience in the nineteenth century
1975 Cambridge University Press *Cambridge*

This collection of essays exemplified the emergence of econometric techniques to understand the economics of technical change. David's case topics are nineteenth century mechanisation in cotton textiles and farming; labour scarcity as a determinant of technical change; and an expert debunking of Robert

Fogel's claim that railways contributed little to the production potential of nineteenth-century America. The author stresses economies of scale, learning-by-doing, and localised technical practices in explaining technical change.

4255
Dosi, Giovanni
Technical Change and Industrial Transformation: The theory and an application to the semiconductor industry
1984 Macmillan *London*

A complex attempt to apply a theory of the determinants of the innovative process to the semiconductor industry. In relation to the industry, the book focuses on the impact of American military and space policies, the cumulativeness of technological advantages, and 'learning-by-doing'. There is an extensive comparison of the US and Japanese industries.
Firms: Bell Labs; Texas Instruments

4256
Dosi, Giovanni; Giannetti, Renato; Toninelli, Pier Angelo (Editors)
Technology and Enterprise in a Historical Perspective
1992 Clarendon Press, *Oxford*

A collection of twelve essays, this volume gives a number of well-known scholarly authors, mostly economists or historians of technology, an opportunity to summarize or apply work explored earlier. Some essays are theoretical. The remaining five are case studies either of the chemical industry or of Italy. Authors include Sidney Pollard, Nathan Rosenberg, Thomas P. Hughes, William Lazonick, Richard Nelson, David J. Teece, Sidney Winter, Keith Pavitt, and David A. Hounshell.
Firms: Du Pont; Montecatini

4257
Dummett, G. A.
From Little Acorns: A history of the A.P.V. Company Limited
For main entry, see 1352

4258
Dutton, H. I.
The Patent System and Inventive Activity During the Industrial Revolution, 1750–1852
1984 Manchester University Press *Manchester*

This is the posthumously published work of Harry Dutton, whose early death robbed British business history of a fine scholar. Based on his PhD thesis, the book surveys the development of the British patent system to the amending Act of 1852 and shows in particular how the law was modified in favour of the inventor in the 1830s. It contains a useful section on the inventors themselves and on the economics of invention, and should be used in conjunction with Macleod (qv).

4259
Edgerton, David E. H.; Horrocks, Sally M.
British Industrial Research and Development before 1945
Economic History Review, vol. 47, no. 2, 1994: pp 213–38

Important reassessment of the view that Britain's R&D effort was historically weak.

4260
Fitzgerald, Deborah
The Business of Breeding: Hybrid corn in Illinois, 1890–1940
For main entry, see 214

4261
Graham, Margaret B.
RCA and the VideoDisc: The business of research
For main entry, see 1547

4262
Graham, Margaret B. W.; Pruitt, Bettye H.
R&D for Industry: A century of technical innovation at Alcoa
1990 Cambridge University Press *Cambridge*

This is a massive study of strategy and technical innovation in R&D that ranks alongside Hounshell and Smith on Du Pont (qv).

4263
Habakkuk, H. J.
American and British Technology in the

Nineteenth Century: The search for labour saving inventions
1962 Cambridge University Press *Cambridge*

This is a highly influential, though dense and theoretical work which argues that technical choices rested on an economy's factor proportions. Thus, the USA with its shortage of labour before the 1840s opted for labour-saving, capital-intensive technologies while the reverse happened in contemporary labour-abundant Britain.

4264
Higonnet, Patrice; Landes, David S.; Rosovsky, H. (Editors)
Favourites of Fortune: Technology, growth and economic development since the Industrial Revolution
1991 Harvard University Press *Cambridge, MA*

This is an important collection of essays from an established team (Bairoch, Chandler, Crouzet, David, Fischer, Fogel, Lazonick, Mokyr, Rostow, Temin, et al.) which explores the relationship between technology and growth. The book is divided into three parts: technology; 'entrepreneurialism'; and paths of economic growth. Useful for business historians in discussing in more general terms the environment in which technological innovation occurs.

4265
Hoke, Donald R.
Ingenious Yankees: The rise of the American system of manufactures in the private sector
For main entry, see 1331

4266
Hounshell, David A.
From the American System to Mass Production, 1800–1932: The development of manufacturing technology
1984 Johns Hopkins University Press *Baltimore, MD*

This is a splendidly-researched and written analysis of the development of production technologies, from interchangeability to Fordism. It demonstrates how armory methods of production spread to the production of other light consumer durables like sewing machines, reapers, bicycles, and cards.
Firms: Brown & Sharpe; Cold; Ford; General Motors; McCormick; Singer; Wilcox & Gibbs

4267
Hounshell, David A.; Smith, John Kenly
Science and Corporate Strategy: Du Pont R&D, 1902–1980
1988 Cambridge University Press *Cambridge*

The authors present a comprehensive and critical study of one of the first American companies to emulate German corporate research techniques. The book deals in detail with the major issues facing company strategists in charge of the management of research.
Firms: Du Pont

4268
Hughes, Thomas P.
Networks of Power: Electrification in western society, 1880–1930
For main entry, see 2722

4269
Hughes, Thomas P.
American Genesis: A century of invention and technological enthusiasm, 1870–1970
1989 Viking Penguin *New York, NY*

This is an exploration of how the American nation became involved in technological endeavour and what the repercussions have been for American society, particularly for politics, business, architecture and art. It is more optimistic than pessimistic about the impact of technology.

4270
Hughes, Thomas P.; Hughes, Agatha C. (Editors)
Lewis Mumford: Public Intellectual
1990 Oxford University Press *New York, NY*

An important collection of studies which examine the contribution of Mumford, author of *Technics and Civilisation* and *The Myth of the Machine*, and a pioneer in the study of technology as cultural history. The volume was based on a conference convened at the University of Pennsylvania, which houses the Mumford archive.

4271
Jeremy, David J.
Transatlantic Industrial Revolution: The diffusion of textile technologies between Britain and America 1790–1830s
1981 Basil Blackwell *Oxford*

An extensive empirical study of the westwards migration of textile workers and technologies from Britain during the early industrial period. Using a stage model, it finds strong evidence for the critical roles of emigrant skilled workers and indigenous entrepreneurs in successfully transferring new technologies to a follower economy. A seminal work on the diffusion of technology, it contains an extensive glossary and is replete with diagrams and illustrations.
Firms: Boston Manufacturing Co.; Dover Manufacturing Co.; Merrimack Manufacturing Co.

4272
Jeremy, David J. (Editor)
International Technology Transfer: Europe, Japan and the USA, 1700–1914
1991 Edward Elgar Publishing *Aldershot*

This is the first of two volumes of case studies of technology transfer, in which economic and business contexts are considered.

4273
Jeremy, David J. (Editor)
The Transfer of International Technology: Europe, Japan and the USA in the twentieth century
1992 Edward Elgar Publishing *Aldershot*

This is the second of two volumes of case studies.

4274
Jeremy, David J. (Editor)
Technology Transfer and Business Enterprise
1993 Edward Elgar Publishing *Aldershot*

This reprint collection of 26 articles and excerpts provides examples of a number of the major theoretical and empirical studies of the complex interactions between technology transfer and business.

4275
Juma, Calestous
The Gene Hunters: Biotechnology and the scramble for seeds
1989 Zed Books *London*

While almost exclusively concerned with biotechnology, especially in Africa, this gives an insight into the interest of many chemical companies in the provision of improved seeds for agriculture.

4276
Kenney, Martin
Biotechnology: The university-industrial complex
For main entry, see 783

4277
Kogut, Bruce (Editor)
Country Competitiveness: Technology and the organizing of work
1993 Oxford University Press *New York, NY*

Based on a conference held at EIASM in Brussels, this edited collection offers business historians many useful ideas about approaches to technological change, R&D, and organizational and labour management responses, including flexible specialization in several countries, including the US, Japan, UK, France and Germany. Contributors include Dosi, Dunning, Fruin and Nishiguchi.
Firms: General Motors; Toyota

4278
Leslie, Stuart W.
The Cold War and American Science: The military-industrial-academic complex at MIT and Stanford
1993 Columbia University Press *New York, NY*

Studying how two major American universities became powerhouses of defence-related R&D, Leslie also shows how federal government support shaped science itself. His case studies include microwave electronics and the forerunners of Silicon Valley at Stanford, and Charles Stark Draper's Instrumentation Lab at MIT. Leslie disproves that academics were passive partners and shows that peaceful applications of Cold War science were hard to achieve.

4279

Mackenzie, Donald

Inventing Accuracy: An historical sociology of nuclear missile guidance systems

1990 MIT Press *Cambridge, MA*

This is a pathbreaking study of the social, cultural and political dynamics which determined the choice of technology in the arms race.

4280

MacLeod, Christine

Inventing the Industrial Revolution: The English patent system, 1660–1800

1988 Cambridge University Press *Cambridge*

Important study of what might be termed the 'proto-patent period' in British business history, which explores the relationship between patents and inventions before the 19th century and warns against inferring too much from the patent data. Because the book is concerned more with the intellectual and philosophical underpinnings of patent activity, it should be used in conjunction with works which assess the economic impact of patents e.g. Dutton (qv).

4281

Millard, André

Edison and the Business of Innovation

1990 Johns Hopkins University Press *Baltimore, MD*

Drawing on the enormous, but increasingly accessible Edison archives, this study illuminates Edison's role as an R&D manager, countering the myth of Edison as the heroic lone inventor. Valuable for its portrayal of the machine shop culture.

Firms: Edison

4282

Mokyr, Joel

The Lever of Riches: Technological creativity and economic progress

1990 Oxford University Press *Oxford*

This is an important contribution to the literature dealing with technological change over the long run.

4283

Mowery, David C.; Rosenberg, Nathan

Technology and the Pursuit of Economic Growth

1989 Cambridge University Press *Cambridge*

This study debunks several myths about technical change, including the idea that new science is needed to achieve technological advances, that spin-offs from military R&D enhance civilian technologies, and that government support for large-scale, high-risk technical programmes is a successful strategy.

Firms: IBM

4284

Musson, A. E.

Joseph Whitworth and the Growth of Mass-Production Engineering

Business History, vol. 17, no. 2, 1975: pp 109–49

The role of Joseph Whitworth in the creation of the rudiments of mass-production in the nineteenth century, especially his role as a technical innovator and propagandist, is examined here.

Firms: W. & J. Crighton & Co.; Whitworth & Co.; Maudslay Sons & Field

4285

Myllyntaus, Timo

Finnish Industry in Transition, 1885–1920: Responding to Technological Challenges

1989 Museum of Technology *Helsinki, Finland*

At the turn of the century technological development provided great opportunities for the modernization of manufacturing. This book focuses on how three major Finnish manufacturing groups in sawmilling, papermaking and engineering took advantage of new technology. Special attention is paid to an examination of the use of mechanical energy and the introduction of electrical technology. Both quantitative and qualitative methods have been applied in comparing the three groups.

Firms: A. Ahlström Ab; Karhula Oy; W. Rosenlew & Co.

4286

Noble, David F.

America by Design: Science, technology, and the rise of corporate capitalism

1977 Alfred A. Knopf *New York, NY*

This describes how a managerial elite, trained in engineering universities (above all,

the MIT), took over the factory, the corporation, even the economy of the USA. The study's weaknesses spring from its confinement to science-based industries, its neglect of business schools, and its 'failure to distinguish between the operational requirements of a technology and those of capitalism, whatever the variety.' (A. D. Chandler, in *Technology and Culture* vol.19, 1978, p. 571).
Firms: General Electric; AT&T

4287
Noble, David F.
Forces of Production: A social history of industrial automation
1984 Alfred A. Knopf *New York, NY*
The core of this book is an investigation of the origins of numerical control in the 1940s and 1950s which sets Air Force-funded, arrogant academics at large R&D institutions like MIT against common-sense entrepreneurs who offered cheaper and more practical approaches. Alongside the numerical control study is a radical polemic urging 'reflection and revolution' (p. xiii). The social history of industrial automation never materializes.

4288
Okochi, Akio
Hatsumei Koi to Gijutsu Koso: Gijutsu to Tokkyo no Keiei-shi-teki Isou [Inventive Activity and Technological Imagination]
1992 Tokyo Daigaku Shuppan-kai *Tokyo, Japan*
The author reviews technological development and patents and their influence on industrialization; he links this analysis to Schumpeter's theories on innovation.

4289
Ozawa, Terutomo
Japan's Technological Challenge to the West, 1950–74: Motivation and accomplishment
1974 MIT Press *Cambridge, MA*
A study of technology transfer in postwar Japanese industrialization. The book focuses on state support for selective import of technologies for key industries, and the efforts of individual Japanese firms to choose, adapt and perfect imported technologies.

4290
Pavitt, Keith (Editor)
Technical Innovation and British Economic Performance
1980 Macmillan *London*
A collection of eighteen essays, this influential volume, from the Science Policy Research Unit at Sussex University, explores the relationships between technical innovation and business, as well as government policies towards innovation, and innovation within particular industries. Of especial value are the international comparisons of relationships between innovative activities and export shares (by K. Pavitt and L. Soete) and British attitudes to engineering education (by A. Albu).

4291
Reich, Leonard S.
The Making of American Industrial Research: Science and business at GE and Bell, 1876–1926
For main entry, see 3235

4292
Rose, Mark
Authors and Owners: The invention of copyright
For main entry, see 1692

4293
Rosenberg, Nathan (Editor)
The American System of Manufactures: The report of the committee on the machinery of the United States, 1855; and the special reports of George Wallis and Joseph Whitworth, 1854
1969 Edinburgh University Press *Edinburgh, Scotland*
Re-set from the text in the Parliamentary Papers, these two reports which first described to British readers the new interchangeable techniques of manufacture pioneered in the USA are prefaced by a long and valuable contextual essay by the editor. To be read with Hounshell and Roe Smith (qqv).

4294
Rosenberg, Nathan
Technology and American Economic Growth
1972 Harper *New York, NY*

This book is a good introduction to the interactions between technology and economic activity in the USA, chiefly in the nineteenth century, but needs to be revised in the light of two decades of new literature, both in the history of technology and the history of business.

4295
Rosenberg, Nathan
Inside the Black Box: Technology and economics
1982 Cambridge University Press *New York, NY*

Rosenberg, who has done much to clarify at a conceptual level the relationship between technological and economic change, here presents a collection of papers (some jointly authored) dealing with views of technical progress; characteristics of technologies; market determinants of technical change and technology transfer.

4296
Schaumann, Ralf
Technik und technischer Fortschritt im Industrialisierungsprozess: Dargestellt am Beispiel der Papier-, Zucker- und chemischen Industrie der nördlichen Rheinländer: 1800–1875 [Technology in the Process of Industrialization: Paper, sugar, chemicals]
1977 Rohrscheid *Bonn, Germany*

This 500-page detailed monograph has copious statistical data on labour, technology and finance.

4297
Schedvin, C. B.
Shaping Science and Industry: A history of Australia's Council for Scientific and Industrial Research, 1926–49
1987 Allen & Unwin *Sydney, Australia*

This is a comprehensive and authoritative history of Australia's major governmental research institution during its first quarter century. Schedvin discusses the genesis of the CSIR and its major research areas, which included mainly agricultural subjects or applied science for agricultural purposes. Industrial interests became more important later on, especially in the context of the Second World War. The book is also an excellent analysis of the science political context of CSIR and an evaluation of its scientific and practical impact. It is to be followed by a second volume leading up to the 1970s.

4298
Schmookler, Jacob
Invention and Economic Growth
1966 Harvard University Press *Cambridge, MA*

This is a seminal work which argues that technological change in the form of invention and innovation results from increased investment: that is, invention is a rational process, responding to economic opportunity. Drawing on patent statistics starting in 1837, Schmookler might have modified his view had he, like Christine MacLeod (qv), gone back to Britain in the seventeenth and eighteenth centuries.

4299
Smith, George David
From Monopoly to Competition: The transformation of Alcoa, 1880–1986
1988 Cambridge University Press *Cambridge*

A large-scale official history, stressing continuous innovation in technology and marketing, and the history of Alcoa's long-running antitrust problems. Also covers managerial structure and labour relations.

4300
Smith, Merritt Roe
Harper's Ferry Armory and the New Technology: The challenge of change
1977 Cornell University Press *Ithaca, NY*

Elegantly written and thoroughly researched, this study was one of the early ones to place technical change in its social setting. Political intrigue in Washington and a web of self-interest at the Ferry impeded technical change and the upset in social relations it brought. To be read with Hounshell (qv).
Firms: Harper's Ferry Federal Armory

4301
Sumida, Jon Tetsuro
In Defence of Naval Supremacy: Finance, technology and British naval policy, 1889–1914
For main entry, see 1415

4302
Teitelman, Robert
Gene Dreams: Wall Street, academia, and the rise of biotechnology
For main entry, see 793

4303
Thomas, Donald E. Jr
Diesel: Technology and society in industrial Germany
1987 University of Alabama Press *Tuscaloosa, AL*

Based on the Diesel archives and family papers this book is both a biography of Eugen Diesel and a study of his revolutionary innovation in relation to entrepreneurship and German science and technology. Case studies of attempts by businesses to develop and market the engine (largely unsuccessfully) are a major feature.

Firms: Augsburg Engine Works; Krupp; Diesel Engine Company of Augsburg; General Society for Diesel Engines

4304
Usher, Abbot P.
A History of Mechanical Inventions
1954 Beacon Press *Boston, MA*

An impressively wide-ranging and very long-term history. It traces the development of significant technologies and power applications within a framework informed by cultural history and includes a discussion of the process of invention and the diffusion of ideas between China and the West over two thousand years.

4305
von Hippel, Eric
The Sources of Innovation
1988 Oxford University Press *New York, NY*

Aimed at corporate R&D managers and government policy makers, this book argues that the sources of innovation are traceable through the functional relationships that firms and individuals have to a particular innovation. Innovation is 'predictably distributed' among firms on the basis of the expected economic benefit to be derived from their functional relation to the innovation–which von Hippel demonstrates in a series of case studies.

4306
Wetzel, Walter
Natural Science and the Chemical Industry in Germany
For main entry, see 749

4307
Whittaker, D. H.
Managing Innovation: A study of British and Japanese factories
1990 Cambridge University Press *Cambridge*

In the tradition of Dore's *British Factory - Japanese Factory* (qv), this book is a comparative study of the use of CNC technology in comparable factories in the two countries. The emphasis is on differences in training and employment relations influencing the application of technologies.

Business & Government

4308
Aitken, Hugh G. J.
The Continuous Wave: Technology and American Radio, 1900–1932
For main entry, see 3332

4309
Arana Pérez, Ignacio
La Liga Vizcaína de Productores y la política económica de la Restauracíon 1894–1914: Relaciones entre el empresariado y el poder político [The Liga Vizcaína de Productores and Economic Policy in the Restoration Period, 1894–1914: Relations between business and political power]
1988 Caja de Ahorros Vizcaína *Bilbao, Spain*

This book is a comprehensive study of one of the most important interest groups in the late nineteenth century in Spain, the Liga Vizcaína de Productores, which represented the interests of the Biscayan iron and steel industry.

4310
Armstrong, Christopher; Nelles, Henry V.
Monopoly's Moment: The organisation and regulation of Canadian utilities, 1830–1930
For main entry, see 2712

4311
Baker, W. J.
A History of the Marconi Company
For main entry, see 3213

4312
Becker, William H.
The Dynamics of Business-Government Relations: Industry and exports 1893–1921
University of Chicago Press *Chicago, IL*
A masterly analysis of business-government relations at a critical stage in America's corporate history.

4313
Bennett, Douglas C.; Sharpe, Kenneth E.
Transnational Corporations versus the State: The political economy of the Mexican auto industry
For main entry, see 912

4314
Berghahn, Volker R.
The Americanisation of West German Industry, 1945–1973
1986 Berg *Leamington Spa*
This book makes a detailed examination of German business leaders' attitudes to post-war restructuring of business and the European economy.

4315
Bishop, Matthew; Kay, John
Does Privatization Work?: Lessons from the UK
1988 London Business School *London*
This is a useful review of the quantitative evidence on the effects of Mrs Thatcher's privatization programme on British industry.

4316
Blank, Stephen
Government and Industry in Britain: The Federation of British Industries in politics, 1945–1964
1974 Saxon House *Farnborough*
A valuable study which finds little evidence that the Federation exerted much direct influence on political attitudes or decisions.
Firms: Federation of British Industries

4317
Bonin, Hubert
Suez: Du canal à la finance (1858–1987) [Suez: From canal to financial services (1858–1987)]
For main entry, see 3128

4318
Broehl, Wayne G. Jr
Cargill: Trading the World's Grain
For main entry, see 3934

4319
Burgess, Giles H. Jr (Editor)
Antitrust and Regulation
For main entry, see 50

4320
Burk, Robert F.
The Corporate State and the Broker State: The du Ponts and American national politics, 1925–1940
For main entry, see 771

4321
Cabrera, M.
La patronal ante la II República: Organizaciones y estrategias [Employers and the Second Republic: Organizations and strategies]
1983 Siglo XXI *Madrid, Spain*
This book offers a complete study of the relations between the entrepreneurship and the political power during the Second Republic in Spain (1931–1936).

4322
Castaneda, Christopher James
Regulated Enterprise: Natural gas pipelines and northeastern markets, 1938–1954
For main entry, see 2765

4323
Castaneda, Christopher James; Pratt, Joseph A.
From Texas to the East: A strategic history of Texas Eastern Corporation
For main entry, see 2958

4324
Chester, Sir Norman
The Nationalisation of British Industry, 1945–51
1975 HMSO *London*
A massive and authoritative peacetime official history of the nationalization programme of the Attlee government.

4325
Chick, Martin (Editor)
Governments, Industries and Markets: Aspects of government-industry relations in the UK, Japan, West Germany and the USA since 1945
1990 Edward Elgar *Aldershot*
Offers a conceptual approach to government–industry relations in the modern period, with the major focus on Britain (8 out of 12 contributions). However, the case studies, which deal with banking, motor manufacturing, whisky, chemicals, electricity, and iron and steel, tend to be rather self-contained.

4326
Clark, John G.
Energy and the Federal Government: Fossil fuel policies, 1900–1946
For main entry, see 387

4327
Comín, F.; Martín Aceña, P.
Historia de la empresa pública en España [History of Public Enterprise in Spain]
1991 Espasa-Calpe *Madrid, Spain*
This book is a complete summary of recent work done about state-owned enterprises in Spain during the eighteenth to twentieth centuries.

4328
Cruikshank, Ken
Close Ties: Railways, government and the Board of Railway Commissioners, 1851–1933
1991 McGill-Queen's University Press
Kingston and Montreal, Canada
This is a careful study of an important regulatory nexus which draws on considerable unpublished evidence about state institutions and the railway industry.

4329
Curran, James; Seaton, Jean
Power without Responsibility: The press and broadcasting in Britain
For main entry, see 1711

4330
d'Angio, Agnès
La politique des travaux publics du groupe Schneider de 1895 à 1949 [The Politics of Public Works in the Schneider Group 1895–1949]
1993, PhD Thesis, École des Chartes
This thesis describes the public works branch of the Schneider metallurgy group.
Firms: Schneider

4331
Davila, Carlos et al
La CAR 25 Años en el Desarrollo Regional [A Colombian Regional Planning Agency (CAR), 1961–1986]
1987 Universidad Javeriana *Bogotá, Colombia*
This is a commissioned company history that traces the first 25 years of a Colombian regional planning agency. Some of the topics dealt with are: the evolving institutional and development context of the agency, strategy and structure among its nine executive directors and the evolution of inter-institutional relations. It relies on the agency's archives, abundant secondary sources, interviews with former and present employees at different levels, as well as with selected customers.

4332
Del Rey Reguillo, Fernando
Propietarios y patrons: La política de las organizaciones económicas en la España de la Restauracíon (1914–1923) [Landowners and Employers: The economic organizations' policy in Restorationist Spain (1914–1923)]
1992 Ministerio de Trabajo y Seguridad Social *Madrid, Spain*

A comprehensive work on the main interest groups of Spanish entrepreneurs and their relations with the political power.

4333
Dewar, Margaret E.
Industry in Trouble: The federal government and the New England Fisheries
For main entry, see 316

4334
Diefendorf, Jeffry M.
Businessmen and Politics in the Rhineland, 1789–1834
1980 Princeton University Press *Princeton, NJ*
This is a detailed study of the 'political education' of the business community on the Left Bank of the Rhine during the period between 1789 and the Customs Union of 1834. Diefendorf focuses on merchants, bankers and manufacturers in Cologne, Crefeld and Aachen.

4335
Doria, M.
Ansaldo: L'impresa e lo Stato [Ansaldo: The enterprise and the state]
For main entry, see 686

4336
Dunnett, Peter J. S.
The Decline of the British Motor Industry: The effects of government policy, 1945–1979
For main entry, see 809

4337
Eichler, Ned
The Thrift Debacle
For main entry, see 2647

4338
Evans, Peter
Dependent development: The alliance of multinational, state, and local capital in Brazil
1979 Princeton University Press *Princeton, NJ*
The book is an important source for the study of the role played by multinationals in the process of industrialization in developing countries. It examines the relationship between multinationals, Brazilian entrepreneurs, and state companies in Brazil during the 1970s.
Firms: Banco Nacional de Desenvolvimento Economico; CEME; Companhia Vale do Rio Doce

4339
Faundez, Julio; Picciotto, Sol
The Nationalisation of Multinationals in Peripheral Economies
1978 Macmillan *London*
Seven chapters deal with the modern business history of multinational enterprise, including the Tanzanian experience in the late 1960s, the nationalization of copper in Chile, and the Norwegian oil industry.

4340
Foreman-Peck, James; Millward, Robert
Public and Private Ownership of British Industry 1820–1990
1994 Clarendon Press *Oxford*
Important new work taking a long view of the nationalization and privatization of British industries and seeking to give perspective to the privatization activity of the 1980s.

4341
Freyer, Tony
Regulating Big Business: Antitrust in Great Britain and America, 1880–1990
1992 Cambridge University Press *Cambridge*
This is a welcome synthesis of the main trends in regulation in the United States and Britain, which argues that since the 1920s the regulatory regimes of the two countries, together with the entrepreneurial and managerial responses of large-scale corporations, have tended to converge.
Firms: American Tobacco; ALCOA; US Steel; Mogul Steamship Co.

4342
Friedman, David
The Misunderstood Miracle: Industrial development and political change in Japan
For main entry, see 1328

4343
Genther, Phyllis
A History of Japan's Government–Business Relationship: The passenger car industry
For main entry, see 1002

4344

Glimstedt, Henrik

Mellan teknick och samhalle: Stat, marknad och produktion i svensk bilindustrie, 1930–1960 [Between Technology and Society: State, markets and production in the Swedish transport industry, 1930–1960]

For main entry, see 874

4345

Goodrich, Carter

Government Promotion of American Canals and Railroads 1800–1890

1960 Columbia University Press *New York, NY*

This is not really a business history per se but is invaluable and pathbreaking on the role of government in the USA–federal, state and city–in trying to promote economic development via infrastructural projects, namely the construction of canals and railroads. It focuses on the paradox that resort to government action was so extensive 'in the most individualistic of countries in its most individualistic period'. It is good on the motives of the various interest groups, the sources of finance and the impact on the economy.

Firms: Baltimore & Ohio Railroad; Pennsylvania Railroad; Erie Canal

4346

Grant, Wyn; Marsh, David

The CBI

1977 Hodder & Stoughton *London*

The authors argue that the CBI has been a weak institution, lacking a common strategy. Accordingly, it had little influence on government. The authors are therefore sceptical of 'corporatist' interpretations of British business-government relations.

Firms: Confederation of British Industry

4347

Hadley, Eleanor M.

Antitrust in Japan

1970 Princeton University Press *Princeton, NJ*

Written by an academic economist who was also a former member of General MacArthur's staff in charge of zaibatsu dissolution in occupied Japan in the late 1940s, this is a seminal study of the attempt to break up Japan's family-owned zaibatsu. Hadley studies the deconcentration programme, the reasons for its partial failure, and its economic consequences.

Firms: Dai-Ichi Bank; Mitsubishi; Mitsui; Sumitomo

4348

Hague, Douglas C.; Wilkinson, Geoffrey

The IRC: An Experiment in Industrial Intervention: A history of the Industrial Reorganisation Corporation

1983 Allen & Unwin *London*

A good official history that contains case studies of interventions in the automobile, ball-bearing and machine-tool industries.

Firms: BL; Alfred Herbert

4349

Hanscher, Leigh

Regulating for Competition: Government, law and the pharmaceutical industry in the United Kingdom and France

For main entry, see 723

4350

Harris, Nigel

Competition and the Corporate State: British Conservatives, the state and industry, 1945–1964

1972 Methuen *London*

A study of the gradual replacement of policies of decontrol by a more interventionist and corporatist policy in the course of the 1950s.

4351

Harris, Richard A.

Coal Firms Under the New Social Regulation

1985 Duke University Press *Durham, NC*

This book is a study of the impact of the Surface Mining Control and Reclamation Act (1977) on the American coal industry. Grounded in political theory, the book provides excellent insights into the development of environmental legislation and business lobbying against it.

4352
Heston, Thomas J.
Sweet Subsidy: The economic and diplomatic effects of the US Sugar Acts, 1934–1974
1987 Garland *New York, NY*

Based on a 1975 PhD thesis, this work focuses on the American government's deep long-term involvement in the sugar industry, both in domestic subsidies and in foreign economic policy, especially towards Cuba. It is scholarly and detailed.

4353
High, Jack (Editor)
Regulation: Economic theory and history
1991 University of Michigan Press *Ann Arbor, MI*

A useful collection of theoretically informed historical essays which cover many aspects of the history of regulation in the United States, including the airlines, telecommunications, baseball and electric utilities.
Firms: American Airlines; AT&T

4354
Hills, Jim
Information Technology and Industrial Policy
For main entry, see 3224

4355
Horwitz, Robert B.
The Irony of Regulatory Reform: The deregulation of American telecommunications
For main entry, see 3346

4356
Hovenkamp, Herbert
Enterprise and American Law, 1836–1937
1991 Harvard University Press *Cambridge, MA*

This is a monograph which deals with the legal ideas underpinning the regulation of American business. Due attention is given to the railroads, antitrust, the trade unions, and market failure.

4357
Hughes, Jonathan R. T.
The Governmental Habit Redux: Economic controls from colonial times to the present
2nd Edition
1991 Princeton University Press *Princeton, NJ*

This is a valuable survey and analysis of governmental intervention in American business. Distinguishing between industry and intrusive agencies, it shows that American business has rarely been free from government, and that the current illogical arrangements are the product of history.

4358
Jack, Doug
Beyond Reality: Leyland Bus – the twilight years
For main entry, see 817

4359
Jacquemin, Alexis P.; Jong, Henry W. de
European Industrial Organisation
For main entry, see 3521

4360
Jenkin, Michael
British Industry and the North Sea: State intervention in a developing industrial sector
For main entry, see 432

4361
Johnson, Arthur M.
The Development of American Petroleum Pipelines: A study in private enterprise and public policy, 1862–1906
For main entry, see 2959

4362
Johnson, Arthur M.
Petroleum Pipelines and Public Policy 1906–1959
For main entry, see 2960

4363
Johnson, Chalmers
MITI and the Japanese Miracle: The growth of industrial policy, 1925–1975
For main entry, see 3454

4364
Jones, Geoffrey; Kirby, Maurice
Competitiveness and the State: Government and business in twentieth-century Britain
1991 Manchester University Press *Manchester*

A product of the Lancaster-Reading business history meetings, this collection, with its interest in industrial policy and competitiveness, offers further perspectives on the 'decline of Britain' issue.

4365
Kay, John; Mayer, Colin; Thompson, David (Editors)
Privatisation and Regulation: The UK experience
1986 Clarendon Press *Oxford*
A good collection of essays on the development of privatization, deregulation and contracting out after 1979. It contains a number of case studies and a substantial bibliography.

4366
Kobayashi, Masa-aki
Nippon no Kogyo-ka to Kangyo Haraisage: Seifu to Kigyo [Japanese Industrialization and the Disposal of Government Enterprises: Government and business]
1977 Toyo Keizai Shinpo-sha *Tokyo, Japan*
This work is a detailed history of the disposal of government enterprises covering the period from the 1870s to the 1910s. It includes case studies on Takashima Coal Mining, Miike Coal Mining, Kamaishi Iron Works, Nagasaki Shipyard, Tomioka Silk Mill et al.
Firms: Kamaishi Iron; Miike Coal; Nagasaki Shipyard; Takashima Coal; Tomioka Silk

4367
Kolko, Gabriel
Railroads and Regulation, 1877–1916
For main entry, see 2874

4368
Komiya, Ryutaro; Okuna, Masahiro; Suzumura, Kotaro (Editors)
Industrial Policy of Japan
1988 Academic Press *New York, NY*
A comprehensive investigation of Japanese industrial development since 1945 by a team of leading Japanese economists. It discusses industrial policy, trade, growing and declining industries and mergers, and contains case studies of steel, autos, computers, textiles, shipbuilding, and aluminium.

4369
Latham, Earl
The Politics of Railroad Co-ordination, 1933–1936
For main entry, see 2876

4370
Leslie, Stuart W.
The Cold War and American Science: The military-industrial-academic complex at MIT and Stanford
For main entry, see 4278

4371
Lockwood, W. W. (Editor)
The State and Economic Enterprise in Japan
1965 Princeton University Press *Princeton NJ*
A well-known collection of articles focusing on the role of the state in Japanese development since the Meiji era.

4372
Martin, Albro
James J. Hill and the Opening of the Northwest
For main entry, see 2878

4373
Martin, Albro
Railroads Triumphant: The growth, rejection and rebirth of a vital American force
For main entry, see 2879

4374
Martín Aceña, P.; Comín, F.
INI: Cincuenta años de industrialización en España [INI Fifty years of industrialization in Spain]
1991 Espasa-Calpe *Madrid, Spain*
The latest monograph published about the Instituto Nacional de Industria, the Spanish industrial state-owned group recently (1995) dismantled for private sector involvement. It is a commissioned history launched on the 50th anniversary of its foundation (1942). The authors supply a comprehensive study of the main enterprises in the group.

Firms: INI

4375

Mason, Mark

American Multinationals and Japan: The political economy of Japanese capital controls, 1899–1980

For main entry, see 3410

4376

Matsumoto, Koji

The Rise of the Japanese Corporate System: The inside view of a MITI official

1991 Kegan Paul International *London*

Written by a former high-ranking MITI official, this is an examination of government-corporate relations in postwar Japan. Although it seeks to propound a particular view, it is illuminating on the ideas of Japan's bureaucracy.

4377

McCraw, Thomas K. (Editor)

Regulation in Perspective: Historical essays

1981 Harvard University Press *Cambridge, MA*

An overview of the American experience of regulation, influenced by cultural, industrial and political factors, developed from a Harvard Business School conference.

4378

McCraw, Thomas K. (Editor)

America vs. Japan: A comparative study

For main entry, see 3612

4379

Mercer, Helen; Rollings, Neil; Tomlinson, J. D. (Editors)

Labour Governments and Private Industry: The experience of 1945–51

1992 Edinburgh University Press *Edinburgh, Scotland*

This is a useful, if sometimes polemical, collection of essays dealing with the relationship between the Attlee governments and private industry. An important contribution to the study of British government–business relations, the book has more to say about government than about firms. There are thought-provoking chapters on cotton and motor manufacturing which challenge Correlli Barnett's thesis in the *Audit of War* (qv).

4380

Middlemas, Keith

Industry, Unions and Government: Twenty-one years of the National Economic Development Office

1983 Macmillan *London*

The official history of NEDO since its creation in 1961, written with full access to reports and records. A useful work on this important tripartite body on which government, employers and unions were represented through a period of intense economic crisis and debate.

4381

Millward, Robert; Singleton, John (Editors)

The Political Economy of Nationalisation in Britain 1920–1950

1995 Cambridge University Press *Cambridge*

An important collection of essays which explore the antecedents of the British nationalization policies of the 1940s. There are case studies of coal, civil air transport, the motor vehicle industry, railways, gas, water, the arms of industry and cotton, and a section on government–industry relations in the 1940s.

Firms: Bank of England; British European Airways Corporation; British Overseas Airways Corporation; Central Electricity Board; Iron & Steel Corporation of Great Britain

4382

Morikawa, Hidemasa (Editor)

Nippon no Kigyo to Kokka: Nippon Keiei-shi Koza, Vol. 4 [Business and Government in Japan: Japanese Business History Series, Vol. 4]

1976 Nippon Keizai Shinbun-sha *Tokyo, Japan*

This is a wide-ranging history on relations between Government and business in Japan. There are chapters on Japan Incorporated, Shibusawa Eiichi, the nationalization of railways, the munitions industry, Toyota and Honda, cartels, business circles as power elite groups, and Japan Incorporated and postwar democracy.

Firms: Toyota; Honda

4383
Mowery, David C.; Rosenberg, Nathan
Technology and the Pursuit of Economic Growth
For main entry, see 4283

4384
Olson, Mancur
The Rise and Decline of Nations: Economic growth, stagflation and social rigidities
For main entry, see 3467

4385
Parris, Henry
Government and the Railways in Nineteenth-Century Britain
For main entry, see 2811

4386
Pryke, Richard
Public Enterprise in Practice: The British experience of nationalization over two decades
For main entry, see 3622

4387
Ripley, William Z.
Railroads, Rates and Regulation
For main entry, see 2887

4388
Rose, Mark H.
Interstate: Express highway politics 1941–1956
For main entry, see 3006

4389
Sapelli, G.; Carnevali, F.
Uno sviloppo fra politica e strategia: ENI (1953–1985) [Development Between Politics and Strategy: ENI (1953–1985)]
For main entry, see 2730

4390
Schweitzer, Arthur
Big Business in the Third Reich
2nd Edition
1977 Indiana University Press *Bloomington, IA*

First published in 1964, this is a major work which examines the relationship between big business and the Nazi regime in Germany.

4391
Self, Peter; Storing, H. J.
The State and the Farmer
For main entry, see 189

4392
Sklar, Martin J.
The Corporate Reconstruction of American Capitalism, 1890–1916: The market, the law, and politics
1988 Cambridge University Press *New York, NY*

This richly researched study of antitrust presents new empirical material on its legislative origins, judicial construction and political shaping.

Firms: American Tobacco; Standard Oil

4393
Smith, Martin J.
The Politics of Agricultural Support in Britain: The development of the agricultural policy community
For main entry, see 190

4394
Smith, Thomas C.
Political Change and Industrial Development in Japan: Government enterprise, 1868–1880
1955 Stanford University Press *Stanford, CA*

A classic text examining the role of the Meiji state in early Japanese industrialization. Smith considers the state a central actor and initiator and despite much further research his views have not been overturned.

Firms: Mitsubishi; Mitsui

4395
Sumida, Jon Tetsuro
In Defence of Naval Supremacy: Finance, technology and British naval policy, 1889–1914
For main entry, see 1415

4396
Temin, Peter
Taking Your Medicine: Drug regulation in the United States
For main entry, see 794

4397
Temin, Peter; Galambos, L.
The Fall of the Bell System
For main entry, see 3239

4398
Tiratsoo, Nicholas; Tomlinson, Jim
Industrial Efficiency and State Intervention: Labour 1939–51
1993 Routledge *London*

This is a welcome attempt to challenge received wisdom about the Labour Government's apparent failure to encourage industrial modernisation after the Second World War. It also provides information on the role of British managers and trade unions as well as shedding light on the 'Americanisation' of productivity debate.

Firms: Anglo-American Council on Productivity; British Employers Confederation; British Institute of Management; Federation of British Industries; ICI

4399
Tolliday, Steven W. (Editor)
Government and Business
For main entry, see 60

4400
Traves, Tom
The State and Enterprise: Canadian Manufacturers and the Federal Government, 1917–1931
1979 University of Toronto Press *Toronto, Canada*

This book contains several case studies of the relationship among businessmen's organizations, regulatory agencies and market forces from the Great War to the Great Depression.

4401
Tripathi, Dwijendra (Editor)
State and Business in India: A historical perspective
1987 Manohar Publications *New Delhi, India*

The book is a collection of essays, written specially for this volume dealing with the role played by various state systems from the Mughals down to our own times in promoting or thwarting private business. The book also describes the manner in which the big and organized enterprises responded to the constraints and opportunities generated by different political systems in India.

4402
Tripathi, Dwijendra (Editor)
Business and Politics in India: A historical perspective
1991 Manohar Publications *New Delhi, India*

Based on solid scholarship, the volume is a product of a joint endeavour of some of the leading scholars. Covering the period from the Great Mughals until after independence, it seeks to analyse the continuity and change in the attitude of Indian business towards political twists and turns and how these influenced the course of Indian business and vice versa.

4403
Turner, Henry A. Jr
German Big Business and the Rise of Hitler
1985 Oxford University Press *New York, NY*

Turner explores the part played by Germany's businessmen in undermining the authority of the Weimar Republic by supporting the emerging Nazi party.

4404
Turner, John (Editor)
Businessmen and Politics: Studies of business activity in British politics 1900–1945
1984 Heinemann *London*

In this welcome set of essays, the relationship between British businessmen and politics is analysed. Topics covered include pre-1914 attacks on municipal socialism, the politics of oil, and the growth of industrial organisation.

Firms: Bankers' Industrial Development Co.; ICI; National Confederation of Employers' Organisations; Securities Investment Trust; Shell

4405
Vietor, Richard H. K.
Energy Policy in America Since 1945: A study of business–government relations
For main entry, see 396

4406
Vietor, Richard H. K.
Contrived Competition: Regulation and deregulation in America

1994 Belknap Press of Harvard University *Cambridge, MA*

This major work on change in American regulation of industry, contains case studies on four leading firms: American Airlines, El Paso Natural Gas, AT&T, and Bank America. It shows how each was challenged by the post-1978 environment of deregulation, and how each responded.

Firms: AT&T; American Airlines; Bank America; El Paso Natural Gas

4407

Whale, John

The Politics of the Media

For main entry, see 1743

4408

Wilks, Stephen R. M.

Industrial Policy and the Motor Industry

For main entry, see 852

4409

Wilks, Stephen; Wright, Maurice (Editors)

The Promotion and Regulation of Industry in Japan

1991 Macmillan *London*

An important collection of essays on bureaucratic intervention in Japanese industry, focusing on the promotion of new industries (pharmaceuticals, biotechnology), the management of decline (shipbuilding), and the regulation of the telecommunications sector.

Firms: AT&T; NTT

4410

Wurm, Clemens A.

Politics and Industrial Relations: Steel, cotton and international cartels in British politics, 1924–1939

1993 Cambridge University Press *Cambridge*

A study of commercial diplomacy, analysing the responses of British industry and government to competition, sectoral depression and decline. In particular it analyses the British steel industry's response to the International Steel Cartel, and the Lancashire cotton industry's attempts to reach a market-sharing agreement with Japan. It contrasts the powerful state support enlisted by the steel industry with the restricted response forthcoming for Lancashire cotton. Based on wide-ranging primary research. Published in German by De Gruyter in 1988.

4411

Young, Stephen C.

An Annotated Bibliography on Relations Between Government and Industry in Britain, 1620–1982

For main entry, see 41

4412

Young, Stephen; Lowe, A. V.

Intervention in the Mixed Economy: The evolution of British industrial policy, 1964–1972

1974 Croom Helm *London*

A careful study of Labour Government interventions in the private sector.

4413

Zysman, John

Governments, Markets and Growth: Financial systems and the politics of industrial change

1983 Cornell University Press *Ithaca, NY*

A valuable comparative study of different national systems of industrial finance, covering France, USA, UK and Japan, contrasting the differing roles of banks and markets.

Employers' Associations - Japan

4414

Fletcher, William Miles, III

The Japanese Business Community and National Trade Policy, 1920–42

1989 University of North Carolina Press *Chapel Hill, NC*

Fletcher examines the collective responses of the Japanese business community to economic crisis in the 1920s and 1930s, notably the turn to international cartels. Businessmen were not always unified but did develop a working consensus with state agencies to form policies and develop cohesive attitudes.

4415

Hazama, Hiroshi

Nippon no Shiyo-sha Dantai to Roshi Kankei [Employers' Associations and Industrial Relations in Japan]

1981 Nippon Rodo Kyokai *Tokyo, Japan*

Covering the period from the 1780s to the 1970s, this work is a detailed study of the evolution and functions of employers' associations. There is a valuable chronological table at the end of the book, showing the development of the Japanese employers' associations.

4416

Japan Association of Corporate Executives

Keizai Doyu-kai Sanju-nen-shi [A 30-Year History of the Japan Association of Corporate Executives]

1976 Japan Association of Corporate Executives *Tokyo, Japan*

This is an authoritative history of the Japan Association of Corporate Executives which was set up in April 1946 by younger executives for the purpose of contributing to Japan's postwar rehabilitation.

4417

Japan Business History Institute

Keizai Dantai Rengo-kai Sanju-nen-shi [A 30-Year History of the Federation of Economic Organizations]

1978 Federation of Economic Organization *Tokyo, Japan*

This is the authoritative history of the Federation of Economic Organizations established in August 1946, which represents the collective opinion of the Japanese economic world.

4418

Japan Federation of Employers' Associations

Nikkeiren Sanju-nen-shi [A 30-Year History of the Japan Federation of Employers' Associations]

1981 Japan Federation of Employers' Associations *Tokyo, Japan*

This is an authoritative history of the Japan Federation of Employers' Associations. This organization was set up in April 1948 by employers to cope with labour problems. It is useful for information on both cooperation between capital and labour and labour-management disputes in postwar Japan.

4419

Japan Industry Club

Nippon Kogyo Kurabi Goju-nen-shi [Half a Century of the Japan Industry Club]

1972 Japan Industry Club *Tokyo, Japan*

This is an official history of the Japan Industry Club which was formally established in 1917; its members had represented the collective opinion of the economic world in the 1910s. After the Japan Federation of Economic Associations was founded in 1922 as a central organization, the Japan Industry Club became a social centre for the business world.

4420

Osaka Chamber of Commerce and Industry

Osaka Shoko Kaigi-sho Hyakunen-shi [A Centenary History of the Osaka Chamber of Commerce and Industry]

1979 Osaka Chamber of Commerce and Industry *Osaka, Japan*

This is a well-documented history of the Osaka Chamber of Commerce and Industry covering the period from the 1870s to the 1970s including the position during the Tokugawa era before 1868.

4421

Tokyo Chamber of Commerce and Industry

Tokyo Shoko Kaigi-sho Hyakunen-shi [A Centenary History of the Tokyo Chamber of Commerce and Industry]

1979 Tokyo Chamber of Commerce and Industry *Tokyo, Japan*

This is an authoritative history of the Tokyo Chamber of Commerce and Industry covering the period from the 1870s to the 1970s including earlier activities in the Tokugawa era.

Index of Authors

Index of Firms